# Strategies & Tactics for the Finz Multistate Method

## Fourth Edition

**STEVEN R. FINZ**

This Edition Edited by

**Alex Ruskell, Esq.**

Director of Academic Success and Bar Preparation
University of South Carolina School of Law

Published by Wolters Kluwer in New York.

Wolters Kluwer Legal & Regulatory US serves customers worldwide with CCH, Aspen Publishers, and Kluwer Law International products. (www.WKLegaledu.com)

To contact Customer Service, e-mail customer.service@wolterskluwer.com,
call 1-800-234-1660, fax 1-800-901-9075, or mail correspondence to:

Wolters Kluwer
Attn: Order Department
PO Box 990
Frederick, MD 21705

Printed in the United States of America.

1 2 3 4 5 6 7 8 9 0

ISBN 978-1-4548-7314-3

SUSTAINABLE FORESTRY INITIATIVE    Certified Sourcing
www.sfiprogram.org
SFI-00756

## About Wolters Kluwer Legal & Regulatory US

Wolters Kluwer Legal & Regulatory US delivers expert content and solutions in the areas of law, corporate compliance, health compliance, reimbursement, and legal education. Its practical solutions help customers successfully navigate the demands of a changing environment to drive their daily activities, enhance decision quality and inspire confident outcomes.

Serving customers worldwide, its legal and regulatory portfolio includes products under the Aspen Publishers, CCH Incorporated, Kluwer Law International, ftwilliam.com and MediRegs names. They are regarded as exceptional and trusted resources for general legal and practice-specific knowledge, compliance and risk management, dynamic workflow solutions, and expert commentary.

# Dedication

To Iris

To Jimmy and Mary Frances

# TABLE OF CONTENTS

# How to Use This Book

This book contains a collection of questions (called "items") in the Multistate Bar Exam format, accompanied by answers (called "options") and explanations. Each of the explanations is intended to be a mini-dissertation on the topic involved.

The chapter entitled **Strategies & Tactics: Playing the MBE Game to Win** (what we call the **Multistate Method**) sets forth a detailed method for approaching and dealing with items in this format. You should study the chapter diligently before beginning to practice with the items that follow it. By the time you have worked your way through 50 or 60 items, you should have become so familiar with this Multistate Method that its use is second nature.

The questions are divided into the seven subject areas tested on the Multistate Bar Examination: Civil Procedure, Constitutional Law, Contracts, Criminal Law, Evidence, Real Property, and Torts. If you are still in law school, you can use the separate sections to review the material that you are studying in each of the subject areas. Each section is accompanied by a subject matter outline and a question index. Using the question index, you can look for questions dealing with the particular topics and subtopics that you wish to review.

The items that appear in this book are similar in content and form to the questions that appear on the Multistate Bar Examination (MBE). On the MBE, each item tests only one general subject area but is likely to cover several topics and subtopics within that area. A Torts question, for example, may test knowledge of intentional torts, negligence, nuisance, and proximate cause, all in the same set of answers (options).

For this reason, most questions (items) in this book may be listed in several different places in the question index. If you have just completed your study of intentional torts and wish to field questions that test your newly acquired knowledge, you can find them by looking at the appropriate place in the Torts question index. You may discover, however, that the same questions also test knowledge of topics that you have not yet studied. This need not prevent the questions from being useful to you.

The Multistate Method game plan suggests that, in answering Multistate items, you treat each option (*i.e.*, proposed answer) as a separate true-false question. Using this approach, you can choose to deal only with the options for which your studies have prepared you. The explanation accompanying each item analyzes why the answer we pick is correct and why each of the incorrect options is incorrect. You can use these analyses to check your responses to the options.

If you are preparing for the MBE, you should work on the items in each of the subject areas after completing your review of those areas. If your review has not prepared you for all the options, you will know what areas need further review. The explanations can help you complete your study.

In addition, this book contains a 200-question practice exam in which the items are shuffled, as they are on the MBE, so that the seven subjects are tested in random order. If you need additional questions to review, or want Strategies & Tactics on each MBE subject, you should purchase a copy of *Strategies & Tactics for the MBE*, also published by Aspen and available at your local bookstore. For each MBE subject, *Strategies & Tactics for the MBE* delivers detailed advice on what to study and what traps to watch for, as well as actual released MBE questions with detailed answers.

For substantive MBE review, you should check out the *Law in a Flash* MBE Set, which contains flash cards on all MBE subjects (Civil Procedure, Constitutional Law, Contracts, Criminal Law, Criminal Procedure [tested on the MBE as part of Criminal Law], Evidence, Future Interests [tested as part of Property], Real Property, Sales [tested as part of Contracts], and Torts) as well as a copy of *Strategies & Tactics for the MBE*. The MBE Set is available at your local bookstore.

If you are preparing for the bar exam, you should wait until you have completed your review of all seven Multistate subjects before taking the practice exam contained in this book. It may be a good idea to simulate examination conditions when taking it. Turn off your phone, lock your door, tell the rest of the world to go away, and give yourself three uninterrupted hours for each half of the exam.

GOOD LUCK!

# Strategies & Tactics® —Playing the MBE Game to Win

## TERROR AND THE MBE

It's given on the last Wednesday of February and July in almost every one of the 50 states, and it has become a significant factor in the bar admitting standards of most states. It evokes loathing and paranoia from the souls of embryonic attorneys across the land. It's the Multistate Bar Examination (the MBE), an all-day challenge consisting of 200 questions on seven important subjects. It scares the devil out of most of us.

The reason it's so frightening to us is that our profession attracts people who learned as they were growing up that they could talk their way into and argue their way out of most situations. I'm one of these people. You probably are, too. Much of the time, people like us treat life as a game. The trouble with the MBE is that it doesn't give us a chance to talk or argue, which is what we believe we do best. We find it too structured, too restrictive. There's not enough game in it. It cramps our style.

When we think that, though, we're forgetting that the people who create the MBE are cut from the same cloth as we are. They are law professors and practitioners who have argued their way into and out of trouble all their lives. They've been playing the same game with their lives that we've been playing with ours. The ideas that appeal to them also appeal to us. The only difference is that they specialize in testing and finding out what other lawyers are made of. Their exam does a pretty good job of it, but we have to approach it the way we approach other problems in our lives—as a game that must be played from a position of strength.

It helps to realize that, by its very nature, the MBE has certain aspects that work in our favor. First, because it is given in most of the states, it can test only general principles of law—no petty details. Second, because its multiple choice format eliminates the options of argument or explanation, each issue must be so precisely drawn that only one of the four possible answers satisfies the requirements of the question. Most important, because it is given to budding lawyers, the most argumentative and litigious people in the world, it must be scrupulously fair and unassailable.

To assure that the exam will be just and to protect it against attack, the creators of the MBE have developed a method for constructing questions. They stick to a policy that requires that there be no trick questions and no trick answers. No problem will be solved on the basis of a subtle turn of word or phrase. They even have rules to assure the effective use of apostrophes and to eliminate the confusing misuse of pronouns. Questions are screened repeatedly before they are used, and then screened again.

After the exam has been given, the answers are analyzed. Questions that proved too tricky to be fair are invalidated and eliminated from further consideration. Questions that show themselves to have no correct answer or more than one correct answer are also invalidated. Applicants are not supposed to be asked to select the best of four bad answers or four good answers. There is only one demonstrably correct answer to each question. The others are clearly incorrect. That is, it's clear if we follow the right analytical steps.

Since they have a method for creating the exam, we need a method for taking it. This chapter provides a unique Multistate Method. To develop our method, we must begin by understanding theirs.

## STRUCTURE OF QUESTIONS

Questions, or "items," as the examiners call them, can be broken into three distinct parts: the root, the stem, and the options.

The *root* is the part of the item containing the underlying facts.

The *stem* is the part of the item containing the call of the options or assigning a task. Sometimes it is in the form of a question; sometimes it calls for the completion of a sentence.

The *options* are the answer choices. Sometimes they state conclusions and nothing more; sometimes they link a conclusion with a reason to support it. Sometimes two or more of the options seem to be related to each other; sometimes each of the four is independent of the other three. One of them is always the correct option; three of them are always incorrect.

Exhibit A shows a typical item.

## *DISTRACTORS* AND *FOILS*

The examiners spend a lot of time and energy creating three wrong options for each item. They call the incorrect options "distractors" or "foils." In using those names, they have unwittingly tipped their hand. According to Webster, a "distractor" is something that compellingly and confusingly attracts in the wrong direction. A "foil" is something that serves to set off another thing to advantage or disadvantage by contrasting with it. By definition, some of the incorrect options are there to make the others look good, and some of them are there to make the correct option seem bad.

Here, again, the nature of the exam works in our favor. The examination is supposed to be a test of knowledge. The correct choice must be somewhere among the four options, but it can't be left exposed for everyone to see; it has to be hidden. According to their own rules, the examiners can't use tricky devices or puzzling language, so they have to hide it behind a screen of distractors and foils. Like a magician's banter, these are designed to make us look away from the real action. That's how the game is played.

Exhibit A

# Construction of an MBE question or "Item"

**Root of the question**
(Facts)

Congress passes a law providing that no one who has been a member of an organization that uses unlawful means to deprive any group or person of their rights under the United States Constitution is eligible for employment by the federal government.

**Stem of the question**
("Call" of options)

If the constitutionality of that law is challenged, it should be held

**Options**
(Answer choices)

  (A)  unconstitutional, because it is an *ex post facto* law.

  (B)  unconstitutional, because it prohibits members of certain organizations from holding public office whether or not they knew the purpose of the organizations.

  (C)  constitutional, because employment by the federal government is not a right but a privilege.

  (D)  constitutional, because the federal government has the right to protect itself by not employing persons who hold views inconsistent with the United States Constitution.

Many of the people who create the MBE are law professors or former law professors. In creating distractors and foils, they use insight that comes from their experience with law students. After all, the main purpose of the exam is to find out whether we are finished studying the law and ready to start practicing it. Their foils and distractors are usually based on anticipating the errors that law students are likely to make.

Their method gives all the options a look of superficial plausibility. At first glance, every option appears to be correct. Our response to their bag of tricks must therefore include a careful reading of the language that they use.

## Incomplete definitions and arguments

No one needs to be more precise in the use of language than a lawyer. Learning to communicate precisely is one of the goals of a law school education. A first-semester law student may define "murder" as the unjustified killing of a human being, but a lawyer knows that an unjustified killing isn't murder unless it's an unjustified killing of **another** human being **with malice aforethought**.

Some of the foils and distractors that appear on the MBE consist of incomplete or imprecise statements, like those made by beginners in the classroom. An option that says, "John is guilty of murder because he committed the unjustified killing of a human being," is wrong because it is based on an incomplete definition. Don't assume that the examiners left out the rest of the definition by mistake, or that they expect you to know what they really mean. Don't allow yourself to complete the argument or definition in your mind and conclude that it is correct.

## Dealing with the facts

Lawyers must be very careful with facts. They must assume nothing in addition to what has been established or given. In summing up to a jury, for example, trial counsel may not refer to any facts that have not been proven. Frequently, distractors and foils are designed to find out whether we have the ability to play the game the way a lawyer plays it. If a prosecutor proved only that the defendant shot the victim and that the victim died an hour later, the defendant's prosecution for murder would have to be dismissed unless the prosecutor had also proven that the defendant's bullet caused the victim's death. If the facts in the root of the item do not say that the victim died as a result of the defendant's bullet, don't assume or infer that she did. Only a medical expert is competent to draw such a conclusion, and you are probably not a doctor. Without such proof, we must conclude that the defendant's guilt has not been established.

On the other hand, lawyers can't get away with ignoring facts that have been established. In arguing appeals, for example, lawyers may not claim that the facts proven at the trial should be ignored. They are restricted to making arguments about the legal effects of the proven facts. Since examiners are out to determine whether we can do a lawyer's job, they are likely to fill the root with implausible facts in an effort to trick us into rejecting or disbelieving them. Falling for their ploy can be disastrous. In taking the MBE, we must accept the facts that are given to us, no matter how unlikely or implausible they may seem.

We may have been taught, for example, that an intoxicated person is not capable of driving her car in a reasonable manner. If, however, an item's root tells us that after the defendant drank two quarts of whiskey, she was driving her car in a reasonable manner when she collided with the plaintiff, we must accept this as true. Since negligence is unreasonable conduct, and since we are told that the defendant was driving her car in a reasonable manner, we must conclude that she was not negligent.

## Common errors

Some areas of the law are so confusing to law students that they furnish the examiners with a fertile field in which to cultivate foils and distractors. The literature distributed by the examiners indicates that incorrect options contained in MBE items are frequently based on common errors made by law students. Often, these common errors result from misunderstandings about the significance of legal expressions that have different meanings for lawyers than for laypersons.

The doctrine of "last clear chance" is an example of how this common confusion can be used to create an effective foil or distractor. "Last clear chance" is a doctrine that can be raised only by a plaintiff; its only effect is to eliminate the consequence of the plaintiff's contributory negligence. Thus, even in a jurisdiction that applies the "all-or-nothing" rule of contributory negligence, a plaintiff who goes to sleep in the middle of the road and is struck by a defendant who sees her in time but fails to take reasonable steps to avoid striking her may still win her case. In finding for the plaintiff, the court is likely to say that the plaintiff's negligence does not bar her recovery because the defendant had the "last clear chance" to avoid the accident.

Knowing that many students are confused about this doctrine, the examiners may create a distractor that says, "The defendant wins because the plaintiff had the last clear chance to avoid the accident." It sounds logical, but not to someone who understands that "last clear chance" is a doctrine available only to plaintiffs.

Similarly, a foil or distractor may be based on the "dead man's rule," which excludes evidence of certain conversations with a person now deceased. Although the "dead man's rule" sometimes keeps evidence out, it never justifies the admission of evidence. Thus, an option that says, "The evidence is admissible under the dead man's rule" has to be incorrect, even though at first glance it sounds logical.

## Overlooking the obvious

Some lawyers lose cases because they overlook the obvious. Perhaps that's why the examiners occasionally create an option that is so obviously correct that there is no rational excuse for missing it. It's amazing how many applicants reject such an option in the belief that nothing so important could possibly be so easy.

Items regarding the sufficiency of a deed description are good examples of this technique. The general rule is that a description in a deed is sufficient if it adequately identifies the realty conveyed. Usually, it is impossible to decide whether a description satisfies this requirement without knowing something about surveying in general and the geographical area involved in particular. Since the MBE is not a test of surveying or geographical knowledge, however, its creators cannot expect us to determine the validity of a particular description. Instead, they are likely to give the language of a deed description, tell you that it adequately identifies the realty conveyed, ask whether it is valid, and then create an option that says, "The description is valid because it adequately identifies the realty conveyed." Can anything be more obviously correct? Don't miss a gift like that one.

## Plausible creations

Some applicants are so intimidated by the examination process that they are sure the correct options will involve concepts they never heard of before. This not only leads them to reject options that are obviously correct, it causes them to select options that consist of meaningless garbage. Knowing this, the examiners occasionally indulge their sense of whimsy by building foils and distractors around Latin words or phrases that sound momentous but are used in a context that makes them meaningless.

*Post hoc ergo propter hoc* is an example of a Latin phrase that may be at the core of one of these seemingly plausible creations. The expression translates as "after which, therefore because of which," and is a name given to the error in reasoning that leads people to offer such arguments as "It always rains after I wash my car, so washing my car makes it rain" (*i.e.*, it rains after (and, therefore, because) I wash my car). This is likely to show up as a foil or distractor in an option that says something like, "John will win under the doctrine of *post hoc ergo propter hoc*."

If that kind of bluff fools us, we will end up at the examiners' mercy. In a question that actually appeared on a past MBE, many applicants were taken in by a double-talk option that stated that a plaintiff could not be the holder of a certain easement because "an incorporeal hereditament lies only in grant." One way to avoid falling for such seemingly plausible creations is to remember that after passing all your law school finals, taking a bar review course, and cramming for the exam, you probably are familiar with any rule of law that will matter to the examiners. If an option cites a doctrine or rule that you never heard of, it's probably incorrect.

## Unfamiliar phrases

This doesn't mean that all the correct options will use familiar language. One of the goals of the exam is to determine whether we really understand the law that we've learned or whether we've just been trained like parrots to spout phrases. To accomplish this goal, the examiners may describe familiar concepts in nontraditional words. Instead of saying, for example, that the defendant owed the plaintiff a duty of reasonable care because he created a foreseeable risk to her, they may say, "The defendant owed an obligation to the plaintiff because it appeared that the defendant's conduct would injure her." Instead of saying that strict liability is imposed on one who engages in an ultra-hazardous activity, they may say that "a defendant is liable without regard to fault because his or her occupation is extremely dangerous." Remember that there are many ways of saying anything, and that substance is far more important than form.

## PLAYING THE RIGHT ROLE

In the real world, lawyers play various roles. Sometimes they are judges, deciding the outcome of an issue or selecting the winner of a case. Sometimes they are advocates, making the best argument possible for one of the parties, even though there's no telling whether that party is going to win. Sometimes they are scholars, unconcerned about who wins or loses, interested only in seeing the legal significance of a fact or in selecting the most applicable rule of law, without caring whose interest will be served. It is natural that the items appearing in the MBE game should cast us in each of these three roles. This makes knowing how to act in each of the roles an important part of our Multistate Method.

### Acting as the judge

[*Typical stem:* If the plaintiff sues the defendant for battery, the court should find in favor of . . . ]

In the real world, the judge starts out with no particular result or conclusion in mind. He or she does not decide questions of fact but is always alert for misstatements about the facts in lawyers' arguments. If an argument does not accurately characterize the facts, is based on an inference not justified by the facts, or is based on a rule of law that is not correctly stated, the judge rejects it. He or she rules in favor of the argument in which accurate statements about the facts and law are consistent with the conclusion with which they are coupled.

When you are asked to act as judge, do not decide questions of fact. Do not try to determine who should win or how the issue should be resolved until you have considered all the arguments presented in the options. Examine each option in turn. First, see whether the facts and law are accurately stated. If not, reject the option. See whether the conclusion offered is consistent with the argument advanced. If not, reject the option. There will be only one option in which the argument advanced is based on accurate statements of fact and law and is consistent with the conclusion offered. This is the correct choice. Select it, even though you may not like the result. After all, you're a judge.

### Acting as the advocate

[*Typical stem:* Which of the following is the most effective argument in favor of the defendant's position?]

Unlike the judge, the advocate works toward a particular result—the one he or she's been paid or assigned to accomplish. It doesn't matter whether he or she believes that the client will win. So long as there is any question at all for either the judge or jury, he or she understands that a client is entitled to representation. The advocate assumes that the client can win and then makes the argument that is most likely to bring about the victory. He or she doesn't invent facts but presents and interprets in the light most favorable to the client those facts that have been established.

When an item asks you to be an advocate, examine each of the options in turn to see whether the law is accurately stated and whether the inferences on which the option is based are justified by the facts that are given. If not, reject it. See whether the option presented could possibly result in victory for the client the stem has assigned you to represent. If not, reject it. There will be only one option in which the argument advanced is based on accurate statements of law and fact and which supports your client's position. Choose it, even if you don't really believe that your client can win. After all, you're an advocate.

## Acting as the scholar

[*Typical stem:* The interest in the land that the son had on the day after the landowner's death is best described as a . . . ]

The scholar doesn't try to decide or influence the outcome of a case. The scholar uses his or her knowledge of the law to recognize the legal significance of a particular fact or to select the most applicable rule. He or she sees an intellectual challenge and nothing more. Like a professor asking a question in the classroom, he or she doesn't care who wins or loses. He or she focuses on a specific and limited issue, listens to each of the options chosen by the students, and then smiles at the student whose choice comes closest to the one he or she had in mind when he or she asked the question.

Do the same with an item that casts you in the role of a scholar. Forget about who will win or lose. Don't worry whether the option you select will result in justice. Just focus on the specific issues involved and try to resolve them in your mind. Then examine each of the options carefully and select the one that comes closest to the selection you have already formulated.

## TIMING

Our Multistate Method must teach the most efficient possible use of time. Most people barely manage to answer all the items in the allotted time. **You probably will not have an opportunity to go back and check your choices**. It's wise to get them right on the first pass because that's probably the only chance you will get.

According to the Examiners, seven subjects are tested. The test presents 200 questions total—28 questions in Contracts, and 27 questions each in Constitutional Law, Criminal Law, Evidence, Real Property, Torts, and Civil Procedure (10 questions are being "tested" by the Examiners that do not form part of your score, but you won't be able to distinguish these questions). You should recognize, however, that in reality, *10* law school subjects are tested—the section on Contracts includes questions on Sales, the section on Property includes questions on Future Interests, and the section on Criminal Law includes questions on Criminal Procedure.

There are usually two or more versions of each exam so that, although everyone gets the same questions, the questions are not in the same order. They are randomly shuffled in each version. Therefore, you may see two real property items in a row and then not see another until 10 or 20 items later.

Everyone feels stronger in some of the subjects than in others, and there will be a powerful temptation to go looking for those questions that deal with your best subjects. Resist that temptation. **Answer the questions in the order in which they appear**.

There are three good reasons why you should take this advice. First, the tough ones aren't going to get any easier with the passage of time. If anything, fatigue will make them seem even tougher, so there's no point in putting them off. Second, if you read item #3, for example, and decide not to answer it until later, part of your mind will still be working on it when you try to answer subsequent items. This will keep you from devoting all your energy to the item before you and may even cause you to base a choice in one question on facts that you still remember from item #3. Third and most important, if you skip item #3, there will be a blank space on your answer sheet, and you may become confused into putting the answer to item #4 in the space for item #3. Once you do that, every choice that follows will be written in the wrong space.

This potential pitfall alone makes it better to guess than to leave a blank space. But there's more. The examiners give you one point for every correct choice and don't subtract any points for a wrong choice. This means that a wrong choice is certainly no worse than a blank space. In most states, you can get 60 or more wrong and still pass the exam. If you can't come up with the correct option, guess and move ahead. You have at least a 25 percent chance of guessing correctly.

After the exam is over, the examiners usually determine that some of the items— sometimes as many as 10—were invalid. When this happens, they often give credit for any option chosen. This means that you may receive a point even if you guessed wrong. If you left it blank, though, you'll get nothing.

You won't really be guessing anyway, because a "guess" is a choice that is based on no real knowledge. By the time you get to the bar exam, your head will be so filled with information that there won't be any item that you don't know at least something about. Even if it's buried deep in the unconscious recesses of your mind, this knowledge will increase the probability that the option you choose is correct.

Time is not on your side. You'll have two three-hour sessions with 100 items in each. That breaks down to 33.3 items per hour, about 17 items per half hour, or 1.8 minutes per item. It is important to stay on schedule. Each item is worth one point. You don't get anything extra for the ones you spend extra time on. Every extra second you spend on one item is a second less that you'll have to spend on the next.

## THE TEST BECOMES A GAME

After observing a courtroom proceeding for the first time, the layperson typically scratches his or her temple and says, "It's a game. Nothing but a game." We, on the other hand, say it's serious business. But when we reflect on the origins of the adversary system, we see knights in armor jousting on a field of battle in the belief that the righteous was assured of winning the contest.

It started out as a game, and we're kidding ourselves if we try to believe that there isn't any game left in it. In a way, the phrase "adversary system" is a euphemism for a complex and exciting game that society plays, with lawyers as its game pieces. It is fitting, therefore, that the bar examination, which tests competency to practice law, is, itself, a kind of game, testing, among other things, the applicant's ability to play.

All games involve a combination of knowledge and strategy. A craps shooter has no control over the numbers that come up on the dice; he or she wins or loses by making bets based on his or her knowledge of the odds. A card player decides "when to hold 'em and when to fold 'em" by knowing what cards are in the deck and remembering which ones have already been dealt. Trivial Pursuit champions win by moving their game pieces in the most advantageous way, but they don't get to move them at all unless they know the answers to the questions that appear on the game cards.

The MBE is a game that can't be won without knowledge but knowledge isn't everything. Given enough time, any decent lawyer who approaches the MBE seriously enough to prepare for it adequately can get a passing score. But the exam is long and the hours are short. Without an effective strategy, an applicant is likely to be cut down by the clock. Ding dong. Game over.

To avoid running out of time, move through every item as swiftly as possible. To avoid being foiled and distracted, however, read every relevant word patiently and carefully. At first, these goals seem to be inconsistent with each other. By beginning with an orientation, our Multistate Method provides us with a strategy for accomplishing both of them.

## ORIENTATION

The fact pattern in an item's root may raise dozens of issues, some of which can be resolved and some of which won't ever be resolved. Usually, however, the stem is more narrowly drawn to eliminate all but one or two of the possible issues. If we waste time answering questions that weren't asked, we won't have a chance of answering the ones that were.

To avoid being drawn in to a series of false directions, ***always begin with a quick reading of the stem*** to determine the call of the question. Look for the role that each stem assigns and the task that it sets before you. It may specify a particular cause of action, it may name a crime, it may point to a clause of the United States Constitution, or it may designate the parties, plaintiff, and defendant.

After the stem, **quickly** read the root. We're still not ready to begin choosing among the options, so we aren't sure what we're looking for, even though the stem gave us a pretty good idea. This first reading of the root is part of our orientation.

Don't struggle too hard at this point to understand all the facts. Don't worry about keeping the chronology straight. Don't begin drawing those little diagrams you learned about in law school or bar review. Some facts in the root may not even be relevant to the options, and attempting to deal with them at this point may turn out to be a waste of time. If necessary, you can always return to the root to check the facts again.

## MAKING THE PLAY

Our first reading of the stem and root was an orientation, designed to find out what role we've been assigned to play and what task we've been asked to accomplish. Now it's time to accomplish it. Read the stem again, more carefully this time.

### Basic game plan

Because the examiners' game plan includes options that make us look in the wrong direction, our Multistate Method must adopt a game plan that will keep us from being foiled and distracted. Since the wrong options are supposed to make the other options look either good or bad by comparison, don't compare one option to the others. Treat each as a separate option and as if it were the only one before you. Recall that, according to the examiners' policy, only one can be correct. To play it safe, even if you have found one that you think is true, don't stop until you have checked all four options.

With pencil in hand, examine each option carefully, returning to the root to confirm facts if necessary. Mark the option with a "T" if it is true, with an "F" if it is false, and with a "?" if you can't make up your mind. When you're done, you should have three "F"s and one "T." So long as you have a good clear "T," count "?"s as "F"s. If you have no "T"s at all, treat a "?" as a "T." The option with the "T" next to it is the correct answer.

Although this basic game plan works for all MBE item types, there are a few variations that may help us deal more efficiently with particular kinds of items.

### Negative response

Occasionally a stem asks for a "reverse" response, such as "Which of the following is LEAST likely to violate the Fourteenth Amendment?" When that happens, restate the stem in the reverse: "Would the following violate the Fourteenth Amendment?" You should end up with three "T"s (yes) and one "F" (no). Choose the one that got the "F."

### Overlapping options

Sometimes some of the options contain parts of others. Typical options:

The defendant is guilty of

(A) Burglary only.

(B) Robbery only.

(C) Burglary and Robbery.

(D) Neither Burglary nor Robbery.

Instead of trying to deal with these overlapping options in combination, break them down into the individual components (*e.g.*, Burglary and Robbery). Give each of the individual choices a "T" or "F," and then find the option that contains the correct combination of choices.

## Three-to-one options

In some items, three of the options offer one conclusion coupled with different reasons for it, while the fourth offers the opposite conclusion with no reason at all. A typical question:

The defendant will

(A) lose.

(B) win, because . . . .

(C) win, because . . . .

(D) win, because . . . .

Since the odd option is unaccompanied by a reason, it is impossible to select it without eliminating the other three first. For this reason, when confronted by a three-to-one options item, always consider the odd option last. Then choose it only if all of the others have received "F"s.

## What-if options

Sometimes the options offer additional facts and the stem calls for selection of the fact pattern that would be most likely to bring about a particular result. This kind of item is like the classroom game in which the professor changes the facts in a case under discussion by saying, "Now, what if . . . ?"

[*Typical stem:* Which of the following additional facts or inferences, if it was the only one true, would be most likely to result in a judgment for the plaintiff?]

It is important to remember that this kind of item does not require you to decide whether the additional fact or inference in the "what if" option is true; it directs you to assume that it is. If you encounter one of these, combine the stem with each "what-if" option in turn, accepting as true the facts that it contains. In assigning a "T" or "F," don't ask whether the facts are true or the inference is justified; assume that they are. Then decide whether the existence of these additional facts or inferences would be likely to bring about the particular result (*e.g.*, in the previous item, ask, "If this fact were true or this inference were justified, would it result in a judgment for the plaintiff?").

# SELECTING THE CORRECT OPTION

Selecting the correct option is easy once you've placed three "F"s and one "T" next to the given options. The hard part is deciding whether to give an option a "T" or "F." This becomes easier if an appropriate strategy is applied. Although the MBE will present you with 800 options (*i.e.*, four for each question), all options fall into only two categories. Our Multistate Method provides a strategy to use for each of the categories.

## Simple options

Some options only state possible conclusions. These are called "simple options." Here's a typical simple-option item:

> A man took a diamond ring to a pawnshop and borrowed $20 on it. It was agreed that the loan was to be repaid within 60 days, and if it was not, the pawnshop owner, the defendant, could sell the ring. A week before the expiration of the 60 days, the defendant had an opportunity to sell the ring to a customer for $125. He did so, thinking it was unlikely that the man would repay the loan and that if he did, the defendant would be able to handle him somehow, even by paying for the ring if necessary. Two days later, the man came in with the money to reclaim his ring. The defendant told him that it had been stolen when his shop was burglarized one night and that therefore he was not responsible for its loss. Larceny, embezzlement, and false pretenses are separate crimes in the jurisdiction.
>
> Which of the following crimes has the defendant most likely committed?
>
> (A) Larceny.
> (B) Embezzlement.
> (C) Larceny by trick.
> (D) Obtaining by false pretenses.

These options are "simple" rather than "complex," but not "simple" rather than "difficult." Since nothing is given but a bare conclusion, simple options usually require the most work. In dealing with each simple option, it is necessary to remember the essential elements of whatever rule of law is applicable and to check the root to see whether every one of those elements is satisfied by the facts given.

In the previous example, to decide whether to mark option (A) with a "T" or "F," it is first necessary to remember that larceny is the trespassory taking and carrying off of personal property known to be another's with the intent to permanently deprive. Then it is necessary to return to the root to see whether the defendant trespassorily took the ring, whether he carried it off, whether he knew that the ring belonged to another, and whether he had the intent to permanently deprive. The option can receive a "T" only if all the elements of the crime are satisfied by the facts.

In the real world, it is likely that some of these elements will raise questions of fact for a jury to determine or questions of law that ultimately will be decided by an appellate court. Different juries may come up with different answers to the questions of fact, and different appellate courts may come up with different answers to the questions of law. An MBE item must have three options that are clearly incorrect, however, and one that is clearly correct. This means that the facts must be structured so as to make it clear that at least one of the elements of the rule applicable in each option is unsatisfied.

In the previous example, the defendant's act cannot be larceny (option A) because there was clearly no trespassory taking. A defendant trespassorily takes when he or she receives possession contrary to the rights of the owner. Since the defendant received possession of the ring lawfully, with the man's consent, and with no improper purpose, he did not trespassorily take it and cannot be guilty of larceny. Larceny by trick (option C) is committed by fraudulently obtaining temporary possession of personal property known to be another's. Since the defendant was not planning to do so when he obtained the ring from the man, he cannot be guilty of larceny by trick. Obtaining by false pretenses (option D) is committed by fraudulently inducing another to transfer title to a chattel. Since the man never transferred title to the ring, the defendant cannot be guilty of obtaining it by false pretenses. As can be seen, options A, C, and D are clearly incorrect.

At the same time, the facts must establish that all the elements of the rule supporting the correct option are satisfied. Embezzlement (option B) is committed by criminally converting property of which the defendant has lawful custody. Since the man delivered the ring to the defendant before the defendant developed the intent to steal it, the defendant's custody was clearly lawful. Because only a person with the right to do so is entitled to sell a chattel, and because the defendant did not have the right to sell it, his sale of the ring was clearly a criminal conversion. Since all the elements of embezzlement are clearly satisfied, (B) must be the correct option.

## Complex options

Most of the time, an option will consist of two parts: a conclusion and a reason giving rise to the conclusion. Here's a typical complex-option item:

> The plaintiff was eating in a restaurant when he began to choke on a piece of food that had lodged in his throat. The defendant, a physician who was dining at a nearby table, did not wish to become involved and did not render any assistance, although prompt medical attention would have been effective in removing the obstruction from the plaintiff's throat. Because of the failure to obtain prompt medical attention, the plaintiff suffered severe brain injury from lack of oxygen. The jurisdiction had a statute that relieved physicians of malpractice liability for emergency first aid. When the defendant saw the plaintiff choking, he knew the plaintiff was substantially certain to sustain serious injury.
>
> If the plaintiff asserts a claim against the defendant for his injuries, the court should find for
>
> (A) the defendant, because the defendant did not cause the piece of food to lodge in the plaintiff's throat.

> (B) the plaintiff, because a reasonably prudent person with the defendant's experience, training, and knowledge would have assisted the plaintiff.
>
> (C) the plaintiff, because the jurisdiction has a statute which relieves physicians of malpractice liability for emergency first aid.
>
> (D) the defendant, because the defendant knew that the plaintiff was substantially certain to sustain serious injury.

## "Because" as a conjunction

It is important to understand what an option built around the conjunction "because" or its synonym "since" means. An option of this kind actually makes two statements. If I say, "The street is wet *because* it is raining," my conclusion is "the street is wet," and my reason is "it is raining." If it isn't raining, my whole statement is false. Even if it is raining, my statement is true only if the rain is what is making the street wet.

To decide whether to give the option a "T" or "F," we must first determine whether the reason given is based on an accurate statement. In the real world, we can find out whether it is raining by looking out the window. In an MBE option, if the reason given involves a statement about the facts, we must return to the root to see whether the facts are accurate. If the reason involves a statement about the law, we must search our bank of knowledge to see whether it states the law accurately. If the reason is based on an inaccurate statement of either facts or law, the option gets an "F."

But even if the reason given is based on an accurate statement of the facts or law (*i.e.*, it is actually raining), we cannot give the option a "T" unless the reason logically justifies the conclusion. Since rain does make the street wet, the reason given in the previous statement (*i.e.*, it is raining) justifies the conclusion (*i.e.*, the street is wet), and the entire statement is correct. If the statement is, "The street is wet because the sun is shining," the statement is incorrect even if the sun is shining, because sunshine does not make the street wet.

Option (A) in the previous item says that the court should find for "the defendant, because the defendant did not cause the piece of food to lodge in the plaintiff's throat." Since the reason given (*i.e.*, the defendant did not cause the piece of food to lodge in the plaintiff's throat) is a statement about the facts, we must return to the root to see whether it is accurate. According to the root, the defendant happened to be dining at a nearby table when the plaintiff began choking on food. Since there is no fact indicating that the defendant had anything to do with the food in the plaintiff's throat, the reason is based on an accurate statement about the facts. So far, option A is valid.

Next, we must decide whether the fact that the defendant did not cause the food to lodge in the plaintiff's throat justifies the conclusion that the court should find for the defendant. Here, of course, it is necessary to rely on our knowledge of the law. Under the law of negligence, a defendant is generally not under a duty to assist a plaintiff in peril unless the defendant did something to cause that peril. Since the defendant did not cause the food to lodge in the plaintiff's throat, the defendant had no obligation to help remove it, and his failure to do so cannot result in liability. Since the reason is an accurate statement, and since it logically justifies the conclusion with which it is coupled, option A should receive a "T."

If option A states the reason as follows: "The court should find for the defendant *because the plaintiff's brain injury resulted from a lack of oxygen*," the option would be incorrect. The root states that the plaintiff's brain injury was caused by a lack of oxygen, and this establishes that the reason is based on an accurate statement of the facts. But the medical cause of an injury does not necessarily determine whether a particular defendant is liable. Thus, the reason given does not justify the conclusion to which it is coupled, and the option should receive an "F."

Option (B) is incorrect because it is a misstatement of the law. Since a defendant is generally not under a duty to assist a plaintiff in peril unless the defendant did something to cause the peril in the first place, the defendant's liability is not measured by what any other person would have done. Since the fact that a reasonably prudent person with the defendant's experience, training, and knowledge would have assisted the plaintiff would not justify the conclusion that the court should find for the plaintiff, option (B) should receive an "F." Option (C) references a statute that is in effect in the jurisdiction (a common distractor in MBE questions). Here, the question tells you that the jurisdiction has a statute that relieves physicians of malpractice liability for emergency first aid. Where they exist, statutes of the kind described (*i.e.*, Good Samaritan laws) protect a physician who renders aid, but they do not require that he or she render aid. For this reason, the existence of such a statute would not impose a duty on the defendant and would not be relevant to the defendant's liability. Its existence would not make him or her liable. For this reason, this option should receive an "F." Option (D) also relies upon our knowledge of the law. A defendant who performs a voluntary act with the knowledge that it is substantially certain to result in injury intends that injury and may be liable for causing it. Intentional tort liability cannot be based on a failure to act, however, unless there was an obligation to act in the first place. Because of the rule that provides that a defendant has no duty to assist a plaintiff in peril unless the defendant caused that peril, the defendant had no obligation to assist the plaintiff. Thus, even if he was substantially certain that his failure to do so would result in injury, he is not liable for the injury. The option should receive an "F."

## PRACTICE MAKES BETTER

Anyone who says that practice makes perfect is telling a tall tale; no one and nothing can be perfect. Practice does lead to improvement, though. No matter how good you are at answering Multistate-type questions now, the more you practice, the better you'll get at it. If you know your law, practicing our Multistate Method will equip you with a strategy for achieving success on the MBE.

People who think that there is a way to get the actual MBE questions in advance are dreaming. It's true that each MBE contains 50 questions that have been used before. But the examiners publish only the ones that they will not use again. So if you have a compilation of released questions, such as *Strategies & Tactics for the MBE*, don't expect to see any of them on your exam.

Some publishers and bar reviewers take the exam every time it is given and tell you that their books contain verbatim copies of all the questions that were on it. This is an empty promise. There's no such thing as a fully photographic memory. Nobody can take a six-hour exam and come out of it remembering even a single question word for word. MBE questions are written so precisely that even a slight change of wording alters the effect of the entire question.

Instead of trying to find out what the questions are going to be, concentrate on mastering the Method so that you'll be ready for whatever comes. The questions in this book are similar to those that the Multistate Bar Examiners use.

Try to deal with each item by using the Method outlined in this chapter. Start by orienting yourself to the item with a quick reading of the stem and root, paying careful attention to the role that each assigns to you. Then apply the basic game plan, treating each option as a separate true-false choice and marking it with a "T," "F," or "?."

The MBE is a very special game because it's a game played only by prospective lawyers. Some will be winners, and others will be losers. Decide in advance which you intend to be and build your whole attitude from that basic decision. When you've learned to think of the MBE as a game, you may even find that you look forward to playing it. Afterwards, you may hear yourself saying that it was fun. Nevertheless, it's a game you don't want to play more than once. So practice, practice, practice.

# QUESTIONS
## CIVIL PROCEDURE

# CIVIL PROCEDURE
# TABLE OF CONTENTS
**Numbers refer to Question Numbers**

# CIVIL PROCEDURE

1. A woman was injured when her car collided with a man's vehicle in State A. The woman was a citizen of State B, and the man was a citizen of State C. The woman filed her complaint in federal court in State C based on diversity jurisdiction. Because the man was deceased, she named the man's executor as defendant. The executor was also a citizen of State C. Because the executor was not home at the time the woman served her complaint, she left it with the executor's wife as allowed under the applicable federal rule. However, both the State C rule and the State A rule required personal service of process on executors of estates. The executor moved for summary judgment, arguing service was invalid because the woman failed to personally serve him with the complaint.

   The court should

   (A) grant the motion, because the federal court must apply the law of the state in which it is sitting.

   (B) grant the motion, because the federal court must apply the law of the state in which the claim arose.

   (C) deny the motion, because the motion for summary judgment will affect the woman's substantive rights.

   (D) deny the motion, because the rule is arguably procedural.

2. A man sued a company in federal court for claims based on the federal National Labor Relations Act. Thirty days after the service of the last pleading, the man's lawyer filed and served a demand for a jury trial. The court granted the demand, finding juries normally tried such claims and there was no compelling reason not to do so.

   Is the court's decision correct?

   (A) Yes, because the court has the discretion to allow an untimely request for a jury trial.

   (B) Yes, because there is no indication the man intended to waive his right to a jury trial.

   (C) No, the right to a jury trial is waived unless demand is made within 14 days after service of the last pleading.

   (D) No, a jury trial demand must be made in the initial complaint.

3. A musician, a citizen of State A, sued a company in federal court, claiming the company violated his federal copyright in a song he had written when the company used it as an advertising jingle without his permission. The company was incorporated in State B, and all of its executives and other decision-makers were headquartered in State C. The musician sought $30,000 in damages. Later, the woman who co-wrote the song, who was a citizen of State B, was allowed to join the lawsuit. She claimed $100,000 in damages.

   The company moved to dismiss the lawsuit for lack of subject-matter jurisdiction. How should the court rule?

   (A) Deny the motion, because the woman's claim can be added to the musician's to meet the amount in controversy requirement.

   (B) Deny the motion, because the musician is making a federal copyright claim.

   (C) Grant the motion, because the woman is a citizen of State B.

   (D) Grant the motion, because the musician is only claiming $30,000 in damages.

4. After a man, a citizen of State A, was injured in an automobile accident, he sued several

defendants for $100,000 in damages in state court in State B. The man sued a truck driver, a citizen of State B, a doctor, a citizen of State C, and a company, incorporated in State C and had headquartered in State D. The doctor filed a notice of removal to federal court in State B. Neither the truck driver nor the company objected to removal.

Can the suit be removed to federal court?

(A)  Yes, because neither the truck driver nor the company objected.

(B)  Yes, because the case could have originally been brought in federal court.

(C)  No, because no federal question is involved.

(D)  No, because the truck driver is a citizen of State B.

5.  A doctor, a citizen of State A, sued a pharmaceutical company, incorporated in State B and with its primary place of business in State B, in federal court in State B. The doctor claimed $500,000 in damages based on breach of contract and tortious interference claims, arguing the actions of the company made it impossible for him to make necessary contracts with medical suppliers in State C, where he also had a practice.

In deciding the doctor's claims, what law regarding contracts and torts should the court apply?

(A)  The law of State A, because a plaintiff is the master of his or her claim.

(B)  The law of State B, because jurisdiction is based on diversity.

(C)  The law of State C, because this is where the claim arose.

(D)  The federal common law, because the doctor chose to sue in federal court.

6.  After being injured by faulty construction work that was done on her home, a woman, a citizen of State A, sued a contractor, a citizen of State B, in federal court in State B. The

woman claimed $30,000 for personal injuries, $40,000 for breach of contract, and $10,000 for negligence. After a trial, the jury only awarded $10,000 in damages for the woman's personal injuries, and $10,000 in damages for negligence. The contractor then challenged the verdict, arguing the federal court lacked jurisdiction over the claim. Did the federal court have proper jurisdiction?

(A)  Yes, because the amount in controversy was over $75,000.

(B)  Yes, because the contractor waived jurisdiction by not challenging it when the complaint was filed.

(C)  No, because the woman was only awarded $20,000 total.

(D)  No, because no individual claim was in excess of $75,000.

7.  A freelance writer sued a magazine in federal court claiming federal civil rights violations. The court believed the claims made in the writer's complaint put the magazine on notice and supported a possible claim, but not a plausible one.

Does the writer's complaint fulfill the applicable requirements of the federal rules?

(A)  Yes, because it put the magazine on notice.

(B)  Yes, because it supported a possible claim.

(C)  No, because it did not contain detailed assertions of the facts underlying the claim.

(D)  No, because it did not support a plausible claim.

8.  A man was called as a juror in a case brought in federal court against his boss. During voir dire, he stated that he was positive he could be fair and impartial, was planning to start a new job in a few months in a different state, and had no strong feelings or prior knowledge regarding the issues brought in the plaintiff's complaint.

Would it be proper for the juror to be excused?

(A) Yes, because his boss was one of the parties.

(B) Yes, because it is likely he had an actual bias in favor of his boss.

(C) No, because he was positive he could be fair and impartial.

(D) No, because he had no strong feelings or prior knowledge regarding the issues brought in the complaint.

9. A filmmaker from State A filed suit against a producer from State B in State B federal court. The filmmaker claimed $100,000 in damages related to business dealings between the two men. The state rules for service of process were identical to the federal ones. In order to serve the summons and complaint, the filmmaker first went to the producer's business office, but the producer was not there. Two adult employees, members of the company's executive team working on the new video game that was at the heart of the lawsuit, were at the office, and offered to accept service. Just as the employees made their offer, the producer's administrative assistant, who had just turned 18 years old that day, returned from lunch and offered to accept service. At the same time, the producer's wife arrived at the office and said she would take it. The filmmaker declined the offers and went to the producer's home to see if he was there. When he knocked on the door, the producer's adult sister answered the door. Although she had nothing to do with the producer's business, she told the filmmaker she had been living with her brother for two years and would accept service of the complaint.

Who would be the most appropriate person to accept service?

(A) The members of the executive team, because they are company decision makers.

(B) The sister, because she lives with the producer.

(C) The administrative assistant, because she has implied authority to act on the producer's behalf.

(D) The wife, because she is married to the producer.

10. A woman, a citizen of State A, sued a doctor, a citizen of State B, in federal court in State B, claiming $200,000 in damages after she had an adverse reaction to a drug the doctor prescribed her. The doctor filed a motion for summary judgment, arguing State B's statute of limitations for claims such as the woman's had already expired. The woman countered that her claim was filed well within the federal statute of limitations.

The court should rule in favor of

(A) the woman, because statutes of limitation are arguably procedural.

(B) the woman, because the federal court applies federal common law in determining the appropriate statute of limitations.

(C) the doctor, because statutes of limitations are substantive law.

(D) the doctor, because the federal court should apply the law of the state in which it is sitting.

11. A company filed a diversity action in federal district court in State A against a man for breach of contract. After a trial, the district court found the applicable law of contracts in State A was unsettled. However, the district court ultimately determined that the highest court in the state would likely rule in favor of the company on that particular issue. The man appealed, arguing the district court misinterpreted state law. The court of appeals affirmed, stating it would defer to the district court's determination of state law since it was seated in that state.

Was the court of appeals decision correct?

(A) Yes, because the challenged law is substantive.

(B) Yes, because the district court sits in State A.

(C) No, because the district court was determining unsettled state law.

(D) No, because the district court should have sent the question to the state's highest court for a determination.

12. A man, a citizen of State A, sued a company, incorporated in State B and with its primary headquarters in State C, in federal district court in State A for $100,000 in damages after he was injured by one of the company's products. The company filed a pre-answer motion to dismiss, arguing the court lacked jurisdiction based on diversity because it was unlikely a court would award the man more than $500. The court denied the motion. In its subsequent answer, the company argued the case should be dismissed because the court lacked personal jurisdiction over it since it had never tried to make money in State A or use any of State A's roads.

If the company is correct in its assertion, the court should

(A) dismiss the action, because the company did not purposefully avail itself of the privilege of conducting activities within the forum state.

(B) dismiss the action, because exercise of jurisdiction would not be fair and reasonable.

(C) not dismiss the action, because the company did not raise the issue in its first motion.

(D) not dismiss the action, because the company put a product into the stream of commerce.

13. An independent contractor, a citizen of State A, sued a company, incorporated in State B and with its primary place of business in State C, in federal district court. The contractor claimed $100,000 for false imprisonment, stating "the contractor was confined in a storage room overnight when a company employee negligently locked the door with the contractor still inside." The contractor did not suffer any physical harm caused by his time in the storage room.

The company filed a motion to dismiss. How should the court rule?

(A) Grant the motion, because the contractor failed to state a claim.

(B) Grant the motion, because it is unlikely a court would award over $75,000 in damages in this case.

(C) Deny the motion, because the complaint puts the company on notice of the claim being asserted.

(D) Deny the motion, because there is no indication that it is impossible for recovery to be over $75,000.

14. A man owned a home in State A and lived there for 30 years. After meeting a woman online, he decided to sell his house and move to her home in State B for the foreseeable future to "give love a try." Three days later, the man was involved in an accident with a doctor who was domiciled in State B. He sued the doctor for $100,000 in federal district court in State B. Shortly after filing his suit, the man moved back to State A when his relationship with the woman unexpectedly ended after a fight. The doctor moved to dismiss for lack of subject matter jurisdiction.

Does the district court have jurisdiction over the claim?

(A) Yes, because the man was a citizen of State A when the injury occurred.

(B) Yes, because the man was a citizen of State A when the suit was filed.

(C) No, because the man was a citizen of State B when the injury occurred.

(D) No, because the man was a citizen of State B when the suit was filed.

15. A man, a citizen of State A, bought a life insurance online from a company based in State B. Several years later, a company based in State C agreed to assume the obligations of the State B company and mailed a reinsurance certificate to the man. The man accepted the new offer and paid premiums by mail from State A to the company's office in State C. The State C company had no other contacts with State A. When the man died, the company refused to pay the beneficiary of the policy because it believed the man had committed suicide, which wasn't covered under the policy. The beneficiary sued the company in State A pursuant to State A's long arm statute. The company argued the State A court had no personal jurisdiction over it.

Does the State A court have personal jurisdiction over the company?

(A) Yes, because of State A's interest in protecting its residents in cases like this.

(B) Yes, because the original policy was purchased online.

(C) No, because the company did not have sufficient minimum contacts with State A.

(D) No, because any judgment would violate the company's due process rights.

16. A truck driver from State A sued a trucking company in State A court for violations of the state's wage and hours laws. The truck driver claimed over $200,000 in damages. The trucking company moved to have the case removed to federal district court. The trucking company was incorporated in State B and all of its directors and top management who directed the company worked in State B. However, the company had 60 percent of its trucking fleet, its truck-driving school, and all of its repair centers in State A.

Is removal of the claim to federal district court appropriate?

(A) Yes, because the company is incorporated in State B.

(B) Yes, because the company is directed from State B.

(C) No, because the company has done a significant amount of business in State A.

(D) No, because the truck driver's claims are based on State A law.

17. A woman sued a company in federal court, claiming several violations of federal patent law. During discovery, the woman's attorney inadvertently disclosed a draft report written by one of the woman's expert witnesses to the opposing party.

May the attorney still claim work-product protection for the draft report?

(A) Yes, by notifying the company of the accidental disclosure.

(B) Yes, by asking the court for a protective order.

(C) No, because the attorney waived work-product protection by disclosing the report.

(D) No, because the report was not the final report intended for trial.

18. In 2016, a woman sued a company in federal court after a remote-controlled toy sold by the company exploded and severely injured her. She sent a discovery request to the company asking for "all electronically stored sales records relating to sales of the toys from 2006–2016." Although the company could produce the records for 2013–2016, the remaining sales records had been deleted a month before the woman had filed suit. The company said that under a new cost-saving initiative, it had started routinely deleting all sales records more than three years old to free up space on the company's computers. However, now that the suit had been filed, it had suspended the deletions. The woman contacted a computer expert, who said it might be possible to recover the lost records if the company had an old machine that had been retired from use before the routine

deletions, but that finding the records would be very expensive and might not recover anything. The woman argued the company should pay for the necessary experts to find the missing information.

If the company does not produce the missing information, should the court order it to do so?

(A) Yes, because the company intentionally deleted the requested information.

(B) Yes, because the information was potentially recoverable.

(C) No, because the deletions were done as part of the company's cost-saving initiative.

(D) No, because it was reasonable for the company to delete sales records that were more than three years old.

19. A man sued a doctor in federal court. The doctor decided to answer the complaint. Which of the following potential defenses will not be waived if doctor does not include the defense in his answer?

(A) Insufficient service of process.

(B) Improper venue.

(C) Lack of personal jurisdiction.

(D) Lack of subject matter jurisdiction.

20. After staying in a hotel in State A, a woman, a resident of State B, sued the hotel for breach of contract in a state court in State B. The hotel was incorporated and located in State A. The hotel did not do any business in State B, nor did it have any bank accounts or employees in State B. However, the hotel did advertise on a billboard in State B and its Internet site gave driving directions from several cities in State B, advertised its proximity to State B, and accepted reservations and credit card payments from people all over the world (including people in State B).

Is the hotel subject to personal jurisdiction in State B?

(A) Yes, because its advertising and Internet site targeted State B consumers.

(B) Yes, because it advertised on a billboard in State B.

(C) No, because it did not do any business in State B.

(D) No, because the injury occurred in State A.

21. A woman, a shareholder of a company, brought a class action lawsuit on behalf of herself and all other shareholders against the company in federal district court. The woman claimed $10,000 in damages, and noted that there were approximately 50 shareholders of company stock. If all 50 claims were aggregated, the amount in controversy would be $500,000 dollars.

Would the federal district court have subject matter jurisdiction over the claim?

(A) Yes, because it is being brought as a class action.

(B) Yes, because the aggregated amount in controversy exceeds $75,000.

(C) No, because there is no indication all shareholders will agree to join the action.

(D) No, because there is no indication any individual claim exceeds $75,000.

22. In 2016, a man, a citizen of State A, sued a woman, a citizen of State B, in federal district court in State B. The man and woman had been married for 10 years in State A before they were granted a divorce by a court in State A. The woman moved to State B in 2015. During the original divorce proceedings, the woman was granted custody of the couple's children, who were born in State A. The man now seeks custody of the children and alimony in excess of $75,000.

Does the federal court have jurisdiction over the case?

- (A) Yes, because the woman moved to State B.

- (B) Yes, because the children were born in State A.

- (C) No, because the divorce was granted by State A.

- (D) No, because the man is seeking custody of the children and alimony.

23. A student, who is a citizen of Ireland, sued a restaurant, incorporated in State A and with all of its offices in State A, in federal district court in State A. The student claimed $50,000 in personal injury and $50,000 for breach of contract.

    Does the federal court have jurisdiction over the claim?

    - (A) Yes, because the student is a foreign national.

    - (B) Yes, because the amount in controversy is over $75,000.

    - (C) No, because the personal injury and contract claims cannot be aggregated.

    - (D) No, because there is no indication the defendant consented to the federal court's jurisdiction.

24. A man, a citizen of State A, sued a woman, a citizen of State B, for $100,000 in personal injuries caused by an automobile accident between the two. After a trial in federal district court, the court ruled in favor of the woman and awarded no damages to the man. The woman then filed suit in the same federal district court for $100,000 in personal injuries she suffered in the same accident. Soon thereafter, the man moved to State B, intending to stay there indefinitely.

    May the woman file her claim in the federal court?

- (A) Yes, because the federal court had subject matter jurisdiction over the first action regarding the accident.

- (B) Yes, because citizenship is determined at the time the suit is filed.

- (C) No, because the woman's claim is barred under the compulsory counterclaim rule.

- (D) No, because the woman's claim is barred by res judicata.

25. A man sued a company in federal court claiming violations of federal civil rights and employment laws. Ten days after service of the last pleading directed to an important fact issue, the man filed a written demand for a jury trial on that issue with the court and served it on the company. Ten days after his demand, the man reconsidered and moved to have his jury demand withdrawn. The company opposed the man's motion.

    How should the court rule on the man's motion?

    - (A) Allow the motion, because the man made the original jury demand.

    - (B) Allow the motion, because the man made the motion within 21 days of the last pleading directed to the issue.

    - (C) Deny the motion, because the man did not request withdrawal within seven days of the jury demand.

    - (D) Deny the motion, because the company did not consent to the withdrawal.

26. State A sent a certified letter to a homeowner informing him that if he did not pay his delinquent tax bill his property would be put up for public sale. By state law, the homeowner was required to keep his mailing address updated, but he had failed to do so when he had moved out of the home and into an apartment he owned in a nearby city. Consequently, the letter was returned as "unclaimed" to the state. The state took no

further action before putting the property up for public sale 20 days later.

After his property was sold, the homeowner sued, claiming the state had violated his due process rights by failing to notify him of the sale. Was the state's notification of the sale sufficient?

(A) Yes, because the state sent notification by certified mail to the homeowner's last known address.

(B) Yes, because the state sent notification by certified mail to the property that was subject to the delinquent tax bill.

(C) No, because the letter was returned undelivered.

(D) No, because the property was put up for sale less than 60 days after the letter was returned.

27. After a jury trial in federal district court based on diversity jurisdiction, the court believed the jury's compensatory damage award met the state standard for excessiveness. Consequently, the court offered the plaintiff the choice of either accepting a lower award than that given by the jury or submitting to a new trial.

May the court do so?

(A) Yes, because the court believed the award was excessive under the state standard.

(B) Yes, because the court could simply lower the jury's award if it chose to do so.

(C) No, because there was no indication the jury's award was so excessive as to "shock the conscience."

(D) No, because forcing the plaintiff to accept a potentially lower award violates the Seventh Amendment.

28. In what situation may a court grant a party relief from a final judgment on the basis that the final judgment is void?

(A) When the party discovers new evidence that by due diligence could not have been discovered in time to move for a new trial.

(B) When the party is deprived of due process by failure to give notice.

(C) When fraud has been committed by the adverse party.

(D) When there has been a clerical omission in the court's judgment.

29. The owner of a gas station, who was a citizen of State A, sued a trucking company in federal district court. The trucking company was incorporated in State B, had its entire fleet of trucks and all of its repair centers in State C, and operated its trucks in 48 states. However, the company's CEO and other decision-making officers were based in State A. The gas station owner claimed $20,000 in actual damages and $1 million in punitive damages, arguing the trucking company violated federal trucking laws by habitually using a vacant strip of land adjoining the owner's gas station as a place to move hazardous cargo from one truck to another as trucks passed through the state.

Does the federal district court have subject matter jurisdiction over the owner's claim?

(A) Yes, because the claim involves a question of interstate commerce.

(B) Yes, because the owner's claim is based on federal law.

(C) No, because the owner is only claiming $20,000 in actual damages.

(D) No, because the trucking company is also a citizen of State A.

30. A songwriter sued a singer in federal court, claiming violation of federal copyright laws. The songwriter notified the singer that he

planned to depose him for trial. However, on the day of the singer's deposition, the singer failed to appear.

Was the notice of deposition sufficient to compel the singer's appearance at the deposition?

(A) Yes, because the singer is an adverse party.

(B) Yes, because there is likely substantial need for the singer's deposition.

(C) No, because the songwriter did not subpoena the singer.

(D) No, because the singer will likely be called to testify at trial.

31. A woman sued a man in federal district court, claiming his use of her artwork on his blog constituted a violation of federal copyright law. The man defended himself by arguing that his use of the artwork met the legal definition of "fair use" under the applicable law because his blog was educational and he was writing critically about the artwork. The federal district court ruled in favor of the man, finding the way he used the artwork met the legal definition of "fair use." The woman appealed the decision.

What standard of review will the appellate court use in making a decision regarding whether the use of the artwork was "fair use"?

(A) De novo, because whether the use meets the legal definition of "fair use" is a question of fact.

(B) De novo, because whether the use meets the legal definition of "fair use" is a mixed question of law and fact.

(C) Abuse of discretion, because whether the use meets the legal definition of "fair use" is a question of fact.

(D) "Clearly erroneous," because whether the use meets the legal definition of "fair use" is a matter of law.

32. A city in State A sued the county claiming that the county's occupation tax violated both the State A and Federal Constitutions. The court ruled in favor of the county, finding the tax was lawful under both constitutions. Several county employees in State A then brought a class action suit against the county, challenging the same tax on the same basis as the prior claim. The county employees received no notice of the earlier lawsuit nor were they represented in the prior claim.

Are the employees barred from asserting their claim?

(A) Yes, because their claim is barred by res judicata.

(B) Yes, because their claim is barred by claim preclusion.

(C) No, because the employees did not receive notice of the earlier suit.

(D) No, because the employees are bringing their claim as a class action.

33. A man believed his business partner was stealing money from their business. Consequently, he sought a temporary restraining order from the court. Which of the following four requirements are not necessary for the court to grant a temporary restraining order without notice of a hearing to the man's business partner?

(A) The man must provide some security to pay for any costs or damages if the partner is wrongfully restrained.

(B) The man must certify in writing the efforts he made to give notice to his business partner and the reasons why the court should not require notice.

(C) The man must have first moved for and been granted a preliminary injunction against his partner.

(D) The man must give the court specific facts showing he will suffer immediate and irreparable injury.

34. An alternative energy company, incorporated in State A, placed 100 large wind turbines five miles off the coast of State B for the purpose of generating electric power for the citizens of State A, B, and C. After a hurricane, many of the turbines were destroyed. Much of the wreckage ended up in a State B city's harbor, making the harbor inaccessible to its large scallop and fishing fleet for several weeks. While some of the ships were able to sail farther up the coast to another harbor in State C, several tons of seafood were lost or spoiled because the ships couldn't offload their cargo fast enough. Although there was no way to clearly calculate the damages, city accountants estimated that the city lost at least $1 million in port fees and fish processing costs.

The city sued the energy company in federal court, and the company moved to dismiss for lack of subject matter jurisdiction. Does the federal court have jurisdiction over the city's suit?

(A) Yes, because the city's claim is substantially related to interstate commerce.

(B) Yes, because the incident was substantially related to maritime activity.

(C) No, because all of the company's turbines were off the coast of State B.

(D) No, because all of the company's turbines were less than 10 miles offshore.

35. After severe flooding in State A, the Federal Emergency Management Association issued a check to a woman in State A to fix her home's air conditioning and heating units. Before the woman received the check, it was stolen from her mail carrier and cashed with the woman's forged signature at a small check-cashing business. The check was then turned over to a bank in State A, and the bank collected the funds owed on the check from the Federal Reserve. Eight months later, when the United States learned the check had been stolen, it sued the bank in federal district court in State A to recover the amount of the check. The bank responded that the applicable statute of limitations in State A barred the lawsuit because the federal district court was located in State A and there was no federal statue on point regarding the issue. The United States argued that there was no applicable statute of limitations under federal common law.

The federal district court ruled that State A law applied to the action and the United States was barred from bringing its suit. Is the district court's decision correct?

(A) Yes, because federal courts cannot create federal common law.

(B) Yes, because the federal court must follow the substantive law of State A.

(C) No, because the law is arguably procedural.

(D) No, because the action involves the obligations of the United States.

36. A man from the Northern District of State A got in an auto accident in the Eastern District of State B with a truck driver from the Western District of State C, a security guard from the Western District of State C, and a doctor from the Southern District of State D. The man sued the truck driver, the security guard, and the doctor in federal court based on diversity jurisdiction.

In which judicial districts would venue be proper for the man's action?

(A) The Eastern District of State B.

(B) The Northern District of State A, the Western District of State C, and the Southern District of State D.

(C) The Western District of State C and the Southern District of State D.

(D) The Western District of State C.

37. Which of the following motions is lost if a party fails to make it before filing an answer to a complaint?

(A) Motion to dismiss for lack of subject matter jurisdiction.

(B) Motion to dismiss for lack of personal jurisdiction.

(C) Motion for a more definite statement.

(D) Motion to dismiss for insufficient service of process.

38. A football player sued a doctor in federal district court. If the complaint was mailed to her and she waived formal service, how long does the doctor have to answer the complaint?

   (A) Within 14 days after receipt of the complaint.

   (B) Within 21 days after receipt of the complaint.

   (C) Within 21 days after the complaint was mailed.

   (D) Within 60 days after the request for waiver was mailed.

39. A man was a huge fan of a science fiction movie franchise. He owned every piece of merchandise that had ever been produced, every single book, and was the founding member of a group of people who dressed up as the franchise's characters and went to sporting events, carnivals, and other events. Finally, he named all of his children after franchise characters and turned his car into a life-size model of one of the franchise's spaceships. After a 20-year gap between movies, the franchise finally released a new film. The man went to go see it and thought it was terrible. In fact, he thought it was so terrible that it ruined everything he had ever liked about the franchise. Consequently, he sued the franchise's owners in federal court for damages to compensate him for having to buy a new car, rename his children, and sell all of his merchandise.

How should the franchise's owners respond to the man's complaint?

(A) Make a motion for a more definite statement.

(B) Make a motion for summary judgment.

(C) Make a motion for declaratory judgment.

(D) Make a motion to dismiss for failure to state a claim.

40. A poet sued a playwright in federal district court in State A, claiming the playwright copied a play written by the poet and produced it in a theater in State A. The poet claimed violations of both federal copyright law and State A unfair competition laws. The playwright moved to dismiss the unfair competition claim for lack of subject matter jurisdiction.

Does the federal district court have jurisdiction over the state claim?

   (A) Yes, because success on the federal claim is a prerequisite to success on the state claim.

   (B) Yes, because both claims arose out of production of the play in State A.

   (C) No, because the federal claim does not create pendent jurisdiction over the state claim.

   (D) No, because the unfair competition claim is governed by State A substantive law.

41. A model, a citizen of State A, sued a lawyer and an accountant in state court in State A for injuries sustained during a fight at a baseball game. The lawyer was a citizen of State A, and the accountant was a citizen of State B. The model claimed $100,000 in damages for cuts to his face and a broken nose that cost him several important modeling jobs. A year after filing suit, a surveillance tape at the stadium was discovered. It showed that the lawyer was not involved in the fight at all, so the model dismissed his claim against him. Twenty days after the dismissal, the accoun-

tant sought removal of the case to federal district court in State A.

Can the accountant have the case removed to federal court?

(A) Yes, because the lawyer's dismissal was based on newly discovered evidence.

(B) Yes, because the accountant sought removal within 30 days of the lawyer's dismissal.

(C) No, because the accountant sought removal more than 14 days after the lawyer's dismissal.

(D) No, because the accountant sought removal more than one year after the state court case was commenced.

42. A man, a 55-year-old native of Italy, filed suit in federal district court against his former employer alleging discrimination based on age and national origin. The federal district court dismissed the complaint, finding it failed to allege specific facts constituting a prima facie case of employment discrimination.

Was the federal district court's decision correct?

(A) Yes, because the man needed to show he had a prima facie case before the former employer would be required to answer.

(B) Yes, because the action was based on a federal question.

(C) No, because the man only needed to make a short and plain statement of his claim.

(D) No, because there was no indication that there was no set of facts on which relief could be granted.

43. A marine mechanic finished repairing a boat that was left in his care. After the repairs were done, a man, his ex-wife, and a mortgage lender all claimed to be the true owner of the boat. The mechanic does not want to

keep the boat, and he fears that if he gives it to the wrong person, the other two will sue him for damages.

Under the circumstances, what would be the mechanic's best course of action?

(A) File an interpleader action.

(B) File a declaratory judgment action.

(C) File an impleader action.

(D) File an intervention of right action.

44. A plane traveling from State A to State B crashed in State A, killing all of the passengers. One hundred wrongful death actions against the airline were filed in federal district court in State A. Fifty wrongful death actions against the airline were filed against the airline in State B. State A and State B had very different laws regarding the amount of damages available in wrongful death actions. The airline requested a transfer of the 50 State B actions to State A federal district court based on convenience, noting the crash occurred in State A and the majority of those killed in the crash were State A residents.

If the State B actions are transferred to federal court in State A, what law will the federal court in State A apply to the State B actions?

(A) State A, because the federal district court is sitting in State A.

(B) State A, because the crash occurred in State A.

(C) State B, because the actions originated in State B.

(D) Federal common law, because there is a conflict between the laws of State A and State B.

45. A woman, a citizen of State A, underwent surgery in State B. During the surgery, a medical device that was being implanted in her back snapped and damaged her spine. The woman sued the manufacturer of the device in federal district court in State B and sued

the doctor and the hospital in State B state court. The manufacturer moved to dismiss the woman's action for failure to join the doctor and hospital as necessary parties under Fed. R. Civ. P. 19(a).

Should the federal district court dismiss the woman's case?

(A) No, because the doctor and hospital are joint tortfeasors.

(B) No, because the doctor and hospital are potential defendants in the woman's action.

(C) Yes, because the doctor and hospital are necessary and indispensable parties.

(D) Yes, because the doctor and hospital are likely jointly and severally liable.

46. A cellphone company sued an Internet provider for patent infringement in federal district court. The Internet provider filed a motion to dismiss, and the district court ruled in the Internet provider's favor and awarded attorney's fees and costs. In granting the motion, the court found that the president and sole shareholder of the cellphone company had acted in an inequitable way and that his inequitable conduct was chargeable to the cellphone company. Because it was afraid it would be unable to collect the court's award, the Internet provider moved to amend its pleading to add the president personally under Fed. R. Civ. P. 15 and to amend the judgment to make him immediately liable for the award under Fed. R. Civ. P. 59(e).

Should the court grant the Internet provider's motion?

(A) No, because the president has not had an opportunity to respond to the claim for personal liability.

(B) No, because there is no indication that the new claim was the result of newly discovered evidence.

(C) Yes, because the president was president and sole shareholder of the cellphone company.

(D) Yes, because the president's actions are chargeable to the cellphone company.

47. A man sued a carpenter for negligence in federal district court after a ceiling repaired by the carpenter collapsed and injured the man. The district court ruled in the carpenter's favor, finding he was not negligent in making the repairs. The man then sued the company that employed the carpenter in federal district court, arguing its employee was negligent in repairing the roof.

May the man do so?

(A) No, because his claim is barred by res judicata.

(B) No, because his claim is barred by issue preclusion.

(C) Yes, under the doctrine of *respondeat superior.*

(D) Yes, because the company was not a party to the claim against the carpenter.

48. A processor sued a retailer for violation of one of its patents. Pursuant to Fed. R. Civ. P. 50(a), the retailer moved for judgment as a matter of law, arguing that there was insufficient evidence to support the processor's claim. The court denied the motion and sent the case to the jury. The jury ruled in favor of the processor. The retailer appealed, again arguing that there was insufficient evidence to support the claim. The processor responded that the retailer could not raise the evidence question on appeal because it did not move for either a renewed judgment as a matter of law under Fed. R. Civ. P. 50(b) or for a new trial under Fed. R. Civ. P. 59.

May the court of appeals review the sufficiency of the evidence?

(A) No, because the retailer failed to move for a renewed judgment as a matter of law or a new trial.

(B) No, because the processor received a final judgment from the jury.

(C) Yes, because questions regarding the sufficiency of the evidence may be brought at any time.

(D) Yes, because the retailer had moved for judgment as a matter of law before the jury's verdict.

49. Under which of the following situations is a court LEAST likely to find proper service of process?

(A) The plaintiff personally hands the summons and complaint to the defendant.

(B) A U.S. Marshal leaves the summons and complaint against a company with a company vice president.

(C) An 18-year-old college student leaves the summons and complaint at the defendant's house with the defendant's 18-year-old daughter.

(D) A 21-year-old woman leaves the summons and complaint at the defendant's house with an 18 year old who rents a room there.

50. Which of the following does not require leave of the court or stipulation of the parties?

(A) Deposing a witness more than once.

(B) Deposing a witness from 9–5 on a Monday.

(C) Deposing less than 12 witnesses.

(D) Deposing a witness over the telephone.

51. A student sued a university for racial discrimination in federal district court. During discovery, the student asked for "all items concerning university admission practices." Several years earlier, a professor at the university had written a highly critical internal memorandum concerning the university's admission policies. After the receipt of the memorandum, the university immediately turned it over to the university's attorneys, who were now representing the university in the student's action and used the memorandum in preparing the university's defense. Due to its inflammatory nature and the amount of hearsay it contained, the memorandum was inadmissible at trial.

Does the university have to provide the memorandum to the student?

(A) No, because it is inadmissible evidence.

(B) No, because it is privileged work product.

(C) Yes, because it could lead to the discovery of admissible evidence.

(D) Yes, because it would likely be impossible for the student to obtain the information in any other way.

52. A man, a citizen of State A, and a woman, a citizen of State B, sued a company, incorporated in State B and with its primary place of business in State C, in federal district court in State C after one of the company's trucks got in an auto accident with the man and woman in State C. The man claimed $100,000 in damages, while the woman claimed $30,000 in damages.

Does the federal district court have subject matter jurisdiction over the woman's claim?

(A) Yes, because the man is claiming $100,000 in damages.

(B) Yes, the woman's claim arose from the same auto accident.

(C) No, because the company is incorporated in State B.

(D) No, because the woman's claim is less than $75,000.

53. An artist, a citizen of State A, sued a writer, a citizen of State B in state court in State B for injuries sustained during a fistfight in State B. The artist claimed $30,000 in damages. The writer filed a counterclaim for $80,000 in damages based on the same fight.

   The artist would like to remove the action to federal court based on diversity jurisdiction. May the artist do so?

   (A) No, because the writer's counterclaim is permissive.

   (B) No, because the artist filed the action against the writer.

   (C) Yes, because the amount in controversy is now over $75,000.

   (D) Yes, because the writer's counterclaim is compulsory.

54. A man sued a company for civil rights violations. When the man's attorney failed to comply with a discovery order, the company moved for sanctions under Fed. R. Civ. P. 37(a)(4). The federal district court granted the motion and also disqualified the attorney as counsel. The attorney immediately appealed the order for sanctions. The appellate court dismissed the appeal for lack of jurisdiction.

   Is the appellate court's decision correct?

   (A) No, because the sanctions are immediately appealable under the collateral order doctrine.

   (B) No, because the attorney was disqualified as counsel.

   (C) Yes, because there has been no final decision in the case.

   (D) Yes, because appellate review of the order for sanctions is discretionary.

55. A professor sued an engineer in state court in State A for injuries he received during an auto accident. The court found that the engineer was negligent and ruled in favor of the professor. A woman who was also involved in the accident then sued the engineer in federal court in State B. The woman sought to use issue preclusion to stop the engineer from denying his negligence based on the State A decision. The laws of State A would allow her to do so, but the laws of State B would not.

   May the woman use issue preclusion to stop the engineer from denying his negligence?

   (A) No, because the federal court must follow the laws of State B.

   (B) No, because the woman was not part of the first lawsuit.

   (C) Yes, because the state courts of State A would allow it.

   (D) Yes, because the State A decision would have res judicata effect.

56. A man, who was a citizen of State A, sued a corporation for violations of federal copyright law in state court in State B. His claim was for an injunction that he valued at over $100,000. The corporation, which was incorporated in State B and had its primary place of business in State C, filed a petition to remove the action to federal district court in State B.

   Should the action be removed to federal district court in State B?

   (A) Yes, because the man is suing for violations of federal copyright law.

   (B) Yes, because there is complete diversity of citizenship.

   (C) No, because the corporation is a citizen of State B.

   (D) No, because the amount in controversy requirement was not met.

57. A man sued a company for violation of federal employment discrimination laws, claiming he was unlawfully terminated from his job. During discovery, the company asked in an interrogatory when, where, and by whom

the man was fired from his position. The company's president answered the interrogatory, saying the company vice president fired the man in person in the man's office on December 1. However, after filing his answer, the president learned that the man was actually fired the day before, by the director of personnel, in the director's office, and that the vice president only happened to speak to the man on December 1 because he walked by when the man was cleaning out his office.

Under the circumstances, does the company need to amend its answer?

(A) No, because the man has not filed a response challenging the answer.

(B) No, because the company demonstrated good faith in filing its initial response.

(C) Yes, because the company's response was not based on the president's personal knowledge.

(D) Yes, because the company's response was materially incorrect.

58. A woman, a citizen of State A, was the editor of a magazine that was incorporated and had its primary place of business in State A. A rival magazine, incorporated in State B and with its primary place of business in State B, wrote several editorials in its magazine making fun of the woman. The woman sued the rival magazine for libel in federal district court in State C because it was the only state in the nation where the statute of limitations had not yet run out. Each magazine was sold nationally, and each magazine sold around 10,000 copies per month in State C.

The federal district court in State C dismissed the woman's claim, finding State C did not have jurisdiction. Is the federal district court's decision correct?

(A) No, because the rival magazine was marketed and sold in State C.

(B) No, because the only forum available was State C.

(C) Yes, because the woman did not have sufficient minimum contacts with State C.

(D) Yes, because the rival magazine did not have sufficient minimum contacts with State C.

59. A motorcyclist brought an action in federal district court in the Northern District of State A against a company after he was injured by one of the company's trucks. The action was filed shortly before the statute of limitations ran out on the motorcyclist's claim. The company moved to dismiss on the grounds that the federal court lacked personal jurisdiction over the company and that the venue was incorrect. The federal district court agreed with both of the company's claims. However, because the statute of limitations on the claim has run out, the district court believed it would be unfair to the motorcyclist to dismiss the claim.

What can the court do in regards to the motorcyclist's claim?

(A) The court can only dismiss the case, because it lacks personal jurisdiction.

(B) The court can only dismiss the case, because venue is incorrect.

(C) The court does not have to dismiss the case because it will lead to an unfair result.

(D) The court can transfer the case to a proper venue.

60. A fireman sued a landlord for negligence in federal district court in State A based on diversity jurisdiction. The fireman wanted to depose one of the landlord's former tenants as a witness because he was the only witness to some of the landlord's allegedly negligent actions. However, the tenant, who was not a party to the lawsuit, now lived 500 miles away in State B. The fireman's attorney served a notice of deposition at the tenant's residence, which stated that the deposition would take place in State A and that

the attorney would pay the tenant's travel expenses. The tenant refused to travel to State A.

Can the fireman's attorney subpoena the witness to compel him to attend the deposition in State A?

(A) No, because there is no indication the fireman's attorney is licensed in State B.

(B) No, because the tenant now lives 500 miles away.

(C) Yes, because the tenant was the only witness.

(D) Yes, because the attorney is willing to pay the tenant's travel expenses.

61. A bar owner sued a doctor in state court in State A for damages related to an alleged assault and battery. Pursuant to State A law, the bar owner applied for an attachment of $76,000 on the doctor's home in order to protect his ability to receive a monetary judgment if he was successful in his suit. The relevant statute authorized the attachment of real property without notice or opportunity for a prior hearing, although a defendant could request a hearing within 30 days after the property was attached. To receive an attachment, the plaintiff had to file an affidavit regarding his or her good faith belief that the claim would be successful. The state court granted the attachment and immediately informed the doctor.

The doctor filed suit in federal district court in State A, arguing the attachment violated his rights under the United States Constitution. How should the court rule?

(A) In favor of the bar owner, because the amount is over $75,000.

(B) In favor of the bar owner, because the doctor has 30 days in which to request a hearing.

(C) In favor of the doctor, because he must be awarded a hearing within 14 days of the attachment of real property.

(D) In favor of the doctor, because the attachment was granted based on the bar owner's allegations.

62. An engineer sued an oil company for injuries the engineer sustained during an oilfield explosion. The engineer learned a truck driver who was nearby was the only physical witness to the explosion, although a security camera recorded a video of the explosion as well. Twenty days after filing the complaint, the engineer served the truck driver with a set of interrogatories asking the truck driver to describe what he saw. The truck driver doesn't want to answer because he wasn't supposed to be at the oilfield that day.

Is the truck driver subject to sanctions if he fails to answer the interrogatories?

(A) Yes, because he was the only witness to the explosion.

(B) Yes, because he was served within 60 days of the suit being filed.

(C) No, because he is not a party to the action.

(D) No, because the engineer can get the same information from the security camera.

63. A man sued a woman in federal district court in State A for injuries he sustained from a fight. The woman moved for summary judgment and provided evidence that she was at work in another city at the time the fight was alleged to have occurred. In opposition to the motion, the man submitted an affidavit giving more detailed information about the fight with the woman. The federal district court believed that there was very little chance the man wasn't either mistaken or lying regarding the woman's involvement in a fight with him on the date and time the man alleged it occurred.

Should the federal district court grant summary judgment?

(A) No, because there is still some chance the man's claim is valid.

(B) No, because the man only submitted an affidavit in opposition.

(C) Yes, because the court believes the man is likely mistaken or lying.

(D) Yes, because the court believes there is very little chance the man's claim will be successful.

64. A banker went into an attorney's office seeking representation against a bus company. The banker claimed a company bus ran over him while he was crossing the street, causing serious injuries that led him to being in a coma for several weeks. The banker said the lingering effects of the coma made him unable to work. The attorney had a good faith belief that the banker was telling him the truth, so he filed a complaint against the company for $5 million in damages on the banker's behalf without getting a copy of the police report or any other evidence. During trial, the police report regarding the bus accident was produced. It showed that it was the banker's brother who was hit by the bus and that he only suffered minor injuries. It was also shown that the banker was never hospitalized and had never stopped working. Ultimately, the company won the case, but it spent a considerable amount of money in attorney's fees to do so.

Can the company recover the lost attorney's fees from the banker or the banker's attorney?

(A) No, because it won the case.

(B) No, because the fees represent a valid contract between the company and its attorney.

(C) Yes, because the attorney and the banker conspired to commit fraud.

(D) Yes, because the attorney did not make a reasonable inquiry into the banker's claim.

65. A man sued a woman in federal court for injuries he sustained in an auto accident. The court ordered the attorneys involved in the action to attend a pretrial conference. Sometime later, the court ordered a second pretrial conference. This time, the court required the man and woman to be present. The man did not want to attend the second conference because he did not want to see the woman any more than he had to.

Does the man have to attend the second conference?

(A) No, because a party cannot be ordered to attend a pretrial conference.

(B) No, because a court cannot order more than one pretrial conference.

(C) Yes, because the court may require him to be available to consider possible settlement.

(D) Yes, because the man is the plaintiff in his suit.

66. A software manufacturer sued a computer company in federal district court in State A for breach of contract. The court's jurisdiction was based on diversity. At the close of the computer company's case, the computer company asked the judge to instruct the jury regarding certain points of State A contract law. The judge failed to do so, and the computer company's attorney failed to notice the omission. The jury found in the software manufacturer's favor. The computer company appealed, arguing the judge's failure to give the requested instruction constituted reversible error. The court of appeals believed the judge was wrong in failing to give the requested instruction.

How should the appellate court rule?

(A) Reverse the decision, because the computer company had requested the proper instruction.

(B) Reverse the decision, because the requested instruction was based on State A law.

(C) Affirm the decision, because the requested instruction was based on State A law.

(D) Affirm the decision, because the computer company's attorney failed to object.

67. A woman sued a doctor in federal district court for injuries she sustained during a surgical procedure. Her attorney hired an 18-year-old process server, who served the summons and complaint by leaving it at the doctor's home with his 17-year-old son. The doctor failed to file any response with the court.

If the woman moves for a default judgment, how should the court rule?

(A) Grant the motion, because the doctor had to respond within 21 days.

(B) Grant the motion, because the doctor had to respond within 60 days.

(C) Deny the motion, because the doctor's son was only 17 years old.

(D) Deny the motion, because the process server was only 18 years old.

68. A civil rights activist filed a class action in federal district court in State A against the State A Board of Education. The suit alleged that the school district engaged in discrimination against low-income students, specifically by giving more funding to schools in richer areas than to schools in poorer areas. A woman, who was the parent of a child who attended a school in one of the poorer areas, sought to intervene as of right in the action as a co-plaintiff.

May the woman intervene as of right?

(A) Yes, because there is no indication the existing parties will adequately represent her interest.

(B) Yes, because she has a child attending a school in a poorer area.

(C) No, because the action is being brought as a class action.

(D) No, because the action is being brought against a government entity.

69. A woman sued a psychiatrist for damages she claimed resulted from the psychiatrist hypnotizing her during a counseling session. The woman's attorney wanted to know whether the psychiatrist had any malpractice insurance that might cover the woman's claim, and whether that insurance might have an exclusion for alternative methods of treatment.

What does the woman's attorney need to do to find out whether the psychiatrist has an insurance policy?

(A) Serve the psychiatrist with an interrogatory asking the relevant question.

(B) Depose the psychiatrist regarding whether she has an insurance policy.

(C) File a request for production with the court.

(D) Nothing.

70. Two members of a local golf club wanted to bring a federal class action lawsuit against the club for racial discrimination. One of the members was a lawyer, and the other member was a doctor. The member who was a lawyer would serve as class representative. The two members claimed that the club systematically denied membership perks to black members. The doctor and the lawyer each claimed $100,000 in damages. There were 10 other black members of the club, who likely had damages of around $10,000 each.

May the group proceed as a class action?

(A) Yes, because the doctor and the lawyer are each claiming $100,000 in damages.

(B) Yes, because a class action serves the interest of judicial economy.

(C) No, because joinder of the class members is not impracticable.

(D) No, because each of the other 10 potential members likely had damages of around $10,000 each.

71. The U.S. Securities and Exchange Commission (SEC) filed suit against a company, alleging that its proxy statement was false and misleading. The federal district court ruled in favor of the SEC. A shareholder than filed an action for securities fraud against the company in federal district court. The shareholder moved for partial summary judgment against the company, arguing that the company was collaterally estopped from re-litigating the question of validity of the proxy statement.

How should the court rule?

(A) Grant the motion, because the issue was decided in the SEC action.

(B) Grant the motion, because it is unlikely the shareholder could have intervened in the SEC action.

(C) Deny the motion, because to grant it would violate the company's right to a jury trial on that issue.

(D) Deny the motion, because the shareholder was not a party to the SEC action.

72. A singer sued a company in federal district court seeking an injunction to prevent the company from selling any copies of an album the singer recorded when he was a child. The singer would like to have his claim decided by a jury.

What does the singer need to do to have a jury hear his claim?

(A) Nothing, because the singer is not entitled to a jury.

(B) Serve the company with a separate written demand within 14 days of the last pleading directed to the issue.

(C) Serve the company either a separate written demand or a demand included within another pleading within 14 days of the last pleading directed to the issue.

(D) File a written demand with the court within 14 days of filing the complaint.

73. A man sued a company in federal district court in State A for injuries he received after riding on one of the company's rollercoasters. The case was tried in front of a seven-member jury. The jury returned a verdict 5-2 in favor of the man.

May a verdict be entered in the man's favor?

(A) No, because the verdict was not unanimous.

(B) No, because the jury had less than 12 members.

(C) Yes, because the majority of the jury ruled in the man's favor.

(D) Yes, because a super majority ruled in the man's favor.

74. A computer manufacturer shipped 100 computers to a store through a special delivery service. When the computers arrived at the store, all of them had cracked screens, and the store refused to pay. The manufacturer then filed suit against both the store and the delivery company in federal district court. The manufacturer was incorporated and had its primary place of business in State A. The delivery company was incorporated in State B and had its primary place of business in State B. The store was incorporated in State

C and had its primary place of business in State B. The store wanted to make a claim against the delivery service for the damaged computers, but it wanted to file its own claim in State B state court after the manufacturer's claim is over.

May the store do so?

(A) No, because the issue of liability will already be fully litigated.

(B) No, because the claim arises from the same transaction or occurrence.

(C) Yes, because the store's claim is optional.

(D) Yes, because both the store and the delivery service are citizens of the same state.

75. A sporting goods company sued a supplier in federal district court in State A. The supplier moved to dismiss the claim for lack of jurisdiction, arguing it did not have sufficient minimum contacts with State A for State A to have personal jurisdiction over it. The supplier only had one salesman in State A, and that salesman worked out of his home and was paid through commissions. Importantly, the supplier noted it owned no property in State A and derived only a small part of its total revenue from State A. The sporting goods company countered that orders and samples were subject to the supplier's approval and shipped directly from the supplier to buyers.

Does the court in State A have jurisdiction over the supplier?

(A) Yes, because the salesman solicited orders for the supplier in State A.

(B) Yes, because the supplier shipped directly to buyers.

(C) No, because the supplier only had one salesman in the state.

(D) No, because the salesman worked out of his home and was paid through commissions.

# ANSWERS
# CIVIL PROCEDURE

# ANSWERS TO
# CIVIL PROCEDURE QUESTIONS

1. **D**   While federal courts sitting in diversity apply the substantive law of the state in which they are sitting, they apply federal procedural law if the law is valid and on point. Importantly, under *Hanna v. Plumer, 380 U.S. 460 (1965)*, a federal court sitting in diversity will apply the applicable federal rule if it is "arguably procedural." Here, the conflicting rules in question cover the procedure necessary for service of process, so the federal law is on point.

    **A** is incorrect because while a federal court sitting in diversity is required to apply the state's substantive law, it is not required to apply the state's procedural law. Consequently, the statement in **A** is too broad. **B** is incorrect because the law of the state in which the claim arose would be irrelevant in this case. **C** is incorrect because although the motion for summary judgment itself may affect the woman's substantive rights, the issue regarding service is a procedural one.

2. **A**   Rule 38 states that failure to demand a jury trial within 14 days after service of the last pleading directed to the issue on which a jury is sought results in a waiver of the right to a jury trial. However, Rule 39 gives a court the discretion to grant a belated motion. Importantly, a court should do so in the absence of compelling reasons to the contrary. *See Cox v. Masland & Sons, Inc., 607 F.2d 138 (5th Cir. 1979)*. Therefore, **C** is incorrect.

    **B** is incorrect because although there is no indication the man intended to waive his right, the decision to allow a jury trial is still within the discretion of the court. **D** is incorrect because the demand for a jury trial does not need to be made in the initial complaint.

3. **B**   Under 28 U.S.C. §1331, federal courts have subject matter jurisdiction over claims arising under federal law. Here, since the musician is making a federal copyright claim, the jurisdiction of the federal court is proper.

    If a claim arises under federal law, there is no amount in controversy requirement and the citizenship of the parties is irrelevant. Consequently, the woman's addition to the lawsuit and her citizenship and damage claim will not change the court's federal question jurisdiction in any way. Therefore, **A** and **C** are incorrect. **D** is incorrect because there is no amount in controversy requirement for federal question jurisdiction, so it doesn't matter that the musician is only claiming $30,000 in damages.

4. **D**   If an action that is brought in state court could have originally been brought in federal court, it can be removed to federal court under 28 U.S.C. §1441(a). Only defendants can remove, and if there is more than one defendant, all defendants must consent to the removal. However, if federal jurisdiction is based only on diversity, a case cannot be removed to federal court if one of the defendants is a citizen of the state in which the case was originally brought. Here, although the man could have brought the case in federal court based on diversity, the truck driver is a citizen of State B, where the state action was brought. Consequently, the case cannot be removed to federal court. Therefore, A and B are incorrect.

C is incorrect because actions with jurisdiction based on diversity can also be removed to federal court, not simply actions based on a federal question.

5.   B   When exercising jurisdiction based on diversity, a federal court is required to apply the substantive law of the state in which it is sitting. Here, the federal court is sitting in State B.

A is incorrect because the plaintiff does not get to choose which laws the federal court will follow simply because he or she brought the claim. C is incorrect because choice of law issues are not based upon what state the claim arose in. D is incorrect because although there is federal common law, federal courts cannot use federal common law to decide state law claims.

6.   A   For diversity jurisdiction to be proper under 28 U.S.C. §1332, the amount in controversy must be in excess of $75,000, exclusive of interest and costs. In meeting the jurisdictional threshold, all of the plaintiff's claims against a single defendant can be aggregated. Here, the woman's three claims total $80,000, so the jurisdictional amount is met.

B is incorrect because the federal court's jurisdiction can be challenged at any time, not just at the time the complaint is filed. C is incorrect because the amount in controversy is determined by the plaintiff's complaint, not by what is actually awarded. D is incorrect because the woman could aggregate all of her claims against the contractor.

7.   D   The federal rules generally require only that a complaint put the other side on notice of the claim and they generally do not require detailed assertions of the facts underlying the claim. However, under *Bell Atlantic Corp. v. Twombly, 550 U.S. 544 (2007)* and *Ashcroft v. Iqbal, 556 U.S. 662 (2009)* the facts in the complaint need to support a plausible claim, not just a possible one.

Therefore, **A, B,** and **C** are incorrect.

8.   A   During voir dire, potential jurors are asked questions to determine whether they have some potential bias in the case. If questioning reveals a juror is biased, the juror may be excused for cause. There are two types of biases. An actual bias is when a juror indicates he or she would use predetermined beliefs or principles instead of the facts presented to determine a case. Implied bias is when it is very likely an average person in the same position as the juror would be partial to one of the parties. Even if the juror states he or she can still be fair and impartial, he or she must be excused from the case. Here, since the juror's boss is one of the parties, bias can be implied and the juror should be excused. Therefore, **C** and **D** are incorrect.

B is incorrect because the facts state an implied bias, not an actual one.

9.   B   Under Fed. R. Civ. P. 4, service is proper if the service is (i) personal, (ii) left at the defendant's usual place of abode with a person of suitable age and discretion who resides therein, or (iii) served upon the defendant's authorized agent. Here, since the sister is an adult living with the producer at his home, and there is no indication she does not have suitable discretion, leaving the complaint with her at the producer's home is proper.

A and C are incorrect because there is no indication either the assistant or the members of the executive team are acting as agents for the producer, whatever their job titles may be. **D** is incorrect because the simple fact the producer and his wife are married would not make service of process on the wife proper.

10. **C**     Under *Erie Railroad v. Tompkins, 304 U.S. 64 (1938)*, a federal court in a diversity case must apply the substantive law of the state in which it is sitting, but it follows federal procedural law. The United States Supreme Court has ruled that statutes of limitations are substantive law when determining whether to apply federal or state rules. *See Guaranty Trust Co. v. York, 326 U.S. 99 (1945)*. Consequently, the federal court must follow the statute of limitations rules of State **B**.

A is incorrect because statutes of limitation are substantive law for *Erie* purposes. **B** is incorrect because there is no rule stating that federal courts will follow federal common law in determining an appropriate statute of limitations. **D** is incorrect because federal courts may apply federal procedural law, so this statement is too broad to be correct.

11. **C**     When determining state law, the federal court must apply the substantive law that would be applied by the state's highest court. If the state law is unsettled, the federal court may determine what the highest court of the state would likely do if faced with the issue. Importantly, federal courts of appeal review the district courts' decisions as to unsettled state law *de novo*. Therefore, since the district court was determining state law, the court of appeals should not have deferred to the district court's decision.

A is incorrect because deferral to the district court's decision would still be incorrect even if the law is substantive. **B** is incorrect because the court of appeals should not defer to the district court's decision simply because it sits in the same state the claim was brought in. **D** is incorrect because although the federal court could have abstained from hearing the state law claim or possibly certified the issue to the state courts to obtain a ruling, it could also have made a determination itself regarding how the state courts would rule.

12. **C**     If a defendant files a pre-answer motion to dismiss and does not raise personal jurisdiction in that motion, the defendant waives any objection to personal jurisdiction. Here, the company should have asserted this defense in its first response to the complaint.

While it is true that under *Hanson v. Denckla, 357 U.S. 235 (1958)*, a defendant must purposefully avail himself or herself of the privilege of conducting activities within the forum state, and that this can be shown through a defendant's attempts to make money in the state or use its roads, the issue here is that the company did not claim lack of personal jurisdiction in its first response. Therefore, **C** is the best answer and **A** is incorrect. While exercise of jurisdiction should be fair and reasonable, the issue here is the company's mistake in not bringing up the issue immediately. Therefore, **B** is incorrect. **D** is incorrect because merely putting a product into the stream of commerce without more is not enough for personal jurisdiction.

13. **A**     Under Fed. R. Civ. P. 12(b)(6), a court will dismiss a claim if the complaint contains an allegation that negates one of the elements of the cause of action. False imprisonment is an intentional tort, and the contractor's complaint states he was locked in the storage room through an

employee's negligence. Consequently, the allegation of negligence negates the intent necessary for a successful claim of false imprisonment, and the court should dismiss the claim.

**B** is incorrect because the amount in controversy requirement for diversity jurisdiction requires a good faith allegation of damages, not probability of those damages being awarded. **C** is incorrect because although a complaint should put the defendant on notice, the issue here is that the complaint itself negates one of the elements of a false imprisonment claim. **D** is incorrect because the issue here is the failure of the complaint to state a claim, not whether the amount in controversy requirement was met.

14.  **D**    Federal courts have subject matter jurisdiction based on diversity so long as no plaintiff is a citizen of the same state as any defendant. Citizenship of the parties is determined on the date the suit is filed. If a person moves to a state and intends to stay there indefinitely, the person becomes a citizen of that new state. Here, at the time of filing, the man had moved to State B and intended to stay there for the foreseeable future. Consequently, the man was a citizen of State B when the action was filed, meaning both the doctor and the man were citizens of the same state.

Therefore, **A**, **B**, and **C** are incorrect.

15.  **A**    Most states have long arm statutes that grant in personam jurisdiction over nonresidents in certain situations. However, even if a state has such a long arm statute, the constitutionality of that jurisdiction must still be determined. In a similar scenario to the situation posed by the question, the United States Supreme Court ruled in *McGee v. International Insurance Co., 355 U.S. 220 (1957)* that the forum state's strong interest in protecting its citizens from the potential bad acts of insurance companies gave the forum state personal jurisdiction over the out-of-state insurance company. Importantly, the court noted the company renewed the insurance policy in question with the forum state resident and continued to accept premiums from the forum state resident. Consequently, **A** is the best answer choice, and **C** and **D** are incorrect.

**B** is incorrect because the fact the policy was originally purchased online would not change the analysis.

16.  **B**    If an action brought in a state court could have originally been brought in federal court, a defendant can have it removed to federal court under 28 U.S.C. §1441. Federal courts have subject matter jurisdiction over claims where the plaintiff and defendant are citizens of different states and the amount in controversy is over $75,000. Here, the truck driver is claiming $200,000 in damages, so the amount in controversy is met. Also, the truck driver is a citizen of State A. Consequently, federal jurisdiction will be appropriate so long as the company is not a citizen of State A. The citizenship of a corporation is any state where it is incorporated and the state where its principal place of business is located. A corporation's principal place of business is the place where the corporation's directors and top management direct the corporation's business activities. *See Hertz Corp. v. Friend, 559 U.S. 77 (2010).* While the company does a significant amount of business in State A, since the company is directed in State B, it will be deemed a citizen of State B for both its place of incorporation and because that's where the decisions regarding the company are made.

Therefore, A and C are incorrect. **D** is incorrect because the claim can still be removed to federal court even though it is based on state law.

17. **A**   Work product made in anticipation of litigation is privileged and is not discoverable by an opposing party unless that party makes a showing of substantial need and undue hardship in getting the materials in some other way. Under Fed. R. Civ. P. 26, if a party inadvertently discloses such material to the opposing party, he or she can notify the opposing party of the disclosure and the basis for claiming work-product protection. If the disclosing party does so, the other party cannot use the material until the court makes a determination regarding the validity of the claim. Therefore, **C** is incorrect.

   **B** is incorrect because the attorney does not need to ask for a protective order to claim work-product protection. **D** is incorrect because work product includes the draft reports of trial experts, and any final report intended for trial is likely not protected as work product.

18. **C**   Under Fed. R. Civ. P. 37, a party is not subject to sanctions if it deletes or loses electronically stored data in the routine and good faith operation of its electronic data systems. However, a party must take reasonable steps to protect the data once it becomes clear it would be discoverable in litigation. Here, since the deletion was part of a new, routine cost-saving initiative, and there was no indication the company deleted the information in anticipation of litigation, it would not be subject to any sanctions, such as paying for recovery experts, for failing to produce the requested information.

   **A** is incorrect because although the deletion wasn't a mistake, the company is still protected by Fed. R. Civ. P. 37's safe harbor provision for electronically stored data since the deletion occurred as a routine part of maintaining its information systems. **B** is incorrect because there is no rule stating that electronically stored data must be absolutely unrecoverable before the safe harbor provision comes into play. **D** is incorrect because the operative question is whether the deletion was part of the routine and good faith operation of the information system, not whether the deletion itself was reasonable.

19. **D**   The defense of lack of subject matter jurisdiction can be raised at any time, even on appeal. However, under Fed. R. Civ. P. 12(b), insufficient service of process, improper venue, and lack of personal jurisdiction must be raised at the time a party responds to the complaint either by filing a motion or an an-swer. Therefore, **A, B,** and **C** are incorrect.

20. **A**   In determining personal jurisdiction, *International Shoe Co. v. Washington, 326 U.S. 310 (1945)* established that a party must have sufficient minimum contacts with a state that it would be fair and reasonable for the state to exercise jurisdiction over that party. In *Snowney v. Harrah's Entertainment Inc., 112 P.2d 28 (2006)*, the California court found that a hotel in Nevada that focused advertising on California residents through billboards and its Internet site was subject to personal jurisdiction in California because it targeted and solicited business from California residents.

   **B** is incorrect because the mere fact that a party advertised on a billboard located in a state would likely not be enough to subject it to personal jurisdiction in that state. **C** is incorrect because although it did not do any business in State B, the hotel did solicit business from State B residents by using a billboard in State B, giving driving directions from State B, and noting its proximity to State B. **D** is incorrect because personal jurisdiction is not based on where the injury at issue occurred.

21.  **D**    For a federal court to have subject matter jurisdiction over a claim, the amount in controversy must exceed $75,000. While aggregation of separate claims is allowed in the case of a single plaintiff suing a single defendant, aggregation is not allowed in the case of several plaintiffs against one defendant (unless the plaintiffs are seeking to enforce a single title or right in which they share an undivided interest). In the case of class actions, the claims of the separate class members cannot be aggregated if their claims are not joint or common. Here, the claims all involve different shares of company stock, so the claims are not joint or common. In that case, the court would only have subject matter jurisdiction over the claim if one of the claims exceeded $75,000. Here, there is no indication that one does.

Importantly, although the Class Action Fairness Act of 2005 loosened certain jurisdictional requirements for some class actions, the Act only applies when there are at least 100 proposed members in a class and the aggregate amount in controversy exceeds $5 million dollars.

Therefore, **A, B,** and **C** are incorrect.

22.  **D**    Federal courts will not take jurisdiction over claims involving the issuance of a divorce, alimony, or a child custody decree. *See Akenbrandt v. Richards, 504 U.S. 689 (1992).* Here, the man is seeking custody of the children and alimony.

**A** is incorrect because although there is apparently diversity of citizenship, the issue is that the man is seeking custody and alimony. **B** is incorrect because although the children were born in State A and now reside in State B, this does not create any kind of special federal jurisdiction over the claim. **C** is incorrect because the issue is not that the divorce was granted by State A, it's that the man is asking the federal court to make a decision regarding custody and alimony.

23.  **A**    28 U.S.C. §1332(a)(2) grants subject matter jurisdiction over any dispute between a citizen of a U.S. state and a citizen of a foreign country. Here, the question states that the student is an Irish citizen, so the federal court has subject matter jurisdiction over his claim.

**B** is incorrect because although the amount in controversy is met, the specific issue presented by the question is that the student is a citizen of a foreign country. If the student had been a citizen of a U.S. state other than State A, **B** would have been an appropriate answer. **C** is incorrect because all claims brought by a single plaintiff against a single defendant can be aggregated for the purpose of meeting the amount in controversy requirement. **D** is incorrect because subject matter jurisdiction is not dependent upon a defendant's consent to suit.

24.  **C**    If a counterclaim arises out of the same transaction or occurrence as the plaintiff's claim, it is a compulsory counterclaim that must be asserted by the defendant. Otherwise, the

counterclaim is barred. Here, since the woman's claim arises out of the same automobile accident, it was a compulsory counterclaim that had to be raised at during the first action.

**A** is incorrect because the fact the man sued in federal court in the first action involving the accident would not automatically confer jurisdiction to federal courts for subsequent actions involving the accident. **B** is incorrect because, although citizenship is determined at the time the suit is filed, the issue here is the fact the woman should have brought her injury claim as a compulsory counterclaim. **D** is incorrect because res judicata applies to situations where the same cause of action is brought by the same plaintiff against the same defendant. Here, the woman's claim would turn her into the plaintiff and the man into the defendant, so res judicata would not apply.

25.　**D**　Fed. R. Civ. P. 38 requires a party who desires a jury trial on a fact issue to file a written demand with the court and serve it on the opposing party within 14 days after the service of the last pleading directed to that issue. Once a jury demand is made, it cannot be withdrawn unless all parties consent to the withdrawal. Here, since the company opposes withdrawal, the court should deny the man's motion.

　　**A** is incorrect because the mere fact the man made the original jury demand does not give him free reign to withdrawal it. **B** and **C** are incorrect because the question of whether withdrawal is appropriate is not dictated by when the withdrawal is made.

26.　**C**　In its decision in *Jones v. Flowers, 547 U.S. 220 (2006)*, the United States Supreme Court ruled that the Fourteenth Amendment's Due Process Clause requires the government to take additional reasonable steps after mailed notice of a pending action is returned undelivered. Although the Federal Rules do not require actual notice, a party cannot proceed with his or her claim if he or she knows the opposing party did not receive notice and there are practical alternatives to informing the opposing party (such as remailing the notice or posting it on the property's door). Here, since the state took no further action to try to notify the homeowner before selling the property, the state violated the homeowner's due process rights.

　　**A** and **B** are incorrect because the state took no further action to try to notify the homeowner after the letter was returned undelivered. **D** is incorrect because the notice issue is not affected by when the property was actually put up for sale.

27.　**A**　When a court believes a jury award is excessive, remittitur allows a court to offer a plaintiff the choice of a reduced award or a new trial. If the suit is in federal court based on diversity jurisdiction, the court can look at whether the award meets the state standard for excessiveness.

　　**B** is incorrect because a court cannot simply reduce a jury award without giving a plaintiff the option of a new trial. *See Hetzel v. Prince William County, 523 U.S. 208 (1998)*. **C** is incorrect because the award does not necessarily have to "shock the conscience." If the federal court is sitting in diversity, the court can look to the state standard. **D** is incorrect because remittitur does not violate the Seventh Amendment (however, additur, or offering a defendant the choice between a higher award or a new trial when damages are inadequate, does).

28.  **B**   A judgment is void only when there was a fundamental flaw such as a lack of jurisdiction or a party's deprivation of his or her due process rights through failure to give notice or an opportunity to be heard. *See United Student Aid Funds, Inc. v. Espinosa, 559 U.S. 260 (2010).*

While parties can be relieved from final judgments based on new evidence or fraud, such situations do not make the judgment void. Therefore, **A** and **C** are incorrect. Under Fed. R. Civ. P. 60(a), courts can correct clerical errors at any time, and such errors do not make a judgment void. Therefore, **D** is incorrect.

29.  **B**   Federal courts have subject matter jurisdiction over claims based on federal law. Here, since the owner's claim is based on federal trucking laws, the federal court would have subject matter jurisdiction.

**A** is incorrect because questions of interstate commerce do not necessarily involve questions of federal law. **C** is incorrect because there is no amount in controversy requirement for federal claims. **D** is incorrect because the citizenship of the parties is irrelevant if the claim is based on federal law.

30.  **A**   A notice of deposition is sufficient to compel the deposition appearance of an adverse party.

**B** is incorrect because a party does not have to show substantial need in order to depose a witness or adverse party. **C** is incorrect because subpoenas are only necessary if the witness to be deposed is not a party to the lawsuit. **D** is incorrect because the likelihood of a party's testimony at trial does not affect whether or not that party may be compelled to attend a deposition.

31.  **B**   Appellate courts review mixed questions of law and fact de novo. In general, whether a situation meets a legal standard is a mixed question of law and fact. However, you do not need to know whether the issue presented here is a matter of law, question of fact, or mixed question of law and fact to get the correct answer. Importantly, the other three answer choices are incorrect because they pair an incorrect legal question with each standard.

**A** is incorrect because Fed. R. Civ. P. 52(a)(6) states that a court's findings regarding questions of fact are not disturbed unless they are "clearly erroneous." **C** is incorrect because abuse of discretion is the standard applied to a trial court's decisions regarding discretionary matters, such as leaves to amend. **D** is incorrect because matters of law are reviewed de novo.

32. **C**    If a party receives no notice and is not represented in a prior party's unsuccessful litigation, that party is not barred from asserting the same claim in a subsequent lawsuit. *See Richards v. Jefferson County, 517 U.S. 793 (1996).*

Res judicata applies only in situations where the first and second cases are brought by the same plaintiff against the same defendant. Therefore, **A** is incorrect. Claim preclusion is another term for res judicata. Therefore, **B** is incorrect. **D** is incorrect because under the circumstances the fact the second claim is being brought as a class action has no bearing on whether the second claim is barred.

33. **C**    A party can request a temporary restraining order when an injury will occur before the grant of a preliminary injunction. Consequently, the correct order for such actions is temporary restraining order first, preliminary injunction second. In addition, a preliminary injunction cannot be issued without notice to the adverse party.

To receive an ex parte temporary restraining order, a party must provide security in case the adverse party is wrongfully restrained, certify efforts to notify the adverse party, and state specific facts showing the party will suffer immediate and irreparable injury. Therefore, **A, B,** and **D** are incorrect.

34. **B**    If an action involves a "potentially disruptive effect on maritime commerce" and the activity giving rise to the action has a "substantial relationship to traditional maritime activity," federal courts have original jurisdiction over the action because of its maritime nexus. *See Jerome B. Grubart, Inc. v. Great Lakes Dredge & Dock Co., 513 U.S. 527 (1995).* Here, the turbine wreckage has shut down the harbor for several weeks, and made it inaccessible to the fishing fleet. Consequently, it appears to have the necessary connection to maritime activity, making **B** the best answer.

**A** is incorrect because the mere fact an action involves interstate commerce is not enough to give a federal court subject matter jurisdiction. **C** is incorrect because this action can be brought into federal court based on its relationship to maritime activity, making the citizenship of the opposing parties irrelevant. **D** is incorrect because there is no minimum offshore mileage requirement for an action to arise under maritime law.

35. **D**    Under the rule provided in *Clearfield Trust Co. v. United States, 318 U.S. 360 (1943)*, the federal courts are allowed to make federal common law when the rights and obligations of the United States are at issue. Here, since the action is based on the federal government's obligations to pay on its check, the federal court would use federal common law to make its determination. Therefore, **B** is incorrect.

Although *Erie Railroad v. Tompkins, 304 U.S. 64 (1938)* found that federal courts cannot make federal common law when ruling on state law claims, federal courts are allowed to make federal common law when dealing with the rights and obligations of the United States. Therefore, **A** is incorrect. **C** is incorrect because the deciding issue here is not whether the rule is substantive or procedural, but that the rights and obligations of the United States are being determined by the court.

36.  **A**    Under 28 U.S.C. §1391, venue is proper in (a) the judicial district where any defendant resides, so long as all defendants are residents of the state in which the district is located; (b) a judicial district where a substantial part of the events giving rise to the claim occurred; or, (c) if no district in the United States satisfies either (a) or (b), a judicial district where any defendant is subject to the court's personal jurisdiction in regards to such action. Here, since not all the defendants are citizens of the same state, the only appropriate venue would be the Eastern District of State B, where the accident occurred.

Therefore, **B, C,** and **D** are incorrect.

37.  **C**    Under Fed. R. Civ. P. 12(e), if a party finds that a complaint is so vague or ambiguous that the party cannot reasonably frame a response, the party may move for a more definite statement. However, such a motion must be made before the party responds by filing an answer or other reply.

**A** is incorrect because lack of subject matter jurisdiction can be raised at any time, even on appeal. **B** and **D** are incorrect because they can be raised at the time the party files a motion or his or her answer.

38.  **D**    If a Rule 12 motion is not made, a defendant who was mailed the complaint and who waived formal service must answer within 60 days after the request for waiver was mailed. If a defendant is served formally with a summons and complaint, he or she must answer within 21 days after service. If the court grants a motion for a more definite statement, the answer is due within 14 days. Therefore, **A, B,** and **C** are incorrect.

39.  **D**    Under Fed. R. Civ. P. 12(b), a defendant can make a motion to dismiss for failure to state a claim upon which relief can be granted. This means that even if all of the plaintiff's allegations are true, there is still no claim for which the court can grant relief. Here, even if the man is correct that the movie is so terrible that it ruins the franchise for him, this would not entitle him to any type of judicial relief. If the franchise owners are granted this motion, they will not need to file any type of answer to the complaint.

**A** is incorrect because the issue here is not that the complaint is too vague, the issue is that hating a terrible movie does not create any kind of legal action for the viewer. **B** is incorrect because a motion for summary judgment requires the court to look at all the evidence presented by the parties. Here, the matter can be deposed of much more quickly with a motion to dismiss for failure to state a claim. **C** is incorrect because declaratory judgments are used to determine the rights and status of the parties involved in a case, and such a ruling does not require that any action be taken. Here, the issue is that the man is suing because he hates a movie, which is not something he can be granted relief for, so the court should just dismiss his claim without requiring the parties to do anything else.

40.  **B**    If jurisdiction is based on a question of federal law, the federal court will also have jurisdiction over state law claims arising from the same case or controversy. *See Hurn v. Oursler, 289 U.S. 238 (1933).* Here, both the federal and state claims arise from the playwright putting on the play in State A.

**A** is incorrect because it is unclear whether the federal claim is actually a prerequisite to the state claim. In any event, it would not matter since both claims arise out of the same case or controversy. **C** is incorrect because, as stated above, the federal court would have supplemental or pendent jurisdiction over the state law claim because it is part of the same controversy as the federal claim. **D** is incorrect because the mere fact a claim might be governed by state law does not remove that claim from potential federal jurisdiction.

41.  **D**    Under 28 U.S.C. §1446(b), an action cannot be removed to federal court based on diversity more than one year after the action was commenced in state court. Here, the claim became removable when the model dismissed his claim against the lawyer because the opposing parties are now citizens of different states. However, a year has already passed since the beginning of the action in state court, so it cannot now be removed.

A case must be removed no later than 30 days after the defendant discovers the case is removable. However, because of the one-year rule, **A, B,** and **C** are incorrect.

42.  **C**    Under Fed. R. Civ. P. 9, a complaint only needs to provide a short and plain statement of the claim. The Federal Rules only require heightened and more specific pleading when the claim involves fraud, mistake, or special damages. Here, the man's employment discrimination claim would not need to meet the heightened pleading requirements, and the federal courts cannot require more specific pleading outside the narrow group of situations provided for in the Rules. *See Swierkiewicz v. Sorema N.A., 534 U.S. 506 (2002).* Therefore, **A** is incorrect.

**B** is incorrect because not all federal questions require more specific pleading. **D** is incorrect because this answer choice refers to the standard required under Fed. R. Civ. P. 12(b) for a motion to dismiss for failure to state a claim.

43.  **A**    Under Fed. R. Civ. P. 22 and 28 U.S.C. §1335, a person who is in possession of property claimed by more than one party (known as a "stakeholder") can file an interpleader action to require the property claimants to litigate amongst themselves to determine who owns the property. In this way, the stakeholder can avoid liability.

**B** is incorrect because a declaratory judgment is generally used to determine the rights, duties, or obligations of parties without ordering any action or awarding damages. **C** is incorrect because impleader refers to the ability of a party to bring a non-party into the action if that non-party may be liable for any part of the judgment. **D** is incorrect because intervention of right refers to when a non-party claims an interest in the subject matter of an action and demands to join the action.

44.  **C**    Under 28 U.S.C. §1404, for the convenience of parties or witnesses, the federal district court may transfer a civil action to any other district or division where the action might have been brought or to any district or division to which all of the parties have consented. If a transfer is made purely on the grounds of convenience, the transferee court will apply the law that would have been applied in the original court. *See Van Dusen*

*v. Barrack, 376 U.S. 612 (1964).* Consequently, the State A court will apply the law of State B.

Therefore, **A, B,** and **D** are incorrect.

45.  **A**  Joint tortfeasors with potential joint-and-several liability are permissive parties to an action. Consequently, they are not "necessary and indispensable" parties subject to compulsory joinder under Fed. R. Civ. P. 19. *See Temple v. Synthes Corp., 498 U.S. 5 (1990).* Therefore, the federal case should not be dismissed simply because the woman failed to join the doctor and the hospital.

**B** is incorrect because the mere fact that the doctor and hospital are potential defendants does not make them subject to Fed. R. Civ. P. 19. **C** is incorrect because the United States Supreme Court has held that joint tortfeasors are not necessary and indispensable parties. **D** is incorrect because the fact the doctor and hospital are likely jointly and severally liable does not make them parties necessary for the federal adjudication.

46.  **A**  A pleading cannot be amended if the amendment violates a party's due process rights. The United States Supreme Court has ruled that amending a pleading and simultaneously making the new party liable violates due process because the new party does not have a chance to respond before the entry of judgment against him or her. *See Nelson v. Adams USA, Inc., 529 U.S. 460 (2000).*

**B** is incorrect because a pleading can be amended for other reasons besides the discovery of new evidence. **C** is incorrect because the mere fact that the president was president and sole shareholder of the cellphone company would not automatically make him personally liable for the cellphone company's liability. **D** is incorrect because although his actions are chargeable to the cellphone company, this does not mean he had a chance to contest his potential personal liability.

47.  **B**  Issue preclusion (also known as collateral estoppel) bars a party from re-litigating issues that were actually litigated and necessary for the judgment in the first action. Here, since the man was unsuccessful in his negligence claim against the carpenter, who was primarily liable for his alleged negligence, he cannot now re-litigate the same claim against the company, who was secondarily liable for the alleged negligence.

**A** is incorrect because res judicata usually applies to a situation where the same claimant is suing the same defendant for the same cause of action. **C** is incorrect because the doctrine of *respondeat superior* does not address the fact that the issue of the carpenter's negligence was already litigated. **D** is incorrect because even though the man did not sue the company in the prior action, this fact does not mean the man can now sue the company.

48.  **A**  A motion for judgment as a matter of law is made before the case is submitted to a jury and asks the court for judgment in the moving party's favor based on the argument that no reasonable person could come to a different conclusion. A renewed motion for judgment as a matter of law comes after entry of judgment and can only be made if the moving party made a motion for judgment as a matter of law during the trial. A motion for a new trial

is made after judgment and may be granted because of trial error, juror misconduct, or problems with the verdict.

The United States Supreme Court has ruled that if a party wishes to raise the issue of the sufficiency of the evidence on appeal, the party making the appeal must have already moved for either a renewed judgment as a matter of law or a new trial. *See Unitherm Food Systems, Inc. v. Swift-Eckrich, Inc., 546 U.S. 394 (2006).* Therefore, **B, C,** and **D** are incorrect.

49. **A**    Under Fed. R. Civ. P. 4, service is proper if (a) a party is served personally, (b) service is left at the defendant's usual place of abode with a person of suitable age and discretion who resides within, or (c) service is made upon the defendant's authorized agent. Service can be made by any person who is at least 18 years old and is not a party to the action. Consequently, the plaintiff could not personally serve the defendant.

**B** is incorrect because service may be made by a U.S. Marshal at a party's request and it is likely an executive officer of the company is an authorized agent of the company. **C** is incorrect because the process server is at least 18 years old, and the defendant's daughter likely resides at the defendant's home. **D** is incorrect because the process server is over 18 years of age and the 18-year-old renter resides in the defendant's home.

50. **D**    Oral depositions are governed by Fed. R. Civ. P. 30. They can be taken over the telephone or by other electronic means.

**A** is incorrect because leave of the court or stipulation of the parties is required to depose the same person more than once. **B** is incorrect because a deposition cannot be longer than "one day of seven hours" without leave of the court or stipulation of the parties. **C** is incorrect because a party cannot take more than 10 depositions without leave of the court or stipulation of the parties.

51. **C**    Under the discovery rules in Fed. R. Civ. P. 26(b)(1), a party must provide "any nonprivileged matter that is relevant to any party's claim or defense." Additionally, information "need not be admissible in evidence" if it is likely to lead to the discovery of admissible evidence. Consequently, the university should provide the memorandum to the student. Therefore, **A** is incorrect.

**B** is incorrect because work product is material made in anticipation of litigation. Here, the memorandum was written several years earlier. **D** is incorrect because it is not necessary for the student to show it is impossible for him to obtain the information in any other way.

52. **C**    Although claims that fail to meet the amount in controversy requirement of $75,000 can be heard based on supplemental jurisdiction if they arise from a common nucleus of fact, supplemental jurisdiction does not override the rules regarding complete diversity of citizenship. Here, the woman is a citizen of State B, and the company is incorporated in State

B, so the court would not have subject matter jurisdiction over the claim because both the woman and the company are citizens of the same state. Importantly, a corporation is a citizen of both the state in which it is incorporated and its primary place of business.

Therefore, **A, B,** and **D** are incorrect.

53. **B**    Only defendants may remove an action to federal court. Here, since the artist brought the action, he is the plaintiff and cannot request removal.

A is incorrect because the writer's counterclaim is a compulsory counterclaim since it arises from the same transaction or occurrence. **C** is incorrect because the fact the plaintiff is now facing a claim for over $75,000 would not allow the plaintiff to remove the case to federal court. Additionally, the fact the defendant's counterclaim is compulsory would not allow the plaintiff to remove an action to federal court. Therefore, **D** is incorrect.

54. **C**    Except for certain interlocutory orders such as injunctions, only final decisions are reviewable by an appellate court. In *Cunningham v. Hamilton County, 527 U.S. 198 (1999)*, the United States Supreme Court found that an order imposing sanctions on an attorney was not a final decision regarding the case despite the fact the attorney was no longer involved in the litigation. Therefore, **B** is incorrect.

A is incorrect because the collateral order doctrine refers to a narrow exception to the final decision rule that allows parties to appeal certain interlocutory rulings without waiting for a final decision. **D** is incorrect because there has not been a final decision in the case. Consequently, the appellate court's inability to hear the appeal was not simply discretionary.

55. **C**    Under 28 U.S.C. §1738, a federal court must give state court judgments the same effect as the state itself would give to the judgment. In regards to issue preclusion, this rule applies in all but a few narrow situations delineated by Congress. Here, since State A would allow the judgment to be used this way, the federal district court in State B must do so as well.

A is incorrect because this question does not focus on what law the federal court should apply, but on what effect the State A state court judgment should have in the woman's litigation. **B** is incorrect because issue preclusion does not require the woman to be a party to the first lawsuit. **D** is incorrect because res judicata and issue preclusion are two different legal concepts, and this answer choice is simply lumping them together.

56. **A**    If a plaintiff raises a federal question, a defendant may remove the action to federal court even if that defendant is a citizen of the state in which the claim was originally brought. This differs from the rule for an action that may be removed to federal court based on diversity jurisdiction. In that case, if the defendant is a citizen of the state where the action was brought, he or she cannot remove the action to federal court. Here, because the man's claim raised a federal question, any issue regarding the removal's appropriateness based on diversity jurisdiction is irrelevant. Therefore, **B, C,** and **D** are incorrect.

57.  **D**    Under Fed. R. Civ. P. 26(e)(1), if a party learns that a response to an interrogatory was materially incomplete or incorrect, that party must supplement or correct the response. Here, the response was materially incorrect regarding the time, place, and person who fired the man from his position.

A is incorrect because the responding party's duty to correct the response is not dependent upon the other party challenging the answer. B is incorrect because even though the company seemed to have answered the question in good faith, this would not relieve it of the duty to amend the response once it discovered it was incorrect. C is incorrect because whether the response was based on the president's personal knowledge is immaterial to the question.

58.  **A**    In *Keeton v. Hustler Magazine, 465 U.S. 770 (1984)*, the United States Supreme Court ruled that a state had personal jurisdiction over a defendant magazine for a libel suit because the magazine sold 10,000 copies per month in that state. This was true even though neither the plaintiff nor the defendant were citizens of the forum state or had any other contacts with the forum state. Importantly, by exploiting the state's market, the Court found the magazine should have reasonably anticipated "being haled into court there in a libel action based on the contents of its magazine." Therefore, D is incorrect.

B is incorrect because the mere fact State C was the only state in which the statute of limitations had not yet run out would not give State C jurisdiction over the claim. C is incorrect because the fact the woman did not have much contact with the state would not affect whether the state had personal jurisdiction over the rival magazine.

59.  **D**    Under 28 U.S.C. §1406(a), if a case is filed in an improper venue, the court may transfer the case to any district or division it could have been brought in "if it be in the interest of justice." Consequently, if the court believes dismissing the case would be unfair to the motorcyclist, it can transfer the case to the proper district.

A and B are incorrect because this rule applies even though the federal district court does not have proper jurisdiction over the claim. C is incorrect because the fact dismissal would lead to an unfair result does not give the federal district court jurisdiction.

60.  **B**    A subpoena for a deposition may command a witness who is not a party to the lawsuit to attend a deposition that is "within 100 miles of where the person resides, is employed, or regularly transacts business in person." *See Fed. R. Civ. P. 45(c).* Here, since the tenant lives 500 miles away, he cannot be compelled to attend.

The issue here is that the attorney can depose the tenant, she just needs to travel to State B to do it. A is incorrect because the fireman's attorney can subpoena the witness to attend a deposition in State B even if she is not licensed in State B. C is incorrect because if she wants the deposition, she can travel to State B to get it. D is incorrect because it doesn't matter that the attorney is willing to pay the costs of the tenant's travel.

61.  **D**      In *Connecticut v. Doehr, 501 U.S. 1(1991)*, the United States Supreme Court found that
a statute allowing prejudgment attachment without a showing of extraordinary circumstances violated the Due Process Clause of the Fourteenth Amendment. In determining
the process necessary before a state can deprive a person of his or her property through
a prejudgment attachment, courts should look at (1) the interest that will be affected, (2)
the risk of erroneous deprivation, and (3) the interest of the party seeking the prejudgment
remedy. Here, the State A statute allows attachment based only on an affidavit provided
by the requesting party, which creates a high risk of erroneous deprivation.

**A** is incorrect because amount in controversy is an issue for subject matter jurisdiction,
which is not an issue created by this question. **B** and **C** are incorrect because the Due
Process issue in this case would not be solved by a hearing after the attachment.

62.  **C**      Under Fed. R. Civ. P. 33(a), only parties to an action are required to respond to interrogatories. Non-party witnesses are subject to being deposed. Consequently, the truck driver
does not need to answer the interrogatories.

Therefore, **A, B,** and **D** are incorrect.

63.  **A**      Under Fed. R. Civ. P. 56(a), summary judgment is appropriate only when "there is no
genuine dispute as to any material fact and the movant is entitled to judgment as a matter
of law." Here, since the court believes that there is still some chance that the man's claim
might be valid, it would be inappropriate for the court to grant summary judgment.

**B** is incorrect because the issue here isn't the sufficiency of the evidence; it is whether
there is no genuine dispute as to any material fact. **C** is incorrect because the standard for
summary judgment is not focused on whether the non-moving party is mistaken or lying.
**D** is incorrect because summary judgment is only appropriate when the court believes that
as a matter of law all issues should be decided in the movant's favor.

64.  **D**      Under Fed. R. Civ. P. 11, when an attorney files a pleading, motion, or other paper with
the court, that attorney certifies that "after an inquiry reasonable under the circumstances
. . . the factual contentions have evidentiary support." If an attorney violates this rule, he
or she is subject to sanctions. Here, since the attorney did not do any investigation into the
factual contentions regarding the banker's claim (such as getting the police report), it is
likely the company could move for Rule 11 sanctions and receive a court order requiring
the attorney and/or the banker to pay the lost attorney's fees.

**A** is incorrect because even though the company won the case, this does not fix the harm
caused by the lost attorney's fees. **B** is incorrect because the fee agreement between the
company and its attorney is not at issue. **C** is incorrect because there was no indication
the banker's attorney was acting in bad faith, so they did not conspire together to commit
fraud.

65.  **C**      Under Fed. R. Civ. P. 16, a court may order the attorneys to appear for one or more
pretrial conferences for several reasons, such as expediting the action, discouraging
wasteful pretrial activities, and facilitating settlement. Importantly, under Fed. R. Civ.

P. 16(c)(1), "if appropriate, the court may require that a party or its representative be present or reasonably available by other means to consider possible settlement." In fact, if the man fails to attend, he could be subject to sanctions. Therefore, **A** and **B** are incorrect.

**D** is incorrect because the fact the man is the plaintiff does not change the analysis.

66. **D**    If a party believes that the court has failed to give a proper jury instruction, Fed. R. Civ. P. 51(d) states that a party may assign error to "failure to give an instruction, if that party properly requested it and—unless the court rejected the request in a definitive ruling on the record—also properly objected." Here, since the computer company's attorney did not object, the computer company waived its right to the instruction.

Therefore, A, B, and **C** are incorrect.

67. **A**    If a party has "failed to plead or otherwise defend," the opposing party can move for a default judgment under Fed. R. Civ. P. 55(a). Generally, a defendant must serve an answer "within 21 days after being served with the summons and complaint." *See Fed. R. Civ. P. 12.*

**B** is incorrect because a defendant has 60 days to respond if he or she has waived service. Here, since there is no indication that the doctor waived service, he would have had 21 days to respond. This makes A the stronger answer. Under Fed. R. Civ. P. 4, service is proper if (a) a party is served personally, (b) service is left at the defendant's usual place of abode with a person of suitable age and discretion who resides within, or (c) service is made upon the defendant's authorized agent. There is no strict age requirement regarding who service can be left with, so the 17-year-old son was probably appropriate. Therefore, **C** is incorrect. Service can be made by any person who is at least 18 years old and is not a party to the action. Therefore, **D** is incorrect.

68. **A**    Under Fed. R. Civ. P. 24, "the court must permit anyone to intervene who . . . claims an interest relating to the property or transaction that is the subject of the action, and is so situated that disposing of the action may as a practical matter impair or impede the movant's ability to protect its interest, unless existing parties adequately represent that interest." As the mother of a student in a poor-area school, the woman clearly has an interest in the action and could lose her ability to protect that interest if the civil rights activist loses the case. The important point here is that there is no indication the existing parties will adequately represent her interests.

**B** is incorrect because if the court found that the existing parties would adequately protect the woman's interest, she would not be allowed to intervene as of right. **C** and **D** are incorrect because the underlying nature of the action is irrelevant.

69. **D**    "A party must, without awaiting a discovery request, provide to the other parties . . . any insurance agreement under which an insurance business may be liable to satisfy all or part of a possible judgment." *See Fed. R. Civ. P. 26(a)(1)(A).* Consequently, the attorney does not have to do anything to get the information she wants.

Therefore, **A, B,** and **C** are incorrect.

70. **C**    For a class action to be brought, the class must meet four requirements. First, the class must be so numerous that joinder of all its members is impracticable. Second, there must be a common question of law or fact. Third, the representatives must have a claim or defense typical to the other members of the class. Fourth, the representatives must fairly and adequately protect the interests of the class. *See Fed. R. Civ. P. 23*. Here, since there are only 12 potential class members, it is unlikely a court would find the class so numerous that joinder is impracticable. Therefore, **A** and **B** are incorrect.

    **D** is incorrect because it is not necessary in a class action that each of the unnamed members of the class claim over a certain amount in damages.

71. **B**    Collateral estoppel (also known as issue preclusion) refers to the situation where a particular issue of fact or law has been determined in a prior proceeding, and a party seeks to use that determination in a subsequent proceeding. In that case, courts state that a party is collaterally estopped from re-litigating the issue. In *Parklane Hosiery Co. v. Shore, 439 U.S. 322 (1979)*, the United States Supreme Court ruled that in a similar situation a party could use collateral estoppel offensively against another party when it was unlikely that the party seeking estoppel could have intervened in the first action. Here, since it was unlikely the shareholder could have intervened in an action brought by the SEC, he can use collateral estoppel to prevent re-litigation of the issue in his suit against the company.

    **A** is incorrect because its not enough that the issue was decided in the prior action—there must be some indication that the party seeking to use collateral estoppel in this way would not have been able to intervene in the prior lawsuit. **C** is incorrect because such use of collateral estoppel does not violate a party's Seventh Amendment right to a jury trial even if the prior action involves equitable claims. **D** is incorrect because the shareholder can use the prior ruling even if he was not a party to the SEC action.

72. **A**    The Seventh Amendment of the United States Constitution gives a right to a jury for suits "at common law." Consequently, with only a few exceptions, there is only a right to a jury trial for claims that are "legal" (those claims that involve a claim for damages). There is generally no right to a jury trial for claims that are "equitable" (claims that involve an injunction). Here, since the singer is seeking an injunction, he is not entitled to a trial by jury.

    Therefore, **B, C,** and **D** are incorrect.

73. **A**    Under Fed. R. Civ. P. 48, "a jury must begin with at least six and no more than 12 members." In addition, "unless the parties stipulate otherwise, the verdict must be unanimous and must be returned by a jury of at least six members." Since there is no indication the parties stipulated otherwise, the jury's verdict has to be unanimous before it can be entered in the man's favor. Therefore, **C** and **D** are incorrect.

    **B** is incorrect because, as stated above, a jury can have between 6 and 12 members.

74.  **C**    **A** crossclaim is when a party makes a claim against a co-plaintiff or co-defendant. Under Fed. R. Civ. P. 13(g), a crossclaim must be part of the same transaction or occurrence. However, a crossclaim is always optional. Consequently, the store can file its own claim against the delivery service.

                **A** and **B** are incorrect because the crossclaim is still optional even if it is fully litigated in the other action and even if it arises out of the same transaction or occurrence. **D** is incorrect because the citizenship of the parties does not change the analysis regarding the crossclaim.

75.  **A**    In *International Shoe v. Washington, 326 U.S. 310 (1945)*, the United States Supreme Court ruled that an out-of-state company had sufficient minimum contacts with the forum state when that company purposely availed itself of the chance to do business there, and should have anticipated being required to litigate claims in the forum state. Here, by having a salesman in the state, the supplier purposefully availed itself of the chance to do business there and should have anticipated the possibility of litigation.

                Therefore, **B**, **C**, and **D** are incorrect.

# QUESTIONS
# CONSTITUTIONAL LAW

# CONSTITUTIONAL LAW
# TABLE OF CONTENTS
Numbers refer to Question Numbers

# CONSTITUTIONAL LAW

1. A state enacts the Continuing Professional Education Act, which provides that all persons licensed by the state to practice any profession other than medicine are required to complete 10 units per year of state-approved continuing education studies as a condition for renewal of their professional licenses.

   The day after the statute goes into effect, a law school graduate, who has applied for but not yet received a license to practice law, sues in federal court seeking a declaratory judgment that the Continuing Professional Education Act is unconstitutional. Which of the following is the clearest ground for dismissal of this action by the court?

   (A) No substantial federal question is presented.

   (B) The suit presents a non-justiciable political controversy.

   (C) The student lacks standing to attack the statute.

   (D) The validity of the statute has not yet been determined by a state court.

2. A state law declares a wild pig to be an endangered species and prohibits the killing or shooting of any wild pig within the state. A new national park was established by the federal government to preserve plants and animals native to the region, and is located entirely within the state. The wild pig is so hardy that it has begun to displace other wildlife in the national park. Because the wild pig is actually descended from European stock, the United States Department of the Interior has contracted with an exterminator, a resident of another state, to kill all wild pigs living within the national park. The contract with the exterminator is specifically authorized by federal statutes regulating the operation of national parks.

If the exterminator is prosecuted by the state for violating the law that prohibits the killing of wild pigs, which of the following is the exterminator's strongest argument in defense against that prosecution?

   (A) Only the federal government can declare a species to be endangered.

   (B) As applied, the state statute unduly interferes with interstate commerce.

   (C) As applied, the state statute violates the Obligation of Contracts Clause of the United States Constitution.

   (D) As applied, the state statute violates the Supremacy Clause of the United States Constitution.

3. A state statute prohibits the killing of any animal "in a manner which causes unnecessary pain or suffering of said animal." The defendant is prosecuted for violating the statute by strangling a chicken as part of a religious ritual in which he participated. The defendant defends on the ground that the state statute as applied in his case unconstitutionally interferes with his free exercise of religion.

Which of the following may the court NOT consider in determining the constitutionality of the statute?

   (A) Whether the statute is necessary to protect a compelling state interest.

   (B) Whether the religious belief that requires the strangling of a chicken is reasonable.

   (C) Whether the religious ritual involving the strangling of chickens has been practiced for a long period of time.

   (D) Whether the defendant is sincere in the religious belief that requires the strangling of a chicken.

4. Congress passes a law regulating the wholesale and retail prices of "every purchase of an
automobile in the United States." The strongest argument in support of the constitutionality of such a statute is that

   (A) taken as a whole, the domestic purchases
   and sales of such products affect interstate commerce.

   (B) the United States Constitution expressly
   authorizes Congress to pass laws for the
   general welfare.

   (C) Congress has the authority to regulate the
   prices of products purchased and sold
   because commerce includes buying and
   selling.

   (D) Congress has the right to regulate interstate transportation and the importation
   of products from abroad.

5. A federal statute directs payment of federal
funds to states for use in the improvement and
expansion of state hospital facilities. The terms
of the statute provide that "No state shall
award a contract for hospital improvement
or expansion financed in whole or in part by
funds received under this section unless said
contract requires that the contractor pay its
employees a minimum wage of $10 per hour."

A state contracted with a builder for the construction of a new wing on the State Hospital,
after receiving funds for that purpose under the
federal statute. The contract did not require the
builder to pay its employees a minimum wage
of $10 per hour. Upon learning this, federal
officials demanded that the state either modify
its contract with the builder or return the funds
received under the statute. When the state
refused, the federal government sued the state
in federal court for return of the money.

In the action by the United States against the
state, the court should find for

   (A) the state, because fixing the minimum
   wage of employees is a traditional state
   function.

   (B) the state, because the regulation of hospitals and of construction practices are
   traditional state functions.

   (C) the United States, because Congress has
   the power to regulate the way in which
   federal funds are spent.

   (D) the United States, because some of the
   materials used in hospital construction
   are traded in interstate commerce.

6. A bird is a rare species of quail found only
in the state. Because its flesh is tasty, it was
hunted nearly to extinction until 30 years ago.
At that time, the state instituted conservation
and game management programs designed to
preserve the bird. These programs included
the establishment of breeding preserves, the
employment of ornithologists to study the
bird's habits, the passage of laws restricting
the hunting of the birds, and the employment
of game wardens to enforce those laws. The
expense of maintaining the programs was
financed in part by the sale of hunting licenses.
A recent statute passed by the state legislature
fixes the fee for a hunting license at $10 per
year for state residents, and $20 per year for
nonresidents. A hunter who resides outside the
state was arrested in the state and prosecuted
for hunting without a license in violation of
the statute. He defended by asserting that the
statute is unconstitutional because the hunting
license fee for nonresidents is higher than for
residents.

Which of the following correctly identifies
the clause or clauses of the United States
Constitution violated by the state hunting
license statute?

   (A) The Privileges and Immunities Clause of
   Article IV.

   (B) The Privileges and Immunities Clause of
   the Fourteenth Amendment.

   (C) Both the Privileges and Immunities
   Clause of Article IV and the Privileges
   and Immunities Clause of the
   Fourteenth Amendment.

(D) Neither the Privileges and Immunities Clause of Article IV nor the Privileges and Immunities Clause of the Fourteenth Amendment.

7. An organization asserts that government should be abolished. Its slogan is, "What if they made a law and nobody obeyed?" Its published literature urges all persons to violate laws, no matter how logical they might seem, and in this way to help bring about the abolition of government.

   While in law school, a student joined the organization for the purpose of acquiring material for a book that he was writing. Although he had heard that the organization was dangerous and subversive, the student thought its members to be fools and believed their slogan and literature to be too ridiculous to ever convince anybody of anything. So that he could have access to the organization's records, he volunteered to be Party Secretary. In his capacity as such, he frequently typed handbills written by the organization's Propaganda Chairperson and arranged to have them printed for subsequent distribution, although he did not intend for anybody to be convinced by them. All of these handbills contained the organization's slogan and urged the deliberate violation of laws. Eventually, the student wrote a book about the organization. When he finished law school and applied for admission to the bar, his application was rejected. The state bar examiners stated that the only reason for the rejection of the student's application was a state law that provided that "No person shall be licensed to practice law who has belonged to any organization advocating unlawful activity." If the student brings an appropriate judicial proceeding for an order directing the state bar examiners to admit him to practice law, should the student win?

   (A) Yes, because he joined the organization for the purpose of gathering information for a book that he was writing.

   (B) Yes, because he did not intend for the organization to succeed in convincing people to violate laws.

(C) No, because he knew that the organization advocated unlawful conduct when he joined the organization.

(D) No, because he played an active role in the organization's activities.

8. A state statute requires cable television stations to set aside one hour of airtime per week to be made available without charge for the broadcasting of spiritually uplifting programs produced by recognized religious organizations. The statute further provides that airtime thereby made available shall be equally divided among Jewish, Roman Catholic, and Protestant organizations. A religious organization known as the American Buddhist League produced a spiritually uplifting program but was advised by several cable television stations that it could not be broadcast under the statute. The American Buddhist League has instituted a proceeding in federal court challenging the constitutional validity of the state statute.

   The clearest reason for finding that the statute is unconstitutional is that it violates

   (A) the Free Exercise Clause, in that it treats religions unequally.

   (B) the Establishment Clause, in that it is not closely fitted to furthering a compelling governmental interest.

   (C) the Equal Protection Clause, in that it applies only to cable television stations.

   (D) the Supremacy Clause, in that broadcasting is an area already subject to extensive federal regulation.

9. When revolutionaries seized control of the government of a foreign republic, they confiscated and nationalized several privately owned businesses, including some belonging to citizens of the United States. The President of the United States ordered the Secretary of Defense to prepare to send troops into the country to protect United States interests there. When the Secretary of Defense began giving appropriate orders to military leaders, action was instituted in a federal court for an injunction prohibiting

the Secretary of Defense from sending troops to the country. The plaintiff in that action asserted that the President's order to invade the country violated a federal statute that limited the President's power to invade such nations. The Secretary of Defense asked the court to dismiss the case, on the ground that it lacked jurisdiction.

Does the federal court have jurisdiction to issue the requested injunction?

(A)  No, because the President is Commander-in-Chief of the Army and Navy.

(B)  No, because the federal courts lack the power to review the constitutional validity of a presidential order.

(C)  Yes, because federal officials are subject to the jurisdiction of the federal courts even when carrying out presidential orders.

(D)  Yes, because the President lacks the power to order the invasion of a foreign nation without a declaration of war.

10.  A federal statute prohibits male employees of the United States Census Bureau from wearing beards or moustaches, although no such prohibition exists for employees of other federal agencies. The plaintiff was discharged from his employment with the U.S. Census Bureau for violating the statute by refusing to remove his moustache. If the plaintiff asserts a claim on the ground that the statute was invalid, his most effective argument is that the law

(A)  denies him a privilege or immunity of national citizenship.

(B)  invidiously discriminates against him in violation of the Fifth Amendment to the United States Constitution.

(C)  invidiously discriminates against him in violation of the Fourteenth Amendment to the United States Constitution.

(D)  deprives him of a property right without just compensation.

11.  A state constitution contains an equal protection clause identical in language to the Equal Protection Clause in the Fourteenth Amendment to the United States Constitution. The state legislature passed a law empowering insurance companies within the state to charge different rates for males and females where actuarial analysis revealed a relationship between gender and increased risk. Shortly after its passage, the plaintiff sued in the state court for a judgment declaring that the statute violated the Equal Protection Clause of the state constitution. The trial court found the statute to be valid, and the plaintiff appealed to the Court of Judicial Appeals, the highest court of the state. The Court of Judicial Appeals affirmed the ruling of the lower court.

If the plaintiff seeks United States Supreme Court review of the state Court of Judicial Appeals decision, United States Supreme Court review is available

(A)  by appeal only.

(B)  by certiorari only.

(C)  either by appeal or by certiorari.

(D)  neither by appeal nor by certiorari.

12.  Congress passes the Federal Humane Act prohibiting the interstate transportation of dogs for use in dogfighting competitions or exhibitions. The defendant is prosecuted in a federal court for violating the Federal Humane Act, and defends by asserting that the statute is not constitutionally valid because it was enacted for purposes that were entirely noncommercial. The most effective argument in support of the constitutionality of the statute is that

(A)  Congress is empowered to prohibit cruelty to animals under the federal police power.

(B)  the power to regulate interstate commerce includes the power to completely exclude specified items from interstate commerce without regard to congressional motives.

(C) under the "Cooley Doctrine," the federal and state governments have concurrent power to prohibit cruelty to animals.

(D) acts of Congress are presumptively constitutional.

13. A woman who was not a citizen of the United States applied for temporary employment with the state. She was rejected, however, because the Civil Service Law of the state prohibits temporary state employment of a person who is not a United States citizen. The woman sued in a state court for an order directing the state Civil Service Commission to reconsider her application, on the ground that the section of the Civil Service Law that prohibited the temporary employment of noncitizens was unconstitutional.

The woman asserted that the section in question was invalid under the Supremacy Clause. In determining the constitutionality of the section in question, which of the following would be most relevant?

(A) The unemployment rate in the state.

(B) Federal civil service laws.

(C) The immigration laws and treaties of the United States.

(D) The percentage of persons residing in the state who are not citizens of the United States.

14. Congress enacts the Truth in Selling Act, requiring that certain disclosures be made by sellers in interstate sales transactions, and fixing civil damages for failure to make the requisite disclosures. The Act authorizes parties allegedly damaged by violations of the Truth in Selling Act to sue in either state or federal courts. The Act further provides that any decision of a lower state court construing a section of the Truth in Selling Act

may be appealed directly to the United States Supreme Court.

The provision of this statute that authorizes appeal of a lower state court decision directly to the United States Supreme Court is

(A) constitutional, because Congress has the power to regulate interstate commerce.

(B) constitutional, because Congress may establish the manner in which the appellate jurisdiction of the United States Supreme Court is exercised.

(C) unconstitutional, because Article III of the United States Constitution does not authorize the United States Supreme Court to directly review the decisions of lower state courts.

(D) unconstitutional, because it infringes the sovereign right of a state to review decisions of its own lower courts.

15. Congress enacts the Aid to Education Act, which authorizes the direct expenditure of federal tax funds for the purchase of computers and audiovisual equipment that are then to be donated to private schools for educational purposes. The Act makes the equipment available on equal terms to religiously oriented and non-religiously oriented private schools. However, a provision of the Act states that the equipment so purchased and donated must be used solely for non-religious purposes and non-religious education.

The parents of several students at public schools located in the state have sued in federal court for an order enjoining the use of federal tax funds for the purchase of equipment to be used by religious schools, on the ground that such expenditure is unconstitutional.

Should the court issue the injunction?

(A) Yes, because expenditures of public funds for the purchase of equipment to be used by religious schools violates the Establishment Clause.

(B) Yes, because regulation of education is solely a function of the states.

(C) No, because the petitioners lack standing to challenge the expenditure of funds by the federal government.

(D) No, because the Aid to Education Act permits such expenditures only for non-religious purposes.

16. An ordinance of the city provides for the election of a mayor every four years. The ordinance makes all persons living in the city for one year eligible to vote in mayoral elections. It specifies how a candidate may have his or her name placed on the ballot, and provides that a voter may vote for a person whose name is not on the ballot by writing that person's name onto the ballot at a place provided for that purpose.

Although she was not associated with any political party, a lawyer decided to run for the office of mayor. It was too late for the lawyer to have her name placed on the ballot, so she campaigned for write-in votes. Because many of the people she regarded as her constituents were not United States citizens and did not read or write English, the lawyer furnished prospective voters with self-adhesive stickers imprinted with her name and told them that they could cast a "sticker vote" for her by placing the sticker in the appropriate place on the ballot. Because he feared that stickers would separate from the ballots to which they were attached and attach themselves to other ballots, the City Elections Commissioner advised the lawyer before the election that sticker votes would not be counted.

The lawyer instituted a judicial proceeding for an order compelling the City Elections Commissioner to count sticker votes on the ground that his refusal to do so violated the constitutional rights of voters. Which of the following would be the City Elections Commissioner's most effective argument in support of the constitutionality of his refusal to count sticker votes?

(A) The lawyer is not entitled to assert the constitutional rights of others.

(B) The use of sticker votes would interfere with the accuracy and convenience of ballot counts.

(C) Persons who are unable to read and write English should not be permitted to vote.

(D) The use of sticker votes would enable a person to vote who was not familiar with the issues or candidates.

17. The federal Interstate Riverboat Act provides that the minimum wage for persons employed on river boats engaged in interstate commerce shall be $6.50 per hour and authorizes the United States Department of Labor to impose sanctions for violations of its provisions.

As part of a new tourism campaign, the state runs scenic cruises on a river that serves as a border between it and another state. Persons employed by the state as crew members are regulated by the state Civil Service Code. Employees making less than $6.50 per hour assert a claim against the state in a federal court for money damages consisting of the difference between the wages they have been receiving and $6.50 per hour as required under the federal Interstate Riverboat Act. If the state moves to dismiss the action, should the motion to dismiss be granted?

(A) Yes, under the doctrine of abstention.

(B) Yes, because the Eleventh Amendment to the United States Constitution grants the states immunity from such actions.

(C) No, because the state employs the plaintiffs to engage in the business of tourism, which is not a traditional state function.

(D) No, under the Supremacy Clause.

18. The defendant purchased several pornographic videotapes by mail from a distributor of "adult" products and showed them to friends who attended a barbecue at his home.

The defendant was arrested and charged with presenting an obscene performance in violation of state penal code section 123. The distributor was charged with being an accessory to the defendant's violation.

The defendant pleaded guilty and received a suspended sentence in return for his promise to testify against the distributor in its prosecution for being an accessory to the defendant's violation. In defense against that prosecution, the distributor contended that, as applied, penal code section 123 unconstitutionally violated the defendant's constitutional rights. Does the distributor have standing to assert a violation of the defendant's constitutional rights in its own defense?

(A) Yes, because the videotapes the defendant had been prosecuted for showing were purchased from the distributor.

(B) Yes, because any person may challenge the validity of a statute regulating freedom of expression.

(C) No, because the defendant waived his constitutional rights by pleading guilty to the prosecution.

(D) No, because no person may defend against a criminal charge by asserting the constitutional rights of third persons.

19. To finance federal aviation services, a federal statute requires the payment of an annual federal tax of $1,000 on every aircraft of a certain size. The state Department of Farming owns an airplane that it uses for aerial surveying of agricultural land in the state. Although the size of the airplane makes it subject to the tax, the state paid the tax under protest. If the state sues in an appropriate federal court for the return of the tax payment that it made to the federal government, the court should find for

(A) the state, because the power to tax is the power to destroy.

(B) the state, under the doctrine of state immunity.

(C) the federal government, under the doctrine of state subordination.

(D) the federal government, because the state receives benefit from federal aviation services.

20. The honors program of the state's flagship university appealed to the state, claiming that the large size of the program was starting to hurt its effectiveness. In response, the state passed a new law limiting enrollment in the program to only students who are in the top 5 percent of their high school class or who score in the top 5 percent of the SAT or ACT. Importantly, admissions officers are no longer able to take any other factors into account, such as race, gender, economic disadvantage, or sports and club membership. A group of concerned citizens sues, arguing the honors college will not have as diverse of a student body because race will no longer be taken into account in determining enrollment. Is the new law constitutional?

(A) Yes, because courts will defer to institutional judgment in matters of education.

(B) Yes, because it does not mention race or target racial minorities.

(C) No, because the law has a discriminatory effect.

(D) No, because the state has not shown the law is necessary to achieve a compelling state interest.

21. The federal Protected Shellfish Act provides that contractors hired to enforce the Act shall be exempt from the payment of state income taxes. The state imposes a personal income tax on the income of persons residing within the state. A contractor employed by the federal government to enforce the Act derives his entire income from his contract with the federal government. Although the contractor

resides in the state, he has refused to pay the state income tax.

If the contractor is prosecuted in a state court for failing to pay the state income tax, which of the following would be the contractor's most effective argument in defense against the prosecution?

(A) Income from federal employment is exempt from taxation by the state.

(B) The state income tax imposes a burden on the federal government, since it is likely to increase the costs of enforcing the Protected Shellfish Act.

(C) The state does not have the power to tax income derived from activities conducted on the high seas.

(D) Under the Necessary and Proper Clause, Congress has the power to exempt federal contractors from the payment of state tax.

22. The state requires persons applying for state welfare assistance, driver's licenses, admission to the state university, or certain other state benefits to list their federal social security numbers as part of their applications. In this connection, state agencies refer to an applicant's social security number as his or her "Central File Number." The plaintiff has brought an action in a federal court against certain specified state officials for an order enjoining them from using social security numbers in this fashion. In support of his position, the plaintiff argues that at some time almost all citizens of the state apply for some form of state benefit, and that the compilation of a central file on each citizen of the state is likely to have a chilling effect on the exercise of rights granted by the First Amendment to the United States Constitution.

The clearest reason for the dismissal of the plaintiff's suit is that

(A) the action is unripe.

(B) the question presented is moot.

(C) under the Eleventh Amendment to the United States Constitution, state officials are immune to lawsuits of this kind.

(D) the creation of a central file on each person applying for state benefits involves the resolution of political questions.

23. The city council passed an ordinance making it illegal to sell meat that had not been certified by the city health department. A grocer was soon arrested after selling uncertified meat. The grocer admitted violating the ordinance but argued that the ordinance was not valid under the United States Constitution.

Does the city's municipal court have jurisdiction to determine the constitutionality of the ordinance?

(A) No, if determining the constitutionality of the ordinance requires interpretation of the United States Constitution.

(B) No, because the grocer will not have standing to challenge the constitutionality of the ordinance until he has been convicted of violating it.

(C) Yes, because any court has the power to interpret the United States Constitution.

(D) Yes, only if the municipal court is a state court under the laws of the state.

24. After severe flooding in several states, Congress passed a law creating grants available to state governments that could only be used to fund new flood-control projects on state rivers and streams. The money could not be used for any other purpose. A citizen group challenged the law, arguing it was unconstitutional because it took away fiscal decision-making from the states. Is the new law constitutional?

(A) Yes, because it necessarily affects interstate commerce.

(B) Yes, because Congress may tax and spend for the general welfare.

(C) No, because there is no indication the grants are limited to federal property.

(D) No, because there is no indication the rivers and streams are navigable waters.

25. In which of the following fact situations has there most clearly been a violation of the plaintiff's rights under the Fourteenth Amendment to the United States Constitution?

(A) Plaintiff is a black person whose application for state employment was rejected because he failed to pass the state Civil Service examination. Statistics reveal that 10 percent of the black applicants and 60 percent of the white applicants who have taken the exam have passed it.

(B) Plaintiff is an American of Mexican descent who was denied admission to a privately owned hospital solely because of her ethnic background, but who received competent professional treatment at a state hospital instead.

(C) Plaintiff is a Jewish person who resided in a federally operated housing project, and who was excluded from a prayer breakfast held by the federal agency that ran the project solely because of his religion.

(D) Plaintiff is a woman whose application for employment as a deputy sheriff was rejected by the county solely because of her sex.

26. The state recently passed a law that prohibits the drivers of trucks over a certain length from driving within the state for more than four hours without stopping to rest for at least 30 minutes. A trucker was prosecuted for violating the law while driving a truck through the state on an interstate run. As part of his defense, he asserted that the state statute was unconstitutional in that it unduly burdened interstate commerce. The trial court took judicial notice that there is no federal law requiring interstate truck drivers to stop for rest breaks.

In view of the absence of a federal law requiring interstate truck drivers to stop for rest breaks, which of the following is the state's most effective argument in support of the constitutionality of the statute?

(A) The absence of a federal law indicates that Congress does not regard the matter as one requiring national uniformity.

(B) The requirement that truck drivers stop for rest breaks is largely a matter of local concern.

(C) The statute requiring truck drivers to stop for rest breaks is enforceable only within the state.

(D) In the absence of preemptive legislation by Congress, a state is free to impose restrictions on interstate commerce.

27. A state statute known as the Unlawful Assembly Law contains the following provision:

Section I—It shall be a misdemeanor for any group of three or more persons to gather on a public sidewalk and to deliberately conduct themselves in a manner that is offensive to passersby.

When the governor of the state refused to grant a pardon to a college student who had been convicted of destroying state college property during a campus protest, members of a student organization decided to disrupt state government operations by conducting a loud and boisterous demonstration outside a state government office building that they selected at random. About 30 members gathered on the sidewalk outside the building with noisemakers and musical instruments and began marching while making a loud and disturbing noise. Several persons who had business inside the building were unable to get past the crowd of demonstrators to enter. The defendant, one of the participants, was arrested for marching and shouting obscene words that many passersby found offensive.

The defendant is prosecuted for violating Section I of the Unlawful Assembly Law. He defends by asserting that the section is over-broad. The court should find him

(A)   guilty, because his conduct was in fact offensive to passersby.

(B)   guilty, because the reasonable pass-erby would have been offended by the defendant's conduct.

(C)   guilty, because the reasonable person in the defendant's position would have known that his or her conduct would be offensive to passersby.

(D)   not guilty, because some of the conduct that the law prohibited is constitution-ally protected.

28.  In a certain presidential election, relations between the United States and a foreign republic were the basis of a substantial dis-agreement between the candidates, each supporting the view of his political party. After taking office, the new President com-municated with the U.S. ambassador to the republic, who had been appointed by the former President (a member of the oppos-ing party) with the advice and consent of the Senate. The new President demanded that the ambassador either agree to support the for-eign policy contained in his party's platform or resign. When the ambassador refused to do either, the new President told him that he was dismissed from the office of ambassador.

Given the facts, did the new President have the power to remove the ambassador from office?

(A)   Yes, because ideological differences constitute cause for dismissal from ambassadorial office.

(B)   Yes, because the President has the power to dismiss ambassadors without cause.

(C)   No, because an ambassador appointed with the advice and consent of the Senate cannot be dismissed from office without the advice and consent of the Senate.

(D)   No, because removal of an ambassador is a ***de facto*** withdrawal of diplomatic relations with a foreign power.

29.  The Assembly Appropriations Committee of the State Assembly of the state was consider-ing a bill that would appropriate state funds for advertising the availability of abortion to indigent women. Prior to discussion of the bill, the Committee directed the state attor-ney general to seek an advisory opinion from the state court regarding the validity of the proposed bill under both the state and the federal constitutions. The attorney general made the appropriate ex parte motion pur-suant to the state procedure code before the Court of Errors, the highest court in the state. The Court of Errors rendered an advisory opinion in which it stated that the proposed bill did not violate the state constitution, but that it did violate the First Amendment to the United States Constitution.

The Assembly Appropriations Committee voted to reject the proposed legislation in reliance on the advisory opinion of the Court of Errors. Does the United States Supreme Court have jurisdiction to review the advi-sory opinion rendered by the state Court of Errors?

(A)   Yes, because it interpreted a section of the United States Constitution.

(B)   Yes, because the decision did not rest on an adequate state ground.

(C) No, because an advisory opinion is not a case or controversy under the United States Constitution.

(D) No, because there has been no opportunity for appellate review by a state court.

30. A city is home to a large state college, and many students rent houses together in the city neighborhoods. Due to problems with noise, trash, and other complaints, the city passes an ordinance making it illegal for any one household to have more than five people under the age of 23 living under the same roof. A family with five children, ages 22, 21, 19, 15, and 14, challenges the law, arguing the law violates their constitutional rights. Is the ordinance constitutional?

(A) Yes, because three of the children are legally adults and not part of a protected class.

(B) Yes, because the ordinance is valid as a means of protecting the health and welfare of city residents.

(C) No, because it violates the family's right of privacy.

(D) No, because there is no indication the law's effect will be limited to students attending the state college.

31. In the Mutual Aid Treaty of 1957, the United States and a foreign republic agreed to defend each other against aggression. In connection with a century-old border dispute, one of the republic's neighbors recently threatened to attack the republic if the republic did not relinquish its claim to a certain peninsula. At the request of the republic's prime minister, the President of the United States has ordered United States troops to be flown to the republic immediately for the purpose of defending the republic against attack.

If the President's order is challenged in an appropriate proceeding in a federal court, the strongest argument in support of the validity of the order is that the President

(A) has the power to declare war.

(B) has the power to commit United States armed forces to foreign hostilities to satisfy treaty obligations.

(C) has the power to make treaties with the advice and consent of the senate.

(D) is the Commander-in-Chief of the Army and Navy.

32. A student attended a privately owned medical college. One weekend during the school semester, the student was arrested by city police for participating in a demonstration against the government's position on nuclear disarmament. When the student was brought before a judge for arraignment, however, the court dismissed the charge with the consent of the public prosecutor. The following day, the dean of college called the student into her office. The dean referred to the arrest and said that because his conduct had embarrassed the school, the student was expelled. The student subsequently sued the college for damages resulting from his dismissal.

The most effective argument in support of the student's claim is that the dismissal violated the student's right

(A) to an administrative hearing.

(B) to due process.

(C) to freedom of expression.

(D) under an implied contract with the college.

33. In which of the following fact situations is the plaintiff most likely to have standing in a federal court to challenge the statute involved on the ground that it is unconstitutional?

(A) The plaintiff is the chairperson of an organization dedicated to preventing cruelty to animals. She sues in that capacity to enjoin the enforcement of a state statute that permits state officials to seize and destroy unlicensed dogs without notice to their owners.

(B) The plaintiff is a state in which mining is a major industry. It is suing for a judgment declaring unconstitutional a federal statute that imposes a tax on the mining of certain specified metals on the ground that the tax invidiously discriminates against members of the mining industry.

(C) The plaintiff is a federal taxpayer. He sues to recover taxes paid by him under protest on the ground that the money so paid is being used to support military activities against a nation with which the United States is not at war, and that the statute authorizing its use for that purpose is therefore unconstitutional.

(D) The plaintiff is a state taxpayer whose taxes are used, among other purposes, to support the activities of local school districts. Although she has no children of school age, the plaintiff is suing to enjoin enforcement of a state law, the terms of which permit counselors employed by local school districts to advise students about Acquired Immune Deficiency Syndrome (AIDS).

34. After examining the effects of diesel exhaust on the environment, Congress enacts a statute requiring the owners of diesel-powered trucks used in interstate commerce to pay a diesel-powered vehicle use tax of $800 per vehicle. A trucking company that operates more than 1,000 trucks in interstate commerce refuses to pay the diesel-powered vehicle use tax and sues in a federal court for an injunction prohibiting the enforcement of the tax statute. Which of the following is the company's most effective argument in opposition to the tax?

(A) The tax is regulatory in nature.

(B) Imposition of the tax violates the company's right to Equal Protection under the Fifth Amendment to the United States Constitution.

(C) The tax is so burdensome as to amount to a taking of private property, for which just compensation is required.

(D) The tax is coercive in nature, since it is likely to discourage the use of diesel-powered vehicles in interstate commerce.

35. Several years ago, the state legalized certain forms of gambling and began issuing licenses for the operation of gambling casinos. Since then, legal gambling has become the state's most economically significant industry. People travel to the state from all over the United States to visit nearly 2,000 licensed casinos located within the state. All of the casinos discourage the use of cash at gaming tables and sell chips for gamblers to use when participating in the games that they operate. For this reason, many visitors to the state find themselves to be in possession of chips when returning home. For the convenience of tourists, the state legislature passed the Casino Chip Law requiring restaurants and retail business located at state airports, train stations, and bus terminals to accept chips from customers in lieu of cash, at two-thirds the face value of the chips so tendered. The owner of a restaurant located at an airport in the state was prosecuted in a state court for violating the state law by refusing to accept casino chips from a customer who attempted to use them to pay for food purchased at the restaurant.

If the restaurant owner defends by asserting that the law violates the United States Constitution, which of the following arguments would most effectively support his position?

(A) The law denied the restaurant owner due process, since it required him to give up merchandise without receiving cash in return.

(B) By its terms, the law violated the Commerce Clause, since the businesses that were subject to it were all involved in interstate travel.

(C) The power to coin and fix the value of money is exclusively that of Congress.

(D) Requiring the restaurant to accept casino chips in return for merchandise is a taking of private property without just compensation.

36. After several studies show United States students are falling behind on their math scores when compared to other nations, Congress passes a provision providing for the distribution of free math textbooks to students in both public and private schools. The books contain no mention of religion or religious instruction. The vast majority of private schools in most states are religiously affiliated. A concerned federal taxpayer challenges the provision, arguing it unconstitutionally supports religious entities. Does the taxpayer have standing to make the challenge?

(A) Yes, because any federal taxpayer can challenge congressional spending authorizations.

(B) Yes, because the taxpayer's claim is based on a possible violation concerning the limits of congressional spending authority.

(C) No, because there is no proof that any money freed up by the free textbooks will be spent for religious purposes.

(D) No, because the taxpayer hasn't shown a sufficient nexus between his claim and the book expenditures.

37. In 2009, the United States and a foreign republic entered into a treaty by which each country agreed not to tax citizens of the other. Pursuant to that treaty, Congress enacted the National Tax Immunity Act, which exempts nationals of the republic residing in the United States from the obligation to pay income tax to the United States. Recently, however, a United States citizen living in the republic was prosecuted by the republic's government for failing to pay the republic's income tax. Last week, the President of the United States issued an executive order requiring the Internal Revenue Service to begin collecting income tax from the republic's citizens residing in the United States.

Which of the following persons would be most likely to have standing to challenge the constitutional validity of the presidential order in a federal court?

(A) An organization dedicated to the principle that the United States should keep its promises.

(B) A United States citizen who owns land both in the United States and in the republic.

(C) A citizen of the republic living in the United States.

(D) A representative of the republic's government suing on behalf of the republic.

38. In an attempt to reduce air pollution caused by the use of fossil fuels, Congress passes the Fossil Fuel Use Tax Act, which imposes a tax upon the owners of buildings heated by burning fossil fuels. The state owns an office building which was once used to house state government offices. Since the state government moved to new quarters, offices in the building have been rented by the state to tenants engaged in various aspects of private enterprise. Although the building is heated by fossil fuels, the state has refused to pay the tax imposed by the Fossil Fuel Use Tax Act. The federal government has commenced a proceeding against the state for taxes due under the Fossil Fuel Use Tax Act as a result of the use of fossil fuel to heat the building.

Which of the following is the most effective argument in support of the federal government's position?

(A) Under Article I of the United States Constitution, Congress has unlimited power to impose taxes.

(B) Protection of the environment is a legitimate reason for imposing a tax.

(C) The states owe the federal government the obligation of paying those taxes fixed by federal law.

(D) As applied, the Fossil Fuel Use Tax Act taxes the state's activities as a landlord rather than as a state.

39. After examining studies indicating that chewing gum was directly related to the incidence of tooth decay, the state legislature enacted a law prohibiting the advertising of chewing gum in all media. Which of the following is the clearest reason for holding the law to be unconstitutional?

(A) A state may not interfere with commercial speech.

(B) The sale of chewing gum frequently involves interstate commerce.

(C) The law imposes a prior restraint on publication.

(D) There are less restrictive ways of protecting the public against tooth decay that would be equally effective.

40. Congress enacted a statute making education through the 12th grade compulsory. Which one of the following facts or inferences, if it was the only one true, would be most likely to lead to finding that the statute is constitutionally valid?

(A) The majority of people living in states that have inadequate compulsory education requirements are members of ethnic minorities.

(B) Educational levels in England, France, China, and Russia are superior to those in several states in the United States.

(C) By its terms, the statute is applicable only to residents of the District of Columbia and of United States military bases.

(D) The majority of schoolchildren in the United States move from one state to another at some time during the first 12 years of their education.

41. While serving a 10-year sentence for murder in state prison, the defendant was accused of leading a riot that resulted in the death of a prison guard. Without a hearing, the warden ordered the defendant placed in solitary confinement for the remainder of his sentence. The defendant sued in a United States district court for an order directing his removal from solitary confinement on the grounds that he was deprived of due process and that solitary confinement for the remainder of his sentence was a cruel and unusual punishment. The district court rendered judgment against the defendant, who appealed to the United States Court of Appeals. The United States Court of Appeals affirmed, and the defendant petitioned for certiorari to the United States Supreme Court. While the defendant's petition was pending, parole officials voted to release him from prison although it was three years before the end of his sentence, on condition that he meet with a federal probation officer once per month, that he seek gainful employment, that he refrain from consorting with criminals, and that he be returned immediately to prison upon violation of any of the conditions of parole. In opposing the defendant's petition for certiorari, the state's attorney asserted that his release from prison made the issue moot.

Which of the following is the strongest reason for finding that the issues presented by the defendant's petition are **NOT** moot?

(A) The defendant is no longer a prisoner.

(B) In granting parole, parole officials have acknowledged a violation of the defendant's constitutional rights.

(C) The defendant's claim is capable of repetition if it evades judicial review.

(D) The defendant might be returned to solitary confinement if he is re-incarcerated for violating the conditions of his parole.

42. A state statute provides that no person can be elected to state office who is not a citizen of the United States. The constitutionality of the statute is challenged in an appropriate action by the plaintiff.

If the court hearing the plaintiff's challenge takes judicial notice of the treaties and immigration laws of the United States, it will be because they are relevant to the validity of the statute under

(A) the Supremacy Clause.

(B) the Privileges and Immunities Clause.

(C) the due process requirement.

(D) the doctrine of separation of powers.

43. Under which of the following circumstances is a court most likely to uphold the constitutionality of a statute that requires the taking of a loyalty oath by public employees?

(A) Only persons appointed to state office by the governor are required by law to take the loyalty oath.

(B) The statute requires that the loyalty oath be taken by all state employees.

(C) The loyalty oath required by the statute consists entirely of a promise "to uphold the United States Constitution and to oppose the overthrow of the state or federal government by unlawful means."

(D) The loyalty oath is required only of persons appointed to positions with the state militia that are likely to expose them to classified information.

44. In an attempt to improve air quality, several states pass laws providing that vehicles powered by diesel engines of more than a certain size must be equipped with a specified smog-elimination system to be driven on highways within the state. A trucking company challenges such a law in the state on the ground that it unreasonably burdens interstate commerce. Which of the following is the state's best argument in support of the law?

(A) The law applies to intrastate as well as interstate shipments.

(B) The law applies to all vehicles traveling through the state, including those that are garaged primarily in the state.

(C) The law is necessary to protect the health and safety of residents of the state.

(D) Other states have similar requirements.

45. A coastal state has enacted the Ocean Fishing License Act, which regulates the right to fish in coastal waters. Section 1 of the Act provides that no person shall fish in the ocean from a vessel registered in the state who has not obtained an ocean-fishing license from the state Department of Fish and Game. Section 2 of the Act sets the fees for ocean-fishing licenses at $10 per year for residents of the state and $20 per year for nonresidents. Section 3 of the Act provides that if any section of the Act is found invalid for any reason, such finding should not affect the validity of any other section of the Act.

Which of the following would provide the strongest basis for declaring Section 1 of the Ocean Fishing License Act to be **INVALID**?

(A) A federal law that authorizes a federal agency to issue licenses for fishing in coastal waters of the United States.

(B) The absence of any federal law regulating fishing in coastal waters of the United States.

(C) The Equal Protection Clause of the Fourteenth Amendment to the United States Constitution.

(D) The Due Process Clause of the Fifth Amendment to the United States Constitution.

46. The state enacts legislation appropriating several million dollars of state funds to be spent on conservation of agricultural lands within the state. The statute directs the distribution of such funds to Agricultural Conservation Districts geographically equivalent to the counties of the state, authorizes the creation of such Agricultural Conservation Districts, and empowers them with responsibility for administering funds assigned to them. The statute provides that fiscal decisions of each District shall be made by a Board of Governors to be elected by its residents. The statute also provides that participation in district elections is open only to persons who are able to pass a simple test of reading and writing in the English language and who own agricultural land within the geographic boundaries of the District, and that voters in such elections may cast one vote for each acre of agricultural land that they own within the District.

The constitutionality of the statute has been challenged by a litigant who claims that it violates the "one person, one vote" principle. The best argument in response to that claim is that the principle

(A) applies only to elections for statewide and federal office.

(B) does not apply where property rights are involved.

(C) does not apply because of rights reserved to the states by the Tenth Amendment.

(D) does not apply because results of District elections will principally affect the owners of agricultural land.

47. In a case where the constitutionality of a state law regulating the sale of birth control devices is in issue, which party will have the burden of persuasion?

(A) The state, because procreation involves a fundamental right, and the law may have a substantial impact on that right.

(B) The state, because the state law is more likely to have a substantial impact on women than on men.

(C) The person challenging the statute, since there is a rebuttable presumption that all state laws are constitutional.

(D) The person challenging the statute, since the regulation on non-expressive sexual conduct is reserved to for the states by the Tenth Amendment.

48. A state law makes it a crime to interfere with "any right conferred by the Equal Protection Clause of the Fourteenth Amendment to the United States Constitution." In which one of the following cases is the defendant **LEAST** likely to be convicted of violating the law?

(A) The defendant, the manager of an apartment building funded and operated by a federal housing agency, refused to rent an apartment to a black family solely because of their race.

(B) The defendant, the commissioner of police of a large city, refused to hire homosexuals as police officers solely because of their sexual preference.

(C) The defendant, threatening violence, induced a school bus driver, employed by a public school district, to refuse Jewish students rides solely because of their religion.

(D) The defendant, the proprietor of a restaurant located in a state office building and rented from the state, refused to serve Vietnamese immigrants solely because of their place of national origin.

49. After the state raised property taxes, the defendant became active in an organization against tax raises. As part of a protest, the defendant paraded nude in front of the tax collector's office, carrying a sign that read, "Soaring taxes take the clothes off our backs!" The defendant was arrested under a statute newly enacted by the state legislature. The complete text of the law was, "No person shall behave in a shocking or offensive manner in a public place. Any violation of this section shall be punished by a term not to exceed six months in a county detention facility."

If the defendant defends by asserting that the statute is unconstitutional, his most effective argument would be that

(A) under the First and Fourteenth Amendments, expressive conduct may not be punished by the state.

(B) the statute is vague.

(C) the reasonable person is not likely to have been shocked or offended by the defendant's conduct.

(D) conviction under a newly enacted statute is a violation of due process.

50. A law permitting the payment of public funds as financial aid to schools operated by religious organizations is most likely to be constitutionally valid if it directs payment to

(A) primary schools, for enhancement of the salaries of teachers who do not instruct on religious subjects.

(B) primary schools at which no more than 10 percent of the instructional time is spent on religious subjects, for the purchase of laboratory equipment.

(C) secondary schools, for the purchase of textbooks on secular subjects.

(D) colleges, for the purchase of athletic equipment.

51. Because a river is wide, deep, and flows through several states, it is an important thoroughfare for interstate commercial cargo ships. The state, through which the river flows, has passed a law imposing strict water pollution controls on ships using rivers within the state. A transport company that operates ships on the river has challenged the statute, asserting that it violates the Commerce Clause of the United States Constitution.

Which one of the following facts or inferences, if found to be true, would be most likely to result in a finding that the statute is constitutionally valid?

(A) The river is a source of water for agricultural irrigation in all the states through which it passes.

(B) Congress has not prohibited state regulation of water pollution.

(C) Congress has enacted laws regulating water pollution in interstate rivers.

(D) The company operates only within the state.

52. The defendant was a member of an organization that worshipped 12 different deities, each said to be in charge of a different field of worldly activity. Each month of the year, the organization conducts a festival dedicated to a different one of the deities. In March, a festival was held to honor the goddess of love. As part of the festival, members met to engage in activities involving nudity and group sexual intercourse. Along with other members of the organization, the defendant, who participated in the festival, was arrested by police from the county vice squad. He was convicted of violating a state law that made it a crime "for any adult to engage in sexual intercourse with another while any third person is present."

If the defendant appeals, the conviction

(A) must be overturned, because the group sexual activity was required by a reasonable interpretation of the organization's religious beliefs.

(B)  must be overturned, because the conduct was part of the free exercise of a religion.

(C)  may be upheld, on the ground that an organization that worships multiple deities is not a "religion" for First Amendment purposes.

(D)  may be upheld, even if the group sexual activity was required by the defendant's sincere religious beliefs.

53.  A state statute made the distribution of birth control illegal. The law had been on the books for 80 years, with one reported prosecution. Ten married couples and a doctor challenged the law's constitutionality in federal court. In doing so, they alleged that they violated the law repeatedly. The court believed that it was very unlikely that the state would enforce the law. The court should find

(A)  the case cannot be decided because it is not yet ripe.

(B)  the case cannot be decided because it is moot.

(C)  the case can be decided because violation of the law is capable of repetition.

(D)  the case can be decided since the couples and the doctor have admitted to violating the law.

54.  A small political organization advocates racial segregation and occasionally runs a candidate for election to office in the state. The organization planned to hold a campaign rally at the state capitol two weeks prior to the last statewide election. Because anonymous threats of violence were received by the state police, however, a state court issued an injunction prohibiting the organization from conducting any public rallies until after the election. After the election was over, the organization sought United States Supreme Court review of the state court's decision.

The United States Supreme Court should

(A)  review the state court's decision if the organization desires to hold future rallies in the state.

(B)  review the state court's decision, because any interference with the right to assemble violates the First Amendment to the United States Constitution.

(C)  not review the state court's decision, since the question presented has become moot.

(D)  not review the state court's decision, since the aims of the organization violate the Equal Protection Clause of the Fourteenth Amendment to the United States Constitution.

55.  In 1999, the state enacted the Energy Conservation Tax Rebate Act, creating a state income tax credit for persons who installed solar and/or wind-powered generators in residential realty. The plaintiff began to install a solar generator in his home in the state in November 2012, but did not complete the installation until February 2013. In December 2012, however, the state legislature repealed the Energy Conservation Tax Rebate Act, effective January 1, 2013.

If the plaintiff challenged the repeal of the Act on the ground that it was constitutionally invalid, his most effective argument would be that repeal of the statute violated the

(A)  Obligations of Contracts Clause.

(B)  Due Process Clause of the Fifth Amendment.

(C)  Privileges and Immunities Clause.

(D)  Just Compensation Clause.

56.  Congress passes a law requiring all females who are 18 years of age to register for a new draft. A nonprofit organization advertises that it will provide an attorney and defend without charge any female prosecuted for failing

to register. State statutes prohibit advertising by attorneys. If the Bar Association of the state sues to enjoin further publication of the advertisement in that state, the injunction should be

(A) granted, because state statutes prohibit advertising by attorneys.

(B) granted, since the advertisement could have the effect of encouraging young women to violate the law.

(C) denied, since the advertisement constitutes commercial speech.

(D) denied, under the First Amendment to the United States Constitution.

57. Congress passes the Schools Construction Act, providing for grants of federal funds to states to help finance the construction of new school buildings. A section of the Act provides that states that do not alter their building codes to prohibit the use in school construction of certain substances listed as carcinogenic (cancer-causing) are ineligible for federal funds under the law. The state is the home of an industry that produces one of the materials listed in the federal law as carcinogenic. Its legislature has refused to alter the state building code to conform to the requirements of the Schools Construction Act.

In a federal court, which of the following potential plaintiffs is most likely to be able to obtain a judicial determination of the validity of the section of the Schools Construction Act dealing with state building codes?

(A) The parent of a child who currently attends a public school in the state and who fears that the quality of education in the state will decline if the state does not receive federal funds for school construction.

(B) An organization dedicated to protecting the concept of "states rights" against encroachment by the federal government.

(C) A taxpayer of the United States and the state, who fears that if the state does not receive federal funds for school construction, her state taxes will be increased to pay for school construction that would otherwise have been federally funded.

(D) A building contractor who has been hired by the state to construct a school building, under a contract that is contingent upon receipt by the state of federal school-construction funds to which it would otherwise be entitled.

58. A law in the state requires any person doing business in that state to obtain a business license from the state's Department of Commerce. A recently enacted amendment to that statute prohibits convicted felons in the state from doing business in that state and authorizes the state's Department of Commerce to deny a business license to any such person.

The plaintiff, a convicted felon who was released from a state prison after completion of his sentence, applied for a business license after the passage of the amendment described above. He brings an action in a federal court to enjoin the state's Department of Commerce from enforcing the amendment against him on the ground that it is constitutionally invalid.

The plaintiff's strongest argument is that

(A) states are forbidden by the Obligation of Contracts Clause from interfering with the rights of felons to do business.

(B) the statute unreasonably interferes with the right of felons to travel from one state to another.

(C) the statute violates the Equal Protection Clause of the Fourteenth Amendment to the United States Constitution.

(D) he has already paid his debt to society and should be given the opportunity to make a fresh start in life by engaging in a lawful occupation.

59. Congressional legislation abolishing all legal penalties for gambling could most easily be upheld

(A) as a regulation of interstate and international commerce.

(B) under the Supremacy Clause of the United States Constitution.

(C) if scientific studies showed gambling to be a harmless activity.

(D) if it applied only to the District of Columbia.

60. The plaintiff, a resident of the state, recently lost her job when her employer went out of business. While employed, the plaintiff worked on the night shift and attended college during the day. She applied for unemployment compensation benefits under the state's Unemployment Compensation Act. Although she was otherwise entitled to benefits, she was denied them under a provision of the Act that prohibits the payment of benefits to any person who attends school between the hours of 8 A.M. and 6 P.M. After exhausting all administrative remedies, the plaintiff appealed the denial of benefits, asserting that the prohibition against payment of benefits to day students violated the Equal Protection Clause.

Which of the following is the minimum finding that would result in a ruling that the statute is constitutionally valid?

(A) The classification is a reasonable way of protecting a compelling state interest.

(B) The classification has a rational basis.

(C) The receipt of unemployment benefits is a privilege rather than a right.

(D) The payment of benefits to day students would result in a clear and present danger.

61. The state requires all public and private hospitals to be accredited by the state Department of Health, which is empowered to inspect hospital facilities prior to accreditation and as a condition of continued accreditation. All hospital employees are required to be licensed by the Department of Health. The Department is also responsible for the distribution of funds under a state law that provides financial aid to all accredited hospitals for the purchase of equipment. The state law makes each hospital's share proportional to the number of patients that it treated the previous year.

A privately operated hospital accredited by the state denies admission to whites except under emergency circumstances. An organization has brought an action against the hospital in a state court for an injunction directing it to discontinue its racially exclusionary policy on the ground that it violates the Equal Protection Clause of the Fourteenth Amendment. Which of the following is the strongest argument in support of the position taken by the organization?

(A) Under the Fourteenth Amendment, no place of public accommodation may discriminate against persons because of their race.

(B) The licensing of hospital employees by the state requires the hospital to act as the state would act in complying with requirements of the Fourteenth Amendment.

(C) The Equal Protection Clause of the Fourteenth Amendment requires the state court to eliminate racial discrimination in places of public accommodation.

(D) The state's involvement in hospital regulation and support makes the Equal Protection Clause of the Fourteenth Amendment applicable to the hospital.

62. In which of the following cases is the defendant's conviction most likely to be reversed on constitutional grounds?

(A) The defendant is convicted of operating a theater showing pornographic films in violation of a zoning ordinance that prohibits such activity from being conducted within 500 feet of a school.

(B)   The defendant is convicted of giving weekly parties at his home at which obscene films are shown to persons who pay an entrance fee, in violation of a county ordinance that prohibits the display to groups of three or more persons of materials defined by state law as obscene.

(C)   The defendant, a professional book-seller, is convicted of selling an obscene book to an undercover police officer, in violation of a state law that provides: "It shall be a misdemeanor for any person to sell or to possess for the purposes of sale any obscene book, magazine, or other publication."

(D)   The defendant, a magazine publisher, is convicted of sending obscene materials through the mails in a trial at which the court permitted the introduction of evidence that the defendant advertised his magazine in a way that pandered to the prurient interests of readers.

63.   Relations between the United States of America and another country have been strained for the past four decades. In an attempt to improve these relations, the President of the United States and the Premier of the other country enter into a series of executive agreements. One of these agreements requires the government of each country to discourage its press from mak-ing derogatory references about the other country. At the President's request and in support of that agreement, Congress enacts the Friendly Nations Publications Act, which prohibits the publication of certain specified disparaging statements about the other country in any magazine or newspaper published by the armed forces of the United States.

Which of the following would be the stron-gest argument against the constitutionality of the Friendly Nations Publications Act?

(A)   The President lacked the power to make an executive agreement requiring the United States to discourage its press from making derogatory references to the other country.

(B)   The executive agreement could have been implemented in a less burden-some manner.

(C)   The executive agreement violates the First Amendment to the United States Constitution.

(D)   The Friendly Nations Publications Act violates the First Amendment to the United States Constitution.

64.   A police officer frequently visited a website where random users could video chat with each other. After five minutes, the video chat would switch to another random user in the system. Most users engaged in sexually explicit conduct while on the site. The police officer also engaged in sexually explicit conduct on the site, often while in his uni-form. The police department discovered that the officer was using the site and fired him. The officer sued, arguing that the firing vio-lated his First Amendment rights. The police department firing

(A)   violated his right to freedom of speech.

(B)   violated his right to freedom of association.

(C)   violated his right to freedom of assembly.

(D)   did not violate his First Amendment rights.

65.   Congress passes a law that provides that whenever the President of the United States delegates any person to travel to a foreign nation for the purpose of negotiating an exec-utive agreement, the President must desig-nate a member of the United States Senate to accompany and advise that person. The President vetoes the law, but the presidential veto is overridden by a two-thirds majority of both houses of Congress. The President subsequently delegates an ambassador to

travel to a foreign nation for the purpose of negotiating an executive agreement without appointing a member of the United States Senate to accompany and advise the ambassador.

Which of the following arguments would most effectively justify that action by the President?

(A) The President has sole and exclusive power over foreign affairs.

(B) The law unconstitutionally discriminates against members of the House of Representatives.

(C) The law violates the principle of separation of powers by interfering with the President's power to delegate authority in the field of foreign affairs.

(D) A presidential veto of a law relating to foreign affairs is final, and may not be overridden by Congress.

66. When the plaintiff declared herself to be a candidate for election to the United States Senate from the state, the state Commissioner of Elections refused to place her name on the ballot. The commissioner said that his decision was based on the fact that state records indicated that the plaintiff was only 27 years of age. The plaintiff subsequently instituted a proceeding against the commissioner in a state court. After examining state birth records, and after taking the testimony of the plaintiff's mother and of a physician who was present at the plaintiff's birth, the court found that the plaintiff was 30 years of age and directed the commissioner to list her as a candidate. The plaintiff won the election, but after she began her term of office, the Senate expelled her, declaring that she did not meet the constitutional age requirement.

If the plaintiff institutes a proceeding in a federal court for an order reinstating her to her seat in the Senate, which of the following would be the most effective argument in support of a motion to dismiss her proceeding?

(A) The plaintiff should be collaterally estopped from maintaining the proceeding.

(B) No substantial federal question is presented.

(C) The plaintiff has already had her day in court.

(D) The plaintiff's claim presents a nonjusticiable political question.

67. Congress passes the Federal Aid to Scholars Act, providing for grants of federal funds to college and university students who meet certain financial and scholastic standards. A provision of the Act, however, restricts such payments to citizens of the United States. The plaintiff is a foreign national studying at a university located in the United States under an appropriate visa granted by the Department of State. If the plaintiff challenges the constitutionality of the citizenship requirement of the Federal Aid to Scholars Act, the court should rule that provision

(A) valid, because Congress has plenary power to regulate the rights of aliens.

(B) valid, because resident aliens are not protected by the United States Constitution.

(C) invalid, because it violates the Equal Protection Clause of the Fourteenth Amendment.

(D) invalid, because resident aliens are entitled to the same constitutional protections as citizens.

68. After several natural disasters, a new state law required property owners to permit cable television companies to install cable lines in their buildings so that all state residents would have immediate and reliable access to government notices, news, and other emergency information. A landlord sued, arguing that the mandatory cabling resulted in a taking. The landlord belonged to a church that believed television violence was the main cause of several recent school

shootings. During trial, the state showed that the encroachment on landowners' properties only consisted of cables less than ½ inch in diameter and had a minimal economic impact on the property owner. In determining the existence of a taking, the court should rule in favor of

(A) the landlord, because there was a physical invasion of the property.

(B) the landlord, because he belonged to a church that was anti-television.

(C) the state, because there was an important countervailing interest in informing the public during natural disasters.

(D) the state, because the physical invasion and economic impact of the statute was minimal.

69. The Clean Roads Act authorized the state Department of Transportation to determine without a hearing the identity of persons spilling toxic chemicals on state highways and to order the removal of such chemicals by such persons. The law also provided that failure to comply with such an order within 30 days after receiving it was a crime. On May 1, state investigators submitted a report stating that a leak in the defendant's truck had caused the deposit of chemical residues on roads within the state during the period from January 2012 through January 2013. The same day, the Department of Transportation ordered the defendant to remove all chemical residues from the roads of the state. The defendant refused to do so, and on August 15 he was convicted of violating the Clean Roads Act by failing to comply with the Department of Transportation order.

If the defendant appeals his conviction, his most effective argument would be that the Clean Roads Act

(A) was an **ex post facto** law.

(B) was a bill of attainder.

(C) violated the Due Process Clause of the Fifth Amendment to the United States Constitution.

(D) violated the Due Process Clause of the Fourteenth Amendment to the United States Constitution.

70. A recently enacted state statute provides that no person shall be granted a high school diploma without first passing a series of examinations designed to test minimum competency in reading, writing, mathematics, and United States history. The statute requires that the examinations are to be written by the state Board of Regents and are to be administered on the same day throughout the state. It further provides that each high school in the state may elect to have the examinations administered either by its own employees or, without cost, by agents of the state.

The plaintiff, a taxpayer of the state, has sued in a federal court to enjoin the state from enforcing the statute on the ground that the administration of the examinations in religious schools by agents of the state violates the Establishment Clause of the First Amendment to the United States Constitution. Which of the following is the most effective argument against the plaintiff's claim?

(A) The plaintiff lacks standing to challenge the constitutionality of the statute.

(B) The law does not discriminate among religions.

(C) The law has neither the effect nor the primary purpose of advancing religion.

(D) The state has a compelling interest in the competency of high school graduates.

71. A city ordinance provides as follows:

Section 1—No person shall conduct a public speech or demonstration in the city without first obtaining an assembly permit from the city mayor, who shall not issue such a permit if, in his or her opinion, the speech or demonstration is likely to result in a breach of the public peace.

The defendant desired to hold a rally in the city. After submitting his application for an assembly permit, the defendant stated in a radio interview that he planned to lead the people at the rally to raid and burn an abortion clinic operated by the city. Upon hearing the radio broadcast, the mayor of the city denied the defendant's application.

The defendant conducted the rally, calling for the immediate destruction by fire of the city abortion clinic. He passed flaming torches to people in the crowd, saying, "Follow me, and we'll burn out that nest of evil!" However, he was arrested as the crowd began to follow him toward the abortion clinic, and he was subsequently convicted of conducting a public rally without an assembly permit in violation of the above ordinance. On appeal, the defendant's conviction should be

(A)  reversed, because prior restraint of speech or assembly is inconsistent with the First Amendment to the United States Constitution.

(B)  reversed, because although punishment of the defendant's conduct may be constitutionally valid, his conduct cannot be punished under this ordinance.

(C)  affirmed, because as a result of the defendant's attempt to incite unlawful action, he lacks standing to challenge the constitutionality of the ordinance.

(D)  affirmed, because an ordinance that requires a permit for the conduct of a public meeting is constitutionally valid.

72.  A state statute provides that:

No producer of unrefined petroleum within the state may sell more than half its annual production to buyers outside the state.

The plaintiff is a producer of unrefined petroleum within the state and operates a trucking company for the transportation of his product.

There is no federal statute concerning the right of a state to regulate the sale of unrefined petroleum produced within that state. If the plaintiff challenges the constitutionality of the statute in an appropriate proceeding, which of the following would be the plaintiff's most effective argument?

(A)  The production and sale of unrefined petroleum is a matter of national concern, requiring uniform federal regulation.

(B)  The unrefined petroleum sold by the plaintiff remains in its original package until it reaches the ultimate consumer.

(C)  The state's attempt to regulate the sale of unrefined petroleum in interstate commerce violates the Full Faith and Credit Clause of the United States Constitution.

(D)  Regulation of the sale of unrefined petroleum is preempted by congressional silence.

73.  Congress passes the State Highway Subsidy Act, which makes matching federal funds available to states for the construction of state highways on condition that states receiving such funds prohibit trucks longer than a specified size from operating on state highways. The state has refused to amend its statutes to comply with the Act.

Which of the following persons is most likely to have standing to challenge the constitutionality of the State Highway Subsidy Act?

(A)  A taxpayer of the state who believes that if the state does not receive matching federal funds for the construction of new highways, the state's roads will soon become inadequate for use by its residents.

(B) A federal taxpayer who believes that if the state does not receive matching federal funds for the construction of new highways, its roads will soon become inadequate for use in interstate commerce.

(C) A non-partisan political-action membership organization dedicated to the preservation of "states' rights" that believes that the State Highway Subsidy Act interferes with the state's right to regulate the size of trucks using its highways.

(D) A road construction company that has a contract to build a road for the state and that believes that without matching federal funds, the state will be unable to honor its contract.

74. The defendant was convicted of murder in a state court after a trial in which evidence was admitted over the defendant's objection that it was obtained in violation of his Fourth Amendment rights. On appeal to the highest court in the state, the defendant's conviction was affirmed. After the defendant's petition for certiorari was denied by the United States Supreme Court, he filed a petition for habeas corpus in the appropriate United States District Court on the ground that the evidence used to convict him was obtained in violation of his Fourth Amendment rights. The defendant's petition for habeas corpus should be

(A) granted, because the United States District Court may consider de novo a constitutional challenge to the admissibility of evidence in a state court.

(B) granted, because the defendant has exhausted all available state remedies.

(C) denied, because the United States Supreme Court did not grant certiorari.

(D) denied, because the state court has already determined that the defendant's Fourth Amendment rights were not violated by admission of the evidence.

75. The plaintiff's application for employment as a state police officer was rejected pursuant to a state law that prohibited state employment of "sexual deviates," on the ground that he was a homosexual. The plaintiff subsequently challenged the validity of the state law in a state court, asserting that it violated the Equal Protection Clauses of the constitutions of the United States and of the state, the language of which is substantially the same. No state court has ever interpreted the phrase "sexual deviates" as used in the state law.

While his state court action was pending, the plaintiff instituted a proceeding in a United States district court seeking an order enjoining the state police commissioner from enforcing the law described above on the grounds that it violates the federal constitution's Equal Protection Clause. If the court declines to grant the plaintiff relief, it will most likely be

(A) based on the abstention doctrine.

(B) based on the Eleventh Amendment to the United States Constitution.

(C) on the ground that the question is moot.

(D) on the ground that the plaintiff lacks standing.

76. A state statute requires hairdressers to be licensed by the State Department of Education. The statute further provides that no person shall qualify for a hairdresser's license who has not completed a prescribed program of study, including a two-semester-unit course in biology. The plaintiff, who held a valid hairdresser's license from another state, moved to the state and applied to the state Department of Education for a hairdresser's license. The plaintiff's application was rejected on the ground that, although he had completed all other requirements for a state hairdresser's license, he had never studied biology as required by the state law. If the plaintiff seeks judicial review of the denial of his application, his most effective argument would be that the law

(A) has no rational basis.

(B) violates the Full Faith and Credit Clause of the United States Constitution.

(C) discriminates against out-of-staters.

(D) violates the Privileges and Immunities Clause of the Fourteenth Amendment to the United States Constitution.

77. The defendant placed the following advertisement in a magazine:

> STEAMY FORBIDDEN SEX! The United States Supreme Court has said that nobody can interfere with the private possession of pornography for private viewing in the privacy of your own home. SO, NOW, FOR THE FIRST TIME EVER, we are offering films TOO HOT for commercial showing. Fill out this coupon and SEND NOW for porno too sizzling to be legal in theaters or clubs. THIS OFFER AVAILABLE ONLY FOR PRIVATE POSSESSION FOR PRIVATE VIEWING IN THE PRIVACY OF YOUR OWN HOME.

A federal police officer ordered films from the defendant by sending a check to the address given in the advertisement.

After the officer received the films, the defendant was charged in a federal court with violating a federal statute that prohibits sending obscene films through the mail.

At the defendant's trial, an attempt is made by the prosecution to offer into evidence a copy of the advertisement to which the officer had responded. Upon timely objection by the defendant, the court should rule the advertisement

(A) admissible, because pandering is not protected by the First Amendment.

(B) admissible as evidence that the films sold by the defendant appeal primarily to prurient interest.

(C) inadmissible as constitutionally protected commercial speech.

(D) inadmissible, because the advertisement is not itself obscene.

78. A United States ambassador was appointed by a former President with the advice and consent of the Senate. Three days after taking office, a new President requests the ambassador's resignation after the ambassador posted a photo of himself online in the nude. Upon the ambassador's refusal to resign, the President issues an order purporting to remove the ambassador from office. Is the presidential order valid?

(A) Yes, because there was cause for the ambassador's removal from office.

(B) Yes, because the President has the power to remove ambassadors without cause.

(C) No, because the President may not remove an ambassador without the advice and consent of the Senate.

(D) No, because the Senate has not ratified the order by consenting to the appointment of a new ambassador.

79. The city, as part of an economic development plan for the city's waterfront area, condemned 15 houses owned by the plaintiffs. The properties were not blighted and were not run-down in any way. The plan was to give the properties to a private developer to create new office space. The plaintiffs challenged the city's action. The court should rule in favor of

(A) the plaintiffs, because the houses were being given to a private party.

(B) the plaintiffs, because the houses were in good repair.

(C) the city, because the houses were condemned as part of an economic development plan.

(D) the city, because the condemnation resulted in mere land use regulation.

80. A state statute provides that no license shall be issued for the marriage of any male person below the age of 19 years or any female person below the age of 17 years. An 18-year-old male desires to marry an 18-year-old female. Because of the provisions of the statute, however, the boy has not yet asked the girl to marry him. If the boy challenges the statute in a state court, asserting that it violates his rights under the United States Constitution, which of the following would be the most effective argument in opposition to the boy's claim?

    (A) He lacks standing to challenge the statute.

    (B) The statute has a rational basis.

    (C) Females mature earlier than males.

    (D) The right to regulate marriage is reserved to the states by the Tenth Amendment.

81. A policy of the State University prohibits use of campus facilities by persons or organizations without a permit from the University Chancellor. The plaintiff, a student at State University, is president of a student organization. On three occasions, the plaintiff's applications for permits to use a classroom for meetings of the organization were denied by the University Chancellor. The reason given by the Chancellor was that the organization advocates interference with freedom of speech as protected by the state's constitution.

    Following the most recent denial of her application, the plaintiff commenced a proceeding in a U.S. district court seeking an injunction prohibiting denial of permits to the organization on the ground that it violates the organization's constitutional right to freedom of assembly. Before a hearing could be held on the plaintiff's claim, the University Chancellor reversed his prior decision and granted the organization a permit for the use of campus facilities, declaring that the philosophy embraced by a student organization would no longer be considered in deciding whether that organization would receive a permit for use of campus facilities. If the

University attorney moves to dismiss the plaintiff's claim, the motion should be

    (A) denied, because none of the University Chancellor's decisions were based on an adequate state ground.

    (B) denied, because the plaintiff's claim is one that is capable of repetition and likely to evade judicial review.

    (C) denied, because the plaintiff was damaged by past denials of her application.

    (D) granted, because the claim is moot.

82. After archaeologists discovered the fossil remains of a Stone Age society in the state, Congress passed a law establishing "the National Museum of Prehistoric Artifacts for the enjoyment and education of all residents of the United States." Under the statute, the museum was to be built in the state, near the site of the archeological find. It was to be funded entirely by the federal government, using revenues derived from the national income tax. The federal law provided that the museum was to display prehistoric artifacts and fossils gathered from all parts of the United States, in addition to those artifacts that had been discovered in the state. The attorney general of another state instituted a proceeding in a federal district court for an injunction against the use of federal funds to establish the National Museum of Prehistoric Artifacts in the state, asserting that such expenditure would be an unconstitutional disbursal of federal funds. Which of the following is most likely to support a finding in favor of the constitutionality of the federal statute?

    (A) The congressional spending power.

    (B) The Commerce Clause.

    (C) The Eleventh Amendment to the United States Constitution.

    (D) The doctrine of state sovereign immunity.

83. Because of a series of destructive forest fires in the state, the National Preserve Service issues a regulation closing a national preserve to public use from dusk to dawn. The national

preserve is located entirely within the state. Although the national preserve is a tract of land owned by the federal government, people who have state fishing licenses are permitted to fish in the preserve. As a result of the closing, there is a reduction in the number of persons applying for state fishing licenses and this causes a decline in state revenues. For this reason, the state Department of Fish and Game institutes a proceeding in a federal court, challenging the constitutionality of the regulation.

Which of the following would provide the National Preserve Service with its strongest argument in support of the constitutionality of its regulation?

(A) The Commerce Clause of Article I of the United States Constitution.

(B) The Property Clause of Article IV of the United States Constitution.

(C) The federal police power.

(D) The federal government's right of eminent domain.

84. A state's economy was falling apart because of widespread home foreclosures. The state passed legislation temporarily ordering a moratorium on mortgage repayments. A local bank challenged the law, arguing that the state was unlawfully interfering with private contracts. During trial, the court found that the state was acting reasonably, and the moratorium was in pursuit of a legitimate public purpose. The court should rule in favor of

(A) the bank, because the state may not pass a law impairing the obligation of private contracts.

(B) the bank, because the state may only pass laws impairing the obligation of public contracts.

(C) the state, because the state is acting reasonably in pursuit of a legitimate public purpose.

(D) the state, because only the federal government is subject to the Contract Clause.

85. Because a revolution in a Central American republic threatens to topple its government, the President of the United States orders federal troops to invade the republic. Congress subsequently passes a resolution directing the President to recall the troops. When the President refuses to do so, a proceeding is instituted in a United States district court seeking an order compelling the President to comply with the congressional directive. Which of the following would be the President's most effective argument in opposition to that proceeding?

(A) United States district courts lack power over the President.

(B) The President is Commander-in-Chief of the armed forces.

(C) The matter is a non-justiciable political question.

(D) The presidential order sending troops to the republic amounted to a declaration of war.

86. A state statute makes it a felony for a person over the age of 21 years to engage in sexual intercourse with a person under the age of 16 years. The statute further provides that if persons who are unrelated to each other by blood or marriage spend more than three hours in the same hotel room together, they are conclusively presumed to have engaged in sexual intercourse.

The defendant was charged with violating the statute by engaging in sexual intercourse with a girl under the age of 16 years. The defendant and the girl were not related to each other by blood or marriage. In its instructions to the jury, the court said, "If you find that the defendant and the girl spent more than three hours in the same hotel room, you must find that they engaged in sexual intercourse." The jury found the defendant guilty.

If the defendant subsequently challenged the constitutionality of the statute in an appropriate proceeding, the defendant's most effective argument would be that the statute violated

(A) procedural due process requirements.

(B) substantive due process requirements.

(C) the Equal Protection Clause of the Fourteenth Amendment.

(D) the prohibition against bills of attainder.

87. The defendant, an alien convicted of murder in a state court, appeals his conviction on the ground that aliens were systematically excluded from serving on the jury.

A federal law prohibits aliens from serving on juries in state court proceedings, but there is no state law creating such a prohibition. If the defendant's appeal results in a reversal of his conviction, it will probably be because the federal law

(A) violates the Equal Protection Clause of the Fourteenth Amendment.

(B) violates the Due Process Clause of the Fifth Amendment.

(C) is invalid under the doctrine of separation of powers.

(D) is invalid under the Supremacy Clause of Article VI.

88. A state law provides that the names of prospective jurors in county courts shall be drawn from the list of county residents holding state driver's licenses. The plaintiff, a county resident, is a 22-year-old black woman who does not hold a driver's license. She has never been called as a prospective juror in the county court. In a federal court, the plaintiff challenges the constitutional validity of the state law, claiming that it violates the Equal Protection Clause of the Fourteenth Amendment. In support of her challenge, the plaintiff offers proof that black women between the ages of 18 and 23 make up a large portion of the population of the county, but that no member of this group holds a state driver's license or has ever been called as a prospective juror in the county court.

Evidence that no black women between the ages of 18 and 23 who reside in the county hold state driving licenses should be

(A) excluded, because a state law does not violate the Equal Protection Clause on its face unless its purpose is to discriminate.

(B) excluded, because a state law does not violate the Equal Protection Clause as applied unless it is applied with a discriminatory purpose.

(C) admitted, because a law that has a discriminatory effect may violate the Equal Protection Clause even if its purpose is not to discriminate and it is not applied with a discriminatory purpose.

(D) admitted, because the exclusion of black women between the ages of 18 and 23 years may be evidence that the law had a discriminatory purpose or was applied with a discriminatory purpose.

89. In an attempt to improve the position of United States companies in the world pleasure-cruise market, Congress voted to sell five former battleships to a cruise line for $1 each. If a competitor of the cruise line challenges the constitutionality of the congressional action in an appropriate proceeding, the sale will probably be found

(A) invalid as a denial of equal protection under the Fourteenth Amendment.

(B) invalid as a bill of attainder.

(C) valid under the Property Clause of Article IV.

(D) valid under the general police powers of Congress.

90. Under authority granted by Congress, the United States Department of Defense awarded a contract to a company for the production of airborne bombsights. The contract called for all work to be performed at the company factory located on the banks of Winding River in the state. A clause of

the contract prohibited the company from discharging more than three units per day of a pollutant into Winding River as a result of bombsight production.

While producing bombsights pursuant to its contract with the Department of Defense, the company routinely discharged between two and three units of the pollutant per day into Winding River. Subsequently, the state prosecuted the company for violating a state statute that prohibits any person or business entity from discharging more than two units of the pollutant per day into any river or stream located in the state. In defense, the company asserted that as a federal contractor, it was immune to regulation by the state.

Which one of the following additional facts or inferences, if it were the only one true, would most effectively support the state's argument?

(A) Winding River is located entirely within the state.

(B) Prohibiting the discharge of more than two units of the pollutant per day into Winding River would not increase the cost of producing the bombsights called for by the contract.

(C) Congress has not expressly exempted the company from compliance with state water pollution statutes.

(D) Winding River is not a navigable river.

91. Congress authorizes the National Park Service to sell trees grown in the national parks. A logging company who also sells trees complains that the National Park Service is engaging in unfair competition because it sells trees for half the price charged by commercial growers. The logging company files suit in federal court. In response, the National Park Service immediately raises tree prices to the level charged by commercial growers. The National Park Service then moves to dismiss the proceeding on the ground that it is moot.

The National Park Service's motion should be

(A) granted, because the issue has been rendered moot by the price change.

(B) granted, because Congress has the power to dispose of property belonging to the United States.

(C) dismissed, because the National Park Service might lower its prices again in the future.

(D) dismissed, because the proceeding involves the application of Article IV of the United States Constitution.

92. Congress passes the Securities and Exchange Court Act, establishing the federal Securities and Exchange Court. Under the Act, the new court is to hear civil actions for damages resulting from federal securities and exchange law violations. The Act also provides that there is no right of appeal from decisions of the Securities and Exchange Court, and that the Court will cease to exist at the end of six years unless Congress specifically authorizes it to continue for an additional period. If a defendant against whom a judgment is rendered by the new court challenges the constitutionality of the Securities and Exchange Court Act, which of the following arguments would be most likely to result in a finding that the Act is unconstitutional?

(A) The Securities and Exchange Court Act does not require that judges be appointed to serve for life.

(B) The provision that there is no right of appeal violates the Due Process Clause of the Fifth Amendment.

(C) The United States Constitution does not provide for the establishment of a federal court to hear prosecutions for federal securities and exchange violations.

(D) The United States Constitution gives the Supreme Court the power of judicial review over all inferior federal courts.

93. After negotiation, the President of the United States and the President of the Republic of Ruritania reached an executive agreement. Under the terms of the agreement, profits earned by Ruritanian corporations in the United States would not be subject to taxation in the United States, and profits earned by United States corporations in Ruritania would not be subject to taxation in Ruritania. The plaintiff is a Ruritanian corporation operating in the state. A state statute imposes a tax on all income earned within the state and designates the State Revenue Service as the agency that collects it.

    The State Revenue Service demands that the plaintiff pay income tax as required by state law. If the plaintiff challenges the state law, the plaintiff's most effective argument would be that, as applied to the plaintiff, the law is unconstitutional

    (A) because no state may tax imports or exports without the consent of Congress.

    (B) under the Supremacy Clause.

    (C) under the Necessary and Proper Clause.

    (D) because the power to tax is the power to destroy.

94. Following an investigation by a congressional committee, an impeachment proceeding was brought against a federal judge before the United States Senate. The judge was not permitted to be represented by counsel at the proceeding, although she asked for representation and offered to pay for the services of her own attorney. The Senate found that the judge engaged in improper acts and entered a judgment of impeachment, removing the judge from office. The judge subsequently asked a federal court to set aside the judgment on the grounds that the denial of her request for representation by counsel at the impeachment proceeding was a violation of her constitutional rights. If the federal court refuses to grant the relief requested by the judge, it will probably be

    (A) because the Right to Counsel applies only to criminal prosecutions.

    (B) under the doctrine of separation of powers.

    (C) under the abstention doctrine.

    (D) because a judgment of impeachment cannot extend further than to removal and disqualification from office.

95. A city ordinance requires any person desiring to use public streets for a parade to first obtain a parade permit from the Police Commissioner. The ordinance sets forth procedures and requirements for obtaining such a permit. The defendant challenged these procedures and requirements in a federal court, and they were found to be constitutional on their face. The defendant subsequently applied to the Police Commissioner for a permit to conduct a street parade. Although the defendant complied with all the requirements contained in the ordinance, the Police Commissioner denied the application, saying, "You look like a rebel to me." Two months later, the defendant conducted the parade and was arrested for parading without a permit in violation of the ordinance described above. In defense, the defendant asserted that the ordinance was unconstitutional as applied to him because the Police Commissioner had arbitrarily and capriciously denied his application for a parade permit. Which of the following would be the most effective argument in response to the defendant's assertion?

    (A) There was sufficient time for the defendant to seek judicial review of the Police Commissioner's denial of his application.

    (B) The constitutionality of the statute is *res judicata.*

    (C) The statute imposes a time, place, and manner regulation that is not based on message content.

    (D) The street is a traditional public forum.

96. Congress passes a law making it a crime in the District of Columbia to operate any commercial motor vehicle that is not equipped with a specified noise suppression device. If the constitutionality of the law is challenged in an appropriate proceeding, the law should be declared

   (A) valid as an exercise of the congressional police power over the District of Columbia.

   (B) valid as a reasonable exercise of the congressional power to protect the environment.

   (C) invalid under the Equal Protection Clause of the Fourteenth Amendment.

   (D) invalid under the Necessary and Proper Clause.

97. The state enacts a law imposing a one-cent tax on each use of any video arcade machine located within the state. All such existing machines are equipped with coin slots that accept only quarters. Since it would be too expensive to convert the coin slots to accept additional pennies, the practical effect of the new law will be to require the tax to be paid by video arcade operators. All such machines are manufactured outside the state. Which of the following would be most likely to have standing to challenge the constitutionality of the statute?

   (A) A child who regularly plays video arcade amusement machines.

   (B) An association of video arcade operators.

   (C) An out-of-state manufacturer of video arcade amusement machines.

   (D) A corporation located within the state that is in the business of converting the coin slots on video arcade amusement machines.

98. Congress passes a law imposing a tax on the owners of buildings containing insulating materials made of asbestos. The law provides that funds derived from the tax shall be used to help finance research into the treatment of diseases caused by exposure to asbestos. The constitutional validity of the statute is challenged in an appropriate proceeding on the ground that one of the purposes of the tax is to discourage the use of asbestos insulation in buildings. The statute should be declared

   (A) constitutional, as a valid exercise of the congressional taxing power.

   (B) constitutional under the general federal police power.

   (C) unconstitutional, because Congress does not have the power to regulate the use of building materials.

   (D) unconstitutional, because the law was passed for a purpose other than to raise revenue.

99. A state law prohibits the ownership of land within three miles of the coast by any person who is not a citizen of the United States.

   Which of the following is most likely to have standing to challenge the constitutional validity of the state law?

   (A) An association of persons owning land in a community located within three miles of the coast that asserts that the statute will prevent the cultural growth of the community.

   (B) A citizen who seeks to sell his property to a non-citizen and asserts that the statute will prevent the sale.

   (C) A state taxpayer who asserts that the statute will affect the price of real estate, thereby reducing tax revenue.

   (D) A real estate broker who asserts that the statute will reduce the number of prospective purchasers of realty.

100. The plaintiff was a clerk in the back office of the State Department of Motor Vehicles where he had minimal contact with the public. He was strictly a clerical staff member

and had no policy-making role. The plaintiff read on his computer that someone had just tried and failed to assassinate the President. The plaintiff turned to a co-worker and said, "Hopefully the next guy will be a better shot." The Department of Motor Vehicles then tried to fire the plaintiff, claiming the remark reflected poorly on the Department. The plaintiff claimed that such a firing would violate his First Amendment rights. Can the Department of Motor Vehicles lawfully fire the plaintiff for making the remark?

(A) Yes, because the remark had to do with a matter of public concern and the plaintiff was a public employee.

(B) Yes, because the plaintiff's remark advocated the assassination of the President.

(C) No, because the plaintiff had no contact with the public and no policy-making role.

(D) No, because the plaintiff's statement did not signal any significant job unfitness.

101. Which of the following state laws is **LEAST** likely to be declared unconstitutional?

(A) A law that imposes a tax on all owners of real property within the state, including the federal government.

(B) A law that imposes a registration tax on all vehicles garaged within the state, including those owned by the federal government.

(C) A law that imposes a tax on all building contractors operating within the state, including those who work exclusively for the federal government.

(D) A law that imposes a tax only on persons who lease grazing land from the federal government.

102. A local church was well known for going door-to-door ringing doorbells and handing out flyers condemning homosexuality. Because they wanted to make sure people were home to listen to their message, church members would arrive on people's doorsteps either early in the morning or late at night. After months of ruined breakfasts, dinners, and bedtimes, an overwhelming majority of city residents signed a petition asking the city to outlaw the passing out of handbills door-to-door. A second petition signed by people who worked at night and slept during the day asked the city to ban doorbell ringing for political purposes. In their petition, the nightworkers showed that their productivity was way down from lack of sleep, which adversely affected the city economy. In response to the petitions, the city passed an ordinance that stated "All doorbell ringing for the purpose of handing out handbills is strictly forbidden." The church challenged the new ordinance, claiming it was unconstitutional. Is the new ordinance constitutional?

(A) Yes, because the church can spread its message in other ways.

(B) Yes, because an overwhelming majority of city residents wanted to outlaw the passing out of handbills door-to-door.

(C) Yes, because the city ordinance allowed nightworkers to sleep during the day, which was a public benefit.

(D) No.

103. Because there were limited facilities in the state for disposing of toxic wastes, the state enacted a law prohibiting the disposal within the state of toxic wastes generated outside the state. A manufacturing company located outside the state had previously contracted for the disposal of toxic wastes at a disposal center located inside the state. If the manufacturing company brings an appropriate proceeding challenging the constitutionality of the state law, the argument **LEAST**

likely to result in a finding that the law is invalid is that it violates the

(A) Obligations of Contracts Clause.

(B) Commerce Clause.

(C) Equal Protection Clause of the Fourteenth Amendment.

(D) Privileges and Immunities Clause of Article IV.

104. A disastrous earthquake in Mexico resulted in the loss of thousands of lives and the destruction of millions of dollars' worth of property. Following the disaster, the President of the United States issued an executive order sending U.S. military troops into Mexico to assist in the evacuation of earthquake victims and in general recovery efforts. Congress was not in session at the time. If the constitutionality of the presidential order is challenged, which of the following arguments is most likely to result in a finding that the President's action was constitutional?

(A) The order was a valid exercise of the President's emergency powers.

(B) The order was required by the humanitarian obligations of the President.

(C) The President is Commander-in-Chief of the armed forces.

(D) The President has power over foreign affairs.

105. Congress passes a law that grants federal funds to states for the purchase of equipment to be used in public hospitals for the treatment of diseases caused by cigarette smoking. Paragraph 7 of the law provides that "no state shall be eligible to receive such funds unless said state shall have imposed a tax of seven cents on every package of cigarettes sold in such state in addition to whatever cigarette tax is already in existence at the time that this act takes effect." From which of the following does Congress derive the power to enact paragraph 7 of the law?

(A) The congressional taxing power.

(B) The congressional spending power.

(C) The general federal police power.

(D) The congressional power to regulate interstate commerce.

106. Because of extremely high unemployment in the state, the state requires that state residents be given absolute preference over non-residents for all jobs on the state oil pipeline. The requirement is

(A) valid, under the Contract Clause.

(B) valid, under the interstate Privileges and Immunities Clause.

(C) invalid, under the Contract Clause.

(D) invalid, under the interstate Privileges and Immunities Clause.

107. The Followers of the Holy Flame is a religious organization. According to its religious philosophy, fire is symbolic of the presence of the Creator in all living things. As part of their system of worship, members of the Followers of the Holy Flame attend meetings once per month at which all sit in a circle around a blazing campfire to sing hymns and recite prayers. Usually, they attempt to conduct their meetings on top of the highest mountain in the region, in the belief that such a location is closest to Heaven. For the past several years, they have conducted their monthly meetings on a mountain located in Mountain Range National Park, a preserve owned and maintained entirely by the federal government. This year, because of the danger of wildfire, Congress passed a law prohibiting campfires anywhere within Mountain Range National Park. An attorney representing the Followers of the Holy Flame has commenced an appropriate proceeding on behalf of that organization challenging the validity of the law on the ground that it violates the First Amendment to the United States Constitution by interfering with the free exercise of religion.

Which of the following would be the most effective argument in support of the constitutionality of the law?

(A) The use of fire is not a traditional religious practice.

(B) In view of the danger of wildfire, the use of fire is not a reasonable religious practice.

(C) The prohibition of fires within Mountain Range National Park does not discriminate between religions and has a primarily secular effect.

(D) The law is a valid exercise of the power granted to Congress under the Property Clause of the Constitution.

108. After intense lobbying by an organization made up of professional personal trainers, the state passed a law barring gyms from employing any personal trainer who did not have a college degree in either physical therapy or sports medicine. The legislature's stated intent behind the law was to protect people from injury. A woman who had been employed as a personal trainer for 15 years was fired from the privately-owned gym she worked at because she did not have a college degree. She filed suit to challenge the law, arguing the law clearly disadvantaged people without the financial ability to attend college.

Which statement is correct?

(A) The court will uphold the law because it involves issues of health and safety.

(B) The court will uphold the law because it does not involve a suspect classification.

(C) The court will hold the law invalid because a classification based on financial ability is not substantially related to an important government interest.

(D) The court will hold the law invalid because it regulates the activities of privately owned gyms.

109. The state enacts the Continuing Professional Education Act, which provides that all persons licensed by the state to practice any profession other than medicine are required to complete 10 units per year of state-approved continuing education studies as a condition for renewal of their professional licenses.

An action is brought in a state court by an attorney in the state for an injunction prohibiting enforcement of the Continuing Professional Education Act and an order declaring it to be unconstitutional on the ground that it violates the Equal Protection Clause of the Fourteenth Amendment to the United States Constitution. Which one of the following additional facts or inferences, if it were true, would most effectively support a finding that the statute is constitutional?

(A) Competency in law is based upon the knowledge of principles that change more quickly than those upon which competency in medicine is based.

(B) A license to practice law is a privilege rather than a right.

(C) The power to license professionals is reserved to the states by the Tenth Amendment of the United States Constitution.

(D) The state bar association passed a resolution approving of the requirements contained in the Continuing Professional Education Act.

110. A federal statute directs payment of federal funds to states for use in the improvement and expansion of state hospital facilities. The terms of the statute provide that "No state shall award a contract for hospital improvement or expansion financed in whole or in part by funds received under this section unless said contract requires that the contractor pay its employees a minimum wage of $10 per hour."

A state contracted with a builder for the construction of a new wing on the State

Hospital after receiving funds for that purpose under the federal statute. The contract did not require the builder to pay its employees a minimum wage of $10 per hour.

Several employees of the builder who received less than $10 per hour while working on the State Hospital expansion instituted an action for damages against the state in a federal court, and the state moved to dismiss their cause of action. Which of the following is the clearest reason for dismissal of the suit?

(A) The state is immune from such an action under the Eleventh Amendment to the United States Constitution.

(B) No federal question is involved.

(C) The state did not employ the plaintiffs.

(D) The plaintiffs voluntarily accepted the wage that the builder paid them.

111. A state statute requires cable television stations to set aside one hour of airtime per week to be made available without charge for the broadcasting of spiritually uplifting programs produced by recognized religious organizations. The statute further provides that airtime thereby made available shall be equally divided among Jewish, Roman Catholic, and Protestant organizations. A Buddhist organization produced a spiritually uplifting program, but was advised by several cable television stations that it could not be broadcast under the statute. The organization has instituted a proceeding in federal court challenging the constitutional validity of the state statute.

The state moved to dismiss the proceeding on the ground that the organization lacked standing to challenge the constitutional validity of the statute. Should the motion be granted?

(A) Yes, because an intellectual interest in the outcome of a constitutional

challenge is not a sufficient personal stake to confer standing.

(B) No, because Buddhism is a recognized religion.

(C) No, because the organization produced a spiritually uplifting television program that will not be broadcast because of the statute's provisions.

(D) No, because the religious sensibilities of the organization are offended by the statute.

112. A state constitution contains an equal protection clause identical in language to the Equal Protection Clause in the Fourteenth Amendment to the United States Constitution. The state legislature passed a law empowering insurance companies within the state to charge different rates for males and females where actuarial analysis revealed a relationship between gender and increased risk. Shortly after its passage, the plaintiff sued in the state court for a judgment declaring that the statute violated the equal protection clause of the state constitution. The trial court found the statute to be valid, and the plaintiff appealed to the Court of Judicial Appeals, the highest court of the state. The Court of Judicial Appeals affirmed the ruling of the lower court.

After the decision by the state Court of Judicial Appeals, the owner of an automobile registered in the state sued in a United States district court for an injunction prohibiting the state Insurance Commissioner from authorizing different rates for males and females on the ground that the statute empowering him to do so violates the Equal Protection Clause of the Fourteenth Amendment to the United States Constitution. If the insurance commissioner moves to dismiss the proceeding, the motion to dismiss should be

(A) granted, because adequate state grounds exist for the validity or invalidity of the statute in question.

(B)   granted, under the abstention doctrine.

(C)   denied, because the United States district court is empowered to determine the validity of a state statute under the United States Constitution.

(D)   granted, because the Eleventh Amendment to the United States Constitution prevents a federal court from hearing claims against a state brought by citizens of that state.

113.   A woman who was not a citizen of the United States applied for temporary employment with the state. She was rejected, however, because the Civil Service Law of the state prohibits temporary state employment of a person who is not a United States citizen. The woman sued in a state court for an order directing the state Civil Service Commission to reconsider her application, on the ground that the section of the Civil Service Law that prohibited the temporary employment of non-citizens was unconstitutional.

The woman asserted that the section in question was invalid because it violated the Equal Protection Clause of the Fourteenth Amendment to the United States Constitution. Which of the following would be her most effective argument in support of that position?

(A)   The right to earn a living is a fundamental interest.

(B)   All state discrimination against aliens is invidious since alienage is a suspect classification.

(C)   The section has no rational basis and is not necessary to serve a compelling state interest.

(D)   An alien is not a "person" for purposes of the Equal Protection Clause.

114.   A city ordinance provides for the election of a mayor every four years. The ordinance makes all persons living in the city for one year eligible to vote in mayoral elections.

The City Elections Commissioner advised a voter, who is not a citizen of the United States but has been living in the city for 10 months, that he will not be permitted to vote in the mayoral election because he fails to meet the one-year residency requirement of the city ordinance. Is the one-year residency requirement imposed by the ordinance constitutionally valid as applied to the voter?

(A)   Yes, because a municipality has a compelling interest in assuring that voters will be interested in and familiar with the issues.

(B)   Yes, because aliens have no constitutional right to vote.

(C)   No, because a state may not make durational residency a prerequisite for eligibility to vote.

(D)   No, because although a state may establish durational residency requirements for eligibility to vote, a requirement of one year does not serve a compelling state interest.

115.   The federal Interstate Riverboat Act provides that the minimum wage for persons employed on river boats engaged in interstate commerce shall be $6.50 per hour. However, the state's Civil Service Code provides that crew members of riverboats engaged in interstate commerce are paid from $6 to $8 per hour depending on seniority.

Persons employed by the state as riverboat crew members at wages less than $6.50 per hour assert a claim in state court for money damages consisting of the difference between the wages they have been receiving and $6.50 per hour as required under the federal Interstate Riverboat Act. The court should find for

(A)   the employees, because as to them, the state Civil Service code is superseded by the federal Interstate Riverboat Act.

(B)  the employees, because the federal government has the power to set minimum wages to promote the general welfare.

(C)  the state, because fixing the wages of state employees is a traditional state function.

(D)  the state, because the state is immune from wage regulations under the Eleventh Amendment to the United States Constitution.

116.  The defendant purchased several pornographic videotapes by mail and showed them to friends who attended a barbecue at his home. The defendant was arrested and charged with presenting an obscene performance in violation of state law.

The defendant pleaded not guilty and asserted in his defense that, as applied, the state statute violated his rights under the United States Constitution. Which of the following would be the defendant's most effective argument in support of his position?

(A)  The statute violates the defendant's rights to freedom of speech and the press because the right to hear, see, or read is part of the freedom of expression.

(B)  Application of the statute to the defendant is unconstitutional because it violates the filmmaker's rights to freedom of speech and the press.

(C)  The defendant's constitutional right of privacy was violated because it includes his right to privately possess obscene materials.

(D)  The law that the defendant is charged with violating was intended to punish the publishers rather than the purchasers of obscenity.

117.  To enforce the Protected Shellfish Act, the federal government contracts with private enforcement agencies. The state imposes a Building Rental Tax of $10 per year on tenants occupying rented commercial space within the state. A contractor employed by the federal government rents space for the conduct of his business in a federal office building located in the state at an annual rental of $1.

If the contractor is prosecuted in a state court for failing to pay the state Building Rental Tax, which of the following would be the contractor's most effective argument in defense against the prosecution?

(A)  The Building Rental Tax violates the Equal Protection Clause of the United States Constitution.

(B)  The state may not tax the landlord-tenant relationship with the federal government.

(C)  The contractor's tenancy is specifically authorized by the Protected Shellfish Act.

(D)  The contractor is a federal contractor.

118.  A grocer was convicted of violating a food safety ordinance by a city municipal court. State laws do not permit appeal from judgments of the city municipal court. The grocer seeks direct review by the United States Supreme Court. Does the United States Supreme Court have jurisdiction to review the decision of the city municipal court?

(A)  Yes, because by convicting the grocer, the city municipal court has, in effect, declared the ordinance to be valid under the United States Constitution.

(B)  Yes, because state laws do not permit appeal from judgments of the city municipal court.

(C)  No, because state law does not specifically authorize appeal of city municipal court judgments directly to the United States Supreme Court.

(D)  No, because under Article III of the United States Constitution, the United States Supreme Court may only review decisions of federal courts and of the highest state courts.

119. A state statute known as the Unlawful Assembly Law contains the following provision:

> It shall be a misdemeanor for any group of three or more persons to engage in a public demonstration on a public sidewalk in front of any state government office during regular business hours unless said demonstration is related to matters under consideration by officials employed in said government office.

The defendant took part in a public demonstration that prevented those with business inside a state government office building from entering. The defendant is prosecuted for violating the Unlawful Assembly Law, and he defends by asserting that the section violates the First Amendment to the United States Constitution. The court should find him

(A) not guilty, because the public sidewalk in front of a government building is traditionally regarded as a public forum.

(B) not guilty, because the statute unlawfully regulates the subject matter of demonstrations conducted outside government offices.

(C) guilty, because the state has a compelling interest in the orderly conduct of governmental affairs.

(D) guilty, because the demonstration in which the defendant participated kept persons with lawful business from entering government offices to transact it.

120. The state legislature adopted a law allowing for the use of state funds to advertise the availability of abortions to indigent women. The plaintiff, a state taxpayer and the chairperson of an organization dedicated to campaigning for the rights of unborn children, instituted a proceeding in the federal district court for an injunction prohibiting

state officials from disbursing funds under the new law. Which of the following is the best reason for the court to conclude that the plaintiff has standing to challenge the statute?

(A) Any person has standing to challenge a statute on the ground that it violates a First Amendment right.

(B) Unborn children are a discrete and insular class that cannot be represented in any other way.

(C) The law involves a direct expenditure of state tax funds.

(D) The plaintiff is chairperson of a special-interest political group that has a philosophical and moral interest in preventing enforcement of the statute.

121. A youth organization with chapters and members in all 50 states rejected a girl's application solely on the basis of her race, advising her in writing that membership was open only to white children.

A federal statute makes it a crime for an organization with members in more than one state to deny membership to any person on the basis of that person's race.

The organization is prosecuted in a federal court for violation of the federal statute. The organization asserts that the statute is invalid under the United States Constitution. Which of the following would be the prosecutor's most effective argument in supporting the constitutional validity of the federal statute?

(A) The policy of the organization violates the spirit of the Commerce Clause.

(B) The policy of the organization establishes a badge of servitude in violation of the spirit of the Thirteenth Amendment.

(C) The United States Supreme Court has found racial discrimination to violate the United States Constitution.

(D)  Racial discrimination is inimical to the general welfare of the citizens of the United States.

122.  A student passed his state's licensing examination and petitioned the state Board of Medical Licensing Examiners for a license to practice medicine. Solely because of an arrest by the city police, the Board refused to issue him a license. When the student was brought before a judge for arraignment after the arrest, the court dismissed the charge with the consent of the public prosecutor.

Because of the Board's refusal to license him, the student sued the Board in state court and was unsuccessful. If the student sues the Board in a federal court for an order directing the Board to license him, the court should find for

(A)  the Board, because a license to practice medicine is a privilege rather than a right.

(B)  the student, because the student first attempted to sue in a state court and was unsuccessful.

(C)  the student, because the Board's action was arbitrary and capricious.

(D)  the student, because the Board's decision deprives the student of property without due process.

123.  After examining the effects of diesel exhaust on the environment, Congress enacts a statute requiring the owners of diesel-powered trucks used in interstate commerce to pay a Diesel-Powered Vehicle Use Tax of $800 per vehicle. A trucking company that operates more than 1,000 trucks in interstate commerce refuses to pay the Diesel-Powered Vehicle Use Tax and sues in a federal court for an injunction prohibiting the enforcement of the tax statute.

Which of the following is the federal government's strongest argument in opposition to the trucking company's claim that the Diesel-Powered Vehicle Use Tax is invalid?

(A)  The tax protects the general welfare by discouraging the use of diesel-powered vehicles in interstate commerce.

(B)  Protection of the environment is part of the federal police power.

(C)  The tax is a valid exercise of the spending power since it enables Congress to assure that the money that it gives states for the construction of roads will be most efficiently spent.

(D)  The trucking company lacks standing since it has not yet paid the tax.

124.  In 1999, the United States entered into a treaty with another country by which each country agreed not to tax citizens of the other. Pursuant to that treaty, Congress enacted the National Tax Immunity Act, which exempts that country's nationals residing in the United States from the obligation to pay income tax to the United States. Last week, the President of the United States issued an executive order requiring the Internal Revenue Service to begin collecting income tax from the country's citizens residing in the United States.

If the constitutional validity of the presidential order is challenged by a person with standing to do so, the court should find that the order is

(A)  valid, since the nation must speak with one voice in matters of foreign affairs.

(B)  valid, since the President has broad discretionary powers in matters of foreign affairs.

(C)  invalid, since the President may not abrogate foreign treaties without the advice and consent of the Senate.

(D)  invalid, since the President lacks the power to suspend enforcement of the National Tax Immunity Act.

125. A state statute provides that no person can be elected to state office who is not a citizen of the United States. The constitutionality of the statute is challenged in an appropriate action by the plaintiff.

    The plaintiff's challenge was heard by the highest appellate court of the state, and the court declared the statute to be unconstitutional on the ground that it violated the equal protection clause of the state constitution. If the state seeks review by the United States Supreme Court, which of the following statements is most accurate?

    (A)  The United States Supreme Court can properly review the decision by certiorari.

    (B)  The United States Supreme Court can properly review the decision by appeal.

    (C)  The United States Supreme Court can properly review the decision by certiorari or appeal.

    (D)  The United States Supreme Court cannot review the decision.

126. A coastal state has enacted the Ocean Fishing License Act, which regulates the right to fish in coastal waters. Section 1 of the Act provides that no person shall fish in the ocean from a vessel registered in the state who has not obtained an ocean-fishing license from the state Department of Fish and Game. Section 2 of the Act sets the fees for ocean-fishing licenses at $10 per year for residents of the state and $20 per year for nonresidents.

    An action is brought in a federal court by a resident of the state for an injunction to prohibit the state from enforcing Section 2 of the Ocean Fishing License Act. Which of the following arguments would be **LEAST** likely to lead to a finding that the provisions of that section are invalid?

    (A)  The Act violates the Commerce Clause.

    (B)  The Act violates the Equal Protection Clause.

    (C)  The Act violates the Necessary and Proper Clause.

    (D)  Section 1 of the Act is constitutionally invalid.

127. The state enacts legislation providing that participation in certain elections is open only to persons who are able to pass a simple test of reading and writing in the English language.

    The constitutionality of the statute has been challenged by a litigant who objects to the literacy requirement. If that challenge is successful, it will probably be because the requirement violates

    (A)  the Equal Protection Clause of the Fourteenth Amendment.

    (B)  the "race, color, or previous condition of servitude" clause of the Fifteenth Amendment.

    (C)  freedom of the press under the First Amendment.

    (D)  the Twenty-Sixth Amendment (granting the right to vote to persons 18 years of age and above).

128. Congress passes the Schools Construction Act, providing for grants of federal funds to states to help finance the construction of new school buildings. A section of the Act provides that states that do not alter their building codes to prohibit the use in school construction of certain substances listed as carcinogenic (cancer-causing) are ineligible for federal funds under the law. The state is the home of an industry that produces one of the materials listed in the federal law as carcinogenic. Its legislature has refused to alter the state building code to conform to the requirements of the Schools Construction Act.

    In *defending* the validity of the section, which of the following arguments would be most effective?

(A)  The section is a necessary and proper extension of the congressional power to regulate education.

(B)  The states surrendered their authority over school construction by accepting federal funds for that purpose in the past.

(C)  The federal government can regulate school construction without limitation because the federal government is paying for some of the construction costs.

(D)  It was reasonable for Congress to believe that compliance with the section will assure that the federal money spent on school construction will result in greater benefit than harm to the general public.

129.  A law in the state requires any person doing business in that state to obtain a business license from the state's Department of Commerce. A recently enacted amendment to that statute prohibits convicted felons in the state from doing business in that state and authorizes the state's Department of Commerce to deny a business license to any such person.

The plaintiff, a convicted felon who was released from a state prison after completion of his sentence, applied for a business license after the passage of the amendment described above. He brings an action in a federal court to enjoin the state's Department of Commerce from enforcing the amendment against him on the ground that it is constitutionally invalid.

A federal court will probably

(A)  dismiss the action, because no federal question is involved.

(B)  dismiss the action, since the plaintiff is a resident of the state against which the action is being brought.

(C)  hear the action, since the plaintiff is a resident of the state against which the action is being brought.

(D)  hear the action, since the plaintiff has asserted that the statute is constitutionally invalid.

130.  A recently enacted state statute provides that no person shall be granted a high school diploma without first passing a series of examinations designed to test minimum competency in reading, writing, mathematics, and United States history.

A religious high school in the state sues in a federal court to enjoin enforcement of the statute. In support of its petition, the school asserts that its students belong to a religion that opposes all secular education, and therefore the statute violates their rights and those of the school under the Free Exercise Clause of the First Amendment to the United States Constitution. Which of the following would be the most effective argument in opposition to that claim?

(A)  The school lacks standing to challenge the constitutionality of the statute.

(B)  Opposition to all secular education is not a reasonable religious belief.

(C)  The law is not primarily intended to interfere with a religious belief.

(D)  The state has a compelling interest in the competency of high school graduates.

131.  A city ordinance provides as follows:

Section 1—No person shall conduct a public speech or demonstration in the city without first obtaining an assembly permit from the city mayor, who shall not issue such a permit if, in his or her opinion, the speech or demonstration is likely to result in a breach of the public peace.

Section 2—A fee of $10 shall accompany every application for an assembly permit, unless the application is for a permit to conduct a political campaign rally, in which case no fee shall be required.

Section 3—The provisions of this ordinance are severable, and a judicial declaration that one section hereof is unconstitutional shall not affect the validity of any other section.

Which of the following is the **LEAST** likely reason for holding that Section 2 of the ordinance is *invalid?*

(A) Section 2 violates the Necessary and Proper Clause of the United States Constitution.

(B) Section 2 discriminates against speech on the basis of its content.

(C) Section 2 is vague and/or overbroad.

(D) Section 1 is vague and/or overbroad.

132. A state statute provides that every carrier transporting unrefined petroleum over roads within the state is required to pay a state highway use tax based upon a formula that combines the quantity transported and the distance over which it is moved within the state.

The plaintiff is a producer of unrefined petroleum within the state and operates a trucking company for the transportation of his product.

If the plaintiff challenges the constitutionality of the statute in an appropriate proceeding, which of the following additional facts or inferences, if it was the only one true, would be the most likely to result in a finding that the statute is unconstitutional?

(A) More than 50 percent of the transportation of unrefined petroleum over roads in the state is connected with interstate commerce.

(B) There is no federal statute concerning the right of a state to tax the transportation of unrefined petroleum within that state.

(C) The state imposes no tax on the transportation of any other product within the state.

(D) The other states bordering the state have indicated an intention to impose similar taxes on transportation over their highways.

133. Congress passes the State Highway Subsidy Act, which makes matching federal funds available to states for the construction of state highways on condition that states receiving such funds prohibit trucks longer than a specified size from operating on state highways. The state has refused to amend its statutes to comply with the Act.

The State Highway Subsidy Act is most likely to be held constitutional

(A) as an exercise of the general police power of the federal government.

(B) as an exercise of the spending power of Congress.

(C) under the Property Clause of Article IV of the United States Constitution.

(D) under the Eleventh Amendment to the United States Constitution.

134. A man applied for a job as a city clerk. He was later rejected based on a state law that gave employment preference to graduates of state colleges and universities. The man sued, arguing the law violated the Equal Protection Clauses of both the United States and state constitutions. The state court found the law valid under both constitutions, and the state appellate court affirmed. The man appealed to the highest court in the state, but his petition for certiorari was denied. He now seeks judicial review from the United States Supreme Court.

May the United States Supreme Court grant review?

(A) Yes, because the state court found the law was valid under the United States Constitution.

(B) Yes, because the highest court in the state denied certiorari.

(C) No, because classification based on attendance at a college or university is not a suspect classification.

(D) No, because there has been no determination on the merits by the highest court in the state.

135. A federal police officer ordered pornographic films from the defendant by sending a check to the address given in an advertisement. After the officer received the films, the defendant was charged in a federal court with violating a federal statute that prohibits sending obscene films through the mail.

Which of the following may the court properly consider in determining whether the films sold by the defendant are obscene?

(A) Expert testimony that the films have serious value as works of erotic art.

(B) Expert testimony that activities in the films are likely to appeal to the prurient interest of persons under the age of 18 years.

(C) Expert testimony that the films have serious value as art, and expert testimony that the films are likely to appeal to the prurient interest of persons under the age of 18 years.

(D) No expert testimony.

136. A state law sets the mandatory retirement age for public high school teachers at 60 years for physical education teachers of either gender.

A 60-year-old public high school physical education teacher challenges the law, asserting that it violates the Equal Protection Clause of the Fourteenth Amendment. Which of the following additional facts or inferences, if it were the only one true, would be most likely to result in a finding that the statute is constitutional?

(A) The teacher is not as vigorous and healthy as he was at the age of 50 years.

(B) Physical education teachers must engage in strenuous physical activities likely to be hazardous to the health of a person over the age of 60 years.

(C) The state has the right to set the retirement age for teachers and other state employees.

(D) State law provides that physical education teachers who reach the age of 60 years must be given first preference in being hired for other teaching positions for which they qualify.

137. The defendant, an alien convicted of murder in a state court, appeals on the ground that aliens were systematically excluded from serving on the jury.

A state law prohibits aliens from serving on juries in state court proceedings, but there is no federal law creating such a prohibition. If the defendant's appeal results in a reversal of his conviction, it will probably be because

(A) a state law may not discriminate on the basis of alienage.

(B) the state law violates the Privileges and Immunities Clause of the Fourteenth Amendment.

(C) the state law violates the prohibition against discrimination on the basis of race, color, or previous condition of servitude contained in the Fifteenth Amendment.

(D) the state law is invalid under the Supremacy Clause of Article VI.

138. A state law provides that police rescue divers must be males between the ages of 25 and 30. In its preamble, the law justifies itself by noting the physical strength and stamina necessary to be able to perform the job, including swimming in flood waters, lifting heavy objects off the bottom of lakes, and breaking open submerged cars. A 32-year-old woman challenges the state law, claiming it violates the Equal Protection Clause of the Fourteenth Amendment. Specifically, she argues that the law discriminates against people based on sex and age.

Which of the following statements is correct?

(A) The woman's claim for sex discrimination should fail if the law is necessary to achieve a compelling state interest.

(B) The woman's claim for age discrimination should fail if the law is substantially related to an important government interest.

(C) The woman's claim for sex discrimination should fail if the law has a rational basis.

(D) The woman's claim for age discrimination should fail if the law has a rational basis.

139. The state commences an appropriate proceeding to challenge the constitutionality of an executive agreement between the United States and a foreign country. Under the agreement, neither country can tax the other country's corporations. Which of the following additional facts or inferences, if it was the only one true, would be most likely to result in a finding that the executive agreement was unconstitutional?

(A) The executive agreement was self-executing.

(B) If the state does not collect taxes from the other country's corporations doing business in the state, the tax burden

imposed on other state residents will be increased.

(C) No federal statute authorizes the President to make executive agreements with the foreign country.

(D) Prior to the agreement, Congress enacted a statute prohibiting the President from agreeing not to tax foreign corporations without the advice and consent of the Senate.

140. A federal act prohibited federal executive-branch employees from getting involved in "political management or . . . political campaigns." The plaintiffs, a group of federal civil servants, attacked the constitutionality of the act. In their complaint, the plaintiffs stated that they wanted to engage in prohibited political activities, although they were not specific as to what they were planning to do. However, they conceded that they had not yet engaged in such activities. The court should find

(A) the act is constitutional because the plaintiffs are federal employees.

(B) the act is unconstitutional because it violates the plaintiffs' freedom of expression.

(C) the act is unconstitutional because it violates the plaintiffs' freedom of association.

(D) the plaintiff's action should be dismissed.

141. The plaintiff, who was employed as fire chief by a municipality of the state, was required to retire under a state statute that mandated the retirement of all fire department personnel at the age of 55 years.

The plaintiff institutes a proceeding against the state in a federal district court, seeking an order enjoining the enforcement of the state's mandatory retirement law on the ground that it violates the Equal Protection Clause of the Fourteenth Amendment. The plaintiff's application for an injunction should be

(A) denied, because the proceeding is barred by the Eleventh Amendment.

(B) denied, because the law has a rational basis.

(C) denied, because the law is substantially related to important government interests.

(D) granted, because the statute discriminates against a suspect class.

142. A city council passed an ordinance prohibiting the sale in the city of meat processed at a processing plant not certified by the City Health Department.

A person with standing to do so sues in an appropriate federal court for an order enjoining enforcement of the city ordinance on the ground that it is invalid under the Commerce Clause of the United States Constitution. Which of the following is the best argument in support of granting the injunction?

(A) As applied, the ordinance interferes with interstate commerce.

(B) Regulation of the purity of food is not a matter of local concern.

(C) The concurrent power to regulate commerce does not apply to municipalities.

(D) There are equally effective and less burdensome ways of regulating the purity of food sold in the city.

143. Congress passes the Schools Construction Act, providing for grants of federal funds to states to help finance the construction of new school buildings. A section of the Act provides that states that do not alter their building codes to prohibit the use in school construction of certain substances listed as carcinogenic (cancer-causing) are ineligible for federal funds under the law.

The section in question is probably

(A) constitutional, on the basis of the federal police power.

(B) constitutional, on the basis of the spending power.

(C) constitutional, under both the federal police power and the spending power.

(D) unconstitutional.

144. After severe flooding caused a deficit in the city's budget, the city council imposed a new fee on users of city pools. In the past, the pools had been free for all city residents. Under the new fee system, city pool users could either buy a yearly membership for $500 or pay $5 per entry. The city pools were primarily used by low-income residents who would likely be unable to afford the new fees.

Which group or person is most likely to have standing to challenge the constitutionality of the new fee?

(A) A wealthy doctor who owns his own pool, but uses a city pool to swim laps every day because it is closer to his office.

(B) A low-income family who does not use city pools, but fears the fee will prevent them from using the pools in the future.

(C) An organization dedicated to promoting free access to city services for low-income residents.

(D) An organization of city lifeguards that claims many of its members will lose their jobs or have their hours cut if the new fee is not put in place.

145. Traditionally, a park next to the local elementary school was used for art fairs, concerts, political speeches, and other public functions. After a political rally used posters and imagery that frightened several children, the city passed an ordinance requiring all political speeches to be moved to another

city park one mile away. Non-political functions were unaffected by the ordinance.

Which statement regarding the ordinance is most likely to be true?

(A) The ordinance is valid because it is a valid time, place, and manner restriction.

(B) The ordinance is valid because the park is government property.

(C) The ordinance is valid if it is substantially related to an important government interest.

(D) The ordinance is valid if it is narrowly tailored to achieve a compelling governmental interest.

146. A state law provides that the names of prospective jurors in county courts shall be drawn from the list of county residents holding state driver's licenses. The plaintiff is a 22-year-old black woman who does not hold a driver's license. She has never been called as a prospective juror in a county court. In a federal court, the plaintiff challenges the constitutional validity of the state law, claiming that it violates the Equal Protection Clause of the Fourteenth Amendment. In support of her challenge, the plaintiff offers proof that no black woman in the county between the ages of 18 and 23 holds a state driver's license or has been called as a prospective juror.

If a motion is made to dismiss the plaintiff's claim on the ground that she lacks standing, the motion should be

(A) granted, because the plaintiff does not hold a state driver's license.

(B) granted, because the plaintiff has never been called as a prospective juror.

(C) denied, because being deprived of the opportunity to serve on a jury is a concrete harm.

(D) denied, because the exclusion of black women between the ages of 18 and 23 could deprive the plaintiff of due process if she is ever a litigant in a county court.

# ANSWERS
## CONSTITUTIONAL LAW

# ANSWERS TO
# CONSTITUTIONAL LAW QUESTIONS

1.  **C**  The "case or controversy" requirement of the United States Constitution requires a person attacking the constitutionality of a statute in a federal court to satisfy the burden of showing some actual or immediately threatened concrete personal injury that would be prevented if his or her challenge were sustained. Since the student has not yet been licensed to practice law, the Continuing Professional Education Act does not affect him; declaring it unconstitutional will not protect him against immediately threatened injury. He therefore lacks standing to challenge it.

    A challenge to the validity of a statute on the ground that it violates the United States Constitution is a federal question. **A** is therefore incorrect. A claim is said to present a non-justiciable political controversy if its adjudication would unduly interfere with the exercise of powers of co-equal branches of government or with national policy. **B** is therefore incorrect. **D** is incorrect because the federal courts are not required to wait until the state courts have acted before determining the constitutionality of a state statute.

2.  **D**  Under the Supremacy Clause, an otherwise valid state statute may be superseded by federal legislation to the extent that the two are inconsistent. The contract to kill the wild pigs in the national park was authorized by federal statutes. Since the Property Clause gives Congress the power to control federal property, the federal statutes are valid, and so the state law that prohibits the killing of the wild pigs is superseded, at least as to killings within the national park.

    The power to protect the environment is held by both the federal and state governments, so states do have the power to declare a species to be endangered and to enact legislation protecting it. **A** is therefore incorrect. Since the state statute prohibits the killing of wild pigs only within the state, and since there is no indication that anyone other than the exterminator is interested in coming from outside the state to kill them or that killing them is commerce, the statute probably does not unduly interfere with interstate commerce. **B** is therefore incorrect. The Obligation of Contracts Clause prevents the state from interfering with rights acquired under existing contracts but does not prevent the state from prohibiting activities that parties might otherwise contract to perform. **C** is therefore incorrect.

3.  **B**  Basic to freedom of religion is the rule that a court may not inquire into the truth or reasonableness of a particular religious belief.

    **A** is incorrect because in free exercise cases, the state's pursuit of a compelling state interest would certainly be sufficient (though not necessary) to lead to the upholding of the statute. In *Wisconsin v. Yoder,* 406 U.S. 205 (1972), the United States Supreme Court examined the sincerity of a claimant's religious beliefs in determining whether a state statute as applied violated the Free Exercise Clause. In doing so, the court referred to the fact that the belief involved was of longstanding tradition. **C** and **D** are therefore incorrect.

4.  **A**  Under the Commerce Clause, Congress has the power to regulate commerce among the states. The Necessary and Proper Clause permits Congress to do whatever is reasonably

necessary to the exercise of its enumerated powers. It has been held that if in the aggregate a particular industry has an impact on interstate commerce, Congress may regulate even those aspects of it that are completely intrastate.

**B** is incorrect because no provision of the United States Constitution gives Congress the power to legislate for the general welfare (*i.e.*, federal police power). **C** is incorrect because the congressional power to regulate commerce is limited to interstate commerce, or at least to trade that has an impact on interstate commerce. **D** is a correct statement, but it would not furnish an argument in support of the constitutionality of the statute in question since the statute regulates "every purchase of an automobile in the United States," and this may include those that are sold domestically and intrastate.

5.   **C**      Under the Necessary and Proper Clause, Congress has the power to make laws regulating the use of federal money disbursed pursuant to the spending power. This may enable Congress to control functions that are traditionally those of the state.

A and **B** are therefore incorrect. An intrastate activity may be controlled by Congress under the Commerce Clause if its impact on interstate commerce justifies regulation to protect or promote interstate commerce. **D** is incorrect, however, because the fact that some of the materials used are traded in interstate commerce is not, alone, sufficient to establish such an impact.

6.   **D**      The Privileges and Immunities Clause of Article IV requires each state to treat nonresidents in the same manner as it treats residents. An exception has been made, however, for a law that makes it more burdensome for nonresidents than for residents to exploit a state's natural resources for recreational purposes. See *Baldwin v. Montana Fish and Game*, 436 U.S. 371 (1978) (holding that charging nonresidents a higher fee than residents for hunting licenses was consistent with the Privileges and Immunities Clause of Article IV). The Privileges and Immunities Clause of the Fourteenth Amendment protects only those rights that persons enjoy as citizens of the United States (*e.g.*, the right to travel from state to state, to vote for federal officials, to sue in federal courts, etc.). Since there is no federal right to hunt, the Privileges and Immunities Clause of the Fourteenth Amendment does not apply.

7.   **B**      A person in an organization that advocates illegal conduct can be punished or disqualified for a state benefit only when he or she is an active member of it, knows that it advocates illegal conduct, and has the specific intent to bring about the accomplishment of its illegal goal. Although the student was an active member of the organization and knew that it advocated illegal conduct, he did not intend for it to succeed in accomplishing its illegal goal. He therefore cannot constitutionally be punished for his membership in it.

C and **D** are therefore incorrect. **A** is incorrect because freedom of the press applies only to the communication of ideas, and not to the conduct involved in acquiring the information to be communicated.

8.   **B**      A state law that discriminates among religions violates the Establishment Clause unless it is closely fitted to furthering a compelling governmental interest. It is unlikely that the

statute in question would satisfy that test, but, in any event, the argument contained in **B** is the only one listed that could possibly support the challenge. **B** is therefore correct.

A statute does not violate the Free Exercise Clause unless it interferes with a practice required by a religious belief. Since there is no indication that the religious beliefs of the American Buddhist League require the broadcasting of their program, **A** is incorrect. Although the statute's discrimination against cable television stations might violate the Equal Protection Clause, **C** is incorrect because only a victim of that discrimination (*i.e.*, a cable television station) would have standing to assert that challenge. **D** is incorrect for two reasons: First, the power to regulate use of the airwaves is, to some extent, shared by the federal and state governments, and second, the Supremacy Clause makes a state law invalid only when it is inconsistent with some valid federal statute affecting the same subject matter. Since there is no indication that there is a federal statute that differs from the state law in question, **D** cannot be the correct answer.

9. **C**    Although there is some question about the court's ability to enforce orders directed at the President, it is clear that the court may exercise control over the conduct of executive officials even when they are carrying out presidential orders.

B is therefore incorrect. Although the power to commit troops to foreign hostilities without consulting Congress is one of the emergency powers of the President, it may be limited in advance by federal statutes. If the presidential order was, in fact, a violation of the federal statute cited by the plaintiff, it may be held invalid. **A** is therefore incorrect. **D** is incorrect because the president may mobilize troops against foreign nations in the protection of the national interest without a declaration of war.

10. **B**    By the process of "reverse incorporation," the Due Process Clause of the Fifth Amendment has been held to require equal protection from the federal government similar to what the Fourteenth Amendment requires of state governments. The plaintiff may argue that since the statute applies only to employees of the Census Bureau and not to other federal employees who deal with the public, it arbitrarily discriminates against him.

A is incorrect because the Fourteenth Amendment prohibits states from abridging the privileges or immunities of national citizenship but does not prohibit the federal government from doing so, and because the right to wear a moustache is probably not protected by the Privileges and Immunities Clause because it is not fundamental. **C** is incorrect because the Fourteenth Amendment prohibits invidious discrimination by the states, but not by the federal government. The Fifth Amendment prohibits the taking of private property for public use without just compensation, but is inapplicable here since no property has been taken from the plaintiff for a public purpose. **D** is therefore incorrect.

11. **D**    The decision of the state court was based solely on its determination of whether the statute in question violated the state constitution. Since the United States Supreme Court has no jurisdiction to interpret state constitutions, it has no power to review the decision of the state court interpreting its own constitution.

A, **B**, and **C** are therefore incorrect.

12.  **B**    The congressional power to regulate interstate commerce has been held to include the power to exclude whatever items Congress wants to exclude from commerce between the states. The courts do not usually examine congressional motives in determining the constitutionality of such a statute.

A is incorrect because there is no federal police power. The "Cooley Doctrine" provides that the commerce power, at least in part, is held concurrently by the state and federal governments. **C** is incorrect because the "Cooley Doctrine" has nothing to do with the prohibition against cruelty to animals. Although acts of Congress are presumptively constitutional, **D** is not an effective argument because the presumption of constitutionality is a rebuttable one.

13.  **C**    Under the Supremacy Clause, an otherwise valid state law is invalid if it is inconsistent with a federal law covering the same subject matter. Since the immigration laws and treaties of the United States might contain provisions that are inconsistent with a state law restricting the employment of aliens, they would be relevant to determining its validity under the Supremacy Clause.

If the state law is invalid under the Supremacy Clause, it is unconstitutional no matter what the unemployment rate in the state is and no matter how many noncitizens reside there. **A** and **D** are therefore incorrect. **B** is incorrect because federal civil service laws regulate employment by the federal government and, therefore, do not cover the same subject matter as the state's Civil Service Law.

14.  **B**    Article III of the United States Constitution gives the Supreme Court appellate jurisdiction over all controversies arising under the laws of the United States, and authorizes Congress to determine the ways in which that jurisdiction shall be exercised. Since the Truth in Selling Act is a federal law, the court has jurisdiction to hear appeals from decisions construing it, and Congress may authorize appeals directly from lower state courts.

The power to regulate interstate commerce may empower Congress to authorize a statute requiring disclosures in interstate transactions, but **A** is incorrect because the power to regulate interstate commerce is separate from and unrelated to the power to regulate the exercise of appellate jurisdiction by the Supreme Court. **C** is incorrect because Article III gives the Supreme Court jurisdiction over cases involving federal laws, and empowers Congress to determine how that jurisdiction should be exercised. Although a state has the right to review the decisions of its own courts, the United States Constitution gives the Supreme Court the power to review decisions relating to federal laws. Its exercise of that power is thus constitutionally valid, and not an infringement on the sovereignty of the states. **D** is therefore incorrect.

15.  **D**    The United States Supreme Court upheld such a program against Establishment Clause attack in *Mitchell v. Helms*, 530 U.S. 793 (2000). A majority of the Court believed that the fact that the program treated religious and non-religious schools identically was enough to avoid Establishment Clause problems, so long as there was no evidence that the equipment was actually being diverted for religious purposes.

**A** is incorrect for the same reason that **D** is correct. **B** is incorrect because the power to spend for the general welfare includes the power to subsidize education. Since the use of tax money for religious schools is likely to reduce the amount of tax money available for use by non-religious schools, **C** is incorrect because the petitioners have the necessary standing.

16. **B**    Since the right to vote has been held to be a fundamental interest, state interference with the right to vote is unconstitutional unless it can be shown to serve a compelling state interest. Since the state has a compelling interest in the accuracy and facility of ballot counts, the refusal to count sticker votes will be valid if the City Elections Commissioner shows that it serves that interest. Although it is not certain that this argument will be successful, it is the only one listed that could possibly support the Commissioner's position.

The existence of certain relationships has been held to justify the assertion by one person of another's constitutional rights. **A** is incorrect since the relationship between candidate and voter probably is one of these, and because, as a voter, the lawyer is asserting her own rights. A federal statute prohibits the use of literacy tests in determining eligibility to vote. Even without it, however, **C** is incorrect because it would not eliminate illiterate voters until after they had cast what they believed to be a vote. **D** is a non sequitur since familiarity with issues and candidates does not logically require the ability to write a person's name on a ballot, and because most traditional voting methods (*i.e.*, marking an "X" or flipping a lever) require no more literacy than the sticker vote method.

17. **B**    The Eleventh Amendment provision that the judicial power of the federal government shall not be extended to suits brought against a state by residents of another state has been held to prohibit the federal courts from entertaining suits for money damages against a state by its residents, unless authorized by valid federal statute. For this reason, the federal court action against the state by its employees must be dismissed.

The doctrine of abstention prohibits a federal court from deciding constitutional issues that are premised upon unsettled questions of state law upon which the determination of the action would depend. Since no such unsettled question exists, **A** is incorrect. Tourism is not a traditional state function, and since under the Commerce Clause the federal government has the power to regulate interstate commerce, the Supremacy Clause makes the federal Interstate Riverboat Act supersede the state Civil Service Code. **C** and **D** are incorrect, however, because under the Eleventh Amendment, the federal court lacks jurisdiction to hear an action for damages against a state.

18. **A**    Although a party challenging the validity of a statute is not ordinarily permitted to assert the constitutional rights of third persons, the distributor may do so for two reasons: First, if the statute as applied violated the defendant's constitutional rights, the defendant could not be guilty of violating it, and the distributor could not be called an accessory to the commission of a crime, and second, vendors have been held to have standing to assert the constitutional rights of their customers.

**B** is incorrect because a person challenging the validity of any statute on any constitutional ground must have standing to do so. **C** is incorrect because although the defendant can waive his own constitutional rights, he cannot waive those of the distributor. If the statute's application to the defendant was unconstitutional, convicting the distributor of being an accessory to it would violate the distributor's constitutional rights. **D** is incorrect because it is overbroad. Several exceptions to this general rule exist, including one that permits a vendor to assert the constitutional rights of its customers.

19. **D**     Although the doctrine of state immunity prevents Congress from exercising its commerce or taxing power in a way that substantially interferes with traditional state functions, there is no reason why a state should not have to carry its share of the burdens of government by paying taxes for benefits that it receives. Since the federal tax in question is applied to all who derive benefit from federal aviation services, and since it does not interfere with a traditional function of the state, it is valid.

The power to tax may be the power to destroy, and for this reason states may not freely tax the federal government. **A** is incorrect, however, because the federal government is not under the same restraint in taxing the states. **B** is incorrect because the doctrine of state immunity does not protect the state against paying its fair share for the federal services that it receives. **C** is a fabrication; there is no "doctrine of state subordination."

20. **B**     For a law to trigger strict or intermediate scrutiny, it must have a discriminatory intent. A mere discriminatory effect is not enough to trigger the higher levels of scrutiny under the Equal Protection Clause. There is no indication in the facts that the law is meant to have a discriminatory intent, nor is there any indication or mention of race in the law. In fact, it also bans admissions officers from taking into account many other factors, such as gender, economic disadvantage, and sports and club membership. Therefore, **C** and **D** are incorrect.

**A** is incorrect because there is no rule allowing an institution to do whatever it wants in the name of education.

21. **D**     Under the Necessary and Proper Clause, Congress has the right to make whatever laws are necessary and proper in implementing its other powers. This right has been held to include the power to grant immunity from state taxation.

Although the federal government is itself immune from state taxation, the immunity is not derivative. For this reason, federal employees and contractors are not automatically immune from state taxation, even though such taxation may indirectly burden the federal government. **A** and **B** are therefore incorrect. **C** is an incorrect statement of law since it has been held that a nondiscriminatory state income tax may be imposed on state residents who derive their income from out-of-state activities.

22. **A**     A controversy is not "ripe" for decision unless the issues are fully developed and clearly defined, and not merely speculative, conjectural, or premature. Usually, this requires a showing that objective harm will occur if the issues are not decided. Mere general allegations of a possible subjective "chill" are not sufficient to satisfy this requirement.

A case is "moot" when no unresolved contested questions essential to the effective disposition of the particular controversy remain for court decision. **B** is incorrect because all the issues raised by the action are unresolved. **C** is incorrect because the Eleventh Amendment does not prevent lawsuits to enjoin state officials from enforcing laws claimed to be invalid. A question is political if its resolution would unduly interfere with the operation of a co-equal branch of the federal government or with national policy. **D** is therefore incorrect.

23. **C** Since the United States Constitution is the supreme law of the land, every court must determine whether the laws that it enforces violate the Constitution either by their terms or by the way in which they are applied. This necessarily involves interpretation of the Constitution.

**A** is therefore incorrect. **B** is incorrect for two reasons: First, the municipal court determines who has standing to appear or make particular arguments before it, and second, even if the municipal court's rules regarding standing were identical to the federal rules, the grocer would have standing because the *possibility* of his conviction is sufficient to give him a personal stake in the outcome of the constitutional argument. **D** is incorrect because every court has the power to interpret the Constitution.

24. **B** Article I, Section 8 the power to spend for public purposes that provide for "the common defense and general welfare," so long as that spending does not adversely affect other constitutional rights. Here, providing funding for flood-control projects is clearly beneficial for the general welfare, and there is no indication that any other constitutional right is involved.

**A** is incorrect because, although Congress's actions might affect interstate commerce (for example, the rivers and streams might be used for interstate travel and commerce), the Commerce Clause generally deals with federal laws that directly regulate state action. Here, Congress is merely providing money, which makes **B** a better answer. **C** is incorrect because there is no requirement that a federal program like this be limited to federal property. **D** is incorrect because there is no requirement that a federal program like this be limited to navigable waters.

25. **D** The Equal Protection Clause of the Fourteenth Amendment provides that "no state shall . . . deny to any person within its jurisdiction the equal protection of the laws." Actions of a county or other political subdivision of a state are regarded as state actions. The fact that plaintiff's application was rejected solely because of her sex would probably make that rejection invidious, and a violation of her Fourteenth Amendment rights.

In **A**, the disparity between the pass rates of black persons and white persons might be evidence that a law is being applied in a discriminatory manner, but it does not establish it conclusively. **A** is therefore incorrect. Although discrimination based solely on ethnic background may violate the Equal Protection Clause, **B** is incorrect because the Fourteenth Amendment prohibits state action only, and the discrimination in **B** was practiced by a privately owned hospital. **C** is incorrect for the same reason since the discrimination was practiced by a federal agency rather than a state one.

26. **B**      Under the Cooley Doctrine, the state's power to regulate commerce is held concurrently with the federal government's commerce power. If an activity is one largely of local concern, the state may regulate it in the absence of a federal statute indicating congressional intention to preempt the field. On the other hand, if the activity is one requiring national uniformity, the state may not regulate it in the absence of a federal statute specifically authorizing regulation by the states. For these reasons, the absence of a federal statute would establish that the state regulation is constitutional only if the activity regulated is one largely of local concern. Although it is not certain that the argument in **B** would succeed, it is the only one that could possibly support the constitutionality of the statute.

            **A** is incorrect because the absence of a federal statute might mean that Congress regards the matter of rest breaks for truck drivers as one requiring national uniformity but does not consider a statute requiring such breaks to be a good idea. Although the statute is enforceable only within the state, it clearly has an effect on interstate commerce. **C** is therefore incorrect. **D** is a correct statement if the activity involved is not one requiring national uniformity. If, however, it does require national uniformity, the states are not free to impose restrictions upon it unless authorized to do so by Congress.

27. **D**      A statute is void for overbreadth if it punishes expression that is constitutionally protected along with expression that can validly be punished. Although certain types of offensive expression (including, perhaps, the defendant's) may be prohibited by statute, a law that prohibits "offensive" conduct is so vague that it may also end up punishing constitutionally protected speech. Such a law is therefore overbroad.

            **A, B,** and **C** are incorrect because a person whose conduct can be constitutionally punished under a statute has standing to assert the rights of persons whose conduct is unconstitutionally prohibited by the statute. Thus, although it might have been constitutional to punish the defendant's conduct, the law is constitutionally invalid because of other conduct that it might reach, and if invalid, cannot be enforced even against the defendant.

28. **B**      Although the Constitution requires the advice and consent of the Senate for ambassadorial appointments, the United States Supreme Court has held that the President may dismiss an ambassador at will and without cause.

            **A** and **C** are therefore incorrect. Whether the removal of an ambassador constitutes a withdrawal of diplomatic relations depends on the reason for the ambassador's removal. **D** is incorrect for this reason, and because the President has the power to withdraw diplomatic relations with a foreign government.

29. **C**      The "case or controversy" requirement of Article III of the United States Constitution prevents the United States Supreme Court from exercising jurisdiction in anything but a concrete dispute in which the Court may effectively remedy damage to a legal right by rendering a judicial decree. Since an advisory opinion does not determine the rights of any person, the opinion of the state Court of Errors is not a case or controversy, and the Supreme Court has no jurisdiction to review it.

**A** is therefore incorrect. If a state court's decision that a state law is invalid rests on an adequate state ground, it is not subject to review by the Supreme Court because such review would be futile. If a state court's decision in a matter that qualified as a case or controversy were based on its interpretation of the federal Constitution, the United States Supreme Court could review it. **B** is incorrect, however, because the advisory opinion of the Court of Errors was not a case or controversy. Where a constitutional issue is involved, the Supreme Court may review the decision of a state's highest court, even though that decision was based on an exercise of original jurisdiction. **D** is therefore incorrect.

30. **C**  The right to marry is a fundamental liberty interest, and the United States Supreme Court has held that the Due Process Clause's right of privacy protects the integrity of the family. People who are related by blood or marriage have a right to live together in a common household. Here, the only way for the family to comply with the ordinance is to have at least one of the children move out. Consequently, the ordinance clearly impinges on the family's right of privacy, and is thus unconstitutional.

**A** is incorrect because the fact that some of the children are over 18 and may be considered legally adults does not change the fact that the family's right to live together is being impinged by the ordinance. **B** is incorrect because the ordinance's apparent intention of protecting health and welfare doesn't change the fact it impinges the integrity of the family. **D** is incorrect because limiting the law's effects to state college students doesn't necessarily keep it from violating a family's right to live together.

31. **B**  The emergency powers of the President have been held to include the power to commit United States military personnel to foreign hostilities in satisfaction of existing treaty obligations.

**A** is incorrect because Article I of the Constitution grants the power to declare war to Congress rather than the President. **C** is incorrect because the validity of the treaty is not in issue. As Commander-in-Chief, the President is the ultimate maker of military policy. **D** is incorrect, however, because the decision to send troops to the republic is a matter not of military policy, but of foreign policy.

32. **D**  Constitutional guarantees of due process and freedom of expression protect only against government action. Since the college is privately owned, it is not bound to give the student due process or to avoid interfering with his freedom of expression. Common law and contract rights are thus the only ones that he may hope to enforce against the university.

**A**, **B**, and **C** are therefore incorrect.

33. **C**  To have standing to litigate the constitutionality of a statute, a plaintiff must show that he or she has a personal stake in the action. Federal taxpayers do not usually have standing to challenge an expenditure of federal money because their interest in the taxes that they pay into the federal treasury is too remote to be regarded as substantial. If the federal taxpayer is suing to recover taxes paid under protest, however, he or she has the right to urge any appropriate objections to the validity of the tax — including a constitutional challenge to the law that imposed the tax or directed disbursement of tax money collected.

**A** is incorrect because a moral or intellectual interest in the outcome of litigation is not sufficient to satisfy the requirement of a personal stake in the action. **B** is incorrect because a state does not ordinarily have standing to bring an action as a representative of its citizens since they are said to be protected by their political representation in Congress. State taxpayers have standing to challenge a direct and substantial expenditure of their tax money. But where the activity involved has only a tenuous relationship to an expenditure of funds, it is necessary for the plaintiff to show a direct injury to his or her financial interest. **D** is incorrect because no such injury is shown to exist.

34.  **B**    The Due Process Clause of the Fifth Amendment prohibits arbitrary discrimination by the federal government. Since the law requires the payment of a tax by diesel-powered vehicle users that is not required from non-diesel-powered vehicle users, it is possible to argue that the law discriminates against the operators of diesel vehicles. The argument is very likely to fail since the prohibition falls before an overriding national interest, but it is the only one listed that has any chance of success whatsoever.

**A** is incorrect because the fact that the tax has a regulatory effect is not, alone, enough to make it invalid. The argument that a tax is so burdensome as to constitute an unconstitutional taking has been held to be a political question for which appropriate judicial standards of judgment are not available. **C** is therefore incorrect. The use of a tax to discourage certain activities has been upheld if it is imposed to accomplish an objective within the scope of some other delegated power. **D** is incorrect because the tax is probably justified under the Commerce Clause.

35.  **C**    Article I, Section 8 of the United States Constitution grants Congress the exclusive right to "coin money and regulate the value thereof." Since the state statute requires certain businesses to accept casino chips in payment for merchandise and services, in effect it makes those chips legal tender (*i.e.*, money), thus exercising a function that exclusively belongs to Congress.

Ordinarily, the requirement of due process applies only to governmental deprivations. **A** is incorrect for this reason, and because the Casino Chip Law provides a method for the persons affected to be paid, and even to receive a profit (of one-third) for the handling of the chips. According to the Cooley Doctrine, the commerce power is held concurrently by the state and federal governments. **B** is incorrect because under the Cooley Doctrine, the fact that state law affects interstate commerce is not, alone, sufficient to make it invalid. Since the Casino Chips Law requires licensed casinos to redeem the chips at face value, the "taking" (if there is one) is not without compensation. Although the restaurant owner might argue that the compensation is not "just," the argument in **D** is not nearly as strong as the one raised by **C**, to which there is really no possible response.

36.  **B**    Generally, federal taxpayers do not have standing to challenge the spending of tax dollars because their interest is too attenuated. However, a taxpayer can challenge a spending measure if he or she can show the challenged measure was enacted under Congress's taxing and spending power and exceeds the specific limitations on this power. The United States Supreme Court has stated that the Establishment Clause is such a limit on the

power. Consequently, since the challenge concerns the Establishment Clause and its limit on congressional spending, the taxpayer bringing the challenge will have standing.

**A** is incorrect because it is too broad. A federal taxpayer does not have standing to challenge any and all spending authorizations for any and all reasons. **C** is incorrect because the issue regarding how the money will be spent does not affect the taxpayer's standing. **D** is incorrect because the term "nexus" usually applies to state taxation of interstate commerce, which is not the situation here.

37.  **C**    Standing to challenge the constitutionality of a law or an executive order requires a "personal stake" in the outcome. This requires that the plaintiff be threatened with immediate damage to his or her rights that can be avoided if the court grants the requested relief. A citizen of the republic living in the United States was immune from taxation until the presidential order was issued, and under that order he will be required to pay taxes. Sufficient personal stake thus exists.

**A** is incorrect because an intellectual or political interest is not sufficient to give a plaintiff the personal stake required. **B** is incorrect because a United States citizen was not immune from taxation before the order and therefore has no personal stake in having it declared unconstitutional. **D** is incorrect because foreign governments have no rights under the United States Constitution and therefore have no right to seek its enforcement.

38.  **D**    A federal tax on state activities is valid so long as it is non-discriminatory and does not seriously interfere with the functioning of state government as a sovereign entity. If the activity on which a federal tax is imposed is not one unique to the state government, the tax probably does not interfere with the functioning of state government as a sovereign entity. Since the building is rented to private tenants much as any other commercial office building, the state's activity in operating it is not one that is unique to state government.

**A** is incorrect because Congress's power to tax is subject to all constitutional limitations. Although protection of the environment is a legitimate reason for imposing a tax, a state will be immune from such a tax if it interferes with the functioning of the state as a sovereign entity. **B** is therefore incorrect. **C** is incorrect for the same reason.

39.  **D**    Although the state may interfere with commercial speech to serve a substantial governmental interest, it must not do so in a way that is unnecessarily restrictive. Thus, even though the state may have a substantial interest in protecting the public against tooth decay, the law prohibiting the advertising of chewing gum would be constitutionally invalid if there are less restrictive ways of accomplishing the same objective (*e.g.*, by requiring a warning). Although it is not certain that the argument in **D** would result in a finding that the law is invalid, it is the only one listed that could possibly support such a finding.

**A** is an incorrect statement of law since freedom of expression is not absolute and may be interfered with to serve a substantial government interest. The mere fact that a state law will have an effect on interstate commerce is not enough to make that law invalid unless it imposes an unreasonable burden on interstate commerce. **B** is therefore incorrect.

Although the United States Supreme Court is wary of laws that impose prior restraint on publication, it is far less concerned when those laws affect commercial speech only. **C** is incorrect because the speech involved is commercial, and the fact that the law imposes a prior restraint is therefore not sufficient alone to render it constitutionally invalid.

40.  **C**     Congress has the power to make laws regulating conduct on federal property and in the District of Columbia, virtually without limitation.

A is incorrect because the police powers of the states include the power to regulate education. Although states must do so in a way that does not deny equal protection to persons within their jurisdiction, there is no constitutional requirement that each state do so in an identical way. Some highly imaginative argument might lead a court to conclude that if **B** were true, the statute would be valid under the war and national defense powers of Congress, or that if **D** were true, the statute would be valid under the Commerce Clause. No such stretch of the imagination is necessary in **C**, however, so **B** and **D** are incorrect.

41.  **D**     A question is moot when the issues that it raises have ceased to exist. Although the defendant has been released from physical custody, violations of the conditions of his parole would result in his re-incarceration for the remainder of his sentence. Since the warden ordered his confinement to be solitary for the rest of his sentence, a return to prison would subject him to enforcement of the warden's order. The issues raised by his petition have therefore not ceased to exist.

A is incorrect because although the defendant is no longer in prison, he was paroled on a conditional basis and could be returned to prison for the remainder of his sentence. **B** is incorrect because there are many reasons why parole might be appropriate even if the defendant's rights were not violated. Sometimes the nature of the judicial process makes it impossible for the court to reach a decision in a particular kind of claim before it becomes moot (*e.g.*, challenges to a law prohibiting abortion could never reach the Supreme Court before the birth of a petitioner's baby). In such cases, if the claim is one that is capable of being repeated but likely to evade judicial review, it will not be moot even though the petitioner is unable to show that specific damage will result from a refusal to hear it. The defendant's petition is not such a case, however, because there is no indication that the warden's order was part of a policy that would lead to repetition of claims like the defendant's, and, even if it were, there is no indication that subsequent claims by other prisoners are likely to become moot before being reached by the Court. **C** is therefore incorrect.

42.  **A**     Under the Supremacy Clause, state legislation is invalid if it is inconsistent with federal law. In a challenge to the constitutionality of a statute excluding non-citizens from public office, the treaties and immigration laws of the United States might be relevant to determine whether federal legislation has already addressed the subject, and, if it has, to determine whether the state law is inconsistent with it.

B is incorrect since the treaties and immigration laws of the United States are not relevant to determine what the privileges and immunities of citizenship are. **C** is incorrect because substantive due process has not been held to include the right to hold public office, and procedural due process does not prevent the enactment of a law. The doctrine of separation of powers refers to the relationship between the three branches of the federal government, not to the relationship of state governments to the federal government, so **D** is also incorrect.

43.  **C**        An oath to uphold the United States Constitution and to oppose the unlawful overthrow of government is nothing more than a promise to do something that public employees are legally obligated to do.

**A**, **B**, and **D** are incorrect because some loyalty oaths (such as those that require a disclaimer of membership in organizations referred to as subversive) have been held to deny the freedom of assembly to public officials who are required by statute to take them.

44.  **C**        A state law that burdens interstate commerce is valid if the state interest that the law is designed to protect outweighs the burdens that the law imposes on interstate commerce. Although not enough facts are given to allow a determination of whether this is so in the instant case, **C** is the only argument that offers any support at all to the state's argument.

**A** and **B** are incorrect because the law is likely to discourage commerce from out of state, even though it applies equally to intrastate shipments and vehicles garaged within the state. If all or most other states have similar requirements, that fact might be relevant in determining that the burden on interstate commerce is not an unreasonable one. But the fact that some other states have such a requirement is not enough alone to establish that it is reasonable. **D** is therefore incorrect.

45.  **A**        Under the Supremacy Clause, a state law that is otherwise valid may be declared invalid if it is inconsistent with a federal law concerning the same subject matter. If there is a federal law like the one described in **A**, the Ocean Fishing License Act may be inconsistent with it. If so, the Act will be invalid.

In the absence of any conflicting federal law, the state law might be a valid exercise of police powers or revenue-raising powers. **B** is therefore incorrect. **C** is incorrect because there is no indication that enforcement of Section 1 results in discrimination. **D** is incorrect because the Fifth Amendment imposes restrictions on the federal government, but it is irrelevant to state action.

46.  **D**        Because the activities of Agricultural Conservation Districts will affect only owners of agricultural land, and because such owners constitute a narrow class of persons, elections do not have to be conducted according to the "one person, one vote" principle.

**A** and **B** are under-inclusive since the "one person, one vote" principle applies to all elections that affect the general public. **C** is incorrect because states may not exercise their own powers in a manner inconsistent with the requirements of the United States Constitution.

47.  **A**        In a challenge to state interference with a "fundamental right," or to a state law that allegedly discriminates against a "suspect classification," the state has the burden of establishing that the law is necessary to serve a compelling state interest. The United States Supreme Court has characterized marriage and procreation as fundamental rights.

**B** is incorrect because although gender-based classification is subject to heightened scrutiny, the Supreme Court has not held gender to be a suspect classification. **C** is incorrect because interference with fundamental rights is presumed to be unconstitutional. **D** is incorrect for the same reason, and because state exercises of powers reserved under the Tenth Amendment must be consistent with other requirements of the federal constitution.

48.  **A**    The Equal Protection Clause prohibits *states* from engaging in invidious discrimination. In **A**, the discriminatory action was by a federal officer rather than by a state officer.

Convictions in **B** and **C** are likely since the clause has been held to apply to municipal as well as state action. A conviction in **D** is possible if it is found (and it has been in similar cases) that because of its location in a state office building, and because of the fact that it is rented from the state, the restaurant is so closely linked to the state that the Equal Protection Clause should apply to its management.

49.  **B**    Statutory language that does not allow the person of ordinary intelligence to know what conduct is prohibited by the statute is vague and therefore unconstitutional. Language such as that given here has frequently been held to be vague. Although it is not certain that a court would come to that conclusion, **B** is the only argument that could possibly support the defendant's position.

Although it may be expressive, conduct like the defendant's can be prohibited as part of "time, place, and manner" restrictions not aimed at the content of the symbolic speech. **A** is therefore incorrect. **C** is incorrect for two reasons: First, it may not be an accurate appraisal of the reasonable person's response to the defendant's conduct, and second, the constitutionality of a statute depends on how the person of ordinary intelligence would understand it without regard to any particular conduct. If the language of a statute can be understood by the person of ordinary intelligence, it is not vague and a conviction under it does not violate due process for the sole reason that the statute has been newly enacted and not yet judicially construed. **D** is therefore incorrect.

50.  **D**    The Supreme Court has been permissive of public aid to religious colleges since the restraint imposed by the academic disciplines of their instructors and the age of their students make it unlikely that they are primarily devoted to religious indoctrination.

Almost all direct aid to primary and secondary schools operated by religious organizations has been held to violate the Establishment Clause. **A** and **B** are incorrect for this reason, and because investigation and classification of the teachers and curricula of schools seeking such aid would necessarily result in excessive entanglement of the state with religious schools. Although the Supreme Court has approved the loan of textbooks purchased with public funds to students at religious schools, **C** is incorrect since it would involve the payment of public money directly to the school, and this, too, would probably result in excessive entanglement.

51.  **B**    Because problems of water pollution tend to vary from place to place, it is generally understood that, in the absence of congressional mandates to the contrary, states are free to exercise inconsistent pollution controls in the interest of local health and safety.

**A** is incorrect because problems of pollution may differ, even though the water is used for the same purpose in various states. **C** is incorrect because if Congress has enacted laws regulating water pollution in interstate rivers, inconsistent state regulations are likely to be invalid under the Supremacy Clause. **D** is incorrect because the intrastate nature of the company's business is not relevant to the effect that the statute may have on interstate commerce.

52. **D**    A state interference with the free exercise of a religious belief is constitutionally valid if it is necessary in light of a compelling state interest. Since a court might find that a prohibition of the kind of activity described by the statute serves a compelling interest of the state, **D** is correct.

**A** and **B** are therefore incorrect. **C** is incorrect because in considering a challenge to the constitutionality of a state interference with religion, the court may not consider the validity of the religious beliefs in question.

53. **A**    A case cannot be heard by a federal court unless it is ripe. A case is not ripe if it has not become sufficiently concrete to be easily adjudicated. If a court believes that it is very unlikely that a statute will be enforced, the court will likely treat the case as not being ripe. This is so even if the plaintiff has admitted to violating the statute and is likely to do so again.

**D** is therefore incorrect. A case is moot if it no longer involves an actual controversy because events occurring after the filing have deprived the litigant of an ongoing stake in the controversy (for example, someone suing a school for discriminatory admissions policies who is allowed to attend and manages to graduate before the case is heard). **B** is therefore incorrect. In a few situations, courts will hear a case that is moot—for instance, if the issue is capable of repetition, yet will likely continue to evade review. This is a situation where, if the case was declared moot, a different person might be injured in the same way by the same defendant, and that different person's claim would become moot before review. **C** is therefore incorrect.

54. **A**    The proper means of attacking an injunction is by judicial proceeding. Because of the short time period involved, however, it would have been impossible to obtain judicial review before the election. If the organization desires to hold rallies in the future, there is a likelihood that similarly issued injunctions will likewise evade review. Where a problem is capable of repetition but likely to evade review—even though, as here, the injunction being challenged is no longer in effect—Supreme Court review is available.

**B** is incorrect because some state interference with the right to assemble is permitted, as in the case of valid time, place, and manner restrictions. **C** is incorrect because the possibility that similar future claims will evade review prevents the question from being regarded as moot. **D** is incorrect because the Fourteenth Amendment is not relevant to anything but *state* action, and the organization is a private organization.

55. **A**    If the Rebate Act was an offer for a unilateral contract, and if the plaintiff's commencement of performance can be regarded as an acceptance of that offer (or as a condition that

prevents its withdrawal), then the repeal of the Act may be found to impair the obligations of a contract. Although it is unlikely that the Act will be found to constitute an offer, this is the only one of the arguments that could possibly benefit the plaintiff.

**B** is incorrect because the Due Process Clause of the Fifth Amendment applies only to federal action. There are two Privileges and Immunities Clauses, but neither is applicable here. That of Article IV prohibits discrimination against out-of-staters, while that of the Fourteenth Amendment prevents states from denying persons the rights conferred by United States citizenship. **C** is therefore incorrect. **D** is incorrect since the Just Compensation Clause requires payment for private property that is taken for public use, and here no private property was taken.

56. **D**    It has been held that the First Amendment protects the right of nonprofit organizations who use litigation as an instrument of political expression to solicit prospective clients.

**A** is incorrect since the Supreme Court has held that nondeceptive advertising of legal services is protected by the First Amendment. **B** is incorrect because the fact that the advertisement "could have the effect" of inciting illegal conduct is not sufficient. For that argument to be valid, there must be both an intention that the expression will cause illegal conduct and an imminent probability that such illegal conduct will occur. **C** is incorrect for two reasons: First, although commercial speech is entitled to First Amendment protection, the fact that speech is commercial does not in itself mean that laws regulating it are invalid, and second, the communication in this case is more likely to be regarded as political expression rather than commercial speech since it does not relate solely to economic interests.

57. **D**    Since the results of litigation become part of the law, the requirement of standing is designed to assure that the person challenging the constitutionality of a statute has an incentive to litigate all issues fully and vigorously. Ordinarily, this requires that the plaintiff show some actual or imminent concrete personal injury that would be remedied or prevented if his or her claim were sustained. The building contractor in **D** stands to lose the economic benefits of his contract with the state unless the section in question is invalidated.

**A** and **C** are incorrect because the damage apprehended is less direct and imminent than that in **D**. **B** is incorrect since it is generally understood that a mere political or intellectual interest does not satisfy the requirement of a personal injury.

58. **C**    The Equal Protection Clause provides that "No state shall . . . deny to any person within its jurisdiction the equal protection of the laws." A statute that invidiously discriminates against members of a particular class violates its requirements. Although some questions might exist as to whether the statute's discrimination against felons is "invidious," there is no need to make a determination because, of the arguments listed, **C** is the only one with which the plaintiff stands any chance at all.

**A** is incorrect because the statute in question did not interfere with rights under a preexisting contract. Since the statute applies only to persons convicted of felonies within the state, it does not discourage the interstate travel of felons, so **B** is incorrect. **D** is little more than a statement of moral philosophy and has no basis in constitutional law.

59. **D**    Since the United States Constitution gives Congress the exclusive power of legislation over the District of Columbia, there could be no question about the validity of a federal law applicable only there.

Although legalizing gambling would probably promote certain interstate economic activity, state concerns for public morals would probably outweigh the federal interest in protecting such commerce. This is especially true since all states prohibit or regulate gambling. **A** is therefore not as effective an argument as **D**. The Supremacy Clause applies only where state legislation conflicts with federal law enacted within the scope of the powers delegated to Congress. Whether a federal gambling law would be within the scope of these powers presents a serious question. **B** is therefore not the best of the four arguments. Since there is no general federal police power, Congress lacks the power to substitute scientific opinion (or congressional opinion) for that of the state regarding the public morality. **C** is therefore incorrect.

60. **B**    In cases of economic regulation, the proper test of constitutional validity is whether there was a rational basis for the law. This means that if any situation can be imagined in which the law would be a reasonable way of accomplishing a legitimate purpose, it is valid.

**A** is incorrect since the "compelling state interest" standard is ordinarily applied only in cases involving interference with a "suspect classification" or a "fundamental right." **C** is incorrect since the distribution of any entitlements, whether they are classified as "privileges" or "rights," must be consistent with the requirements of the Fourteenth Amendment. **D** is incorrect because the "clear and present danger" test has been applied only to interference with First Amendment rights.

61. **D**    It has been held that significant state involvement in a particular private activity might make the Equal Protection Clause applicable to the private activity. It is possible that the state's licensing, funding, inspection, and oversight of the hospital operation would be sufficient to have this effect. While it is not certain that a court would come to that conclusion, the argument in **D** is the only one listed that could possibly support the position of the organization.

**A** is incorrect because the Fourteenth Amendment relates only to state action or to private action in which the state is significantly involved. **B** is incorrect because cases have held that licensing alone is not sufficient state involvement. Although the Equal Protection Clause prevents state courts from enforcing private policies of racial discrimination, it does not require state courts to eliminate privately practiced discrimination. **C** is therefore incorrect.

62. **C**    A statute that makes the possession or sale of obscene material by a bookseller a crime without imposing any requirement of scienter is unconstitutional because it is likely to have a chilling effect on booksellers, who probably cannot familiarize themselves with all the books that they sell.

Statutes like that described in **A** have been declared valid on the ground that they are justified by a municipality's interest in land-use planning. Although the United States Supreme

Court has held that no person may be punished for private possession of materials judged to be obscene unless they involve child pornography, showing films for a fee is not private possession, even when done in the home. **B** is therefore incorrect. **D** is incorrect because the Court has held that evidence of pandering may be relevant to the questions of whether material alleged to be obscene appeals primarily to prurient interest and whether it lacks serious value, two elements of the Supreme Court's definition of obscenity.

63.   **D**   Since the First Amendment provides that "Congress shall make no law . . . abridging the freedom of . . . the press," a statute that prohibits certain publications probably violates it.

**A** is not the strongest argument since the President's power to make executive agreements is broad and may cover any area of international concern. **B** is incorrect because there is no constitutional requirement that an executive agreement must be implemented in the least burdensome manner possible. The executive agreement simply calls for the government of each country to "discourage" the press from making certain statements. Since this can be accomplished without violating the First Amendment, **C** is not a correct statement.

64.   **D**   In some cases where a public employee's expressive activities lead to dismissal, the employee will be protected by his or her First Amendment rights and reinstated to his or her position. Here, because the police officer's activities did not involve political news or public information about the police department's functioning, his expression was not a matter of public concern worthy of First Amendment protection. Importantly, the officer's speech purposefully exploited the police department and likely harmed its missions and functions. **A** is therefore incorrect. Freedom of association is not specifically mentioned in the First Amendment, but is derived from individuals' rights of speech and assembly. Freedom of association refers to the idea that if an individual has a First Amendment right to engage in particular expressive activities, a group has the freedom of association to engage in that same activity. Here, as stated above, the officer's expressive conduct did not rise to the level of conduct that would cause the First Amendment to protect him in his job. Consequently, **B** and **C** are therefore incorrect.

65.   **C**   Since the President has broad authority as the chief spokesperson for the United States in the area of foreign affairs, delegations of authority by the President in this field are constitutionally valid. On the other hand, the President's broad powers to delegate authority in this area make interference by Congress with such delegations a violation of the principle of separation of powers.

**A** is incorrect because the United States Constitution specifically gives Congress the power to exercise some control over foreign affairs (*e.g.*, the senatorial power to "advise and consent" in the execution of treaties), thus preventing the President's power in this area from being truly "sole" or "exclusive." **B** is incorrect because the Constitution gives the Senate, not the House of Representatives, power over foreign affairs. Likewise, **D** is incorrect since any presidential veto can be overridden by a two-thirds vote of Congress.

66.   **D**   A case presents a non-justiciable political question when a decision would unduly interfere with the operation of a co-equal branch of government. Article I of the United States

Constitution provides that each house of Congress "shall be the Judge of the Elections, Returns, and Qualifications of its own members." Since the order that the plaintiff seeks would interfere with this power of the Senate, her petition might be said to present a non-justiciable political question.

Collateral estoppel prevents the re-litigation of an issue identical to one that has already been judicially determined. There is some doubt about whether the doctrine would apply to determinations by non-judicial bodies (such as the Senate). In any event, **A** is incorrect because if the doctrine were applied, it would aid the plaintiff's case rather than lead to its dismissal since the issue of her age was determined in her favor. Since the qualifications of a United States Senator are established by the United States Constitution, any question about whether a person is qualified to be a United States Senator is a federal one. **B** is therefore incorrect. The fact that the plaintiff has already had her day in court might lead to a dismissal of her claim if the state court's decision had been unfavorable to her. Since it found in her favor, however, its decision should not justify a dismissal of her case. **C** is therefore incorrect.

67.  **A**    Article I, Section 8, clause 4 gives Congress the power to "establish an uniform Rule of Naturalization." This has been held to grant Congress plenary power over aliens that includes the power to treat non-citizens differently from citizens so long as the discrimination bears some rational relationship to national policy. Since the provision in question could have the effect of encouraging naturalization, it is probably justified by the plenary power of Congress over aliens.

**B** and **D** are incorrect because resident aliens are entitled to many of but not all the protections guaranteed by the United States Constitution. Since the Equal Protection Clause applies only to action by the states and is inapplicable to federal action, **C** is incorrect.

68.  **A**    The Fifth Amendment "Taking" Clause states that private property cannot be taken for public use without just compensation. Consequently, while the government may take private property in certain circumstances, it must pay a fair price for it. Importantly, if the government makes or authorizes a permanent physical occupation of private property, this action automatically results in a taking no matter how minor the interference with the owner's use and no matter how important the government interest. **C** and **D** are therefore incorrect. **B** is incorrect because the landlord's religious beliefs do not become part of the takings analysis.

69.  **D**    The Due Process Clause of the Fourteenth Amendment prevents the states from depriving any person of life, liberty, or property without due process of law. Since the Clean Roads Act made violation of an administrative order a crime, it violated Fourteenth Amendment due process by permitting the order to be issued without giving the defendant an opportunity to be heard.

An *ex post facto* law is one that punishes as criminal an act that was not prohibited when it was performed. The Clean Roads Act was not an *ex post facto* law because it did not impose punishment for an act that had already been committed. Instead, it permitted the issuance of an administrative order, the *future* violation of which would be a crime. **A** is therefore incorrect. A bill of attainder is a law that punishes a person without the benefit of a judicial trial. Since the defendant's conviction was the result of a trial, the Clean Roads Act cannot be called a bill of attainder, making **B** incorrect. **C** is incorrect because the Due Process Clause of the Fifth Amendment applies only to the federal government and has no application to the states.

70.  **C**     The United States Supreme Court has held that state aid to religious schools is constitutionally valid if it has a secular purpose, a primarily secular effect, does not result in undue entanglement between state and religion, and does not produce political divisiveness along religious lines. Since the examinations are designed to test competence in secular subjects and are to be given in all high schools, their administration in religious schools by state employees is not likely to result in entanglement or political divisiveness. Therefore, if the law has a purpose and effect that are primarily secular, it does not violate the Establishment Clause.

  **A** is incorrect because the courts have generally held that a state taxpayer has standing to challenge the constitutionality of a statute that will directly result in an expenditure of state funds. **B** is incorrect because even a law that does not discriminate between religions may be found to violate the Establishment Clause if it serves to advance religion in general. If a law violates any of the four prongs of the test outlined above, the fact that it was enacted to serve a compelling state interest does not prevent it from being unconstitutional under the Establishment Clause. **D** is therefore incorrect.

71.  **B**     The defendant advocated an act of arson; the fact that the crowd—carrying flaming torches—began following him toward the clinic indicates that unlawful conduct was immediately probable. Speech that advocates illegal conduct may be constitutionally prohibited if it advocates action and involves incitement of immediate and probably unlawful conduct. The defendant's conduct may, therefore, be constitutionally prohibited. A law that requires a permit for the conduct of a public assembly but provides vague standards for the granting of such a permit violates the First Amendment, however. Since this ordinance granted the mayor unfettered discretion in granting permits, it was unconstitutional.

  **A** is incorrect because speech that advocates unlawful action and is probable to immediately incite such unlawful action may be subject to prior restraint that is constitutionally permissible. Although the defendant probably did not have a constitutional right to engage in the conduct described, the requirement of standing is relaxed in a constitutional challenge based on vagueness or overbreadth. Thus, even though the defendant's constitutional rights were not violated by the ordinance, he has standing to challenge it on the ground that its vagueness or overbreadth might result in a violation of the constitutional rights of others. **C** is therefore incorrect. **D** is incorrect because it is over-inclusive. Some permit requirements (like those that regulate the time, place, and manner of speech) are constitutionally valid. Others (like this one, which is based on vague standards) are constitutionally invalid.

72.  **A**     Although the Commerce Clause of the United States Constitution gives Congress the power to regulate interstate commerce, it is understood that the states may exercise some regulation as well. If, however, the interstate activity in question is of national concern

and requires uniform federal regulation, then the states may not regulate it in the absence of a federal statute specifically authorizing them to do so. Since this question calls for the assumption that there is no such federal statute, the state's attempt to regulate the interstate sale of petroleum produced within the state would be unconstitutional if that activity is of a national concern and requires uniform federal regulation.

Whether an imported product remains in its original package may be relevant to determining a state's right to *tax* it under Article I, Section 10(2), which prohibits the states from taxing imports or exports. **B** is incorrect, however, because the "original package doctrine" has never been relevant to determining whether a state may regulate a particular activity. Under the Full Faith and Credit Clause, a state is required to enforce judgments and decrees of the courts of other states. Since the facts in this case do not involve an attempt to enforce the judgment or decree of the court of another state, the Full Faith and Credit Clause is inapplicable, and **C** is incorrect. Under the Supremacy Clause, a state law is invalid if it conflicts with a federal law dealing with the same subject matter. In such cases, the field is said to be "preempted" by the existence of a federal statute dealing with the same subject matter. Here, since there is no federal statute, there has been no "preemption," and the Supremacy Clause is inapplicable. **D** is therefore incorrect.

73. **D**    Because the determination of any constitutional issue is likely to become an important part of U.S. law, the requirement of standing is designed to assure that persons litigating constitutional issues have incentive to litigate them vigorously and effectively. For this reason, standing requires that a party seeking to assert a constitutional issue must have a personal stake in the outcome. Usually, this takes the form of an actual or immediately threatened concrete injury that would be prevented by a favorable determination of the claim. Since the construction company in **D** will lose profits if the state is unable to honor its contract, it has the necessary personal stake to confer standing.

Although a state taxpayer may have standing to challenge the constitutionality of an outlay of state funds, **A** is incorrect because the challenge in this case is to a federal statute, not to the expenditure of state funds. The relationship between a federal taxpayer and the federal treasury is regarded as too indirect to confer standing on a federal taxpayer seeking to challenge an outlay of federal funds. **B** is therefore incorrect. An interest that is purely intellectual or political is generally not held to be sufficiently "personal" to confer standing, making **C** incorrect.

74. **D**    The primary purpose of the exclusionary rule is to deter police misconduct in gathering evidence. The United States Supreme Court has held, however, that after a person has had a full and fair hearing in a state court on his or her claim that evidence against him or her was seized illegally, additional review by the federal court would be of minimal use in deterring police misconduct. For this reason, in a habeas corpus proceeding, the federal court is bound by the state court's finding regarding a claimed Fourth Amendment violation.

**A** is therefore incorrect. Although a habeas corpus petition based on an asserted violation of the United States Constitution can be heard in a federal court only after all state court remedies have been exhausted, the exhaustion of state remedies alone is not sufficient reason for the federal court to grant the petition. **B** is therefore incorrect. **C** is incorrect because a denial of certiorari by the United States Supreme Court indicates only that fewer than four judges wanted to hear the claim. It does not reflect any finding on the merits by the United States Supreme Court, and it does not affect the power of any other court — state or federal — to hear the claim.

75.  **A**      The abstention doctrine prevents federal trial courts from deciding constitutional issues that are premised on unsettled questions of state law. Since the constitutionality of the state statute would likely depend on the meaning of the term "sexual deviates," and since the facts say that the state courts have never interpreted that term, the United States District Court should refrain from considering the validity of the statute until the state court has had an opportunity to determine the meaning of the term.

Although the Eleventh Amendment prevents federal courts from entertaining damage claims against a state by its citizens or by those of another state, it does not prevent those courts from issuing an injunction ordering a state official not to violate federal law (including the United States Constitution). **B** is therefore incorrect. A question is said to be moot if there is no longer an issue the judicial determination of which would affect the rights of the parties. Since the rejection of the plaintiff's application was based on the state law described, an order enjoining the state from enforcing it could result in the hiring of the plaintiff. The question is therefore not moot, so **C** is incorrect. A person has standing to assert a constitutional claim if a judicial determination would prevent a concrete and direct injury to him or her. Since a favorable decision could result in the plaintiff's being hired, he does have standing. **D** is therefore incorrect.

76.  **A**      A statutory system of classification is unconstitutional if it lacks a rational basis. Whether or not this statutory requirement has a rational basis is uncertain, but of the arguments listed, **A** is the only one with any possibility of success.

While the Full Faith and Credit Clause requires a state to honor the judgments of the courts of other states, it has never been held to require that states honor professional licenses issued by other states. **B** is therefore incorrect. Since biology may be studied anywhere, and since the statute makes the study of biology a requirement for all persons — state residents and non-residents alike — there is no indication that the statute discriminates against out-of-staters. **C** is therefore incorrect. The Privileges and Immunities Clause of the Fourteenth Amendment prevents states from interfering with the rights that flow from the relationship between a United States citizen and the federal government. Since the right to be a hairdresser does not arise from that relationship, **D** is incorrect.

77.  **B**      Material is obscene if it appeals primarily to prurient interest, depicts sexual activity in a way that offends contemporary community standards, and, on the whole, is lacking in serious artistic or scientific value. Although a "pandering" advertisement used to sell allegedly obscene material might not itself be obscene, the United States Supreme Court has held that its contents may be admitted as evidence relevant to a determination of whether the material so advertised appeals primarily to prurient interest and whether it is lacking in serious value.

The defendant has not been charged with publishing an obscene advertisement, so it does not matter whether the advertisement is constitutionally protected. Its admissibility depends not on whether the advertisement can be constitutionally punished, but on whether it is relevant to a material issue in the case. **A** and **C** are therefore incorrect. **D** is incorrect because, even though not itself obscene, the advertisement may be relevant to determining whether the film is obscene.

78. **B**    Although many presidential appointments are subject to the advice and consent of the Senate, it has been held that the president may remove appointees at will so long as they do not perform judicial or quasi-judicial functions. Since ambassadors perform functions that are strictly executive, the President may remove them at will.

**A**, **C**, and **D** are therefore incorrect.

79. **C**    Under the Fifth Amendment "Takings" Clause, the government cannot take property without fair compensation. Importantly, private property can only be taken for a public use. Consequently, the government cannot simply take private property and hand it to another private owner without some sort of public use. However, the property does not have to be generally open to the public after a taking, and it can be given over to a private party so long as the public can be expected to receive some benefit from its use. Here, since the houses were condemned as part of an economic development plan benefiting the public, the condemnation was a legal taking even though a private party was developing the property.

**A** and **B** are therefore incorrect. In some circumstances, a land use regulation can result in a taking. **D** is therefore incorrect.

80. **A**    Because the determination of any constitutional issue is likely to become an important part of United States law, the requirement of standing is designed to assure that persons litigating constitutional issues have incentive to litigate them vigorously and effectively. For this reason, standing requires that a party seeking to assert a constitutional issue must have a personal stake in the outcome. Usually, this takes the form of an actual or immediately threatened concrete injury that would be prevented by a favorable determination of the claim. Since the girl has not yet consented to marry the boy, the state law does not injure or imminently threaten to injure him.

**B** is incorrect because marriage is a fundamental right, and a statute that interferes with a fundamental right is valid only if it is necessary to serve a compelling state interest. Unless males under the age of 19 are not sufficiently mature for marriage and females over the age of 17 are sufficiently mature for marriage, the fact that females mature earlier than males—even if accurate—is irrelevant. **C** is therefore incorrect. **D** is incorrect because the exercise of a power reserved to the state—even a reserved power under the Tenth Amendment—must be consistent with the United States Constitution.

81. **D**    A claim is moot when there are no unresolved questions for the court to determine. Since the injunction that the plaintiff seeks has been made unnecessary by the change

in University policy, there is no longer a need for judicial determination. **D** is therefore correct.

Federal courts lack the power to interpret state constitutions. For this reason, a federal court may not review a state court decision that is based on an interpretation of the state constitution (*i.e.*, based on an adequate state ground). This principle does not prevent a federal court from hearing a challenge to state action, however, if that challenge is based on the United States Constitution. Since the plaintiff's federal court proceeding asserts that the United States Constitution prohibits the Chancellor's act, the existence or absence of an adequate state ground for the Chancellor's act is irrelevant. **A** is therefore incorrect. A court may hear a claim even though it has become moot if the nature of it is such that the question may come up again and that it is likely to evade judicial review. (For example, the constitutionality of a statute preventing the abortion of a child could not possibly be determined by the United States Supreme Court before the birth of the child.) **B** is incorrect, however, because, in view of the change in University policy, there is no reason to believe that the claim will come up again. Since the Eleventh Amendment prevents federal courts from hearing damage claims against a state, the fact that the plaintiff had been damaged by past denials of her application would not give the court a reason to hear the claim that is otherwise moot. **C** is therefore incorrect.

82.   **A**   The spending power authorizes Congress to expend funds to promote the general welfare. Since the museum was intended to serve all residents of the United States, the congressional decision to establish and fund it is probably justified under the spending power.

The Commerce Clause authorizes Congress to regulate the interstate movement of people or commodities. Although the museum is to serve Americans from all states, the statute makes no attempt to regulate their movement or that of the artifacts to be displayed. **B** is therefore incorrect. The Eleventh Amendment prevents federal courts from hearing claims against a state. Since this claim is against the United States, and not against any individual state, **C** is incorrect. The doctrine of state immunity relieves states of the obligations imposed by certain federal laws. **D** is incorrect because the statute in question imposes no obligations on a state.

83.   **B**   Article IV provides, in part, that Congress shall have the power to make all needful rules and regulations respecting property belonging to the United States. This has been construed to mean that Congress—or an agency authorized by Congress—may exercise power over federal lands substantially, without limitation.

The Commerce Clause is inapplicable here because there is no indication that the national preserve is involved in interstate commerce or movement. **A** is therefore incorrect. **C** is incorrect because, although Congress is empowered to spend for the general welfare, there is no general federal police power. The power of eminent domain permits the government to take private property for public use (subject to the Fifth Amendment requirement of "just compensation"). Since there has been no taking of private property, **D** is incorrect.

84.   **C**   The Contract Clause (Article I, Sec. 10) provides that no state shall pass any law impairing the obligation of contracts. The Clause applies both to federal and state governments.

While state attempts to rewrite public contracts are subject to strict scrutiny, judicial review is not so stringent for private contracts. Consequently, if a state is acting reasonably in pursuit of a legitimate public purpose, "mere rationality" review applies and even substantial modifications to private contracts will be allowed. Here, the court has found that the state's action to save its economy is reasonable and in pursuit of a legitimate public purpose, so the legislation will be upheld.

**A**, **B**, and **D** are therefore incorrect.

85. **C**    An issue presents a non-justiciable political question when a decision would unduly interfere with the exercise of powers vested by the Constitution in other co-equal branches of government. Although it is by no means certain that this is such an issue, **C** is the only one of the arguments listed that has any possibility of success.

It is not clear how a federal court could go about enforcing process against the President if he or she refused to obey a judicial order, but it is generally understood — and was so held in *U.S. v. Nixon*, 418 U.S. 683 (1974) — that the federal courts have jurisdiction over the President. **A** is therefore incorrect. **B** is incorrect because, although the President is Commander-in-Chief of the armed forces, his or her power as such is subject to limitations imposed by Congress. The United States Constitution gives Congress — not the President — the power to declare war. Thus, if the presidential order sending troops to the republic was a declaration of war, it would be constitutionally invalid. **D** is therefore incorrect.

86. **A**    Procedural due process requires, among other things, a jury trial on issues of fact. For this reason, the United States Supreme Court has held that an arbitrary statutory presumption violates procedural due process by depriving the defendant of his or her right to a jury trial on the issue involved. The state statute creates an irrebuttable presumption that persons who spent more than three hours together in a hotel room had sexual intercourse. If that presumption is an arbitrary one, it violates the requirements of procedural due process.

Substantive due process requirements are said to be violated when a statute interferes with certain constitutionally protected individual freedoms. This statute forbids sexual intercourse with persons under the age of 16 years. Since there is clearly no constitutionally protected right to engage in sexual intercourse with such persons, **B** is incorrect. The Equal Protection Clause is violated by a state law that invidiously discriminates. Since statutes designed to protect young people against their own lack of mature judgment — particularly with respect to sexual intercourse — have been held not to be invidious, **C** is incorrect. A bill of attainder is a law that has the effect of punishing specific individuals without benefit of a trial. When the law in question does not name the specific individuals to be punished, it is a bill of attainder if it mandates a punishment based on preexisting and unalterable characteristics. Since the state statute does not impose punishment without a trial, it is not a bill of attainder. **D** is therefore incorrect.

87. **B**    The Fifth Amendment provides in part that no person shall be deprived of life, liberty, or property without due process of law. Due process includes the right to a fair trial. Since it

is possible to argue that the systematic exclusion of aliens from the jury denied the defendant a fair trial, it is possible that the federal statute excluding aliens from juries violated his due process rights. It is, of course, far from certain that a court would come to this conclusion, but of all the arguments listed, that set forth in **B** is the only one that could possibly lead to a reversal of the defendant's conviction.

**A** is incorrect because the Equal Protection Clause of the Fourteenth Amendment prohibits discrimination only by the state and cannot, therefore, be the basis of a decision that *a federal* law is unconstitutional. The doctrine of separation of powers requires that the duties of the federal government be divided among the three branches created by the United States Constitution (*i.e.*, executive, legislative, and judicial). It is not applicable here because there is no claim that Congress interfered with any other branch of the federal government by passing the law in question. **C** is therefore incorrect. Under the Supremacy Clause, when a state law is inconsistent with a valid federal law, the state law is invalid. For this reason, it could not support a conclusion that a federal statute was unconstitutional. **D** is therefore incorrect.

88.  **D**     The Equal Protection Clause prohibits invidious discrimination by the state. Since not all discrimination is invidious, a series of standards have been developed to determine whether a particular form of discrimination is constitutionally valid. If a discriminatory purpose (*i.e.*, a desire to exclude black women between the ages of 18 and 23 from county court juries) was a motivating factor in enacting the law, or if the law is deliberately applied for that purpose, it is necessary to turn to the standards mentioned above. If, however, a law is neutral on its face and is not purposely applied in a discriminatory way, it does not violate the Equal Protection Clause, even though it may have a discriminatory effect. Thus, the fact that a law has a discriminatory effect is not sufficient to result in its invalidity under the Equal Protection Clause unless it is shown that the law had been or was applied with a discriminatory purpose. The fact that the law effectively excluded a particular group may be circumstantial evidence that it was intended—either on its face or in its application—to have that effect.

A and **B** are therefore incorrect. **C** is incorrect because the fact that an otherwise neutral law had a discriminatory effect is not enough to make it invalid unless there was a discriminatory purpose.

89.  **C**     Article IV, Section 3 of the United States Constitution provides in part that Congress shall have the power "to dispose of . . . property belonging to the United States." Since the battleships are property belonging to the United States, Congress has the power to dispose of them under this constitutional provision.

A is incorrect because the Equal Protection Clause of the Fourteenth Amendment prohibits certain discrimination by the states, but it is not applicable to the federal government. A bill of attainder is a legislative act punishing an individual or a group of individuals without a judicial trial. Since the sale of battleships did not punish anyone, it could not be a bill of attainder. **B** is therefore incorrect. Although Congress has the power to spend for the general welfare, it is generally understood that there is no general federal police power. **D** is therefore incorrect.

90. **B**  Under the Supremacy Clause of the United States Constitution, a state law is invalid if it conflicts with a valid federal law dealing with the same subject matter. This principle is frequently used to support the conclusion that a state attempt to regulate the federal government or a federal activity is invalid. A state is free to regulate federal contractors, however, so long as such regulations do not interfere with federal purposes or policies. If the state pollution law were likely to have the effect of increasing the cost of producing bomb sights for the Department of Defense, it could successfully be argued that it is invalid under the Supremacy Clause. If, on the other hand, the state pollution law would not significantly increase the costs of the bombsights, it would probably not interfere with any federal policy and would therefore be valid.

If Winding River is located entirely within the state, it might not be subject to valid congressional regulation under the Commerce Clause. **A** is incorrect, however, because Congress has other powers that might justify federal regulation concerning Winding River. Congress may exempt federal contractors from compliance with a state regulation on the ground that the regulation unduly interferes with a federal activity. Since Congress may create such an exemption impliedly, however, the fact that it has not expressly done so would not be conclusive. **C** is therefore incorrect. The question of whether a river is "navigable" is relevant in determining whether the federal courts have admiralty jurisdiction over it. **D** is incorrect, however, because congressional power to regulate activities on the banks of Winding River may come from other sources (*e.g.*, the power to provide for the common defense).

91. **C**  When an issue appears to be moot as the result of the voluntary conduct of the party moving for dismissal, the party must show that there is no reasonable expectation that the wrong will be repeated. Otherwise, parties could avoid litigation simply by temporarily changing their actions and then repeating their prior actions as soon as the case was dismissed. Since the National Park Service has not shown that the wrong will not be repeated, **C** is the best answer.

A claim is moot when there are no longer any contested questions essential for the disposition of the controversy. However, **A** is incorrect because, as stated above, there is no indication that the National Park Service will not cut tree prices in the future. Although Congress does have the power to dispose of property belonging to the United States under Article IV, this power has no relation to whether a claim is moot or not. Consequently, since the question specifically states the National Park Service is moving to dismiss on the ground that the issue is moot, both **B** and **D** are incorrect.

92. **B**  The Fifth Amendment to the United States Constitution provides in part that no person shall be deprived of life, liberty, or property without due process of law. Although "due process" is an elusive term, it is generally held to include the right of appeal. For this reason, the provision of the Securities and Exchange Court Act that provides that there shall be no right of appeal probably violates the Due Process Clause.

Article III of the United States Constitution provides that federal judges shall hold their offices during good behavior. This has been held to mean that so long as a judge does not act improperly, he or she may not be removed from office during his or her lifetime. This does not mean that the office itself may not be abolished, however. **A** is therefore incorrect. **C** is incorrect because Article III of the United States Constitution specifically empowers Congress to ordain and establish federal courts inferior to the United States Supreme Court. Although the United States Constitution vests the judicial power of the United States in the United States Supreme Court, it provides that the Court's appellate jurisdiction is subject to such exceptions as Congress shall make. **D** is therefore incorrect.

93.  **B**     Under the Supremacy Clause of Article VI of the United States Constitution, the statutes and treaties of the United States are the supreme law of the land. This means that a state law that is inconsistent with any valid federal law or treaty is invalid. Although an executive agreement is not a treaty, it has the same effect as a federal law under the Supremacy Clause. Since the application of the state income tax law is inconsistent with the executive agreement that prohibits the taxation of Ruritanian corporations within the United States, the Supremacy Clause may make the state law invalid as applied to the plaintiff.

Although the United States Constitution prohibits the states from taxing imports or exports without congressional consent, **A** is incorrect because the state income tax is not a tax on imports or exports. The Necessary and Proper Clause gives Congress the power to do whatever is necessary and proper in carrying out its other powers. **C** is incorrect because the constitutionality of an act of Congress is not in question. It has been said that states are prevented from taxing the federal government because "the power to tax is the power to destroy." This argument is not applicable in this case because the state is making no attempt to tax the federal government. **D** is therefore incorrect.

94.  **B**     A federal court may refuse to hear a case because it presents a "non-justiciable political question." An issue is non-justiciable if a decision would unduly interfere with the exercise of powers vested by the Constitution in a co-equal branch of government, or if it involves a matter that the text of the Constitution commits to one of the other branches of government. Since this concept is designed to keep the judiciary from interfering with the activities of the executive and legislative branches of government, it derives from the doctrine of separation of powers. Since the United States Constitution provides that cases of impeachment shall be tried by the Senate, the doctrine of separation of powers could result in the court's refusal to hear the judge's challenge.

The Sixth Amendment provides that defendants in criminal proceedings shall enjoy the right to counsel. **A** is incorrect, however, because the Due Process Clause protects the right to counsel at other proceedings as well. The abstention doctrine prevents a federal court from considering a constitutional question based on an unsettled question of state law. Since the judge's right to counsel at an impeachment proceeding does not depend on state law, **C** is incorrect. Article II, Section 3 of the United States Constitution provides that a judgment of impeachment cannot extend beyond removal and disqualification from office. Federal employment may be a "property" interest, however, to which the Due Process Clause applies. Thus, the fact that the impeachment proceeding results in no more than loss of a job is not sufficient to prevent the Due Process Clause from requiring the right to counsel.

95.  **A**     If a law requiring a permit for the exercise of First Amendment rights is invalid *on its face*, its constitutionality may be attacked as a defense against a charge of violating it. If, on the

other hand, the law is invalid *as applied*, the unconstitutionality of its application may not be raised as a defense against a charge of violating it. Instead, the appropriate course is to apply for a permit and then seek judicial review of the denial of the application, unless there is no time for such judicial review. Since the law was already held to be valid on its face, and since the only claim made by the defendant is that the law was unconstitutionally *applied*, this claim may not be raised by the defendant as a defense unless two months would not have been sufficient time to obtain judicial review. The facts do not disclose whether this is so, but the argument set forth in **A** is the only one listed that could possibly be an effective response to the defendant's claim.

Although the constitutionality of the ordinance on its face has already been decided by a federal court (and is therefore *res judicata*), the defendant's claim is that the ordinance is being applied in an unconstitutional manner. Since even a valid ordinance may be applied in an invalid way, **B** is incorrect. To promote the public order or other public good, a law may impose time, place, and manner restrictions on expressive conduct so long as these restrictions are not based on the message content of the expression. Since the ordinance was found to be constitutional on its face, it probably did constitute a valid time, place, and manner restriction. Like **B**, however, **C** is incorrect because the *application* of the ordinance is being challenged. Although laws may regulate expressive conduct even in traditional public forums, **D** is not a good response to the defendant's claim because not all such regulations are valid. (*Note:* Actually, regulations applicable to traditional public forums must face a stricter test than other such regulations.)

96. **A**    The Constitution gives Congress the exclusive power of legislation over the District of Columbia. Thus, although there is no general federal police power, Congress does have police power over the District of Columbia. **A** is therefore correct.

        **B** is incorrect because there is no general federal police power and no specific congressional power to protect the environment. The Equal Protection clause of the Fourteenth Amendment provides that no state shall deny equal protection of the law to any person within its jurisdiction. Since it applies only to state action and not to action by the federal government, **C** is incorrect. The Necessary and Proper Clause gives Congress the power to do whatever is necessary and proper in exercising its enumerated powers under the United States Constitution. Although it may result in a finding that an act of Congress is valid, it cannot be used to justify a finding that an act of Congress is invalid. **D** is therefore incorrect.

97. **B**    The requirement of standing exists to assure that all constitutional issues will be vigorously and thoroughly litigated. To have standing to challenge the constitutionality of a statute, it is necessary for the challenger to have a personal stake in the outcome of the challenge. In general, one who is likely to sustain concrete harm that could be avoided by a declaration that the statute is invalid has sufficient personal stake to challenge its validity. Since the statute will have the effect of requiring video arcade operators to pay the tax, and since they will not have to pay the tax if the statute is declared unconstitutional, a video arcade operator would have sufficient personal stake to challenge the statute's validity. Since an association has standing to assert the rights of its members, **B** is correct.

Since the arcade operators would be paying the tax, persons who use video arcade machines will not lose anything if the statute is declared constitutional. For this reason, **A** is incorrect. Since there is no indication that the new statute will have any effect at all on the manufacturers of video arcade amusement machines, the manufacturers of such machines have no personal stake in the outcome of the challenge and thus lack standing to assert it. **C** is therefore incorrect. If the statute has any effect on a corporation that is in the business of converting coin slots, it would be to increase rather than decrease its earnings. For this reason, **D** is incorrect.

98.  **A**    Under the United States Constitution, direct taxes must be allocated among the states in proportion to population, all customs duties and excise taxes must be uniform throughout the United States, and no tax may be imposed on exports from any state. Except for these limitations and prohibitions, the congressional power to tax is plenary. For this reason, **A** is correct.

Although the United States Constitution gives Congress the power to *spend* for the general welfare, **B** is incorrect because there is no general federal police power. So long as a tax is within the lawful power of Congress, a court may not inquire into the congressional motive for the imposition of that tax. For this reason, **C** and **D** are incorrect.

99.  **B**    To assure that constitutional issues will be thoroughly and vigorously litigated, the requirement of standing makes it necessary for a person challenging the constitutionality of a statute to have a personal stake in the outcome of the challenge. A challenger has sufficient personal stake when he or she has suffered or is about to suffer some concrete harm that can be remedied or prevented by the court. Since the challenger in **B** asserts that the statute will prevent the sale of his property, he faces imminent concrete harm. Since a declaration that the statute is unconstitutional will permit the sale of his property, thus preventing that harm, he has sufficient personal stake and has standing to assert the challenge.

Although an association may have standing to assert the rights of its members, it is necessary that its members would have standing to sue on their own. **A** is incorrect because the harm faced by the association members is not sufficiently concrete to give any of them standing to challenge the constitutionality of the statute. A state taxpayer lacks standing to challenge any statute except one that provides directly for an expenditure of public funds. **C** is therefore incorrect. **D** is incorrect because the harm that the challenger asserts is neither concrete nor imminent.

100.  **C**    Under the First Amendment, a public employee receives limited protection for speech or associational activities. Specifically, the employee may receive protection for activities that are critical of superiors or that the employer believes are inappropriate for the workplace. If the speech involves a matter of public concern, the court will balance the speech rights of the employee and the government's interest as an employer in promoting efficiency on the job. Importantly, if the employee has a relatively non-public and non-policy-making role, the court is less likely to find that the speech justifies dismissal. Here, the plaintiff may not be fired because his statement was on a matter of public concern, and his non-public and non-policy-making role meant the statement did not show

any significant job unfitness outweighing his right to comment on public matters as a private person. **A**, **B**, and **D** are therefore incorrect.

101. **C**  Although the federal government is immune from state taxation, that immunity does not shield persons working for the federal government, even where the cost of such taxation will eventually be borne by the federal government. For this reason, a tax on building contractors who work for the federal government is constitutionally valid so long as it does not discriminate against them. **C** is therefore correct.

Because the power to tax is the power to destroy, it has been held that any attempt by a state to impose a tax directly on the federal government or its activities is constitutionally invalid. **A** and **B** are therefore incorrect. Although persons doing business with the federal government may be taxed by a state, the state law may not constitutionally discriminate against people doing business with the federal government. **D** is incorrect because the law taxes only those persons leasing land from the federal government.

102. **D**  Under the First Amendment, a speaker's right to canvass, ring doorbells, and give out handbills receives substantial protection. While an individual homeowner is always free to tell the speaker that he or she doesn't want to listen to the speaker, the government cannot tell the speaker that he or she cannot speak in advance. Consequently, even if an ordinance is content-neutral and merely designed to protect unwilling listeners, the government cannot ban all canvassing even if a majority of people wishes it would do so.

**B** is therefore incorrect. **A** is incorrect because a total ban on canvassing violates the First Amendment whether or not the speaker has other ways to spread his or her message. **C** is incorrect because an outright ban is not made lawful simply because it causes a public benefit. The best the city could do here is to pass an ordinance limiting canvassing to certain times.

103. **A**  A state law regulating private contracts violates the Obligations of Contracts Clause only if it is limited to altering contractual rights and remedies. Thus a law, such as this one, that regulates private conduct does not violate the Obligations of Contracts Clause merely because it incidentally reduces the value of existing contracts. Since the statute is not limited to altering contract rights and remedies, it does not violate this clause, and **A** is correct.

The Commerce Clause has been held to prohibit discrimination by a state against out-of-staters since this would have the effect of preventing the free movement of persons and things between the states. Since the state law permits the disposal of wastes generated inside the state while prohibiting the disposal of wastes generated outside the state, a court could find that it violates the Commerce Clause. **B** is therefore incorrect. The Equal Protection Clause prohibits a state from denying to any person within its jurisdiction the equal protection of the laws. Since the state law in question denies to out-of-staters a benefit that is available to state residents, it could be held to violate equal protection. **C** is therefore incorrect. The Privileges and Immunities Clause of Article IV requires a state to accord out-of-staters within a state the same treatment as residents. Since this statute does not, it could be held to violate the Privileges and Immunities Clause. **D** is therefore incorrect.

104.   **C**    Although there are few cases regarding the extent of the President's powers as Commander-in-Chief, it is clear that they include the command of the military forces of the United States. While it is not certain that this includes the power to send troops into a foreign country in the absence of any military threat to United States interests, **C** is correct because it is the only argument listed that could possibly justify the presidential order.

            **A** is incorrect because the President's emergency powers apply only when there is some threat to the national interest. **B** is incorrect because the United States Constitution recognizes no humanitarian power or obligation of the President. The President's power over foreign affairs generally is understood to refer only to diplomatic matters, such as the negotiation of treaties and executive agreement and the receiving of foreign diplomats. **D** is therefore incorrect.

105.   **B**    The United States Constitution grants to Congress the power to spend for the general welfare. The Necessary and Proper Clause adds the power to do whatever is necessary and proper to the execution of Congress's other powers. It has been held that in spending for the general welfare, the Necessary and Proper Clause permits Congress to impose conditions to assure that it gets its money's worth. Since the federal funds covered by the law are to be used for the treatment of diseases caused by smoking, it is possible to argue that a required tax that makes cigarettes more expensive and thus discourages people from using them is a necessary and proper way of protecting the investment of federal funds. While it is not certain that a court would come to this conclusion, **B** is the only principle listed that could possibly justify the provision in question.

            The taxing power is the power to lay and collect revenues for the federal government. Since the challenged provision would not require any payment to the federal government or result in any federal revenue, **A** is incorrect. **C** is incorrect because there is no general federal police power under the United States Constitution. The congressional power to regulate interstate commerce is the power to control the movement of people and things across state lines. Since there is no indication that the addition of a seven-cent tax by states would have any effect at all on movement across state lines, **D** is incorrect.

106.   **D**    Article IV of the Constitution states that the citizens of each state shall be entitled to all privileges and immunities of citizens in the several states. This is the interstate Privileges and Immunities Clause, which is distinguished from the Privileges and Immunities Clause of the Fourteenth Amendment, which prevents a state from denying certain rights of national citizenship (like the right to travel). The interstate Privilege and Immunities Clause prevents a state from discriminating against non-residents, but it only covers rights that are fundamental to national unity. Rights that are fundamental to national unity are all related to commerce. These include the right to be employed, the right to engage in business, and the right to practice one's profession. Here, since access to employment is a right fundamental to national unity, the state's decision to prefer its own citizens is invalid. **B** is therefore incorrect. The Contract Clause generally involves situations where the government is interfering with a public or private contract that has

already been agreed to. Here, the question doesn't make any specific mention of a current contract being affected by the state preference. **A** and **C** are therefore incorrect.

107. **D**  The Property Clause gives Congress the power to make laws disposing of and making regulations concerning the use of all property of the federal government. This includes the power to make restrictions for the purpose of preventing injury to federal lands. Since Mountain Range National Park is owned and maintained by the federal government, the Property Clause authorizes Congress to prohibit fires within its boundaries. **D** is therefore correct.

One of the factors to be considered in freedom of religion cases is whether the challengers are sincere in their religious beliefs. The United States Supreme Court has indicated that the fact that a religious group has engaged in a particular practice for a long period of time is relevant to determining whether the challengers' beliefs are sincerely held. Except for this limited purpose, however, the fact that a particular practice is or is not a traditional one is of no importance. Since no question has been raised regarding the sincerity of the beliefs held by the Followers of the Holy Flame, **A** is incorrect. **B** is incorrect because courts may not inquire into the reasonableness of any religious belief or practice. A law that interferes with the free exercise of religion is valid if necessary to achieve a compelling state interest, considering the weight of the government interest, the degree of interference with a religious practice, and the availability of alternate means of protecting the government interest. Although discrimination between religions and the primarily secular effect of a law are factors to be considered in Establishment Clause cases, they play no role in free exercise challenges. For this reason, **C** is incorrect.

108. **A**  Under the police power, states may regulate the health, safety, and welfare of their citizens. The regulation requiring personal trainers to have a college degree in physical therapy or sports medicine does not involve a suspect classification, so the rational basis test would apply. The goal of protecting citizens from injury is clearly legitimate. A court will uphold the classification if there is any conceivable purpose served by the classification. Here, it is rational for the state to believe limiting the employment of personal trainers to those with college degrees in physical therapy or sports medicine would protect the health and safety of state citizens. Consequently, **A** is the best answer.

**B** is incorrect because even though no suspect classification is involved, a court will not uphold the law if there is no rational basis for it. **C** is incorrect because financial ability is not a suspect classification, and thus would not be held to the standard of substantially related to an important government interest. **D** is incorrect because the fact this law will regulate the activities of privately-owned gyms will not change the analysis.

109. **A**  The Equal Protection Clause of the United States Constitution prohibits classifications based on invidious discrimination. Not all classifications are invidious, however (*e.g.*, persons licensed as attorneys are not permitted to perform surgery, but persons licensed as physicians are). A system of economic classification is not invidious if it has a rational basis. If it is more important for lawyers to keep up to date on the law than it is for doctors to keep up to date on developments on medicine, then the system of classification

adopted by the Continuing Professional Education Act is not invidious and does not violate the Equal Protection Clause.

**B** is incorrect because even where a state has the right to determine conditions for a license, it may not do so in a way that denies equal protection. **C** is incorrect because the states may not exercise their powers in a way that violates constitutionally protected rights. Although the United States Constitution does not specifically protect the right to practice a profession, it does protect the right to equal protection. If the statute invidiously discriminates against certain professionals, it violates that right. **D** is incorrect because the state bar association does not have the power to waive the constitutional rights of its members.

110. **A** The Eleventh Amendment bars action against a state for money damages in a federal court by a resident or non-resident of the state if a judgment in the action would have to be paid out of the state's general treasury.

    **B** is incorrect because the suit arises under a federal statute. **C** is incorrect because this question does not depend on who the plaintiff's employer was, since the action by employees of the builder is for damages resulting from the state's failure to require the builder to pay the $10 wage. Unless the employees were aware of their rights, they could not have waived them. **D** is incorrect because there is no indication that the employees knowingly waived their rights.

111. **C** Standing to challenge the constitutional validity of a state statute requires a personal stake in the outcome. The fact that the organization's production will not be shown so long as the statute is enforced is a sufficient personal stake to confer standing.

    **A** is incorrect because the personal stake thus created is more than an intellectual interest. **B** is incorrect because a non-recognized organization would be denied benefits under the statute and thus has the necessary personal stake. **D** is incorrect because an affront to religious sensibilities is insufficient to confer standing except in a challenge to the validity of a tax or spending law.

112. **C** Article III of the United States Constitution gives the federal courts the power to decide questions arising under the federal Constitution. Since the action in the United States district court is for an injunction based on the invalidity of a state statute under the United States Constitution, the United States district court has jurisdiction.

    A state court decision that rests on an adequate state ground may not be appealed to the United States Supreme Court, but **A** is incorrect because this is a new action, not an appeal of a state court decision. The abstention doctrine may prevent a federal court from taking a question regarding the constitutionality of a state law when the meaning of the state law is uncertain and may be cleared up by a state court decision. **B** is incorrect because there is no uncertainty about the meaning of the state statute in question, and therefore there is no reason to wait for interpretation by a state court. **B** is also incorrect because no relevant state proceeding is pending. **D** is incorrect because although the

Eleventh Amendment prohibits a federal court from hearing a claim for damages against a state, it does not prevent a constitutional challenge to a state law.

113. **C**   Three tests exist to determine whether a state system of classification violates the Equal Protection Clause, depending on the basis of the classification. Most statutes that regulate economic or social interests are constitutionally valid if they have a rational basis. Statutes that discriminate against suspect classes or that interfere with a fundamental right are valid only if they are necessary to achieve a compelling state interest. Statutes that discriminate against classes that are close to being suspect or that interfere with rights that, although not fundamental, are very important, are valid only if they are substantially related to an important government interest. Although alienage is ordinarily regarded as a suspect classification requiring application of the compelling state interest test, the rational basis test is applied when the discriminatory legislation involves standards for employment in executing public policy or performing functions that go to the heart of representative government. The argument in **C** is effective in either event.

So far, the right to earn a living has not been found to be a fundamental interest. **A** is therefore incorrect. **B** is incorrect because systems of classification that serve a compelling state interest are not invidious even if based on alienage. **D** is an incorrect statement of the law; aliens are "persons" under the Equal Protection Clause. Even if it was a correct statement, however, **D** would not support the woman's position.

114. **D**   It has been held that a state may establish durational residency requirements to assure that voters will have sufficient interest in the outcome of an election. It has also been held, however, that overly long durational requirements serve no compelling state interest and are therefore invalid. The United States Supreme Court has specifically held one year to be too long. See *Dunn v. Blumstein*, 405 U.S. 330 (1972).

**A** and **C** are therefore incorrect. The United States Constitution sets requirements for determining eligibility to vote in national elections but is silent about the right of aliens to vote in local elections. **B** is incorrect, however, because the city ordinance extends the right to *all* persons who satisfy the residency requirement.

115. **A**   Under the Supremacy Clause, a state law is invalid to the extent that it is inconsistent with a valid federal law affecting the same subject matter. Although in paying its employees, the state may be immune from federal regulation, this is so only when the state is engaging in a traditional state function. The United States Supreme Court has held, however, that engaging in interstate commerce is not a traditional state function. For this reason, federal law fixing the wages of persons employed in interstate commerce is applicable to state employees, and, under the Supremacy Clause, supersedes inconsistent state law.

**B** is incorrect because there is no general federal police power (*i.e.*, power to legislate for the general welfare). In determining whether the state is engaging in a traditional state function, and thereby possibly immune from federal regulation, it is necessary to be more specific than the argument in **C** would suggest. Although paying employees is a traditional state function, paying them to operate interstate cruise boats is not. **C**

is therefore incorrect. **D** is incorrect because the immunity granted to states under the Eleventh Amendment is applicable only in federal courts.

116. **C**   The United States Supreme Court has held (*Stanley v. Georgia*, 394 U.S. 557 (1969)) that there is a constitutional right to privacy that protects the private possession of obscene materials for noncommercial use.

A is incorrect because the First Amendment freedoms of expression protect the rights to speak or print, offering only indirect protection to the rights to see, read, or hear. **B** is incorrect for two reasons: First, one is not ordinarily permitted to assert the constitutional rights of third persons. Although vendors may assert the rights of their customers, no rule has developed that permits vendees to assert the right of their suppliers. Second, freedom of speech and the press does not protect the publication of obscenity. **D**, too, is incorrect for two reasons: First, there is no indication that the statute in question was not designed to punish purchasers of obscenity, and, second, if the defendant presented an obscene performance as charged, he *is* a publisher of obscenity.

117. **A**   The Equal Protection Clause of the Fourteenth Amendment to the United States Constitution provides that no state shall deny to any person within its jurisdiction the equal protection of the laws. Since the Building Rental Tax is imposed on those who occupy rented space, but not on those who occupy space that they own, it is possible to argue that the law denies equal protection. This argument might fail, but it is the only one listed that has any chance at all of success.

Although the federal government is immune from taxation by the states, that immunity is not enjoyed by persons doing business with the federal government, even though their business is specifically authorized by federal statute. **B**, **C**, and **D** are therefore incorrect.

118. **B**   Federal statutes limit the Supreme Court's review of state court decisions to those of the highest state court to which appeal is possible. If no appeal is possible in the state courts, then there is no reason why the United States Supreme Court cannot review decisions of the municipal court.

A is incorrect, however, because if appeal to a higher state court were possible, the case would not be ripe for consideration by the Supreme Court until the highest state court decided it. **C** is incorrect because under Article III of the United States Constitution, the appellate jurisdiction of the Supreme Court is regulated by Congress and not by the states. At present, applicable federal statutes limit Supreme Court review to decisions of federal courts and of the highest state courts. **D** is incorrect, however, because this limitation does not appear in the Constitution.

119. **B**   The state may impose "time, place, and manner" restrictions on expression in protection of its interest in promoting free access to government buildings and the orderly conduct of governmental activities. These restrictions may not, however, be based on message content because such restrictions unconstitutionally interfere with freedom of speech.

Since the statute permits demonstrations involving one kind of message and prohibits demonstrations involving a different kind of message, it violates the First Amendment.

Although the United States Supreme Court has held that a statute may not completely prohibit expression in traditional public forums like streets and parks, **A** is incorrect because this statute is directed only at the sidewalks in front of government office buildings and does not prevent the use of other parts of the public forum for purposes of expression. The state's compelling interest in the orderly conduct of governmental affairs and in the protection of free access to government buildings would probably justify a law prohibiting noise or demonstrations in front of government office buildings. **C** and **D** are incorrect, however, because the statute imposes restrictions on the message content of such demonstrations.

120. **C**   Federal taxpayers are usually regarded as being too remote from the expenditure of federal funds to have standing to challenge them, but state taxpayers are not. If a state law involves a direct expenditure of funds, as this one does, any state taxpayer may have standing to challenge it.

**A** is incorrect because standing requires a personal stake even if the challenge is based on an alleged violation of the First Amendment. **B** is incorrect for several reasons, but the simplest is that a statute that authorizes the advertising of services that already exist does not threaten the rights of unborn children. **D** is incorrect because philosophical, moral, intellectual, or political interest is insufficient to confer standing on a person challenging a law.

121. **B**   The Thirteenth Amendment abolishes slavery and gives Congress the power to make laws enforcing its provisions. Discrimination based solely on race has been held to involve a "badge" of slavery that the Thirteenth Amendment authorizes Congress to abolish.

The Commerce Clause gives Congress the power to regulate interstate commerce but imposes no obligations on anyone. The organization's policy could not, therefore, violate "the spirit of the Commerce Clause," so **A** is incorrect. **C** is incorrect because racial discrimination violates the United States Constitution only when practiced by government. **D** is incorrect because there is no federal police power, and thus there is no congressional power to legislate for the general welfare.

122. **D**   Whether it is classified as a right or a privilege, a license to practice medicine is an *entitlement* of which a person cannot be deprived without due process. **A** is therefore incorrect. Since the denial of this entitlement was based on an arrest that did not involve a hearing, it has been accomplished without due process and thus violates the student's constitutional right.

**B** is incorrect because the federal courts have jurisdiction to adjudicate federal questions, and an asserted violation of rights under the United States Constitution obviously raises a federal question. The deprivation of property interest without a hearing violates the due process requirement, even though not arbitrary or capricious. **C** is therefore incorrect.

123.   **A**   If diesel exhaust is harmful to the environment, a tax discouraging the use of the diesel-powered vehicles might be beneficial to the general welfare. Since Article I, Section 8 of the United States Constitution gives Congress the power to impose taxes to provide for the general welfare, **A** is the best argument in support of the tax.

Although Congress may tax for the general welfare, **B** is incorrect because there is no "federal police power." **C** is incorrect because the tax is not tied to spending, and there is no indication either that it is applicable only in states that have received federal highway funds or that it will result in more efficient use of such funds. A taxpayer has standing to challenge the validity of a tax that, if valid, will require payment from the one challenging it since he or she has the necessary personal stake in the outcome of the litigation. **D** is therefore incorrect.

124.   **D**   The President may have the power to abrogate treaties when certain circumstances make such abrogation necessary for protection of the national interest. He or she does not have the power to suspend enforcement of laws enacted by Congress, however, except in extraordinary circumstances (*e.g.*, wartime emergencies, etc.). Once Congress enacted the National Tax Immunity Act, the immunity of the country's nationals was protected by law, rather than by treaty.

**A**, **B**, and **C** are therefore incorrect.

125.   **D**   Since the United States Supreme Court does not have jurisdiction to determine whether a statute violates the provisions of a state constitution, it could not overturn the state court's finding that the statute in question violates the state constitution. **A**, **B**, and **C** are therefore incorrect.

126.   **C**   The Necessary and Proper Clause permits Congress to do what is necessary and proper in carrying out the powers delegated to it by the Constitution. It is therefore irrelevant to the constitutionality of this state statute.

**A** might lead to the conclusion that the section is invalid since it obviously discriminates against interstate commerce. **B** might lead to the same conclusion since the higher license fee imposed on nonresidents could constitute invidious discrimination. If Section 1, which requires a license, is constitutionally invalid, Section 2, which sets the fees for such licenses, could not be validly enforced. For this reason, **D** might likewise justify the conclusion that Section 2 is invalid.

127.   **A**   The Equal Protection Clause prohibits invidious discrimination. Although a literacy requirement in a voting statute is not necessarily invidious, **A** is the only reason listed that could result in a judgment that the statute is unconstitutional.

Literacy tests have sometimes been found to be a tool of racial discrimination, but such a finding generally leads to the conclusion that there has been a denial of equal protection rather than a violation of the somewhat narrower prohibitions of the Fifteenth Amendment. **B** is therefore incorrect. **C** is incorrect because the literacy requirement does not prohibit or otherwise regulate the written use of foreign languages. **D** is incorrect because the Twenty-Sixth Amendment prohibits only discrimination in the franchise based on age.

128. **D**   Since the United States Constitution grants Congress the power to spend for the general welfare, Congress is entitled to attach conditions to its grants to assure that such spending does, in fact, promote the general welfare. The use of federal funds in a way that is likely to give cancer to schoolchildren would not promote the general welfare, and so Congress is empowered to guard against it.

   **A** is incorrect because Congress does not have the power to regulate education. **B** is incorrect because receipt of federal funds does not result in a surrender by the states of the powers reserved to them under the Constitution. **C** is incorrect because Congress's power to regulate by attaching conditions to federal spending programs is limited, at least, to conditions that are themselves constitutionally valid.

129. **D**   The United States Constitution gives the federal courts jurisdiction over all cases arising under the Constitution.

   Since the plaintiff's argument is that the statute violates the United States Constitution, and thus involves a federal question, **A** is incorrect. The Constitution does not give the federal courts jurisdiction over cases between a state and a citizen of that state, so **C** is incorrect. But because a federal question is involved, **B** is also incorrect.

130. **D**   In deciding whether an interference with an activity required by religious belief violates the Free Exercise Clause, the courts apply the compelling state interest standard. Thus, if a statute serves a compelling state interest and is sufficiently narrow to be the least burdensome method of achieving that interest, it may be constitutionally valid even though it interferes with a particular religious practice.

   **A** is incorrect for two reasons: First, associations are frequently held to have standing to assert the constitutional rights of their members, and second, since the statute may necessitate a change in the school's curriculum with attendant financial outlays, the school has a personal stake in the outcome. Although the *sincerity* of a professed religious belief may be examined in a free exercise challenge, **B** is incorrect because the Establishment Clause prevents a court from inquiring into the *reasonableness* of a religious belief. Even a law that is not primarily intended to interfere with a religious belief may violate the Free Exercise Clause if it has that effect. **C** is therefore incorrect.

131. **A**   The Necessary and Proper Clause authorizes Congress to do whatever is necessary and proper in carrying out its other powers, and is therefore irrelevant to the given facts, which involve a municipal ordinance.

   Although certain regulations concerning the time, place, and manner of holding public meetings are constitutionally permissible, such regulations may not be directed against or in favor of particular types of message content. **B** might, therefore, be a good argument since the ordinance requires a fee for a permit to conduct an assembly for some purposes, but not for others. A law is vague or overbroad if the person of reasonable intelligence would not be able to understand its terms. Since Section 2 makes special provision for "political campaign" rallies without defining them, it is possible to argue that it is vague or overbroad. **C** might, therefore, be a valid argument. If Section 1 is vague or overbroad (which it probably is in view of the unfettered discretion that it grants to the mayor), it cannot be enforced. If Section 1 — which requires a permit — cannot be enforced then, obviously, neither can Section 2 — which fixes a fee for the permit application. Thus, in spite of Section 3, which purports to make Sections 1 and 2 severable, **D** is a good argument.

132.  **C**     The Equal Protection Clause of the Fourteenth Amendment prohibits invidious discrimination by the state. If the state imposes a tax on the transportation of unrefined petroleum, but not on the transportation of any other product, it is possible to conclude that it is invidiously discriminating against transporters of unrefined petroleum. While it is not certain that a court would come to this conclusion, the argument in **C** is the only one listed that could possibly result in a finding that the statute is unconstitutional.

Although the United States Constitution is silent as to the rights of states to tax interstate commerce, it is generally understood that a state tax is valid if it requires interstate commerce to pay its fair share of the value of state services without discriminating in favor of local commerce. Thus, the fact that the tax is imposed on interstate transporters as well as local ones is not enough to make it invalid, and **A** is therefore incorrect. The state's power to tax activities performed within the state does not depend on a statutory grant of authority by the federal government. Thus, unless a federal statute specifically prohibits a particular form of state taxation, it is presumed valid. **B** is therefore incorrect. A state tax on interstate commerce is ordinarily valid if it bears a fair relationship to services provided by the state to the taxpayer and will not produce cumulative tax burdens. Since transporters of petroleum receive the benefit of using state roads, a tax based on distance and the quantity of cargo transported bears a fair relationship to that benefit.

Although neighboring states may impose similar taxes, there is no danger of duplicative taxing since the amount of the tax is related to activity actually performed within the state. **D** is therefore incorrect.

133.  **B**     Article I, Section 8 of the United States Constitution empowers Congress to spend money for the general welfare. Under the Necessary and Proper Clause, this spending power includes the power to impose conditions designed to assure that Congress will get its money's worth for sums spent. Since the size of the vehicles that use a highway could affect its longevity, the condition contained in the State Highway Subsidy Act is probably a valid exercise of the spending power.

**A** is incorrect because there is no general federal police power. The Property Clause (Article IV, Section 3) empowers Congress to make needful rules and regulations concerning *federal property*. Since the State Highway Subsidy Act applies to the construction of *state* highways, the Property Clause is inapplicable and **C** is incorrect. The Eleventh Amendment prevents federal courts from hearing certain claims against states. It is therefore inapplicable to determining the constitutionality of a federal law. **D** is therefore incorrect.

134. **A**    The United States Supreme Court may review a decision when a state court has held a state law valid under the United States Constitution. Here, the state court has held the law was valid under the Equal Protection Clause of the United States Constitution, so review is available.

**B** is incorrect because the important point is that the state court has found the law to be constitutional under the United States Constitution, not that the highest court in the state denied certiorari. **C** is incorrect because whether a particular classification is suspect determines the burden of proof to be met for a constitutional challenge, not the availability of Supreme Court review. **D** is incorrect because the state supreme court's denial of certiorari means the appellate court was the highest state court available to the man's challenge.

135. **A**    Although expert testimony is not necessary to establish that a work does or does not have serious value, it is admissible for that purpose, so **A** is correct and **D** is incorrect. Unless the material is targeted to a specific group, however, the standards of the *adult* community must be applied.

**B** and **C** are therefore incorrect.

136. **B**    A statute that discriminates on the basis of age is constitutional if its system of classification has a rational basis (*i.e.*, if facts can be imagined that would make the statute a reasonable means of accomplishing a legitimate purpose). Protection of public health is a legitimate legislative purpose. Thus, if the work of physical education teachers is hazardous to the health of older persons, the statute's age classification is a reasonable means of achieving a legitimate legislative purpose.

**A** is incorrect because the physical condition of one 60-year-old person is not sufficient to establish a rational basis for a statute that discriminates against all persons of that age. Even when exercising its legitimate powers, a state must do so in a way that is consistent with requirements of the United States Constitution. **C** is therefore incorrect. Since some physical education teachers may be unqualified for other teaching positions, the fact assumed in **D** would leave them no better off than they would be without it. **D** is therefore incorrect.

137. **D**    Under the Supremacy Clause of Article VI, a state law is invalid if it is inconsistent with a valid federal law covering the same subject matter. It is easy to decide whether a state law that specifically contradicts a federal law is invalid under the Supremacy Clause. It becomes more difficult when, as here, the state law prohibits something that the federal law does not mention at all. The fact that the federal law is silent about aliens serving on state juries might mean that Congress has permitted aliens to serve on state juries by not

prohibiting such service. It could also mean, however, that Congress deliberately left the matter to regulation by the states. In deciding which conclusion to draw, it is necessary to consider the dominance of federal interest. Since Congress has primary authority to determine the legal status of aliens, state legislation that affects aliens is likely to be pre-empted by congressional silence. While it is not certain that a court would come to this conclusion, the argument set forth in **D** is the only one listed that could support a reversal of the defendant's conviction.

Although state laws that discriminate on the basis of alienage are unconstitutional unless they are necessary to serve a compelling state interest, they are not per se invalid. (Also remember that there's an important exception to the general rule that a compelling state interest must be served: Where the government job involves a "traditional government function," even just a rational basis is enough to make the restriction of the job to citizens valid.) **A** is therefore incorrect. The Privileges and Immunities Clause of the Fourteenth Amendment prohibits a state from interfering with rights that result from United States citizenship. It is inapplicable to this case since aliens are not United States citizens. **B** is therefore incorrect. **C** is incorrect for two reasons: First, discrimination against aliens is not necessarily based on race, color, or previous condition of servitude, and second, the Fifteenth Amendment prohibits such discrimination only in denying the right to vote.

138.  **D**    The United States Supreme Court has held that age is not a suspect classification. Consequently, a claim of age discrimination will be unsuccessful if the government can show the challenged law has a rational basis. Therefore, **B** is incorrect.

A is incorrect because the "achieve a compelling state interest" standard only applies to classifications based on race, alienage, and national origin, not gender. For classifications based on gender, the law will only be upheld if it is substantially related to an important government interest. Therefore, **C** is incorrect.

139.  **D**    Like treaties, executive agreements are the supreme law of the land. Unlike treaties, however, executive agreements do not stand on the same footing as acts of Congress. Thus, while a treaty supersedes prior inconsistent federal statutes, an executive agreement does not. For this reason, Congress may, by statute, limit the president's power to make executive agreements. If Congress had done so by a prior law that prohibited the President from making this kind of agreement, the agreement may be declared void.

Some executive agreements require subsequent congressional action to operate. Others, called "self-executing," require no subsequent act of Congress to become operative. This distinction is related to the effect of an executive agreement, but not to its validity. For this reason, **A** is incorrect. As the Equal Protection Clause of the Fourteenth Amendment prevents invidious discrimination by the states, the Due Process Clause of the Fifth Amendment bars arbitrary discrimination by the federal government. When federal regulation (to which an executive agreement is equivalent) has nationwide impact, however, the existence of overriding national interests may permit regulation that would be forbidden to the states. For this reason, the fact that the executive agreement imposes an increased tax burden on other corporations is not by itself sufficient to make it invalid. **B** is therefore incorrect. **C** is incorrect because the President's power to make executive agreements is inherent, and therefore it does not require specific authorization from Congress.

140. **D**     A case is not yet ripe and is therefore not yet decidable by a federal court if it has not yet become sufficiently concrete to be easily adjudicated. Here, since the plaintiffs have not been specific about the precise acts that they wish to carry out, a court will likely find the case is not yet ripe. When a federal court determines an action is unripe, it must dismiss the action entirely.

**A**, **B**, and **C** are therefore incorrect.

141. **B**     In deciding equal protection cases, the United States Supreme Court has developed three levels of scrutiny. State regulations of social or economic interests are valid if they have a rational basis. Statutes that discriminate against a suspect class or that interfere with a fundamental right are not valid unless they are necessary to achieve a compelling state interest. Statutes that discriminate against a group that is close to being a suspect class are valid only if they are substantially related to important government interests. It has been held that discrimination based on age does not involve a suspect class or a group that is close to being a suspect class. For this reason, the statute is valid if it has a rational basis. **C** is therefore incorrect.

The Eleventh Amendment prevents the federal courts from hearing damage claims against a state. Since this proceeding is not an action for damages, however, the Eleventh Amendment does not prevent it from being heard. **A** is therefore incorrect. **D** is incorrect because age is not a suspect class, and because even a statute that does discriminate against a suspect class may be valid if it is necessary to achieve a compelling state interest.

142. **D**     Under its police power, a state may enact laws to protect the welfare of its residents, even though those laws impose a burden of some kind on interstate commerce, so long as there is no reasonable, less burdensome way of accomplishing that purpose. If, however, the burden that it imposes on interstate commerce is an unreasonable one, the statute will be invalid under the Commerce Clause. Although it is not certain that the argument in **D** would succeed, it is the only one listed that could possibly support granting of the injunction.

**A** is incorrect because the fact that a statute interferes in some way with interstate commerce is not by itself sufficient to make it invalid. Since the state's police power permits it to enact laws for the welfare of its residents, the purity of food is clearly a matter of local concern. **B** is therefore incorrect. Powers reserved to the states may be delegated by them to their municipalities and agencies. **C** is incorrect because the state's power to regulate commerce is concurrent with the federal commerce power and may thus be exercised by municipal governments within the state.

143.  **B**    **A** and **C** are inaccurate statements since there is no general federal police power. **B** is an accurate statement since the spending power entitles the federal government to take steps to assure that its spending benefits the public welfare.

144.  **A**    In order to assert a constitutional claim, a person or organization must have standing. This means the person or organization must have a personal stake or direct interest in the outcome. To have standing, the person or organization must be in danger of suffering some concrete injury that would be prevented or remedied if the court grants the requested relief. Because the doctor actually uses the city pools, and the new fee will increase his cost in doing so, he will suffer a concrete injury if the new fee is put in place. If a court finds the new fee unconstitutional, the doctor will not suffer that injury. Consequently, he has standing to challenge the new fee. His wealth and ownership of his own pool are irrelevant.

    **B** is incorrect because the family only fears that an increase could affect them in the future. Unless the family could show the feared effect is likely to occur, they have no concrete injury. **C** is incorrect because a mere intellectual interest in the outcome is not sufficient for standing. Unless the organization can show its members actually use the city pools, it lacks the personal stake necessary for standing. **D** is incorrect because a declaration that the fee is unconstitutional would likely cause the very harm the organization of city lifeguards fears. Consequently, such a declaration would not prevent them from suffering an injury.

145.  **D**    A restriction on speech in a traditional public forum such as a public park or street corner is subject to strict scrutiny. This means the restriction must be narrowly tailored to achieve a compelling governmental interest. The government can impose time, place, and manner restrictions on speech, but those restrictions must be content-neutral. This ordinance specifically targets political speech, so **A** is incorrect. **B** is incorrect because the government may not limit speech on property simply because it is the property owner. **C** is incorrect because it states the wrong level of scrutiny.

146.  **C**    To assure that constitutional challenges will be fully and vigorously prosecuted, the concept of standing requires that a person challenging the constitutionality of a statute have some personal stake in the outcome. Usually this means that the challenger must face some imminent concrete harm that would be avoided if the court grants the relief that he or she requests. Since the plaintiff's complaint is that the law effectively prevents her from serving on a jury, she lacks standing unless being deprived of an opportunity to serve on a jury constitutes concrete harm.

    Since the plaintiff does not have a driver's license, the existing law makes her ineligible for jury service. Since a declaration that the law is invalid would remove the disability imposed by the statute, the plaintiff's failure to have a driver's license is more likely to result in a finding that she has standing than a finding that she does not. **A** is therefore incorrect. Under the existing law, the plaintiff will not be called as a prospective juror so long as she does not have a driver's license. On the other hand, a declaration that the law is invalid would have the effect of making her eligible to be called as a prospective juror. Since this would eliminate the harm that the existing statute causes, the fact that she has never been called is more likely to defeat than to support the motion to dismiss her claim. **B** is therefore incorrect. Since there is no fact indicating that the plaintiff is or is about to become a litigant in the County Court, the possibility that she will be denied due process if she ever does become one is not harm that is imminent or concrete. **D** is therefore incorrect.

# QUESTIONS
## CONTRACTS

# CONTRACTS
# TABLE OF CONTENTS

**Numbers refer to Question Numbers**

**VIII. Remedies**

# CONTRACTS

1. Immediately after his graduation from college in June, the plaintiff announced his plan to begin law school the following September and to marry his girlfriend in December. The plaintiff's father was afraid that marriage during the plaintiff's first year of law school might cause him to fail or drop out of school. He called the plaintiff on the phone and said that if the plaintiff postponed his wedding plans until after the completion of his first year of law school, he would give him a cash bonus of $1,000 and would pay the plaintiff's tuition for the second year of law school. The plaintiff agreed and called his girlfriend to tell her that he wanted to postpone the wedding. She became so angry at him that she broke off their engagement. Two months later, the plaintiff's girlfriend married someone else.

The plaintiff's father died soon after the plaintiff began school, but the plaintiff successfully completed his first year. Although the plaintiff earned excellent grades, he decided that he was not really interested enough in the law to want to continue his legal education. After failing to register for a second year of law school, he notified his father's administrator of his decision. The plaintiff said that although there would be no tuition expense, he expected to be paid the $1,000 cash bonus that his father had promised him. The administrator refused to pay anything.

If the plaintiff brought suit against the administrator of his father's estate for $1,000, the plaintiff would probably be

(A) unsuccessful, because his contract with his father violated public policy.

(B) unsuccessful, because the plaintiff failed to register for a second year of law school.

(C) unsuccessful, because the plaintiff's death terminated his offer.

(D) successful.

2. A furniture dealer had 500 chairs for sale. The chairs had a fair market value of $100 each. The manufacturer had discontinued production of the chairs, however, and they were the last ones the dealer had. For that reason, the dealer advertised them at $75 each, even though at that price, her profit would be only $10 per chair. An interior decorator had contracted with the dealer to provide furniture for a new hotel. On May 4, after seeing the chairs advertised, the decorator wired the dealer, "Please ship me 500 chairs as advertised at $75 per chair COD." On May 5, immediately upon receipt of the telegram, the dealer wired the decorator, "Accept your offer. Will ship 500 chairs tomorrow." The decorator telephoned the dealer immediately upon receipt of the dealer's telegram on May 6, saying that, after discussing the chairs with his client, he had decided to cancel the order. On May 7, the dealer sold all the chairs to another buyer at $75 each. If the dealer sued the decorator for breach of contract, the court should award the dealer

(A) $5,000 (500 chairs at $10 profit per chair).

(B) $37,500 (500 chairs at $75 per chair).

(C) $12,500 (fair market value of $100 minus contract price of $75 times 500 chairs).

(D) nothing, since the dealer sustained no damage.

3. On March 12, the plaintiff hired the defendant to construct a three-car garage on the plaintiff's realty. After negotiation, they entered into a valid written contract that fixed the

price at $8,000. According to the terms of the contract, the plaintiff was to pay $4,000 when the work was half completed, on or before April 25, and to pay the balance upon completion. All work was to be completed by June 1. On April 10, when the work was one-quarter complete, the partial structure was totally destroyed in a fire that started without fault by either party. The damage done by the fire made it impossible to complete construction on time. Because he was committed to begin construction on a hotel on June 1, the defendant notified the plaintiff on April 12 that he would perform no further work for the plaintiff. The plaintiff subsequently hired another contractor to build the garage at a price of $9,000. The plaintiff instituted an action against the defendant for damages resulting from breach of contract, and the defendant asserted a defense based on impossibility of performance. The court should find for

(A)   the defendant, because the fire was not his fault.

(B)   the defendant, because he has not yet received any compensation from the plaintiff.

(C)   the plaintiff, because the work was only one-quarter complete when fire destroyed the structure.

(D)   the plaintiff, because the defendant's obligation was to work for the plaintiff until June 1.

4.   The buyer agreed to purchase 250 2" × 4" construction-grade wooden studs from the seller by a written contract that provided that the buyer would make payment prior to inspection. The studs were delivered to the buyer by truck and were covered with a canvas tarpaulin when they arrived at the buyer's work site. The driver demanded payment before he would unload or uncover the studs.

The buyer refused to pay for the studs before inspecting them, and the driver returned them

to the seller. If the seller asserts a claim for breach of contract against the buyer, the court should find for —

(A)   the seller, because the buyer's refusal to pay prior to inspection was a breach.

(B)   the seller, because the buyer's refusal to pay prior to inspection was an anticipatory repudiation.

(C)   the buyer, because the contract provision calling for payment prior to inspection was unconscionable.

(D)   the buyer, because the seller failed to deliver the studs.

5.   A manufacturer of computer hardware and software was seeking a way to speed up the operation of its Basic Computer Program. On March 1, it posted the following notice in the employees' lounge:

The stockholders of this company are offering a cash prize of $200 to any employee who develops a modification of the Basic Computer Program that will double its operating speed. Design modification entries should be submitted to the head of the Basic Program Department prior to June 1. In the event that modifications are submitted by more than one employee, the prize will go to the employee who submits the design which, in the opinion of the Basic Program Department, can be used most economically.

An engineer employed by the company read the notice on March 5, and immediately began working on program modifications in his spare time. On March 8, he wrote and signed a memo that said, "I accept the stockholders' offer of a $200 prize for redesigning the Basic Computer Program. I am hard at work on the project and expect to submit my modification design within a week or two." The engineer sent the note to the head of the Basic Program Department by the interoffice correspondence system, but it was somehow diverted and was never received by the department head. The notice that was posted on March 1 constituted

(A) an offer for a unilateral contract.

(B) an offer for a bilateral contract.

(C) an offer for a unilateral contract that ripened into a bilateral contract when the engineer wrote the memo on March 8 and deposited it in the interoffice correspondence system.

(D) a preliminary invitation to deal, analogous to a newspaper advertisement for the sale of goods.

6. When he moved into a new condo, the owner entered into a written contract with a gardener. Pursuant to its terms, the gardener was to perform certain specified gardening services in the yard of the condo each week for a period of one year, for which the owner was to pay the sum of $50 per month. The contract contained a clause that stated, "The condo owner hereby agrees not to assign this contract without the written permission of the gardener." Three months after entering into the agreement, the owner informed the gardener that he was selling the condominium to the plaintiff, and asked the gardener to consent to the owner's assignment of the contract to the plaintiff. Because the costs of landscaping materials had increased dramatically in the last three months, the gardener was glad for an opportunity to be relieved of his obligations under the contract and refused to consent to the assignment. The owner assigned the contract to the plaintiff anyway, but the gardener refused to perform any further work on the yard. After formally demanding performance from the gardener, the plaintiff hired another gardener to do the same work for $75 per month, which was the best price the plaintiff could negotiate.

In an action by the plaintiff against the gardener for breach of contract, the court should find for

(A) the plaintiff, because the gardener had no right to unreasonably withhold consent to the assignment.

(B) the plaintiff, because the assignment was valid in spite of the gardener's refusal to consent.

(C) the gardener, because the contract prohibited assignment by the owner without the gardener's consent.

(D) the gardener, because the contract was for personal services.

7. On June 1, after arson fires had damaged several city buildings, the city council voted to offer a reward to aid in apprehension of the arsonists. On June 2, by order of the city council, signs were posted in various locations throughout the city. The posters identified the buildings that had been burned and stated: "$1,000 REWARD is hereby offered by the city to any person furnishing information leading to the conviction of persons responsible for setting fire to said buildings." A police officer employed by the city saw the posters on June 5 and resolved to make a special effort to catch the arsonists. Although he was not officially assigned to the case, he notified his fellow police officers and his usual underworld informants that he was especially interested in the case. As a result, another police officer and an underworld informant passed information to the police officer that they thought might relate to the arson crimes. The tip the first police officer received from the other officer proved to be of no assistance, but the tip he received from the informant led him to conduct a further investigation. His efforts eventually resulted in the arrest of two men who pleaded guilty to setting fires in public buildings. The first police officer demanded that the city council pay him $1,000, but the council refused.

If the police officer institutes a lawsuit against the city for the $1,000 reward offered in the signs posted on June 2, which of the following would be the city's most effective argument in defense?

(A) The reward should go to the informant, since it was his information that eventually led to the arrest of the arsonists.

(B)   The reward was not accepted, since the arsonists were not convicted but pleaded guilty.

(C)   The police officer gave no consideration for the city's promise to pay a reward, since he was already obligated to attempt the apprehension of the arsonists.

(D)   There was no enforceable promise by the city, since the offer was for a gratuitous cash award.

8.   A foreign country is an English-speaking republic on the continent of Europe. Its unit of currency is the "dollar," which is worth about 85 U.S. cents. While on a business trip in the United States, the plaintiff, who owned a glue factory in the foreign country, entered into a written contract with the defendant. According to the contract, the defendant was to purchase 30 tons of liquid glue from the plaintiff, to be delivered on or before July 10. The contract stated the total price of the glue to be "NINE THOUSAND ($9,000) DOLLARS." After receiving the shipment, the defendant sent the plaintiff an international money order for 9,000 of the foreign country's dollars. The plaintiff wrote to the defendant, claiming that the agreement called for the payment of 9,000 U.S. dollars, but the defendant refused to make any further payment. The plaintiff instituted an action against the defendant in the United States and offered to testify that, prior to executing the written memorandum, she and the defendant agreed that the price expressed in the writing was to be in U.S. dollars.

If the defendant objects to the testimony, the objection should be

(A)   sustained, since the oral agreement about which the plaintiff is offering to testify was made prior to the execution of the written memorandum of sale.

(B)   sustained, only if the written memorandum was prepared by the defendant.

(C)   overruled, unless the writing is found to be a complete integration of the agreement between the defendant and the plaintiff.

(D)   overruled, because the evidence that the plaintiff is offering to present does not modify or contradict the terms of the writing.

9.   The plaintiff was fishing on her boat when she heard a call for help. Looking around, she saw a man drowning and flailing his arms over his head. The plaintiff jumped into the water and swam toward the man, dropping her fishing gear into the lake and losing it in her effort to aid the man. She grabbed the man by the hair and swam to the shore, dragging him out of the water. The man was unconscious, but she gave him mouth-to-mouth resuscitation until he regained consciousness. When the man opened his eyes, he said, "I know I can never repay you for saving my life, but I promise to pay you $100 the first of next month as a token of my gratitude." A few days later, the man died from causes not related to the incident.

The following month, the plaintiff made demand upon the man's executor for the $100 that the man promised her and for an additional $100, which was the value of the fishing gear that she lost in her attempt to rescue the man. The executor rejected both demands. If the plaintiff institutes an action for the value of her fishing gear against the executor of the man's estate, the court should find for

(A)   the plaintiff, on a theory of *quantum meruit*.

(B)   the plaintiff, because danger invites rescue.

(C)   the plaintiff, because the reasonable person in the man's position would have offered to pay for the loss of the fishing gear in exchange for the plaintiff's attempt to rescue him or her.

(D)   the executor of the man's estate.

10. A woman's hobby was restoring and collecting antique automobiles. After acquiring an antique automobile, she contacted a body shop about having the car repainted. The body shop said that it would paint the car for $700 and would sell the woman a new bumper for an additional $150. Using an order blank from a pad that he purchased at a stationery store, the body shop's owner wrote out all the terms of the agreement. On a printed line marked "PAYMENT," he wrote, "Paint job—$700, payable $300 in advance and $400 on completion. Bumper—$150, payable on delivery." Both the body shop's owner and the woman signed at the bottom of the form. Which of the following statements most correctly describes the obligations set forth in the writing signed by the woman and the body shop owner?

(A) Payment by the woman of the initial $300 is a condition precedent to the body shop's obligation to paint the car, and the body shop's painting of the car is a condition precedent to the woman's obligation to pay the additional $400.

(B) Payment by the woman of the initial $300 is a condition precedent in form and substance to the body shop's obligation to paint the car, and the body shop's painting of the car is a condition precedent in form, but subsequent in substance to the woman's obligation to pay the additional $400.

(C) Payment by the woman and painting of the car by the body shop are concurrent conditions.

(D) Neither party's obligation to perform is conditioned upon performance by the other party.

11. The plaintiff was employed by the defendant as department manager pursuant to a written contract. The contract was for a five-year term and fixed the plaintiff's compensation at $2,000 per month. The plaintiff's work was satisfactory, but two years after entering into the contract with him, the defendant reorganized the company. As a result of the reorganization, the plaintiff's department was eliminated, and the defendant terminated the plaintiff's employment. The plaintiff advertised in the "jobs wanted" section of the newspaper, but he did not find a job until six months after his discharge, when he went to work for another company doing the same general sort of work that he had been doing for the defendant and earning the same salary. In an action by the plaintiff against the defendant for damages resulting from breach of the employment contract, the court should give judgment to

(A) the defendant, since the plaintiff's position was eliminated.

(B) the plaintiff, for severance pay in a sum equivalent to two months' salary.

(C) the plaintiff, in a sum equivalent to the salary that the plaintiff lost between the time of his discharge and the time he began working for the new company, plus the cost of advertising in the "jobs wanted" section of the newspaper.

(D) the plaintiff, in a sum equivalent to the salary that the plaintiff would have received during the balance of the contract term.

12. The plaintiff was the owner of a fleet of taxis that he leased to independent drivers in return for 60 percent of the fares that they collected. All the leases were scheduled to expire on December 31. Because the cars in his fleet were beginning to look shabby, the plaintiff decided to have them all painted during the first week of January, before negotiating new leases with the drivers. At the beginning of December, he called the defendant's auto-painting company to inquire about his price for painting all the cars in the plaintiff's fleet. The defendant said he would do the job for $150 per car.

The plaintiff said, "I'm talking about 60 cars. That's a lot of business. I'll give you the job if you'll do it for $125 per car."

"I'd really like to have your business," replied the defendant.

"See you the first week in January," the plaintiff said.

On January 3, the plaintiff brought one of his taxis to the paint shop and offered to make arrangements for bringing in the rest of the cars to be painted. The defendant said that he had just obtained a contract to paint some school buses and that he was too busy to do any work for the plaintiff. The plaintiff subsequently asserted a claim for damages against the defendant.

Which of the following additional facts or inferences, if it were the only one true, would be most helpful to the plaintiff in his action against the defendant?

(A)  The defendant's statement, "I'd really like to have your business," implied a promise to paint all the cars in the plaintiff's fleet at $125 per car.

(B)  The plaintiff relied on the defendant's statement by bringing the taxi to the shop.

(C)  Immediately prior to January 3, the plaintiff could have had the taxis painted at another shop for $125 each, but immediately after January 3, the lowest price he could find was $150.

(D)  On January 3, when the defendant told the plaintiff that he was too busy to do the work, the plaintiff offered to pay the defendant $150 per car and tendered payment of that sum.

13.  When the plaintiff's uncle died, he left her a 10-story office building that had a motion picture theater on its ground floor. The offices in the building were all occupied when the plaintiff acquired title to it. The motion picture theater was vacant, however, so she advertised for a tenant. The defendant had researched the neighborhood and decided that it was a good location for a pornographic

movie theater. When he saw the plaintiff's advertisement, he contacted her and said that he was interested in leasing the theater. He did not tell her what type of films he intended to show because he thought that she might be unwilling to rent it to him for that purpose. On April 1, they entered into a written rental agreement for the theater, occupancy to begin on May 1. On April 15, the city council passed an ordinance prohibiting the showing of pornographic films in the neighborhood where the theater was located. As a result, the defendant advised the plaintiff that he was canceling the rental agreement.

If the plaintiff sues the defendant for breach of contract, the court should find for

(A)  the defendant, under the doctrine of frustration of purpose.

(B)  the defendant, under the doctrine of impossibility of performance.

(C)  the defendant, because after the contract had been formed, government action made its subject matter unlawful.

(D)  the plaintiff.

14.  A builder contracted to add a room to a homeowner's house for $3,000, with the understanding that the materials used by the builder were to be included in that price. The day before work was to begin, the homeowner wired the builder, "The deal is off. Do not begin work." The builder subsequently asserted a claim against the homeowner for breach of contract. The homeowner raised non-compliance with the Statute of Frauds as a defense. Which of the following statements is most correct about the application of the Statute of Frauds to the contract between the homeowner and the builder?

(A)  The contract was required to be in writing if the materials that would have been required had a price in excess of $500.

(B)  The contract was required to be in writing if, at the time of contracting, the parties intended that the materials required would have a price in excess of $500.

(C) The contract was required to be in writing if the materials that would have been required had a price in excess of $500, and the parties intended that the materials required would have a price in excess of $500 at the time of contracting.

(D) The contract was not required to be in writing.

15. After the plaintiff said that the defendant owed him $3,000, the defendant promised to pay $2,000, which the plaintiff agreed to accept as payment in full. Subsequently, the defendant refused to make payment, and the plaintiff asserted a claim for $2,000 based on the defendant's promise. If it was the only one true at the time of the defendant's promise, which of the following additional facts or inferences would be most likely to result in a judgment for the plaintiff?

(A) The defendant honestly believed that he owed the plaintiff $3,000, but the plaintiff did not believe that the defendant owed him the money.

(B) The plaintiff honestly believed that the defendant owed him $3,000, but the defendant did not believe that he owed the plaintiff the money.

(C) The plaintiff was threatening to institute a lawsuit against the defendant for $3,000 plus costs and interest.

(D) The plaintiff had already commenced a lawsuit against the defendant for $3,000 plus costs and interest.

16. A building contractor's daughter was about to celebrate her 21st birthday, and the contractor wanted to give her a gift that would express his sentiments for her. He was a wealthy and successful contractor, but he had begun his career as an assistant bricklayer. Instead of purchasing something for his daughter, he

decided to give her a gift with the labor of his hands. The contractor entered into a written contract with the defendant. According to its terms, the contractor agreed to build a brick fireplace for the defendant, performing all the labor himself. In return, the defendant agreed to pay the sum of $1,000 to the contractor's daughter on her birthday, February 12, upon completion of the work by the contractor to the defendant's satisfaction. The daughter did not learn of the transaction until February 12. Before signing the written contract, the defendant and the contractor agreed orally that the defendant would make a reasonable effort to obtain a loan to pay for the work, but that if the defendant was unsuccessful in doing so by January 1, the agreement between them would be of no effect. The defendant made efforts to obtain the loan but could not do so. On January 1, the defendant informed the contractor that because he was unable to obtain the loan, he was calling off the deal. In an action for breach of contract brought against the defendant by the proper party, will the defendant be successful in asserting as a defense his inability to obtain a loan?

(A) Yes, because obtaining a loan was a condition precedent to the existence of an enforceable contract.

(B) Yes, because a modification of a construction contract may be by oral agreement.

(C) No, because the defendant is estopped from denying the validity of the written agreement.

(D) No, because the agreement concerning the loan is an oral agreement that was made prior to the writing and it contradicts the terms of the writing.

17. Assume that the defendant in each of the following fact patterns objects to enforcement of the agreement on the ground that it violates the Statute of Frauds. In which of the following fact patterns is the agreement between the plaintiff and the defendant **LEAST** likely to be enforced over the defendant's objection?

(A) The defendant orally agreed to purchase a series of porcelain figurines from the plaintiff to be delivered one per week for 15 weeks at a price of $100 per figurine. Prior to the first delivery, the defendant advised the plaintiff that he was no longer interested in receiving the figurines.

(B) The defendant orally agreed to purchase a hand-carved entry door for the defendant's home with the defendant's coat of arms on it for a price of $600. After the plaintiff completed the rough carving of the defendant's coat of arms, the defendant changed her mind and notified the plaintiff that she would not accept delivery of the door.

(C) The defendant's pleadings admitted making an oral agreement to purchase a painting from the plaintiff for $900 but asserted as an affirmative defense that the agreement was unenforceable under the Statute of Frauds.

(D) The defendant orally agreed to a price of $1,200 for the purchase of 100 lawn-trimmers manufactured by the plaintiff for resale in the defendant's store. The plaintiff then sent the defendant a memorandum signed by the plaintiff and outlining the terms of their agreement. The defendant did not sign the memorandum or respond to it in any way.

18. The plaintiff, a minor, purchased a used car from the defendant for $1,200. The reasonable rental value of the car was $150 per month. After she had owned the car for two months, the steering failed while she was driving it, causing it to collide with a tree. Although the plaintiff was unhurt, the car sustained $400 worth of damage. The plaintiff returned the damaged car to the defendant and demanded her money back, but the defendant refused to refund her money. If the plaintiff asserts a claim against the defendant,

the court should award her a judgment in the amount of

(A) $1,200 (the full purchase price of the car).

(B) $900 (the purchase price of the car less its reasonable rental value).

(C) $800 (the purchase price of the car less the damage that it sustained).

(D) nothing.

19. The seller and the buyer were neighbors who owned homes on adjoining parcels of realty. They were both in the business of selling art supplies, each operating an art supply store that engaged in friendly competition with the other. The seller owned a garden tractor that he used for cultivating vegetables in the backyard of his home. The buyer, who wanted to plant a garden in his own backyard, sent the seller a note in which he offered to buy the tractor from the seller for $500. The seller responded on February 15 by sending the buyer a letter that stated, "I will sell you my garden tractor for $600 and not a penny less. To give you time to think it over, I promise to hold this offer open until March 15." On March 5, the buyer noticed a similar garden tractor in the yard of another neighbor. He called that neighbor on the phone and offered to buy it for $500, but he said, "Are you kidding? I just bought it from [the seller] for $600." On March 6, the buyer went to the seller's store with $600 in cash, and said, "I've decided to buy that tractor from you. Here's the money." The seller refused the money and told the buyer that he had already sold the tractor to the other neighbor. If the buyer asserts a claim against the seller for damages resulting from the seller's refusal to sell the tractor on March 6, the court should find for

(A) the buyer, because the seller's offer of February 15 was irrevocable until March 15.

Let's look at some specific parts of Program 1-1 (the pay-calculating program) to see examples of each element listed in the table above. For your convenience, Program 1-1 is listed again.

## Program 1-1

```
1    // This program calculates the user's pay.
2    #include <iostream>
3    using namespace std;
4
5    int main()
6    {
7        double hours, rate, pay;
8
9        // Get the number of hours worked.
10       cout << "How many hours did you work? ";
11       cin >> hours;
12
13       // Get the hourly pay rate.
14       cout << "How much do you get paid per hour? ";
15       cin >> rate;
16
17       // Calculate the pay.
```

(B) the buyer, because the seller did not notify him that he was withdrawing his offer to sell the buyer the garden tractor until after the buyer accepted it.

(C) the seller, because the buyer learned of the sale to the other neighbor on March 5.

(D) the seller, because his letter of February 15 was a rejection of the buyer's original offer to purchase the garden tractor.

20. The seller and the buyer entered into a written contract for the sale of 200 electric power drills. Although they orally agreed on a price, they inadvertently failed to include it among the terms of the written agreement. In an action for breach of the contract, the court should

   (A) admit oral testimony to establish the price that the parties intended.

   (B) refuse to enforce the contract if it is one that the Statute of Frauds required to be in writing.

   (C) conclude that the contract calls for the payment of a reasonable price.

   (D) disregard the writing since it fails to contain all the essential terms of the agreement.

21. On May 15, after negotiation, a painter and a homeowner entered into a written agreement for the painting of the homeowner's home. The writing stated that the price was to be $300 plus the cost of materials, that the work was to begin on June 2 and be completed by June 12, that stucco portions of the house were to be painted yellow and wood trim was to be painted brown, and that the written memorandum was a full and final expression of the agreement between the painter and the homeowner. During litigation between the painter and the homeowner to enforce the contract, the homeowner offered to testify to the following additional facts. Which is the **LEAST** likely to be admitted into evidence over timely objection by the painter?

   (A) Prior to signing the memorandum, the painter and the homeowner orally agreed that the contract would have no legal effect if the homeowner sold his house prior to June 2.

   (B) Prior to signing the memorandum, the painter and the homeowner orally agreed that the homeowner would use no paint without first submitting it for the homeowner's approval.

   (C) While signing the memorandum, the painter and the homeowner orally agreed that any promises made by either of them during negotiations were to be enforceable, even if they were omitted from the memorandum.

   (D) While signing the memorandum, the painter and the homeowner orally agreed that the painter would spend no more than $10 per gallon for paint.

22. On May 20, on a form provided by an air-conditioning company, the defendant agreed to purchase from the company 100 described air-conditioning units at a price of $250 each, FOB the company's factory. The contract contained a clause that prohibited either party from assigning its rights or obligations under the contract without the consent of the other party. On June 1, the company's employees loaded the units on a truck owned and operated by an independent trucking company. When the loading was complete, the air-conditioning company phoned the defendant that the shipment was on its way. Later that day, the company executed a document that contained the following language: "In consideration of $20,000 to me in hand paid by the plaintiff this date, I hereby assign to the plaintiff all rights under my contract with the defendant dated May 20." On June 2, while en route to the defendant's warehouse, the truck containing the air-conditioning units overturned, and the entire shipment was destroyed.

   The defendant did not consent to the company's assignment of rights to the plaintiff. In an action by the plaintiff against the defendant, the plaintiff will probably recover

(A)  the contract price of $25,000 (100 air-conditioning units at $250 each).

(B)  the difference between the contract price and the market value of the air-conditioning units.

(C)  nothing, since recovery from the defendant would unjustly enrich the plaintiff.

(D)  nothing, since the contract between the defendant and the plaintiff prohibited assignment.

23.  A world-renowned artist's will left a collection of 30 of his paintings to his niece, an art dealer. The paintings inherited by the niece were untitled, but they were identified by the numbers 1 through 30. The niece had a catalog printed containing photographs and descriptions of each painting in the collection. On August 1, she sent a copy of the catalog to another art dealer, with the following cover letter:

> I know how much you like my uncle's work, so I'm giving you an opportunity to buy some of these paintings before I offer them to any other dealers. The price is $2,000 per painting, no matter how many you buy. Telegraph your order within two weeks, or I'll put them on the market.
>
> (signed)

On August 2, the art dealer sent the niece a telegram that said, "I accept your offer to sell painting Number 30 for $2,000. I will come to your gallery in two days to pick up the painting, and will pay cash at that time."

On August 3, after receiving the telegram, the niece telephoned the dealer and said that because of favorable publicity that the collection had received, she would not sell painting Number 30 for less than $3,000. The dealer agreed on the telephone to pay $3,000 for

painting Number 30. Between August 1 and August 3 the fair market value of the painting increased by $1,000.

On August 4, the dealer sent and the niece received a telegram that said, "I accept your offer to sell your uncle's paintings 1 through 29 for $2,000 each. I will pick up the paintings tomorrow, and will pay for them at that time."

On August 5, the dealer presented herself at the niece's gallery and tendered payment of $2,000 each for all 30 paintings. However, the niece refused to sell her any of the paintings except Number 30, for which the niece insisted the agreed price was $3,000. The dealer left without buying it, saying that the niece would be hearing from her lawyer.

If the niece asserts a claim against the dealer for breach of a contract to purchase painting Number 30 for $3,000, the court should find for

(A)  the dealer, because her promise to pay $3,000 for the painting was not in writing.

(B)  the niece, because the fair market value of painting Number 30 increased by $1,000 between August 1 and August 3.

(C)  the niece, because she relied on the dealer's promise to pay $3,000 for painting Number 30.

(D)  the niece, because she had not received payment from the dealer prior to their conversation on August 3.

24.  On March 1, an aluminum siding contractor entered into a written contract with the homeowner for the installation of aluminum siding on the exterior of the homeowner's home. The contract called for completion of the job by April 1 and contained a clause that prohibited assignment by either party without the other party's written consent. The contractor started work immediately upon the signing of

the contract. On March 15, the homeowner sold his house, assigning to the new owner his contract with the contractor.

In which of the following fact situations is the plaintiff **LEAST** likely to succeed in his action against the defendant?

(A)  The contractor finished the job in a workmanlike manner on March 29 and demanded but did not receive payment. The contractor instituted an action against the original homeowner for payment.

(B)  The contractor finished the job in a workmanlike manner on March 29 and demanded but did not receive payment. The contractor instituted an action against the new owner for payment.

(C)  When the contractor learned of the homeowner's assignment to the new owner, he refused to do any further work. The original homeowner instituted an action against the contractor for breach of contract on April 15.

(D)  When the contractor learned of the original homeowner's assignment to the new owner, he refused to do any further work. The new owner instituted an action against the contractor for breach of contract on April 15.

25.  On August 1 a wholesaler of office supplies contracted by telephone to sell 50 cases of typewriter ribbons to a business equipment retailer at a total price of $450. On August 15, the wholesaler telephoned the retailer and told him that because of a shortage of materials, the price that the wholesaler had to pay for typewriter ribbons had increased drastically. The wholesaler said that if he delivered the ribbons at the price of $450, he would lose a great deal of money. He asked the retailer to consent to a higher price, suggesting that the retailer pass the increase along to his customers. After further discussion, the retailer and the wholesaler agreed to change the price of the order from $450 to $650. On

August 18, the retailer succeeded in purchasing 50 cases of typewriter ribbons from another supplier for $500. On September 1, the wholesaler delivered 50 cases of typewriter ribbons to the retailer, together with a bill for $650. The retailer rejected the delivery.

In an action by the wholesaler against the retailer for breach of contract, which of the following would be the retailer's most effective argument in defense?

(A)  The wholesaler's demand for more money was unconscionable, since typewriter ribbons were available at a lower price.

(B)  The August 15 agreement increasing the price was not in writing.

(C)  The retailer's promise to pay $650 was unsupported by consideration.

(D)  An increase in the wholesaler's cost resulting from a shortage of materials was foreseeable on August 1.

26.  The seller was an importer of arts and crafts products from Mediterranean countries, selling mainly to large department stores and import shops. To keep his sales force down to a minimum, the seller did most of his selling by sending catalogs describing products and prices to prospective customers and taking orders by mail on forms provided with the catalogs. The phrase "10 percent discount on COD orders only" appeared on the order form and on each page of the catalog. After receiving one of the seller's catalogs, the buyer decided to order 1,000 Greek coffeepots for sale in her import shop. On April 25, she typed the following across the seller's order form: "Send immediately 1,000 Greek coffeepots (Catalog #6047) at 10 percent discount. Payment within 10 days of receipt and acceptance." The seller received the order on April 27. On April 28, the seller shipped 1,000 Greek coffeepots to the buyer, who received and accepted them on May 2. On April 29, the seller wrote to the buyer,

"I am shipping pursuant to your request and will expect payment within 10 days. Since discounts apply only to COD shipments, you are herewith billed at full price." The buyer received the letter and enclosed bill on May 3. On May 4, the buyer sent the seller a check in payment of the amount billed, less 10 percent.

When was a contract for sale of the coffeepots formed?

(A) On April 25, when the buyer sent the order to the seller.

(B) On April 27, when the seller received the order from the buyer.

(C) On April 28, when the seller shipped the coffeepots to the buyer.

(D) On May 2, when the buyer received the shipment of coffeepots.

27. After lengthy negotiations, the plaintiff purchased a car from the defendant, a car dealer. The plaintiff was driving it the following day when the brakes failed due to a defect that existed at the time the defendant delivered the car to the plaintiff. As a result, the car collided with a pole and was damaged. The plaintiff asserted a claim against the defendant for damages resulting from breach of the implied warranty of merchantability. Which one of the following additional facts, if it were the only one true, would be most likely to result in a judgment for the defendant?

(A) At the time of the sale, both the defendant and the plaintiff signed a document stating that the car was being sold "as is."

(B) The car that the plaintiff bought from the defendant was a used car.

(C) The defect that caused the brakes to fail could not have been discovered by reasonable inspection prior to the sale.

(D) The plaintiff purchased the car in reliance on the advice of a mechanic

whom she hired to inspect it prior to making the purchase.

28. The defendant, who broke his leg falling from a ladder, was treated by a doctor. At the time treatment began, the defendant explained that he was short of cash, but that his treatment was covered by group insurance. The doctor agreed to wait for his fee until the insurance company made payment and offered to bill the insurance company directly for the services that he rendered to the defendant. The defendant provided the doctor with claim forms from the company that insured the defendant's union. The doctor filled out the form, had the defendant sign a portion of it authorizing the insurance company to make payment directly to the doctor, and submitted the form to the company. Because of an error by employees of the insurance company, the payment was sent to the defendant, who failed to make any payment at all to the doctor.

If the doctor asserts a claim against the defendant to recover the amount of the unpaid bill, the court will probably find for

(A) the doctor, because he is a creditor third-party beneficiary of the group insurance policy that covered the defendant.

(B) the doctor, because the defendant impliedly promised to pay the doctor for his services.

(C) the defendant, because the doctor agreed to accept payment from the insurance company.

(D) the defendant, because the doctor billed the insurance company directly.

29. A landowner wanted to open an amusement park on a parcel of real estate that he owned. After negotiation, the landowner hired a contractor to build a roller coaster and several other amusement devices on the land according to specifications furnished by the landowner. The landowner and the contractor entered into a written contract by which

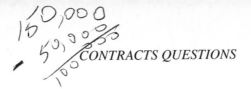

the contractor agreed to begin construction on August 1, to be finished with everything but the roller coaster by November 1, and to complete construction of the roller coaster by December 15. The contract price was $150,000, to be paid as follows: $50,000 on August 1, $50,000 upon completion of everything but the roller coaster, and the balance of $50,000 upon completion of the roller coaster. The contractor began work on August 1, after receiving $50,000 from the landowner. By November 1, the contractor completed construction of everything but the roller coaster in accordance with the specifications.

On November 1, the contractor demanded the landowner pay him $50,000, but the landowner refused to do so. Which of the following statements is most correct concerning the rights of the contractor?

(A) The contractor is entitled to damages limited to the sum of $50,000.

(B) The contractor is entitled to damages in the sum of $100,000.

(C) The contractor may refuse to perform any further work without incurring liability for breach of contract.

(D) The contractor may not sue the landowner for breach of contract until he completes construction of the roller coaster.

30. A landowner was suffering from a terminal disease and did not expect to live much longer. She was the owner of a parcel of realty known as Blackacre and wanted her son to have it. Blackacre was worth $500,000, but it was subject to a non-assumable mortgage securing a note with a balance of $100,000. For this reason, the landowner offered to sell Blackacre to her son for $100,000. Her son said that he would like to buy it, but that it would take him a while to raise the money. Fearful that she would die before the transaction could be completed and that her administratrix would

be unwilling to sell the realty to her son for that price, the landowner wrote and signed a document that said, "In consideration of $20 paid to me by my son, I hereby promise to convey my realty known as Blackacre to him for the sum of $100,000 if he pays the entire purchase price within one month." Two days later, the landowner died. One week after that, her son tendered the sum of $100,000 to the administratrix of the landowner's estate, demanding that she convey Blackacre to him, but the administratrix refused.

If the son instituted a proceeding against the landowner's administratrix for an order directing her to sell Blackacre to him for $100,000, the court should find for

(A) the son, because the document written and signed by the landowner was a valid option contract.

(B) the son, because the document written and signed by the landowner was intended to be a testamentary substitute.

(C) the landowner's administratrix, because $20 is not sufficient consideration for a $100,000 option.

(D) the landowner's administratrix, because $100,000 is not sufficient consideration for realty valued at $500,000.

31. The plaintiff, a minor who looked older than he was, wished to purchase a motorcycle. The plaintiff went to the defendant's motorcycle shop and looked at some of the models on display. Selecting a motorcycle he liked, he began negotiating with the defendant. The defendant offered to sell him the motorcycle that was on display in the showroom, but the plaintiff said that he wanted a new one. The defendant explained that the display model was the only one she had, but she said that she was planning to order some new motorcycles from the manufacturer anyway and would order one for the plaintiff if he agreed to purchase it. The plaintiff and the defendant entered into a written contract for the sale

of a new motorcycle at a price of $1,000, to be paid on delivery within two weeks. The following day, the defendant ordered 10 new motorcycles from the manufacturer, and the plaintiff purchased materials and began building a storage shed for the motorcycle.

One week after contracting with the plaintiff, the defendant notified the plaintiff that the new motorcycle was ready for delivery, but that the defendant would not deliver it to the plaintiff unless the plaintiff either proved himself to be over the age of majority or found an adult to act as co-purchaser of the motorcycle. If the plaintiff immediately commenced an action against the defendant for breach of contract, the court should find for

(A) the defendant, because if she delivered the motorcycle to the plaintiff, the plaintiff might subsequently disaffirm the contract and demand the return of the purchase price.

(B) the defendant, because the plaintiff lacked contractual capacity.

(C) the plaintiff, because he purchased materials for and began construction of a storage shed for the motorcycle in justified reliance on the defendant's promise to deliver it.

(D) the plaintiff, because one who contracts with a minor is obligated to perform.

32. On March 22, by a written memorandum signed by both parties, the seller agreed to sell and the buyer agreed to buy a described parcel of realty. The buyer and seller were both in the business of buying and selling real estate. The contract called for closing of title on May 30 and fixed all other terms, but it did not indicate the price to be paid. On May 30, the buyer tendered $60,000 cash, but the seller refused to convey the realty. The buyer subsequently instituted an action against the seller for specific performance of the contract and offered evidence that $60,000 was the fair market value of the realty both on March 22 and on May 30. In defense, the seller

asserted that the memorandum failed to satisfy the requirements of the Statute of Frauds. The buyer's suit against the seller should

(A) succeed, because the buyer and the seller are both in the business of buying and selling real estate.

(B) succeed, because under the UCC, a contract that is silent as to price is presumed to call for payment of fair market value.

(C) fail, because the written contract did not fix the price to be paid.

(D) succeed, because there is likely evidence establishing that the parties orally agreed that the price to be paid was the fair market value of the realty.

33. A rescuer saved the life of a man's wife, who subsequently promised to change her will to leave $500 to the rescuer. The wife later died intestate, however, survived only by her husband. After the wife's death, the husband executed a document that read as follows:

In consideration of my wife's promise to leave the rescuer $500, of the rescuer's saving my wife's life, and of the rescuer's promise not to assert any claim against the estate of my wife, I hereby promise to pay the rescuer the sum of $500.

The husband died two months after signing the above agreement. The rescuer submitted a claim for $500 to the administrator of the husband's estate, but the administrator denied the claim.

Is the fact that the rescuer saved the wife's life sufficient consideration for the husband's promise to pay him $500?

(A) Yes, because it is recited as consideration in the document that the husband signed.

(B) Yes, because it materially benefited the husband.

(C) No, because the husband did not ask the rescuer to save his wife.

(D) No, because the value of the service rendered by the rescuer to the husband was speculative.

34. A woman, who was dying, wanted to leave her house to her niece. The woman's will left the house to her husband. Because the woman was unlikely to live long enough for a new will to be drafted, her husband promised her that if she kept the will the same, he would leave the niece enough money in his will to make up for the niece not getting the house. The woman died, and the husband failed to make any changes to his will. The niece then sued his estate for the value of the house. Will she recover?

(A) No, because she is not a creditor beneficiary of the agreement between the wife and her husband.

(B) No, because a will speaks on death, and neither the wife nor the husband ever changed theirs.

(C) Yes, because she was an intended beneficiary of the agreement between the wife and her husband.

(D) Yes, because she was a donee beneficiary of the agreement between the wife and her husband.

35. In preparation for an annual convention that was to be held on January 9, the buyer ordered 500 ballpoint pens from the seller at a total price of $285, paying for them in advance. Because the pens were to be given to conventioneers as souvenirs, they were to be imprinted with the name and slogan of the association and were to be delivered to the buyer on or before January 8. The seller and the buyer entered into a written contract containing the above terms on November 16. The seller tendered 475 ballpoint pens to the buyer on January 8.

Which of the following correctly states the legal relationship between the buyer and the seller on January 8?

(A) The buyer must accept the tendered delivery of 475 pens but may successfully sue for damages resulting from breach of contract.

(B) The buyer may elect to accept the tendered delivery of 475 pens but may not successfully sue for breach of contract if it does so.

(C) The buyer may reject the tendered delivery of 475 pens but may successfully sue only for the return of its advance payment if it does so.

(D) The buyer may reject the tendered delivery of 475 pens and may successfully sue for the return of its advance payment and for damages resulting from breach of contract if it does so.

36. A man texted his friend, "I really want to sell my motorcycle. I would consider $2,000 for it." His friend immediately texted back, "I accept! I'll give you a check immediately!" The friend then went to his bank and had a cashier's check for $2,000 prepared. He also went out and bought a motorcycle helmet, motorcycle leathers, and a shed in which to store his new motorcycle. The next day when the friend showed up for the motorcycle, the man refused to give it to him. If the friend sues for specific performance, the court should find for

(A) the friend, because he accepted the man's offer.

(B) the friend, because he detrimentally relied on the man's offer.

(C) the man, because he merely made a statement of future intention.

(D) the man, because he was merely soliciting bids.

37. On June 1, the plaintiff, a licensed real estate broker, entered into a written contract with the defendant. According to the contract, the plaintiff was given the exclusive right to sell the defendant's home at a price of $100,000 for a period of three months. The defendant

agreed to pay the plaintiff a 7 percent commission "upon transfer of title." On July 1, as a result of the plaintiff's efforts, a buyer agreed to purchase the defendant's home at a price of $100,000. According to the terms of the contract, the defendant was to deliver evidence of clear title prior to July 20. At the defendant's request, an abstract company researched the chain of title and delivered an abstract to the defendant on July 15 showing clear title. The defendant did not deliver the abstract to the buyer, however, because his neighbor was unhappy with the prospect of having the buyer move into the defendant's home and asked the defendant to try to get out of the deal. On July 21, the buyer notified the defendant that he would not go through with the transaction because of the defendant's failure to deliver the abstract of title as agreed.

The plaintiff sued the defendant for a 7 percent commission based on the defendant's contract with the buyer. Which of the following would be the plaintiff's most effective argument in support of her claim?

(A)  The plaintiff delivered a buyer "ready, willing, and able" to purchase the defendant's property.

(B)  But for a willful breach by the defendant, the buyer would have taken title to the realty.

(C)  The defendant and the buyer entered into a contract for the sale of the defendant's realty as a result of the plaintiff's efforts.

(D)  The defendant's refusal to deliver the abstract frustrated the purpose of the contract between the defendant and the plaintiff.

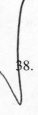

38.  The seller and the buyer entered into a written contract for the sale of 500 bicycles at a total price of $50,000. The contract required delivery by the seller prior to June 1 and payment by the buyer within 30 days after delivery. On May 15, the seller delivered

the bicycles to the buyer, who received and accepted them. On May 21, because the seller was having cash flow problems, he telephoned the buyer, asking whether the buyer could pay for the bicycles immediately. The buyer said that he would pay by May 25 if the seller was willing to accept 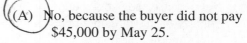 $45,000 in cash as payment in full. The seller agreed, but by June 20, the buyer had made no payment at all. The seller subsequently instituted an action against the buyer for $50,000. The buyer admitted the existence of the contract, the delivery of the bicycles, and his non-payment; but he asserted that he was liable for only $45,000 because of the agreement that he made with the seller on May 21.

Is the buyer's assertion correct?

(A)  No, because the buyer did not pay $45,000 by May 25.

(B)  No, because a promise to perform a preexisting obligation is not valuable consideration.

(C)  Yes, because there has been a valid novation.

(D)  Yes, because there has been a valid agreement of accord.

39.  A publisher mailed an offer to publish a writer's first book for $25,000. The writer immediately mailed back her acceptance. The acceptance was properly addressed with the correct amount of postage. However, the post office lost the letter and the publisher never received it. Is there a contract?

(A)  No, because the post office lost the letter.

(B)  No, because the publisher was excused from performance since he did not receive the letter.

(C)  Yes, because the acceptance was properly addressed with the correct amount of postage.

(D)  Yes, because the writer mailed her acceptance.

40. When the plaintiff was admitted to law school, her mother was so proud of the plaintiff that she said, "If you successfully complete your first year, I'll buy all your books for the following two years. In addition, I'll give you $250 for every 'A' that you earn in your first year." The plaintiff made extra efforts to earn "A"s. The plaintiff's mother died while the plaintiff was in her first year of law school, but the plaintiff succeeded in earning two "A"s in her first year, and completed school in two additional years. The plaintiff demanded that her mother's executrix pay her $250 for each of the two "A"s that she received in her first year, and pay for the books that she had purchased in her second and third year, but the executrix refused.

If the plaintiff asserts a claim against the executrix for $500 for the two "A"s that she received in her first year of law school, will the plaintiff's claim be successful?

(A) No, because she was already obligated to use her best efforts while in law school.

(B) No, because the plaintiff's mother died before the plaintiff received the "A" grades.

(C) Yes, because prior to her mother's death, the plaintiff made extra efforts in an attempt to earn "A"s.

(D) Yes, because the plaintiff got into law school.

41. In a transaction involving the sale of a bicycle, which of the following persons is **NOT** a merchant under the UCC?

(A) The owner of a bicycle store who sells her own personal bicycle after using it for 14 months by placing an advertisement under the heading "Used Merchandise" in the classified section of the newspaper.

(B) The owner of an automobile dealership who buys a bicycle for use by employees of the dealership's parts department in making deliveries.

(C) A bicycle mechanic who buys a new bicycle from a retail store to give as a gift to his nephew.

(D) The owner of a messenger service who employs a full-time bicycle mechanic to maintain bicycles used in her business, and who sends the mechanic to inspect a new bicycle before buying it for use by messengers in her employ.

42. The defendant was the owner and operator of a summer resort located at a high elevation in the northern part of the country. Because the hotel was open only during the summer, the defendant usually employed a single resident caretaker to live and work at the hotel during the winter months. On August 1, after applying for the job of winter caretaker, the plaintiff entered into a valid written contract with the defendant. According to its terms, the plaintiff was to take up residence at the hotel on October 1, and to remain in residence until the following April 1, at which time the defendant was to pay him $10,000. During the plaintiff's period of residence, he was to receive free room and board and to perform certain maintenance tasks. On August 15, the plaintiff enlisted in the U.S. Navy, his period of service to begin on September 25 and to continue for three years. Mention of the plaintiff's enlistment appeared in the "Hometown Gossip" section of a local newspaper and was seen by executives of the defendant. The defendant immediately began seeking another winter caretaker and hired another caretaker on September 15, entering into a valid written contract with him on that date that contained terms identical to those in the contract with the plaintiff.

On September 20, the plaintiff failed the physical examination performed by Navy physicians and was rejected for naval service. The plaintiff reported for work at the hotel on October 1 but was advised that his services were not required.

If the plaintiff asserts a claim against the defendant for damages resulting from breach of contract, the court should find for

(A) the plaintiff, since he was ready, willing, and able to perform as agreed on October 1.

(B) the plaintiff, since he never informed the defendant that he would not be reporting to work as agreed.

(C) the defendant, since the plaintiff's enlistment was an anticipatory repudiation of his contract with the defendant.

(D) the defendant, since the defendant hired another caretaker in reliance on the reasonable belief that the plaintiff would be unable to perform as agreed.

43. On May 1, the defendant hired the plaintiff to reshingle the roof of his house at an agreed price of $5,000, to be paid within 10 days after completion, and with all work to be completed by July 1. The plaintiff began work on May 2 and worked diligently until May 15. At that time, the plaintiff had performed services that were worth $1,500, and which increased the value of the defendant's house by $1,500. On May 16, through no fault of either party, the house caught fire and was totally destroyed. Although the proceeds that the defendant received from his fire insurance policy were sufficient to cover the cost of building a new house, the defendant decided to sell the property instead. The plaintiff demanded payment under the contract, but the defendant refused to pay.

If the plaintiff asserts a claim for payment against the defendant, a court should award judgment to the plaintiff in the sum of

(A) $5,000, since it was the price on which the plaintiff and the defendant agreed.

(B) $1,500, since it was the value of the plaintiff's work.

(C) $0, since the defendant derived no benefit from the plaintiff's work.

(D) $5,000, because the defendant could have rebuilt the house with the proceeds from the fire insurance policy.

44. At the age of 14, the plaintiff designed a program for a computer game. He demonstrated the program to the defendant, a company in the business of marketing computer software. The defendant executives were so impressed by the program designed by the plaintiff that they hired him as a game program consultant at a salary of $30,000 per year. In addition, they offered to purchase marketing rights to the game by a separate contract. According to the terms of the contract that they offered, the defendant would have the exclusive rights to copy and market the program for the game and would pay the plaintiff 30 percent of all revenues derived from the exercise of those rights. After consulting with his parents and their attorney, the plaintiff accepted the defendant's offer and signed the contract. Three months later, before the defendant had begun marketing the plaintiff's game program, the plaintiff needed cash to purchase expensive computer equipment. For a large cash payment, he assigned his rights under the contract to his friend. His friend intended to inform the defendant of the assignment but neglected to do so. One month later, the plaintiff assigned the same rights to another software company as security for a credit purchase of additional computer equipment. The other company was unaware of the assignment to the plaintiff's friend and never notified the defendant that the plaintiff had assigned the rights to it. Two months later, the defendant began marketing the game, realizing high profits from its sale. Although the plaintiff has demanded payment pursuant to the terms of his contract, the defendant has refused to make any payments.

If the plaintiff commences an action against the defendant for royalties equivalent to 30 percent of the revenues generated by the sale of the game, which of the following would be the defendant's most effective argument in defense?

(A) The plaintiff was a minor at the time he contracted with the defendant.

(B) The plaintiff has made at least one effective assignment of the contract rights.

(C) Neither the friend nor the other company notified the defendant about the assignment from the plaintiff.

(D) An assignment of wages is invalid.

45. A woman and her sister lived together in the woman's house in the town of Wildwood. On March 1, the woman called her daughter on the telephone and said that she was beginning to have premonitions of her own death. The woman said that she was willing to deed her home to her daughter while she was alive rather than put her daughter through probate expenses. The woman said, however, that she would do so only if her daughter agreed to permit her aunt to stay in the house for the rest of her life and to permit her brother, who resided in another state, to live in the house for as long as he wanted if he should ever decide to come to Wildwood. The daughter promised to do so, and on March 15, the woman deeded the home to her as agreed. At the time, the home had a value of $100,000. The daughter called her brother on March 10, and told him that their mother had deeded her the house but did not tell him about her promise to allow her brother to live there. On March 15, the aunt wrote to the brother:

"I don't think that either your mother or I have much longer to live, and we both miss you terribly. If you agree to come and live here in Wildwood for as long as either of us lives, I will leave you my entire estate.

Love,

(signed)

On March 17, the brother called his sister and told her about the note that he had received from their aunt. He said that he was thinking of moving to Wildwood, and that if his sister promised to allow him to live in the house that their mother had deeded to her until their aunt died, he would give her 50 percent of the inheritance. The daughter agreed, and her brother immediately wrote to their aunt, telling her that he was moving to Wildwood in response to her offer. Their aunt received the brother's letter on March 20. The brother made arrangements to move to Wildwood, and did so, at an expense of $800. Both their mother and their aunt died on March 22, but the brother did not learn of their deaths until he arrived in Wildwood on March 24. At that time, his sister refused to allow him to move into the house.

The brother instituted an action against his sister for damages resulting from her refusal to allow him to move into the house, and the only defense asserted by the sister was that her promises were not in writing. Which of the following would be the sister's most effective argument in support of her position?

(A) Her promises to her mother and her brother were promises to create an interest in land.

(B) It was possible that the promise that she made to her mother and her brother would not be performed within a year.

(C) The house had a value in excess of $500.

(D) She received no consideration from her brother for either promise.

46. A painter entered into a contract to paint the homeowner's house for $5,000. After painting the doors and the trim, the painter got a job offer in a different state that he had to accept immediately or would lose. He asked the homeowner if he could get out of the agreement, and the homeowner, realizing the spot the painter was in, agreed. The painter then asked if he could be paid for the amount

of painting he did do. The homeowner refused. Can the painter sue to recover the value of the partial performance he rendered?

(A) No, because the painter was the one who requested to end the agreement.

(B) No, because there was a mutual rescission of the contract.

(C) Yes, because the homeowner received value from the painter.

(D) Yes, because the painter was entitled to be paid for his part performance.

47. The defendant, a manufacturer of widgets, entered into a valid written contract that called for the sale of 2,000 widgets to the plaintiff at a price of $10 per widget. Several weeks prior to the date set for delivery, the defendant telephoned the plaintiff and advised her that because of difficulty in locating a sufficient supply of frammis rods, the defendant would be unable to deliver more than 1,000 widgets. After discussion, the plaintiff agreed to accept 1,000 widgets at $10 per widget instead of 2,000 as originally agreed. After the defendant delivered 1,000 widgets, however, the plaintiff brought an action against him for damages resulting from breach of contract. In adjudicating the plaintiff's claim, the court should find for

(A) the plaintiff, because her agreement to accept 1,000 widgets was not in writing.

(B) the plaintiff, because her promise to accept 1,000 widgets was not supported by consideration.

(C) the defendant, because the plaintiff agreed to accept 1,000 widgets.

(D) the defendant, because there has been an accord and satisfaction.

48. A man and the plaintiff were neighbors in a recently created subdivision. Since both wanted to have landscaping work done, they decided to join forces in hopes of getting a better price. They hired a landscaper to plant grass and shrubs in their yards, directing him to bill each of them for the labor and materials attributable to his separate realty. After the landscaper completed the work, he submitted his bills to the man and the plaintiff, who paid them immediately. The following week, however, the man concluded that the landscaper had erroneously billed him for some work done on the plaintiff's land. He showed his calculations to the plaintiff, asking that the plaintiff reimburse him for the amounts that he claimed to have paid on the plaintiff's account. The plaintiff was certain that his neighbor was incorrect, but because he did not want to come to bad terms with his new neighbor, he offered to hire a gardener to keep the man's lawn mowed and trimmed for the next two years. The man agreed to accept the offered services in lieu of payment.

The plaintiff hired the defendant to maintain his lawn and the man's lawn for the next two years, agreeing to pay him $50 per month for certain specified services. The plaintiff and the defendant signed a memorandum of agreement, and the plaintiff gave a photocopy of it to his neighbor. Two months later, the plaintiff sold his house. At the closing of title, the plaintiff handed the new homeowner the original memorandum of his agreement with the defendant and executed an assignment to the new homeowner of his rights thereunder. The defendant continued rendering services as agreed for an additional six months, receiving a check for $50 from the new homeowner each month. Then, the defendant notified the man and the new homeowner that he would no longer be able to work on their lawns. The man wrote to the plaintiff and the new homeowner, demanding that they make arrangements to have his lawn maintained for the remaining 16 months pursuant to his agreement with the plaintiff, but neither responded.

The plaintiff sued the defendant for breaching their agreement regarding maintenance of the lawns. Which one of the following facts or inferences, if it were the only one true, would furnish the defendant's most effective argument in defense against the plaintiff's claim?

(A) There are equally competent gardening services in the area which, for $50 per month, would perform work comparable to that which the defendant agreed to perform.

(B) The value of labor and materials used in lawn maintenance has increased dramatically since the signing of the memo.

(C) The agreement between the man and the plaintiff was oral.

(D) The defendant's inability to work on the lawns was the result of a serious heart attack that led his doctors to advise him against ever working again.

49. In response to an advertisement that he saw in the newspaper, the homeowner telephoned the contractor and asked him to come to the homeowner's home to estimate the cost of providing and installing new aluminum screens for all the homeowner's windows. After taking measurements, the contractor returned to his shop and prepared a written estimate, in which he said that he would do the entire job for $350. When the homeowner received the contractor's written estimate, he wrote across it with a red felt-tipped pen, "I'll pay $300, but not a penny more," and mailed it to the contractor. When the contractor received the estimate with the homeowner's statement written on it, he wrote on the estimate, "I'll do it for $325." He sent the estimate back to the homeowner on September 5, but on September 12, having received no response, he sent the homeowner a note that said, "All right, you win. I'll do the job for $300. Unless I hear from you to the contrary, I'll be there with the new screens on September 28. Signed, the contractor."

The homeowner received the note on September 14, but made no response. On September 28, without the homeowner's knowledge and while the homeowner was at work, the contractor went to the homeowner's home and installed new aluminum window screens.

Which of the following best characterizes the legal relationship between the homeowner and the contractor **AFTER** installation of the window screens on September 28?

(A) A contract was formed when the homeowner failed to respond to the contractor's letter of September 12 within a reasonable time after he received it.

(B) A contract was formed when the contractor began to install the screens on September 28.

(C) A quasi-contract was formed when the contractor finished installing the screens on September 28, obligating the homeowner to pay a price equivalent to their reasonable value.

(D) No contractual relationship existed between the homeowner and the contractor.

50. The defendant signed a five-year contract with the plaintiff. According to the contract, the plaintiff would bag apples produced in the defendant's orchard. There was a fixed price for each pound bagged, with a minimum of 5,000 pounds to be bagged each year. A liquidated damages clause provided that if the defendant requested less than the 5,000-pound minimum, the defendant would still pay the per-pound bagging price for each pound by which the defendant's order was less than the minimum. This was so regardless of whether the plaintiff was required to do any work. In the second year, the defendant requested significantly less than the 5,000-pound minimum of bagged apples. If the plaintiff sues for breach and requests damages based on the liquidated damages clause, the court should find for

(A) the defendant, because the liquidated damages clause is a poor estimate of actual losses.

(B)  the defendant, because the liquidated damages clause was an unenforceable penalty.

(C)  the plaintiff, because the liquidated damages clause was a reasonable estimation of damages under the contract.

(D)  the plaintiff, because damages in this situation would be difficult to calculate.

51  A woman knew that a local writer often gave private lessons in memoir writing for $50 an hour. The market rate for such courses was closer to $30 an hour, but the writer had already published two memoirs and was somewhat famous. One day, the woman ran into the writer at the grocery store. The woman told the writer how much she admired her memoir writing. The writer then said, "I can come by your house tomorrow to give you some lessons." The woman said nothing. The next day, the writer showed up at the woman's house and the two of them worked on some of the woman's writing for an hour. For four weeks, the writer showed up at the woman's house at the same time, on the same day, and the two of them worked for an hour. At the end of the month, the writer asked the woman to pay her. How much does the woman owe?

(A)  Nothing, because the woman never agreed to pay the writer.

(B)  $120, the fair market value of the writer's lessons since the two of them never had a formal agreement.

(C)  Nothing, because by showing up at the woman's house, the writer was making a gratuitous gift.

(D)  $200, since this represented the writer's standard fee.

52.  A boxer, the son of a poor family, grew up on his family's small farm just outside of town. Despite the handicaps of poverty and lack of education, the boxer eventually became the world's heavyweight boxing champion. Proud of the boxer's accomplishments, the town council voted to erect a statue commemorating the boxer's victory over his social and economic disadvantages. Pursuant to town ordinances and regulations, bids were accepted from several sculptors, including the plaintiff. Because the plaintiff's work was relatively unknown, she attempted to make her bid more attractive to the council by including a guarantee that her work would be satisfactory. On February 1, the town council entered into a written contract with the plaintiff, hiring her to create the statue, and agreeing to pay her $5,000 upon its installation on the steps of the town hall on or before June 30. A clause in the contract provided, "It is expressly understood that the personal satisfaction of the Mayor is a condition precedent to the council's obligation to make payment hereunder. Upon completion of the statue, it shall be made available for inspection by said mayor. If said mayor is unsatisfied with the work, he shall notify the plaintiff immediately, and the contract shall be canceled without liability of any party."

The plaintiff sculpted a likeness of the boxer in farmer's overalls with his hands in boxing gloves clasped victoriously over his head, which she completed on June 10. The boxer had been arrested in another state on May 30, however, and charged with possession of a dangerous drug. His trial was scheduled for September 10. The town council was fearful that the boxer would be convicted and that the statue would embarrass the town.

The mayor went to the plaintiff's studio on June 11 after receiving notice that the statue was ready for inspection. When he arrived, the statue was covered with a canvas tarpaulin. When the plaintiff removed the cover, the mayor said, "It's too small. The deal is off." The mayor truly believed the statue was too small, even though he was also fearful of the conviction. The plaintiff subsequently demanded that the town council pay for the statue, but the council refused. In an action by the plaintiff against the town council, the court should find for

(A) the plaintiff, because a reasonable person would have found the plaintiff's work to be satisfactory.

(B) the plaintiff, because the mayor was fearful that the statue would embarrass the town if the boxer was convicted.

(C) the town council, because the contract gave the mayor the absolute right to reject the plaintiff's finished work.

(D) the town council, because the mayor actually believed that the statue was too small.

53. The plaintiff worked for a corporation for 40 years. The corporation told the plaintiff that the plaintiff would be given the right to retire at any time with a lifetime pension. The plaintiff continued to work for a few more years, then retired after downsizing her home so that her expenses could be covered by the pension. She received the pension for several years. After the founder of the corporation died, the corporation stopped paying the pension. The plaintiff then sued. The court should rule in favor of

(A) the plaintiff, because she chose to retire when she could have kept on working.

(B) the plaintiff, because she received the pension in recognition of her 40 years of service.

(C) the plaintiff, because she worked for a few more years after receiving the pension promise.

(D) the defendant, because there was no consideration supporting the promise of the pension.

54. By a written contract, the plaintiff, the operator of a natural foods store, agreed to purchase 200 pounds of large nuts from the defendant at a specified price. A term of the contract provided that "payment shall be due immediately on delivery and prior to inspection of the shipment." When a box containing the nuts was delivered, the plaintiff paid the agreed price without inspecting its contents. One hour later, the plaintiff opened the box and discovered that it contained small nuts instead of large nuts. When the plaintiff telephoned the defendant to ask that the defendant exchange the small nuts for large ones, the defendant refused. The plaintiff repackaged the nuts and returned them to the defendant. Subsequently, the plaintiff asserted a claim against the defendant for breach of contract.

In considering the contract provision that required payment prior to inspection, a court is most likely to hold that

(A) it is unconscionable and therefore not subject to enforcement.

(B) it constitutes a waiver of the buyer's right to inspect prior to acceptance.

(C) it does not impair the buyer's right to inspect prior to acceptance.

(D) it was not enforceable when the contract was made, but since the plaintiff did pay before inspecting the goods, he waived his right to a preacceptance inspection.

55. The buyer and the seller were members of the graduating class of a college. The buyer, who was planning to go to law school, told the seller that he might need some law books. The seller had recently inherited a law library, so he compiled a list of the books in the collection and mailed it to the buyer on July 5 with a note that said, "Interested in buying?" The buyer wrote the following letter on a copy of the booklist and mailed it to the seller on Tuesday, July 8:

Dear seller,

I will buy your law library consisting of the books on this list for $2,600 cash if you deliver the books to my home by the time I start law school in mid-September. I promise to hold this offer open until September 1.

Yours truly,
[signed] the buyer

In the buyer's letter of July 8, what was the legal effect of the statement, "I promise to hold this offer open until September 1"?

(A) The language did not prevent the buyer from revoking the offer.

(B) At common law, the language creates an irrevocable option in the seller's favor.

(C) Under the UCC, the buyer was prevented from revoking the offer until September 1.

(D) The language created an option in favor of the seller, subject to the condition that the buyer actually begin law school.

56. Which of the following is most likely to be regarded as valid consideration for a man's oral promise to pay his neighbor $1,000?

(A) The fact that his neighbor had saved the man's house from a fire the day before the man's promise was made.

(B) The fact that at the same time the man made the promise to pay, his neighbor promised to deliver to the man fire-fighting equipment valued at $1,000.

(C) The fact that after the man made the promise, his neighbor relied upon it by committing himself to the purchase of fire-fighting equipment at a price of $1,000.

(D) The fact that immediately after the man made the promise, his neighbor sent the man a written memorandum of their agreement, to which the man did not object within 30 days.

57. An airline agreed to buy all of its jet fuel requirements from a jet-fuel supplier. The supplier committed to supply those requirements at a price pegged to the industry-wide posted price for crude oil. Then, because of a war, the price increased dramatically. The supplier reneged on the agreement. The airline sued. The court should rule in favor of

(A) the supplier, because the war was not foreseeable at the time of contracting.

(B) the supplier, because the plaintiff was not bound to buy any goods at all.

(C) the airline, because it bound itself to act reasonably and in good faith in estimating the quantity of fuel it required.

(D) the airline, because a mere price increase would not invalidate the agreement.

58. After the commercial success of a rock music group, its lead singer entered into a contract with the defendant. According to its terms, the singer, singing alone, was to record a song for the defendant. The defendant was to pay $2,000 to the singer 30 days after the record was made, whether or not it was ever commercially released. If the record was released, the singer was to receive additional compensation depending on the number of copies of the record that were sold.

The singer made the record required by the contract on March 1. On March 15, the singer bought a piano, promising to pay for it when he received payment from the defendant. As security for his promise, the singer assigned to the piano seller his right to collect the $2,000 that the defendant owed him for making the record. The piano seller immediately notified the defendant of the assignment. On April 1, the singer purported to assign the same right to his landlord to induce him to refrain from instituting eviction proceedings based on non-payment of rent. The landlord immediately notified the defendant of the assignment. On April 20, the singer sued the defendant for non-payment of the $2,000.

Which of the following additional facts or inferences, if it were the only true, would be most likely to result in a judgment for the defendant?

(A) The singer was an infant at the time of all the transactions described above.

(B) The singer made at least one effective assignment of the right to collect the $2,000.

(C) The singer's performance at the March 1 recording session was so bad that the record can never be commercially released.

(D) A statute in the jurisdiction prohibited the assignment of future wages by employees.

59. In an agreement made on April 15, the plaintiff agreed to design a coat of arms for the defendant and to fabricate a wooden door with the coat of arms carved into it for the front of the defendant's home. The defendant agreed to pay $650 for the door, but it was understood that if the defendant was not completely satisfied with the coat of arms and the door, he would be under no obligation to go through with the deal. Before the plaintiff completed the door, the defendant came to the conclusion that he did not really want a coat of arms. When the plaintiff brought the finished door to the defendant, the defendant took a quick glance at it. Although the coat of arms was properly designed and carved, and although the door had been fabricated in a workmanlike manner, the defendant said, "I just don't like it," and refused to accept it.

In an action by the plaintiff against the defendant, which of the following would be the defendant's best defense?

(A) The agreement was not in writing as required by the Statute of Frauds.

(B) The agreement was an offer for a unilateral contract that the defendant rejected by refusing to accept the finished door.

(C) The defendant's subjective satisfaction was a condition precedent to his obligation to accept the door.

(D) Since the coat of arms was not yet associated with the defendant, it was possible for the plaintiff to find another buyer for it.

60. Because its property was filling up with a lot of unwanted recycled plastic it didn't want to pay to have removed, a landfill gave a construction firm free recycled plastic for use in its construction work. All the firm had to do was come to the landfill and pick it up. The plastic turned out to be defective, and the firm sued the landfill for breach of contract. The landfill argued that there were no contractual obligations to the firm because any promise it made was not supported by consideration. The landfill argued it had merely made a gift of the plastic on the condition that the firm come and pick it up. Can the firm successfully sue for breach of contract?

(A) Yes, because the firm relied on the landfill's promise to its detriment.

(B) Yes, because the landfill wanted the firm to take the plastic and benefited when it did so.

(C) No, because the landfill did not bargain for the firm's performance.

(D) No, because the unwanted plastic was a gift.

61. When the buyer's employer prepared to transfer him to its plant located in Twin Oaks, the buyer contracted with the seller for the purchase of the seller's home located in Twin Oaks. According to the contract, title was to close and the home was to be vacant and ready for occupancy by the buyer no later than April 20. Because the buyer was arranging to move his family to Twin Oaks on April 20, at the buyer's insistence the contract contained a liquidated damages clause. The clause provided that if the house was not ready for occupancy on April 20, the seller would pay the buyer $75 for each day thereafter that it

remained unavailable for occupancy. When the buyer and his family moved to Twin Oaks on April 20, the home was not ready for occupancy. As a result, the buyer and his family had to stay at a motel. On May 1, the seller advised the buyer that he did not intend to go through with the sale of this house. On May 10, the buyer instituted an action against the seller for specific performance and damages.

With respect to the buyer's demand for specific performance, a court

(A) may find for the buyer, whether or not the liquidated damages clause is held to be enforceable.

(B) may find for the buyer, because the liquidated damages clause is unenforceable.

(C) may find for the buyer, because the liquidated damages clause is enforceable.

(D) must find for the seller.

62. On June 11, the homeowner asked a local handyman whether the handyman would be interested in painting the homeowner's house. Following their conversation, they entered into the following handwritten agreement, which the handyman wrote on the back of an old envelope and which both signed:

> The homeowner and the handyman hereby agree that the handyman will paint the outside of the homeowner's house for $700 as follows: wood trim brown; doors and window frames green; siding yellow (two coats).

The handyman painted the siding yellow and gave it two coats of paint. He painted the wood trim brown and the doors and window frames green, but gave them only one coat of paint. The homeowner refused to pay unless the handyman gave the wood trim, doors, and window frames a second coat. The handyman instituted an action against the homeowner for $700. At the trial, the homeowner attempted to testify that prior to executing

the agreement, he and the handyman agreed orally that the handyman would apply two coats of paint to the wood trim, doors, and window frames, as well as to the siding.

The trial judge should rule the homeowner's testimony

(A) admissible only for the purpose of establishing that the phrase "(two coats)" is ambiguous.

(B) admissible for the purpose of establishing that the phrase "(two coats)" is ambiguous and for the additional purpose of explaining the ambiguity.

(C) admissible, because the agreement was written by the handyman.

(D) inadmissible, since the writing was a complete expression of the agreement of the parties.

63. A man who had been studying the writings of various mystical philosophers, decided to sell all his worldly possessions, give the money to charity, and wander about in the desert for a while to seek insight and spiritual fulfillment. After about a month in the desert, the man became ill and collapsed into unconsciousness. When he woke, he was in the home of a retired surgeon who now lived like a hermit in the desert, and who had found him in a helpless condition. As the doctor fed soup to the man, the man said, "I have no money. I can never pay you for any of this." The doctor replied, "I'm not doing this for money."

During the next week, the doctor fed the man and gave him medical treatment. When the man was well enough to travel, the doctor borrowed an old pickup truck from a distant neighbor and drove the man to the house of the man's mother. The following week, after the man told his mother what the doctor did for him, the man's mother wrote the doctor: "In gratitude for the services that you rendered my son, I hereby promise to pay you $350.00 when I get my dividend check next month." Before the dividend check arrived, however, both the man's mother and the doctor died. The plaintiff, the doctor's administrator, advised the mother's husband of the letter that his wife had sent and indicated that he intended to make a claim against her estate for $350.

After a discussion with the plaintiff, in which the plaintiff agreed not to assert a claim against the mother's estate, the husband prepared a document that read, "In consideration of services rendered by the doctor to my wife's son, and of the plaintiff's promise to make no claim against the estate of my wife, I hereby agree to pay $350.00 to the doctor's estate." After signing the document, the husband handed it to the plaintiff. The husband never paid anything to the estate, however, and the plaintiff instituted suit against him. The husband defended on the ground that his promise to pay $350 was not supported by consideration.

If the plaintiff's lawsuit against the mother's husband is successful, it will most likely be for which of the following reasons?

(A) The document that the husband executed was an offer for a unilateral contract that the plaintiff accepted by not making a claim against the mother's estate.

(B) A judgment for the husband would result in his being unjustly enriched.

(C) The husband is estopped from denying the validity of his agreement with the plaintiff.

(D) The husband's agreement with the plaintiff was a compromise.

64. On September 10, the company, a well-known publisher of law books, posted the following notice on the bulletin board at a law school:

> As an incentive to research and scholastic excellence, the company announces the institution of an award. The award will consist of a complete set of the company's encyclopedias and will be presented to the student in each graduating class of the law school who attains the highest overall cumulative Grade Point Average. In the event two or more students graduate with the same Grade Point Average, the dean will be asked to select the winner from among them based on school service and community involvement.

A student, who had just begun her final year at the law school, saw the notice. Her grades already placed her toward the top of her class, but she resolved to work harder than ever before in an attempt to win the company's award. On September 20, she mailed a letter to the company saying, "I accept your offer for the award and will do my best to win it." Her letter was received by the company, but it was lost in the mailroom before any company officials had an opportunity to see it.

Which of the following statements is most correct about the company's notice?

(A) It was an offer for a unilateral contact.

(B) It was an offer for a bilateral contract.

(C) It was an offer for either a unilateral contract or a bilateral contract at the offeree's option.

(D) It was an offer for a unilateral contract that ripened into a bilateral contract when the student achieved the highest grade point average in her class.

65. The defendant's 20-year-old son became ill while traveling. The plaintiff, a youth hostel operator, let the son stay in one of the hostel's rooms and nursed the son back to health. The plaintiff contacted the defendant, who thanked the plaintiff and promised to pay the plaintiff for any of his expenses. The plaintiff then sent the defendant a bill. The defendant refused to pay. What result?

(A) There was an enforceable contract based on the plaintiff's promise to pay the defendant's expenses.

(B)   There was no enforceable contract because the defendant's promise was not supported by consideration.

(C)   There was an enforceable contract because the plaintiff detrimentally relied on the defendant's promise.

(D)   There was no enforceable contract because the plaintiff had a moral obligation to give aid to the son.

66.   The plaintiff was a manufacturer of sewing supplies, including thread, needles, thimbles, and patterns. The defendant was an engineer employed by the plaintiff in its product design department. Working at home on his days off, the defendant invented a device that could be used to increase the fuel efficiency of automobile engines. Without telling his employer anything about it, the defendant obtained a patent on the device and sold the patent rights for $100,000 to a motor vehicle manufacturer. The plaintiff subsequently learned about the defendant's invention and demanded the money that the defendant had received from the manufacturer. In support of its demand, the plaintiff referred to a provision of the defendant's employment contract that required him to devote all his working time and energies to his employment. The plaintiff's attorneys argued that because of this provision, the device had been invented on company time, and that the patent rights therefore belonged to the plaintiff. At a conference with the plaintiff's attorneys, the defendant signed a promissory note for $50,000, payable to the plaintiff, and the plaintiff agreed to abandon its claim. When the note came due, the defendant refused to pay it.

In an action by the plaintiff against the defendant on the promissory note, which of the following additional facts or inferences, if it was the only one true, would be most helpful to the defendant's defense?

(A)   The employment contract was oral, although the Statute of Frauds required it to be in writing.

(B)   At the time the defendant signed the promissory note, the plaintiff did not honestly believe that it was entitled to the patent rights, but the defendant believed that the plaintiff was entitled to the patent rights.

(C)   At the time the defendant signed the promissory note, the plaintiff honestly believed that it was entitled to the patent rights, but the defendant did not believe that the plaintiff was entitled to the patent rights.

(D)   The plaintiff was not entitled to the patent rights under the employment contract.

67.   The plaintiff was a manufacturer of wood-finishing products with a plant in the city. The defendant was a manufacturer of wooden furniture with a factory located in the town. Pursuant to a written agreement, the defendant agreed to purchase 50 gallons of wood stain from the plaintiff at $5 per gallon, "FOB the defendant's factory." The plaintiff delivered the wood stain to a trucking company that loaded it safely onto a truck in the city. While en route to the town, however, the truck was hijacked by thieves. Its contents were never recovered.

In an action by the plaintiff against the defendant for the agreed price of the stain, which of the following comments is most correct?

(A)   The plaintiff fulfilled her obligation to the defendant when the stain was loaded safely aboard a truck in the city.

(B)   The risk of loss passed to the defendant when the plaintiff delivered the stain to the trucking company, although title to the stain never actually passed to the defendant.

(C)   The risk of loss did not pass to the defendant.

(D)   The risk of loss was not on the plaintiff, since the loss was the result of action by the public enemy.

68. When a landowner's daughter and a painting contractor's son announced that they were getting married, the landowner and the contractor decided to give them a house as a wedding present. On January 1, the two men entered into a written agreement with each other, pursuant to which they were to have a house built on the landowner's lot, with the landowner and the contractor each paying half the cost. It was further agreed that after completion of the house, the contractor would pay the landowner $10,000 as his share of the cost of the lot, and the landowner would convey the lot to their children.

On February 2, the two men entered into a written contract with the plaintiff, a builder. The contract called for payment in installments, each payment being due upon completion of a specified stage of building. In addition to its other terms, the contract contained a clause providing that as each payment came due, the plaintiff would bill and collect half of it from the landowner and half of it from the contractor. In the contract, the plaintiff agreed that neither would be responsible to him for more than half of the price.

On March 3, the contractor entered into a separate contract with the plaintiff. Pursuant to this contract, the plaintiff hired the contractor as a subcontractor to do all the painting required in connection with the construction of the house. Because the house was being built for his son, the contractor agreed to do the job for $3,000 although his work was worth $5,000. The $3,000 was to be deducted from the final payment that the contractor would owe the plaintiff for construction of the house.

In April, the contractor became ill. Because he could no longer work, he sold his painting business to his son, a competent and licensed painting contractor, for about half of what it was actually worth. As one of the terms of the contract of sale, the contractor's son promised to do all the painting work on the house that the plaintiff was constructing. The contractor notified the plaintiff of his

agreement with his son. When the house was ready to be painted, however, the contractor's son informed the plaintiff that he would not paint it.

The plaintiff hired another painting subcontractor to do the job at a price of $5,000 and asserted a claim for breach of contract against the contractor's son. If there was an enforceable contract between the contractor and his son, the court should find for

(A) the contractor's son, because there was no privity between the plaintiff and him.

(B) the contractor's son, because a contract for personal services is not assignable.

(C) the plaintiff, because the plaintiff was an intended donee beneficiary of the contract between the contractor and his son.

(D) the plaintiff, because the plaintiff was an intended creditor beneficiary of the contract between the contractor and his son.

69. The seller and the buyer had been friends for years. The seller was the owner of a rare antique sports car, which the buyer had offered to buy from her on several occasions but which the seller had never been willing to sell. On the buyer's birthday, the seller and the buyer went out for dinner and drinks. After dinner, the seller continued drinking until she was somewhat intoxicated. During their conversation, the seller said, "As a birthday present, I've decided that I'm going to sell you my sports car for $500. And just to make sure that I don't change my mind after I sober up, I'll put it in writing." With that, she wrote on a paper napkin, "We agree to the sale of my sports car to the buyer for $500, COD," and signed her name at the bottom. The buyer also signed the napkin and put it in her purse. The following day, the buyer tendered $500 in cash to the seller, but the seller refused to sell her the car, claiming that she had been drunk when she made the offer.

In an action by the buyer against the seller for breach of contract, which of the following additional facts, if it was the only one true, would be most helpful to the seller's defense?

(A) The seller was so drunk when she wrote on the napkin that she did not know the legal consequences of her act.

(B) The seller would not have offered to sell the car to the buyer for $500 if she had not been drunk.

(C) The car was worth more than $500.

(D) The seller changed her mind about selling the car before the buyer tendered the cash.

70. The defendant was the owner and operator of a store that sold exotic birds and aviary supplies. The plaintiff was the owner and operator of a pet shop in which dogs, cats, tropical fish, and exotic birds were sold. The defendant kept a trained Amazon parrot on a perch near the sales counter in his store. The bird had an extensive vocabulary and did tricks on his perch to the great amusement of the defendant's customers. The plaintiff wished to have the parrot for his own personal pet and had attempted to purchase him from the defendant on numerous occasions, but the defendant always indicated that he was unwilling to sell. On January 5, the plaintiff again asked the defendant if he would sell the parrot, to which the defendant replied, "I'd consider selling him to you, but I don't even know what a bird with this parrot's training is worth." The plaintiff said that he would do some research to find out, if the defendant would promise to seriously consider selling the parrot for whatever they found the proper price to be. Based on their conversation, the plaintiff and the defendant executed the following document:

The defendant hereby agrees to sell to the plaintiff one trained Amazon parrot for a price to be paid in cash and on delivery, said price to be agreed upon after determining the reasonable value of a bird with the parrot's training.

The plaintiff contacted five generally acknowledged experts in trained exotic birds and received opinions from them regarding the parrot's value that ranged from $700 to $1,000. When the plaintiff attempted to buy the parrot from the defendant for $1,000, however, the defendant indicated that he was unwilling to sell the parrot at any price.

In an action by the plaintiff against the defendant for specific performance of the agreement made on January 5, the plaintiff will

(A) win, because he offered to pay $1,000 for the parrot.

(B) win, but he will be required to pay a price for the parrot that the trier of fact finds to be reasonable in light of expert and other evidence presented at the trial.

(C) lose, since the January 5 document does not manifest an intent to be bound.

(D) lose, since specific performance is not available in an action for breach of a contract for the sale of a chattel.

71. The plaintiff was the owner of an air-conditioning repair company. His employees did all the repair jobs, but the plaintiff himself did the estimating and made price quotes to customers. The plaintiff maintained a fleet of pickup trucks for use by his employees when traveling to and from repair jobs, but the plaintiff usually drove his own personal station wagon when going out to give a potential customer an estimate.

On February 15, the plaintiff ordered a new station wagon from the defendant, a new-car dealer. Prior to signing the sales contract, the salesperson who sold him the car explained that the new car could be obtained by the defendant only from the manufacturer. For this reason, she said, it might be as long as two weeks before the defendant could deliver the new car to the plaintiff. The plaintiff said that this would be all right, but that he definitely needed the car by March 10 for use in his business. Based on this discussion, it was agreed that the new car would be ready for him no later than March 5.

Immediately following the signing of the sales contract by the plaintiff and the defendant, the salesperson contacted the manufacturer's sales department and placed the order for the plaintiff's car. She explained to the sales representative at the manufacturer that she had contracted to deliver the car to the plaintiff no later than March 5, and that if she was unable to do so, she would probably lose the sale. The sales representative assured her that the car would be delivered on time.

On March 4, the plaintiff sold his old station wagon because he believed that he would be receiving the new one the following day. The manufacturer failed to deliver the new car to the defendant until March 30, making it impossible for the defendant to deliver it to the plaintiff on time.

The plaintiff instituted an action for breach of contract against the defendant, and he alleged damages that included lost profits resulting from his inability to travel to the premises of potential customers for the purpose of estimating jobs and selling his company's services. Which of the following would be the defendant's most effective argument in response to that allegation?

(A) At the time the contract was formed, it was not foreseeable that late delivery of the automobile would result in business losses.

(B) Late delivery by the manufacturer made performance of the sales contract by the defendant impossible.

(C) The plaintiff could have mitigated damages by renting another vehicle or using one of the company pickup trucks while waiting for delivery of the station wagon.

(D) Consequential damages are not available for the breach of a contract of sale.

72. A licensed physician was driving home from the hospital where she worked when she saw a pedestrian fall unconscious to the pavement. The doctor stopped her car, examined the pedestrian, and diagnosed that he was experiencing cardiac arrest. After attempting to render medical treatment, the doctor carried the pedestrian to her car and drove him to the hospital. There, she continued attempting to treat him for an hour, after which the pedestrian died without ever having regained consciousness. At the time she assisted the pedestrian, the doctor reasonably expected to be compensated for her services. The doctor subsequently sent the administratrix of the pedestrian's estate a bill for medical services, but the administratrix refused to pay it.

The jurisdiction had a "Good Samaritan" statute. If the doctor asserts a claim against the pedestrian's administratrix for the reasonable value of her medical services, the court should find for

(A) the doctor, because at the time she assisted the pedestrian, she reasonably expected to be compensated for her services.

(B) the doctor, because a contract was implied-in-fact.

(C) the pedestrian's administratrix, because the pedestrian received no benefit as a result of the doctor's services.

(D) the pedestrian's administratrix, because the jurisdiction has a "Good Samaritan" statute.

73. The plaintiff was a professional gambler who made his living by accepting illegal bets on horse races and other sporting events. Because he suspected that the police had discovered his operation, he began looking for a new location for his illegal activities. Finding an empty storefront building on Main Street, he contacted the defendant, its owner. On December 12, they entered into a lease of the premises for a six-month period. According to the lease, the plaintiff's occupancy was to begin on the first of January, at a rent of $200

per month. The plaintiff paid the first month's rent upon signing the lease.

On December 17, the plaintiff was arrested on charges of illegal bookmaking. He pleaded guilty and received a nine-month sentence. The following day, his attorney advised the defendant that the plaintiff would not be moving into the leased premises after all. The defendant agreed to release the plaintiff from the lease and immediately rented the premises to another tenant for $300 per month, occupancy to begin on December 20. When the plaintiff was released from prison nine months later, he demanded that the defendant return his $200. The defendant refused on the ground that the contract that the plaintiff had made with her had an illegal purpose.

If the plaintiff institutes an action against the defendant, a court should find for

(A) the defendant, since the courts will not aid either party to an illegal contract.

(B) the defendant, since she and the plaintiff were not *in pari delicto* regarding the illegality of the lease agreement.

(C) the plaintiff, since the lease agreement was not illegal.

(D) the plaintiff, since his sentence to serve nine months in prison made performance by him impossible as a matter of law.

74. The defendant, an 84-year-old woman, suffered from Parkinson's disease. She asked the plaintiff, a woman who rented space in her home, to quit her job so she could care for the defendant. The plaintiff agreed and quit her job in return for the defendant's promise that when the defendant died she would leave the house and surrounding farm to the plaintiff. Three days after the agreement was made, the defendant made an appointment to see her lawyer to change her will. However, before she could keep the appointment, she fell ill and was hospitalized. The plaintiff spent a lot of time with her at the hospital, but a few days later, the defendant died. The plaintiff

sued the defendant's estate for specific performance of the promise to convey the house and farm. The court should rule in favor of

(A) the plaintiff, because she gave up her employment and agreed to take care of the defendant.

(B) the plaintiff, because the defendant showed her intent to honor the agreement by making the appointment with her lawyer.

(C) the defendant's estate, because the house and farm are worth much more than the services actually performed by the plaintiff.

(D) the defendant's estate, because a will speaks at death.

75. The buyer received an advertising brochure from the seller in the mail. The brochure contained a photograph of a computer, and above it the statement, "While they last. All computers on sale at 25 percent below manufacturer's list price." The buyer immediately contacted the company that manufactured the computer pictured in the seller's brochure and determined that the manufacturer's list price for the 410 was $1,000. She then sent her check for $750 ($1,000 less 25 percent) to the seller with a cover letter that stated, "I hereby accept your offer for the sale of a computer. My check is enclosed herewith." The seller threw the buyer's letter and check away.

The brochure that the seller sent the buyer is best described as

(A) an invitation for offers.

(B) an invitation for offers that ripened into an offer when the buyer learned the list price for the computer.

(C) an invitation for offers that ripened into an offer when the buyer relied on it by sending her check and cover letter.

(D) an offer for the sale of a computer.

76. A group of workmen signed contracts at a fixed rate to work on a ship during the

salmon-canning season, as the ship went from San Francisco to Alaska and back. When the ship arrived in Alaska, the workmen told the captain that they would not do any more work unless the captain gave them a very substantial increase in salary. Since the captain had nowhere to go to get replacement men, he agreed. The workmen then worked on the way back to San Francisco. When the captain refused to pay the extra money, the workmen sued. The court should rule in favor of

(A) the workmen, because they relied on the captain's promise of an increased salary.

(B) the workmen, because parties can renegotiate a contract based on a change in conditions.

(C) the captain, because he agreed to the salary increase while under duress.

(D) the captain, because the workmen had a pre-existing duty to work on the way back to San Francisco.

77. The seller was the owner of a lot and building that contained two residential apartments. The seller resided in the upstairs apartment and rented the downstairs apartment to a tenant and his family on a month-to-month basis. The buyer was interested in purchasing the realty from the seller. After negotiations, the buyer and the seller entered into a written contract that provided that the seller would sell the house to the buyer for $60,000 and that delivery of title was to occur on or before August 1. The seller promised that at the time title was delivered, the upstairs apartment would be vacant and that the downstairs apartment would be vacant within three months thereafter. The buyer promised to pay $58,000 upon delivery of title, and the balance of $2,000 three months after delivery of title. The contract provided that "The buyer's obligation to pay $2,000 three months after delivery of title shall be voided if the downstairs apartment has not been vacated by that time."

Which of the following statements concerning the order of performances is **LEAST** accurate?

(A) The seller's delivery of title on or before August 1 and the buyer's payment of $58,000 are concurrent obligations.

(B) Vacancy of the upstairs apartment is a condition precedent to the buyer's obligation to pay $58,000 upon delivery of title.

(C) Payment by the buyer of $58,000 is a condition precedent to the seller's obligation to deliver title to the premises.

(D) Payment by the buyer of $2,000 is a condition subsequent to the seller's obligation to have the downstairs apartment vacated within three months after the delivery of title.

78. Article 2 of the UCC applies

(A) only to transactions in goods.

(B) only to transactions involving merchants.

(C) to all commercial transactions.

(D) only to transactions in goods or services.

79. After seeing the small airplane that the pilot was flying go down in stormy seas, the pilot's wife stood on the shore screaming, "Oh, God, won't somebody please save my husband?" Upon hearing her appeal for help, the plaintiff went out in his rowboat and succeeded in rescuing the pilot. The plaintiff subsequently asked the pilot's wife to pay him for his trouble, but she refused.

If the plaintiff asserts a claim for payment against the pilot's wife on a theory of promissory estoppel, which of the following would be the pilot's wife's most effective argument in defense?

(A) The plaintiff was an officious intermeddler.

(B)   The value of the pilot's life is too speculative.

(C)   No promise of payment can be reasonably inferred from the wife's cry for help.

(D)   There was no consideration for the wife's promise.

80.   The buyer was a collector of antiques who had purchased many expensive pieces from the seller, an antiques dealer. Knowing that the seller was traveling to Europe, the buyer wrote to him on March 11, "If you should come across a good piece in your travels, please purchase it for me. I don't care about the cost."

On April 17 the seller wrote to the buyer, "I have found an excellent settee. The price is $15,000, but I think it's a good buy. Are you still interested? If so, let me know if the price is acceptable to you."

The buyer received the seller's letter on April 21, and, on that same day, texted the seller, "Fifteen thousand is OK. Buy the piece on my account."

Soon thereafter, the seller sold the piece to another collector who offered more money.

In litigation between the buyer and the seller, if a court determines that the seller's letter of April 17 was not an offer, it will most likely be because that letter

(A)   was an acceptance of the offer contained in the buyer's letter of March 11.

(B)   did not specify the terms of payment.

(C)   did not manifest a willingness to be bound.

(D)   did not specify a manner of acceptance.

81.   The defendant, who resided in the city, was the owner of a chain of dry cleaning stores. Because his stores had been financially successful, he began selling franchises. By the terms of his franchise agreements, the defendant permitted franchisees to use the name of his store in return for an initial fee of $50,000 and 10 percent of the gross revenues.

The plaintiff lived in a distant state. When she heard about the financial success of the stores, she wrote to the defendant, asking him to sell her a franchise to operate a dry cleaning store in her state. Because the defendant had great affection for the plaintiff and wanted her to live near him, he sent her a letter in which he said, "If you will come and live here, I will give you a franchise to operate in the city without any initial fee. All you will have to pay is 10 percent of the gross revenues."

The plaintiff immediately wrote the defendant to tell him that she was coming to live in the city as he requested, and that she was looking forward to operating a store there. After the plaintiff moved to the city, however, the defendant told her that his contract with another franchisee prevented him from giving her a franchise to operate a store in the city.

If the plaintiff asserts a claim against the defendant for breach of contract, the court should find for

(A)   the plaintiff, on a theory of bargained-for exchange.

(B)   the plaintiff, because she detrimentally relied on the promise made by the defendant.

(C)   the defendant, because his promise was for a conditional gift.

(D)   the defendant, because his affection for the plaintiff is not sufficient to support his promise to her.

82.   The seller is a manufacturer of wall-coverings that he ordinarily sells to retailers in boxes containing 10 packages per box. By a valid written contract, the buyer agreed to purchase, and the seller agreed to sell, 10 boxes of 107-Blue. When the boxes arrived,

the buyer inspected them and found that 2 of the boxes contained 109-Red instead of 107-Blue. The buyer immediately notified the seller, who informed the buyer that he no longer produced 107-Blue and had sent the buyer his last 8 boxes. The seller said that he had sent 2 boxes of 109-Red as an accommodation, and that the buyer did not have to accept them unless he wanted to.

Which of the following correctly states the buyer's rights regarding the shipment?

(A)  The buyer may reject the entire shipment.

(B)  The buyer may reject the entire shipment, or accept the 8 boxes containing 107-Blue and reject the 2 boxes containing 109-Red.

(C)  The buyer may accept the 8 boxes containing 107-Blue and reject the 2 boxes containing 109-Red, or accept the entire shipment and collect damages resulting from its nonconformity to the terms of the contract.

(D)  The buyer may reject the entire shipment, accept the 8 boxes containing 107-Blue and reject the 2 boxes containing 109-Red, or accept the entire shipment and collect damages resulting from its nonconformity to the terms of the contract.

83.  By a valid written contract formed on May 7, the builder agreed to construct a warehouse for the landowner. Pursuant to the terms of the contract, the building was to be completed no later than November 30. The agreed price was $60,000, of which the landowner was to pay $20,000 when the construction was 50 percent complete and the balance upon completion. The builder began work on May 11 and had completed 25 percent of the construction by June 5, when the partially finished structure was struck by lightning and completely destroyed in the resulting fire. No payment had yet been made by the landowner to the builder. On June 7, the builder notified

the landowner that he was too busy to rebuild the structure and that he would not continue to work on the project. The landowner subsequently hired another contractor to build the warehouse at a lower price and rejected all the builder's demands for payment. If the builder asserts a claim against the landowner, the builder is entitled to recover

(A)  the difference between $60,000 and the price that the landowner paid to have the warehouse built by another contractor.

(B)  the reasonable value of the work performed by the builder prior to the destruction of the structure by lightning and fire.

(C)  25 percent of $60,000 ($15,000).

(D)  nothing.

84.  When the defendant's employers transferred him to the West Coast, they promised to pay all his relocation expenses, including any commission that he might have to pay for the sale of his home. The defendant contacted the plaintiff, a real estate broker, and entered into a written contract with her on September 1. Under its terms, the defendant agreed that if the house was sold to any buyer who made an offer during the following two months, he would pay the plaintiff upon the closing of title a commission equivalent to 6 percent of the actual selling price of the house. In return, the plaintiff agreed to make reasonable efforts to find a buyer for the house at a price of $80,000.

On September 15, after the plaintiff showed the defendant's home to the buyer, the buyer offered to purchase it for $75,000, on condition that title would close on or before December 1. On September 18, the defendant accepted the buyer's offer. On September 19, the buyer gave the defendant $10,000 as a deposit.

On November 15, the buyer notified the defendant that he had changed his mind and would not go through with the purchase of the house, agreeing to forfeit the deposit that he had paid in return for the defendant's agreement not to sue for damages. The following day, the defendant entered into a contract to sell the house to another buyer for $80,000. The defendant subsequently rejected the plaintiff's demand for payment.

If the plaintiff institutes a claim against the defendant for her commission, she is entitled to collect

(A)  $4,800 (6 percent of $80,000).

(B)  $4,500 (6 percent of $75,000).

(C)  $600 (6 percent of $10,000).

(D)  nothing.

85.  A trash collector contracted with the city to collect garbage. Although the contract entitled the collector to $150,000 for five years, the collector requested an additional $10,000 a year from the city council because his operating costs had substantially increased due to an unanticipated explosion of new houses. The city made the payments. A citizen then sued to have the additional payments refunded to the city. The court should rule in favor of

(A)  the collector, because the city council agreed to the additional $10,000 a year.

(B)  the collector, because there was a valid modification of the contract.

(C)  the citizen, because the collector had a pre-existing duty to collect the city's garbage.

(D)  the citizen, because the collector took unfair advantage of the city by requesting more money to pick up the trash.

86.  The defendant and his wife were co-owners of a parcel of realty. After 25 years of marriage, they decided to execute wills. Before executing the wills, they agreed in writing that each would leave a life estate in his or her share of the realty to the other, and that the survivor would leave a fee interest in the realty to their son, the plaintiff. After executing their wills, they told the plaintiff about their agreement. The plaintiff had recently contracted for the purchase of a residence but subsequently canceled the contract. Shortly afterwards, the defendant's wife died, leaving a life estate in her share of the realty to the defendant. One year later, the defendant remarried and changed his will to leave the realty to his second wife. When the defendant died, the plaintiff learned that the defendant's will left the realty to his second wife, so he sued the executrix of the defendant's estate for damages resulting from the defendant's breach of his agreement with his first wife.

The court should find for

(A)  the plaintiff, because he canceled his contract for the purchase of a residence in reliance on the agreement between the defendant and his first wife.

(B)  the plaintiff, because after his mother's death, the plaintiff became a creditor beneficiary of the agreement between the defendant and his first wife.

(C)  the defendant's executrix, because the plaintiff is a donee beneficiary of the agreement between the defendant and his first wife.

(D)  the defendant's executrix, because by its terms, the agreement between the defendant and his first wife might be capable of being performed within one year.

87.  The plaintiff, an unmarried woman, became pregnant. Before the child was born, she told the defendant that he was the father. The defendant agreed to pay the expenses of having the child in return for the plaintiff's promise not to bring a paternity suit. After the child was born, the defendant refused to pay. A blood test then proved that the child could not be the defendant's. The plaintiff sued the defendant, claiming the defendant still needed to live up to the settlement since

she had truly believed he was the father of the child. The court should rule in favor of

(A) the plaintiff, because she detrimentally relied on the defendant's promise.

(B) the plaintiff, because the plaintiff had a reasonable subjective belief that her claim was valid.

(C) the defendant, because forbearance to bring suit cannot count as consideration for a settlement.

(D) the defendant, because the plaintiff merely surrendered an invalid claim.

88. When they decided to computerize their paperwork, a law firm contacted a specialist in the application of computer technology to the practice of law. After negotiations, the firm entered into a written contract with the specialist on June 1. According to the terms of the contract, the specialist was to immediately deliver and install in the office of the firm a computer and other specified hardware. The specialist was also required to design and install, by October 15, software consisting of a computer program that would suit the special needs of the firm's practice. In addition, the specialist agreed to service and maintain the hardware for a period of six years from the date of the contract. In return, the firm agreed to pay $5,000 within 30 days after delivery of the hardware, $5,000 within 30 days after delivery of the software, and $1,000 on the first day of each year that the contract remained in effect.

The firm also agreed to furnish specifications for the software at least 30 days before the date for its installation. The hardware referred to in the contract was standard equipment, readily available from and serviceable by any reputable computer supplier. The software was not standard, however, and its design required special skill and knowledge regarding the application of computer technology to the practice of law. The contract specified that the price of the hardware was $6,000, the price of the software was $4,000, and

the charge for service and maintenance was $1,000 per year. On June 15, the specialist installed the agreed hardware in the office of the firm. On June 20, in satisfaction of an antecedent debt, the specialist assigned to another computer programmer her rights to receive payment for hardware already delivered under the contract with the firm. On August 1, before beginning to work on the design for the agreed software, the specialist sold her business to an established and reputable computer dealer. By the terms of the sale, the specialist assigned to the computer dealer all her rights under the contract with the firm.

The firm failed to make any payment following the installation of the hardware, and on August 15, the specialist instituted a claim against them for $5,000. Which of the following would be the firm's most effective argument in defense against that claim?

(A) The specialist has not begun work on designing the software required by the contract.

(B) The specialist has made at least one effective assignment of her rights under the contract.

(C) The firm has no assurance that the specialist's obligations under the contract will be fulfilled.

(D) The contract between the specialist and the firm was divisible.

89. A drug manufacturer made vaccines and sold them to various distributors. Just before the drug manufacturer was about to raise the price of its vaccines, one of the distributors learned of the pending price increase. On May 19, the distributor placed a large order for 1,000 vials. The distributor's order stated that the distributor was to receive a price of $64 per vial (the old price), compared with the new price of $171. On June 3, the manufacturer shipped 50 vials at the old price, and simultaneously notified the distributor that the remainder of this order would be priced

at the new price. The notice said the manufacturer was shipping the 50 vials as a favor, and acceptance of the order was expressly conditioned on the manufacturer's terms. The notice also said that if the distributor wanted to cancel the balance of the order, it could do so on or before June 13. The distributor sued for an order of specific performance compelling the manufacturer to sell it the remaining 950 vials at the old price. The court should rule in favor of

(A) the distributor, because the manufacturer accepted the offer by shipping 50 vials.

(B) the distributor, because the manufacturer breached the contract by sending only 50 vials.

(C) the manufacturer, because the distributor's actions were unreasonable.

(D) the manufacturer, because it made a counteroffer.

90. The defendant was a veterinarian who specialized in the treatment of livestock, including pigs, horses, cows, and sheep. The plaintiff was a farmer who raised various species of livestock. In addition, the plaintiff kept a private collection of exotic animals. Because the plaintiff's livestock frequently needed the attention of a veterinarian, he entered into a written contract with the defendant on January 1. Under the terms of the contract, the plaintiff was to pay the defendant $250 per month for one year, in return for which the defendant would render whatever treatment the plaintiff's livestock required during that period.

On February 10, the local zoo telephoned the defendant, offering to give her a surplus tiger. Although the defendant had no experience with exotic animals, she accepted the tiger and put it in a cage in the back of her office. On February 22, having heard that the defendant had acquired a tiger, the plaintiff called her. When he asked the defendant if she was interested in selling the tiger for $450, she said, "I was hoping to get $1,000 for the

tiger, but I'll throw it in under our existing contract without charging you anything at all for it." On March 10, the defendant was at the plaintiff's farm for the purpose of inoculating some of his cattle. When the plaintiff asked why she had not brought the tiger, the defendant said, "I've changed my mind. If you want the tiger, you'll have to pay $450 for it."

The plaintiff asserts a claim against the defendant because of her refusal to deliver the tiger as promised. The court should find for

(A) the plaintiff, because although the defendant was not a merchant as to the sale of a tiger, she was a merchant as to the sale of veterinary services.

(B) the plaintiff, because his conversation with the defendant on February 22 resulted in a valid modification of the existing contract.

(C) the defendant, because her promise to give the plaintiff the tiger was unsupported by consideration.

(D) the defendant, because her promise to give the plaintiff the tiger was not in writing.

91. On January 3, a lumber retailer ordered from a lumber wholesaler 1,000 2" × 4" fir boards, each 8 feet in length, for delivery by January 15. When the wholesaler delivered the fir boards on January 15, they were received by the retailer's manager, who informed the retailer that delivery was made but that the boards delivered by the wholesaler were only 7 feet long. The retailer intended to notify the wholesaler immediately, but he was busy and forgot to do so.

On February 20, the retailer received the wholesaler's bill for the boards, but he did not pay the bill or communicate with the wholesaler in any way. On May 15, the wholesaler instituted a claim against the retailer for the price of the boards, and, in defense, the retailer contended that the boards delivered did not conform to the contract of sale. The court should find for

(A) the wholesaler, because the retailer failed to inform him that the boards were only 7 feet in length.

(B) the wholesaler, because a merchant buyer who accepts delivery of nonconforming goods is bound to pay for them at the contract price.

(C) the retailer, because the boards did not conform to the contract of sale.

(D) the retailer, because a merchant seller is not entitled to the price of nonconforming goods if a reasonable inspection prior to shipment would have disclosed the nonconformity.

92. A manufacturer of tractors had purchased hundreds of motors from an engine maker in the past at a price of $5,000 each. In 2011, the engine maker ceased production of the motor. By April 15, 2012, the engine maker found that she had only three motors left in her warehouse. Because she wanted to make room for the newer models, the engine maker signed and sent the following letter to the tractor manufacturer on April 15, 2012:

> I have only three motors left in stock and have stopped manufacturing them. If you are interested, I will sell you any or all of them for $1,000 each, a fraction of their usual price. Because we have done business in the past, I promise to hold this offer open until June 1, 2012.

Because the engine maker told the tractor manufacturer that she would hold the offer open until June 1, the tractor manufacturer went away on vacation without responding. On May 15, 2012, not having heard from the tractor manufacturer, the engine maker sold two of the motors to a car dealer for $1,000 each. Afraid to lose out on any more motors, the tractor manufacturer then bought the remaining motor when he returned.

Was the engine maker's statement, "I promise to hold this offer open until June 1," supported by consideration?

(A) Yes, because it was a firm offer under the UCC.

(B) Yes, because the tractor manufacturer detrimentally relied upon it by not responding before May 15.

(C) Yes, because the tractor manufacturer subsequently purchased one of the motors from the engine maker.

(D) No, because the tractor manufacturer gave nothing in return for the promise.

93. The defendant and her assistant were working alone late one night when the defendant had a heart attack that rendered her unconscious and caused her to fall down an airshaft. The assistant believed the defendant to be dead, but he called for an ambulance and leaped into the airshaft, sustaining serious injury himself. Finding that the defendant was still alive, the assistant gave her first aid consisting of cardiopulmonary resuscitation. When the ambulance arrived, paramedics used stretchers and pulleys to get the defendant and the assistant out of the airshaft, and then they brought them to the hospital. Several days later, while she was still in the hospital, a doctor told the defendant that she would probably have died if not for the assistant's quick and effective action. The defendant wrote the assistant a note that said, "In return for your saving my life, I'm going to pay all your hospital bills. In addition, I'm going to add a bonus of $3,000 per month to your salary for the rest of your life. If you choose to retire right now, I'll pay you $3,000 per month for the rest of your life as a retirement pension." The defendant paid the assistant's hospital bills, but because her business took an unexpected downturn, she never paid him $3,000, and subsequently she informed him that she would not be able to pay him a bonus or a retirement pension. If the assistant asserts a claim against the defendant for her failure to pay him the bonus of $3,000 per

month, which of the following would be the assistant's most effective argument in support of his claim?

(A)  The defendant's promise to pay the bonus was in writing.

(B)  The assistant detrimentally relied on the defendant's promise.

(C)  The defendant's promise was supported by an underlying moral obligation.

(D)  The assistant's rescue of the defendant resulted in a contract implied-in-fact.

94.  An art dealer employed several agents who traveled throughout the world purchasing art for her to sell in her gallery. One of her agents sent her a painting that she said was by a famous artist. The dealer had just received the painting and was about to place it on display when the buyer, a collector of art, came into the gallery. Seeing the new painting, he said, "An interesting painting by the famous artist." The dealer replied, "Yes, it is. I'm asking $50,000 for it." The buyer agreed to the price and immediately wrote a check for the sum of $50,000 payable to the order of the dealer, writing the words "Payment in full for the painting by the famous artist" on the back of the check. The dealer accepted the check and delivered the painting to the buyer. If the painting had actually been by the famous artist, it would have been worth $50,000. The same day, however, the buyer discovered that the painting was a forgery, worth only a few hundred dollars, and he stopped payment on his check before the dealer could cash it.

If the dealer asserts a claim against the buyer for breach of contract, which of the following would be the buyer's most effective defense?

(A)  The contract of sale was not evidenced by a writing signed by both parties.

(B)  At the time of sale, the buyer and the dealer both believed that the painting was by the famous artist.

(C)  It is unconscionable to make the buyer pay $50,000 for a painting worth only a few hundred dollars.

(D)  The painting was not adequate consideration for the buyer's promise to pay.

95.  On February 1, the landlord and the tenant entered into a written contract. By its terms, the landlord was to rent the tenant a building for use by the tenant as a "sports book," which is an establishment where bets are made on horse races and other sporting events. The tenant's tenancy was to commence on April 1 and to continue for a period of two years. Rent was to be $1,000 per month, plus 20 percent of the tenant's gross profits. Prior to occupancy by the tenant, the landlord was to remodel the building's interior so that it would be suitable for the tenant's purpose. Specifically, the contract required the landlord to install a "tote-board" that could instantaneously compute and display gambling odds on specified sporting events, a series of projection-screen televisions with cable connections for the broadcast of sporting events as they happened, and other equipment suitable only for use in a "sports book" establishment. Upon signing the contract on February 1, the tenant gave the landlord a deposit of $2,000. At that time, neither party could have reasonably anticipated that existing state law would be changed. On April 1, the landlord had not made the agreed improvements in the interior of the building and refused to comply with the tenant's demand for the return of his deposit.

On February 1, existing state law prohibited the operation of a "sports book," but on April 1, existing state law permitted the operation of a "sports book." If the tenant sues the landlord for the return of his deposit, the court should find for

(A)  the landlord, because public policy prohibits the enforcement of gambling contracts.

(B) the landlord, because the agreement of February 1 had an illegal purpose.

(C) the tenant, because he and the landlord were *in pari delicto*.

(D) the tenant, under the doctrine of frustration of purpose.

96. In January, a farmer planted a field of beans that would be ready for harvest in June. Because she expected the harvest to yield more than 5,000 bushels of beans, she entered into a written contract with a buyer on March 1, wherein the farmer agreed to sell and the buyer agreed to buy 2,000 bushels of beans at $2 a bushel to be delivered during the month of June. On March 2, the farmer entered into an identical written contract with a restaurant.

In the first week of April, heavy rains inundated the farmer's field, destroying part of her crop. As a result, she doubted that she would be able to fulfill her contract with both the buyer and the restaurant. On April 15, she called the restaurant and said that because of the storms, she would not be able to deliver more than 1,000 bushels. The restaurant said "I'll take whatever you deliver, but I intend to hold you to the terms of our contract."

On June 15, the farmer harvested her field. The American Bean Exchange price on June 15 was $2 per bushel and beans were readily available at that price. The farmer's harvest yielded 2,000 bushels of beans, and on June 15 she delivered 1,000 bushels to the restaurant. If the restaurant institutes a claim against her for damages resulting from breach of contract, which of the following would be the farmer's most effective argument in defense?

(A) Her inability to deliver 2,000 bushels was the result of an Act of God.

(B) She notified the restaurant on April 15 that she would be unable to deliver more than 1,000 bushels.

(C) The restaurant sustained no substantial damage, since the contract price equaled the market price on the day of delivery.

(D) Her obligation to the buyer was greater than her obligation to the restaurant, since her contract with the buyer was formed before her contract with the restaurant.

97. The homeowner went into his garage one morning and found that someone had broken in during the night and stolen a hand-carved milking stool that had been stored there. The stool did not have much intrinsic worth, but it was a family heirloom and had great sentimental value for the homeowner. The angry homeowner ran into a bar that was located near his home. Entering the bar, he said in a loud voice, "I'll pay $1,000 to anyone who finds the thief that stole a hand-carved stool out of my garage last night." The owner of the bar heard the homeowner's statement and said, "I'll catch that thief for you."

Which of the following statements most correctly describes the position of the homeowner and the owner of the bar following the incident in the bar?

(A) The homeowner has made an offer for a unilateral contract that became irrevocable when the owner of the bar said, "I'll catch that thief for you."

(B) The homeowner has made an offer for a unilateral contract that the owner of the bar can accept only by catching the thief before the homeowner makes an effective revocation of the offer.

(C) The homeowner and the owner of the bar are parties to a bilateral contract.

(D) The homeowner has not made any offer that can be accepted by the owner of the bar.

98. The landowner was the owner of two adjoining parcels of unimproved realty. Although she was interested in improving and selling the realty, she did not have the necessary capital. After negotiation, the landowner

entered into a written contract with a building contractor. According to the terms of the contract, the builder was to provide labor and materials for the construction of a building on one of the parcels according to certain specifications. All construction was to be completed by a certain date, at which time the landowner was to convey the other parcel of realty to the builder as his sole compensation for the labor and materials supplied. The contract contained a clause providing for liquidated damages in the event of a breach by either party.

After the builder completed construction as agreed, the landowner refused to convey the other parcel of realty to him. As a result, the builder appropriately asserted alternative claims for relief against the landowner, demanding liquidated damages as provided in the contract, actual damages, or an order directing the landowner to perform as agreed.

Which of the following correctly describes the builder's rights against the landowner?

(A)  If the liquidated damages clause established a penalty, the court can properly enter judgment for any actual damages that resulted from the landowner's breach.

(B)  If the liquidated damages clause did not establish a penalty, the court can properly direct the landowner to perform as agreed.

(C)  If the liquidated damages clause established a penalty, the court can enter a judgment for any actual damages; if it did not, the court can direct the landowner to perform as agreed.

(D)  The builder has no enforceable rights.

99.  An automobile dealer sold an expensive line of imported automobiles. The company that manufactured the vehicles in Germany sold them to the dealer at the wholesale price for resale by the dealer at the retail price.

On January 12, a buyer ordered a new automobile from the dealer, executing a written contract of purchase and sale at the specified retail price. The car was to be equipped with certain optional equipment and was to be delivered on or before March 15. Immediately after contracting with the buyer, the dealer ordered the car from the company in Germany.

On February 28, another buyer ordered from the dealer a car identical to that which had been ordered by the first buyer at an identical price. The following day, before ordering a car for the second buyer from the company, the dealer received the car ordered by the first buyer. When the first buyer was notified, however, he said that he had changed his mind and would not go through with the transaction. The dealer therefore delivered the car to the second buyer and did not order a car for the second buyer from the manufacturer.

If the dealer asserts a claim against the first buyer for damages resulting from breach of contract, the dealer is entitled to recover

(A)  nothing, because the car was sold to the second buyer at the same price that the first buyer agreed to pay.

(B)  the difference between the wholesale price of the car and its retail price.

(C)  the difference, if any, between the price that the first buyer agreed to pay for the car and its reasonable market value.

(D)  the difference, if any, between the price that the dealer paid for the car and its reasonable market value.

100.  For several years following his graduation from college, the plaintiff made no attempt to find employment. During this period, he was usually intoxicated, and spent most of his time drinking alcohol at the bar owner's tavern. On September 1, 2012, the plaintiff's mother stated orally

that if the plaintiff promised to go to law school and to stop drinking for the rest of his life, she would give him $10,000 on July 1, 2013. The plaintiff promised that he would never drink alcohol again and that he would enroll in law school as soon as possible.

The plaintiff began attending a law school two weeks later. In December 2012, however, he withdrew from the school, deciding that he did not like it.

On July 1, 2013, the plaintiff's mother refused to pay, and the plaintiff asserted a claim against her for $10,000. Which of the following would be the plaintiff's mother's most effective argument in response to that claim?

(A) The plaintiff's completion of law school was an implied condition precedent to his mother's promise to pay $10,000.

(B) The plaintiff's remaining in law school until July 1, 2013, was an implied condition precedent to his mother's duty to pay.

(C) The plaintiff's mother's promise was not supported by consideration.

(D) The plaintiff's mother's promise was not in writing.

101. The defendant's father earned his living as a crop-duster, using an airplane to dust farmers' fields with insecticides for a fee. When he died, he left the business to the defendant. Although the defendant did not know how to fly an airplane and did not personally participate in crop-dusting, she continued to run the business by hiring pilots to fly the crop-dusting planes. Soon after inheriting the business, the defendant entered into a business contract with the plaintiff, a farmer. The terms of the contract required the defendant's company to dust the plaintiff's crop four times per year for a period of four years, at a total price of $10,000 that the plaintiff paid upon signing the contract.

The defendant's company performed as agreed for two years. At the end of that period, the defendant sold the entire business to a local pilot, assigning to the pilot the balance of her contract with the plaintiff. All the defendant's employees agreed to work for the pilot.

After being notified of the assignment, the plaintiff sued the defendant, asserting that the defendant's sale of the business to the pilot was a breach of the defendant's obligation under the contract because crop-dusting involves a personal service. Which of the following would be the defendant's most effective argument in response to that claim?

(A) An assignment of contract rights includes a delegation of contract duties.

(B) The pilot had more expertise at crop-dusting than the defendant did.

(C) The defendant had never personally participated in dusting the plaintiff's fields.

(D) The defendant's assignment of the plaintiff's contract to the pilot did not impose an additional burden on the plaintiff since there was no change in price.

102. The shareholder was a major shareholder of the corporation, a retail company. In January, the corporation had cash-flow problems that placed it in danger of insolvency. On January 15, the corporation applied to the bank for a loan, but the bank said that it would lend the money requested only if the shareholder agreed to guarantee payment by the corporation. Fearful of losing her investment in the corporation, the shareholder promised the bank on January 16 that if the corporation did not repay the loan as agreed, the shareholder would do so. On January 17, the bank made the requested loan to the corporation.

On May 1, the corporation defaulted in payment, and the bank threatened to force the corporation into bankruptcy. On May 11, in an attempt to save the company, the corporation officials offered to turn some of the corporate assets over to the bank for sale at their market value, with the understanding that if the market value exceeded the amount that the corporation owed the bank, the bank would refund the excess to the corporation.

The bank rejected the corporation's offer of May 11 and asserted a claim against the shareholder for repayment of the loan. Which of the following additional facts or inferences, if it were the only one true, would be most likely to lead a court to find in favor of the shareholder?

(A) The shareholder's January 16 promise to pay the corporation's debt was induced by the fear that the corporation could not continue to exist without the loan.

(B) The shareholder's January 16 promise to pay the corporation's debt was not in writing.

(C) The shareholder received nothing of value in return for her January 16 promise to pay the corporation's debt.

(D) The assets that the corporation offered to turn over to the bank on May 11 were sufficient to repay the loan.

103. The landlord was the owner of a storefront building that she leased to the tenant for a three-year period. The tenant paid the rent for two years, and then he assigned the balance of his lease to a woman, advising the landlord in writing that the woman would be paying the rent from that point on. For the following five months, the woman paid the rent directly to the landlord. Then the woman moved out and stopped paying rent. If the landlord asserts a claim against the tenant for unpaid rent, which of the following arguments would be most effective in the tenant's defense?

(A) The landlord's accepting rent from the woman resulted in a novation.

(B) The landlord's accepting rent from the woman resulted in an accord and satisfaction.

(C) By accepting rent from the woman, the landlord impliedly consented to the tenant's assignment to the woman.

(D) A prohibition against assignment of a leasehold interest is a restraint against alienation.

104. The defendant owned a trucking company. His wife, the plaintiff, was a freelance book illustrator. When a book publisher contacted the defendant to discuss the transportation of his products, the defendant promised the plaintiff that he would get the publisher to employ her as a book illustrator for a year. During negotiations with the publisher, the defendant offered the publisher a lower rate if the publisher would do so.

The defendant and the publisher subsequently entered into a written one-year contract for the defendant to transport all the publisher's products at a specific low rate. At the same time, the publisher orally agreed that in return for the low rate that the defendant was giving him, he would employ the plaintiff for a year as his book illustrator, starting immediately.

When the plaintiff learned of the agreement, she notified all her clients that she could no longer work for them because illustrating books for the publisher would take all her time. For the next six months, the plaintiff did a satisfactory job as the publisher's book illustrator. Then, she and the defendant were divorced. Following the divorce, the defendant told the publisher that he was releasing him from his promise to employ the plaintiff and would give him the same low rate even if the publisher did not continue to employ the plaintiff for the rest of the year. The publisher thereupon discharged the plaintiff from his employ.

The plaintiff asserted a claim against the defendant for damages that resulted from his releasing the publisher from the promise to employ the plaintiff for a year. If the defendant's only defense is that he received no consideration for promising the plaintiff that the publisher would employ her for a year, which of the following would be the plaintiff's most effective argument in response to that defense?

(A) The publisher's promise to employ the plaintiff for one year was obtained by the defendant as a gift from the defendant to the plaintiff.

(B) The defendant made an irrevocable assignment to the plaintiff of rights under his contract with the publisher.

(C) No consideration is required to support a promise between husband and wife.

(D) The publisher's promise to hire the plaintiff for one year was given in return for the low rate that the defendant gave him.

105. When the seller inherited a valuable painting, he asked the buyer, an art dealer, if she was interested in buying it. On January 15, after looking at the painting, the buyer said that she would not have enough cash to purchase the painting until February 1. At the buyer's request, the seller signed a document containing a written offer to sell the painting to the buyer for $50,000 and a written promise to hold the offer open until February 2.

On January 20, the seller sold the painting to someone else for $45,000. The following day, after the buyer read about the sale in a newspaper, she went to the seller's home with $50,000 in cash and demanded that the seller sell her the painting for that price. The seller refused, saying that he was withdrawing his offer.

If the buyer asserts a claim for damages resulting from the seller's sale of the painting to another, the court should find for

(A) the buyer, because she accepted the seller's offer before the seller withdrew it.

(B) the buyer, because the seller promised in writing to hold the offer open until February 2.

(C) the seller, because a judgment for damages is not an appropriate remedy for breach of a contract to sell a unique chattel.

(D) the seller, because when the buyer tendered payment, she knew that the seller had already sold the painting.

106. The buyer operated a grocery store in which he sold fresh fish and other food items. The seller was a wholesaler of fresh fish. By a written contract, the buyer and the seller agreed that the buyer would purchase from the seller 100 kilograms per week of a fish known as "rock lurgid" at a specified price that was higher than the market price of "scmods," another type of fish. When the seller made the first delivery under the contract, however, the buyer refused to accept it, complaining that the fish delivered by the seller was scmods, a species unrelated to lurgid. The buyer was aware of the fact that scmods is frequently referred to as "rock lurgid."

The seller subsequently asserted a breach of contract claim against the buyer. At the trial, the seller attempted to testify that in the fresh fish industry, scmods is frequently referred to as "rock lurgid."

If the buyer objects, this testimony should be

(A) excluded, because it modifies the terms of a written contract that the buyer and the seller intended to be a complete record of their agreement.

(B) excluded, because the price to which the buyer and the seller agreed is higher than the market price of scmods.

(C) admitted, because the buyer was aware of the fact that scmods is frequently referred to as "rock lurgid."

(D) admitted, to explain the meaning of the term "rock lurgid" as used in the contract.

107. After serving in the military for 10 years, the plaintiff informed her father that she had gotten married and was retiring from military service. Glad to hear the news, the plaintiff's father said, "Because that's what I always hoped you would do, I'm going to give you a home as a wedding present." He showed the plaintiff plans for the construction of a house and promised that he would have it built on a lot that he owned and would deed it to her as soon as it was complete. The plaintiff was so pleased with the plans that her father showed her that she immediately canceled a contract that she had already made for the purchase of a home.

The following week, the plaintiff's father contacted the defendant, a builder. The plaintiff's father showed the defendant the plans and asked her to build a house according to those plans so that he could give it to his daughter as a wedding present. By a written contract, the plaintiff's father and the defendant agreed that the defendant would build on the father's lot according to the plans on a cost-plus-profit basis. The plaintiff's father immediately sent a copy of the contract and plans to the plaintiff.

The defendant subsequently informed the plaintiff's father that soil conditions would make it necessary to drive piles for the foundation, increasing costs by approximately 600 percent. At the defendant's suggestion, the plaintiff's father and the defendant agreed to the construction of a less expensive house instead, to be based on different plans. When the plaintiff learned about the change, she informed her father and the defendant that she was dissatisfied with their new agreement.

If the plaintiff asserts a claim against the defendant as a third-party beneficiary of the original contract between the plaintiff's father and the defendant, the defendant's most effective argument in defense would be that

(A) the plaintiff was a donee beneficiary because the house was being built as a wedding present for her.

(B) the plaintiff was a creditor beneficiary because the contract between her father and the defendant was made after her father promised the plaintiff that he would give her the house.

(C) the plaintiff did not rely to her detriment on her father's promise to give her a house built according to any particular plans.

(D) the plaintiff was not an intended third-party beneficiary of the contract between her father and the defendant.

108. On January 5, because he needed money to pay the rent on his store, the storeowner sent copies of the following letter to four possible buyers:

> I need to sell my heart-shaped diamond ring by January 15 for $1,500. I am making this offer to four possible buyers because all of you have admired the ring. If interested, please contact me before January 15.

On January 14, the storeowner received a letter from the first buyer agreeing to pay $1,500 for the ring. The storeowner did not respond to letter. On January 17, the storeowner received a letter from the second buyer agreeing to pay $1,700 for the ring. On January 17, the storeowner wrote to the second buyer saying, "I agree to the terms of your letter."

The first buyer asserts a claim against the storeowner on account of the storeowner's refusal to sell the ring to the first buyer for $1,500. The court should find for

(A) the storeowner, because the offer contained in the storeowner's letter of January 5 was revoked by his letter to the second buyer on January 17.

(B) the storeowner, because he did not accept the offer contained in the first buyer's letter.

(C) the first buyer, because the first buyer complied with the terms of the storeowner's offer.

(D) the first buyer, because the second buyer's letter was not received by the storeowner until after January 15.

109. The defendant was a retailer of home-gardening supplies. On March 1, the defendant entered into a written contract with a wholesaler of seeds. According to the terms, the wholesaler was to furnish the defendant with seeds in 10-pound bags at a specified price. The contract provided that for a period of one year, the defendant would purchase all its seeds from the wholesaler and that the wholesaler would furnish all the seeds required by the defendant. It provided further that the defendant would advise the wholesaler of its requirements by the first of each month, and that the wholesaler would make delivery by the end of that month. The contract was silent about the right to assign or delegate.

Upon signing the contract on March 1, the defendant notified the wholesaler of its seed requirements for that month. The wholesaler made a delivery to the defendant on March 17. Prior to April 1, the defendant notified the wholesaler of its requirements for April. On April 20, the wholesaler sold its entire business to the plaintiff, including its contract with the defendant, and notified the defendant of the sale the same day. On April 24, after the defendant received notice of the assignment, the plaintiff delivered the seed that the defendant ordered from the wholesaler.

The next day, the defendant wrote to the plaintiff, enclosing a check for the seeds

the plaintiff had delivered and demanding that the plaintiff assure the defendant that it would be able to meet the defendant's seed requirements in the future. On June 1, not having heard from the plaintiff, the defendant notified the wholesaler and the plaintiff that it was canceling the contract.

If the plaintiff asserts a claim against the defendant for breach of contract, the court should find for

(A) the plaintiff, because the defendant failed to order seeds as required by contract.

(B) the plaintiff, because there was no indication that the terms of the contract would not be performed by the plaintiff.

(C) the defendant, because the plaintiff failed to furnish assurances as demanded by the defendant.

(D) the defendant, because requirements contracts are not assignable without consent of the purchaser.

110. The homeowner hired a painting contractor to paint the homeowner's residence, entering into a valid written contract with the contractor that fixed the price of the job at $5,000 and provided that the contractor would deliver a "satisfactory result." Because the contractor wished to give his daughter the money that he received from the job as a wedding gift, a clause of the contract directed the homeowner to pay the money directly to the daughter. After the contractor finished painting the house, he sent the homeowner a bill for $5,000. When the homeowner received the bill, he called the contractor and complained about the paint job, saying that he did not think it was "satisfactory" as required by the contract. He said, "I've got half a mind not to pay you at all, but if you'll take $4,500, I'm willing to call it square." The contractor reluctantly agreed to accept $4,500 payable directly to him because he needed cash. The

homeowner paid the $4,500 to the contractor, who did not give any part of it to the daughter.

The daughter learned about the contract between the contractor and the homeowner after the contractor received payment from the homeowner. Which of the following most accurately describes the rights of the daughter?

(A) The daughter is entitled to collect $5,000 from the homeowner.

(B) The daughter is entitled to collect $4,500 from the contractor.

(C) The daughter is entitled to collect $5,000 from the homeowner or $4,500 from the contractor, but not both.

(D) The daughter is not entitled to collect anything from either party.

111. When the landowner's daughter told him that she was getting married, the landowner was so happy that he promised to deed her a parcel of realty that he owned and to have a house built on it for her as a wedding present. The following day, the landowner entered into a written contract with the defendant, a building contractor, for the construction of a house on the landowner's land. The landowner later gave his daughter a copy of the contract, and, as a result, she canceled a contract into which she had previously entered for the purchase of a home. As a result of an argument between the landowner and the defendant, the defendant never built the house.

The landowner later deeds the land to his daughter, and she asserts a claim against the defendant for failure to fulfill the obligations under his contract with the landowner. The court should find for

(A) the daughter, because the landowner intended for her to benefit from his contract with the defendant.

(B) the defendant, because the contract called for personal services.

(C) the defendant, because the daughter is an incidental beneficiary.

(D) the defendant, because the daughter is a donee beneficiary.

112. The defendant was an investor who frequently bought and sold real estate on his own account. He had purchased a parcel of realty for $100,000 and was considering selling it. On September 1, the plaintiff, another real estate investor, asked whether the defendant would be willing to accept $125,000 for the property. The defendant said that he would, but only if payment was in cash. When the plaintiff said that he would need a month or two to raise that kind of money, the defendant wrote the following on a sheet of paper and signed it:

> I hereby offer to sell my realty to the plaintiff for $125,000 cash. I promise to hold this offer open until November 1, and I further promise that I will not sell the property to anyone else before then. This is a firm offer.

On October 20, the defendant sold the property to another person for $110,000 and wrote the plaintiff a note in which he said, "I hereby withdraw my offer to sell you the property for $125,000." On October 25, the plaintiff purchased the property from the other person for $135,000.

If the plaintiff asserts a claim against the defendant for damages resulting from the defendant's sale of the property to the other person, the court should find for

(A) the defendant, because he received no consideration for his promise to keep the offer open.

(B) the defendant, because he sold the realty to the other person more than 30 days after promising the plaintiff to keep the offer open.

(C) the plaintiff, because the document that the defendant signed on September 1 was a firm offer in writing.

(D) the plaintiff, because the plaintiff customarily engaged in buying and selling real estate.

113. When he won the state lottery, the defendant bought a new home and decided to have it landscaped by a well-known landscape architect. After investigating several sources, the defendant learned that the landscaper was one of the most famous landscape architects in the world. Following a series of discussions, the defendant and the landscaper entered into a written contract that called for the landscaper to design and execute a landscaping plan for the defendant's property at a total price of $90,000. Upon completion of the job, the defendant was to pay $80,000 of this sum directly to the landscaper. The defendant agreed to pay the balance of $10,000 to the plaintiff because the landscaper was indebted to the plaintiff for that sum. A clause of the contract provided that "there shall be no assignment of rights under this contract."

The landscaper's design called for a moat to be dug around the defendant's house and planted with aquatic plants. Although the landscaper completed the rest of the job himself, he hired an earthmoving subcontractor to dig the moat, which the earthmoving subcontractor did in complete conformity with the landscaper's plan. When the job was completed, the plaintiff executed a document purporting to assign his rights under the contract to another person. The entire job was completed in a reasonably workmanlike manner, but the defendant refused to make any payment under the contract.

The plaintiff asserts a claim against the defendant for $10,000, which the plaintiff claims the defendant owes him under the contract. Which of the following would be the defendant's most effective argument in defense against that claim?

(A) The plaintiff has made a valid assignment of his rights under the contract.

(B) The plaintiff was not a party to the contract.

(C) The plaintiff was a mere incidental beneficiary of the contract.

(D) There was no mutuality of obligation between the defendant and the plaintiff.

114. A manufacturer needed a new factory and purchased a parcel of realty on which he wished to have it constructed. After negotiation, the manufacturer entered into a valid written contract with a licensed builder. Pursuant to its terms, the builder was to construct a two-story building on the manufacturer's realty according to specifications furnished by the manufacturer, at a total price of $250,000 to be paid in full upon completion of the building. The builder completed the building, and the manufacturer paid him $250,000, but subsequently the manufacturer learned that the building failed to conform to the specifications. As a result, it would not serve the manufacturer's purpose. The building had the same value as if constructed in conformity with the specifications, but it would cost the manufacturer $12,000 to make it conform to the specifications. Because of an increase in the costs of construction, it would cost $350,000 to construct a new building in conformity with the specifications.

If the manufacturer asserts a claim against the builder for breach of contract, the manufacturer should recover

(A) nothing, because the building had the same value as if built in conformity with the specifications.

(B) $12,000 (the cost of making the building conform to the specifications).

(C) $100,000 (the difference between the contract price and the cost of having a new building constructed in accordance with the specifications).

(D) $250,000 (the contract price).

115. The seller wanted to sell his piano. Because four buyers had all expressed interest in it, the seller wrote and signed the following letter on May 1, sending a photocopy to each of the persons named:

> Dear Four Potential Buyers:
>
> I know that you are all interested in buying my piano and I need to sell it. I therefore promise to sell it to whichever of you makes the highest offer prior to June 15.
>
> (signed)

The seller's letter of May 1 to the four buyers is best described as

(A) a firm offer.

(B) an invitation for offers.

(C) an option to purchase that was given to Able, Baker, Carr, and Davis but could only be exercised by the first to respond.

(D) an auction.

116. On January 17, a homeowner hired a builder to build a new greenhouse on his property. After negotiation, they entered into a valid written contract that fixed the price at $8,000. Work was to be completed by March 1. On February 1, when the greenhouse was one-quarter complete, it was totally destroyed in a freak snowstorm. The damage made it impossible to complete construction by March 1. Because he was scheduled to begin construction on a new hotel on March 2, the builder informed the homeowner that he would perform no further work on the greenhouse. The homeowner subsequently hired a second builder, who agreed to build the greenhouse for $9,000. The first builder sued the homeowner on a quasi-contract theory, seeking compensation for the services that he rendered prior to the storm. The first builder is entitled to receive

(A) the reasonable value of the work performed by the first builder, less the difference between the price that the homeowner had agreed to pay the first builder and the price that the homeowner agreed to pay the second builder.

(B) the reasonable value of the work performed by the first builder.

(C) one-quarter of the price that the homeowner agreed to pay the first builder for the completed greenhouse.

(D) nothing, since the homeowner has received no benefit from the first builder's work.

117. The buyer agreed to purchase 300 commercial-grade metal screws from the seller by a written contract that provided that the buyer would make payment prior to inspection. The screws were delivered by truck and were in a closed box. The buyer paid the truck driver before inspecting the screws. Upon subsequent inspection, however, the buyer discovered the screws were of domestic rather than commercial grade. The buyer called the seller, offering to return the screws and demanding return of his money. The seller refused to take the screws back or give the buyer a refund. Which of the following is most correct about the effect of the buyer's payment prior to inspection?

(A) The terms of the contract required an unconditional acceptance prior to inspection, and payment constituted unconditional acceptance.

(B) Even if the contract provision calling for payment prior to inspection was invalid, payment resulted in a waiver of the right to inspect prior to acceptance.

(C) Payment did not impair the buyer's right to inspect the goods prior to acceptance.

(D) Payment constituted acceptance, but the buyer was entitled to revoke acceptance within a reasonable time thereafter.

118. On August 1, a cell phone manufacturer posted a notice in the employee lounge offering $200 to any employee who could design a "killer app" by November 1, in time for the Christmas gift-buying season. A designer employed by the manufacturer saw the notice and immediately began working on a new phone application in his spare time. On September 1, the manufacturer removed the old sign and posted a new notice that said, "The offer of a cash prize for a 'killer app' is hereby withdrawn." On October 1, the designer submitted his design for a "killer app," which was eventually adopted for use by the manufacturer. The manufacturer refused to pay any money to the designer. If the designer asserts a claim against the manufacturer in a jurisdiction that accepts the view expressed in the Restatement of Contracts, Second, the designer's most effective argument will be that

(A) a bilateral contract was formed when the designer submitted the design that the manufacturer eventually adopted.

(B) the designer relied on the offer contained in the first notice by working on the design in his spare time prior to September 1.

(C) the promises contained in the first notice could not be withdrawn until November 1.

(D) the company's attempt to withdraw its offer was unconscionable.

119. A hiker was hiking in the woods when she heard a cry for help. She then saw a climber hanging from the edge of a cliff, clearly about to fall. The hiker ran to the cliff's edge and pulled the climber to safety. The climber was so happy that he said, "In token for saving my life, I promise to pay you $100 the first of next month." A few days later, the climber died falling from another cliff. The

jurisdiction has a "Good Samaritan" statute. If the hiker institutes an action against the executor of the climber's estate for the $100 that the climber promised to pay her, the court should find for

(A) the hiker, because the jurisdiction has a "Good Samaritan" statute.

(B) the hiker, because she detrimentally relied on the climber's promise to pay her.

(C) the climber's executor, because the climber's promise was unsupported by consideration.

(D) the climber's executor, because it is impossible to calculate the value of the hiker's services.

120. A parts dealer agreed to deliver a special bumper to a car collector's home for $150. After the contract was signed, the dealer called the collector and told him that he would not deliver the special bumper as agreed. The collector succeeded in buying another one like it in another town for $130, incurring reasonable travel expenses of $20 in going to pick it up. In an action by the collector against the dealer, the court should find for

(A) the collector, in the sum of $20.

(B) the collector, in the sum of $40.

(C) the collector, in the sum of $170.

(D) the dealer.

121. When his daughter was about to turn 21, a builder decided he wanted to give her some money so she could buy a new car. Consequently, the builder entered into a written contract with a homeowner to build a new addition. In return, the homeowner agreed to pay the sum of $5,000 to the builder's daughter on her birthday upon completion of the work to his satisfaction. A few weeks before her birthday, the builder's daughter married a circus clown, and the builder did not approve. The

builder asked the homeowner to pay the $5,000 to him directly, which he did. On her birthday, the builder's daughter learned for the first time of the written agreement between her father and the homeowner. The daughter then commences a lawsuit against the homeowner. Will the lawsuit succeed?

(A)  No, because she gave no consideration for the homeowner's promise to pay her.

(B)  No, because the payment by the homeowner to the builder was the result of an effective oral modification of the written contract.

(C)  Yes, because the daughter is an intended donee beneficiary of the contract between the builder and the homeowner.

(D)  Yes, because the written contract between the builder and the homeowner operated as an assignment to the daughter of the builder's right to payment.

122.  By a written agreement, a university agreed to buy 100 air conditioners from a company at a price of $250 each, FOB the company's factory. On June 1, the company loaded the air conditioners on a truck owned by an independent trucking company. The company informed the university that the air conditioners were on their way. Later that day, the company assigned its rights under the contract to a parts manufacturer to which it owed money. The university consented to this assignment. On June 2, en route to the university, the truck fell off a bridge and the entire shipment was destroyed. In an action by the university against the company for damages resulting from the non-delivery of the air conditioners, which of the following would be the company's most effective argument in defense?

(A)  There has been a valid assignment to the parts manufacturer.

(B)  The risk of loss passed to the university when the air conditioners were loaded onto the truck.

(C)  The risk of loss passed to the trucking company when the air conditioners were loaded onto the trucking company's truck.

(D)  Performance of the contract was made impossible by the destruction of the air conditioners.

123.  The seller's grandfather left her a collection of the first 30 Super Jimmy comics, the only Super Jimmy comics in existence. The seller sold some comics and pop art in her art gallery, so she made up a catalog showing pictures of the 30 comics, and on August 1, she sent a copy of the catalog to a comic book dealer with a note:

> I know how much you love Super Jimmy, so I wanted to give you a chance to buy some of the comics before I offer them to any other dealers or collectors. The price is $200 per comic book, no matter how many you buy. E-mail me your order within two weeks, or I'll put them on the market.

On August 2, the dealer sent the seller an e-mail that said, "I accept your offer to sell Super Jimmy Number 30 for $200. I will come to your house in two days to pick up the comic and will pay you cash at that time." On August 3, after receiving the e-mail, the seller telephoned the dealer and said that because of favorable publicity that the collection had received, she would not sell Super Jimmy Number 30 for less than $300. The dealer agreed on the telephone to pay $300 for comic Number 30.

On August 4, the dealer sent an e-mail to the seller that said, "I accept your offer to sell Super Jimmy comics 1 through 29 for $200 each. I will pick up the comic books tomorrow and will pay for them at that time."

On August 5, the dealer showed up at the seller's home and tendered payment of $200 each for all 30 comic books, but the seller refused to sell her any of the comics except for Number 30, for which the seller insisted the agreed price was $300. The dealer left without buying it. The dealer sued for an order directing the seller to sell the dealer comics 1 through 29 for $200 each. Which of the following would be the seller's most effective argument in defense against that action?

(A) Since the dealer is a comic book dealer, there is an adequate remedy at law.

(B) The seller's August 1 promise to keep the offer open for two weeks was unsupported by consideration.

(C) The dealer's e-mail of August 2 was a rejection of the seller's offer to sell comic books 1 through 29.

(D) The catalog and the seller's cover letter were mere invitations to negotiate.

124. An importer of arts and crafts products from Russia sold his products mainly to department stores and import shops. To keep his sales force down, the importer did most of his selling by sending catalogs describing products and prices to prospective customers and taking orders by mail on forms provided with the catalogs. The forms contained the phrase "10 percent discount on COD orders only." After receiving one of the catalogs, a coffee shop owner decided to order some Russian coffeepots for sale in her store. The shop owner had been doing business with the importer on an "open account" basis. On July 27, she typed the following across the importer's order form: "Send immediately 50 Russian coffeepots at 10 percent discount. Payment within 10 days of receipt and acceptance." The importer received the order on July 29. On July 30, the importer shipped 50 coffeepots to the shop owner, who received and accepted them on August 3. On July 31, the importer wrote to the shop owner, "I am shipping pursuant to your request and will expect payment within

10 days. Since discounts apply only to COD shipments, you are herewith billed at full price." The shop owner received the letter and enclosed bill on August 4. On August 5, the shop owner sent the importer a check in payment of the amount billed, less 10 percent. If the importer asserts a claim against the shop owner for the balance of the amount billed, the court should find for

(A) the importer, because the shop owner's order was on the importer's order form.

(B) the importer, because the shop owner was aware that the importer's catalog and order form specified that the 10 percent discount applied only to COD shipments.

(C) the shop owner, because she had been doing business with the importer on an "open account" basis.

(D) the shop owner, because the importer accepted her offer to purchase at a 10 percent discount.

125. A landowner wanted to open a miniature golf course on a parcel of real estate that he owned. After negotiation, the landowner hired a builder to build the golf course and a waterslide. The landowner and the builder entered into a written contract by which the builder agreed to begin construction on August 1, to be finished with everything except the waterslide by November 1, and to complete construction of the waterslide by December 15. The contract price was $150,000 to be paid as follows: $50,000 on August 1; $50,000 upon completion of everything but the waterslide; and the balance of $50,000 upon completion of the waterslide. The builder began work on August 1, after receiving $50,000 from the landowner. By November 1, the builder completed construction of everything but the waterslide in accordance with the specifications. The landowner paid $50,000 to the builder on November 1, and the builder began construction of the waterslide, but before it was completed, the builder

informed the landowner that he would not finish the job. Which of the following statements is correct concerning the landowner's rights against the builder?

(A)   The landowner may recover all payments that he has made to the builder.

(B)   The landowner may recover from the builder the reasonable cost of completing the waterslide.

(C)   The landowner may recover all payments that he has made to the builder and the reasonable cost of completing the waterslide.

(D)   The landowner is not entitled to recover the payments or the reasonable cost of completing the waterslide.

126.   The buyer went to a car dealer to look at some of the cars on display. Selecting a car, he began negotiating with the dealer. The dealer offered to sell him the car that was on display in the showroom, but the buyer said that he wanted to buy a new one. The dealer explained that the display model was the only one she had, but she was planning to order some new ones from the manufacturer anyway and would order one for the buyer if he agreed to purchase it. The buyer and the dealer entered into a written contract for the sale of a new car at a price of $10,000, to be paid on delivery within two weeks. The following day, the dealer ordered 10 new cars from the manufacturer, and the buyer purchased materials and began building a garage for the car.

One week after contracting with the buyer, the dealer notified him that the new car was ready for delivery, and the buyer went immediately to the dealer's showroom to take delivery of it. The buyer tendered his own personal check in payment of the purchase price, but the dealer refused to accept it. Which of the following most accurately describes the legal rights and obligations of the parties upon such refusal by the dealer?

(A)   The buyer's tender of a check discharged the dealer's obligation under the contract, since an agreement that is silent as to the manner of payment is presumed to call for payment in cash.

(B)   The buyer's tender of a check discharged the dealer's obligation under the contract unless the buyer tendered payment in cash immediately upon being informed of the dealer's refusal to accept the buyer's check.

(C)   The buyer's tender of a check did not discharge the dealer's obligation under the contract, but the dealer's obligation will be discharged if the buyer fails to tender cash within a reasonable time.

(D)   The dealer's refusal to accept a check discharged the buyer's obligation under the contract, since an agreement that is silent as to the manner of payment is presumed to call for payment in any manner current in the ordinary course of business.

127.   In preparation for a big convention to be held on June 16, the convention committee ordered 500 bobblehead dolls from the company at a total price of $500, paying for them in advance. Because the bobbleheads were to be given to conventioneers as souvenirs, they were to be imprinted with the name and slogan of the convention and were to be delivered to the committee on or before June 15. The company and the committee entered into a written contract containing the above terms on May 1. The company tendered 475 bobbleheads to the committee on June 15. The committee instituted an action against the company for breach of contract. If only one of the following additional facts were true, which would furnish the company with its most effective defense to that action?

(A)   The company was unable to obtain necessary materials from its suppliers

in time for production of 500 bobbleheads by June 15.

(B) The committee failed to serve the
company with notice of its intention
to sue before instituting the action.

(C) Only 400 conventioneers attended the
convention.

(D) On June 1, the company advised the
committee that it would only be able
to deliver 475 bobbleheads, and the
committee orally agreed to reduce the
order to that number.

128. On June 1, a licensed real estate broker
entered into a written contract with a homeowner. According to the contract, the broker was given the exclusive right to sell the
homeowner's home at a price of $100,000
for a period of three months. The homeowner agreed to pay the broker a 7 percent
commission "upon transfer of title." The
broker went to work looking for a buyer.

On August 1, the homeowner entered into a
written contract with a buyer for the purchase and sale of the homeowner's home
at a price of $98,000, with title to close on
December 1. The broker was unaware of the
transaction and did not participate in it. On
November 1, the buyer informed the homeowner that he would not be going through
with the deal.

The broker sued the homeowner for a 7 percent commission based on the homeowner's
contract with the buyer. Which of the following would be the homeowner's most
effective argument in defense against the
broker's claim?

(A) The price that the buyer agreed to pay
for the purchase of the homeowner's
home was $98,000.

(B) Transfer of title was not to take place
until after the three-month period of
the broker's exclusive right to sell.

(C) As a result of the buyer's conduct,
transfer of title never took place.

(D) The broker did not participate in the
formation of the homeowner's contract with the buyer.

129. When the plaintiff was accepted to law
school, her mother was so proud of the plaintiff that she said, "If you successfully complete your first year, I'll buy all your books
for the following two years and give you
$250 for each 'A.'" The plaintiff's mother
died while the plaintiff was in her first year
of law school, but the plaintiff succeeded in
earning two "A"s in her first year and completed school in two additional years. If the
plaintiff asserts a claim against her mother's
executrix for the cost of the books that she
purchased in her second and third year of
law school, which of the following would be
the executrix's most effective argument in
defense against the plaintiff's claim?

(A) The agreement between the plaintiff
and her mother was divisible.

(B) The agreement between the plaintiff
and her mother was not in writing.

(C) The mother's offer was for payment of
a cash bonus.

(D) The mother's promise was unsupported
by consideration.

130. A man developed a new phone application
that allowed users to follow the records of
their favorite college teams. A company
liked the application and offered the man
a job as an in-house designer and 30 percent of the application's revenues if the man
would give the company the exclusive right
to market and sell the application. The man
and the company agreed to the arrangement.
Soon thereafter, the man assigned his rights
in the contract to the plaintiff in return for
some music equipment. A week after that,
the man assigned his rights under the contract to a software company.

Three months later, the company offered to pay the man $50,000 for all rights to the application if the man would consent to a mutual rescission of the contract. The man accepted the offer and received a payment of $50,000. If the plaintiff subsequently institutes an action against the company for a sum equivalent to 30 percent of the revenues derived from the sale of the application, the court should find for

(A) the company, because the rights under which the plaintiff is claiming were subsequently assigned to the software company.

(B) the company, because the company was unaware of the assignment to the plaintiff at the time it paid $50,000 to the man.

(C) the company, because the right that the man purported to assign to the plaintiff was neither identified nor existing at the time of the purported assignment.

(D) the plaintiff, because he gave value for the right that the man assigned to him.

131. A woman, who had a son and daughter, agreed to deed to her daughter her farm so long as the daughter agreed to allow her brother to live on it for as long as he wished. The daughter agreed, but she did not tell her brother about their mother's condition that he be allowed to live on the farm.

The woman's sister lived in the same town. She had always wanted the woman's son, her only nephew, to live near her, so she wrote him a letter, telling him that if he moved to the town, she would give him her estate when she died. The son, who knew the farm was deeded to his sister, told his sister that if she would let him live on the farm until their aunt died, he would give his sister half of what he received from the aunt. She agreed, and her brother moved onto the farm. The aunt passed away soon thereafter.

The aunt's will left her entire estate to the son, but the son refused to share any portion of it with his sister. If the daughter asserts a claim against her brother for a share of the inheritance that he received from their aunt, a court should find for

(A) the daughter, because her brother is estopped from denying the existence of an enforceable contract between him and his sister.

(B) the daughter, because her brother promised to share the inheritance with her if she promised to allow him to live on the farm until their aunt's death.

(C) the son, because his sister's promise to their mother created an implied condition precedent to her brother's obligation to share the inheritance with his sister.

(D) the son, because his promise to his sister was not supported by consideration.

132. The homeowner hired the defendant to maintain his lawn, agreeing to pay him $50 per month for certain specified services. Two months later, the homeowner sold his house to the plaintiff. At the closing of title, the homeowner handed the plaintiff the original memorandum of his agreement with the defendant and executed an assignment to the plaintiff of his rights thereunder. The defendant continued rendering services as agreed for an additional six months, receiving a check for $50 from the plaintiff each month. Then, the defendant notified the plaintiff that he would no longer be able to work on the lawn.

The plaintiff sued the defendant for breaching the agreement contained in the memorandum. The court should find for

(A) the defendant, because the payment by the plaintiff did not result in a novation.

(B) the defendant, because his only agreement was with the homeowner.

(C) the defendant, because no consideration flowed from the plaintiff to the homeowner in exchange for the memorandum.

(D) the plaintiff, as assignee of the agreement between the homeowner and the defendant.

133. When the homeowner purchased her home, she obtained a fire insurance policy. The policy provided that if the home was destroyed or seriously damaged by fire, the insurance company would pay "living expenses necessitated by the loss" until the homeowner's house was rebuilt or she acquired another house, but in no event for a period in excess of 90 days. The policy stated that since it was often impracticable to distinguish between normal living expenses and those necessitated by fire loss, the insurance company's liability for "living expenses necessitated by the loss" was fixed at $50 per day.

Subsequently, the homeowner's home was seriously damaged by fire. The homeowner moved into a hotel and entered into a written contract with a contractor for repairs to her home. The contract required payment in advance by the homeowner and completion of repairs by the contractor within 60 days. One of its clauses provided that if the contractor failed to complete the job on time, the contractor would pay the homeowner the sum of $50 per day as liquidated damages. It took the contractor 70 days to complete the job.

The insurance company paid the homeowner $3,000 (60 days at $50 per day), but refused to pay the additional $500 for the 10-day period caused by the contractor's late performance. If the homeowner sues the insurance company for $500, the court should find for

(A) the homeowner, because the insurance company agreed to pay $50 per day until the homeowner's house was reconstructed.

(B) the homeowner, because she can establish that her "living expenses necessitated by the loss" exceeded whatever amount she was entitled to receive from the contractor.

(C) the homeowner, because at the time the fire insurance policy was issued to the homeowner, it reasonably appeared that the homeowner would expend approximately $50 per day in "living expenses necessitated by the loss" in the event of fire damage to her home.

(D) the insurance company, because the homeowner is estopped by the liquidated damages clause in her contract with the contractor from asserting that her "living expenses necessitated by the loss" exceeded $50 per day.

134. Proud of a local painter's accomplishments, the town council voted to erect a statue commemorating the painter's victory over his social and economic disadvantages. Pursuant to town ordinances and regulations, bids were accepted from several artists, including the sculptor. Because the sculptor's work was relatively unknown, she attempted to make her bid more attractive to the council by including a guarantee that her work would be satisfactory. On February 1, the town council entered into a written contract with the sculptor, hiring her to create the statue and agreeing to pay her $5,000 upon its installation on the steps of the town hall on or before June 30. A clause in the contract provided, "It is expressly understood that the personal satisfaction of the mayor is a condition precedent to the council's obligation to make payment hereunder. Upon completion of the statue, it shall be made available for inspection by said mayor. If said mayor is unsatisfied with the work, he shall notify the sculptor immediately,

and the contract shall be canceled without liability of any party."

The sculptor sculpted a likeness of the painter in farmer's overalls with a paintbrush in his teeth, which she completed on June 10. The painter had been arrested in another state on May 30, however, and charged with possession of a dangerous drug. His trial was scheduled for September 10.

At the same time, an art collector came to town, saw the statue, and offered to buy it from the sculptor for $6,000. Fearful that the painter's pending trial would induce the mayor to reject her statue, the sculptor immediately accepted the offer, notifying the town council on June 10 that she would not be submitting a statue for the mayor's approval. In an action by the town council against the sculptor, the court should find for

(A)  the town council, because the sculptor has committed an anticipatory breach.

(B)  the town council, because the statue that the sculptor created might have met with the mayor's satisfaction.

(C)  the town council, because the price that she received from the art collector exceeded $5,000.

(D)  the sculptor, because the town council's promise under the contract was illusory.

135.  By a written contract, the owner of a bar agreed to purchase 200 pounds of large pickled eggs from a farmer at a specified price. A term of the contract provided that "payment shall be due immediately on delivery and prior to inspection of the shipment." When a box containing the eggs was delivered, the bar owner paid the agreed price without inspecting its contents. One hour later, the bar owner opened the box and discovered that it contained small eggs rather than large eggs. When the bar owner called the farmer to ask that the farmer exchange the small eggs for large ones, the

farmer refused. The bar owner repackaged the eggs and returned them to the farmer. Subsequently, the bar owner asserted a claim against the farmer for breach of contract.

If the bar owner succeeds in an action against the farmer for breach of contract, a court is most likely to

(A)  issue an order directing the farmer to deliver 200 pounds of large pickled eggs as required by the contract.

(B)  award damages consisting of the difference between the value of large eggs and small eggs.

(C)  award damages consisting of the purchase price plus the difference between the contract price and the market price for large eggs.

(D)  require the farmer to return the money that the bar owner paid.

136.  The buyer, who was planning to go to law school, told the seller that he might need some law books. The seller had recently inherited a law library, so he compiled a list of the books in the collection and mailed it to the buyer on July 5 with a note that said, "Interested in buying?" The buyer wrote back to the seller and told him that he would buy the books if the seller delivered them to his home on September 1.

The seller received the letter on Wednesday, July 9, and immediately responded by writing, "I accept your offer to buy my library and will deliver it to you as you require." He signed the letter and mailed it properly addressed to the buyer, but due to a fire in the post office, it was never delivered. When the seller delivered the books on September 1, the buyer refused to accept them.

If the seller instituted an action against the buyer for breach of contract, which of the following statements is most correct about the seller's letter of July 9?

(A) It bound both parties to a unilateral contract when it was mailed.

(B) It formed a bilateral contract when mailed because the buyer chose the mail as the medium of communication.

(C) The letter would have constituted an acceptance if it had been received, but because it was not received, no contract was formed.

(D) The seller's mailing of the letter did not prevent the buyer from withdrawing his offer.

137. Because the buyer was arranging to move his family across the country on April 20, the buyer insisted that the contract for his new home contain a liquidated damages clause. The clause provided that if the new home was not ready for occupancy on April 20, the seller would pay the buyer $75 for each day thereafter that it remained unavailable for occupancy. When the buyer and his family moved on April 20, the home was not ready for occupancy. As a result, the buyer and his family had to stay at a motel. On May 1, the seller advised the buyer that he did not intend to go through with the sale of this house. On May 10, the buyer instituted an action against the seller for specific performance and damages pursuant to the liquidated damages clause.

With respect to the buyer's demand for damages pursuant to the contract's liquidated damages clause, the court's finding will turn on whether

(A) the motel at which the buyer stayed charged a rate that was commercially reasonable.

(B) the buyer could have avoided staying at a motel by making a reasonable attempt to mitigate damages.

(C) at the time the contract was formed, the sum of $75 per day was reasonably

related to what the parties believed the buyer's living expenses would be.

(D) the buyer's purpose in insisting on a liquidated damages clause was to encourage the seller to vacate the premises on time.

138. A man, who had been studying the writings of various saints, decided to sell all his worldly possessions, give the money to charity, and hike for a while to seek insight and spiritual fulfillment. After about a month, the man became ill and collapsed into unconsciousness. When he awoke, he was in the home of a retired surgeon who now lived like a hermit in the mountains, and who had found him in a helpless condition. As the doctor fed garlic soup to the man, the man said, "I have no money. I can never pay you for any of this." The doctor replied, "I'm not doing this for money."

In the next week, the doctor fed the man and gave him medical treatment. When the man was well enough to travel, the doctor borrowed an old pickup truck from a distant neighbor and drove the man to the house of the man's mother. The following week, after the man told his mother what the doctor did for him, the man's mother wrote the doctor: "In gratitude for the services that you rendered my son, I hereby promise to pay you $350.00 when I get my dividend check next month." Before the dividend check arrived, however, both the man's mother and the doctor died. The doctor's administrator advised the mother's husband of the letter that his wife had sent and indicated that he intended to make a claim against her estate for $350.

After a discussion with the administrator, in which the administrator agreed not to assert a claim against the mother's estate, the husband prepared a document that read, "In consideration of services rendered by the doctor to my wife's son, and of the administrator's promise to make no claim against the estate of my wife, I hereby agree to pay $350.00 to the doctor's estate." After signing the document, the husband handed it to the administrator. The husband never paid anything to the estate, however, and the administrator instituted suit against him. The husband defended on the ground that his promise to pay $350 was not supported by consideration.

Were the services rendered by the doctor sufficient consideration for the husband's promise?

(A) They are sufficient consideration because they imposed a preexisting moral obligation on the husband.

(B) They are not sufficient consideration because they were not requested by the husband.

(C) The question of whether or not they are sufficient consideration depends on whether the husband received any material benefit from them.

(D) The question of whether or not they are sufficient consideration depends upon whether the reasonable value of the services approximated $350.

139. On September 10, the company, a well-known publisher of law books, posted a notice in the law school bookstore that it would award $10,000 to the student with the highest grade point average.

A student, who had just begun her final year at the law school, saw the notice. Her grades already placed her toward the top of her class, but she resolved to work harder than ever before in an attempt to win the company's award. On September 20, she mailed a letter to the company saying, "I accept your offer for the award and will do my best to win it." The following May, because of budget cutbacks, the company posted a new notice at the law school stating that it would not be presenting any awards.

In a jurisdiction that applies the Restatement of Contracts, 2d rule, a court's decision as to

whether the company's offer was effectively revoked by the notice posted in May will most likely depend on whether

(A) the student saw the second notice before taking her exams.

(B) the second notice was as large and as conspicuously posted as the first.

(C) the student's letter of September 20 was effective when mailed or when received.

(D) the student made extra efforts in her studies in reliance on the September 10 notice.

140. When a landowner's daughter and a painting contractor's son announced that they were getting married, the landowner and the contractor decided to give them a house as a wedding present. On January 1, the two men entered into a written agreement with each other, pursuant to which they were to have a house built on the landowner's lot, with the landowner and the contractor each paying half the cost. It was further agreed that after completion of the house, the contractor would pay the landowner $10,000 as his share of the cost of the lot, and the landowner would convey the lot to their children.

On February 2, the two men entered into a written contract with a builder. The contract called for payment in installments, each payment being due upon completion of a specified stage of building. In addition to its other terms, the contract contained a clause providing that as each payment came due, the builder would bill and collect half the payment from the landowner and half from the contractor. In the contract, the builder agreed that neither would be responsible to him for more than half the price.

On March 3, the contractor entered into a separate contract with the builder. Pursuant to this contract, the builder hired the contractor as a subcontractor to do all the painting required in connection with the construction of the house. Because the house was being built for his son, the contractor agreed to do the job for $3,000, although his work was worth $5,000. The $3,000 was to be deducted from the final payment that the contractor would owe the builder for construction of the house.

In April, the contractor became ill. Because he could no longer work, he sold his painting business to his son, a competent and licensed painting contractor, for about half of what it was actually worth. As one of the terms of the contract of sale, the contractor's son promised to do all the painting work on the house that the builder was constructing. The contractor notified the builder of his agreement with his son. When the house was ready to be painted, however, the contractor's son informed the builder that he would not paint it.

The landowner then decided he did not want to convey the property to his daughter and the contractor's son. The contractor's son then sued the landowner. Which of the following arguments would furnish the landowner with his strongest defense?

(A) The contractor's son did not rely or assent to the contract of January 1 between the landowner and the contractor.

(B) The contractor's son's painting of the house was a condition precedent to the landowner's obligation to convey.

(C) The contractor's son was only an incidental beneficiary of the January 1 contract between the landowner and the contractor since the landowner's primary intention was to benefit his daughter.

(D) The contract that the contractor made with the builder on March 3 was a breach of a fiduciary obligation that the contractor owed the landowner.

141. The seller and the buyer had been friends for years. The seller was the owner of a rare guitar, which the buyer had offered to buy from her on several occasions but which the seller had never been willing to sell. On the buyer's birthday, the seller and the buyer went out for dinner and drinks. After dinner, the seller continued drinking until she was somewhat intoxicated. During their conversation, the seller said, "As a birthday present, I've decided that I'm going to sell you my guitar for $500. And just to make sure that I don't change my mind after I sober up, I'll put it in writing." With that, she wrote on a paper napkin, "We agree to the sale of my guitar to the buyer for $500, COD," and signed her name at the bottom. The buyer also signed the napkin and put it in her purse. The following day, the buyer tendered $500 in cash to the seller, but the seller refused to sell her the guitar, claiming that she had been drunk when she made the offer. If the buyer is successful in an action against the seller, a court is most likely to

(A) issue an order directing the seller to sell the buyer the guitar for $500.

(B) award damages equivalent to the reasonable market value of the guitar.

(C) issue an order directing the seller to sell her guitar for $500 and award damages equivalent to the reasonable market value of the seller's guitar less $500.

(D) award damages of $500.

142. The plaintiff had long admired the defendant's dog, which was trained to get the paper and start the coffeepot every morning. The plaintiff finally convinced the defendant to agree to sell him the dog, and the defendant wrote out a contract that said, "I agree to sell my dog to the plaintiff. Price to be decided at delivery." The plaintiff was seeking to purchase the dog for resale. When the plaintiff arrived to pick up the dog a week later, the defendant refused to give the dog to him. The plaintiff then filed suit. Does the

UCC apply to the transaction between the plaintiff and the defendant?

(A) Yes, because this was a transaction in goods.

(B) Yes, because the price and the delivery date terms were missing from the agreement.

(C) No, because, unless it is a farm animal, a living thing does not fit the definition of "goods" under the UCC.

(D) No, because the plaintiff was seeking to purchase the dog for resale.

143. An attorney decided to invest $4,000 in art for her office. On November 1, she decided to purchase a painting from the defendant, with delivery to be made to the attorney on December 28 after the painting was framed.

On November 15, the attorney learned that the defendant had accidentally sold the painting to another buyer. Based on this knowledge, the attorney gave another art dealer $4,000 to purchase another painting.

On November 30, the defendant learned of the mistake and got the painting back from the other buyer. On December 28, when the defendant arrived at the attorney's office with the framed painting, the attorney refused to accept it.

The attorney instituted an action against the defendant on December 29 seeking specific performance of the November 1 agreement. With respect to the attorney's demand for specific performance, a court is most likely to find for

(A) the defendant, since the attorney refused to accept delivery of the painting on December 28.

(B) the defendant, since the attorney has already succeeded in investing $4,000 in art for her office.

(C) the attorney, since the painting is unique.

(D) the attorney, since the defendant's sale to the other person was an anticipatory repudiation of its contract with the attorney.

144. The seller was the owner of a lot and building that contained two residential apartments. The seller resided in the upstairs apartment and rented the downstairs apartment to a tenant and his family on a month-to-month basis. The buyer was interested in purchasing the realty from the seller. After negotiations, the buyer and the seller entered into a written contract that provided that the seller would sell the house to the buyer for $60,000 and that delivery of title was to occur on or before August 1. The seller promised that at the time title was delivered, the upstairs apartment would be vacant and that the downstairs apartment would be vacant within three months thereafter. The buyer promised to pay $58,000 upon delivery of title and the balance of $2,000 three months after delivery of title. The contract provided that "The buyer's obligation to pay $2,000 three months after delivery of title shall be voided if the downstairs apartment has not been vacated by that time."

The seller delivered title to the buyer on August 1, and as of November 15, the downstairs apartment remained occupied by the tenant. Which of the following statements best describes the buyer's rights?

(A) The buyer is entitled to an order directing the seller to commence a legal proceeding against the tenant for the purpose of evicting him from the premises.

(B) The buyer is not required to pay the seller the additional $2,000.

(C) The buyer is entitled to rescind his contract with the seller, reconveying title to her and receiving the return of his $58,000.

(D)   The buyer may bring a legal proceeding for the purpose of evicting the tenant from the premises, and, if successful, is required to pay the seller $2,000 less the expenses he incurred in evicting the tenant.

145.   The buyer was a collector of antiques who had purchased many expensive pieces from the seller, an antiques dealer. Knowing that the seller was traveling to Europe, the buyer wrote to him on March 11, "If you should come across a good piece in your travels, please purchase it for me. I don't care about the cost."

On April 17, the seller wrote to the buyer, "I have found an excellent table. The price is $15,000, but I think it's a good buy. Are you still interested? If so, let me know if the price is acceptable to you." The next day, for personal reasons, the seller decided he did not want to sell to the buyer.

The buyer received the seller's letter on April 21, and, on that same day, e-mailed the seller, "Fifteen thousand is OK. Buy the piece on my account."

The seller later sold the piece to another buyer who offered more money.

In litigation between the buyer and seller, if a court determines that the seller's letter of April 17 was an offer, was a contract formed between the buyer and the seller?

(A)   Yes, because sending an e-mail was a reasonable way for the buyer to accept the seller's offer.

(B)   Yes, because, as a merchant, the seller was obligated to act in good faith.

(C)   No, because an offer sent by mail may be accepted only by mail.

(D)   No, because the seller changed his mind about the piece prior to April 21.

146.   A banking firm hired a computer-banking specialist to update its computer network for $15,000. The specialist then went to work installing hardware and writing special software for the firm. Soon thereafter, to pay off a debt that the specialist owed to a computer programmer, the specialist assigned to the computer programmer her rights to receive payment under the contract. After the work was completed, the firm refused to pay.

The computer programmer instituted a claim against the firm for $15,000. Which one of the following additional facts or inferences, if it were the only one true, would be most likely to lead to a judgment for the firm?

(A)   The programmer was not a specialist in the application of computer technology to the practice of banking.

(B)   The contract between the specialist and the firm did not contain a clause permitting assignment.

(C)   The contract between the specialist and the firm contained language that stated, "This contract may not be modified except by a writing signed by both parties hereto."

(D)   The firm paid $15,000 to the specialist prior to being notified of the specialist's assignment to the programmer.

147.   The defendant was a veterinarian who sometimes acquired exotic animals from local zoos. The plaintiff was the owner of a large livestock ranch.

On March 10, the defendant and the plaintiff agreed that the defendant would sell the plaintiff an aardvark for $450, payment and delivery to be on March 20. On March 15, the plaintiff called the defendant and said, "When you deliver the aardvark, will you throw in a pig for my daughter without charging extra for it?" The defendant said, "Yes," but when she delivered the aardvark on March 20, she refused to give the daughter a pig. If the plaintiff asserts a claim against the defendant because of her failure to deliver the pig as promised, the court should find for

(A)  the plaintiff, because the plaintiff and the defendant were merchants with respect to the sale of a pig.

(B)  the plaintiff, because the plaintiff and the defendant were merchants with respect to the sale of an aardvark.

(C)  the plaintiff, because the plaintiff and the defendant were merchants with respect to the sale of an aardvark and a pig.

(D)  the plaintiff.

148.  On January 3, a retailer of lumber ordered from a lumber wholesaler 1,000 2" × 4" fir boards, each 8 feet in length, for delivery by January 15. When the wholesaler delivered the fir boards on January 15, they were received by the retailer's manager, who informed the retailer that delivery was made but that the boards delivered by the wholesaler were only 7 feet long. The retailer intended to notify the wholesaler immediately but was busy and forgot to do so.

On January 16, economic conditions caused the price of lumber to double, and on January 17, the retailer notified the wholesaler that the boards were only 7 feet long, returned them to the wholesaler, and demanded that the wholesaler furnish 8-foot boards at the contract price. If the wholesaler refuses to do so, and the retailer asserts a claim against the wholesaler for breach of contract, the court should find for

(A)  the retailer, in a sum equivalent to the difference between the contract price and the fair market value of 7-foot boards on January 15.

(B)  the retailer, in a sum equivalent to the difference between the contract price and the fair market value of 8-foot boards on January 15.

(C)  the retailer, in a sum equivalent to the difference between the contract price and the fair market value of 8-foot boards on January 17.

(D)  the wholesaler.

149.  A pawnbroker occasionally sold used jewelry to the buyer, who owned a jewelry store. On June 1, the pawnbroker sold the buyer a ring for $2,500, representing the stone in it to be a diamond. On July 16, the buyer learned that the stone in the ring that he had purchased from the pawnbroker was not a diamond but rather cubic zirconia, making the ring worth only $300.

On July 17, the pawnbroker assigned to a retailer, for $1,500 cash, the sales contract with the buyer. The retailer then requested payment from the buyer. The buyer refused.

The retailer sued the buyer, but in defense, the buyer claimed the stone was not a diamond, and the suit was unsuccessful. If the retailer brings an action against the pawnbroker, the court should find for

(A)  the pawnbroker, because an assignment does not imply a warranty that the obligor will perform.

(B)  the pawnbroker, because the assignment to the retailer caused the retailer to step into the pawnbroker's shoes with respect to the claim against the buyer.

(C)  the retailer, because the buyer's defense existed at the time the assignment was made by the pawnbroker to the retailer.

(D)  the retailer, because an assignment for consideration implies a warranty that the obligor will perform.

150.  In anticipation of changing over to a more "upscale" restaurant, a restaurant entered into a written agreement with a new butcher. Under the agreement, the butcher would

provide "as many top quality steaks at $10 per pound as the restaurant decides to order." A week later, before the restaurant had made its first order, the butcher called the restaurant and said that a sharp rise in the price of cattle feed meant that it was impossible to provide "top quality" steaks for less than $15 per pound. The butcher said he was willing to provide lower quality steaks if the restaurant wanted to keep the price the same. The restaurant responded that it was already planning to host the National Meat Eater's Convention and could only do so if it had top quality steaks. The restaurant sued the butcher for breach.

How should the court rule?

   (A) In favor of the restaurant, because of its detrimental reliance.

   (B) In favor of the restaurant, because this is a valid requirements contract.

   (C) In favor of the butcher, under the doctrine of impossibility.

   (D) In favor of the butcher, because the restaurant's promise is illusory.

151. On February 1, the landlord and the tenant entered into a written contract. By its terms, the landlord was to rent the tenant a building for use by the tenant as a "sports book," which is an establishment where bets are made on horse races and other sporting events. The tenant's tenancy was to commence on April 1 and to continue for a period of two years. Upon signing the contract on February 1, the tenant gave the landlord a deposit of $2,000. At that time, neither party could have reasonably anticipated that existing state law would be changed.

On February 1, existing state law permitted the operation of a sports book, but on April 1, existing state law prohibited the operation of a sports book. If the tenant sues the landlord for the return of his deposit, the court should find for

   (A) the landlord, because public policy prohibits the enforcement of gambling contracts.

   (B) the landlord, because the purpose of the agreement of February 1 has become illegal.

   (C) the tenant, because he and the landlord were not *in pari delicto.*

   (D) the tenant, under the doctrine of frustration of purpose.

152. In January, a farmer planted an orchard of apples that would be ready for harvest in June. The farmer entered into a written contract with a restaurant on March 2, wherein the farmer agreed to sell and the restaurant agreed to buy 2,000 bushels of apples to be delivered during the month of June.

In the first week of April, heavy rains inundated the farmer's orchard, destroying part of her crop. As a result, she doubted that she would be able to fulfill her contract with the restaurant. On April 15, she called the restaurant and said that because of the storms, she would not be able to deliver more than 1,000 bushels. The restaurant said, "I'll take whatever you deliver, but I intend to hold you to the terms of our contract." However, immediately after the call, the restaurant contracted to purchase from another supplier 1,000 bushels of apples with delivery on June 15.

On June 15, the farmer delivered 2,000 bushels to the restaurant, but the restaurant refused to accept any more than 1,000 bushels. If the farmer sues the restaurant for breach of contract, the restaurant's most effective defense would be based on the principle of

   (A) novation.

   (B) anticipatory repudiation.

   (C) *nudum pactum.*

   (D) impossibility of performance.

153. A developer entered into a written agreement with a farmer to buy the farmer's farm for $500,000. The closing was scheduled for September 5. On September 1, the farmer called the developer and said, "I can't go through with this. The farm means too much to me. Can we just forget about the contract?" The developer, who was suddenly interested in buying a different property, said it was fine if the farmer wanted out. On September 2, the other property was sold to a homebuilder. On September 3, the developer called the farmer back and said, "Look, I want to go through with our original closing." The farmer said, "You agreed to cancel our contract, and I'm already talking about selling to someone else for twice the price."

If the developer sues the farmer for breach of contract, may she recover?

(A) Yes, because any contract modification had to be in writing.

(B) Yes, because the farmer did not act in good faith.

(C) No, because the developer told the farmer it was fine if the farmer wanted out.

(D) No, because the farmer acted in reliance on the developer's statements.

154. A sporting goods store called a distributor and ordered 200 football jerseys at $50 a piece. Three days later, the distributor sent the store a signed letter marked "Confirmation." The letter repeated the sales terms from the phone conversation and said, "This confirms your order of 200 football jerseys, total price $10,000." The store received and read the letter on January 3. The jerseys arrived on January 4. On January 14, the store called and told the distributor, "We never agreed to buy these jerseys. We're sending them back."

Is the agreement enforceable?

(A) Yes, because the agreement is between merchants.

(B) Yes, because the distributor provided consideration by sending the jerseys.

(C) No, because the agreement violates the Statute of Frauds.

(D) No, because the store told the distributor it didn't order the jerseys within 14 days of receipt of the letter.

155. A woman's father earned his living as a fumigator, using a fleet of trucks to fumigate office buildings with insecticides for a fee. When he died, he left the business to his daughter. Although his daughter did not know how to drive a truck and did not personally participate in fumigating, she continued to run the business by hiring workers to drive the trucks and fumigate the buildings. Soon after inheriting the business, the woman entered into a business contract with a bank. The terms of the contract required the woman's company to fumigate the bank's building four times per year for a period of four years, at a total price of $10,000 that the bank paid upon signing the contract.

The fumigation company performed as agreed for two years. At the end of that period, the woman sold the entire business to a local trucker, assigning to the trucker the balance of her contract with the bank. All the daughter's employees agreed to work for the trucker.

The bank consented to the assignment, but the trucker subsequently failed to perform as required by the contract. If the bank seeks the return of the unearned portion of the money that it paid to the woman on the signing of their contract, it may collect it from

(A) the woman only.

(B) the trucker only.

(C) either the woman or the trucker.

(D) neither the woman nor the trucker, because the bank's only remedy is a judgment for the difference between the contract price and the price that the bank would have to pay another for the same service.

156. During negotiations with a printing company, a publisher agreed to hire the printing company president's wife as a cover artist for a year in exchange for a lower rate on printing costs. The artist was thrilled and immediately told all her clients that she wouldn't be able to work for them. Six months later, after the president and the artist were divorced, the president called the publisher and said that it could fire the artist if it chose to do so, with no ramifications to the contract. The publisher immediately fired the artist.

If the artist asserts a claim against the publisher for damages resulting from breach of his promise to hire the artist for one year, the court should find for

(A) the artist.

(B) the publisher, because the artist gave nothing in return for his promise.

(C) the publisher, because his promise was not in writing.

(D) the publisher, because he and the president mutually rescinded their contract.

157. After serving in the military for several years, a soldier informed her father that she had gotten married and was retiring from military service. Glad to hear the news, the soldier's father agreed to give the soldier a house built on his land as a present. Thrilled with the gift, the soldier cancelled her contract to buy another house.

The father and a builder signed an agreement to build a new house, and the father showed the plans to the soldier. However, after beginning the work, the builder discovered that the house could not be built for what the father was willing to pay. Consequently, the father and the builder agreed to a smaller plan for the house.

If the soldier asserts a claim against her father for changing the building plans, which of the following would be the most effective argument in support of her claim?

(A) The modification of the father's contract with the builder was unsupported by consideration.

(B) The soldier detrimentally relied on her father's oral promise by canceling the contract that she had already made to purchase a home.

(C) The contract between the father and the builder was a writing signed by the father.

(D) The soldier's marriage and retirement from military service was consideration for her father's promise to give her a house built according to the plans that he showed her.

158. On January 17, a storeowner agreed to sell a penguin-shaped ring to the plaintiff for $2,000. However, when the plaintiff came to pick up the ring on January 18, the storeowner refused to sell it to him. If the plaintiff sues the storeowner, is the plaintiff entitled to specific performance of the sale?

(A) No, because specific performance is not available as a remedy for breach of a contract for the sale of personalty.

(B) Yes, because the storeowner is a merchant with respect to the sale of a diamond ring.

(C) Yes, because the ring is highly unusual.

(D) Yes, because the storeowner could have obtained specific performance in the event of a breach by the plaintiff.

159. The plaintiff was a retailer of home-gardening supplies. On March 1, the plaintiff entered into a written contract with a wholesaler of seeds. According to the terms, the wholesaler was to furnish the plaintiff with pumpkin seeds in 10-pound bags at a specified price. The contract provided that for a period of one year, the plaintiff would purchase all its pumpkin seeds from the wholesaler and that the wholesaler would furnish all the pumpkin seeds required by the plaintiff. It provided further that the plaintiff would advise the wholesaler of its requirements by the first of each month and that the wholesaler would make delivery by the end of that month. The contract was silent about the right to assign or delegate.

Upon signing the contract on March 1, the plaintiff notified the wholesaler of its pumpkin seed requirements for that month. The wholesaler made a delivery to the plaintiff on March 17. Prior to April 1, the plaintiff notified the wholesaler of its pumpkin requirements for April. On April 20, the wholesaler sold its entire business to a new owner, including its contract with the plaintiff, and notified the plaintiff of the sale the same day. On April 24, after the plaintiff received notice of the assignment, the new owner delivered the seeds that the plaintiff ordered from the wholesaler.

The next day, the plaintiff wrote to the new owner, enclosing a check for the seeds that the new owner had delivered, and demanding that the new owner assure the plaintiff that it would be able to meet the plaintiff's pumpkin seed requirements in the future. On June 1, not having heard from the new owner, the plaintiff notified the wholesaler and the new owner that it was canceling the contract.

If the plaintiff asserts a claim against the wholesaler for breach of contract, the court should find for

(A) the plaintiff.

(B) the wholesaler, because the plaintiff impliedly consented to the

assignment by accepting delivery from the new owner.

(C) the wholesaler, because the plaintiff impliedly consented to the assignment by demanding assurances from the new owner.

(D) the wholesaler, because its assignment of rights to the new owner implied a delegation of duties.

160. The homeowner hired a painting contractor to paint the homeowner's residence, entering into a valid written contract with the contractor that fixed the price of the job at $5,000 and provided that the contractor would deliver a "satisfactory result." After the contractor finished painting the house, he sent the homeowner a bill for $5,000. When the homeowner received the bill, he called the contractor and complained about the paint job, saying that he did not think it was "satisfactory" as required by the contract. The paint job had many noticeable drips and missed spots. He said, "I've got half a mind not to pay you at all, but if you'll take $4,500, I'm willing to call it square." The contractor reluctantly agreed to accept $4,500, even though he thought the job was just fine and the homeowner was not entitled to a reduction in price.

The contractor subsequently brought a claim against the homeowner for $500 as the balance due on the agreed price for the paint job, asserting that his agreement to accept $4,500 was unsupported by consideration. If the homeowner defends by claiming that there was an accord and satisfaction, the court should find for

(A) the homeowner, because the homeowner reasonably believed that the result was not "satisfactory" as required by the contract.

(B) the homeowner, because no consideration is required for an agreement to modify a contract.

(C)    the contractor, because the agreement to modify the contract was not in writing.

(D)    the contractor, because the contractor did not believe that the result was not "satisfactory," as required by the contract, or that the homeowner was entitled to a reduction in price.

161.    A home design store contracted with a manufacturer to buy 1,000 drinking cups made of glass. In response, the manufacturer sent 1,000 drinking glasses made of plastic. The store received the goods, paid for them, but failed to discover the cups were plastic instead of glass. A few days later, the store discovered the discrepancy. In the home wares and design industry, a plastic cup is generally worth half as much as a glass cup. At the time the cups were delivered, the cost of a plastic cup was 50 cents, and the cost of a glass cup was $1. However, due to a huge drop in the stock market, the market price for all housewares dropped 50 percent. By the time the store could sell the cups to a discount store, the price for plastic cups was 25 cents.

The home design store sued the manufacturer for damages. The court should find for

(A)    The home design store, for $500.

(B)    The home design store, for $750.

(C)    The home design store, for $1,000.

(D)    The manufacturer.

162.    A manufacturer needed a new factory and purchased a parcel of realty on which he wished to have it constructed. After negotiation, the manufacturer entered into a valid written contract with a licensed builder. Pursuant to its terms, the builder was to construct a two-story building on the manufacturer's realty according to specifications furnished by the manufacturer, at a total price of $250,000, to be paid in full upon completion of the building.

When the structure was partially completed, the manufacturer decided to retire from the business and told the builder to stop work. The builder had already spent $180,000 on materials and labor and would have needed to spend another $35,000 to complete the building in conformity with the specifications. Because of an increase in construction costs, the value of the partially completed structure was $300,000. If the builder asserts a claim against the manufacturer for breach of contract, the builder should recover

(A)    $265,000 (the value of the partially completed structure less the cost of completing construction).

(B)    $250,000 (the contract price).

(C)    $215,000 (the contract price less the cost of completing construction).

(D)    $180,000 (the amount that the builder has expended).

163.    The seller wanted to sell his accordion. Because four buyers had all expressed interest in it, the seller wrote to all of them on May 1, telling them he was selling his accordion, had told all four of them he was doing so, and would sell it for a fair price.

On June 16, the seller received a letter from the first buyer offering to buy the accordion for $1,000. On June 19, the seller received a letter from the second buyer that said, "I received your offer of May 1. Will $2,000 buy the accordion?"

On June 21, the seller wrote to the second buyer, "I accept your offer and will sell you the accordion for $2,000. (signed)."

The seller's letter of June 21 is best described as

(A)    an offer.

(B)    an acceptance.

(C)    an invitation to negotiate.

(D) an anticipatory repudiation of the seller's agreement with the first buyer.

164. The buyer agreed to purchase steel beams from the seller by a written contract. The beams were delivered by truck and were in a closed box. Upon inspection, however, the buyer discovered the beams were iron instead of steel. The buyer sent the seller a letter notifying him that the beams did not conform to the contract. Even so, the buyer kept and used the beams, even though iron beams were not as valuable as steel ones. If the buyer asserts a claim against the seller for breach of warranty, the court should enter judgment in favor of

(A) the buyer, for the difference between the value of steel beams and iron beams.

(B) the buyer, for the return of the price that he paid.

(C) the seller, because the buyer used the beams.

(D) the seller, because he might have been able to sell the beams elsewhere for a higher price.

165. On August 1, the homeowner entered into a written contract with a buyer for the purchase and sale of the homeowner's home at a price of $398,000, with title to close on December 1. On November 1, the buyer informed the homeowner that he was severely ill, and that due to the changes in his financial circumstances, he would not be going through with the deal.

The homeowner instituted an action against the buyer for breach of contract. Which of the following statements is most correct regarding the legal relationship between the homeowner and the buyer?

(A) The homeowner is entitled to a judgment for damages resulting from the buyer's refusal to complete the transaction.

(B) The homeowner is entitled to a judgment for specific performance because every parcel of real estate is unique.

(C) The homeowner is entitled to a judgment for damages resulting from the buyer's refusal to complete the transaction, and he is also entitled to specific performance, because every parcel of real estate is unique.

(D) The buyer is excused from performance because of impossibility.

166. Because he always wanted his nephew to live nearby, the landowner offered to leave his nephew half of his estate if he agreed to move back to the city. The nephew agreed. The nephew then asked his sister if she would let him live in her apartment until the landowner died in exchange for half of what he received from the landowner. The landowner soon passed away.

The landowner's will left his entire estate to the nephew. The nephew refused to share any portion of it with his sister. If there was an enforceable agreement between the nephew and the landowner, his sister is most correctly described as an

(A) intended creditor beneficiary of that agreement.

(B) intended donee beneficiary of that agreement.

(C) incidental beneficiary of that agreement.

(D) assignee of 50 percent of whatever rights the nephew has under that agreement.

167. In exchange for use of his neighbor's boat, the homeowner hired a lawn service to maintain his lawn and his neighbor's lawn for the next two years. The homeowner and the lawn service signed a memorandum of agreement, and the homeowner gave a photocopy of it to his neighbor. The lawn

service rendered services as agreed for six months. Then, the lawn service notified the homeowner and the neighbor that it would no longer be able to work on their lawns. The neighbor sued the lawn service for breaching the agreement contained in the memorandum. The court should find for

(A) the neighbor, because he is a creditor third-party beneficiary of the contract between the lawn service and the homeowner.

(B) the neighbor, because the neighbor is a donee third-party beneficiary of the contract between the lawn service and the homeowner.

(C) the lawn service, because the neighbor is only an incidental third-party beneficiary of the contract between the lawn service and the homeowner.

(D) the lawn service, because there was no privity between the lawn service and the neighbor.

168. On July 1, after hearing that the buyer was going to attend law school, the seller sent the buyer a letter offering to sell his old law books. The buyer wrote back on July 8 and told the seller he would buy the law books for $100 if the seller delivered them to his apartment on September 1. On August 1, the buyer decided that he did not want to go to law school after all and wrote the seller a note telling him that he was no longer interested in buying the law books. He was about to go to the post office to mail it when the seller knocked at his door. As soon as the buyer opened the door, the seller said, "I'll bring you those law books tomorrow. I'll just have to borrow a friend's station wagon to transport them." The buyer said, "Never mind. I don't want them," and handed the seller the note that he had written but not mailed.

The seller's statement on August 1 that "I'll be bringing you those law books tomorrow" was probably

(A) an offer.

(B) a ratification of the acceptance that was mailed on July 8 but was never delivered to the buyer.

(C) an acceptance.

(D) commencement of performance.

169. A homeowner asked a builder to build a new pool in his backyard while he was away on a three-week bus tour of Europe. The homeowner and the builder signed a contract for 10 percent less than the market price, and the homeowner signed a detailed work order for the builder's work crew. Several days later, the work crew went out to do the job described in the work order. By mistake, they installed the pool in a neighbor's yard. Since the neighbor was on the same trip as the homeowner, no one was around to tell the work crew they had the wrong house. When the homeowner returned, he demanded the builder perform the work as agreed. The builder refused, and the homeowner sued.

Which of the following additional facts or inferences, if it was the only one true, would most likely result in a judgment for the builder?

(A) There is another builder who will build a pool for the homeowner for the same price.

(B) The original contract would have resulted in a loss for the builder.

(C) The homeowner had accidentally written the wrong address in the work order.

(D) The builder was unsuccessful in collecting payment from the neighbor.

170. After a fire destroyed a storeowner's store, the storeowner entered into a contract with a builder to rebuild the store for $200,000. The contract called for work to be completed by December 1. After taking a closer look at the work that needed to be done, the

builder contacted the storeowner and said he could not take on the job for less than $275,000.

The storeowner quickly found another builder who was willing to do the job for $250,000. After the second builder began work, the storeowner contacted him and said that if he could finish the building by November 1, the storeowner would pay him an extra $25,000. The second builder completed the work by November 1, and the storeowner paid him $275,000. The storeowner then sued the first builder for damages resulting from breach of the original construction contract. A court would likely award the storeowner

(A) nothing.

(B) $25,000.

(C) $50,000.

(D) $75,000.

171. An entrepreneur entered into a contract with a seller to buy a new office building for his new company. Prior to the date set for closing, the entrepreneur contacted the seller and said he was no longer buying the building because the necessary funding for the company had not come through. The seller did not try to resell the office building. A year later, the seller sued the entrepreneur for breach of contract.

In deciding the lawsuit, the court should rule in favor of

(A) the entrepreneur, because the seller did not try to resell the office building.

(B) the entrepreneur, under the doctrine of impossibility of performance.

(C) the entrepreneur, because he notified the seller prior to the date set for closing.

(D) the seller, for a sum equal to the difference between the contract price and the fair market value of the property on the date set for closing.

172. On June 2, a truck manufacturer and an engine maker entered into an agreement for the sale of a new engine for $1,000. In a telephone conversation with the engine maker on June 5, however, the truck manufacturer said that he would sue the engine maker for breach of contract unless the engine maker agreed to accept $200 as payment in full. Because business was poor, the engine maker agreed to accept that sum, but then she subsequently rejected the truck manufacturer's tender of $200. If the engine maker sues the truck manufacturer for $1,000, the court should find for

(A) the truck manufacturer, because the original agreement was modified in the telephone conversation of June 5.

(B) the engine maker, because her agreement to accept $200 was not evidenced by a writing.

(C) the engine maker, because her agreement to accept $200 was unsupported by consideration.

(D) the engine maker, because her agreement to accept $200 was made under duress.

173. Important as a food commodity, pears are traded on the American Pear Exchange. Although farmers are free to negotiate prices for the sale of their pears, the price received by pear farmers on any given day is generally determined by the American Pear Exchange price.

In January, a farmer planted an orchard of pears that would be ready for harvest in June. Because she expected the harvest to yield more than 5,000 bushels of pears, she entered into a written contract with a buyer on March 1, wherein the farmer agreed to sell and the buyer agreed to buy 2,000 bushels of pears to be delivered during the month of June at the American Pear Exchange price as of June 15. On March 2, the farmer entered into an identical written contract with a restaurant.

In the first week of April, heavy rains inundated the farmer's orchard, destroying part of her crop. As a result, she doubted that she would be able to fulfill her contract. The farmer than called the buyer. When she explained the problem to the buyer, he said that he would accept 1,000 bushels instead of 2,000 if the farmer would agree to accept the American Pear Exchange price as of May 1 instead of June 15. The farmer said, "Well, you've got me over a barrel. I'll never be able to deliver 2,000 bushels in June, so I accept your terms."

On May 1, the price was $2 per bushel. On June 16, the price of pears doubled. The farmer's harvest yielded 4,000 bushels. The farmer delivered 1,000 bushels to the buyer on June 20. The buyer demanded the right to purchase another 1,000 bushels at $2 per bushel, but the farmer refused to sell him an additional 1,000 bushels at that price. If the buyer institutes a claim against the farmer for breach of contract, the court should find for

(A) the farmer, because farmers are free to negotiate prices for the sale of their pears.

(B) the farmer, because her agreement to accept the American Pear Exchange price as of May 1 was consideration for the buyer's agreement to accept 1,000 bushels instead of 2,000 bushels.

(C) the buyer, because the agreement to modify his contract with the farmer was not in writing.

(D) the buyer, because the farmer's harvest was sufficient to permit her to satisfy her original contractual obligations.

174. In August 2012, a bar owner threatened to sue the student for $10,000, claiming that the student owed him that sum for unpaid bar bills. The student asked his mother to lend him money with which to pay the bar owner. On September 1, 2012, the student's mother stated orally that if the student promised to go to law school and to stop drinking for the rest of his life, she would give him $10,000 on July 1, 2013. The student promised that he would never drink alcohol again, and that he would enroll in law school as soon as possible. On September 3, 2012, the student wrote to the bar owner, describing his agreement with his mother and stating that if the bar owner did not sue him, he would pay the bar owner the $10,000 as soon as he received it from his mother.

The student began attending a law school two weeks later. In December 2012, however, he withdrew from the school, deciding that he did not like it.

On July 1, the student's mother paid her son $10,000, but the student refused to pay the bar owner, denying that he owed unpaid bar bills. If the bar owner asserts a claim against the student for breach of the promise contained in the student's letter of September 3, which of the following additional facts, if it were the only one true, would be most likely to result in a judgment for the bar owner?

(A) The bar owner did not respond to the student's letter of September 3.

(B) On September 3, the student reasonably believed that he owed the bar owner $10,000, but the bar owner did not reasonably believe that the student owed him $10,000.

(C) On September 3, the bar owner reasonably believed that the student owed him $10,000, but the student did not reasonably believe that he owed the bar owner $10,000.

(D) On July 1, the bar owner's claim against the student for unpaid bar bills was barred by the statute of limitations.

175. The homeowner hired a famous landscaper to fix up his lawn. The landscaper's design

owner's house and planted with aquatic plants. Although the landscaper completed the rest of the job himself, he hired an earthmoving subcontractor to dig the moat, which the earthmoving subcontractor did in complete conformity with the landscaper's plan. The entire job was completed in a reasonably workmanlike manner, but the homeowner refused to make any payment under the contract.

The landscaper asserted a claim against the homeowner on account of the homeowner's refusal to pay him for his services, and the homeowner defended on the ground that the landscaper breached the contract by hiring a subcontractor to dig the moat. In deciding the claim, the court should find for

(A) the homeowner, because the landscaper hired the earthmoving subcontractor to dig the moat around the homeowner's house.

(B) the homeowner, because the reason that the homeowner contracted with the landscaper was that he wanted the job done by a well-known landscape architect.

(C) the landscaper, because the moat was dug in complete conformity with the landscaper's plan.

(D) the landscaper, because all contract rights are freely assignable.

176. In exchange for use of his neighbor's ski house, the homeowner hired a lawn service to maintain his lawn and his neighbor's lawn for the next two years, agreeing to pay the lawn service $50 per month for certain specified services. The homeowner and the lawn service signed a memorandum of agreement, and the homeowner gave a photocopy of it to his neighbor. Two months later, the homeowner sold his house to a doctor. At the closing of title, the homeowner handed the doctor the original memorandum of his

agreement with the lawn service and executed an assignment to the doctor of his rights thereunder. The lawn service continued rendering services as agreed for an additional six months, receiving a check for $50 from the doctor each month. Then, the lawn service notified the neighbor and the doctor that it would no longer be able to work on their lawns.

The neighbor hired a gardener to continue performing the same services on the neighbor's lawn for a fee of $25 per month. If the neighbor sues the doctor for $400 ($25 per month for the 16 months remaining in the term), the court should find for

(A) the neighbor, because the doctor's monthly payments to the lawn service resulted in an estoppel-type waiver of his rights to deny liability.

(B) the neighbor, because the homeowner's promise to provide lawn maintenance services touches and concerns the land.

(C) the doctor, because he did not agree to pay for the maintenance of the neighbor's lawn.

(D) the doctor, because the price of $25 per month to maintain the neighbor's lawn was equal to one-half the price that the lawn service charged for maintaining both lawns.

177. On April 1, a law firm hired a famous and uniquely skilled software specialist to design and install new computer software specifically for the firm. The new software was to be installed by October 1. On August 15, after winning the state lottery, the specialist sold her business to a computer dealer. The computer dealer agreed to fulfill any existing contracts entered into by the specialist.

On August 16, the specialist informed the firm of her sale to the dealer, stating that the software called for by the contract would be designed and installed by the dealer and not the specialist. If the firm institutes a claim against the specialist on August 18, the court should find for

(A) the firm, since the specialist's statement on August 16 was an anticipatory repudiation.

(B) the firm, since the specialist's sale to the dealer did not impose on the dealer an obligation to design software.

(C) the specialist, since design and installation of the software was not required until October 1.

(D) the specialist, since her sale to the dealer implied a delegation of all her obligations under her contract with the firm.

178. On May 15, a music store telephoned a guitar factory and ordered 50 guitars at a price of $200 per guitar. On May 16, the music store sent a signed letter marked "Confirmation" that read: "This confirms our order of 5 guitars." On May 17, the factory shipped 50 guitars to the store. On May 18, the factory received the letter from the music store. On May 19, the factory sent a bill to the store for $10,000. On May 20, the music store received the bill. On May 21, the music store sent back the 50 guitars with a letter marked "Failure to Order" that read: "We never ordered these." On May 22, the factory received the letter. The factory can make all of the guitars it has customer orders for, and it makes a profit of $50 per guitar.

May the factory recover on the contract against the music store?

(A) Yes, for $10,000.

(B) Yes, for $2,500.

(C) Yes, for $250.

(D) No.

179. A local school held a charity auction where companies and other members of the community donated items for the school to auction off. A local guitar maker agreed to donate a new electric guitar valued at over $1,500. During the auction, the plaintiff bid $50 and was declared the highest bidder. The plaintiff gave the school a check for $50. Because the guitar company was so embarrassed at the low price paid for the guitar, it refused to deliver it to the plaintiff. If the plaintiff asserts a claim against the guitar company for failing to deliver the guitar, the court should find for

(A) the plaintiff, as an assignee.

(B) the plaintiff, as an intended third-party creditor beneficiary.

(C) the guitar company, because there was no agreement between it and the plaintiff.

(D) the guitar company, because the agreement was not supported by consideration.

180. A famous musician was scheduled to play a concert that would be broadcast on national television. A music-streaming service that had an exclusive agreement with the musician contracted with the television network to run a 30-second advertisement on Saturday, October 1, at 8:15 P.M. Although the contract did not state it specifically, the understanding was that the advertisement would run during the last 15 minutes of the concert. The advertisement was designed to promote the music-streaming service by advertising the musician's "surprise" new album that was exclusive to the site.

The day before the concert, the musician was killed in a car accident. The television station offered to run the advertisement at the agreed time for a 20 percent discount, but the music service declined, stating that the entire advertisement and advertising campaign was built around the concert occurring. If the television station sues the music-streaming service for breach of contract, how should the court rule?

(A)  For the television station, because the contract did not specifically state the advertisement would run during the concert.

(B)  For the television station, since there was nothing stopping it from running the advertisement at the agreed time.

(C)  For the music-streaming service, under the doctrine of impossibility.

(D)  For the music-streaming service, under the doctrine of frustration of purpose.

# ANSWERS
## CONTRACTS

# ANSWERS TO
# CONTRACTS QUESTIONS

1. **D**    The plaintiff's father's offer was for a unilateral contract—his promise to pay in return for the plaintiff's postponing the wedding. When the plaintiff postponed the wedding, he accepted his father's offer, and a contract was formed.

   Some cases have held that an agreement never to marry violates public policy, but there is no reason why an agreement to postpone a marriage would do so. **A** is therefore incorrect. **B** is incorrect because the plaintiff's father's promise was to pay if the plaintiff postponed the wedding. His language did not make payment conditional upon the plaintiff's registration for a second year. Although an offer terminates upon the death of the offeror, **C** is incorrect because the plaintiff accepted the offer by postponing the wedding, and, once accepted, an offer is no longer revocable.

2. **D**    Since the dealer sold the chairs to another buyer at the same price that the decorator had contracted to pay, the dealer sustained no damage. Where there is no limit to the availability of the items sold, some cases allow a seller to recover lost profits when a buyer cancels, reasoning that even though the seller resold at the same price, he or she would have made two sales instead of one if the buyer had not breached. Since there were no more chairs to sell, however, the dealer lost nothing.

   **A** is therefore incorrect. An action for the price might be available where traditional calculation of damages would be inadequate, but **B** is incorrect because the dealer has suffered no damages. **C** correctly states the remedy that would have been available to the decorator in the event of a breach by the dealer. Because the fair market value exceeds the contract price, however, the formula expressed in **C** bears no relationship to damages suffered by the dealer as a result of the decorator's breach. **C** is therefore incorrect.

3. **A**    If an event that was not foreseeable to the parties at the time a contract was formed makes performance of the contract impossible, such performance is excused. In the absence of facts that specifically suggest the contrary, destruction of the subject matter of a contract is usually held to have been unforeseeable by the parties at the time of contracting.

   At the time the fire occurred, the plaintiff was not in breach because he was not required to make payment until the garage was half complete, and the defendant was not in breach because he was not required to be half finished until April 25. **B** and **C** are therefore incorrect. It is usually held that impossibility excuses performance only to the extent that performance has been made impossible. **D** is incorrect, however, because the contract was not for labor until June 1, but rather for construction of the garage by June 1, and the fire has made completion by that date impossible.

4. **A**    The UCC provides that where there is no agreement to the contrary, a buyer is entitled to inspect goods prior to making payment or accepting them. It provides further, however, that the parties may agree that payment is required before inspection. If so, failure to make payment upon delivery of the goods is a breach.

Anticipatory repudiation occurs when, *prior to the time when performance is required*, a party indicates by word or deed that he or she will not perform. **B** is incorrect because the buyer's refusal to pay occurred at the time payment was required, and therefore constituted a breach. The UCC provides that even if payment is made prior to inspection, no acceptance occurs until after the buyer has had a reasonable opportunity to inspect. In view of this provision, a promise to pay prior to inspection is not unconscionable, and **C** is incorrect. Since the seller tendered delivery in accordance with the terms of the contract, **D** is incorrect.

5.  **A**     A unilateral contract is a promise to perform in exchange for a specified act by the promisee. Since the company promised to make payment to the employee who submitted the winning design, its offer was for a unilateral contract.

A bilateral contract is an exchange of promises, each given in return for the other. Since the company promised to pay only if the modification design was actually submitted, and asked for no promise in return for its promise to pay, **B** is incorrect. The company's notice made clear its intention to pay only one prize and its obligation to pay only upon receipt of a design that complied with its requirements. Its promise, therefore, could not have been given in exchange for the promise contained in the engineer's March 8 memo, even if that memo had been received. **C** is therefore incorrect. The key difference between an offer and an invitation to negotiate is that an offer creates an immediate power of acceptance in the offeree. Since any employee could have accepted the company's offer of a reward by successfully designing and submitting the required program modification, **D** is incorrect.

6.  **B**     If a promise not to assign a contract is enforceable, it is like any other promise, in that damages may be available as a remedy for its breach. An assignment made in violation of such a promise is usually regarded as valid, however. This means that even though the gardener may be entitled to recover from the owner for damages resulting from the owner's assignment to the plaintiff, the plaintiff may enforce the contract against the gardener.

**C** is therefore incorrect. **A** is incorrect because a promise not to assign without a party's consent does not require that party to act reasonably in deciding whether or not to consent. It is generally understood that a contract involving personal services is not assignable because an assignment of such a contract may increase the obligor's burden. Since the contract between the owner and the gardener specified the tasks that the gardener was to perform, and since a change in obligee (*i.e.*, in the ownership of the condominium) would not alter those tasks, assignment to the plaintiff did not increase the gardener's burden. For this reason, the contract should not be regarded as one calling for personal services, and **D** is incorrect.

7.  **C**     Consideration is a benefit to the promisor or a detriment to the promisee that was bargained for and given in return for the promisor's promise. For this reason, if the police officer did something that he was already obligated to do, his act could not be consideration for the city's promise to pay since no new benefit was given to the city and no detriment was sustained by the police officer in return for that promise. A police officer's obligation to his employer includes the duty to attempt to apprehend criminals, so the police officer's performance was of a preexisting duty.

**A** is incorrect because establishing that the informant is entitled to the reward does not necessarily establish that the police officer (or anybody else) is not entitled to it as well. **B** is incorrect because a guilty plea is a conviction. Since the city's promise was to pay in return for information leading to a conviction, it was an offer to pay for something of value, not an offer for a gratuitous cash award. **D** is therefore incorrect.

8.  **D**    The parol evidence rule prohibits the introduction of extrinsic evidence of prior or contemporaneous agreements offered to contradict, vary, or modify an unambiguous writing that the parties intended to be a full and final expression of their agreement (*i.e.*, a "complete integration"). Since the "dollar" is the unit of currency in both the United States and the foreign country, the contract that specifies a price of 9,000 dollars without identifying which country's dollars are intended is probably ambiguous. The evidence offered by the plaintiff would help explain and clarify the ambiguity. It is not barred by the parol evidence rule since it does not contradict, vary, or modify the writing.

   **A** and **C** are therefore incorrect. Ambiguities in a writing are frequently construed against the party who prepared it, but only if they cannot be clarified in some other way. **B** is incorrect because parol evidence may be introduced to explain an ambiguity, no matter who caused it.

9.  **D**    The man made no express promise to pay for the fishing gear. There was no implied promise because there is no fact indicating that the plaintiff acted with the expectation of compensation or reimbursement for her losses. The executor is therefore not bound to pay for her loss.

   *Quantum meruit* is available to prevent unjust enrichment only where services were rendered under circumstances such that the party from whom payment is sought was aware of the other party's expectation of payment. **A** is therefore incorrect. The phrase "danger invites rescue" has been used in tort cases to explain why one who creates a peril owes a duty of care to a person attempting to rescue another from it. **B** is incorrect, however, because the principle has no application in contract problems. Since there is no indication that the man promised to pay for the fishing gear, the fact that someone else in his position would have is irrelevant, making **C** incorrect.

10. **A**    Performance of one of a series of mutual promises is a condition precedent to others in the series if the circumstances indicate that it should obviously precede the others. Since the writing called for payment of $300 in advance, it is obvious that the parties intended that it should be paid before the work commenced. The woman's payment of $300 was thus a condition precedent to the body shop's obligation to paint. Since the contract called for the payment of an additional $400 after completion, it is obvious that the parties intended that the paint job should be finished before payment of the additional money was required. Completion of the paint job is thus a condition precedent to the woman's obligation to pay the additional $400.

   A condition subsequent is an event the occurrence or non-occurrence of which operates to discharge a duty that had already become absolute. Since the body shop was obligated to paint before receiving the additional $400, and since it could not undo the paint job once it was completed, the woman's payment of the additional $400 cannot be called a condition subsequent to the body shop's obligation to paint the car. **B** is therefore incorrect. Concurrent conditions require the parties to exchange performance simultaneously. **C** is incorrect because the language of the contract makes it obvious that the parties intended a consecutive order of performance (*i.e.*, the woman pays $300, the body shop completes paint job, the woman pays $400). Since the agreement required partial payment in advance and completion of the job before the balance was due, **D** is incorrect.

11. **C**      In an action for breach of an employment contract, a non-breaching employee is entitled to receive the full contract price for the balance of the term plus consequential damages, less damages avoided by mitigation. Since the plaintiff mitigated damages by taking a job with another company at the same salary, he is entitled to what he lost between the discharge and the beginning of his new job. His advertising expenses are collectible as consequential damages.

A is incorrect because the reorganization by the defendant was voluntary. An employment contract may require payment of severance pay in the event of termination, but absent such agreement, there is no such legal requirement. **B** is therefore incorrect. **D** is incorrect because the plaintiff's work for the new company at the same salary mitigated his damages.

12. **A**      If the defendant's statement implied a promise to paint the cars, it was an acceptance of the plaintiff's offer, thus forming a contract of which the defendant's subsequent refusal to paint the cars would be a breach. (*Note:* Although the defendant's statement probably was not a promise, the question requires this to be assumed as an additional fact.)

If, on the other hand, he made no promise to paint the cars, there was no contract and could be no breach. This would be true even though the plaintiff suffered detriment in reliance on his belief that the defendant would paint his cars. **B** and **C** are therefore incorrect. When the plaintiff offered $125 per car, he rejected the defendant's offer to paint them for $150. It was too late for him to accept that offer on January 3, so **D** is incorrect.

13. **D**      None of the reasons given to justify a victory for the defendant is a good one. The doctrine of frustration of purpose may excuse performance of a contract when an unforeseen event destroys its underlying purpose, but only if both parties knew what that purpose was.

A is incorrect because the plaintiff did not know the defendant's purpose. Impossibility of performance discharges a contractual obligation when an unforeseen event makes performance vitally different from that reasonably contemplated by both parties at the time the contract was formed. **B** is incorrect because the plaintiff was unaware of the use contemplated by the defendant. When government action makes the subject matter of a contract unlawful, it may be unenforceable for illegality, because of frustration of purpose, or under the doctrine of impossibility of performance. **C** is incorrect, however, because the subject matter of the contract between the defendant and the plaintiff was the rental of a motion picture theater, and the showing of motion pictures was not made unlawful by the city council's action.

14.  **D**  The Statute of Frauds requires a contract for the sale of goods with a price of $500 or more to be in writing, but it does not apply to a contract for services, even if goods are to be provided by the person performing the services.

15.  **B**  Usually, a promise is unenforceable unless it is supported by consideration. Consideration is a bargained-for exchange of value given for a promise and may consist of benefit to the promisor or detriment to the promisee. If an alleged debt is invalid, a person who promises to pay a sum in settlement of it receives no benefit in return for his or her promise. Similarly, if a person who receives such a promise does not honestly believe that the debt is valid, he or she suffers no detriment by agreeing to accept less in settlement. For this reason, a promise to pay a sum of money to settle a claim for debt is supported by consideration if the debt is valid or the person asserting the claim believes that it is. Thus, if the plaintiff honestly believed that the defendant owed him $3,000, his agreement to accept $2,000 was consideration for the defendant's promise, making the promise enforceable.

On the other hand, if the plaintiff did not believe that the defendant owed him the money, the plaintiff suffered no detriment and the defendant received no benefit in return for the defendant's promise. Since the promise would, thus, be unsupported by consideration, it would be unenforceable. **A** is therefore incorrect. **C** and **D** are incorrect because unless the debt actually existed or the plaintiff believed that it did, his agreement to accept $2,000 would not be consideration for the defendant's promise to pay it.

16.  **A**  Although the parol evidence rule prevents the introduction of extrinsic evidence for the purpose of modifying the terms of certain written memorandums, it does not prevent the admission of such testimony for the purpose of establishing that no contract was ever formed. Since the oral agreement made before execution of the writing establishes a condition precedent to the formation of a contract, it is admissible.

An agreement to modify a contract is one that is made after formation of the contract. **B** is incorrect because the oral agreement regarding the loan was made before execution of the written contract. Since the defendant has not asserted that the written agreement is valid, there is no reason why he should be estopped from denying that it is. **C** is therefore incorrect. **D** is incorrect because the oral agreement relates to the formation of the contract and does not modify or contradict its terms.

17.  **A**  The Statute of Frauds requires a contract for the sale of goods with a price of $500 or more to be in writing. It might be argued that the agreement in **A** was divisible—really 15 separate agreements, each for a single $100 purchase—and therefore not within the Statute of Frauds. (*Note:* Since the agreement was for the purchase of a "series" of figurines, it was probably not a divisible contract, but **A** is the only one of the four fact patterns presented in which the Statute of Frauds *might* prevent enforcement.)

UCC §2-201 specifically excludes from application of the statute a contract for the sale of specifically manufactured goods if the seller has made a substantial beginning in their manufacture. The Statute of Frauds would be inapplicable in **B** since the plaintiff had already completed the rough carving when the defendant attempted to cancel the contract.

Since UCC §2-201 specifies that the Statute of Frauds is satisfied by an admission in the pleadings of the existence of a contract, the statute would not prevent enforcement in **C**. UCC §2-201 provides that between merchants, a written memorandum of a contract that is sufficient to bind the sender binds the receiver also if he or she fails to object to it within 10 days. Since both parties in **D** are merchants, the writing prepared by the plaintiff and not responded to by the defendant satisfies the statute.

18.  **B**    A minor may disaffirm a contract on the ground of incapacity. If, however, the disaffirming minor is the plaintiff in an action for restitution, his or her recovery will be offset by the reasonable value of the benefit that he or she had received. Measuring the benefit in terms of reasonable rental value is a common judicial approach.

A is therefore incorrect. **C** is incorrect because the damage that the car sustained is not related to the benefit that the plaintiff received. **D** is incorrect because it fails to recognize the minor's right to disaffirm the contract.

19.  **C**    An offer may be revoked at any time prior to its acceptance and is effectively revoked when the offeree learns of an act by the offeror that is wholly inconsistent with the offer. The seller's offer to sell the tractor to the buyer was thus revoked when the buyer learned that the seller had sold it to the other neighbor.

The seller's promise to keep the offer open until March 15 was unsupported by consideration and therefore was not enforceable. Although UCC §2-205 makes certain firm offers between merchants enforceable without consideration, **A** is incorrect because the seller and the buyer were not merchants regarding the sale of the tractor. **B** is incorrect because the revocation took effect when the buyer learned of the sale to the other neighbor. **D** is incorrect because the letter of February 15 was an offer to sell the tractor and could have given rise to a contract if accepted by the buyer before the seller revoked it.

20.  **A**    A court may reform a contract to reflect the intentions of the parties if, as a result of inadvertence, the writing does not actually reflect the intentions. In determining the intentions of the parties, the court may admit whatever evidence is relevant and material.

**B** is incorrect because UCC §2-201 declares that a writing may satisfy the Statute of Frauds even though one or more terms (except the quantity term) are omitted. The Universal Commercial Code (UCC) provides that parties may conclude a contract for sale even though the price is not settled, and that if they do, the price is to be the reasonable price at the time of delivery. **C** is incorrect, however, because the seller and the buyer did agree on a price. **D** is incorrect because parol evidence may be admitted for the purpose of determining what the parties intended the price to be.

21.  **C**    The parol evidence rule prohibits the introduction of extrinsic evidence of prior or contemporaneous agreements to contradict, vary, or modify an unambiguous writing that the parties intended to be a full and final expression of their agreement. It is generally understood that in the absence of fraud or mistake, a clause in a written contract that states that the writing is intended to be a complete integration of the agreement between the parties

establishes that it is a complete integration. If so, the agreement in **C** would be barred by the parol evidence rule since it was a contemporaneous agreement that contradicts a term of the writing.

The purpose of the parol evidence rule is to discourage litigation by encouraging parties to put their entire agreement in writing. Since this purpose would not be served by prohibiting parol evidence regarding the question of whether or not the obligations created by the writing ever came into being, parol evidence pertaining to a written contract's becoming effective is admissible. **A** is therefore incorrect. Since the writing requires the homeowner to pay for the paint, the agreements in **B** and **D** do not modify any obligation created by the writing and so would probably be admitted. **B** and **D** are therefore incorrect.

22. **A**　　An agreement for the sale of goods FOB a particular place requires the seller to load the goods on board a carrier at that place. Once the seller has done so, the buyer's obligation to pay the seller for the goods becomes complete. Under UCC §2-210, a seller who has completely performed may assign its rights even if terms of the contract prohibit assignment. Since the seller's rights have been assigned to the plaintiff, the plaintiff now is entitled to collect the price from the defendant.

**B** correctly states the remedy usually available to the *buyer* in the event of the seller's failure to deliver, but it is incorrect as a statement of the seller's remedy. Payment by the defendant might enrich the plaintiff, but since the plaintiff has given value for the assignment of the air-conditioning company's rights, the enrichment would not be unjust. **C** is therefore incorrect. So long as assignment does not impose an additional burden on the obligor, an assignment of contract rights is enforceable in spite of a clause prohibiting it. **D** is therefore incorrect.

23. **A**　　A contract is formed upon acceptance of an offer. An offer is a manifestation of present intent to be bound to specific terms. Since the niece's letter of August 1 clearly expressed her willingness to sell each of the paintings to the dealer for $2,000, it was an offer. An acceptance occurs when the offeree communicates to the offeror that he or she agrees to the terms of the offer. Since the dealer's telegram clearly expressed her willingness to pay $2,000 for painting Number 30, it was an acceptance. A contract for the sale of painting Number 30 at a price of $2,000 was thus formed. For this reason, the niece's action for breach of a contract to purchase the painting for $3,000 must fail unless there has been an enforceable modification of the original contract. Under UCC §2-209(3), a modification of a contract must be in writing if the contract as modified is within the provisions of the Statute of Frauds. Since, as modified, the oral contract between the niece and the dealer calls for the sale of goods with a price in excess of $500, it violates the Statute of Frauds and will not be enforced over the dealer's objection. **A** is therefore correct.

Since an increase in the fair market value of the painting would not satisfy the requirement of a writing, **B** is incorrect. A promise that is not supported by consideration or one that violates the Statute of Frauds may be enforceable if the promisee *justifiably* relies on it *to his or her detriment*. **C** is incorrect, however, because reliance alone is insufficient to have this effect and because there is no indication that the niece changed her position (*i.e.*, relied). Since the niece's offer of August 1 called for acceptance by telegraphed order, the dealer's telegram on August 2 was an acceptance even though payment had not been made. **D** is therefore incorrect.

24.  **C**    Assignment of a contract transfers all the assignor's rights to the assignee. After the assignment, the assignor has no rights in the contract and cannot sue to enforce it.

**A** is incorrect because assignment does not discharge the assignor of his or her obligations under the contract. There is a presumption, however, that an assignment of rights under a contract includes a delegation of duties as well. **B** is therefore incorrect because, as assignee, the new homeowner is obligated to make payment as agreed by the original homeowner. Unless there is a clear agreement to the contrary, a promise not to assign without consent of the other party is usually viewed as a covenant. An obligee who breaches that covenant by assigning may be liable for damages to the obligor, but the assignment is valid in spite of the no-assignment clause so long as it imposes no additional burden on the obligor. Since the contractor's obligation after the assignment is identical to his obligation before the assignment (*i.e.*, to install aluminum sliding on the outside of the building), there is no reason to hold the assignment invalid. **D** is therefore incorrect.

25.  **B**    The UCC treats a modification of a contract as a new contract. For this reason, if the contract as modified falls within the provisions of the Statute of Frauds, the modification must be in writing. UCC §2-209(3). Since the modification resulted in an agreement to sell goods with a price of $500 or more, the Statute of Frauds requires a written memorandum. The absence of a writing makes the contract unenforceable over the objection of the retailer.

A contract is unconscionable if one party is so deprived of free choice that he or she is forced to make a one-sided bargain that favors the other party. Since the free enterprise system sometimes results in different prices being set by different suppliers of the same commodity, the mere fact that the merchandise was available at a lower price than that requested by the wholesaler is not sufficient to make the agreement to pay the wholesaler's price unconscionable. **A** is therefore incorrect. **C** is incorrect because, under UCC §2-209(1), an agreement to modify a contract may be enforceable even if it is unsupported by consideration. **D** would be relevant if the wholesaler attempted to excuse his own non-performance by asserting impossibility or frustration of purpose. Since the retailer agreed to the modification, however, the wholesaler's reason for requesting it is irrelevant to its enforceability.

26.  **C**    A contract is formed upon acceptance of an offer. Since the buyer's order identified the subject of the transaction, specified the quantity, set forth price and terms, and called for shipment, it conferred upon the seller the power to create a contract by accepting and was, therefore, an offer. Under UCC §2-206(1)(b), an order to purchase goods for prompt shipment calls for acceptance either by prompt shipment or prompt promise to ship. Since the seller shipped (*i.e.*, accepted the offer) on April 28, the contract was formed on that date.

Catalogs of the kind used by the seller are mere invitations to negotiate because they are sent to a large number of buyers and do not refer to specific items for sale but rather to types of items. For that reason, the buyer's order could not constitute an acceptance. **A** and **B** are therefore incorrect. **D** is incorrect because the contract had already been formed when the goods were shipped.

27.  **A**     Under UCC §2-314, an implied warranty of merchantability accompanies every sale by a merchant unless disclaimed by unequivocal language. UCC §2-316(3)(a) specifically provides that the phrase "as is" may be used to disclaim the warranty.

**B** is incorrect because the implied warranty may accompany the sale of a used product as well as a new one. **C** is incorrect because liability for breach of warranty does not depend on negligence or fault by the seller. Under UCC §2-315, an implied warranty that the product is fit for the buyer's particular purpose accompanies a sale only if the seller knows the buyer's purpose and knows also that the buyer is relying on the seller's judgment in furnishing a product to suit that purpose. **D** is incorrect, however, because the implied warranty of merchantability does not require reliance on the seller's judgment.

28.  **B**     In the absence of an agreement to the contrary, one who seeks the services of another, knowing that the other expects to be paid for those services, impliedly promises to pay for the services by availing himself or herself of them. Although the doctor agreed to wait for payment and to bill the defendant's insurance company directly, nothing in the conversation between the doctor and the defendant indicates that the doctor was willing to look solely to the insurance company for payment.

If the benefit that a contract confers on a noncontracting party was intended to satisfy a preexisting obligation owed by one of the contracting parties, the person on whom the benefit is conferred is called a creditor third-party beneficiary. Since the defendant's debt to the doctor did not exist at the time the insurance contract was made, the doctor could not have been a creditor beneficiary. **A** is therefore incorrect. **C** and **D** are incorrect because, as noted above, nothing in the conversation between the doctor and the defendant indicates that the doctor agreed to look solely to the insurance company for payment.

29.  **C**     When either party to a contract breaches it, the other party is excused from further performance. Since the landowner breached by refusing to make payment as required, the contractor may refuse to perform any further work.

In addition, the non-breaching party is entitled to damages consisting of the losses that he or she sustained as a result of the breach. This may include profits that he or she would have earned if the breach had not occurred. **D** is therefore incorrect. Ordinarily, lost profits are measured by the balance of the contract price less whatever it would have cost the builder to complete performance. Since the amounts specified in **A** and **B** are not necessarily based on this measure, **A** and **B** are incorrect.

30.  **A**     An option is a promise to keep a particular offer open for a specified period of time. If it is supported by consideration, it is a separate contract and is enforceable during the specified period. Since the document stated that the landowner received $20 in return for her promise to keep the offer open, her promise was supported by consideration and is therefore

enforceable. Many cases hold that consideration that is cited in a writing, but which was never actually given or received, is "sham consideration," and that sham consideration does not support a promise. **A** is correct in spite of this, however, because the facts do not indicate that the landowner did not receive $20 from her son, and because none of the other answers listed could possibly be correct.

An attempted testamentary substitute is an attempt by a person to dispose of his or her property after death without the formality of a will. Since all jurisdictions have statutes that impose certain formal requirements on wills, a testamentary substitute that fails to satisfy these requirements is ineffective. Thus, if the document signed by the landowner is an attempted testamentary substitute, the result would be a judgment for the administratrix. **B** is therefore incorrect. To avoid interfering with the freedom of contract, courts do not ordinarily inquire into the adequacy of consideration. This is particularly true where parties to a contract are related to each other, or where there is some other reason why one of them might be willing to accept less than actual value from the other. For this reason, **C** and **D** are incorrect.

31.  **D**    A minor may disaffirm his contract on the ground that he or she lacked capacity, but the party contracting with him or her may not.

A and **B** are therefore incorrect. Detrimental reliance is sometimes given as a reason for enforcing a promise that was unsupported by consideration. **C** is incorrect because the defendant's promise was supported by consideration (*i.e.*, the plaintiff's promise), making the plaintiff's reliance irrelevant.

32.  **C**    Under the Statute of Frauds, a contract for the sale of any interest in real estate must be in writing, and the writing must contain all the essential terms. The price is an essential term in a contract for the sale of realty, since the court will be unable to fashion a remedy without it.

Although UCC §2-305(1) makes special provision for contracts between merchants, providing that a contract silent as to price is presumed to be for a reasonable price, these provisions apply only to the sale of goods and not to the sale of realty. **A** and **B** are therefore incorrect. Since this contract does not satisfy the requirements of the Statute of Frauds, it is unenforceable over objection, even though oral evidence might establish the intentions of the parties with respect to missing terms. **D** is therefore incorrect.

33.  **C**    Consideration requires a bargained-for exchange. Since the husband did not ask the rescuer to save his wife, the rescuer's doing so was neither bargained for nor given in exchange for the husband's promise.

The fact that a promisor calls something "consideration" for his or her promise does not make it so. **A** is incorrect because the service was not given in exchange for the promise. Even though the service rendered by the rescuer may have materially benefited the husband, it is not consideration for the husband's promise because it was not performed in exchange for the promise. **B** is therefore incorrect. A service given in return for a promise, however, would be consideration for the promise even if the value of the service cannot be specified. **D** is therefore incorrect.

34.  **C**    A beneficiary may sue the promisor only if the beneficiary was an "intended" beneficiary. The test for an "intended" beneficiary is whether the circumstances show that the promisee intended to give the beneficiary the benefit of the promised performance. Here, the woman (the promisee) intended to give her niece the benefit of the value of her house. Consequently, the niece can sue the woman's husband (the promisor) for his failure to live up to his promise to his wife. **A** and **D** are incorrect because the terms "creditor" and "donee" beneficiaries have been rendered obsolete by the Second Restatement's change to the terms "intended" and "incidental" beneficiaries. **B** is incorrect because the failure to change the wills is irrelevant to the analysis.

35.  **D**    The seller's obligation under a contract of sale is to deliver goods that conform in every way to the terms of the contract. Since the contract called for delivery of 500 pens, delivery of anything less is a breach. Since the seller failed to perform as promised, the buyer is entitled to the return of all money already paid. In addition, since the seller breached the contract, the buyer is entitled to damages resulting from the breach.

           **A** is incorrect because the buyer is not required to accept a nonconforming tender. If a buyer chooses to accept a nonconforming tender, he or she must pay the contracted price but is entitled to sue for damages resulting from the seller's defective performance, so long as he or she notifies the seller of his or her intention to do so. **B** is therefore incorrect. On the other hand, if the tender does not conform to the seller's promise, the buyer may reject it. Having done so, the buyer is entitled to damages that resulted from the seller's breach. **C** is incorrect because return of the buyer's advance payment may not be sufficient to compensate the buyer for other damages that it sustained. (*Note:* Damages are traditionally measured by the difference between the contract price and the "cover price" or the fair market value of the goods involved.)

36.  **D**    A party who wishes to make a contract may make statements that are not offers but rather solicitations of bids. These bids are the basis of preliminary negotiations and cannot be accepted. Here, the man saying "I would consider" shows his statement to be a mere solicitation of bids, and not a true offer. Consequently, the friend cannot accept and no contract is formed. This makes **A** incorrect. **B** is incorrect because detrimental reliance usually refers to the other party beginning performance or making costly preparations in anticipation of a contract. Here, the friend buying motorcycle equipment and a shed is unlikely to rise to this level. **C** is incorrect because a statement of future intention is an announcement by a person that he or she intends to contract in the future. The man's statement that he wanted to sell his motorcycle did not show that he necessarily intended to make any contract in the future.

37.  **B**    Under the brokerage contract, transfer of title was a condition precedent to the defendant's obligation to pay a commission. There is always an implied agreement, however, that a party will not willfully prevent the performance of a condition to his or her obligation. If transfer of title was prevented by the defendant's willful breach of his contract with the

buyer, the defendant thus violated the implied agreement with the plaintiff and may be held liable for damages (*i.e.*, the unpaid commission) that resulted.

Although real estate brokerage contracts frequently require payment of the commission when the broker procures a ready, willing, and able buyer, **A** and **C** are incorrect because this contract was conditioned on the transfer of title. "Frustration of purpose" may excuse performance of a contract where an unforeseen event destroys the underlying reasons for performing the contract. **D** is incorrect because the doctrine of frustration of purpose never results in liability but rather excuses a party's failure to perform.

38. **A**    An accord is a new obligation intended to take the place of an existing one. To be enforceable, it must be supported by consideration. To discharge the original obligation, it must actually be performed. Performance of the new obligation is known as "satisfaction," and it is the satisfaction rather than the accord that discharges a contractual obligation. The agreement of May 21 constituted an accord, but since the buyer did not pay $45,000 in cash by May 25, there has been no satisfaction and thus no discharge of his obligation to pay $50,000 as originally agreed.

While a promise to perform a preexisting obligation is not valuable consideration, **B** is incorrect because the buyer's original contractual obligation was to pay before June 14, and his May 21 promise was to pay by May 25. A novation is an agreement to substitute a third party for one of the parties to the contract. **C** is therefore incorrect. **D** is incorrect because accord without satisfaction does not work to discharge contractual obligations.

39. **C**    Under the mailbox rule, an acceptance is effective when sent. However, if the offeror never receives the acceptance, the acceptance has to be properly dispatched in order to create a contract. Here, since the facts state that the writer put the correct address and proper postage on the acceptance, the mailbox rule applies. This makes **A** and **B** incorrect. **D** is incorrect because even if the writer mailed her acceptance, the mailbox rule would not apply if the acceptance was not properly dispatched (*i.e.*, she put the wrong address on it).

40. **C**    Most jurisdictions agree that an offer for a unilateral contract cannot terminate once the offeree begins performance. The plaintiff's extra efforts to earn "A"s while her mother was alive would thus have prevented her mother's death from terminating the offer. Earning the "A"s constituted acceptance of the offer and entitled the plaintiff to the promised bonus.

**A** is incorrect because there is no rule of law requiring a law student to use his or her best efforts while in law school. **B** is incorrect because the plaintiff's efforts would have prevented termination of the offer until she had a reasonable opportunity to complete performance. Since her mother's promise was not made until after the plaintiff got into law school, and since the plaintiff did not apply to law school with any expectation of compensation from her mother, the plaintiff's law school enrollment was not relevant to the enforceability of her mother's promise. **D** is therefore incorrect.

41. **B**    UCC §2-104 defines a merchant as a person who deals in goods of the kind involved in the transaction, one who by his or her occupation holds himself or herself out as having

knowledge peculiar to the goods involved in the transaction, one to whom such knowledge may be attributed by his or her employment, or a person who by his or her occupation holds himself or herself out as having such knowledge. Since the buyer in **B** is not in the bicycle business, does not hold himself or herself out as having special knowledge of bicycles, and does not employ a person who does so, he or she is not a merchant under UCC §2-104.

The seller in **A** is in the bicycle business and therefore deals in bicycles. The buyer in **C** is a bicycle mechanic, and as such holds himself out as having special knowledge of bicycles. Special knowledge of bicycles may be attributed to the buyer in **D** because she employed a bicycle mechanic to assist in making the purchase.

42. **D**    A prospective inability to perform occurs when a party to a contract has, by his or her own conduct, divested himself or herself of the ability to perform. A party who justifiably relies to its detriment on another party's prospective inability to perform is discharged from its obligations under the contract. Since the hotel executives learned that the plaintiff had enlisted, and since this would make it impossible for the plaintiff to perform, they were justified in hiring another caretaker. Since the hotel ordinarily employed only one winter caretaker, hiring the new caretaker was sufficiently detrimental to excuse it from performing its contract with the plaintiff.

A and **B** are incorrect because the hotel justifiably relied to its detriment on the plaintiff's prospective inability to perform when it hired the new caretaker upon learning of the plaintiff's enlistment. An anticipatory repudiation occurs when a party refuses to perform even though he or she is able to do so. **C** is incorrect because the plaintiff never refused to perform.

43. **B**    Ordinarily, when unforeseeable circumstances make performance impossible, that performance is excused. When this occurs after performance has begun, the party who has performed is not entitled to contract remedies, since there has been no breach by the other party. In construction contracts, if the contractor is hired to repair an existing building rather than build a new one, the contractor is entitled to recover in restitution for the reasonable value of the work done prior to the destruction of the building. In contracts involving building a new building, contractors are not permitted any recovery in restitution for the work that was destroyed, because no benefit was conferred on the owner.

A and **D** are incorrect because the plaintiff did not fully perform, such performance having become impossible without fault by either party.

44. **B**    An assignment transfers the assignor's rights to the assignee, thus extinguishing the assignor's rights under the contract. Since the plaintiff has assigned his rights under the contract, he can no longer enforce them.

**A** is incorrect for two reasons: First, lack of contractual capacity makes a contract voidable only at the option of the person who lacked it, and second, a minor has capacity to contract in connection with his or her own business interests. An assignee's failure to notify the obligor that an assignment has been made may result in a discharge of the obligor's obligation to the assignee to the extent of payments that the obligor made to the assignor. **C** is incorrect, however, because the assignee's failure to notify does not alone discharge any obligation owed by the obligor. In some jurisdictions, an assignment of wages is invalid. **D** is incorrect for two reasons: First, if the assignment is invalid, the defendant is liable to the plaintiff, and second, the assignment was of royalties, not of wages.

45.  **A**    The Statute of Frauds requires that a contract to create an interest in land be in writing. Most states agree that this requirement applies to a promise to create a leasehold interest, so it would apply to both promises made by the daughter.

The Statute of Frauds also requires a writing if the contract is one that *by its terms* cannot be performed within one year. The promise that the daughter made to her mother could be performed within one year if her brother died during that period. The promise that the daughter made to her brother could be performed within one year if their aunt died during that period. **B** is therefore incorrect. UCC §2-201(1) requires that a contract for the sale of goods for a price of $500 or more be in writing. **C** is incorrect, however, because a house is realty rather than goods, and because the requirement of a writing is based on the *price* rather than the value of goods sold. Consideration is something of value given in return for a promise, but it is not necessary that the consideration flow from the promisee to the promisor. **D** is incorrect because the woman's conveyance to her daughter was consideration for her daughter's promise to the woman, and because her brother's promise to share the inheritance was consideration for his sister's promise to him. In addition, **D** is incorrect because the lack of consideration does not relate to the assertion that an oral promise is unenforceable.

46.  **B**    As long as neither party has fully performed a contract, the parties may agree to cancel the whole contract. Such an agreement is called a mutual rescission. However, when parties agree to a mutual rescission, most courts hold that neither party is obligated to pay for any benefits already received under the contract. **A** is incorrect because it is irrelevant who asked to get out of the contract first. **C** and **D** are incorrect because parties are not obligated to pay for any benefits they received under the contract before the mutual rescission.

47.  **A**    UCC §2-209(3) provides that an agreement to modify a contract must be in writing if the contract as modified is within the provisions of the Statute of Frauds. Since the contract as modified calls for the sale of 1,000 widgets at $10 per widget for a total price of $10,000, and since the Statute of Frauds requires a contract for the sale of goods with a price of $500 or more to be in writing, the contract as modified falls within the provisions of the Statute of Frauds. Since it is not in writing, it is not enforceable over the objection of the plaintiff.

**C** is therefore incorrect. **B** is incorrect because UCC §2-209(1) provides that an agreement to modify an existing contract may be enforceable without consideration. An accord is an agreement to substitute a new obligation for an existing one. To be enforceable, an accord, like any other agreement, must be supported by consideration. Since consideration is a detriment suffered in exchange for a benefit received, and since the defendant suffered no detriment in return for the reduction in his obligation, the agreement to accept 1,000 widgets instead of 2,000 as originally required by the contract is unsupported by consideration. **D** is therefore incorrect.

48.  **A**    Although the defendant breached his contract with the plaintiff, he is not liable unless the breach resulted in damage. If there are equally competent gardeners in the area who will perform the same work at the same price, the plaintiff has sustained no damage as a result of the defendant's failure to perform.

An increase in the costs of labor and materials would not excuse the defendant from performance, since such increases are usually regarded as foreseeable to the parties at the time they contract. **B** is therefore incorrect. The agreement between the man and the plaintiff may have motivated the plaintiff to contract with the defendant, but **C** is incorrect because the defendant's obligation does not depend on the validity of the plaintiff's motivation. A party's inability to perform does not excuse performance unless the inability was unforeseeable at the time the contract was made. Since the likelihood that one of the parties to a contract will become ill is generally regarded as foreseeable, **D** is incorrect.

49.  **D**    The note that the contractor sent on September 5 demanding $325 was a rejection of the homeowner's offer to pay $300. An offeree who has killed an offer by rejecting it does not have the power to resurrect it by a subsequent acceptance. The contractor's note of September 12 was thus no more than a new offer. Since an offer may not make the offeree's silence an acceptance, the contractor's offer of September 12 was never accepted because the homeowner did not respond to it.

**A** is therefore incorrect. Since there was no existing offer that could be accepted by performance, the contractor's commencement of performance on September 28 could not have resulted in the formation of a contract, making **B** incorrect. Since the homeowner did not know that the contractor was installing the screens, and since the contractor did not have a reasonable expectation of compensation at the time he installed them, the contractor has no quasi-contract remedy, and **C** is incorrect.

50.  **B**    Parties to a contract may make an explicit agreement as to what each party's remedy for a breach of contract will be. However, such "liquidated damages clauses" are invalid if they act as a penalty. The purpose of damages is to put the plaintiff in the same position he or she would have been in had the contract been fulfilled. It is not to punish the defendant for breach. Importantly, where a damage clause is keyed to the plaintiff's lost gross revenues, lost profits, or other figure not necessarily tied to actual losses, the court is likely to find it an unenforceable penalty. Here, the clause is an unenforceable penalty because the plaintiff gets paid the same amount regardless of whether it had to do any work, and thus regardless of whether it incurred operating costs in performing the work. Consequently, the clause has no connection to the nature of the breach, and is an unreasonable estimate of potential losses to the plaintiff. **A** is incorrect because, although the clause is a poor estimate of actual losses, a court will not enforce it because it rises to the level of an unenforceable penalty. **C** is incorrect because the clause was not a reasonable estimation of the

damages. **D** is incorrect because there is no indication this agreement is so complicated or the industry so volatile as to make damages difficult to calculate.

51.   **D**      Even if parties do not expressly exchange an offer and acceptance, if they indicate by their conduct their understanding that a contract was formed, an implied-in-fact contract exists. Importantly, if an offeree silently receives the benefit of the offeror's services, a court will hold that the offeree accepted a contract for those services if he or she had a reasonable opportunity to reject them and knew or should have known that the offeror expected to be compensated. Here, the woman had a reasonable opportunity to reject the writer's services (they met each other for an hour over four weeks), and she knew that the writer was usually compensated at $50 an hour for writing lessons. Consequently, an implied-in-fact contract was formed for the lessons at the writer's usual rate. **A** is incorrect because an implied-in-fact contract was formed under these facts. **B** is incorrect because market value is irrelevant to the analysis. **C** is incorrect because there is no fact indicating that the writer was intending to make a gift of her services.

52.   **D**      Ordinarily, a promise to perform services implies a promise to perform them in a satisfactory manner, judged by an objective standard. A specific agreement that personal satisfaction is required, however, is usually understood to call for subjective satisfaction so long as the party whose satisfaction is required acts in good faith. Thus, if the mayor actually believed that the statue was too small, and he was, therefore, not subjectively satisfied with it, the town is discharged of its obligation under the contract.

A is therefore incorrect. If the mayor liked the statue but rejected it because he feared embarrassment resulting from a conviction, the town would be in breach because the rejection would not be in good faith. If he genuinely did not like the statue, however, the incidental fact that he feared embarrassment if the boxer was convicted would not be relevant. **B** is therefore incorrect. Although the clause called for subjective satisfaction, it did not create an absolute right to reject the work since such an agreement is understood to mean that the decision as to whether or not the work is satisfactory must be made in good faith. **C** is therefore incorrect.

53.   **A**      Promissory estoppel is used by the courts to enforce promises when the promise induces the promisee to rely on it to his or her detriment. Here, the plaintiff relied on the promise to her detriment because she retired when she could have gone on working based on her belief that she would receive a pension. Consequently, the promise can be enforced through promissory estoppel. **B** is incorrect because "past services are not valid consideration for a promise." Consequently, the plaintiff's years of service prior to the awarding of the pension were not consideration for the pension. **C** is incorrect because, although she worked a few more years after receiving the pension, it was clear this service was not a bargained-for exchange for the pension. **D** is incorrect because, although there was no consideration for the pension, it could still be enforced through promissory estoppel.

54.   **C**      UCC §2-512(2) specifically provides that where a contract calls for payment prior to inspection, such payment does not constitute acceptance and does not impair the buyer's right to inspect.

The requirement of payment prior to inspection is not an uncommon one, and therefore not unconscionable, making **A** incorrect. **B** and **D** are incorrect because UCC §2-512(2) prevents preinspection payment from having these effects.

55. **A** Since the promise to keep the offer open is unsupported by consideration, it is a gratuitous one, and therefore unenforceable.

Although UCC §2-205 makes certain "firm offers" between merchants enforceable without consideration, at common law, an option (*i.e.*, promise to hold an offer open) is not enforceable without consideration. **B** is incorrect because it is, thus, based on an inaccurate statement of the law. **C** is incorrect because UCC provisions relating to "firm offers" apply only when they are made by merchants. **D** is incorrect for these reasons and also because nothing in the language of the buyer's letter indicates that the buyer's beginning law school is a condition for any of the obligations that might result from the transaction. It clearly was not a condition *precedent* because performance was to take place prior to the beginning of law school in mid-September.

56. **B** Although the Statute of Frauds might require a contract for the sale of goods with a price of $1,000 to be in writing, the question asks only if the neighbor's promise can be viewed as *consideration* for the man's promise. Consideration is something of value that is bargained for and given in exchange for a promise. Since the neighbor's promise to deliver fire-fighting equipment is of obvious value to the man, if given in return for the man's promise of payment, it is consideration for it.

**A** is incorrect because the neighbor's prior services were not given in exchange for the man's promise. **C** is incorrect because the doctrine of promissory estoppel may make a contract enforceable in the *absence* of consideration, but although detrimental reliance may take the place of consideration, it is not consideration unless bargained for. Although the kind of written memorandum referred to in **D** sometimes satisfies the requirement of a writing, it is not relevant to the question of consideration or the lack of it.

57. **C** UCC §2-306 states that "a term which measures the quantity by the output of the seller or the requirements of the buyer means such actual output or requirements as may occur in good faith, except that no quantity unreasonably disproportionate to any stated estimate or in the absence of a stated estimate to any normal or otherwise comparable prior output or requirements may be tendered or demanded." Comment 2 to §2-306 states that requirements and output contracts do not "lack mutuality of obligation since under this section, the party who will determine quantity is required to operate his plant or conduct his business in good faith and according to commercial standards of fair dealing in the trade so that his output or requirements will approximate a reasonably foreseeable figure." Under a requirements contract, the buyer promises that he or she will buy all of his or her requirements from the seller. This promise, coupled with the buyer's good faith obligation to order reasonable quantities, constitutes consideration for the seller's counter-promise to meet the buyer's needs. Here, the airline bound itself to act reasonably and in good faith in estimating the quantities of fuel it required. Since the airline was bound, the supplier's return promise was not void for lack of mutuality of obligation. Consequently, **B**

is incorrect. **A** and **D** are incorrect because part of the purpose of a requirements contract such as this one is to receive goods at predictable price. Thus, wars pushing up prices and other price increases are likely foreseeable.

58. **B**      An assignment is effective only if the assignor has given up all rights under the assigned contract. Thus, if the singer has made an effective assignment, he no longer has any rights against the defendant.

        **A** is incorrect for several reasons: First, since the contract was for the singer's business, the singer's infancy is probably irrelevant; second, even if the singer's infancy at the time of his contract with the defendant is relevant, it makes the contract voidable at the singer's option, not the defendant's; and, third, if the singer's infancy invalidated the assignments, the defendant would not benefit in the singer's action against it. **C** is incorrect because the agreement was to pay for the recording session whether or not a record was ever released. **D** is incorrect because the singer was probably a contractor rather than an employee and because if the assignments were held invalid, the defendant would have to pay the singer.

59. **C**      A condition precedent is an event that must occur before a party's obligation to perform under a contract becomes absolute. Since the agreement provided that the defendant would be under no obligation to pay unless he was satisfied with the product, satisfaction was a condition precedent to his obligation to accept and pay for the door. Ordinarily, a contract making a buyer's satisfaction a condition precedent to his or her obligation is held to require that the goods be satisfactory to the reasonable person (*i.e.*, objective satisfaction). However, where the agreement calls for the design of something to be personally identified with the buyer, as here, it is more likely that the parties intended the buyer's own personal satisfaction (*i.e.*, subjective satisfaction) to be the standard. If so, the defendant's dissatisfaction with the product, so long as it was based on good faith, would prevent the defendant from being obligated to purchase the door. While it is not certain that a court would come to this conclusion, the argument set forth in **C** is the only one listed that could possibly support the defendant's position.

        **A** is incorrect because the Statue of Frauds does not apply to goods that are specially designed for the buyer and which, therefore, would not be readily salable in the regular course of business. A unilateral contract is one in which the promisor has agreed to do something in return for a specified act by the promisee (*i.e.*, a promise for an act), and, therefore, one in which only one party is bound to perform. **B** is incorrect because the agreement between the defendant and the plaintiff was an exchange of promises, each party's promise being given in exchange for the other party's promise (*i.e.*, a bilateral contract). If the plaintiff were able to sell the door to another buyer, her damages might be mitigated to some extent. **D** is incorrect, however, because the mere possibility that damages might thus be mitigated is not sufficient to defeat the plaintiff's substantive rights.

60. **B**      Even if a defendant can show that a plaintiff never overtly bargained for the defendant's promise to do something, as long as a court concludes that the defendant's promise induced the plaintiff's promise or performance, the fact that the defendant didn't expressly bargain in return for that promise doesn't matter. Here, there was consideration because the

landfill offered the plastic for free because it wanted someone else to come remove it, and thus save the landfill the cost of disposing of the plastic itself.

**A** is incorrect because there is no fact showing that the construction firm detrimentally relied on the landfill's promise (*e.g.,* buying a special machine for the plastic, etc.). **C** is incorrect because the "bargain" theory of consideration does not mean the parties must actually bargain over the terms of the agreement—it just means the promise made by the defendant and the detriment to the plaintiff must induce each other. **D** is incorrect because this was not a gift situation. The landfill wanted to have the plastic hauled away for free, and the construction firm wanted the plastic and agreed to do so.

61. **A** Specific performance is a remedy that may coexist with the remedy of damages. Thus, its availability does not depend on the availability of damages—liquidated or otherwise.

  **B** and **C** are therefore incorrect. **D** is incorrect, since specific performance is available as a remedy for the seller's breach of a contract for the sale of realty.

62. **B** The parol evidence rule prohibits the admission of extrinsic evidence of a prior or contemporaneous agreement to contradict, vary, or modify the terms of an unambiguous written contract that the parties intended to be a final and complete expression of their agreement. Almost all jurisdictions, however, permit extrinsic evidence to be used to establish that the writing is ambiguous, and, if so, to explain the ambiguity.

  **A** is incorrect since it does not recognize that oral testimony may be used to explain the ambiguity. **C** is incorrect for the same reason, in spite of a general rule of construction that requires the resolution of *unexplained* ambiguities against the party who drafted the contract. **D** is incorrect since even if the writing was a complete expression of the parties' agreement, oral testimony is admissible to explain ambiguities.

63. **D** A promise to forbear or abandon a civil claim in return for some payment by the promisee is referred to as a compromise. The promise to forbear is sufficient consideration for the promisee's promise to pay if the claim could have been asserted in good faith. Although the facts do not indicate whether the plaintiff believed in good faith that he had a claim against the mother, **D** is the only theory listed that might have any prospect of success.

  **A** is incorrect since the husband's promise was given in exchange for the plaintiff's "promise to make no claim," and a unilateral contract involves a promise that is given in exchange for an act rather than a promise. **B** is incorrect since the facts do not indicate any *unjust* enrichment, and since, even if they did, unjust enrichment is not, alone, enough to result in liability. **C** is incorrect since promissory estoppel requires detrimental reliance by the promisee, and there is no fact indicating detrimental reliance by the plaintiff.

64. **A** An offer for a unilateral contract involves an offer to exchange a promise for an act. Since the notice offered a prize to the student achieving the highest Grade Point Average and did not ask students to make any promise or agreement that they would do so, it was a promise offered in return for an act.

**B** is therefore incorrect. **C** is incorrect since the offeror has the sole power to decide whether its offer can be accepted by an act or a promise. **D** is incorrect since once the student achieved the highest GPA in her class, there was nothing further for her to do, and so it could not be said that she was now obligated to perform, as she would be under a bilateral contract.

65. **B**     A promise to pay for services received in the past is usually held not to be supported by consideration. Here, since the plaintiff's services were not given at the defendant's request, the promise was unsupported by consideration and could not be enforced as a contract. Thus, **A** is incorrect. **C** is incorrect because the defendant received the plaintiff's promise to pay after he nursed the son back to health. Consequently, he could not have detrimentally relied upon it. **D** is incorrect because there is no moral obligation to treat the injured for free.

66. **B**     Even if a claim is invalid, a promise to abandon it may be consideration for another's promise of payment if the claim could have been asserted in good faith. If the plaintiff did not believe that it was entitled to the patent rights, it could not have asserted its claim in good faith, and its promise to abandon the claim would not have been consideration for the defendant's promise.

 If the plaintiff's claim was asserted in good faith, abandonment of the claim was consideration for the defendant's promise of payment, regardless of whether the employment contract was enforceable. **A** is therefore incorrect. **C** is incorrect since it indicates that the plaintiff's promise to abandon the claim was made in good faith, which would make it good consideration for the defendant's promise. **D** is incorrect because abandonment of an invalid claim may be consideration for a promise to pay, so long as the person abandoning the claim believes in good faith that it is a valid one.

67. **C**     The term *FOB* requires the seller to deliver the goods on board the carrier at the place specified, and the risk of loss does not pass to the buyer until the seller has done so. Since this contract was "FOB the defendant's factory," the plaintiff's obligation was to deliver it there, and the risk of loss did not pass until she did so.

 **A** and **B** are therefore incorrect. **D** is incorrect for two reasons: First, the term "public enemy" refers to a person, group, or nation waging war against the United States, and second, because while interference by a public enemy might relieve a seller of the obligation to deliver, it does not pass the risk of loss to a buyer.

68. **D**     When a promise is made with the intent that its benefit flow to a third person, that person is an *intended* beneficiary of the promise. When that benefit is intended to satisfy an obligation that the promisee owes to the third party, the third party is an intended *creditor* beneficiary. According to the Restatement 2d, a promise is enforceable by an intended creditor beneficiary when he or she relies upon or assents to the arrangement. Since the beneficiary is presumed to have assented when notified of the contract, and since the contractor notified the plaintiff, the plaintiff may enforce the contractor's son's promise even though there is no privity between them.

**A** is therefore incorrect. **B** is incorrect for two reasons: First, because non-assignability would prevent the *assignee* from recovering but could not be raised as a defense by that assignee, and second, because obligations under a construction contract may generally be assigned to any competent contractor. **C** is incorrect because the preexisting obligation that the contractor owed the plaintiff, and which the contractor's contract with his son was designed to satisfy, made the plaintiff a *creditor* rather than a *donee* beneficiary.

69. **A**    Since a contract is a meeting of minds, a person who does not know the legal consequences of his or her act is incapable of contracting. Where the incapacity results from intoxication, some jurisdictions require proof that the other party was aware of the intoxication and the resulting incapacity. Although it is not clear whether the buyer was sufficiently aware of the seller's incapacity, the additional fact in **A** is the only one listed that could help the seller's defense.

So long as the seller knew the legal consequences of her act, her motivation is irrelevant. **B** is therefore incorrect. So long as the consideration given for a promise has value, courts, recognizing that contracting parties may be motivated by factors other than monetary worth, do not usually inquire into the sufficiency of that value. For this reason, **C** is incorrect. Although an offeror may withdraw an offer at any time prior to acceptance, **D** is incorrect for two reasons: First, such withdrawal is not effective until communicated to the offeree, and second, the facts suggest that a contract was formed when the napkin was signed, making a subsequent attempt at revocation ineffective.

70. **C**    Although a court may reform a contract by filling in a missing term in accordance with the manifest intent of the parties, it may not create a contract where the writing fails to indicate that the parties had the intent of creating one. The January 5 document leaves the price term to subsequent agreement after determining reasonable value. It does not indicate that reasonable value will be the price or set forth any method by which the sale price is to be determined. It is an "agreement to agree," and as such, it does not manifest an intention to be bound to any particular terms.

**A** and **B** are therefore incorrect. Specific performance may be available in an action for breach of a contract for the sale of a chattel if the chattel is unique. Since a trained, talking bird is probably unique, **D** is incorrect.

71. **C**    Losses that are normal but not inevitable results of a breach of contract (*e.g.*, the plaintiff's claim of lost business resulting from non-delivery of the station wagon) are called "consequential damages," and they may be recovered if they were foreseeable to the parties at the time the contract was made, and if they could not have been mitigated by the aggrieved party. If the plaintiff could have traveled to the customers' premises by renting a car or by using one of the company pickup trucks, the defendant would not be responsible for damages resulting from his failure to mitigate consequential damages by doing so.

**A** is incorrect because the plaintiff had advised the salesperson that he needed to use the station wagon for his business, making business losses foreseeable. **B** is incorrect because impossibility excuses performance only if it results from factors not within the reasonable contemplation of the parties at the time the contract was formed. Here, both parties knew that the defendant was planning to order the station wagon from the manufacturer and could have anticipated that the manufacturer might not deliver the car on time. **D** is incorrect since consequential damages are available in actions for breach of a sales contract.

72.　**A**　Even though no contract exists, a party can recover from another on a quasi-contract (*i.e.*, a contract implied-in-law) theory when he or she rendered a service to the other with the reasonable expectation of compensation. Thus, if the doctor had a reasonable expectation of payment at the time she rendered medical services to the pedestrian, she may recover on a quasi-contract theory.

　　　　A contract is implied-in-fact when, although the parties have not expressed agreement, their intent to enter into a mutually binding bargain is evident from their conduct and the surrounding circumstances. Since the pedestrian remained unconscious for the entire period during which the doctor rendered services, he could not have acted in a way that manifested the intent to make a binding contract. **B** is therefore incorrect. **C** is incorrect because quasi-contract recovery is usually based on the value of the detriment sustained by the plaintiff, rather than that of the benefit received by the defendant. Where they exist, "good Samaritan" statutes protect physicians against negligence liability in connection with treatment that they render without expectation of compensation at accident or other emergency scenes. Although "good Samaritan" statutes do not extend this protection to a physician who charges for his or her services, they do not prevent him or her from doing so. **D** is therefore incorrect.

73.　**C**　A contract for the lease of realty is not illegal even though the lessee might have an illegal activity in mind when he or she enters into the lease.

　　　　Ordinarily, the courts will not aid either party to an illegal contract unless the party seeking relief was not equally guilty (*i.e.*, *in pari delicto*) with the other party. **A** and **B** are incorrect, however, because the contract to lease realty did not have an illegal purpose. **D** is incorrect because impossibility excuses performance only if it is brought about through no fault of the breaching party.

74.　**A**　Even in equitable claims, courts judge the adequacy of consideration as of the time the contract was made, not as of the time the contract was allegedly breached. Thus, if it appeared fair at the time of contracting, a court will find it enforceable. Here, at the time of contracting, the plaintiff gave up her job and promised to take care of the defendant, a job of unknown difficulty and duration. Consequently, the defendant's promise will be enforced, and the plaintiff is entitled to specific performance. **B** is incorrect because there is no question here regarding the defendant's intent to gift the property. **C** is incorrect because even though the house and farm were worth more than the services actually performed by the plaintiff, the contract as it stood at the time of contracting was not grossly unfair or inequitable. **D** is incorrect because the issue is the agreement between the plaintiff and the defendant, not the will.

75.　**A**　An offer is a manifestation of willingness to be bound to specified terms that gives an offeree the power to create a contract by accepting. Since an advertisement rarely does this, it is usually regarded as a mere invitation for offers rather than as an offer unless the circumstances indicate that the party who published the advertisement did so with the intent of empowering another to turn it into a binding contract simply by accepting it. Usually, such an intent is found only where the advertisement indicates the number of items on sale and contains words indicating an intent to be bound. Here, the phrase "While they last" makes clear that a reader of the advertisement does not have the power to turn it into a binding contract by accepting and therefore indicates an intent not to be bound.

**B, C,** and **D** are incorrect because the language used in the advertisement indicates an intent not to be bound to any person who responds.

76. **D**   Under the pre-existing duty rule, if someone does or promises to do something that he or she is already legally obligated to do, or if he or she forbears or promises to forbear from doing something he or she is not legally obligated to do, he or she has not incurred a sufficient detriment to count as consideration. Most courts hold that where one party promises another that he or she will do what he or she is already legally obligated to do for that person, the promise is not a detriment sufficient for consideration. Specifically, courts want to discourage behavior where a party takes unfair advantage of another party by threatening failure to fulfill his or her obligations. **A** is incorrect because of the pre-existing duty rule. **B** is incorrect because this is not a situation where parties are renegotiating based on any change in conditions. **C** is incorrect because while the captain was likely under some sort of duress when he agreed to the higher salaries, the agreement will not be enforced because of the pre-existing duty rule, making **D** a better answer.

77. **D**   A condition subsequent is an event which, by agreement of the parties, discharges a duty of performance that had already become absolute. The language of the sales agreement makes it clear that the seller's promise to have the downstairs apartment vacated was to be performed prior to payment by the buyer. Since it could not be undone once it was performed, there can be no condition subsequent to it. Thus, **D** is an inaccurate statement.

**A, B,** and **C** are accurate statements since performances that are to be exchanged simultaneously are usually found to be concurrently conditioned on each other.

78. **A**   UCC §2-102 provides that "this Article applies to transactions in goods." Although many of the sections of Article 2 create special rules for transactions involving merchants, many other sections apply to all transactions in goods, whether the parties are merchants or not. Therefore, **B** is incorrect. **C** is incorrect because many commercial transactions (*e.g.*, sales of realty) are not "transactions in goods" and, therefore, are not covered by Article 2. **D** is incorrect because transactions in services are not covered by Article 2.

79. **C**   A promise that is unenforceable for lack of consideration or because it fails to satisfy the requirements of the Statute of Frauds may nevertheless be enforceable under the doctrine of promissory estoppel if the promisee justifiably relied upon it to his or her detriment. If, however, no express or implied promise was made to the plaintiff, then promissory estoppel is not applicable. Although it is not certain that the trier of fact would find that no promise was implied, the argument in **C** is the only one listed that could possibly support the wife's position.

A person who acts without having been asked to and under circumstances such that his or her action was not called for by the situation is sometimes referred to as an "officious intermeddler" and is prevented from receiving compensation for his or her performance. **A** is incorrect because the wife asked for help, and also because the emergency called for the plaintiff's action. In a claim based on promissory estoppel, the promisee's recovery is not based on the value received by the promisor, but on either the promise made by the promisor or the detriment sustained by the promisee. Thus, the value of the pilot's life is not relevant to the plaintiff's claim, and **B** is incorrect. **D** is incorrect because under the doctrine of promissory estoppel, a promise may be enforceable without consideration.

80.  **C**     An offer is a manifestation of the offeror's willingness to enter into a contract on the terms specified. It is sometimes said that a communication is an offer if an acceptance is the only thing necessary to turn it into a binding contract. The language used by the seller—"Are you still interested?"—leaves some doubt about whether the letter expressed a willingness to be bound. Some courts might find that it does; some courts might find that it does not. But if a court held that the letter was not an offer, **C** is the only reason listed that would justify that conclusion.

An acceptance is an unconditional manifestation of willingness to be bound by the terms of an offer, and is, therefore, the last step that must be taken to form a contract. The seller obviously did not intend his letter to result in a contract since he asked the buyer to let him know whether he was still interested and whether the price was acceptable. Thus, even if the buyer's letter of March 11 was an offer—which is doubtful—the seller's letter of April 17 could not have been an acceptance of it. For this reason, **A** is incorrect. Under the UCC, the omission of terms in what would otherwise be a contract implies reasonable terms. Specifically, the omission of a payment term implies that full payment is to be made at the time and place of delivery. **B** is therefore incorrect. Similarly, an offer that fails to indicate how acceptance should be made implies that acceptance may be made by any reasonable means. **D** is therefore incorrect.

81.  **A**     Ordinarily, a promise is not enforceable unless it is supported by consideration. Consideration is something that is bargained for and given in exchange for the promise. Although consideration frequently is found in some benefit conferred upon a promisor in exchange for a promise, it is generally understood that a detriment suffered by the promisee is sufficient consideration for a promise if it was bargained for and given in exchange for that promise. Since the defendant desired for the plaintiff to be near him, he promised to give her a franchise if she would move to the city and live near him. Whether or not the defendant gained any benefit from her move, the plaintiff suffered the detriment of moving from her home to the city. This detriment, having been bargained for in exchange for the defendant's promise, is sufficient to satisfy the requirement of consideration.

A promise that is unsupported by consideration may be enforceable anyway under the doctrine of promissory estoppel if the promisee justifiably relied on it to his or her detriment. **B** is incorrect, however, because the defendant's promise was supported by consideration, and the doctrine of promissory estoppel applies only in the absence of consideration. It is sometimes argued that where a promise is made to confer a benefit on another person in return for some act that is of no benefit to the promisor, the promise is one for a conditional gift and is therefore unenforceable. This argument does not apply, however, where the detriment suffered by the promisee was something that the promisor wanted and was an inducement for the promisor's promise. Since the defendant desired for the plaintiff to live near him in the city, and since it was this desire that motivated his promise to her, **C** is incorrect. Affection is not enough to support a promise and cannot serve as consideration because it is not something bargained for in exchange for a promise. **D** is incorrect, however, because the promise made by the defendant was given not merely out of affection for the plaintiff but to induce the plaintiff to move to the city.

82. **D**  UCC §2-601 provides that if goods delivered fail in any respect to conform to the contract of sale, the buyer may reject the whole, accept the whole, or accept any commercial units (*i.e.*, quantities that may be sold commercially without substantially impairing their value) and reject the rest. UCC §2-607 provides that acceptance does not of itself impair any other remedy for nonconformity. Finally, UCC §2-714 permits a buyer to recover damages resulting from the nonconformity of accepted goods.

83. **D**  If the circumstances that resulted in destruction of the structure excused performance by the builder, his refusal to continue was not a breach. Since, however, he did not perform as promised, his only remedy would be in quasi-contract. If the circumstances did not excuse performance by the builder, his refusal to continue was a breach. Even a breaching builder may be entitled to a quasi-contract remedy, however, if the owner of the premises received some benefit as a result of his or her work. In either event, the builder's recovery would be limited to the value of the benefit received by the landowner. Since this was a contract for a new structure, and the structure was completely destroyed, the landowner received no benefit from the builder's work. The builder is therefore not entitled to any recovery.

A seller's damages for the buyer's breach of a contract for the sale of goods may consist of the difference between the contract price and the market value of the goods. The measure of damages expressed in **A** seems to be based on this rule, but it is incorrect because it is not an accurate statement of that rule and because this is not a contract for the sale of goods. **B** and **C** are incorrect because quasi-contract damages are measured by the benefit received by the defendant, and the landowner received no benefit at all.

84. **D**  A condition precedent to a contractual obligation is an event that must occur before a party will be under a duty to perform. Real estate brokerage contracts frequently make the broker's commission due upon producing a buyer who is "ready, willing, and able" to purchase on the agreed terms. In the contract by which the defendant agreed to pay a 6 percent commission to the plaintiff, however, there were two express conditions precedent to the defendant's obligation to pay. First, the commission was due only if the house was sold to a buyer who made an offer during a two-month period beginning September 1. Second, the commission was due only upon the closing of title. Although the plaintiff found a buyer during the agreed period, the house was not sold to that buyer. In addition, title did not close. Since there was a failure of these conditions precedent, the defendant's obligation to pay the plaintiff's commission never became absolute, and the plaintiff is entitled to no recovery from the defendant.

**A**, **B**, and **C** are therefore incorrect.

85.  **B**     Under Rest. 2d §89(a), a modification is binding if it is "fair and equitable in view of circumstances not anticipated by the parties when the contract was made." Here, the modification was fair and equitable, voluntarily entered into, and motivated by events that were not anticipated at the time the original contract was created. Specifically, an additional $10,000 per year does not seem unreasonable in the face of an "explosion" of new development. **A** is incorrect because the modification is not necessarily enforceable simply because the city council agreed to it. **C** is incorrect because of the rule regarding modification. **D** is incorrect because there is no indication in the facts that the collector took unfair advantage of the city.

86.  **A**     One who will derive a benefit from a contract to which he or she is not a party is a third-party beneficiary of that contract. If the contracting parties meant for their contract to benefit the third party, he or she is an intended third-party beneficiary. At some point, an intended third-party beneficiary may acquire the right to enforce the contract even though he or she was not a party to it. Some jurisdictions hold that he or she acquires that right upon learning of the contract; others hold that he or she acquires that right upon justifiably and detrimentally relying on the contract; and still others hold that he or she acquires the right either upon relying or upon assenting to the contract. All agree, however, that justified and detrimental reliance by an intended third-party beneficiary gives him or her the right to enforce the contract. If the plaintiff relied on the agreement between his parents by cancelling his contract to purchase a residence, he is entitled to enforce the agreement against the defendant's estate.

               If the benefit to a third party was intended to fulfill an obligation that one of the contracting parties owed him, the third party is referred to as a *creditor beneficiary*. Otherwise, the third party is a donee beneficiary. **B** is incorrect because the distinction is based on the intentions of the contracting parties at the time the contract was formed and because neither parent owed the plaintiff an obligation that was to be satisfied by leaving him the realty. The plaintiff was, thus, a donee beneficiary of the contract between his parents. **C** is incorrect, however, because a donee beneficiary may enforce a contract if the contracting parties intended to confer a benefit on him or her (subject to the above rules regarding the rights of intended third-party beneficiaries). If, by its terms, an agreement is not capable of being performed within one year, the Statute of Frauds requires a writing. Since the agreement between the plaintiff's parents was in writing, its enforceability does not depend on whether it could be performed within one year. **D** is therefore incorrect.

87.  **B**     All courts agree that a plaintiff's promise to waive a valid claim constitutes sufficient consideration for the defendant's promise to pay a settlement. Additionally, most modern courts would probably hold that the waiver of an invalid claim constitutes sufficient consideration for a settlement if the plaintiff, at the time of settlement, had a bona fide subjective belief that the claim was valid, and this belief was not unreasonable. Here, the plaintiff had a subjective belief that the defendant was the child's father, and it was likely reasonable, as the defendant was willing to pay a settlement to avoid a paternity suit. **A** is incorrect because there is no evidence of detrimental reliance on the part of the plaintiff. **C** is incorrect because forbearance to bring suit can count as consideration for a settlement. **D** is incorrect because the plaintiff had a bona fide subjective belief that the claim was valid, and her belief was not unreasonable.

88. **B** An effective assignment transfers all the assignor's rights to the assignee. If the specialist made an effective assignment of her rights under the contract with the firm, she can no longer enforce those rights, and the court must find against her.

Since the contract called for payment of $5,000 within 30 days after installation of the hardware and did not require design of the software until several months later, the parties could not have intended design or its commencement to be conditions precedent to payment. **A** is therefore not an effective argument. **C** is incorrect because the contract apportioned $6,000 to the value of the hardware, making the obligation to pay (at least the initial $5,000) unrelated to fulfillment of other obligations under the contract. A divisible contract is one in which separate obligations are regarded as separately enforceable agreements. If this contract was divisible, then the obligation to pay for the hardware already delivered would not be dependent on any other obligation. **D** is incorrect because this argument would hurt, rather than help, the firm's cause.

89. **D** Ordinarily, an order to buy goods for current shipment will be deemed accepted if the seller ships conforming or non-conforming goods. However, "such a shipment of non-conforming goods does not constitute an acceptance if the seller seasonably notifies the buyer that the shipment is offered only as an accommodation to the buyer." UCC §2-206(1)(b). Importantly, when a seller makes an accommodation shipment, the shipment is treated as a counteroffer of the goods that have been shipped as they are. When the buyer receives the nonconforming goods, he or she can: (1) keep the nonconforming goods, in which case there is a contract for the goods as they are, at the price the seller has indicated he or she will charge for them; or (2) the buyer can reject the shipment and thus prevent a contract from coming into existence at all. However, the buyer cannot hold the seller in breach for having shipped nonconforming goods or demand conforming goods. Under the facts here, based on the manufacturer's notice, the manufacturer's shipment of the 50 vials was a counteroffer. Consequently, there was never a contract for the other 950 vials, and the distributor is not entitled to specific performance. Thus, **A** and **B** are incorrect. **C** is incorrect because the issue is whether there was an accommodation, not anything regarding the distributor's business practices.

90. **C** Ordinarily, a promise is unenforceable unless supported by consideration. Since consideration involves a bargained-for exchange, a preexisting obligation cannot serve as consideration for a new promise, since it was not given in exchange for that promise. Except for the $250 per month that the plaintiff was already obligated to pay the defendant, the plaintiff gave nothing in return for the defendant's promise to deliver the tiger. Thus, the defendant's promise was unsupported by consideration and is therefore unenforceable.

**A** is incorrect for two reasons: First, the UCC defines the term *merchant* in terms of the sale of *goods*, not services, so there can be no merchant as to the sale of services, and second, the requirement of consideration is not suspended when one of the parties to a promise is a merchant. UCC §2-209 provides that an agreement modifying a contract under UCC Article 2 needs no consideration to be binding. **B** is incorrect, however, because under UCC §2-102, Article 2 applies only to transactions in goods. Since the original contract between the defendant and the plaintiff was for veterinary *services*, it does not come under Article 2. Therefore, UCC §2-209 does not apply to the attempted modification. **D** is incorrect because an agreement to modify a contract need not be in writing to be valid unless the contract, as modified, comes within the provisions of the Statute of Frauds. Since the Statute of Frauds requires a contract for the sale of goods with a price of $500 or more to be in writing, and since this agreement—even as modified—called for services and goods without a price of $500 or more, it does not fall within the provisions of the Statute of Frauds.

91. **A**    Under UCC §2-606, acceptance occurs when the buyer fails to make an effective rejection. Under §2-602, rejection must be made within a reasonable time after delivery and is ineffective unless the buyer seasonably notifies the seller. Since the retailer was aware of the nonconformity the day the boards were delivered but failed to notify the wholesaler of the nonconformity until the wholesaler sued him four months later, he accepted the boards. Ordinarily, a buyer who accepts the nonconforming goods may claim damages as a setoff against the contract price. Under UCC §2-607, however, a buyer who accepts delivery of nonconforming goods and fails to notify the seller within a reasonable time after discovering the nonconformity is barred from any remedy.

**B** is incorrect because a buyer who notifies the seller within a reasonable time may revoke his or her acceptance or may use damages resulting from nonconformity of the goods as a setoff against the contract price. Although the boards did not conform to the contract of sale, **C** is incorrect because the retailer failed to seasonably notify the wholesaler of the nonconformity. **D** is incorrect because it has no basis in existing law. Even if the seller could have avoided the nonconformity by making a reasonable inspection, he or she is entitled to collect the contract price of goods that the buyer accepts without notifying him or her of the nonconformity.

92. **D**    Consideration usually consists of some legal detriment suffered by the promisee that is given in exchange for the promisor's promise. Since the manufacturer gave nothing in return for the engine maker's promise to keep the offer open, her promise was not supported by consideration.

Under UCC §2-205, an assurance given by a merchant in a signed writing that an offer regarding the sale of goods will be held open is called a "firm offer," and may be enforced without consideration. **A** is incorrect, however, because although such an offer may be binding without consideration, it is not supported by consideration unless the offeree suffers some detriment in exchange for it. **B** is incorrect for a similar reason. Sometimes justified and detrimental reliance may make a promise enforceable even though it was not supported by consideration, but, although detrimental reliance may serve as a substitute for consideration, it is not consideration. Although a subsequent purchase by the manufacturer might constitute legal detriment, it could not be consideration for the engine maker's promise because the engine maker did not require it in exchange for her promise. **C** is therefore incorrect.

93. **C**    Ordinarily a promise is not enforceable unless there was consideration (*i.e.*, something given in exchange for and to induce the promise) for it. Since the assistant's service had already been rendered without expectation of payment, it was not given in exchange for

the promise and is not consideration for it. Some cases have held, however, that a promise to do that which the promisor is morally obligated to do should be enforceable. Since this is an infrequently applied exception to the requirement of consideration, it is unlikely that a court would come to this conclusion. **C** is the only one of the arguments listed, however, that could result in a victory for the assistant.

**A** is incorrect because an otherwise unenforceable promise is not made enforceable simply because it is in writing. Sometimes, a promisee's justified and detrimental reliance makes a promise enforceable, serving as a substitute for consideration. Detrimental reliance means, however, that the promisee changed his or her position for the worse because he or she believed that the promise would be kept. **B** is incorrect since there is no fact indicating that the assistant relied on her promise by changing his position because of it, or that he was worse off as a result. When a person confers a benefit on another with a reasonable expectation of payment, an implied-in-fact contract may result. **D** is incorrect, however, because there is no fact indicating that the assistant had any expectation of payment when he rescued the defendant, particularly because he thought the defendant was dead when he leaped into the shaft.

94.   **B**   If, at the time a contract is formed, the parties to it are operating under a mutual mistake, the resulting lack of mutual agreement excuses non-performance by either party. Thus, if both the buyer and the dealer mistakenly believed that the painting was painted by the famous artist, the buyer's non-performance would not constitute a breach.

A is incorrect for two reasons: First, the Statute of Frauds requirement that the writing be signed by the party to be charged may be satisfied by the buyer's check, and second, delivery by the seller satisfies the Statute of Frauds. UCC §2-302(1) (and some jurisdictions in non-UCC cases) hold that if a contract was unconscionable at the time it was made, the court may refuse to enforce it. **C** is incorrect, however, because the equality of bargaining positions in a contract between experts (such as an art dealer and an art collector) prevents a voluntary agreement from being unconscionable unless one of them deliberately withholds knowledge from the other. To avoid interfering with the freedom to bargain, courts rarely consider the adequacy of consideration except in consumer contracts when equitable relief is sought. **D** is therefore incorrect.

95.   **B**   A contract that had an illegal purpose when it was made is unenforceable by either party. Of course, the fact that one of the parties had an illegal objective in mind when he or she entered into an otherwise lawful contract is not enough to make that contract illegal. These facts indicate, however, that both parties knew the illegal purpose for which the premises were to be used, that the landlord agreed to equip it specifically for that purpose, and that computation of the rent was based on the tenant's profits from his unlawful activity. Under the circumstances, the contract was an agreement to engage in an unlawful activity. Even though the operation of a "sports book" subsequently became lawful, the illegality of the contract at the time of its formation makes it unenforceable. Although refusing to require the return of the tenant's deposit is likely to benefit the landlord, public policy considerations justify such refusal. When asked to enforce a contract with an unlawful purpose, the court will leave the parties as it found them.

The contract between the landlord and the tenant was not a gambling contract since none of the obligations depended upon the outcome of an event over which neither had control. **A** is therefore incorrect, even though public policy does prohibit the enforcement of gambling contracts. Sometimes the courts will come to the aid of one party to a contract with an unlawful purpose, arguing that he or she was not *in pari delicto* (*i.e.*, equally guilty) with the other party. **C** is incorrect, however, because the fact that two parties were *in pari delicto* is never used to justify granting relief to one of them. When an unforeseeable change in circumstances makes a contract fail of its essential purpose, the parties to it may be excused from performance under the doctrine of frustration of purpose. **D** is incorrect because the change in circumstances in this case did not interfere with the essential purpose of the contract but rather aided it.

96. **C**    Generally, a buyer's damages for a seller's non-delivery consist of the difference between the contract price and the market price on the day of delivery. Since the market price and the contract price are identical, the restaurant has sustained no real damage as a result of the farmer's non-delivery of 1,000 bushels. (Although the restaurant may be entitled to *incidental* damages, which include the cost of finding another seller, **C** is still correct because of its emphasis on the restaurant's lack of "substantial" damage.)

Ordinarily a circumstance that prevented a party from performing will excuse non-performance only if its occurrence was not foreseeable to the parties at the time of contracting. This is true whether that circumstance is described as an Act of God or not. (After all, almost everything a farmer does depends on Acts of God.) Since there is no fact indicating that the April storms were unforeseeable, **A** is incorrect. A breach of contract is not excused simply because the breaching party gave notice in advance that there would be a breach. There is a rule that one who treats an anticipatory repudiation as an immediate breach is required to mitigate damages. That rule is inapplicable here, however, because the restaurant did not treat the farmer's statement as an immediate breach, taking no action until the farmer's non-delivery. **B** is therefore incorrect. The rights of contracting parties are not ordinarily relative to the obligations that they may owe under other contracts. Thus, the fact that the farmer owed obligations to the buyer under a separate contract would not affect the obligations that she owed to the restaurant under her contract with it. **D** is therefore incorrect.

97. **B**    A unilateral contract is one in which only the offeror promises to perform, and only if the offeree performs a specified act. Since the homeowner's offer was to pay $1,000 to the person who "finds the thief," he has made an offer for a unilateral contract. As with any offer, an offer for a unilateral contract does not become binding unless it is accepted before it is effectively revoked. Since an offer for a unilateral contract can be accepted only by performing the required act, the bar owner could accept the homeowner's offer only by catching the thief before the homeowner effectively revoked the offer. (*Note:* Many authorities hold that an offeror may not effectively revoke after substantial performance by the offeree in reliance on the offer.)

Some jurisdictions hold that an offer for a unilateral contract becomes irrevocable after an offeree substantially commences performance. The bar owner did not commence performance, however, so his statement alone is not sufficient to make the homeowner's offer irrevocable even in those jurisdictions. **A** is therefore incorrect. A bilateral contract is one in which the parties exchange promises, each promise serving as consideration for the other. Although the bar owner's statement might be construed as a promise, the homeowner's offer made clear that acceptance could be made only by catching the thief. For this reason, the bar owner's promise (if it was a promise) could not be an acceptance of the homeowner's offer, and no bilateral contract could have been formed. **C** is therefore incorrect. An offer is a manifestation of the offeror's intention to enter into a contract with the offeree on the terms specified, which raises in the reasonable person an expectation that nothing more than acceptance is required to create a contract. Since the homeowner's statement expressed an intention to pay the specified amount to any person who performed the specified task, it is an offer. **D** is therefore incorrect.

98. **C**     A liquidated damages clause is a provision in a contract fixing the amount of damages should a breach occur. Courts enforce liquidated damages clauses so long as the amount set is reasonable, the actual damages are difficult to ascertain, and the contract tailors the liquidated damages to the circumstances. If any of these requirements is unfulfilled, the clause is unenforceable as a "penalty." In that event, the parties may collect only the actual damages that resulted from the breach. The purpose of an agreement as to liquidated damages is to eliminate the problems that may arise in establishing or defending against actual damage claims in certain circumstances. For this reason, if the liquidated damages clause is enforceable, it provides the only *damage* remedy. It does not, however, prevent the wronged party from seeking other *non-damage* relief. Thus, even if the liquidated damages clause did not establish a penalty (*i.e.*, was enforceable), the builder may be entitled to the equitable remedy of specific performance. **C** is therefore correct.

99. **B**     The standard measure of damages for a buyer's breach of a sales contract is the difference between the price that the buyer agreed to pay and the reasonable market value or price received by the seller upon resale in a commercially reasonable manner. Under the standard measure for damages, the dealer would not be entitled to recover from the first buyer since it sold the car to the second buyer at the same price that the first buyer agreed to pay. UCC §2-708 provides, however, that where the standard measure of damages "is inadequate to put the seller in as good a position as performance would have done," the seller may recover the profit that it would have made from full performance by the buyer. If the first buyer had performed as agreed, the dealer would have made one profit from the sale of a car to the first buyer and a second profit from the sale of a car to the second buyer. As a result of the first buyer's breach, the dealer made only one profit—the one derived from its sale to the second buyer. The standard measure of damages is thus insufficient to put the dealer in as good a position as if the first buyer had performed as agreed. For this reason, the dealer is entitled to the profit that it would have made upon selling the car to the first buyer. Since its profit consists of the difference between the wholesale price and the retail price, **B** is correct.

A and C are incorrect for the reason discussed above. In addition to being incorrect for this reason, D is incorrect because it is not based on any of the existing rules for measuring damages, and also because it bears no logical relationship to damages actually resulting from the first buyer's breach.

100.  **B**    A contract may make the happening of a particular event a condition precedent to the performance of a contractual duty. If so, the obligation to perform that duty does not become absolute until the condition precedent is fulfilled. Thus, if the plaintiff's remaining in law school was a condition precedent to his mother's obligation to pay, the fact that the plaintiff withdrew in December 2012 would relieve his mother of that obligation. A condition precedent may be express (*i.e.*, stated in words or a substitute for words) or implied (*i.e.*, not stated, but capable of being reasonably inferred from the conduct or language of the parties). The fact that the plaintiff's mother's promise was not to be performed until July 1, 2013, might justify the inference that the plaintiff's remaining in law school until that time was a condition precedent to his mother's obligation. Although it is not certain that such an inference would be drawn, B is the only argument listed that might support his mother's position.

Since it might take longer than one year to complete law school, and since the plaintiff's mother promised to pay within one year, it is obvious that completion of law school could not have been a condition precedent to the plaintiff's mother's obligation. A is therefore incorrect. Consideration may consist of some legal detriment suffered by a promisee in return for the promisor's obligation. A person suffers a legal detriment when he or she does or undertakes to do something that he or she is not already under an obligation to do. Since the plaintiff was not legally obligated to stop drinking or to go to law school, his promises and undertakings to do so were legal detriments, and therefore may serve as consideration for his mother's obligation. For this reason, C is incorrect. The Statute of Frauds makes an oral contract unenforceable over objection if, by its own terms, it cannot be performed within one year. Although the agreement between the plaintiff and his mother required the plaintiff to go to law school and to stop drinking for the rest of his life, these obligations could have been fully performed within one year since the plaintiff could have died within that period. D is therefore incorrect.

101.  **C**    A transfer of contract rights is called an assignment; a transfer of contract duties is called a delegation. In general, contract duties are delegable so long as delegation would not prevent the obligee from getting what he or she bargained for. Duties that involve personal services (*i.e.*, that depend upon the obligor's special skills, training, or expertise) are not delegable because an obligee who bargained for the obligor's special abilities would not be receiving them if the obligor's duties were performed by another. Whether crop-dusting is an activity that depends on the unique skills of the crop-duster (*i.e.*, calls for personal services) is uncertain. But even if it is, the fact that the defendant did not herself participate in the activity would indicate that the plaintiff probably did not bargain for and certainly would not have received her special skills anyway. Thus, the delegation to the pilot would not deprive the plaintiff of what he bargained for, and would therefore not be a violation of the plaintiff's rights.

Although the statement contained in **A** is an accurate one, it would not provide the defendant with an effective response to the plaintiff's claim because if a contract duty requires personal services, it is not delegable. If a contract duty requires the personal services of the obligor, it is generally understood that the obligee bargained for its performance by the obligor himself or herself. **B** is incorrect because such a duty may be non-delegable even if the delegatee possesses skills equal to or greater than those of the delegator. In general, contract rights are assignable so long as the assignment does not increase the burden of the obligor's performance. Although it requires the obligor to pay a different person than the one he or she agreed to pay, an assignment of the right to collect money usually does not increase his or her burden since it does not change the amount of money that the obligor must pay. **D** is incorrect, however, because the plaintiff has not objected to the defendant's assignment of rights but rather to the defendant's delegation of duties.

102.  **B**  Ever since 1677, the Statute of Frauds has required a promise to answer for the debt of another to be in writing. Since the shareholder's promise was to pay the debt of the corporation, it would be unenforceable over the shareholder's objection if it was not in writing.

Although a promise made under duress (*i.e.*, induced by an improper threat) is void, *economic* duress rarely justifies avoidance of a promise. In addition, for any duress to make a promise void, the duress must have resulted from some improper threat made by the promisee. Since the economic distress of the corporation did not result from any conduct or threat by the bank, and since the bank's refusal to lend money without a personal guarantee was not improper, the economic fears that induced the shareholder's promise will not result in its avoidance. **A** is therefore incorrect. A promise is generally not enforceable unless it is supported by consideration. But consideration may consist of either some benefit conferred upon the promisor or some detriment incurred by the promisee. Since the bank lent money to the corporation in return for the shareholder's promise, the bank incurred a detriment that satisfies the requirement of consideration even if the shareholder gained no benefit from it. **C** is therefore incorrect. **D** is incorrect because a surety becomes liable immediately upon default by the principal debtor and is not entitled to have the creditor proceed first against the principal debtor's assets. (Even without applying this principle, however, **D** can be eliminated because the shareholder promised to pay if the corporation did not, and the corporation did not.)

103.  **A**  Novation is the substitution by mutual consent of a third person for a party to a contract. By assigning to the woman, the tenant agreed to substitute the woman for him. It may be argued that by accepting rent from the woman with the knowledge that the tenant had assigned to the woman, the landlord was also consenting to the substitution of the woman for the tenant as a party to the contract. Although it is not certain that a court would come to that conclusion, the argument set forth in **A** is the only one that could possibly be effective in the tenant's defense.

An accord is an agreement by which a new obligation is imposed on one of the parties to a contract in place of one that the contract originally created. Satisfaction occurs when the party on whom that obligation was imposed fulfills it. A party who satisfies the new obligation imposed upon him or her as a result of the accord is discharged from the performance of the original obligation for which the new one was substituted. Since the landlord's accepting rent from the woman did not result in the imposition of any new obligation on the tenant, it was not an accord. Therefore, there could have been no satisfaction. For this reason, **B** is not an effective argument in the tenant's defense. Consent is willingness. Implied consent is willingness that the reasonable person would gather or infer by observing the conduct of a party. Since the landlord accepted rent directly from the woman knowing that the tenant had assigned the balance of the lease to the woman, the reasonable person might gather or infer that the landlord was willing for that assignment to take place. It might, thus, be correct to conclude that the landlord impliedly consented to the assignment. **C** is not an effective argument in the tenant's defense, however, because after an assignment, the assignor remains secondarily liable for performance under the contract. This is so even when the other party has consented, expressly or impliedly, to the assignment. The word *alienation* is sometimes used to mean the transfer of an interest in real property, and since an assignment is a transfer, a prohibition against assigning a leasehold interest is a restraint against alienation. Since the courts look with disfavor on restraints against alienation, they are strictly construed. **D** does not present an effective argument in the tenant's defense, however, for two reasons: First, restraints on alienation, if properly drawn, are enforceable, and second, the secondary liability of an assignor as described above makes the question of whether the assignment was a valid one irrelevant (*i.e.*, if the assignment was invalid, the tenant would be primarily liable; if the assignment was valid, the tenant would be secondarily liable).

104.   **A**   A promise is ordinarily not enforceable unless it is supported by consideration. Thus, a promise to make a gift is not usually enforceable. Once a gift has been completed, however, the donee's rights do not depend on the donor's promise. Thus, although a promise to make a gift may be unenforceable, a completed (or executed) gift creates an irrevocable right in the donee. The completion of a gift requires an intent to create a property right coupled with delivery and acceptance of some symbol of that right. It is clear that the defendant intended to create a right in the plaintiff. Delivery and acceptance probably occurred when the plaintiff was advised of the publisher's promise. While it is not certain that a court would come to that conclusion, **A** is the only argument listed that could possibly provide the plaintiff with an effective response to the defendant's defense of no consideration.

An assignment is a transfer from assignor to assignee of the assignor's right to receive performance under a contract. Since the defendant's contract with the publisher did not give the defendant the right to be hired by the publisher as a book illustrator, the benefit that the plaintiff received could not have been received by assignment. **B** is therefore incorrect. **C** is incorrect because the law of contracts does not recognize any special rule about consideration in agreements between husband and wife. Although **D** addresses consideration that the publisher received for his promise, it is incorrect because it does not address the defendant's defense (*i.e.*, that there was no consideration for the defendant's promise to the plaintiff).

105.  **D**   An offer can ordinarily be accepted at any time prior to its termination. An offer terminates, however, when the offeree becomes aware that the offeror has acted in a manner inconsistent with the offer. When the buyer learned that the seller had sold the painting to someone else, the seller's offer terminated, depriving the buyer of the power to accept it. This is true even though the buyer did not learn of the offer's termination directly from the seller.

**A** is therefore incorrect. Since the buyer gave nothing in return for the seller's promise to keep the offer open until February 2, his promise was unsupported by consideration. Ordinarily, a promise to keep an offer open for a specified period of time is unenforceable unless supported by consideration. Under UCC §2-205, a written promise by a merchant to hold an offer open for a specified period not to exceed three months is a "firm offer," enforceable without consideration. **B** is incorrect, however, because there is no fact indicating that the seller was a merchant. The standard remedy for breach of contract is a judgment for damages. Although specific performance is available in the case of a contract for the sale of a unique chattel, the wronged party may still choose to seek a judgment for damages. **C** is therefore incorrect.

106.  **D**   UCC §2-202 provides that a writing intended by the parties to be a final expression of their agreement cannot be modified by evidence of a prior or contemporaneous agreement. It further provides, however, that its terms may be explained by usage of trade. UCC §1-205 defines the term *"usage of trade"* as a practice or method of dealing that is so regularly observed in a trade as to justify the expectation that it will be observed in a particular transaction. Since the seller's testimony would show that calling scmods "rock lurgid" is a usage of trade, it should be admitted to explain the meaning of that term.

**A** is therefore incorrect. Since the law of contracts does not require contracting parties to agree to the market price, **B** is incorrect. A contract is supposed to be interpreted according to the intentions of the parties. For this reason, usage of trade is admissible because it tends to show what members of a particular trade intended by the use of certain language. If one of the parties to a contract was unaware of a particular trade usage, he or she may attempt to prove this to a court or jury to convince it that the trade usage meaning was not what he or she intended. Since the trade usage may still be evidence of what the other party intended, however, it should be admitted. **C** is therefore incorrect.

107.  **D**   Contracts frequently benefit persons other than the contracting parties (*i.e.*, third-party beneficiaries). In general, contracts can be enforced only by parties to them. Under some circumstances, however, intended third-party beneficiaries can enforce contracts to which they are not parties. Whether a third-party beneficiary is an "intended" beneficiary depends in part on whether the contract called for performance to be made directly to that third party. If not, he or she is merely an "incidental" beneficiary and has no right of enforcement. Although the defendant knew that the plaintiff's father intended to give the house to the plaintiff, the defendant may argue that the plaintiff was not an "intended beneficiary" because the contract did not require the defendant to perform directly for the plaintiff (*i.e.*, the lot was the plaintiff's father's). A court might rule differently, but **D** is the only argument listed that might be effective in the defendant's defense.

When performance is not designed to satisfy a preexisting obligation to a third-party beneficiary, that third-party beneficiary is a donee beneficiary. However, when performance is designed to satisfy a preexisting obligation to a third-party beneficiary, he or she is a creditor beneficiary. Because there is some question about whether the plaintiff's father owed the plaintiff any obligation as a result of his oral promise to her, it is difficult to determine whether she is a donee or creditor beneficiary. **A** and **B** are both incorrect, however, because both donee and creditor beneficiaries may be able to enforce contracts to which they are not parties. **C** is incorrect because the facts indicate that the plaintiff cancelled a contract to buy a house as a result of the plaintiff's father's promise.

108. **B**     An offer is an expression by the offeror of willingness to enter into a contract with the offeree on specified terms. A valid offer creates in the offeree the power of acceptance. To determine whether a particular communication qualifies as an offer, it is thus necessary to decide whether the reasonable person in the position of the offeree would believe that nothing more than his or her acceptance is required to form a contract. Although the storeowner's letter of January 5 used the word "offer," it indicated that it was being made to four different people. Since he had only one diamond ring for sale, it must have been obvious to each of the people who received the storeowner's letter that someone else might purchase it first. For this reason, none of them could reasonably have believed that his or her acceptance was all that was necessary to form a contract. The storeowner's letter was, therefore, not an offer but merely an invitation to negotiate. At best, then, the first buyer's letter was an offer. Since the storeowner did not accept it, no contract was formed between the storeowner and the first buyer.

    **A** is incorrect for two reasons: First, as explained above, the storeowner's letter to the first buyer was not an offer, and second, if it had been an offer, it could not have been revoked after the first buyer accepted it by his letter of January 14. **C** is incorrect because the storeowner's letter was not an offer. Since the storeowner was under no obligation to sell the ring to the first buyer, the date of his negotiation and agreement with the second buyer is irrelevant in the first buyer's case. **D** is therefore incorrect.

109. **C**     UCC §2-609 provides that when one party to a contract has reasonable grounds for insecurity about the other's performance, it may demand assurances and suspend its own performance until they are received. The section also provides that failure to furnish such assurances is a repudiation of the contract. Since UCC §2-210 provides that a delegation of contract duties is a reasonable ground for insecurity, the wholesaler's sale to the plaintiff gave the defendant the right to demand assurances from the plaintiff. Since the plaintiff failed to provide assurances, the defendant was entitled to suspend performance and did not breach by doing so.

    **A** is therefore incorrect. **B** is incorrect because UCC §2-210 specifically provides that delegation of contract duties provides the other party with reasonable grounds for insecurity. **D** is incorrect because UCC §2-210 provides that (except under the special circumstances set forth in that section) a party may perform its contract obligations through a delegate.

110.  **D**  When parties to a contract agree that one of the benefits of the contract will flow directly to a non-contracting party, that person is an intended third-party beneficiary. If the agreement was made for the purpose of satisfying an obligation that one of the contracting parties owed to the third-party beneficiary, he or she is a creditor beneficiary. Otherwise, he or she is a donee beneficiary. Once his or her rights have vested, a donee beneficiary can enforce the contract even though he or she was not a party to it. Some jurisdictions hold that a donee beneficiary's rights vest when he or she learns of the contract; others hold that his or her rights vest when he or she relies on the contract to his or her detriment. All agree, however, that until his or her rights vest, the parties may modify the contract without incurring any liability to the donee beneficiary. Since the daughter did not learn of the contract until after the parties had modified it to eliminate the benefit to her, she has no right to enforce it.

111.  **C**  A non-contracting party who will benefit from a contract between two other persons is a third-party beneficiary. If the contracting parties intended that the benefit flow to him or her when they contracted, he or she is an intended beneficiary. If they did not, he or she is an incidental beneficiary. Although an intended beneficiary may be entitled, under certain circumstances, to enforce the contract, an incidental beneficiary is not. In determining whether a third party is an intended beneficiary, courts usually consider whether a statement to that effect was made during negotiations or in the contract, and whether performance or payment is to flow directly to the beneficiary. Since the contract between the landowner and the defendant called for the construction of a house on property that belonged to the landowner, and since there was no mention made of any contract right flowing to the daughter, the daughter is probably an incidental beneficiary and not entitled to enforce the contract against the defendant.

**A** is therefore incorrect. Although a contract calling for personal services is not ordinarily assignable, **B** is incorrect because the landowner has made no attempt to assign to his daughter his rights under the contract with the defendant. A donee beneficiary is an intended third-party beneficiary to whom neither party was under an obligation at the time the contract between them was formed. Even if the daughter were a donee beneficiary, however, **D** would be incorrect because a donee beneficiary may have rights to enforce the contract.

112.  **A**  Ordinarily, no promise is enforceable without consideration. Consideration consists of some legal detriment suffered by the promisee in return for the promise. Since the plaintiff suffered no legal detriment in return for the defendant's promise to keep the offer open, the defendant's promise is unenforceable.

UCC §2-205 provides that a promise to keep an offer open for a specified period of time is binding without consideration if made by a merchant, in a signed writing, and the transaction involves the sale of goods. This kind of offer is known as a "firm offer." The section also provides that the maximum time for which a firm offer is binding is three months. **B**, **C**, and **D** are all designed to trap examinees who are confused about UCC §2-205. All are incorrect because UCC §2-205 applies only to transactions in goods and has no application to the sale of realty. In addition, **B** is incorrect because the section sets a time limit of three months rather than 30 days. **D** is also incorrect because the section requires only that the offeror be a merchant and fixes no such requirement about the offeree.

113.   **A**   An assignment transfers the assignor's rights to the assignee and extinguishes those rights in the assignor. Thus, if the plaintiff has made a valid assignment of his rights to another person, the plaintiff no longer has those rights and cannot enforce them against the defendant.

A non-contracting party who will benefit from the contract is a third-party beneficiary. If the contracting parties intended him or her to benefit, he or she is an intended third-party beneficiary; if not, he or she is an incidental beneficiary. If they intended him or her to benefit to satisfy an obligation that one of the contracting parties owed him or her, he or she is a creditor beneficiary; if not, he or she is a donee beneficiary. Since the agreement between the landscaper and the defendant specified that part of the price was to be paid directly to the plaintiff, the contracting parties clearly intended that the plaintiff benefit from the contract. For this reason, he was an intended beneficiary. Since they did so to satisfy a debt that the landscaper owed the plaintiff, the plaintiff is a creditor beneficiary. **B** and **D** are incorrect because a creditor beneficiary may enforce the contract even though he or she is not a party to it. **C** is incorrect because the plaintiff is an intended rather an incidental beneficiary.

114.   **B**   Ordinarily, the damages remedy is designed to put the parties in the position in which they would have been had the contract not been breached. If the builder had not breached the contract, the manufacturer would have a building that conformed to his specifications at a price of $250,000. To make the manufacturer whole, then, the builder should be required to pay the cost of making the building conform to the specifications.

Although the building has the same value that it would have had if it conformed to the specifications, it is not the building that the manufacturer contracted for, and it would cost the manufacturer $12,000 to make it so. Since damages should place the parties in the position for which they bargained, **A** is incorrect. Since it would cost only $12,000 to make the building conform to the bargained-for specifications, it would be unjust to permit the manufacturer to receive a windfall by making the builder pay damages based on the difference between the building's value and the value that resulted from an increase in construction costs. **C** is therefore incorrect. **D** is incorrect because the manufacturer has received some value and should not be permitted to keep it without paying for it.

115.   **B**   An offer is a manifestation of present intent to be bound to specified terms. One of the tests of whether a statement should be construed as an offer is whether a reasonable person in the shoes of a person receiving it would believe that only his or her expression of assent is necessary to form a binding contract. Since each of the recipients knew that there were three other recipients, each knew that his or her own expression of assent might not result in a contract because it might not be the highest offer. Also, since the seller's letter referred to the responses that he expected to receive as "offers," a court would probably hold that it was nothing more than an invitation for offers. While it is not

certain that a court would come to that conclusion, **B** is the only option listed that could possibly be correct.

Under UCC §2-205, a "firm offer" is a written promise by a merchant to hold an offer to buy or sell goods open for a specified period of time. Since there is no indication that the seller was a merchant, his letter could not have been a firm offer. **A** is therefore incorrect. An option is an agreement to hold an offer open for a specified period of time, and (except for the provisions of UCC §2-205) is not enforceable without consideration. Since none of the recipients of the seller's letter gave anything in return for it (*i.e.*, consideration), it could not have been an option. **C** is therefore incorrect. An auction is a public sale of property to the highest bidder conducted in the presence of all prospective buyers or their agents. The seller's letter could not have been an auction because it was not a public sale and because the bidders were not present. **D** is therefore incorrect.

116. **D**    Since quasi-contract remedies are essentially designed to prevent unjust enrichment, they are usually unavailable against a non-breaching defendant who has received no benefits from the plaintiff's work.

      **A**, **B**, and **C** are therefore incorrect. In addition, **A** is incorrect because its formula bears no reasonable relationship to the value of either the benefit received by the homeowner or the detriment suffered by the first builder. **C** is incorrect for the additional reason that quasi-contract recovery is based on reasonable value rather than on the contract price.

117. **C**    UCC §2-606 provides that unless the buyer does some act inconsistent with the seller's ownership, acceptance of goods occurs only after the buyer has had a reasonable opportunity to inspect the goods and either notifies the seller of his or her intention to keep them or fails to reject them. Thus, payment did not constitute acceptance because it was made before the buyer was given a reasonable opportunity to inspect the screws.

      **A**, **B**, and **D** are incorrect because the UCC provides that acceptance does not occur until after there has been a reasonable opportunity to inspect.

118. **B**    Under the Restatement of Contracts, Second, an offer for a unilateral contract cannot effectively be withdrawn once the offeree has begun performance. Since the designer began working on the design prior to the manufacturer's attempt to withdraw its offer, the manufacturer's offer will be held to be irrevocable.

      A bilateral contract is an exchange of promises. Since the designer's performance was complete upon his submission of the design, no bilateral contract was created by the submission because no promise by the designer resulted from it. **A** is therefore incorrect. **C** is incorrect because an offer for a unilateral contract can be withdrawn at any time prior to the offeree's commencement of performance. **D** is incorrect for the same reason, and because, under the UCC, "unconscionability" only prevents enforcement of a contract that is found as a matter of law to have been unconscionable at the time that it was made.

119.  **C**    Usually, a promise is unenforceable unless it is supported by consideration, which requires a bargained-for exchange. Since the climber's promise was made after the hiker rendered a service with no apparent expectation of compensation, the service was not given in exchange for the promise and the promise is not supported by consideration. For this reason, the majority of jurisdictions would not enforce it. Although some courts might enforce a promise to fulfill a "moral obligation," **C** is the only answer that could be correct in any jurisdiction.

"Good Samaritan" statutes, where they exist, protect from liability for negligence those who render emergency aid at an accident scene. The statutes do nothing more. **A** is incorrect because they have no application to contract problems. **B** is based on an inaccurate interpretation of the facts: Since the hiker did not change her position after receiving the climber's promise, she did not rely on it, detrimentally or otherwise. **D** is incorrect because if something of value has been given in return for a promise, the promise is supported by consideration even though the value of that consideration may be uncertain.

120.  **A**    Upon breach of the sales contract, the non-breaching party is ordinarily entitled to compensatory, incidental, and consequential damages. A buyer's compensatory damages consist of the difference between the contract price and either the fair market value or the "cover" price (*i.e.*, actual cost of replacement, so long as it is reasonable). If the cover price (or fair market value) is less than the contract price, the buyer is not entitled to compensatory damages, but the saving is not credited to the breaching seller. Incidental damages consist of the reasonable costs of repurchasing. Consequential damages are those that foreseeably arise from the special needs or position of the buyer that result from the breach (*e.g.*, the seller's non-delivery causes the buyer to go out of business). The collector sustained no consequential losses, and since the collector's cover price was less than the contract price, he can receive no compensatory damages. However, since the repurchase involved $20 in reasonable expenses, he is entitled to $20 as incidental damages.

**B** is incorrect because it bears no reasonable relation to the collector's loss. **C** is incorrect because it would award the collector the entire contract price in addition to incidental damages. **D** is incorrect because it would credit the dealer with the savings that resulted from his breach.

121.  **B**    A donee third-party beneficiary of a contract may enforce it. The parties are free to modify that contract, however, any time prior to the donee beneficiary's detrimental reliance on it. Since the daughter did not learn of the contract until after it had been modified, she has no right to enforce the terms that existed prior to the modification.

**A** is incorrect because a third-party beneficiary of a contract may enforce it even though he or she has not given consideration. **C** is incorrect because the rights of a donee beneficiary do not vest until he or she learns of or relies upon the contract, and the daughter did not learn about or rely on the contract until after it had been modified to exclude her. An assignment of contract rights is ineffective until the assignee learns of and accepts it. **D** is incorrect because even if the written contract between the homeowner and the builder was an assignment to the daughter, the daughter did not learn of her father's intent to create rights in her until after he eliminated those rights by modifying his contract with the homeowner.

122.  **B**  In an FOB contract, the risk of loss passes to the buyer as soon as the goods are loaded on a carrier at the place specified. This means that once the air conditioners were loaded onto the trucking company's truck, any loss not resulting from the fault of the seller became the university's. The university is thus not entitled to damages due to non-delivery resulting from such loss.

A is incorrect because assignment does not free the assignor from obligations under the contract, even if the obligee has consented to the assignment. As between parties to a contract, one of them always bears the risk of loss. The fact that a third (*i.e.*, non-contracting) party may also have become liable for such loss does not affect the rights that contracting parties have against each other. **C** is therefore incorrect. After a contract is formed, if a change in circumstances occurs that was not contemplated by the parties at the time of formation and which makes a party's performance impossible, that performance is excused. **D** is incorrect, however, because the destruction of a particular shipment of air conditioners does not necessarily make it impossible for the seller to deliver other units that would satisfy its obligation under the contract.

123.  **C**  Since the seller's offer was for the sale of any or all of the comics, the dealer could accept by promising to purchase any or all of them. Since her telegram specifically agreed to the purchase of only one comic, the seller may successfully argue that she rejected the seller's offer to sell the others.

A is incorrect for several reasons. Specific performance is available as a buyer's remedy when the subject of the contract of sale is unique because no amount of money can replace it. The fact that the dealer was a comic book dealer does not establish that she was buying the comics for resale. Even if she was, damages might not be an adequate remedy since the uniqueness of each comic (they were the only copies in existence) makes it impossible to determine what her damages were. **B** is incorrect because the seller and the dealer are merchants, and under the UCC, a promise between merchants to keep an offer open for a specified period of time may be enforceable even without consideration. Since the language of the seller's letter made it clear that the dealer could create a binding contract for the sale of any or all of the comic books simply by e-mailing her order, the seller's letter was an offer, and **D** is incorrect.

124.  **D**  Since the shop owner's order constituted an offer, and the shipment by the importer constituted an acceptance of that offer, the terms of the offer became the terms of the contract on July 30. The shop owner is thus entitled to the discount for which she contracted.

If there is a discrepancy between printed words in a contract form and typed words on that form, the typed words are presumed to control. **A** is therefore incorrect. Although the importer's catalog made clear his unwillingness to apply a 10 percent discount to any but COD shipments, the shop owner's offer was to purchase at discount with payment within 10 days. When the importer accepted by shipping, his pre-offer unwillingness became irrelevant. **B** is therefore incorrect. An open account is an arrangement between seller and buyer whereby the buyer regularly purchases on credit without executing notes or security agreements. **C** is incorrect because the existence of an open account, while relevant to credit terms, is not relevant to price terms in a contract.

125. **D**     When a builder commits an anticipatory repudiation of a building contract, the person who hired him or her may be entitled to rescind and be free of all obligations under the contract. **A** is incorrect, however, because the builder is then entitled to an offset based on quasi-contract (*i.e.*, the reasonable value of his or her services) for work already performed. If the landowner rescinds, the builder's quasi-contract remedy might exceed the amount that he has received from the landowner. If so, the builder is entitled to credit for the excess as a setoff in the landowner's action for the cost of completion. On the other hand, if the landowner does not rescind but instead sues the builder for the standard remedy, he is entitled to the difference between the contract price and the cost of completion. Since the landowner still holds $50,000 of the contract price, this sum should be deducted from the standard remedy. **B** is therefore incorrect. For the same reasons as **A** and **B**, **C** is incorrect.

126. **C**     Under UCC §2-511, a contract that is silent as to the manner of payment calls for payment in any manner current in the ordinary course of business. The seller is entitled to demand payment in cash, but if he or she does so, the buyer is entitled to a reasonable opportunity to procure the necessary cash.

     **A** is incorrect for the reason stated above. **B** is incorrect because the buyer is entitled to a reasonable time to procure cash. **D** is incorrect because a seller may demand cash.

127. **D**     Under UCC §2-209(1), an agreement to modify a contract is enforceable even though unsupported by consideration. Since, as modified, the agreement does not fall within the provisions of the Statute of Frauds, it need not be in writing. Thus, if the committee agreed to accept 475 bobbleheads instead of 500, the company's delivery of 475 bobbleheads would not be a breach.

     The company's inability to obtain the necessary materials would not excuse performance unless that inability resulted from circumstances that were not within the reasonable contemplation of the parties at the time the contract was formed. Since there is no indication that this is so, **A** is incorrect. A buyer who accepts a nonconforming tender may recover damages only if it notifies the seller of its intention to sue. **B** is incorrect, however, because no notice is required if the buyer rejects the tender. Since the contract called for delivery of 500 bobbleheads, tender of any fewer is a breach in spite of the fact that the committee may not have actually needed 500. **C** is incorrect for this reason (and incidentally, because there is no indication that it was the committee's plan to give only one bobblehead to each conventioneer).

128. **C**     The brokerage contract made transfer of title a condition precedent to the homeowner's obligation to pay the broker. Since title was not transferred, the condition had not been met, and the homeowner's obligation to pay the commission never came into being.

A is not a good defense because the homeowner voluntarily accepted the $98,000 offer, thus waiving the price condition that appeared in the brokerage contract. Since the contract for sale between the homeowner and the buyer was formed on August 1, within the period of the broker's exclusive right to sell, **B** is not a good defense. Since the contract between the broker and the homeowner granted the broker the exclusive right to sell the homeowner's home, the broker would be entitled to a commission upon the transfer of title, even though the sale was made without the broker's participation. **D** is therefore not a good defense.

129. **B**  Under the Statute of Frauds, a promise that by its terms cannot be performed within a year must be in writing. Since the mother's promise to buy books for a two-year period could not be performed within a year, it violated the Statute of Frauds.

Even if the offer made by the mother was divisible, the plaintiff's successful completion of her first year of law school would have been an acceptance of both its parts. **A** is therefore incorrect. **C** is incorrect because there is no special rule governing a promise to pay a cash bonus; such a promise is enforceable according to the rules that govern the enforceability of promises in general. Since the mother's offer to pay for the plaintiff's books was an offer for a unilateral contract (a promise for an act), the plaintiff's successful completion of her first year was both an acceptance of the offer and consideration for her mother's promise. **D** is therefore incorrect.

130. **B**  Before the obligor learns of an assignment by the obligee, if an obligor and obligee agree in a commercially reasonable manner to a valid modification of the contract, the modification is effective as to rights that the assignee has acquired against the obligor. Thus, the plaintiff is bound by the modification. An obligor's duty under a contract is discharged to the extent of payment made to the obligee before learning of the obligee's assignment. Thus, the company should receive credit for any payment that the company made to the man prior to notification of the assignment. Since the company's payment of $50,000 to the man completely discharged the company's obligation under the contract as modified, and since the modification and payment took place prior to notice of the assignment to the plaintiff, the plaintiff's claim will fail.

131. **D**  Ordinarily, no promise is enforceable unless it is supported by consideration. Consideration consists of some legal detriment sustained by the promisee in return for the promisor's promise. Since at the time the sister promised her brother that she would let him live on the farm, she was already obligated to do so, her promise to him was not a legal detriment to her and thus could not be consideration for his promise to share their aunt's estate with her. For this reason, **D** is correct.

Even without consideration, a promise many be enforceable under the doctrine of promissory estoppel if the promisee justifiably relied on it to his or her detriment. **A** is incorrect, however, because there is no indication that the sister relied on her brother's promise to share the estate. **B** is incorrect because the brother's promise was unsupported by consideration. Since the brother was unaware of his sister's promise to their mother, it could not constitute an implied condition precedent to the brother's obligation. **C** is therefore incorrect.

132.  **D**      The assignee of contract rights is entitled to enforce them to the same extent the assignor would have been.

The defendant's breach of his contract with the homeowner gives the plaintiff, as the homeowner's assignee, a cause of action against the defendant. **A** and **B** are therefore incorrect. Contract rights are ordinarily alienable, as are other chattels. Since any chattel or right may be the subject of a gift, the fact that the plaintiff gave no consideration for the assignment of the homeowner's rights would not prevent it from taking effect. **C** is therefore incorrect.

133.  **A**      An insurance contract involves an agreement by the insurer to pay the insured upon the occurrence of an event not within the control of either. The payment agreed upon need not bear any relationship to damage that results from the event (although many policies require that there be such a relationship). Since the insurance company agreed to pay $50 per day in the event of destruction or substantial damage to the house by fire, it is obligated to do so.

**B** is therefore incorrect. The insurance company's agreement to pay $50 per day is not a liquidated damages clause since it does not fix liability in the event of *breach* by the insurance company. **C** is incorrect because it attempts to apply to an insurance contract the rule that determines the validity of a liquidated damages clause. The insurance policy fixes the insurance company's liability for the homeowner's living expenses at $50 per day without regard to whether or not she actually incurred such expenses. **D** is incorrect for this reason.

134.  **A**      An anticipatory breach occurs when, before performance is required, a party to a contract says or does something that indicates that he or she will not perform as required. When an anticipatory breach occurs, the other party need not wait until the time for performance is passed but may immediately avail itself of remedies for breach of contract.

Since the sculptor's obligation under the contract was to submit a statue for approval by the mayor, her failure to do so is a breach whether or not the statue would have met with the mayor's approval when submitted. **B** is therefore incorrect. **C** is incorrect because a breach occurs when a party fails to fulfill his or her contractual obligations, whether or not he or she profits from such failure. Since a contract calling for a party's personal satisfaction is understood to require good faith, that party's promise to pay if satisfied is not illusory. **D** is therefore incorrect.

135.  **C**      Ordinarily, non-delivery by the seller entitles the buyer to damages consisting of the difference between the contract price and either the "cover price" or the reasonable market value of the undelivered goods. Here, because the eggs delivered did not conform to the agreement, the bar owner was entitled to return them. Since he has already paid the contract price and has received nothing for his money, he is entitled to the return of what he paid in addition to damages.

Specific performance, as suggested by **A**, is available only where the subject of the sales contract is unique or cannot otherwise be obtained. Here, there are no facts to suggest that this is so. **B** is incorrect because it is the measure of damages for breach of warranty and is obviously insufficient to compensate the bar owner, since the small eggs have been returned but paid for. **D** is incorrect because it does not permit recovery for damages resulting from the farmer's breach.

136.  **D**    The buyer's offer was for a unilateral contract. According to its terms, it could be accepted only by performance consisting of delivery of the books to the buyer's home. An offer for a unilateral contract can be withdrawn at any time prior to the offeree's performance or commencement of performance.

**A** is incorrect because an offer for a unilateral contract binds only one party (the promisor) until accepted by performance. **B** and **C** are incorrect because an offer for a unilateral contract cannot be accepted by any means other than performance.

137.  **C**    A liquidated damages clause is enforceable (and does not constitute a penalty) if the amount specified is reasonable in light of what the parties contemplated at the time the contract was formed, if the actual damages would be difficult to ascertain, and if the liquidated damages agreed to are tailored to the circumstances of the contract. Since living expenses would be difficult to ascertain, and since the clause calling for liquidated damages was tailored to the contract, the clause is enforceable if $75 per day was reasonable in light of what the parties contemplated at the time the contract was made.

**A** and **B** are incorrect because if the liquidated damages clause is enforceable, the buyer need not show that he actually sustained or could not have avoided or mitigated the damage. **D** is incorrect since a liquidated damages clause does not constitute a penalty just because one of the parties hoped that it would encourage the other to perform on time.

138.  **B**    Although the administrator's forbearance might have been consideration for the husband's promise to pay, the question specifically asks whether *the doctor's services* are sufficient consideration. Consideration involves a bargained-for exchange, and since the husband did not ask the doctor for the services, they cannot be said to have been "bargained for." (*Note:* Although some cases allow recovery on another theory for services like those rendered by the doctor to the extent necessary to prevent injustice, such services are not "consideration" unless bargained for.)

The services rendered may have imposed a moral obligation upon the husband, but **A** is incorrect because it is generally understood that a moral obligation is not sufficient consideration for a promise. **C** is incorrect because even a material benefit is insufficient to serve as consideration unless it was bargained for. **D** is incorrect for two reasons: First, courts do not generally inquire into the adequacy of that which was given as consideration, and second, since there was no bargain, it does not matter whether the services rendered were adequate.

139.  **D**    Although an offer can ordinarily be withdrawn by the offeror at any time prior to its acceptance, the Restatement rule is that an offer for a unilateral contract cannot be withdrawn

once the offeree has begun to perform. Thus, if the student began making extra efforts in an attempt to win the prize, the company was prevented from withdrawing the offer.

**A** and **B** are therefore incorrect. **C** is incorrect because an offer for a unilateral contract can be accepted only by performance, making the student's letter irrelevant.

140. **A**    If a contract is made with the intention of benefiting a third party to whom neither of the contracting parties owes any obligation, that third party is referred to as an intended donee beneficiary of the contract. Since the landowner's intention was to give a wedding gift to his daughter and the contractor's son, the contractor's son is an intended donee beneficiary. In some jurisdictions, a donee beneficiary may enforce only a promise on which he or she has detrimentally relied. In others, he or she may enforce it if he or she has assented to it. The Restatement view is that he or she may enforce it if he or she relied *or* assented. But if, as here, he or she has done neither, he or she has no right to enforce the agreement.

A condition precedent is an event that must occur before a party's obligation to perform becomes absolute. Ordinarily, it results from an express or implied agreement between the parties. Since the contractor's son's agreement to paint the house was made after the landowner's agreement to convey, the contractor's son's performance could not have been intended to be a condition to the landowner's obligation. **B** is therefore incorrect. **C** is incorrect because when the landowner entered into the January 1 contract with the contractor, it was for the purpose of giving a wedding gift to the contractor's son as well as his daughter. **D** is incorrect for two reasons: First, the agreement between the landowner and the contractor probably did not create any fiduciary relationship between them, and second, the contractor's agreement with the builder was not inconsistent with any right or benefit to which the landowner was entitled.

141. **A**    Specific performance of a sales contract will be granted where money damages that would accurately compensate cannot be measured because the subject of the sale is rare or unique. Since the guitar was a rare one, specific performance might be available. Although it is not certain that a court would decide to grant such relief, **A** is the only remedy listed that could possibly be granted.

If a court awarded damages, they would be based on the difference between the contract price and the fair market value of the guitar. **B** is incorrect because it does not accurately measure the damages. **C** is incorrect because, while the buyer may elect damages or specific performance, she may not receive both. **D** is incorrect since there is no relationship between $500 and the damages sustained by the buyer.

142. **A**    By its terms, the UCC applies to all transactions in "goods," which are defined as any things that are movable at the time of the sale.

The UCC provides approaches for filling in certain missing terms, but the absence or presence of any particular terms in a contract does not determine whether the UCC applies. **B** is therefore incorrect. **C** and **D** are incorrect since nothing in the UCC definition of "goods" excludes living creatures or consumer items (*i.e.*, items purchased for the buyer's own use).

143. **A**    Although the attorney's refusal to accept the painting is excused by her reinvestment of the money in reliance on of the defendant's prospective inability to perform, her refusal of the defendant's tender discharges the defendant from further obligation to perform.

B is incorrect since the defendant's obligation to deliver is not dependent on the attorney's reason for making the purchase. **C** and **D** are incorrect since the attorney's refusal to accept delivery constitutes a waiver of any specific performance rights that she otherwise might have had.

144. **B**    When a contract calls for performance by one party prior to performance by the other, the first party's performance is generally held to be a condition precedent to the other party's performance. A condition precedent is an event without which a party's obligation does not become absolute. Since the contract provided that the buyer's obligation was void if the downstairs apartment was not vacant within three months after the transfer of title, vacancy of the downstairs apartment was an express condition precedent to the buyer's obligation to pay the additional $2,000. An obligor's obligation is discharged upon failure of a condition precedent to it.

A is incorrect since the seller is no longer the owner of the premises and therefore lacks standing to bring a proceeding to evict the tenant. **C** is incorrect because the contract specifies that in the event the apartment remained occupied, the buyer's remedy is to avoid his obligation to pay the additional $2,000. **D** is incorrect because the contract specifically provides that the buyer's obligation to pay the additional $2,000 is nonexistent if the apartment is not vacant within three months after the passage of title.

145. **A**    A contract is formed upon acceptance of an offer. Thus, if the seller's letter of April 17 was an offer, a contract was formed if the buyer's acceptance was effective before the offer was revoked. Ordinarily, an acceptance is effective upon dispatch if communicated in a manner authorized by the offer. Since an offer that does not specify a means of communicating acceptance authorizes acceptance in any reasonable manner, a contract was formed on April 21 when the buyer dispatched the e-mail since sending an e-mail was a reasonable way of communicating acceptance.

Good faith means honesty and fair dealing. **B** is incorrect because there is no indication that the seller failed to act in good faith. **C** is incorrect because an offer not specifying a means of acceptance authorizes acceptance in any reasonable manner. Revocation of an offer is effective when notice is received by the offeror. Since the seller did not notify the buyer of his change of mind, it could not have effected a revocation. Thus, **D** is incorrect.

146. **D**    An obligor is discharged of liability to the obligee's assignee to the extent of any payments made to the original obligee prior to notice of the assignment. Thus, if the firm

paid $15,000 to the specialist before being advised that the specialist had assigned her rights to the programmer, it could not be required to pay that sum to the programmer.

Since the $15,000 in question was payment for work that had already been delivered, the fact that the programmer might not be capable of carrying out the obligations under the contract is not relevant to her right to collect. **A** is therefore incorrect. In general, all rights under a contract are assignable, so a contract that is silent about the right to assign impliedly permits assignment. **B** is therefore incorrect. A modification of a contract occurs when the parties agree to change the performance required. An assignment is a transfer of contract rights. Since assignment of a right does not change the performance required, the right asserted by the programmer was not the result of a modification. **C** is therefore incorrect.

147.  **D**    Under UCC §2-209, an agreement to modify a contract for the sale of goods needs no consideration to be binding. Since a contract for the sale of an aardvark is a contract for the sale of goods, the agreement that the defendant made to "throw in a pig" for the plaintiff's daughter is binding and may be enforced by the plaintiff.

A, B, and C are incorrect because the provisions of UCC §2-209 do not distinguish contracts between merchants from contracts between non-merchants.

148.  **B**    A buyer who rightfully rejects nonconforming goods is entitled to damages for non-delivery. Under UCC §2-713(1), these consist of the difference between the contract price and the market price at the time when the buyer learned of the breach. Since the retailer learned of the nonconformity on January 15, **B** is correct.

C is therefore incorrect. **A** would be the correct measure of damage if the retailer had kept the 7-foot boards but is incorrect because he returned them to the wholesaler. Rejection of nonconforming goods may be made within a reasonable time after receiving them. Although the retailer did not act immediately upon discovering the nonconformity, the return of the goods two days later was probably within a reasonable time. Even if two days was not a reasonable time, however, the wholesaler's agreement to their return would prevent him from making that assertion. **D** is therefore incorrect.

149.  **C**    Although an assignment does not imply a warranty that the obligor will perform, an assignment for consideration does imply a warranty that at the time of the assignment, the obligor has no defenses. Since at the time of the pawnbroker's assignment to the retailer, the buyer had a defense based on the nonconformity of the ring delivered by the pawnbroker, the pawnbroker's implied warranty to the retailer was breached. The pawnbroker is therefore liable to the retailer.

A and B are incorrect because there has been a breach of the implied warranty that the obligor has no defenses. **D** is incorrect because no warranty that the obligor will perform is implied by an assignment, even for consideration.

150.  **D**    A party's promise is illusory if that party's promise has not created a binding obligation. If each party has not agreed to a binding obligation, the agreement is not enforceable.

Under the agreement, the butcher agreed to provide meat at $10 per pound, but the restaurant didn't actually promise to do anything. The restaurant could order meat from another supplier or not order any meat at all since it only agreed to order as much meat as "the restaurant decides to order." Consequently, the agreement is not enforceable.

**A** is incorrect because the restaurant hasn't actually done anything to suggest it detrimentally relied on the butcher's promise. The restaurant only said that it needed top quality steaks for a "planned" convention. It didn't say it decided to host the convention based on the agreement, or that it was actually going to have the convention at all. **B** is incorrect because the restaurant did not bind itself to buying meat from the butcher. Under a valid requirements contract, a promisor agrees to buy from a supplier all that he or she requires, and the supplier agrees to supply that amount. If the restaurant had agreed to buy as much "top quality" steaks as it required, it would have been a valid requirements contract under the UCC. Impossibility of performance excuses performance when an event that was unforeseeable at the time of formation occurs prior to the time of performance, making performance impossible. **C** is incorrect because, although it would be costly for the butcher to provide the steaks, it would not be impossible.

151. **D**   When an unforeseeable change in circumstances makes a contract fail of its essential purpose, the parties to it may be excused from performance under the doctrine of frustration of purpose. The essential purpose of the contract between the landlord and the tenant was the operation of a "sports book." Since an unforeseeable change in state law made that activity illegal, the contract has failed of the essential purpose contemplated by both parties at the time it was formed. The tenant is, thus, excused from performance under the doctrine of frustration of purpose. Since his non-performance is, therefore, not a breach, he is entitled to the return of his deposit.

**A** is incorrect because the agreement between the landlord and the tenant was not a gambling contract. **B** is incorrect because the subsequent and unforeseeable illegality of the contract's purpose makes the doctrine of frustration of purpose applicable. "*In pari delicto*" means "equally guilty." **C** is incorrect, because at the time the contract was formed, neither party was guilty.

152. **B**   An anticipatory repudiation occurs when a promisor makes a positive statement to the promisee that he or she will not perform his or her contractual duties. An anticipatory repudiation by a promisor may be treated as an immediate breach by the promisee. One who repudiates before the time for performance may withdraw his or her repudiation unless the other party relied upon it. Since the restaurant relied on the farmer's repudiation by making other arrangements for the purchase of 1,000 bushels, the farmer is prevented from withdrawing her repudiation, and the restaurant is relieved of its obligation to her with respect to 1,000 bushels.

Novation is the substitution by mutual consent of a third party for one of the original parties to contract. Since there has been no such substitution, **A** is incorrect. *Nudum pactum* is a phrase that refers to a promise that is not supported by consideration. Since the promises of the farmer and the restaurant were each given in return for the other, **C** is incorrect. Impossibility of performance excuses performance when an event that was unforeseeable at the time of formation occurs prior to the time of performance, making performance impossible. Its effect is to relieve both parties of their obligations under the contract. The doctrine is inapplicable here because performance was not impossible for either the farmer or the restaurant. **D** is therefore incorrect.

153.   **C**   The Statute of Frauds applies to land sales, so any land sale agreement has to be in writing. However, under Rest. 2d. §148, so long as a contract does not involve a sale of goods, it can be rescinded orally even if the original agreement was in writing. Consequently, even though the original contract had to be in writing (since it involved land), the agreement was validly rescinded when the developer orally said it was fine if the farmer wanted out. **A** is therefore incorrect.

   **B** and **D** are incorrect. While the farmer seems to have lied when he stated he was "talking about selling," there's no indication he actually did anything regarding the resale of the property or that those statements caused the developer to do anything. Consequently, his statements wouldn't change the analysis.

154.   **A**   Under UCC §2-201(2), "between merchants if within a reasonable time a writing in confirmation of the contract and sufficient against the sender is received and the party receiving it has reason to know its contents, it satisfies the requirements [of the Statute of Frauds] against such party unless written notice of objection to its contents is given within 10 days after it is received." Under UCC §2-201(1), a confirmation letter is sufficient against the sender if it is "sufficient to indicate that a contract for sale has been made between the parties and signed by the party against whom enforcement is sought." Here, since both parties appear to be merchants, the confirmation letter was sufficient to bind the sporting goods store when it did not send written objection within 10 days of receipt. Importantly, the store read the letter and the only thing the store has done is phone the distributor. **C** is therefore incorrect.

   **B** is incorrect because the issue here concerns the oral nature of the original agreement and its apparent violation of the Statute of Frauds, not any potential failure of consideration. **D** is incorrect because the store did not send written notice of objection within 10 days. The store merely called the distributor 11 days after it received the letter.

155.   **C**   Although an assignment of contract rights divests the assignor of those rights, a delegation of contract duties does not have the same effect, even when consented to by the obligee. For this reason, the woman will remain liable to the banker for any breach of their contract. On the other hand, a delegatee of contract duties also becomes liable to the obligor for breach since the obligor is an intended third-party creditor beneficiary of the contract of delegation. For this reason, the bank may be entitled to collect from either the woman or the trucker.

   **A** and **B** are therefore incorrect. The standard measure of damage for breach of contract is the difference between the contract price and the reasonable market value of the services contracted for. In the event of a major breach, however, the wronged party may elect the remedy of rescission and restitution. Rescission involves cancellation of the contract. Restitution requires the return to the wronged party of any unearned benefit that he or she conferred on the breaching party. Since the trucker's refusal to perform is obviously a major breach, the bank may seek rescission and restitution. **D** is therefore incorrect for this reason, and because it fails to account for the fact that the bank has paid the woman.

156. **A**  Contracts frequently benefit persons other than the contracting parties. Such persons are called third-party beneficiaries. If the contracting parties meant for those persons to benefit from the contract, they are intended beneficiaries; otherwise, they are incidental beneficiaries. If a promisor's performance is intended to satisfy a preexisting obligation owed by the promisor to the third-party beneficiary, he or she is a creditor beneficiary; if not, he or she is a donee beneficiary. Once an intended third-party beneficiary's rights have *vested*, the contracting parties are no longer free to modify or rescind the portion of their contract that benefits him or her. Since the president and the publisher intended that the artist benefit from the publisher's promise to employ her, and since this was not intended to satisfy a preexisting obligation that the president owed the artist, the artist is an intended donee beneficiary. In some jurisdictions, the rights of a donee beneficiary vest as soon as he or she learns of the contract. In other jurisdictions, his or her rights vest only when he or she detrimentally relies on the contract. In other jurisdictions, his or her rights vest when he or she detrimentally relies or expresses assent. Since the artist learned of the contract, assented to it, and detrimentally relied on it by notifying other clients that she could not work for them, her rights have vested in all jurisdictions, and she may succeed in her claim against the publisher.

**B** is incorrect for two reasons; First, consideration for the publisher's promise was furnished by the president's giving him a low rate, and second, the doctrine of promissory estoppel makes the artist's detrimental reliance a substitute for consideration. The Statute of Frauds requires a promise that cannot be performed within a year to be in writing. **C** is incorrect because the publisher's promise was to employ the artist for one year and was therefore not required to be in writing. **D** is incorrect because after the donee beneficiary's rights have vested, the contracting parties may not rescind without his or her consent.

157. **B**  In attempting to enforce the father's promise, the soldier faces two problems. First, the Statute of Frauds requires a writing for a promise to convey an interest in real estate, and the father's promise was oral. Second, a promise is not ordinarily enforceable if made without consideration, and the soldier gave nothing in return for her father's promise. The doctrine of promissory estoppel might solve both problems, making the soldier's detrimental reliance on the father's promise a substitute for both a writing and consideration. To be more precise, the soldier's reliance might cause her father to be estopped from raising either the lack of a writing or the lack of consideration as a defense. Since the soldier's cancellation of the contract that she had already made could subject her to liability and will cause her to lose the benefits of her previous bargain, it could qualify as detrimental reliance. In any event, **B** is the only argument listed that could possibly support the soldier's claim.

The argument in **A** is not that modification violated the soldier's rights, but that the modification was unenforceable without consideration. It is generally understood, however, that the parties to a fully executory bilateral contract may agree to rescind, the necessary consideration being furnished by each party's giving up the right to the other's performance. The parties are then free to make a new contract by exchanging new promises. Thus, the absence of consideration would not invalidate the new agreement between the father and the builder. **A** is therefore incorrect. **C** is incorrect for two reasons: First, the writing did not contain any promise to the soldier, and second, even if the Statute of Frauds is satisfied, the problem of consideration for the father's promise to the soldier remains unsolved. Consideration is something given in return for a promise. Since the soldier had married and decided to retire from the military before her father's promise was made, her marriage and retirement could not be consideration for his promise. **D** is therefore incorrect.

158.  **C**    Although the usual remedy for breach of a sales contract is a judgment for damages, specific performance is available to a buyer if the subject of the contract was unique or highly unusual. This is nearly always true of contracts for the sale of realty, because every piece of realty is regarded as unique. Though not as common in the sale of chattels, specific performance may be granted in the event of a breach by one who has agreed to sell a highly unusual chattel.

A is therefore incorrect. **B** is incorrect because the award of specific performance does not depend on whether or not the parties to the sales contract are merchants. Since a seller can usually resell a chattel upon the buyer's breach and recover as damages the difference between the contract price and the resale price, specific performance is not usually available to a seller. **D** is incorrect for this reason.

159.  **A**    Ordinarily, a party to a contract may assign its rights or delegate its duties to another. UCC §2-210 provides, however, that delegation does not relieve the delegator of contract duties or of liability for breach. Since the wholesaler delegated its duties to the new owner, and since the new owner breached those duties by failing to provide assurances as required, the wholesaler (as well as the new owner) is liable to the plaintiff for the breach.

An agreement to substitute the performance of a third person for that of the obligor accompanied by a specific agreement to release the obligor from its contractual duties is a "novation," which relieves the released obligor of any further obligation. The plaintiff's consent to the wholesaler's assignment/delegation would not have that effect, however, because the plaintiff did not specifically agree to release the wholesaler. **B** and **C** are incorrect for this reason. **C** is also incorrect because UCC §2-210 provides that a party who demands assurances from a delegatee does not thereby prejudice its rights against the original obligor. Although an assignment of rights implies a delegation of duties, **D** is incorrect because the assignor/delegator is secondarily liable upon breach by the delegatee.

160.  **A**    An accord is an agreement to substitute a lesser obligation for that which existed under a contract. Like any other agreement, it does not ordinarily have binding effect (*i.e.*, does not discharge the original contract obligation) unless supported by consideration.

Consideration usually consists of some legal detriment suffered in return for the benefit received. The benefit received by the homeowner was a reduction in the price of the paint job. If the homeowner did not give anything in return (*i.e.*, consideration) for this reduction, the contractor would be entitled to collect the balance due. If the homeowner did not reasonably believe that the contractor's work was not "satisfactory," he was not entitled to seek damages under the contract and gave up nothing in return for the reduction in price. However, if he did reasonably believe that the contractor's work was not "satisfactory," he had a right to seek damages under the contract. Here, the numerous drips and missed spots likely made his belief reasonable. By giving up this right, he has given consideration for the reduction in price. **B**, **C**, and **D** are therefore incorrect.

161.  **A**  If a buyer accepts defective goods, that buyer generally can sue for breach of warranty. Here, by taking the cups and reselling them, the home design store accepted the goods. Under §2-714(2), the usual damages for breach of warranty are the "difference at the time and place of acceptance between the value of the goods accepted and the value they would have had if they had been as warranted, unless special circumstances show proximate damages of a different amount." Consequently, the home design store is entitled to the difference in value at the time of the shipment, or 50 cents times 1,000 ($500). Although the drop in the stock market caused the home design store to lose even more money when it resold the cups, this does not affect the damage calculation. **B** and **C** are therefore incorrect. **D** is incorrect because the manufacturer sent defective goods, and the buyer of defective goods is entitled to recover under the UCC.

162.  **C**  If the manufacturer had not breached his contract, the builder would have collected $250,000, from which he would have had to pay the costs of completing the building. Since the damages remedy should be designed to place the parties in the positions for which they bargained, the builder should receive the contract price less the cost of completing the building.

A is incorrect because the builder did not bargain for and should not receive the benefit of a windfall resulting from increased construction costs. **B** is incorrect because it fails to take into account the expenses that the builder would have had in earning the contract price. A builder who commits a substantial breach may have no remedy other than quasi-contract for the detriment that he or she has suffered. Since the builder has not committed a breach, however, he should not be restricted to this remedy. **D** is therefore incorrect.

163.  **A**  An offer is a manifestation of present intent to be bound to specified terms. Since the seller's letter expresses an unequivocal intention to sell the accordion to the second buyer for $2,000, it is an offer.

**C** is therefore incorrect. An acceptance is an agreement to be bound to the terms of an offer. The seller's letter could not be an acceptance unless the second buyer's letter was an offer. Since Baker's letter did not actually say that he would pay $2,000 (*i.e.*, did not express a willingness to be bound), but rather asked whether the seller would accept $2,000, it was not an offer, and the seller's response could not have been an acceptance. **B** is therefore incorrect. Since the seller never agreed to sell the accordion to the first buyer, his offer to the second buyer could not be a repudiation of an agreement with the first buyer. **D** is therefore incorrect.

164.   **A**   Under UCC §2-313, a warranty is made by any description of the goods that is given by the seller and which is part of the basis of the bargain. The seller thus warranted that the beams delivered would be steel. Under UCC §2-714, a buyer who has accepted nonconforming goods and who notifies the seller of the nonconformity within a reasonable time is entitled to damages. The measure of damages for breach of warranty is fixed by UCC §2-714 as the difference between the value that the delivered goods had at the time of acceptance and the value that conforming goods would have had at that time.

B is incorrect because it would entitle the buyer to keep the beams without paying anything for them. **C** is incorrect because it would allow the seller to collect the price of steel beams although he delivered iron beams. Although the seller might have been better off selling the beams to another buyer at a price higher than they were worth, he has breached his warranty that the beams delivered would be steel and will be required to compensate the buyer for what the buyer has lost. **D** is therefore incorrect.

165.   **A**   Since the buyer contracted to purchase the homeowner's home, his failure to do so is a breach that entitles the homeowner to any damages that result. **A** is therefore correct.

A buyer can frequently obtain specific performance of a contract to sell realty because the uniqueness of a given parcel of realty makes money damages an inadequate remedy. **B** is incorrect, however, because there is nothing unique about the money that the homeowner was to receive under the contract, making money damages an adequate remedy for the seller. Consequently, **C** is incorrect as well. Impossibility excuses performance only if the circumstance that made performance impossible was unforeseeable at the time the contract was formed. The subsequent illness of a party is usually regarded as foreseeable, making **D** incorrect.

166.   **D**   An assignment is a transfer of a right to receive the benefits of a contract. If there was an enforceable agreement between the nephew and the landowner, the nephew's promise to share some of the rights that he received under that contract could be called an assignment. Although it is not certain that the nephew's conversation with his sister resulted in a valid assignment, **A** is the only answer that could possibly be correct.

The difference between an assignee and a third-party beneficiary of a contract is that an assignee's right is transferred to him or her after a contract has been created, while a third-party beneficiary's right (whether an intended or an incidental beneficiary) is created by the contract itself. Since the agreement between the nephew and the landowner did not require either the nephew or the landowner to give anything to, or do anything for, the sister, the sister's right was not created by it. **A**, **B**, and **C** are therefore incorrect.

167.   **A**   Although a contract is not usually enforceable except by one in privity, a third-party beneficiary may enforce it if the parties to the contract intended that it should benefit him or her. This is true whether the intended third-party beneficiary is a creditor beneficiary or

a donee beneficiary. A creditor beneficiary is one whom the parties intended to benefit to satisfy a preexisting obligation owed by one of them. The neighbor is a creditor beneficiary since the homeowner made the contract to satisfy an obligation that he owed the neighbor.

A donee beneficiary is one whom a contracting party intended to benefit even though he or she owed him or her no obligation. **B** is incorrect since the homeowner owed the man an obligation under their previous agreement. An incidental beneficiary is one who derives benefit from a contract not made with the intention of benefiting him or her. Thus, **C** is incorrect. **D** is incorrect since the man was an intended beneficiary of the lawn service and the homeowner's contract.

168.  **A**  An offer is an expression of willingness to be bound to specified terms. Since both parties were aware of the price and terms set forth in the buyer's letter, the seller's statement could be construed as an offer to sell the books to the buyer under those same terms.

**B** and **C** are incorrect because the buyer's letter of July 8 bound him to purchase only if the books were delivered to his home, so nothing but delivery could be regarded as acceptance. **D** is incorrect because the performance required is delivery of the books, and the seller has, by his statement, made no efforts toward such delivery.

169.  **C**  A condition is an event that must occur before the performance of a contractual obligation is due. Because the builder could not build the pool until the homeowner identified where it should be built, the homeowner's failure to indicate the correct address could be seen as a failure of the condition. Until necessary conditions are fulfilled, an obligor is entitled to suspend performance. If it is too late to fulfill the condition, the obligation is discharged. Here, since the contract called for the pool to be completed before the homeowner returned home, it was too late for the homeowner to fulfill the condition by identifying the correct address and the builder's obligation was discharged.

The standard measure of damages for breach of a contract for services is the difference between the contract price and the market price. Since the standard price was 10 percent higher than the contract price, the homeowner could still recover the difference between the market price and the contract price. This is true whether another builder was willing to build the pool for the same price or not. Consequently, **A** is incorrect. The law of contracts does not guarantee a profit. **B** is incorrect because if the builder's obligation was otherwise enforceable, the fact he would lose money does not relieve him of his obligation. **D** is incorrect because the fact he could not collect payment from the neighbor is irrelevant to the contract between the builder and the homeowner.

170.  **C**  The standard measure for damages for a builder's breach of a construction contract is the difference between the contract price and the owner's actual cost of completing the building as agreed. Here, the original agreement was $200,000 for construction to be completed by December 1. The second builder agreed to complete the building by December 1 for $250,000. Consequently, the damages caused by the breach of the contract were $50,000. Although the storeowner agreed to pay an extra $25,000 if the work

was completed sooner, this would not be part of the standard calculation for damages. Consequently, **B** and **D** are incorrect.

**A** is incorrect because although the project ended up costing $275,000 (which was the amount the first builder said he could do the job for), this fact does not excuse the initial breach of contract.

171.  **D**    The standard measure for damages for breach of a sales contract is the difference between the contract price and the fair market value on the date performance was required.

It is generally understood that a non-breaching party has a duty to mitigate damages after a breach. This means that he or she cannot sit by and watch those damages increase when reasonable conduct would have prevented damages from increasing. Here, the seller's failure to attempt to resell the building has done nothing to increase the damages he has suffered due to the breach of contract. Thus, **A** is incorrect. Although unforeseeable circumstances that make performance of contractual duties impossible may excuse performance of a contract, the failure of the company's funding did not make the purchase of the office building impossible (maybe inconvenient or foolhardy, but not impossible). Thus, **B** is incorrect. **C** is incorrect because the fact the entrepreneur informed the seller prior to the date set for closing did not excuse the breach.

172.  **A**    UCC §2-209 provides that the modification of a sales contract is valid, even without consideration. The engine maker's agreement to accept $200 as payment in full is, therefore, enforceable as a modification of the original contract.

**B** is incorrect because a modification need not be in writing unless, as modified, the contract comes under the Statute of Frauds. Since the modification set a purchase price of $200 (*i.e.*, less than $500), the fact that it was not written does not affect its enforceability. **C** is incorrect because UCC §2-209 specifically dispenses with the need for consideration. Duress is a compulsion or constraint that deprives a party of the ability to exercise free will, and it generally involves physical threats. Economic pressures do not constitute duress unless the one exerting them brings about a desperate economic situation of the other party. Even then, most jurisdictions refuse to call such pressure duress. **D** is therefore incorrect.

173.  **C**    Under UCC §2-209, a modification of a contract is valid even though unsupported by consideration. That same section provides, however, that the Statute of Frauds applies to a contract which, as modified, is within its provisions. Since the agreement made on April 15 between the buyer and the farmer called for the purchase of 1,000 bushels at the American Pear Exchange price as of May 1, and since that price was $2 per bushel, the contract called for the sale of goods with a price of $2,000. Since the Statute of Frauds applies to the sale of goods with a price of $500 or more, this oral contract as modified falls within its provisions, and is therefore unenforceable over the objection of the buyer.

Although farmers are generally free to negotiate prices for the sale of pears, the farmer is bound by the price that she already negotiated. **A** is therefore incorrect. **B** is incorrect for two reasons: First, no consideration is required for the modification of a contract under the UCC, so the fact that each promise was consideration for the other is irrelevant, and second, the Statute of Frauds requires this contract to be in writing, whether it is supported by consideration or not. Since liability for breach of contract is imposed regardless of fault, a party's liability is not dependent on his or her ability to perform. **D** is therefore incorrect.

174. **C**   Under modern law, forbearance to assert a claim against another party is consideration for the other party's promise to pay money if the party who forbears reasonably believes his or her claim to be valid. Thus, if the bar owner reasonably believed his claim for unpaid bar bills to be valid (whether or not the student believed this), his forbearance to assert that claim is valid consideration for the promise to pay that the student made in his letter of September 3. Under these circumstances, that promise would be enforceable.

A unilateral contract is one in which a party exchanges his or her promise for the other party's act. An offer for a unilateral contract can be accepted only by performing the act for which the offeror called. Since the student's letter offered to pay if the bar owner would refrain from suing him (*i.e.*, to exchange the student's promise for the bar owner's act of forbearance), it was an offer for a unilateral contract. As such, it could be accepted only by the bar owner's performance (*i.e.*, forbearance to sue). For this reason, the bar owner's failure to respond to the student's letter would not be relevant to the issue of whether or not the student's offer was accepted. **A** is therefore incorrect. If the bar owner did not reasonably believe that the student owed him $10,000, he suffered no legal detriment by forbearing to assert a claim for that sum. His forbearance could not, therefore, be consideration for the student's promise. The student's promise would thus be unenforceable, and **B** is therefore incorrect. The bar owner's claim is not based on the promise the student made when he incurred the alleged bar bills, but on the promise that the student made in the letter of September 3. If that promise is enforceable, it is independent of the original claim for unpaid bar bills. For this reason, the enforceability of the claim for unpaid bar bills is not relevant. **D** is therefore incorrect.

175. **C**   In general, contract obligations are freely delegable unless the obligee has a special interest in having the obligations performed personally by the obligor. It is usually held that construction contracts are delegable, since any reputable builder can construct whatever was contracted for if provided with the proper plans. Since a moat is simply a hole in the ground, and since the earthmoving subcontractor completed the moat in complete conformity with the landscaper's plans, the landscaper's delegation of the digging work was probably not a breach of contract.

**A** is therefore incorrect. **B** is incorrect because the homeowner's interest in having the job done by a well-known architect is probably satisfied by the fact that the landscaper designed the plan and executed most of the work himself, coupled with the fact that the moat was dug in complete conformity with the landscaper's plan. **D** is incorrect for two reasons: First, contract rights are not freely assignable if the assignment would impose an additional burden on the assignor's obligor, and second, a transfer of contractual obligations is a delegation, not an assignment.

176.   **C**      Since the doctor did not, by word or deed, express or imply a willingness to pay for the maintenance of the neighbor's lawn, he is under no obligation to do so. (*Note:* It is generally understood that an assignment of contract rights includes a delegation of contract obligations. Since the homeowner assigned to the doctor his rights under the contract between the homeowner and the lawn service, the lawn service would have been entitled to enforce against the doctor any rights that the lawn service had under that contract. Since the homeowner did not assign to the doctor any rights under the homeowner's contract with the neighbor and did not delegate to the doctor any obligations under his contract with the neighbor, however, the neighbor may not enforce those rights against the doctor.)

**A** is incorrect because there is no indication that the neighbor has suffered any detriment as a result of reliance on the payments made by the doctor to the lawn service. A covenant contained in the record of title to realty may be enforceable against subsequent owners of the realty if it touches and concerns the land involved. **B** is incorrect, however, because there is no indication that the homeowner's promise was noted in the record of title to his realty. As has been noted above, the doctor is not liable to the neighbor because the doctor made no express or implied promise that would be enforceable by the neighbor. Although **D** correctly concludes that the doctor is not liable to the neighbor, it suggests that the reason is that the neighbor sustained no damage. This is incorrect, however, because the neighbor is now paying $25 per month, while previously he was paying nothing.

177.   **A**      An anticipatory repudiation is an unequivocal statement that he or she will not perform made by a party before performance is due under a contract. Upon a party's anticipatory repudiation, the other party has an immediate right to sue for breach of contract. In general, all duties under a contract are delegable except those that call for personal services or special skills. Since the design of the software program required special skills and knowledge, the specialist lacked the right to delegate that duty to the dealer, and the specialist continued to be under an obligation to perform. Her statement on August 16 was, thus, an anticipatory repudiation, giving the firm an immediate right of action against her.

**B** is incorrect because an assignment of all rights under a contract is generally understood to delegate all duties under that contract. Since anticipatory repudiation results in an immediate right of action, the fact that performance is not yet due does not prevent a suit for breach on that ground. **C** is therefore incorrect. **D** is incorrect because the duty to design a program involved personal services and special skills, so even though it was delegated by the specialist's sale to the dealer, the delegation did not relieve the specialist of her duties under the contract.

178.   **C**      Under UCC §2-201(1), a contract can be enforced against a party if that party has sent the other party a memorandum. To be enforceable, the memorandum has to be a "writing sufficient to indicate that a contract for sale has been made between the parties and signed by the party against whom enforcement is sought . . . A writing is not insufficient because it omits or incorrectly states a term agreed upon but the contract is not

enforceable under this paragraph beyond the quantity of goods shown in the writing." Nearly all courts have held the absence of a price term does not make a memorandum insufficient. Here, the music store's "confirmation" letter is sufficiently complete to serve as a memorandum. However, since the letter says "5 guitars," the factory can only enforce the agreement to this amount. Thus, the factory is entitled to the profit it would make on selling five guitars, or $250. Importantly, the facts state that the factory can make all of the guitars ordered by its customers, so it is not losing anything except profits on this failed sale.

**A**, **B**, and **D** are, therefore, incorrect.

179.  **A**    In an assignment, the assignor transfers to an assignee the assignor's right to receive a benefit from a third person. Here, the company promised to give the school a guitar, and the school transferred its right to receive it to the plaintiff when the plaintiff submitted the highest bid. Importantly, the company made a promise to the school to donate the guitar. That promise was supported in one of two ways. Either there was consideration because the guitar company would receive free publicity by donating the guitar, or there was detrimental reliance because the school "sold" the guitar. Consequently, because the school can enforce the guitar company's promise, the plaintiff can also enforce the promise as the school's assignee.

**B** is incorrect because an intended third-party creditor beneficiary of a contract is a third party to whom one of the contracting parties owed a preexisting debt and to whom the other party therefore agreed to render performance. Here, there is no indication the school owed a debt to anyone. **C** is incorrect because although there was no direct agreement between the guitar company and the plaintiff, the plaintiff can enforce the guitar company's promise to the school as an assignee. **D** is incorrect because the promise was likely supported by consideration, as stated above.

180.  **D**    Under the doctrine of frustration of purpose, a party may be discharged from a contract if the party's purpose is completely or almost completely frustrated by events that destroy the party's purpose in entering the contract. The television station could broadcast the advertisement, but since the music-streaming service's primary reason for running the advertisement at that particular time was to reach the musician's audience with its musician-themed ad and exclusive content, and since that purpose has been frustrated by the musician's death, the music-streaming service will be discharged from the contract. Importantly, the musician's death was an unforeseeable event that occurred through no fault of the music-streaming service. Consequently, **B** is incorrect.

**A** is incorrect because the understanding between the parties was that the ad would run during the concert, and the doctrine of frustration of purpose would still apply. **C** is incorrect because it is not impossible for the ad to run, it is simply that the purpose for running the ad has been completely frustrated by the musician's death and lack of the televised concert.

# QUESTIONS
## CRIMINAL LAW

# CRIMINAL LAW
# TABLE OF CONTENTS
Numbers refer to Question Numbers

# CRIMINAL LAW QUESTIONS

1. The public prosecutor had information that unlawful gambling activities were being conducted at a tavern known as the Second Bedroom on Main Street. She obtained a warrant for the search of the Second Bedroom by presenting an affidavit that stated that she had received information regarding the illegal activities from an informant who had observed the reported activities while present at the tavern. The affidavit stated that the informant frequently gave information to the police and prosecutor and that the information received from the informant in the past had always been found to be accurate. It did not give the name of the informant, however, because it stated that his anonymity needed to be preserved both for his own protection and to continue his effectiveness as an informant.

The warrant that was issued authorized the search of "the premises known as the Second Bedroom and located at 481 Chambers Street" and of "all persons in said premises at the time of the execution of the warrant who are found to be in possession of gambling records." There was a furniture store known as the Second Bedroom located at 481 Chambers Street, but the officers assigned to execute the warrant went to the Second Bedroom tavern on Main Street. Upon searching the premises, they found gambling records in a cash drawer located behind the bar.

The owner of the tavern was charged with violating the state's gambling law. He moved to suppress the use of gambling records found in the cash drawer. His most effective argument in support of that motion is that

(A) the affidavit submitted in support of the application for the warrant was based entirely on hearsay.

(B) the affidavit submitted in support of the application for the warrant did not identify the informant.

(C) the information contained in the affidavit submitted in support of the application for the warrant was uncorroborated.

(D) the information contained in the affidavit submitted in support of the application for the warrant did not properly identify the defendant's premises.

2. The defendant checked her suitcase when she made a cross-country airplane flight. Police officers had a warrant for the defendant's arrest. When the plane landed, a police dog that was trained to recognize the smell of marijuana was allowed to sniff all checked baggage as part of a routine inspection procedure. Upon sniffing the defendant's bag, the dog gave signs that it had been trained to give when it recognized the smell of marijuana. The defendant was allowed to claim the suitcase when she got off the plane. After she claimed it, a police officer arrested her for possession of a dangerous drug as she carried the suitcase through the airport. The arresting officer then searched the suitcase and found a package of marijuana.

After her conviction for drug possession, the defendant made a timely appeal to suppress the use of the marijuana as evidence against her. The trial court had found that the arresting officer had probable cause to believe she was in possession of marijuana. Should the motion be granted?

(A) Yes, because allowing the dog to sniff the defendant's luggage was an unreasonable search.

(B) No, because the arresting officer had a warrant for the defendant's arrest.

(C) No, because the possibility of airline hijacking makes the routine examination of passengers' luggage necessary to protect the public against a clear and present danger.

(D)   No, because when the defendant was arrested, the arresting officer had probable cause to believe that she was in possession of marijuana.

3.   The defendant met the victim in a bar where both were drinking. Because the defendant was too drunk to drive, the victim offered him a ride home. In the victim's car, the defendant put his arms around the victim and attempted to kiss her. The victim told him that she wasn't interested and tried to push him away, but the defendant overpowered her and succeeded in having sexual intercourse with her. The victim was 17 years old.

The defendant was charged with forcible rape under the common law. If only one of the following facts or interferences were true, which would be most likely to lead to the defendant's acquittal on that charge?

(A)   The defendant was so drunk that he believed the victim was willing to have sexual intercourse with him.

(B)   The defendant was so drunk that he did not realize that he was engaging in sexual intercourse.

(C)   The victim was so drunk that she did not realize that the defendant was engaging in sexual intercourse with her.

(D)   The victim was so drunk that immediately after intercourse began, she forgot who the defendant was and believed him to be her husband.

4.   In which of the following fact patterns is the defendant's motion to suppress the evidence most likely to be granted?

(A)   The defendant was riding in a car owned by his friend. Police stopped the car and asked to see the friend's driver's license. After the friend showed it to them, they asked his permission to search the car. The friend said, "Sure, go ahead." Upon searching under the seat in which the defendant had been

sitting, the police found a package of heroin, which was offered at the defendant's trial for illegally possessing narcotics.

(B)   The defendant was staying at a hotel, but he was two weeks behind on his room charges. The hotel desk clerk permitted the police to search the defendant's room while he was out. Upon doing so, the police found narcotics, and the defendant was subsequently charged with possession.

(C)   The defendant was arrested for driving while intoxicated. After he was taken to jail, his car was towed to the police auto pound. There, a police officer taking inventory of the car's contents found a weapon in the car that had been used in the commission of a crime with which the defendant was subsequently charged.

(D)   While the defendant was driving, police officers stopped him for going through a red light. A routine check of his license through the police department computer indicated that a bench warrant had been issued for his arrest for failing to appear in connection with four parking tickets that had been issued to vehicles registered to him. The officers advised him that he was under arrest. Although they did not handcuff him, they ordered him to empty his pockets onto the hood of the police car. A marijuana cigarette that was in one of his pockets was subsequently offered against him at his trial for possession of a controlled substance.

5.   The defendant had lost her job and needed to make some money quickly. While visiting a local tavern, she ran into an old friend. When the defendant told the friend about her financial problems, the friend pointed to an expensive-looking coat that was hanging on a coat rack and said, "Why don't you steal that coat? It looks like you should be able to sell

it for at least $100." Because the defendant said that she was afraid the owner of the coat would see her, the friend agreed to sing in a loud voice to create a diversion so that the defendant could steal the coat while everyone was watching the friend. As soon as the friend began to sing, the defendant took the coat from the coat rack and ran from the tavern. In fact, the coat actually belonged to the friend, who had been joking when he told the defendant to steal it.

Of which of the following crimes may the defendant be properly convicted?

(A)  Larceny only.

(B)  Conspiracy only.

(C)  Larceny and conspiracy.

(D)  Neither larceny nor conspiracy.

6.  The defendant knew that his neighbor, the victim, had a weak heart and that the victim had suffered several heart attacks in the past. Because he was angry at the victim, the defendant decided to try to frighten him into another heart attack. He watched the victim's house, and when he saw the victim leaving through the front door, he ran toward him shouting, "Look out! Look out! The sky is falling!" Although the defendant was not sure that this would kill the victim, he hoped it would. When the victim saw the defendant running toward him shouting, he became frightened, had a heart attack, and died on the spot.

The jurisdiction has statutes that define first degree murder as "the deliberate and premeditated killing of a human being," and second degree murder as "any unlawful killing of a human being with malice aforethought, except for a killing that constitutes first degree murder." In addition, its statutes adopt common law definitions of voluntary and involuntary manslaughter.

Which of the following is the most serious crime of which the defendant can properly be convicted?

(A)  First degree murder.

(B)  Second degree murder.

(C)  Voluntary manslaughter.

(D)  Involuntary manslaughter.

7.  The defendant was having dinner in a restaurant with his employer, the victim, when the victim left the table to go to the restroom. As the victim walked away, the defendant noticed that the victim's wristwatch had fallen off his wrist onto the table. Since it looked like a rather valuable watch, the defendant decided to steal it. Picking up the watch, he put it into his pocket. A few moments later, he began to feel guilty about stealing from his employer, so when the victim returned to the table, the defendant handed him the watch and said, "Here, you dropped this, and I put it into my pocket for safekeeping."

Which is the most serious crime of which the defendant can be properly convicted?

(A)  Larceny.

(B)  Attempted larceny.

(C)  Embezzlement.

(D)  No crime.

8.  A 15-year-old girl undressed a 15-year-old boy and attempted to have sexual intercourse with him. Although at first the boy was unwilling to have intercourse, the girl gave him marijuana to smoke until he became so intoxicated that he was willing to try. By then, however, his intoxication made him physically unable to perform. A statute in the jurisdiction provides that "A person is guilty of rape in the third degree when, being 17 years of age or more, he or she engages in sexual intercourse with a person under the age of 16 years."

If the girl is charged with attempting to commit rape in the third degree as a result of her attempt to have intercourse with the boy, she should be found

(A) guilty, because she overcame his resistance by the use of an intoxicating substance and would have completed the act of intercourse but for the boy's physical inability to perform.

(B) guilty, because the boy was under the legal age of consent.

(C) not guilty, because the girl was under the age of 17.

(D) not guilty, because the girl was a female.

9. A store owner wanted to erect a new storage building so that he could expand his business of selling animal food and veterinary supplies. He was afraid, however, that the building department would not issue him a permit to begin construction. A building department clerk said that she would make a false entry in the official records to indicate that a permit had already been issued if the store owner would pay her $500. The store owner agreed and said that he would bring the money the following day. The next day, however, when the store owner went to the clerk's office with $500, he was told that she had been fired.

A statute in the jurisdiction provides that "Any person who shall give or accept a fee not authorized by law as consideration for the act of any public employee is guilty of bribery, a felony. Any person who shall offer to commit a bribery is guilty of bribery in the second degree, a felony."

If the jurisdiction applies the common law definition of conspiracy, of which of the following crimes can the clerk properly be convicted?

(A) Bribery in the second degree only.

(B) Conspiracy to commit bribery only.

(C) Bribery in the second degree or conspiracy to commit bribery, but not both.

(D) Bribery in the second degree and conspiracy to commit bribery.

10. The defendant called her attorney and asked whether it would be a crime to burn down her own home. The attorney said that arson was defined as the intentional burning of any dwelling and that arson was a serious crime. In fact, the defendant's attorney was incorrect: The applicable statute in the jurisdiction defines arson as "the intentional burning of the dwelling of another." Believing what the attorney told her, however, the defendant burned down her own home for the purpose of collecting the proceeds of her fire insurance policy.

If the defendant is charged with attempted arson, she should be found

(A) guilty, because a mistake of fact does not prevent a person from being guilty of a criminal attempt.

(B) guilty, because her mistake of law resulted from reasonable reliance on the advice of an attorney.

(C) not guilty, because the defendant did not intend to burn the dwelling of another.

(D) not guilty, because the defendant's attempt is subsumed in the substantive crime of insurance fraud.

11. Angry because her coworker had insulted her, the defendant decided to get revenge. Because she worked for an exterminator, the defendant had access to cans of a poison gas that was often used to kill termites and other insects. She did not want to kill the coworker, so she carefully read the user manual supplied by the manufacturer. The manual said that the gas was not fatal to human beings, but that exposure to it could cause serious ailments, including blindness and permanent respiratory irritation. When she was sure that no one would see her, the defendant brought a can of the gas to the parking lot and released the poison gas into the coworker's car. At lunchtime, the coworker and his friend sat together in the coworker's car. As a result of their exposure to the gas in the car,

the friend died, and the coworker became so ill that he was hospitalized for over a month.

If the defendant is charged with the murder of the friend, she should be found

(A) guilty, because the friend's death resulted from an act that the defendant performed with the intent to cause great bodily harm to a human being.

(B) guilty, because the use of poison gas is an inherently dangerous activity.

(C) not guilty, because she did not know that the friend would be exposed to the poison gas.

(D) not guilty, because she did not intend to cause the death of any person.

12. The defendant was charged with the attempted murder of the victim. If only one of the following facts or inferences were true, which would be most likely to result in an acquittal?

(A) The victim was already dead when the defendant shot him, although the defendant believed him to be alive.

(B) The victim was alive when the defendant shot him, although the defendant believed that the victim was already dead.

(C) The defendant's gun was unloaded when he aimed it at the victim and pulled the trigger, although the defendant believed it to be loaded.

(D) Intending to poison the victim, the defendant put a harmless substance into the victim's drink, although the defendant believed that the substance was lethal.

13. The defendant had been arraigned on a charge of burglarizing the home of the victim. The day before the defendant's trial, the defendant was told that he was to appear in a lineup. The defendant asked for his lawyer to be present at the lineup but was told that

he had no right to his lawyer's presence. When he refused to appear in the lineup, the officers said "Things will go bad for you if you refuse." The defendant then appeared in the lineup. There were five other men in the lineup, and all were of approximately the same height, weight, and skin color as the defendant.

At the defendant's trial, the victim testified that she had been returning home on the night of the burglary when she saw a man running from her house. She said that she recognized the defendant as the man whom she had identified as the burglar at a lineup the day before.

If the defendant's attorney makes a timely objection to the identification made by the victim, the court should

(A) sustain the objection, because the defendant was entitled to have his attorney present at the lineup.

(B) sustain the objection, because the defendant's refusal to participate in the lineup was overcome by force or the threat of force.

(C) overrule the objection, because there were five other men in the lineup and all were of approximately the same height, weight, and skin color as the defendant.

(D) overrule the objection, because any taint connected with the lineup procedure has been purged by the victim's subsequent re-identification of the defendant in the courtroom.

14. Because many neighborhood residents had been complaining about the exploitation of tenants by absentee landlords and about the lack of law enforcement in their poor neighborhood, the City Attorney instituted a campaign of neighborhood reform. The City Attorney obtained a series of warrants for inspection of buildings in the neighborhood. He accomplished this by presenting an affidavit that stated that many health and

safety violations had been observed in buildings located in the neighborhood by police and building inspectors traveling through the neighborhood. Pursuant to the warrants, police officers and building inspectors were ordered to inspect certain buildings. As a result, an apartment building owned by the defendant was found to have more than 20 violations of the city's building code. The defendant was prosecuted under a state law that made it a felony for any landlord to willfully fail to correct health and safety violations in a building that he or she owned.

If the defendant moves to suppress the evidence against him that was obtained as a result of the inspection of his building, his motion should be

(A) granted, because the inspections were part of a general scheme to enforce the law in a particular neighborhood only.

(B) denied, because the affidavit that was submitted in support of the request for a warrant specifically stated that violations had been observed in the defendant's building.

(C) denied, because no warrant is needed to inspect buildings for health or safety violations.

(D) denied, because there was probable cause to believe that violations would be found in some of the buildings.

15. On the defendant's birthday, his friend gave him a new television as a gift. The following day, when the defendant opened the box and began using the television, he noticed that there was no warranty document with it. The defendant phoned his friend and asked the friend for the missing warranty document. The friend said, "I can't give it to you because the television was stolen." The defendant kept the television and continued using it.

The defendant was guilty of

(A) receiving stolen property only.

(B) larceny only.

(C) receiving stolen property and larceny.

(D) no crime.

16. In which of the following fact situations is the defendant most likely to be convicted of the crime charged? Assume that the jurisdiction applies the common law definition of all crimes.

(A) The defendant offered an acquaintance $1,000 to burn down the defendant's factory, but the acquaintance refused. The defendant was charged with solicitation to commit arson.

(B) The defendant deliberately burned down his home and collected the proceeds of his fire insurance policy. The defendant was charged with larceny by trick.

(C) The defendant deliberately burned down the victim's store because he wanted to put the victim out of business. The defendant was charged with arson.

(D) The defendant attempted to burn down his neighbor's house because he disliked his neighbor. He poured gasoline on the door of the house and threw a match onto it. The flames had just charred the door when it started to rain and the fire went out. The defendant was charged with arson.

17. The defendant was arrested and driven to police headquarters. A police officer gave the defendant his *Miranda* warnings and the defendant said he wanted to speak with his lawyer before talking to anyone. Just then, the police officer was called away to help deal with a drunken man that was fighting in one of the holding cells. An hour later, another officer leaned in the room asked the defendant, "Do you need anything?" The defendant replied, "Yeah — a good lawyer because everyone knows I stabbed that guy."

At trial, the defendant filed a motion to prevent the introduction of his statement. How should the court rule?

(A) The court should deny the motion, because the defendant volunteered the statement.

(B) The court should deny the motion, because there was no indication the delay in contacting the lawyer was intentional.

(C) The court should grant the motion, because the statement was the product of an unlawful "two-step" interrogation.

(D) The court should grant the motion, because the defendant's request for an attorney should have been granted immediately.

18. A small but valuable piece of jewel-encrusted statuary had been stolen from an antiques shop, and all foot patrol officers in the area were notified by walkie-talkie to look for the thief. When an officer saw the defendant running down the street away from the direction of the antiques shop, she became suspicious of him. The officer stopped the defendant and asked him his name and his reason for running down the street. When the defendant said, "Just jogging," the officer ordered him to raise his hands and then frisked him to see if he was in possession of the stolen statue. She felt a hard object in his pocket and, believing it to be the statue, reached inside. The object that she felt turned out to be a pistol, for which the defendant did not have a permit as required by law.

Prior to the defendant's trial on the charge of unlawfully possessing a concealed weapon, he moved to suppress the use of the pistol. His motion should be

(A) granted, because it was obtained as the result of an unlawful search.

(B) granted, because it was not the item that the officer was seeking when she frisked him.

(C) denied, because the officer reasonably suspected him of stealing the statue.

(D) denied, because it was discovered as part of a valid pat-down search.

19. A boy overheard two other boys talking about killing the victim by hiding his asthma medicine.

The boy hoped that the other boys' plan would succeed. He decided to help them without saying anything about it. Going into the victim's room, the boy searched until he found the medicine. Then he put it on a night table so that the other boys would be sure to find it. One of the two boys decided not to go through with the plan and ran away. However, the other boy went to the room and threw away the medicine. The victim had an asthma attack and died.

A statute in the jurisdiction provides that persons the boy's age are adults for purposes of criminal liability.

If the boy is charged with conspiracy, a court will probably find him

(A) guilty, because he knowingly aided and abetted in the commission of a crime.

(B) guilty, because he committed an overt act in furtherance of an agreement to throw away the victim's medicine.

(C) not guilty, because he did not agree to commit any crime.

(D) not guilty, because one of the boys effectively withdrew from any conspiracy that existed.

20. As part of her campaign for reelection, the President of the United States was driving through the main street of a city in a car with a bubble-shaped roof made of bulletproof glass. Intending to shoot the President, the defendant crouched on the roof of a building and aimed a high-powered rifle at the glass top of his car. He fired three times, striking the glass with each bullet. None of the

bullets penetrated the glass, and because of the noise of the cheering crowd, the President was unaware that any shots had been fired. A police officer observed the defendant firing at the President, however, and placed him under arrest. The defendant was subsequently charged with violating a federal statute that makes it a crime to attempt to assassinate the President, and he was acquitted in a federal court.

If the defendant is prosecuted in the state court and charged with criminal assault under state law, a court should find him

(A) not guilty, because he has already been acquitted in the federal court.

(B) not guilty, because the President was unaware that shots had been fired.

(C) guilty, because the defendant intended to hit the President with the bullets.

(D) guilty, because the defendant's conduct would cause the reasonable person to be placed in fear of his or her life.

21. A man had just been released from prison after serving a three-year term for aggravated assault. In need of money, he called his old friend, the defendant, and asked whether the defendant would be interested in joining him in the robbery of a pawnshop. The defendant agreed, but only after making the man promise that there would be no violence. Upon the defendant's insistence, they carried realistic-looking toy guns, and when they entered the pawnshop, they drew their toy guns and ordered the store owner to give them all the money in his cash register and all the gems in his safe. The store owner took a gun from the safe and shot the man, killing him. The store owner then aimed the pistol at the defendant, who fled from the store. By statute, the jurisdiction has adopted the felony-murder rule.

If the defendant is charged with the murder of the man, the defendant's most effective argument in defense is that

(A) the man was not a victim of the felony that resulted in his death.

(B) the store owner was justified in shooting the man.

(C) the use of toy guns made it unforeseeable that the robbery would result in the death of any person.

(D) the defendant lacked malice aforethought.

22. Although the defendant had been licensed to drive for 15 years, he allowed his license to expire while he was temporarily out of the country. When he returned, he meant to get it renewed or reinstated but did not get around to doing so. Although a statute made it a misdemeanor to drive without a license, the defendant continued to drive. One day, he accidentally dropped his cigarette while driving his car. He felt around for it while he drove, until his fingers encountered its glowing tip. Taking his eyes off the road for a moment to pick up the still-burning cigarette, he failed to see the victim, who stepped out from between parked cars. The defendant struck the victim, who died instantly.

If the defendant is charged with homicide as a result of the victim's death, which of the following would be the prosecutor's most effective argument?

(A) The victim's death resulted from the defendant's commission of a dangerous misdemeanor.

(B) The defendant's violation of the statute that required a driver's license made him guilty of culpable negligence per se, since the statute was designed to protect users of public roads against unqualified drivers.

(C) While mere negligence is insufficient to sustain a murder charge, it is sufficient to sustain a charge of involuntary manslaughter where it results in death.

(D) The defendant created a high and unreasonable risk of death or serious injury when he took his eyes off the road while driving.

23. A lifeguard worked from 5 P.M. to 10 P.M. every night at a public swimming pool operated by the city. When she arrived at work Wednesday evening, she asked her supervisor whether she could leave early because she had a date. Since there were only a few people at the pool, the supervisor said that the lifeguard could leave at 8 P.M. At 8 P.M., the lifeguard told the supervisor she was going and left, although the pool had become quite crowded with adults and young children. At 9 P.M., a nine-year-old girl fell into the pool, striking her head against its edge. One of the adults swimming in the pool saw the girl fall and realized that the child would drown if someone did not rescue her. The adult had seen the lifeguard leave and knew that there was no lifeguard present, but she made no effort to rescue the girl, although the adult was a strong swimmer and could easily have done so with no risk to herself. The girl drowned.

If the lifeguard is charged with criminal homicide in the death of the girl, which of the following would be her most effective argument in defense?

(A) She was not present at the time of the drowning.

(B) Her duty to assist people in the swimming pool terminated when the supervisor permitted her to leave at 8 P.M.

(C) The girl's death resulted from the adult's failure to render aid.

(D) She did not intend the girl's death.

24. The victim was addicted to heroin and frequently committed acts of prostitution to obtain the money she needed to buy drugs. One night, she was out looking for customers for prostitution when she was approached by the defendant, who asked what her price was. When she told him that she would have intercourse with him for $20, he said that he

would get the money from a friend and see her later. When the victim went home several hours later, the defendant was waiting inside her apartment. He said that he wanted to have sex with her, but when the victim repeated her demand for $20, he said that he had no money. She told him to get out or she would call the police. The defendant took a knife from his pocket, saying that if she did not have intercourse with him, he would kill her. Silently, the victim took off her clothes and had intercourse with him. Afterwards, when the defendant fell asleep, the victim beat him with a lamp.

If the defendant is charged with rape, the court should find him

(A) guilty, because he overcame the victim's refusal to have intercourse with him by threatening to kill her with his knife.

(B) not guilty, because the victim's demand for $20 made her resistance conditional and therefore less than total.

(C) not guilty, because the victim offered no resistance and the defendant did not use physical force.

(D) not guilty, because of the injuries inflicted by the victim.

25. A woman was in her eighth month of pregnancy when her husband left her. Unwilling to face life as a single parent, she asked her doctor to perform an abortion. Her doctor refused, explaining that abortion so late in pregnancy could be dangerous. The woman's cousin, the defendant, had graduated from medical school and was waiting for news about whether she had passed the state medical board's licensing exam. The woman asked the defendant to abort the pregnancy, saying that she would kill herself if the defendant refused. Reluctantly, the defendant agreed to perform the abortion in the woman's kitchen. The defendant performed a surgical procedure that usually resulted in abortion, but because the pregnancy had advanced as far as it did, the baby was alive when separated from the woman's

body. The defendant held the baby's head under water in an attempt to end his life, but after a short time, her conscience bothered her. She pulled the baby from the water and gave him mouth-to-mouth resuscitation, directing the woman to call an ambulance. When the ambulance arrived, the baby was breathing on his own. He was taken to a hospital where, because of brain damage, he remained in a coma until he died five years later.

If the defendant is charged with murdering the baby, her most effective argument in defense would be that

(A) the woman had a constitutional right to an abortion.

(B) the defendant attempted to save the baby's life by giving him mouth-to-mouth resuscitation.

(C) the baby's death five years later after the defendant's act was not proximately caused by the defendant's act.

(D) the defendant lacked the necessary state of mind to be guilty of criminal homicide, because the surgical procedure that she performed usually resulted in abortion.

26. The defendant shot the victim to death. She was subsequently charged with voluntary manslaughter. Which of the following additional facts, if true, would lead to an acquittal on that charge?

(A) At the time of the shooting, the defendant believed that the victim was going to stab her, but the reasonable person in her place would not have held that belief.

(B) At the time of the shooting, the reasonable person in the defendant's place would have believed that the victim was going to stab the defendant, but the defendant did not hold that belief.

(C) At the time of the shooting, the defendant did not know whether the victim was going to stab her.

(D) At the time of the shooting, the defendant mistakenly, but reasonably, believed that the victim was going to stab her.

27. Two students were law students in the same Contracts class. Knowing that the professor kept his lecture notes in a cabinet in his office, they planned to break into the office for the purpose of copying his notes. The first student purchased a miniature camera for this purpose after discussing the purchase with the second student and collecting half the cost from her. When they saw the professor leave his office at lunchtime, they went there. The second student opened the locked door by slipping a strip of plastic under its latch. Once inside the office, the first student found the professor's notes and photographed them with the camera that he had purchased.

Of which of the following crimes may the first student properly be convicted?

(A) Conspiracy to commit burglary.

(B) Conspiracy to commit larceny.

(C) Both conspiracy to commit burglary and conspiracy to commit larceny.

(D) Neither conspiracy to commit burglary nor conspiracy to commit larceny.

28. The defendant and his friend were trying to become stuntmen, so they filmed several stunt videos and posted them to the Internet. To continue to attract views, they made the stunt videos increasingly elaborate. In their latest video, the defendant's friend ran in front of a concrete wall while the defendant shot at him with a pistol. After the first take, the friend said, "You need to shoot closer to me, so it looks a lot cooler." In the second take, the defendant shot as close as he could to his friend. One of the bullets ricocheted off the wall and struck the friend in the head. He was killed instantly.

What is the most serious crime the defendant can be charged with?

(A)  Murder.

(B)  Voluntary manslaughter.

(C)  Involuntary manslaughter.

(D)  No crime.

29.  A hunter earned his living by catching poisonous reptiles for sale to zoos and private collectors. He had been commissioned to capture a rare, highly poisonous species of snake. The hunter hired a professional chemist to develop and manufacture a drug that he could take before handling this particular snake, and which would protect him against the reptile's poison in the event that he was bitten. Although the chemist knew that the bite of the snake was usually fatal, and that there was no defense against its venom, she welcomed the opportunity to earn some easy money. She sold the hunter a bottle of tablets, telling him that they were based on her secret formula and that they would protect him against the snake's venom. Actually, the tablets were made of nothing more than sugar, but the chemist thought that if the hunter believed strongly enough in their power, he would handle the snakes so confidently that he would not be bitten. The hunter caught a snake and took one of the chemist's tablets before handling it, following the instructions that she had given him. While he was handling the snake, it bit him. Because the tablets did not protect him against the venom, the hunter became ill as a result of the snakebite and almost died.

If the chemist is prosecuted for her sale of the tablets to the hunter, she may properly be found guilty of

(A)  attempted murder only.

(B)  obtaining property by false pretenses only.

(C)  attempted murder and obtaining property by false pretenses.

(D)  neither attempted murder nor obtaining property by false pretenses.

30.  The defendant purchased an ounce of cocaine and divided it into 50 packets of about one-half gram each. She was selling them outside the local high school when a drug addict noticed her and saw the opportunity to get some free drugs. The drug addict stepped up beside her. With his hand in the pocket of his jacket, he thrust his finger forward inside the pocket and jabbed her in the ribs with it. Snarling, he said, "I've got a gun. Give me the dope or I'll blow you away." The defendant reached into her purse, drew a small pistol that she kept there, and shot the drug addict, killing him.

If the defendant is charged with the murder of the drug addict, she should be found

(A)  guilty, because it was unreasonable for her to use deadly force to protect illegal contraband.

(B)  guilty, because the drug addict was unarmed.

(C)  guilty, because the defendant was committing a crime and therefore had no privilege of self-defense.

(D)  not guilty, because it was reasonable for her to believe that her life was in danger.

31.  The defendant and his brother ran a methamphetamine lab in their home. An undercover officer went to the home and tried to buy a large quantity of drugs. As the undercover officer was paying, his police radio went off. The defendant's brother yelled, "Police!" and grabbed a nearby shotgun the brothers kept to defend their lab. He then shot the undercover officer in the leg. Other officers stormed the house and arrested both the defendant and his brother. Both of them were charged with conspiracy to sell methamphetamine and battery for the shooting of the officer.

At trial, the defendant argued he was not guilty of battery because he was not the one who shot the officer. How should the court rule?

(A) Guilty, because the brother was defending the lab when he shot the officer.

(B) Guilty, because the defendant acted with reckless indifference in keeping the shotgun on the property to defend the lab.

(C) Not guilty, because the defendant did not shoot the undercover officer.

(D) Not guilty, because the sale of methamphetamine is not an inherently dangerous crime.

32. After looking at a car that the seller had advertised for sale, the buyer agreed to purchase it for $3,000. The buyer gave the seller $100 cash, promising to bring the balance and to pick up the car the following day. In fact, the seller was a thief who had no intention of selling the car and had been collecting cash in down payments from buyers all over the state. As soon as the buyer left, the seller ran off with the $100. One week later, the seller was arrested and charged with embezzlement and larceny by trick. He can properly be convicted of

(A) embezzlement only.

(B) larceny by trick only.

(C) embezzlement and larceny by trick.

(D) neither embezzlement nor larceny by trick.

33. A wife was extremely hot-tempered and very possessive of her husband. She frequently flew into a hysterical rage if he even looked at another woman. One evening, the wife and the husband were in a bar when they began arguing. Wanting to hurt his wife, and knowing that it would infuriate her, the husband asked a waitress, who was sitting at the next table, to dance with him. The waitress accepted, but as she and the husband began to dance, the wife became enraged and ran at them, striking the husband over the head with a wine bottle. Later that night, the husband died of a head injury resulting from the blow. The wife was charged with murder, but her lawyer argued that the charge should be reduced to voluntary manslaughter because the wife was acting out of extreme passion when she struck the husband. Is the wife's lawyer correct?

(A) Yes, on the theory of deliberate provocation.

(B) Yes, because of the wife's extreme feelings of possessiveness regarding her husband.

(C) No, because the ordinary person in the wife's situation would not have become violently enraged by the husband's dancing with the waitress.

(D) No, on the theory of mistaken justification.

34. The company was a retailer of computer hardware and software. It frequently sold its products on credit, and credit customers were required to execute security agreements giving the company, in the event of default in payment, the right to repossess the goods sold without resort to judicial proceedings. The defendant was employed by the company as a collection agent. As such, his job was to contact customers whose payments were past due and to repossess computer hardware when necessary.

One night, the defendant went to a customer's home to demand that she either make her payments or return the computer hardware. Although he heard a radio playing inside the apartment, no one answered his knock. The defendant tried the door, thinking that his knock might not have been heard over the sound of the radio. Finding the door unlocked, he opened it and entered the apartment. He called the customer's name as he walked from room to room, but found that nobody was home. He was about to leave when he saw the computer hardware that the customer had purchased from the company on a table. He left a signed note that said, "Because of non-payment, I have repossessed your computer." He then took the equipment with him.

If the defendant is charged with common law burglary, which of the following would be his most effective argument in defense?

(A) He did not use force to make an entry.

(B) He did not enter by "breaking" since the door was not locked.

(C) When he opened the door and entered the apartment, he had no intention of committing a crime.

(D) He left a note explaining his actions.

35. The defendant suffered a severe head injury in an accident that occurred three years ago. As a result, she experienced eight incidents of sudden unconsciousness, each lasting approximately two minutes. All the incidents occurred within a three-month period immediately following the accident, and all occurred while the defendant was at home. Last week, she was driving her automobile in a lawful manner when she suddenly lost consciousness as a result of the head injury. Her car swerved out of control onto the sidewalk, striking and permanently injuring a pedestrian. The defendant was charged with violating a state statute that defines the crime of "reckless maiming" as "causing permanent injury to another person by acting in knowing disregard of the plain and strong likelihood that death or serious personal injury will result."

Which of the following is the defendant's most effective argument in defense against the charge of reckless maiming?

(A) The defendant's head injury was not the result of any culpable conduct by the defendant.

(B) After losing consciousness while driving, the defendant was no longer capable of exercising control over the operation of her vehicle.

(C) The defendant reasonably believed that she would not have any further incidents of unconsciousness.

(D) The defendant did not know that her driving would lead to death or serious injury.

36. During a trip across the United States, a man used an Internet company that allowed people to rent out their homes to travelers. The man picked a nice home near the Grand Canyon that the defendant was renting out while he was away on business. While staying in the home, the man stumbled across a used syringe in a trash can. Because he suspected the defendant was engaged in criminal activity, the man searched the home and discovered several bags of heroin in the defendant's closets. The man took the drug evidence to the local police. Based on this evidence, the police arrested the defendant as soon as he returned.

If the defendant makes an appropriate motion to suppress the evidence, the motion should be

(A) granted, because by turning the evidence over to the police, the man acted as a *de facto* agent of the government.

(B) granted, because the man intentionally searched for drug evidence while staying in the home.

(C) granted, because the police used the evidence in arresting the defendant.

(D) denied.

37. The defendant came home from work to find that his wife and two of his children had been slashed and cut and were lying dead in a pool of blood. His third child was also cut and bleeding severely. As the defendant approached, the child said, "Our neighbor killed Mommy." The defendant said, "I'll kill that son of a bitch." Then he loaded his shotgun and went next door to the neighbor's house. He knocked on the door, and the neighbor opened the door and said, "I killed your family, what are you going to do about it?" The defendant shot and killed him. State statutes codify the common law definitions of

voluntary and involuntary manslaughter, and define first degree murder as "the deliberate and premeditated killing of a human being," and second degree murder as "the killing of a human being with malice aforethought."

If the defendant is charged with voluntary manslaughter, the court should find him

(A) guilty, because he intended the death of the neighbor because he believed that the neighbor had killed his wife and children,

(B) guilty, because the killing of the neighbor was deliberate and premeditated.

(C) not guilty, because the killing of the neighbor was deliberate and premeditated.

(D) not guilty, because the neighbor was the killer of the defendant's wife and children.

38. The defendant was the chief cashier at a supermarket. As part of her duties, she deposited the day's receipts in the company safe each night. One Friday night, when the store was to be closed for the entire weekend, after depositing the day's receipts in the safe, the defendant removed $500 from the safe without permission. She knew that no one would be looking for the money in the safe during the weekend and planned to take it with her on a gambling junket to Las Vegas. Her intentions were to gamble with the money, and, if she won, to return it on Monday morning. If she lost, she planned to alter the store records to hide the fact that the money was missing.

On Monday morning, the defendant returned to the supermarket. Having won a few hundred dollars during her weekend gambling trip, she returned the money that she had taken from the safe. One of her coworkers saw her returning the money and questioned her about it until the defendant admitted what she had done. The coworker stopped her before she closed the safe and said that unless the defendant gave him $25 of the store's

money, he would tell the boss. The defendant knew that she could get away with taking $25 because the store records were frequently off by that much and the boss never worried about it. Thus, she took out $25 from the safe and gave it to the coworker.

If the defendant is charged with larceny for taking $500 from the safe on Friday night, she should be found

(A) not guilty, because the owner of the supermarket was not deprived of its use.

(B) not guilty, because when she took the money, she intended to return it if she won.

(C) guilty, because she withheld $25 on Monday morning.

(D) guilty, because she planned to keep the money if she lost.

39. A statute provides as follows: "Any person who knowingly sells an intoxicating substance to a person under the age of 21 years shall be guilty of a misdemeanor." The owner of a cocktail lounge hired the defendant to work as her bartender. Before the defendant began working, the owner read him the above statute and explained the need for him to check the identification of all persons who appeared to be under the age of 21 years. She also told him that if she ever heard of his violating the statute, she would fire him immediately. Later that night, a 17-year-old teenager who looked like he was 25 ordered a glass of wine. The teenager showed the defendant an altered driver's license that falsely stated his age to be 22. The defendant was not sure whether the phrase *intoxicating substance* in the statute included wine, and he served it to the teenager. An undercover police officer who was at the bar observed the transaction. Hoping to make an arrest, the officer deliberately waited until after the wine was served. He then showed his badge, demanding to see the teenager's identification. Recognizing the driver's license as a forgery, he arrested the defendant.

If the defendant is charged with violating the statute, his most effective argument in defense is that

(A) he did not know whether the statutory phrase *intoxicating substance* included wine.

(B) he reasonably believed the teenager to be over the age of 21 years.

(C) the undercover police officer entrapped him.

(D) the wine was not an intoxicating substance because the teenager never got a chance to drink it.

40. A state law requires automobiles to be equipped with a device to reduce the emission of air-polluting substances and provides that any person who knowingly removes such a device from an automobile shall be guilty of a misdemeanor. The defendant was the operator of an automobile service station at which she conducted minor repairs. The victim brought her car to the defendant's station and asked whether there was anything that the defendant could do to improve the car's fuel economy. The defendant said that removing the air-pollution control device would make the car use less fuel, and she offered to do so for a fee. The victim paid the fee, and the defendant removed the device. Although the defendant worked carefully, she accidentally loosened a connection in the exhaust system without knowing she had done so. However, she did know that such leaks could result in death. When the victim drove away, exhaust gases were leaking from the exhaust system into the victim's car. After driving for a short time, the victim was poisoned by the gases and died.

If the defendant is prosecuted for the homicide of the victim, she should be found

(A) guilty of involuntary manslaughter under the unlawful act doctrine, because the victim's death would not have occurred but for the defendant's

removal of the air-pollution control device.

(B) guilty of voluntary manslaughter, because she knew there was a possibility that death could result from a leak in the exhaust system.

(C) guilty of involuntary manslaughter, because an automobile is a dangerous instrumentality and the defendant was culpably negligent.

(D) not guilty.

41. After closing down his restaurant at 3 A.M. the defendant was getting in his car to go home when he felt something sharp and metal jab him in the back. A low voice growled, "I've got a gun. Give me your wallet or I'll shoot you right here." Because of several recent thefts in the area, the defendant habitually carried a large kitchen knife in his coat pocket. The defendant spun around and stabbed the "robber" in the chest. The "robber" fell down to the ground dead. The defendant then realized that the "robber" was actually the owner of the competing restaurant next door, who was well known for playing practical jokes, and the "gun" was simply the round handle of a metal spatula. The defendant was arrested and charged with murder.

If the defendant asserts that he acted in self-defense, he should be found

(A) not guilty, because the defendant was justified in believing he was about to be robbed.

(B) not guilty, because the defendant's belief that the "robber" would shoot him was reasonable.

(C) guilty, because the defendant did not turn around and verify that the "robber" was actually holding a gun.

(D) guilty, because it was unreasonable to spin around and stab an unknown person with a kitchen knife.

42. The defendant was a narcotics addict in desperate need of a shot. He offered to permit a drug dealer to have sexual intercourse with his wife in return for drugs. The drug dealer accepted the offer and went home with the defendant. When the defendant told his wife about the arrangement, however, she refused to have any contact with the drug dealer. The defendant struck her several times and held her down while the drug dealer had intercourse with her forcibly. Afterwards, the drug dealer handed a packet of heroin to the defendant.

Which of the following is the most serious crime of which the defendant can be found guilty?

(A) Rape.

(B) Battery.

(C) Procuring for prostitution.

(D) Possession of narcotics.

43. The defendant was about to go to his sister's wedding when he remembered that he had inadvertently left his camera at his friend's house. Although he knew that his friend was out of town, the defendant went to his friend's house in the hope of finding some way to get the camera so that he could take pictures at the wedding. The door was locked, but when the defendant shook the doorknob vigorously with his hand, the door opened. The defendant entered and searched for his camera, but he could not find it. As he was leaving, he saw a silver candy dish on a shelf with several other items and took it to give his sister as a wedding present. He subsequently changed his mind, however, and returned it to his friend.

Of which of the following crimes may the defendant properly be convicted?

(A) Larceny.

(B) Burglary.

(C) Attempted burglary.

(D) No crime.

44. The defendant was a nightclub performer who was billed as "the man with second sight." As part of his nightclub act, he would put on a blindfold and walk between the tables, identifying the contents of pockets and purses of members of the audience. One day, as a publicity stunt, he had himself blindfolded and attempted to drive an automobile in rush-hour traffic. Because he was unable to see the road, he collided with the vehicle in front of him. As a result of the impact, the other vehicle burst into flames and three of its occupants were severely burned, one so badly that he permanently lost the use of his legs. If they had not been rescued by a fire company that happened to be passing by, all three would have died.

On a charge of attempted involuntary manslaughter, the defendant should be found

(A) guilty, since his reckless behavior nearly resulted in the death of another human being.

(B) guilty, since he had completed all steps necessary to result in guilt for involuntary manslaughter, and the deaths of the victims were prevented by an independent agency.

(C) not guilty, since he lacked the requisite state of mind to be liable for an attempt.

(D) not guilty, since the crime of involuntary manslaughter is a lesser offense included in murder.

45. A state statute provides that "any person who brings about the death of another human being with the intent to cause said death or in the course of committing burglary, rape, robbery, or kidnapping shall be guilty of murder in the first degree." The jurisdiction applies common law definitions for the four enumerated felonies. The defendant was attempting to use dynamite to blow open the door of a warehouse so that he could enter to steal its contents. His accomplice was waiting in the getaway car parked at the curb. When the

defendant detonated the charge, the resulting explosion damaged the building wall, causing bricks and chunks of mortar to fly through the air. A brick crashed through the windshield of the getaway car, striking the accomplice in the head and killing him.

If the defendant is charged with murder in the first degree, which of the following arguments would be his most effective defense?

(A) The statute was not intended to protect the accomplice of a felon.

(B) Burglary as defined by common law is not a dangerous felony.

(C) The accomplice's death was not proximately caused by the defendant's attempt to commit any of the crimes enumerated by the statute.

(D) The accomplice assumed the risk by participating in the commission of a felony.

46. The defendant, who had applied for employment with a company, learned that the decision as to whether to hire him would be made by the company's personnel manager. Anxious to receive the job, the defendant offered to give the personnel manager his first week's pay if the personnel manager would hire him. The personnel manager accepted the defendant's offer and hired him, later accepting the payment. Subsequently, the defendant and the personnel manager were both charged with violating a state law that provided that "it shall be a felony for any person with responsibility for hiring others to solicit, demand, or receive anything of value from persons hired in exchange for hiring said persons." They were tried jointly, the personnel manager as a principal and the defendant as an accessory.

The defendant's best argument for a dismissal of the charge against him is that

(A) a person cannot be tried as an accessory until the principal has first been tried and convicted.

(B) he did not assist the personnel manager in the commission of the crime.

(C) no person can be charged as an accessory if the crime could not have been committed without his or her participation.

(D) the law was intended to protect people in the defendant's position against people in the personnel manager's position.

47. The defendant, in need of money, waited in an alley until the victim walked by on the street. Then, stepping out of the alley, he stuck his hand in his pocket with his finger thrust forward and said, "I've got a gun in this pocket." Snatching the victim's purse with the other hand, he ran away. Because she thought that he had a gun, the victim did not attempt to stop him.

Of which of the following offenses would the defendant be most likely to be properly convicted?

(A) Robbery.

(B) Larceny by trick.

(C) Embezzlement.

(D) False pretenses.

48. When a doctor went away on vacation, he left the key to his apartment with his neighbor, the defendant, who promised to water the doctor's plants until he returned. One day, as the defendant was watering the doctor's plants, she suspected one of them to be marijuana. She watered the rest of the plants and then went to the public library, where she consulted a reference book and found that the suspicious plant was indeed marijuana. She went back to the doctor's apartment and let herself in with the key. Then she pulled the marijuana plant out by its roots and destroyed it by stuffing it into the garbage disposal in her own apartment.

The jurisdiction applies the common law definition of larceny and has a statute defining burglary as "breaking and entering into the premises of another for the purpose of committing larceny." If charged with larceny and burglary, the defendant should be found guilty of

(A) larceny only.

(B) burglary only.

(C) larceny and burglary.

(D) neither larceny nor burglary.

49. In the course of robbing a bank, the defendant pointed a gun at three bank tellers and the bank manager and ordered them to go from the bank lobby to the back room while his confederate attempted to open the safe. Threatening to shoot them if they refused, he then ordered one of the bank tellers to undress and commanded the bank manager to have sexual intercourse with her. Fearful that they would be killed otherwise, the manager and teller obeyed the defendant's commands without protesting.

Of which of the following crimes is the defendant guilty?

(A) Solicitation to commit rape.

(B) Rape.

(C) Both solicitation to commit rape and rape.

(D) Neither solicitation to commit rape nor rape.

50. The defendant sold a pistol to a man. Later, the man was stopped by police who were routinely checking the licenses of motorists. The man objected to a search of his car, but the officers ignored him. The officers thoroughly searched the man's car and discovered the pistol in the glove compartment. Subsequently, the defendant was charged with violating a statute that makes it a crime for any person "to sell or offer for sale any firearm that has not been properly registered pursuant to law."

The defendant's motion to prevent introduction of the pistol into evidence will most likely be

(A) denied, since the routine license check was not a violation of the man's rights.

(B) denied, because the defendant has no standing to object to the search of the man's car.

(C) granted, because the man objected to the search of his car at the time it took place.

(D) granted, because the search of the man's car was excessive in scope.

51. A man broke into a church in order to desecrate it. He planned to do so by sacrificing a squirrel on top of the altar. When he got inside the church, the squirrel bit him on the finger and escaped. The man believed desecrating a church was a felony, but there were actually no laws at all regarding desecration. If the man is charged with burglary, he should be

(A) convicted, because he intended to commit a felony when he broke into the church.

(B) convicted, because he would have completed his intended crime if the squirrel hadn't escaped.

(C) acquitted, because he could only be charged with attempted burglary.

(D) acquitted, because what he intended to do was not a crime.

52. The defendant belonged to a sorority. Members of the sorority who paid a rent of $100 per semester were entitled to a single-occupancy bedroom in the sorority house. Although house residents shared kitchen and dining room facilities, the bedrooms were not communal and were normally kept locked by their occupants. With the knowledge of its members, the sorority kept duplicates of all keys so that copies could be made in the event that a resident lost her key. A student,

a member of the sorority, suspected that the defendant was selling marijuana. One weekend, when she knew that the defendant had gone home to visit her parents, the student called the police and told them of her suspicions. In response to her call, two officers came to the sorority house to interview the student. During the course of their conversation, the student stated that she was the defendant's roommate and offered to let them into the defendant's room. In fact, the student was not the defendant's roommate. The key that she used to open the door was actually one of the duplicates kept by the sorority. Upon entering, the police officers saw a tobacco pipe containing traces of marijuana residue on a night table. The defendant was subsequently prosecuted for possession of marijuana. Prior to trial, she made an appropriate motion to suppress the use of the pipe and its contents as evidence.

Which of the following would be the prosecution's strongest argument in opposition to the defendant's motion?

(A) The student had apparent authority to permit the entry into the room.

(B) The student had probable cause to believe that the officers would find marijuana in the room.

(C) The defendant did not have a reasonable expectation of privacy since she knew that the sorority kept a duplicate of her room key.

(D) The Fourth Amendment prohibition against unreasonable search and seizure should not be strictly applied to students at educational institutions.

53. Because they were bigots, a man and a woman were angry when a black family moved into a house on their street. Deciding to drive them away and to set an example that would discourage other black people from moving into the neighborhood, they agreed to set fire to the family's home. They went to the house, and the man started pouring gasoline around it. A crowd of onlookers began to gather. The defendant, one of the onlookers, shouted, "Burn their house down!" intending that the man and the woman would do so. After the man finished pouring the gasoline, the woman lit a match and set it afire, burning the house to the ground.

On a charge of arson, the defendant is

(A) guilty, because he aided and abetted in the crime by his presence, coupled with his criminal intent.

(B) guilty, because, intending that the man and the woman would burn the house down, he shouted encouragement.

(C) not guilty, because his words did not create a clear and present danger that did not already exist.

(D) not guilty, because words alone are not sufficient to result in criminal liability.

54. The defendant was a resident patient at the state mental hospital, where he had been receiving treatment for a mental illness diagnosed as chronic paranoid schizophrenia. As a result of his illness, he believed that the governor of his state was part of a nationwide plot to turn all voting citizens into drug addicts. He felt that the only way to foil the plot was to kill the governor, but he realized that the law prohibited such an act. He knew that if he was caught making any attempt on the governor's life, he would be punished, but he concluded that it would be better to be convicted and punished for a crime than to be turned into a drug addict. Ultimately, he was unable to resist his impulse to kill the governor, and, in the context of his delusion, his conduct seemed reasonable.

On the governor's next visit, the defendant placed poison in food he knew would be served to the governor, intending to cause the governor's death. The governor ate the food and died as a result. If the defendant is charged with murder in a jurisdiction that has adopted only the M'Naghten test of insanity, the defendant should be found

(A)  guilty, since he knew the nature of his act and that it was prohibited by law.

(B)  not guilty, because the defendant can establish that his mental illness made him unable to resist the impulse to kill the governor.

(C)  not guilty, since the defendant's conduct was the result of mental illness.

(D)  not guilty, because his delusion was the result of mental disease and if his conduct was reasonable within the context of that delusion.

55.  In which of the following situations is the defendant's claim of intoxication most likely to result in his or her being found not guilty?

(A)  In a jurisdiction that applies the common law definition, the defendant is charged with involuntary manslaughter for the death of a pedestrian whom she struck while driving an automobile. The defendant asserts that at the time of the accident, she was so drunk that she did not see the pedestrian in the roadway.

(B)  In a jurisdiction in which the statutory age of consent is 18, the defendant is charged with statutory rape after having sexual intercourse with a female who was 17 years of age. The defendant asserts that he was so intoxicated that he did not realize that he was engaging in sexual intercourse.

(C)  In a jurisdiction that applies the common law definition, the defendant is charged with murder for the death of a person whom she struck with her automobile. The defendant asserts that, without her knowledge, an unknown person put alcohol in her fruit juice, as a result of which she became so intoxicated that she could not see

clearly or control the movements of her hands and feet. She further asserts that, unaware that she was drunk, she believed the visual and physical difficulties to be the result of illness and was attempting to drive to a hospital when the accident occurred.

(D)  In a jurisdiction that applies the common law definition, the defendant is charged with voluntary manslaughter after killing his wife. He asserts that he was so drunk that he imagined that he saw another man in bed with her, and that he killed her in the drunken rage that resulted.

56.  In which one of the following situations is the defendant **LEAST** likely to be guilty of murder?

(A)  Having been hired by a third person to beat the victim severely enough to "put her in the hospital," the defendant struck the victim repeatedly with a baseball bat in the knees. Although the defendant intended only to break the victim's legs, she died of shock.

(B)  Because he suffers from mental disease, the defendant believed the victim to be Adolf Hitler. Intending to kill him, the defendant shot him to death.

(C)  Believing the victim to be asleep, the defendant fired 10 bullets into his head. In fact, the victim had died of a heart attack moments before the defendant entered the room and was already dead when the defendant shot him.

(D)  The defendant stole a check from the victim's mailbox and attempted to cash it in a bank by masquerading as the victim. Suspecting forgery, the bank teller signaled to the bank guard. As the guard approached, the defendant shot at him. When the guard returned the defendant's fire, one of the guard's bullets ricocheted off a wall and struck a customer, killing him.

57. A landlord was the owner of a three-unit residential building. One day, while the defendant and his wife were out of town, the landlord and a police officer were having coffee together in the landlord's apartment. During the course of their conversation, the landlord said that she was worried about the defendant because once, while visiting him, she saw a substance in his apartment that she believed to be cocaine. Since she really did not know what cocaine looked like, however, she was not sure. The officer said, "Don't worry. For all you know, the stuff you saw was talcum powder. I'm a cop, so I know coke when I see it. If you'd like, I'll have a look and let you know whether or not there is anything for you to worry about."

Using her key to open the door to the defendant's apartment, the landlord brought the officer inside. Lying on a table in the entrance hall inside the apartment was a plastic pouch containing white powder. The officer sniffed it and said, "That's coke, all right," putting it in his pocket. Eventually, the defendant was charged with criminal possession of dangerous drugs.

On the charge of possessing dangerous drugs, if the defendant makes an appropriate motion to suppress use of the plastic pouch of cocaine that the officer found in his apartment, his motion should be

(A) denied, since the plastic pouch was in plain sight when the officer entered the apartment.

(B) denied, since the landlord, the owner of the building, had given the officer permission to enter.

(C) denied, since the defendant was not under suspicion at the time that the officer entered the apartment.

(D) granted.

58. When he was 19 years old, the defendant pleaded guilty to petty larceny. Because of his age, he was not sentenced to prison, but he was required to report to a Youth Supervision Officer every month for one year. At the end of that period, he was discharged from supervision. At the time, his attorney advised him that he was pleading guilty to a "Youthful Offense" rather than to a crime, and that because he was assigned to a Youth Supervision Officer, he would have no criminal record as a result of the proceeding. The defendant believed this advice, but it was in fact false, in that the charge to which he pleaded guilty was a criminal one.

Twenty years later, the defendant applied for employment with the state. In his application, he stated under oath that he had never been convicted of a crime.

A state statute reads as follows:

"Perjury in the second degree consists of making any statement under oath with the knowledge that such statement is false. Perjury in the second degree is a felony punishable by a term not to exceed five years in the state prison."

If the defendant is charged with perjury in the second degree, the court should find him

(A) not guilty, because he lacked the mental state required by the statute.

(B) not guilty, because reliance on the advice of counsel is a complete defense.

(C) not guilty, because a plea of guilty is not the same as a conviction.

(D) guilty.

59. A woman was a collector of antique automobiles. One day, she took her infant daughter for a ride in one of the most valuable cars in her collection. On her way, she stopped to buy a newspaper. Because her daughter had fallen asleep in the backseat, the collector left her in the car when she got out. The defendant, a professional car thief who happened to be at the newspaper stand, jumped into

the collector's car and drove it away without noticing the daughter in the backseat.

The defendant realized that he would not be able to sell a stolen car as unusual as this one, so he parked it in a friend's garage, still unaware of the presence of the sleeping child. Getting the collector's name and phone number from some papers in the glove compartment of the car, the defendant phoned her and left a message on her voicemail, telling her that if she did not immediately bring $1,000 in cash to a certain location, he would set the car on fire.

Upon hearing the message, the collector brought $1,000 to the location specified. The defendant, who was waiting for her, took the money and returned the car. The daughter was still sleeping quietly in the backseat.

If the defendant is charged with kidnapping, he should be found

(A) guilty, since he confined and moved the daughter without her consent.

(B) guilty, since the asportation of the daughter resulted from his commission of a serious felony.

(C) not guilty, since his primary purpose was to steal the car, and the movement of the daughter was only incidental to his accomplishing that purpose.

(D) not guilty, since he did not know that the daughter was in the car.

60. The defendant was driving across the border from Mexico. He arrived at the border station. The border inspector asked him to open the trunk of his car and began searching it. In the course of the search, the inspector discovered three pounds of marijuana. The defendant was subsequently charged with the illegal importation of a controlled substance and was tried in a federal court. While his trial was pending, the state charged him with violation of a state statute that provided that "any person in possession of more than one ounce of marijuana shall be guilty of

a felony." While the federal court trial is in progress, if the defendant moves to dismiss the state court prosecution on the ground that it violates the double jeopardy clause of the United States Constitution, his motion should be

(A) granted, since both the prosecutions resulted from the same transaction.

(B) granted, since the supervisor did not have probable cause for the search.

(C) denied, since he has not yet been placed in jeopardy in the federal court.

(D) denied, since the two prosecutions are not by the same sovereign.

61. Because he was a professional thief, the defendant owned a skeleton key that could be used to open many different locks. One evening, when he knew that the victim was away on vacation, the defendant went to her home for the purpose of stealing cash that he believed was hidden inside. While he was trying unsuccessfully to use his skeleton key to open the victim's door, the defendant was arrested by a police officer. In fact, the victim had placed her cash in a bank safety deposit box before going on vacation, and her house contained nothing of value.

If charged with violating a statute that makes it a crime to "possess any skeleton key with the intent to use it for the purpose of committing an unlawful entry onto the property of another," he should be found

(A) guilty, because the statute was designed to protect the public against professional thieves.

(B) guilty, because he possessed a skeleton key with the intent to use it for the purpose of committing an unlawful entry.

(C) not guilty, because the crime defined by the statute is merged into the crime of attempted burglary.

(D) not guilty, because to convict him would be to punish him merely for having a guilty mind.

62. A statute provides that "If the death of any person proximately results from the commission of or attempt to commit any misdemeanor or non-forcible felony, the person committing said misdemeanor or non-forcible felony shall be guilty of third degree manslaughter."

Because he had been convicted three times of driving while under the influence of alcohol, the defendant's driving license was revoked. One night, while driving home from a party, the defendant lost control of his automobile and collided head-on with a vehicle traveling in the other direction. Two occupants of the other car were killed. The defendant was charged with driving without a license, which was a misdemeanor, and with third degree manslaughter under the above statute. Should the court find the defendant guilty of third degree manslaughter?

(A) No, because driving without a license is not *malum in se*.

(B) Yes, because the deaths were proximately caused by his operation of a motor vehicle without a license.

(C) Yes, because driving while intoxicated is a dangerous act.

(D) Yes, because he knew or should have known that driving without a license could result in loss of life.

63. A student and the defendant were college students who needed money. One night, the student suggested that they hold up a local convenience store. When the defendant told her that she was afraid to get involved in a robbery, the student offered to go into the store alone if the defendant would wait outside in the car with the engine running so that they could make a getaway after the robbery. The defendant agreed on the condition that they split the take. The following day, they went together to a sporting goods store, where the student purchased a shotgun. That night, the defendant drove the student to the convenience store and waited in the parking lot with the engine running. The student went

into the store with the shotgun hidden in a paper bag. Once inside, she pointed it at the store clerk and made him give her the contents of the cash register. Then she ran out to the car. When the defendant saw the student running toward the car, she became frightened and drove away without waiting for the student.

The defendant is guilty of

(A) conspiracy only.

(B) robbery only.

(C) conspiracy and robbery.

(D) either conspiracy or robbery, but not both.

64. In which of the following fact situations is the defendant **LEAST** likely to be properly convicted of murder?

(A) The defendant came home to find his wife lying on the floor of their apartment semi-conscious and severely bruised. When he asked her what happened, she said that their neighbor had raped and beaten her. The following morning, the defendant hid behind some bushes waiting for the neighbor to leave his home. When the neighbor stepped out of his door, the defendant, intending to kill him, shot him, causing his death.

(B) A state law required every motor vehicle registered within the state to be covered by a valid policy of liability insurance. The defendant was operating a vehicle for which no liability insurance policy had been issued when he struck a pedestrian, who later died of the resulting injuries.

(C) The defendant placed a small quantity of ant poison in a cup of coffee that he was serving to a date. He did not intend to cause any serious injury, but he hoped that the poison would make her slightly ill so that he could induce her to spend the night in his apartment rather than to go home. His date drank the coffee and died as a result.

(D) The defendant's daughter was suffering from a lingering, incurable, fatal disease. One day, while the defendant was visiting her in the hospital, she screamed and writhed in pain. Wanting to end her suffering, the defendant placed a pillow over her face and held it there until she died of suffocation.

65. A rare migratory bird is protected by international treaty. For this reason, hunting of the bird is restricted to seasons fixed by a law known as the Protection Act. Until recently, the Act permitted hunting of the bird only during the months of March and April. The law was changed last year, however, to permit bird hunting during the additional months of May and June.

The defendant did not know that the law fixing the hunting season had been changed. Because he did not like to compete with other hunters, he planned to go bird hunting in May, believing that the season ended in March. He invited his friend to join him, but the friend refused. The friend, who was also unaware that the law had been changed, informed a game warden about his conversation with the defendant. The defendant went bird hunting on May 15. He shot at several birds and missed before he succeeded in killing one of them. As soon as he did, the game warden arrested the defendant. If the defendant is charged with attempting to violate the Protection Act, which of the following would be his most effective argument in defense?

(A) He actually succeeded in killing a bird prior to his arrest.

(B) The act that he intended to commit was not a crime.

(C) The friend was *in pari delicto* with the defendant because he was unaware that the law had been changed.

(D) The attempted crime merged with the completed act.

66. The defendant had suspected for some time that his wife was unfaithful to him. One night, when she came home later than usual, the defendant confronted her, demanding to know where she had been. Tearfully, the wife confessed that she had been out with a male friend and that she had sexual intercourse with him. The defendant flew into a rage, striking the wife repeatedly about the face and head with his clenched fist. The following day, the wife died as a result of the injuries that the defendant had inflicted. The defendant was subsequently charged with murder. At the defendant's trial, his attorney asserted that, under the circumstances, the defendant should not be convicted of any crime more serious than voluntary manslaughter.

Which of the following would be the prosecuting attorney's most effective argument in response to that assertion?

(A) The defendant's conduct indicated an intent to kill the wife.

(B) The defendant's conduct indicated an intent to inflict great bodily harm on the wife.

(C) The defendant did not catch the wife *in flagrante delicto*.

(D) In the defendant's position, a person of ordinary temperament would not have become angry enough to lose normal self-control.

67. Because of a series of early morning burglaries that had been committed in a suburban neighborhood, police officers assigned to patrol the area were instructed to stop and question all persons traveling through the neighborhood between the hours of 2 A.M. and 5 A.M. One morning at 3:30 A.M., a police officer noticed the defendant running along a street in the area. The officer pulled his patrol car against the curb and ordered the defendant to stop. The defendant said, "What for? Am I under arrest?"

The officer responded, "No. I just want to talk to you." The officer got out of the car and opened the back door, pointing his finger at the back seat. When the defendant got into the back of the patrol car, the officer said, "Now, I think you'd better tell me why you're running here at this hour."

The defendant said, "I guess you already know. I just broke into a house around the corner."

The officer arrested the defendant, who was subsequently charged with burglary. At the trial, two witnesses testified that they saw the defendant leaving the burglarized house shortly before his arrest. In addition, the prosecution offered the testimony of the officer regarding his conversation with the defendant in the back of the patrol car. The defendant moved to exclude evidence of his statement.

Which of the following would be the prosecution's most effective argument in response to the defendant's motion?

(A) Independent evidence tends to establish that the defendant did commit the burglary with which he is charged.

(B) The defendant was not in custody at the time of the conversation.

(C) The defendant was not a suspect at the time of the conversation.

(D) The officer's questioning of the defendant was part of a routine investigation.

68. The defendant was invited to a party at the home of the homeowner. Because he wanted to help make the party a success, the defendant purchased fireworks and brought them to the party. A state statute requires that any person engaging in the use of fireworks have a license and provides that the license may be issued only upon successful completion of a safety course conducted by the fire department. Although the defendant had never completed the safety course and had no license to engage in the use of fireworks, he believed that he was competent to do so without

causing any danger. During the party, the defendant set off some of the fireworks in the homeowner's backyard with the homeowner's consent. Although the defendant acted reasonably, one of them exploded prematurely, causing a fire that completely destroyed the homeowner's home.

If the defendant is charged with arson, he should be found

(A) guilty, because he violated the statute requiring a license for the use of fireworks.

(B) guilty, because the fire resulted from his conduct.

(C) not guilty, because the homeowner consented to the defendant's use of the fireworks.

(D) not guilty, because the defendant did not intend damage to the homeowner's home.

69. Because he was convicted of driving while intoxicated, the defendant's driver's license was suspended. One day, he made a series of repairs to the engine of his car. That night, after coming home from a party, the defendant decided to test his car by driving it on a quiet residential street on the outskirts of town. Traveling north toward an intersection, he accelerated until he was driving at a speed of 100 miles per hour. The victim, who was driving west, proceeded across the intersection in violation of a red traffic signal light. The defendant saw the victim's car, but because of the speed at which the defendant was traveling, was unable to avoid striking it. The victim was killed in the collision. A statute in the jurisdiction provides "No person shall operate a motor vehicle on any public road or highway in this state unless such person shall be the holder of a valid driving license. Violation of this section shall be punishable by a maximum of 30 days in the county jail."

If the defendant is convicted of the murder of the victim, it will most likely be because

(A) driving while intoxicated is evidence of culpable negligence.

(B) his speed was evidence of a wanton disregard for human life.

(C) the jurisdiction applies the misdemeanor-manslaughter rule.

(D) the victim's death resulted from the defendant's unlicensed operation of a motor vehicle.

70. When the owner of a hardware store went away on vacation, she left her assistant in charge of the store. One day, while the assistant was alone in the store, the defendant entered and pointed a realistic-looking toy pistol at the assistant, demanding all the money in the cash register. The assistant believed that the pistol in the defendant's hand was real and complied with the defendant's demand because he was afraid that if he did not, the defendant would shoot him.

The following day, the owner returned from her vacation. When the assistant told her about the holdup, the owner became so upset that she suffered a cerebral hemorrhage and died.

The jurisdiction has a statute that provides that "Any person who causes the death of another human being with the intent to cause such death or in the course of committing a dangerous felony shall be guilty of murder." If the defendant is charged with the murder of the owner, he should be found

(A) guilty, because robbery is a dangerous felony.

(B) guilty, because it was foreseeable that the robbery would result in the death of the owner.

(C) not guilty, because the owner's death did not occur while the defendant was committing a dangerous felony.

(D) not guilty, because the toy pistol that the defendant used could not foreseeably

have inflicted an injury upon another person.

71. Which of the following fact situations is the defendant's claim of intoxication **LEAST** likely to be an effective defense?

(A) Charged with rape, the defendant asserts that immediately before the act, he drank a great deal of liquor, and that as a result, he was so intoxicated that he believed the victim to be his wife.

(B) Charged with murder, the defendant asserts that immediately before she shot the victim, an unknown person put alcohol in her orange juice without her knowledge, and that as a result she was so intoxicated that she believed her gun to be a harmless toy.

(C) Charged with attempted robbery, the defendant asserts that at the time she pointed her pistol at the victim and demanded money, she was so intoxicated that she thought the victim was a friend of hers and would know that she was joking.

(D) Charged with larceny of an automobile, the defendant asserts that after injecting heroin into his bloodstream, he was so intoxicated that he believed the automobile to be his own.

72. In which of the following fact situations is the defendant most likely to be convicted of criminally receiving stolen property?

(A) After a woman was arrested for car theft, the district attorney offered to let her plead guilty to a lesser offense in return for her cooperation in the apprehension of the defendant. At the district attorney's request, the woman offered to sell the defendant the car that she had been caught stealing, telling the defendant that it was stolen. The defendant agreed to purchase it for $300 and was arrested as he handed the cash to the woman.

(B) A man told the defendant that the police were after him for stealing a car, and that he wanted to get rid of the car as soon as possible. When he offered to give the car to the defendant, the defendant said, "Give it to my brother, but don't tell him it's stolen." The man gave the car to the defendant's brother without telling him that it was stolen.

(C) An undercover police officer contacted the defendant saying, "Are you interested in buying stolen cars?" The defendant said, "If the price is right, I'll take all you can get." Requisitioning a car from the police department's property division, the officer showed it to the defendant, telling him that the car was stolen. The defendant agreed to purchase the car and was arrested as he handed cash to the officer.

(D) Intending to make a fraudulent claim under his automobile theft insurance policy, a man sold his car to the defendant, telling him that the car was stolen. When the man was subsequently arrested and charged with insurance fraud, he told the police about the circumstances of his sale to the defendant, who was then charged with receiving stolen property.

73. After observing the defendant for several weeks, police officers concluded that he was engaged in the illegal sale of a dangerous drug. Two officers obtained a warrant and searched the defendant's kitchen while the defendant was present. Finding an ounce of the substance, the officers arrested the defendant and advised him of his rights. While driving to the police station, one officer said to the other, "I'll bet the defendant has the rest of the drugs stashed somewhere. If some kids get their hands on it, it could kill them. Then we'll have the SOB on a murder rap."

The defendant, who overheard the officer's statement from the back of the police car,

said, "Wait, I've got 10 pounds of the stuff hidden in the tool shed behind my garage." The officers returned to the defendant's house and found the rest of the drugs in the tool shed. The defendant was charged with violating a statute that made it a felony to possess more than eight ounces of drug. Prior to trial, the defendant moved to suppress the drugs found in his tool shed.

Which of the following additional facts or inferences, if it were the only one true, would provide the prosecution with its most effective opposition to the defendant's motion?

(A) When he told the officers where to find the drugs, the defendant fully understood his Fifth Amendment right to remain silent.

(B) The officers were unaware that the defendant could overhear their conversation from the back of the police car.

(C) The defendant's statement about the location of the drugs was voluntary.

(D) The search of the defendant's kitchen and the arrest of the defendant for possession of one ounce of drugs were lawful.

74. The defendant was employed as store manager by a retailer of tools and equipment. One day, as part of her duties, the defendant was re-arranging merchandise in the storeroom while examining store inventory records. After moving a gasoline-powered lawnmower to a position next to the rear door inside the storeroom, the defendant discovered that the lawnmower was not listed in the inventory records. Realizing that the lawnmower would therefore not be missed, the defendant decided to steal it. She planned to take the mower out onto the loading dock behind the store just before the store closed, and from there to put the mower in her car after the store closed. Before removing it from the storeroom, however, the defendant changed her mind, leaving it where she had placed it and adding it to the store inventory list.

Of which of the following crimes may the defendant be properly convicted?

(A) Larceny only.

(B) Embezzlement only.

(C) Larceny and embezzlement.

(D) Neither larceny nor embezzlement.

75. The defendant and victim, both scientists working on a new laser gun for the military, were drinking in a bar when they got into an argument about the merits of their work. The two men got off their bar stools and started shoving each other. The victim reached into his pocket and started to take out his cellphone saying, "You know what? I've actually got a laser gun to work and now you are dead!" The victim had an app on his phone that made a sound like a laser charging up. The victim turned on the sound while the cellphone was still in his pocket. Because the defendant was intoxicated, he mistook the glow of the cellphone screen and the noise as the charging of a real laser gun. He grabbed a glass from the bar, shattered it, and then stabbed the victim. The victim then bled to death. The defendant was charged with murder. At trial, the defense showed that the defendant genuinely but unreasonably believed that the victim was about to shoot him with a laser gun. Consequently, the defendant claimed self-defense. In the majority of states, if the court believes the defendant's claim regarding the circumstances of the victim's death, the defendant's self-defense claim will result in the defendant being found

(A) not guilty of any crime.

(B) guilty of murder.

(C) guilty of voluntary manslaughter.

(D) guilty of depraved heart murder.

76. The defendant was charged with first degree murder under a statute that defines that crime as "the deliberate and premeditated unjustified killing of a human being." At his trial,

the defendant offered the testimony of a psychiatrist who attempted to testify that the defendant had a violent temper and that, at the time of the killing, the defendant was so enraged that he was not in control of his acts.

In a jurisdiction that has adopted only the M'Naghten test of insanity, is the testimony of the psychiatrist admissible?

(A) Yes, because it tends to establish that the defendant was insane at the time of his act.

(B) Yes, because it tends to establish that the killing was not "deliberate and premeditated."

(C) No, because it does not tend to establish insanity under the M'Naghten rule.

(D) No, because in a prosecution for criminal homicide, provocation should be measured by an objective standard.

77. A state police officer was investigating a series of car thefts. A federal officer was assigned to assist under a federal statute that permits the U.S. Department of Justice to aid local police departments in investigating certain crimes. Because of the defendant's criminal record, the state police officer went to the defendant's home and questioned him regarding the recent thefts. During the course of the questioning, the state police officer drew her gun and threatened to shoot the defendant if the defendant did not immediately admit his guilt. The defendant confessed to the thefts and identified his partner. The state police officer left the defendant, saying, "I'll be back for you later." Then, after obtaining the necessary warrant, the state police officer arrested the defendant's partner.

Unaware of the state police officer's activity, the federal officer examined a stolen vehicle that had been recovered by the state police. Using a U.S. Department of Justice computer, the federal officer identified fingerprints as the defendant's. The federal officer obtained the necessary warrant and arrested the defendant. The defendant's partner and the defendant were charged in a state court with car theft.

The defendant moves to dismiss the prosecution on the ground that his constitutional rights were violated by the state police officer. His motion should be

(A) granted, because the state police officer failed to advise him of his *Miranda* rights.

(B) granted, because the state police officer threatened to shoot him if he did not confess to the crimes.

(C) denied, because the officers were employed by different sovereigns.

(D) denied, because his arrest resulted from an independent investigation by the federal officer.

78. The defendant's roommate heard of someone in a nearby town who bought stolen cars. Because they needed money to pay their rent, the roommate proposed to the defendant that they steal a car and sell it. The defendant agreed, and the two of them went out immediately looking for a car to steal. The roommate got behind the wheel of a car they found and drove the car while the defendant sat beside him. Later, the defendant climbed into the backseat and went to sleep.

While the defendant was sleeping, the roommate thought that he noticed a police car following them. Hoping to avoid contact with the police, he turned off onto a road that led into a neighboring state. Shortly after crossing the state line, the roommate and the defendant were arrested by federal police. They were subsequently charged in a federal court with violating the Dyer Act, which makes the interstate transportation of stolen vehicles a federal crime, and with conspiracy to violate the Dyer Act.

On the charge of violating the Dyer Act, the defendant should be found

(A) not guilty, because he could not have anticipated that the roommate would drive the car across the state line.

(B) not guilty, because he did not agree to transport the car across a state line.

(C) not guilty, because transportation of the car across the state line was not necessary to the success of the criminal enterprise.

(D) guilty.

79. The defendant, an attorney, was vice president of a corporation that made children's pajamas. After several children were burned to death while wearing the corporation's product, both the defendant and the corporation were charged with criminal negligence. After placing the defendant under arrest and informing her of the charge against her, the arresting officer said, "Now your answers may be used against you, so you don't have to give any, and you're entitled to an attorney." The defendant said, "I am an attorney," and answered questions that the officer then put to her regarding her corporate duties. At her trial, the defendant moved to exclude evidence of her answers to those questions, although she conceded that her statement was not coerced.

Read the summaries of the decisions in the four cases (A–D) below. Which is most applicable as a precedent?

(A) After hearing gunshots, a police officer ran toward the sound. Finding the victim lying dead in a pool of blood, the officer asked a group of persons who were standing nearby what happened. The defendant, who was among the bystanders, replied, "I shot the son of a bitch." At the defendant's murder trial, the court denied a motion to exclude the officer's testimony regarding the defendant's statement.

(B) A recently arrived immigrant from Southeast Asia was arrested for burglary. After the arresting officer read him his *Miranda* rights, she asked, "Do you understand what I just said?" The defendant replied, "Yes. I break in the house for steal." The defendant's pretrial motion to exclude evidence of his confession was granted.

(C) Following a series of assaults, police officers went to the defendant's home. The officers told the defendant that she was not under arrest, but that they would appreciate her cooperation in answering their questions. The defendant said, "I'm innocent, and I'm willing to prove it by standing in a lineup." She then accompanied the police officers to the police station where two assault victims picked her out of a lineup. At the defendant's trial on a charge of assault, her motion to exclude evidence of the lineup identification was denied.

(D) When the defendant was awakened at 3 A.M. by the sound of knocking on his front door, he opened it to find three uniformed police officers. One of them said, "We have reason to believe that there is stolen property in your house. Do you mind if we search?" The defendant let the officers in. During the course of their search, they seized a stereo set that had been stolen from a local appliance store. At his trial for criminally receiving stolen property, the defendant's motion to suppress use of the stereo as evidence was granted.

80. After a man was arrested for selling large quantities of illegal substances, he agreed to assist the police in return for a promise that the charges against him would be reduced. In furtherance of their agreement, the police set the man up in the used car business and spread the rumor that the man dealt in stolen vehicles. Subsequently, a woman came to the man's lot offering to sell the man a stolen car. After conferring with a police officer assigned to the investigation, the man purchased the car from the woman. When he had done so, the police arrested the woman and notified the car's owner that it had been recovered. The following day, the defendant came to the man's lot and said that he wished to purchase a stolen car. At the direction of an undercover police officer, the man sold the defendant the car that he had purchased from the woman.

If the defendant is charged with receiving stolen property, which of the following would be his most effective argument in defense?

(A) The defendant was entrapped by an agent of the police.

(B) The car that the defendant purchased was not stolen property.

(C) The man's cooperation with the police was coerced.

(D) The police cannot bargain away a defendant's rights in an agreement with a third person.

81. The defendant and his girlfriend had been living together and sharing a bedroom for five months when they began arguing regularly. After one such argument, the defendant stormed out of the apartment. Angry at him, the girlfriend called the police to report that the defendant was in possession of nearly a kilogram of marijuana. Two officers came to talk to the girlfriend in the apartment. When they asked how she knew that the defendant had that much marijuana, the girlfriend said, "I've seen it. He keeps it in our closet. Would you like to look?" One of the officers said that they would, and the girlfriend led them to the closet in the bedroom that she shared with the defendant. When the girlfriend opened the closet door, a plastic bag containing one and one-half pounds of marijuana fell from the shelf. One of the officers took it. Later, the defendant was arrested and charged with the unlawful possession of a dangerous drug. If the defendant makes a timely motion to suppress use of the marijuana as evidence, which of the following would be the prosecution's most effective argument in opposition to his motion?

(A) Their conversation with the girlfriend gave the police officers probable cause to believe that there was marijuana in the closet.

(B) Failure to seize the marijuana immediately might have given the defendant time to dispose of it before the police officers could obtain a search warrant.

(C) The girlfriend invited the police officers to search the closet.

(D) The marijuana was in plain view when the closet door was opened.

82. The defendant was waiting for a bus on a street corner shortly after midnight when three young men approached him and demanded that he give them some money. Fearing that they would attack and injure him, the defendant drew a pistol from his pocket. The three men began running away, but the defendant shot each of them in the back, seriously injuring two and killing the third. As a result, the defendant was charged with two counts of aggravated assault and one count of murder. By the time a grand jury was convened, the incident had received a great deal of media attention, several newspapers referring to the defendant as "The Vigilante Hero." The defendant presented no evidence to the grand jury, but after hearing the prosecution's evidence, the grand jury refused to indict. Following the proceeding, the prosecuting attorney stated that she believed that the grand jury's decision resulted from publicity surrounding the incident, and that she intended to bring the matter before another grand jury. Three weeks later, a second grand jury issued an indictment against the defendant. If the defendant moves to dismiss the indictment on the ground that it violates his rights under the Double Jeopardy Clause of the United States Constitution, his motion should be

(A) granted, because the first grand jury's failure to indict is *res judicata*.

(B) granted, if the charges brought before the second grand jury were identical to the charges brought before the first grand jury.

(C) denied, unless the decision of the first grand jury was motivated by sympathy or undue prejudice.

(D) denied, because no trial has begun.

83. The defendant fired a pistol through the ceiling of her apartment because the neighbors had refused several requests to stop making so much noise at their party. She did not intend to hit anyone with the bullet, but she hoped that the shot would frighten her neighbors and chill the atmosphere. After passing through the floor of the apartment above the defendant's, the bullet struck a piece of furniture and ricocheted. It struck the victim, lodging in his shoulder and injuring him.

An ambulance was called to transport the victim to a hospital for treatment. Because the ambulance driver was driving negligently, the ambulance was involved in a collision that resulted in the victim's death. If the defendant is acquitted on a charge of murdering the victim, it will most likely be because the court finds that

(A) the defendant did not intend to strike anyone with the bullet.

(B) the victim's death was proximately caused by the negligence of the ambulance driver.

(C) the defendant was privileged to abate a nuisance by self-help.

(D) the defendant's conduct did not show a wanton disregard for human life.

84. The victim and the defendant were roommates until they began arguing bitterly. During one argument, the victim moved out of the apartment that they shared. As she left, she said, "I'm going to get even with you for all the grief you've caused me." The following day, the defendant's friend told the defendant that the victim had purchased a gun. The friend also said that the victim told her that

she was going to shoot the defendant the next time she saw her. As a result, the defendant began carrying a loaded pistol. Several days later, realizing that she still had the key to the defendant's apartment, the victim went back to return it. The defendant was leaving her apartment when she saw the victim walking toward her. As the victim reached into her pocket for the apartment key, the defendant drew her pistol and shot the victim, aiming to hit her in the chest. The bullet grazed the victim's shoulder, inflicting a minor injury. The victim immediately drew her own pistol and shot the defendant with it, striking her in the thigh and inflicting a serious injury.

If the defendant is charged with attempted murder, which of the following would be her most effective argument in defense?

(A)  The victim's injury was not serious enough to result in death.

(B)  The defendant did not succeed in striking the victim in the chest as she intended.

(C)  It was reasonable for the defendant to believe that the victim was reaching into her pocket for a gun.

(D)  The force that the defendant used was not deadly.

85.  Two men were members of a militant political group. As a protest against the use of harmful agricultural chemicals, they planned to burn down a factory that produced such chemicals. To be certain that no persons would be injured in the explosion, they chose a time when they knew that the factory was closed. At 10 P.M., they broke into the factory and wired a fire bomb to a timer that was set to detonate at 11 P.M. At 10:45 P.M., they telephoned the local police and told them that the factory would be bombed in 15 minutes, warning them to evacuate any persons who might happen to be in the area. At 11 P.M., the bomb detonated, causing flames that totally destroyed the factory. Two transients

who had broken into the factory at 10:30 P.M. in search of a place to sleep were killed by the blast.

If the two men are charged with murder, they should be found

(A)  not guilty, because they did not desire or know that their act would result in the death of a human being.

(B)  not guilty, because the deaths of the transients were totally independent of their purpose in blowing up the factory.

(C)  guilty, because it was not reasonable to believe that the police could successfully evacuate the area in 15 minutes.

(D)  guilty, because the deaths resulted from their commission of a dangerous felony.

86.  There were three employees and three customers in a bank when the defendant entered and drew a pistol from his pocket. Waving the pistol in the air, the defendant shouted, "Freeze! This is a holdup!" Threatening to shoot him if he did not obey, the defendant ordered one of the tellers to open the vault. After the teller had done so, the defendant directed everyone present to lie down on the floor. The defendant then removed all the cash from the vault and left the bank, forcing one of the customers at gunpoint to accompany him into his car as a hostage. After driving for about 15 minutes, the defendant opened the car door and permitted the hostage to get out.

Of how many kidnappings may the defendant properly be convicted?

(A)  Zero.

(B)  One.

(C)  Two.

(D)  Six.

87. Undercover police officers received an anonymous tip that the defendant was engaged in buying and selling stolen cars. They decided to catch the defendant by pretending to be criminals. One of the officers arranged to meet the defendant, telling the defendant that his friend was looking for a buyer for stolen cars. When the defendant said that he might be interested in purchasing one for resale, the officer offered to put up half the money and to buy it with him as a partner. The defendant agreed, and the officer gave him $1,000 in cash as his share. The officer had requisitioned the money from the police department for that purpose and had it marked in a way that would permit its subsequent identification. The officer then introduced the defendant to the other officer, saying that the other officer was a car thief. The other officer offered to sell the defendant a car that he said he had stolen, but which he had actually requisitioned from the police department for that purpose. After agreeing on a price for the car, the defendant paid the other officer with the marked money that the first officer had given him. The officers immediately placed the defendant under arrest.

The defendant is charged with criminally receiving stolen property. Which of the following would be his most effective argument in defense against that charge?

(A) The car that the defendant purchased from the other officer had been requisitioned from the police department.

(B) The money that the defendant used to purchase the car from the other officer had been requisitioned from the police department.

(C) The two officers entrapped the defendant into purchasing the car.

(D) The anonymous tip received by the officers was not sufficient to give them probable cause to believe that the defendant was guilty of a crime.

88. Four weeks after breaking her engagement with her boyfriend, the defendant was angry because her boyfriend still had not returned a stereo that he had borrowed from her. She went to his house one night to demand its immediate return. When she got there, the boyfriend was not at home and his door was unlocked. The defendant entered to look for her stereo but could not find it. While searching, she noticed that the boyfriend had a new couch. Thinking that the couch was worth as much as her stereo, she tore open one of its cushions and set it on fire before leaving. The fire destroyed the couch completely and charred the walls and ceiling of the room, although the house itself was not seriously damaged. The defendant was subsequently prosecuted. Statutes in the jurisdiction adopt the common law definitions of burglary, larceny, and arson.

If the defendant is charged with burglary and arson, she can properly be convicted of

(A) burglary only.

(B) arson only.

(C) burglary and arson.

(D) neither burglary nor arson.

89. After being arrested and charged with bribery, the defendant spent one night in a detention cell at the county jail. The informant, who had been arrested on a charge unrelated to the defendant's case, was assigned to the same detention cell as the defendant. Before putting the informant in the cell, the police asked for his help. The following morning, the defendant and the informant were released on bail. Leaving the jail together, they stopped for breakfast and chatted about the charges against them. During the course of their conversation, the defendant told the informant that he was in fact guilty of bribery, and that he had paid unlawful fees to several public officials. At the defendant's trial, the informant was called as a prosecution witness. The informant stated that he spoke to

the defendant about the bribery case because the police had offered to drop charges against him in return for help in getting evidence against the defendant. The informant then attempted to testify to the conversation in which the defendant admitted his guilt. If the defendant's attorney objected and moved to exclude the testimony on the ground that the defendant was not warned that anything he said to the informant might be used against him, should the informant's testimony regarding the defendant's admission of guilt be excluded on that ground?

(A) Yes, because the police asked for the informant's help before putting him in a cell with the defendant.

(B) Yes, because at the time of the informant's conversation with the defendant, the informant was acting as an agent of the police.

(C) No, because the prosecution may not bargain away the rights of one defendant in a deal with another.

(D) No, because the defendant was not in police custody when he admitted his guilt to the informant.

90. As a result of mental illness, the defendant was obsessed with the delusion that his wife, the victim, was building a bomb in the basement of their house, and that she was going to use it to blow up the world. Because he twice tried to kill the victim, he had been confined to a state mental hospital on two occasions. After his most recent release from confinement, the defendant discussed his belief with the police, but they did not take him seriously. Although he knew that he would be imprisoned for murder if he was caught, he pushed the victim down a flight of stairs, thinking that he would save the world by killing her. The victim died of injuries that she sustained in the fall.

If the defendant is prosecuted for the murder of the victim, his most effective argument in

defense would be that, as a result of mental illness,

(A) he did not know that his act was wrong.

(B) he lacked criminal intent.

(C) he was unable to control his conduct.

(D) he did not appreciate the nature and quality of his act.

91. A teacher at a privately operated high school found an anonymous note on his desk stating that the writer had heard through the grapevine that the defendant, one of the teacher's students, was unlawfully selling drugs to other students. The teacher immediately showed the note to the school administrator, who ordered the defendant to report to her office. When the defendant did so, the administrator reached into the defendant's trouser pocket, where she found 23 capsules containing drugs. The defendant was subsequently prosecuted for unlawful possession of a controlled substance. In an appropriate proceeding, the defendant moved to suppress evidence of the capsules found by the administrator on the ground that she had violated his Fourth Amendment rights by searching him.

Which of the following is the most effective argument in opposition to the defendant's motion?

(A) The administrator was not working for the government.

(B) The special relationship between a high school administrator and a student implies the student's consent to a search by the administrator.

(C) Special concern for the well-being of young people justifies a warrantless search of a student suspected of selling drugs to other students.

(D) The administrator had probable cause to believe that the defendant was in possession of dangerous drugs.

92. A teenager, who was 15 years of age, entered the sporting goods department and asked the employee to sell her ammunition for a pistol. The employee placed a box of ammunition on the counter and said, "That'll be $9, please." The employee usually worked in another department. Realizing that she did not have any money with her, the teenager left the store without the ammunition, saying that she would return for it later. A statute in the jurisdiction provides as follows: "Any person who sells ammunition for a firearm to a person below the age of 16 years shall be guilty of a felony. The employer of any person who violates this section during the course of such employment shall be guilty of a misdemeanor punishable by a fine not to exceed $250. It shall not be a defense to a violation of this section that the defendant had no knowledge of the age of the person to whom the sale was made."

The teenager did not return to the store. If the employee is charged with attempting to violate the above statute, which of the following would be the employee's most effective argument in defense against that charge?

(A) The employee did not know of the statute or its provisions.

(B) The employee did not know that the teenager was below the age of 16 years.

(C) The owner should be prosecuted under the statute, since she was the employee's employer.

(D) The employee is customarily employed in another department and should not be held to the same standard as a person in the business of selling firearms and ammunition.

93. The defendant and his ex-girlfriend had hated each other for years. One day, the defendant waited outside his ex-girlfriend's office building with a loaded pistol, planning to kill his ex-girlfriend. When the defendant saw the victim leave the building, he believed the victim was his ex-girlfriend and shot at her, aiming to kill her. The victim was struck by the bullet and died of the bullet wound. If the defendant is charged with the victim's murder in a jurisdiction that applies the common law definition and the doctrine of transferred intent, the defendant should be found

(A) guilty, because the jurisdiction applies the doctrine of transferred intent.

(B) guilty, because the defendant intended to bring about the death of the person at whom he shot.

(C) not guilty.

(D) guilty, because the defendant created an unreasonable risk that a human being would die.

94. Federal agents arrested the defendant and others pursuant to a warrant issued by a federal court. At the time of the arrest, federal officers seized a quarter-ounce of heroin that was in the defendant's possession. As a result, the defendant was convicted of violating a federal statute that prohibits the possession of heroin with the intent to engage in interstate distribution thereof. Following her conviction in the federal court, federal officials offered to permit the state to use the seized heroin as evidence in a state prosecution of the defendant. The defendant was subsequently charged in a state court with conspiracy to sell a controlled substance in violation of a state statute. If the defendant moves to dismiss the state prosecution on the sole ground that it violates her rights under the double jeopardy clause of the United States Constitution, her motion should be

(A) granted, because the same evidence that was used to convict her in the federal prosecution will be used to convict her in the state prosecution.

(B) granted, because the crime of conspiracy is a lesser offense that was constructively included in the federal prosecution.

(C) denied, because she is being charged in the state court with the violation of a different statute than that which she was convicted of violating in the federal court.

(D) granted, because a person may not be prosecuted by different sovereigns for the same offense.

95. After the defendant entered a tavern and sat on a stool at the bar, a friend sitting beside him said, "Did you ever have this special drink?" The defendant ordered the special drink, although he had never heard of it before. While he realized that the drink had some alcohol in it, he was unaware that it was 90 percent alcohol. When the bartender placed the drink in front of the defendant, the defendant drank it quickly. A few moments later, the defendant fell off his bar stool because he was overcome by the alcohol. He fell against an elderly man, knocking him against the wall and causing the elderly man to fracture several ribs. If the defendant is charged with committing a criminal battery against the elderly man, which of the following additional facts or inferences, if it was the only one true, would provide the defendant with his most effective argument in defense?

(A) The defendant did not intend to become intoxicated by drinking the drink.

(B) The defendant did not know that drinking the drink would cause him to fall off the bar stool.

(C) The defendant did not intend to make contact with the elderly man.

(D) The defendant had never before been overcome by the alcohol in one drink.

96. The defendant was the owner of a tavern. On two occasions in the recent past, thieves entered the defendant's tavern after closing time and stole several thousand dollars worth of liquor. In an attempt to protect himself against further thefts, the defendant began sleeping in the tavern at night with a loaded pistol by his side. One night, while on his rounds, a police officer noticed that one of the defendant's windows was open and climbed through the window to investigate. Hearing the sound of someone moving about his tavern, the defendant stood up and cocked his pistol. When the officer heard the sound and saw the outline of a person standing by the bar with a pistol in his hand, the officer shouted, "Drop that gun or I'll shoot!" The defendant and the officer fired their pistols at each other. Each was struck by the other's bullet.

If the defendant is charged with attempted murder because of his shooting of the officer, the court should find him

(A) not guilty, because the defendant reasonably believed that his life was in danger.

(B) guilty, because deadly force is not permitted in defense of property.

(C) guilty, because the intent to kill or inflict great bodily harm can be inferred from the defendant's conduct.

(D) guilty, because at the time of the shooting, the officer was a police officer acting within the scope of his official duties.

97. The defendant and a bank robber had been in the same cell together while serving time in prison. Soon after their release, the bank robber asked the defendant to join him in robbing a bank. The defendant refused, stating that he did not want to go back to prison. The bank robber said he wouldn't use deadly force, then said that he would rob the bank himself if the defendant would provide him

with a place to hide afterwards. The defendant agreed that the bank robber could hide in the defendant's apartment following the robbery in return for one-fourth of the proceeds of the robbery. The following day, the bank robber robbed the bank. While he was attempting to leave the bank, a security guard began shooting at him, and the bank robber fired back, killing a bystander. One week later, the bank robber was arrested at the defendant's apartment, where he had been hiding, and was charged with robbery and felony murder.

The defendant was subsequently charged with felony murder on the ground that he was an accomplice to the robbery committed by the bank robber that resulted in the death of a bystander. The court should find the defendant

(A) not guilty, because he was an accessory after the fact.

(B) not guilty, because he did not know that the bank robber was going to use deadly force to accomplish the robbery.

(C) guilty, only if it was foreseeable that someone would be shot during the course of the robbery.

(D) guilty, because an accomplice is responsible for all crimes committed in furtherance of the crime to which he or she is an accomplice.

98. After being advised by an informant that the defendant was growing marijuana in a large field, two police officers flew over the field in an airplane and observed marijuana growing there. Because of particularly dense cloud formations, it was necessary for them to use special equipment to photograph the field. The following day, the officers drove to the field and looked through the barbed wire fence that surrounded it. Although nothing was growing in the field, they observed that something had recently been harvested. They also observed a series of footprints leading to a barn located in the field. After obtaining a search warrant, the officers entered the field and searched the barn, where they found two suitcases containing marijuana. The defendant was later arrested.

The defendant's attorney made an appropriate motion to exclude the marijuana contained in the suitcases. Should the evidence be excluded?

(A) Yes, because the police used special equipment to photograph the field.

(B) No, because the reliability of the informant can be established.

(C) Yes, because it was reasonable for the defendant to believe that nobody would look into his field.

(D) No, because the officers had a warrant to search the barn.

99. A statute prohibited the sale of liquor between the hours of midnight and 8 A.M. When a customer came into the defendant's liquor store and asked to buy a bottle of liquor, the defendant looked at the clock and saw that it said five minutes past eleven, so he sold the liquor to the customer. The defendant believed that the clock was correct and did not realize that the previous day the state had changed from standard time to daylight saving time. In fact, the correct time was five minutes past midnight.

If the defendant is charged with attempting to violate the statute, he should be found

(A) guilty, because he sold liquor between midnight and 8 A.M.

(B) guilty, because he should have known the actual time.

(C) guilty, because the statute did not require specific intent.

(D) not guilty, because he believed that the time was five minutes past eleven.

100. The victim borrowed $50 and a watch worth an additional $50 from the defendant. Although the defendant repeatedly requested that the victim return the watch and the money, the victim refused to do so. The defendant and the victim belonged to the same exercise club. One day, while the victim was in the shower, the defendant opened the victim's locker and took $100 from the victim's wallet, returning the wallet to the locker. It was the defendant's intention to keep $50 of the money to pay himself back for the money he had loaned the victim and to keep the other $50 to pay himself for the watch that the victim had refused to return. A statute in the jurisdiction adopts the common law definition of larceny and provides that a larceny of $50 or less is a misdemeanor, while a larceny of more than $50 is a felony. The defendant is guilty of

(A) one misdemeanor only.

(B) two misdemeanors only.

(C) a felony.

(D) no crime.

101. Because he wanted to run away with his mistress, a man decided to murder his wife by poisoning her. He slipped a lethal dose of poison into her morning coffee and went to work. When the wife came down to the kitchen and drank it, she immediately fell facedown on the counter. A few minutes later, the mistress came to the kitchen backdoor and saw the wife facedown on the counter. The mistress thought the wife was sleeping, but the wife was really about two hours away from death by the poison. Believing this was her chance to kill the wife, the mistress broke into the house and stabbed the wife in the back with a cleaver. The wound would not have killed the wife except for the fact that she was weakened by the poison. She died 10 minutes later, although she would have lasted a few more hours if she hadn't been stabbed.

May the mistress be held criminally liable for the murder?

(A) Yes, because the stabbing sped up the wife's death.

(B) Yes, because the mistress had unlawfully entered the house.

(C) No, because the wife would have died anyway based on the poison.

(D) No, because the stabbing could not have killed the wife on its own.

102. The defendant and two other men met while in prison and decided that when they were released, they would rob a bank together. Soon after their release, they planned the robbery, agreeing that the defendant would steal and drive the getaway car and that the two other men would commit the actual robbery. The defendant stole a car for the robbery and brought it to one of the men's house, but the day before the robbery was to be committed, the defendant was arrested for violating the conditions of his parole and was returned to prison. The following day, the two other men went ahead with the plan, entering the bank and threatening to shoot the cashiers if they did not hand over all available cash. A teller pushed a button that alerted the police, and the two men were arrested before leaving the bank.

Of which of the following crimes is the defendant guilty?

(A) Attempted robbery.

(B) Conspiracy to commit robbery.

(C) Attempted robbery and conspiracy to commit robbery.

(D) No crime.

103. The public prosecutor had information that unlawful gambling activities were being conducted at a tavern. She obtained a warrant for the search by presenting an affidavit that stated that she had received information regarding the illegal activities

from an informant who had observed the reported activities while present at the tavern. The affidavit stated that the informant frequently gave information to the police and prosecutor and that the information received from the informant in the past had always been found to be accurate. It did not give the name of the informant, however, because it stated that his anonymity needed to be preserved both for his own protection and to continue his effectiveness as an informant. The warrant was issued.

Upon searching the premises, the police found gambling records in a cash drawer located behind the bar. In addition, the defendant, who was in the tavern, was searched and found to be in possession of unlawful gambling records.

The warrant was properly issued and executed with respect to the tavern. The defendant was charged with gambling, and he moved to suppress the use of gambling records found on his person. The court should

(A) grant the motion, because the court that issued the warrant did not have probable cause to believe that any customers in the tavern were engaging in unlawful gambling activities.

(B) grant the motion, because the warrant did not properly identify the persons to be searched.

(C) deny the motion, because a warrant that authorizes a search of premises may also authorize the search of persons present on those premises.

(D) deny the motion, because the fact that the defendant was found to be in possession of unlawful gambling records corroborated the information contained in the affidavit that the public prosecutor submitted in support of the application for the warrant.

104. The defendant met a girl in a bar where both were drinking. Because the defendant was too drunk to drive, the girl offered him a ride home. In the girl's car, the girl consented to intercourse. A statute provided that it was unlawful to engage in sexual intercourse with a female under the age of 18 years, and the girl was 17 years old. If the defendant believed that the girl was over the age of 18 years, is he guilty of statutory rape?

(A) No, because he believed the girl to be over the age of 18 years.

(B) No, if the reasonable person who was not intoxicated would have believed the girl to be over the age of 18 years.

(C) Yes, unless the girl assured him that she was over the age of 18 years.

(D) Yes, but only if the defendant realized that he was having intercourse.

105. Three friends were hanging out while their parents were not home. The first boy was 17 years of age; the girl and the second boy were each 15. Since the girl had engaged in sexual relations with several other boys at the high school, she and the first boy secretly agreed that she would try to seduce the second boy. The girl had some marijuana in her purse, and she and the second boy smoked some of it. Soon, however, the second boy's intoxication made him physically unable to perform. A statute in the jurisdiction provides that "A person is guilty of rape in the third degree when, being 17 years of age or more, he or she engages in sexual intercourse with a person under the age of 16 years."

Laws in the state define a conspiracy as "An agreement to commit a crime between two or more persons with the specific intent to commit a crime." If the first boy is charged with conspiracy based on his agreement with the girl regarding the seduction of the second boy, the first boy's most effective argument in defense would be that

(A) the seduction of the second boy would not have been possible without the girl's participation.

(B) the first boy did not commit any overt act that was likely to accomplish the seduction of the second boy.

(C) the girl was unsuccessful in having intercourse with the second boy.

(D) intercourse between the girl and the second boy would not have been a crime.

106. A store owner wanted to erect a new storage building so that he could expand his business of selling diet food and health supplies. He was afraid, however, that the building department would not issue him a permit to begin construction. A building department clerk said that she would make a false entry in the official records to indicate that a permit had already been issued if the store owner would pay her $500. The store owner agreed and said that he would bring the money the following day. The next day, however, when the store owner went to the clerk's office with $500, he was told that she had been fired.

A statute in the jurisdiction provides that "Any person who shall give or accept a fee not authorized by law as consideration for the act of any public employee is guilty of bribery, a felony. Any person who shall offer to commit a bribery is guilty of bribery in the second degree, a felony."

If the defendant is prosecuted for attempted bribery in the second degree, the court should find him

(A) not guilty, because bribery in the second degree is an attempt crime, and there can be no liability for attempting to attempt.

(B) not guilty, because it was the clerk who made the initial offer.

(C) not guilty, because the defendant committed bribery in the second degree

when he agreed to pay the clerk for altering the records, and the attempt merged with that crime.

(D) guilty, because attempting to commit bribery in the second degree is a lesser offense included in that crime.

107. Angry because her coworker had insulted her, the defendant decided to get revenge. Because she worked for an exterminator, the defendant had access to cans of a poison gas that was often used to kill termites and other insects. She did not want to kill the coworker, so she carefully read the user manual supplied by the manufacturer. The manual said that the gas was not fatal to human beings, but that exposure to it could cause serious ailments, including blindness and permanent respiratory irritation. When she was sure that no one would see her, the defendant brought a can of the gas to the parking lot and released the poison gas into the coworker's car. At lunchtime, the coworker and his friend sat together in the coworker's car. As a result of their exposure to the gas in the car, the friend died and the coworker became so ill that he was hospitalized for over a month.

If the defendant is charged with the attempted murder of the coworker, she should be found

(A) guilty, because the coworker suffered a serious illness as the result of a criminal act that she performed with intent to cause him great bodily harm.

(B) guilty, because her intent to cause great bodily harm resulted in the death of the friend.

(C) not guilty, because she did not intend to cause the death of any person.

(D) not guilty, because the crime of attempted murder merges with the crime of murder.

108. The defendant had been arraigned on a charge of burglarizing the home of the

victim. He was assigned a public defender and pleaded not guilty, but because he was unable to post bail, he was in jail awaiting trial. After the police received a warrant to do so, they had an undercover police officer placed in the same cell as the defendant. The officer was instructed not to question the defendant about the charge against him.

While walking through the corridor of the jail, the defendant told the officer that he had committed the burglary with which he was charged. At trial, the officer testified to the conversation that he had with the defendant in which the defendant admitted his guilt.

If the defendant's attorney objects to the testimony of the officer regarding the statement that the defendant made to him in the corridor, the objection should be

(A) sustained, because the statement was made to a police officer in the absence of and without the consent of the defendant's attorney.

(B) sustained, because the officer entrapped the defendant into making the statement.

(C) overruled, because the officer was placed in the defendant's cell pursuant to a warrant.

(D) overruled, because the defendant made the statement voluntarily.

109. Two boys decided to kill another boy that they did not like. To do so, they planned to steal the victim's asthma medication. As the two boys were walking toward the victim's room, one of the boys decided not to go through with the plan. Because he was afraid that the other boy would make fun of him for chickening out, he said nothing to him about his change of mind. Instead, saying that he needed to use the bathroom, he ran away. The other boy then went into the victim's room by himself, found the medicine, and threw the medicine away. Later

that night, the victim had an asthma attack and died because he was unable to find his medicine.

A statute in the jurisdiction provides that persons the age of the two boys are adults for the purposes of criminal liability.

If the boy who ran away is charged with the murder of the victim, a court will probably find him

(A) guilty, because he and the other boy agreed to throw away the victim's medicine in the hope that doing so would cause the victim's death.

(B) guilty, because he aided and abetted in causing the victim's death.

(C) not guilty, because he did not physically participate in throwing away the victim's medicine.

(D) not guilty, because he withdrew from the conspiracy before any overt act was committed.

110. A man had just been released from prison after serving a three-year term for aggravated assault. In need of money, he called his old friend, the defendant, and asked whether the defendant would be interested in joining the man in the robbery of a pawnshop. The defendant agreed, but only after making the man promise that there would be no violence. Upon the defendant's insistence, they carried realistic-looking toy guns. When they entered the pawnshop, they drew their toy guns and ordered the pawnshop owner to give them all the money in his cash register and all the gems in his safe. The pawnshop owner took a gun from the safe and shot the man, killing him. The pawnshop owner then aimed the pistol at the defendant, who fled from the store. As the pawnshop owner ran out into the street with his pistol in his hand, the defendant jumped into the car that he and the man had left parked at the curb. Speeding away from the scene without looking or caring where he

was going, the defendant accidentally struck a pedestrian, who died of her injuries. By statute, the jurisdiction adopted the felony-murder rule.

If the defendant is charged with the murder of the pedestrian, the court should find him

(A) guilty, because the pedestrian's death resulted from the defendant's attempt to commit a robbery.

(B) guilty, because he drove the car in a criminally negligent manner.

(C) not guilty, because he was in reasonable fear for his own life when attempting to flee in the automobile.

(D) not guilty, because the pedestrian's death did not occur during the commission of a felony.

111. A nine-year-old girl fell into a public pool, striking her head against its edge. Her aunt saw the girl fall and realized that the child would drown if someone did not rescue her. The aunt knew that there was no lifeguard present, and that no one else had seen the girl fall, but she made no effort to rescue the girl although the aunt was a strong swimmer and could easily have done so with no risk to herself. The girl drowned.

If the aunt is charged with criminal homicide in the death of the girl, the court should find her

(A) guilty, because she could have saved the girl without any risk to herself.

(B) guilty, because she knew that she was the only person present who was aware of the girl's plight and who was able to rescue her.

(C) guilty, because she was related to the girl.

(D) not guilty, because she had no duty to aid the girl.

After a man raped the defendant in her apartment, he fell asleep. The defendant tied his hands and feet to the four corners of the bed and woke him. She said, "Now you are going to be punished for what you have done. I should kill you, but I won't because I want to make sure that you suffer for the rest of your life." Using the man's own knife, she began to cut and jab him with it, planning to torture but not to kill him. She stabbed and blinded him in both eyes, then cut off his sex organs. She also severed the tip of his nose and made a series of cuts across his face and chest.

112. The man died as a result of the injuries inflicted by the defendant. She was charged with first degree murder in a jurisdiction that defines that crime as "the unlawful killing of a human being committed intentionally, with deliberation and premeditation." The court should find the defendant

(A) not guilty, because the defendant did not intend to cause the man's death.

(B) not guilty, because the defendant was acting in self-defense.

(C) guilty, because the man's death resulted from the defendant's commission of a dangerous felony.

(D) guilty, because the man's death resulted from torture.

113. The defendant noticed a gold-plated pen on her professor's desk and put it into her pocket. She did so with the intention of returning the pen in a week or two. The following day, however, the pen was stolen from the defendant's briefcase. The jurisdiction applies the common law definitions of larceny and burglary.

If the defendant is charged with larceny as a result of her taking the gold-plated pen, she should be

(A) acquitted, because theft of the pen from her briefcase was a superseding cause.

(B) acquitted, because she intended to return the pen in a week or two.

(C) convicted, because the professor was permanently deprived of the pen.

(D) convicted, because theft of the pen from her briefcase was foreseeable.

114. Between flights, a woman set her briefcase down beside her seat in the airport waiting room. The defendant saw this and walked past her in a casual fashion, picking up the briefcase and walking off with it as he went by. The woman, believing that he had taken it by mistake, ran to him and said, "Pardon me, sir. You've taken my bag." The defendant drew a realistic-looking toy pistol, pushed her into a seat, and ran away. The defendant was charged with robbery.

Read the summaries of the decisions in the four cases (A–D) below. Then decide which is most applicable as a precedent to this case.

(A) The victim was walking on a crowded street with her purse hanging from a strap over her shoulder when the defendant yanked the purse with sufficient force to break the strap. The defendant then ran off with it into the crowd. The defendant's conviction for robbery was reversed.

(B) The defendant took a package of meat from a showcase in a supermarket and slipped it under his shirt. He left the store without paying for it. The store cashier ran after him into the parking lot and stepped in front of him, blocking his path. The defendant took a straight razor from his pocket and grabbed another customer. He held the razor to the customer's throat, telling the store cashier to get out of the way. The cashier stepped aside, and the defendant ran away, releasing the other customer. The defendant's conviction for robbery was affirmed.

(C) A schoolteacher took her sixth grade class to visit a display of medieval torture devices at the museum. She sat in a wooden torture chair and had herself shackled into it to demonstrate its operation to her students. The defendant, who worked at the museum, surreptitiously photographed her with an instant camera. He then went to the office of the teacher's husband and showed the husband the photograph of the teacher in the torture chair. The defendant said that his confederates would torture her unless he called them on the phone and told them that the husband had given him $500. The husband gave him the money. The defendant's conviction for robbery was reversed.

(D) When the victim purchased a ticket at the airport for his flight, he checked his baggage. Later, the defendant, wearing a mask and carrying a gun, entered the room where checked baggage was stored. While forcing the room attendant to lie face down on the floor, the defendant opened the victim's suitcase and removed several hundred dollars worth of negotiable securities. The defendant's conviction for robbery was affirmed.

115. A supermarket cashier borrowed money from the company safe to get through the weekend, then returned it on Monday morning after she was paid. One of her coworkers saw her returning the money and questioned her about it until the cashier admitted what she had done. The coworker stopped her before she closed the safe and said that unless the cashier gave him $25 of the store's money, he would tell the boss. The cashier knew that she could get away with taking $25 because the store records were frequently off by that much and the

boss never worried about it. Thus, she took out $25 from the safe and gave it to the coworker.

Of which one of the following crimes is the coworker most likely to be guilty as a result of his conduct on Monday morning?

(A) Robbery, because he obtained money from the cashier by threat and intimidation.

(B) Larceny, because he obtained money by inciting and encouraging the cashier to steal $25 from the safe.

(C) Embezzlement, because he obtained his employer's money by violating his duty to report the cashier's conduct.

(D) Fraud, because he obtained money by withholding information that he had a duty to disclose.

116. A statute provides as follows: "Any person who knowingly sells an intoxicating substance to a person under the age of 21 years shall be guilty of a misdemeanor." The owner of a cocktail lounge hired a new bartender. Before the bartender began working, the owner read him the above statute and explained the need for him to check the identification of all persons who appeared to be under the age of 21 years. She also told him that if she ever heard of his violating the statute, she would fire him immediately. Later that night, a 17-year-old teenager who looked like he was 25 ordered a glass of wine. The teenager showed the bartender an altered driver's license that falsely stated his age to be 22. The bartender was not sure whether the phrase *intoxicating substance* in the statute included wine, and he served it to the teenager. An undercover police officer who was at the bar observed the transaction. He then showed his badge, demanding to see the teenager's identification. Recognizing the driver's license as a forgery, he arrested the bartender.

The owner is charged with violating the statute, and the prosecutor asserts that she should be held vicariously liable for the bartender's act. Which of the following would be the owner's most effective argument in defense?

(A) The owner did not have personal knowledge of the sale to the teenager.

(B) The owner cautioned the bartender against violation of the statute.

(C) The bartender is not guilty of violating the statute.

(D) The bartender was not acting within the scope of his employment when he sold wine to a minor in violation of the statute.

117. The defendant was an avid deer hunter. His favorite place to hunt was a small cemetery in the middle of a densely populated suburban neighborhood. Because the neighborhood had grown so quickly within the past decade, deer were forced to congregate in a few wooded patches in the cemetery, making the likelihood of seeing a deer extremely high. One morning when the defendant was in the cemetery, he saw a deer standing near the cemetery gates about 80 yards away. The defendant shot at the deer. The bullet missed and went through the front window of a nearby house, killing the victim. What is the most serious crime for which the defendant can be convicted?

(A) Battery.

(B) Involuntary manslaughter.

(C) Voluntary manslaughter.

(D) Murder.

118. In the course of robbing a bank, the defendant pointed a gun at three bank tellers and the bank manager and ordered them to go from the bank lobby to the back room while his confederate attempted to open the safe.

If the defendant is charged with kidnapping the bank manager, his most effective argument in defense would be that

(A) he did not demand a ransom.

(B) he released the bank manager as soon as the robbery was completed.

(C) ordering the bank manager to go from the bank lobby to the back room was incidental and necessary to the commission of the robbery.

(D) the bank manager was an adult.

119. The police believed the defendant was engaged in drug dealing, so they obtained a warrant to search her home. When they arrived, a man was working in the front yard. He told the officers that he was the defendant's ex-husband and that she had moved out. He led the officers inside and took them to a back bedroom where he said the defendant had "left some of her stuff." The officers searched the back bedroom and found several shoeboxes of marijuana. The man then told the officers the defendant had moved to another house down the street. He said the defendant was still at work, but would be home soon, so they should hurry and search the house before the defendant destroyed the evidence. The officers went down the street and found the front door unlocked. They then searched the house, and discovered a large marijuana grow operation.

At trial, the defendant argued that the search that uncovered the marijuana grow operation was unlawful. How should the court rule?

(A) The search was lawful based on exigent circumstances.

(B) The search was lawful based on consent.

(C) The search was unlawful because the officers did not have a warrant.

(D) The search was unlawful based on the fruit of the poisonous tree.

120. Because they were bigots, two men were angry when a Chinese family moved into a house on their street. Deciding to drive them away and to set an example that would discourage other Chinese people from moving into the neighborhood, they agreed to set fire to the family's home. They went to the house, and one of the men started pouring gasoline around it. A crowd of onlookers began to gather. The defendant, one of the onlookers, hoped that the men would burn down the house but said nothing. After the first man finished pouring the gasoline, the second man lit a match and set it afire, burning the house to the ground.

On a charge of arson, the defendant is

(A) guilty, because she made no attempt to stop the crime from being committed.

(B) guilty, because her hope that the men would burn the house down amounted to criminal intent.

(C) not guilty, because mere presence coupled with silent approval is not sufficient to result in liability as an accessory.

(D) not guilty, because she was, at most, an accessory after the fact.

121. A landlord was the owner of a three-unit residential building. She lived in an apartment on the third floor; her son, the defendant, lived with his wife in an apartment on the second floor; and the ground floor apartment was rented to a police officer and his family. One day, while the defendant and his wife were out of town, the landlord and the officer were having coffee together in the landlord's apartment. During the course of their conversation, the landlord said that she was worried about the defendant because once, while visiting him, she saw a substance in his apartment that she believed to be cocaine. Since she really did not know what cocaine looked like, however, she was not sure. The officer said, "If you'd like, I'll

have a look and let you know whether or not there is anything for you to worry about."

Using her key to open the door to the defendant's apartment, the landlord brought the officer inside. Lying on a table in the entrance hall inside the apartment was a plastic pouch containing white powder. The officer sniffed it and said, "That's coke, all right," putting it in his pocket. Then he noticed a television in the living room that looked like one stolen from an appliance store in the neighborhood. Without saying anything about the television to the landlord, the officer obtained a search warrant by submitting an affidavit indicating that he had seen certain items in the defendant's apartment that he had probable cause to believe were stolen. Later, he returned, entered, and thoroughly searched the apartment pursuant to the warrant. The television that he had seen on his first visit was not stolen, but during the course of his search, he found several items that were stolen. Eventually, the defendant was charged with burglary.

On the charge of burglary, if the defendant makes an appropriate motion to suppress the use of stolen items found in his apartment, his motion should be

(A)  denied, since the stolen items were obtained as the result of a lawful search.

(B)  denied, since it would not serve the interests of justice to require a police officer to ignore a discovery that he or she has probable cause to believe is contraband.

(C)  granted, because the search warrant was issued as the result of information obtained in an unlawful search.

(D)  granted, since his possession of stolen items is not necessarily proof that he stole those items.

122.  A woman was a collector of antique automobiles. One day, she took her infant

daughter for a ride in one of the most valuable cars in her collection. On her way, she stopped to buy a newspaper. Because her daughter had fallen asleep in the backseat, the collector left her in the car when she got out. The defendant, a professional car thief who happened to be at the newspaper stand, jumped into the collector's car and drove it away without noticing the daughter in the backseat.

The defendant realized that he would not be able to sell a stolen car as unusual as this one, so he parked it in a friend's garage, still unaware of the presence of the sleeping child. Getting the collector's name and phone number from some papers in the glove compartment of the car, the defendant phoned her and left a message on her telephone answering machine, telling her that if she did not immediately bring $1,000 in cash to a certain location, he would set the car on fire.

When the collector realized that her car, with her daughter in the backseat, was gone, she became frantic and rushed home. When she picked up her phone to call the police, her answering machine played the defendant's message. Upon hearing it, the collector brought $1,000 to the location specified. The defendant, who was waiting for her, took the money and returned the car. The daughter was still sleeping quietly in the backseat.

Which of the following additional facts or inferences, if it were the only one true, would be most likely to lead to a conviction of the defendant on a charge of robbery of $1,000 from the collector?

(A)  The car was in the collector's possession when the defendant took it.

(B)  The collector paid the money to prevent injury to her daughter.

(C)  The collector paid the money to prevent damage to her automobile.

(D) By the time the collector showed up with the money, the defendant had discovered the daughter sleeping in the backseat.

123. A state police officer was investigating a series of car thefts. A federal officer was assigned to assist under a federal statute that permits the United States Department of Justice to aid local police departments in investigating certain crimes. Because of a man's criminal record, the state officer went to the man's home and questioned him regarding the recent thefts. She did not inform the federal officer that she was going to do so. During the course of the questioning, the state officer drew her gun and threatened to shoot the man if the man did not immediately admit his guilt. The man confessed to the thefts and identified the defendant as his partner. The state officer left the man, saying, "I'll be back for you later." Then, after obtaining the necessary warrant, the state officer arrested the defendant.

Unaware of the state officer's activity, the federal officer examined a stolen vehicle that had been recovered by the state police. The federal officer found fingerprints in locations that indicated that they were made by a person breaking into and starting the car. Using a U.S. Department of Justice computer, the federal officer identified the fingerprints as the man's. The federal officer obtained the necessary warrant and arrested the man. The man and the defendant were charged in a state court with car theft.

The defendant moved to dismiss the prosecution against him on the ground that his identification was obtained during the course of an unlawful interrogation of the man. Which of the following would be the prosecution's most effective argument in opposition to the defendant's motion?

(A) The discovery of the defendant's identity was inevitable.

(B) The discovery of the defendant's identity was the result of an independent investigation that purged any taint resulting from the illegality of the interrogation of the man.

(C) The interrogation of the man did not violate the defendant's constitutional rights.

(D) The defendant was not in custody at the time of the man's interrogation.

124. The defendant placed a large wager on a football game that he had to win or he was going to have his home foreclosed on. He decided to watch it at a local bar. During the very close game, the defendant was so nervous that he drank several beers and became drunk. At the last minute, the team he bet on scored a touchdown and won the game. The defendant cheered. He then noticed two big men sitting at the other end of the bar who worked for the bookie he had placed the bet with. Fearing the men were going to hurt him because of his win, the defendant got in his car and drove home. A police officer saw him driving erratically and tried to pull him over. A reasonable sober driver would have recognized the car as a police car, but the defendant thought it was the bookie's employees coming to kill him. The defendant made a quick turn onto a busy side street. A pedestrian was crossing the street with his headphones on and without looking. The defendant hit him with the car, and the pedestrian died immediately. The defendant was charged with involuntary manslaughter. The defendant should be found

(A) not guilty, because the pedestrian was contributorily negligent in crossing the busy street without looking and with his headphones on.

(B) not guilty, because the defendant did not intend to cause the pedestrian's death.

(C) not guilty, because the defendant genuinely believed he was fleeing for his life.

(D) guilty.

125. The defendant and his friend decided to rob a woman at an ATM. When the woman withdrew her money, the defendant hit her with a brick and his friend grabbed her purse. As the two men were fleeing the scene, a police officer yelled for them to stop. When they did not do so, he shot them both. The defendant's friend later died from his injuries.

If the defendant is put on trial for felony murder, how should the court rule?

(A) Guilty, because his friend died during the commission of a felony.

(B) Guilty, because his friend died during the commission of a dangerous felony.

(C) Not guilty, because his friend was killed by a police officer.

(D) Not guilty, because the felony was completed when his friend was shot.

126. The defendant, who was a law student, was attempting to study for her final examinations. She was having difficulty concentrating because the people in the apartment above hers were having a loud party, and the defendant found the noise distracting. She telephoned, asking her neighbors to stop making so much noise, but they refused to do so. Finally, the defendant fired a pistol through the ceiling of her apartment. She did not intend to hit anyone with the bullet but hoped that the shot would frighten her neighbors and chill the atmosphere. After passing through the floor of the apartment above the defendant's, the bullet struck a piece of furniture and ricocheted. It struck the victim, lodging in his shoulder and injuring him.

Which of the following is the most serious crime of which the defendant may be properly convicted?

(A) Battery.

(B) Attempted involuntary manslaughter.

(C) Attempted voluntary manslaughter.

(D) Attempted murder.

127. The defendant and her friend were roommates until they began arguing bitterly. During one argument, the defendant moved out of the apartment that they shared. As she left, she said, "I'm going to get even with you for all the grief you've caused me." The following day, a neighbor told the friend that the defendant had purchased a gun. The neighbor also said that the defendant told her that she was going to shoot the friend the next time she saw her. As a result, the friend began carrying a loaded pistol. Several days later, realizing that she still had the key to the apartment, the defendant went back to return it. The friend was leaving the apartment when she saw the defendant walking toward her. As the defendant reached into her pocket for the apartment key, the friend drew her pistol and shot the defendant, aiming to hit her in the chest. The bullet grazed the defendant's shoulder, inflicting a minor injury. The defendant immediately drew her own pistol and shot the friend with it, striking her in the thigh and inflicting a serious injury.

The defendant is charged with attempted murder. If the defendant asserts the privilege of self-defense, she will most probably be found

(A) guilty, because it was reasonable for the friend to believe that the defendant was reaching into her pocket for a gun.

(B) guilty, because the defendant's injury was not serious enough to result in death.

(C) guilty, because the fact that the defendant was carrying a pistol is evidence of premeditation.

(D) not guilty.

128. Two men were members of a militant political group. As a protest against the use of harmful agricultural chemicals, they planned to burn down a factory that produced such chemicals. A few days later, they set off a bomb that burned the factory to the ground.

The jurisdiction has a statute that extends the common law definition of arson to buildings other than dwellings. Of which of the following crimes may the men be properly convicted?

(A) Arson only.

(B) Conspiracy only.

(C) Arson or conspiracy, but not both.

(D) Both arson and conspiracy.

129. The defendant's toolbox was stolen out of the back of his pickup truck. The next day, the defendant saw the victim walking down the street carrying what the defendant believed was his stolen toolbox. The defendant jumped out of his truck and grabbed the toolbox from the victim, yelling "If you don't give the toolbox to me, I'm going to shoot you dead!" The victim gave the defendant the toolbox and the defendant drove away. At the next stop sign a block away, the defendant opened the toolbox and realized that the toolbox wasn't in fact his missing toolbox. A police officer who saw the defendant grab the victim's toolbox pulled up in his police car and immediately arrested the defendant.

The defendant is charged with robbery. At trial, the prosecution shows that because the victim's toolbox was much larger than the defendant's, the defendant was unreasonable in the belief that the toolbox was his stolen toolbox. However, the defendant shows that he honestly believed the toolbox was his. The court should find the defendant

(A) guilty, because the defendant's belief that the toolbox was his missing toolbox was unreasonable.

(B) guilty, because the defendant threatened to shoot the victim if he didn't give him the toolbox.

(C) not guilty, because the defendant honestly believed the toolbox was his missing toolbox.

(D) not guilty, because there was no indication that the defendant could carry out on his threat.

130. Four weeks after breaking her engagement with her boyfriend, the defendant was angry because her boyfriend still had not returned a stereo that he had borrowed from her. She went to his house one night to demand its immediate return. When she got there, the boyfriend was not at home and his door was unlocked. The defendant entered to look for her stereo but could not find it. While searching, she noticed that the boyfriend had a new couch. Thinking that the couch was worth as much as her stereo, she tore open one of its cushions and set it on fire before leaving. The fire destroyed the couch completely and charred the walls and ceiling of the room, although the house itself was not seriously damaged. The defendant was subsequently prosecuted. Statutes in the jurisdiction adopt the common law definitions of burglary, larceny, and arson.

If the defendant is charged with larceny as a result of the destruction of the couch, which of the following would be her most effective defense against that charge?

(A) The boyfriend's door was unlocked when she entered.

(B) She believed the couch to be equal in value to her stereo.

(C) She did not physically move the couch.

(D) She did not intend to benefit from the destruction of the couch.

131. One day, the owner of a department store asked an employee in the store's shoe department to temporarily replace a sporting

goods salesman who did not show up for work. A teenager, who was 15 years of age, subsequently entered the sporting goods department and asked the employee to sell her ammunition for a pistol. The employee placed a box of ammunition on the counter and said, "That'll be $9, please." Realizing that she did not have any money with her, the teenager left the store without the ammunition, saying that she would return for it later. A few hours later, while the owner was helping the employee stock handguns, the teenager returned and bought the ammunition.

A statute in the jurisdiction provides as follows: "Any person who sells ammunition for a firearm to a person below the age of 16 years shall be guilty of a felony. The employer of any person who violates this section during the course of such employment shall be guilty of a misdemeanor punishable by a fine not to exceed $250. It shall not be a defense to a violation of this section that the defendant had no knowledge of the age of the person to whom the sale was made."

If the owner is prosecuted under the statute, the owner should be found

(A) guilty, because her employee sold ammunition to a person under the age of 16 years.

(B) guilty, because it was unreasonable for the owner to assign the employee to the sporting goods department without properly instructing him regarding the statute.

(C) guilty, because the owner was present when the employee made the sale to the teenager.

(D) not guilty, because holding one person vicariously liable for the crime of another violates the constitutional right to due process of law.

132. A man was scared of heights. To cure him, his friend, a psychiatrist and experienced mountain climber, convinced him to go mountain climbing with her on Mount Smoke, the highest peak in the state. The mountain was known as a tough and dangerous climb. It was also known for the large amount of poisonous volcanic gases that escaped from vents at the top. These gases were known to cause problems with people's nervous systems. At the top of the mountain, the man and the woman stood on the edge of a cliff to take a selfie. As they were about to take the picture, a freak gust of wind blew a cloud of volcanic gas over them. The toxins in the gas caused both the man and the woman to lose voluntary control of their arms and legs. The woman punched the man, knocking him off the cliff to his death.

Is the woman criminally liable for the man's death?

(A) Yes, because her punch was the proximate cause of his death.

(B) Yes, because she voluntarily put herself in contact with a gas known to cause nerve problems.

(C) No, because the wind gust was a freak occurrence and unforeseeable.

(D) No, because the gas made the woman lose control of her arms and legs.

133. The defendant and a bank robber had been in the same cell together while serving time in prison. Soon after their release, the bank robber asked the defendant to join him in robbing a bank. The defendant refused, stating that he did not want to go back to prison. The bank robber then said that he would rob the bank himself if the defendant would provide him with a place to hide afterwards. The defendant agreed that the bank robber could hide in the defendant's apartment following the robbery in return for one-fourth of the proceeds of the robbery. The following day, the bank robber robbed the bank. One week later, the bank robber was arrested at the defendant's apartment.

The defendant was charged with conspiracy to commit robbery. The court should find the defendant

(A) not guilty, because he did not agree to participate in the actual perpetration of the robbery.

(B) not guilty, because the defendant's agreement to permit the bank robber to stay at his apartment following the robbery was not per se unlawful.

(C) guilty, because he was an accessory to the robbery.

(D) guilty, because he agreed to furnish the bank robber with a place to hide in return for a portion of the proceeds of the robbery.

134. After his arrest for drug possession, the defendant asked to have his attorney present and telephoned her office, leaving a message that he had been arrested. When the attorney received the message, she telephoned the county sheriff, asking where the defendant was being held. The sheriff said that he did not know. However, this was a lie. As a result of the lie, it took the attorney several hours to find the defendant. While waiting for the attorney, one of the officers said to the defendant, "Why don't you tell us about it?" whereupon the defendant admitted growing marijuana. The defendant was subsequently charged with violating a state law that prohibits growing marijuana.

The defendant's attorney made an appropriate motion to prevent the use of the defendant's statement as evidence against him. The motion should be

(A) granted, because the defendant asserted his right to have an attorney present.

(B) granted, because the sheriff actually knew the defendant's whereabouts when he said that he did not.

(C) granted, because the sheriff lied to the attorney.

(D) denied, because the defendant waived his right to remain silent when he admitted growing the marijuana.

135. A man asked his friend, a doctor, for help killing his wife. The doctor gave his friend a bottle of "deadly poison pills," and told his friend to give his wife two of them for "certain death." The pills were actually common muscle relaxants, and were widely available with a prescription. The doctor did not think the pills could kill anyone, although it would probably make his friend's wife go to sleep for a little while. He thought that if his friend gave the pills to his wife and believed he had killed her, he would regret his actions and change his mind. That night, the man slipped the pills into his wife's wine glass. His wife had a severe allergic reaction and almost died.

The man was prosecuted for conspiracy to murder his wife. How should the court rule?

(A) Guilty, because he believed the pills were deadly poison.

(B) Guilty, because his wife almost died.

(C) Not guilty, because his wife did not die.

(D) Not guilty, because the doctor did not think the wife would die.

136. After a fight at a bar, police officers arrested one of the women involved and drove her to the station. On the way, the police officers advised the woman that she had the right to remain silent, that anything she said might be used against her, that she was entitled to have an attorney present during questioning, and that if she could not afford an attorney, one would be furnished without cost. The woman said she didn't want to answer any questions without her attorney present. The officers allowed the woman to contact her attorney, who stated he would get to the station when he could.

Several hours passed. The officers went to breakfast at a diner. At the diner, the owner told them the diner had recently been robbed by a woman. He described the woman and said one of his employees had seen her later at a bar. The owner's description matched the woman the officers had just arrested. When the officers returned, they gave the woman breakfast they had brought from the diner and asked her if she knew anything about the diner being robbed. The woman immediately admitted robbing the diner.

At trial, the woman moved to exclude her confession. How should the court rule?

(A) The confession should be excluded, because the woman said she wouldn't talk without her attorney present.

(B) The confession should be excluded, because the officers did not tell the woman they suspected her of robbing the diner before questioning her.

(C) The confession should be admitted, because the woman received *Miranda* warnings before admitting to the robbery.

(D) The confession should be admitted, because the woman waived her *Miranda* rights by answering the officers' questions.

137. While playing baseball, the defendant and the victim got into an argument when the victim, an umpire, called a strike on the defendant. Enraged at what he perceived as unfair treatment, the defendant swung as hard as he could and hit the victim in the head with the metal bat he was using. The victim died instantly. The defendant then yelled, "Geesh, I didn't mean to kill him!"

If the defendant is prosecuted for criminal homicide, the most serious crime the defendant can be found guilty of is

(A) murder.

(B) voluntary manslaughter.

(C) involuntary manslaughter.

(D) battery.

138. A man was first in line for a new edition of an extremely popular cellphone. Just as the doors to the store were opening, the victim stepped in front of the man and said, "Too bad—I'm too important to wait." The defendant, who was standing in line behind the man, yelled, "Hey, don't let him do that to you! Kill that jerk!" The man took a knife from his pocket and stabbed the victim to death.

The defendant is charged with murder. He should be found

(A) guilty, because he yelled "Kill that jerk!"

(B) not guilty, because the defendant did not physically help the man in any way.

(C) not guilty, because words alone are not enough for criminal liability.

(D) not guilty, because there was no indication the defendant actually intended the man to kill the victim.

139. Two undercover police officers received an anonymous tip that the defendant was engaged in buying and selling stolen cars. The two officers got a car from the police impound lot and then met with the defendant. After the officers told the defendant that the car was stolen, the defendant offered to buy it. When the defendant handed the officers the money, they placed him under arrest.

The defendant is charged with conspiracy to receive stolen property. The jurisdiction follows the common law view. The court should find him

(A) guilty, because he believed the car was stolen.

(B)  guilty, because the officers told him the car was stolen.

(C)  not guilty, because neither officer intended to participate in the purchase or sale of a stolen vehicle.

(D)  not guilty, because the car that he agreed to purchase from the officers was not actually stolen.

140.  The defendant hired a hitman to kill a business rival. When the defendant was out of town, the hitman went to the business rival's home. The hitman looked through the window and saw the business rival sleeping in a chair. The hitman fired five shots into the business rival's chest and ran away. Unbeknownst to the hitman, the business rival had died of a heart attack five minutes earlier. The shots would have been fatal if the business rival was still alive. Two minutes after fleeing the scene, the hitman checked his cellphone and found an earlier message from the defendant stating that he was thinking of calling off the hitman's contract. The defendant is arrested and charged with attempted murder. The defendant should be found

(A)  guilty, because the defendant hired the hitman to kill the business rival.

(B)  not guilty, because the defendant was out of town.

(C)  not guilty, because the defendant attempted to withdraw from the conspiracy.

(D)  not guilty, because it was factually impossible to murder the business rival.

# ANSWERS
## CRIMINAL LAW

# ANSWERS TO
# CRIMINAL LAW QUESTIONS

1.  **D**     An officer executing a warrant for the search of premises is limited to a search of the place described in the warrant. A misidentification will invalidate the search unless the officer could not mistake the place to be searched. The officer executing the warrant could not have been certain whether it was for a tavern known as the Second Bedroom located on Main Street or for premises known as the Second Bedroom located at 481 Chambers Street (but which contained a furniture store rather than a tavern). It may therefore be successfully argued that the warrant did not properly identify the defendant's premises, and the search was invalid. While it is not certain that a court would come to this conclusion, **D** is the only argument listed that could possibly support the motion to suppress.

      **A** is incorrect because an affidavit submitted to establish probable cause may be based entirely on hearsay. If it establishes the credibility of the informant and the reliability of his or her information, it may serve as the basis for the warrant, even though it does not name the informant. **B** is incorrect because the affidavit indicated that the informant had given information in the past that had always proved to be accurate (thus establishing his credibility) and that he had observed the activities himself (thus establishing the reliability of his information). Even without establishing credibility and reliability, an affidavit that fails to identify the informant could support the issuance of a warrant if the information that it contains is corroborated by other independent evidence. **C** is incorrect, however, because if credibility and reliability are established, corroboration is unnecessary.

2.  **D**     A police officer who has probable cause to believe that the defendant is in the process of committing a crime may arrest the defendant without a warrant. Upon making a lawful arrest, the police officer may search the defendant's person and packages within the defendant's control to prevent the loss of evidence and to protect the officer.

      Some courts have held that one who ships baggage on an airline has no reasonable expectation of privacy with respect to the contents of the baggage; other courts hold that sniffing of baggage by a dog does not violate the reasonable expectation of privacy because it is nonintrusive. Either way, most agree that such an inspection is not an unreasonable search. **A** is therefore incorrect. **B** is incorrect because if probable cause existed, the arrest was lawful even without a warrant. Since the dog sniffed the baggage after the plane had landed, and since it was sniffing for marijuana rather than weapons, **C** is a non sequitur and therefore is incorrect.

3.  **B**     Under the common law, rape is forced sexual intercourse with a female, who is not the spouse of the defendant, without her consent. Modern statutes have expanded this definition to include male victims, spouses, and other acts not amounting to sexual intercourse. Rape is a "general intent" crime, which means that a conviction may be had even though the defendant did not intend to engage in intercourse without the female's consent if he acted recklessly or was criminally negligent in determining whether or not she consented. It is necessary, however, that the defendant intend to engage in intercourse. If the defendant did not intend to have intercourse, he cannot be convicted.

**A** is incorrect because it may have been reckless or criminally negligent for the defendant to believe that the victim consented. Since the victim initially attempted to resist the defendant's advances, it may be found that the intercourse was without her consent even though she was so drunk that she was unaware that it took place or unaware of the defendant's identity. **C** and **D** are therefore incorrect. **C** is also incorrect since most courts agree that sexual intercourse with a woman who lacks the capacity to consent because she is unconscious or intoxicated is done without her consent and therefore is rape. In addition, **D** is incorrect because a rape takes place when penetration occurs without consent and is not undone if the victim subsequently consents.

4.  **B**    Although a warrantless search is usually invalid, it may be valid if consented to by one with authority to consent. Since a guest in a hotel is entitled to exclusive possession of the room that he or she occupies, the hotel keeper does not have the power to consent to the search of a guest's room, even if the guest is overdue in his or her payments. The motion in **B** would probably be granted for this reason.

On the other hand, the owner of an automobile does have the power to consent to a search of it, so the motion in **A** would fail. After a defendant's automobile has been impounded by the police, they have the right to search it for the purpose of making an inventory of its contents. Although the reason for the inventory search is to protect the police against possible subsequent claims that contents of the impounded vehicle were taken or converted while the vehicle was in police custody, evidence that is incidentally discovered during the course of such a search is admissible against the defendant. The motion in **C** would therefore fail. In **D**, the search did not take place until the defendant was placed under arrest. A search of the defendant's person conducted incidentally to a lawful arrest is not a violation of his Fourth Amendment right to be secure against unreasonable search and seizure, so the motion in **D** would fail.

5.  **D**    Larceny is defined as a trespassory taking and carrying off of personal property known to be another's with the intent to permanently deprive the owner thereof. A taking is trespassory if it violates the rights of the owner. Since the coat was the friend's and since the friend told the defendant to take it, the taking did not violate the friend's rights and was therefore not trespassory. **A** and **C** are therefore incorrect.

A criminal conspiracy is committed when two or more persons with the specific intent to commit a crime agree to commit that crime. Since the friend knew that the coat was his, he did not have the specific intent to commit a crime when he agreed to help the defendant take it. **B** and **C** are therefore incorrect.

6.  **A**    A killing is intentional if the defendant desired or knew to a substantial degree of certainty that it would result from his or her act. A killing is deliberate and premeditated if the defendant was capable of reflecting upon it with a cool mind and did in fact do so. Since the defendant hoped for (*i.e.*, desired) the victim's death, the killing was intentional. Since he reflected on it in advance with a cool mind, it was deliberate and premeditated.

Since first degree murder is the most serious crime listed, **B**, **C**, and **D** are incorrect. Voluntary manslaughter is an intentional killing resulting from extreme emotional disturbance or in the mistaken belief that it is justified. **C** is also incorrect because there is no indication that the defendant was emotionally disturbed or mistakenly believed that his act was justified. Involuntary manslaughter is an unintended killing that results from criminal negligence. **D** is incorrect because the defendant intended the death of the victim.

7. **A**   Larceny is defined as a trespassory taking and carrying off of personal property known to be another's with the intent to permanently deprive the owner thereof. A trespassory taking is an acquisition of possession contrary to the rights of the owner and without the owner's consent. Since the defendant acquired possession without the victim's permission, he committed a trespassory taking. A carrying off occurs when the defendant moves the property, even slightly, with the intention of exercising dominion over it. Since the defendant moved the watch from the table to his pocket with the intention of keeping it, he carried it off. Since he knew that the watch belonged to the victim and intended to keep it for himself, he had knowledge that the property was another's and intended to deprive the owner of it. He therefore committed a larceny, making **A** correct.

A person is guilty of a criminal attempt when, with the specific intent to bring about a criminally prohibited result, he or she comes substantially close to bringing it about. Although the defendant is probably guilty of attempted larceny, **B** is incorrect because larceny is a more serious crime. Embezzlement is defined as a criminal conversion of personal property by one in lawful custody of that property. Employees who steal property from their employers while in custody of it because of the employment relationship may be guilty of embezzlement. **C** is incorrect, however, because the defendant did not come into possession of the watch as a result of his employment relationship with the victim. **D** is incorrect because the defendant is guilty of larceny for the reasons stated above.

8. **C**   At common law, rape can be committed by using intoxicants to overcome the victim's resistance. Under the given statute, however, third degree rape is committed only when a person over the age of 17 has sexual intercourse with a person under the age of 16. Since the girl was only 15, she cannot be guilty of committing it.

**A** and **B** are therefore incorrect. **D** is incorrect because the statute specifically provides that the crime can be committed by a female.

9. **A**   The clerk is obviously guilty of bribery in the second degree because she offered to alter the official records for $500. She cannot be guilty of conspiracy, however, because of Wharton's Rule, which provides that there can be no conspiracy unless the agreement involves at least one person who is not essential to the commission of the crime to which the conspirators agreed. The Wharton Rule applies to the crimes of bigamy, incest, gambling, bribery, adultery, and dueling. Since the crime of bribery could not have been committed by either the clerk or the store owner acting alone, neither can be found guilty of conspiring with the other to commit it.

B, C, and D are therefore incorrect. C is additionally incorrect because conspiracy is a separate crime that does not merge with the crime that the conspirators agreed to commit.

10.  C    A person is guilty of a criminal attempt when, with the specific intent to bring about a result that is criminally prohibited, he or she comes substantially close to bringing about that result. Since under the applicable statute, burning down one's own house is not arson, the result that the defendant specifically intended to bring about was not criminally prohibited by the arson statute. For this reason, the defendant could not be guilty of attempted arson. C is therefore correct.

Even though it was factually impossible for a defendant to commit a particular crime, he or she may be convicted of attempt if the crime would have been committed had the facts been as the defendant thought them to be. For example, if the defendant burned her own house believing it to be the dwelling of another, she could be convicted of attempted arson. Thus, A is an accurate statement of the law. A is incorrect, however, because the defendant did not make a mistake of fact (*i.e.*, she knew that the dwelling was her own). Since guilt for attempt requires the specific intent to accomplish a purpose that is criminally prohibited, a person cannot be guilty if what he or she intended to accomplish was not criminally prohibited. This is true even if he or she believes that it is criminally prohibited, no matter how that mistaken belief was formed. B is therefore incorrect. D is incorrect for two reasons: First, while a defendant cannot be convicted of both a substantive crime and an attempt to commit that substantive crime, he or she can be convicted of the attempt instead of the substantive crime, and second, the defendant is charged with attempted arson, not attempted insurance fraud.

11.  A    Murder is the unjustified killing of a human being with malice aforethought. Malice aforethought includes the intent to cause great bodily harm to a human being. A defendant "intends" a particular consequence if he or she desires or knows to a substantial degree of certainty that it will occur. Since the defendant desired and/or knew that exposure to the gas was likely to result in great bodily harm to the coworker, she intended to cause great bodily harm to a human being. Since the friend died, the defendant may be found guilty of his murder. A is therefore correct.

B is incorrect because engaging in an inherently dangerous activity is not equivalent to malice aforethought. C is incorrect because the defendant's intent to cause great bodily harm to any human being is sufficient to make her guilty of murder in causing the death of the friend. Although the intent to kill is a form of malice aforethought, D is incorrect because the intent to cause great bodily harm is also a form of malice aforethought.

12.  B    A person is guilty of a criminal intent when, with the specific intent to bring about a criminally prohibited result, he or she comes substantially close to achieving that result. Thus, all attempts are "specific intent" crimes. This means that, although murder may be committed without the intent to kill, attempted murder may not. If the defendant believed that the victim was already dead, he could not have intended to kill him and so could not be guilty of attempted murder.

A defendant with the specific intent to commit a particular crime may be guilty of attempting it even though accomplishing the intended result was factually impossible. **A** is incorrect because the defendant's intent to kill the victim could make him guilty of attempted murder even though the fact that the victim was already dead made murder factually impossible. **C** is incorrect because the defendant's belief that the gun was loaded could establish that he had the specific intent to kill the victim, even though the fact that the gun was unloaded made it factually impossible for him to accomplish the result that he intended. **D** is incorrect because the defendant's belief that the substance was a poison could help establish that he had the specific intent to kill the victim, even though the fact that the substance was harmless made it impossible for him to accomplish the intended result.

13.  **A**    Because of the possibility that manipulation of the circumstances of a lineup will result in a likelihood of inaccurate identification, the United States Supreme Court has held that after the filing of formal charges against him or her, a prisoner is entitled to the presence of counsel at a lineup.

Since all prisoners are expected to obey the commands of their jailers, no prisoner is required to resist violations of his or her constitutional rights by those in apparent legal authority. **B** is incorrect because it suggests that failure to resist results in waiver. **C** is incorrect because requirements as to lineup procedures are more flexible than those listed. It has even been held that a one-person "show-up" may be valid if it is conducted properly. The taint of an improper lineup procedure may be purged by evidence that the in-court identification was arrived at by means distinguishable from the lineup. **D** is incorrect, however, because the victim's courtroom identification of the defendant was nothing more than a repetition of the lineup identification.

14.  **D**    Even in the absence of probable cause to believe that health and safety violations exist in a particular building, a warrant to search it for such violations may be issued upon probable cause to believe that such violations exist in buildings in the neighborhood.

**B** is therefore incorrect. **A** is incorrect because such a scheme justifies the issuance of warrants like those issued here, rather than invalidating it. Although the courts have considerable leeway in issuing warrants for health and safety inspections, **C** is incorrect because warrants are required by the Fourth Amendment to the United States Constitution.

15.  **D**    The crime of receiving stolen property consists of acquiring stolen property with the knowledge that it was stolen and the intent to permanently deprive the owner thereof. Since the defendant did not know that the television was stolen when he acquired possession of it, he cannot be guilty of receiving stolen property. **A** and **C** are therefore incorrect.

The crime of larceny consists of the trespassory taking and carrying off of personal property known to be another's with the intent to permanently deprive the owner thereof. Since the defendant did not know that the television was the property of another when he took it (*i.e.*, received it from his friend), he cannot be guilty of larceny. **B** and **C** are therefore incorrect.

16. **D**　　At common law, arson is defined as the intentional or malicious burning of the dwelling of another. Any burning that chars some actual part of the structure is sufficient to result in a conviction. Since the door was charred, there was sufficient burning to establish the defendant's guilt.

Although modern statutes prohibit the acts described in **A**, **B**, and **C**, the question specifies that the jurisdiction applies common law definitions of all crimes. Since common law arson involves a burning of the dwelling of another, and since the structure that the defendant attempted to burn was not a dwelling and was his own, **A** is incorrect. At common law, larceny by trick is committed when the defendant defrauds another into parting with temporary possession of personal property. Since the insurance company gave the defendant title to rather than temporary possession of the policy proceeds, **B** is incorrect. Since the building that the defendant burned in **C** was not a dwelling, **C** is incorrect.

17. **A**　　If a defendant makes a voluntary incriminating statement that is not induced by police interrogation, *Miranda* does not apply and the statement can be used against the defendant in court. Here, the defendant said "everyone knows I stabbed the guy" in response to "Do you need anything?" Interrogation occurs when the police ask a question that they should know is reasonably likely to elicit an incriminating response from the suspect. "Do you need anything?" is unlikely to be viewed as such a question.

**B** and **D** are incorrect because the rule is that once a defendant requests an attorney, any interrogation must cease. There is no rule requiring that the attorney be produced immediately. In this case, no interrogation had taken place yet. A "two-step" interrogation is where a police officer questions a suspect, gets a confession, gives the suspect *Miranda* warnings, and then questions the suspect to get the confession again. Here, there is no indication any interrogation had begun, and the second officer's question, "Do you need anything?" is unlikely to be viewed as any type of interrogation. **C** is therefore incorrect.

18. **A**　　An officer who reasonably suspects a person of a crime may be justified in questioning that person about his or her identity and activity. If during the course of the conversation, he or she has reason to suspect that he or she may be armed, he or she is justified in frisking him or her for weapons. If during the course of a legitimate frisk for weapons, he or she discovers contraband in his or her possession, it may be seized and used as evidence against him or her. The defendant was not frisked for weapons, however, but for the stolen statue. In the absence of a warrant or valid arrest, such a search violates the Fourth Amendment guarantee against unreasonable search and seizure.

**B** is incorrect because if a frisk is valid, items discovered during its course may be seized and used as evidence, even though they were not what the officer was seeking. **C** is incorrect because there is no fact to indicate that the officer's suspicion was reasonable, and because even a reasonable suspicion does not justify any warrantless search other than a frisk for weapons. **D** is incorrect because the search was for contraband, not for a weapon, so it was not a valid pat-down search.

19. **C**　　A criminal conspiracy is an agreement to commit a crime, and it is complete when two or more persons make such an agreement. Although the boy privately decided to assist the

other boys in the commission of a crime, he did not agree with them that he would do so. He is therefore not guilty of conspiracy, and **C** is correct.

One who knowingly aids and abets in the commission of a crime is guilty of that crime as an accessory. For this reason, the boy might be guilty of murder. **A** is incorrect, however, because the boy is charged not with murder but with conspiracy. Some jurisdictions hold that to convict for conspiracy, it is necessary to prove an overt act in addition to an agreement to commit a crime. Even in these jurisdictions, however, the boy would not be guilty of conspiracy because he did not agree to commit a crime. **B** is therefore incorrect. Co-conspirators are guilty of the crime of conspiracy when their agreement is made and are not rendered innocent by the withdrawal of one or more of them from the conspiracy. **D** is incorrect for this reason, and because the boy was never part of the conspiracy in the first place.

20. **C**    There are two different forms of criminal assault — conduct that intentionally induces fear, and attempted battery. Criminal battery is the intentional or reckless application of force to the body of another. A person is guilty of a criminal attempt when, with the specific intent to bring about a criminally prohibited result, he or she comes substantially close to achieving that result. Since the defendant shot at the President with the intention of hitting him, he attempted a battery. Since he did not succeed, his crime was assault.

A is incorrect because the crime of which he was acquitted in the federal court was not the same crime with which he is charged in the state court. It is generally held that the constitutional protection against double jeopardy is not offended by separate prosecutions for violating the laws of two different sovereigns (*i.e.*, federal and state governments) even though both arise from the same act. Assault based on intentionally inducing fear requires that the victim was aware of the defendant's conduct, and that as a result, the victim experienced reasonable apprehension of contact. **B** and **D** are incorrect, however, because assault based on attempted battery requires no such awareness or apprehension.

21. **B**    Many jurisdictions hold that the defendant will not be guilty of the murder of a co-felon under the felony-murder rule if the co-felon's death resulted from a justifiable attempt by the victim to prevent the crime. Although this is not the law in all jurisdictions, it is the only argument listed that would provide the defendant with any defense at all.

A is incorrect because the felony-murder rule is applied to deaths that occur during the commission of a felony, even though the person killed is not the intended victim. **C** is incorrect because the normal reactions of victims, bystanders, and police make violence a foreseeable result of any robbery. **D** is incorrect because jurisdictions that apply the felony-murder rule regard the intent to commit a felony as a form of malice aforethought.

22. **D**    Involuntary manslaughter is an unintended killing that results from conduct that created a high and unreasonable risk of death or serious injury or from the commission of a *malum in se* misdemeanor. If the defendant's conduct created such risk, he could thus be guilty of involuntary manslaughter. While it is not certain that a court would come to this conclusion, **D** is the only argument listed that could possibly support the prosecution.

The unlawful act doctrine (also called the misdemeanor-manslaughter rule) might make a death resulting from the commission of a misdemeanor involuntary manslaughter, but only if the misdemeanor involved is inherently dangerous or *malum in se*. Since driving without a license is neither, **A** is incorrect. **B** is incorrect because it is based on a perversion of a rule of tort law that provides that the violation of a statute that was designed to protect a class of persons to which the plaintiff belongs from the risk that resulted in harm may be described as negligence per se. There is no counterpart in the criminal law, however. **C** is not an accurate statement since mere negligence will not result in a criminal conviction.

23. **B**    Ordinarily, an omission (*i.e.*, failure to act) does not lead to criminal responsibility unless it violated a legal duty to act. The lifeguard's duty to aid people at the swimming pool existed only because she was employed as a lifeguard, and therefore it was in force only during her hours of employment. Since her supervisor allowed her to leave at 8 P.M., her hours of employment ended at that time. For this reason, she may successfully argue that she had no duty to rescue someone who came into peril after she left the pool.

If she did have a legal duty to render aid, her absence could be a violation of that duty. **A** is therefore incorrect. Since any death may have more than one cause, the fact that the adult's inaction was a cause of the girl's death does not establish that criminal conduct by the lifeguard was not also a cause. **C** is therefore incorrect. **D** is incorrect because, at common law and under statutes, there are many forms of criminal homicide that can be committed without the intent to cause the death of a person.

24. **A**    Under the common law, rape is committed when the defendant intentionally has sexual intercourse with a female, not his wife, without her consent. Although it is necessary that the victim be unwilling, it is not necessary for her to put up a fight if it would be futile for her to do so or if she reasonably believes that resisting will cause her to sustain serious injury. Since the victim's refusal was overcome by a threat that would have led a reasonable person in her place to fear for her life, the intercourse was without her consent.

If her resistance had been overcome by payment, the intercourse would not have been against her will. But the fact that she was willing to accept payment does not mean that she consented to intercourse with one who did not offer payment, or even with one who did. **B** is therefore incorrect. **C** is incorrect because the victim's resistance was overcome by the defendant's threat of physical force. Since the victim inflicted the injuries after the intercourse occurred, her conduct in inflicting them could not possibly relate to whether she consented to the intercourse. **D** is therefore incorrect.

25. **C**    Murder is the unjustified killing of a human being with malice aforethought. Since malice aforethought includes the intent to kill, and since the defendant held the baby's head under water in an attempt to end his life, the defendant had the necessary mental state and committed the necessary act to make her criminally responsible for murder. It is also necessary, however, for the prosecution to show that her act was a proximate cause of the baby's death. Since there is no clear indication that this is so, it is possible that the defendant may be acquitted of murder. In addition, many states have rules that fix a period of

time (usually one to three years) following a defendant's act and provide that no death occurring after that time is proximately caused by the act. Although it is not certain that her argument will succeed, it is the only one listed that could possibly provide her with an effective defense.

**A** is incorrect because no constitutional right to an abortion has been found to exist in the last three months of pregnancy, and because the baby was born alive. The defendant's attempt to save the baby's life after she tried to kill him is not sufficient to relieve her of criminal liability for his death if his death was proximately caused by her previous conduct. **B** is therefore incorrect. Even though the surgical procedure that the defendant performed did not usually result in the death of a human being, her attempt to kill the baby after he was born makes **D** incorrect.

26. **D**   One who intentionally kills another under the mistaken but reasonable belief that he or she was defending himself or herself against imminent bodily harm may be protected by the privilege of self-defense and therefore be found not guilty of any criminal homicide. If his or her belief was unreasonable, however, he or she is still guilty of voluntary manslaughter, although not of murder. **A** is incorrect, because if the reasonable person would not have had held the belief, the defendant is guilty of voluntary manslaughter. **B** is incorrect because if the defendant did not hold the belief, she is not only guilty of voluntary manslaughter but of murder as well.

27. **D**   Persons are guilty of conspiracy to commit a particular crime when they agree to commit it. At common law, burglary is defined as breaking and entering into the dwelling of another at night for the purpose of committing a larceny or any felony therein. Since the agreement was to break into an office rather than a dwelling, and to do so at lunchtime rather than nighttime, it was not a conspiracy to commit burglary. At common law, larceny is defined as intentionally taking and carrying off the personal property of another with the intent to permanently deprive the owner of it. Since the agreement was to copy but not carry off the professor's notes, it was not a conspiracy to commit larceny. **A**, **B**, and **C** are thus incorrect.

28. **A**   Murder is the unlawful killing of another with malice aforethought. Even if there is no intent to kill, malice aforethought can be implied when there is a reckless indifference to an unjustifiably high risk to human life. This is also known as depraved heart murder. Here, because the defendant shot as close as he could to his friend as his friend ran in front of a concrete wall, a court would likely find he acted with reckless indifference to an unjustifiably high risk to human life. Consequently, he could be charged with murder. **D** is therefore incorrect.

In most cases, voluntary manslaughter requires the defendant to kill in the "heat of passion." This requires some type of provocation that causes the defendant to lose self-control. **B** is incorrect because there was no provocation. A defendant can be found guilty of involuntary manslaughter when his or her behavior is grossly negligent and an accidental death results. As stated above, a court would likely find the defendant's actions to be more than negligence, so **C** is incorrect.

**29. B**    Obtaining property by false pretenses is committed when, with the intent to cause the victim to transfer title to personal property, the defendant makes a fraudulent misrepresentation that causes the victim to do so. Since the chemist told the hunter that the pills were made from a secret formula that would protect him against the venom when she knew that statement to be false, and since she did so for the purpose of obtaining money from him and succeeded in doing so, she is guilty of false pretenses.

Attempted murder requires a specific intent to cause the death of a human being. Intent to cause death requires either the desire or substantial certainty that death will result. Since the chemist believed that the hunter would not be bitten if he took the sugar pills, she lacked the intent necessary to make her liable for attempted murder. **A, C,** and **D** are therefore incorrect.

**30. D**    Self-defense is a privilege to use reasonable force to protect oneself against aggression. In determining whether force was reasonable, courts usually balance the danger likely to result from its use against the benefit of using it. If the benefit that would be apparent to the reasonable person in the defendant's situation outweighs the danger that would be apparent to the reasonable person in the defendant's situation, the force that the defendant used was reasonable. Since it is generally understood that the reasonable person would consider the benefit of saving his or her own life to be of greater weight than the danger of killing an assailant, it is usually held that lethal force (*i.e.*, force likely to kill or do serious bodily harm) is reasonable if used by a person who reasonably believes that he or she is being attacked with lethal force. Thus, if it was reasonable for the defendant to believe that her life was in danger, it was probably reasonable for her to use lethal force to protect it.

**A** is incorrect because the defendant was attempting to protect herself rather than the cocaine. Even if the drug addict was actually unarmed, the defendant's reasonable belief that he had a pistol might have privileged her use of lethal force in self-defense. **B** is therefore incorrect. A person who is committing a crime has no right to defend himself or herself against a lawful arrest. Since the drug addict was not attempting to arrest the defendant, however, the fact that she was committing a crime at the time of his attack is irrelevant. **C** is therefore incorrect.

**31. A**    Battery is an intentional harmful or offensive touching of another person. Shooting someone with a shotgun is clearly a battery. A co-conspirator in a criminal operation is liable for any crimes committed by another co-conspirator if the crime was foreseeable and committed in furtherance of the conspiracy. Here, the brothers conspired to run a methamphetamine lab. The shooting was foreseeable because the brothers kept the shotgun around to protect the lab. The shooting was committed in furtherance of the conspiracy because the defendant's brother was protecting the lab when he shot the undercover officer. Consequently, the defendant would be liable for the battery. **C** is therefore incorrect.

**B** is incorrect because the defendant would be liable based on the conspiracy, not because he acted with any type of reckless indifference. **D** is incorrect because the question of whether drug dealing is dangerous or not has no effect on the relevant analysis.

32.  **D**   Embezzlement is the conversion of personal property known to be another's with the intent to defraud, by a person in lawful possession of the property. Since the seller's possession was the result of fraud and therefore not lawful, he is not guilty of embezzlement. **A** and **C** are therefore incorrect. Larceny by trick is committed when the defendant fraudulently induces the victim to deliver *possession* of personal property to the defendant. If the victim transfers title to the property involved, the crime of larceny by trick has not been committed. Since the buyer's intention was to make the seller the owner of the money, he transferred title to the money, and therefore **B** and **C** are incorrect.

33.  **C**   Although killing with the intent, at least, to cause great bodily harm is ordinarily classified as murder, it may be reduced to voluntary manslaughter if the defendant was acting in the heat of passion. This is only so, however, if the provocation that produced the passion would have done so in the person of ordinary temperament.

   **A** is a fabrication; there is no "theory of deliberate provocation." **B** is incorrect because the objective standard described above (*i.e.*, the person of ordinary temperament) makes the wife's emotional peculiarities irrelevant. **D** is based on a misinterpretation of the law. An intentional killing may be reduced from murder to manslaughter if the defendant was acting under the mistaken belief that the killing was justified. This is known as the theory of mistaken justification. **D** is incorrect because the wife did not act in the mistaken belief that she was justified, and because **D** would erroneously apply the theory to *prevent* reduction to manslaughter.

34.  **C**   At common law, burglary is defined as breaking and entering into the dwelling of another at night with the intent to commit a larceny or felony therein. If, at the time the defendant entered, he did not intend to commit an act that would amount to a crime, he cannot be guilty of burglary.

   A "breaking" occurs when the defendant creates the opening through which he or she enters, even though no force is used. **A** and **B** are incorrect, because by opening the door to the victim's apartment, the defendant created the opening through which he entered, thus committing the necessary breaking. The crime of burglary is committed, if at all, at the time the unlawful entry takes place with the requisite state of mind. Conduct performed subsequently (*i.e.*, leaving a note) does not undo a crime that has already been committed. **D** is therefore incorrect.

35.  **C**   Since all the incidents of unconsciousness occurred within three months after the accident and nearly three years ago, it was probably reasonable for the defendant to believe that they would not occur again. If she entertained that belief, and if it was reasonable, she cannot be said to have knowingly disregarded the plain and strong likelihood of harm as required by the statute. Although it is not certain that a court would come to that conclusion, **C** contains the only argument listed that could possibly support the defendant's defense.

   **A** is incorrect because if the defendant did knowingly disregard the plain and strong likelihood of further blackouts, it would not matter what caused them. **B** is incorrect because the crime, if any, took place when the defendant drove in knowing disregard, and so would have already been committed by the time the defendant passed out. **D** is incorrect because the statute does not require knowledge that death or serious injury will result, but only knowledge that there is a strong likelihood that it will.

36. **D**    The Fourth Amendment only protects people from searches and seizures that are carried out by or on behalf of the government. Consequently, if the government is not involved in the search, the Fourth Amendment does not apply. Importantly, the Fourth Amendment is not violated if a private person, acting alone, conducts a search or seizure and then passes the evidence along to the government. Here, the man was acting purely as a private citizen. The fact that he then gave the evidence he discovered to the police does not turn him into a government agent answerable to the Fourth Amendment.

**A**, **B**, and **C** are therefore incorrect.

37. **A**    Voluntary manslaughter is committed when the defendant, with the intent to cause death or great bodily harm, causes the death of a human being under circumstances such that the defendant is acting in the "heat of passion." The belief that the neighbor brutally murdered his family probably is sufficient to furnish the heat of passion that reduces the crime from murder to manslaughter.

**B** is incorrect for two reasons: First, deliberation and premeditation require a mind that is capable of thinking coolly and rationally, and under the circumstances, the defendant probably wasn't, and second, deliberation and premeditation are not elements of voluntary manslaughter. Since voluntary manslaughter is a lesser offense included in first degree murder, the defendant could be convicted of voluntary manslaughter even if he were guilty of first degree murder. **C** is incorrect because it suggests that guilt of first degree murder would prevent a conviction for voluntary manslaughter. Convicting and sentencing for crime are functions of the court, not of the family of the crime's victim. **D** is incorrect because it suggests a law of vendetta (*i.e.*, that if the neighbor was the killer, the defendant could punish him without incurring criminal responsibility).

38. **D**    Larceny is a trespassory taking and carrying off of personal property known to be another's with the intent to permanently deprive the owner of it. Although the defendant planned to return the money in the event of one contingency, she planned not to return it in the event of another. This contingent intent to permanently deprive is sufficient to make her guilty of larceny when she took and carried off the money on Friday night.

**A** is incorrect because she took the money with the intent (contingent at least) to permanently deprive the owner. **B** is incorrect because she intended not to return it if she lost. Since the crime was committed when she took the money, the fact that she did or did not return it all on Monday morning is irrelevant. **C** is therefore incorrect.

39. **B**    Although most statutes that forbid the sale of alcohol to minors impose strict liability (*i.e.*, defendant's knowledge is not an element), this one does not because it prohibits only the *knowing* sale. If the defendant reasonably believed that the teenager was over the age of 21, he lacked the knowledge that is requisite to a conviction.

Not knowing whether wine was an intoxicating substance under the statute would not be a defense because all persons are conclusively presumed to know the law. Ignorance of the law is not a defense. **A** is therefore incorrect. Entrapment is available as a defense only when a police officer induced the defendant to commit a crime that he or she was not already disposed to commit. **C** is incorrect because the police officer did nothing to encourage the sale. The statute prohibits the sale of intoxicating substances without regard to whether or not anyone becomes intoxicated by them. **D** is therefore incorrect.

40. **D**    Under the "unlawful act doctrine" (also known as the "misdemeanor-manslaughter rule"), a person may be guilty of involuntary manslaughter if a death results from his or her commission of a crime that is *malum in se* or inherently dangerous. Neither of these factors exists here. Therefore, **A** is incorrect. **B** is incorrect because voluntary manslaughter requires the intent to kill or cause great bodily harm, and the knowledge that death is possible is not sufficient to constitute such intent. Most jurisdictions hold that criminal or culpable negligence that results in death may support a conviction for involuntary manslaughter. In some of those jurisdictions, culpable negligence is defined as unreasonable conduct in the face of a foreseeable risk. In others, more is required: either that the defendant knew of the risk and willfully disregarded it, or that under the circumstances known to the defendant, his or her conduct created a high degree of risk of death or serious bodily injury. Since the facts do not indicate that the defendant engaged in unreasonable conduct in the face of a foreseeable risk, willfully disregarded a known risk, or under the circumstances knew her conduct created a high risk of death or serious bodily injury, **C** is incorrect because there is no evidence of criminal negligence.

41. **B**    Self-defense involves a privilege to use reasonable force to prevent what is reasonably perceived as a threat of imminent bodily harm. If a defendant makes a mistake regarding the need for self-defense, courts will look at whether such a mistake was reasonable. If the mistake was reasonable, the defendant is entitled to claim he or she acted in self-defense. Here, the recent robberies, time of day, robber's threat, and the metal spatula handle in the back likely made it reasonable for the defendant to believe he was in danger of being shot. **A** is incorrect because the primary question is whether the defendant's actions were *reasonable*, not whether they were *justified*. **C** is incorrect because self-defense does not require a defendant to verify the truth of his or her belief; it just requires that that belief is reasonable. **D** is incorrect because the circumstances here likely made the defendant's actions reasonable.

42. **A**    A person is guilty as an accessory to a crime when he or she aids and abets in its perpetration. At common law, a defendant commits rape when he or she has sexual intercourse with a woman who is not his wife without the woman's consent. Although under this definition a husband cannot be guilty as a principal of raping his wife, he can be guilty as an accessory if he aids and abets another to have sexual intercourse with her without her consent. Since the defendant assisted the drug dealer in committing rape (*i.e.*, having intercourse with the wife without her consent), he is guilty of rape as an accessory.

Depending on the statutory definitions of procuring for prostitution and possession of narcotics, the defendant may be guilty of all the crimes listed. **B**, **C**, and **D** are incorrect, however, because rape is clearly the most serious of them.

43.  **A**    Larceny is defined as the trespassory taking and carrying off of personal property known to be another's with the intent to permanently deprive the owner thereof. Since the defendant's taking and carrying off of the candy dish was inconsistent with his friend's rights, it was trespassory. Since the defendant knew that the candy dish was his friend's, and since giving it to his sister as a wedding present would permanently deprive his friend of it, he committed larceny, and **A** is correct.

Burglary is the breaking and entering into the dwelling house of another for the purpose of committing a felony therein. Since the defendant entered to recover his own camera, his purpose was not to commit a felony, and he is not guilty of burglary, **B** is therefore incorrect. A person is guilty of a criminal attempt when, with the specific intent to bring about a result that is criminally prohibited, he or she comes substantially close to bringing about that result. Since the defendant did not have the purpose of committing a felony inside his friend's home, he lacked the intent necessary for burglary and therefore could not be convicted of attempted burglary. **C** is therefore incorrect. **D** is incorrect because the defendant is guilty of larceny as explained above. The larceny was committed at the moment that the defendant carried off the candy dish with the requisite intent, and it was not uncommitted when he returned the item.

44.  **C**    A person is guilty of attempting to commit a crime when, *with the specific intent* to bring about a criminally prohibited result, he or she comes substantially close to achieving that result. Since involuntary manslaughter is *unintended* homicide, there can be no attempt to commit it because the requisite state of mind cannot exist.

**A** and **B** are therefore incorrect. Since there is no requirement that a person be prosecuted for the highest possible crime that he or she committed, **D** is incorrect.

45.  **C**    The defendant obviously did not have the intent to cause the death of the accomplice and was obviously not engaged in committing rape, robbery, or kidnapping at the time that the accomplice was killed. Under the common law definition, burglary is a breaking and entering into the dwelling of another at night for the purpose of committing a felony therein. Since the defendant was not attempting to enter a dwelling house, he was not committing a burglary either.

**A** is incorrect because most jurisdictions apply the felony-murder rule to the killing of one felon by another. **B** is incorrect because the statute does not require that the felony being committed is a dangerous one. While assumption of the risk is a defense in tort actions, it is not in criminal prosecutions. **D** is therefore incorrect.

46.  **D**    The victim of a crime does not share the guilt of the perpetrator, even though the victim's participation was necessary to the crime's commission. If the law was designed to protect people in the defendant's position against people in the personnel manager's position, the defendant can be regarded as the victim of the personnel manager's act and thus escape criminal liability. While it is not certain that a court would be persuaded by this argument, it is the only one listed that could possibly result in dismissal.

Although the statement contained in **A** was correct at early common law, it is no longer true in a majority of jurisdictions. **B** is factually incorrect, since the personnel manager could not have committed the crime if the defendant had not paid him the money. Under Wharton's Rule, persons who agree to commit a crime cannot be convicted of conspiracy unless at least one of them was not essential to the commission of that crime. Wharton's Rule applies to bigamy, incest, gambling, bribery, adultery, and dueling. Since the crime created by the statute could not have been committed by one person alone, Wharton's Rule would prevent the conviction of the personnel manager and the defendant for conspiracy to commit it. **C** is incorrect, however, because the defendant is not being charged with conspiracy, but with being an accessory to the substantive crime, and because accessories frequently are people without whom the crime could not have been committed.

47.  **A**  Robbery is larceny accomplished by force or a threat of force directed at the lawful possessor of the property taken. The defendant's snatching of the purse was accomplished by force, and the hand in his pocket coupled with his words constituted a threat of force.

Larceny by trick requires that the victim give up the property in reliance on the defendant's fraud. Since the victim's purse was taken by force, **B** is incorrect. Embezzlement is criminal conversion of personal property by one in lawful possession. **C** is incorrect because the defendant did not obtain possession of the property lawfully. Larceny by false pretenses involves a misrepresentation of fact that is intended to and does in fact cause the victim to transfer title to property. **D** is incorrect because the victim did not transfer title to the defendant.

48.  **A**  Larceny is a trespassory taking and carrying off of property known to be another's with the intent to permanently deprive. There is no requirement that the victim's possession of the property be lawful. The defendant's taking of the plant was trespassory, and therefore a larceny, because she had been authorized to water it, not to carry it off. The defendant could not be guilty of burglary since her use of the key that the doctor gave her prevents her entry from constituting a breaking, which requires force against the premises.

49.  **B**  Rape is sexual intercourse without consent of the female. Since the bank teller's resistance was overcome by the defendant's threat and her resulting fear of death, the intercourse occurred without her consent. One who commands another to do an act is responsible for the criminal consequences thereof. Although the defendant did not himself have sexual intercourse with the teller, he is guilty of rape because he commanded the bank manager to do so. Solicitation is committed by encouraging, ordering, or commanding another to commit a crime. If the person solicited actually commits the crime, however, solicitation merges with the substantive crime and is not subject to separate prosecution.

50.  **B**  Ordinarily, no person has standing to assert the constitutional rights of another. For this reason, a defendant who seeks to suppress evidence seized as the result of the search of another person may not successfully argue that the search and seizure were unconstitutional unless he or she had a sufficient possessory or proprietary interest in the thing searched to give him or her a reasonable expectation of privacy that was violated by the

search. Since the car and the pistol were both the man's, and since the defendant thus could not have a reasonable expectation of privacy, the defendant has no standing to object to the search, and his motion should be denied.

For the reasons stated above, **C** and **D** are incorrect. Usually, a search without a warrant violates the rights of the person searched unless it is incident to a lawful arrest. Since the facts do not indicate that the man was arrested prior to the search of his glove compartment, the search probably did violate his rights. **A** is therefore incorrect.

51.  **D**    Under the common law, burglary is the breaking and entering into the dwelling house of another, at night, with the intent to commit a felony therein. Most states have changed burglary to include entry into any kind of structure at any time of the day. Here, since what the man was intending to do wasn't a crime, he can't be convicted of burglary.

**A** is incorrect because the issue is whether what the man intended to do was a felony, not that the man intended to commit a felony by doing something that wasn't actually a crime. **B** is incorrect because the burglary would have been complete the minute he entered the church if what he was doing was actually a felony. Importantly, burglary requires the intent to commit a felony, not its actual completion. **C** is incorrect because his underlying actions did not actually add up to burglary, so he clearly could not be liable for attempt.

52.  **A**    A search may be lawful if consent is given by one in apparent authority to do so. If the student actually was the defendant's roommate, she would have had authority to consent to a search of common areas of their room. Since she told the police that she was, and since she had a key to the room, it was probably reasonable for them to believe her. Her apparent authority might, thus, justify the search. While a court might not find it to be so, the argument in **A** is the only one listed that could possibly result in denial of the defendant's motion.

**B** is incorrect because although information received from an informant might furnish probable cause sufficient to permit the issuance of a warrant, the informant's belief is not sufficient to justify a warrantless search. **C** is incorrect because the defendant had no expectation that any other person would enter the room in her absence. Although she knew that the sorority retained a copy of her room key, she knew also that this was done to facilitate duplication in the event that a resident lost her key. **D** is incorrect because even though there are some cases indicating that a primary or secondary school administrator can consent to a search of a locker used by a student, this view has not been applied to college students or to searches of a student's room, and the student was not a school administrator.

53.  **B**    One who, with the intent that a crime will be committed, encourages another to commit that crime, is liable for it as an accessory.

**A** is incorrect because mere presence at the scene of a crime is not sufficient, even if the defendant intended or was willing for the crime to be committed. **C** is incorrect because the words of encouragement need not create a new danger for liability to be imposed. **D** is incorrect for two reasons: First, under some circumstances, words alone might be sufficient, and second, here, the words were coupled with intent.

54. **A**    Under the M'Naghten test, a person may be found not guilty by reason of insanity only if mental illness prevented him or her from knowing the nature and quality of his or her act or from knowing that the act was legally wrong. Since the defendant knew what he was doing (*i.e.*, that he was poisoning the governor), and he knew that it was against the law, he was not insane.

B refers to the irresistible impulse supplement, and it is incorrect because the facts indicate that the jurisdiction has adopted only the M'Naghten test. C is incorrect because it refers to the Durham Rule, which is no longer applied in any jurisdiction. In some jurisdictions, a defendant is insane under the M'Naghten rule if mental disease caused him or her to suffer from a delusion within the context of which the defendant's act would be lawful. D is incorrect, however, because even within the context of the defendant's delusion, the defendant knew that killing the governor was an unlawful act.

55. **B**    Although statutory rape is sometimes called a strict liability crime, this means only that liability can be imposed even though the defendant was not aware that the female with whom he was having intercourse was underage. No liability can be imposed, however, unless the defendant had intent to engage in intercourse.

A is incorrect because liability for involuntary manslaughter may be imposed if the victim's death resulted from reckless conduct by the defendant. Driving while drunk may be sufficiently reckless to result in liability. C is incorrect because even if the defendant did not know that she was drunk, it may have been reckless for her to drive while she knew that her vision and motor abilities were impaired. Since voluntary manslaughter is the killing of a human being with the intent to kill or to cause great bodily harm under circumstances of great emotional distress, D is incorrect because the facts asserted by the defendant would inculpate rather than exculpate him.

56. **C**    Murder is defined as criminal homicide with malice aforethought. Since homicide involves an act that causes the death of a human being, and since the victim's death in C did not result from the defendant's act, the defendant could not be guilty of murdering the victim.

Malice aforethought is the intent to kill, the intent to cause great bodily harm, the intent to commit a felony, the intent to escape from lawful custody, or acting with wanton disregard for human life. A is incorrect because the defendant's desire to cause the victim great bodily harm might constitute malice aforethought. B is incorrect because knowledge of the victim's identity is not a material element of either murder or of malice aforethought. Since the defendant did intend to cause the victim's death, he had the requisite *mens rea*, even though he believed the victim to be someone else. D is incorrect for two reasons: First, shooting at the bank guard was a felony, and the intent to commit a felony may constitute malice aforethought in a prosecution for the death of any person killed during the course of that felony, and second, starting a gun battle in a bank can be regarded as wanton disregard for human life, which may also constitute malice aforethought.

57. **D**    An examination of a defendant's effects is a search if it is conducted under circumstances that violate the defendant's reasonable expectation of privacy. Ordinarily, a person has a

reasonable expectation that an apartment that he or she has the exclusive right to occupy will remain private. For this reason, the inspection of the defendant's apartment probably violated his reasonable expectation of privacy and therefore was a search. Ordinarily, a search of a defendant's effects violates his or her Fourth Amendment rights unless it is conducted pursuant to a warrant. Since the examination of the defendant's apartment was conducted without a warrant, it violated the defendant's rights. Evidence seized in violation of a defendant's Fourth Amendment rights is inadmissible under the exclusionary rule.

**A** is incorrect because the plastic pouch was not in plain sight until the officer entered, and the entry itself violated the defendant's rights. **B** is incorrect because a landlord does not have the power to waive his or her tenant's constitutional rights — even if he or she is the tenant's mother. At one time, *Miranda* warnings were not required until a person became a suspect. No such qualification ever applied to the right to be secure against unreasonable search and seizure, however. **C** is therefore incorrect.

58.  **A**  Since the statute requires knowledge that the statement is false, and since the defendant believed the statement to be true, he lacked the required mental state to be guilty of perjury.

**D** is therefore incorrect. If, as the result of his attorney's advice, the defendant believed that he had not been convicted of a crime, he lacked the knowledge necessary to make him guilty under the statute. However, the defendant's reliance on the advice of counsel would not, in itself, have prevented him from being guilty unless he actually believed that advice, so **B** is incorrect. Since a guilty plea is equivalent to a conviction, **C** is incorrect.

59.  **D**  Kidnapping is defined as the intentional asportation and confinement of a person against that person's will, by force or threat, and without lawful authority. Since the defendant did not know that the daughter was in the car when he drove it away, he lacked the requisite intent.

**A** is therefore incorrect. **B** is incorrect because kidnapping has no equivalent of the felony-murder rule. **C** is incorrect since if he knew that the daughter was in the car, the defendant could be guilty of kidnapping even if the asportation of the daughter was secondary to his stealing of the car.

60.  **D**  The double jeopardy clause prevents a person from being placed twice in jeopardy for the same offense. This does not prevent prosecution by two separate sovereigns for crimes arising out of the same transaction, however, because a different offense has been committed against each sovereign. In addition, the two crimes with which the defendant is charged are not identical. (The federal prosecution is for illegal importation; the state prosecution is for illegal possession.)

**A** is therefore incorrect. **B** is incorrect since it has been held that customs agents have probable cause to search the car of any person entering the United States. **C** is incorrect because it is generally understood that jeopardy begins as soon as a trial commences.

61. **B**    Since the statute prohibits possession of a skeleton key with the intent to commit an unlawful entry, and since the defendant was, in fact, attempting to effect an unlawful entry with his skeleton key, he is guilty of violating the statute.

    **A** is incorrect because the fact that the defendant was a professional thief is not enough to make him guilty of violating any law, even one designed to protect the public against professional thieves. The crime defined by the statute would merge into the crime of attempted burglary if the defendant was charged with or convicted of attempted burglary. But in the absence of an attempted burglary charge, there is no reason why the lesser crime cannot be prosecuted. **C** is therefore incorrect. A careful reading of the statute discloses that it punishes conduct (*i.e.*, possession of a skeleton key) coupled with a guilty mind. **D** is therefore incorrect.

62. **B**    Since the statute defines as third degree manslaughter any death that proximately results from the commission of a crime, the defendant cannot be found guilty under the statute unless the victim's death proximately resulted from his crime.

    Although the common law misdemeanor-manslaughter rule is applied only to deaths resulting from the commission of misdemeanors that are *mala in se*, the statute given makes no such requirement. **A** is therefore incorrect. **C** is incorrect for the same reason, and because there is no indication that the defendant was driving while intoxicated at the time the accident occurred. **D** is incorrect because neither the common law rule nor the statute requires that the risk be a foreseeable one.

63. **C**    One who intentionally aids or facilitates the commission of a crime is guilty of the crime as an accessory. Robbery is larceny committed by force or threat of force. Although the defendant did not point a gun and demand money, she aided and abetted the student by operating the getaway car. She is thus guilty as an accessory. Conspiracy is an agreement to commit a crime made by two or more people who have specific intent. The defendant and the student committed the crime of conspiracy when they agreed on the commission of the robbery.

    **A**, **B**, and **D** are incorrect because the crime of conspiracy is separate from and does not merge into the substantive crime that the conspirators agreed to commit.

64. **B**    A defendant is guilty of murder when he or she proximately causes the death of another human being unlawfully and with malice aforethought. Malice aforethought consists of the intent to kill, the intent to cause great bodily harm, escape from lawful custody, the commission of a felony, or reckless disregard for human life. Since there are no facts indicating that the defendant in **B** intended to kill or cause harm, was escaping from lawful custody, or engaged in conduct demonstrating a reckless disregard for human life, the only way he could be convicted of murder would be if the pedestrian's death proximately resulted from the commission of a felony. There is no fact indicating that violation of the insurance statute was a felony. Even if it was, the violation was not causally related to the pedestrian's death since the death would have occurred whether or not the vehicle was insured. For this reason, the defendant could not be convicted of murder.

An unlawful killing committed with the intent to kill or inflict great bodily harm might be voluntary manslaughter if the defendant was acting under extreme emotional distress or mistaken justification. The defendant in **A** might still be convicted of murder, however, because the lapse of time between his discovery of the atrocity that the neighbor committed and his killing of the neighbor could prevent a court from finding that he was acting under extreme emotional distress. **A** is therefore incorrect. Although the defendant in **C** did not have an intent to kill, his conduct might be regarded as sufficiently reckless to result in a conviction for murder. Although it is possible that the defendant in **D** was acting under sufficient emotional distress for the killing to be regarded as voluntary manslaughter rather than murder, courts rarely make special allowances for "mercy" killings. **D** is therefore incorrect.

65.  **B**    A person is guilty of a criminal attempt when, with the specific intent to bring about a criminally prohibited result, he or she performs some act that comes substantially close to achieving that result. Many jurisdictions hold that if the result that the defendant specifically intended to bring about was not a crime, the defendant cannot be guilty of a criminal attempt. This is sometimes known as the doctrine of legal impossibility. Although not all jurisdictions recognize this defense, it is the only argument listed that could furnish the defendant with an effective defense in any jurisdiction.

Since the elements of criminal attempt are often included among the elements of the substantive crime that was attempted, criminal attempts are often lesser included offenses of the substantive crimes. Lesser offenses are said to merge with the crime in which they are included, which means that a person who is convicted of a substantive crime cannot also be convicted of attempting it. There is no requirement that a defendant be prosecuted for the highest or most serious crime resulting from his or her act, however. This means that a prosecutor may choose to charge a defendant with attempting a crime, even if a conviction for the substantive crime could have been obtained. For this reason, the fact that the defendant actually succeeded in killing a bird would not prevent his conviction for attempting to do so, and **A** and **D** are incorrect. A person is *in pari delicto* with another when they are equally guilty. Since the friend did not commit or attempt to commit a crime, he is not guilty of anything and therefore is not *in pari delicto* with the defendant. **C** is therefore incorrect.

66.  **D**    Voluntary manslaughter is the killing of a human being with the intent to kill or inflict great bodily harm, under circumstances of extreme emotional distress (or mistaken justification). Frequently, the rage that accompanies a discovery of infidelity by a spouse has been held to be sufficient emotional distress to reduce an intentional homicide from murder to voluntary manslaughter. Most jurisdictions apply an objective standard, however, in judging a defendant's emotional distress. Thus, if a person of ordinary temperament would not have lost self-control, the defendant's emotional distress would not have been sufficient to result in a reduction of his crime from murder to manslaughter.

**A** and **B** are incorrect because although a killing with the intent to kill or inflict great bodily harm *may* be murder, extreme emotional distress may reduce it to voluntary manslaughter even though the defendant intended to kill or inflict great bodily harm. Although anger that results from the defendant's catching his spouse *in flagrante delicto* (*i.e.*, in the act) may justify reducing a murder charge to one of manslaughter, **C** is incorrect because there is no requirement that defendant's emotional distress result from this particular circumstance.

67. **B**   Evidence obtained in violation of a defendant's constitutional rights may not be used against him or her. The United States Supreme Court has held that *Miranda* warnings must be given before questioning a person in custody. An interrogation conducted without giving the required *Miranda* warnings thus violates a defendant's rights, making confessions so obtained inadmissible. The warnings are required only when the person being questioned is in custody, however. Thus, if the defendant was not in custody at the time his statement was made, his rights have not been violated, and his statement should not be excluded. A person is in custody when the police deprive him or her of his or her freedom of action in any significant way. It is possible that a court would find that the officer's pointing toward the back seat of the patrol car was an order coupled with an implied threat sufficient to deprive the defendant of his freedom, and that he was therefore in custody. It is also possible, however, that the defendant's entry into the police car was voluntary, and that it did not, therefore, amount to custody. Of all the arguments listed, however, this is the only one with any possibility of success.

Even if a defendant's confession is excluded because of a failure to give the required *Miranda* warnings, he or she may be convicted on the basis of other evidence. The existence of such independent evidence, although it may convict the defendant, does not make admissible the confession that was obtained in violation of his or her rights. **A** is therefore incorrect. Prior to the *Miranda* decision, the Supreme Court's *Escobedo* decision required that a suspect be given certain warnings as soon as he or she became the *focus* of a police investigation. **C** is incorrect, however, because *Miranda* subsequently changed the "focus" test to a "custody" test, requiring that warnings be given only after the suspect was in custody. Whether or not the investigation was routine, *Miranda* warnings are required whenever the person interrogated is in custody. **D** is therefore incorrect.

68. **D**   Arson is the intentional or reckless burning of the dwelling of another. Although the defendant caused the burning of the homeowner's dwelling, he did not do so intentionally since he believed that there would be no damage. (**Note:** Although some jurisdictions hold that a reckless burning may be arson, the facts indicate that the defendant acted reasonably.)

Although violation of a statute may be *evidence* of negligence or even of recklessness, a statutory violation is not in itself sufficient to satisfy the *mens rea* requirement for arson. **A** is therefore incorrect. **B** is incorrect because it would impose criminal liability without the necessary *mens rea*. **C** is incorrect because consent by the homeowner to the defendant's use of fireworks is not equivalent to consent to the burning of his home.

69. **B**   Murder is a killing with malice aforethought. Malice aforethought includes wanton disregard for human life, which means acting in deliberate disregard of the plain and strong likelihood that death or great bodily harm would result. Operating a motor vehicle at a speed of 100 miles per hour might or might not be found to constitute wanton disregard

for human life, but of the reasons listed, **B** is the only one that could result in a conviction for murder.

**A** is incorrect for two reasons: First, culpable negligence is insufficient to constitute malice aforethought, and second, the facts do not indicate that the defendant was intoxicated at the time the accident occurred. Under the misdemeanor-manslaughter rule, a death resulting from the commission of a misdemeanor might be classified as *manslaughter*. Since driving without a license carries a maximum sentence of less than one year (*i.e.*, 30 days), it is properly classified as a misdemeanor. **C** and **D** are incorrect, however, because the misdemeanor-manslaughter rule cannot lead to a conviction for *murder*.

70.   **C**        All jurisdictions that recognize a felony-murder rule apply it only when the victim's death (or the injury that leads to it) occurs during the commission of a felony. Since the stroke that caused the owner's death did not occur until the day after the defendant robbed the store, it did not occur during the perpetration of a felony by the defendant, and the felony-murder rule does not apply.

**A** and **B** are therefore incorrect. **D** is incorrect because many cases have held that since the victim of a robbery is likely to respond with force, even a robbery with a toy gun is a dangerous felony.

71.   **A**        "Specific intent" crimes are those that require a state of mind amounting to a desire or knowledge by the defendant that his or her conduct will result in a consequence that is criminally proscribed. "General intent" crimes are those for which conviction may be based on recklessness or criminal negligence. Voluntary intoxication may provide a defense to crimes requiring specific intent since it may prevent its formation. Awareness of the effect that alcohol is likely to have on the capacity to assess risks, however, prevents voluntary intoxication from serving as a defense to crimes involving general intent. Since rape may consist of recklessly having intercourse without the victim's consent, it is a general intent crime, and voluntary intoxication is not a defense to it.

Involuntary intoxication, on the other hand, may be a defense to crimes involving recklessness, as well as to specific intent crimes. The defendant's assertion in **B** might therefore provide her with an effective defense. Since attempted robbery requires the specific intent to commit a larceny by force or threat of force, the defendant's intoxication in **C** may have prevented her from having the intent required and may thus provide her with an effective defense. In **D**, the defendant's assertion is that he lacked the intent to deprive the rightful owner of possession of the automobile. Since this specific intent is an essential element of larceny, his intoxication may provide him with an effective defense.

72.   **B**        Receiving stolen property consists of the acquisition of stolen property with the knowledge that it has been stolen and with the intent to permanently deprive its owner of it. Acquisition occurs when the defendant takes possession of the property himself or herself, or when he or she directs that possession be delivered to another. Thus, although the defendant did not personally take possession of the car that the man stole, he received it when he directed that it be delivered to his brother.

In **A**, the car that the defendant received had already been recovered by the police and was therefore not stolen at the time of the sale. In **C** and **D**, there is no indication that the cars sold to the defendant ever had been stolen. **A**, **C**, and **D** are therefore incorrect.

73. **B**    After being advised of his or her *Miranda* rights, a suspect in custody cannot be subjected to police interrogation unless he or she voluntarily and intelligently waives those rights. If the officers were unaware that the defendant could overhear their conversation, the first officer's comment was not an interrogation of the defendant, and the defendant's statement was not obtained in violation of his rights.

If the defendant's statement was the result of an interrogation, it violated his rights unless he waived them voluntarily and intelligently. **A** is incorrect because it would make the defendant's waiver intelligent but not necessarily voluntary (*e.g.*, he may have been intimidated by the presence of police). **C** is incorrect because it would make the defendant's waiver voluntary, but not necessarily intelligent (*e.g.*, he might not have understood his rights). The U.S. Constitution protects the defendant against custodial interrogations, even if the custody itself is lawful. **D** is therefore incorrect.

74. **D**    Larceny is the trespassory taking and carrying off of personal property known to be another's with the intent to permanently deprive. In this definition, "trespassory" means without the consent of the owner. Since rearranging the merchandise in the storeroom was part of the defendant's duties and therefore done with the store's consent, her moving of the lawnmower was not trespassory. *Taking* means acquiring possession. Since the defendant did not transfer the lawnmower from her employer's possession to her own, she did not take it. Although any exercise of dominion accompanied by even a slight movement may constitute a "carrying off," the defendant moved the lawnmower as part of her duties and without any intention — at that time — of making it her own. She therefore did not carry it off. For a person to be guilty of larceny, the intent to permanently deprive must exist at the time she took and carried off the chattel involved. Although the defendant did decide to permanently deprive the store of the lawnmower, she did not perform any act that might be taking or carrying off after making that decision. For these reasons, the defendant is not guilty of larceny. Embezzlement is a criminal conversion of personal property by one in lawful custody of it. Conversion takes place when the defendant seriously interferes with the rights of the owner, usually by exercising dominion or control over the chattel. Because the defendant never did anything inconsistent with the store's rights in the lawnmower and never exercised dominion or control over it, she cannot be said to have converted it. She is not therefore guilty of embezzlement.

75. **C**    In the majority of states, if a defendant made an unreasonable mistake as to the need for force in self-defense, the defendant's crime can be reduced from murder to voluntary manslaughter even though such a claim does not completely excuse a defendant's actions. This is referred to as a claim of "imperfect" self-defense. Here, the question states that the defendant honestly but unreasonably believed that he needed to use deadly force to protect himself from the victim's laser gun. Given the circumstances of the victim's job, the defendant's intoxication, and the particulars of the cellphone, such a belief could be honest yet unreasonable. Importantly, the question tells you to assume that the court believes

the defendant's version of events, whether or not you believe the defendant's belief to be ridiculous. **A** is incorrect because self-defense requires a reasonable belief as to the need for force. Here, the question states that the defendant's belief was unreasonable. **B** is incorrect because the defendant's unreasonable belief will have an effect on his case. **D** is incorrect because depraved heart murder has to do with situations where a defendant acted with such great recklessness that he or she can be said to have extreme indifference to the value of human life. In these situations, the defendant is not necessarily intending to kill anyone, but is acting in such a way as to make someone's death likely.

76.  **B**   When the words *deliberate* and *premeditated* appear in a murder statute, *deliberate* means that the defendant was possessed of a cool mind capable of reflection, and *premeditated* means that the defendant actually did reflect on his or her act before committing it. Since the psychiatrist's testimony indicates that the defendant may have been incapable of cool reflection at the time of his act, it may be admitted for the purpose of showing that the killing was not deliberate and premeditated.

A is incorrect because under the M'Naghten test, a defendant is insane only if mental disease made him or her incapable of knowing the nature and quality of his or her act, or that it was wrong. **C** is incorrect because the testimony may be admitted to establish lack of deliberation and premeditation, even though it does not establish that the defendant was insane. An intentional killing may be reduced from murder to voluntary manslaughter if the defendant was acting in the heat of passion caused by sufficient provocation. For this purpose, the provocation and defendant's response to it are usually judged by an objective standard. **D** is incorrect, however, because, as explained above, psychiatric evidence of the defendant's state of mind may be relevant to the elements of deliberation and premeditation.

77.  **D**   If the only evidence against the defendant was excluded because it was obtained by coercing his confession, his motion to dismiss might be granted. But although a coerced confession cannot be used in a criminal prosecution against the person who made it, evidence that was obtained independently of the coerced confession can be used. Since the federal officer obtained evidence of the defendant's identity without knowledge of the defendant's statement, the defendant's motion must be denied.

A and **B** are therefore incorrect. **C** is incorrect because if the federal officer's discovery of the evidence against the defendant resulted from a violation of the defendant's constitutional rights, it might be excluded in spite of the fact that the federal officer was employed by the federal government and the state police officer by the state.

78.  **D**   A conspiracy is an agreement to commit a crime. Conspirators are vicariously liable for crimes committed in furtherance of the conspiratorial goal by other members of the conspiracy. This is so even if those crimes were unforeseeable, not included in the original plan, or unnecessary to the success of the conspiracy, so long as they were committed in furtherance of the conspiratorial goal. Since the roommate transported the car across a state line for the purpose of aiding their escape, it was in furtherance of the conspiratorial goal. **A**, **B**, and **C** are therefore incorrect.

79. **B**    A statement made in response to a custodial interrogation of a suspect is admissible against him or her only if, after being advised of his or her *Miranda* rights, he or she makes a voluntary and intelligent waiver. Since the defendant concedes that her statements were voluntary, the only remaining issue is whether she had sufficient knowledge and understanding of her rights to intelligently waive them. The same issue was resolved in **B**, in which the defendant's response to the officer's question made it doubtful that the defendant understood his constitutional rights.

In **A**, since the defendant was not in custody at the time he answered the officer's questions (and since the question was probably not an "interrogation"), the issue of waiver did not arise. Although a person who has been formally charged with a crime is entitled to counsel at a lineup, **C** is not applicable since the defendant had not been formally charged with any crime, and since, therefore, she was not entitled to counsel, no issue of waiver arose in her case. The Fourth Amendment protects against warrantless search, but this protection may be waived by a person who voluntarily and intelligently consents to such a search. Waiver was, therefore, an issue in **D**. Although the officer's statement might not have been sufficient to make the defendant's waiver intelligent, the circumstances — an unexpected, middle-of-the-night visit by three uniformed police officers — also raise serious doubts about its voluntariness. For this reason, **B** (in which the only issue was the knowledge and understanding of the waiver) is more applicable as a precedent. [**Note:** Case-summary analysis questions are usually as uncertain as this one. Fortunately, they are no longer common on the MBE.]

80. **B**    The crime of receiving stolen property is committed when the defendant receives stolen property with the knowledge that it is stolen and with the intent to permanently deprive the owner of it. Since the car that the defendant purchased was in the lawful custody of the police, it could be argued that it was no longer stolen. Although it is not certain that this argument would succeed, it is the only one listed that could possibly be effective in the defendant's defense. **B** is therefore correct.

Since the police are supposed to prevent crime rather than instigate it, many jurisdictions hold that a defendant who was induced by the police or an agent of the police to commit a crime that he or she was not otherwise disposed to commit is entrapped and has a valid affirmative defense to the crime charged. **A** is incorrect, however, because the defendant came looking for a stolen car and was therefore already disposed to commit the crime with which he was charged. Ordinarily, a defense may not be based on the assertion of another's rights. If the man's cooperation was coerced, the man's rights may have been violated. **C** is incorrect, however, because the defendant may not base his defense on the invasion of the man's rights. **D** is incorrect because no right of the defendant's was bargained away.

81. **C**    If a warrantless search violates a reasonable expectation of privacy held by the person whose property is searched, it violates that person's Fourth Amendment rights. Since each person who shares property with another knows that the other has access to it, neither of them has a reasonable expectation that the property will remain private. For this reason, a search is generally valid if authorized by one of the persons who share the property that is searched. Since the girlfriend shared the apartment, the bedroom, and the closet with

the defendant, the defendant could have no reasonable expectation that these areas would remain private, and the girlfriend's consent to the search made it valid.

Although a search warrant may not be issued without probable cause, probable cause does not justify a search without a warrant. **A** is therefore incorrect. If police discover contraband during hot pursuit of a suspect, they may be permitted to seize it without a warrant if necessary to prevent disposal or destruction. **B** is incorrect, however, because the police were not in hot pursuit of the defendant when they discovered the marijuana. The seizure of contraband "in plain view" might be valid because its discovery was not the result of a search. **D** is incorrect, however, because the police officers had already begun their search (*i.e.*, by having the girlfriend open the closet door for them to look inside it) when the marijuana fell into view.

82. **D**    The Double Jeopardy Clause provides that no person shall be placed twice in jeopardy for the same offense. It is generally understood, however, that jeopardy does not begin until the commencement of a trial, which occurs when a jury is impaneled. Since a grand jury proceeding is not "jeopardy," there is no constitutional reason why a matter should not be brought before a grand jury several times.

A and B are therefore incorrect. In addition, **A** is incorrect because the term *res judicata* is applied only to a final determination by a court. **C** is incorrect because jeopardy has not yet begun, so the motion must be denied, whether or not the first grand jury's decision was motivated by prejudice.

83. **D**    Murder is the unjustified killing of a human being with malice aforethought. Malice aforethought means a wanton disregard for human life, or an intent to kill, inflict great bodily harm, commit a felony, or resist a lawful arrest. Since it is clear that the defendant did not intend to commit a felony, to resist a lawful arrest, or to strike anyone with the bullet, she can be found guilty of murder only if her conduct showed a wanton disregard for human life. Thus, if she is acquitted, it can only be because the court found that her conduct did not show a wanton disregard.

**A** is incorrect because malice aforethought may exist without an intent to kill. Since any result may have many proximate causes, the fact that the ambulance driver's conduct was a proximate cause of the victim's death does not establish that the defendant's conduct was not also a proximate cause of that death. **B** is therefore incorrect. The privilege to abate a nuisance permits the use of reasonable force only. Although the conduct of the defendant's neighbors may have constituted a nuisance, it is obvious that the use of a deadly weapon was not a reasonable response to it. **C** is therefore incorrect.

84. **C**    A person is privileged to use reasonable force to protect himself or herself from what he or she reasonably believes to be a threat of imminent bodily harm. Potentially lethal force is reasonable when used in response to what the defendant reasonably perceives to be a threat of potentially lethal force. Thus, if the defendant reasonably believed that the victim was reaching for a gun, her use of a gun in response may have been reasonable and therefore privileged. While it is not certain that a court would come to this conclusion,

the argument in **C** is the only one listed that could possibly provide the defendant with an effective defense.

A person is guilty of a criminal attempt when, with the intent to bring about a criminally prohibited result, he or she comes substantially close to achieving it. **A** is incorrect because the fact that a death did not actually occur will not prevent a conviction for attempting to cause one. If the defendant had the intent to kill the victim when she aimed her pistol at the victim's chest, she would be guilty of attempted murder if she came subsequently close to causing the victim's death. This might be so even if she did not strike the victim in the chest, or even if she did not strike the victim at all. For this reason, **B** is incorrect. **D** is incorrect because deadly force is force that is likely to result in death or great bodily harm. The use of a pistol thus constitutes deadly force even though the harm that it actually causes happens to be slight.

85. **D**    Murder is the unjustified killing of a human being with malice aforethought. In addition to reckless disregard for human life, and the intent to kill, to cause great bodily harm, or to resist a lawful arrest, malice aforethought includes the intent to commit a dangerous felony. Since arson is a dangerous felony, **D** is correct.

A is incorrect because malice aforethought may exist even though the defendants did not intend to kill. Some jurisdictions have held that the felony murder rule cannot be applied *unless* the deaths were totally independent of the defendants' purpose in committing a felony. **B** is a misstatement of this rule and is therefore incorrect. **C** is incorrect because unreasonable conduct is not sufficient to constitute malice aforethought.

86. **B**    Kidnapping consists of intentionally transporting and confining a person against that person's will by force or threat and without legal authority. The essential difference between kidnapping and criminal false imprisonment is the requirement of asportation: Unless the defendant has moved the victim to the place of confinement, there is no kidnapping. Since the defendant forced the hostage to accompany him to his car, where he confined her for a period of 15 minutes, he has kidnapped her. Because he did not move any of the other victims to the place of their confinement, he did not kidnap them.

**A**, **C**, and **D** are therefore incorrect.

87. **A**    A defendant is guilty of criminally receiving stolen property when he or she acquires stolen personal property with knowledge that it is stolen and with the intent to permanently deprive its owner. Since the car that the defendant purchased from the other officer had been requisitioned from the police department, it was not stolen property. Since the defendant never received stolen property, he cannot be guilty of this crime.

**B** is incorrect because guilt does not require that the defendant pay for stolen property with his own money (or that he pay for it at all). Police officers are supposed to prevent crime, not to cause it. For this reason, many jurisdictions hold that a defendant who was entrapped (*i.e.*, induced by a police officer to commit a crime that he or she was not otherwise inclined to commit), cannot be convicted of committing it. The officers did not entrap the defendant because the defendant indicated his inclination to purchase a stolen car before either officer suggested that he do so. **C** is therefore incorrect. A search or arrest warrant may not be issued without a showing of probable cause, but no such showing is required before beginning an investigation. For this reason, **D** is incorrect.

88.  **B**  Arson is the intentional or malicious burning of the dwelling of another. Since even the slightest charring of the walls or ceiling is regarded as a burning, there was a burning of the boyfriend's dwelling. Since malice includes recklessness, and since it was clearly reckless to set fire to a couch while it was inside the house, the necessary state of mind is present. The defendant is therefore guilty of arson.

Burglary is the trespassory breaking and entering of the dwelling of another at night with the intent to commit a larceny or any felony therein. The defendant entered the boyfriend's dwelling at night. The unauthorized opening of a closed door can constitute a breaking, and any unauthorized entry is trespassory. Although the defendant did commit a felony inside (*i.e.*, arson), she cannot be guilty of burglary unless she intended to do so when she entered. Since at the time the defendant entered the boyfriend's house, she meant only to retrieve her own property, she did not have the requisite intent to make her guilty of burglary. **A** and **C** are therefore incorrect. **D** is incorrect because the defendant is guilty of arson as explained above.

89.  **D**  Because of the inherently coercive nature of police custody, the United States Supreme Court held (in *Miranda*) that inculpatory statements resulting from custodial interrogation of a defendant are inadmissible unless the defendant received certain warnings prior to making the statements. Among the required warnings is a caution that anything that the defendant says may be used against him or her. Because the informant was working for the police, it is possible that his conversation with the defendant amounted to a police interrogation. Thus, if the defendant was in custody at the time, his statement might be inadmissible because he had not received *Miranda* warnings. The *Miranda* rule applies only to custodial interrogations, however. So, since the defendant was not in custody at the time of his conversation with the informant, the lack of *Miranda* warnings would not make his statement to the informant inadmissible.

**A** is incorrect because even though the informant might have been an agent of the police at the time he and the defendant shared a cell (*i.e.*, while the defendant was clearly in custody), the statements in question were not made at that time. **B** is incorrect because *Miranda* warnings are required for custodial interrogations only. The issue to be determined is whether the conversation between the informant and the defendant was a custodial interrogation and therefore a violation of the defendant's rights. **C** assumes that the defendant's rights were violated and uses that assumption to prove that the defendant's rights were violated. This is circular reasoning and is therefore incorrect.

90.  **C**  Under the "irresistible impulse" test, a person is not guilty by reason of insanity if mental disease made him or her incapable of controlling his or her conduct at the time of the alleged criminal act. Although not all jurisdictions accept this definition of insanity, under the facts given, **C** is the only argument listed that would serve as an effective defense in any jurisdiction.

The M'Naghten rule provides that a person is not guilty by reason of insanity if, at the time of the allegedly criminal act, mental disease prevented him or her from knowing either the nature and quality of his or her act or that it was wrong. A defendant is said to know that his or her act is "wrong," however, if he or she is aware that it is prohibited by law. Since the defendant knew that if he was caught, he would be imprisoned for murder, he had sufficient understanding that his act was wrong to make him sane under this rule. **A** is therefore incorrect. The concept of "intent" relates to the defendant's state of mind regarding the immediate consequences of his or her act, quite apart from the concept of "motive," which refers to a defendant's purpose in bringing that consequence about. Since the defendant desired to kill the victim, he had the necessary intent to make him guilty of murder, in spite of his noble motive (*i.e.*, to save the world). **B** is therefore incorrect. A person who, by reason of mental illness, is incapable of understanding the nature and quality of his or her act is insane under the M'Naghten rule discussed above. The phrase *nature and quality of the act,* however, refers to the physical character of the act and to its physical consequences. Since the defendant understood that he was pushing the victim down the stairs and that this could result in her death, he did understand the nature and quality of his act. **D** is therefore incorrect.

91. **A**     The Fourth Amendment to the United States Constitution protects against unreasonable search and seizure. Ordinarily, a warrantless search is regarded as unreasonable and therefore unlawful under this clause. This constitutional provision applies only to searches conducted by the police or by other *government officials*, however. For this reason, the fact that the administrator was not a government employee — and was not working in conjunction with any government employee — would make the Fourth Amendment protection absolutely inapplicable here.

As to **B**, there is some Supreme Court support for the proposition that a student's consent to an administrative search may sometimes be implied from the special relationship between students and administrators. But that consent would be unlikely to extend to something as intrusive as a body search (which is what occurred here when the administrator reached into the defendant's pocket) on only the weak hearsay evidence that was present here. And, in any event, this explanation is not as good as **A**, which resolves the issue automatically. Therefore, **B** is wrong. Similarly, **C**'s "special concern for the well-being of young people" rationale might support certain types of searches, but it wouldn't support a body search with the much-less-than-probable-cause, hearsay-type evidence here. **D** is incorrect for three reasons: First, an anonymous note does not ordinarily give anyone probable cause to believe its contents, especially where the note is itself based on hearsay; second, probable cause does not justify a warrantless search by a government official; and third, the administrator's search of the defendant did not violate his Fourth Amendment rights even if she did not have probable cause because, as explained in **A**, the defendant was not a government actor.

92. **B**     A person is guilty of a criminal attempt when, with the specific intent to bring about a criminally prohibited result, he or she comes substantially close to bringing about that result. Thus, while certain crimes may be committed without intending the prohibited consequences, criminal attempt always requires the specific intent to bring about the

prohibited result. Although the employee could be convicted of violating the statute if he actually sold ammunition to the teenager, he could not be convicted of attempting to violate the statute unless he knew that the teenager was under the age of 16 and intended to sell her the ammunition.

For obvious practical reasons, there is usually an irrebuttable presumption that all persons know the law. Ignorance of the law, therefore, would not provide the employee with a defense. **A** is therefore incorrect. The fact that the owner is vicariously liable under the statute would not furnish the employee with a defense since the statute imposes liability on both employee and employer. **C** is incorrect for this reason, and because the statute imposes vicarious liability on the employer only if the employee actually makes a sale, which the employee did not do. **D** is incorrect because the statute does not make knowledge or experience an element of guilt.

93.  **B**     At common law, murder is the unlawful killing of a human being with malice aforethought. One state of mind that constitutes malice aforethought is the intent to kill a human being. Since knowledge of the victim's identity is not an essential element of murder, the fact that the defendant was mistaken about the identity of the person at whom he was shooting does not prevent him from having the necessary state of mind (*i.e.*, intent to kill). For this reason, the defendant may be convicted even without application of the doctrine of transferred intent.

A is therefore incorrect. **C** is incorrect because the defendant unlawfully killed the victim with the intent to kill a human being and is therefore guilty of murder. Although a wanton disregard for human life may constitute malice aforethought, mere negligence does not. Since the creation of an unreasonable risk is merely negligent, this fact is not sufficient to justify a finding that the defendant had malice aforethought, which is necessary to a conviction for murder. **D** is therefore incorrect.

94.  **C**     The Fifth Amendment to the United States Constitution provides, in part, that "no person shall . . . be subject for the same offense to be twice put in jeopardy of life or limb." This prevents a defendant from being charged twice with the same crime. The charge against the defendant in the state court involves the violation of a statute that is different from the one that she was convicted of violating in the federal court, however. The state prosecution is thus not for the same offense. For this reason, the double jeopardy clause does not require its dismissal even though the same evidence will be used in both prosecutions.

A is therefore incorrect. A criminal conspiracy consists of an agreement between two or more persons to commit a crime and is complete when the agreement is made. It is a crime separate from the substantive crime that the conspirators agreed to commit and does not merge with that substantive crime. **B** is incorrect for this reason, and because prosecutions for violating state and federal statutes are not for the same offense, even though based on a single act by the defendant. **D** contains an incorrect statement since violations of the statutes of different sovereigns constitute different offenses; therefore, separate prosecutions are not barred by the double jeopardy clause.

95.   **D**   Criminal battery consists of the intentional, reckless, or criminally negligent application of force to the body of another. Since it is thus a general intent crime, it may be committed without the intent to make contact with the victim. While voluntary intoxication is no defense to a general intent crime, involuntary intoxication ordinarily is. A person has become involuntarily intoxicated when his or her intoxication was the result of an unpredictable and grossly excessive reaction to an intoxicating substance. Thus, if the defendant had never before been overcome by the alcohol in one drink, it may be that his intoxication was involuntary and that it will provide him with a defense to the charge of criminal battery. It is not certain that this defense would be successful, since a court might find that although the response was unpredictable, it was not grossly excessive. The fact set forth in **D**, however, is the only one listed that might possibly provide the defendant with an effective defense.

A person may become "voluntarily" intoxicated even without the intent to become drunk so long as he or she is aware that the substance that he or she is taking has an intoxicating potential. Since the defendant was aware that the drink had some alcohol in it, his intoxication may be called voluntary even if he did not intend to become drunk. **A** is therefore incorrect. If the defendant's conduct in drinking the drink was reckless or criminally negligent, he could have the necessary *mens rea* to be guilty of battery (*i.e.*, general intent), even though he did not specifically know what risk he was creating (*i.e.*, that he would fall off the bar stool). **B** is therefore incorrect. **C** is incorrect because battery is a general intent crime, and therefore it does not require the intent to make contact with another human being.

96.   **A**   A person is privileged by self-defense to use reasonable force to protect himself or herself against what reasonably appears to be an imminent threat of bodily harm. In this connection, reasonable force is the force that would appear necessary to the reasonable person. Even deadly force is reasonable if the person using it reasonably believes that he or she is being threatened with deadly force. Thus, since the defendant reasonably believed that his life was in danger, the force that he used in self-defense was probably reasonable, making the defendant not guilty of attempted murder.

Although deadly force is not ordinarily considered reasonable in defense of mere property, **B** is incorrect because the defendant's shot was probably fired in response to a threat against his person and may have been justified by self-defense. Although the intent to kill or inflict serious injury can be inferred from the fact that the defendant fired at the officer, **C** is incorrect because, if reasonable, his conduct was privileged by self-defense. Since the defendant had no way of knowing that the person threatening him was a police officer, the officer's status as such can have no bearing on the reasonableness of the defendant's actions. **D** is therefore incorrect.

97.   **C**   One who intentionally aids, abets, or facilitates the commission of a crime is criminally responsible for the crime as an accomplice. In addition, an accomplice is criminally responsible for all the foreseeable consequences of the crime that he or she facilitated. Since the use of the defendant's apartment to escape detection was part of the bank robber's plan in preparing for the robbery, the defendant's agreement to permit the bank robber to use it

facilitated the robbery, making the defendant an accomplice to it. As such, the defendant may be guilty of felony murder in the death that resulted from the robbery, but only if it was foreseeable that such a death would occur.

One who becomes an accessory after a crime has been committed (*i.e.*, accessory after the fact) by knowingly harboring the person who committed it is not criminally responsible for prior acts committed by the person harbored. A person who facilitates the commission of a crime by agreeing in advance that he or she will harbor the perpetrator after the crime is committed is guilty as an accomplice (*i.e.*, accessory before the fact), however. As such, he or she is criminally responsible for all foreseeable consequences of the crime to which he or she was an accomplice. **A** is therefore incorrect. Since an accomplice is criminally responsible for those consequences that were foreseeable, the fact that the defendant did not actually know that the bank robber would use a gun does not protect him from liability if the bank robber's use of a gun was foreseeable. **B** is therefore incorrect. A conspirator is criminally responsible for all crimes committed by co-conspirators in furtherance of the subject of the conspiracy. **D** is incorrect, however, because an accessory is criminally responsible only for consequences that were foreseeable.

98.  **C**      The United States Constitution protects criminal defendants against unreasonable search and seizure. To give this protection meaning, the courts exclude evidence obtained as the result of an unreasonable search. Not every observation or inspection by police officers is properly classified as a search, however. In general, it is understood that a search occurs only when the police inspect a place in which the defendant has a reasonable expectation of privacy. If the field was such a place, the overflight and subsequent visit by police constituted searches, and, since they were performed without a warrant, the evidence obtained as a result of those searches should be excluded. On the other hand, if the field was not a place in which the defendant had a reasonable expectation of privacy, the overflight and visit were not searches and the evidence should not be excluded.

**A** is incorrect because if the defendant had no reasonable expectation of privacy, the use of special equipment to photograph what the police observed would not be a search. The United States Constitution provides that a warrant may be issued only upon a showing of probable cause. For this reason, a warrant obtained solely on the basis of information received from an informant may be invalid unless the reliability of the informant can be properly established. **B** is incorrect, however, because the warrant in this case might have been issued on the basis of the police officers' observations. The constitutional protection against unreasonable search and seizure prevents the use of evidence obtained directly or indirectly as a result of an improper search (*i.e.*, "fruit of the poisonous tree"). Thus, if the warrant was issued as the result of observations that the officers made in violation of the defendant's constitutional rights, the evidence will be excluded even though it was discovered after the warrant was issued. **D** is therefore incorrect.

99.  **D**      A person is guilty of a criminal attempt when, with the specific intent to bring about a result that is criminally prohibited, he or she comes substantially close to accomplishing that result. Since the defendant believed that the time was five minutes past eleven, and since it would have been lawful to sell liquor at that time, he did not have the specific

intent to bring about a result that was criminally prohibited. For this reason, he could not be guilty of attempting to violate the statute.

**A** and **B** are therefore incorrect. Attempt always requires specific intent, even where the substantive crime does not. Thus, even if the statute did not require specific intent, the defendant could not be guilty of *attempting* to violate it without specifically intending to sell liquor after midnight. **C** is therefore incorrect.

100. **A** At common law, larceny is defined as a trespassory taking and carrying off of personal property known to be another's with the intent to permanently deprive the owner thereof. A person who is reclaiming his or her own property is not committing larceny since he or she is not carrying off the property of another. Thus, the defendant's taking of $50 to pay himself back for the money that the victim owed him was not a larceny. Except in the case of fungible goods, however, this rule does not protect a defendant who takes something that is not his or her own, even though it is equivalent in value to the property that he or she seeks to reclaim. Thus, the defendant's taking of $50 cash to pay himself for the watch that the victim refused to return is a larceny.

Since the statute provides that a larceny of $50 or less is a misdemeanor, **A** is correct, and **B**, **C**, and **D** are incorrect.

101. **A** A person has to be the "cause-in-fact" of a death in order to be convicted for it. The mistress is not a "but-for" cause-in-fact of the wife's death since the wife would have died anyway from the poison. However, a person can meet the cause-in-fact requirement if he or she is a "substantial factor" in causing the death. Here, the mistress's actions significantly sped up the death, so she was a substantial factor in causing the death. Consequently, she would fulfill the cause-in-fact requirement and could be found guilty of the murder. Therefore, **C** and **D** are incorrect. **B** is irrelevant because the fact the mistress was in the house unlawfully does not change the analysis.

102. **C** A criminal conspiracy is an agreement to commit a crime and is complete when the agreement is made. Since the defendant agreed to commit a robbery with the two other men, he is guilty of conspiracy. A person is guilty of a criminal attempt when, with the specific intent to bring about a result that is criminally prohibited, he comes substantially close to bringing about that result. Since the two other men intended to rob the bank and came substantially close to doing so, they are guilty of attempted robbery. Co-conspirators are vicariously liable for crimes committed in furtherance of the agreement. Since the attempted robbery was committed in furtherance of the agreement between the defendant and the two other men, the defendant is criminally liable for the attempt even though he did not physically participate in it.

103. **B** A warrant authorizing the search of persons must clearly identify the particular persons to be searched, although it is not necessary that they be identified by name. This warrant identified them in terms of a fact that could not be determined until they had been searched, however (*i.e.*, "all persons . . . who are found to be in possession of unlawful gambling records"). It therefore lacked the required particularity. If there was probable

cause to arrest a person, a search performed incident to that arrest would be valid. While it is uncertain whether a court would find that there was probable cause to arrest the defendant, **B** is the only answer listed that could possibly be correct.

Probable cause means that facts are known that would lead the reasonable person to believe that a crime was being committed. If the reasonable person would believe that gambling activities were being conducted in the tavern, he or she would certainly be justified in believing that some of the people present were engaging in them. **A** is therefore incorrect. Although a warrant that authorizes the search of premises may also authorize the search of persons present on said premises, **C** is incorrect because this warrant does not identify the people to be searched with sufficient particularity. **D** is incorrect because if corroboration is required, it must exist prior to the issuance of the warrant, not after its execution.

104.   **D**      Some courts say that statutory rape is a strict liability crime, requiring no intent at all; other courts say that it is a general intent crime requiring only the intent to have sexual intercourse. Under either view, this means that a defendant who has sexual intercourse with a female who is too young to consent is guilty if he was aware that he was engaging in intercourse. This is so even though he did not know that she was underage, even though the reasonable person would not have known it, and even though she told him that she was over the age of consent.

A, **B**, and **C** are therefore incorrect.

105.   **D**      Under the state's definition, conspiracy requires an agreement to commit a crime with the specific intent to commit a crime. If the act that the first boy and the girl agreed to commit was not a crime, the first boy lacked the specific intent required. Since neither the common law nor the statute prohibits sexual intercourse between persons of the second boy's and the girl's ages, intercourse between them would not have been a crime, and therefore the agreement between the first boy and the girl was not a conspiracy.

For certain crimes, Wharton's Rule provides that there can be no conviction for conspiracy unless one of the parties to the agreement was not logically essential to the commission of the act that they agreed to commit. **A** is incorrect, however, because although the girl's participation was essential to the seduction of the second boy, the first boy's participation was not. In addition, Wharton's Rule does not apply to statutory rape. Conspiracy is a separate crime and is committed when the conspiratorial agreement is made. Some jurisdictions also require that there have been an overt act in furtherance of the conspiracy. **B** is incorrect, however, because such an act need only be committed by one of the co-conspirators, and the girl's acts would suffice. Since the crime is committed when the agreement is made, the fact that the act that the parties agreed to commit never actually took place is not a defense. **C** is thus incorrect.

106.   **D**      A lesser included offense is an offense the elements of which are completely included among the elements of a more serious crime. Attempting to commit a crime is always a lesser included offense since its elements are always included among the elements of the completed crime. One who commits a crime is guilty of all lesser included offenses.

Since the defendant offered to commit bribery, he is guilty of bribery in the second degree, and since the attempt is included in the completed crime, he is guilty of attempting to commit bribery in the second degree.

A person is guilty of attempting to commit a crime when, with the specific intent to commit that crime, he or she comes substantially close to committing it. **A** is incorrect because bribery in the second degree is not an "attempt" crime. It is statutorily defined as offering to commit bribery and is committed when the offer is made. **B** is incorrect because although the clerk first offered to accept the money, the defendant's subsequent agreement was also an offer to pay the money. In addition, the defendant's trip to the clerk's office the following day was for the purpose of offering to pay the money. **C** is based on a misinterpretation of the law. A lesser included crime is said to "merge" with the more serious one, but this means only that a defendant cannot be convicted of both. There is no reason why he or she cannot be convicted of the lesser one only.

107. **C**  A person is guilty of a criminal attempt when, with the specific intent to bring about a prohibited result, he or she comes substantially close to doing so. Thus, all attempts are "specific intent" crimes. This means that although murder does not require a specific intent to cause the death of a person, attempted murder does. Since the defendant did not intend to cause the death of a human being, she lacks the intent required to make her guilty of attempted murder.

**A** is therefore incorrect. The death of the friend does not satisfy the specific intent requirement unless the defendant intended to bring it about. For this reason, **B** is also incorrect. Although the attempt to murder a person may merge with the actual murder of the person, **D** is incorrect because the coworker did not die and so could not have been murdered.

108. **A**  A criminal suspect may not be interrogated in the absence of his or her attorney once formal charges have been brought. It has been held that placing a secret police agent to elicit incriminating statements violates this rule, even though the officer asks no questions.

**B** is incorrect because "entrapment" refers only to conduct by a police officer that induced the defendant to commit a crime that he or she was not otherwise inclined to commit. **C** is incorrect because a warrant does not justify a police interrogation in violation of the above rule. **D** is incorrect because even a voluntary statement violates the above rule if made as a result of a police interrogation conducted without the presence or consent of the defendant's attorney.

109. **A**  Murder is the unjustified killing of a human being with malice aforethought. Malice aforethought includes the intent to kill, which means the desire or knowledge that the defendant's act will bring about the death of another person. Since the other boy threw away the victim's medicine with the desire that doing so would bring about the death of the victim, and since the victim died as a result, the victim was murdered. A criminal conspiracy is an agreement to commit a crime. Since the two boys agreed to kill the victim, they were involved in a criminal conspiracy. Co-conspirators are vicariously liable for any crimes committed in furtherance of the conspiracy. Since the murder of the

victim was committed by the other boy in furtherance of his agreement with the boy who ran away, the boy who ran away is vicariously liable for it. **A** is therefore correct.

Since the boy who ran away did no physical act that enabled the other boy to bring about the victim's death, he did not aid or abet him in bringing it about. **B** is therefore incorrect. **C** is incorrect because the principle of vicarious liability as explained above makes it unnecessary for the boy who ran away to physically participate in the commission of the crime with which he is charged. One who effectively withdraws from a conspiracy before its goal is accomplished may avoid vicarious guilt for the substantive crime, although not for the crime of conspiracy. For a withdrawal to be effective, however, the withdrawing conspirator must at least do something that places his or her co-conspirator on notice of his or her withdrawal. Since the boy who ran away did not do so, he has not effectively withdrawn from the conspiracy, and **D** is incorrect.

110. **A**    The felony-murder rule provides that the intent to commit a felony is malice aforethought, and that a death that results from the perpetration of a felony is therefore murder. For this purpose, the perpetration of a felony continues during the defendant's attempt to escape to a place of seeming safety. The pedestrian's death thus occurred during the perpetration of a robbery, and the defendant could be convicted of murder even if he was driving carefully at the time it occurred.

       **B**, **C**, and **D** are therefore incorrect.

111. **D**    In the absence of special circumstances, no person is under a legal duty to render aid to another. Since a failure to act can lead to criminal responsibility only in the face of a duty to act, the adult's failure to rescue the girl was not a crime.

       This is true even though she could have saved the girl without risk to herself, even though she knew that there was no one else who could rescue the child, and even if she was related to the girl. **A, B,** and **C** are therefore incorrect.

112. **A**    Since the statute requires intent, and since the defendant did not intend the man's death, she is not guilty of first degree murder under the statute.

       **B** is incorrect because once the man was asleep (and certainly once he was tied to the bed), the defendant was no longer in danger and therefore not privileged to use force in self-defense. Although some first degree murder statutes include deaths resulting from the commission of dangerous felonies, this particular statute does not. **C** is therefore incorrect. Many first degree murder statutes include death resulting from torture, but this one does not. **D** is therefore incorrect.

113. **B**    At common law, larceny is defined as intentionally taking and carrying off the personal property of another with the intent to permanently deprive the owner of it. Since the defendant planned to return the pen to the professor in a week or two, she lacked the intent to permanently deprive him of it.

**A** is incorrect because if she had the requisite intent at the time she took the pen, the fact that it was later taken from her would not undo the crime that she had already committed. **C** is incorrect because the defendant lacked the requisite intent. There are no facts justifying the inference on which **D** is based, but even if there were, the defendant's taking would not be a larceny unless she intended (*i.e.*, was substantially certain) that the professor would be permanently deprived of the pen.

114. **B**  Robbery is larceny accomplished by physical force or threat. The defendant clearly committed a larceny. Although he acquired possession and carried off the briefcase without the use of force, the issue is whether his subsequent use of force to retain possession was sufficient to make him guilty of robbery. **B** is the only case in which this issue arose.

In **A**, no force was used after acquisition of the purse. In **C** and **D**, although force was used to acquire the stolen property, none was used thereafter.

115. **B**  One who incites and encourages another to commit a crime may be guilty as an accomplice or accessory, especially when he or she derives some direct benefit from the crime. Since the coworker demanded $25 to cover up the cashier's crime while they were standing in front of the open safe and then watched as the cashier reached into the safe and handed it to him, he can be found guilty as an accessory to larceny.

Robbery is larceny committed by force or threat of force. **A** is incorrect because the threat that the coworker made was not of force. Embezzlement is the fraudulent taking of property that is lawfully in the defendant's possession. Since the $25 that the coworker took from the cashier was not lawfully in the coworker's possession to begin with, he did not embezzle it. **C** is therefore incorrect. Crimes characterized by the term *fraud* involve takings that are committed by making misrepresentations that induce the owner to willingly part with possession or title. **D** is incorrect because the owner of the supermarket was not induced to part with the money by reliance on a misrepresentation.

116. **C**  Vicarious liability refers to responsibility that is imposed on one person for a crime committed by another. If the bartender was not guilty of violating the statute, there has been no crime for which the owner can be held vicariously liable. Although it is not certain that this argument will succeed, it is the only one listed that could possibly support the owner's defense.

**A** is incorrect because when vicarious liability is imposed, the fault (or lack of fault) of the person on whom it is imposed is irrelevant. **B** is similarly incorrect because vicarious liability may be imposed for the crime committed by an agent even though the agent violated specific instructions in committing it. **D** is incorrect because a bartender selling drinks to a bar customer is acting in the scope of employment, since his or her conduct is designed to benefit his or her employer and since he or she is subject to the employer's right of control while doing so.

117. **D**  In nearly all states, the defendant is liable for murder if he or she causes a death while acting with a "depraved heart" or an extreme indifference to the value of human life.

For depraved-heart murder, the risk of death or serious bodily injury has to be so great that the defendant can be said to act with great recklessness. Importantly, negligence or even gross negligence won't suffice. Here, hunting deer in a "densely populated suburban neighborhood" is likely so reckless as to reach the level required for depraved-heart murder.

**A**, **B**, and **C** are therefore incorrect.

118. **C**    Kidnapping is the intentional asportation and confinement of a person against the person's will by means of force or threat and without lawful authority. Although it is obvious that the defendant intentionally confined the bank manager against his will by means of force and threat and without lawful authority, there is some question as to whether there was an asportation. Ordinarily, any moving of the victim satisfies the requirement of asportation. Many jurisdictions now hold, however, that there is no asportation if the movement of the victim was incidental to and a necessary part of the commission of some other substantive crime. Although it is not certain that a court would accept that view, the argument in **C** is the only one listed that could possibly support the defendant's defense.

In some jurisdictions, a ransom demand makes the defendant guilty of a more serious degree of the crime, but no jurisdiction requires a ransom demand as an essential element of kidnapping. **A** is therefore incorrect. **B** is incorrect because, once committed, a crime cannot be uncommitted. **D** is incorrect because the crime of kidnapping can be committed against an adult as well as a child.

119. **C**    The search of the other house was unlawful because the officers did not have a warrant and no exception to the warrant requirement applied.

Under the exigent circumstances exception to the warrant requirement, police may enter a home without a search warrant to prevent harm to persons, prevent the imminent destruction of evidence, or while in pursuit of a suspect. Here, although the ex-husband warned the officers that the woman would be coming home soon and could destroy the evidence, there was no indication that the officers did not have time to secure a warrant before the woman came home or that it was likely the evidence was in imminent danger of being destroyed. **A** is therefore incorrect. Under the consent exception, if officers receive valid consent to search a home, they do not need a search warrant. Here, the ex-husband didn't actually tell the officers they had permission to search the other house. In addition, even if he had given permission, there was no indication that the ex-husband had any authority to consent to a search of his ex-wife's house. **B** is therefore incorrect. "Fruit of the poisonous tree" refers to the doctrine that illegally obtained evidence cannot be used for the purpose of obtaining other evidence. Here, the officers had a warrant for the woman's original home. Consequently, there is no issue with the evidence obtained during the first search, and the "fruit of the poisonous tree" doctrine would not apply. **D** is therefore incorrect.

120. **C**    Unless a defendant was ready, willing, and able to give affirmative assistance in the commission of the crime, his or her presence and silent acquiescence are not sufficient to result in criminal liability.

Ordinarily, one is not under any obligation to attempt to prevent a crime from being committed. **A** is therefore incorrect. **B** is incorrect because, even with criminal intent, mere presence at the scene of a crime is not sufficient to satisfy the requirement of *actus reus*. The defendant was not an accessory at all since her presence was not sufficient participation, but in any event, she could not have been an accessory *after* the fact since the crime was committed after her involvement began. **D** is therefore incorrect.

121. **C**   Since one purpose of the exclusionary rule is to deter police officers from violating the Fourth Amendment, information obtained as a result of an unlawful search may not be used to justify the issuance of a warrant authorizing further search.

Such a warrant is invalid, and anything found pursuant to it is excluded as one of the fruits of the original unlawful search. **A** is therefore incorrect. **B** is incorrect for the same reason, even though it seems sound. Although possession of stolen items is not in itself sufficient to permit the conclusion that the possessor was the thief, it is certainly acceptable as circumstantial evidence to be considered by a jury. **D** is therefore incorrect.

122. **D**   Robbery is a larceny that is committed by force or threat to use force against the lawful possessor of the property taken or any other person. If the collector gave the defendant $1,000 because he knowingly threatened to injure the daughter if she did not, his taking of the money was robbery. Although he did not know that the daughter was in the car when he first made the threat, it could be found that the threat was continued by his conduct. Thus, if he knew that the daughter was in the car when he received the money from the collector, it might be concluded that he obtained the money by a threat to burn the daughter, not just the car.

**A** is incorrect for two reasons: First, he did not take the car by force, and second, he is charged with robbery of the cash, not of the car. **B** would not make him guilty of robbery unless he knew that the daughter was in the car when he threatened to burn it. **C** is incorrect since in most jurisdictions, robbery requires that the threat be directed against a person.

123. **C**   Statements obtained from a suspect in violation of his or her constitutional rights (and, some authorities suggest, the fruits of such statements) cannot be used against him or her. Only the person from whom the statement was obtained, however, has standing to assert the constitutional violation. Since the interrogation of the man did not violate the defendant's rights, the defendant lacks the necessary standing to assert its unconstitutionality.

**A** and **B** are incorrect because there are no facts indicating that the defendant's complicity would have been discovered without the man's statement. Since the interrogation of the man did not violate the constitutional rights of the defendant, it does not matter whether the defendant was in custody at the time it took place. **D** is therefore incorrect.

124. **D**   A defendant may be liable for involuntary manslaughter if his or her conduct results in the accidental death of another person. Involuntary manslaughter is particularly applicable to cases where the defendant causes a drunk-driving accident that kills someone. As

long as the intoxication was a significant contributing factor to the accident, the defendant is almost certainly guilty of involuntary manslaughter. Importantly, most states require only a mental state of gross negligence, and driving while drunk constitutes recklessness (a higher mental state than gross negligence). Additionally, in a jurisdiction applying the misdemeanor-manslaughter rule, drunk driving will at least be a misdemeanor. Here, since defendant's drunk driving constituted recklessness and his intoxication proximately caused the crime by leading to his mistaken belief that he was being chased, the defendant is guilty of involuntary manslaughter. The fact that the victim may have been contributorily negligent is not a defense to involuntary manslaughter. **A** is therefore incorrect. **B** is incorrect because involuntary manslaughter does not require the defendant to intend to cause the death of the victim. **C** is incorrect because his belief that he was being chased would not provide a defense for the defendant.

125. **C**    Felony murder is a foreseeable killing that occurs during the course of a felony. In the majority of states, a person cannot be found guilty of felony murder for the death of a co-felon if that co-felon is killed by the police. Here, since the defendant's friend was shot by a police officer, it is unlikely he would be found guilty of felony murder. Therefore, **A** and **B** are incorrect.

**D** is incorrect because a death that occurs while fleeing the scene still meets the requirements of felony murder, whether or not the felony itself is technically completed.

126. **A**    Criminal battery consists of the intentional, reckless, or criminally negligent application of force to the body of another. The defendant's act of shooting through the ceiling into an apartment in which she knew there were people probably was at least criminally negligent, and so it probably constituted a battery.

A person is guilty of attempting to commit a crime when, with the specific intent to bring about a criminally proscribed result, he or she comes substantially close to accomplishing that result. Since involuntary manslaughter is an unintended homicide, no person can have the specific intent to commit it. Thus, there can be no attempt to commit it, and **B** is therefore incorrect. Attempted murder and attempted voluntary manslaughter both require an intent to kill. Since the defendant did not intend to strike anyone with the bullet, **C** and **D** are incorrect.

127. **D**    A person is privileged to use reasonable force to protect himself or herself from what he or she reasonably believes to be a threat of imminent bodily harm. Since the friend fired a pistol at the defendant and was (or appeared to be) capable of firing it again, it was reasonable for the defendant to believe herself threatened with imminent bodily harm and was probably reasonable for her to respond with deadly force.

If the friend's belief that the defendant was about to shoot her was a reasonable one, the friend's use of force may have been privileged. **A** is incorrect, however, because although an aggressor has no right of self-defense against a reasonable response to his or her initial aggression, the defendant committed no act of aggression until after the friend fired at her. Self-defense may privilege the use of deadly force in response to what is reasonably perceived as deadly force. Even though the force used by the friend had not yet caused death or serious injury, it was capable of doing so, and can therefore be regarded as deadly force. **B** is therefore incorrect. **C** is incorrect because even a premeditated killing may be privileged by self-defense.

128.  **D**  At common law, arson was defined as the intentional burning of another's dwelling. Under the statute given, the definition includes buildings other than dwellings as well. Since the men desired to burn down the factory, they had the necessary intent. Since they succeeded in doing so, they are guilty of arson. Conspiracy consists of an agreement to commit a crime. Since the men agreed to commit arson, they are guilty of conspiracy. Conspiracy does not merge with the substantive crime and may be the basis of separate prosecution and conviction. **D** is therefore correct.

129.  **C**  Robbery is a larceny where the property is taken from the person or presence of the owner, and the taking is accomplished by force or threat. Importantly, a larceny is the trespassory taking and carrying away of the personal property of another with intent to steal. Consequently, if the defendant is reclaiming his or her own property, then the defendant is not committing robbery. This is true even if the defendant honestly but unreasonably believes that what he or she is taking is his or her own property. Here, the defendant has not committed larceny because he is taking back "his" own property, not property of another.

   **A**, **B**, and **D** are therefore incorrect.

130.  **C**  Larceny is a trespassory taking and carrying off of personal property known to be another's with the intent to permanently deprive the owner. Since the defendant did not physically move the couch, she may successfully argue that because there was no asportation (*i.e.*, carrying off), there was no larceny.

   It is sometimes argued that one who enters through an unlocked door committed no breaking and, therefore, is not guilty of burglary. **A** is incorrect, however, because breaking is not an element of larceny. If a defendant carried off personal property that actually was his or her own, he or she could not be guilty of larceny because he or she did not take the property of another. If he or she mistakenly believed that it was his or her own, he or she still would not be guilty of larceny because he or she did not carry off property known to be another's. The couch was not the defendant's, however, and she knew that it was not hers. The fact that it was equal in value to her stereo would not, therefore, justify her taking or carrying it off. **B** is therefore incorrect. A person who takes and carries off personal property known to be another's with the intent to permanently deprive is guilty of larceny without regard to whether or not he or she intended to benefit by doing so. **D** is therefore incorrect.

131.  **A**  Some cases have held that the imposition of a prison term on the basis of vicarious liability for a strict-liability crime committed by a defendant's employee is a violation of due process. It is generally understood, however, that the imposition of a fine on this basis is constitutionally valid. Since this statute makes an employer vicariously liable for

the payment of a fine if an employee sells ammunition to a minor, and since the owner's employee sold ammunition to a minor, the owner may be convicted.

**B** and **C** are incorrect because of the specific language of the given statute: **B** because the statute imposes strict liability and does not make negligence or unreasonable behavior a basis of guilt, and **C** because the statute does not make the employer's presence an element of guilt. **D** is incorrect because it is over-inclusive: There are many situations in which criminal law may validly impose vicarious liability for the crime of another (*e.g.*, co-conspirators are vicariously liable for each other's crimes committed in furtherance of the conspiracy).

132.  **D**    One of the elements of every crime is the actus reus, or the requirement that the defendant's conduct be a voluntary act. If a defendant acts reflexively or while in a state of unconsciousness, his or her actions do not fulfill the actus reus requirement and he or she will not be held criminally liable. Here, the toxic gas caused the woman to lose voluntary control of her arms or legs, and she had no control over them when she punched the man. Consequently, she cannot be held criminally liable for his death.

Therefore, **A**, **B**, and **C** are incorrect.

133.  **D**    A conspiracy is an agreement by two or more persons to commit a crime. Ordinarily, one who agrees to furnish services to another that the other will use in committing a crime is not guilty of conspiracy merely because he or she knows the purpose to which the services will be put. Where, however, the supplier has a stake in the criminal enterprise, his or her agreement to furnish services may constitute a conspiracy to commit the crime. Since the defendant knew that the bank robber would be using his apartment as a hideout following the robbery, and since the bank robber's promise to compensate the defendant by paying him a percentage of the loot gave the defendant a stake in the criminal enterprise, the defendant may be guilty of conspiracy.

**A** is therefore incorrect. **B** is incorrect for two reasons: First, the defendant's agreement probably was per se unlawful, since he knew that the bank robber would be hiding in his apartment to escape detection (*i.e.*, that he would be harboring a felon), and second, the defendant had a personal stake in the bank robber's crime. The crime of conspiracy to commit robbery is complete when the defendant agrees with another to commit the robbery, and is a separate crime from the robbery itself. Thus, the fact that a defendant is guilty of robbery is not relevant to the issue of whether he or she conspired (*i.e.*, agreed) to commit it. For this reason, **C** is incorrect.

134.  **A**    Once a criminal defendant has asserted his or her right to have an attorney present, further interrogation in the absence of the attorney makes any incriminating statements by the defendant inadmissible. Since the defendant was questioned after asserting his right to counsel, the statement that he made in response to that questioning should be excluded.

**B** and **C** are therefore incorrect. Even after asserting his or her right to counsel, a defendant may waive that right by making incriminating statements during a discussion that the defendant initiates. Since the defendant's statement was made in response to a question by the police officer, however, it does not constitute a waiver of his rights and is therefore inadmissible. **D** is therefore incorrect.

135. **D**    Conspiracy occurs when two or more people with the specific intent to commit a crime agree to commit it. Here, since the doctor did not think the wife would die, he did not really agree to commit murder. Consequently, there was no conspiracy.

    **A** is incorrect because even if the man believed the pills were deadly poison, he'd still have to reach an agreement to commit a crime with someone else in order to be prosecuted for conspiracy. Here, no one actually agreed to help him kill his wife. **B** and **C** are incorrect because the crime of conspiracy is complete when the unlawful agreement is made. The success or failure of the substantive crime the parties agree to do is irrelevant.

136. **A**    The Fifth Amendment protects a defendant from being coerced into answering police questions. Police must give *Miranda* warnings to a person in custody before questioning him or her. If the person in custody then asserts his or her right to have an attorney present during questioning, all interrogation must stop until the attorney arrives or the person gives a valid waiver. Here, while the woman received her *Miranda* warnings, her attorney was not present and she had not waived her rights before officers started questioning her about the robbery. Because police interrogation is coercive, a confession given under the circumstances here would not be admissible. Therefore **D** is incorrect.

    **B** is incorrect because officers are only required to advise a person in custody of his or her rights. Officers are not required to tell the person about their suspicions. **C** is incorrect because the issue here is that the officers continued to question her after giving her *Miranda* warnings.

137. **A**    Murder is the unlawful killing of a human being with malice aforethought. Malice aforethought may consist of intent to cause great bodily harm. A defendant has intent to cause great bodily harm when he or she desires or knows that his or her act will result in serious injury. Here, by hitting the victim as hard as he could in the head with a metal bat, the defendant at least knew his act was going to result in serious injury. Voluntary manslaughter is the unlawful killing of a human being with the intent to cause death or great bodily harm, but under circumstances where the defendant is suffering from great emotional distress or mistaken justification. **B** is incorrect because having a strike called on a person during a baseball game does not result in great emotional distress or mistaken justification sufficient to reduce murder to voluntary manslaughter. Involuntary manslaughter occurs when the defendant's behavior is grossly negligent and results in the accidental death of another person. **C** is incorrect because the defendant intended to hit the victim with the bat. Battery is where the defendant intentionally or recklessly causes either bodily injury or offensive touching. **D** is incorrect because the defendant's actions are sufficient to result in the defendant being found guilty of murder, a much more serious crime.

138. **A**    Accomplice liability means that one who aids, abets, encourages, or assists another to perform a crime will himself or herself be liable for that crime. Importantly, if a defendant's

words encourage or approve of the crime, and thereby assist commission of the crime, then the speaker is liable even if he or she did not take any physical acts. The defendant is an accomplice to the killing of the victim and is consequently guilty of murder. This is because the defendant encouraged the man in the man's commission of the murder. The fact that the defendant's involvement consisted of words alone doesn't lessen his liability. **B** and **C** are therefore incorrect. **D** is incorrect because the defendant's actions encouraged the man to kill the victim, whether or not the defendant truly intended that the man kill the victim.

139.  **C**     Under the common law, a criminal conspiracy is an agreement between two or more persons to commit a crime. Without such an agreement, there can be no conspiracy. Since neither officer actually intended to commit a crime, the defendant never made such an agreement with either of them, even though he believed he did. For this reason, he cannot be guilty of conspiracy.

**A**, **B**, and **D** are therefore incorrect.

140.  **A**     The impossibility defense can be raised where the defendant has done everything in his or her power to accomplish a crime, but, due to other circumstances, no substantive crime has been committed. A factual impossibility arises out of a defendant's mistake of fact. The factual impossibility defense is always unsuccessful today. Here, the fact that the business rival was already dead before the hitman shot him made it factually impossible to murder him, but it does not supply the hitman with a defense against attempted murder. Under the principles of accomplice liability, since the defendant aided and encouraged the hitman to kill the business rival by hiring him, the defendant is liable for any crime the hitman committed at his urging as long as he had the requisite intent for that crime. Here, the defendant had the requisite intent for attempted murder because he wanted the business rival killed. Since the hitman cannot defend himself by claiming factual impossibility, the defendant cannot either. **D** is therefore incorrect. **B** is incorrect because accomplice liability does not require the defendant to be physically present at the scene of the crime. **C** is incorrect because withdrawal is only effective when the defendant has in some sense undone the effects of his or her assistance and encouragement. Here, the hitman didn't receive the message until after the crime was committed.

# QUESTIONS
# EVIDENCE

# EVIDENCE
# TABLE OF CONTENTS

**Numbers refer to Question Numbers**

# EVIDENCE QUESTIONS

1. The defendant operated a chain of fast food restaurants that specialized in fried fish. The defendant entered into a valid written contract with the plaintiff for the purchase of "6,000 pounds of frozen fish filets of frying quality," to be delivered by the plaintiff over a period of six months. One week after the plaintiff made its first delivery pursuant to the contract, however, the defendant notified the plaintiff that the product delivered was unacceptable because the filets delivered weighed only eight ounces each, and that they were cut from Grade B fish. The plaintiff subsequently brought an action against the defendant for breach of contract. At the trial of that action, the plaintiff offered the testimony of a chef. The chef testified that he was the head chef at a leading hotel, that he was an expert on the preparation of fried fish in fast food restaurants, and that he had been employed as a chef in fine restaurants for more than 30 years. He testified further that in that time, he had purchased large quantities of fish on numerous occasions and was familiar with the terminology used in the wholesale fish industry. The chef stated that when the phrase "fish filets of frying quality" is used in the wholesale fish business, it means boneless pieces from six to nine ounces in weight and cut from Grade A or B fish. For the purposes of the trial, the parties specifically agreed to be bound by the terminology of the wholesale fish industry. Upon proper objection by the defendant's attorney, the chef's testimony as to the meaning of the phrase should be

   (A) admitted as evidence of trade terminology.

   (B) admitted, because the chef is an expert on the preparation of fried fish in fast food restaurants.

   (C) admitted, because the parties specifically agreed to be bound by the terminology of the wholesale fish industry.

   (D) excluded, since it is an opinion.

2. While visiting the United States from a Central American republic, the plaintiff purchased a sweater at a department store and paid for it at the appropriate cash register. In ringing up the sale, however, the store employee neglected to remove a security tag that was still affixed to the sweater to prevent theft. As a result, the tag caused an electronic security alarm to ring as the plaintiff attempted to exit the store with the purchased merchandise. Security guards immediately accosted her and placed her under citizen's arrest. Eventually, the police were called, and a more thorough investigation was instituted. As a result, it was determined that the plaintiff had paid for the merchandise. Authorities of the department store apologized to the plaintiff and permitted her to leave.

   Subsequently, a magazine erroneously reported that the plaintiff had been arrested, charged with shoplifting at the department store, and taken into police custody. Because the plaintiff was a candidate for political office in the Central American republic, newspapers in that country reprinted the magazine article. The plaintiff lost the election, and she instituted an action against the magazine for damages resulting from defamation. At the trial of the plaintiff's action, the magazine called as a witness a man who resided in the republic, who testified that he was familiar with the plaintiff's reputation in that country. He stated that, in the republic, the plaintiff was generally known as a thieving and corrupt politician. If the plaintiff's attorney moves to strike that testimony, the motion should be

(A) granted, since reputation evidence is not admissible for the purpose of establishing a party's conduct at any particular time.

(B) granted, since evidence of a party's character is admissible only in criminal cases.

(C) denied, since evidence of the plaintiff's reputation is relevant to her claim for damage resulting from defamation.

(D) denied, since the evidence is relevant to the truth or falsity of the statements made in the magazine article.

3. At the trial of an action by the plaintiff against the defendant for breach of contract, the plaintiff alleged that the defendant failed to deliver 3,000 filters as agreed. The plaintiff asserted further that, as a result, it was required to purchase filters on the open market at a price substantially higher than that agreed upon in its contract with the defendant. As part of its case, the plaintiff offered the testimony of the witness, who stated that she was the plaintiff's purchasing agent. She said that when the defendant breached its contract with the plaintiff, she had been assigned to purchase filters elsewhere. In answer to a question, she said, "I recall buying 3,000 filters at a price of $23 per hundred." The plaintiff's attorney then showed her a paper that the witness identified as a photocopy that she personally had made of the plaintiff's file on that purchase, explaining that the original was kept in the plaintiff's home office, which was located in another state. Upon objection by the defendant's attorney, which of the following should the court admit into evidence?

(A) The witness's testimony as to her recollection of the purchase price.

(B) The copy that the witness authenticated.

(C) The witness's testimony as to her recollection of the purchase price, and the copy that the witness authenticated.

(D) Neither the witness's testimony as to her recollection, nor the authenticated copy.

4. A city newspaper printed an article claiming that a local university president was a "horrible racist" who "looked down on minority groups and would prefer not to have any at the university." The university president filed suit for defamation. During the university president's presentation of the case, he sought to put the mayor on the stand. The mayor was prepared to testify that when he asked the university president for a personal donation to help city relief services during a recent flood, the university president wrote a large check from his own account. Since several substantially minority neighborhoods were flooded along with other neighborhoods in the city, the check helped many minority citizens. The newspaper's lawyer objected.

How should the court rule regarding the mayor's testimony?

(A) Admissible, because the university president's character is at issue.

(B) Admissible, because it shows the university president supports minorities.

(C) Inadmissible, because a specific incident is not enough to establish one's character.

(D) Inadmissible, because it is not probative of any material issue in the case.

5. At the trial of a personal injury action, the plaintiff claimed that he had sustained a shattered elbow when he was knocked from his bicycle by the defendant's car. A doctor testified for the plaintiff, stating that she examined him for the first time on the morning of the trial and that her examination was made specifically in preparation for her testimony.

The doctor stated that during the course of the examination, the plaintiff said, "My arm hurts so much, I don't see how I'll ever be able to go back to work." Which of the following would be the defendant's strongest argument in support of a motion to strike the testimony?

(A) The plaintiff's statement was made in contemplation of litigation.

(B) The doctor was not examining the plaintiff for the purpose of treatment.

(C) The plaintiff's statement was self-serving.

(D) Evidence of the plaintiff's statement is more prejudicial than probative.

6. A witness saw the fatal shooting of the victim. The witness told a grand jury investigating the shooting that, "The defendant was the shooter! I was standing 10 feet away when I saw the defendant murder the victim!" The defendant was arrested and charged with murder. At trial, the witness could not be found. Eventually, the police discovered that the witness had moved out of the country and left no forwarding address. Since the witness is unavailable, the prosecution attempts to offer his grand-jury statement into evidence. The trial court is convinced that the grand-jury testimony has circumstantial guarantees of trustworthiness. Upon objection by the defendant, the witness's statement should be

(A) admitted, because the witness is not available to testify at trial.

(B) admitted, because the use of the evidence is consistent with the general interests of justice.

(C) admitted, because the trial court is convinced the grand-jury testimony has circumstantial guarantees of trustworthiness.

(D) excluded.

7. The plaintiff sued an amusement park after the plaintiff was injured on a rollercoaster. At trial, the plaintiff called a witness who testified that she was at the amusement park and, after the plaintiff was injured, the man employed by the amusement park to run the rollercoaster came over and said, "I'm sorry! I didn't secure your seatbelt right!" The amusement park objected.

The court should

(A) overrule the objection, because the statement is attributable to the amusement park.

(B) overrule the objection, because the statement is a declaration against interest.

(C) sustain the objection, because the statement is inadmissible against the amusement park.

(D) sustain the objection, because the statement is inadmissible hearsay.

8. A woman was the mother of a four-year-old girl. One day, because the woman had an appointment, she left the girl in the care of the defendant. While in the defendant's custody, the girl began to cry. In an attempt to quiet her, the defendant beat her severely, striking her repeatedly across the back and raising a series of welts and bruises. Soon afterwards, the woman returned and took the girl home. As the woman was undressing the girl to prepare her for bed, she noticed the marks on the girl's body and asked, "What happened?" The girl responded by saying that the defendant had spanked her. The defendant was subsequently arrested and charged with child abuse. At the defendant's trial on that charge, the woman was called as a witness by the prosecution on the presentation of its direct case. When the woman attempted to testify to the above conversation between herself and the girl, the defendant's attorney objected on the ground that the girl's statement was hearsay.

The prosecutor's most effective argument in opposition to the objection would be that the statement is admissible as

(A) a present sense impression.

(B) an excited utterance.

(C) a statement of present physical condition.

(D) an identification.

9. At the trial of the defendant for receiving stolen property, the prosecution called a man to the witness stand. The man testified that in a conversation that he had with the defendant in jail shortly after the defendant's arrest, the

defendant admitted that he knew that the car that he had been driving was stolen. Which of the following facts or inferences would best support the defendant's motion to exclude the man's testimony?

(A) At the time of their conversation, the man told the defendant that he was an attorney.

(B) At the time of their conversation, the defendant reasonably believed that the man was employed as an investigator for the defendant's attorney.

(C) The man had offered to recommend an attorney to the defendant and had asked the defendant to tell him the facts of the case.

(D) The man had been charged with a crime, and on the day of the defendant's trial, had negotiated a favorable plea bargain in return for his testimony.

10. The plaintiff was injured when she fell down a flight of steps at a bartending school. She subsequently sued the school for damages, asserting that the accident resulted from the school's negligence in allowing parts of the stairway to become loose. At the trial, a doctor testified that he had examined and treated the plaintiff following the accident. On direct examination, he stated that, in his opinion, the plaintiff had sustained a spinal injury. He also stated that in making the diagnosis, he did not take a spinagram.

On cross-examination, the school's attorney asked the doctor whether he had ever read the work of a noted specialist in spinal injuries. The doctor replied that he had heard of the specialist, but that he had never read any of her work. The school's attorney then opened a book by the specialist and said, "In this book, the specialist says that it is impossible to diagnose spinal injuries without taking a spinagram. How do you justify your diagnosis in view of that statement?" If the plaintiff's attorney objected to the question, the court should

(A) sustain the objection, since the specialist has not testified in the proceeding.

(B) sustain the objection, since no proper foundation has been laid.

(C) overrule the objection, since an expert may be cross-examined regarding the works of other experts in the field.

(D) overrule the objection, since the doctor admitted having heard of the specialist.

11. A witness, testifying on behalf of the prosecution, stated that he saw the defendant shoot the victim three times in the back. During the defendant's case, the defendant's attorney offered two properly authenticated judgments of conviction. One showed that the witness had been convicted two years ago of attempted murder, which was a felony. The other showed that the witness had been convicted one year ago of knowingly making false statements in an application for a business license, which was a misdemeanor. Over objection by the prosecution, the court should admit the judgment(s) of conviction of

(A) attempted murder only.

(B) knowingly making false statements in an application for a business license only.

(C) both crimes.

(D) neither crime.

12. An inspector employed by the State Aeronautics Bureau was assigned to investigate the crash of an airline flight. During the course of his investigation, the inspector questioned an airline mechanic who had worked on the plane just before it took off on its last flight. The mechanic said that while going over the plane, he had discovered some dangerous cracks in its engine parts, but that when he called them to the attention of his supervisor, he was told to forget about them. He stated also that after the crash, he was fired as part of a cover-up. The inspector included a verbatim transcript of the mechanic's statement in the report that he filed as required by

Bureau procedure. Soon thereafter, the inspector and the mechanic both died. In an action brought against the airline under the state's wrongful death statute by the surviving spouse of a passenger who died in the crash, the plaintiff offered the inspector's written report into evidence. Upon objection by the airline, the portion of the report containing the transcript of the mechanic's statement should be

(A) admitted, because the inspector is dead.

(B) admitted, because the mechanic is dead.

(C) admitted, as a vicarious admission by the airline.

(D) excluded, since it is hearsay.

13. The defendant was charged with stealing three valuable figurines from the home of the victim while painting the interior of that home.

At the defendant's trial, the victim testified that he first noticed that the figurines were missing about an hour after the defendant left his home. He stated that he looked the defendant's number up in the telephone book and properly dialed the number listed therein. Over objection by the defendant's attorney, the victim stated that a man answered the phone and said he was the defendant. The victim stated that he then said, "Where are the figurines?" and that the person at the other end of the line said, "I'm sorry. I took them." The objection by the defendant's attorney should be

(A) sustained, because there was no independent evidence establishing that the defendant was the person to whom the victim was speaking.

(B) sustained, since the victim did not actually see the person to whom he was speaking.

(C) sustained, since the statement is hearsay.

(D) overruled.

14. A statute provides that the owner of a motor vehicle is vicariously liable for the negligence of any person driving with said owner's permission. In an action for personal injuries brought by the plaintiff against the defendant, the plaintiff alleges that she was injured as a result of the negligent driving of a woman who was operating the defendant's car with the defendant's permission at the time of the accident. The defendant denies ownership of the vehicle in question. Over the objection of the defendant's attorney, the plaintiff offers into evidence an insurance policy issued by an insurance company. The policy is authenticated by the testimony of an officer of the company, who states that the policy was purchased by and issued to the defendant, and that on the day of the accident, the policy was in force on the vehicle in question. The policy and authenticating testimony should be

(A) admitted, since it tends to establish that the defendant was the owner of the vehicle at the time of the accident.

(B) admitted, since it is relevant to the defendant's ability to pay a judgment rendered against her.

(C) excluded, because policy prohibits the introduction of evidence that a party did or did not have liability insurance on the day of an accident.

(D) excluded, because it has no probative value relative to the issues in the case.

15. Two defendants were charged with committing an armed robbery that occurred on a Saturday. Although they were being tried together, the defendants were represented by different attorneys. Both asserted that they were together at a rock concert in another state on the day of the robbery. At the trial, a witness testified on behalf of the defendants. On direct examination, the first defendant's attorney asked the witness about a conversation he had with the first defendant on the Thursday before the robbery. The witness stated that during that conversation, the first defendant told him that she and the second defendant were planning to leave for the

rock concert together on Friday morning and would not be back in town until Monday. Upon timely objection by the prosecution, the testimony of the witness should be

(A) admitted, only insofar as it refers to the first defendant.

(B) admitted, only insofar as it refers to the second defendant.

(C) admitted, insofar as it refers to both defendants.

(D) excluded as hearsay.

16. The defendant was charged with murdering the victim, a prominent union leader, by throwing him off the roof of an office building. At the defendant's trial, the prosecution offered the testimony of a police officer who arrived at the scene moments after the victim's death.

    The officer testified that as he was getting out of his cruiser, he heard an unidentified person in the crowd shout, "A tall man pushed him off the roof!" The defendant's objection to the statement should be

    (A) overruled, since it does not establish with certainty that the defendant was the person referred to in the declarant's statement.

    (B) overruled, since the person making the statement did so while in a state of excitement resulting from what he had just observed.

    (C) sustained, since the identity of the person making the statement is unknown.

    (D) sustained, because there are likely eyewitnesses available to testify in court.

17. The publisher of a large daily newspaper printed an article by a journalist in its employ. The article accused the plaintiff of misusing church funds. The plaintiff commenced a defamation action against the publisher.

    At the trial of the defamation action, the publisher's attorney called a bartender who worked in a bar near the publisher's office. The bartender stated that on the day after the journalist's article appeared in the newspaper, the journalist told him, "When I wrote that piece on the plaintiff, I believed every word of it." On objection by the plaintiff's attorney, the bartender's testimony should be

    (A) admitted as evidence that the article was published without malice.

    (B) admitted as a declaration of the journalist's state of mind.

    (C) admitted as a self-serving declaration.

    (D) excluded as hearsay.

18. The defendant was an orderly employed by the hospital in which the patient died. The administrator of the patient's estate sued the defendant, seeking the return of a watch that he claimed that the defendant had taken from the patient's hospital room after the patient died. At the trial, the defendant testified that about one week prior to the patient's death, the patient called him into his room and handed him the watch, saying, "You've been kind to me. This is for you." If the administrator objects to the testimony, the court should

    (A) overrule the objection, since the statement is an admission.

    (B) overrule the objection under the applicable Dead Man's Act.

    (C) overrule the objection, since the patient's statement had a direct legal effect on the defendant's right to possess the watch.

    (D) sustain the objection, since the statement is hearsay, not within any exception to the hearsay rule.

19. Following his arrest on New Year's Eve, the defendant was charged with reckless driving and driving while under the influence of intoxicating liquor. The arresting officer testified at the defendant's trial on those charges.

The officer stated that she was a highway patrol officer, that she was familiar with the stretch of state highway on which the defendant was arrested, and that she had extensive experience observing and estimating the speed of moving vehicles. She said that she was in her patrol car observing traffic from behind some bushes when she saw the defendant drive by at what appeared to be an excessive rate of speed. When asked by the prosecuting attorney whether she formed an opinion of the defendant's speed at that time, she replied that she had. When the prosecutor asked her to state that opinion, the defendant's attorney objected. The objection should be

(A) sustained, because the officer did not claim she was an expert on the speed of moving vehicles.

(B) sustained, since no proper foundation was laid.

(C) overruled, since a police officer is regarded as an expert on the speed of moving vehicles.

(D) overruled, since a layperson may express an opinion regarding the speed of moving vehicles.

20. Charged with forcible rape, the defendant relied on a defense of alibi. At the trial, the victim testified that the defendant was the man who accosted her on the street, dragged her into the basement of an apartment building, and forced her to submit to sexual intercourse. During the case, the defendant's attorney offered the testimony of a witness who stated that she was familiar with the victim's reputation in the community and that the victim was thought of as a prostitute. The defendant's attorney also offered into evidence a certified court record indicating that the victim had been convicted of prostitution, a misdemeanor, two months prior to the alleged rape.

Upon proper objection by the prosecution, which of the following should the court admit?

(A) The witness's testimony only.

(B) The court record only.

(C) The witness's testimony and the court record.

(D) Neither the witness's testimony nor the court record.

21. On January 15, after receiving a brochure from the company advertising a sale of blank DVDs at an especially reduced price, a store ordered 2,000 blank DVDs from the company for resale. When the DVDs were delivered, however, the store's manager refused to accept delivery, asserting that she had expected the DVDs to be packaged in plastic cases, but that those delivered were packaged in paper boxes. The company sued the store for breach of contract.

At trial, the store manager testified that it is easier to sell DVDs when they are packaged in plastic cases. She attempted to testify further that she had ordered blank DVDs from the company on three previous occasions, and that the DVDs received in response to each order had been packaged in plastic cases. If the company's attorney objects to this testimony, which of the following would be the company's most effective argument in support of the objection?

(A) Evidence of past conduct is not admissible for the purpose of establishing a party's conduct on any particular occasion.

(B) The order was in writing and made no mention of the way in which the products were to be packaged.

(C) The DVDs were being sold at an especially reduced price to permit resale at a lower price.

(D) DVDs are commonly packaged in paper boxes like those in which the blank DVDs had been delivered to the store.

22. A statute provides that "No person shall operate a motor vehicle on the public roads

of this state who is not covered by a policy of automobile liability insurance with a limit of not less than $15,000. Any person in violation of this section shall be guilty of a felony." Following an automobile accident in which a vehicle driven by the defendant collided with a vehicle driven by the plaintiff, the defendant was charged with operating an uninsured vehicle in violation of the statute. After trial, the defendant was found guilty of violating the section and sentenced to a term of imprisonment. Subsequently the defendant died, and the plaintiff commenced an action against the defendant's estate for personal injuries sustained in the collision. In selecting the jury, the plaintiff's attorney asked each of the prospective jurors whether he or she owned stock in any automobile liability insurance carrier. During the trial of the action, the defendant's attorney offered into evidence a judgment of the defendant's conviction for driving an uninsured vehicle. Upon objection by the plaintiff's attorney, the judgment should be

(A) admitted, since the plaintiff's attorney has falsely suggested that the defendant was insured at the time of the accident.

(B) excluded, since evidence that a party is or is not covered by liability insurance is inadmissible to establish fault or freedom from fault.

(C) excluded, since it is self-serving.

(D) excluded, since it is hearsay, not within any exception to the hearsay rule.

23. During the trial of a personal injury claim arising from an automobile accident, the defendant offered a videotape into evidence after properly marking it for identification and testifying that it was an accurate representation of the accident scene. On *voir dire* examination by the plaintiff's attorney, the defendant stated that he hired a man to make a videotape of the place where the accident occurred and that the tape that had been offered in evidence was a copy of the tape made by the man. He stated further that after the man gave the copy to him, he mislaid it for several months, and that his wife found it only a few days before the trial. When asked about the location of the original videotape, the defendant said that he did not know where it was or even whether it still existed.

Upon objection by the plaintiff's attorney, the court should rule that the videotape copy is

(A) inadmissible, because the original videotape has not been shown to be unavailable.

(B) inadmissible, because there is a period of time during which custody of the videotape cannot be established.

(C) inadmissible, because the man has not authenticated it.

(D) admissible.

24. After his vehicle collided with the plaintiff's on March 1, the defendant retained an attorney to represent him in any possible litigation that might develop. The attorney hired a private investigator to interview the plaintiff regarding the facts of the accident. On March 5, the investigator followed he plaintiff into a bar, sat next to him, and engaged him in conversation. During the conversation, the plaintiff described the accident that he had with the defendant, and said, "Just between you and me, I drank a six-pack of beer just before the accident happened. It's a good thing nobody smelled my breath." Eventually the plaintiff commenced a personal injury action against the defendant. At the trial of the action, the plaintiff testified on direct examination that he had been driving at a slow rate of speed when the defendant's vehicle suddenly pulled out of a driveway into his path.

On cross-examination, the defendant's attorney asked the plaintiff whether he had drunk alcohol during the hour prior to the accident. The plaintiff answered that he had not. The defendant's attorney then asked, "Didn't you tell an investigator from my office that you had consumed an entire six-pack of beer just before the accident?" If the plaintiff's attorney objects to the question, the court should

(A) sustain the objection, since the plaintiff's prior statement was not made under oath.

(B) sustain the objection, since it was unethical for the defendant's attorney to make contact with the plaintiff through an investigator.

(C) sustain the objection, since the statement is hearsay not within any exception to the hearsay rule.

(D) overrule the objection.

25. In an action by the seller against the buyer for breach of contract, the seller's manager testified that after the buyer refused to accept delivery of merchandise as agreed, he personally arranged for the resale of the goods at a price that was $3,000 less than that which the buyer had agreed to pay.

On cross-examination, the buyer's attorney asked, "Didn't you once plead guilty to violating Penal Code section 22.9(a)?" Which of the following additional facts or inferences, if it were the only one true, would most effectively support the seller's objection to the question?

(A) The manager's plea of guilty was the result of a plea bargain after he had originally been charged with a more serious crime.

(B) The manager subsequently withdrew the guilty plea.

(C) Penal Code section 22.9(a) prohibits operating an automobile without proper liability insurance coverage.

(D) The manager was not in the employ of the seller at the time of his guilty plea.

26. The plaintiff was a student at a private high school. One day, while leaving the school building in the rain, the plaintiff slipped on the wooden steps that led from the school to the street. He immediately experienced pain in his elbow, but he got up and went home. Later, the pain became so severe that he went to see a doctor, who X-rayed the elbow and told him that it was fractured. Eventually, the plaintiff commenced an action for negligence against the school, claiming that the paint that had been used on the wooden steps became extremely slippery when wet with rain, and that the school was negligent in using it.

At trial, the plaintiff subpoenaed the school's maintenance manager. The manager testified that he stripped the old paint from the wooden steps the day after the plaintiff's accident and repainted the steps with a paint that did not become slippery when wet with rain. He said he did so before the school learned of the plaintiff's accident. The plaintiff offered this testimony as proof that the steps were in a dangerous condition at the time of the accident. Upon objection by the school's attorney, the manager's testimony should be

(A) admitted, since it is an admission.

(B) admitted, because the steps were stripped and repainted before the school learned about the plaintiff's accident.

(C) excluded, because it is being offered for the purpose of proving that the steps were in a dangerous condition at the time of the accident.

(D) excluded, since evidence of subsequent repair is not admissible in an action for negligence.

27. The plaintiff was crossing the street on foot when she was struck by a delivery van driven by an employee of the defendant while the employee was in the process of making a delivery. Following the accident, the employee was charged with reckless driving and pleaded not guilty. At the trial on the charge of reckless driving, the employee testified in his own defense. He stated that at the time of the accident, he had taken his eyes off

the road to look for the address of the place to which he had to make his delivery, and that as a result, he didn't see the plaintiff crossing the street.

The plaintiff subsequently brought an action against the defendant under the theory of *respondeat superior* for personal injuries resulting from the employee's negligence. At the trial, the plaintiff proved that the employee remained in the defendant's employ until the employee died from causes not related to the accident. The plaintiff then offered a transcript of the employee's testimony at the reckless driving trial. Upon objection by the defendant's attorney, the transcript should be

(A) admitted, under the prior testimony exception to the hearsay rule.

(B) admitted, under the past recollection recorded exception to the hearsay rule.

(C) admitted as a vicarious admission, under the public record exception to the hearsay rule.

(D) excluded as hearsay not within any exception to the hearsay rule.

28. The defendant went to see a lawyer. After the lawyer closed her office door and only the defendant and the lawyer were in the room, the defendant asked, "Let's say I was to shoot someone. Would it make a difference if I tried to pick a fight with him first? If he tried to hit me or something, would that mean I could maybe claim self-defense?" The lawyer explained the self-defense privilege to the defendant, and the defendant went on his way. A week later, the defendant shot the victim during a bar fight.

At trial, the defendant claimed he shot the victim in self-defense. The prosecution called the lawyer to testify about his conversation with the defendant. The defendant's attorney objected on the ground of attorney-client privilege. The objection should be

(A) overruled, because the defendant did not pay the lawyer a fee.

(B) overruled, because the communication related to the carrying out of a future crime.

(C) sustained, because the lawyer gave the defendant legal advice.

(D) sustained, because the conversation was confidential.

29. The victim was found dead in his garage, hanging by the neck from a rope tied to a roof beam. His widow brought an action against the victim's psychiatrist under the state's wrongful death statute. In her complaint, the widow alleged that the psychiatrist was negligent in his treatment of the victim, whom he knew or should have known to be suicidal. In his answer, the psychiatrist denied that he knew the victim to be suicidal, denied that he had treated him negligently, and denied that the victim's death was a suicide. At the trial of the wrongful death action, a nurse employed by the psychiatrist testified that the day before the victim's death, she heard the victim say to the psychiatrist, "I think suicide is the only way out." Upon objection by the psychiatrist's counsel, which of the following statements is most correct?

(A) The statement should be admitted for the purpose of establishing that the victim's death was a suicide.

(B) The statement should be admitted for the purpose of establishing that the psychiatrist knew or should have known that the victim was suicidal.

(C) The statement should be admitted both for the purpose of establishing that the victim's death was a suicide and that the psychiatrist knew or should have known that the victim was suicidal.

(D) The statement should not be admitted.

30. The defendant, a police officer who had recently joined the police department, was charged with the murder of his wife. At the

trial, the prosecution claimed that while on a visit to the country, the defendant's wife was walking across a meadow when the defendant shot her from three-quarters of a mile away with a rifle equipped with a telescopic sight. The defendant admitted firing the rifle, but he maintained that his wife's death was an accident. On the presentation of the defendant's case, his attorney called a firearms expert, who testified that the rifle was not reliably accurate at any distance in excess of a half-mile.

On direct examination, the defendant's attorney showed the expert a treatise on guns and asked him whether he had ever heard of it. The expert said that he had, that the treatise was a recognized authority in the field of firearms and ballistics, and that he used it in forming his own opinion regarding the capabilities of the rifle. Over objection by the prosecutor, the defendant's attorney read the expert a passage of the treatise that stated that the accurate range of the rifle was a half-mile and asked whether the expert agreed with that statement. When the expert said that he did, the defendant's attorney offered the treatise in evidence. The trial court will most likely

(A) sustain the objection, since direct examination of an expert regarding the materials that he used in forming his opinion is not permitted.

(B) sustain the objection, since although the questioning was proper, the treatise itself is not admissible in evidence.

(C) overrule the objection, since the expert's testimony that the treatise was a reliable authority laid a proper foundation for admission of the treatise in evidence.

(D) overrule the objection, since the expert's testimony that he relied on the treatise in forming his opinion laid a proper foundation for admission of the treatise in evidence.

31. After the plaintiff was injured in an automobile accident, the plaintiff sued the defendant for $50,000. Two weeks before trial, the plaintiff went to the defendant's home and said, "Listen, you were negligent, but I'm sick of worrying about this and I was texting when the wreck happened. I'll dismiss my case against you for $10,000." The defendant refused the plaintiff's offer and would now like to testify regarding the plaintiff's statement. May she do so?

(A) Yes, because it is admissible as a party admission.

(B) Yes, because it is admissible as a declaration against interest.

(C) No, because it is inadmissible hearsay.

(D) No, because it is inadmissible as an offer to compromise.

32. The defendant was on trial for vandalizing a national monument. The defendant testified that she did not do it. The defendant wanted to call a witness who would testify that she has known the defendant for at least 20 years and, in her opinion, the defendant has always been an honest person. Is the witness's statement admissible?

(A) Yes, because the defendant testified she did not vandalize the monument.

(B) Yes, because it is admissible to prove defendant's credibility as a witness in her own defense.

(C) No, because the defendant's character for truthfulness has not been attacked.

(D) No, because the witness is merely stating her opinion regarding the defendant's truthfulness.

33. The landlord was the owner of a three-story professional building. The entire second floor of the landlord's building was rented to an optometrist. Persons visiting the office of the optometrist either rode in an elevator located inside the building or climbed a stairway that was fastened to the outside of the building and that led from the street level to the second floor only. The plaintiff was a patient

of the optometrist. One day, upon leaving the optometrist's office and descending the stairway on the outside of the building, the plaintiff fell, sustaining serious injuries. She commenced an action against the landlord, alleging that the stairway was dangerous in that it was too steep, it lacked a handrail, and the stair treads were too narrow. The landlord denied that the stairway was dangerous. In addition, as an affirmative defense, he denied control over the stairway, asserting that it had been leased to the optometrist as part of the second-floor office.

At the trial, the plaintiff called a manager who had been employed by the landlord as building manager at the time of the accident, but who was presently unemployed. The manager testified that two days after the accident, the landlord instructed him to install a handrail on the stairway and to post a sign that read, "CAUTION: Steep and narrow stairway!" The landlord's attorney objected to the testimony and moved that it be stricken. Which of the following would be the plaintiff's most effective argument in response to the objection and in opposition to the motion to strike?

(A)  The manager is no longer in the landlord's employ.

(B)  The testimony is relevant to establish that the stairway was dangerous.

(C)  The testimony is relevant to establish that the landlord was aware that the stairway was dangerous.

(D)  The testimony is relevant to establish that the landlord was in control of the stairway.

34.  The plaintiff and the defendant were employed as clerks in the law office of an attorney. They disliked each other intensely. On February 6, they argued bitterly, almost coming to blows. Later, the plaintiff went to the company parking lot and discovered that the tires and canvas top on his car had been slashed with a knife. Angrily, he returned to

the office and accused the defendant of the vandalism in the presence of the attorney, saying, "I dare you to deny it." The plaintiff subsequently instituted a tort action against the defendant for damage to his car. At the trial, the attorney testified on behalf of the plaintiff. After describing the events that took place in his office on February 6, he stated that when the plaintiff dared the defendant to deny damaging his car, the defendant said nothing. The attorney stated that he, the attorney, then said, "If I thought you did this, I'd have to fire you. Now, did you?" and that the defendant still said nothing. The attorney testified further that he gave the defendant another opportunity to deny the plaintiff's accusation, and that after the defendant refused once again to answer, the attorney fired him. If the defendant's attorney objected to the testimony, the court should

(A)  overrule the objection, because the reasonable person in the defendant's situation would have denied slashing the tires and canvas top.

(B)  overrule the objection, since the defendant is a party to the action and will have an opportunity to deny making the statement.

(C)  sustain the objection, since silence cannot be used as an admission or form the basis for civil liability.

(D)  sustain the objection, since answering the attorney's question might have tended to incriminate the defendant.

35.  In an action by the plaintiff against the defendant, the plaintiff alleged that it had entered into a written contract with the defendant for the purchase of satin material that the plaintiff intended to use in manufacturing its products, and that the defendant failed to deliver the material as promised. At the trial, an employee testified that he worked in the plaintiff's legal department, and that he had negotiated the contract in question. He stated further that, although the original and all copies of the contract had been destroyed

in an office fire, he knew the substance of its contents. When the plaintiff's attorney began to question the employee about the contents of the contract, the defendant objected. The trial court should

(A) sustain the objection, since the employee's testimony would violate the parol evidence rule.

(B) sustain the objection, since the employee's testimony would violate the best evidence rule.

(C) overrule the objection, since the absence of the original document has been explained.

(D) overrule the objection, since the Statute of Frauds is satisfied by the fact that a written memorandum of agreement was made.

36. The plaintiff sued the defendant, claiming that she slipped on a puddle of water in the defendant's grocery store. The plaintiff called a witness who the plaintiff's lawyer expected to say that she had seen the puddle 40 minutes before the plaintiff slipped, and that she informed the store manager of the puddle. Instead, the witness said, "I never saw any puddle." Surprised, the plaintiff's lawyer then called the witness's neighbor, who proposed to testify that the day after the accident she was working in her backyard when the witness leaned over the fence and told her, "That puddle was there for over an hour — and I told the store manager about it!" The neighbor's testimony is admissible

(A) as truth of the matter asserted.

(B) only to impeach the witness.

(C) as evidence of material fact.

(D) because there are other "circumstantial guarantees of trustworthiness" regarding the neighbor's statement.

37. Suspecting that some students were trafficking in illegal drugs, a college chancellor requested assistance from the state police in apprehending the traffickers. In response to the request, an undercover police officer registered at the college as a student. While attending classes, the officer became friendly with the defendant, who was rumored to be involved in the illicit drug traffic. One day, while chatting with the defendant, the officer said, "Hey, how about selling me some heroin?" The defendant responded by saying, "I don't know what you're talking about." But the officer said, "Come on, everybody knows about it. And I really need the stuff." The defendant again denied knowing anything about drugs, but the officer insisted, displaying a $50 bill. "I'm really strung out," the officer said. "I'll give you $50 for stuff worth $25. Come on. How about it?" At this, the defendant handed the officer a packet of heroin and took the $50 bill. The defendant was subsequently arrested and charged with the unauthorized sale of a dangerous drug. At his trial, he asserted the defense of entrapment. The prosecution offered the testimony of several other students, who stated that on various occasions in the past, they had purchased heroin from the defendant. The defendant's attorney objected to the introduction of the testimony of the students. The objection should have been

(A) sustained, since character evidence is not admissible against a defendant in a criminal proceeding.

(B) sustained, since proof of unconvicted bad acts is not admissible for the purpose of establishing a person's character.

(C) overruled, since such evidence would tend to prove that the defendant was predisposed to commit the crime with which he has been charged.

(D) overruled, since evidence of past conduct is relevant to establish that a defendant engaged in criminal behavior on a particular occasion.

38. The plaintiff slipped on a wet spot on the floor of the produce department in a

supermarket. He commenced an action for damages two years and 11 months later, just before the three-year statute of limitations would have run out. In her opening statement at the trial of the action, the supermarket's attorney said that it was her client's contention that the delay in instituting action indicated that the plaintiff had not sustained any real injury and that the damages claimed by the plaintiff were fabricated.

The plaintiff testified in his own behalf. During cross-examination, the supermarket's attorney asked him when he consulted for the first time with an attorney regarding the accident. The plaintiff answered, "Not until a few months ago, because a man from the supermarket offered to settle for $3,000, and I was trying to get a better offer."

If the supermarket's attorney moved to strike that part of the answer that referred to settlement negotiations, the motion to strike should be

(A) denied, since evidence of the settlement negotiations is admissible to explain the plaintiff's delay in instituting the action.

(B) denied, since the settlement offer is relevant to establish that the supermarket believed itself to be at fault.

(C) granted, since a policy rule prevents evidence of settlement negotiations from being admitted.

(D) granted, since that portion of the answer was not responsive to the question asked.

39. Executing a valid warrant, police raided an adult theater, lawfully arresting its owner and lawfully seizing a copy of the film that he was showing. The owner was subsequently charged with "conducting an obscene film performance" in violation of a state law.

At trial, the prosecution called a professor to the stand. The professor testified that she was a professor of film arts and the author of several books on the art of erotic filmmaking. She said that although she believed the erotic film to be a valid art form, she found the film at issue to be devoid of any literary or artistic merit. She stated further that in her opinion it was obscene. In objecting to this testimony, which of the following would be the owner's most effective argument?

(A) The professor's opinion relates to an ultimate issue in the prosecution.

(B) The professor's opinion is stated in legal terms.

(C) The professor does not qualify as an expert.

(D) Since the matter at issue is a subjective one, expert testimony is inadmissible.

40. After bonds that the plaintiff purchased from the defendant proved to be worthless, the plaintiff instituted an action against the defendant for breach of contract and misrepresentation. At the trial, the plaintiff's attorney subpoenaed the defendant's chief bookkeeper. The bookkeeper appeared in court in response to the subpoena but refused to take the stand. The trial judge told the bookkeeper that unless he took the stand, he would be held in contempt of court. The bookkeeper continued to refuse, asserting his privilege against self-incrimination under the Fifth Amendment to the United States Constitution. He reasonably believed that his testimony could tend to incriminate him. Should the bookkeeper be held in contempt?

(A) Yes, since the privilege against self-incrimination applies only to testimony at criminal proceedings.

(B) Yes, since the bookkeeper was not a party to the proceeding.

(C) Yes, since the privilege against self-incrimination does not justify a refusal to take the stand in a civil proceeding.

(D) No, since the bookkeeper reasonably believed that his testimony could tend to incriminate him.

41. The plaintiff sued the defendant claiming that she was bit when the defendant's dog escaped from the defendant's yard and attacked her. The defendant argued that she didn't own a dog. The plaintiff's lawyer called the witness, expecting the witness to say that the defendant had owned the dog for at least three years, and that her dog was the dog that bit the plaintiff. Instead, the witness testified, "I've never seen a dog around the defendant's property. In fact, the defendant is allergic." Surprised, the plaintiff's lawyer introduced a statement made by the witness at deposition where the witness said, "The defendant has owned that crazy dog for three years. And it has bitten everyone, including the plaintiff." The witness's deposition statement is admissible as

(A) proof that the defendant owned the dog that bit the plaintiff.

(B) for impeachment purposes only.

(C) because the statement is necessary in the interests of justice.

(D) as a statement against interest.

42. The defendant, who was charged with armed robbery, retained an attorney. In preparing the defense of his client, the attorney interviewed the defendant's friend. The friend told the attorney that he and the defendant had been together at a baseball game at the time of the robbery. At the defendant's trial, the attorney called the friend to the stand and asked if he had seen the defendant on the day of the robbery. The friend said that he had not. The attorney subsequently called another witness to testify that he had seen the friend and the defendant together at the baseball stadium at the time of the robbery. The trial judge should rule that the witness's testimony is

(A) inadmissible, because the attorney cannot impeach his own witness.

(B) inadmissible, because the attorney is bound by the testimony of his own witness.

(C) admissible, because the friend is a hostile witness.

(D) admissible, because the witness's testimony is relevant to material issues.

43. A man and woman were in a car accident. Although the woman was unhurt, the man was severely injured. The man looked at the woman and said, "I know I'm about to die. I never told you this, but me and [the defendant] murdered the doctor last year. He owed us money." The man then died. The defendant was later prosecuted for the murder, and the prosecution called the woman to testify to the above statement by the man. The man's statement is

(A) inadmissible hearsay.

(B) admissible under the excited utterance exception.

(C) admissible as a dying declaration.

(D) admissible as a present sense impression.

44. The plaintiff sued the defendant for damage that resulted from a collision between the plaintiff's motorcycle and one of the defendant's trucks. After receiving the summons, the president and sole stockholder of the defendant notified the company attorney. The attorney said that she wanted to meet with the president and the driver of the truck. At the attorney's request, the president went to the attorney's office with the driver who had been driving the truck at the time of the accident. While discussing the case with the attorney in the presence of the driver, the president said that on the day before the accident, he was aware that the truck's brakes were not working properly but that because of his heavy workload, he postponed making the necessary repairs.

At the trial of the plaintiff's suit against the defendant, the plaintiff attempted to have the driver testify to the statement that the president made to the attorney about the brakes. The defendant's attorney objected on the ground of the attorney-client privilege.

Should the driver be permitted to testify to the president's statement?

(A) Yes, because the attorney-client privilege does not apply to testimony by one who does not stand in a confidential relationship with the person against whom the evidence is offered.

(B) Yes, because it is presumed that a communication made in the presence of third persons is not confidential.

(C) Yes, because communications made by or on behalf of corporations are not privileged.

(D) No.

45. At trial, a witness testified that on the day of the incident, she looked up the defendant's number in the phone book and dialed it, and that a male voice answered and said he was the defendant. The witness stated further that she then asked, "Are you the animal that exposed his privates to my daughter?" to which the voice replied, "Yes, I couldn't help myself." Finally, the witness testified that she was familiar with the defendant's voice and recognized it when she was speaking to him on the phone.

If the defendant's attorney objects to the witness's testimony regarding the identification of the defendant's voice, the judge should rule this testimony

(A) admissible, since the usual accuracy of the telephone directory, coupled with the self-identification of the person who answered, makes it likely that the person who answered was the defendant.

(B) admissible, since there is a presumption that a person who gratuitously identifies himself or herself when answering a telephone will do so accurately.

(C) admissible, because the witness testified that she was familiar with the defendant's voice and recognized it when speaking to him on the phone.

(D) inadmissible, as a violation of the defendant's privilege against self-incrimination.

46. The plaintiff was in a motorcycle accident that shattered his leg. The leg became severely infected after the defendant surgeon replaced the plaintiff's shattered bone with cadaver bone. The infection led to the eventual amputation of the plaintiff's leg. The plaintiff sued the defendant for medical malpractice. At trial, the plaintiff called the defendant as a witness. The only question that the plaintiff asked was, "Did you perform the cadaver bone operation?" The defendant answered "yes." The plaintiff turned the defendant over to the defendant's lawyer, who asked the defendant, "Wasn't the leg damage so severe that it would have been amputated anyway even if you hadn't tried to insert the cadaver bone?" The plaintiff's lawyer objected. The court should

(A) sustain the objection, because the direct examiner has the right to control the presentation of his or her case.

(B) sustain the objection, because the question goes beyond the scope of direct.

(C) overrule the objection, because the question involves the defendant's credibility.

(D) overrule the objection, because the question is within the scope of the direct examination.

47. The defendant was on trial for the murder of his wife. The prosecution wants to put the defendant's neighbor on the stand, who will testify that she was watching television one evening when a friend of hers banged on her front door and shouted, "I was jogging by and your neighbor just came outside covered in blood and told me he shot his wife!" The friend was then in an auto accident a few days later and now lies in a coma.

Can the neighbor testify regarding her friend's statement?

(A) Yes, because it was an excited utterance.

(B) Yes, because the friend is now in a coma and cannot testify herself.

(C) No, because it is inadmissible hearsay.

(D) No, because the statement is being offered for its truth.

48. In a personal injury action by the plaintiff against the defendant, the plaintiff claimed that the accident occurred because the defendant, who was operating a blue Ford sedan, was driving at an excessive rate of speed. At the trial, the plaintiff's attorney called the witness as a witness on the plaintiff's direct case. The witness testified that after hearing a broadcast on a police radio on the day of the accident, she looked out her window and saw the defendant's blue Ford sedan strike the plaintiff's red convertible on Main Street. The witness said that she did not have a present recollection of what she had heard on the police radio, but that she made a written note of it immediately following the broadcast. The plaintiff's attorney showed her a piece of paper that had been marked for identification, and the witness said that she now remembered that she had heard a police dispatcher saying that officers were in pursuit of a blue Ford sedan that was traveling down Main Street at an excessive rate of speed.

If the defendant's attorney objects to the testimony of the witness regarding what she heard on the police radio, the court should hold that her testimony is

(A) inadmissible as hearsay, not within any exception.

(B) admissible as a sense impression.

(C) admissible as a past recollection recorded.

(D) admissible as present recollection refreshed.

49. At the trial of a personal injury action instituted by the plaintiff against the defendant, the defendant testified on his own behalf as part of his direct case. In response to a question by his attorney, the defendant stated that shortly after the accident, he told a police officer that the traffic signal light had been red against the plaintiff. Upon objection by the plaintiff's attorney, the court should hold that the defendant's testimony regarding his statement to the police officer is

(A) inadmissible hearsay.

(B) admissible, because the defendant's testimony was based on firsthand knowledge.

(C) admissible as a prior consistent statement.

(D) admissible, because the defendant was on the witness stand and available for cross-examination.

50. Charged with the rape of the victim, the defendant claimed that he and the victim had frequently engaged in sexual intercourse in the past, and that they sometimes played a game in which the victim pretended to resist him and he pretended to overcome her resistance by force. He asserted that on the day of the alleged rape, either the victim consented to the intercourse or her conduct led him to reasonably believe that she consented. At his trial, the victim testified that the defendant forced her to have sexual intercourse with him on the day in question. On cross-examination, the defendant's attorney asked the victim whether she ever had sexual intercourse with the defendant willingly before the alleged rape. If the prosecutor objects to this question, the objection should be

(A) sustained, since past sexual behavior of the complainant is not material to the allegations of a rape prosecution.

(B) sustained, since the probative value of her answer is likely to be outweighed by its prejudicial effect.

(C)  overruled, in the absence of a statute prohibiting the inquiry, since the
complainant's past sexual behavior is
logically relevant to the elements of a
rape prosecution.

(D)  overruled, since the question and the
testimony that it will elicit are relevant to the defendant's defense of
consent.

51.  A state statute provides that the owner of any
motor vehicle operated on the public roads
of the state is liable for damage resulting
from the negligence of any person driving
the vehicle with the owner's permission. The
plaintiff was injured when a vehicle operated
by a man struck her while she was walking
across the street. At the scene of the accident, the man apologized to the plaintiff,
saying, "I'm sorry. It isn't my car. I didn't
know that the brakes were bad." The plaintiff
subsequently instituted an action against the
defendant for her damages, asserting that the
defendant owned the vehicle. She alleged that
the defendant was negligent in permitting the
vehicle to be driven while he knew that the
brakes were in need of repair and that he was
vicariously liable under the statute for the
negligence of the man. The defendant denied
ownership of the vehicle. At the trial, the
plaintiff offered testimony by a mechanic that
on the day after the accident, the defendant
hired him to completely overhaul the brakes.
Upon objection by the defendant, the evidence is

(A)  admissible, to show that the defendant
was the owner of the vehicle.

(B)  admissible, to show that the brakes were
in need of repair on the day of the
accident.

(C)  inadmissible, because the condition of
the vehicle on any day other than that
of the accident is irrelevant to show
its condition at the time the accident
occurred.

(D)  inadmissible, under a policy that
encourages safety precautions.

52.  A hidden videotape camera at the office of a
finance company routinely records all transactions taking place during business hours.
At the trial of the defendant, a black man
charged with robbing the company, the prosecution offers a videotape made by the hidden
camera at the time the robbery occurred. The
defendant's attorney objects to introduction
of the videotape on the ground that, while it
is clear from the tape that the robber was a
black man, there is no certainty that the man
pictured was the defendant. Should the objection be sustained?

(A)  Yes, since use of the tape violates the
defendant's privilege against self-
incrimination.

(B)  Yes, because the tape's value is outweighed by unfair prejudice.

(C)  No, because if the defendant is pictured in the tape, it is admissible as an
admission.

(D)  No, because the tape would tend to
prove that the defendant was the
robber.

53.  During a road rage incident, the victim was
punched in the face. The defendant was then
prosecuted for assault. At trial, a witness
was called by the prosecution to testify. The
witness stated that the victim came to her
apartment two days after the incident and
told her, "[the defendant] punched me in the
face because he thought I was talking on my
cellphone and not paying attention to my
driving." The witness's testimony is

(A)  admissible as an excited utterance.

(B)  admissible as a present sense
impression.

(C)  admissible as a declaration against the
defendant's interest.

(D)  inadmissible.

54.  At the defendant's trial for murder, the witness testified that he heard three gunshots
immediately after hearing the defendant

shout, "I'll kill you!" The defendant's attorney asked no questions on cross-examination but reserved the right to call the witness back to the stand at a later time. Subsequently, the defendant's attorney offered the testimony of a police officer who stated that, in an interview at the scene of the shooting, the witness said that he did not hear any gunshots. The police officer's testimony is

(A) admissible for impeachment purposes only.

(B) admissible as substantive evidence only.

(C) admissible for impeachment purposes and as substantive evidence.

(D) inadmissible, since it is hearsay not within any exception.

55. After derailment of a passenger train, the train corporation was charged with criminal negligence under a statute that made corporations criminally liable for the criminal negligence of their employees. At trial, a state railroad inspector testified that on the day of the derailment, the driver of the derailed train was operating the train while intoxicated. The jury found the corporation not guilty of criminal negligence. A passenger on the derailed train subsequently instituted an action against the corporation for personal injuries that he sustained as a result of the derailment. Although the passenger's attorney properly served the inspector with a subpoena, he failed to appear at the trial. If the passenger's attorney offers evidence of the testimony that the inspector gave at the criminal proceeding, the evidence is most likely to be admissible as

(A) an admission.

(B) past recollection recorded.

(C) former testimony.

(D) a present sense impression.

56. The defendant had been a member of a professional crime organization for 20 years and had participated in many crimes during that period of time. Because the defendant's testimony was crucial to the district attorney's attempt to break the crime organization, the defendant was offered transactional immunity if he would testify against other members of the organization. He did so, and his testimony resulted in several convictions. The defendant subsequently wrote and published a book in which he described in detail many of the crimes that he committed, including the shotgun murder of the victim. Following the publication, the victim's wife commenced an action against the defendant for damages resulting from the wrongful death of her husband. At the trial, a police officer who had been called to the scene of the victim's shooting testified that just before the victim died, he heard him say, "I'm dying. I saw [the defendant] pull the trigger on me." The jurisdiction has a "dead man's statute." If the defendant moves to strike the police officer's testimony, his motion should be

(A) granted, since a dying declaration is admissible only in a trial for criminal homicide.

(B) granted, since the defendant received transactional immunity.

(C) denied, since the victim believed himself to be dying when he made the statement.

(D) denied, since the jurisdiction has a "dead man's statute."

57. After the crash of an airplane, an action for wrongful death was brought by the husband of a passenger killed in the crash. During the trial, the plaintiff called an employee of the State Aviation Agency that investigated the circumstances surrounding the crash.

The witness testified that during the course of his investigation, he questioned a mechanic on the day of the crash. He said that the mechanic stated that he and another mechanic had been assigned by the airport supervisor to inspect the flight before takeoff, but that they did not inspect the plane as directed. He also testified that the mechanic claimed to be an employee of the airline. Independent evidence indicated that the mechanic was employed by the airline and authorized to speak for it at the time the statement was made. The mechanic was unavailable to testify. If the witness's testimony is objected to, the judge should rule it admissible

(A)  because the witness testified that the mechanic claimed to be an employee of the airline.

(B)  because independent evidence indicated that the mechanic was employed by the airline at the time the statement was made.

(C)  because independent evidence indicated that at the time the statement was made, the mechanic was authorized to speak for the airline.

(D)  because the mechanic is unavailable to testify.

58.  The plaintiff was injured when the ladder on which she was standing collapsed without warning. Immediately following the accident, the plaintiff was taken to the hospital, where she remained for approximately six hours. At the trial of the plaintiff's action against the manufacturer of the ladder, a nurse employed by the hospital was called to the stand by the plaintiff's counsel.

The nurse testified that he was on duty when the plaintiff was brought into the hospital, and that the plaintiff complained of pain almost continually from the time she arrived until the time she left. Upon proper objection by the defendant, this testimony should be

(A)  admitted, as a part of a pertinent medical history.

(B)  admitted, as a statement of present physical sensation.

(C)  not admitted, since pain is a purely subjective matter and not a proper subject

of testimony by anyone but the injured party.

(D)  not admitted, since it is hearsay.

59.  The defendant's dog frequently dug holes in the lawn of the plaintiff, who had telephoned the defendant to complain in a loud voice on several occasions. One day, after the dog dug up the plaintiff's prize rosebush, the plaintiff ran to the defendant's house and banged on the defendant's front door. When the defendant opened the door, the plaintiff shouted, "You jerk!" The defendant struck him in the face with his fist and closed the door. The plaintiff later sued the defendant for battery, and the defendant asserted the privilege of self-defense. At the trial, the defendant offered the testimony of a local shopkeeper, who stated that he knew the plaintiff's reputation in the neighborhood and that the plaintiff was known as "a bad actor who will fight at the drop of a hat."

If the plaintiff's attorney objects to the testimony of the shopkeeper, the objection should be

(A)  sustained, since evidence of the plaintiff's character is not relevant to his action for battery.

(B)  sustained, since the plaintiff is not the defendant.

(C)  overruled, since the testimony is relevant to the defendant's assertion of the privilege of self-defense.

(D)  overruled, since the plaintiff placed his character in issue by bringing the lawsuit.

60.  At the trial of a negligence action, a doctor testified that she was the orthopedic surgeon who treated the plaintiff. She stated that, at her direction, technicians in her office X-rayed the plaintiff's left leg. She stated further that, based upon her examination of the plaintiff's leg and upon her study of the X-ray, it was her opinion that the plaintiff

had suffered a fracture of the tibia (a bone in the leg). She said she would have formed the same opinion without inspection of the X-ray. The X-ray was unavailable. Upon proper objection by the defendant, the doctor's opinion should be

(A) excluded, because the X-ray was hearsay and she stated that her opinion was based on it.

(B) admitted, because the X-ray is unavailable.

(C) admitted, because she testified that she would have formed the same opinion without inspection of the X-ray.

(D) admitted, since the opinion of an expert may be based on matters not in evidence.

61. While walking down a stairway that led to the women's restroom at a theater, the plaintiff fell and sustained serious injuries to her shoulder. She sued the theater for damages, alleging that it had negligently permitted the stairway to be littered with scraps of paper and that she had slipped on one of them.

At trial, the witness testified that he had been employed as the theater's manager for a period of three weeks prior to the accident, that as such, he was the person to whom accidents would ordinarily be reported, and that in the three-week period preceding the accident, he had received no reports of accident or injury occurring on those particular stairs. The judge should rule this testimony

(A) admissible, because it tends to prove that the plaintiff did not use the care that would have been exercised by a reasonable person.

(B) admissible, because it tends to prove that the theater was generally careful about maintaining the stairway.

(C) inadmissible, because it is self-serving.

(D) inadmissible, because it is not probative of the theater's exercise of due care on this particular occasion.

62. A man was dying of cancer, and his doctors only gave him a few moments to live. The man gathered his family around his bed, including his brother, and said, "I'm dying. I want all of you to know that [the defendant] and I were the ones who murdered the police chief last year." Soon thereafter, against all odds, the man recovered and fled to a small island off the coast of South America. The defendant was later prosecuted for the murder, and the prosecution called the man's brother to testify to the above statement by the man. The man's statement is

(A) admissible as a dying declaration.

(B) admissible as an excited utterance.

(C) inadmissible because the man did not die.

(D) inadmissible because it was hearsay not within any exception.

63. At the trial of an action for personal injuries resulting from an automobile accident that occurred in the city, a witness testified for the defendant. He stated that he was standing on a street corner at the time of the accident and observed the plaintiff's car go through a red light. The plaintiff's attorney had information indicating that the witness was not even in the city on the day of the accident and had actually been observed on that day committing an armed robbery in another city located at the other end of the state. On cross-examination, she asked, "Weren't you actually robbing a store in another city on the day this accident occurred?" The witness refused to answer, invoking the privilege against self-incrimination under the Fifth Amendment to the United States Constitution. Over objection by the defendant's attorney, the judge ordered that the witness's entire testimony be stricken. Subsequently, the defendant appealed from a judgment for the plaintiff, asserting that the trial court erred in striking the witness's

testimony. Which of the following would be the plaintiff's most effective argument in response to the defendant's assertion?

(A) The privilege against self-incrimination is effective only in criminal proceedings.

(B) The trial record, independent of the witness's testimony, does not indicate that the witness's answer would incriminate him.

(C) Since the trial determined the rights of persons other than the witness, the requirement of due process outweighed the witness's privilege against self-incrimination.

(D) The witness's refusal to answer prevented adequate cross-examination.

64. The defendant, a college student, was charged with the attempted murder of the victim, a fellow student, outside one of the college classrooms. At trial, the defendant's attorney called the school's dean of students to the witness stand. The dean testified that immediately following the stabbing that led to the prosecution, she interviewed the defendant, and he stated that when the victim insulted him, he stabbed the victim in anger. She testified further that she had taken notes of the conversation, which she then placed in the defendant's student file. If the prosecutor offered the defendant's student file in evidence as a business record, which of the following would be the defendant's most effective argument in support of an objection to the admission of the file?

(A) The dean had an independent recollection of the events and was present in court to testify.

(B) The investigation of crimes is not a regularly conducted business activity for the college.

(C) The business record exception to the hearsay rule does not apply in criminal trials.

(D) The defendant's statement is second-level hearsay.

65. In a challenge to the will of the deceased, opponents of the will called the deceased's next-door neighbor to the stand. The neighbor testified that she had observed the deceased acting strangely for several months before and after the date on which his will had been executed. When asked to specify in what way his behavior was strange, she said that he frequently appeared in his front yard wearing nothing but a towel and a football helmet, turning his face to the sky and shouting, "Bring on the saucers! I'm ready to do battle!" She said that there were also times when she found him wandering about the street in a daze, and that on several occasions she had to take him home because he told her that he didn't know where he was. In rebuttal, proponents of the will called a doctor to the stand. The doctor testified that he had seen the deceased only three days before the execution of the will for his semiannual medical checkup and that he did not observe any strange behavior at that or any other time. If opponents of the will seek to exclude the doctor's statement from evidence, the statement should be

(A) excluded, since evidence that abnormal behavior was not observed is inadmissible to establish the sanity or competence of a decedent.

(B) excluded, because the doctor's testimony does not indicate a sufficient opportunity to observe the deceased's behavior.

(C) admitted, because the opponents of the will opened the door by introducing the testimony of the neighbor.

(D) admitted, since a medical doctor may qualify as an expert on the sanity of a patient.

66. At the trial of the plaintiff's personal injury action against the defendant, the witness was called as a witness on the plaintiff's direct

case. The witness, a police officer, testified that he arrived at the scene of the accident about 10 minutes after it occurred. He stated that when he got there, he had a conversation with another police officer who was already on the scene. When the witness said that he had no independent recollection regarding the nature of their conversation, the plaintiff's attorney showed him a copy of an official police report and asked whether he recognized it. The witness identified it as the report that he filed following his investigation of the accident. The plaintiff's attorney offered the report in evidence. The defendant's attorney objected to its admission on the ground that it contained the following statement:

The other officer reports that an unidentified witness told him that the defendant went through a red light without stopping.

Should the police report be admitted into evidence?

(A) Yes, because the witness used it to refresh his recollection while testifying.

(B) Yes, because it is a business record.

(C) No, because a police report is not a record kept in the usual course of business.

(D) No, because neither the witness nor the other officer saw the accident.

67. The buyer, a United States importer, contracted with the seller, a Dutch manufacturer, for the purchase of trivets to be manufactured in the Netherlands by the seller. When the seller delivered the trivets, however, the buyer refused to accept them, asserting that he had contracted for genuine porcelain and that the trivets delivered by the seller were imitation porcelain. The buyer died shortly afterwards. The seller sued the buyer's estate in the United States for breach of contract, claiming that he explained to the buyer during negotiations that the trivets would be made of imitation porcelain.

At trial, the attorney for the buyer's estate called the buyer's brother as a witness. The brother testified that he was an expert in Dutch and had been present at the negotiations between the buyer and the seller. He said that the seller and the buyer asked him to assist by translating when necessary because neither spoke the other's language very well. He stated further that when the trivets were being discussed, the seller said something in Dutch that the buyer said he did not understand. The buyer then asked his brother to translate, and the brother replied, "He says that the trivets will be genuine porcelain." The jurisdiction has a "dead man's statute." The seller's attorney objected to the brother's last statement and asked the court to exclude it from the record.

The brother's statement should be

(A) admitted, because it is relevant to the buyer's intention at the time the contract was formed.

(B) admitted, because the jurisdiction has a "dead man's statute."

(C) admitted, because the brother qualified as an expert on the Dutch language.

(D) excluded, because it is hearsay not within any exception.

68. After receiving a tip, police officers stopped a car being driven by the defendant and forced him to open the trunk. In it, the officers discovered a canvas bag containing seven pounds of cocaine. They seized the car and the cocaine as evidence and placed the defendant under arrest. Without advising him of his rights to remain silent and to consult with an attorney, they questioned him about the cocaine. During the questioning, the defendant said, "I don't know anything about it. It isn't even my car."

The defendant was charged with illegal possession of a controlled substance. Subsequently, the defendant's motion to suppress the use of the cocaine as evidence was granted, and the charges against him were dismissed. The defendant thereupon commenced an appropriate proceeding against the police department for recovery of his automobile. On presentation of his direct case, the defendant testified that he owned the seized automobile but had registered it to a friend for purposes of convenience. On cross-examination, the attorney representing the police department asked, "After your arrest, did you tell the arresting officers that it wasn't your car?"

If the defendant's attorney objects to this question, the objection should be

(A) sustained, because the defendant's interrogation was in violation of his *Miranda* rights.

(B) sustained, because the defendant's motion to suppress was granted.

(C) overruled, because the automobile in which the cocaine was transported is "fruit of the poisonous tree."

(D) overruled, because his denial that he owned the car was a prior inconsistent statement.

69. In an action by the plaintiff against the defendant for breach of contract, the attorney for the plaintiff called an employee as a witness. The employee testified that she was the employee of the plaintiff in charge of the defendant's account. She said that on May 17, she had supervised a shipment of dyes to the defendant. She stated that she did not personally inspect the shipment but that immediately after the company shipping clerk inspected the shipment, he told her its contents and she listed them on an invoice and signed it. A copy of the invoice was then sent to the defendant in accordance with standard company practice. She said that she no longer had any independent recollection of what the shipment contained, but that the original invoice was now in the hands of the company attorney. When the attorney representing the plaintiff showed her a document and asked her to identify it, she said that it

was the invoice to which she had referred, and that the signature on it was her own. When the attorney for the plaintiff offered it in evidence, the attorney for the defendant objected.

If the court admits the invoice into evidence, it will most probably be as

(A) past recollection recorded.

(B) a record kept in the usual course of business.

(C) an original document under the best evidence rule.

(D) present recollection refreshed.

70. The plaintiff was a commercial furniture-finisher. The defendant was a manufacturer of commercial furniture-finishing supplies. In an action by the plaintiff against the defendant for breach of contract, a dispute arose as to the meaning of the term "unit of lacquer," which appeared in a contract between the parties. The witness, an officer of the plaintiff, testified on her company's direct case.

The witness testified that in the furniture-finishing industry the term "unit of lacquer" means 55 gallons of lacquer. If the defendant's attorney objects, the witness's testimony should be

(A) excluded as a self-serving statement.

(B) excluded as hearsay, not within any exception to the hearsay rule.

(C) admitted as evidence of business habit.

(D) admitted, because it serves to establish a trade usage.

71. At the defendant's trial on a charge of rape, the victim testified that after meeting him in a bar, she accompanied the defendant to his apartment, where he forced her to have sexual intercourse with him against her will. The defendant's attorney did not cross-examine the victim.

In his opening statement, the defendant's attorney said that although his client admitted to having sexual intercourse with the victim shortly after they first met on the night in question, he intended to prove that the victim consented to the intercourse. Then, on direct presentation of the defendant's case, his attorney attempted to offer evidence of the victim's prior sexual conduct with other men.

Upon objection by the prosecution, this evidence should be

(A) admitted for the purpose of impeachment only.

(B) admitted as substantive evidence only.

(C) admitted as substantive evidence and for the purpose of impeachment.

(D) excluded.

72. In the trial of a tort action in a United States district court, if the substantive law of the state is being applied, which of the following statements is correct regarding confidential communications between psychotherapist and patient?

(A) The United States district court **MUST** recognize the psychotherapist-patient privilege if it is recognized by the law of the state.

(B) The United States district court **MAY** recognize the psychotherapist-patient privilege even if it is not recognized by the law of the state.

(C) The United States district court **MAY** recognize the psychotherapist-patient privilege if it is recognized by the law of the state.

(D) The United States district court does not need to make any notice of state law.

73. In an action by the plaintiff against the defendant for personal injuries resulting from negligence, the plaintiff's attorney called the witness as a witness on the plaintiff's direct case. The witness's testimony was offered to prove that the plaintiff suffered physical pain from his injuries. The witness testified that she was the plaintiff's mother, and that during the weeks following the accident, she observed the plaintiff taking pink pills on several occasions. The plaintiff's attorney then asked the witness if she knew why the plaintiff was taking the pink pills. When the defendant's attorney objected, the plaintiff's attorney withdrew the question and asked whether the witness was present when the doctor examined the plaintiff the day after the accident. The witness responded that she heard the plaintiff say, "My neck hurts," and that the doctor handed the plaintiff the pink pills and said, "These pink pills are very effective for pain."

If the defendant's attorney moves to exclude the witness's testimony about what the doctor said, that testimony should be

(A) admitted as a declaration of present physical sensation.

(B) admitted as a declaration of past physical sensation.

(C) excluded as hearsay, not within any exception to the hearsay rule.

(D) admitted as evidence of a medical history.

74. The defendant pleaded not guilty to a charge of committing an armed robbery of a bank. When the defendant appeared in court on the day of the trial, his head was completely bald.

The prosecuting attorney called the employee as a witness on the prosecution's direct case. The employee testified that she was employed by the bank, and that she was present when the robbery was committed. She stated that the robber had bushy red hair. When asked whether the defendant was the robber, she looked at him sitting in the courtroom and said that she was not sure. The prosecuting attorney then asked her whether she had identified the defendant as the robber at a lineup conducted on the day of the robbery. If the defendant's attorney objects to that question, the objection should be

(A) sustained, since her statement is hearsay not within any exception.

(B) sustained, since the prosecuting attorney may not impeach his own witness.

(C) overruled, since the employee is on the witness stand and available for cross-examination.

(D) overruled, since the employee is a disinterested witness.

75. The plaintiff sued the defendant, alleging that the defendant was negligent in building a new office building. The plaintiff called a well-known engineer as an expert witness. During the engineer's direct testimony, the engineer identified a book as a reliable authority in the field. How may the book be used at trial?

(A) It may be given to the jury to examine in the presence of the judge.

(B) The engineer may read relevant passages to the jury.

(C) The jury may take the book with them into the jury room.

(D) While the engineer may have relied on the book in forming his opinion, he may not read from the book or give it to the jury.

76. The defendant was charged with the second degree murder of the victim under a statute that defined that crime as "the unlawful killing of a human being with malice aforethought, but without premeditation." The defendant's attorney asserted a defense of insanity and called the defendant as a witness on his own behalf. After the defendant testified on direct examination and cross-examination, his attorney called a doctor to the witness stand. The doctor stated that he was a psychiatrist, had practiced for 30 years, had treated thousands of patients with illnesses like the defendant's, and had testified as an expert in hundreds

of criminal homicide trials. He testified, "After listening to the defendant's testimony, I am of the opinion that the defendant did not have malice aforethought as our law defines it on the day of the victim's death." On cross-examination, the doctor admitted that he had never spoken to or seen the defendant before, and that his opinion was based entirely on his observations of the defendant's testimony.

Which of the following would be the prosecuting attorney's most effective argument in support of a motion to exclude the doctor's statement?

(A) The doctor's testimony embraces the ultimate issue.

(B) The doctor's opinions were based entirely upon courtroom observations.

(C) The doctor had insufficient opportunity to examine the defendant.

(D) Whether the defendant had "malice aforethought" is a question to be decided by the jury.

77. At the trial of her negligence action against the defendant, the plaintiff exhibited her leg to the jury and testified that following the accident, her leg was so badly mangled that she believed that she was going to die. The plaintiff's attorney then called a witness, who testified that he arrived at the scene of the accident moments after it occurred and found the plaintiff lying in the roadway in a pool of blood. The witness stated that he heard the plaintiff scream, "Oh, God, I had the green light in my favor and now I'm dying!" The defendant's attorney made timely objection to the witness's testimony.

Which of the following is the best reason for concluding that the plaintiff's statement was **NOT** a dying declaration?

(A) The plaintiff's statement did not identify the person who she believed to be responsible for her death.

(B) The plaintiff was in court when the witness testified to her statement.

(C) The proceeding was a civil one.

(D) The plaintiff was not dying at the time her statement was made.

78. The plaintiff retained the defendant, an attorney, to represent him in connection with a boundary dispute between the plaintiff and his neighbor. Subsequently, the plaintiff sued the defendant for malpractice, alleging that the defendant negligently failed to institute an action to quiet title before such action was barred by the statute of limitations. At the trial, the defendant testified that he advised the plaintiff to commence an action to quiet title, but that the plaintiff instructed the defendant not to do so, stating that he feared that because of the litigation, his neighbor might find out that the plaintiff had once been convicted of a felony. The plaintiff objected on the ground that his communication with the defendant was confidential. In a jurisdiction that recognizes the common law attorney-client privilege, the plaintiff's objection should be

(A) sustained, because the plaintiff's statement was related to the reason for his consultation with the defendant.

(B) sustained, because the plaintiff's statement was necessary to his consultation with the defendant.

(C) overruled, because the defendant's testimony is relevant to the issue of the defendant's negligence.

(D) overruled, because an adversary proceeding between attorney and client terminates the confidential relationship between them.

79. The defendant, a 16-year-old child, was involved in an accident while driving a friend's car. At the request of the plaintiff, who was injured in the accident, a court designated the defendant's father as the defendant's legal guardian for the purpose of defending the plaintiff's lawsuit against the defendant. The plaintiff then sued the defendant, joining her father as a defendant as required by state law. The defendant and her father consulted an attorney about the lawsuit. The father was present when the defendant told the attorney that she had been driving over the speed limit at the time of the accident. The attorney refused to represent the defendant, and her father thereafter retained another attorney. At the trial of the plaintiff's action against the defendant and her father, the attorney was called as a witness on the plaintiff's direct case. When the plaintiff's attorney attempted to question him regarding the conversation that he had with the defendant, the defendant's attorney objected on the ground that the conversation was privileged. In a jurisdiction that recognizes the common law attorney-client privilege, should the objection to the attorney's testimony be sustained?

(A) Yes, because the father's designation as the defendant's legal guardian made his presence at the consultation necessary.

(B) Yes, because all communications made by a client to an attorney while seeking advice are privileged.

(C) No, because the defendant and the father are joint defendants.

(D) No, because the attorney never agreed to represent the defendant and the father.

80. Section 481 of the City Code of Municipal Ordinances provides in part, "In any municipal parking lot operated by the City, it shall be a misdemeanor for any person to park a vehicle more than 17 feet in length in a space marked 'Compact Car Only.'" At the defendant's trial on a charge of violating that section, the public prosecutor rested after proving that the defendant's car was more than 17 feet in length and that it had been parked in a municipal parking lot operated by the city in a space marked "Compact Car Only." Without offering any

evidence, the defendant moved to dismiss on the ground that the public prosecutor had failed to prove the contents of Section 481 of the City Code of Municipal Ordinances. In response to the defendant's motion, the public prosecutor asked the court to take judicial notice of that section. The jurisdiction permits a court to take judicial notice of municipal ordinances. The defendant's motion to dismiss should be

(A) granted, because the jurisdiction permits a court to take judicial notice of municipal ordinances.

(B) granted, because the alleged violation of Section 481 of the Code of Municipal Ordinances is an ultimate issue to be determined by the trier of fact.

(C) granted, because the court qualifies as an expert on the contents of the City Code of Municipal Ordinances.

(D) denied, because the contents of local law need not be proven in a criminal prosecution.

81. The State Police Commissioner was subpoenaed to appear before a state grand jury investigating corruption in state law enforcement agencies. After being sworn, the commissioner refused to answer any questions, asserting his privilege against self-incrimination under the Fifth Amendment to the United States Constitution. After the state prosecutor granted him use immunity, however, the commissioner testified that for years he had been aware that his assistant, the defendant, and certain other members of his department were receiving bribes from members of nationwide organized crime syndicates. The defendant was subsequently charged in a state court with receiving bribes. At the defendant's trial, the commissioner was called as a witness for the defense. On direct examination, the commissioner testified that he had never heard of the defendant or any other member of his department engaging in corrupt acts.

On cross-examination, the prosecuting attorney asked the commissioner, "Didn't you testify at a grand jury proceeding that you had been aware for years that the defendant had been taking bribes?" The commissioner refused to answer on the ground that he had received immunity before testifying at the grand jury proceeding. Should the court compel the commissioner to answer the question?

(A) Yes, but the answer is admissible only for the purpose of impeaching the commissioner's credibility.

(B) Yes, but the answer is admissible only as substantive evidence against the defendant.

(C) Yes, and the answer is admissible for the purpose of impeaching the commissioner's credibility and as substantive evidence against the defendant.

(D) No.

82. While crossing a street in the city, the plaintiff was struck by a northbound hit-and-run motorist and severely injured. In a subsequent negligence action against the city, the plaintiff asserted that there was a dangerous curve on the street just south of the place where the accident occurred, and that the city was negligent in failing to post signs warning pedestrians and motorists of the danger. During trial, the court issued a special instruction to the jury regarding the dangers of negative evidence.

As part of its defense, the city called the city traffic commissioner as a witness. The witness testified that she had been the city traffic commissioner for the past 20 years and that the street south of the accident location was substantially unchanged during the period of the witness's employment. The witness stated that because of her official position, all reported traffic accidents in the city were brought to her attention whether or not they resulted in lawsuits. She stated further that although the street was a busy thoroughfare, she had never heard of an accident on the street prior to the plaintiff's injury.

Upon proper motion by the plaintiff's attorney, the testimony of the witness should be

(A) admitted, because the street south of the accident location was substantially unchanged during the period of the witness's employment.

(B) admitted, because the court issued a special instruction to the jury regarding the dangers of negative evidence.

(C) excluded, because it is possible that accidents occurred that were not reported.

(D) excluded, because of the inherent unreliability of negative evidence.

83. In a negligence action against a hotel, the plaintiff asserted that while she was a guest at the hotel, she slipped on wet pigeon droppings in an alley located next to the hotel, sustaining injury. In defense, the hotel denied that it was negligent and denied ownership and control of the alley in which the accident occurred. At the trial, the plaintiff called a hotel maintenance employee as a witness. The witness testified that although employees of the hotel had never before cleaned pigeon droppings from the alley, they began doing so after the plaintiff commenced her lawsuit against the hotel. If the hotel objects to the testimony of the witness, the testimony should be

(A) admitted.

(B) excluded, because subsequent cleaning of pigeon droppings may have been nothing more than a response to the litigation.

(C) excluded, because of a policy that encourages the taking of remedial measures following an accident.

(D) excluded, because the hotel denied that it was negligent.

84. At the trial of a personal injury action, a doctor testified that she examined the plaintiff on the day of the trial, and that at that time, the plaintiff told her that she felt pain in her knee.

On cross-examination, the defendant's attorney asked the doctor whether she had ever met the plaintiff before the day of the trial. The doctor responded that she had not, and that her sole purpose in examining the plaintiff was to prepare for testifying at the trial. The defendant's attorney then moved to strike that portion of the doctor's testimony that referred to the plaintiff's complaint of pain. In a jurisdiction that applies the common-law rule regarding confidential communications between patient and physician, should the defendant's motion be granted?

(A) Yes, because the examination was solely for the purpose of litigation.

(B) Yes, because the probative value of the statement is outweighed by the possibility of prejudice.

(C) Yes, because statements made to a physician are privileged.

(D) No, because the statement described what the plaintiff was feeling at the time.

85. At the trial of the defendant on a charge of criminal battery, the prosecutor called the victim as a witness. The victim testified that he had argued with the defendant in a bar shortly before he was struck in the head from behind. He said that he did not see who struck him, but that a moment before the blow, he heard a voice that he did not recognize shout, "Watch out for [the defendant]!"

If the defendant's attorney objects to the victim's statement about what he heard, that statement should be

(A) excluded, because the victim could not identify the person who shouted.

(B) excluded, because the victim's testimony is self-serving.

(C) admitted.

(D) excluded, because there was no proof that the person shouting had personal knowledge of the assailant's identity.

86. Procedural delays caused five years to pass before the plaintiff's personal injury claim against the defendant was ready for trial. At the trial, the plaintiff's attorney called the witness, an eyewitness to the accident. The witness testified that before coming to court, she had refreshed her recollection by looking at written notes of her interview with the plaintiff's attorney that took place the week after the accident. On proper motion by the defendant's attorney, the court

   (A) should strike the witness's testimony, unless it is shown that the notes themselves are unavailable.

   (B) may direct that the notes be brought into court for inspection by the defendant's attorney.

   (C) may not properly direct that the notes be brought into court because they have not been offered into evidence.

   (D) should admit the notes into evidence as an admission of a party.

87. During the presentation of the plaintiff's direct case in a personal injury action, the plaintiff's attorney called a doctor to the stand for the purpose of establishing that the plaintiff had sustained an injury to one of her glands.

   When the plaintiff's attorney began to question the doctor about her qualifications, the defendant's attorney conceded on the record and in the presence of the jury that the doctor was an expert on injuries of the glands and objected to any further questions regarding the qualifications of the doctor. The court was satisfied that the doctor qualified as an expert on glands. Should the plaintiff's attorney be permitted to continue questioning the doctor regarding her qualifications?

   (A) No, because the qualifications of the doctor are no longer in issue.

   (B) No, because the court is satisfied that the doctor is qualified as an expert on diseases and injuries of the glands.

   (C) Yes, because the court must determine for itself whether a witness qualifies as an expert and cannot allow the matter to be determined by stipulation of the parties.

   (D) Yes, because the jury may consider an expert's qualifications in determining his or her credibility.

88. The plaintiff was a passenger in a car driven by the defendant when the car struck a pole. The plaintiff subsequently asserted a claim against the defendant, alleging that injuries that resulted from the defendant's negligent driving caused the plaintiff to be hospitalized for more than a month. At trial, on the presentation of the plaintiff's direct case, the plaintiff testified that immediately after the accident, while the defendant was extremely nervous and upset, the defendant said, "Don't worry, I've got plenty of insurance."

   Upon objection by the defendant's attorney, that portion of the plaintiff's testimony should be

   (A) excluded, because it is not relevant to a material issue.

   (B) excluded, because it relates to a compromise offer.

   (C) admitted as evidence of an admission of a party.

   (D) admitted as evidence of an excited utterance.

89. At the defendant's trial on charges of criminal assault and battery, the witness was called by the prosecutor. The witness testified that while he was walking through a parking lot at night, the defendant attacked and beat him. The witness stated further that although there were no artificial lights of any kind in the vicinity of the parking lot, he was able to see the defendant clearly in the light of the full moon. After direct examination of the witness by the prosecutor, the defendant's attorney waived cross-examination, and the witness left the courtroom.

The defendant's attorney subsequently called an expert witness to testify that there was no moon at all on the night of the alleged crime. The prosecutor conceded the expert's qualifications.

Upon timely objection by the prosecutor, the expert's testimony should be

(A) admitted to show that the witness's testimony is not worthy of belief.

(B) admitted, because it is part of the *res gestae*.

(C) excluded, because the witness was not given an opportunity to explain his testimony in view of the additional evidence.

(D) excluded as extrinsic evidence of a collateral matter.

90. The defendant was arrested after she used a credit card bearing the name "Timothy Nolan" to pay for a purchase. The defendant was subsequently charged with fraudulent use of a credit card. At her trial, a police officer testified that when she arrested the defendant, she found her to be in possession of 5 credit cards bearing the name "Timothy Nolan" and 36 other credit cards bearing a total of 36 different names. In addition, the officer stated that the defendant's wallet contained driver's licenses to match each of the various names on the credit cards.

If the defendant's attorney moves to exclude evidence that the defendant possessed credit cards or driver's licenses other than that which she was charged with fraudulently using, which of the following would be the prosecutor's most effective argument in opposition to that motion?

(A) The number of credit cards and driver's licenses in the defendant's possession tends to establish a criminal plan.

(B) The number of credit cards in the defendant's possession makes it likely that she had stolen them.

(C) The defendant should be required to explain why she possessed so many credit cards belonging to other people.

(D) The defendant's possession of 41 credit cards bearing names other than her own is an admission by conduct.

91. The plaintiff brought a negligence action against the defendant for damages resulting from personal injuries sustained in an automobile accident. Prior to trial, the parties and their attorneys attended a settlement conference in the judge's chambers. During the course of the settlement conference, the judge asked the defendant how fast she was going at the time of the accident, to which the defendant replied, "I really don't know, Your Honor." The defendant was not under oath.

At the trial, the defendant testified on her own behalf. In response to a question by her attorney, the defendant said, "When the accident occurred, I was definitely not exceeding the speed limit." On cross-examination, the plaintiff's attorney asked the defendant, "Did you ever say that you didn't know how fast you were going at the time of the accident?" The defendant's attorney objected to the question.

The objection of the defendant's attorney should be

(A) sustained, because a proper foundation was not laid.

(B) sustained, because the defendant was not under oath at the settlement conference.

(C) overruled, because the statement that the defendant made at the settlement conference tends to establish that the defendant is not worthy of belief.

(D) sustained, because the plaintiff's attorney failed to confront the defendant prior to asking her about the statement.

92. The defendant was arrested for driving under the influence of alcohol while operating a car

that he borrowed from a friend earlier that day. After the arrest, the police conducted an inventory search of the vehicle and found a container of marijuana in the trunk. As a result, the defendant was charged with violating a state law that made it a crime to knowingly possess marijuana. Testifying on his own behalf at the trial, the defendant stated that he was not aware there was marijuana in the trunk. On cross-examination, after properly marking it for identification, the prosecutor showed the defendant a letter that had been taken from his coat pocket following his arrest, and he asked whether he recognized it. When the defendant said that it was a note from his wife, the prosecutor showed it to the defendant's attorney and offered it in evidence. Among other things, the note said, "We sure got high on that stuff we smoked last night."

The jurisdiction recognizes the common law spousal privilege. If the defendant's attorney objects to admission of the letter, his objection should be

(A) sustained, because the letter is hearsay not within any exception to the hearsay rule.

(B) sustained, because the letter is not relevant to a material issue.

(C) sustained, because the jurisdiction recognizes the common law spousal privilege.

(D) overruled, because the letter is a declaration against the penal interest of the defendant's wife.

93. At the trial of an action for breach of contract brought by the plaintiff against the defendant, the plaintiff's attorney called the plaintiff as a witness on her own behalf. The plaintiff was an expert in dog behavior. On direct examination, the plaintiff's attorney asked, "Do you own a German shepherd with a white forepaw?" The plaintiff said that she did. No other questions were asked on direct examination. On cross-examination, the defendant's

attorney asked the plaintiff, "Your dog is generally known to be gentle, isn't that correct?"

If the plaintiff's attorney objects to the question, the objection should be

(A) sustained, because the question went beyond the scope of cross-examination.

(B) sustained, because the question is leading.

(C) overruled, because the plaintiff is a hostile witness.

(D) overruled, because the plaintiff is an expert in dog behavior.

94. Which of the following is **NOT** self-authenticating?

(A) A will with the attestation of witnesses affixed to it.

(B) A newspaper.

(C) A directory of public service telephone numbers issued by the state civil services administration.

(D) A copy of a divorce decree prepared by the attorney for one of the divorced spouses and certified correct by the clerk of the court.

95. The plaintiff was riding a motorcycle manufactured by the defendant when he collided with an automobile, sustaining serious personal injuries. Following the accident, examination of the motorcycle revealed that its fork was severely bent. The plaintiff claimed that the fork bent when he drove the motorcycle over a bump in the road, and that the bending of the fork caused him to lose control and strike the automobile. The plaintiff asserted a personal injury claim against the defendant on the ground that the motorcycle was equipped with a fork that was not strong enough to withstand the pressures of normal operation and was therefore defective in design. The defendant denied that

the motorcycle was defective and claimed that the accident resulted from the plaintiff's negligent operation of the motorcycle and that the fork did not bend until the motorcycle collided with the automobile. During trial, the judge gave the jury a special instruction regarding the uncertainty of negative evidence.

The defendant called the witness, who was employed by the defendant as vice president in charge of safety. The witness was the person to whom all complaints of product failure would be reported. The witness testified that he had held that position for six years, that in that time the company had sold more than 10,000 motorcycles identical to the one ridden by the plaintiff, and that the witness had never heard about a fork bending in normal operation. If the plaintiff's attorney objects, the witness's testimony should be

(A) admitted, because the judge gave the jury a special instruction regarding the uncertainty of negative evidence.

(B) admitted, because the witness was the person to whom all complaints of product failure would be reported.

(C) excluded, because it is possible that accidents occurred that were never reported to the company.

(D) excluded, because negative evidence is inherently unreliable.

96. While visiting the United States from a Central American republic, the plaintiff purchased a sweater at a department store and paid for it at the appropriate cash register. In ringing up the sale, however, the store employee neglected to remove a security tag that was still affixed to the sweater to prevent theft. As a result, the tag caused an electronic security alarm to ring as the plaintiff attempted to exit the store with the purchased merchandise. Security guards immediately accosted her and placed her under citizen's arrest. Eventually, the police were called, and a more thorough investigation was instituted.

As a result, it was determined that the plaintiff had paid for the merchandise. Authorities of the department store apologized to the plaintiff and permitted her to leave.

Subsequently, a magazine erroneously reported that the plaintiff had been arrested, charged with shoplifting at the department store, and taken into police custody. Because the plaintiff was a candidate for political office in the Central American republic, newspapers in that country reprinted the magazine article. The plaintiff lost the election, and she instituted an action against the magazine for damages resulting from defamation.

On cross-examination, the plaintiff's attorney asked a witness whether he and the plaintiff were political rivals, and the witness answered that they were not. The plaintiff's attorney subsequently offered the testimony of a republic official, who stated that, in a recent election, the witness ran against the plaintiff for political office, and that the witness won the election by engaging in a campaign of false accusations against the plaintiff. Upon appropriate motion of the magazine's attorney, the testimony of the official should be

(A) admitted, since it tends to attack the witness's credibility by showing bias.

(B) admitted, since the magazine opened the door by bringing the plaintiff's reputation into question.

(C) admitted, since it is evidence of an admission.

(D) excluded.

97. At the trial of a personal injury action, the plaintiff claimed that he had sustained a shattered elbow when he was knocked from his bicycle by the defendant's car. A doctor testified for the plaintiff, stating that she examined him for the first time on the morning of the trial and that her examination was made specifically in preparation for her testimony.

The doctor then stated that during the course of the examination, the plaintiff also said, "When I was struck by the car, my right elbow struck the ground so hard that I heard a sound like a gunshot." If the defendant objects to this testimony, the court should

(A) sustain the objection, since the statement is hearsay.

(B) sustain the objection, since the examination was not performed for the purpose of diagnosis or treatment.

(C) overrule the objection, since the statement was part of a pertinent medical history.

(D) overrule the objection, since the statement described a former sense impression.

98. After a minor impact caused an automobile to explode, killing all its occupants, the company that manufactured the car was charged with criminal negligence and prosecuted by the state. At the trial, an automobile safety design expert testified under oath on behalf of the prosecution. He stated that in his opinion the car was poorly designed, and that because of the construction of its engine, an explosion was inevitable if the front end of the car collided with any object at an impact speed in excess of 35 miles per hour.

Subsequently, the plaintiff was injured when the car that he was driving exploded after striking another vehicle in the rear. The plaintiff brought an action in a neighboring state against the company for personal injuries.

Pursuant to a subpoena that had been served on the company, the plaintiff's attorney called upon the company to produce records of tests that it had performed on the car before marketing it. The company's attorney objected, on the ground that the company had turned the test records over to its attorney in preparation for trial. Should the trial court require production of the records?

(A) No, since they are privileged as an attorney's work product.

(B) No, since they are privileged as materials prepared for litigation.

(C) No, since they are privileged as a confidential communication to an attorney.

(D) Yes, since they are relevant to the issues and not protected by privilege.

99. The plaintiff was injured when she fell down a flight of steps at a bartending school. She subsequently sued the school for damages, asserting that the accident resulted from the school's negligence in allowing parts of the stairway to become loose.

On the defendant's case, the school's attorney called a doctor to the stand. After establishing that she was an expert in the field of spinal injuries, the school's attorney asked her whether, in her opinion, it was possible for a person to sustain a herniation of the spine in a fall down a flight of steps. The doctor stated that in her opinion it was not possible to sustain such an injury in that way. On cross-examination, the plaintiff's attorney asked the doctor whether she had ever examined or treated the plaintiff. The doctor answered, "I have never even met the plaintiff." The plaintiff's attorney then moved to strike the testimony that the doctor had given on direct examination. The motion should be

(A) granted, since the doctor's opinion is not based on matters within her personal knowledge.

(B) granted, since the doctor's opinion is based on matters not in evidence.

(C) denied, since the doctor was testifying in response to a hypothetical question.

(D) denied, since an expert's testimony may be based on observations made in the courtroom.

100. The defendant was charged with murdering the victim, a prominent union leader, by throwing him off the roof of an office building. At the defendant's trial, the prosecution offered the testimony of a police officer who arrived at the scene moments after the victim's death.

The prosecuting attorney asked the officer whether he interviewed any of the people in the crowd. The officer replied that he interviewed an eyewitness, but that he no longer remembered her name or what she told him. He then said that he had accurately recorded the contents of the eyewitness's statement in his notebook as she was making it and that he had brought the notebook to court with him. The prosecuting attorney asked the officer to read the contents of the statement to the jury. If the defendant's attorney objected, the court should

   (A)  sustain the objection, since the statement of the eyewitness is hearsay, not within any exception to the hearsay rule.

   (B)  overrule the objection, since the statement is a past recollection recorded.

   (C)  overrule the objection, since the statement is part of the *res gestae.*

   (D)  overrule the objection, since the officer's notebook is a business record.

101. The plaintiff sued a newspaper publisher for stating that the plaintiff had misused church funds. The publisher's attorney offered the testimony of an editor employed by the publisher. The editor testified that it was his job to note retraction demands in an office file, and that as a matter of company policy and practice, all such demands were promptly reported to him for that purpose and promptly noted by him. He said that on the morning of the trial he had searched the file for notes of any retraction demand made by the plaintiff and found none. If the publisher's attorney offers the file in evidence, the plaintiff's objection should be

   (A)  sustained, since the absence of a notation cannot be used as evidence that an event did not occur.

   (B)  sustained, since the file is self-serving.

   (C)  overruled, since the file itself is admissible as a business record.

   (D)  overruled, since the editor used the file to refresh his recollection.

102. Following his arrest on New Year's Eve, the defendant was charged with reckless driving and driving while under the influence of intoxicating liquor. The arresting officer testified at the defendant's trial on those charges.

The officer stated that she chased the defendant in her patrol car, apprehended him, and ordered him out of his car. The prosecutor asked, "Did you notice anything in particular about his breath at that time?" The officer answered, "Yes, it smelled like alcohol." The defendant's attorney objected to the question and moved to strike the answer. The motion should be

   (A)  granted, because the question was leading.

   (B)  granted, since the officer's answer was a conclusion.

   (C)  granted, since the officer's statement went to an ultimate issue in the case.

   (D)  denied.

103. At trial for breach of contract, the defendant offered the testimony of a store manager who stated that blank DVDs from the plaintiff always came in plastic cases. In response, the plaintiff offered the testimony of a witness, who stated that he was the plaintiff's shipping manager and in charge of filling orders for blank DVDs received by the plaintiff. Over objection by the defendant's attorney, the witness stated that in the past four months the plaintiff had shipped DVDs packaged in paper boxes to 20 other customers and that none had rejected them.

He also testified that the 20 customers were of the same general size and class as the defendant. The objection should have been

(A) overruled, since evidence of previous dealings is usually admissible for the purpose of establishing the parties' state of mind at the time the contract was formed.

(B) overruled, since the defendant opened the door by offering the testimony of the store manager.

(C) overruled, because the 20 customers to which the witness referred were of the same general size and class as the defendant.

(D) sustained, since such transactions are not relevant to the agreement between the plaintiff and the defendant.

104. After his vehicle collided with the plaintiff's on March 1, the defendant retained an attorney to represent him in any possible litigation that might develop. The attorney hired a private investigator to interview the plaintiff regarding the facts of the accident. On March 5, the investigator followed he plaintiff into a bar, sat next to him, and engaged him in conversation. During the conversation, the plaintiff described the accident that he had with the defendant, and said, "Just between you and me, I drank a six-pack of beer just before the accident happened. It's a good thing nobody smelled my breath." Eventually the plaintiff commenced a personal injury action against the defendant. At the trial of the action, the plaintiff testified on direct examination that he had been driving at a slow rate of speed when the defendant's vehicle suddenly pulled out of a driveway into his path. During cross-examination, the plaintiff stated that he had not been drinking prior to the accident.

During presentation of the defendant's case, the defendant's attorney called the investigator to the stand. Over objection by the plaintiff's attorney, the investigator described the conversation that he had with the plaintiff in the bar on March 5 and stated that the plaintiff told him that he had consumed a six-pack of beer just prior to the accident. The investigator's testimony was

(A) admissible for impeachment purposes only.

(B) admissible as substantive evidence only.

(C) admissible for impeachment purposes and as substantive evidence.

(D) inadmissible.

105. In an action by the seller against the buyer for breach of contract, the seller's manager testified that after the buyer refused to accept delivery of merchandise as agreed, he personally arranged for the resale of the goods at a price that was $3,000 less than that which the buyer had agreed to pay.

On cross-examination, the buyer's attorney asked, "Didn't you once plead guilty to violating Penal Code section 22.9(a)?" The manager denied ever pleading guilty to the code section. The buyer's attorney subsequently offered a transcript of the manager's conviction for violating the code section. If only one of the following facts or inferences were true, which would most effectively support the seller's objection to its admission into evidence?

(A) The manager's violation of the code section is unrelated to his duties as an employee of the seller.

(B) The manager's conviction was subsequently reversed on the ground that the evidence used against him was obtained in violation of the Fourth Amendment to the United States Constitution.

(C) The crime of which the manager was convicted was a misdemeanor.

(D) The crime of which the manager was convicted was a *malum prohibitum* felony.

106. The plaintiff was crossing the street on foot when she was struck by a delivery van driven by an employee of the defendant while the employee was in the process of making a delivery. Following the accident, the employee was charged with reckless driving and pleaded not guilty. At the trial on the charge of reckless driving, the employee testified in his own defense. He stated that at the time of the accident, he had taken his eyes off the road to look for the address of the place to which he had to make his delivery and that as a result, he didn't see the plaintiff crossing the street.

The plaintiff subsequently sued the defendant under the theory of *respondeat superior*. The plaintiff proved that the employee was in the defendant's employ until the employee died of natural causes unrelated to the accident. The plaintiff then offered the transcript of the employee's testimony at the reckless driving trial.

The court refused to admit the transcript of the employee's testimony. Upon presentation of the defendant's case, the defendant's attorney offered into evidence a properly certified transcript of a court record indicating that the employee had been acquitted after trial on the charge of reckless driving. Upon objection by the plaintiff's attorney, the transcript should be

(A) admitted, as an official record.

(B) admitted, to raise a conclusive presumption that the employee was not driving recklessly at the time of the accident.

(C) excluded, since the employee is not available for cross-examination regarding his guilt or innocence of the charge of reckless driving.

(D) excluded, since it is not relevant to the issues on trial.

107. A young couple was driving home from a party when they collided with the plaintiff's car. The police arrived at the scene and arrested the driver for driving while intoxicated. He was later tried and acquitted. Several months after the trial, the plaintiff instituted an action against the driver for personal injuries resulting from the accident.

The couple married after the criminal trial but divorced before the civil trial. If the plaintiff's attorney asks the driver's ex-wife to state how much alcohol she had observed the driver consume at the party, the driver's objection should be

(A) sustained, since the ex-wife's testimony would involve a confidential marital communication.

(B) sustained, under the spousal privilege.

(C) sustained, since a rule of policy prevents the testimony of a former spouse from being used against a party.

(D) overruled.

108. The defendant, a police officer who had recently joined the police department, was charged with the murder of his wife. At the trial, the prosecution claimed that while on a visit to the country, the defendant's wife was walking across a meadow when the defendant shot her from three-quarters of a mile away with a rifle equipped with a telescopic sight. The defendant admitted firing the rifle but maintained that his wife's death was an accident. On the presentation of the defendant's case, his attorney called a firearms expert, who testified that the rifle was not reliably accurate at any distance in excess of a half-mile.

In rebuttal, the prosecutor called a police officer who joined the police force at the same time as the defendant. The officer testified that he and the defendant had attended firearms classes together at the police academy, and that the defendant had been with him in a firearms class when their instructor said that the rifle was capable of remarkable accuracy at distances of up to two miles if fired by a good marksman. On objection by the defendant's attorney, the testimony of the officer should be

(A) admitted, only for the purpose of proving that the defendant believed the rifle to be accurate at the distance involved.

(B) admitted, only for the purpose of proving that the rifle was accurate at the distance involved.

(C) admitted for the purpose of proving that the defendant believed the rifle to be accurate at the distance involved, and for the purpose of proving that it was accurate at that distance.

(D) excluded as hearsay.

109. The defendant was arrested for murder. While he was being held in the county jail, he shared a cell with the witness, who was being held on misdemeanor vandalism charges. During the defendant's trial, the prosecutor called the witness to the stand to authenticate the defendant's voice on an audio clip posted to the Internet the day of the murder. After the prosecutor laid the proper foundation, the witness testified that although he never knew the defendant before his arrest, he spoke with the defendant when they were sharing the cell together and the voice on the audio file was the defendant's. The defendant's attorney objected, arguing the witness could not properly authenticate the defendant's voice.

The court should

(A) sustain the objection, because the witness's testimony is inadmissible hearsay.

(B) sustain the objection, because the witness had never heard the defendant's voice until after his felony arrest.

(C) overrule the objection, because the witness spoke with the defendant while they shared the cell.

(D) overrule the objection, because the witness can be qualified as a special expert in a criminal trial.

110. At trial, a witness testified that on the day of the incident, she looked up the defendant's number in the phone book and dialed it, and that a male voice answered, "[Defendant] speaking." The witness stated further that she then asked, "Are you the animal that exposed his privates to my daughter?" to which the voice replied, "Yes, I couldn't help myself."

The witness testified further that she knew it was the defendant on the phone because she had once chatted with him outside the grocery store and recognized his "really deep" voice. If the defendant moves to strike this testimony, the motion should be

(A) granted, since one conversation is not sufficient to justify testimony as to voice identification.

(B) granted, since expert testimony is required for the identification of a voice.

(C) denied, since a voice may be identified by a layperson who testifies that he or she recognized it because he or she had heard it before under circumstances connecting it with the alleged speaker.

(D) denied, because the witness testified to a distinctive characteristic about the defendant's voice that permitted her to recognize it.

111. In a personal injury action by the plaintiff against the defendant, the plaintiff claimed that the accident occurred because the defendant, who was operating a blue sedan, was driving at an excessive rate of speed. At the trial, the plaintiff's attorney called a witness who testified that she was walking on the street at the time the accident occurred and that, although she did not see the vehicles before the collision, she knew that the defendant's vehicle was traveling at a high rate of speed because of the screeching sound made by his tires immediately before

the impact. If the defendant's attorney objects to this testimony, the court should

(A) permit the witness to testify, but should give the jury a cautionary instruction regarding lay opinions.

(B) permit the witness to testify, because a layperson is competent to form an opinion regarding the speed of a moving automobile.

(C) exclude the witness's testimony, because a layperson is not competent to form an opinion as to the speed of a moving automobile.

(D) exclude the witness's testimony, because the witness did not have an adequate opportunity to form an opinion regarding the speed of the defendant's automobile.

112. After the crash of an airplane, an action for wrongful death was brought by the husband of a passenger killed in the crash. During the trial, the plaintiff called an employee of the State Aviation Agency that investigated the circumstances surrounding the crash.

The witness read aloud from an investigation report that quoted an unidentified witness to the crash as stating that she heard an explosion several seconds before she saw the plane burst into flames. He testified that the report from which he was reading was one kept in the regular course of business by the State Aviation Agency, that the entry from which he was reading had been made by another investigator who worked for the Agency, that the investigator who made the entry was sworn to investigate airplane crashes and to keep honest and accurate records of the results of those investigations, and that the investigator who made the entry was now dead. Upon appropriate objection, the evidence should be ruled

(A) admissible as a business record.

(B) admissible as an official written statement.

(C) admissible as past recollection recorded.

(D) inadmissible as hearsay not within any exception.

113. The plaintiff was injured when the ladder on which she was standing collapsed without warning. Immediately following the accident, the plaintiff was taken to the hospital, where she remained for approximately six hours. The plaintiff later sued the manufacturer of the ladder. At the trial, the plaintiff's attorney next offered a properly authenticated hospital record. After examining the record, the defendant's attorney, outside the presence of the jury, moved to exclude a portion of the record that read: "History: Ladder collapsed. Patient fell." The motion to exclude that portion of the record should be

(A) granted, because it can be excluded without causing any physical damage to the record.

(B) granted, because it has no bearing on the plaintiff's medical condition.

(C) denied, because the history was taken for the purpose of diagnosis or treatment.

(D) granted, since hospital personnel are not experts in determining the causes of accidents.

114. The plaintiff sued the defendant for battery. At trial, the defendant offered the testimony of the local parish priest, who stated that he had known the defendant for years and that he and everyone else in the community thought of him as a peaceable man who would never resort to violence except in self-protection. The defendant offered the testimony as circumstantial evidence to prove that he did not strike the plaintiff without justification.

If the plaintiff's attorney objects to the testimony of the parish priest, the testimony should be

(A) excluded, because it is being offered as circumstantial evidence to prove that the defendant did not strike the plaintiff without justification.

(B) admitted, because the priest testified that his own opinion of the defendant coincided with what the community thought about him.

(C) admitted, because it states the reputation of the defendant.

(D) admitted, for the limited purpose of establishing the defendant's state of mind at the time of the occurrence.

115. While walking down a stairway that led to the women's restroom at a theater, the plaintiff fell and sustained serious injuries to her shoulder. She sued the theater for damages, alleging that it had negligently permitted the stairway to be littered with scraps of paper and that she had slipped on one of them.

At trial, the theater manager testified that immediately following the accident, a crowd formed around the fallen plaintiff, and he heard a friend of his in the crowd shout, "She was taking the stairs three at a time and she missed one!" He stated that the speaker was a good friend of his, who offered to testify if need be. The judge should rule this testimony

(A) admissible as an excited utterance.

(B) admissible, because the manager can identify the person who made the statement.

(C) admissible, because the person who made the statement offered to testify to it herself.

(D) inadmissible as hearsay.

116. The plaintiff was a commercial furniture-finisher. The defendant was a manufacturer of commercial furniture-finishing supplies. In an action by the plaintiff against the defendant for breach of contract, a dispute arose as to the meaning of the term "unit of lacquer," which appeared in a contract between the parties. The witness, an officer of the plaintiff, testified on her company's direct case.

The plaintiff's attorney asked the witness whether the plaintiff and the defendant had ever done business in the past. In response, the witness said, "Definitely. In fact, before coming to court today, I refreshed my recollection by looking at company files. Then, based on my own knowledge, I prepared a chart, which accurately indicates the dates of the occasions we have done business together." After the witness testified to those dates, the plaintiff's attorney offered the chart that the witness had prepared into evidence. Should the chart be admitted into evidence over the objection of the defendant's attorney?

(A) Yes, as a summary of a business record.

(B) Yes, as an illustration of the witness's testimony.

(C) No, because it is not the best evidence of the contents of the plaintiff's files.

(D) No, because a witness may not refresh his or her recollection by reference to materials unless they are in court and marked for identification.

117. The defendant pleaded not guilty to a charge of committing an armed robbery of a bank. When the defendant appeared in court on the day of the trial, his head was completely bald. Witnesses stated that the bank was robbed by a man with bushy red hair.

The prosecuting attorney called a guard as a witness. The guard testified that she was employed as a guard in the county house of detention where the defendant had been in custody since the day of his arrest. She stated that when she saw the defendant on the day of his arrest he had bushy red hair. She stated further that, at the defendant's request, she provided the defendant with shaving articles on the morning of the trial and remained outside his cell, where she watched while he shaved his head. If the defendant's attorney objects to this testimony, the testimony should be

(A) excluded, as extrinsic evidence of a collateral matter.

(B) excluded, under the defendant's privilege against self-incrimination.

(C) admitted, to explain why the defendant no longer has bushy red hair.

(D) admitted, as evidence of an admission by conduct.

118. Soon after his election as labor union president, the defendant raised his presidential salary from $135,000 to $160,000 per year. As a result, he was subsequently charged with violating a state law making it a felony for union officials to knowingly misappropriate union funds. The defendant admitted granting himself the pay raise but claimed as a defense that when he did so, he believed the union rules authorized such action.

The defendant's attorney called the former president of the union. The former president testified to a conversation that took place between him and the defendant before the defendant ordered the pay raise. The former president stated that when the defendant asked him whether the union president was permitted to raise his own salary, the former president told him that the president could do so whenever he deemed it necessary. If the prosecuting attorney objects to the former president's testimony on the ground that it is hearsay, the former president's testimony should be

(A) admitted, as evidence of the defendant's state of mind.

(B) excluded, as hearsay, not within any exception.

(C) excluded, because the former president likely does not qualify as an expert on the union's rules.

(D) admitted, because the out-of-court assertion was made by the witness himself.

119. At the trial of her negligence action against the defendant, the plaintiff exhibited her leg to the jury and testified that following the accident, her leg was so badly mangled that she believed that she was going to die. The plaintiff's attorney then called a witness, who testified that he arrived at the scene of the accident moments after it occurred and found the plaintiff lying in the roadway in a pool of blood. The witness stated that he heard the plaintiff scream, "Oh, God, I had the green light in my favor and now I'm dying!" The defendant's attorney made timely objection to the witness's testimony.

The witness's testimony is

(A) admissible as evidence of an excited utterance.

(B) inadmissible as hearsay, not within any exception.

(C) admissible as evidence of a declaration of present state of mind.

(D) admissible as evidence of a declaration of past state of mind.

120. The defendant was charged in a state court with third degree arson on the allegation that he set fire to his own house for the purpose of collecting benefits under a fire insurance policy. At his trial, the defendant called the witness as a witness in his favor. On direct examination by the defendant's attorney, the witness testified that at the time of the fire, he and the defendant were together at a baseball game 50 miles away from the defendant's home.

The prosecuting attorney then offered proof that the witness had been arrested as an accessory to the burning of the defendant's house and that the charge against him was still pending. If the defendant's attorney objects to this evidence, the objection should be

(A) sustained, because evidence of unconvicted bad acts is inadmissible to extrinsically impeach a witness.

(B) sustained, because the arrest of the witness is not material to the charge against the defendant.

(C) overruled, because the pending charge against the witness is evidence that the witness is a biased witness.

(D) overruled, because the arrest is evidence that the witness has a bad reputation for honesty and truthfulness.

121. The plaintiff appeared as a chef on a televised cooking contest. After the plaintiff was eliminated and left the room, the defendant, a judge on the show, turned to another one of the judges and said, "That guy was totally on drugs and his cooking tastes like it." The plaintiff didn't know about the defendant's statements until he watched the show on television. Concerned that the defendant's statement could damage the success of his new restaurant, the plaintiff sued the defendant for defamation. At trial, the plaintiff testified as to what the defendant said on the television show. The defendant's attorney objected.

The objection should be

(A) granted, because a recording of the show would be the best evidence regarding what was said.

(B) granted, because the testimony is inadmissible hearsay.

(C) denied, because it is a declaration against interest.

(D) denied, because the plaintiff saw the television show where the defendant made his statements.

122. At the trial of the defendant on a charge of criminal battery, the prosecutor called a witness who testified that he was working as a bartender at the time and place where the victim was attacked. In answer to a question by the prosecutor, the witness said that he did not remember whether he shouted anything immediately before the attack. The prosecutor showed the defendant's attorney a written report of a conversation between the witness and an investigator and had it marked for identification. Then the prosecutor showed the report to the witness and asked whether it refreshed his recollection. If the defendant's attorney objects to this procedure, the objection should be

(A) sustained, unless the report has been admitted into evidence.

(B) sustained, because the report is inadmissible hearsay.

(C) overruled, because the witness testified that he did not remember whether or not he shouted anything prior to the attack.

(D) overruled, but only if the prosecutor offers the report into evidence.

123. During the presentation of plaintiff's direct case in a personal injury action, the plaintiff's attorney called a doctor to the stand for the purpose of establishing that the plaintiff had sustained an injury to her skull.

On direct examination, the doctor testified that after receiving a positive result in a test known as a skullogram, she concluded that the plaintiff had sustained an injury to her skull. On cross-examination, the defendant's attorney showed the doctor a book and asked whether she relied on it in forming her diagnosis. The doctor stated that she did not, but she admitted that it was a well-respected work in the field. The defendant's attorney then asked the doctor to read aloud a passage from the book that stated that a positive result in a skullogram almost always indicated that there was no injury to the patient's skull. If the plaintiff's attorney objects, can that passage be read to the jury?

(A) Yes, for the purpose of impeachment only.

(B) Yes, as substantive evidence only.

(C) Yes, for the purpose of impeachment and as substantive evidence.

(D) No.

124. The plaintiff was a passenger in a car driven by the defendant when the car struck a pole. The plaintiff subsequently asserted a claim against the defendant, alleging that injuries that resulted from the defendant's negligent driving caused the plaintiff to be hospitalized for more than a month. At trial, on the presentation of the plaintiff's direct case, the plaintiff testified that following his release from the hospital, the defendant's insurance company paid the plaintiff's hospital bill of $20,000. Upon objection by the defendant's attorney, this portion of the plaintiff's testimony should be

(A) excluded, because the payment of the plaintiff's hospital bill is an offer of compromise.

(B) excluded.

(C) admitted, because reference to the fact that the defendant was insured can be severed from the rest of the plaintiff's statement.

(D) admitted, as circumstantial evidence that the defendant regarded himself to be at fault in causing the accident.

125. The plaintiff brought a negligence action against the defendant for personal injuries that the plaintiff sustained when she was struck by the defendant's car while she was a pedestrian. In defense, the defendant asserted that he was not negligent and that the plaintiff was contributorily negligent in that she was not in the area designated as a crosswalk at the time of the accident. The plaintiff's attorney called the witness as a witness on the plaintiff's behalf.

The witness testified that she held a valid driver's license, that she had been driving an automobile for 40 years, that she had seen the defendant's car just before it struck the plaintiff, and that, in her opinion, it was moving at a speed in excess of the speed limit, 35 miles per hour. If the defendant's attorney objects to the witness's testimony regarding the speed of the defendant's vehicle, which of the following would be the most effective argument in support of that objection?

(A) The witness did not qualify as an expert on the speed of a moving automobile.

(B) The witness's statement of opinion concerned an ultimate fact in the litigation.

(C) The witness did not have sufficient opportunity to form an opinion regarding the speed of the defendant's vehicle.

(D) The speed of the defendant's vehicle was a fact, and therefore it cannot be established by opinion evidence.

126. At the trial of an action brought by the plaintiff against the defendant for breach of contract, a witness was called by the plaintiff's attorney. The witness identified the signature on a document as the defendant's, testifying that he knew the defendant's signature because he and the defendant had once been partners and that he had seen the defendant's signature many times during the course of their partnership.

The witness then testified to other matters, and on cross-examination, the defendant's attorney asked the witness, "Didn't the partnership between you and the defendant break up because the defendant accused you of dishonesty?" If the plaintiff's attorney objects to that question, the objection should be

(A) sustained, because the question seeks to elicit hearsay not within any exception to the hearsay rule.

(B) overruled, because the question seeks to elicit an admission.

(C) overruled, because the question seeks to elicit evidence that is admissible for purposes of extrinsic impeachment.

(D) overruled, because the question seeks to elicit evidence that would tend to establish that the witness is a biased witness.

127. A federal officer had been informed that a person arriving from Europe on a particular airline flight would be carrying cocaine in his baggage. The officer went to the airport and stood at the arrival gate with a dog that had been specially trained to recognize the scent of cocaine. When the defendant, carrying his bag, walked by, the dog began barking and scratching the floor in front of him with his right paw. The officer stopped the defendant and searched his bag. In it, he found a small brass statue with a false bottom. Upon removing the false bottom, the officer found one ounce of cocaine. The defendant, who was arrested and charged with the illegal importation of a controlled substance, claimed he had purchased the statue as a souvenir and was unaware that there was cocaine hidden it its base.

At the defendant's trial, the prosecution offered to prove that the defendant had been convicted 15 years earlier of illegally importing cocaine by hiding it in the base of a brass statue. If the defendant's attorney objected, the court should rule that proof of the defendant's prior conviction is

(A) admissible, as evidence of habit.

(B) admissible, because it is evidence of a distinctive method of operation.

(C) inadmissible, because evidence of previous conduct by a defendant may not be used against him or her.

(D) inadmissible, because the prior conviction occurred more than 10 years before the trial.

128. The plaintiff was riding a motorcycle manufactured by the defendant when he collided with an automobile, sustaining serious personal injuries. He claimed the fork on the motorcycle bent when he was riding it.

The defendant's attorney attempted to offer a film into evidence. The film showed a test being conducted on a motorcycle fork identical to the one on the plaintiff's motorcycle. In the test, the fork was subjected to the application of more than 15,000 pounds of pressure and did not bend. However, while the plaintiff's accident took place on a hilly dirt road, the test took place on a flat test track. If the plaintiff's attorney objects, the film should be

(A) excluded, because it has not been properly authenticated by the photographer who made the film.

(B) excluded, because it is not the best evidence of the test that was performed.

(C) excluded, because the test conditions were not identical to the conditions that the plaintiff claims existed at the time of the accident.

(D) admitted.

129. The defendant was charged with murdering the victim, a prominent union leader, by throwing him off the roof of an office building. At the defendant's trial, the prosecution offered the testimony of a police officer who arrived at the scene moments after the victim's death.

The prosecuting attorney asked the officer whether he knew the defendant. The officer said that prior to the death of the victim, he had arrested the defendant three times for aggravated assault, and that the defendant had been convicted each time. The prosecutor offered properly authenticated court records of the convictions. Upon timely objection by the defendant's attorney, the court should admit into evidence

(A) the officer's testimony only.

(B) the court records only.

(C) both the officer's testimony and the court records.

(D) neither the officer's testimony nor the court records.

130. The plaintiff sued a hedge fund, claiming the fund made certain trades he did not think were prudent, resulting in a large financial loss. In defense, the hedge fund pointed to a state law that limited damages for trading losses based on a hedge fund trade unless a client protest was made within 30 days of the trade.

The hedge fund's attorney offered the testimony of one of its managers, who testified it was his job to note any client protests. He said any protests were promptly reported to him and noted by him as a matter of company policy. He said he had searched the relevant file for any note regarding a protest made by the plaintiff and could not find one. The hedge fund's attorney then offered the file in evidence. The plaintiff objected.

The court should

(A) sustain the objection, because the evidence is inadmissible hearsay.

(B) sustain the objection, because the lack of a note does not prove the plaintiff did not protest the trade.

(C) overrule the objection, because the file was kept by the manager as a regularly conducted business activity.

(D) overrule the objection, because the file was used to refresh the manager's recollection.

131. The plaintiff sued the defendant for damages after the defendant hit the plaintiff with his car while the plaintiff was riding his bicycle. The plaintiff called his first witness, who had been riding in the car with the defendant, believing he would testify that the defendant was texting when the accident occurred. However, during the first witness's testimony, the first witness denied seeing the defendant texting and said, "I've never claimed anything different!" The plaintiff now wants to call a second witness. The second witness would testify that the first witness told her about the accident and said that the defendant was "texting the entire time and wasn't even looking at the road."

Is the second witness's testimony admissible?

(A) Yes, to impeach the first witness and to prove the defendant was texting.

(B) Yes, to impeach the first witness.

(C) No, because it is inadmissible hearsay.

(D) No, because the first witness was testifying for the plaintiff.

132. The defendant was on trial for murder. The defendant wants to testify that after the murder a witness told her, "I saw the guy that did it." The defendant wants to use this statement to prove she did not commit the murder because she is female. May the defendant do so?

(A) Yes, because it is relevant non-hearsay.

(B) Yes, because it is a declaration against interest.

(C) No, because it is hearsay.

(D) No, because the probative value is substantially outweighed by the danger of unfair prejudice.

# ANSWERS
## EVIDENCE

# ANSWERS TO
# EVIDENCE QUESTIONS

1. **A**    Under both common law and the UCC, evidence of trade terminology is admissible for the purpose of establishing the meaning of a particular term in a contract between parties in the trade. Since the contract calls for the sale of fish at wholesale, evidence of trade terminology used in the wholesale fish industry is relevant to establish the meaning of the term in question.

Ordinarily, a witness is not permitted to testify to his or her opinion. A witness who qualifies as an expert in a particular field, however, may be permitted to testify to an opinion regarding his or her field of expertise. Since the chef is not offering an opinion regarding the preparation of fried fish in fast food restaurants, he need not qualify as an expert in that particular field. **B** is therefore incorrect. **C** is incorrect because even if parties have not specifically agreed to be bound by the terminology of a particular industry, that terminology may be relevant in determining the meaning of unexplained terms in a contract so long as both parties are likely to have been aware of the meaning of the trade terminology. **D** is incorrect because an expert may offer an opinion regarding his or her field of expertise.

2. **C**    Damages in a defamation action are supposed to compensate the plaintiff for an injury to her reputation. Since the injury would be less severe if the plaintiff's reputation was not a good one to begin with, evidence of the plaintiff's reputation in the republic is relevant to the issue of damages and is therefore admissible.

**A** is incorrect because the evidence was not offered for the purpose of proving that the plaintiff engaged in any particular conduct. If proper, character evidence may, with some limitations, be used in any litigation, whether civil or criminal. **B** is therefore incorrect. **D** is incorrect because evidence of reputation is not usually admissible for the purpose of establishing that the person in question did or did not act in a particular way on a particular occasion.

3. **C**    The best evidence rule requires production of an original or qualified duplicate when the terms of a writing are in dispute or when a writing is offered as evidence of a fact and the writing is not shown to be unavailable. The witness's testimony can be admitted because it was based on her own recollection and was not dependent on the plaintiff's file on the purchase. The copy can also be admitted because a photocopy is admissible as a qualified duplicate.

4. **D**    Under FRE 401, evidence has to be relevant to be admissible. Relevant evidence is evidence that tends to make any fact of consequence to the determination of a case more probable than it would be without the evidence. Here, relevant evidence would be evidence tending to prove the university president is not racist. However, the fact he granted mayor's request for a donation to a general flood relief fund does not do anything to show he's not a racist. While minority neighborhoods may have been helped by the donation, there is no indication he knew minority citizens would receive aid or that he intended minority citizens

to receive aid. At most, the donation shows he is charitable, a question that is not at issue. **B** is therefore incorrect.

**A** is incorrect because only facts related to the university president's alleged racism may be admitted. Facts related to other parts of his character are irrelevant. **C** is incorrect because evidence of specific acts may be used to prove character under FRE 405(b). However, as stated above, his donation does not prove anything regarding his alleged racism.

5.  **D**    Hearsay is an out-of-court assertion offered for the purpose of proving the truth of the matter asserted. Thus, if the plaintiff's statement to the doctor is being offered to prove that the plaintiff was experiencing pain in his arm, the statement would be hearsay. An exception to the hearsay rule, however, permits the admission of statements made as part of a medical history given in connection with a medical examination made for the purpose of treatment or diagnosis. Since the doctor's examination was being made for the purpose of diagnosis, the patient's statement should be admissible. Under FRE 803(4), the circumstances surrounding the medical examination in which a patient's statement was made go to the weight rather than to the admissibility of that statement. Thus, the fact that the examination was not made for the purpose of treatment or that it was made in contemplation of litigation is not in itself sufficient to prevent admission unless the prejudicial effect of the statement is likely to outweigh its probative value. While a court might not come to that conclusion, the argument in **D** is the only one listed that could possibly support the motion to strike.

A and **B** are incorrect because unless the probative value is likely to be outweighed by the prejudicial effect, the fact that the examination was not being made for the purpose of treatment or that it was being made in contemplation of litigation would not be sufficient to result in its exclusion. **C** is incorrect because there is no rule that prevents the admission of self-serving statements.

6.  **D**    FRE 807 allows courts to admit hearsay evidence that does not fall within any well-defined exclusion, if it is highly reliable and badly needed in the case. There are five requirements: 1. The statement must have circumstantial guarantees of trustworthiness; 2. the statement must be offered as evidence of a material fact; 3. the statement must be more probative on the point for which it is offered than any other evidence that is available through reasonable efforts; 4. use of the evidence must be consistent with the general purposes of the FRE and the interests of justice; and 5. the proponent of the evidence must give notice of his or her intention to offer the statement sufficiently in advance of the trial or hearing to provide a fair opportunity to prepare to meet it. However, because of the Sixth Amendment's Confrontation Clause, grand jury testimony cannot be used against a criminal defendant (other than the testifier) unless the testifier takes the stand and is available for cross-examination. Here, since the witness is not available to be cross-examined by the defendant's lawyer at trial, and since the defendant did not have the opportunity to cross-examine the witness at the time of the grand jury, the witness's grand jury testimony can't be used against the defendant.

**A**, **B**, and **C** are therefore incorrect.

7.  **A**    Under FRE 801, a statement made by the party's agent or employee on a matter within the scope of the relationship can be offered against the opposing party as an admission. Such statements are not considered hearsay under the Rules. Here, since the man works for the amusement park, the witness's testimony regarding his statement can be admitted as an admission of negligence in not securing the plaintiff's seatbelt. Therefore, **C** and **D** are incorrect.

        **B** is incorrect because the declaration against interest rule only applies when a declarant is unavailable. Here, there is no indication the rollercoaster operator is not available to testify.

8.  **B**    Since hearsay is an out-of-court statement offered for the purpose of proving the matter asserted in that statement, and since the girl's statement that the defendant struck her is offered for the purpose of proving that the defendant struck her, the statement is hearsay. FRE 803(2) provides, however, that an excited utterance may be admissible as an exception to the hearsay rule. An excited utterance is a statement made about a startling event while the declarant is under stress caused by the event. The common law equivalent—spontaneous declaration—could not ordinarily be applied if the statement was made in response to a question. The Federal Rules of Evidence have eliminated that condition, however. While the passage of time might lead a court to conclude that the girl was no longer under stress produced by the beating and hold that the statement is not admissible, **B** is the only argument listed that could possibly be effective in response to the objection.

        Although a witness is permitted to make statements regarding her own sense impressions, and these statements may include identification of other persons, there is no hearsay exception for such statements when they are made out of court. **A** and **D** are therefore incorrect. Similarly, while a witness may make statements regarding her own physical condition, including explanations of the causes for that condition, **C** is incorrect because the girl's statement was made out of court and was not given in connection with a medical examination done for the purpose of treatment or diagnosis.

9.  **B**    The attorney-client privilege applies to communications made to an attorney by a person seeking legal advice. Generally, the privilege of confidential communication with an attorney extends also to the employees or agents of that attorney who are acting in furtherance of the attorney-client relationship. Some jurisdictions hold that where one mistakenly confides in another, believing the other to be an attorney, there is a privileged relationship so long as that mistaken belief was reasonable. Thus, if the defendant reasonably believed that he was communicating with an agent of his attorney, the conversation may have been privileged. While it is not certain that a court would come to that conclusion, the argument in **B** is the only one listed that could possibly support the motion.

        **A** is incorrect because the man's statement would not result in a privilege unless the defendant was speaking with the man for the purpose of obtaining legal advice. **C** is incorrect because the man's offer would not make disclosure of the facts to him essential to the relationship between the defendant and his attorney. Police interrogation of a person in custody might violate the man's constitutional rights. Unless the man had been sent by the police for the purpose of obtaining a statement from the defendant, however, the fact that he negotiated a plea bargain on the day that his testimony was given would not violate the defendant's rights and would not prevent the man's testimony from being admissible as an admission. **D** is therefore incorrect.

10. **B**      In many jurisdictions, an expert witness may be cross-examined in reference to a text not in evidence only if his or her opinion was based upon it. Under FRE 803(18), it is not necessary to show that the witness relied on the text involved, but it is necessary to establish that it is a reliable authority. **B** is correct because neither of these two foundations has been laid.

**A** is incorrect because there is no requirement that the author of a text used on cross-examination be a witness at the proceeding. **C** is only partially correct, since it is necessary to show such works to be reliable authorities before they can be used in cross-examination. Since the doctor's admission that he has heard of the specialist is not sufficient to establish that her work is a reliable authority, **D** is incorrect.

11. **C**      Under FRE 609, convictions may be used to impeach the credibility of a witness. A court may not exclude proof of such convictions if they are for felonies or for misdemeanors involving dishonesty. Since attempted murder is a felony, and since the other crime was a misdemeanor involving dishonesty, evidence of both was admissible.

Therefore, **A, B,** and **D** are all incorrect.

12. **D**      Hearsay is an out-of-court assertion offered to prove the truth of the matter asserted. Since the mechanic's statement was made out of court and is offered to prove the truth of what it asserts, it is inadmissible as hearsay.

Although the record filed by the inspector might qualify as either a business record or an official document, the transcript that it contains of a statement made by the mechanic makes this a multiple hearsay problem. While the record itself might be admissible under one of the two named exceptions to the hearsay rule, only that information that was within the inspector's personal knowledge may be admitted. The fact that either the declarant or the person who made the record is dead is not in itself sufficient to make the statement admissible. **A** and **B** are therefore incorrect. Under both the common law and FRE 801(d)(2)(D), a statement by an employee may be admissible as a vicarious admission of the employer only if the statement was made within the scope of employment and while the employment relationship existed. Since the mechanic had been discharged before making the statement in question, **C** is incorrect.

13. **D**      Under FRE 901(5), voice identification can be made by a witness who testifies that he or she properly dialed a number listed in the telephone book, and that circumstances including self-identification show that the person listed was the one who answered.

**A** and **B** are therefore incorrect. Since the defendant's statement is contrary to his interests, it is an admission, which is not hearsay under the Federal Rules of Evidence and is admissible as an exception to the hearsay rule under common law. **C** is therefore incorrect.

14.　**A**　Although evidence of insurance is not admissible for the purpose of showing fault or wrongful conduct, it is admissible for other purposes if relevant to them. Evidence is logically relevant if it tends to prove or disprove a fact of consequence. Since a person would probably not purchase liability insurance on a vehicle that he or she does not own, the fact that the defendant purchased the policy and that it was in force on the day of the accident tends to establish that she was the owner of the vehicle on that day. It is thus relevant to the issue of ownership and therefore admissible.

**B** is incorrect since a defendant's ability to pay a judgment against him or her is not relevant to either liability or damages in a negligence case. **C** is incorrect because the policy mentioned prevents such evidence only if offered to establish fault or wrongful conduct. **D** is incorrect because the evidence tends to establish ownership, which has been disputed by the defendant.

15.　**A**　Under FRE 803(3), declarations of a declarant's then-existing intentions are described as statements of present state of mind and are admissible as exceptions to the hearsay rule. They may be relevant to establish that the declarant acted in a way that was consistent with those stated intentions; however, such evidence is relevant only to establish the conduct of the declarant himself or herself. The view taken by the majority and by the FRE is that they are not relevant to establish the conduct of others. Courts generally admit such statements with limiting instructions directing the jury to consider them only on the issue of the declarant's actions.

**B**, **C**, and **D** are therefore incorrect.

16.　**B**　Under FRE 803(2), a statement relating to a startling event that was made while the declarant was under the stress of excitement from that event is admissible under the excited utterance exception to the hearsay rule.

**A** is incorrect because the uncertainty of the identification goes to the weight of the evidence rather than to its admissibility. **C** is incorrect because a statement may be admissible as an excited utterance even though the identity of the person making it is unknown. An excited utterance is admissible as an exception to the hearsay rule whether or not other evidence is available. **D** is therefore incorrect.

17.　**D**　Hearsay is defined as an out-of-court statement offered to prove the truth of the matter asserted in that statement. Since the publisher can only be offering the bartender's statement to prove that the journalist believed in his story, it is hearsay.

**A** is therefore incorrect. **B** is incorrect, because under FRE 803(3), a statement of a declarant's past state of mind is admissible only in a will contest. That a statement is self-serving may keep it from being admitted under certain exceptions to the hearsay rule, but it is never grounds for its admission. **C** is therefore incorrect.

18.　**C**　Hearsay is an out-of-court statement offered to prove the truth of the matter asserted in that statement. If offered for any other purpose, it is not hearsay. If an out-of-court statement has a direct legal effect apart from its communicative effect, it is not hearsay since it is offered not to prove the truth of any matter asserted but to prove its direct legal effect. Since the defendant is attempting to establish that the watch was a gift to him, and since the patient's words coupled with delivery by handing the defendant the watch would have the legal effect of creating an executed gift, the statement is admissible.

An admission is a statement made by a party and offered against that party. Since the patient is not a party to the proceeding, his statement cannot be termed an admission. **A** is therefore incorrect. The Dead Man's Act, where it exists, prevents evidence of a conversation with a decedent from being offered against the interests of that decedent. **B** is incorrect, however, since the Dead Man's Act, if it existed, would require that the objection be sustained, not overruled. The patient's statement was not hearsay since it is offered to establish its direct legal effect apart from its communicative effect. **D** is therefore incorrect.

19. **D**    Most modern courts, and FRE 701, allow laypersons to give opinions regarding matters within the competence of the ordinary person so long as a proper foundation is laid. This foundation requires a showing that the witness had experience that would enable him or her to form an opinion, that he or she had an opportunity to perceive, and that he or she formed an opinion based on that perception. Since the officer has so testified, her testimony regarding the defendant's speed should be admitted as a lay opinion.

**A** and **B** are therefore incorrect. Although some police officers might qualify as experts on the speeds of moving vehicles, **C** is incorrect for two reasons: First, a witness to the speed of a vehicle need not be an expert, and second, not all police officers qualify as experts.

20. **D**    Under FRE 412, reputation evidence of the past sexual behavior of the victim is not admissible in a trial for rape under any circumstances. Evidence of the victim's past is not admissible except for conduct with the defendant offered to support a defense of consent, or conduct with others offered to show that the defendant was not the source of semen or the victim's injury. Since the court record is not offered for these purposes, it is not admissible.

**A** and **C** are therefore incorrect. Under the FRE, evidence of conviction for a crime is admissible for the purpose of impeaching a witness's credibility if the crime was a felony or a misdemeanor involving dishonesty. Since prostitution is neither, the conviction is not admissible to impeach the victim's credibility. **B** is therefore incorrect.

21. **C**    Evidence of past dealings between the parties to a contract is usually admissible to prove the intentions of the parties at the time the contract was formed. This is only so, however, if conditions at the time the previous dealings took place are substantially the same as conditions that existed at the time the contract was formed. If the DVDs were being sold at an especially low price, evidence of past sales at the regular price might not be relevant in determining the intentions of the parties.

**A** is incorrect because the evidence is not being offered for the purpose of establishing the company's conduct, but rather for the purpose of establishing the store's intentions. The parol evidence rule prohibits the introduction of oral testimony of prior or contemporaneous agreements for the purpose of contradicting the terms of an unambiguous written contract. **B** is incorrect, however, since the absence of any reference to the way in which the product was to be packaged would make the contract ambiguous, and oral evidence could be offered to explain the ambiguity. **D** is incorrect because the common practice would not in itself be sufficient to overcome the expectations that might have resulted from past transactions between the parties.

22.　**A**　Evidence that a party is insured is inadmissible to establish fault or damage because insurance coverage or the lack of it is not logically or legally relevant to those issues. For this reason, it is ordinarily improper for either party to comment on insurance or the lack of it during the trial of a negligence action. If a plaintiff falsely suggests that the defendant is insured, however, a defendant may be permitted to counter the suggestion by proving that he lacked insurance. Since the plaintiff's attorney asked jurors whether they owned stock in an automobile liability insurance carrier, a court might conclude that a false suggestion of insurance coverage has been made and that the defendant should therefore be permitted to prove that he had none. While it is not certain that a court would come to this conclusion, **A** is the only option that could possibly be correct.

**B** is incorrect because the evidence involved was not offered for the purpose of establishing fault or freedom from it. **C** is incorrect because there is no prohibition against the offer of evidence that is self-serving (a party's evidence almost always is). The FRE specifically authorize the admission of a judgment of conviction when it is relevant. **D** is therefore incorrect.

23.　**D**　If relevant, photographs and films are admissible if a witness testifies that they are accurate representations of what they purport to be. Since the defendant has identified the videotape copy as a fair and accurate representation of the accident scene, and since the appearance of the accident scene is relevant in the trial of an accident claim, the videotape is admissible and **D** is correct.

Under the best evidence (*i.e.*, original document) rule, where the contents of a document are in issue, secondary evidence of its contents is inadmissible unless the original or a qualified duplicate is shown to be unavailable. Although a videotape could be regarded as a document for this purpose, **A** is incorrect because the contents of the videotape are not in issue; the tape is offered to show what the accident scene looked like. Since the defendant testified that the tape is an accurate representation of the accident scene, it is admissible without regard to its custody and whereabouts since made. **B** is therefore incorrect. **C** is incorrect because any witness may authenticate a pictorial representation by testifying that it is an accurate representation of what it purports to be.

24.　**D**　Since a person who makes statements that contradict each other might not be worthy of belief, a witness may be impeached on cross-examination by inquiry regarding prior inconsistent statements.

If a prior inconsistent statement is offered as substantive evidence, it must have been made under oath and at a trial. But a prior inconsistent statement used merely to impeach does not need to fulfill those requirements. Since only impeachment use is being made here, **A** is incorrect. Although it may be unethical for an attorney to make contact directly with an adversary known to be represented by counsel, information obtained by such a contact is not necessarily inadmissible. In any event, **B** is incorrect because there is no reason to believe that the plaintiff was represented by counsel at the time of his conversation with the investigator, or, if he was, that the attorney knew him to be. A statement of a party offered against that party is admissible as an admission. Under FRE 801(d)(2), an admission is not hearsay; under the common law, an admission is an exception to the hearsay rule. **C** is therefore incorrect.

25.  **B**    Under FRE 410(4), a withdrawn guilty plea cannot be used in any subsequent action or proceeding, so if the plea was withdrawn, the buyer's attorney can properly be prevented from asking about it.

A and **C** are incorrect because the circumstances and the crime to which the plea was given go to the weight rather than to the admissibility of the evidence. **D** is incorrect because the impeachment of the seller's witness does not depend on the seller's employment of that witness.

26.  **C**    Because of a policy to encourage repairs of dangerous conditions, evidence that a defendant repaired a condition subsequent to the occurrence of an accident is inadmissible for the purpose of establishing negligence or that the condition was dangerous at the time of the accident.

**A** is incorrect for that reason, and because the term *admission* ordinarily describes an *out-of-court* statement made by a party. **B** is incorrect because the rule of policy applies whether or not the defendant has received notice of the accident and pending lawsuit. **D** is incorrect because it is over-inclusive. Such evidence is admissible for some purposes (like establishing ownership or control).

27.  **C**    Since an employer is vicariously liable for the negligence of an employee committed within the scope of employment, statements tending to establish that the accident resulted from the employee's negligence are relevant in the plaintiff's action against the defendant. The evidence should thus be admitted unless excluded under the hearsay rule. Hearsay is an out-of-court statement offered to prove the truth of the matter asserted. These facts raise what is sometimes called a multiple-level hearsay problem (*i.e.*, a problem involving an out-of-court statement that contains another out-of-court statement). This is so because the employee's testimony at the reckless driving trial was not made during the negligence trial and so is an "out-of-court" statement, and because the evidence of his statement is contained in a transcript that was also not made as part of the negligence trial and so is an "out-of-court" statement. For multiple-level hearsay (*i.e.*, the transcript containing the employee's statement) to be admissible, each level must be separately admissible. The first level of hearsay is the testimony by the employee at the reckless driving trial. Under the common law, statements by an employee are admissible against the employer only if the employee had the authority to make them. But FRE 801(d)(2)(D) requires only that the employee's statement concerned a matter within the scope of his or her employment

and was made while the employment relationship existed. The employee's statement is therefore a vicarious admission, which is an exception to the hearsay rule at common law and is not hearsay at all under the FRE. The second level of hearsay is the transcript. Since it was made by a public official (the court reporter), regarding "matters observed pursuant to duty imposed by law as to which matters there was a duty to report" (that the employee made the admission), the transcript qualifies as a public record or report under FRE 803(8). **C** is therefore correct.

Under FRE 804(b)(1), prior testimony is admissible as an exception to the hearsay rule only if the party against whom it is offered had an incentive and an opportunity to cross-examine when the testimony was first given. Since the defendant was not a party to the proceeding at which the employee's testimony was given, the testimony does not qualify for admission under this exception. **A** is therefore incorrect. The past recollection recorded exception requires that the record was made from the recorder's own knowledge and requires the recorder to authenticate the record in court. **B** is incorrect because the employee's statement was not authenticated or recorded by the employee. **D** is incorrect for the reasons stated above.

28. **B**    Under the attorney-client privilege, the client has a right not to disclose (and the right to prevent his or her attorney from disclosing) any confidential communication between the attorney and the client relating to the professional relationship. However, the privilege does not apply to a communication that is related to carrying out a future crime or wrong. Here, the communication relates to the defendant's apparent plan to shoot the victim, which was then carried out.

The attorney-client privilege applies to a professional attorney-client relationship. Importantly, such a relationship does not require the paying of a fee. **A** is therefore incorrect. **C** and **D** are incorrect because although the lawyer gave the defendant legal advice and the conversation between them was confidential, it involved the carrying out of a future crime.

29. **C**    Under FRE 803(3), statements of a declarant's then-existing state of mind are admissible as an exception to the hearsay rule. Since it is likely that a suicidal state of mind such as that indicated by the victim's statement to the psychiatrist would continue until the following day, and since it is likely that a person with that state of mind would commit suicide, the fact that the victim was of a suicidal state of mind on the day before his death is relevant to the question of whether his death was a suicide. Hearsay is an out-of-court statement offered to prove the truth of the matter asserted in that statement. If the victim's statement to the psychiatrist is offered for the purpose of establishing that the psychiatrist knew or should have known that the victim was suicidal, it is not hearsay since it is not offered to prove the truth of the matter asserted (*i.e.*, that suicide is the only way out).

30. **B**    Under FRE 803(18), statements contained in a published treatise may be called to the attention of an expert on direct examination or cross-examination, and, if the treatise is established to be a reliable authority, may be read into the record. To prevent the jury from misunderstanding and misapplying a work written by and for experts, however, the treatise itself is not admissible.

**A**, **C**, and **D** are therefore incorrect.

31.  **D**     Under FRE 408, offers of compromise are excluded as evidence and cannot be used to prove or disprove the validity or amount of any disputed claim. Here, there is clearly a disputed claim since the plaintiff and defendant are in court regarding potential liability for the automobile accident.

A party admission is any statement made by a party to a lawsuit that another party wants to use as evidence against that party. Here, while the plaintiff's statement is clearly a party admission, it is excluded under FRE 408 because the plaintiff offered to compromise by dismissing the suit for $10,000. Therefore, **A** is incorrect. A declaration against interest is a statement made by an unavailable declarant. This is an exception to the hearsay rule. Here, there is no indication the plaintiff is not available. Therefore, **B** is incorrect. Hearsay is an out-of-court statement offered in court to prove the truth of the matter asserted. Here, the issue is that the plaintiff offered $10,000 to dismiss the case, not whether the statement was hearsay or not. Therefore, **C** is incorrect.

32.  **C**     Under FRE 608(a), attempts to prove a defendant's character for truthfulness with opinion evidence regarding honesty are not admissible unless the defendant's character for truthfulness has been attacked. Even though the defendant testified in her own defense and claimed she didn't vandalize the monument, there is no indication that the defendant's character has been attacked. Therefore, **A**, **B**, and **D** are incorrect.

33.  **D**     Although evidence of subsequent repairs is inadmissible to establish that a condition was dangerous or that the defendant was negligent, it may be admitted if relevant to some other issue. Since it is not likely that the landlord would have taken the action indicated if he were not in control of the stairway, the evidence may be admitted for the purpose of establishing control.

**A** is incorrect because it suggests that some rule of privilege prevents testimony by the defendant's employee, when no such rule exists. The admissibility of the manager's testimony does not, therefore, depend on his employment status. **B** and **C** are incorrect because of the policy rule that prohibits evidence of subsequent repairs to establish fault.

34.  **A**     Silence may be regarded as a tacit admission of a fact asserted in the presence of the person remaining silent under circumstances such that a reasonable person would have denied the assertion. Evidence of the defendant's refusal to answer the plaintiff's assertion is therefore admissible as an admission so long as a reasonable person would have denied the assertion.

If it were not otherwise admissible, however, the mere fact that the defendant was a party and able to deny it would not be sufficient to make the testimony admissible. **B** is therefore incorrect. **C** is incorrect because silence may constitute an admission as stated above. The Fifth Amendment privilege against self-incrimination might prevent an inference of guilt from being drawn in a criminal case from the silence of a defendant, but it does not prevent such an inference from being drawn in a civil case. **D** is therefore incorrect.

35.  **C**     Under the best evidence rule, where the terms of a writing are in issue, the writing itself must be offered into evidence unless the writing is shown to be unavailable through no action in bad faith. Since the original and all copies of the contract were destroyed in a fire, oral testimony as to its contents is admissible.

The parol evidence rule prohibits oral testimony of prior or contemporaneous agreements to alter the terms of a contract intended to be a complete integration of the parties, but it does not prevent oral testimony regarding the contents of a written agreement. **A** is therefore incorrect. **B** is incorrect because the writing has been shown to be unavailable. The Statute of Frauds provides that certain contracts are unenforceable unless in writing, but it does not relate to the evidence used to establish the existence of a contract. **D** is therefore incorrect.

36.  **B**     Certain prior inconsistent statements of a trial witness are substantively admissible if the witness's prior statement is inconsistent with the witness's trial testimony and was given under oath subject to the penalty of perjury at a trial, hearing, or other proceeding, or in a deposition. Importantly, a prior inconsistent statement that was not made under oath, or not given at a formal proceeding, is not substantively admissible. In that case, the prior inconsistent statement can be used for impeachment purposes only. Here, the witness's statement was not made under oath or in any type of proceeding—it was made the day after the accident to her neighbor in the backyard, so it can only be used to impeach the witness. **A** and **C** are therefore incorrect. "Circumstantial guarantees of trustworthiness" come into play when determining whether FRE 807's residual exception applies. Therefore, **D** is incorrect.

37.  **C**     The defense of entrapment applies if the police were responsible for inducing the defendant to commit a crime that he was not otherwise likely to commit, and it does not apply if the defendant was predisposed to commit the crime charged. Since the defendant has raised the defense of entrapment, evidence that he had previously sold heroin is relevant to establish his predisposition to do so at the time when the officer made the purchase.

Although character evidence is not admissible for the purpose of showing that a criminal defendant committed a certain act, it may be admissible against him or her for other purposes. **A** is therefore incorrect. **B** is incorrect because the evidence was being offered not to establish the defendant's character but to establish that the officer provided the opportunity for the crime (which is not entrapment) rather than that he induced the defendant to commit it (which would have been entrapment). **D** is incorrect because character evidence may not be used for that purpose.

38.  **D**     Since an attorney is entitled to control the direction of his or her examination, an answer that is otherwise admissible may be stricken if it is not responsive to the question asked. Since the supermarket's attorney did not ask why the plaintiff delayed consulting with counsel, the plaintiff's explanation is unresponsive to the question and may be stricken. **D** is therefore correct.

Although policy prevents admission of settlement negotiations to prove damage, the rule of limited admissibility permits admission of such evidence if it is offered for some other purpose, such as to explain the delay in instituting an action. **A** is incorrect, however, because although otherwise admissible, that portion of the answer may be stricken as unresponsive. **B** is incorrect because a policy rule specifically prohibits the admission of settlement negotiations for the purpose of establishing fault. **C** is incorrect because the policy rule does not apply if the evidence is offered for a proper purpose.

39.  **B**     At one time, the courts recognized a prohibition against opinion testimony relating to an ultimate issue in the case on trial. Now, however, it is recognized that such testimony may be admitted in evidence so long as the opinion is not couched in legal terms. Since the word *obscene* has special legal significance, the professor may not state an opinion that the film was obscene.

A is incorrect for the reason stated above. **C** is not the best argument. Since a witness may qualify as an expert by a showing of his or her knowledge, skill, experience, training, or education in a particular area, the fact that the witness is a professor of film arts and an author of several books on the topic of erotic filmmaking would probably be sufficient to qualify her as an expert. **D** is incorrect because FRE 702 abandons the requirement of strict necessity for expert testimony and permits it whenever the witness's specialized knowledge will assist the jury to understand the evidence or to determine a fact in issue.

40.  **C**     Although the Fifth Amendment privilege against self-incrimination protects a witness in a civil or criminal case against being required to give testimony that might tend to incriminate him or her, it does not justify a complete refusal to take the stand except by a defendant in a criminal prosecution.

The privilege applies to any testimony anywhere if it might subsequently be used in a criminal proceeding against the person who gave it. **A** and **B** are therefore incorrect. **D** is incorrect because the bookkeeper's belief would justify his refusal to answer certain questions, but not his complete refusal to take the stand.

41.  **A**     Certain prior inconsistent statements of a trial witness are substantively admissible if the witness's prior statement is inconsistent with the witness's trial testimony and was given under oath subject to the penalty of perjury at a trial, hearing, or other proceeding, or in a deposition. Here, because the prior inconsistent statement was made at a deposition, it is substantively admissible to prove the truth of the matter asserted. **B** is therefore incorrect. While the statement may be necessary in the interests of justice, that consideration comes into play when courts determine whether the residual exception might apply. **C** is therefore incorrect. A statement against interest references declarations which, at the time they are made, are so against the declarant's interest that it is unlikely that they would have been made if they were not true. Here, as far as the facts provided in the question go, the witness's prior statement seems to have nothing to do with her own interests. **D** is therefore incorrect.

42.  **D**     Evidence is admissible if relevant, and relevant if it tends to prove or disprove a fact of consequence. Since the defendant could not have committed the crime if he was elsewhere

at the time, evidence of his whereabouts tends to establish his guilt or innocence and is therefore relevant.

**A** and **B** are incorrect statements because FRE 607 expressly permits a party to impeach his or her own witness. A hostile witness is one who manifests hostility to the attorney questioning him or her, not just one who gives unexpected answers. Since the friend did not manifest hostility, **C** is incorrect.

43.  **A**  Hearsay is a statement, other than one made by the declarant while testifying at the trial or hearing, offered in evidence to prove the truth of the matter asserted. Here, the woman's statement is hearsay since it is being offered to prove that the defendant really did murder the doctor. The statement is not admissible under the excited-utterance exception because the man's statement did not relate to the event causing the man's stress and excitement (namely, the car wreck). **B** is therefore incorrect. The statement is not admissible under the dying declaration exception because it doesn't concern the cause or circumstances of the declarant's impending death. **C** is therefore incorrect. A "present sense impression" refers to circumstances where the statement is describing or explaining an event or condition made while the declarant was perceiving the event or condition, or immediately thereafter. **D** is therefore incorrect.

44.  **D**  A client is privileged to prevent another from disclosing the contents of a confidential communication with his or her attorney. Although the presence of third persons usually results in a finding that the communication was not intended to be confidential, this is not so if the presence of those persons was essential to the communications with the attorney. The driver's presence does not prevent the president's communication with the attorney from being confidential since, as the driver of the truck, she was essential to the conference between the president and the attorney.

**A** is incorrect since if the communication was confidential, the client's privilege applies to any attempt to disclose it. **B** is incorrect because the driver's presence was essential to the purpose of the conference. **C** is incorrect because corporations are entitled to the privilege, which clearly applies to communications between lawyers and high-ranking officers of the corporation.

45.  **A**  Under FRE 901(b)(6), voice identification can be made if the witness testifies that she properly dialed a number listed in the directory and circumstances, including self-identification, show the person answering to be the one listed and called.

**B** is a fabrication; although the combination of a listing in the telephone directory and self-identification by the person answering the phone may result in an inference regarding that person's identity, there is no presumption that the person who answered identified himself or herself accurately. **C** is incorrect since the FRE make independent recognition unnecessary under the circumstances described above. The privilege against self-incrimination protects against "testimonial communications" but does not prevent testimony by others than the defendant concerning admissions made by the defendant. **D** is therefore incorrect.

46.    **A**    Cross-examination is normally limited to the subject matter of the direct examination and matters concerning the credibility of the witness. The court does have discretion to allow cross-examination that goes beyond the scope of direct, but judges are extremely unlikely to allow questions that will disturb a party's tactical decisions in presenting his or her case. Here, the plaintiff has decided to use the defendant's testimony only to establish that the defendant did the operation. Consequently, the objection should be sustained for this reason. **B** is therefore incorrect.

   **C** is incorrect because the examiner's question does not have to do with credibility. **D** is incorrect because the question goes outside the scope of direct since the defendant was only asked one question on direct that only involved whether he was the one who did the surgery.

47.    **A**    Under FRE 803's excited utterance exception to the hearsay rule, a statement made during or soon after a startling event is admissible so long as the declarant makes the statement while the declarant is still excited by the event. Here, seeing the defendant covered in blood and saying he shot his wife is clearly a startling event, and the fact the neighbor shouted the statement while banging on the witness's door shows she was still under the stress of the excitement. Therefore, **C** and **D** are incorrect.

   **B** is incorrect because FRE 803 does not require an excited declarant be unavailable to testify.

48.    **A**    Hearsay is an out-of-court statement offered to prove the truth of the matter asserted in that statement. Since the statement that a blue sedan was traveling at an excessive speed was made out of court, and since it was offered to prove that the defendant's blue sedan was traveling at an excessive speed, it is hearsay. **A** is therefore correct.

   A witness may testify to his or her sense impression, even though that testimony is stated as an opinion. Since the witness is not testifying to her own sense impression but rather to something that she heard another person say, **B** is incorrect. Under the hearsay exception known as "past recollection recorded," a witness may read from a written note if he or she made it himself or herself based on information that he or she knew of his or her own knowledge while the information was fresh in his or her mind. The note that the witness read does not qualify, however, because it was not based on something that she knew of her own knowledge but rather on something she had heard another person say. **C** is therefore incorrect. A witness may refresh his or her recollection while testifying by examining almost anything that will have that effect. He or she may then testify from his or her refreshed recollection, but only if his or her testimony is otherwise admissible. Since the statement to which the witness is attempting to testify is hearsay, it is inadmissible and is not made admissible by the fact that she refreshed her recollection by looking at a writing. **D** is therefore incorrect.

49.    **A**    Hearsay is defined as an out-of-court statement offered to prove the truth of the matter asserted in that statement. Since the defendant's statement that the light was red was made out of court, and since it apparently was offered to prove that the light was red, it

is hearsay and therefore inadmissible. Although the defendant may testify to facts that he knows of his own knowledge (*i.e.*, that the light was red against the plaintiff), he may not testify to an out-of-court statement for the purpose of proving the truth of the matter asserted in that statement (*i.e.*, hearsay).

Since his testimony is not that the light was red but rather that he told the police officer that it was red, **B** is incorrect. Evidence of a prior consistent statement may be admissible to rebut a claim of recent fabrication. **C** is incorrect, however, because there is no indication that the plaintiff has claimed that the defendant's statement about the color of the light is a recent fabrication. Hearsay is inadmissible even though the declarant is present in court and available for cross-examination. **D** is therefore incorrect.

50. **D**   Under FRE 412, a rape victim's past sexual conduct is generally not admissible in a prosecution for her rape. An exception is made, however, for evidence of past sexual conduct between the defendant and the complainant if offered to support the defense of consent. Since evidence regarding past sexual conduct between the defendant and the victim might tend to support the defendant's assertion that he reasonably believed that the victim consented, it should be admitted.

**A** and **B** are therefore incorrect. **C** is incorrect because the complainant's past sexual conduct does not ordinarily tend to establish that defendant did or did not have sexual intercourse with her against her will on the occasion in question.

51. **A**   The law seeks to encourage safety precautions by prohibiting evidence of subsequent remedial measures from being used for the purpose of showing fault. Such evidence may be admissible for other purposes, however. Here, the defendant had denied ownership of the vehicle. Since it is unlikely that anyone other than the owner would arrange to have the brakes overhauled, the testimony of the mechanic is relevant to establish the defendant's ownership and should therefore be admitted.

**B** is incorrect because of the above-stated policy rule. **C** is incorrect because the evidence is being used to establish that the defendant was the owner of the vehicle, not to establish the condition of the brakes. **D** is incorrect since the evidence is admissible to establish ownership.

52. **D**   Evidence is relevant if it would tend to establish a fact in issue. If the tape would tend to prove that the defendant was the robber, it is logically relevant. It should, therefore, be excluded only if it violates some other rule of evidence or if its probative value is substantially outweighed by its prejudicial impact.

**A** is incorrect because the privilege against self-incrimination applies only to "testimonial communications" and does not prevent evidence based on observations of the defendant. Whether or not it is certain that the person pictured in the videotape was the defendant is a question for the jury. The robber's skin coloring (like his height, weight, and walk) is relevant to his identification. Since there are many people with the same skin color, the fact that the robber's was the same as the defendant's is not in itself enough to result in prejudice that outweighs the probative value of the videotape. **B** is therefore incorrect. An admission by conduct is an act by a defendant from which the logical inference may be drawn that he or she believes himself or herself to be criminally liable. Usually, it refers to flight, the use of an assumed name, fabrication of evidence, or some other act committed after the crime. **C** is therefore incorrect.

53.  **D**     Hearsay is a statement, other than one made by the declarant while testifying at the trial or hearing, offered in evidence to prove the truth of the matter asserted. Here, the witness is repeating the victim's out-of-court statement, and the statement is being used to prove the defendant was the assailant.

**A** is incorrect because the "excited utterance" exception only applies when the statement relates to a startling event or condition, and the statement is made while the declarant is still under the stress of excitement caused by the event or condition. **B** is incorrect because the "present sense impression" exception is an exception for statements describing or explaining an event or condition made while the declarant is perceiving the event or condition, or immediately thereafter. Here, the statement was made two days later, so the witness was no longer under the stress of excitement caused by the event, nor was the witness describing the event while the witness was perceiving it. The "declaration against interest" exception applies when the declaration, at the time it is made, is so against the declarant's interest that it is unlikely it would have been made if it was not true. Importantly, the exception involves looking at the declarant's interest, and this answer choice is asking you to consider the defendant's interest instead of the witness's interest. **C** is therefore incorrect.

54.  **A**     Hearsay is defined as an out-of-court assertion offered for the purpose of proving the truth of the matter asserted. The fact that a witness made a prior contradictory statement is relevant to his or her credibility as a witness, whether or not the prior statement was actually true, since people who tell different stories on different days may not be worthy of belief. If offered for that purpose, and not to prove the absence of gunshots, the officer's testimony is not hearsay. If offered to prove that there were no gunshots (*i.e.*, as substantive evidence), however, it is hearsay.

**B** and **C** are therefore incorrect. **D** is incorrect, since for purposes of impeachment, the statement is not hearsay because it is not offered to prove the truth of what it asserted.

55.  **C**     Former testimony is admissible if it was given under oath by a presently unavailable declarant in a proceeding where the party against which it is now offered had an opportunity and incentive to cross-examine. Since the inspector did not respond to the subpoena, he is presently unavailable. Since his testimony was given at a criminal prosecution of the corporation, at which the corporation had opportunity and incentive to cross-examine, the former testimony is admissible. Although the facts do not indicate how the inspector knew that the driver was intoxicated or why he was permitted to so testify at the criminal negligence trial, **C** is the only reason listed that could result in the admission of his statement.

An admission is a statement made by a party that is offered against that party. Since the inspector is not a party, **A** is incorrect. A past recollection recorded must have been prepared by the witness while the information was fresh in his or her mind and requires the witness to testify that the record was true when made. Since the inspector did not record the statement and is not present to testify, **B** is incorrect. A present sense impression is a statement describing an event that was made while or soon after the declarant perceived the event. Since there is no indication that the inspector perceived the event, **D** is incorrect.

56. **C** Under FRE 804(b)(2), a statement is admissible as a dying declaration in a civil or criminal case if it was made by a person now unavailable, about the cause of his or her death, upon personal knowledge, and under a sense of immediately impending death. Since the victim is presently unavailable and said that he saw the defendant shoot him, his statement is admissible if he made it with a sense of impending death.

Although the common law made such statements admissible in cases of criminal homicide only, **A** is incorrect because the FRE extend the exception to civil litigation as well. Transactional immunity prevents criminal prosecution but does not prevent civil litigation. **B** is therefore incorrect. Where it exists, the effect of the "dead man's statute" is to exclude certain evidence, not to make it admissible. **D** is therefore incorrect.

57. **B** Hearsay is an out-of-court statement offered to prove the truth of the matter asserted in that statement. An admission is an out-of-court statement made by a party that is offered against that party. Under the common law, admissions are admissible as exceptions to the hearsay rule. Under FRE 801(d)(2), admissions are admissible because they are not hearsay. If an employee of a party makes a statement that is offered against the employer, the statement may be admissible as a vicarious admission of the employer if it was made while the employment relationship existed and concerned a matter within the scope of the declarant's employment. If the mechanic was employed by the airline as a mechanic, his statement that he failed to inspect the plane does concern a matter within the scope of his employment. It would not be admissible as a vicarious admission of the airline, however, unless it can be established that the mechanic was so employed. If the mechanic made an out-of-court statement that he was so employed, it would be hearsay if offered to prove his employment by the airline. For this reason, independent evidence of the employment relationship is required.

**A** is therefore incorrect. Although the common law requires that the declarant be one authorized to speak for the party, **C** is incorrect because the FRE have abolished that requirement. **D** is incorrect because the unavailability of a declarant is not in itself sufficient to make his or her out-of-court assertion admissible.

58. **B** Under FRE 803(3), an assertion of a declarant's then-existing physical sensation is admissible as an exception to the hearsay rule.

Statements made as part of a medical history may be admissible if made for purposes of diagnosis or treatment. Ordinarily, "medical history" refers to statements made by a declarant about physical sensations and events in the past. **A** is incorrect for this reason, and because the nurse's testimony does not indicate that the plaintiff's complaints were made for the purpose of facilitating a diagnosis or treatment. **C** is incorrect because others than the injured party may testify to objective signs of pain or to the injured party's statements about the pain if they fit into exceptions to the hearsay rule. **D** is incorrect because of the present physical sensation exception.

59.    **C**     Evidence is relevant if it tends to prove or disprove a fact of consequence. Relevant evidence is ordinarily admissible. Self-defense is a privilege to use force that the reasonable person in the defendant's shoes would have considered necessary to prevent an attack upon himself or herself. Evidence of the plaintiff's reputation for unprovoked violence is relevant because it tends to establish whether the reasonable person in the defendant's shoes would have believed himself or herself to be under attack.

       **A** and **B** are incorrect because the evidence is relevant to the reasonableness of the defendant's fear. **D** is incorrect because the plaintiff's character is not related to the essential elements of a battery action.

60.    **D**     An expert may testify to an opinion based upon material not in evidence so long as it is material upon which the reasonable expert would have based an opinion, even if the material itself would be inadmissible.

       **A** is therefore incorrect. An X-ray is regarded as a writing, and if a witness is testifying only to its contents, it may be covered by the best evidence rule. If so, such testimony may be excluded unless it can be shown that the X-ray itself is not available. In this case, however, the witness was not testifying solely to the contents of the X-ray, but to an opinion that she formed based upon examination of the plaintiff's leg, in addition to study of the X-ray. **B** is therefore incorrect. **C** is incorrect because an expert may base his or her opinion testimony on material not in evidence.

61.    **D**     Evidence of the non-occurrence of similar accidents might be admissible to prove that the area was not dangerous, but only if the condition during the period testified to was substantially the same at the time of the accident. Since there is no indication that the stairs were littered with paper during the period described by the witness, the fact that no similar accidents occurred does not prove that the condition was not unsafe when the plaintiff fell.

       **A** and **B** are therefore incorrect. **C** is incorrect because it is perfectly permissible and proper for witnesses to give self-serving testimony. (That they often do is illustrated by the fact that criminal defendants frequently say, "I didn't do it!")

62.    **A**     If the declarant is unavailable as a witness, a statement made under the belief of impending death is admissible under an exception to the hearsay rule. While the declarant must be aware of his or her impending death, he or she does not have to actually die. The only requirement is that the declarant is unavailable. Here, since the man has fled and moved beyond the court's subpoena power, the exception applies. **C** and **D** are therefore incorrect. An excited utterance is an exception for certain statements made under the influence of a startling event. Here, the declarant is in bed dying from cancer, which is not a "startling event" (*e.g.*, a car crash, shooting, etc.). **B** is therefore incorrect.

63. **D**   Since cross-examination about the witness's whereabouts is directly relevant to impeachment of his direct testimony, his refusal to answer makes meaningful cross-examination impossible. When a witness cannot be subjected to full cross-examination, his direct testimony should be stricken.

**A** is incorrect because the privilege is available whenever testimony of the witness might lead to criminal prosecution of the witness, even though the matter in which the testimony is elicited is not a criminal proceeding. The privilege against self-incrimination would offer little protection if it was necessary for the person invoking it to show how the statement might be incriminating. Thus, unless it is impossible to conceive of circumstances in which the answer called for would be incriminating, the witness may invoke the privilege. **B** is therefore incorrect. **C** is a fabrication without any basis in law; in any event, it is patently incorrect since the issue is not whether the witness should have been allowed to invoke the privilege but whether his direct testimony should have been stricken.

64. **B**   A writing may be admitted under the business record exception to the hearsay rule if it was made in the course of a regularly conducted business activity from the recorder's own knowledge or from an inherently reliable source and was accurate when made. If the investigation of crimes is not a regularly conducted business activity for the college, its record of such an investigation would not be admissible as a business record. Although it is not certain that a court would come to that conclusion, the argument in **B** is the only one listed that could possibly support the defendant's objection.

**A** is incorrect because a business record may be admissible even though the person who made it is available and has testified. **C** is incorrect because it is an inaccurate statement of law; the exception applies in all trials. Hearsay is an out-of-court statement offered to prove the truth of the matter asserted in that statement. The phrase "second-level hearsay" is sometimes used to describe a hearsay that is included in another statement that is also hearsay. Here, for example, the defendant's statement was made out of court and is offered to prove that the defendant stabbed the victim (*i.e.*, the matter asserted). The file that includes the statement is also an out-of-court statement that is offered to prove the truth of what it asserts (*i.e.*, that the defendant said he stabbed the victim). **D** is incorrect, however, because the defendant's statement is an admission, which FRE 801(d)(2) defines as a statement made by a party and offered against that party, and which that rule specifically provides is not hearsay.

65. **B**   Evidence that the witness never observed strange behavior in a testator is admissible to prove he or she was competent, but only if the nature of the witness's experience with the testator is such that he or she is likely to have observed such behavior if it occurred. Semiannual examinations of the testator probably are not frequent enough to permit the inference that behavior that did not occur on those visits did not occur at other times.

**A** is incorrect since if a witness does have sufficient opportunity to observe, the testimony will be admitted. **C** is incorrect since the door is thus opened only to testimony that is not otherwise inadmissible. **D** is incorrect because the doctor is not testifying to his opinion but to his observations.

66.  **D**     The FRE recognize an exception to the hearsay rule for business records. Some courts interpret the FRE in a way that makes police records inadmissible under this exception to the hearsay rule. Other courts interpret the FRE in a way that makes police records admissible under this exception. Under FRE 803(6), a written report is admissible as a business record if it was made in the regular course of business, while the transaction recorded was fresh in the entrant's mind, regarding facts within his or her own knowledge or from an inherently reliable source. The statement contained in the police record filed by the witness was not based on a fact known by the witness of his own knowledge. It might still be admissible, however, if it had been received from an inherently reliable source. Although the other officer may be regarded as such a source, he did not have personal knowledge either. Since the source of the recorded fact was an unidentified witness, and since an unidentified witness is not an inherently reliable source, the record is not admissible.

Although a testifying witness may refresh his or her recollection by reference to documents that are not in evidence, his or her doing so does not make those documents admissible. **A** is therefore incorrect. **B** is incorrect for the reason given above. Since the police are in the business—among other things—of investigating accidents, a police report may be regarded as a record kept in the usual course of business and may be admissible as such if all the other requirements are met. **C** is therefore incorrect.

67.  **A**     Unless it is excluded by some rule of law, evidence is admissible if it is relevant to a material issue. Since contracts are interpreted in accordance with the intentions of the parties, the buyer's intentions are material to the seller's action for breach of contract. Since the buyer did not understand the seller's statement, the brother's translation of that statement would tend to establish (*i.e.*, is relevant to) the buyer's intentions. It should therefore be admitted.

In jurisdictions that have a "dead man's statute," that law may prohibit the admission of evidence regarding a transaction with a decedent. **B** is incorrect because, although the "dead man's statute" may result in the exclusion of evidence, it is never used as a justification for its admission. If the brother were testifying to the meaning of a Dutch word or expression, his testimony would not be admissible unless he qualified as an expert on the Dutch language. **C** is incorrect, however, because the brother's testimony is not offered for the purpose of explaining the meaning of the seller's language but for the purpose of showing what the buyer believed it to mean. Hearsay is an out-of-court statement offered for the purpose of proving the truth of the matter asserted in that statement. Since the brother's statement to the buyer was made out of court, it would be hearsay if offered for the purpose of proving the truth of anything that it asserted. **D** is incorrect, however, because the statement is offered not to prove the truth of what was asserted by either the seller or the brother, but to establish the buyer's state of mind at the time of the negotiation. It is therefore not hearsay.

68.  **D**     The fact that a witness made prior statements that were inconsistent with his or her testimony indicates that he or she may not be a credible witness, or at least that his or her testimony may not be worthy of belief. Thus, for the purpose of impeachment, a witness may be cross-examined about prior inconsistent statements. Since the defendant's statement to

the arresting officers was inconsistent with his statement on the witness stand, he may be cross-examined about it.

Statements obtained in violation of a prisoner's *Miranda* rights cannot be used against him or her in a criminal prosecution. Because use of such statements for impeachment in a civil proceeding is not ordinarily contemplated by the police, prohibiting such use is not likely to affect police conduct. For this reason, it has been held that statements obtained in violation of a prisoner's *Miranda* rights may be used for purposes of impeachment in civil proceedings. **A** is therefore incorrect. **B** is incorrect for two reasons: First, the defendant's motion was to suppress the use of the physical evidence rather than the use of statements made during the interrogation, and second, even an order suppressing the use of his statements in the criminal prosecution would not prevent their use in this civil proceeding. If statements are obtained from a prisoner in violation of his or her constitutional rights, the same policy that prohibits their use as evidence prohibits the use of leads obtained as a result of those statements. This is the "fruit of the poisonous tree" doctrine. Although this doctrine may result in the exclusion of evidence, it is never used to justify the admission of evidence. **C** is therefore incorrect.

69. **B**    Under FRE 803(6), a properly authenticated written record qualifies as an exception to the hearsay rule if it was made as part of the regular course of business while the transaction recorded was fresh in the entrant's mind regarding facts within his or her personal knowledge or from an inherently reliable source. This invoice was kept in the regular course of business and has been authenticated by the employee. Although the employee did not personally know the contents of the shipment, the shipping clerk's business duty to report accurately makes him an inherently reliable source, and the employee made the entries immediately upon receiving the information from him.

**A** is incorrect because the past recollection recorded exception applies only if the record was prepared from the witness's own knowledge, and permits it to be read to the jury, but not admitted into evidence. The best evidence rule provides that where the contents of a writing are in issue, secondary evidence of the writing is inadmissible unless the original is shown to be unavailable. **C** is incorrect because the effect of the best evidence rule is to exclude certain classes of evidence and not to make admissible evidence that would otherwise be inadmissible. A witness whose present recollection has been refreshed by reference to a document may testify from his or her refreshed recollection. **D** is incorrect because the employee stated that she had no present recollection and because the attorney for the plaintiff sought to introduce the document itself.

70. **D**    Under the UCC, evidence of the usage of trade terminology is admissible to prove the meaning of such terms in a contract between parties in the trade. Since both the plaintiff and the defendant are in commercial industry, the witness's evidence of trade usage should be admissible.

Witnesses frequently make self-serving statements. In fact, almost anything said by a party-witness is likely to be self-serving (*e.g.*, a criminal defendant's testimony that she is "not guilty," or a personal injury plaintiff's testimony that the defendant went through a red light). **A** is incorrect because there is no rule of law that excludes self-serving statements from evidence. Hearsay is defined as an out-of-court statement offered for the purpose of proving the truth of the matter asserted in that statement. Since the witness's testimony is not of an out-of-court statement, it cannot be hearsay. **B** is therefore incorrect. Although proof of an established business custom may be offered as evidence that it was followed on a particular occasion, **C** is incorrect because the witness has not testified to any particular custom of her company.

71.  **D**    Under FRE 412, evidence of specific acts involving the victim's past sexual behavior is admissible in a rape trial only if it is relevant to an issue regarding the source of semen, or if it involves past sexual behavior between the victim and the defendant and is offered for the purpose of establishing the defense of consent. Since the defendant admits to having sexual intercourse with the victim, there is no issue regarding the source of semen. Although the defendant has asserted a defense of consent, the evidence offered by his attorney does not relate to prior sexual contact between the defendant and the victim. The evidence is thus inadmissible.

A, **B**, and **C** are therefore incorrect.

72.  **A**    FRE 501 provides that in the trial of a civil proceeding in which state law provides the rule of decision, the rules of privilege shall be determined in accordance with state law. Thus, if a civil action is being tried in a federal court under the substantive law of a state, the federal court must apply the state law of privilege. If the state law recognizes a psychotherapist-patient privilege, the federal court must recognize it as well. Consequently, **C** and **D** are incorrect. If the state law does not recognize a psychotherapist-patient privilege, the federal court may not. **B** is therefore incorrect.

73.  **C**    Hearsay is an out-of-court assertion offered for the purpose of proving the truth of the matter asserted. Since the witness's testimony referred to the doctor's assertion that the pink pills were for pain and was offered for the purpose of proving that the plaintiff took them for pain, that assertion is hearsay.

A declaration of the *declarant's* present physical sensation is admissible as an exception to the hearsay rule. The plaintiff's statement, "My neck hurts," might thus be admissible. **A** is incorrect, however, because the doctor's statement did not declare anything about his own physical state. **B** is incorrect for the same reason. Statements of a declarant's past physical sensation are admissible under the medical history exception if made to a doctor for the purpose of diagnosis and treatment. **D** is incorrect, however, because the objection was to testimony regarding a statement by the doctor.

74.  **C**    Under FRE 801(d)(1)(C), evidence of prior identification is not hearsay, if the declarant is on the witness stand and available for cross-examination.

A is therefore incorrect. **B** is incorrect for two reasons: First, a party is permitted to impeach his or her own witness, and second, to impeach means to attack the witness's credibility, which the prosecuting attorney has not attempted to do to the employee. **D** is incorrect because although a jury may consider the fact that a witness is interested or disinterested in weighing the value of his or her testimony, the interest of a witness does not affect the admissibility of his or her testimony.

75.  **B**    Under FRE 803(18), so long as the judge believes the passages are relevant to some issue, the engineer may read those passages, and they will be admissible to prove the assertions they make regarding proper building and engineering techniques. However, a "learned writing," such as the book, may not be admitted as an exhibit. The jury may only hear the appropriate portions read to it, and interpreted for it by the expert on the stand at the time.

**A**, **C**, and **D** are therefore incorrect.

76.  **D**    It is the jury's job to determine whether the evidence proves facts sufficient to satisfy the requirements of law as charged by the court. Expert opinion may be admitted to *assist* the trier of fact to understand the evidence or to determine a fact in issue, but it may not be stated in a way that would deprive the jury of its power to determine facts. Since the jury must decide whether the defendant had malice aforethought, expert testimony regarding the defendant's mental capacity would be admissible. The doctor's statement, however, did not express an opinion regarding the defendant's mental condition but rather his opinion whether the defendant had malice aforethought.

Although the common law once prohibited expert testimony that "embraced the ultimate issue," **A** is incorrect because FRE 704 (and the laws of many states) have eliminated this restriction. The opinions of an expert may be based solely on courtroom observations (or may even be based on assumed facts contained in a hypothetical question). The fact that a testifying psychiatrist has never spoken to the subject or even seen him or her outside a courtroom may reflect on the weight (*i.e.*, persuasive value) of his or her testimony but not on its admissibility. **B** and **C** are therefore incorrect.

77.  **B**    Under FRE 804(b)(2), a statement qualifies for the dying declaration exception to the hearsay rule if it was made by a presently unavailable person under a sense of immediately impending death upon personal knowledge respecting the cause and circumstances of death and is offered in a criminal homicide trial or a civil action. Since the plaintiff was in court, she is not presently unavailable, and her statement does not qualify as a dying declaration.

**A** is incorrect because it is sufficient that the statement concerned a cause or circumstance of what the plaintiff believed was her impending death. Although the common law restricted the use of dying declarations to criminal homicide trials, **C** is incorrect because the FRE specifically authorize their admission in civil proceedings. The FRE do not require that the declarant actually be dying to qualify his or her statement as a dying declaration, so long as he or she believed himself or herself to be dying at the time he or she made it. **D** is therefore not sufficient reason to prevent the plaintiff's statement from being admissible as a dying declaration.

78.  **C**    In general, evidence is admissible if it is relevant to a material issue. Since the defendant's negligence is a material issue in a malpractice action against him, testimony that

is relevant to the defendant's negligence is admissible unless excluded under one of the rules of evidence. The common law attorney-client privilege prevents an attorney from testifying, over his or her client's objection, to confidential communications by the client that were related to the professional relationship. The privilege does not prevent such testimony, however, in litigation relating to a breach of duty arising from the relationship.

Thus, **A** is incorrect. **B** is incorrect for the above reason, and because even unnecessary statements may be privileged if they relate to the purpose of the consultation. Ordinarily, the attorney-client privilege survives the relationship, protecting the confidentiality even after the attorney-client relationship ceases to exist. Thus, **D** is incorrect.

79.  **A**    At common law, a confidential communication made to an attorney by a person seeking legal advice is generally privileged. If the communication is made in the presence of a third person, an inference may be drawn that the person speaking did not intend for the communication to be confidential. However, if the presence of the third person was necessary, such an inference cannot be drawn and the communication remains privileged. Since state law provided for the designation of the father as the defendant's legal guardian and required his joinder as a defendant in an action against her, his presence at the consultation with the attorney was necessary so that he could assure that the defendant's rights were protected.

**B** is incorrect because it is over-inclusive; only those communications that the client intended to be confidential are privileged. Where two or more clients have consulted an attorney together on a matter of common interest, their communications are not privileged if one client seeks to offer them as evidence against the other. **C** is incorrect, however, because unless the father is seeking to offer the attorney's testimony against the defendant (or vice versa), the mere fact that the defendant and the father are joint defendants is not sufficient to destroy the privilege. A confidential communication made to an attorney while seeking legal advice is privileged at common law, whether or not the attorney actually gives advice or agrees to represent the person who made the communication. **D** is therefore incorrect.

80.  **A**    Judicial notice is a doctrine that permits courts to accept as true facts or propositions of law without specific evidence. A fact that has been judicially noticed becomes part of the record and requires no further proof. Although judicial notice is commonly taken of the statutes of the state in which a particular court is sitting, most jurisdictions do not permit municipal ordinances to be judicially noticed, requiring that their contents be proven as facts. However, because this jurisdiction permits a court to take judicial notice of municipal ordinances, the court could judicially notice the section in question and deny the defendant's motion for dismissal.

In determining whether there has been a violation, the trier of fact may consider facts that have been judicially noticed by the court. **B** is therefore incorrect. Ordinarily, judicial notice is taken of facts that are commonly known. This may include the contents of laws, since all are presumed to know them. **C** is incorrect for two reasons: First, the judge's personal expertise or knowledge of particular facts is not sufficient to justify his judicially noticing them, and second, judicial notice may be taken of commonly known or readily verifiable facts, even though the judge lacks personal expertise. The contents of relevant law must be proven unless they are judicially noticed by the court. Since courts frequently refuse to take judicial notice of municipal ordinances, **D** is over-inclusive and therefore incorrect.

81.　**C**　A witness who testifies under a grant of use immunity is protected against use of that testimony in any subsequent criminal proceeding against him or her. Since the commissioner was not a defendant in the prosecution, use immunity did not prevent the use of his statement. FRE 613 permits the admission of prior inconsistent statements of a witness for the purpose of intrinsically or extrinsically impeaching the credibility of that witness. Evidence of the commissioner's prior statement is thus admissible for the purpose of impeachment. FRE 801 permits the use of a witness's prior inconsistent statement as substantive evidence if it was given under oath subject to the penalty of perjury at a trial, hearing, or other proceeding. Since the commissioner's statement was made under oath at a grand jury proceeding, it is admissible as substantive evidence as well.

　　　　　**A**, **B**, and **D** are therefore incorrect.

82.　**A**　If a proper foundation is laid, evidence that a place has been used over a period of time without any accident is logically relevant to prove that the place was not dangerous. The foundation for such negative evidence requires proof, however, that the place was used a substantial number of times under substantially similar conditions. The witness's testimony that the street was a busy thoroughfare is probably sufficient to establish its use a substantial number of times. Unless, however, it is established that the street was substantially unchanged, proof that there were no prior accidents is irrelevant to the plaintiff's claim that there was a dangerous curve in the road.

　　　　　**B** is incorrect because if a proper foundation is laid for the introduction of negative evidence, there is no requirement that the court issue a special instruction to the jury. The argument in **C** is one that the plaintiff's attorney may make to the jury in an attempt to persuade it not to draw from the witness's testimony an inference that the street is safe. **C** is incorrect, however, because if a proper foundation for the evidence is laid, that argument goes to its weight rather than to its admissibility. Although negative evidence presents severe relevancy problems, the laying of a proper foundation resolves them, making such evidence admissible. **B** is therefore incorrect.

83.　**A**　Unless otherwise provided by law, all evidence is admissible that has a tendency to prove or disprove a fact of consequence (*i.e.*, that is relevant). Since the hotel has denied ownership and control of the alley, evidence relevant to ownership or control is therefore admissible. The testimony of the witness is relevant to ownership or control since it is unlikely that hotel employees would clean the alley if the hotel did not own or control it. His testimony is therefore admissible.

　　　　　Hotel employees might have begun cleaning the alley even though the hotel did not own or control it, and the hotel attorney may try to convince a jury not to infer ownership or control from the remedial measure. **B** is incorrect, however, because the argument that it states goes to the weight rather than the admissibility of the evidence. Although a policy seeks to encourage safety by prohibiting evidence of subsequent remedial measures for the purpose of proving fault, **C** and **D** are incorrect because the testimony of the witness is admissible for the limited purpose of proving ownership or control.

84.  **D**    Under FRE 803(3), an assertion of the declarant's then-existing physical sensation is admissible as an exception to the hearsay rule. The common law makes a distinction that prohibits the admission of such statements if they were made in contemplation of litigation. The FRE do not make such a distinction, however, allowing the circumstances under which the statement was made to go to the weight rather than the admissibility of the evidence.

**A** and **B** are therefore incorrect. Where it is recognized, the physician-patient privilege may prevent the admission of testimony by a doctor regarding confidential communications with the patient over objection by the *patient.* **C** is incorrect because an objection based on the privilege would not be available to anyone but the patient.

85.  **C**    Under FRE 803(2), a statement relating to a startling event made while the declarant was under the stress of excitement caused by the event is admissible as an excited utterance. This is so even if the declarant's identity is unknown.

**A** is therefore incorrect. The term *self-serving declaration* usually refers to an out-of-court statement made by a party and which is offered by that party to prove an element of his or her case. Like any other hearsay, it is inadmissible unless it falls into one of the exceptions to the hearsay rule. (For example, a document containing self-serving declarations might be admissible as a business record.) Since the victim is not a party to the prosecution, it is probably not correct to call his testimony self-serving. More important, although self-serving declarations made *out-of-court* may be excluded from evidence as hearsay, there is no rule prohibiting self-serving *testimony*. For these reasons, **B** is incorrect. Although an excited utterance is admissible only if made by a declarant with personal knowledge, such knowledge is presumed. **D** is therefore incorrect.

86.  **B**    A witness is permitted to refresh her recollection before testifying by reviewing past notes, depositions, and other statements. FRE 612 gives the trial court discretion to require the production at trial of any writings that were used to refresh a witness's recollection before trial.

Secondary evidence to prove the contents of a writing is inadmissible under the best evidence rule unless the original or a qualified duplicate is shown to be unavailable. Thus, if the witness were testifying to the contents of the notes, her testimony would be inadmissible unless the notes were shown to be unavailable. She is not testifying to the contents of the notes, however, but from her memory after refreshing it by looking at the notes. For this reason, the best evidence rule is inapplicable, and **A** is incorrect. Although the notes have not been offered into evidence, they have been used to refresh the witness's recollection before trial. For this reason, the court may require their production under FRE 612. **C** is therefore incorrect. An admission is a statement by a party that is offered against that party. Since the witness is not a party to the proceeding, her statements cannot be admissions. **D** is therefore incorrect.

87. **D**    Although the court decides whether evidence is admissible and whether a witness is competent to testify, it is for the jury to decide what weight to give testimony that the court has admitted. In doing so, the jury must determine how credible it finds a particular witness to be. If that witness is an expert testifying to his or her opinions, it would be impossible for the jury to make that determination without knowing the witness's qualifications. The concession by the defendant's attorney is not sufficient, since it is very likely that the jury will hear contrary opinions given by other experts. To decide which of the experts it believes, the jury must be able to compare their qualifications. For this reason, the details of the doctor's qualifications remain an issue even though the defendant's attorney concedes that she is sufficiently qualified to testify to her opinions.

**A** and **B** are therefore incorrect. If all parties agree to a fact, a court may accept it as true without requiring further proof. Thus, if all parties agree that a particular witness qualifies as an expert, the court may—on the basis of that stipulation—dispense with the *requirement* of further proof (although it may not prevent the party offering the testimony of that witness from questioning him or her about his or her qualifications). **C** is therefore incorrect.

88. **A**    In general, evidence is admissible if it is relevant to a material issue (*i.e.*, tends to establish some fact of consequence) in the litigation. Since liability for negligence does not depend on whether the defendant was insured, the fact that the defendant was or was not insured is not of consequence (*i.e.*, not relevant to a material issue) in the litigation. It is therefore not admissible.

A compromise consists of a payment or a promise to pay given in return for a promise to discontinue or not to assert a claim. Since the defendant was not offering anything in return for a promise not to assert a claim, his statement was not a compromise offer. **B** is therefore incorrect. Admissions are words or acts of a party offered against that party. Under the common law, admissions of a party may be admissible as exceptions to the hearsay rule; under FRE 801(d)(2), admissions of a party are not hearsay at all. Like all other evidence, however, admissions may be admitted only if relevant to a material issue. Since the fact that the defendant was or was not insured is not material, his statement—even if it could be regarded as an admission—is inadmissible. (**Note:** It might be argued that the defendant's statement implies that he knew himself to be at fault. This argument would not make the statement admissible, however, because FRE 411 specifically provides that evidence that a party was insured is not admissible for the purpose of establishing that party's fault or liability.) FRE 803(2) provides that an excited utterance may be admissible as an exception to the hearsay rule and defines an excited utterance as a statement relating to a startling event or condition that is made while the declarant is under stress or excitement caused by that event or condition. **D** is incorrect for two reasons: First, the defendant's statement that he had plenty of insurance is not related to the accident that produced his excitement, and second, like any other evidence, an excited utterance is not admissible unless it is relevant to a material issue.

89. **A**    The credibility of a witness may be impeached extrinsically (*i.e.*, by evidence that does not come from the witness's own mouth) by evidence that tends to show that his or her

testimony is not worthy of belief because he or she was incapable of perceiving accurately. Since the witness stated that his identification of the defendant was by the light of the full moon, evidence that there was no moon that night would tend to show that the witness's identification is unworthy of belief because he was incapable of making accurate observations.

The phrase *res gestae* was formerly used to refer to statements made under stress resulting from a startling event. Its use has largely been replaced by the "excited utterance" concept. **B** is incorrect because the testimony of the expert did not refer to any statement made while under stress or excitement. Except for evidence of prior statements, the FRE do not require confrontation as a foundation for the introduction of extrinsic evidence offered to impeach a witness. **C** is therefore incorrect. A matter is described as "collateral" if it is not material to issues in a case. **D** is incorrect because a witness's ability to perceive or remember is always regarded as material.

90.  **A**    Although evidence of unconvicted bad acts is generally inadmissible to extrinsically impeach a witness, FRE 404 provides that it may be admissible for other purposes. One of the most common permissible uses of such evidence is to create an inference that the defendant is guilty of the crime charged by showing that it was part of a general criminal plan or scheme. Since the defendant's possession of 41 different credit cards bearing 36 different names suggests that she planned to make fraudulent use of them all, evidence of that fact may be admissible. Such circumstantial evidence must be subjected to close examination to determine whether its probative value is outweighed by its prejudicial effect, so it is not certain that a court would admit the evidence. Of all the arguments set forth, however, **A** is the only one that could possibly provide the prosecutor with an effective argument in opposition to the motion to exclude.

Since the defendant is not charged with stealing credit cards, an inference that she did so is not relevant to any fact of consequence in the prosecution. For this reason, **B** is incorrect. (**Note:** It might be logical to argue that such an inference is relevant because a person who would steal credit cards is probably disposed to make fraudulent use of them. Such an argument would fail, however, because evidence of unconvicted acts is inadmissible for the purpose of proving a mere criminal disposition.)

Under the Fifth Amendment privilege against self-incrimination, a criminal defendant cannot be required to explain his or her conduct. **C** is therefore incorrect. An admission by conduct occurs when a party engages in conduct that indicates his or her own belief that he or she is guilty of the crime charged (*e.g.*, attempting to bribe an arresting officer to let the defendant go free or attempting to flee after being charged with a crime). Since possession of credit cards bearing other names does not indicate that the defendant believed herself to be guilty of fraudulently using the card bearing the name "Timothy Nolan," it is not an admission by conduct. **D** is therefore incorrect.

91.  **C**    The fact that a witness has previously made a statement that is inconsistent with his or her testimony indicates that he or she is not always honest and that, therefore, his or her testimony is not worthy of belief. For this reason, a witness may be cross-examined about

prior inconsistent statements. Although the common law requires that the witness first be told when and to whom the statement was made, the FRE have dispensed with this requirement.

For the above reason, **A** and **D** are incorrect. Under some circumstances, former testimony given under oath may be admissible as substantive evidence, but prior inconsistent statements are admissible for purposes of impeachment even if not made under oath. **B** is therefore incorrect.

92. **B**  In general, evidence is admissible only if it is relevant to a material issue. Evidence is relevant to a material issue if it tends to establish some fact of consequence. Since the defendant is charged with knowingly possessing the marijuana found in the trunk, the only material issue is whether the defendant knew it was there. The note from his wife may indicate that they smoked marijuana together on some other occasion (although her use of the word "stuff" makes even this questionable), but it does not tend to establish anything about the defendant's knowledge of what was in the trunk of the borrowed car. For that reason, it is not relevant to a material issue and should be excluded.

Hearsay is an out-of-court statement offered to prove the truth of the matter asserted in that statement. There is some doubt about the reason for offering the note from the defendant's wife. If it is offered for any reason other than to prove that they "got high on the stuff [they] smoked last night," it is not hearsay. Even if it is offered for that purpose, however, it probably falls under an exception to the hearsay rule since it is a declaration against the penal interests of the defendant's wife. Although declarations against the penal interest are not exceptions to the hearsay rule at common law (which makes an exception only for declarations against financial interest), they are exceptions under FRE 804(b)(3). **A** is therefore incorrect. Under the common law spousal privilege, one spouse may not give evidence against another in a criminal case. Thus, if the jurisdiction recognizes the common law spousal privilege, it would probably result in the exclusion of the note from the defendant's wife. **C** is incorrect, however, because its language indicates that this would be the only reason for excluding the note, and, as explained above, the note would be excluded even if the jurisdiction did not recognize this privilege. Although the statement contained in the note from the defendant's wife is a declaration against her interest and therefore an exception to the hearsay rule, it is not admissible because, as explained above, it is not relevant to a material issue. **D** is therefore incorrect.

93. **A**  Most jurisdictions hold that cross-examination should be limited to inquiry into matters to which the witness testified on direct examination. Some jurisdictions grant broader latitude. All agree, however, that questions that go beyond the scope of cross-examination are improper. Thus, if the question went beyond the scope of cross-examination, the objection should be sustained.

**B** is incorrect because leading questions are permitted on cross-examination. A hostile witness is one who has demonstrated anger or hostility to the attorney questioning him or her. **C** is incorrect because there is no indication that the plaintiff has done so. Since the question is not whether the dog is gentle, but whether the dog is generally known to be gentle, the plaintiff's expertise (or lack of it) on the subject of dog behavior is irrelevant. **D** is therefore incorrect.

94.  **A**        Ordinarily, a will must be authenticated by witnesses who testify to its execution. **A** is therefore correct. FRE 902 provides that periodicals, publications issued by public authorities, and certified copies of public records are self-authenticating. **B**, **C**, and **D** are therefore incorrect.

95.  **B**        If a proper foundation is laid, evidence that a particular product has been used many times without accident is admissible as circumstantial evidence that its condition is not dangerous. The required foundation includes evidence that the conditions under which the product was used were identical to those that existed at the time of the accident and that the witness would have heard if there had been any accidents. Since the witness testified that more than 10,000 of the motorcycles were sold, since presumably they were used on roads, and since most of these roads have bumps, the requirement of use in identical conditions has probably been satisfied. To complete the required foundation, it is thus necessary only to show that the witness was the person to whom all complaints of product failure would have been made.

                  **A** is incorrect because although a judge may choose to give a special instruction regarding the uncertainty of negative evidence, there is no rule of law requiring such an instruction. **C** is incorrect because the objection that it raises goes to the weight rather than the admissibility of the evidence. **D** is incorrect because under conditions such as those described above, negative evidence is admissible.

96.  **A**        Evidence that tends to impeach a witness's credibility by showing bias is admissible. The facts that the witness and the plaintiff were political rivals, and that the witness had used smear tactics in campaigning against the plaintiff in the past, would tend to show bias and are therefore likely to be admitted.

                  **B** is incorrect because the fact that the magazine brought the plaintiff's reputation into issue is not in itself sufficient to require the admission of evidence of a type that would otherwise be inadmissible. An admission is a statement by a party that is offered against that party. Since the official is not a party, nothing said by him could be regarded as an admission. **C** is therefore incorrect. **D** is incorrect, since the evidence was admissible to show bias.

97.  **C**        Under FRE 803(4), statements purporting to describe the way in which a physical condition came about are admissible as part of a medical history if made for the purpose of diagnosis, and if pertinent to diagnosis. The term *diagnosis* refers to the nature and origin of an injury. Even though the doctor's examination was performed to enable her to testify, she was attempting to form a diagnosis. Since the sound made by the plaintiff's elbow striking the pavement might be pertinent to a determination of the nature and origin of the plaintiff's injury (*i.e.*, a diagnosis), the statement is admissible.

                  **A** is incorrect because a statement made as part of a medical history is admissible as an exception to the hearsay rule. **B** is incorrect because even though the examination was performed in contemplation of the doctor's testimony, one of its purposes was to allow the doctor to diagnose (*i.e.*, determine the nature of) the plaintiff's injury. Although a witness might be permitted to testify to his or her own former sense impression, there is no exception to the hearsay rule for a witness's repetition of a declarant's former sense impression. **D** is therefore incorrect.

98.  **D**    The records are relevant to the issues since they would tend to establish what knowledge the company had regarding the effects of the car's design. They are not privileged for the following reasons:

They are not an attorney's work product because they do not contain mental impressions formed by an attorney. **A** is therefore incorrect. They are not materials prepared for litigation since they were made before the car was even marketed. **B** is therefore incorrect. They were not prepared for the purpose of communicating with the company's attorney, so **C** is incorrect.

99.  **C**    An expert may testify in answer to a hypothetical question so long as the facts assumed in that hypothetical have been established (or will be established) by the evidence offered. Since the plaintiff's case involves the assertion that her fall down the stairs resulted in her injury, it was proper for the school's attorney to ask for the doctor's opinion as to whether such an injury was possible given such facts.

The expert's answer may be based on the facts assumed in the hypothetical and need not be based on facts actually in evidence or known by him or her. **A** and **B** are therefore incorrect. Although an expert's opinion may be based on observations made in the courtroom, **D** is incorrect because the doctor's was not.

100.  **A**    The statement of the eyewitness fits the classic definition of hearsay: an out-of-court statement offered to prove the truth of the matter asserted in that statement.

Exceptions to the hearsay rule are made for past recollection recorded and business records, but only if the person recording the information knew it to be true of his or her own knowledge when the record was made. Since the officer could not have known of his own knowledge whether the statement of the eyewitness was true, **B** and **D** are incorrect. *Res gestae* is sometimes used as a synonym for "excited utterance," but **C** is incorrect because the fact that the statement resulted from an interview would probably prevent it from being an excited utterance and because there is no indication that the witness made the statement under stress.

101.  **C**    Under both FRE 803(7) and the majority rule, if a business record is otherwise admissible, the absence of entries in it may be used to establish non-occurrence of a particular event if it was the practice of the business to promptly record all such events.

**A** is therefore incorrect. **B** is incorrect because the fact that evidence is self-serving is not in itself sufficient to make it inadmissible. Although almost anything may be used by a witness to refresh his or her recollection, the fact that a document was so used is not sufficient to permit its admission into evidence. **D** is therefore incorrect.

102.  **D**      Laypersons may testify to their sense impressions in terms of opinion when there is
                 no other practical way to describe these sense impressions. The only possible way of
                 describing the smell of alcohol is to say that it smells like alcohol, and testimony so
                 describing it is admissible.

                 A leading question is one that would cause the reasonable person to believe that the
                 questioner was seeking one specific answer rather than another. **A** is incorrect because
                 the question did not indicate what answer it sought. **B** is incorrect because under the
                 circumstances, a conclusion was the only possible way of describing the officer's sense
                 impression. Although it was once held that opinion testimony was not admissible if it
                 went to an ultimate issue in the case, the prohibition has been abandoned under the FRE
                 and in a majority of common law jurisdictions. **C** is therefore incorrect.

103.  **D**      In interpreting terms in a contract, courts attempt to determine what the parties had in
                 mind when they agreed to those terms. Since evidence of prior transactions between the
                 same parties may be relevant indications of what they were thinking or expecting when
                 they formed the agreement, such evidence is ordinarily admissible. However, evidence
                 of transactions that did not involve the defendant would not give any indication of the
                 defendant's state of mind unless the defendant was aware of those transactions. Since
                 the facts do not show that the defendant was aware of the transactions in question, **D** is
                 correct.

                 **A** is incorrect because such evidence is admissible only if it involved the same parties.
                 **B** is incorrect because the witness's statement is not directly relevant to any statement
                 made by the store manager. Even if the 20 customers were of the same general size and
                 class as the defendant, evidence of their responses does not tend to establish anything at
                 all about the defendant's intentions or expectations at the time the contract was formed.
                 **C** is therefore incorrect.

104.  **C**      Hearsay is an out-of-court statement offered to prove the truth of the matter asserted in
                 that statement. If the plaintiff's statement is offered to impeach the plaintiff by showing
                 that he is not worthy of belief because he tells different stories on different days, it is
                 not hearsay. His statement is therefore admissible for impeachment. At common law, a
                 statement of a party offered against that party (*i.e.*, an admission) is hearsay but is admis-
                 sible under an exception to the hearsay rule. Under FRE 801(d)(2), an admission is not
                 hearsay at all. Either way, the plaintiff's statement would be admissible as substantive
                 evidence. **C** is therefore correct, and **A**, **B**, and **D** are incorrect.

105.  **B**      Proof that a witness was convicted of a felony or a misdemeanor involving dishonesty
                 may be admissible for the purpose of extrinsically impeaching the credibility of the wit-
                 ness, but not if the conviction was subsequently reversed for any reason.

                 **A** is incorrect because the evidence is offered to impeach the manager's credibility as a
                 witness, and this is not related to his employment by the seller. The fact that the convic-
                 tion was for a misdemeanor would not prevent its admission if the misdemeanor was one
                 that involved dishonesty. **C** is therefore incorrect. **D** is incorrect because if the crime of

which the witness was convicted was a felony, it may be admissible without regard to the nature of the felony.

106. **D**    A plaintiff in a negligence action is not required to prove that the defendant or its employee acted recklessly or committed any crime. The employee's acquittal on the criminal charge or reckless driving is therefore irrelevant to the issues in the plaintiff's action.

Thus, even though a court record might be admissible as an official written statement, **A** is incorrect because this record is not relevant. **B** is incorrect for two reasons: First, the fact that the employee was not driving recklessly is not relevant to the plaintiff's claim, and second, since the burden of proof in a criminal case differs from the burden of proof in a civil case, acquittal in the criminal court cannot determine the issues in a civil case. If a court record were covered under an exception to the hearsay rule, the unavailability of the person who was the subject of the proceeding from which the record emanated would not prevent its admission. **C** is therefore incorrect.

107. **D**    **A** is incorrect for two reasons. First, a confidential marital communication is one that takes place during the course of the marriage, and the couple was not married at the time of the party. Second, the privilege protects only confidential communications, and the driver's consumption of alcohol at the party would not be determined to be a confidential communication. Although the common law spousal privilege might prevent adverse testimony by a party's spouse even though it concerns events that preceded the marriage, **B** is incorrect because the privilege does not survive the marriage and would have terminated with the couple's divorce. **C** is a fabrication, with no basis in law. **D** is therefore correct.

108. **A**    Hearsay is defined as an out-of-court statement offered to prove the truth of the matter asserted in that statement. The statement of the firearms instructor is relevant to establish what the defendant believed, since the defendant was present when he said it and it is likely that he believed what his instructor said. If offered to prove the defendant's state of mind rather than the range of the rifle, it is not hearsay because it is not offered to prove the truth of what was asserted (*i.e.*, that the rifle is accurate at two miles).

On the other hand, if offered to prove the range of the rifle (*i.e.*, the matter asserted in the statement), it would be inadmissible as hearsay. **B** and **C** are therefore incorrect. **D** is incorrect because the statement is not hearsay if used to prove the defendant's state of mind.

109. **C**    Any witness who is familiar with an alleged speaker's voice may authenticate a recording of that speaker's voice. Since the witness spoke with the defendant while they shared the cell, he is now familiar with the defendant's voice and can properly authenticate it.

**A** is incorrect because hearsay is defined as an out-of-court assertion offered for the purpose of proving the truth of the matter asserted. Here, the witness is offering his opinion regarding whether the speaker on the audio file is the defendant. Importantly, he is not saying anything regarding any of the defendant's particular statements. **B** is incorrect because there is no special prohibition or rule that takes into account when the witness became familiar with the alleged speaker's voice. Therefore, it doesn't matter that the witness only became familiar with the defendant's voice after arrest. Under FRE 702, expert testimony is only appropriate when the subject matter requires scientific, technical, or other specialized knowledge. The witness's identification of the voice does not require any of these things. Therefore, **D** is incorrect.

110.  **C**    Any person who recognizes a voice because of experience that he or she has had with that voice may testify as to the identification of the speaker. Since the witness had experience with the defendant's voice in a face-to-face conversation and claims to recognize it as a result, her testimony identifying the defendant as the speaker is admissible.

**A** is incorrect because the extent of the experience that a witness had with the voice he or she is identifying goes to the weight of the evidence rather than to its admissibility. **B** is incorrect because everyday experience with speech places the identification of a voice within the capacity of a layperson who has experience with the voice sufficient to recognize it. Although a witness may testify to a distinctive characteristic that helped him or her to recognize a voice, **D** is incorrect because he or she is not required to do so.

111.  **D**    A lay witness may be permitted to testify to opinions if those opinions are rationally based on the personal perceptions of the witness. This requires, of course, that the witness have an adequate opportunity to perceive that on which his or her opinion is based. Since the witness did not see the defendant's car before the accident, and since tires may screech even when vehicles are being operated at reasonable speeds, the witness's opinion as to the speed of the defendant's car is probably not based on sufficient opportunity to perceive and should be excluded.

**A** and **B** are therefore incorrect. **C** is incorrect because if he or she had sufficient opportunity to perceive and form an opinion, a layperson is competent to form and testify to some opinions.

112.  **D**    Hearsay is defined as an out-of-court assertion offered for the purpose of proving the truth of the matter asserted. Since there appears to be no reason for offering the statement of the unidentified witness except to prove the truth of the matter that it asserts, it is hearsay. A business record may be admitted under an exception to the hearsay rule only if it was made by one who had personal knowledge of the information recorded or received it from an inherently reliable source. Since the investigator did not have personal knowledge and there is no indication that the witness interviewed by the deceased investigator was an inherently reliable source, **A** is incorrect. An official written statement may be admitted as an exception to the hearsay rule only as to information that the public official who recorded it knew of his or her own knowledge. Since the quote from the unidentified witness concerns information that the investigator did not know of his own knowledge, **B** is incorrect. Past recollection recorded is also admissible only if the record was made from the recorder's own knowledge and if the recorder is present in court to authenticate it. **C** is incorrect for these reasons, and because even if it were

admissible, past recollection recorded can be read to the jury but not physically introduced into evidence.

113.   **C**   FRE 803(4) and (6) permit the introduction of hospital records containing statements made by the patient for purposes of diagnosis. Since the circumstances that led to the injury are relevant to a diagnosis of the injury, they may be included in the record offered in evidence.

**A** and **B** are therefore incorrect. **D** is incorrect since the statements in the record were not opinion and therefore do not require the testimony of experts.

114.   **A**   Character evidence is not ordinarily admissible for the purpose of proving a person's conduct on a particular occasion. Thus, if evidence of the defendant's character is offered to prove anything about his conduct on the occasion of the incident in question, it is not admissible.

**B** is incorrect because a witness who testifies to a person's reputation is not required to know that person or to have any personal opinion about him. **C** is applicable only in criminal prosecutions. If the evidence were allowed for the purpose stated in **D**, it would be to prove that the defendant did not strike the plaintiff without justification. **D** is therefore incorrect for the same reasons that make **A** correct.

115.   **A**   Under FRE 803(2), a statement is admissible under the excited utterance exception to the hearsay rule if it was about a startling event and made while under the stress of excitement resulting from that event. The FRE further provide that the statement may be admissible even if the identity of the declarant is unknown.

**B** and **C** are therefore incorrect. **D** is incorrect because an excited utterance is admissible as a hearsay exception.

116.   **B**   Physical illustrations of a witness's testimony are admissible to illustrate that testimony if the witness testifies from personal knowledge that the illustration is a fair representation of what it purports to be. Since the witness testified from her own knowledge that the chart was an accurate representation of the dates on which her company had done business with the defendant, it may be admitted for that purpose.

FRE 803(6) permits the admission of business records if they were kept in the regular course of business and made while the transaction recorded was fresh in the entrant's mind regarding facts within her personal knowledge or from an inherently reliable source. This exception to the hearsay rule applies only to the record itself, however, and not to any summary of it. **A** is therefore incorrect. Under the best evidence rule, secondary evidence of a writing is not admissible to prove the terms of the writing unless the original or a qualified duplicate is shown to be unavailable. However, this rule is applicable only when the terms of the writing are in dispute. Since the contents of the plaintiff's files are not in dispute, the best evidence rule is inapplicable. Introduction of the chart might be said to place the contents of the chart in issue. Since the chart is an original, however, the best evidence rule does not exclude it. **C** is incorrect for these reasons. Materials used by a witness to refresh his or her recollection while he or she is testifying *must* be shown to opposing counsel and marked for identification. The court *may* also require the production of materials that were used to refresh a witness' recollection before trial. **D** is incorrect, however, because FRE 612 leaves this requirement to the court's discretion.

117.  **C**    Unless excluded by a rule of law, all evidence is admissible that tends to prove or disprove a fact in issue. The robber's identification is obviously a fact in issue. Since the guard's testimony tends to establish that at the time of his arrest, the defendant's physical appearance fit the description of the robber given by witnesses, her testimony is admissible for the purpose of explaining why the defendant no longer has bushy red hair.

A rule of evidence prohibits impeachment of a witness by extrinsic evidence of a collateral matter. **A** is incorrect, however, because the guard's testimony is not offered for the purpose of impeaching the defendant and because the identity of the robber is not a collateral matter. The Fifth Amendment privilege against self-incrimination protects a person from being compelled to give evidence that might be used against him or her in a criminal proceeding. **B** is incorrect, however, because the privilege relates only to testimonial evidence and does not prevent another from testifying to what he or she has seen the defendant do. An admission by conduct occurs when a defendant does some act that logically indicates that he or she believes himself or herself to be guilty. Although the defendant's attempt to change his appearance might suggest such a conclusion, the fact that there are many other legitimate reasons for the defendant to shave his head makes this a weak argument in this case. **D** is therefore incorrect.

118.  **A**    Hearsay is an out-of-court statement offered to prove the truth of the matter asserted in that statement. If the former president's statement was offered to prove that the president was permitted to raise his own salary (*i.e.*, the matter asserted), it would be hearsay. Since the defendant's defense is that he believed the union rules permitted him to act as he did, evidence of his state of mind is material. Since what he heard from the former president is likely to have affected his state of mind, the former president's testimony is relevant to the defendant's state of mind. Thus, it is not hearsay if offered to prove what the defendant thought, rather than to prove the truth of the former president's statement (*i.e.*, that the defendant was entitled to raise his own salary).

**B** is therefore incorrect. **C** is incorrect because the former president is not telling the jury his opinion but rather testifying that he stated that opinion in a conversation that he had with the defendant. This is offered not to prove that his opinion was correct but to establish the defendant's state of mind as a result of hearing the former president's opinion. An out-of-court statement offered to prove the truth of the matter asserted in that statement is inadmissible as hearsay even if the person who made that statement testifies to it himself or herself. **D** is therefore incorrect.

119.  **A**    Under FRE 803(2), an excited utterance is a statement relating to a startling event made while the declarant was under the stress of excitement caused by that event, and it is admissible as an exception to the hearsay rule.

**B** is therefore incorrect. Statements of a declarant's then-existing state of mind also fall under FRE 803(3)'s hearsay exception for descriptions of the declarant's intention, attitude, emotional condition, or mental feeling. **C** is incorrect, however, because although "I'm dying" might qualify as a declaration of the plaintiff's state of mind, "I had the green light in my favor" does not, since it does not describe her mental state. **D** is incorrect for two reasons: First, the plaintiff's statement said nothing about her past mental state, and second, FRE 803(3) permits declarations of past state of mind to be admitted only in certain will cases.

120. **C**  Although evidence of unconvicted bad acts is inadmissible for the purpose of proving bad character, if relevant, it may be admissible for the purpose of attacking a witness's credibility by showing bias. An acquittal of the defendant would affect the prosecution of the witness on the charge of being his accessory. Thus, the pending prosecution against the witness is relevant evidence of bias and is admissible for impeachment purposes.

    **A** is therefore incorrect. The bias of a witness is always material to his or her credibility. For this reason, evidence of such bias is admissible even though it may relate to a matter that is not material to the charge against the person on trial. **B** is therefore incorrect. **D** is incorrect because although it may be used to establish bias, extrinsic evidence of unconvicted bad acts is not admissible for the purpose of proving that a witness has a bad or dishonest character.

121. **D**  For a witness to be competent, he or she must simply have personal knowledge of the matter and be willing and able to testify truthfully. Here, the plaintiff saw the television broadcast, and nothing in the question implies he would be unable to tell the truth.

    **A** is incorrect because the fact a recording of the show likely exists would not preclude the plaintiff's oral testimony regarding the defendant's defamatory statements. **B** is incorrect because the defendant's statement is not an out-of-court statement being used to prove the truth of the matter asserted. Even if the defamatory statement itself is untrue, it is still legally actionable simply because it was made. **C** is incorrect because there is no indication the defendant is unavailable to testify, which is required under the rule regarding declarations against interest.

122. **C**  To get the whole story, a direct examiner or cross-examiner may attempt to refresh a witness's present recollection by showing the witness's physical objects or writings. If the purpose is to refresh the witness's recollection (rather than to expose the item to the jury), any item may be used, so long as it is first shown to opposing counsel and marked as an exhibit (*i.e.*, for identification). Before refreshing items can be used, however, the witness must have exhausted his or her unrefreshed memory. Since the witness stated that he could not remember whether he shouted (*i.e.*, that his present memory was exhausted), the prosecutor was permitted to attempt to refresh his recollection in the manner described.

    Since the report was used only to refresh the witness's recollection but was not itself being used to prove anything, it need not be admitted, admissible, or offered into evidence. **A**, **B**, and **D** are therefore incorrect.

123.   **C**      In some jurisdictions, a learned treatise can be used on the cross-examination of an expert witness only if the witness relied upon that treatise in forming his or her opinion. FRE 803(18) dispenses with that requirement, however, making the contents of a learned treatise an exception to the hearsay rule to the extent that they are called to the attention of a witness during cross-examination. This provision makes portions of learned treatises on medicine admissible both for impeachment and as substantive evidence. *(***Note:** Such portions may be read aloud, but a copy may not be physically admitted into evidence.)*

**A** and **B** are incorrect because they are under-inclusive. **D** is incorrect because the above section makes the contents of a learned treatise an exception to the hearsay rule.

124.   **B**      Under FRE 409, offers to pay or actual payments of medical or hospital bills are inadmissible for the purposes of proving negligence, liability, or the value of a claim. Although there are purposes for which such evidence might be admissible, none are listed among the options.

**A** is incorrect because FRE 409 excludes evidence of payment of hospital bills whether or not such payments are part of an offer of compromise. **C** is incorrect for this reason, and because a statement that is otherwise admissible may remain admissible even though it is inseparable from a statement about insurance. **D** is incorrect because FRE 409 specifically excludes such evidence if it is offered for the purpose of establishing fault.

125.   **C**      It is generally understood that a lay witness may testify to opinions regarding matters within the contemplation of the ordinary person so long as the opinion is rationally based on the witness's personal perception. For an opinion to be rationally based on the witness's personal perception, however, it is necessary to show that the witness had sufficient opportunity to perceive the matter about which he or she formed an opinion. Since the witness testified that she first saw the defendant's car just before it struck the plaintiff, her opportunity to perceive was probably not adequate to support her opinion. While it is not certain that a court would sustain the objection, the argument in **C** is the only one listed that could possibly support the objection.

**A** is incorrect because the ordinary driver is competent to form an opinion regarding the speed of a moving vehicle. FRE 704 specifically provides that if opinion testimony is otherwise not objectionable, it is not objectionable simply because it concerns an ultimate issue to be determined by the trier of fact. **B** is therefore incorrect. It is sometimes said that witnesses must testify to facts, and inferences are to be drawn by the jury. For this reason, lay opinions are usually not admissible if it would be reasonably practical for the witness to state the separate facts that caused him or her to form that opinion so that the jury could draw whatever inferences it deems proper. On the other hand, if it is not reasonably practical to express the separate factors that caused the witness to form a particular opinion, the witness may be permitted to state the opinion that he or she formed. Since the factors that go into an opinion regarding the speed of a moving vehicle cannot ordinarily be expressed as separate facts, a witness who is competent to form an opinion as to that speed will be permitted to express that opinion. **D** is therefore incorrect.

126. **D**   A cross-examiner is given broad leeway in attempting to impeach a witness intrinsically (*i.e.*, by eliciting testimony from that very witness). In general, a cross-examination question is proper if it has a logical tendency to discredit the testimony of the witness being cross-examined. A witness thus may be questioned about any facts that tend to show that the nature of his or her relationship to a party gives him or her a bias (*i.e.*, motive to be less than objective in his or her testimony). Since the defendant's accusation that the witness was dishonest would be likely to result in making the witness angry at the defendant and therefore biased, the question is proper and the objection should be overruled.

Hearsay is an out-of-court statement offered to prove the truth of the matter asserted in that statement. If the defendant's statement that the witness was dishonest were offered to prove that the witness was dishonest, it would be hearsay. Since it is offered for another purpose (*i.e.*, to show that the witness is biased), however, it is not hearsay. **A** is therefore incorrect. An admission is a declaration by a party that is offered against that party. Since the defendant's declaration that the witness was dishonest would be offered in favor of the defendant, it is not an admission. **B** is therefore incorrect. Extrinsic impeachment is evidence tending to impeach a witness that does not come from that witness's own testimony. Since the evidence that would tend to impeach the witness is sought from the witness himself, it cannot be called "extrinsic." **C** is therefore incorrect.

127. **B**   In general, evidence of a defendant's character or disposition is inadmissible for the purpose of proving that he or she acted in a particular way on a particular occasion. An exception is made, however, for evidence that shows a definite, particular, and strong inference that the defendant did the precise act charged. Included in this exception is evidence tending to establish that the defendant uses a distinctive *modus operandus* (MO), or method of operation. For this reason, the fact that the defendant previously smuggled cocaine using a brass statue with a false bottom could be admissible. Although it is not certain that a court would admit the evidence for this purpose, **B** is the only answer listed that could possibly be correct.

FRE 406 permits evidence of habit to be used as circumstantial evidence that on a particular occasion, the defendant's conduct was consistent with his or her habit. **A** is incorrect, however, because habit evidence requires a showing that the actor in question consistently acts in a particular way, and one prior experience is not sufficient to establish a habit. Although evidence of a defendant's previous conduct is inadmissible if offered against him or her for some purposes, it may be admissible if offered against him or her for others. **C** is thus incorrect because it is over-inclusive. Evidence of a prior conviction is not usually admissible for the purpose of impeaching a witness if the conviction occurred more than 10 years prior to the trial at which it is offered. **D** is incorrect, however, because the defendant's prior conviction is not being offered to impeach his credibility but rather to establish a distinctive MO.

128.  **C**   Evidence of a scientific test or experiment is admissible only if a foundation is laid that indicates the substantial identity of material conditions. Thus, if the test conditions were not substantially the same as the conditions that existed at the time of the accident, evidence of the test and its results should be excluded.

**A** is incorrect because a film may be authenticated by anyone who knows it to be an accurate representation of what it purports to be. The best evidence rule provides that when the contents of a document are in dispute, secondary evidence is not admissible in the absence of a showing that the original or a qualified duplicate is not available. Since there is no dispute about the contents of any document, the best evidence rule is not applicable, and **B** is incorrect. **D** is incorrect for the reasons given above.

129.  **D**   Evidence of past crimes might be admissible to impeach a witness's credibility but never solely for the purpose of showing that a criminal defendant had a disposition to commit a particular kind of crime. Since there is no indication that the defendant testified, there is no reason to impeach his credibility.

**A**, **B**, and **C** are therefore incorrect.

130.  **C**   Under FRE 803, records "kept in the course of a regularly conducted business activity" can be admitted if they are made at or near the time of the event, by a person with knowledge, who makes the record as a regular practice, and there is no indication of the record's untrustworthiness. Here, the manager testified he regularly made notes of client protests as part of his job, and there is no indication in the facts that the file is untrustworthy. Therefore, **C** is the best answer. **B** is incorrect because FRE 803(7) allows business records to be used to prove the nonoccurrence of an event. Because this is an exception to the hearsay rule, **A** is incorrect.

**D** is incorrect because the fact the manager used the file to refresh his recollection would not make the file admissible evidence.

131.  **B**   Prior inconsistent statements made by a witness may be used to attack that witness's testimony because those statements tend to show that the witness's testimony is not believable. Therefore, **C** is incorrect. However, since the second witness's statement was not made under oath and does not invoke any hearsay exception, it can only be used for impeachment and not to prove that the defendant was texting. Therefore, **A** is incorrect.

**D** is incorrect because FRE 607 allows the credibility of a witness to be attacked by any party.

132.  **C**   Hearsay is an out-of-court assertion offered for the purpose of proving the truth of the matter asserted. Thus, if the witness's statement is being offered to prove a man killed the victim instead of the female defendant, it is inadmissible hearsay. Therefore, **A** is incorrect.

A declaration against interest is a statement made by an unavailable declarant that is against the declarant's interest when made. This is an exception to the hearsay rule. Here, there is no indication the witness is not available. Therefore, **B** is incorrect. **D** is incorrect because the issue here is that the statement is hearsay, not that it might be unfairly prejudicial.

# QUESTIONS
# PROPERTY

# PROPERTY
## TABLE OF CONTENTS
**Numbers refer to Question Numbers**

# PROPERTY QUESTIONS

1. The landowner owned a five-acre tract of land in fee simple. In desperate need of money, the landowner prepared a deed purporting to convey the realty in fee simple to "Bearer" and took it to the office of a real estate investor. For a cash payment of $500 that the real estate investor paid him on the spot, the landowner signed the deed and handed it to the real estate investor saying, "You own it now."

   A statute in the jurisdiction provides that no document purporting to convey any interest in real property shall be recorded unless it is in writing; clearly identifies the grantor, the grantee, and the interest conveyed; and is signed and acknowledged by the grantor.

   The real estate investor subsequently instituted a proceeding to eject the landowner from the land. The landowner defended by asserting that he held a fee simple in the land and was therefore entitled to possess it. Which of the following arguments would most effectively support the landowner's assertion?

   (A) The deed was unrecordable.

   (B) The deed failed to identify the grantee.

   (C) $500 was inadequate consideration.

   (D) The landowner acted under economic duress in selling the land to the real estate investor.

2. Twenty-two years ago, a farmer built a chicken coop near the edge of his yard. In fact, about one-third of the structure was built on the neighboring parcel of land. The neighbor has demanded that the farmer remove the part of his chicken coop that encroaches upon his land. The farmer has refused to do so, claiming that he has become the owner of that part

   of the neighbor's land by adverse possession. A statute in the jurisdiction fixes the period of time for acquiring title to land by adverse possession at 20 years. The neighbor has instituted legal proceedings against the farmer for an order directing the farmer to remove the encroachment, and the farmer has filed a counterclaim, requesting a judgment declaring him to be the owner of the portion of the neighbor's land on which his chicken coop encroaches.

   Which of the following additional facts, if it were the only one true, would be **LEAST** likely to result in a judgment for the neighbor?

   (A) Ever since he built the chicken coop, the farmer has given the owner of the neighbor's land one dozen eggs per week in return for permission to encroach on the land.

   (B) After a portion of the chicken coop had been built on the neighbor's land, the owner of the neighbor's land told the farmer that it could remain there so long as the farmer used it to house chickens.

   (C) Soon after building the chicken coop, the farmer told the owner of the neighbor's land that he realized that he was encroaching, and that he would remove the encroachment whenever the owner of the neighbor's land asked him to.

   (D) The neighbor purchased the land from the prior owner 15 years after the chicken coop was built and commenced the action against the farmer 6 years after acquiring title.

3. In 1996, the landowner bought Blackacre. A doctor owned the neighboring parcel,

Whiteacre. The doctor used a path over Blackacre every day to walk from his home to his office in town. He did so for eight years, and many of the neighbors jokingly referred to it as the "doc's path," although he was using it without the landowner's permission. When the doctor faced some money problems, the landowner bought Whiteacre and held it for one year. During that year, the doctor continued to occupy Whiteacre as a tenant and use the path. The landowner then sold Whiteacre to a dentist, who used the path for another seven years. In 2012, the landowner decided to put a swimming pool across the path. The dentist claimed the landowner could not do so because he had gained an easement by prescription. The statutory period was 10 years. Did the dentist have a prescriptive easement to use the path?

(A) Yes, because there can be tacking on the dominant side of a prescriptive easement.

(B) Yes, because the doctor's and dentist's use of the path was hostile.

(C) Yes, under the doctrine of easement by estoppel.

(D) No, because the doctor's use was not hostile when the landowner owned Whiteacre.

4. A landowner, who was ill, executed a deed to her home naming her sons as joint tenants with full right of survivorship. Because her older son was on an extended trip out of the country, she handed the deed to her younger son, saying that she wanted him to let the older son know about it as soon as possible. She told her younger son that she was conveying the property while she was alive because she did not want her sons to be responsible for inheritance tax, but that she wished to continue living in the house until her death. The younger son had the deed duly recorded and then returned it to the landowner, asking that she keep it for him in her safe deposit box. The landowner

continued living in the home until the time of her death one month later. The younger son died the following week without occupying the realty and without telling the older son about the conveyance. The landowner's will left all her property to her sister. The younger son's will left all his property to his friend. Who is entitled to the realty?

(A) The friend, because the landowner delivered the deed only to her younger son, and the younger son devised the property to the friend.

(B) The sister, because the landowner delivered the deed to her younger son in an attempt to avoid tax liability while making a testamentary disposition.

(C) The sister, because the younger son never occupied the realty and the deed was in the landowner's possession at the time of her death.

(D) The older son, because the younger son received the deed as the older son's agent and the older son succeeded to the younger son's interest on the younger son's death.

5. A landowner sued to quiet title to a certain parcel of realty, seeking judgment declaring her as its owner. A farmer opposed her claim, asserting that she had delivered to the farmer a deed purporting to convey all her interest in the realty. Which of the following additional facts or inferences, if it was the only one true, would provide the landowner with the most effective argument in response to the farmer's assertion?

(A) The farmer gave no consideration for the conveyance.

(B) The deed did not indicate what interest was being conveyed.

(C) The deed was not signed by the landowner or her agent.

(D) The deed was not recorded.

6. After looking at most of the real estate in the county, a real estate investor decided that a rancher's ranch would be ideal for the golf course and country club that he wanted to build. Since the two-story ranch residence building was in good condition, the real estate investor planned to renovate and convert it into the club restaurant. The other buildings on the ranch were old and run-down, and it was the real estate investor's intention to tear them down. After negotiations, the real estate investor and the rancher entered into a contract for the sale of the farm, describing it as follows: "All that realty known as The Flying L Ranch, and identified as Tract 14, Lot 249, Parcel 61 in the Tract Index maintained by the office of the Recorder of the County of Parsons; said realty consisting of 240 acres more or less, one two-story residential building, one 60-foot-by-140-foot cattle barn, and nine small wooden sheds measuring approximately 50 square feet each." The contract set the purchase price at $240,000, with title to close two months from the date that the contract was signed. Two weeks after signing the contract, the real estate investor experienced a drastic change in his financial position and decided not to go through with the purchase of the ranch.

Before the real estate investor had a chance to contact the rancher about his change in plans, a severe windstorm blew down two of the small wooden sheds on the property. Immediately after the destruction of the two sheds, the real estate investor notified the rancher that he would not purchase the ranch on the ground that part of the realty had been destroyed. In a jurisdiction that has rejected the doctrine of equitable conversion, if the rancher sued the real estate investor for damages resulting from the real estate investor's refusal to conclude the sale, the court should find for

(A) the real estate investor, because the realty no longer conforms to the description of it in the contract of sale.

(B) the real estate investor, because the risk of loss from causes not the fault of either party remained with the rancher until the closing of title.

(C) the rancher, because the risk of loss from causes not the fault of either party passed to the real estate investor immediately upon execution of the contract.

(D) the rancher, because the sheds were not essential parts of the realty and abatement of the purchase price would have been a suitable remedy.

7. The plaintiff orally gave permission for defendant to build a road across the plaintiff's land so the defendant could get from his land to the public highway. The defendant hired a construction crew and bought materials to dig and pave the road. Six months after the road was completed, the plaintiff told the defendant he was revoking his permission. He then sued the defendant for trespass. In determining the defendant's rights to the road, the court should find

(A) the defendant had a revocable license.

(B) the defendant had no right to the road because the license to use it violated the Statute of Frauds.

(C) the defendant had an irrevocable license.

(D) the defendant had an irrevocable easement.

8. The developer was the owner of a tract of realty that she divided into 40 lots in accordance with the state's subdivision statute. When the developer prepared deeds to all the lots in the subdivision, the deeds to all lots numbered 21 through 40 contained language restricting the use of the land to one-story single-family residences, but the deeds to lots numbered 1 through 20 contained no

such restriction. The developer sold Lot 1 to the first buyer, conveying it by a deed that contained no restrictions. A second buyer subsequently purchased lots numbered 25 through 30 from the developer for investment purposes, receiving deeds containing the above restriction. Before construction began on any of the lots in the subdivision, the second buyer sold Lot 25 to a third buyer, conveying it by a deed that contained no restrictions. Lots 1 and 25 were located across the street from each other, each visible to the other.

The third buyer began construction of a three-story, three-family residence on Lot 25, and the first buyer sued for an injunction to prevent its construction. Which of the following would be the third buyer's most effective argument in defense?

(A) The deed that she received did not mention any restriction in the use of Lot 25.

(B) The deed that the first buyer received did not mention any restriction in the use of Lot 25.

(C) The first buyer was not aware of the restriction contained in the deed to Lot 25 and did not rely on it in purchasing Lot 1.

(D) The restriction in the deed to Lot 25 did not touch and concern the land.

9. As part of a divorce settlement between husband and wife, the wife conveyed a parcel of realty "to my ex-husband for life; remainder to my children who survive my ex-husband." Which of the following interests does the ex-husband have the power to convey to the buyer?

(A) The right to possess the realty until the ex-husband's death.

(B) The right to possess the realty until his ex-wife's death.

(C) The right to possess the realty until the death of the buyer.

(D) No right to possess the realty.

10. The landowner was the owner of six acres of land, the northern boundary of which fronted on a road, and the southern boundary of which fronted on a lake. The landowner's house was located in the middle of the property, about halfway between the road and the lake. Pursuant to the laws of the jurisdiction, he divided the land into three lots. Lot 1, the northernmost lot, fronted on the road. Lot 3, the southernmost lot, fronted on the lake. Lot 2, which contained the landowner's house, was located between Lots 1 and 3, with no frontage on either the road or the lake. The only ingress and egress to Lot 2 was over a clearly marked and graded dirt driveway that crossed Lot 1, connecting Lot 2 with the road.

The landowner continued to live in his house on Lot 2, but he sold Lot 1 to a man. The deed to the man reserved an easement over the dirt driveway that connected Lot 2 with the road.

Five years after the landowner's conveyance to the man, the county constructed a new road along the westernmost boundary of Lots 1, 2, and 3. The new road led from the old road to the lake. The landowner began using the new road for ingress and egress to his property, maintaining but not using the dirt driveway that crossed Lot 1. If the man, desiring to sell Lot 1, brought an action to enjoin the landowner from further use of the right of way across Lot 1, the court should find for

(A) the landowner, because his easement was created by express reservation.

(B) the landowner, because an implied easement by necessity does not terminate upon the termination of the necessity.

(C) the man, because an implied easement by necessity terminates upon termination of the necessity.

(D) the man, because continued use of the easement by the landowner will unreasonably reduce the value of Lot 1.

11. A landowner was the owner in fee simple absolute of a parcel of land. He executed a valid will in which he devised the land to "those of my children who survive me, to hold equally, share and share alike, as joint tenants and not as tenants in common, with full right of survivorship." The landowner's son and daughter, both adults, were his only living children at the time his will was executed. Three months later, the son borrowed money from a financial institution, executing a note secured by a mortgage on the land. Soon afterwards, the son committed suicide without repaying the loan. The following year, the landowner died, survived only by his daughter.

The jurisdiction has a statute that provides that a mortgagee of realty holds equitable title to the realty. Which of the following statements best describes the daughter's interest in the land following the death of the landowner?

(A) The daughter holds the land as a joint tenant with the financial institution.

(B) The daughter holds the land as a tenant in common with the financial institution.

(C) The daughter is the sole owner of the land, subject to the financial institution's lien for the amount owing by the son.

(D) The daughter is the sole owner of the land, and her interest is not subject to any lien on behalf of the financial institution.

12. A woman was the owner of a parcel of undeveloped land. When she died, her will devised the land to her husband, "for life, remainder to such person as my husband shall designate by his will." Three months after the woman's death, the husband married his second wife. As a wedding present, he executed a deed purporting to convey the land to his second wife in fee simple absolute. The day after executing the deed, the husband died intestate, survived only by his second wife. The second wife subsequently agreed to sell the land to a buyer by a contract that required the conveyance of marketable title. The deed tendered by the second wife did not contain a covenant of general warranty. On the day set for closing, the buyer refused to accept the deed tendered by the second wife and demanded the return of his deposit. In litigation between the second wife and the buyer, a court should find for

(A) the buyer, because the deed tendered by the second wife did not contain a covenant of general warranty.

(B) the buyer, because the land reverted to the woman's estate upon the death of the husband.

(C) the second wife, because the husband's conveyance to his second wife was a valid exercise of the power of appointment that he received under the woman's will.

(D) the second wife, because she was the only person qualified to inherit from the husband under the laws of intestacy.

13. A donor executed a deed to his land that contained the following clause:

To Senior Center, for so long as the realty shall be used as a home for the elderly, but if racial discrimination is practiced in the admission of residents to said home, to Senior Life for so long as the realty shall be used as a home for the elderly.

Senior Center and Senior Life were both charitable institutions devoted to the needs of indigent elderly persons.

On the day after the deed was executed, the donor's interest in the land is best described as

(A) a valid reversion.

(B)  a valid possibility of reverter.

(C)  a valid right of reentry.

(D)  void under the Rule Against Perpetuities.

14.  A landowner sold a parcel of land to a buyer. The land consisted of 100 acres, of which 30 acres were wooded and the rest was livestock pasture. The purchase price was $100,000, of which the buyer paid $50,000 in cash. The balance of $50,000 was to be paid in full 10 years after the closing of title, with interest of 8 percent per annum to be paid on a monthly basis until then. After receiving title to the land, the buyer entered into possession and paid the interest to the landowner as agreed. In addition, the buyer paid real estate taxes of $1,000 per year as they came due. After occupying the realty with his wife for nine years, the buyer died. His will devised the land to his wife for life, remainder to the buyer's brother. After the buyer's death, his wife remained on the land, making monthly interest payments to the landowner. The next year, the balance of the purchase price became due, and the wife received a tax bill from the county assessor for $1,000.

As between the wife and the buyer's brother, which of the following correctly states their respective obligations regarding payment of the real estate taxes and principal balance owed by the buyer?

(A)  The wife is obligated to pay the real estate taxes and to pay $50,000 to the landowner.

(B)  The wife is obligated to pay the real estate taxes, but the brother is obligated to pay $50,000 to the landowner.

(C)  The brother is obligated to pay the real estate taxes, but the wife is obligated to pay $50,000 to the landowner.

(D)  The brother is obligated to pay the real estate taxes and to pay $50,000 to the landowner.

15.  The landowner willed her realty "to my nephew for 20 years, remainder to my niece if she is living at that time; but if my niece is not living at the termination of my nephew's estate, to the oldest child of my niece who is living at the time of my death." The landowner died in January 1990, survived by her nephew, her niece, and the niece's son, who was 14 years old. In January 1991, a hunter moved onto the realty, living in a shack that he constructed from discarded packing crates. The niece died in 1999. In January 2010, 20 years after the death of the landowner, the niece's son discovered that the hunter had been in possession of the realty for 19 years. He made no attempt to have the hunter removed from the realty until January 2012, when the hunter had been in possession for 21 years. A statute in the jurisdiction fixes the period for acquisition of title by adverse possession at 20 years. Another statute fixes the age of majority at 18 years.

If the niece's son sued to have the hunter removed from the realty in January 2012, the court should find for

(A)  the son, because the period of adverse possession began running against him when he became the owner of the realty in 2010.

(B)  the son, because the period of adverse possession began running against him when the niece died in 1999.

(C)  the son, because the period of adverse possession began running against him when he was no longer an infant under the laws of the jurisdiction.

(D)  the hunter.

16.  A man owed a bank $50,000 in credit card debt. When the man fell behind on his payments, the bank told him that if he did not arrange to give the bank adequate security, the bank would sue him. The man's father thereafter signed a mortgage to the bank of his home to secure repayment by the man of the debt to the bank. However, the man's

father did not sign any documents that made him personally liable on the man's debt to the bank. Is the mortgage valid?

(A) No, because the man's father cannot mortgage his property to secure repayment of the debt of another.

(B) No, because the man's father did not receive any direct benefit for granting the mortgage.

(C) No, because the man's father did not guarantee the debt.

(D) Yes.

17. A brother and sister inherited a single-family home from their father. The property was left to both of them in equal parts and said nothing about who had the right to occupy the property. The sister chose to live in the home, while the brother decided to stay in his apartment. The fair market value of the home was $20,000 a year. The brother asked for $10,000 in yearly rent from the sister, who refused to pay him. Instead, she said he was welcome to live with her and her family in the home.

Is the brother entitled to receive rent from his sister?

(A) No, because the father's will said nothing about rental proceeds.

(B) No, because the sister said the brother was welcome to live with her in the home.

(C) Yes, because the sister is occupying the entire home.

(D) Yes, because the home was left to the brother and sister in equal parts.

18. On January 3, a seller and a buyer entered into a written contract for the sale of the seller's land. At the time the contract was signed, the buyer handed the seller a check drawn on a foreign bank in payment of the entire purchase price. Pursuant to the contract, the seller executed a deed to the realty and deposited it with a commercial escrow company, with instructions to deliver the deed to the buyer as soon as the buyer's check cleared the bank. The buyer's check cleared the bank on January 15, but because of a strike by certain bank employees, the escrow company did not learn that the check had cleared until January 21 and did not deliver the deed to the buyer until January 22. On January 17, the buyer executed a deed purporting to convey the realty to a developer. A statute in the state makes it a misdemeanor for any person "to execute any document purporting to convey an interest in real estate that the person executing said document did not actually hold at the time the document was executed, regardless of whether the person executing said document was aware that he or she did not hold the interest that the document purported to convey." If the buyer is charged with violating the above statute by executing a deed to the developer on January 17, he should be

(A) convicted, because he did not become the owner of the realty until the deed was delivered on January 22.

(B) convicted, because he did not become the owner of the realty until January 21, when the escrow company learned that the check had cleared.

(C) acquitted, because his title to the property relates back to January 15, when his check cleared the bank.

(D) acquitted, because when his check cleared the bank, his title to the property related back to January 3 when the contract of sale was executed.

19. After working 20 years for a company, a man was promoted from assistant manager to manager of a branch located in another state. When he learned that a new employee was moving to the branch to replace him as assistant manager, the man offered to sell the new employee his home for $260,000. After inspecting the premises, the new employee accepted the offer. They entered into a written contract of sale calling for closing of title

six weeks after the signing of the contract. Because their employer was eager to have them both start at their new positions as soon as possible, the contract contained a clause permitting the new employee to move into the house immediately. The new employee did so a few days after signing the contract of sale. The man kept the fire insurance policy on the house in effect, planning to cancel it upon conveying title to the new employee. In addition, the new employee purchased a policy of fire insurance on the house immediately after contracting for purchase of the house. Two weeks after the new employee moved in, a fire of unknown origin partially destroyed a portion of the roof, the entire kitchen, and parts of the exterior of the house. The new employee immediately notified the man that he was unwilling to complete the transaction at the price originally agreed upon, but that he would be willing to renegotiate to determine a new price based on the diminished value of the real estate as the result of the fire.

If the man sues for damages based upon the new employee's anticipatory repudiation of the contract of sale, the man's most effective argument would be that the court should find for him because

(A) the risk of loss passed to the new employee when he took possession of the premises pursuant to the contract.

(B) the new employee purchased a policy of fire insurance covering the premises prior to the contract.

(C) the man had a policy of insurance insuring him against fire damage to the house.

(D) a fire is presumed to be the fault of the person who is in possession at the time it occurs.

20. A developer was the owner of a 40-acre tract of land. Complying with the state's subdivision law, he subdivided the tract, creating 20 building lots in addition to the necessary

public areas. The developer retained 5 acres, on which he installed a well and water-purifying equipment. He laid pipes from his water-purifying plant to all the other lots in the subdivision. Every conveyance of land in his subdivision contained a restriction requiring the grantee to purchase from the developer all water used on the realty. A homeowner contracted to purchase a lot in the subdivision from the developer by a written agreement in which the homeowner agreed that after the closing of title, he would purchase all water used on the realty from the developer at a specified price for a period of 10 years. At the closing, the developer delivered a deed with the aforementioned restriction, but the homeowner did not sign it. Three years after closing, the homeowner installed his own well and stopped buying water from the developer. If the developer asserts a claim for damages against the homeowner, the court should find for

(A) the developer, because the homeowner contracted to purchase water from the developer for a period of 10 years.

(B) the developer, because a discrepancy between a contract for the sale of realty and a conveyance is resolved by looking to the contract.

(C) the homeowner, because the agreement to purchase water did not touch and concern the land of the developer.

(D) the homeowner, because the homeowner did not sign the deed.

21. A landowner owned a parcel of real estate that fronted on a major road. At the other end of the property, mountains rose majestically toward the sky. The landowner divided the parcel into Lot 1, which fronted on the road, and Lot 2, which did not. He sold Lot 1 to the homeowner, conveying title by a deed that reserved a 30-foot-wide ingress and egress easement for the benefit of Lot 2. The homeowner immediately constructed a house on Lot 1, taking advantage of the spectacular view of the mountains by installing a picture

window in his living room on the wall facing Lot 2. A developer then purchased Lot 2 from the landowner, receiving a deed that included the aforementioned easement over Lot 1.

The developer executed a deed to the electric company, granting it the right to erect poles on and string wires over his right of way across Lot 1 for the purpose of bringing power to Lot 2. If the homeowner sues for an injunction preventing the electric company from erecting poles on or stringing wires over Lot 1, the court should find for

(A) the homeowner, since an appurtenant easement is not alienable.

(B) the homeowner, since the electric company's proposed activity is outside the scope of the easement.

(C) the developer, since an appurtenant easement may be divisible for purposes incidental to its contemplated use.

(D) the developer, since every appurtenant easement contains and includes an easement in gross.

22. A landowner inherited from her grandfather an old building located in the city. Upon her death, she willed it "to the city, for as long as the building is used as a theater for the presentation of dance, drama, and the arts." Subsequently, the city council passed a valid resolution empowering the mayor to authorize temporary use of the theater building by an appropriate production company. The mayor orally authorized a ballet company to occupy the theater without charge and to use it for the presentation of dance productions. Three months after moving into the building, the director of the ballet company advertised for bids from contractors for the renovation of the building. In requesting the bids, the director announced that it was his intention to remove all interior walls from the building, thus converting the building into a "theater-in-the-round." The city instituted a

proceeding in which it sought an injunction to prevent the ballet company from permitting any permanent alteration in the structure of the building. If the city is successful, it will probably be because the ballet company

(A) paid no rent to the city.

(B) has not entered into any lease with the city.

(C) was a tenant at sufferance.

(D) was guilty of ameliorating waste.

23. A landlord was the owner of a two-bedroom house that he rented to the tenant pursuant to a three-year lease that provided, "Tenant agrees that he or she will not assign or sublet the premises without the written permission of the landlord." Seven months after taking possession under the lease, the tenant asked the landlord's permission to sublet the house for a period of three months. Although the tenant offered to submit the names of potential subtenants to the landlord for approval, the landlord said that he would not approve the sublease to any person under any circumstances. The tenant thereafter sublet the premises to a sublessor. Which of the following statements is most correct regarding the rights of the landlord?

(A) The landlord may elect to terminate the lease and evict the sublessor.

(B) The landlord may successfully assert a claim against the tenant for breach of covenant.

(C) The landlord may elect to terminate the lease and evict the sublessor, and the landlord may also successfully assert a claim against the tenant for breach of covenant.

(D) The landlord cannot evict the sublessor, nor may he sue the tenant for breach of covenant.

24. The landowner died, leaving a will that contained the following clause:

CLAUSE X — I hereby devise my realty located on Main Avenue to my wife for life, remainder to those of my children who achieve the age of 21 years. If any child of mine shall predecease me, or if any child of mine shall survive me but shall die before achieving the age of 21 years, that child's share shall be distributed equally among any of that child's children who shall marry, but if such child of mine shall die without issue, then his or her share shall be distributed among my children who achieve the age of 21 years.

At the time of the landowner's death, he had no grandchildren and was survived by three children. Two years after the landowner's death, the youngest daughter gave birth to a child. One week after the baby's birth, the youngest daughter died at the age of 20.

If the baby marries at the age of 18, will she be entitled to share in the Main Avenue property?

(A)  Yes, because her interest vested within 21 years after the death of the landowner.

(B)  Yes, because her interest vested within 21 years after the death of her mother.

(C)  No, because at the time of the landowner's death, it was possible that the baby's interest would not vest until more than 21 years after the deaths of the landowner's three children.

(D)  No, because at the time of her mother's death, it was possible that a grandchild would subsequently be born who would marry more than 21 years after the deaths of the landowner's three children.

25.  When a woman married her husband, he had a child from a previous marriage and had acknowledged himself to be the father of an illegitimate child. Together, the woman and her husband had a child. When the woman died, her will left a parcel of realty "to all children of my husband, including those children not born of our marriage, and whether legitimate or illegitimate." At the time of the woman's death, the child born to both the woman and her husband has an interest in the realty that can be described as

(A)  vested subject to partial divestment, since the husband may have more children in his lifetime.

(B)  absolutely vested, since the class of persons to whom the realty was devised closed immediately upon the woman's death.

(C)  contingent, since the husband may subsequently acknowledge his paternity of other illegitimate children in being at the time of the woman's death.

(D)  void, since the birth of a person not in being at the time the interest was created may affect the child's right in the realty.

26.  Forty years ago, the city built a dam on a creek for improvement of the city water supply. The city already owned the realty on which the dam was to be built, but before commencing construction, it obtained from all downstream owners grants of the right to interfere with the creek water. Each of these grants included a conveyance of the right to completely stop the flow of the creek by erecting the dam, and of the right to release water from the dam into the creek when necessary in the city's discretion for proper management of the dam. All such grants were properly recorded. Since construction of the dam, the city has not released water from the dam into the creek. As a result, the creek has been completely dry for the past 40 years. This year, because of an extremely wet winter, city hydrologists in charge of dam management have decided to release water from the dam into the creek. A landowner is the owner of a 250-acre parcel of realty downstream from the dam and crossed by the creek.

If the landowner institutes an action for an injunction to prevent the city from releasing water into the creek, the court should find for

(A)  the landowner, because no easement is valid that purports to authorize the maintenance of a private nuisance.

(B)  the landowner, because the right to release water in the creek was terminated by the city's non-use of it for 40 years.

(C)  the city, because an incorporeal hereditament lies only in grant.

(D)  the city, because it obtained the right to release water into the creek from all downstream owners before constructing the dam.

27.  A tenant leased property from the landlord for two years, ending January 1, 2013. The tenant paid rent at the end of every month. There were no communications between the parties during the entire tenancy. On December 31, the tenant sent a messenger to deliver a rent check for the same amount as the tenant paid under the prior lease. The tenant also included a note that read, "I've loved living here. By giving you this check, I hereby renew my tenancy for one year." The landlord refused to accept the check or note and told the messenger to take it back. On February 1, the landlord told the tenant that he was evicting the tenant. The tenant argued that he never received any notice of lease termination. Does the landlord have the right to evict the tenant on February 1?

(A)  No, because the landlord failed to give proper notice.

(B)  No, because the tenant indicated his intent to renew and offered payment.

(C)  Yes, because the landlord has the right of election.

(D)  Yes, because the landlord constructively evicted the tenant by refusing his rent payment.

28.  The seller and the buyer entered into a written contract for the sale of the seller's realty. The contract was complete in all other respects, but it failed to indicate the quality of title to be conveyed or the type of deed to be used. If the other party failed to perform, who could successfully sue for breach of contract?

(A)  The seller only, because the contract is clear as to the buyer's obligations.

(B)  Either the seller or the buyer, because the contract requires conveyance of marketable title by whatever deed is customarily used in the area.

(C)  Either the seller or the buyer, because parol evidence is available as to the intentions of the parties regarding the quality of title to be conveyed and the type of deed to be used.

(D)  Neither the seller nor the buyer, because of lack of mutuality of obligation.

29.  Several years ago, a chemical company developed a plan to use underground pipes for the purpose of transporting non-poisonous chemical wastes to a waste storage center located several miles away from its plant. At that time, it began negotiating for the right to lay an underground pipeline for that purpose across several tracts of realty. In return for a cash payment, the owner of a parcel of land executed a right-of-way deed for the installation and maintenance of the pipeline across his land. The right-of-way deed to the chemical company was properly recorded. The land passed through several intermediate conveyances until it was conveyed to the seller about 15 years after the right-of-way deed was recorded. The intermediate deeds were recorded, but none mentioned the right of way.

Two years later, the seller agreed to sell the land to the buyer by a written contract in which, among other things, the seller agreed to furnish the buyer with an abstract of title. The seller hired a reputable abstract company to prepare the abstract. The abstract company prepared an abstract and delivered it to the seller. The abstract omitted any mention of the right-of-way deed. The seller delivered the abstract of title to the buyer. After examining the abstract, the buyer paid the full purchase price to the seller, who conveyed the land to the buyer by a deed that included covenants of general warranty and against encumbrances. At the time of closing, the seller, the buyer, and the abstract company were all unaware of the existence of the right-of-way deed. After possessing the land for nearly a year, the buyer was notified by the chemical company that it planned to begin installation of an underground pipeline on its right of way across the land.

The buyer subsequently asserted a claim against the abstract company for damages that the buyer sustained as a result of the existence of the right of way. The court should find for

(A)  the abstract company, because it was unaware of the existence of the right-of-way deed.

(B)  the abstract company, because the right-of-way deed was outside the chain of title.

(C)  the buyer, because the buyer was a third-party beneficiary of the contract between the seller and the abstract company.

(D)  the buyer, because the deed executed by the seller contained a covenant against encumbrances.

30.  Immediately after World War II, the return of thousands of servicemen to the city resulted in a severe housing shortage. To ease the problem, an area at the east end of town that had been used primarily for agriculture was rezoned for residential use. As soon as the change in zoning took place, the developer purchased a 200-acre farm located in that part of the city and subdivided it in accordance with applicable laws. Setting aside space for public streets, a public school, drainage, and utility easements, he created 500 building

lots. He constructed a single-family residence on each lot and sold them all. Every deed contained a covenant restricting the land to single-family residential use. In addition, a subdivision plan containing a description of the subdivision and of the deed restrictions was filed and a copy furnished to all buyers. Many of the residences in the subdivision have since changed ownership, but all conveyances have contained restrictions similar to those originally used. Because the developer was primarily interested in a quick profit, he built the houses cheaply. As a result, most of them are now in decaying condition. Several of the owners have reconstructed their homes. A few have torn them down completely and replaced them with new single-family dwellings. A builder is the owner of a lot in the subdivision, having inherited it from his father, who was one of the original purchasers from the developer. The builder has torn down his house and is about to begin construction of a three-story professional building in which he is planning to rent office space to doctors, lawyers, and dentists. A majority of homeowners oppose any change in the development. If a group of homeowners in the subdivision sue for an injunction to prevent the builder from building the office building, are they entitled to the injunction?

(A)  Yes, because of the restrictions contained in the deeds.

(B)  Yes, because the majority of homeowners oppose any change in the development.

(C)  No, because most of the buildings in the subdivision are in a state of decay and therefore require reconstruction.

(D)  No, because of the changing character of the neighborhood.

31.  The landlord completed construction of a new office building and rented the entire ground floor to the tenant, an attorney, under a three-year lease that fixed rent at $600 per month. The landlord was unable to obtain a tenant to rent any other space in the building.

Six months later, the tenant vacated the premises. In a claim by the landlord against the tenant for rent for the balance of the term, which one of the following additional facts, if it were the only one true, would be most likely to result in a judgment for the tenant?

(A) The day after the tenant vacated, the landlord rented the ground floor to another attorney on a month-to-month basis at a rent of $500 per month.

(B) The day after the tenant vacated, the landlord began using the ground floor as a management office for the building.

(C) The reason the tenant vacated was that the building was located in a part of town not easily accessible by public transportation, and as a result, many of the tenant's clients refused to travel to see him there.

(D) The reason the tenant vacated was that he had been disbarred and was disqualified from the practice of law.

32. The seller agreed to sell the buyer a tract of land by a written contract that said nothing about the interest to be conveyed. The seller subsequently delivered a deed that was complete in all other respects but failed to indicate the interest conveyed. The buyer received the deed and had it duly recorded. Which of the following statements is most correct about the effect of the deed?

(A) It conveys a fee simple absolute, resulting in liability for damages if the seller did not in fact hold such an interest at the time the deed was delivered.

(B) It conveys whatever interest the seller had at the time the deed was delivered.

(C) It conveys whatever interest the seller had at the time the contract of sale was formed.

(D) It does not effectively convey any interest in the realty.

33. When the landowner died, he was the owner of 200 acres of undeveloped land. His will devised the land to his three daughters as joint tenants with full right of survivorship.

Shortly after the landowner's death, one of the daughters became ill and died. Her will devised her entire interest in the realty to the youngest daughter. Which of the following most correctly states the proportional interests that the surviving daughters would hold as a result?

(A) The surviving daughters would be tenants in common with equal interests in the realty.

(B) The surviving daughters would be joint tenants with equal interests in the realty.

(C) The surviving daughters would be tenants in common, with the youngest daughter holding a two-thirds interest and the other daughter holding a one-third interest in the realty.

(D) The surviving daughters would be joint tenants, with the youngest daughter holding a two-thirds interest and the other daughter holding a one-third interest in the realty.

34. The landowner purchased a 10-acre tract of land from the seller, paying one-half the purchase price upon closing and giving the seller a note for the balance secured by a purchase money mortgage. Although the landowner never missed a payment on the note, the seller foreclosed on the land six months later by falsely certifying that the landowner was in default, and by falsely swearing that notice of the foreclosure proceeding had been given to the landowner as required by statute. A buyer purchased the land at the resulting foreclosure sale, receiving a sheriff's deed. The buyer immediately recorded the deed and took possession of the realty. He constructed a residence on the land and put a fence up around the building and a small area

surrounding it. Since then, he has openly and continuously occupied the land enclosed by the fence, but made no use of the land outside it.

The landowner continued making payments to the seller according to the terms of his note. Because he lived in a distant part of the state, he was unaware of the foreclosure sale until 11 years later, when he attempted to sell the realty. Then, when an abstract company informed him of the sale, he sued for an order setting aside the sheriff's deed to the buyer and ejecting the buyer from the land. The buyer counterclaimed for a judgment declaring him to be the owner of the land by adverse possession.

A statute in the jurisdiction sets the period for acquiring title to realty by adverse possession at 10 years. If the court decides that the sheriff's deed should be set aside, which of the following comments is most correct about the buyer's interest in the land?

(A)  The buyer has no lawful interest in the land since he possessed it under color of a title that proved to be defective.

(B)  The buyer is the owner of the area surrounded by his fence but has no lawful interest in the land outside the fence since he did not occupy or possess it.

(C)  The buyer is the owner of all the land, since adverse possession cannot result in a subdivision of realty.

(D)  The buyer is the owner of all the land, since he occupied part of it under color of title to the entire tract.

35.  Several years ago, the landowner conveyed land to the first buyer. The first buyer immediately resold the land to her partner, the second buyer, without recording the deed that she had received from the landowner. The second buyer duly recorded the deed that he received from the first buyer and resold the land two years later to the third buyer, who immediately recorded his deed. One year after the third buyer's purchase of the land, the landowner purported to convey it to the fourth buyer, who immediately recorded his deed. The jurisdiction has a statute that provides that no conveyance of real estate is effective against a subsequent purchaser for value without notice unless it shall have been recorded. The official recording office does not maintain a tract index.

If the fourth buyer asserts that his title is superior to the third buyer's and sues the third buyer to quiet title to the land, which of the following would be the fourth buyer's most effective argument?

(A)  The deed from the first buyer to the second buyer was recorded outside the chain of title.

(B)  The first buyer did not have the power to convey the land.

(C)  The landowner was guilty of intentional misrepresentation in the sale of the land to the fourth buyer.

(D)  The second buyer had constructive notice that the first buyer had not recorded the deed that she received from the landowner.

36.  The landowner owned a small parcel of real estate that fronted on a lake, with a dock providing access to the lake. Because his friend owned a boat and enjoyed fishing on the lake, the landowner told him orally that he could launch his boat from the dock whenever he wanted. The landowner subsequently sold the realty to the buyer, advising him that his friend, the fisherman, had permission to launch his boat from the dock. When he took title, the buyer assured the landowner that he would continue to permit the fisherman to use the dock. The next time the fisherman attempted to do so, however, the buyer ordered him off the realty and told him not to enter it again.

If the fisherman sues for an order directing the buyer to permit him to continue using the dock for launching his boat, the court should find for

(A) the fisherman, because the buyer purchased the realty with knowledge of the fisherman's right.

(B) the fisherman, because an easement in gross survives the sale of the servient estate.

(C) the buyer, because the fisherman's right to use the dock terminated or was revoked.

(D) the buyer, because an easement appurtenant does not survive the sale of the servient estate.

37. In January, the landowner executed a will leaving a tract of land to "my brother for life, remainder to be divided equally among my brother's children, share and share alike." At the time of the will's execution, the brother had two daughters. In March, his daughters were killed in a boating accident. The following June, the landowner died. Fifteen years later, the brother executed a deed to a buyer purporting to convey "all my right, title, and interest in the land." A year after he executed that deed, the brother died without a will. The brother was survived by his six-year-old son.

Which of the following correctly describes the brother's son's interest in the land immediately **BEFORE** the death of the brother?

(A) Vested remainder subject to complete divestment.

(B) Vested remainder subject to partial divestment.

(C) Contingent remainder.

(D) No valid interest.

38. The landlord rented a warehouse to the tenant pursuant to a lease that fixed the rent at $500 payable at the beginning of each month. The lease contained a provision stating that in the event the tenant failed

to pay rent as agreed, the landlord had the right to terminate the tenancy and reenter the premises. After the tenant missed two rent payments, the landlord threatened to institute an eviction proceeding unless the unpaid rent was paid immediately. The following day, the tenant moved out, sending the landlord a check for $1,000 in payment of rent already owing. Also enclosed was an additional check for $500 in payment of the following month's rent and a letter that stated that it was the tenant's intention to surrender the premises immediately. The landlord made no attempt to re-rent the warehouse, and it remained vacant for the balance of the term of the tenant's lease. Upon its expiration, the landlord asserted a claim against the tenant for unpaid rent from the date the tenant vacated until the end of the lease term.

In deciding the landlord's claim against the tenant, the court should find for

(A) the landlord, since the tenant failed to pay the rent as agreed.

(B) the landlord, since the lease reserved a right of reentry.

(C) the tenant, since the lease reserved the landlord's right of reentry.

(D) the tenant, since, in effect, he gave the landlord a month's notice of his intention to vacate.

39. The landowner lived on 40 acres of land in a remote area. He split the land into two 20-acre parcels: Lot 1, which contained his house, and Lot 2, on which there were no buildings. He subsequently negotiated for the sale of Lot 2 to a developer. During the course of their discussions, the developer told the landowner that he planned to build a small cannery on the land for the commercial processing of locally grown produce. They subsequently entered into a written contract for the sale of Lot 2, which contract contained no mention of restrictions regarding the use of the subject land.

The landowner thereafter realized that the construction of a commercial cannery on land adjacent to his home might disturb his peace and quiet and reduce the value of his property. At the time scheduled for the closing of title, the landowner delivered a deed that stated: "Grantee does hereby covenant for himself, his successors, and his assigns that the realty conveyed herein shall not be used for any purpose other than the construction of a single-story residential building." The developer read the deed and accepted it, paying the full purchase price as agreed, but when the landowner asked him to sign the deed, the developer refused to do so. The following day, the developer had the deed recorded in accordance with the law. Several months later, the developer completed construction of a commercial cannery on the land.

If the landowner sues the developer for damages resulting from the developer's construction of the cannery on the land adjacent to the landowner's, the court should find for

(A)  the landowner, because the operation of a commercial cannery adjacent to a private residence constitutes a private nuisance.

(B)  the landowner, because of the restrictive covenant contained in the deed.

(C)  the developer, because at the time the contract was made, the landowner knew that the developer intended to use the land for the construction of a commercial cannery.

(D)  the developer, because he did not sign the deed containing the restrictive covenant.

40.  A company was a holding company that owned controlling interests in several agricultural enterprises. Because many of the company's holdings were expanding rapidly, the company retained a consultant to project and predict the company's real estate needs for the next 50 years. Based on advice that it received from its consultant, the company

began looking for more land. Because a farmer owned a 400-acre farm in the vicinity of one of the company's holdings, the company offered to purchase the land from him. The farmer refused to sell, saying that he planned to work the land until he retired from farming. Instead, the farmer and the company entered into a written option agreement pursuant to which, for an immediate cash payment, the farmer granted the company the right to purchase the land at a fixed price 30 years from the date the agreement was executed. The company did not record the option. The following year, the farmer had a heart attack and sold the land to a buyer. When he sold the land, the farmer told the buyer about the company's option.

In subsequent litigation, a court should declare that the company's interest under the option agreement was

(A)  invalid, because the company did not record the option agreement.

(B)  invalid, under the Rule Against Perpetuities.

(C)  valid, because the buyer had actual notice of the option when he purchased the land from the farmer.

(D)  valid, because the company gave consideration for the option.

41.  The tenant rented commercial office space from the landlord for a rent of $3,000 a month. As part of the lease, the tenant was given the right to exclusive occupancy of the basement of the building to use as storage. When the tenant moved into the building, it found that the entire basement was filled with building materials belonging to the landlord. The landlord promised to move the materials, and the tenant kept sending requests to the landlord to do so. After six months without the materials being removed from the basement, the tenant withheld the entire seventh month's rent but remained in the premises. The landlord sued the tenant for the month's $3,000 rent. The landlord should recover

(A) $0.

(B) $3,000 minus that part of the rent that can be apportioned to the basement.

(C) $3,000 minus the cost of cleaning the basement.

(D) $3,000.

42. A landowner owned two pieces of property. The landowner mortgaged the first property to the bank, and the second property to a finance company. The landowner fell behind in his payments on the first property. The bank got a judgment lien against the landowner because the loan on the first property went into default and there was not enough brought in during foreclosure to satisfy the loan. The landowner then fell behind on his payments on the second property. The finance company foreclosed on the second property, which, after satisfying the amount owed to the finance company, resulted in a surplus of $3,000. The landowner still owed $2,000 to the bank. How should the surplus be distributed?

(A) The landowner should get $3,000.

(B) The bank should get $2,000, and the finance company should get $1,000.

(C) The bank should get $2,000, and the landowner should get $1,000.

(D) The bank should get $3,000.

43. When the landowner died, among her personal effects was found a deed by which she purported to convey an interest in her ranch to her nephew. Based on the deed, the nephew claimed to have an interest in the realty, but the administratrix of the landowner's estate denied the claim. Which of the following facts or inferences, if it was the only one true, would provide the nephew with his most effective argument in support of his claim?

(A) Before she died, the landowner told the nephew that he would become the owner of the ranch after she was gone.

(B) The nephew was out of the country on the day that the landowner executed the deed.

(C) The deed names as grantees, "The landowner and the nephew as tenants in common."

(D) The landowner signed the deed two hours prior to her death.

44. Because it was her niece's birthday, a landowner duly executed a deed by which she conveyed her land to her niece. The landowner was elderly and had been chronically ill for several years. On days when she did not feel well enough to go out, she frequently sent her chauffeur to run errands for her. One morning, she called the chauffeur into her room and handed him an envelope. "I want you to give this deed to my niece," she said. "I also want you to go to the bank and the grocery store. Be sure and call me before you come home." The chauffeur went first to the bank, and then to the grocery store. Then, before going to the niece's house, he called the landowner to ask whether there was anything else she wanted him to do. He was advised on the telephone that the landowner had died soon after he left the house. Upon hearing this news, he returned immediately, without giving the deed to the niece. Eventually, the niece learned about the deed and claimed title to the land.

Which of the following is the most effective argument in opposition to the niece's claim?

(A) Title does not pass until there is a physical delivery to the grantee or his or her agent.

(B) The landowner died before the deed could be recorded.

(C) The deed remained in the landowner's control until her death.

(D) The deed was an attempted testamentary substitute.

45. In 1984, the landowner died, leaving a will that devised his land, "to my friend for life, and then to my neighbor." The friend, who lived in a distant state, never took possession of the land. In 1986, the friend's brother moved onto the lands without informing the friend or obtaining his permission. The friend's brother fenced most of the land, paid the real estate taxes as they came due, and lived in a house that he constructed on the land. He continued to occupy the realty until 2012, when the friend died without ever having learned of his brother's possession of the land. Under the jurisdiction's applicable statute of limitations, title by adverse possession may be acquired after 10 years of continuous, open, notorious, and hostile possession of realty. In 2012, the neighbor discovered that the friend's brother was in possession of the land and commenced an action to eject him. The friend's brother counterclaimed, seeking a judicial decree that he had acquired title by adverse possession.

Which of the following arguments is most likely to result in a victory for the neighbor?

(A) The friend's brother's possession of the land was not hostile, since he was the friend's brother.

(B) The friend's brother's possession of the land was not open and notorious, since the friend did not know that he was occupying it.

(C) The period of limitations did not begin running against the neighbor until the friend's death in 2012.

(D) Absent a unity of possessory right, no tacking of successive periods of adverse possession is permitted.

46. In 2012, the landowner died, leaving a will that in pertinent part read as follows: "I hereby give, devise, and bequeath my land to my husband for life, remainder to my children. If, however, any of my children shall predecease my husband, said child's share shall pass to said child's children to be distributed equally among them, share and share alike." When the will was executed in 2004, the landowner was married to her first husband, and they had two sons. Her first husband died in 2005, in an automobile accident that also killed her eldest son. Her eldest son had no children. The following year, the landowner married her second husband. At the time of her death in 2012, the landowner was survived by her second husband, her youngest son, and her daughter. Her daughter, who had been born in 2011, was her child by her second husband.

In a jurisdiction that has abolished the Rule in Shelley's Case but which applies the common law Rule Against Perpetuities, which of the following most accurately describes the interests held by the landowner's children and grandchildren?

(A) The remainder to the landowner's children is valid, but the substitutionary gift to her grandchildren is void since the size of the class was not determinable at the time the interest was created.

(B) The remainder to the landowner's children and the substitutionary gift to her grandchildren are void since it was possible for the landowner to marry a person who was unborn at the time their interests were created.

(C) The remainder to the eldest son is valid, but the remainder to the daughter and the substitutionary gift to her children are void since their lives were not in being at the time the interest was created.

(D) The remainder to the landowner's children and substitutionary gift to her grandchildren are valid.

47. The seller conveyed a parcel of land to the buyer by a deed that contained the following provisions:

The seller hereby conveys the described realty to the buyer in fee simple, in return for the buyer's agreement that he shall use the land for residential purposes only, and that he will require any person to whom he grants an estate in said land to make the same promise.

The buyer used the land for residential purposes for a period of 22 years, after which he commenced construction of a supermarket on the land. If the seller institutes an appropriate action in which he seeks a judgment declaring that the land has reverted to him because of the change in use, the seller should

(A) win, because the language of the deed created a fee simple subject to an executory limitation.

(B) win, because the buyer has violated a covenant contained in the deed by which the seller conveyed the property to him.

(C) lose, because the restrictive language of the deed violated the Rule Against Perpetuities.

(D) lose, because the language of the deed created no more than a contractual obligation.

48. In a will that is offered for probate today, realty is devised "to my children, but if my friend is still alive 30 years after my death, to my friend." The interest of the friend is

(A) a valid contingent remainder.

(B) a valid executory interest.

(C) an invalid contingent remainder.

(D) an invalid executory interest.

49. A landowner was the owner of a 200-acre parcel of unimproved realty located on the edge of a town. In 2007, when the area was largely uninhabited, she platted and obtained government approval for a subdivision of 100 acres. It was divided into 200 building lots, with necessary streets, utilities, and drainage easements. All lots were conveyed during 2007, every deed containing provisions restricting use of the lots to single-family, one-story residences. Each deed contained the following language:

The restrictions contained herein are binding on the grantee, and his or her heirs and assigns, and may be enforced by the owner or lawful occupant of any lot in the development.

A developer purchased a lot in 2007 and sold it to a homeowner, who built a one-story single-family residence thereon in 2008. The house burned down in 2012, and the homeowner applied for a building permit for the construction of a three-family dwelling on the same site. In 2010, local zoning laws were changed to allow multiple family dwellings. If a resident of the subdivision brings an appropriate action to prevent the construction of a multiple-family dwelling, the court will most probably

(A) not prevent the construction, since zoning laws supersede restrictions contained in deeds.

(B) not prevent the construction, unless the developer's deed to the homeowner contained a restriction like that contained in the landowner's deed to the developer.

(C) prevent the construction, because the restriction contained in the deeds to the lots runs with the land.

(D) prevent the construction, since a building destroyed by fire must be replaced, if at all, by a building of the same general character and use.

50. The landowner held a tract of land in fee simple absolute. On March 1, she sold it to the first buyer for $30,000 cash, executing and delivering a deed of general warranty. On April 1, discovering that the first buyer had never recorded his deed, the landowner purported to sell the realty to the second buyer, who was unaware that it had been previously

sold to the first buyer. The second buyer recorded her deed on April 13, after conducting a title search. The third buyer, who knew of the previous sale to the first buyer, told the second buyer about it on April 15, offering her $28,000 if she would quitclaim the property to him. Fearful that she might lose the property to the first buyer, the second buyer accepted the offer, executing and delivering to the third buyer a quitclaim deed that same day. The first buyer recorded on April 16. The third buyer recorded on April 17.

The jurisdiction has a recording statute that provides that "No conveyance of an interest in realty shall be good against subsequent purchasers unless it shall have been recorded." Whose interest is superior?

(A) The first buyer's, since his recording of April 16 placed the third buyer on constructive notice of his right.

(B) The first buyer's, since the third buyer had actual notice of the sale to the first buyer.

(C) The third buyer's, since the third buyer purchased for value before the first buyer recorded his deed.

(D) The third buyer's, since the first buyer acquired no rights in the land until April 16, which was after the third buyer's purchase from the second buyer.

51. The landowner was the owner of a 100-acre tract of land. After obtaining the necessary government approval, he platted a 75-acre subdivision consisting of 135 building lots, with streets and utilities easements. He then sold the subdivision to a developer, retaining the other 25 acres for his own residential use. After the developer began building houses on the subdivision, the telephone company asked the landowner to grant it an easement across a corner of his land so that it could bring service to the lots in the subdivision. The landowner agreed and, by an appropriate written document that the telephone company

duly recorded, granted the telephone company an easement over a described strip of his land "for the erection of such poles, and the placement of such wires, as the telephone company shall require for the purpose of providing telephone service."

Two years later, a cable television company entered into a contract with the telephone company pursuant to which it was licensed by the telephone company to transmit the cable company's television signals through the telephone company's wires, in return for which it agreed to pay the telephone company a substantial fee. The cable company signals sent through the wires were similar to telephone signals, and neither increased the wear and tear on the telephone company's wires nor increased the burden on the landowner's land.

If the landowner brings an action against the telephone company for an order enjoining it from permitting the cable company's use of the wires, which of the following statements most accurately explains why the landowner will lose?

(A) All easements appurtenant are freely alienable.

(B) All easements in gross are freely alienable.

(C) Although noncommercial easements in gross are not alienable, commercial easements in gross are alienable.

(D) The landowner derived commercial benefit from the easement that he granted the telephone company.

52. On January 1, 2013, a farmer borrowed $15,000 from the bank, signing a note secured by a mortgage on her farm. The following August 1, the farmer entered into a valid written contract to sell the farm to the buyer. The contract contained a provision by which the farmer promised to deliver title free from encumbrances on or before October 10. On October 10, 2013, the farmer executed

and delivered to the buyer a deed that contained a covenant against encumbrances. On October 11, 2013, the bank duly recorded its mortgage on the farm. On October 14, 2013, the buyer recorded her deed.

A statute in the jurisdiction states: "In the event of a dispute between parties claiming conflicting interests in realty, the interest which shall first have been recorded shall have priority."

Using funds that she had received from the buyer upon the sale of the farm, the farmer paid her debt to the bank in full on October 16, 2013, receiving and duly filing a satisfaction of mortgage. If the buyer institutes an appropriate action against the farmer for breach of the covenant against encumbrances, the buyer is entitled to

(A) rescission of the deed, since the covenant was breached at the time the deed was delivered.

(B) damages for breach of contract, since the covenant was breached at the time the contract was made.

(C) nominal damages only, since the buyer sustained no actual damages as a result of the existence of the bank's interest.

(D) nothing, since there has been no breach of the covenant.

53. The tenant was in the business of manufacturing furniture and occupied a factory building that he rented for that purpose from the landlord. When the landlord told the tenant that he was thinking of selling the building, the tenant discussed with his brothers the possibility of purchasing it as an investment. After negotiation, they bought the building from the landlord, who conveyed it by a deed that referred to the grantees but did not specify the tenancy created. The purchase price was $100,000, of which the three brothers paid half in cash at the time the deed was delivered. At the same time, the three brothers executed and delivered a deed of trust to secure a note for the balance of the purchase price. It was the intention of the three brothers to hold the building until rising real estate prices made it possible for them to sell it at a profit. Until then, it was understood that the tenant would continue to occupy and use it for his business.

Subsequently, after requesting but not receiving contributions from his brothers, the tenant spent $6,000 to improve the building by adding another bathroom, and $3,000 to preserve the building by repairing the roof, which had begun to leak. In addition, the tenant alone paid principal and interest on the outstanding trust deed obligation and all real estate taxes on the property.

If the tenant does not sue for partition but brings an appropriate action for contribution against his brothers, which of the following statements most accurately describes the rights of the parties?

(A) The brothers must pay a portion of the sum that the tenant spent on improving the property.

(B) The brothers must pay a portion of the sum that the tenant spent to pay principal, interest, and taxes on the property.

(C) The brothers must pay a portion of the sum that the tenant spent to pay principal, interest, and taxes on the property, and any right that the tenant has against the brothers is subject to a setoff for the reasonable rental value of the premises.

(D) The brothers must pay a portion of the sum that the tenant spent on improving the property; the brothers must pay a portion of the sum that the tenant spent to pay principal, interest, and taxes on the property; and any right that the tenant has against the brothers is subject to a setoff for the reasonable rental value of the premises.

54. A woman owned a home with a large backyard. Once a year or so, the woman would
hire a company to rake and trim the plants on
her property. Afterwards, the woman always
used her truck to dump the clippings and
leaves in a large pile of leaves and branches
that her neighbor already had on a remote
part of his five-acre parcel. The woman's
property was too small to have any reasonable place to dump the clippings and leaves.
The neighbor did not give the woman permission to do this, but he knew about it. The
woman did this most years for 40 years. The
neighbor then sold his property to his daughter. This year, when the woman tried to dump
her leaves and branches on the property, the
daughter told her she could no longer do so.
The state has a 20-year adverse possession
statute.

Is the woman entitled to continue using the
property to dump her leaves and branches?

(A) Yes, because she did so for 40 years.

(B) Yes, because the woman had no other
place to dump the clippings and
leaves.

(C) No, because the neighbor knew she was
dumping the clippings and leaves.

(D) No, because the woman only dumped
clippings and leaves most years.

55. The landowner conveyed a tract of land to a
man and woman. In which of the following
circumstances are they most likely to hold the
land as tenants by the entirety?

(A) They were not married, but the landowner, believing them to be married,
executed a deed "to [the man and
woman] as tenants by the entirety."

(B) They had been living together for 20
years but were not married. The landowner, knowing that they were not
married, executed a deed "to [the
man and woman] as tenants by the
entirety."

(C) They were not married but believed
themselves to be married. After the
landowner executed a deed "to [the
man and woman] as joint tenants,"
They re-conveyed the land to themselves "as tenants by the entirety."

(D) They were married, and the landowner
executed a deed "to [the man and
woman]."

56. In 2001, the landowner, who owned a tract
of land in fee simple absolute, executed
and delivered a valid deed that conveyed
the land "to my sisters as joint tenants and
not as tenants in common, with full right of
survivorship." The older sister died in 2005,
leaving a will that devised "all my interest
in the land to my daughter for life, then to
her daughters for life, then to all children of
her daughters whenever born." The younger sister died in 2007, leaving a will that
devised "all my interest in the land to my
friend." In 2008, the friend quitclaimed the
land to her doctor in return for payment of
$20,000.

In 2013, the doctor contracted to sell the
land to a dentist, promising to convey marketable title. When she tendered a general
warranty deed on the date that title was
to close, the dentist refused to accept it
on the ground that the doctor's title was
unmarketable.

In an appropriate action by the doctor against
the dentist for damages resulting from his
breach of contract, the court should find for

(A) the doctor, since the younger sister
became the sole owner of the land
upon the death of the older sister in
2005.

(B) the doctor, since her tender of a general
warranty deed gave the dentist sufficient protection, even if her title was
unmarketable.

(C) the dentist, since a title granted by quitclaim deed is unmarketable.

(D) the dentist, since the devise contained in the will of the older sister gave interests in the land to her daughter, her granddaughters, and any potential great-grandchildren.

57. When the tenant graduated from business college, he decided to go into the retail shoe business. He leased a small store for this purpose from the landlord for a period of three years. The written lease contained a clause that prohibited subletting without the written permission of the landlord. The lease did not contain an express reservation of the landlord's right to terminate the leasehold in event of a breach. After six months, the tenant found the shoe business unsatisfactory. He asked the landlord to release him from the lease, but the landlord refused to do so. One month later, the tenant assigned the balance of the lease to an attorney, who moved in immediately. When the landlord learned of the assignment, he demanded that the attorney vacate the premises.

If the landlord commences an appropriate proceeding to remove the attorney from the premises on the ground that the assignment to her was void, the landlord should

(A) win, since the lease prohibited alienation of the leasehold interest.

(B) win, since in the absence of a specific agreement to the contrary, a tenant may not assign without the landlord's express permission.

(C) lose, since the lease did not contain an express reservation of the landlord's right to terminate the leasehold in the event of a breach.

(D) lose, since restraints on alienation of estates in land are strictly construed.

58. The builder constructed an office building and leased it to the tenant for a period of 20 years. A clause of the lease provided that "nothing herein shall be construed to prevent the assignment of rights or obligations hereunder by either the landlord or the tenant." Three years later, the tenant assigned his interest under the lease to an investment company, notifying the builder of the assignment. The assignment agreement was signed by both the tenant and the investment company and contained a promise by the investment company to make rent payments directly to the builder.

If the investment company defaults in rent payments, which of the following statements is most correct about the rights of the builder?

(A) The builder can recover from the investment company as a third-party beneficiary of the assignment agreement.

(B) The builder cannot recover from the tenant under the lease.

(C) The builder can recover from the investment company but not from the tenant.

(D) The builder cannot recover from anyone.

59. Assume that a life tenant is in possession of realty, the reasonable rental value of which exceeds the sum necessary to pay principal and interest on an obligation secured by an encumbrance on the realty. Which of the following correctly states the rule regarding the obligations of the life tenant and remainderman with respect to payment of an obligation secured by an encumbrance on the realty?

(A) The life tenant must pay both principal and interest.

(B) The life tenant must pay interest, and the remainderman must pay the principal.

(C) The life tenant must pay the principal, and the remainderman must pay interest.

(D) The remainderman must pay both principal and interest.

60. A landowner was the owner of a three-acre parcel of undeveloped land on Barrett Road. This was the only land that he owned on Barrett Road. On his son's birthday, the landowner executed a deed naming his son as grantee and containing the following description: "All my property located on Barrett Road, consisting of four acres of undeveloped land."

As soon as he finished executing the deed, the landowner handed it to his son, saying, "Consider this a birthday present." The son examined the deed, thanked his father, and handed it back to him, asking that the landowner hold the deed for safekeeping. The landowner took it and locked it in the drawer of his desk. The following day, the landowner died. The executor of the landowner's estate has refused to deliver the deed to the son and claims that there has been no valid conveyance of any land by the landowner to his son.

If the son commences an action to quiet title to the realty on Barrett Road, the son should

(A) lose, since a deed that purports to convey more land than the grantor owns is void.

(B) lose, since there has been no delivery of the deed.

(C) lose, since there was no consideration for the transfer.

(D) win.

61. A state statute provides that:

No fire insurance proceeds shall be payable under any policy issued in this state except to a person who holds an insurable interest in the insured property at the time a fire loss occurs. For purposes of this section, an insurable interest in realty is held only by the person suffering the risk of loss.

On May 10, the seller contracted with the buyer for the sale of the seller's home, title to close on or about July 1. According to the terms of the contract, the buyer was to move into the house on June 1 and to pay rent of $350 per month until title closed. On May 11, the buyer purchased a policy of fire insurance on the house from the insurance company. The buyer moved in as planned on June 1. On June 10, the buyer fell asleep while smoking in bed. His cigarette ignited the bedclothing, causing a fire that severely damaged the house. The buyer filed the appropriate proof of loss with the insurance company, but the insurance company refused to pay on the ground that the buyer lacked the necessary insurable interest. The buyer sued the insurance company for breach of contract. If the jurisdiction recognizes the doctrine of equitable conversion, a court should find for

(A) the buyer, since the risk of loss passed to him as soon as he contracted to purchase the house.

(B) the buyer, since the fire resulted from his negligence.

(C) the insurance company, since the seller was the legal owner of the realty.

(D) the insurance company, since at the time the buyer purchased the policy of insurance, he had no insurable interest in the realty.

62. When the landowner was 78 years of age, her doctors advised her that she had a terminal disease. She immediately arranged to have a will prepared in which she devised her realty "to my twin brother for life, remainder to his children in fee simple." At the time of the landowner's death, her brother was alive and had two living children. The jurisdiction has a statute permitting the alienation of all future interests in land.

Which of the following most correctly describes the interest held by the two children at the time of the landowner's death?

(A) Contingent.

(B) Indefeasibly vested.

(C)   Vested subject to complete divestment.

(D)   Vested subject to partial divestment.

63.   The landowner was the owner in fee simple of a rectangular parcel of real estate, the north edge of which fronted on the street. He subdivided it into three lots, identified as Lots 1, 2, and 3. Lot 1 was the northernmost lot, and it fronted on the street. Lot 3 was the southernmost lot, with Lot 2 located between Lots 1 and 3. After the subdivision, the landowner conveyed Lot 1 to the first buyer and Lot 2 to the second buyer, and he retained Lot 3 for himself. Since there was no access to Lots 2 and 3, the deed to the first buyer created an easement across Lot 1 for access in favor of the occupants of Lots 2 and 3, and the deed to the second buyer created an easement across Lot 2 for access in favor of the occupants of Lot 3.

As soon as she received title, the first buyer constructed a residence on Lot 1. When it was completed, she sold the property to the third buyer. The second buyer subsequently built a residence on Lot 2. Twenty-five years after the second buyer constructed the house, a new public road was dedicated and built along the westernmost boundary of Lots 1, 2, and 3, providing convenient access to all three parcels. When the new public road was completed, the third buyer informed the second buyer and the landowner that he would no longer allow them to cross his land to get to theirs, and he erected a barrier across the access road that they had been using.

The landowner then began construction of a three-story, single-family residence on his lot. In an action by the landowner to enjoin the third buyer from interfering with his continued use of the right of way across Lot 1, the court should find for

(A)   the landowner, since the removal of the need for the easement did not affect the right to the easement.

(B)   the landowner, since to hold otherwise would adversely affect the rights of the occupants of Lot 2.

(C)   the third buyer, since an easement by necessity terminates when the need for it ceases to exist.

(D)   the third buyer, since the construction of a three-story building by the landowner will increase the burden of the servient estate.

64.   The homeowner's employer transferred him to a branch of the firm located in another state, so the homeowner listed his home for sale with a licensed real estate broker. Since the house had not been sold by the time the homeowner was to move, he signed and delivered to the broker a power of attorney that stated, "I hereby appoint the broker as my attorney-in-fact and authorize her to contract for the sale of my home." Three weeks later, the buyer offered to buy the homeowner's home. After showing the buyer the power of attorney that the homeowner had given her, and after negotiations, the broker prepared a contract for the sale of the homeowner's home. The contract was complete in every other respect but said nothing about the kind of deed that was to be executed. The buyer and the broker both signed the contract. At the time when title was to pass, the homeowner executed and tendered a quitclaim deed to the realty, but the buyer refused to accept it. The use of general warranty deeds is customary in the area. If the homeowner institutes an action against the buyer for breach of contract, a court should find for

(A)   the homeowner, since the power of attorney was silent as to the type of deed that the homeowner was willing to execute.

(B)   the homeowner, since the title that he held at the time that the deed was tendered was, in fact, marketable.

(C)   the buyer, since the use of general warranty deeds is customary in the area.

(D)   the buyer, since a quitclaim deed does not convey valid title to realty.

65.   On March 1, the seller and the buyer entered into a valid written contract for the sale of

the seller's home to the buyer at a price of $380,000, with title to close on June 15. It was further agreed that the buyer could move into and occupy the premises until title passed, at a rent of $500 per month to be added onto the purchase price and paid to the seller at the time of closing. On April 15, before the closing, a fire completely destroyed the house. The fire was not the result of fault by either party.

The jurisdiction applies the doctrine of equitable conversion. In litigation between the parties, which of the following statements best describes the rights of the parties?

(A) The buyer is obligated to purchase the premises at the price agreed in the contract.

(B) The buyer is obligated to purchase the premises, with the price reduced by the value of the house that was destroyed.

(C) The buyer may choose either to purchase the premises with the price reduced by the value of the house that was destroyed, or to cancel the contract and receive a refund of any monies paid by him to the seller.

(D) The sales contract is canceled by operation of law, and the buyer is entitled to the return of any monies paid by him to the seller.

66. By a will executed in 2011, the landowner devised a parcel of commercial land "to my niece and her heirs for as long as the property is not used for the sale of alcohol; but if the property is ever used for the sale of alcohol, to the National Cancer Association, a charitable organization." The landowner died on July 7, 2013.

In a jurisdiction that applies the common law Rule Against Perpetuities, permits the alienation of all future interests in land, and has abolished the destructibility rule, which of the following most correctly describes the

interest of the National Cancer Association in the land on July 8, 2013?

(A) Valid contingent remainder.

(B) Valid executory interest.

(C) Void executory interest.

(D) Void contingent remainder.

67. On January 15, 2013, the landowner executed a deed conveying a parcel of realty "to my friend and his heirs, but if the property is ever used as a base to help the United States go to war, then to my dentist and her heirs."

On January 16, 2013, the friend's interest in the realty is best described as

(A) a fee simple absolute.

(B) a fee simple subject to an executory interest.

(C) a quasi-life estate subject to a condition subsequent.

(D) void under the Rule Against Perpetuities.

68. The landowner was the owner of a 40-acre tract of realty, the northern boundary of which lay along the shore of a lake, and along the southern boundary of which lay a road. Twenty years ago, the landowner split the tract into two equal parcels. Parcel 1 fronted on the lake, and Parcel 2 fronted on the road. Ten years later, the landowner sold a lot consisting of a three-acre portion of Parcel 1 to the buyer. The buyer's lot fronted on the lake and was surrounded on its other three sides by the balance of Parcel 1. Because ingress and egress to the lot without crossing the landowner's land was impossible, the landowner granted the buyer an easement from the road to the lot. The easement crossed Parcels 1 and 2 at a location that was described by metes and bounds in the grant deed. The buyer built a cabin on the lot and constructed a driveway leading from the cabin to his easement.

Five years later, the landowner sold the remaining land to the developer.

The developer subdivided it into 60 building sites, dedicating roads and drainage easements as required by state law. None of the roads in the developer's subdivision followed the path of the buyer's easement, but two paved roads led from the road to the buyer's driveway. The buyer began using the paved roads as soon as they were completed to gain ingress and egress to his property. Two months later, the developer began building a house on the site of the buyer's easement.

If the buyer asks a court to stop the developer from building over his easement, the court should find for

(A) the developer, because the dedication and construction of roads leading to the buyer's driveway removed the strict necessity for the initial right of way.

(B) the developer, because unity of ownership resulted in a destruction by merger of the easement.

(C) the buyer, because he did not consent to relocation of his easement.

(D) the buyer, because an easement in gross is freely alienable by the holder of the dominant estate.

69. The landowner was the owner in fee simple of a parcel of land. On May 1, the landowner executed two deeds. Deed #1 purported to grant an undivided one-quarter interest in the land to the landowner's chauffeur. Deed #2 purported to grant an undivided one-quarter interest in the land to the landowner's nephew.

On May 1, the landowner handed the chauffeur Deed #1, saying, "Because you have been a good and faithful chauffeur for all these years, I'm giving you this deed. But it isn't to take effect until after my death." The chauffeur thanked the landowner and took the deed.

On May 10, the landowner died, leaving no will.

If the chauffeur seeks a judicial declaration that he held a possessory interest in the land on the landowner's death, which would be his most effective argument?

(A) The chauffeur's possession of Deed #1 raises an irrebuttable presumption that the conveyance was effective at the time the deed was delivered.

(B) On May 1, the chauffeur received a remainder interest in the land.

(C) The deed was a testamentary substitute.

(D) The landowner's death completed delivery of the deed.

70. Due to periodic flooding, the city stopped using a storage yard and bridge 30 years ago. At that time, a hermit built a wooden shack on that portion of the city's land that had formerly been used as a dirt road between the storage yard and the bridge. Since then, the hermit has been living in the shack and has been raising donkeys on the land formerly used as a dirt road. In addition, he planted a vegetable garden that produced food for himself and his donkeys.

Earlier this year, the city decided to begin using the storage yard again and demanded that the hermit remove himself and his possessions. The hermit refused, asserting that by adverse possession, he had become the owner of the land that he occupied. A statute in the jurisdiction conditions ownership by adverse possession on 20 years of continuous, hostile, open, and notorious possession.

If the city institutes a proceeding to eject the hermit, the outcome is most likely to turn on whether

(A) the city had knowledge that the hermit was in possession of part of the city's land.

(B) the jurisdiction permits the acquisition of city property by adverse possession.

(C) the hermit paid taxes on the land that he occupied.

(D) the hermit occupied the land under color of title.

71. Soon after a husband and wife married, they became interested in the purchase of a home with a price of $375,000. Because neither of them had been employed for very long, they were unable to find a bank to lend them money for the purchase. The seller indicated that he would be willing to accept a note for part of the purchase price if the husband and the wife could obtain an acceptable co-signer.

The wife's mother said that she would give them the money for the down payment and co-sign the note if the wife and the husband promised to make all payments on the note as they came due, and if the three of them took title to the property as joint tenants with right of survivorship. All agreed. On the day that title closed, the wife's mother paid $25,000 cash to the seller, and she, the husband, and the wife all signed a note promising to pay the balance, secured by a mortgage on the realty that they all executed. The seller executed a deed conveying the realty to the husband, the wife, and the wife's mother as joint tenants with right of survivorship.

The husband and the wife moved into the house, but the wife's mother never did. The following year, the wife's mother died, leaving a will purporting to devise her interest in the realty to her friend. The year after that, the wife and the husband were divorced. The wife subsequently executed a deed purporting to convey her interest in the realty to her tennis coach. The husband subsequently executed a deed purporting to convey his interest in the realty to his neighbor.

Which of the following best describes the interests of the friend, coach, and neighbor in the realty?

(A) The friend, coach, and neighbor are tenants in common, each holding a one-third interest.

(B) The coach and neighbor are tenants in common, each holding a one-half interest.

(C) The coach and neighbor are joint tenants as to a two-thirds interest, and tenants in common as to a one-third interest.

(D) The friend, coach, and neighbor are joint tenants, each holding a one-third interest.

72. The landowner was the owner in fee simple absolute of a tract of land. On January 10, 2013, the landowner borrowed $20,000 from the bank and executed a note secured by a mortgage on the land. On April 30, 2013, as a 21st-birthday present, the landowner executed a grant deed conveying the land to his son. The deed made no mention of the mortgage held by the bank. On May 15, 2013, the bank duly recorded its mortgage. On May 17, 2013, the son duly recorded his deed. Neither the landowner nor the son ever made any payments to the bank.

The jurisdiction has a statute that provides that "No conveyance, transfer, or mortgage of real property shall be good and effectual in law or equity against creditors or subsequent purchasers for value and without notice, unless the same be recorded." If the bank attempts to foreclose on the mortgage, will it succeed?

(A) Yes, because the landowner executed the mortgage to the bank before executing the deed to the son.

(B) Yes, because the bank recorded his mortgage before the son recorded his deed.

(C) No, because the son did not take the land "subject to" the bank's mortgage.

(D) No, because the bank is not a purchaser for value.

73. A tenant leased property from a landlord for one year at a monthly rent of $3,000. During his tenancy, the tenant built a large outside fireplace. The fireplace cost $1,000 to build, but was worth $2,000. However, two months before the end of the lease, the tenant vacated the property. On the same day, the landlord sold the property to a buyer, who immediately moved onto the property. The buyer then received a court order stating the fireplace had become part of the realty.

The tenant sued both the landlord and the buyer, claiming the fireplace belonged to him and they were unjustly enriched by its sale. How should the court rule?

(A) Neither the landlord nor the buyer owes the tenant anything.

(B) The buyer owes the tenant $1,000.

(C) The buyer owes the tenant $2,000.

(D) The landlord owes the buyer any profit on the land sale that can be attributed to the fireplace.

74. The landowner was the owner of two parcels of land, one known as Greenacre and the other known as Redacre. By a deed dated January 1, she granted Greenacre "to First Foundation for as long as the realty is used as a home for the elderly, but if said realty shall ever cease to be used as a home for the elderly, to Second Foundation." By a deed dated January 2, she granted Redacre "to my nephew for life, remainder to my niece, but if the realty shall ever be used for any purpose other than residential, to Second Foundation." First Foundation and Second Foundation are both charitable organizations.

Second Foundation has a valid future interest in

(A) Greenacre only.

(B) Redacre only.

(C) Greenacre and Redacre.

(D) Neither Greenacre nor Redacre.

75. The landlord leased an office to the tenant for a period of five years by an agreement that prohibited assignment by the tenant without the landlord's written permission. Two years after taking occupancy, the tenant requested the landlord's permission to assign the balance of his leasehold to a store owner. After checking the store owner's credit, the landlord wrote the tenant that the assignment was acceptable to him so long as the store owner personally assumed all obligations of the lease. The tenant's attorney prepared an agreement by which the tenant assigned all his rights under the lease to the store owner and the store owner agreed to personally assume all obligations under the lease. After the agreement was signed by the tenant and the store owner, the tenant's attorney sent a copy of it to the landlord. The store owner moved into the premises and began paying rent to the landlord.

After paying rent for six months, the store owner abandoned the premises and made no further payment. If the landlord asserts a claim against the tenant for damages resulting from the store owner's non-payment of rent, the court should find for

(A) the tenant, because the landlord consented to the tenant's assignment to the store owner.

(B) the tenant, because there was a novation.

(C) the tenant, because the store owner personally assumed all obligations under the lease.

(D) the landlord.

76. Pursuant to a written lease, the tenant rented a two-acre parcel of realty from the landlord for a period of two years. During the period of his tenancy, the tenant made substantial and valuable improvements to the realty. Prior to the termination of the lease period, the tenant told the landlord that he intended to remove the improvements. The landlord objected, asserting that the improvements had become part of the realty and threatening

to sue the tenant if he made any attempts to remove the improvements. The tenant thereupon sued for a judicial declaration that he was entitled to remove the improvements.

Which of the following additional facts or inferences, if it was the only one true, would be most likely to result in a judgment for the tenant?

(A) The value of the improvements made by the tenant exceeded $20,000.

(B) The improvements made by the tenant were not of a kind that the reasonable landlord would have expected a tenant to make.

(C) The written lease was silent regarding the tenant's right to make or remove improvements.

(D) The improvements made by the tenant could be removed without causing any damage to the realty.

77. The landowner was the owner in fee simple of a rectangular parcel of realty that was 500 feet deep with 100 feet of frontage on the street. He divided it into two building lots, each 45 feet wide by 500 feet deep, with a strip 10 feet wide and 500 feet deep between them. He sold one lot to a doctor and the other to a lawyer, deeding the 10-foot strip between the lots to both of them as tenants in common. The doctor and lawyer both wish to construct commercial buildings toward the rear of their lots and plan to use the 10-foot strip between the lots as a driveway for access to the buildings in the rear. Each fears, however, that the other will sell and that the new owner will sue to partition the 10-foot strip, cutting off access to the rear of the lot.

If the doctor and lawyer seek your advice as to how best to prevent this from happening, you should suggest that they

(A) enter into a contract not to partition, inserting language that specifically

makes the agreement binding on the heirs, assigns, and successors of each.

(B) convey the property to themselves as joint tenants with right of survivorship.

(C) take no legal action, since tenants in common have no right of partition.

(D) partition the strip into two five-foot-wide strips, each granting the other an easement over his or her strip and recording the right-of-way deeds.

78. In 2004, the landowner executed a will by which he devised his land "to my eldest daughter for life; and upon the death of my eldest daughter, as follows: a one-third interest to the children of my eldest daughter, a one-third interest to the children of my youngest daughter, and a one-third interest to the children of my nephew, but if any of my nephew's children should fail to survive to the age of 25 years, then the interest of such child or children of my nephew shall pass to all grandchildren of my nephew equally, share and share alike."

At the time the will was signed, the eldest daughter had a son. In 2008, the son was heavily in debt to the bank, who was threatening to commence an involuntary insolvency proceeding against him. To induce the bank to refrain from commencing the proceeding, the son executed a quitclaim deed conveying his interest in the land to the bank.

The landowner died in 2010. In January 2013, the eldest daughter died. Statutes in the jurisdiction abolish the Rule in Shelley's Case and permit the alienation of future interests in land.

In August 2013, the son contracted to sell a one-third interest in the land to the buyer, agreeing to convey marketable title. On the day that title was to pass, the son tendered a general warranty deed, but the buyer refused to accept it, asserting that the quitclaim that the son had executed in 2008 was a cloud on the title. If the son sues the buyer for breach of contract, the court should find for

(A) the buyer, since a quitclaim deed conveys whatever interest the grantor possesses at the time of its execution.

(B) the buyer, since the son received no valid interest in the land.

(C) the son, since even if title was not marketable, his tender of a general warranty deed gave the buyer sufficient protection.

(D) the son, since he held marketable title to a one-third interest in the land.

79. By grant deed, a landowner conveyed a parcel of realty "to the Church of the Lord so long as the property is used for church purposes."

Which of the following best describes the interest held by the landowner in the realty on the day after his grant to the Church of the Lord?

(A) Contingent remainder.

(B) Reversion.

(C) Possibility of reverter.

(D) Shifting executory interest.

80. The landowner bequeaths his land "to my son for life, then to his surviving children for life, then to the surviving children of my daughter." At the time of conveyance, the landowner's daughter had three children, and she was 80 years old. The son then died, leaving no surviving children. The daughter's three children then claimed possession of the property. The jurisdiction followed the common law Rule Against Perpetuities. The court should find that

(A) the daughter's three children share the property equally, because it is impossible for the daughter to have any more children.

(B) the daughter's three children share the property equally, subject to any later born children.

(C) the daughter's three children share the property equally, because they were alive at the moment the gift was created.

(D) the daughter's three children have no interest in the property.

81. The landowner was the owner of a parcel of realty that he subdivided into three lots. Lot 1 was the only one that fronted on the road. Lot 2 was north of Lot 1, and Lot 3 was north of Lot 2. To ensure that the occupants of Lots 2 and 3 would have access to their property, the deeds created a 12-foot-wide easement from the road across Lot 1 for the benefit of Lots 2 and 3, and across Lot 2 for the benefit of Lot 3. The landowner sold Lot 1 to the first buyer, Lot 2 to the second buyer, and Lot 3 to the third buyer. The second and third buyers used the easement for three years, creating by their use a bare dirt road across Lots 1 and 2. They found, however, that whenever there were heavy rains, the dirt road became muddy and passage became difficult. Because the third buyer was in the construction business, he offered to construct a 24-foot-wide paved road across Lots 1 and 2, at his own expense, for use by all persons with a legal right to the easement. The first buyer consented to its construction across Lot 1, but the second buyer stated that he would not permit the third buyer to construct such a road on Lot 2. If the third buyer institutes a proceeding for an order compelling the second buyer to permit the construction across Lot 2, the court should find for

(A) the third buyer, if the construction is necessary to prevent the road from becoming muddy after heavy rains.

(B) the third buyer, because he is willing to construct the road at his own expense.

(C) the third buyer, because the construction of a paved road would improve the values of Lots 2 and 3.

(D)   the second buyer, because the con-
      struction of such a road would impose
      an additional burden on the servient
      estate.

82.  When a couple married, the groom's mother
     decided to give them a parcel of land as a
     wedding present. She executed a deed con-
     veying the land "to husband and wife, as
     joint tenants and not as tenants in common,
     with full right of survivorship" and handed
     it to them at the wedding reception. Two
     years later, the couple separated. Although
     she and the husband did not divorce, the wife
     began living with another man. At the man's
     request, the wife executed a quitclaim pur-
     porting to convey her interest in the land to
     him. In a jurisdiction that recognizes tenancy
     by the entirety, which of the following state-
     ments is most correct about the interest that
     the man received as a result of the quitclaim
     executed by the wife?

     (A)   The man received no valid interest,
           since a quitclaim extinguishes the
           rights of the person executing it but
           does not necessarily confer any rights
           on the person receiving it.

     (B)   The man became a joint tenant with the
           husband, since a quitclaim conveys
           whatever title the grantor held at the
           time of its execution.

     (C)   The man became a tenant by the entirety
           with the husband, since a quitclaim
           conveys whatever title the grantor held
           at the time of its execution.

     (D)   The man became a tenant in common
           with the husband, since conveyance
           by a joint tenant severs the joint
           tenancy.

83.  The landowner was the owner of a 200-acre
     parcel of land. Because he knew that he was
     dying, the landowner executed a deed pur-
     porting to convey a portion of the land to his
     sister, who lived in another state. The deed
     described the realty conveyed as "a portion
     of the land 200 feet by 200 feet in size, with

its northeastern corner located at the eastern
end of the northern border of the land." On
Sunday, the landowner placed the deed in
an envelope with the proper postage affixed,
addressed it to his sister, and placed it on
his dining-room table with the intention of
mailing it the following day. That night, the
landowner died. The following morning,
unaware that his father had died, the landowner's son found the envelope on the table
and mailed it. The sister died on Tuesday.
The letter carrier delivered the envelope
containing the deed to the sister's house
on Wednesday. Without opening the envelope, the sister's daughter wrote the word
"deceased" across it and handed it back to
the letter carrier, asking him to return it to
the sender. The envelope reached the landowner's house on Friday. When it did, the
landowner's son opened the envelope and
tore up the deed that it contained. The landowner's will left everything he owned to
his son. The sister's will left everything she
owned to her daughter. Subsequently, both
the landowner's son and the sister's daughter
asserted ownership of the realty described in
the deed.

Assume the description was sufficient. In litigation between the sister's daughter and the
landowner's son regarding title to the realty
described in the deed, the court should find
for

(A)   the landowner's son, because the sister
      died before the envelope containing
      the deed reached her house.

(B)   the landowner's son, because the
      landowner died before the envelope
      containing the deed was mailed to the
      sister.

(C)   the sister's daughter, because she did
      not know that the envelope contained a
      deed when she asked the letter carrier
      to return it to the sender.

(D)   the sister's daughter, because when
      the deed was mailed to the sister, the
      sender relinquished control over it.

84. The lessee leased a parcel of realty from the landlord for a term of five years. During that term, the entire parcel was taken by eminent domain. Which of the following statements is correct about the rights of the lessee?

(A) The lessee may continue to occupy the premises for the balance of the term unless the leasehold interest was specifically mentioned in the condemnation award.

(B) The lessee is freed of the obligation to pay rent for the balance of the term.

(C) The lessee is entitled to a share of the condemnation award based on the value of the unexpired term of the leasehold less rent that would have become due during that term.

(D) The lessee is freed of the obligation to pay rent for the balance of the term, and is also entitled to a share of the condemnation award based on the value of the unexpired term of the leasehold less rent that would have become due during that term.

85. In 1997, without the landowner's permission, an artist moved onto the landowner's realty and constructed a dwelling. Since then, she has lived there continuously, openly, and notoriously. In 2004, the landowner died, leaving the realty to his two-year-old son. At that time, an uncle was appointed as the son's legal guardian. In 2007, the uncle became aware that the artist was in possession of the realty that the son had inherited from the landowner. In 2013, after the artist had been in possession of the realty for 16 years, the uncle sued on the son's behalf to eject the artist. In her defense, the artist asserted that she had become the owner of the realty by adverse possession.

A statute in the jurisdiction fixes the time for acquiring title by adverse possession at 15 years.

Has the artist become the owner of the realty by adverse possession?

(A) No, because the statutory period will not begin to run against the son until he achieves majority at the age of 18 years.

(B) No, because the statutory period began to run against the son when he inherited the realty in 2004.

(C) No, because the statutory period began to run against the son when the uncle became aware that the artist was in possession of the realty in 2007.

(D) Yes.

86. The seller was an architect and interior designer. She lived in a house that she had designed, and she frequently invited potential clients to her home so that she could show them the quality of her work. The house was located on a 20-acre parcel of realty that the seller had inherited from her grandmother. Because the land had once been part of a farm, there were many old farm buildings on it, most of which were in a badly deteriorated condition. The seller used one of these old buildings as a barn for a horse that she kept as a hobby.

When the seller was offered a position working for a real estate developer in another state, she decided to sell her realty. She entered into a valid contract to sell the property to the buyer for $250,000. She also offered to sell the buyer her horse, but the buyer said that he was not interested in keeping any animals. Since the seller needed to relocate to her new job location immediately, she gave the buyer permission to move onto the realty before the closing of title. After the buyer had done so, and prior to the closing, the building that the seller had used for a barn burned down as the result of a fire that did no other damage.

Prior to the date set for closing, the buyer claimed that the purchase price should be reduced by a sum equivalent to the value of the barn.

If the seller consults you regarding the buyer's claim, you should advise her that she is entitled to collect the full $250,000

(A) because the barn was not an essential part of the realty.

(B) because the buyer's possession of the realty when the barn burned down raises a presumption that he was at fault.

(C) if the jurisdiction applies the doctrine of equitable conversion.

(D) unless the barn burned without any fault by the buyer.

87. The landowner was the owner of two adjacent parcels of realty known as Lot A and Lot B. The northern boundary of Lot A was the southern boundary of Lot B. An old dirt road crossed both parcels, providing access to a river that flowed along the southern boundary of Lot A. The landowner sold Lot B to a doctor by a grant deed containing a river access easement permitting the holder of Lot B to use the dirt road that crossed Lot A. Subsequently, the landowner divided Lot A in half. He retained the southern portion, conveying the northern portion to a dentist. The deed to the dentist contained no mention of an easement for river access over the property that the landowner retained. At the closing, however, the landowner told the dentist that she was welcome to use the dirt road across his property for river access.

During the next 10 years, the doctor and the dentist frequently used the dirt road across the landowner's property for gaining access to the river. Then, because weather conditions made it necessary, the doctor paved that portion of the road.

A statute in the jurisdiction provides that all holders of an easement shall share equally the expenses of maintaining it.

When the doctor asked the dentist to contribute to the cost of paving the dirt road, the

dentist refused on the ground that she was not the holder of an easement. If the doctor asserts a claim against the dentist under the above statute, the doctor's most effective argument would be that the dentist held an easement by

(A) dedication.

(B) implication.

(C) express reservation.

(D) express grant.

88. The farmer is the owner of a hillside parcel of land, on which he grows apples for sale to a company that makes juice from them. For several years, the farmer has been irrigating his apple trees with water from a stream that flows across the land. After flowing across the land, the stream flows through a valley. A homeowner, who owns the valley, lives there with his family. The homeowner's family uses water from the stream for household purposes. This year, the farmer informed the homeowner that he was planning to build a small dam across the stream so that he would be able to pump water out of it more easily for irrigating his apple trees. The homeowner immediately instituted a proceeding to prevent the farmer from constructing the dam.

The jurisdiction determines water rights by applying riparian law.

If it were the only one true, which of the following additional facts or inferences would be most likely to cause a court to grant the relief requested by the homeowner?

(A) Construction of a dam will increase the farmer's consumption of water from the stream.

(B) Construction of a dam will change the natural flow of the stream.

(C) Construction of a dam will cause the farmer to consume more water from the stream than is reasonably necessary for the enjoyment of the farmer's land.

(D) The farmer can continue to pump water from the stream without constructing a dam.

89. The landowner executed a document purporting to lease a parcel of real estate to the tenant for 50 years at an annual rent of $1,000. Twenty years before the scheduled expiration of the lease, the entire parcel was taken by the state for the construction of a reservoir. At a condemnation proceeding, the trier of fact found that the balance of the tenant's leasehold was valued at $30,000. Of the total condemnation award, the tenant should receive

(A) $30,000, but the tenant will be required to pay the landowner a sum equivalent to the rent for the balance of the lease term.

(B) nothing, because the tenant's interest violates the Rule Against Perpetuities.

(C) $30,000, and the tenant will have no further obligation to the landowner.

(D) $30,000, minus a sum equivalent to the rent for the balance of the lease term, and the tenant will have no further obligation to the landowner.

90. Because he wanted a new boat, the landowner borrowed $50,000 from the bank and executed a note and mortgage on his realty for that amount in favor of the bank. The bank did not record the mortgage. Five years later, because he needed money to go into business, the landowner borrowed $20,000 from the lender, executing a note and trust deed on his realty for that amount in favor of the lender. The lender recorded the trust deed immediately. Two years later, the landowner defaulted on both notes. As a result of a foreclosure proceeding brought jointly by the bank and the lender, a court approved the sale of the landowner's realty for $50,000.

The jurisdiction has a recording statute that provides, "No transfer of an interest in real property shall be good against subsequent transferees for consideration and without notice unless it is recorded."

If the bank and the lender both claim a right to the proceeds of the foreclosure sale, whose claim should receive priority?

(A) The lender, because the mortgage held by the bank was not recorded.

(B) The lender, because the bank had constructive notice of the trust deed in favor of the lender.

(C) The bank, because the priority of security interests is not governed by recording statutes.

(D) The bank, because the mortgage held by the bank was a purchase money mortgage.

91. Soon after they were married, a wife and her husband purchased a house, taking title as tenants by the entirety. They made a $20,000 down payment and executed a note and mortgage for the balance, agreeing to make payments of $600 per month. Three months later, realizing that it would be difficult for them to make the payments, the wife offered to make her grandmother a part owner if she would help them pay for the house. The grandmother agreed to contribute $300 per month toward the payments, and at the grandmother's request, the wife and her husband executed a deed reconveying the property to themselves and the grandmother as joint tenants with right of survivorship. A statute in the jurisdiction permitted a joint tenancy to be created in this manner. The wife subsequently died, leaving a will that named her husband as her sole distributee.

Which of the following most correctly describes the relationship between the husband and the grandmother following the death of the wife?

(A) Joint tenants, with each holding a one-half interest in the realty.

(B)  Joint tenants, with each holding a one-third interest in the realty, and tenants in common as to the other third.

(C)  Tenants in common, with the husband holding a two-thirds interest in the realty and the grandmother holding a one-third interest in the realty.

(D)  Tenants in common, with each holding a one-half interest in the realty.

92.  A farmer was the owner of a large tract of land on which he grew crops. Because his income was declining, he decided to subdivide and sell his land. With government approval, he platted a subdivision consisting of 50 parcels of land with necessary access and utility easements. Soon afterwards, he conveyed one of the parcels to his neighbor by a properly recorded deed that they both signed and that contained the following language:

> The parties hereto hereby covenant for themselves, their heirs, successors, and assigns, that the realty herein conveyed shall not be used for any purpose other than residential, and that all conveyances of realty in the subdivision shall contain this covenant.

The neighbor subsequently sold half of his parcel to a friend, conveying it by a deed that contained no covenants or restrictions. Six months later, because he was unable to sell any of the other parcels, the farmer resumed agricultural activities on his remaining land. At the same time, the friend began construction of a gas station on the realty that he had purchased from the neighbor.

The friend commenced a proceeding to prevent the farmer from engaging in agricultural activities on the land, on the ground that such activities are not for residential purposes. Which of the following would be the farmer's most effective argument in opposition to the friend's proceeding?

(A)  The friend's deed contained no language of covenant or restriction.

(B)  The farmer did not covenant to refrain from using the land for agricultural purposes.

(C)  The friend and the farmer were not in privity.

(D)  The covenant in the farmer's deed to the neighbor did not touch and concern the land.

93.  On January 1, the landlord and the tenant entered into a written agreement by which the tenant rented a furnished apartment from the landlord. According to their agreement, the tenant was to occupy the apartment for one month at a rental of $250 payable in advance. The agreement further provided that its terms were to be automatically renewed at the end of each month unless either party terminated it by giving 20 days of written notice to the other. Upon signing the agreement and pursuant to its terms, the tenant paid the landlord $150 as a security deposit, with the understanding that the landlord could elect to apply it to any unpaid rent upon termination of the agreement.

Which of the following best describes the tenant's interest in the realty after executing the written agreement on January 1?

(A)  Tenancy for years.

(B)  Tenancy at will.

(C)  Periodic tenancy.

(D)  Tenancy at sufferance.

94.  When a farmer died, he left his farm to his son for life, with remainder to a church. The son tried farming the land for a while but found the work unpleasant. Although gravel had never before been mined or removed from the land, the son learned that he could derive a substantial income by doing so. He therefore dug a deep and extensive pit on the land from which he began removing gravel

for sale to builders and other commercial purchasers.

If the church asserts a claim against the son because of his removal of gravel, the court should

(A) grant the church a proportionate share of any profits derived from the sale of gravel removed from the land.

(B) issue an injunction against further removal of gravel and order the son to account to the church for profits already derived from the sale of gravel removed from the land.

(C) deny relief to the church, because no right of action will accrue until the church's interest becomes possessory at the termination of the son's estate.

(D) deny relief to the church, because a life tenant is entitled to remove minerals from an open pit.

95. The landowner's will devised a parcel of realty "to all the children of my son equally, share and share alike." At the time of the landowner's death, his son had two sons. One year after the landowner's death, the son's third child, a daughter, was born. Because the estate was sizable, probate court procedures were not completed until several months after the daughter's birth.

Who received a valid interest in the realty under the landowner's will?

(A) The sons only.

(B) All three children.

(C) All three children, and any other children of the son born subsequently.

(D) None of the children because the devise of an interest to them is void under the Rule Against Perpetuities.

96. The landlord, who was the owner of a commercial office building, leased an office in the building to a lawyer pursuant to a 10-year lease calling for rent in the sum of $1,000 per month. The lawyer occupied the premises for a period of two years, paying the rent as it became due each month. At the end of that period, he assigned the balance of the leasehold to a dentist by a document in which the dentist agreed to be personally liable for all obligations under the lease and which was signed by the lawyer and the dentist. Immediately following execution of the assignment, the lawyer sent a copy of it to the landlord. The dentist occupied the premises for several years, paying the rent as it came due. When seven months of the lease period remained, the dentist assigned the balance of the leasehold to a chiropractor. The chiropractor did not agree to be personally liable for all obligations under the lease, and the landlord was not informed of the assignment. The chiropractor occupied the premises for two months but did not pay rent. At the end of that period, the chiropractor assigned the balance of the lease to a psychic. The psychic occupied the premises for five months without paying rent, abandoning the premises when the lease expired. When the premises were vacated, a total of seven months' rent remained unpaid.

The landlord asserted a claim against the lawyer for unpaid rent. The court should award judgment for the landlord in the sum of

(A) nothing, since the dentist agreed to be personally liable.

(B) $2,000, the rent that accrued while the chiropractor occupied the premises.

(C) $5,000, the rent that accrued while the psychic occupied the premises.

(D) $7,000, all unpaid rent.

97. In January 20012, three buyers took title to a parcel of realty as joint tenants with right of survivorship. In March of that year, after obtaining the written consent of the two other buyers, the first buyer purported to convey her interest in the realty to her daughter. In January 2013, the second buyer died, leaving

a will in which he purported to leave his interest in the realty to his son.

Which of the following most accurately states the interests of the parties in the realty?

(A) The third buyer, the first buyer's daughter, and the second buyer's son are tenants in common, each holding an undivided one-third interest.

(B) The third buyer and the first buyer's daughter are joint tenants and the second buyer's son is a tenant in common, each holding an undivided one-third interest.

(C) The third buyer and the first buyer's daughter are joint tenants, each holding an undivided one-half interest.

(D) The third buyer and the first buyer's daughter are tenants in common, with the third buyer holding an undivided two-thirds interest and the first buyer's daughter holding an undivided one-third interest.

98. The landowner, the owner of a summer beach cabin, conveyed it to his daughter as a gift for her 16th birthday. Two years later, on her 18th birthday, the daughter went to the cabin for the first time and found a man in possession of it. When she asked what he was doing there, the man said, "Anyone who lives around here can tell you that I've been coming here every summer. I got the landowner's permission." In fact, the man had occupied the beach cabin every summer for the past 10 years but had not occupied the cabin during other seasons. The daughter instituted a proceeding to evict the man. In defense, the man claimed that he had acquired title to the cabin by adverse possession. Statutes in the jurisdiction fix the period for acquiring title to realty by adverse possession at 10 years and the age of majority at 18 years.

Has the man acquired title by adverse possession?

(A) No, because computation of the period of adverse possession begins anew each time there is a change in ownership of the realty.

(B) No, because for the past two years, the owner of the cabin was under a legal disability.

(C) Yes, because occupancy only during the summer was consistent with the appropriate use of the cabin.

(D) Yes, because the man had the landowner's permission to occupy the cabin during the summers.

99. A landowner was the owner of a parcel of land. On January 11, the landowner borrowed money from a bank, executing a note secured by a mortgage on the land. The following March, the landowner conveyed the land to his niece as a gift by a deed that made no mention of the bank's mortgage. The niece recorded the deed on March 15. The bank recorded the mortgage on March 18. The jurisdiction has a recording statute that provides that "no interest in realty shall be good against a subsequent purchaser for value and without notice unless it shall first have been recorded." Payment to the bank was not made as required by the note, and the bank attempted to foreclose on the land.

When the niece received notice of the foreclosure proceeding, she opposed it on the ground that her interest was superior to the bank's. Is the niece correct?

(A) No, because the landowner executed the mortgage to the bank before executing the conveyance to the niece.

(B) No, because a mortgage is not regarded as an interest in realty under recording statutes.

(C) Yes, because the niece recorded the deed before the bank recorded the mortgage.

(D) Yes, because the conveyance to the niece made no mention of the mortgage.

100. The landowner conveyed a parcel of land "to my son for life, but if my son should ever use liquor on the premises, to my daughter for life; then to my grandson." The grandson's interest is best described as

(A) a reversion.

(B) a contingent remainder.

(C) a vested remainder.

(D) void under the Rule Against Perpetuities.

101. Three brothers held Blackacre as joint tenants. Faced with serious credit card debt, the eldest brother conveyed his interest to a friend of his who agreed to pay off the debt. What is the effect of the conveyance to the friend?

(A) The two younger brothers and the friend hold the property as joint tenants.

(B) The two younger brothers and the friend hold the property as tenants in common.

(C) The two younger brothers hold a two-thirds interest in the property as joint tenants.

(D) The friend holds a one-third interest as a joint tenant with the brothers

102. The landlord was the owner of a commercial building that he leased to a friend for use as a retail shoe store for a period of five years. In the lease, the friend covenanted not to assign the premises without the landlord's written consent. A clause of the lease reserved the landlord's right to terminate the lease in the event of a breach of this covenant. Two years after the friend began occupancy, he sold the business to his store manager. After obtaining the landlord's

written consent, the friend assigned the balance of the lease to the manager. The manager operated the shoe store for several months and then sold it to his neighbor. As part of the sale, the manager executed a document purporting to transfer to the neighbor all remaining rights under the lease. The manager did not obtain the landlord's permission for this transfer. When the landlord learned of this transfer to the neighbor, he instituted a proceeding in which he sought the neighbor's eviction on the ground that the covenant not to assign had been violated.

Which of the following would be the neighbor's most effective argument in opposition to the landlord's claim?

(A) The covenant against assignment is void as a restraint against alienation.

(B) The landlord's only remedy is an action against the manager for damages resulting from breach of the covenant.

(C) The landlord waived his rights under the covenant by consenting to the assignment by the friend to the manager.

(D) The transfer by the manager to the neighbor was not an assignment but a sublease.

103. A business owner owned a lumberyard and a lumber mill. Because a woman's property was between the lumberyard and the mill, the business owner bought a 20-foot-wide easement through the woman's property so his trucks could drive back and forth between the lumberyard and the mill. Several years later, the business owner called the woman and said, "I won't need that easement anymore." Shortly thereafter, the business owner sold the lumberyard and mill to a buyer. The buyer relied on the business owner's assertion that he could still drive trucks over the easement when he bought the property. On the first day the buyer owned the two properties, the buyer

tried to drive his trucks across the easement. However, the woman had put up a barricade and told the buyer that she would not allow the trucks to pass without a new agreement. The buyer sued the woman for use of the easement.

The court should rule in favor of

(A)  the buyer, because the business owner only told the woman he wouldn't need the easement anymore.

(B)  the buyer, because the buyer relied on the business owner's assertion when he bought the properties.

(C)  the woman, because the easement was revocable at the will of the grantor.

(D)  the woman, because there is no indication she received any benefit from the sale.

104.  Zoning laws provided that all land on the north side of Main Street was restricted to residential use, and that commercial use was permitted on all land on the south side of Main Street. No business could be operated on land zoned for residential use.

A subdivision was located on the north side of Main Street. The subdivision plan that had been filed when the subdivision was created provided that persons occupying realty in the subdivision were permitted to operate small businesses in their homes, so long as such operation did not interfere with or annoy other residents in the subdivision.

A typist operated a typing service from an office in her home in the subdivision. A buyer entered into a contract to buy the home and the business. After entering into the contract of sale, however, the buyer learned of the zoning law that prohibited the operation of any business in a residential zone. He could not have discovered the zoning violation by reasonable inquiry prior to entering into the contract of sale.

He immediately informed the typist that he would not go through with the purchase of the typist's home because of the zoning violation. If the typist asserts a claim against the buyer for breach of contract, the court should find for

(A)  the buyer, because the purchaser of realty cannot be forced to buy potential litigation.

(B)  the buyer, because he could not have discovered the zoning violation by reasonable inquiry prior to entering into the contract of sale.

(C)  the typist, because the zoning law that prohibited the operation of the typist's business existed before the contract of sale was formed.

(D)  the typist, because her business was permitted by provisions of the subdivision plan.

105.  The landowner conveyed a parcel of realty "to my friend so long as liquor is not sold on the premises, but if liquor is sold on the premises, then to the Foundation for Hereditary Diseases." Two years later, the friend began selling liquor on the premises.

Which of the following best describes the friend's interest in the realty on the day before he began selling liquor on the premises?

(A)  void, since the interest of the Foundation for Hereditary Diseases could have vested more than 21 years after the death of all persons who were in being at the time of the conveyance.

(B)  fee simple absolute.

(C)  fee simple subject to an executory interest, since the friend's interest will terminate if liquor is ever sold on the premises.

(D)  fee simple subject to a condition subsequent.

106. When the seller said that she was interested in selling her home and the lot on which it stood, the buyer expressed interest in purchasing it. After negotiations, the buyer and the seller entered into a written contract that provided that the seller would sell the realty to the buyer for $260,000 and that delivery of title was to occur on or before August 1. The seller further promised that at the time title was delivered the house would be vacant. A clause in the contract provided that "The risk of loss from non-negligent causes shall remain with the seller until delivery of title." On July 15, through no fault of the seller or the buyer, the house burned down. The seller had not yet moved out of the house, and title had not yet been transferred to the buyer. The jurisdiction does not recognize the doctrine of equitable conversion.

Following the destruction of the house, if the buyer seeks to rescind the contract, he

(A) can, since the parties agreed that the risk of loss would not shift to the buyer until passage of title.

(B) can, since the jurisdiction has rejected the doctrine of equitable conversion.

(C) cannot, since the jurisdiction does not recognize the doctrine of equitable conversion.

(D) cannot, because the risk of loss passed to the buyer immediately upon execution of the contract to purchase.

107. After looking at most of the real estate in the county, a builder decided that the landowner's ranch, The Dancing L, would be ideal for the golf course and country club that he wanted to build. After negotiations, the builder and the landowner entered into a contract for the sale of the farm, describing it as follows: "All that realty known as The Dancing L Ranch, and identified as Tract 14, Lot 249, Parcel 61 in the Tract Index maintained by the office of the Recorder of the County of Stinson; said realty consisting of 240 acres more or less, one two-story residential building, one 60-foot by 140-foot cattle barn, and nine small wooden sheds measuring approximately 50 square feet each." This property was the only parcel in the county known as The Dancing L and identified by these Tract, Lot, and Parcel numbers. Even so, it was standard practice in the area to use a different method when describing parcels of land. The contract set the purchase price at $240,000, with title to close two months from the date that the contract was signed. Two weeks after signing the contract, the builder experienced a drastic change in his financial position and decided not to go through with the purchase of The Dancing L.

At the time and place of closing, the landowner tendered a deed containing a description of the realty that was identical to that which appeared in the contract of sale, but the builder refused to accept it. In a subsequent action by the landowner against the builder for damages resulting from breach of contract, the court should find for

(A) the landowner, because his land was the only realty in the county that was known as The Dancing L, and the only parcel identified by the Tract, Lot, and Parcel numbers used in the contract description.

(B) the landowner, because the builder waived any objection to the validity of the description by signing a contract containing an identical description.

(C) the builder, because the contract and deed lacked a metes and bounds description.

(D) the builder, because it was not standard practice in the area to use descriptions like the one contained in the contract and deed.

108. A brother and sister owned a farm as joint tenants. When the brother lost his job, he

granted a mortgage to the bank, giving the bank a lien against all of the property. His sister did not know about the mortgage. The brother then died, and the bank contacted the sister, offering to let her take over the mortgage payments in her brother's name. When the sister refused to do so, the bank foreclosed on the property. May the bank do so?

(A)  Yes, because the brother gave it a lien against all of the property.

(B)  Yes, because the bank gave the sister an opportunity to assume the mortgage.

(C)  No, because the brother and sister were joint tenants.

(D)  No, because the sister did not know of the mortgage until after her brother's death.

109.  The landowner was the owner of six acres of land, the northern boundary of which fronted on a road and the southern boundary of which fronted on a lake. The landowner's house was located in the middle of the property, about halfway between the road and the lake. Pursuant to the laws of the jurisdiction, he divided the land into three lots. Lot 1, the northernmost lot, fronted on the road. Lot 3, the southernmost lot, fronted on the lake. Lot 2, which contained the landowner's house, was located between Lots 1 and 3, with no frontage on either the road or the lake. The only ingress and egress to Lot 2 was over a clearly marked and graded dirt driveway that crossed Lot 1, connecting Lot 2 with the road.

The landowner continued to live in his house on Lot 2, but he sold Lot 1 to the first buyer and Lot 3 to the second buyer. The deed to the first buyer reserved an easement over the dirt driveway that connected Lot 2 with the road. The landowner had never used the lake, and there was no clearly marked road or path to it across Lot 3. The deed to the second buyer, however, reserved an easement described by metes and bounds across Lot 3 for the purpose of access to the lake from Lot 2.

Two years after the landowner's conveyance to the second buyer, the second buyer sold Lot 3 back to the landowner. One month later, the landowner conveyed Lot 3 to the third buyer by a deed that made no mention of any easement over Lot 3. The landowner subsequently sold his home and Lot 2 to the fourth buyer, executing a deed that granted the fourth buyer a right of way over Lot 3 for access to the lake, identical to the easement described in the original grant from the landowner to the second buyer. When the fourth buyer attempted to cross Lot 3, however, the third buyer refused to permit him to do so. If the fourth buyer institutes an action for an injunction directing the third buyer to refrain from interfering with the fourth buyer's right of way over Lot 3, the court should find for

(A)  the fourth buyer, because the right to cross Lot 3 was expressly granted by the landowner in the deed to Lot 2.

(B)  the fourth buyer, because the easement to cross Lot 3 was created by the deed that conveyed Lot 3 to the second buyer.

(C)  the third buyer, because the landowner's non-use of the easement across Lot 3 resulted in its termination.

(D)  the third buyer, because the easement to cross Lot 3 terminated when the landowner repurchased Lot 3 from the second buyer.

110.  A donor executed a deed to his realty, which contained the following clause:

To Family Center, for so long as the realty shall be used as a home for families, but if racial discrimination is practiced in the admission of residents to said home, to Family Life for so long as the realty shall be used as a home for families.

Family Center and Family Life were both charitable institutions devoted to the needs of indigent families.

On the day after the deed was executed, Family Life's interest in the land is best described as a

(A) valid contingent remainder.

(B) valid executory interest.

(C) void contingent remainder.

(D) void executory interest.

111. A landowner sold a parcel of land to a buyer. The realty consisted of 100 acres, of which 30 acres were wooded and the rest was livestock pasture. The purchase price was $100,000, of which the buyer paid $50,000 in cash. The balance of $50,000 was to be paid in full 10 years after the closing of title, with interest of 8 percent per annum to be paid on a monthly basis until then. After receiving title to the land, the buyer entered into possession and paid the interest to the landowner as agreed. In addition, the buyer paid real estate taxes of $1,000 per year as they came due. After occupying the realty with his wife for nine years, the buyer died. His will devised the land to his wife for life, remainder to the buyer's brother. After the buyer's death, his wife remained on the land, making monthly interest payments to the landowner.

The fences surrounding the livestock pastures on the realty were in decaying condition, and the wife made arrangements to have some of the trees cut down for use in repairing the fences. When the buyer's brother learned of the wife's plan, he brought a proceeding for an injunction to prevent her from doing so. In response to the buyer's brother's petition, a court should find for

(A) the wife, because the cutting of trees on the land was a reasonable way of maintaining the fences.

(B) the wife, because a life tenant has an unlimited right to make use of natural resources of the realty.

(C) the buyer's brother, because destruction of trees on a parcel of realty constitutes ameliorating waste.

(D) the buyer's brother, because the fences were permitted to decay during the buyer's lifetime.

112. A landowner willed her realty "to my nephew for 20 years, remainder to my niece if she is living at that time; but if my niece is not living at the termination of my nephew's estate, to the oldest child of my niece who is living at the time of my death." The landowner died in January 1993, survived by her nephew, her niece, and the niece's two children — a son, who was 14, and a daughter, who was 7.

Which of the following correctly describes the interest that the niece's daughter had in the realty on the day after the death of the landowner?

(A) Vested remainder subject to complete divestment.

(B) Contingent remainder.

(C) Springing executory interest.

(D) No valid interest in the realty.

113. On March 1, a landowner conveyed a tract of realty to her son and daughter as joint tenants with right of survivorship. On April 1, the landowner purported to sell that same tract to a buyer by general warranty deed. The buyer paid cash for the property and was unaware of the prior conveyance to the landowner's children. The son and daughter recorded their deed on April 3. The buyer recorded his deed on April 5. The son died on April 7.

The jurisdiction has a statute that provides, "In determining the priority of conflicting interests in land, the first such interest

to have been recorded shall have priority."
Who has priority on April 8?

(A)  The daughter, because the conveyance
      to the son and daughter was recorded
      before the conveyance to the buyer
      was recorded.

(B)  The daughter, because the realty was
      conveyed to the son and daughter
      before the conveyance to the buyer
      was recorded.

(C)  The buyer, because the daughter's
      interest did not ripen until after the
      buyer's interest was recorded.

(D)  The buyer, because the landowner
      conveyed to him by general warranty
      deed.

114.  A farmer was the owner of a dairy farm,
      which included a large processing plant.
      About five years ago, the farmer decided to
      build a new barn for his animals and bor-
      rowed $30,000 for that purpose from the
      bank. At the time he made the loan, the
      farmer executed a note requiring monthly
      payments of a specified sum and secured
      by a mortgage on the farm. The following
      year, the farmer sold the farm to a dairyman,
      conveying it by a deed that stated, "The
      realty described herein is conveyed subject
      to an existing note and mortgage held by the
      bank."

      Several months after buying the farm, the
      dairyman purchased a new cooling tank for
      the processing plant. The tank had a 5,000-
      gallon capacity and weighed several tons
      when empty. In installing the cooling tank,
      the dairyman had the wooden floor of the
      farm's processing plant torn out and replaced
      with concrete. Brackets were placed in the
      wet concrete so that when it hardened they
      could not be removed. The new tank was
      then permanently fastened to the brackets.
      The dairyman made several monthly pay-
      ments to the bank on the mortgage note but
      then missed three consecutive payments.

The bank was unsuccessful at collecting on
the note, and it instituted foreclosure proceedings. As a result, an appropriate court
directed the sale of all property subject
to the mortgage. Should the cooling tank
purchased and installed by the dairyman be
included in the foreclosure sale?

(A)  Yes, because installation of the tank
      converted it to a fixture.

(B)  Yes, because the dairyman made sev-
      eral of the monthly payments.

(C)  No, because the cooling tank was
      brought onto the realty after the exe-
      cution of the note and mortgage.

(D)  No, because the dairyman took the
      property "subject to" the mortgage.

115.  A landowner owned a parcel of real estate
      that fronted on a major road. At the other
      end of the property, mountains rose majesti-
      cally toward the sky. The landowner divided
      the parcel into Lot 1, which fronted on the
      road, and Lot 2, which did not. He sold Lot
      1 to the homeowner, conveying title by a
      deed that reserved a 30-foot-wide ingress
      and egress easement for the benefit of Lot
      2. The homeowner immediately constructed
      a house on Lot 1, taking advantage of the
      spectacular view of the mountains by install-
      ing a picture window in his living room
      on the wall facing Lot 2. A developer then
      purchased Lot 2 from the landowner, receiv-
      ing a deed that included the aforementioned
      easement over Lot 1. Several years later, the
      developer began construction of a home on
      Lot 2.

      The house that the developer was con-
      structing on Lot 2 was to be three stories
      tall and would block the view from the
      homeowner's picture window of the moun-
      tains. If the homeowner seeks an injunction
      to prevent the construction of the develop-
      er's house in a manner likely to obstruct
      the homeowner's view, the court should
      find for

(A) the homeowner, because the home-owner's house was built before the developer began construction.

(B) the homeowner, because the construction of the developer's house as planned will interfere with the homeowner's natural easement for air, light, and view.

(C) the developer, because the homeowner has no right to an undisturbed view of the mountains.

(D) the developer, because there was no proof he was aware of the view from the homeowner's picture window when he purchased the property from the landowner.

116. The landowner died leaving a will that contained the following clause:

I further direct that my realty be sold, and that the proceeds of such sale be given to a charity to be selected by my executor from among those to which I made contributions during the year immediately prior to my death, provided, however, that out of said proceeds $2,000 shall first be given to each of my children and grandchildren who survive to the age of 22 years.

At the time of the landowner's death, he had no grandchildren and was survived by three children, one of whom was 22 years old.

The landowner's realty was sold by the executor of the landowner's will for a price in excess of $1 million. The 22-year-old demanded the executor pay her $2,000 under the clause of the landowner's will, but the executor refused to pay, asserting that the 22-year-old's interest was void under the Rule Against Perpetuities. The 22-year-old should

(A) lose, because the interests of a charity cannot be made to depend upon the happening of an event that might

occur after expiration of the period of perpetuities.

(B) lose, because it is possible that a grandchild will be born whose interest will not vest until more than 21 years after the death of all persons in being at the time of the landowner's death.

(C) win, because her interest vested upon the landowner's death and is not dependent upon the number of children or grandchildren who survive to the age of 22 years.

(D) win, because she is the first person who can possibly qualify to take under the clause.

117. Several years ago, a chemical company developed a plan to use underground pipes for the purpose of transporting non-poisonous chemical wastes to a waste storage center located several miles away from its plant. At that time, it began negotiating for the right to lay an underground pipeline for that purpose across several tracts of realty. In return for a cash payment, the owner of Westacre executed a right-of-way deed for the installation and maintenance of the pipeline across his land. The right-of-way deed to the chemical company was properly recorded. Westacre passed through several intermediate conveyances until it was conveyed to the seller about 15 years after the right-of-way deed was recorded. The intermediate deeds were recorded, but none mentioned the right of way.

Two years later, the seller agreed to sell Westacre to the buyer, by a written contract in which, among other things, the seller agreed to furnish the buyer with an abstract of title. The seller hired a reputable abstract company to prepare the abstract. The abstract company prepared an abstract and delivered it to the seller. The abstract omitted any mention of the right-of-way deed. The seller delivered the abstract of title to the buyer. After examining the abstract, the buyer paid the full purchase price to the seller, who conveyed Westacre to the buyer by a deed that included covenants of general warranty and against encumbrances. At the time of closing, the seller, the buyer, and the abstract company were all unaware of the existence of the right-of-way deed. After possessing Westacre for nearly a year, the buyer was notified by the chemical company that it planned to begin installation of an underground pipeline on its right of way across Westacre.

If the buyer sues the seller because of the presence of the right of way, the most likely result will be a decision for

(A) the seller, because the buyer relied on the abstract of title prepared by the abstract company in purchasing Westacre.

(B) the seller, because the seller was without knowledge of any defects in the title to Westacre.

(C) the buyer, because the covenants in the seller's deed to the buyer were breached.

(D) the buyer, because the seller negligently misrepresented the condition of title to Westacre.

118. When the landowner died, he was the owner of 200 acres of undeveloped land. His will devised the land to his three daughters as joint tenants with right of survivorship.

One of the daughters subsequently sold her share of the land to a friend by a valid deed containing covenants of general warranty. Which of the following statements would correctly describe the relationships between the parties?

(A) The two daughters and the friend hold the land as joint tenants.

(B) The two daughters and the friend hold the land as tenants in common.

(C) The two daughters and the friend hold the land as tenants in common, but the daughters have rights of survivorship as to each other's interests.

(D) The two daughters hold equal shares of a two-thirds interest in the land as joint tenants, and the friend holds a one-third interest in the land as a tenant in common.

119. Several years ago, the landowner sold a one-acre parcel of realty to a prospector, who immediately moved onto the land, built a cabin, and set up a mechanical apparatus for removing gold from the stream that flowed across the realty. The prospector never recorded the deed because he heard that he could save money on taxes that way. Two years later, the landowner, who was aware that the prospector had not recorded the deed, purported to sell the land to a policeman by a deed that the policeman immediately recorded. As a gift, the policeman subsequently conveyed the land to a grocer, who recorded the conveyance. Neither the policeman nor the grocer ever saw or inspected the land. Last month, the grocer sold the land to a lawyer, delivering a quitclaim deed that the lawyer immediately recorded. The jurisdiction has a statute providing in essence that no conveyance is valid against a subsequent purchaser for value without notice unless it is recorded.

A court declared the lawyer's interest to be inferior to the prospector's. If the lawyer instituted an action against the grocer for damages, the court should find for

(A) the grocer, unless at the time the grocer conveyed the land to the lawyer, the grocer was aware that the prospector was in possession of the land.

(B) the grocer, since his conveyance to the lawyer contained no covenants of title.

(C) the lawyer, since the grocer did not give value for the land.

(D)   the lawyer, if a reasonable inspection by the grocer would have revealed that the prospector was in possession of the land.

120.  A landowner was the owner of a 200-acre parcel of unimproved realty located on the edge of town. In 2004, when the area was largely uninhabited, she platted and obtained government approval for a subdivision of 100 acres to be known as Olde Estates. It was divided into 200 building lots, with necessary streets, utilities, and drainage easements. All lots in Olde Estates were conveyed during 2004, every deed containing provisions restricting use of the lots to single-family, one-story residences. Each deed contained the following language:

The restrictions contained herein are binding on the grantee, and his or her heirs and assigns, and may be enforced by the owner or lawful occupant of any lot in the Olde Estates development.

The second parcel, known as Olde Heights, remained undeveloped. In 2007, the zoning laws were changed to restrict the use of land in the areas known as Olde Estates and Olde Heights to residential use for one-, two-, or three-family dwellings.

The landowner now seeks to develop the parcel known as Olde Heights as a residential subdivision of 75 lots. She wishes to place restrictions in the deeds limiting the use of lots in the subdivision to residential, and she wants to make the restrictions enforceable by residents of Olde Estates. Under which of the following circumstances would her scheme be most likely to succeed?

(A)   Restrictions in deeds to lots in Olde Heights limit their use to one-, two-, or three-family dwellings.

(B)   Restrictions in deeds to lots in Olde Heights are consented to by all purchasers of lots contained therein.

(C)   All deeds to lots in Olde Heights contain a clause providing that the restrictions contained therein can be enforced by any resident of either Olde Heights or Olde Estates.

(D)   Olde Heights is regarded as a part of a common development scheme that includes the land known as Olde Estates.

121.  On January 1, 2011, a farmer borrowed $15,000 from the bank, signing a note secured by a mortgage on her farm. The following August 1, the farmer entered into a valid written contract to sell the farm to the buyer. The contract contained a provision by which the farmer promised to deliver title free from encumbrances on or before October 10. On October 10, 2011, the farmer executed and delivered to the buyer a deed that contained a covenant against encumbrances. On October 11, 2011, the bank duly recorded its mortgage on the farm. On October 14, 2011, the buyer recorded her deed.

The farmer did not pay the bank, and two years later, the buyer conveyed the farm to a developer by a deed dated October 30, 2013, that contained a covenant against encumbrances. The bank instituted foreclosure proceedings one month after the developer took title to the land. The developer satisfied the bank's mortgage on December 10, 2013, by paying the debt contracted by the farmer. The statutory period of limitations on actions for breach of any covenant contained in a deed is one year. If the developer instituted an action against the farmer on December 20, 2013, for breach of the covenant against encumbrances, which of the following would be the farmer's **LEAST** effective argument in defense?

(A)   The developer has an adequate remedy against the buyer.

(B)   An action for breach of a covenant contained in a deed can be brought only by the grantee named in that deed.

(C) The developer had constructive notice of the mortgage.

(D) The statute of limitations bars the developer's action against the farmer.

122. A landowner was the owner of a rectangular 200-acre parcel known as The Retreat located outside of town. The Retreat was famous as the most desired property in town. On his son's birthday, the landowner executed a deed naming his son as grantee, and containing the following description:

Five acres of The Retreat, being those five acres that lie at the northeast corner of said realty, and constituting a square with its northernmost and easternmost sides lying on the north and east boundaries of The Retreat, respectively.

Is the description legally sufficient to result in a conveyance if all other requirements are found to have been satisfied?

(A) Yes, because it adequately identifies the realty described.

(B) Yes, but all that it can convey is an unidentified fractional portion of the land known as The Retreat.

(C) No, since it lacks either metes and bounds or reference to existing government surveys.

(D) No, since a deed cannot convey less than the entire parcel of realty to which it refers.

123. On May 10, the seller contracted with the buyer for the sale of the seller's home, title to close on or about July 1. According to the terms of the contract, the buyer was to move into the house on June 1 and to pay rent of $350 per month until title closed. The buyer moved in as planned on June 1. On June 10, the buyer fell asleep while smoking in bed. His cigarette ignited the bedclothing,

causing a fire that severely damaged the house.

The jurisdiction does not recognize the doctrine of equitable conversion. Which of the following correctly states the rights of the buyer and the seller?

(A) The buyer is not required to purchase the property, and the seller must return any monies already received from the buyer in connection with the purchase.

(B) The buyer is not required to purchase the property, but the seller may retain any monies already received from the buyer in connection with the purchase.

(C) The buyer is required to purchase the property and must pay the full price agreed upon in the contract of sale.

(D) The buyer is required to purchase the property, but the purchase price should be abated to the extent of the damage.

124. The landowner was the owner in fee simple of a rectangular parcel of real estate. He subdivided it into two lots and sold one of the lots to the buyer, keeping the other lot for himself. At the time of the purchase, the buyer told the landowner about his plans to install a large picture window. Soon after the sale, the buyer began to install the window. At the same time, the landowner began construction of a three-story building on his lot.

In an action by the buyer to enjoin the landowner from completing construction of the three-story building in such a way as to obstruct the view from the buyer's picture window, the court should find for

(A) the buyer, because upon purchasing the lot from the landowner, he received an implied easement for light, air, and view.

(B) the buyer, because he acquired by prescription an easement to an unobstructed view from the picture window.

(C) the buyer, because he notified the land-owner of his intention to build the picture window at the time of his purchase of the lot from the landowner.

(D) the landowner.

125. On March 1, the seller and the buyer entered into a valid written contract for the sale of the seller's home to the buyer at a price of $180,000, with title to close on June 15. It was further agreed that the buyer could move into and occupy the premises until title passed, at a rent of $500 per month to be added onto the purchase price and paid to the seller at the time of closing. On April 15, before the closing, a fire completely destroyed the house. The fire was not the result of fault by either party.

The jurisdiction does not apply the doctrine of equitable conversion. In litigation between the parties, which of the following additional facts, if it was the only one true, would be most likely to result in a finding that the buyer is obligated to purchase the premises at the price agreed upon in the contract of March 1?

(A) On March 1, the buyer purchased a policy of fire insurance on the premises that was in force on the day that the house was destroyed by fire.

(B) In accordance with an agreement between the parties, the buyer was in possession of the house on the day of the fire.

(C) On March 1, it was foreseeable to the parties that fire could damage the realty prior to the closing of title.

(D) Destruction of the house resulted in a relatively minor reduction in the value of the realty.

126. The landowner was the owner in fee simple of a parcel of land. On May 1, the landowner executed a deed that purported to grant an undivided one-quarter interest in the land to the landowner's nephew.

On May 2, the landowner sent for her nephew. She said, "I was planning to leave you an interest in the land in my will, but I see no reason why you should have to pay inheritance tax. So I'll give it to you while I'm still alive if you promise to move in here with me sometime during the next year." The nephew promised that he would do so, and the landowner gave him the deed, saying, "Then it's yours." The nephew read the deed, thanked the landowner, and handed the deed back to the landowner for safekeeping. The landowner placed it in a drawer of her desk.

On May 7, the landowner argued with her nephew. Angry, the landowner tore the deed into eight pieces and returned them to her desk drawer. On May 10, the landowner died, leaving no will.

In an appropriate proceeding, should a court find that the nephew held a possessory interest in the land on the landowner's death?

(A) No, because the deed was an attempted testamentary substitute.

(B) No, because the landowner's possession of the deed raises an irrebuttable presumption that there was no effective delivery.

(C) Yes, because there was an effective conveyance to the nephew on May 2.

(D) Yes, because the nephew detrimentally relied by promising to move in with the landowner.

127. The landowner was the owner in fee simple absolute of a tract of land. On January 10, 2013, the landowner borrowed $20,000 from the bank and executed a note secured by a mortgage on the land. On April 30, 2013, as a 21st birthday present, the landowner executed a grant deed conveying the land

to his son. The deed made no mention of the mortgage held by the bank. On May 15, 2013, the bank duly recorded its mortgage. On May 17, 2013, the son duly recorded his deed. Neither the landowner nor the son ever made any payments to the bank.

The jurisdiction has a statute that provides that "Every conveyance of an interest in real estate that shall not be recorded shall be void against any subsequent grantee in good faith of the same real estate or any portion thereof whose conveyance shall be first duly recorded." If the bank attempts to foreclose the mortgage, will it succeed?

(A) No, because the bank's mortgage was recorded outside the chain of title.

(B) No, because the son did not have actual or constructive knowledge of the bank's interest at the time the land was conveyed to him.

(C) Yes, because the bank's interest was recorded prior to the son's interest.

(D) Yes, because the son did not give consideration for the conveyance from the landowner.

128. On April 1, the landowner's grandmother died, leaving a will that purported to devise to the landowner a 90-acre parcel of realty known as Southacre and an adjoining 10-acre parcel known as Northacre.

On May 1, the landowner executed a general warranty deed containing covenants of title and quiet enjoyment, which purported to convey to a lawyer "a 100-acre tract of land consisting of a 90-acre parcel known as Southacre and a 10-acre parcel known as Northacre."

On June 15, the lawyer sold Northacre and Southacre to a doctor, executing a general warranty deed describing both parcels and containing covenants of title.

On July 1, the landowner learned that just before her death, his grandmother had sold

Northacre to a builder. Unaware of the lawyer's conveyance to the doctor, the landowner offered the builder $10,000 to convey Northacre to the lawyer. On July 2, the builder accepted the landowner's offer and conveyed Northacre to the lawyer by general warranty deed containing covenants of title.

The doctor institutes an appropriate proceeding for an order declaring himself to be the owner of Northacre. Which of the following would be the doctor's most effective argument in support of his claim?

(A) The builder's conveyance of Northacre to the lawyer was the result of an attempt by the landowner to conform the title to the covenant.

(B) The lawyer has an effective remedy against the landowner.

(C) The lawyer's intention was to convey Northacre to the doctor on July 1.

(D) The lawyer's conveyance to the doctor on June 15 estops the lawyer from asserting his title to Northacre.

129. The landowner was the owner of Redacre. By a deed dated January 2, she granted Redacre "to my nephew for life, remainder to my niece, but if the realty shall ever be used for any purpose other than residential, to Sunrise Foundation." Sunrise Foundation is a charitable organization.

If Sunrise Foundation's interest in Redacre is valid, it is best described as a

(A) vested remainder subject to divestment.

(B) contingent remainder.

(C) shifting executory interest.

(D) springing executory interest.

130. The landlord leased an office to the tenant for a period of five years by an agreement that prohibited assignment by the tenant without the landlord's written permission. Two years after taking occupancy, the tenant

requested the landlord's permission to assign the balance of his leasehold to a store owner. After checking the store owner's credit, the landlord wrote the tenant that the assignment was acceptable to him so long as the store owner personally assumed all obligations of the lease. The tenant's attorney prepared an agreement by which the tenant assigned all his rights under the lease to the store owner and the store owner agreed to personally assume all obligations under the lease. After the agreement was signed by the tenant and the store owner, the tenant's attorney sent a copy of it to the landlord. The store owner moved into the premises and began paying rent to the landlord.

After paying rent for six months, the store owner assigned the balance of the leasehold to an accountant. The accountant paid rent directly to the landlord for two additional months and then stopped paying rent and abandoned the premises. In an action by the landlord against the store owner for unpaid rent, the court should find for

(A) the landlord.

(B) the store owner, because the accountant paid rent directly to the landlord for two months.

(C) the store owner, because there was no privity of contract between the landlord and the store owner.

(D) the store owner, because the store owner was only obligated to pay rent so long as he remained in possession of the premises.

131. By grant deed, a landowner conveyed a parcel of realty "to the Church of the Lord so long as the property is used for church purposes, but if the grantee permits the property to be used for any purpose other than a church purpose, the property shall revert to the grantor." Two weeks after receiving title, the Church of the Lord filed an application with the county Building Department for a permit to construct a house of worship on the parcel. Prior to issuing the permit, the Building Department published notice of the church's application as required by state law. Upon seeing the notice, a homeowner who owned an adjacent parcel advised church officials that he had been driving across the parcel to gain access to his land for more than 30 years. He claimed that he had thus acquired an easement by prescription and threatened to commence an action to quiet title to the realty for the purpose of having his easement judicially recognized. The county Building Department informed officials of the Church of the Lord that no building permit could be issued while an action to quiet title was pending. Because it could take several years for such an action to reach conclusion, and because the easement claimed by the homeowner would not significantly interfere with building plans, the church attorney advised granting him the easement that he claimed to hold. Church officials subsequently executed a deed granting the homeowner the easement that he claimed.

On the day after the Church of the Lord granted an easement to the homeowner, the landowner asserted that the homeowner's use of the premises was other than for church purposes and instituted an action for an order declaring that he was the owner of the realty. Which of the following would be the Church of the Lord's most effective argument in opposition to the landowner's claim?

(A) The Church of the Lord acted in good faith on the advice of its attorney.

(B) The language of the deed created a fee simple determinable.

(C) The homeowner's easement preexisted the landowner's grant to the Church of the Lord.

(D) The landowner's interest violated the Rule Against Perpetuities.

132. When the homeowner purchased her home, she borrowed part of the purchase price

from a bank. Simultaneously with receipt of title to the realty, she executed a note payable to the bank and secured by a mortgage on the realty. Subsequently, the homeowner sold the realty to the first buyer, who took it subject to the mortgage and assumed the mortgage. Two years later, the first buyer sold the property to the second buyer, who also took it subject to the mortgage and assumed the mortgage. The following year, the second buyer sold the property to the third buyer, who took it subject to the mortgage but did not assume the mortgage.

For two years, the third buyer made payments on the note to the bank. Then, because of changes in the area, the property decreased sharply in value, and the third buyer stopped making payments.

The mortgage executed by the homeowner contained a clause that specifically permitted buyers of the premises to take them "subject to the mortgage" and/or to "assume the mortgage." If the bank sues the homeowner, the first buyer, and the second buyer on the note, from which of them is it entitled to recover?

(A)  The homeowner only.

(B)  The second buyer only.

(C)  The homeowner and the second buyer only.

(D)  The homeowner, the first buyer, and the second buyer.

133.  The landowner was the owner of a 200-acre parcel of realty known as Westacre. Because he knew that he was dying, the landowner executed a deed purporting to convey a portion of Westacre to his sister, who lived in another state. The deed described the realty conveyed as "A portion of Westacre 200 feet by 200 feet in size, with its northeastern corner located at the eastern end of the northern border of Westacre." Westacre was a famous piece of property, with a giant plastic lobster at the eastern end of its northern border.

There were no government survey markers in the area.

If the deed were enforceable in all other respects, would the description that it contains be sufficient to effect a conveyance?

(A)  No, because it does not set forth metes and bounds.

(B)  Yes, because there is an artificial monument at the eastern end of the northern border of Westacre.

(C)  Yes, because it identifies the realty conveyed with reasonable clarity.

(D)  Yes, because there are no government survey markers in the area.

134.  A man purchased a home from a development company. The deed from the development company stated that the man would have the right to use a small private neighborhood beach near the property that the development company had built to attract buyers to the neighborhood. However, the deed did not state whether these beach rights were transferable. Twenty-one years later, the man sold the home to a woman. By then, the development company had sold the beach to a nearby golf course. When the woman went to use the beach, the golf course kicked her off. The woman brought suit to enforce the beach rights included in the deed. The court should rule in favor of

(A)  the woman, because she gained use of the beach by adverse possession.

(B)  the woman, because the deed created an easement appurtenant.

(C)  the golf course, because it did not create the original deed.

(D)  the golf course, because the deed did not say whether the beach rights were transferable.

135.  The landowner is the owner of a hillside parcel of realty known as Slopeacre, on which he grows oranges for sale to a company

that makes juice from them. For several years, the landowner has been irrigating his orange trees with water from a stream that flows across Slopeacre. After flowing across Slopeacre, the stream flows through Flatacre, a parcel of realty located in the valley below Slopeacre. A homeowner, who owns Flatacre, lives there with his family. The homeowner's family uses water from the stream for household purposes.

The jurisdiction determines water rights by applying riparian law.

Because of a drought, there was enough water in the stream to satisfy the needs of either Flatacre or Slopeacre, but not both. There were no other riparian owners. Who is entitled to use the water?

(A) The landowner, because he is the upstream owner.

(B) The landowner, because he needs the water for agricultural use.

(C) The homeowner, because he needs the water for household use.

(D) The homeowner, because he is the downstream owner.

136. A farmer was the owner of a large tract of land on which he grew crops. Because his income was declining, he decided to subdivide and sell his land. With government approval, he platted a subdivision consisting of 50 parcels of land with necessary access and utility easements. Soon afterwards, he conveyed one of the parcels to the first buyer by a properly recorded deed that they both signed and that contained the following language:

> The parties hereto hereby covenant for themselves, their heirs, successors, and assigns, that the realty herein conveyed shall not be used for any purpose other than residential, and that all conveyances of realty in the subdivision shall contain this covenant.

The first buyer subsequently sold half of his parcel to the second buyer, conveying it by a deed that contained no covenants or restrictions. Six months later, because he was unable to sell any of the other parcels, the farmer resumed agricultural activities on his remaining land. At the same time, the second buyer began construction of a gas station on the realty that he had purchased from the first buyer.

The farmer commenced a proceeding to prevent the second buyer from constructing a gas station on the realty. Should the court grant the relief requested by the farmer?

(A) No, because the farmer did not sell any of the other land in the subdivision.

(B) No, because the second buyer did not agree to refrain from non-residential use of the land.

(C) Yes, because the covenant in the farmer's deed to the first buyer ran with the land.

(D) Yes, because the construction of a gas station by the second buyer was likely to inhibit sale of the remaining parcels in the subdivision.

137. The landlord, who was the owner of a commercial office building, leased an office in the building to the first lessee pursuant to a 10-year lease calling for rent in the sum of $1,000 per month. The first lessee occupied the premises for a period of two years, paying the rent as it became due each month. At the end of that period, he assigned the balance of the leasehold to the second lessee by a document in which the second lessee agreed to be personally liable for all obligations under the lease and which was signed by the first lessee and the second lessee. Immediately following execution of the assignment, the first lessee sent a copy of it to the landlord. The second lessee occupied the premises for several years, paying the rent as it came due. When seven months of the lease period remained, the second lessee

assigned the balance of the leasehold to the third lessee. The third lessee did not agree to be personally liable for all obligations under the lease, and the landlord was not informed of the assignment. The third lessee occupied the premises for two months but did not pay rent. At the end of that period, the third lessee assigned the balance of the lease to the fourth lessee. The fourth lessee occupied the premises for five months without paying rent, abandoning the premises when the lease expired. When the premises were vacated, a total of seven months' rent remained unpaid.

The landlord asserts a claim against the third lessee for unpaid rent. The court should award judgment for the landlord in the sum of

(A) nothing, since the third lessee did not agree to be personally liable.

(B) $2,000, since the third lessee and the landlord are not in privity of contract.

(C) $2,000, the amount of rent that remains unpaid for the period during which the third lessee occupied the premises.

(D) $7,000, the amount of rent that remains unpaid for the period during which the third lessee and his assignee, the fourth lessee, occupied the premises.

138. A woman leased a parcel of land from a landlord for one year. The rent was $1,000 a month, with an option to buy at lease termination. While living on the property, the woman erected a small garage. The garage cost $2,000 to build, but was worth $3,000 when it was completed. The woman vacated the property three months before the expiration of the lease, telling the landlord she would not exercise her purchase option. On the same day, the landlord conveyed the property to a developer, although the property remained vacant for the remainder of the lease term.

The landlord sued the woman for $3,000 in unpaid rent. How should the court rule?

(A) The woman owes the landlord $3,000.

(B) The woman owes the landlord $1,000, because the cost of the garage was $2,000.

(C) The woman does not owe the landlord anything, because he conveyed the property to the developer the day the woman left.

(D) The woman does not owe the landlord anything, because the garage she built is worth $3,000.

139. A buyer put down a deposit in order to buy several acres of forested land from a landowner. The contract provided that the landowner would deliver marketable title. Prior to closing, the buyer discovered a man had built a cabin on the land without the landowner's permission or knowledge. It was unclear how long the man had been on the land. On the day of closing, the buyer refused to accept the deed on the ground that the landowner's title was not marketable and demanded his deposit back. The landowner refused to return the deposit but offered to furnish the buyer with title insurance that specifically insured against adverse possession claims. If the buyer sues the landowner, who is most likely to win?

(A) The buyer, because the man may have acquired title by adverse possession.

(B) The buyer, because there is no indication the deed has been recorded.

(C) The landowner, because he is willing to provide title insurance to the buyer.

(D) The landowner, because the man may not have a valid claim for adverse possession.

140. The landowner conveyed a parcel of realty "to my friend and his heirs, so long as liquor is not sold on the premises, but if liquor is sold on the premises, then to

the Foundation for Heart Diseases." The Foundation for Heart Diseases was a charity. Two years later, the friend began selling liquor on the premises.

Which of the following best describes the interest of the Foundation for Heart Diseases in the realty on the day after the friend began selling liquor on the premises?

(A) Fee simple absolute, because the Foundation for Heart Diseases is a charity.

(B) Right of reentry.

(C) No interest, since at the time of the conveyance, it was possible that the interest that the deed purported to grant to the foundation would not vest within a period measured by a life or lives in being plus 21 years.

(D) Valid shifting executory interest.

141. A landowner allowed an artist to live on her land for free. The artist built a large machine on the property that was used to excavate and carve stones removed from the landowner's land for the artist's work. The machine weighed two tons and was the size of a small garage. Ten years later, the landowner sold the land to a buyer. The sales contract referred to the subject of sale as "all the realty located at . . ." followed by a metes and bounds description. Prior to closing, the artist removed the machine. The buyer discovered the machine was removed and demanded that the selling price of the realty be abated. The artist told the buyer she never intended the machine to become part of the property, and the landowner concurred that she never considered the machine part of the property. The jurisdiction's applicable statute provides that if part of the realty that is subject to the sales contract is removed or destroyed, the buyer may elect to take title subject to the appropriate abatement of the purchase price.

Should the selling price be abated?

(A) Yes, because the contract referred to "all the realty."

(B) Yes, because the size and purpose of the machine made it a fixture.

(C) No, because the artist did not intend for the machine to become a fixture.

(D) No, because the machine was not fastened to the ground.

142. When the landowner died, he was the owner of 200 acres of undeveloped land. His will devised the land to his three daughters as joint tenants with right of survivorship. All three of them lived in a distant state, but after the landowner's death, the youngest daughter moved onto the land and began cultivating it. She grew grain and beans, realizing substantial profits from these farming activities almost immediately.

The land had a reasonable rental value of $12,000 per year. After the youngest daughter began realizing a profit from her farming enterprise, the eldest daughter asserted a claim against the youngest daughter for $4,000 per year, equivalent to one-third of the reasonable rental value. Which of the following facts or inferences, if it were the only one true, would be most likely to result in a judgment for the eldest daughter?

(A) Farming was the best and highest use of the land.

(B) A real estate developer had offered to purchase the land for substantially more than its reasonable market value, but the youngest daughter refused to sell her interest.

(C) The eldest daughter had attempted to move onto the land, but the youngest daughter prevented her from doing so.

(D) The youngest daughter erected permanent structures on the land that she occupied for residential and agricultural purposes.

143. In January, a farmer sold a large tract of land to a developer for $100,000. The developer paid $50,000 when he received the deed, and executed a note for the balance secured by a mortgage on the land. Neither the deed nor the mortgage was recorded. The developer failed to make any of the required mortgage payments. In March, the farmer purported to sell the land to a builder for $100,000. In April, after the farmer contacted the developer regarding the missing mortgage payments, the developer reconveyed the title back to the farmer. In June, the builder learned of the earlier land sale and the reconveyance to the farmer.

If the builder brings an action against the farmer to quiet title, the court should rule in favor of

(A) the farmer, because he did not hold title to the land when he made the sale to the builder.

(B) the farmer, because there is no indication the builder recorded the farmer's deed to him.

(C) the builder, because the farmer's sale to the builder was fraudulent.

(D) the builder, because the farmer is estopped from denying the builder's title.

144. A landowner owned a large tract of undeveloped land. In 1995, a man built a cabin on the landowner's land without the landowner's knowledge. Five years later, in June 2000, the landowner discovered the man's presence and forced him to move away. A month later, the man moved back to the cabin without the landowner's knowledge. The man remained in possession for another 16 years. In 2016, the landowner discovered the man again and filed an action to eject him. The relevant statutory period for acquiring title by adverse possession is 20 years.

The court should find for

(A) the landowner, because the landowner removed the man in June 2000.

(B) the landowner, because the landowner did not give the man permission to return.

(C) the man, because there was no indication he was removed in June 2000 by a court order.

(D) the man, because his removal in June 2000 was only temporary.

# ANSWERS
## PROPERTY

# ANSWERS TO
# PROPERTY QUESTIONS

1.  **B**    Under common law, a conveyance of real estate is not valid unless it identifies the grantor, the grantee, and the property conveyed. The statute simply codified this rule. Realty cannot be conveyed by the use of negotiable paper (*i.e.*, to bearer). For this reason, the document conveyed no interest.

    **A** is incorrect because even an unrecordable deed may affect the rights of grantor and grantee as against each other. **C** is incorrect for two reasons: First, consideration is not required to make a deed effective, and second, courts do not generally inquire into the adequacy of consideration. Although a claim of economic duress has occasionally been used to avoid the legal effect of documents that are otherwise valid, it is not applied consistently enough to make **D** the correct answer, and it is not applied unless the duress was created by the party against whom it is asserted.

2.  **D**    So long as the adverse possessor has remained openly, notoriously, hostilely, and continuously in possession for the statutory period, he or she may acquire title to the land even though it changed ownership during the period of his or her adverse possession. Thus, the fact that the neighbor bought the land from a prior owner during the period of the farmer's possession would not result in a judgment for the neighbor.

    Possession of realty is hostile if it is contrary to the rights of the owner. Since occupying realty that has been rented from the owner is not contrary to his or her rights, the payment of rent would have prevented the farmer's possession from being hostile. Since a dozen eggs per week could be construed as rent, **A** might result in a judgment for the neighbor and is therefore incorrect. Permission from the owner of the neighbor's land would have had the same effect, making **B** incorrect. If the farmer said that he would remove the chicken coop whenever the owner of the neighbor's land asked him to, and the owner of the neighbor's land did not, it might likewise be concluded that the chicken coop remained by permission of the owner of the neighbor's land. The farmer's possession would not therefore be hostile, making **C** incorrect.

3.  **D**    An easement by prescription is an easement that is gained under the principles of adverse possession. Consequently, a person who uses another's land for more than the applicable statutory period, gains an easement by prescription. However, in order to gain such an easement, the use must be without the servient land holder's permission, and the use must be continuous and uninterrupted through the statutory period. Different landholder's uses can be tacked together to reach the required number of years in the statutory period. However, in the case where a dominant tenement comes to be owned by the same person who owns the servient tenement, even if the tenant on the dominant property uses the easement, this use will not be hostile, and the requisite hostile use will therefore be interrupted. Here, during the one-year period when the landowner owned Whiteacre (the dominant parcel), the doctor's use was not hostile since it will be deemed to be with the permission of the landowner, who is now the doctor's landlord.

Therefore, there will be not tacking from the doctor to the landowner to the dentist, and the dentist will not have completed the 10-year statutory period. **A** and **B** are therefore incorrect.

An easement by estoppel is created when one landowner allows another to use his or her land under circumstances where the landowner should reasonably foresee that the other landowner will substantially change position believing this permission will not be revoked, and the other landowner does in fact change position. Here, there is no indication that the doctor or dentist did so. **C** is therefore incorrect.

4.   **D**   A deed is effective upon delivery to and acceptance by the grantee or the grantee's agent. Delivery of a deed to one co-tenant is usually viewed as delivery to all co-tenants. Thus, the delivery to the younger son was a delivery to the older son as well. If a conveyance is beneficial to a named grantee, acceptance by that grantee is presumed. Since the transfer was beneficial to the older son, it is presumed that the older son accepted delivery of the deed. These facts, coupled with recording by the older son's co-tenant, are sufficient to result in an effective conveyance to the older son of a joint tenancy in the land. Since joint tenants have the right of survivorship, the younger son's interest passed to the older son upon the younger son's death.

An **A** is incorrect because the delivery to the younger son was a delivery to his co-tenant as well, and because the older son's right of survivorship made the younger son's devise to the friend ineffective. A testamentary disposition is a transfer made by will. Since the landowner conveyed the realty *inter vivos* (*i.e.*, while alive), **B** is incorrect. **C** is incorrect because occupancy by a grantee is not necessary to make the grant effective, and because the conveyance was effective upon delivery and acceptance of the deed and was not undone by the grantee's return of the deed to the grantor for safekeeping.

5.   **C**   Unless a deed is signed by the grantor or the grantor's agent, it does not effectively convey an interest in realty.

A gift is a transfer without consideration. **A** is incorrect because an interest in realty may be conveyed as a gift and such a conveyance is valid even though no consideration was given for it. **B** is incorrect because a deed that is silent as to the interest being conveyed is presumed to convey whatever interest the grantor holds. Recording a deed gives the world constructive notice of the grantee's interest but does not affect the validity of the deed. **D** is incorrect because an unrecorded deed is effective at least against the grantor.

6.   **D**   Under the doctrine of equitable conversion, the risk of loss of realty passes to the buyer as soon as a contract of sale is executed. In jurisdictions that have rejected the doctrine of equitable conversion, the risk of loss of realty subject to a contract for sale remains with the seller until the transfer of either title or possession to the buyer. Most jurisdictions agree, however, that if destruction of an *immaterial* part of the realty occurs prior to that time, the seller may enforce the contract after the price is abated to account for the damage. Since

the facts make it clear that the sheds were inconsequential and that the real estate investor intended to demolish them after taking title to the realty, they may be regarded as immaterial parts of the realty.

**A** is therefore incorrect. **B** is incorrect because the sheds were not material parts of the realty. In jurisdictions that have rejected the doctrine of equitable conversion, **C** is an inaccurate statement of the law.

7. **C**  A license is a right to use the licensor's land that is revocable at the will of the licensor. However, a license is irrevocable if its use would have been an easement except for failure to meet the Statute of Frauds, and the licensee makes substantial expenditures on the land in reliance on the licensor's promise that the license will be permanent or of long duration. Here, the license, although oral, was irrevocable because of the defendant's substantial reliance expenditures. **A** is therefore incorrect.

A license is not required to satisfy the Statute of Frauds, so it can be created orally. **B** is therefore incorrect. Easements must meet the Statute of Frauds, so they cannot be created orally. **D** is therefore incorrect.

8. **C**  Ordinarily, restrictions contained in a conveyance cannot be enforced to benefit realty in which the grantor has no interest. Since the developer had already conveyed Lot 1, he had no interest in it when he conveyed Lot 25 to the second buyer. For this reason, restrictions contained in the deed for Lot 25 cannot be enforced for the benefit of Lot 1. An exception is sometimes made in the case of a subdivision if it can be shown that a prior purchaser bought in reliance on restrictions to be contained in deeds to subsequent purchasers. Since there is no indication that the first buyer was aware that the deed to Lot 25 would contain a restriction, however, he could not have relied on it when purchasing Lot 1 and cannot enforce it. **C** is therefore correct.

**A** is incorrect because a restriction may be enforced against a covenantor's successor, even though the deed by which the covenantor conveyed to his successor did not mention it. Thus, the fact that the third buyer's deed did not mention the restriction is not sufficient to prevent the issuance of the injunction. **B** is incorrect because, as explained above, if the first buyer knew that the restriction would be contained in the deed to Lot 25 and relied upon that restriction, he may have acquired the right to enforce it even though it was not mentioned in his deed. A covenant is said to "touch and concern" the burdened land if only the possessor of that land may perform it, and it is said to "touch and concern" the benefitted land if the resulting benefit is tied to possession of that land. Since only the possessor of Lot 25 can comply with the use restriction, it touches and concerns Lot 25. Since Lot 1 is in close physical proximity and in full view of Lot 25, its value will be affected by the use to which Lot 25 is put. The restriction, therefore, touches and concerns Lot 1. For these reasons, **D** is incorrect.

9. **A**  The ex-husband may convey the interest that he holds. Since his interest is a life estate, **A** is correct.

Since the ex-wife or the buyer might outlive the ex-husband, **B** and **C** are incorrect. Since life estates are alienable, **D** is also incorrect.

10.   **A**   An easement by express reservation is one for the benefit of the grantor that he or she creates by language contained in the deed by which he or she conveys the servient estate. It does not terminate with non-use unless there is a clear manifestation of the intention to abandon it by the easement-holder. The landowner's maintenance of the right of way across Lot 1 indicates that it was not his intention to abandon it.

An implied easement by necessity terminates when the strict necessity ceases to exist. **B** and **C** are both incorrect, however, because the easement across Lot 1 was by *express* reservation. The existence of an easement generally does diminish the value of the servient estate. **D** is incorrect because this reduction in value, even if unreasonable, is not in itself sufficient to invalidate the easement.

11.   **D**   The landowner's will did not speak until the landowner's death, and it devised an interest in the realty only to those children who survived the landowner. Since the son predeceased the landowner, the son never received an interest in the realty; his purported mortgage to the financial institution did not give the financial institution any interest. For this reason, the landowner's interest was unaffected by the mortgage and was absolute. As the landowner's only surviving child, the daughter received the landowner's interest upon the landowner's death.

Since the financial institution held no interest in the realty, **A**, **B**, and **C** are incorrect.

12.   **B**   The woman has given her husband a power of appointment. A power of appointment is the legal right to designate subsequent transferees of realty. It may be exercised only in the manner specified by the donor of the power. If the donee of the power fails to exercise it, the realty subject to the power of appointment reverts to the estate of the donor. Since the woman specified that her husband's power of appointment could be exercised only by will, and since her husband failed to exercise it by his will, the land reverted to the estate of the woman upon her husband's death. Marketable title is title that is free from claims that would lead a reasonable person to doubt its validity. Since the realty reverted to the woman's estate, the second wife had no interest in it subsequent to the death of the husband. Her inability to deliver marketable title is a breach of her contract with the buyer, entitling the buyer to the relief that he seeks.

Covenants for title in the deed might have given the buyer a lawsuit against the second wife if the title that the deed purported to convey proved to be defective, but they would not have made the title marketable. **A** is therefore incorrect. Since the woman specified that her husband's power could be exercised only by will, his *inter vivos* conveyance to the second wife was without effect. **C** is therefore incorrect. The land did not pass to her husband's heirs under the laws of intestacy because her husband's failure to exercise the power by will resulted in reversion of the land to the estate of the woman. **D** is therefore incorrect.

13. **B**    A reversion is a future interest of the grantor that will automatically follow a prior estate that will inevitably terminate (*e.g.*, a life estate; a leasehold). A possibility of reverter is a future interest of the grantor that will automatically follow a prior estate that will not inevitably terminate (*e.g.*, fee simple determinable). A right of reentry is a future interest of the grantor that does not revert automatically but which requires some act by the grantor for him or her to reacquire a possessory right and which follows an estate that will not inevitably terminate. Since the property was conveyed only for so long as it is used as a home for the elderly, it will automatically revert to the grantor if that use is ever discontinued. It is thus either a reversion or a possibility of reverter. Since it is not certain that it ever will cease to be used as a home for the elderly, however, the prior estate is not one that will inevitably terminate. For this reason, the grantor's interest is a possibility of reverter.

**A** is therefore incorrect. **C** is incorrect because if the property ever ceases to be used as a home for the elderly, no act of the grantor is necessary to make his interest possessory. **D** is incorrect because the Rule Against Perpetuities does not apply to a grantor's interest.

14. **B**    A life tenant is required to pay real estate taxes that become due during the term of her life tenancy. Although a life tenant is required to pay interest on outstanding encumbrances, the remainderman is under an obligation to pay principal.

**A** is incorrect because as life tenant, the wife should not be required to pay principal. **C** is incorrect for this reason, and because as remainderman, the brother should not be required to pay the real estate taxes. **D** is incorrect for the latter reason.

15. **A**    Acquisition of title by adverse possession results from application of a statute of limitations that prevents the record owner from enforcing any rights that he or she might have against the adverse possessor. For this reason, the period does not begin to run until a cause of action by the record owner accrues. Thus, it does not begin running against an infant owner until he or she achieves majority; it does not begin running against a remainderman until the preceding estate terminates. (**Note:** If the realty was held in fee simple when the period of adverse possession began, it may continue in spite of changes in ownership of the fee.) Until the nephew's estate terminated, the son had no right to sue the hunter, although he did have an ownership interest in the land at the time the hunter moved onto the land.

**B** is incorrect because the son's right was not possessory until the termination of the nephew's estate. **C** is incorrect because even after achieving majority (c.1994), the son's interest in the realty was not possessory. **D** is incorrect because the hunter's period of adverse possession against the son did not begin until the son's interest became possessory. Another way of looking at the problem is to recognize that the adverse possessor acquires no greater interest than is held by the person against whom his or her possession is adverse. Thus, the hunter's possession during the nephew's term could not have resulted in more than his acquisition of a 20-year term (*i.e.*, the nephew's interest) by adverse possession.

16.  **D**     A mortgage is a financing arrangement where the person buying property (or one who already owns property) receives a loan and the property is pledged as security to guarantee repayment of the loan. Importantly, a person may grant a mortgage on his or her own property to secure payment of someone else's debt. Consequently, the mortgagor does not need to receive any direct benefit for granting a mortgage. Here, the mortgage is valid. Therefore, if the man does not pay, the bank can sue the man for the balance, and if the man is judgment proof or pays only some of the debt, the bank can foreclose on the house and have it sold at auction to satisfy the man's debt. This is so even though the man's father did not sign any underlying note or make a personal guarantee of repayment, and even though the man's father received no direct personal benefit from granting the mortgage.

**A**, **B**, and **C** are therefore incorrect.

17.  **B**     A co-tenant may occupy the entire premises, subject only to the other co-tenant's right to do so as well. If the occupying tenant does not exclude the other co-tenant from the property, the occupying tenant has no duty to pay the non-occupying co-tenant rent. Here, the brother and sister share in the property equally, so they are co-tenants. Since the sister said the brother was welcome to live with her, he has not been excluded from the property and she does not owe him any rent. Therefore, **C** and **D** are incorrect. **A** is incorrect because the analysis of this question does not depend on the language used in the father's will.

18.  **C**     When a deed is deposited with a commercial escrow agent with instructions to deliver it to the grantee upon the happening of a condition outside the grantor's control, title passes automatically upon the happening of the specified condition. The buyer thus owned the realty as soon as his check cleared on January 15, and he is not guilty of violating the statute.

**A** and **B** are therefore incorrect. In some jurisdictions, the risk of loss passes to the buyer upon execution of a contract for the sale of realty. **D** is incorrect, however, because the passage of title does not relate back to the execution of the contract.

19.  **A**     Whether they apply the doctrine of equitable conversion, the Uniform Vendor and Purchaser Risk Act, or some other system for apportioning the risk of loss under a real estate sales contract, most jurisdictions agree that the risk of loss from causes other than the fault of the vendor passes to the vendee when he or she takes possession of the realty prior to closing. Although a small minority of jurisdictions disagree, **A** is the only argument listed that could possibly support the man's position.

**B** and **C** are incorrect because passage of the risk of loss does not depend on the purchase of fire insurance by either party. **D** is incorrect because no jurisdiction recognizes such a presumption.

20.  **A**     No reason appears in the fact situation why the contract between the developer and the homeowner is not enforceable. Since the contract contains the homeowner's promise to purchase water from the developer, he will be liable to the developer for damages resulting from his breach.

**B** is incorrect because there is no discrepancy between the contract and the deed, and because — at least in determining what estate the grantee has received — discrepancies between a deed and a contract for sale are resolved by looking to the deed. Since only the possessor of the land on which the well and water-purifying plant were located could benefit from the covenant to purchase water, and since only the possessor of the land granted by the developer could comply with it, both the benefit and the burden resulting from the covenant touched and concerned the land. Although this is not relevant to the homeowner's obligations under the contract, the inaccuracy of the statements makes **C** incorrect. **D** is incorrect for two reasons: First, acceptance of a deed containing restrictions may bind the grantee to those restrictions even though he or she did not sign the deed, and second, the homeowner agreed to purchase water in the contract of sale.

21. **B**    The holder of an easement may not use it in a way that goes beyond the scope of use contemplated at the time of its creation. Since the easement across Lot 1 was created for ingress and egress to Lot 2, its use for the purpose of erecting poles and stringing power lines exceeds its scope.

   **A** is incorrect because an appurtenant easement is ordinarily transferred by conveyance of the dominant estate and is therefore alienable. In addition to the fact that calling an easement "divisible" says nothing about it, **C** is incorrect because the stringing of wires was not incidental to the contemplated use of the ingress-egress easement. An easement is appurtenant if it is designed to benefit the holder of a particular piece of realty. An easement in gross is not designed to benefit the holder of a particular piece of realty. Since this easement was for access to Lot 2, it was appurtenant. **D** is incorrect because it is a meaningless and incorrect statement of the law.

22. **B**    A tenancy with no fixed duration is a tenancy at will and can be terminated by either party. Since the mayor's authorization did not specify a duration, it created a tenancy at will. Since the city can terminate the occupancy, it has the right to prevent occupancy other than under conditions that it sets, and, therefore, to obtain an injunction against violations of those conditions.

   Since the ballet company's agreement with the city did not obligate it to pay rent, its non-payment of rent is not a breach that would give the city any rights that it would not have had otherwise. **A** is therefore incorrect. **C** is incorrect because a tenant at sufferance is one who entered under a valid lease that has since expired or terminated. Ameliorating waste is the name given to substantial alterations made by the tenant of leased premises that do not diminish the value of the real estate. **D** is incorrect because the fact that there was no lease probably makes the term inappropriate, because there is no indication that the proposed changes would not diminish the value of the realty and because courts are not always willing to enjoin ameliorating waste.

23. **B**    A tenant's violation of a lease provision prohibiting sublet or assignment of a leasehold is usually regarded as a breach of covenant for which the tenant may be liable for damages. Because courts favor the alienability of estates in land, however, the violation does not ordinarily result in a finding that the assignment or sublease is void. A lease may expressly

reserve the landlord's right to terminate the lease if the covenant against alienation is breached. If so, the landlord may elect to evict the subtenant or assignee as a holdover. The landlord may not elect to terminate the lease and evict the sublessor, however, because the lease between the landlord and the tenant did not expressly reserve that right.

24.  **C**    Under the Rule Against Perpetuities, no interest is good unless it must vest, if at all, during a period measured by lives in being plus 21 years. Since the baby's marriage might have taken place more than 21 years after the deaths of the landowner's three children, her interest might not have vested until after the period prescribed by the Rule expired, and thus violates the Rule.

A and B are incorrect because the interest *might* have vested after the period expired; the fact that it actually did not does not make it valid. The birth of other grandchildren would not affect the interests of the baby since the will provided that the share of a prematurely deceased child should be divided among issue *of that child*, and the youngest daughter could not possibly have any children after her own death. **D** is therefore incorrect.

25.  **B**    If a gift is made to a class of persons, some of whom are in being and ascertained at the time the gift is made, the class opens and closes immediately. Since the gift was made in the woman's will, it became effective at her death. Since some of her husband's children were in being and ascertained at that time, the class closed immediately.

A is incorrect because, as explained above, the class closed upon the death of the woman. An interest is contingent if its vesting is subject to a condition precedent. The child's right to take a share of the realty does not depend on the happening of a condition precedent, so it is not contingent. **C** is therefore incorrect. **D** is incorrect because the class closed immediately upon the death of the woman, and because even if it had not, the child's right would be vested subject to partial divestment and therefore not void.

26.  **D**    An easement by express grant does not terminate by non-use unless there is a clearly manifested intent to abandon it. Since there is nothing to indicate that the city intended to abandon the right to empty water into the creek that crossed the landowner's land, it may exercise that right even though it has not done so for 40 years.

A private nuisance is a tortious interference with the plaintiff's right to use and enjoy realty. Since the easement privileged the city to dump water into the creek, its conduct in doing so is not a violation of any right held by the landowner. **A** is therefore incorrect. **B** is incorrect because there was no manifestation of an intent to abandon the easement. **C** is a fabrication that has no meaning at all.

27.  **C**    A tenancy at sufferance happens when a tenant holds over at the end of a valid lease. Specifically, the tenant must have entered the property legally, the tenant's right to possession must have ended, and the tenant must have remained without the owner's consent. When a tenancy at sufferance comes into existence, the landlord has the right of election between evicting the tenant and holding the tenant to another term as tenant. The election to keep a tenant may be express or implied. Importantly, a landlord will be found to elect a

tenancy renewal when the landlord accepts rent for the new period or gives some affirmative sign that he or she is regarding the lease as continuing for a new period. However, the mere fact that the tenant tenders a rent check, without any affirmative act by the landlord, won't cause such an election. Consequently, the landlord has the right to evict the tenant immediately. **A** and **B** are therefore incorrect.

Constructive eviction is used where the landlord has an obligation and continually breaches that obligation in a way that makes the premises virtually uninhabitable for the intended use. There is no indication of this in the fact pattern. **D** is therefore incorrect.

28. **B**   In the absence of language to the contrary, a contract for the sale of realty is presumed to call for conveyance of marketable title by whatever form of deed is customarily used in the area. Thus, the contract is complete, valid, and enforceable, even though silent about these two requirements.

A and **D** are incorrect because the contract so construed is enforceable by either party. Although parol evidence may be admitted for the purpose of determining the intentions of the parties to a contract, this contract can be enforced without it, based upon the presumption described above. **C** is therefore incorrect.

29. **C**   Some jurisdictions hold that an abstractor of title impliedly warrants the abstract to be accurate; all jurisdictions agree that there is at least an implied warranty that the service will be performed in a reasonable manner. Since the right-of-way deed was properly recorded, the abstract company's failure to include it in the abstract that it furnished was a breach of either the promise to perform reasonably or the implied warranty of accuracy. In either event, since the buyer was an intended creditor beneficiary of the contract between the seller and the abstract company, the buyer can enforce it.

If there was an implied warranty of accuracy, **A** is incorrect because liability is imposed without fault for its breach. If there was no implied warranty of accuracy, **A** is incorrect because liability may be imposed if the abstract company's lack of awareness of the right of way resulted from its failure to act reasonably. Since the right-of-way deed from the owner of the land to the chemical company was properly recorded before any of the grants of the land took place, it was not outside the chain of title, and **B** is incorrect. **D** is incorrect because the liability of the abstract company does not depend on covenants made by the seller.

30. **A**   If a deed contains a restriction or covenant prohibiting the grantee from using the realty in a particular way, that restriction may be equitably enforced (*i.e.*, by injunction) by a successor to the grantor's interest against a successor to the grantee's interest if the restriction constitutes an equitable servitude. A restriction may be held to constitute an equitable servitude if it creates a burden that touches and concerns the land of the original grantor and a benefit that touches the land of the original grantee, if the original parties intended it to run with the land, and if the person against whom enforcement is sought had actual or constructive notice of the burden when he or she received his or her interest. The restriction touches and concerns the land of the builder (against whom enforcement is sought)

because only the occupant of the builder's land can comply with it. The restriction touches the land of the other residents of the subdivision (who seek to enforce it) because the value of their realty will be affected by the use to which the builder's lot and other realty in the subdivision are put. The fact that the subdivision plan that was filed contained a description of the deed restrictions indicates that the original parties intended it to be enforceable by all residents of the subdivision and also serves to give successors to original grantees constructive knowledge of the restriction. Thus, the restriction is enforceable as an equitable servitude against the builder by other residents of the subdivision.

**B** is incorrect because the enforcement of restrictive covenants in the deeds to lots in a subdivision does not depend on the will of other members of the subdivision. Restrictions that touch and concern the land outlive buildings that are on the land and do not cease to be enforceable simply because those buildings have ceased to be operative. **C** is therefore incorrect. Changes in the community may result in a decision to stop enforcing deed restrictions only where the changes are such that it is no longer substantially possible to secure the benefits that the restrictions were intended to create. **D** is incorrect because no facts indicate that such a change has occurred.

31. **B**    Ordinarily, a tenant who abandons the premises before the expiration of the lease is liable for rent for the balance of the term. If, however, the landlord *surrenders* his or her rights under the lease, the tenant will be free from liability for the balance of the term. A surrender generally takes place when the landlord occupies the premises for his or her own purposes.

Re-letting the premises for the balance of the term might be a surrender of the landlord's rights or might be performed on the defaulting tenant's account to mitigate damages, depending on the intent of the landlord. Where, as here, there is a lot of other vacant space in the building, and the landlord has re-let the premises for a rent lower than provided in the lease, and on a month-to-month basis, it is not likely that his intent was to surrender his rights but rather to mitigate damages. **A** is therefore incorrect. The agreement between the landlord and the tenant did not restrict use of the premises to any particular activity. For this reason, the fact that the premises are not well suited to the activity that the tenant had in mind, or that the tenant is no longer licensed in the practice for which he planned to use them, is irrelevant to his liability under the lease. **C** and **D** are therefore incorrect.

32. **B**    If a conveyance of realty is complete in all other respects but silent as to the interest that is being conveyed, it is presumed to convey whatever interest the grantor holds at the time the conveyance is executed.

Thus, **A** and **C** are incorrect. Although a deed to realty should expressly identify the parties, the realty, and the interest conveyed, **D** is incorrect because without language to the contrary, the deed is presumed to convey whatever interest the grantor held.

33. **B**    The distinguishing feature of joint tenancy is that it includes the right of survivorship. This means that, although a joint tenant may sever a joint tenancy during his or her lifetime, if he or she dies without doing so, his or her interest passes to surviving joint tenants. The

result is that unless the joint tenancy is severed by one of the joint tenants, the joint tenant who lives the longest will become the holder of the combined interests of all the original joint tenants. To give effect to this principle, it is understood that upon the death of one of the joint tenants, his or her share passes to the remaining joint tenants, increasing the fractional shares that they hold in joint tenancy. Since a will speaks only upon the death of the testatrix, the deceased daughter's purported devise to the youngest daughter did not occur during the deceased daughter's life and therefore could not sever the joint tenancy. As a result, the surviving daughters continue to be joint tenants, the share of each being increased from one-third to one-half.

**A** and **C** are incorrect because the surviving daughters continue to be joint tenants for the reason given above. **D** is incorrect because the deceased daughter could not sever the joint tenancy by will, and therefore her interest will be divided equally between the surviving joint tenants.

34.  **D**    Ordinarily, an adverse possessor of realty acquires title only to that portion of the realty that he or she actually occupied and possessed. One who occupies any portion of a parcel of realty under "color of title" (*i.e.*, pursuant to a written instrument that appears to convey title), however, is said to occupy it all. Since the buyer openly, notoriously, hostilely, and continuously occupied a portion of the land for the statutory period under color of the title conveyed by the sheriff's deed, he has acquired title to that entire parcel of realty by adverse possession.

Although the document under which the buyer believed himself to have title proved to be defective, **A** is incorrect because of the interest that he acquired by adverse possession. **B** is incorrect because he occupied a portion of the realty under color of title. Although possession of part of the premises under color of title may result in acquisition of title to the whole, the *general* rule is that the adverse possessor may acquire title only to that portion of the premises that he or she has actually occupied. **C** is therefore incorrect.

35.  **A**    A conveyance is recorded outside the chain of title if a reasonable search of the chain of title to the realty conveyed would not disclose that it occurred. A tract index identifies parcels of realty by number and enables a title searcher to trace the chain of title by searching for transactions involving realty identified by the appropriate number. By using a tract index to search for transactions involving the land's parcel number, a title searcher would discover that the land had been conveyed by the first buyer to the second buyer, and by the second buyer to the third buyer. Without a tract index, a title searcher traces the chain of title by searching for transactions involving appropriate grantees and grantors. Without a tract index, a title searcher would have no way of determining that the realty conveyed by the first buyer to the second buyer and by the second buyer to the third buyer was the land, because the landowner's conveyance of the land to the first buyer had never been recorded, so there was nothing in the record to connect the first buyer with the land. Thus, the conveyance from the first buyer to the second buyer was recorded outside the chain of title. For the purpose of determining priorities under a recording statute, a conveyance outside the chain of title is treated as an unrecorded conveyance. Under the statute, no conveyance of realty is effective against a subsequent purchaser without notice of it unless it was recorded. Since

the deed from the first buyer to the second buyer is treated as unrecorded, neither it nor the subsequent deed from the second buyer to the third buyer (which is also outside the chain of title) is effective against the fourth buyer, who purchased without notice.

Recording statutes determine the priority of interests. Under the statute given, the first buyer's conveyance to the second buyer and the second buyer's conveyance to the third buyer are not effective against the fourth buyer for the reasons given above, and, as a result, the fourth buyer's interest takes priority over the third buyer's. This does not mean, however, that the first buyer did not have the power to convey the realty. If the landowner purported to sell to a purchaser who had notice of the landowner's previous conveyance to the first buyer, for example, the first buyer's conveyance to the second buyer would have been effective against that purchaser. For this reason, **B** is incorrect. Intentional misrepresentation by the landowner might make the landowner liable in tort for damages, but it does not affect the rights of the third buyer and the fourth buyer as against each other. **C** is therefore incorrect. Since the fourth buyer is seeking to establish that his title is superior to the third buyer's, knowledge by the third buyer's predecessor is not relevant. **D** is therefore incorrect.

36.  **C**    An easement is an interest in realty. A license is permission to use realty. An interest in realty cannot be conveyed except by written instrument. Thus, the oral permission that the landowner gave the fisherman could not have created an easement and must have created a license. Unless consideration is given for it, a license to use realty is revocable at will by the licensor or his or her successor. In most jurisdictions, a license automatically terminates when the realty is sold by the licensor. In those jurisdictions, the fisherman's license terminated upon the landowner's sale to the buyer. In a few jurisdictions, a license survives the sale of the realty, but if it was a revocable license, it remains revocable. Since the fisherman did not give consideration for the license, it was revocable, and if it survived the sale to the buyer, it was effectively revoked when the buyer ordered the fisherman off the property.

**A** is incorrect because knowledge by a grantee that the grantor created a license to use the realty does not cause the license to survive the sale. **B** and **D** are incorrect because the oral permission could not have resulted in any easement. **D** is also incorrect because an easement appurtenant does survive the sale of the servient estate.

37.  **B**    A remainder is a grantee's future interest that will become possessory upon the termination of a prior estate that is certain to terminate. If the remainder is not subject to any conditions precedent other than the event that terminates the prior estate, it is said to be vested. If it is subject to an additional condition precedent, it is said to be contingent. Since the brother will surely die, the termination of the brother's life estate is inevitable, and the son's interest is a remainder. Since there are no other conditions precedent to the son's interest becoming possessory, it is a vested remainder. Since the gift is to be shared by all the brother's children, however, the interest that the son receives will be diminished if the brother has any more children before his death. It is thus subject to partial divestment.

**A** is incorrect because there is no condition that would result in complete divestment of the son's interest. A gift to an unborn person is usually regarded as contingent (*i.e.*, upon his or her birth). For this reason, the son's interest at the time of the landowner's death could be described as a contingent remainder. When the son was born, however, the contingency was satisfied, and his interest became vested (subject to partial divestment). **C** is therefore incorrect. **D** is incorrect because the son had a vested remainder subject to partial divestment.

38.  **A**   Ordinarily, a tenant who abandons the premises before the expiration of the lease is liable for rent for the balance of the term.

The lease may reserve to the landlord the right to terminate the tenancy and reenter in the event of non-payment, but **B** is incorrect because this is an alternative to the right to collect rent, not the source of it. A landlord who elects to terminate the tenancy will not be entitled to collect rent for the balance of the term. **C** is incorrect, however, because a landlord may elect not to terminate and hold the tenant for rent. **D** is incorrect because neither party to a lease may avoid obligations under it merely by giving notice, unless the lease so provides.

39.  **B**   In determining the extent of the estate conveyed and the restrictions to which it is subject, the courts look to the deed that conveyed it. If there is a disagreement between the contract of sale and the conveyance, the language of the conveyance prevails. Although the Statute of Frauds requires the transfer of an interest in realty to be in writing and signed by the party to be charged, most courts hold that accepting and recording a conveyance containing restrictions in the use of the land conveyed binds the grantee to those restrictions even though he or she did not sign the deed in which they appeared or agree to them in the contract of sale.

The operation of a commercial cannery next to a residence might constitute a private nuisance, depending on the character of the neighborhood and the way in which the cannery is operated. **A** is incorrect, however, because such an operation is not necessarily a nuisance. **C** is incorrect because the restriction in the deed is controlling. **D** is incorrect because the developer accepted and recorded the deed.

40.  **B**   Under the Rule Against Perpetuities, no interest is good unless it must vest, if at all, within a period measured by a life or lives in being plus 21 years. Options to purchase realty are required to meet the requirements of the Rule Against Perpetuities unless they are attached to a lease or other interest in the realty held by the optionee. Since the option purports to convey a right to purchase at a time beyond the period prescribed by the Rule, it is void.

**A** and **C** are incorrect because notice, whether actual or constructive (*i.e.*, by recording), does not make valid an interest that violated the Rule. **D** is incorrect because the option violates the Rule Against Perpetuities.

41.  **A**   If the landlord makes it physically impossible for the tenant to occupy some portion of the premises, the lease has been breached. This is called an actual partial eviction. In that case, the tenant is entitled to withhold the entire rent, not just the part attributable to the portion of the premises from which the tenant has been actually evicted. Importantly, the

tenant can withhold rent without moving out of the rest of the premises. Here, since it is physically impossible for the tenant to occupy the basement, the landlord has committed an actual partial eviction of the tenant. Therefore, the tenant is entitled to withhold all of the month's rent, and he does not need to move out of the premises.

**B**, **C**, and **D** are therefore incorrect.

42.  **C**    In a foreclosure sale, the owner of the equity in the foreclosed property does not receive anything until all persons having a lien or security interest in the property have been satisfied. A judgment lien creditor typically gets an interest that is equivalent to a mortgage, and the priority of that lien dates from the day the lien is filed. Here, since the bank has a judgment lien from the first foreclosure, it is entitled to be paid in full before the landowner gets anything. **A** is therefore incorrect. **B** is incorrect because the finance company has been satisfied through foreclosure and the landowner no longer owes it anything. **D** is incorrect because $3,000 is more than the bank is owed.

43.  **C**    A deed does not effectively convey an interest in realty until it has been "delivered" to the grantee. Delivery to one tenant in common is usually regarded as delivery to all. If the deed named the landowner and the nephew as tenants in common, it can be successfully argued that possession by the landowner indicates delivery to her as a grantee, which would satisfy the requirement of delivery to the nephew, her co-tenant. While it is not certain that a court would come to this conclusion, **C** is the only one of the additional facts listed that could possibly support the nephew's claim.

Delivery of a deed may occur even though the deed is not physically placed in the grantee's hands, but only if there is some act by which the grantor manifests the intention to make the deed presently effective. In **A**, the landowner's words simply indicate her intention that the transfer not take effect until her death. **A** is therefore incorrect. **B** is incorrect because the fact that the nephew was out of the country on the day the landowner executed the deed does not indicate anything about her state of mind when she executed it. **D** is incorrect because when the deed was signed is irrelevant in determining the intent of the grantor.

44.  **C**    Title to realty does not pass by deed unless the deed is delivered to the grantee while the grantor is alive. For delivery to occur, the grantor must perform some act that manifests an intention for the conveyance to be presently effective. Usually, this is done by physically placing the deed in the grantee's hands. Although this is not the only available method of delivery, it is apparently the one that the landowner chose, since she instructed her chauffeur to bring the deed to her niece. Since the chauffeur was the landowner's employee, however, the landowner retained the right and power to change her mind and instruct him not to give the deed to her niece, or even to tear it up. Since she retained this control over the deed, it might be concluded that she never manifested an intention to make a presently effective transfer. While it is not certain that a court would come to this conclusion, **C** is the only argument listed that could possibly be effective in opposition to the niece's claim.

Although physical delivery to the grantee is a common way of manifesting the intention to make a presently effective transfer, **A** is incorrect because it is not the only way. Recording statutes determine the priority of interests in realty but do not determine the validity of those interests. For this reason, a valid transfer of realty can occur without recording. **B** is therefore incorrect. An attempted testamentary substitute is a living person's attempt to make a disposition of property after his or her death without complying with the statutory formalities required for wills. The law regards these formalities as so important that an attempt to make a testamentary disposition without them is usually invalid. **D** is incorrect, however, because if the deed had been delivered to the niece prior to the landowner's death, it would have been effective immediately and would thus have been an *inter vivos* transfer rather than a testamentary disposition.

45. **C**    Title by adverse possession results from the operation of a statute of limitations that prevents an action to recover possession from being brought after a specified period of time. But the statute does not begin to run against a potential plaintiff until he or she has a possessory right in the realty. Since the neighbor had no right to possession during the life of the friend, the statute did not begin running against him until the friend's death. Since the friend did have a possessory interest at the time his brother's occupancy began, the statutory period ran against the friend. As a result, the friend's brother had probably acquired the friend's interest by adverse possession. Since the friend's interest was a life estate, however, his brother's interest terminated upon the friend's death.

**A** is incorrect since *hostile* means against the right of the owner. Possession without the owner's permission is hostile. **B** is incorrect because *open and notorious* means in full view of the world and does not require that the owner have actual knowledge. **D** is a fabrication that lacks any meaning at all. In any event, *tacking* refers to one adverse possessor's getting credit for a previous adverse possessor's time.

46. **D**    Depending on the law of the jurisdiction, the "husband" to whom the landowner's will refers is either her first husband, to whom she was married when the will was executed, or her second husband, to whom she was married when she died. Under the Rule Against Perpetuities, no interest is good unless it must vest, if at all, within a period measured by a life or lives in being plus 21 years. A will is effective upon the death of the testatrix. If the will gave a life estate to the first husband, the rights of the children and grandchildren vested immediately upon the landowner's death, since the first husband is already dead. Since this is within the period described by the Rule Against Perpetuities, their interests are valid. If the will gave a life estate to the second husband, the interests of the children and grandchildren will vest upon the death of the second husband. Since this is within the period described by the Rule Against Perpetuities, their interests are valid.

If a class to which an interest in realty is given can be determined at the time the interest vests, the interest is valid even though the class could not be determined when the interest was created. If the will left a life estate to the first husband, **A** is obviously incorrect since the size of the class was already determined when the interest was created (*i.e.*, on the death of the landowner). If the will left a life estate to the second husband, the only grandchildren who will take the estate are those born to a child of the landowner's who dies before the second husband. Since the deceased child could not have any children after his or her own death, the class of grandchildren who will receive the substitutionary gift can be determined at the time the interest vests. **A**, therefore, would still be incorrect. Since a will is effective upon the death of the testatrix, the interests devised by the landowner's will were created when the landowner died. Since she could not marry after her death, **B** is incorrect. If the will left a life estate to the second husband, the interests of the daughter's children will vest only if the daughter dies before the second husband. Since the daughter's life and the second husband's life were both in being when the interest was created (*i.e.*, when the landowner died), the interests will vest, if at all, during a period measured by a life or lives in being. **C** is therefore incorrect.

47.  **D**    Frequently, deeds contain language restricting the way the realty conveyed may be used. Such language may help to define the estate conveyed by imposing a condition that limits the possessory right of the grantee, or it may simply create a contractual obligation between the grantor and the grantee. A conveyance of realty in fee simple transfers absolute ownership, subject to any limitations that appear in the conveyance. A fee simple may be restricted by language that makes it determinable or which subjects it to defeasance upon the happening of a condition subsequent, or which subjects it to an executory limitation. If the language indicates that the grantor will automatically get the realty back upon the happening of a stated event, it creates a fee simple determinable. If the language indicates that the grantor has a right to do something to get the realty back upon the happening of a stated event, it creates a fee simple subject to a condition subsequent. On the other hand, restrictive language in a deed may simply create a contract between the grantor and the grantee, which, if breached by the grantee, entitles the grantor to damages. Usually, courts hold that the restrictive language creates nothing more than a contract unless it specifically provides for termination of the grantee's estate in the event the restrictions are violated. Since the language of the restriction in the seller's deed to the buyer does not specifically provide for the termination of the buyer's estate in the event that the realty is used for purposes other than residential, it probably created no more than a contractual obligation. While it is not certain that a court would come to this conclusion, **D** is the only answer listed that could possibly be correct.

An executory limitation gives a future interest to someone other than the grantor, so if the language in the deed created an executory limitation, it would not result in judgment for the seller. **B** is incorrect because the violation of a covenant contained in a deed is not sufficient to divest the grantee of the realty. **C** is incorrect because the Rule Against Perpetuities is not applicable to the interest of a grantor.

48.  **B**    A grantee's future interest that will become possessory upon the termination of a prior estate is either a remainder or an executory interest. If termination of the prior estate is inevitable, the interest that follows it is a remainder. The remainder is contingent if there is a condition precedent to it other than termination of the prior estate. If termination of the prior estate is not inevitable, the interest that follows it is an executory interest. Under the language of the will, the estate of "my children" will not terminate unless the friend lives another 30 years after this person's death. Since this is not inevitable, the friend's interest is executory. Under the Rule Against Perpetuities, no interest is good unless it must vest, if at all, within a period measured by a life or lives in being plus 21 years.

Since the friend's interest will vest, if at all, during the friend's lifetime, his executory interest is valid.

**D** is therefore incorrect. The friend's interest is not a remainder since the prior estate will not terminate unless the friend lives another 30 years after the death, and this is not inevitable. **A** and **C** are therefore incorrect.

49.  **C**  For a burden imposed by a deed restriction to be applied to the grantee's (covenantor's) successor, it must be one that runs with the land. A burden runs with the land if it touches and concerns the land; if there is privity of estate between the covenantor and his or her successor, as well as between the covenantor and the covenantee (the original grantor); and if the parties so intended. A restriction touches and concerns the burdened land if only the possessor of that land can comply with it. It touches and concerns the benefitted land if the benefit of the restriction is directly tied to the land. In this case, the building restriction touches and concerns the land because it affects the value of the lot in question and of the surrounding land, and because only the holder of the burdened land can comply with it. The necessary privity exists because the homeowner purchased from the developer and because the developer purchased from the landowner. The language indicates that the parties intended the covenant to run. It therefore may be enforced against the homeowner.

**A** is incorrect because zoning laws supersede deed restrictions only when those zoning laws are more restrictive than the deed restrictions. **B** is incorrect because if the burden runs with the land, a successor to the covenantor is bound by the covenantor's promise. **D** is a fabrication, with no basis in law.

50.  **C**  The recording statute provides that a conveyance that has not yet been recorded is not effective against a subsequent purchaser for value. Since the second buyer purchased before the first buyer recorded, the first buyer's title was inferior to the second buyer's. Since the second buyer's quitclaim to the third buyer conveyed whatever interest the second buyer had, the interest that the third buyer received (*i.e.*, the second buyer's) was superior to the first buyer's. Since the third buyer's purchase occurred before the first buyer recorded, the conveyance from the landowner to the first buyer is not effective against the third buyer.

The effect of the recording statute is that a conveyance is not effective against a subsequent purchaser unless it was recorded prior to that purchase. Since the third buyer purchased on April 15 and the first buyer did not record until April 16, the first buyer's deed is not effective against the third buyer. **A** is therefore incorrect. **B** is incorrect because the statute does not require that the subsequent purchaser be without notice. Although recording statutes determine the priority of interests to realty, they do not determine the rights that exist between a grantor and grantee. It is not accurate to say that the first buyer received no rights until he recorded because the conveyance by the landowner gave him rights at least against the landowner. **D** is therefore incorrect.

51.  **C**  An easement is in gross if it is created for the benefit of a grantee in a status other than that of an owner of a specific piece of realty. Since this easement was created for the benefit of

the phone company rather than for the owner of a specific parcel of realty, it was in gross. It is generally understood that commercial easements in gross may be alienated, so long as such alienation does not increase the burden on the servient estate.

Although the statement in **A** is accurate, it is inapplicable and therefore incorrect because an easement appurtenant is one that is created for the benefit of a grantee in a status as owner of a specific piece of land. **B** is incorrect because noncommercial easements in gross are generally held to be inalienable. Even if it were an accurate statement, **D** would not result in the landowner's defeat. It is not an accurate statement since the landowner sold the subdivision before he created the easement.

52.  **C**    A covenant against encumbrances is a grantor's promise that the title conveyed is free from liens. If a lien exists when the covenant is made (*i.e.*, on delivery of the deed), there is a breach that entitles the grantee to damages. The farmer's satisfaction of the mortgage cut off any rights to the realty that the bank had. Thus, although there has been a breach of covenant, the buyer has sustained no actual damages. Most jurisdictions would allow recovery of nominal damages, however.

A is incorrect because the appropriate remedy for breach of the covenant against encumbrances is an action for damages. **B** is incorrect because the covenant that was contained in the deed was not breached until the deed was delivered. There was a breach, though, because the encumbrance existed at the time when the farmer delivered the deed. **D** is therefore incorrect.

53.  **B**    Unless a contrary intention is shown, a conveyance to two or more persons is presumed to create a tenancy in common. Tenants in common are obligated to share in the payment of principal, interest, and real estate taxes.

Although co-tenants are required to share in the costs of maintenance, **A** is an inaccurate statement because in the absence of a specific agreement, they are not required to share in the costs of improvements. **C** is also an inaccurate statement because unless he or she has ousted (*i.e.*, denied possession to) his or her co-tenants, a tenant in possession is not required to account to co-tenants for the rental value of the property occupied.

54.  **D**    An easement by prescription is obtained when one property owner uses another's property in a manner similar to adverse possession. However, that use must be continuous. If the use is so infrequent that it resembles a minor trespass, the continuous requirement is not met. Here, the woman only dumped her leaves on the neighbor's property at most once a year. This is likely not sufficient to meet the continuous requirement, and the only way the woman could continue to dump the clippings and leaves on the property would be if she had obtained an easement by prescription.

A is incorrect because the woman's infrequent dumping of the clippings and leaves is unlikely to meet the continuous requirement, even if she did this for more than the state's adverse possession period. **B** is incorrect because it appears to be referencing a potential easement by necessity, and there is no indication the properties were ever under common ownership. **C** is incorrect because the neighbor only knew about the dumping. The relevant adverse possession requirement is that the use be hostile, and this requirement would clearly not be met if the neighbor had given his permission. However, the question said specifically that he did not do so.

55.  **D**    In jurisdictions that recognize tenancy by the entirety, a conveyance to a husband and wife is presumed to create a tenancy by the entirety in the absence of a contrary intention.

**A**, **B**, and **C** are incorrect because only persons who are validly married to each other may hold land as tenants by the entirety.

56.  **A**    Marketable title is generally a title that a reasonable buyer, fully informed of the facts and their legal significance, would be willing to accept. It is often impossible to tell in advance whether a third person's claim to an interest in realty will be successful. Since the reasonable buyer is not usually willing to purchase an interest that he or she may lose in later litigation, title is not marketable if anything could give a third person a reasonable chance of successfully asserting a claim to an interest in the realty. Thus, the title tendered by the doctor was marketable only if there was no reasonable doubt about the success or validity of a claim that might then be asserted by persons claiming under the older sister's daughter, grandchildren, or great-grandchildren. The two sisters were joint tenants who have the right of survivorship. Thus, the younger sister received the older sister's interest upon the older sister's death, and the older sister's attempt to will her interest was ineffective. As a result, the friend received an unclouded title from the younger sister, and since a quitclaim conveys the grantor's interest, the doctor received an unclouded title from the friend. While there is nothing to prevent the assertion of a lawsuit by the older sister's daughter, her grandchildren, her great-grandchildren, or persons claiming under them, there is no reasonable chance of success for such a lawsuit. The title that the doctor tendered to the dentist is thus marketable, and the dentist's refusal to accept it was a breach.

**B** is incorrect, since if the title was unmarketable, the dentist would not be required to buy a lawsuit by accepting any deed at all from the doctor. A quitclaim conveys whatever interest the grantor holds. **C** is therefore incorrect. **D** is incorrect because the effect of a joint tenant's right of survivorship is that the interest of a joint tenant cannot be devised by will.

57.  **D**    Assignment of a leasehold interest occurs when the holder of the interest transfers to another all that remains of his or her interest. Sublease of a leasehold interest occurs when the holder of the interest transfers part of but not all his or her remaining interest. Since the tenant transferred all his remaining interest to the attorney, he made an assignment. The lease prohibited subletting. Because courts favor the free alienation of interests in land, contractual restraints on alienation are strictly construed. For this reason, a clause that prohibits subletting does not prohibit assignment.

**A** is therefore incorrect. **B** is an incorrect statement of the rule; assignment of a lease is *permitted* in the absence of an agreement to the contrary. Even if the lease contained an express reservation of the landlord's right to terminate in the event of a breach, the landlord could not terminate the attorney's leasehold since the tenant's assignment did not breach his agreement not to sublet. **C** is therefore incorrect.

58.   **A**     Since the parties to the assignment agreement intended that payments be made by the investment company to the builder, the builder was a third-party beneficiary of the assignment agreement and can enforce it against the investment company. Unless released by the obligee, a party to a lease, like a party to any other contract, continues to be responsible for performance of the obligations thereunder even after assigning rights or delegating duties that exist under the lease. This is true even if the lease permits assignment and even if the obligee consents to the assignment. **B** is incorrect because the builder has not released the tenant from his obligations under the lease and therefore can still collect from the tenant.

59.   **B**     Although all the statements might be logical ways of solving this problem, the law is clear that a life tenant is required to pay interest — to the extent of the reasonable rental value of the realty — and a remainderman is required to pay the principal.

      **A**, **C**, and **D** are therefore incorrect.

60.   **D**     So long as a description is sufficient to identify the realty conveyed, it is legally adequate, even though it contains some error with respect to the size of the parcel. Since the landowner owned only one parcel of realty on Barrett Road, the description can identify only one parcel and is thus adequate.

      **A** is therefore incorrect. **B** is incorrect because delivery occurred when the landowner handed the deed to his son, telling him that it was a birthday present. The fact that his son returned it to the landowner is not relevant since he only asked the landowner to hold it for safekeeping. **C** is incorrect because there is no requirement that a deed be supported by consideration, and because once the deed was delivered, there was an executed gift.

61.   **A**     Under the doctrine of equitable conversion, the risk of loss passes to the buyer of real estate as soon as the contract is made. On the day of the loss, the buyer thus had an insurable interest as defined by the statute.

      Although various jurisdictions disagree about when the risk of loss passes in a sale of realty, all agree that if a party causes a loss, he or she bears the risks that result from it. For this reason, if the fire resulted from the buyer's negligence, he probably bore the risk of loss. **B** is incorrect, however, because it indicates that this is the only way the buyer would bear the risk of loss, and, under the doctrine of equitable conversion, the risk of loss fell upon him as soon as the contract of sale was formed. Under the doctrine of equitable conversion, as soon as the contract of sale is formed, the risk of loss passes to the purchaser despite the fact that the seller continues to be the legal owner until the closing of title. **C** is therefore incorrect. **D** is incorrect because the statute recognizes that an insurable interest is held by the person suffering the risk of loss, and the doctrine of equitable conversion passes the risk to the buyer when the contract is formed.

62.   **D**     A remainder interest is vested if there are no conditions precedent to its becoming possessory other than the termination of the prior estate. If there are additional conditions precedent, the remainder is contingent. Since it is inevitable that the brother will die, and since there are no conditions precedent to the interests of the children, their interests are vested.

It is possible, however, that the brother will have additional children. If so, the children will share in the realty, but their shares will be diminished. Their interests are therefore subject to partial divestment.

**A** is incorrect since there are no conditions precedent to the vesting of their interests. **B** is incorrect because of the possible partial divestment described above. **C** is incorrect because although their shares may be diminished, they will receive some shares.

63.  **A**   An easement created by express grant is not affected by the fact that the reason for its creation no longer exists.

**B** is incorrect because the rights of third persons are not relevant in the consideration of easement disputes between landholders. **C** is based on an accurate statement of the law about implied easements by necessity, but it is incorrect because the easement in question was created by grant, and was therefore not an implied easement by necessity. Since the three-story building is to be a one-family residence, its existence will not appreciably increase the burden on the servient estate. **D** is therefore incorrect.

64.  **C**   Absent an agreement to the contrary, a contract for the sale of realty calls for the execution and delivery of whatever deed is customarily used in the area. Thus, if the use of general warranty deeds is customary, the homeowner's tender of a quitclaim was a breach that would excuse the buyer from performance.

**A** is incorrect because the creation of a power of attorney to sell realty implies the power to contract for whatever deeds are customarily used in the area. Quitclaims are not customarily used anywhere, except under special circumstances. A quitclaim conveys whatever title the grantor held at the time it was executed and thus conveys marketable title if the grantor held same. **B** is incorrect, however, because even if title is marketable, a quitclaim does not give a grantee recourse against the grantor if problems should develop, and because the contract implied a promise to deliver the kind of deed customarily used in the area. **D** is incorrect because a quitclaim conveys valid title if the grantor held valid title.

65.  **A**   Under the doctrine of equitable conversion, a purchaser of realty becomes its equitable owner as soon as the sales contract is formed and suffers the risk of loss resulting from damage to the premises prior to the passage of title. Thus, in a jurisdiction that applies the doctrine of equitable conversion, the loss would be suffered by the buyer. He is, therefore, obligated to pay the full contract price in spite of the fact that the value of the realty has been diminished through no fault of his own.

**B**, **C**, and **D** are therefore incorrect.

66.  **C**   A remainder is a grantee's future interest that is to become possessory after the termination of a prior interest that will inevitably terminate. An executory interest is a grantee's future interest that follows an interest that will not inevitably terminate. Since the interest of the National Cancer Association was to become possessory only if the land was used for the sale of alcohol, and since this event is not inevitable, the interest of the National

Cancer Association must be executory. **A** and **D** are therefore incorrect. Under the Rule Against Perpetuities, no interest is good unless it must vest, if at all, within a period measured by a life or lives in being plus 21 years. Since the land might not be used for the sale of alcohol until after the expiration of the period of perpetuities, and since the interest of the National Cancer Association will not vest until that time, its interest is void under the Rule Against Perpetuities. [**Note:** An exception to the Rule Against Perpetuities is made for a shift from one charity to another. This exception does not apply in this case since the niece is not a charity.] **C** is therefore correct, and **A** is therefore incorrect. [**Note:** The common law "destructibility rule" resulted in a merger of a present possessory interest and a future interest held by the same person, even if there were intervening contingent remainders. Although the question indicates that the jurisdiction has abolished the destructibility rule, its existence or nonexistence has no application to these facts.]

67.  **B**      A grant to a named grantee "and his or her heirs" traditionally conveys a fee interest. A fee simple subject to an executory interest is a fee interest that will terminate automatically upon the happening of a specified contingency. The grant of a fee followed by the words "but if" is usually held to create a fee simple subject to an executory interest, because the language indicates that the grantee's interest will not continue beyond the happening of the specified contingency.

A fee simple absolute is a possessory interest that includes all present and future interests in the realty. **A** is incorrect because the grant limits the interest of the friend, making it terminate upon the happening of a specified event. A life estate is a possessory interest in realty that will terminate at the end of a specified life. Since the interest conveyed to the friend by the deed will not terminate at the end of a specified life, it is not a life estate. The law does not recognize any interest known as a "quasi-life estate." **C** is therefore incorrect. Under the Rule Against Perpetuities, no interest is good unless it must vest, if at all, within a period of time measured by a life or lives in being plus 21 years. Since the interest of the dentist would not vest until the United States went to war and used the property as a base, and since this could have occurred hundreds of years after the conveyance was made, the dentist's interest was void under the Rule Against Perpetuities. The fact that a portion of a grant is void under the Rule Against Perpetuities, however, does not affect the validity of other interests created by that grant. For this reason, and because the friend's interest vested immediately, **D** is incorrect.

68.  **C**      If the location of an easement is precisely indicated by a written instrument, such as the deed that created it, neither the holder of the dominant estate nor the holder of the servient estate may relocate it without the consent of the other. Sometimes, the fact that the holder of an easement has stopped using it for a substantial period of time justifies the conclusion that he or she has abandoned it. This always requires some additional evidence of an intent to abandon, however. Ordinarily, two months is not a sufficient length of time to indicate abandonment, and since there is no additional evidence of the buyer's intent to abandon the easement, his use of the paved road for two months does not imply consent to a relocation. Since this easement was described by metes and bounds in the deed that created it, and since the buyer has not consented to its relocation, it continues to exist in its original location. Since the holder of the servient estate is not permitted to interfere with the easement holder's use of the easement, the buyer is entitled to the relief that he seeks.

Although an implied easement by necessity terminates when the strict necessity for it terminates, an easement created by express grant does not terminate without abandonment, consent, or condemnation. **A** is incorrect because the buyer's easement was created not by implication, but by grant. When the dominant and servient estates come to be owned by the same person, there is said to be a merger, and preexisting easements that the dominant estate held over the servient estate are extinguished. **B** is incorrect, however, because after the buyer's easement was created, the buyer's lot was the dominant estate and Parcels 1 and 2 were the servient estates, and the dominant and servient estates were not owned by the same person. An easement that directly benefits another parcel of realty (*e.g.*, a right of way for ingress and egress) is an easement appurtenant. An easement that benefits an individual regardless of his or her relationship to another parcel of realty (*e.g.*, a power company's right to install power lines) is an easement in gross. Easements appurtenant are freely alienable; easements in gross are not. **D** is incorrect for three reasons: First, the buyer's easement was an easement appurtenant; second, easements in gross are not freely alienable; and third, the case raises no issue regarding alienability.

69. **B**    A deed does not operate to convey any interest in land until it has been delivered. Physical transfer of a deed that is absolute on its face constitutes a delivery only if the grantor intended to make a presently effective transfer of an interest. When the landowner handed the chauffeur a deed and said that it was not to take effect until his death, his intent may have been to make a present transfer to the chauffeur of a future interest that would become possessory upon his death. Such an interest is a remainder. While it is not certain that a court would come to this conclusion, **B** is the only argument listed that could possibly support the chauffeur's position.

Although possession by a grantee raises a presumption that there has been a valid and effective delivery, **A** is incorrect because the presumption is not irrebuttable; it may be rebutted by proof that the grantor did not intend to make a present transfer. A testamentary substitute is an attempt by a living person to dispose of property after his or her death without complying with the formalities that statutes require of valid wills. **C** is incorrect because an attempted testamentary substitute is ineffective. Delivery is complete when the grantor does some voluntary act that manifests his or her intention to make a presently effective transfer. Since there is no indication that the landowner's death was voluntary, it could not have completed delivery. **D** is therefore incorrect.

70. **B**    The hermit has been in continuous possession for more than 20 years. His possession was hostile, because it was contrary to the rights of the city, the land's true owner. It was open and notorious because it was not hidden and knowledge of his possession could have been obtained by anyone who looked. Having fulfilled all the statutory requirements, he would ordinarily be correct in his assertion that he has acquired title by adverse possession. Most jurisdictions, however, prohibit the acquisition of city or state property by adverse possession. This being the only legal obstacle to the hermit's assertion, the outcome will most likely depend on whether the jurisdiction permits the acquisition of city property by adverse possession.

**A** is incorrect because if the possession was open and notorious as described above, it does not matter whether the actual owner ever really knew of it. Some adverse possession statutes establish a condition that the adverse possessor pay taxes on the realty during the period of his or her adverse possession. **C** is incorrect, however, because this statute did not contain such a requirement. An adverse possessor who occupies land under color of title may become the owner of all the land that he or she believed he or she owned, including that which he or she did not actually occupy. Since the hermit asserts ownership only of the land that he occupied, however, color of title is irrelevant, and **D** is incorrect.

71.  **B**    Joint tenancy is a form of co-ownership in which the joint tenants have the right of survivorship. This means that upon the death of one joint tenant, the others receive equal shares in his or her interest. When the wife's mother died, the husband and the wife received equal shares of her interest. The joint tenancy of the husband and the wife continued, but each held a one-half interest in the whole instead of a one-third interest. Joint tenants may convey their interests *inter vivos* without each other's consent, but a joint tenant's grantee takes as a tenant in common with the remaining owners. Thus, upon the wife's conveyance to the coach, the coach and the husband were tenants in common, each with a one-half interest. Upon the husband's conveyance to the neighbor, the neighbor and the coach became tenants in common, each with a one-half interest.

**A** is incorrect because, as a joint tenant with right of survivorship, the wife's mother could not effectively pass her interest by will. Since a conveyance by a joint tenant makes the grantee a tenant in common, neither the coach nor the neighbor received a joint tenancy in any part of the estate. **C** is therefore incorrect. **D** is incorrect for this reason, and because the friend received no interest at all under the wife's mother's will.

72.  **A**    Today, all jurisdictions have recording statutes that determine priorities. In cases not covered by the recording statutes, however, common law rules of priority apply. The statute in this question determined the priority of interests in cases in which the subsequent taker was a purchaser for value and without notice. Since the son received the conveyance as a gift, he gave nothing in return for it, and therefore he was not a purchaser for value. As a result, the statute does not apply, and common law rules of priorities do. At common law, priorities between successive transferees of interests in real property are determined simply on the basis of chronology — "first in time, first in right." Thus, since the bank received its interest before the son received his interest, the bank's is superior.

If the statute was applicable, the bank's interest would have been superior to the son's only if the bank's mortgage was recorded before the land was conveyed to the son. If the mortgage was not recorded before the conveyance occurred, the fact that the mortgage was recorded before the conveyance was recorded would not give priority to the mortgage. **B** is therefore incorrect. Unless an applicable recording statute has a contrary effect, a grantee of mortgaged realty takes subject to the mortgage, whether or not the existence of the mortgage is mentioned in the grantee's deed. Since the recording statute is not applicable to the son's interest, the son took the realty subject to the bank's mortgage. **C** is therefore incorrect. **D** is incorrect for two reasons: First, the statute imposes the requirement of value on junior claimants and the bank is the senior claimant, and second, the bank was a purchaser for value since it gave consideration (*i.e.*, a loan of $20,000) in return for an interest in realty (*i.e.*, the mortgage).

73.  **A**  Under the doctrine of accession, the owner of realty becomes the owner of anything that becomes part of the realty. Consequently, since a court has ruled the fireplace has become part of the realty, the tenant isn't entitled to any compensation.

**B**, **C**, and **D** are therefore incorrect.

74.  **A**  Under the Rule Against Perpetuities, no interest is good unless it must vest, if at all, during a period measured by a life or lives in being plus 21 years. Since it is possible that the change in use would occur after the end of this period, both grants to Second Foundation would appear to violate the Rule. The Rule Against Perpetuities is not applied, however, to shifts from one charity to another, so Second Foundation's interest in Greenacre is valid. Since the nephew and the niece are not charities, Second Foundation's interest in Redacre is invalid. **B**, **C**, and **D** are therefore incorrect.

75.  **D**  While a tenant who vacates after an assignment is no longer in privity of estate with the landlord, he or she continues to be in privity of contract under the initial lease and continues to be liable for rent. The assignor's liability is secondary, while the assignee's liability is primary. Thus, if the landlord is successful in collecting from the tenant, the tenant may seek indemnity from the store owner. This does not, however, protect the tenant from liability to the landlord.

The lease required the tenant to obtain the landlord's permission before assigning. If he had not done so, some jurisdictions might permit the landlord to avoid the assignment. In any event, however, the landlord's consent does not operate to destroy his contract rights against the tenant. **A** is therefore incorrect. A novation is an agreement by which parties to a contract substitute a new party for one of the original parties. For a novation to occur, there must be an agreement by the new party to assume the contractual obligations of the party whom he or she is replacing, *and* an agreement by the original obligee to extinguish the contractual obligations of the party who is being replaced. Although the store owner agreed to personally assume the tenant's obligations under the lease, the landlord did not agree to relieve the tenant of those obligations. Thus, there was no novation, and **B** is incorrect. Usually, an assignee of a tenant's rights under a lease is liable to the landlord only for rent that accrued during the assignment period. An assignee who personally assumes obligations under the lease may also be liable for rent accrued before the assignment took place or after reassignment. The assumption of obligations by an assignee might, thus, impose additional duties on that assignee. It does not, however, relieve the assignor of any of his or her initial obligations to the landlord. **C** is therefore incorrect.

76.  **D**  A fixture is a former chattel which, by reason of its annexation to realty, has become part of the realty. A tenant is entitled to use leased realty but not to remove parts of it when he or she leaves. Thus, if the improvements made by the tenant were fixtures (*i.e.*, became part of the realty), the tenant would not be entitled to the judgment that he seeks. One of the factors considered in determining whether an improvement made by the tenant was so

annexed to the realty as to be a fixture is whether it can be removed without causing any substantial damage to the realty. If so, the improvement may be regarded as a *chattel* that belongs to the tenant, and which he is, therefore, entitled to remove, rather than as a *fixture* that has become part of the realty. Although this factor alone might not be sufficient to keep the improvements from being regarded as fixtures, it is the only one listed that could support the conclusion that they are not.

The value of the improvements is not relevant since even a valuable improvement may be a fixture if it became part of the realty, and if so, it belongs to the landlord. **A** is therefore incorrect. **B** is incorrect because an improvement is a fixture if it has become part of the realty, and this does not logically depend on whether it was foreseeable that the tenant would make it. The general rule is that the tenant may not remove fixtures unless the parties agreed to the contrary. Absent such an agreement, the general rule applies. **C** is therefore incorrect.

77. **D**    An easement is the right to use realty of another. The realty subject to the easement is called the *servient estate*. If the benefit that the holder of an easement receives is associated with his or her ownership of a particular parcel of realty, the easement is appurtenant, and the realty benefitted by that easement is called the *dominant estate*. Easements appurtenant are freely alienable, usually transferred with a conveyance of the dominant estate. If an easement is recorded, subsequent grantees of the servient estate have constructive notice of its existence and take the servient estate subject to the easement. Since according to the advice in option **D**, the easements that the doctor and lawyer would grant each other would be for access to their own parcels of realty, they would be easements appurtenant. The effect of the transaction would be that the doctor and lawyer each would own half of the driveway and hold an easement over the other's half. Since the easements would be appurtenant, they would be transferable to any transferees of the dominant estates. Since they would be recorded, they would bind any transferees of the servient estates. Thus, each property owner would have the right to use the entire driveway (*i.e.*, the half that he or she owns and the half over which he or she has an easement), and neither would have the right to interfere with the other's use.

**A** is incorrect because such a contract would bind only the parties to it. If the successor to either were to partition, the only remedy would be an action for damages against the original promisor. **B** is incorrect since a joint tenant may sell his or her interest, the grantee becoming a tenant in common with the remaining party. This would leave the remaining party in the same position that he or she was in the beginning. **C** is based on an inaccurate statement of the law, since tenants in common do have the right to partition.

78. **D**    Valid title is not necessarily marketable. Since no one should be required to purchase a lawsuit, marketable title means title about which there is no reasonable doubt of validity. To decide whether the son held marketable title in August 2013, it is necessary to determine whether the quitclaim that he executed in 2008 could possibly have affected his title to the realty. A will speaks on the death of the testator. This means that no devise of an interest in realty created by the landowner's will was of legal effect until the landowner's death in 2010. The son, thus, had no interest at all in the land in 2008 when he executed the

quitclaim to the bank. Since a quitclaim conveys only the interest that the grantor holds at the time of its execution, the son gave up no interest in the realty as a result of the 2008 quitclaim. Under the landowner's will, the son received a remainder in a one-third interest in the land that became possessory upon the death of the eldest daughter in June 2013. His title was therefore marketable on the day he tendered the deed to the buyer.

Although a quitclaim conveys whatever interest the grantor possesses at the time of its execution, **A** is incorrect because the son held no interest in the land when he executed the quitclaim to the bank in 2008. A remainder is a future interest that will become possessory upon the termination of a prior estate, the termination of which is inevitable. Since the eldest daughter's death was inevitable, the son received on the death of the landowner a remainder that became possessory on the death of the eldest daughter. The son's interest was therefore valid, making **B** incorrect. A general warranty deed ordinarily contains a grantor's warranty that he or she holds the interest that is conveyed. But no one is required to buy a lawsuit. A warranty of title provides a remedy against the grantor, but it does not make the title marketable. Were title unmarketable at the time that the son tendered the deed, the son would be failing to fulfill his obligation under the contract of sale, and the buyer could not be required to go through with the transaction. **C** is therefore incorrect.

79.  **C**    After granting an interest in realty, a grantor may continue to hold one of three future interests in the realty. If the grantor has conveyed any interest that is less than that which he or she holds, his or her future interest is a reversion (*e.g.*, the grantor, who holds a fee simple absolute, conveys only a life estate or an estate for years. In that case, the grantor retains a reversion.) If the grantor conveys his or her interest in a way that may result in the grantee's eventual loss of the interest conveyed, the grantor's possible future interest is either a possibility of reverter or a right of reentry. If the grantee's interest is to terminate automatically upon the happening of a specified event, the grantee's interest is determinable, and the grantor's future interest is called a possibility of reverter. (*E.g.*, the grantor, who holds a fee simple absolute, conveys "to the grantee for so long as the premises are used for residential purposes." In that case, if the premises ever cease to be used for residential purposes, the grantee's estate will terminate automatically and the fee will revert to the grantor. The conveyance has given the grantee a fee simple determinable, and the grantor retains a possibility of reverter.) On the other hand, if the grantee's interest will not terminate automatically, but the grantor retains the right to terminate the grantee's interest on the happening of a specific event, the grantee's interest is subject to a condition subsequent, and the grantor's future interest is a right of reentry. (*E.g.*, the grantor, who holds a fee simple absolute, conveys "to the grantee, but if the premises ever cease to be used for residential purposes, the grantor may reenter." The conveyance has given the grantee a fee subject to a condition subsequent, and the grantor retains a right of reentry.)

Although the conveyance executed by the landowner contains language that may result in the church's loss of its interest, it does not convey an interest less than that held by the landowner. For this reason, the future interest retained by the landowner cannot be a reversion and must be either a possibility of reverter or a right of reentry. The deed makes use of the realty for non-church purposes an event that results in the church's loss of its interest. Since the church's interest in the land will terminate automatically, and there is no language indicating that the landowner has to do something to take back the land (*i.e.*, no mention of a right to reenter in the deed), **C** is correct.

A remainder is a future interest held by a grantee that will become possessory following the inevitable termination of a prior estate. Since the landowner was the grantor rather than a grantee, his interest cannot be a remainder. **A** is therefore incorrect. **B** is incorrect because the landowner did not convey less than his entire interest. An executory interest is a future interest held by a grantee that will become possessory following the termination of the prior estate when termination is not inevitable. Since the landowner was the grantor rather than a grantee, his interest cannot be executory. **D** is therefore incorrect.

80. **D**     Under the Rule Against Perpetuities, no interest is good unless it must vest, if at all, not later than 21 years after some life in being at the creation of the interest. Importantly, under the common law, if a gift is made to a class, the entire gift fails unless it can be said that each class member must have his or her interest vest or fail within lives in being plus 21 years. This rule is triggered if the class could obtain new members after the testator's death. Importantly, under the "fertile octogenarian" rule, there is a conclusive presumption that any person, regardless of age or physical condition, is capable of having children. Here, it would appear the gift is invalid because the daughter is presumed to be able to have another child, and that child could take after lives in being plus 21 years — for example, all of the son's children might be born after the landowner's death, and might die more than 21 years after the landowner's death. Consequently, in courts taking a strict common-law approach to class gifts, the daughter's three now-living children would not take anything since their interest violates the Rule. Under the "fertile octogenarian" rule, it does not matter that the daughter could not possibly have any further children. However, even courts that generally follow the common-law Rule Against Perpetuities will usually allow the gift to stand as to any member of the class who was alive at the moment the gift is created. Consequently, the daughter's three children will take the property since they were alive at the moment the gift was created.

A, **B**, and **D** are therefore incorrect.

81. **D**     An easement is a right to use, but not to possess, the land of another. The land that is subject to an easement is known as the servient tenement or estate. The holder of an easement may not overburden the servient estate. This means that the easement holder may not change the easement or use it in a way that was not contemplated when it was created. An easement holder has the right and the duty to maintain the easement but may not do so in a way that would overburden the servient estate. Some cases have held that paving an easement that has long existed as a dirt road overburdens the servient estate. Whether or not a court would so hold in this case is unknown. The easement created by the deeds was only 12 feet wide, however, and the third buyer now seeks to widen it to 24 feet. This would undoubtedly overburden the servient estate since it would increase the portion of that estate that is subject to use by the easement holder and reduce the portion available for unlimited use by its owner.

Sometimes a change in circumstance may justify a change in use of an easement. The fact that the road becomes muddy after a heavy rain, for example, might justify paving it. **A** is incorrect, however, because doubling the width of the easement is a change substantial enough to result in an overburdening of the servient estate. The holder of a servient estate has no obligation to maintain an easement running across it, while the user of such easement is required and is entitled to maintain it at his or her own expense. This does not give the easement holder the unilateral right to make changes in the easement, however, simply because he or she is willing to pay for them himself or herself. **B** is therefore incorrect. Even if the construction of the road that the third buyer proposes to build would improve the value of the lots affected, the second buyer is free to reject the improvement in value, choosing to keep his land the way it is. **C** is therefore incorrect.

82.  **D**   Some jurisdictions recognize a special co-tenancy known as tenancy by the entirety, which can be held only by a husband and wife. Where it exists, tenancy by the entirety is like joint tenancy in that it gives each co-tenant the right of survivorship, but it is unlike joint tenancy in that neither co-tenant may sever it without the consent of the other. In those jurisdictions that recognize tenancy by the entirety, it is presumed that any conveyance to a husband and wife creates a tenancy by entirety. Most such jurisdictions hold that the presumption may be rebutted by evidence that some other form of ownership was contemplated by the parties to the conveyance. The conveyance to wife and husband "as joint tenants and not as tenants in common, with full right of survivorship" rebuts the presumption and results in a joint tenancy. Although a joint tenant may convey his or her interest without the consent of the other joint tenant, such a conveyance severs the joint tenancy as to the interest conveyed and makes the grantee a tenant in common. (**Note:** In some jurisdictions, there is an irrebuttable presumption that a conveyance to husband and wife creates a tenancy by the entirety. In these jurisdictions, the wife's purported transfer to the man would be void unless the husband consented to it. Of the answers listed, however, **D** is the only one that could possibly be correct.)

A quitclaim extinguishes the rights of the person executing it by conveying those rights to the person receiving it, although it does not specify what those rights are or warrant that they exist. **A** is therefore incorrect. Although a quitclaim ordinarily transfers whatever interest is held by the person executing it, any transfer by a joint tenant severs the joint tenancy. For this reason, the wife's conveyance to the man severed the joint tenancy, and **B** is incorrect. **C** is incorrect because only a husband and wife may hold title as tenants by the entirety.

83.  **B**   A deed does not effectively convey realty until it is delivered. Although delivery does not always require a transfer of physical possession of the deed by the grantor to the grantee, it does require some word or act by the grantor that manifests his or her intent that the conveyance shall have a present operative effect. When the landowner placed the envelope on the dining-room table, it was with the intention of mailing it the following morning. Since it was always possible for him to change his mind before mailing it, the fact that he planned to mail it is not sufficient to manifest an intent that it would be presently operative. Since he died without doing anything that would manifest such an intent, there was no delivery.

Conveyance by deed is not effective unless the deed is accepted by the grantee, but if the grant is beneficial, the grantee's acceptance is presumed. Thus, if the landowner had manifested the necessary intent (*e.g.*, by mailing the deed), a delivery might have taken place even though the sister died before she became aware of the conveyance. **A** is therefore incorrect. The presumption that a grantee has accepted a deed can be rebutted by proof that he or she rejected it. Such a rejection could not take place, however, unless the grantee knew about the deed. For this reason, if the sister had sent back the envelope containing the deed without knowing its contents, she would not have rejected it by so doing. **C** is incorrect, however, because the sister's daughter was not the grantee and because there was no delivery to the sister. Ordinarily, a grantor's delivery of a deed to a third person with instructions to deliver it to the grantee is a delivery to the grantee so long as the grantor relinquished all control. It may be that mailing a deed has that effect, since the sender ordinarily loses control over an envelope once it is delivered to the postal authorities. **D** is incorrect, however, because the landowner did not relinquish control over the envelope before his death.

84. **D**    The taking of an entire parcel of realty by eminent domain results in acquisition by the taker of all present and future interests in the realty. For this reason, the leasehold interest passes with the rest of the property, whether or not it is specifically mentioned in the judicial decree. **A** is therefore incorrect. Since the lessee thus loses his right to occupy the property, he or she is freed from the obligation of paying rent due under the balance of the lease. Also, a leasehold interest is a non-freehold but possessory interest in real property. As with any property interest, if it is taken for public use, its holder is entitled to "just compensation" under the Fifth Amendment to the United States Constitution. Since taking the realty by eminent domain results in a condemnation of the leasehold as well as the landlord's reversion, the lessee is entitled to a proportionate share of the condemnation award. Since he or she is entitled to be compensated for what he or she has lost, his or her share should be based on the value of the unexpired balance of his or her term. Since he or she is no longer obligated to pay rent, however, the rent that he or she would have otherwise had to pay should be deducted from the value.

85. **D**    A person may acquire title to realty by adverse possession if he or she occupies it without its owner's permission openly, notoriously, and continuously for the statutory period of time. This occurs because the running of a statute of limitations then makes it impossible for the adverse possessor to be judicially ejected. Since a new owner acquires the old owner's right to eject an unlawful possessor, the statutory period of limitations continues to run in spite of changes in ownership. Since the artist has adversely possessed the realty for more than 15 years, she has acquired title by adverse possession.

For the above reason, the fact that the son became the owner in 2004 did not restart the period. If the owner of the realty is under a legal disability (*e.g.*, infancy) at the time the adverse possession begins, commencement of the statutory period is delayed until the legal disability has terminated. If the owner is not under a legal disability at the time the possession begins, however, the fact that he or she subsequently suffers a legal disability or that title subsequently passes to a person who is under a legal disability will have no effect on the running of the statutory period. Since there is no fact indicating that the landowner was under any legal disability in 1997 when the artist began her possession of the realty, the running of the statutory period commenced at that time and continued without interruption upon the passage of title to the son. **A** is therefore incorrect. Since only a person with a right of possession can sue to eject an unlawful possessor, the statute of limitations cannot work against the holder of a future interest. Thus, an adverse possessor acquires only the possessory interest that existed at the time of her possession. If, for example, the landowner had been the holder of a life estate with a remainder in the son, the artist's adverse possession during the landowner's life could have led only to the artist's acquisition of a life estate by adverse possession. Then, upon the landowner's death in 2004, a new period of possession would have begun against the son's fee interest. The will by which the son received title spoke only upon the landowner's death, however. This means that when the artist began possession in 1997, the son had no future interest at all. Since there is no fact to the contrary, the landowner's interest must have been a fee when the artist moved on, and it was this fee that the artist acquired by adverse possession. For this reason, **B** is incorrect. **C** is incorrect for the reasons given above, because at the time the artist's adverse possession began, the holder of the fee interest (the landowner) was under no disability, and because if the possession is open and notorious, it does not matter whether the owner is aware of it.

86. **C**    Under the doctrine of equitable conversion, the risk of loss passes to a buyer of realty as soon as a contract of sale is formed. Thus, if the jurisdiction applies this doctrine, the buyer must sustain the loss resulting from destruction of the barn.

If an essential part of the realty is destroyed prior to passage of the risk of loss, a buyer might be excused from performing his or her obligations under the contract of sale. On the other hand, if a nonessential part of the realty is destroyed, the buyer might be required to go through with the purchase with an abatement of the price to compensate for the loss. Thus, if the risk of loss had not passed to the buyer, the fact that the barn was not an essential part of the realty might prevent him from withdrawing from the transaction but would not permit the seller to collect the full price. **A** is therefore incorrect. Although many jurisdictions hold that the risk of loss passes to a buyer as soon as he or she takes possession of the realty, there is no principle of law by which possession creates a presumption of fault. **B** is therefore incorrect. Once a risk of loss passes to a party, that party suffers the consequence of such a loss even if it did not result from his or her fault. Since there are various theories that might have passed the risk of loss to the buyer (*e.g.*, the doctrine of equitable conversion, possession), the fact that he was without fault would not in itself be sufficient to prevent him from bearing the loss. **D** is therefore incorrect.

87. **B**    Under the facts given, it is possible that the conveyance to the dentist created an implied easement. This may arise when a grantor conveys a portion of his or her land, retaining a part over which an apparent previous use existed that was reasonably necessary to the enjoyment of the portion conveyed and could have been the subject of an easement. Since the existence of a dirt road made previous use across the landowner's land apparent, and since river access might be reasonably necessary to the use and enjoyment of the dentist's land, the deed to the dentist may thus have created an easement by implication. Although it is not certain that a court would come to this conclusion, **B** is the only argument listed that might be effective for the doctor.

An easement by dedication is a use granted to the public either by deed or by operation of law. Since there is no indication that the dirt road ever became a public right of way, **A** is incorrect. An easement by express reservation is created by a deed in which the grantor retains a right to use the realty conveyed. Since the dentist was a grantee, she could not have obtained an easement by express reservation. **C** is therefore incorrect. An easement by express grant is created by a deed that specifically conveys to a grantee the right to use the property of another. Since the landowner's deed to the dentist did not mention the easement, and since there is no fact indicating that the dentist ever received it by conveyance, there was no easement by express grant. **D** is therefore incorrect.

88.  **C**  Those who own land adjacent to a flowing body of water (*i.e.*, riparian owners) have some rights to use that water. Under modern common law, each riparian owner has the right to make reasonable use of the water. If construction of a dam would result in the consumption of more water than is reasonably necessary, a court might hold that the farmer has no right to build the dam.

**A** is incorrect because the farmer's increased use of the water might still be reasonable. At one time, it was said that no riparian owner was permitted a use that altered the natural flow of the stream. If "natural flow" is given a literal meaning, this would make it virtually impossible for anyone but the furthest downstream owner to use the water. For this reason, the natural flow rule has given way to a rule that bases riparian rights on reasonable use. Thus, even if the dam altered the natural flow, the farmer would have a right to construct it so long as his use was reasonable. **B** is therefore incorrect. Under the reasonable use test, the farmer may dam the stream so long as doing so would not make his water use unreasonable. **D** is incorrect because this would be so even if he could accomplish the same without damming the stream.

89.  **D**  If leased realty is taken by eminent domain, the leasehold and the reversion merge in the taker, the leasehold is terminated, and the obligation to pay rent ceases. Since both the lessor and the lessee have had something of value taken for public use, each is entitled to receive just compensation for what he or she has lost. The lessor is entitled to receive the value of the leased premises (including the value of rent to be received), minus the value of the leasehold interest that he has already conveyed. The lessee is entitled to receive the value of the leasehold. If not for the condemnation, however, the lessee would have been required to pay rent to enjoy the benefits of her leasehold. Since the condemnation terminates that obligation, the rent that the lessee otherwise would have been required to pay should be deducted from the value of her leasehold.

**A** is incorrect because the taking terminates the leasehold, and with it, the obligation to pay rent. The Rule Against Perpetuities provides that no interest is good unless it must vest if at all within a period of time measured by a life or lives in being plus 21 years. Since a lessee's interest in leased premises vests at the moment the lease is executed, the Rule Against Perpetuities is inapplicable to it. **B** is therefore incorrect. Since the condemnation terminates the tenant's obligation to pay rent for the balance of the lease term, allowing her to keep the entire $30,000 would result in her receiving more than she has actually lost. For this reason, **C** is incorrect.

90. **A** Proceeds of a foreclosure sale are taken by holders of security interests in the order of the priority of their respective interests. Since mortgages and trust deeds create security interests in realty, the priority of the conflicting claims will be determined in accordance with the recording statute. The statute given is a typical notice statute. According to its terms, the interest held by the bank cannot take priority over the interest held by the lender because the bank's mortgage had not been recorded when the lender received its interest, the lender gave value for its interest, and there is no fact indicating that the lender was aware of the bank's mortgage when the lender received its interest.

Since neither the statute nor the common law makes priority dependent on whether any person has notice of the interests of subsequent takers, **B** is incorrect. Recording statutes generally do apply to security interests in realty. In addition, this statute specifically refers to the transfer of "an interest in realty," and so, by its terms, applies to security interests. **C** is therefore incorrect. **D** is incorrect because a purchase money mortgage is a mortgage given to the borrower to buy the subject real estate. Here, the landowner was only trying to buy a boat.

91. **A** Probably the best-known characteristic of the joint tenancy is the right of survivorship. Under it, when a joint tenant dies, his or her interest is not inherited by his or her heirs and distributees but passes to the remaining joint tenants. At common law, a joint tenancy could not exist unless the shares and possessory rights of the joint tenants were equal, and unless the interests of the joint tenants were created at the same time and by the same document. (These are known as the four unities — unity of interest, possession, time, and title.) Many states have modified these common law requirements by statute, but even in those states, the shares of joint tenants are presumed equal unless there is an agreement to the contrary. For this reason, the reconveyance by the wife and her husband created a joint tenancy, with the wife, her husband, and her grandmother each holding a one-third interest. Upon the wife's death, her third passed to her husband and her grandmother in equal shares, continuing them in joint tenancy with each holding a one-half interest in the realty.

**B**, **C**, and **D** are incorrect because upon the death of a joint tenant, the surviving joint tenants continue in joint tenancy. In addition, **B** and **C** are incorrect because upon a joint tenant's death, his or her share passes equally to the surviving joint tenants.

92. **B** The language of the covenant in the farmer's deed to the neighbor contained two parts. The first part restricted the use of the land conveyed by that deed. Since the farmer was not engaging in any activity on that land, this part of the covenant does not burden him at all. The second part required all further deeds to land in the subdivision to bear the same covenant. Since the farmer has not yet conveyed any of the other land in the subdivision, none of it is burdened by the covenant.

A covenant that runs with the land benefits successors to the original covenantee and burdens successors to the original covenantor. Thus, a covenantee's successor may enforce it even though it was not mentioned in his or her deed, and even though he or she was not in privity with the covenantor. For this reason, **A** and **C** are incorrect. For a covenant to run, it must touch and concern the land. A covenant restricting the use of land in a subdivision touches and concerns the covenantor's estate because it affects the value of the burdened estate and because only the person in possession of that estate can possibly be burdened by it. Such a covenant touches and concerns the covenantee's estate because the permitted uses of land in a subdivision necessarily affect the value of other land in the subdivision. For these reasons, **D** is incorrect.

93.   **C**     A periodic tenancy is a tenancy that will continue for a stated period and for repeated similar periods unless terminated by proper notice from one of the parties. Since the written agreement created a tenancy for one month that was to automatically renew each month unless terminated as provided, it created a periodic tenancy.

A tenancy for years is an estate for a fixed determinable period of time (not necessarily measured in years). Since the written agreement did not fix a time for the expiration of the tenant's tenancy, it did not create a tenancy for years. **A** is therefore incorrect. A tenancy at will is an estate without a fixed duration that will continue until terminated by either party. By its nature, it is continuous until affirmatively terminated. Unlike the periodic tenancy, its continuation does not depend on the automatic renewal of an agreement for a stated period. Since the written agreement of January 1 was for one month subject to automatic renewal, **B** is incorrect. When a tenant fails to vacate at the expiration of his or her leasehold, he or she becomes a tenant at sufferance. **D** is incorrect because a tenancy at sufferance is not created by written agreement.

94.   **B**     Voluntary waste consists of some act by a possessory tenant that diminishes the value of the realty or otherwise "injures the inheritance." One of the ways in which it is committed is by removing minerals from the land. Ordinarily, when a life tenant commits voluntary waste, the holder of a vested remainder is entitled to bring an immediate action at law for damages. In the alternative, the remainderman may be entitled to the equitable remedies of injunction and an accounting for profits already derived from the sale of such minerals. (**Note:** Although it is understood that a possessory tenant may remove minerals from realty that is good for no other purpose, or may continue removing minerals from a mine that was open when his or her tenancy began, neither of these exceptions applies under the facts in this case.)

A possessory tenant who commits voluntary waste is not entitled to retain any of the profits from his or her activity. For this reason, the church is entitled to all profits derived from the sale of gravel, rather than merely to a proportionate share. **A** is therefore incorrect. It is sometimes held that the holder of a contingent remainder or a remainder subject to divestment has no right to sue for waste until his or her interest vests indefeasibly. Since the remainder interest held by the church is already vested, however, **C** is incorrect. The rule that permits a possessory tenant to continue removing minerals from a mine that was open when he or she began his or her tenancy is sometimes known as the "open pit" doctrine. **D** is incorrect, however, because the facts indicate that gravel had never before been mined or removed from the land.

95.   **A**     A class gift is a gift to a group of persons undefined in number when the gift is made. The landowner's will created a class gift since it devised the realty to all children of the

son without specifying their names or their number. A class gift passes to all persons who are in the class at the time the class opens or who enter the class prior to its closing. Ordinarily, a class opens at the time the gift is created. Since the landowner's will spoke at the time of the landowner's death, and since the sons were already in existence at that time, they are obviously within the class and entitled to an interest in the realty. In determining whether the daughter received an interest, it is necessary to decide when the class closed. If there are members of the class in existence at the time the class gift is created, the class opens and closes immediately upon creation of the gift. Since the sons were in existence at the time of the landowner's death, the class closed immediately upon the landowner's death. For this reason, the daughter did not enter the class before its closing and therefore received no interest in the realty.

**B** and **C** are incorrect for the above reason. Under the Rule Against Perpetuities, no interest is good unless it must vest, if at all, within a period of time measured by a life or lives in being plus 21 years. Since the son was in being at the time the landowner's will spoke, and since the son could not have children after his own death, no interest created by the landowner's will could possibly vest after a period measured by the life of the son. **D** is therefore incorrect.

96.  **D**     In the contract between the landlord and the lawyer (*i.e.*, the lease), the lawyer agreed to pay rent of $1,000 per month for the entire term of the lease. The lawyer cannot unilaterally change this obligation by assigning the lease to another. Thus, although the assignment to the doctor might make the doctor responsible for rent, it does not free the lawyer of such liability. For this reason, the landlord is entitled to collect from the lawyer all unpaid rent.

**A** is incorrect because the doctor's liability is additional to the lawyer's and does not free the lawyer from liability. **B** and **C** are incorrect because the lawyer agreed to pay rent for the entire lease period.

97.  **D**     Probably the best known attribute of joint tenancy is the right of survivorship. This means that when one joint tenant dies, the remaining joint tenants inherit the interest of the deceased. Sale of an interest by a joint tenant destroys the joint tenancy as to the seller's interest, and the buyer takes as a tenant in common. The other joint tenants continue to be joint tenants, however. This means that when the first buyer conveyed her interest to the first buyer's daughter, the first buyer's daughter became a tenant in common with a one-third interest, while the second buyer and the third buyer continued to be joint tenants as to the remaining two-thirds. Because of the right of survivorship, the second buyer's attempt to transfer his interest by will was ineffective. As a result, upon the second buyer's death, the third buyer (as the second buyer's joint tenant) survived to the second buyer's interest, and the second buyer's son received no interest at all. Since the third buyer already held a one-third interest and since he inherited the second buyer's interest, the third buyer ended up with a two-thirds interest.

**A** is incorrect because, as a result of the third buyer's right of survivorship, the second buyer's will could not pass an interest to his son. **B** is incorrect for the same reason, and because sale by a joint tenant breaks the joint tenancy as to the seller's interest, which means that the first buyer's daughter took as a tenant in common. **C** is incorrect because the first buyer's daughter took as a tenant in common and therefore did not receive any share of the second buyer's interest upon the second buyer's death.

98. **C** Title to property may be acquired by adverse possession if the person claiming such title occupies the realty openly, notoriously, hostilely, and continuously for the statutory period. Possession is "open and notorious" if the possessor has, in general, behaved as an owner. Since the man occupied the premises every summer, his possession was open and notorious. Possession is "hostile" if it is contrary to the rights of the owner. Since the facts do not indicate that the man had the owner's permission to occupy the cabin, his occupancy was hostile. While possession must be "continuous," it need not be without interruptions if the interruptions are consistent with the appropriate use of the realty. Since this was a summer cabin, occupancy only during the summers might have been consistent with its appropriate use. If it was, the man has acquired title by adverse possession.

Once the period of possession has begun, it continues to run in spite of conveyances or other changes in ownership. Thus, **A** is an inaccurate statement and is therefore incorrect. If the owner of realty is under a legal disability at the time adverse possession begins, computation of the period of possession does not start until the disability ends. If, however, the owner is not under a legal disability at the time adverse possession begins, subsequent legal disability or legal disability of a subsequent owner does not interrupt the running of the period. **B** is therefore incorrect. Because of the requirement that adverse possession be hostile to the rights of the owner, one who occupies with permission of the owner cannot acquire title by adverse possession. **D** is therefore incorrect.

99. **A** By its terms, the given recording statute applies only where the subsequent taker is a "purchaser for value." Since the niece received the realty as a gift, she is not a purchaser for value. The recording statute, therefore, does not apply. In the absence of an applicable recording statute, the common law rule of "first in time — first in right" prevails. Since the bank received his interest before the niece received hers (*i.e.*, the bank is first in time), the bank's interest is superior to the niece's.

By definition, a mortgage is a security interest in realty. **B** is therefore an inaccurate statement and is incorrect. As explained above, the absence of an applicable recording statute makes the niece's interest inferior to the bank's because it was created after the bank's. **C** is therefore incorrect. Since the conveyance to the niece made no mention of the bank's mortgage, the niece is without notice of its existence. The statute only protects a person without notice, however, if he or she is a purchaser for value. **D** is therefore incorrect.

100. **C** A grantee's future interest is a remainder if it follows an estate that is certain to terminate. If there are no conditions precedent to the remainder becoming possessory other than termination of the prior estate, the remainder is vested. If there are additional conditions precedent, the remainder is contingent. Since the grandson's estate becomes possessory

on the death of either the son or daughter, and since these deaths are certain to occur, the grandson's interest is a vested remainder.

**A** is incorrect because only a grantor can hold a reversion. **B** is incorrect because except for the death of the life tenant, there is no condition precedent to the grandson's interest becoming possessory. Under the Rule Against Perpetuities, no interest is good unless it must vest, if at all, during a period measured by a life or lives in being plus 21 years. Since the grandson's interest is vested, it does not violate the Rule Against Perpetuities. **D** is therefore incorrect.

101. **C**     A joint tenancy means that two or more people own a single, unified interest in the property. A joint tenancy also means the parties to the joint tenancy share a right of survivorship (meaning that if one dies, the other joint tenants become owners of the deceased tenant's interest). There are several ways in which a joint tenancy can be destroyed, and severance normally results in a tenancy in common. A tenancy in common has no right of survivorship. Importantly, if there are three or more original joint tenants, a conveyance by one of them to a stranger will create a tenancy in common between the stranger and the original joint tenants. However, the joint tenancy will continue between the original joint tenants. Here, the conveyance creates a tenancy in common between the friend and the two younger brothers for one-third of the property, but the younger brothers' joint interest in the remaining two-thirds of the property survives. Consequently, if the friend dies, his interest will go to his heirs or devisees. If one of the brothers dies, his interest will go to his brother.

**A**, **B**, and **D** are therefore incorrect.

102. **C**     Under the "Rule in Dumpor's Case," many jurisdictions hold that if a landlord consents to an assignment by the tenant, the covenant against assignment is thereafter waived and the assignee may in turn assign to another without being bound by the covenant. Although it is not certain that the court in this jurisdiction would apply the rule, **C** is the only option listed that could possibly be effective in the neighbor's defense.

Courts strictly construe restraints against the alienation of leasehold interests. This means that a covenant against assignments does not prevent subleases, and vice versa. **A** is incorrect, however, because although such covenants are strictly construed, they are not void. Ordinarily, an assignment made in violation of a covenant not to assign is valid, and the landlord has no remedy other than an action for damages resulting from the breach. Where, as here, however, the landlord reserves the right to terminate the lease in the event of a violation of the covenant, the assignment is voidable at the landlord's election. **B** is therefore incorrect. An assignment is a transfer of all remaining rights under a lease; a sublease is a transfer of less than all remaining rights. Since the manager transferred all remaining rights to the neighbor, the transfer was an assignment, and **D** is incorrect.

103. **A**     The extinguishment of an easement must normally satisfy the Statute of Frauds. Consequently, the business owner's oral statement, taken by itself, did not extinguish the

easement. In that case, the easement would pass to the buyer when he purchased the dominant tenement, and the woman cannot now force the buyer to make a new agreement.

**B** is incorrect because the easement was not extinguished, so the buyer's reliance is immaterial. **C** is incorrect because the thing that distinguishes a license from an easement is the fact the license is revocable at the will of the licensor. Here, the question is dealing with an easement, not a license, and this statement is a misstatement of the correct rule. **D** is incorrect because the woman did not have to receive a benefit from the sale for the easement to remain enforceable.

104.   **A**   Every contract for the sale of realty contains an implied covenant by the seller that he or she will deliver marketable title. Marketable title means title that is reasonably secure against attack. It is generally understood that title to property that is being used in violation of a zoning law is not marketable. If a seller is unable to deliver marketable title, the buyer is not required to complete the transaction because no person should be required to purchase potential litigation. Since the buyer's agreement to purchase the house was connected with his purchase of the business, it is likely that a court would find that the zoning violation constitutes a defect that excuses the buyer from going through with the purchase. Although it is not certain that a court would come to this conclusion, **A** is the only option that could possibly be correct.

**B** and **C** are incorrect because the courts usually hold that an existing zoning violation makes title unmarketable. **D** is incorrect because a public law that prohibits a particular activity takes precedence over a private rule that permits it.

105.   **C**   A fee simple subject to an executory interest is a fee interest that is defeased in favor of a third person upon the happening of a specified event. Here, the Foundation for Hereditary Diseases will take the property if the friend ever uses it for the sale of alcohol.

Although an interest that might vest after a period measured by a life or lives in being plus 21 years is void under the Rule Against Perpetuities, this does not affect the validity of any prior estate. For this reason, even if the interest of the Foundation for Hereditary Diseases violates the Rule Against Perpetuities, it has no effect on the validity of the friend's interest. **A** is therefore incorrect. A fee simple absolute is complete ownership that is not subject to defeasance. **B** is incorrect because of the special limitation created by the phrase "so long as." A fee simple subject to a condition subsequent is an interest that is subject to defeasance on the happening of a specified event but which does not terminate until the holder of the future interest takes some step to make his or her interest possessory. **D** is incorrect, however, since there is no indication that the foundation has to do anything to take the property.

106.   **A**   In those jurisdictions that apply the doctrine of equitable conversion, a purchaser under a real estate sales contract becomes the equitable owner of the realty and bears the risk of loss as soon as the contract is formed. In those jurisdictions that have adopted the Uniform Vendor and Purchaser Risk Act, the risk of loss does not pass to the buyer until either title or possession has passed. But both these rules apply only when the parties

have not agreed to the contrary. Parties to a contract are free to agree as to when the risk of loss is to pass. In this contract, the parties agreed that the risk of loss would not pass until title was conveyed.

**B**, **C**, and **D** are incorrect because they ignore the agreement of the parties.

107.  **A**    A contract for the sale of realty is unenforceable unless it adequately describes the subject realty. Similarly, a deed is ineffective unless it adequately describes the realty conveyed. For these purposes, any description of realty is adequate if it clearly identifies the property being conveyed. There can be no doubt that the description would be adequate if the landowner's was the only realty in the county known as The Dancing L and identified by the Tract, Lot, and Parcel numbers given. (**Note:** So long as it clearly identified the property involved, the description in the deed tendered by the landowner would have been adequate even if the property was not the only parcel in the county known as The Dancing L or was not the only parcel known by the Tract, Lot, and Parcel numbers given.) If the description is adequate, the contract of sale is enforceable, and the landowner has fulfilled his obligation under it by tendering the deed. The builder's refusal to accept the deed would thus be a breach that would entitle the landowner to damages.

A contract for the sale of realty, like any other contract of sale, must identify the subject of the agreement. If it does not, it is unenforceable because the court would be unable to fashion a remedy for its breach. **B** is incorrect because it suggests that a contract that is not sufficiently specific to be enforced becomes enforceable simply because the parties entered into it. **C** and **D** are incorrect because any description that clearly identifies the realty is sufficient even if it is not expressed in metes and bounds or the standard form.

108.  **C**    When a joint tenant dies, the interest is extinguished at the moment of the joint tenant's death and the other joint tenant becomes sole owner of the entire property. Consequently, the property interest cannot pass to heirs, devisees, or mortgagee or judgment lien creditors. Here, while the brother purported to give a lien against all of the property, his interest vanished at the time of his death and the bank held nothing.

**A**, **B**, and **D** are therefore incorrect.

109.  **D**    An appurtenant easement is terminated by merger if the dominant and servient estates come into common ownership, and it does not automatically revive if they are severed. Thus, when the second buyer sold Lot 3 back to the landowner, the easement terminated. When the third buyer received Lot 3 from the landowner by a grant that did not mention the right of way, he took it free of the right of way.

Since the third buyer received title to Lot 3 free of the easement, the landowner could not unilaterally revive it. **A** is therefore incorrect. **B** is incorrect because the easement terminated by merger when the landowner reacquired Lot 3. **C** is incorrect because non-use is not in itself sufficient to terminate an easement that was created by express reservation or grant.

110.  **B**    A remainder is a future interest in a grantee that will automatically become possessory following a prior estate that will terminate inevitably (*e.g.*, a life estate). An executory interest is a future interest in a grantee that will not automatically become possessory and which follows a prior estate that will not terminate inevitably. Since the interest of Family Life will become possessory only if racial discrimination is practiced by Family Center, and since this may never happen, the interest of Family Life is best classified as an executory interest. Under the Rule Against Perpetuities, no interest is good unless it must vest, if at all, during a period measured by a life or lives in being plus 21 years. Since Family Center might begin practicing racial discrimination after the period proscribed by the Rule, the interest of Family Life seems to violate the Rule. Because of an exception, however, the Rule Against Perpetuities does not apply to the interest of a charity that follows the interest of a charity. Since Family Center and Family Life are both charitable institutions, the Rule Against Perpetuities does not apply, and the interest of Family Life is valid.

**D** is therefore incorrect. **A** and **C** are incorrect because it is not inevitable that the interest of Family Center will terminate, and the interest of Family Life, therefore, cannot be a remainder.

111.  **A**    A life tenant is entitled to make reasonable use of natural resources for the purpose of maintaining the realty.

**B** is incorrect, however, because this right is limited to reasonable use. The term *waste* is used to describe any substantial change in realty that occurs while it is in the possession of a person holding less than a fee interest. If the change is beneficial to the value of the realty, it is known as *ameliorating waste.* **C** is incorrect for two reasons: First, the destruction of trees on a parcel of realty is not necessarily ameliorating waste since that term would be used only if such destruction benefits the value of the realty, and second, since ameliorating waste benefits the realty, a court is not likely to enjoin it. **D** is incorrect because a life tenant is not required to permit decay to continue simply because it began while the realty was possessed by a prior tenant.

112.  **D**    The landowner's will devised a contingent remainder to the niece and an alternate contingent remainder to the oldest child of the niece living at the time of the landowner's death. Since the niece's daughter was not the oldest child living at the time of the landowner's death, she received no interest.

She did not receive a vested remainder since she had no right at all to take the realty. **A** is therefore incorrect. She did not receive a contingent remainder because there was no condition that would result in her taking the realty. **B** is therefore incorrect. She did not receive an executory interest because there was no condition that would entitle her to divest a previous estate and assert an interest in the realty. **C** is therefore incorrect.

113.  **A**    Under this recording statute (a pure race-type statute), the first interest recorded is superior. The daughter's interest derives from the deed that was recorded on April 3. Since the buyer's deed was not recorded until April 5, the daughter's interest had priority.

**B** is incorrect because under a race-type statute, all that matters is the order in which the interests were recorded. **C** is incorrect because the daughter's interest derives from the deed that was recorded on April 3. The general warranty deed by which the landowner conveyed to the buyer will determine the buyer's rights against the landowner. But **D** is incorrect because the recording statute determines the rights of the buyer and the daughter as against each other.

114. **A**    A mortgage given as a security interest in realty covers all the realty at the place described therein, including parts that are affixed after the mortgage is created. A fixture is a former chattel that has become part of the realty. Once it becomes part of the realty, it is subject to a security interest created by a mortgage on that realty even if the mortgage was given before the fixture became part of the realty. Thus, if the cooling tank was a fixture, the mortgage that the farmer gave the bank includes a security interest in it. [A chattel becomes a fixture when it is permanently affixed to the realty or, even if it is not permanently affixed, when its installation is essential to the use of a particular building. Since both of these conditions were met by the installation of the cooling tank, it was a fixture.]

The question of whether a chattel has become a fixture does not depend on whether the person installing it made payments on a note, so **B** is incorrect. **C** is incorrect because a fixture is subject to a mortgage on the realty even if affixed to the realty after the mortgage was created. The dairyman is not personally liable for payment of the note because the property was conveyed "subject to" the mortgage, but the realty — including fixtures — is subject to enforcement of the mortgagee's rights. **D** is therefore incorrect.

115. **C**    Ordinarily, no person has a right to an unspoiled view. Thus, in the absence of special circumstances (such as those making the interference a nuisance), interference with the view is not actionable even if the person complaining was there first or if the newcomer knew that his or her building would obstruct a view.

**A**, **B**, and **D** are therefore incorrect.

116. **C**    The landowner's will specified the amount to be paid to each child and grandchild who reached 22, and the 22-year-old's share does not depend on the number of children and grandchildren who will meet that condition. Since she was 22 at the time of the landowner's death, she already met the condition, and her interest vested immediately without any possibility of defeasance.

**A** is incorrect for two reasons: First, there are situations in which the interest of a charity might be valid although it does not vest until after the period of perpetuities (as when its executory interest is to vest following termination of the interest of another charity), and second, because the effect that the vesting of her interest has on that of the charity is immediate. **B** is incorrect because the 22-year-old's share is specific, and therefore, it does not depend on the number of people in the class. The validity of the 22-year-old's interest depends on whether it must vest, if at all, before the expiration of the period of perpetuities. **D** is incorrect because there is no reason why this should depend on whether or not she is the first person to qualify.

117.  **C**    The covenant against encumbrances is a representation that there are no easements or liens burdening the realty. If the realty is in fact burdened by such an encumbrance, the covenant is breached and liability is imposed on the covenantor.

This is so even though the purchaser relied on assurances in addition to the covenant, and even though the grantor was unaware of the existence of the encumbrance at the time he or she executed the covenant. **A** and **B** are therefore incorrect. **D** is incorrect because there is no indication that the seller failed to act reasonably (*i.e.*, was "negligent").

118.  **D**    If a joint tenant sells his or her interest, he or she severs the joint tenancy as to his or her interest, but not as to the interests of the other joint tenants. The friend, therefore, acquired a one-third interest in the realty, but as a tenant in common. The two daughters continued to be joint tenants as to their two one-third interests.

**A** is incorrect because the friend is a tenant in common. **B** and **C** are incorrect because the two daughters are joint tenants.

119.  **B**    A quitclaim deed resembles a release since it purports to convey only the interest that the grantor holds at the time of its execution. It includes no implied warranties for title, so the grantor incurs no liability if the title that he or she held proves less than perfect.

This is true even if the grantor knew that this title was defective at the time the quitclaim was executed. **A** is therefore incorrect. Whether the grocer gave value for the realty is not relevant in determining the effect of the grocer's conveyance to the lawyer, since an interest in realty may be acquired without payment of consideration. **C** is therefore incorrect. **D** is incorrect because a quitclaim does not imply a promise by the grantor to act reasonably.

120.  **D**    Ordinarily, a covenant cannot be used to benefit lands owned by third parties. Since the land in Olde Estates is no longer owned by the landowner, the restrictions contained in deeds to lots in Olde Heights would not, therefore, be enforceable by residents of Olde Estates. If, however, it can be shown that when residents of Olde Estates purchased their lots, it was with the expectation that similar restrictions would be imposed on subsequent purchasers of lots in Olde Heights, they will be permitted to enforce the covenants made by Olde Heights purchasers on a theory of implied reciprocal servitudes. The best way of establishing this expectation is by showing that Olde Estates was part of a common development scheme with Olde Heights.

**A** is incorrect since the lack of privity between residents in Olde Heights and those in Olde Estates would prevent the restriction from being enforceable by residents of Olde Estates. Although **B** might result in burdens being imposed on purchasers of lots in Olde Heights, it would not make the restrictions enforceable by residents of Olde Estates. **B** is therefore incorrect. **C** is incorrect because such a clause would bind only the grantees of the deeds but would not burden successors to those grantees since there will be no privity between them and the residents of Olde Estates.

121. **A**  The fact that a plaintiff has an adequate remedy against a third person is no defense for a defendant against whom the plaintiff has an otherwise enforceable right.

**B** might be an effective defense because many jurisdictions hold that the requirement of privity makes a covenant against encumbrances enforceable only by the grantee of the deed containing that covenant. In many jurisdictions, the existence of an encumbrance that is known to the grantee is not a breach of the covenant against encumbrances. **C** might be an effective defense since the bank's mortgage was recorded prior to the buyer's interest. The developer was therefore on notice of it. **D** is an effective defense since a statute of limitations on actions for breach of covenant contained in a deed begins to run upon delivery of the deed containing the covenant.

122. **A**  A description in a deed is legally sufficient if it adequately identifies the realty being conveyed. Thus, although the description used by the landowner is not in the traditional form, it is legally sufficient if it adequately identifies the subject realty.

Where a deed purports to convey a portion of a parcel of realty by a description that clearly states the amount of land conveyed but does not adequately describe it, it is sometimes held that the deed conveys an unidentified fractional portion of the parcel. **B** is incorrect, however, if the description adequately identifies the realty being conveyed. Although metes and bounds and reference to government survey markers are the most commonly used forms of description, **C** is incorrect because they are not the only acceptable forms. **D** is a fabrication with no basis in existing law and is therefore incorrect.

123. **C**  All jurisdictions agree that a party who damages realty bears the risk of the resulting loss. This means that since the destruction of the premises resulted from the buyer's negligence, he will not be relieved of his obligations under the contract.

**A**, **B**, and **D** are therefore incorrect.

124. **D**  The law does not recognize an easement for light, air, or view unless it was created by express grant.

**A** and **B** are therefore incorrect. **C** suggests an estoppel theory, but an easement by estoppel exists only where there is evidence of an attempt to create an express easement that failed for formal reasons. Since the facts indicate no attempt to create an express easement for light, air, or view, **C** is incorrect.

125. **B**  In most jurisdictions that do not apply the doctrine of equitable conversion, the risk of loss remains with the vendor until the transfer of either title to or possession of the premises. If the buyer was living in the house at the time of the fire, his possession would, therefore, result in passage of the risk of loss to him. Although a minority of jurisdictions disagree, **B** is the only additional fact listed that could result in that finding in any jurisdiction.

Although some states hold that a purchaser of realty acquires an insurable interest as soon as the sales contract is formed, his or her purchase of insurance does not cause the risk of loss to pass to him or her. **A** is therefore incorrect. If destruction of the house was foreseeable when the contract was formed, a party might be prevented from asserting a defense based on impossibility of performance. If the risk of loss did not pass to the buyer, however, the fact that such loss was foreseeable would not affect his or her right to cancel the contract or to abate the purchase price in proportion to the damage. **C** is therefore incorrect. Even if the risk of loss has not passed to the purchaser, the vendor in a contract for the sale of real property is entitled to enforce it against the purchaser so long as damage to the premises does not materially affect its value. **D** is incorrect, however, because even under those circumstances, the purchaser is entitled to a proportional abatement of the contract price.

126.　**C**　An otherwise valid conveyance is effective upon delivery. Delivery occurs when the grantor, by words or conduct, manifests an intention that the deed have a present operative effect. Transfer of physical possession of the deed to the grantee raises a presumption that the grantor had such intent. In this case, the landowner's statement, "Then it's yours," supports that presumption.

An attempt to make a gift that is to become effective only after the donor's death may fail because it is essentially a testamentary gift that does not meet the formal requirements for wills. **A** is incorrect, however, because the landowner's language indicated that she intended the transfer of an interest to the nephew to take effect immediately. A grantor's possession of a deed may raise a presumption that there has been no effective delivery. **B** is incorrect, however, because the presumption may be rebutted by proof that there was a delivery and that the grantee thereafter returned the deed to the grantor for safe-keeping only. When consideration is an issue, detrimental reliance may take the place of the required consideration. **D** is incorrect, however, since a deed may be valid without consideration.

127.　**C**　The given statute is a "race-notice" type statute, in that it makes good faith and prior recording conditions for a subsequent grantee's priority. Although the son took the realty in good faith, he did not record before the bank. The bank's interest is therefore superior to the son's.

An interest is said to be recorded outside the chain of title when it was recorded in a way that would have prevented the reasonable title searcher from discovering it. In most jurisdictions, an interest recorded outside the chain of title is regarded as not having been recorded at all. Under the given statute, however, the first interest has priority so long as it was recorded before the subsequent interest was recorded. Since the son's interest was recorded two days after the bank's, and since there was no reason why a title searcher would not have discovered the bank's interest at that time, **A** is incorrect. Although the statute's "good faith" requirement is probably satisfied by the fact that the son lacked actual or constructive notice of the bank's interest at the time the land was conveyed to him, **B** is incorrect because the statute imposes the additional requirement that the subsequent interest be recorded before the earlier one. Most "notice" and "race-notice" statutes establish the payment of value as a condition of the junior claimant's priority. A careful reading of this statute will show that it does not, however. **D** is therefore incorrect.

128. **D**   If a person without ownership purports to convey an estate that he or she does not have, and he or she subsequently acquires title to that estate, the doctrine of estoppel prevents the grantor from asserting his or her title against his or her grantee and causes the after-acquired title to pass directly to the grantee by operation of law.

Since the covenants made by the landowner were breached only by the landowner's delivery of a deed purporting to convey title that he did not have, and since only his grantee could sue for damages resulting from such breach, the landowner's covenants to the lawyer are not relevant in the doctor's action. **A** is therefore incorrect. **B** is incorrect because the doctor's rights against the lawyer are independent of any rights that the lawyer may have against the landowner. Thus, the existence of an effective remedy that the lawyer can exercise against the landowner is not in itself sufficient to entitle the doctor to the relief he seeks from the lawyer. Although the lawyer's intention may have been to convey Northacre to the doctor on June 15, he was incapable of doing so at that time since he had not received title to Northacre from the landowner. For this reason, the lawyer's conveyance to the doctor could not have conveyed an interest in Northacre, no matter what the lawyer intended. **C** is therefore incorrect.

129. **C**   An executory interest is a grantee's future interest in land that will become possessory upon the termination of a prior estate, which termination is not inevitable. If the executory interest replaces the interest of another grantee, it is a shifting interest. Since the termination of the nephew's and the niece's interests in Redacre is not inevitable, Sunrise Foundation holds an executory interest. Since its interest will replace that of the nephew or the niece, it is a shifting executory interest.

**A** and **B** are incorrect because a remainder is a future interest that will become possessory upon the termination of a prior estate, which termination is inevitable, and the terminations of the nephew's and the niece's interests in Redacre are not inevitable. **D** is incorrect because a springing interest is one that does not become presently possessory until sometime after the natural termination of the previous estate.

130. **A**   An assignee of a tenant's rights under a lease is in privity of estate with the landlord and is therefore liable for rent accrued during the period of his or her possession. If he or she personally assumes the obligations of the lease, he or she is also liable for rent accrued before the assignment went into effect and after it terminates. Since, in his agreement with the tenant, the store owner personally assumed the obligations of the lease, he is personally liable for rent accrued throughout the entire duration of the lease. Although the landlord was not a party to this agreement, he can enforce it as an intended creditor third-party beneficiary.

By collecting from subsequent assignees, a landlord does not waive the right to collect rent from an assignor who is obligated to pay it. **B** is therefore incorrect. **C** is incorrect because the landlord was a third-party beneficiary of the contract between the store owner and the tenant and can therefore enforce the promise made by the store owner. Because the store owner agreed to personally assume the obligations of the lease, he was obligated to pay all sums due under it. Since the obligation to pay rent under a lease does not depend on whether the lessee is in possession of the premises, the store owner is liable for all rent that accrued throughout the duration of the lease whether he was in possession of the premises or not. **D** is therefore incorrect.

131.  **C**    If the homeowner's easement preexisted the landowner's grant, it could not be said that the Church of the Lord permitted a use other than for church purposes since it had no power to do otherwise. Since the landowner's right was to become possessory only if the church permitted use other than for church purposes, this argument might defeat the landowner's claim. While it is not certain that a court would come to this conclusion, **C** is the only argument listed that might support the church's position.

     **A** is incorrect because if the church permitted use of the property for other than church purposes, thus violating the limitation contained in the grant, then the interest of the Church of the Lord would terminate, even though there may have been sound motivation for its conduct. It may be true that the language of the deed created a fee simple determinable. **B** is incorrect, however, because this conclusion would result in the termination of the Church of the Lord's interest. Although the landowner's interest under the deed will not necessarily vest within the period prescribed by the Rule Against Perpetuities, **D** is incorrect because the Rule Against Perpetuities does not apply to a future interest of the grantor.

132.  **D**    One who assumes an existing mortgage when purchasing realty personally undertakes to pay the note that the mortgage secures and is thus personally liable for payments on the note. Subsequent sales of the realty, even to other purchasers who "assume" the mortgage, do not relieve prior obligors of personal obligations that they agreed to assume. Since the homeowner promised to pay (by executing the initial note), she continues to be personally liable. Since the first and second buyer promised to pay (by assuming the mortgage), they continue to be personally liable.

     **A**, **B**, and **C** are therefore incorrect.

133.  **C**    Although the most common forms of description involve reference to metes and bounds, artificial and natural markers, government survey markers, or property address, any method of description is sufficient if it establishes the identity of the realty conveyed with reasonable clarity. Since it is a famous piece of property, the description appears to identify the realty conveyed with reasonable clarity.

     **A**, **B**, and **D** are therefore incorrect.

134.  **B**    An easement appurtenant is an easement benefiting a particular dominant estate. The original deed created an easement appurtenant because the beach rights were clearly intended to benefit house purchasers based on their ownership of realty near the beach. Easements appurtenant are freely alienable and usually transferred with a conveyance of the dominant estate. Importantly, both the benefit and burden of an easement appurtenant pass when property is transferred. Here, the benefit passed when the man sold the woman the house, and the burden passed when the development company sold the golf course the beach.

**A** is incorrect because both the man's and the woman's use of the beach was by permission. **C** is incorrect because it does not matter whether the current owner of the beach created the original deed. **D** is incorrect because the deed did not have to specifically state that the beach rights were transferable.

135.  **C**    Under the existing reasonable use doctrine, when it is necessary to determine which riparian owner is entitled to water that is in limited supply, the courts consider many factors. Most important, however, is the use to which each owner puts the water. Although agricultural use is considered "higher" than most other uses, domestic or household use is universally acknowledged to be the "highest" use of all, entitling it to priority over all other uses. Since the choice to be made is between the landowner's agricultural use and the homeowner's household use, the homeowner's rights will prevail.

A is incorrect because upstream owners do not ordinarily have greater rights than downstream owners. **B** is incorrect because household use is a higher use than agricultural use. **D** is incorrect because with the retreat from the natural flow doctrine, downstream owners do not have greater rights than upstream owners.

136.  **C**    Ordinarily, if a covenant would have been enforceable as between the covenanting parties, it is enforceable by and against their successors if it runs with the land. A covenant is said to run with the land if the covenanting parties intended that it would bind their successors, if the covenant touches and concerns the land involved, and if the necessary privity exists between the covenanting parties and between the parties by and against whom enforcement is sought. The language of the covenant, "for themselves, their heirs, successors, and assigns," is the language traditionally used to indicate that the parties intended that their successors be bound. Here, the covenant touches and concerns the land. The necessary privity existed between the farmer and the first buyer because they were grantor and grantee. The necessary privity exists between the farmer and the second buyer because the second buyer succeeded to the first buyer's interest. For these reasons, the covenant contained in the farmer's deed to the first buyer runs with the land, thus binding the second buyer. Although covenants running with the land are usually enforceable only at law (*i.e.*, by a judgment for damages), they may be enforceable as equitable servitudes (*i.e.*, by injunction) if money damages would not be an adequate remedy. Since it was the farmer's intention to create a residential community, the presence of a gas station would probably interfere with the residential character of the community and money damages would not prevent this from happening, the remedy at law is probably not adequate and the covenant is probably enforceable by injunction as an equitable servitude.

This is true whether or not the farmer succeeds in selling the rest of the subdivision. Some cases hold that when passage of time and change of circumstances make restrictive covenants fail of their initial purpose, they may cease to be of effect. Perhaps this could eventually lead a court to find that the restriction, obviously designed to protect the residential nature of the subdivision, is unenforceable because the neighborhood is not really residential in nature. **A** is incorrect, however, because six months is not a sufficiently long period of time to justify such a conclusion. Equitable servitudes may be enforced against successors to the covenantor even though they did not agree to be bound by them. This is particularly so where recording of the deed gives those successors constructive notice of the existence of the restriction. **B** is therefore incorrect. If the covenant runs with the land, it is enforceable against the second buyer whether or not his violation of it will result in actual damage. If the covenant does not run with the land, it is not enforceable against the second buyer, even if its violation would result in actual damage. For this reason, **D** is incorrect.

137.   **A**   An assignment occurs when the tenant transfers to a third person all his or her rights, title, and interest in the leased premises. An assignee comes into privity of estate with the landlord. Importantly, if rent is not paid, the landlord may sue the assignee so long as the assignee remains on the premises. However, the landlord may not sue the assignee after the assignee has transferred the premises to a third party unless the assignee has assumed the duty to pay rent. Here, the third lessee did not agree to be personally liable for all obligations under the lease, and he assigned the balance of the lease to the fourth lessee and no longer remained in possession.

**B**, **C**, and **D** are therefore incorrect.

138.   **A**   A tenant's obligation to pay rent is not terminated if the tenant chooses to vacate the premises before the expiration of the lease term unless the landlord re-lets the premises on the tenant's account. However, a landlord is not required to do so. Consequently, since the property remained vacant, the woman still owes three months rent.

**B** and **D** are incorrect because the lease called for payment in money ("$1,000 per month") and the lessor would not be required to accept payment in any other form. No matter how the garage is valued, the landlord would not be obligated to accept it in lieu of money. **C** is incorrect because conveyance of land to a buyer does not relieve a tenant of the obligation to pay rent. Normally, the grantor of leased property assigns the grantee the right to receive the rents. However, if this right is not passed to the grantee, the tenant must keep paying rent to the original lessor. Consequently, the change in ownership does not change the woman's obligation to pay rent to someone (making **A** the best answer).

139.   **A**   Marketable title is title that a well-informed, reasonably prudent buyer would be willing to accept. Because a reasonably prudent buyer would not want to buy a lawsuit, any doubt about the title held by the landowner would make the title unmarketable. Here, the man's possible adverse possession claim puts the landowner's title in doubt. Therefore, since the contract required the landowner to deliver marketable title, the landlord would be in breach. Therefore, **D** is incorrect.

**B** is incorrect because the issue is the possible adverse possession claim, not any recording statute. **C** is incorrect because an insurance policy would only protect against economic losses cause by the landowner's failure to deliver good title. Importantly, it would not make the title marketable.

140.   C   Under the Rule Against Perpetuities, no interest is good unless it must vest, if at all, during a period measured by a life or lives in being plus 21 years. Since liquor might be sold on the premises after the expiration of this period, it is possible that the interest of the Foundation for Heart Diseases would vest beyond the period of perpetuities. For this reason, it received no valid interest.

The future interest of a charity is not subject to the Rule Against Perpetuities if it follows the estate of another charity. Otherwise, the Rule Against Perpetuities applies as it would to any other grantee. **A** is incorrect because there is no indication that the friend is a charity. **B** is incorrect because only a grantor can hold a right of reentry. An executory interest is a future interest that follows an estate that is not certain to terminate. **D** is incorrect because the interest of the Foundation for Heart Diseases is void as explained above.

141.   C   The contract provided for the sale of "all the realty." Realty is generally defined as land or anything permanently attached to the land or non-moveable property. A fixture is a chattel that has become part of the realty. In deciding whether a chattel is a fixture that has become part of the realty, courts usually look to the intention of the parties. Here, both the artist and the landowner never considered the machine part of the property, so **C** is the best answer. Therefore, **A** is incorrect.

**B** is incorrect because although courts consider the movability of a chattel when considering whether it is a fixture, courts usually make a determination based on party intent. Although the size of the machine likely made it hard to move, it wasn't necessarily immovable. **D** is incorrect because the determination of whether something is a fixture is not based solely on whether it is attached to the realty.

142.   C   Ordinarily, a co-tenant has a right to occupy and possess the premises without being required to account to other co-tenants for rent. A co-tenant who has *ousted* another co-tenant or prevented him or her from occupying the premises may be required to account for profits and the reasonable value of rent, however.

**A** contains a familiar phrase, but it is not related in any way to the rights and obligations that arise from co-tenancy. **B** is incorrect because a co-tenant is not obligated to sell his or her interest, and no new obligations arise from his or her failure to do so. The construction of permanent buildings on the land may increase the value of the interests of other co-tenants but does not obligate the co-tenant who builds them to account for rent. **D** is therefore incorrect.

143.   D   Under the doctrine of estoppel by deed, one who conveys realty in which he or she has no interest is estopped from denying the validity of the conveyance if he or she then acquires the realty. Here, although the farmer did not own the land at the time of the purported sale to the builder, the fact that he later acquired the land through the developer's reconveyance means he is now estopped from denying the sale to the builder. Therefore, **A** is incorrect.

**B** is incorrect because compliance or non-compliance with recording statutes does not relate to a grantee's rights against the grantor. Here, the builder is the grantee and the farmer is the grantor. **C** is incorrect because fraud alone is not sufficient to result in a ruling that title has passed.

144.   **A**   A person acquires title to land by adverse possession if he or she possesses the land with use that is open, notorious, hostile, and continuous for the statutory period. A temporary absence does not break the adverse possessor's continuity of possession if it is consistent with the adverse possessor's claim. However, if the absence is inconsistent with the adverse possessor's claim, it breaks continuity of possession. Here, the landowner "forcing" the man to move is clearly inconsistent with his claim. Consequently, even though he was only gone for a month, the man's period of possession was broken and he has only had continuity of possession for 16 years.

B is incorrect. Adverse possession requires that the adverse possessor's use be hostile. Consequently, the landowner's failure to give permission to the man would actually help the man's adverse possession claim. **C** is incorrect because there is no requirement that removal be by court order. **D** is incorrect because even temporary removals can break continuity of possession if they are inconsistent with the adverse possessor's use.

# QUESTIONS
# TORTS

# TORTS
# TABLE OF CONTENTS
### Numbers refer to Question Numbers

# TORTS QUESTIONS

1. The manufacturer made a product that was sold over the counter for the treatment of dandruff and dry scalp conditions. A doctor purchased a bottle at a drugstore. A statement on the label read, "This product will not harm normal scalp or hair." The doctor used the product as directed. Because of a rare scalp condition making him allergic to one of the ingredients, the product irritated his scalp, causing him much pain and discomfort. In an action for negligence by the doctor against the manufacturer, which of the following additional facts or inferences, if it was the only one true, would be most effective in the manufacturer's defense?

   (A) The doctor did not read the statement on the label.

   (B) The reasonable person in the manufacturer's position would not have foreseen that the product would injure persons with the doctor's allergy.

   (C) The product was manufactured for the manufacturer by another company.

   (D) The manufacturer was unaware that an allergy existed like that suffered by the doctor.

2. The defendant lived in a neighborhood in which the incidence of violent crime had been increasing. The plaintiff and the defendant were having tea together in the defendant's kitchen when there was a knock at the door of the defendant's home. Although the door was equipped with a peephole that would have enabled the defendant to see who was outside before opening, the defendant opened the door without looking. As soon as the door was opened, an armed robber entered with a gun. The robber struck the plaintiff several times with the barrel of his pistol before robbing her of her money and leaving. The plaintiff subsequently asserted a negligence claim against the defendant for injuries resulting from the attack, alleging that it was negligent for the defendant to open the door without looking to see who was there.

   Which of the following additional facts, if it was the only one true, would be most helpful to the plaintiff's claim against the defendant?

   (A) The defendant was aware of the high incidence of crime in the neighborhood.

   (B) The plaintiff was aware of the high incidence of crime in the neighborhood.

   (C) The defendant had invited the plaintiff for tea because she hoped to sell the plaintiff her used living room furniture.

   (D) One of the defendant's neighbors had been robbed and attacked by the robber in a similar manner the previous day.

3. A farmer advertised his farm for sale. A developer had been secretly advised by a friend in the state highway department that a major highway would soon be built adjacent to the farmer's land. Knowing that this would increase the value of the property, the developer contacted the farmer and offered to purchase the farm. The developer said that she would be willing to pay the fair market value as determined by any licensed real estate appraiser selected by the farmer. The farmer hired a licensed real estate appraiser who determined the fair market value to be $400,000. The developer purchased the land, paying that price. Under state law, the developer was required to tell the farmer about the new road, but she failed to do so.

   Three weeks after the closing of title, the state announced plans to build a highway adjacent to the land. This announcement increased the value of the land to $4,000,000. If the farmer institutes an action for misrepresentation against the developer, the court should find for

(A) the developer, because the farmer knew her to be a real estate investor.

(B) the developer, because she allowed the farmer's appraiser to determine the fair market value of the land.

(C) the farmer, because the developer's failure to disclose the coming of the highway was a breach of a fiduciary obligation.

(D) the farmer, because the developer had an obligation to disclose that the state would be building a highway adjacent to the land.

4. A woman was injured when a robber shot her with a pistol manufactured by the gun maker. She asserted a claim against the gun maker, alleging that the pistol with which she had been shot was meant to be sold for a price under $50. Which of the following arguments is most likely to lead to a judgment for the woman?

(A) The gun maker is vicariously liable for battery, since it was foreseeable that a purchaser of the pistol would shoot another person with it.

(B) The gun maker breached an implied warranty that the gun was merchantable, since a pistol that is meant to be sold for under $50 is unfit for ordinary use.

(C) The gun maker is liable for negligence, since the criminal law is designed to protect persons like the woman from becoming the victims of robbers.

(D) The gun maker is liable for negligence, since the low selling price of the pistol made it foreseeable that it would be used in connection with a crime.

5. A man was already intoxicated when he entered the bartender's tavern. At first, the bartender refused to serve him any more alcohol. The man insisted, however, and at his insistence, the bartender served him more drinks.

When the man left the bar, he was unable to start his car. He asked a dentist, who was driving by, to assist him. The dentist, who realized that the man was drunk, determined that the man's battery was weak and started the man's car by connecting a cable to her own battery. Later, while driving, the man struck a pedestrian who was walking across the street.

The pedestrian asserted a claim for his personal injuries against the dentist. Which one of the following facts or inferences, if it was the only one true, would provide the dentist with the most effective defense?

(A) The state had a statute making a barkeeper liable for damage done by a person who purchased alcohol from the barkeeper after already being intoxicated.

(B) The dentist was in the business of rendering road service to motorists having trouble with their cars.

(C) The man drove 200 miles before striking the pedestrian.

(D) The man would not have struck the pedestrian if he had not been intoxicated.

6. The driver was driving at an unreasonably fast rate of speed when, as a result, he collided with a hunter's car that was standing unattended against the curb. The impact caused a loaded rifle that the hunter had left in the back seat of the car to fire. The bullet went through the car window and traveled four blocks before striking a painter, who was leaving a paint factory after work. Although the painter had lost the sight in his left eye in an accident that occurred when he was a child, he was employed by the paint factory as a color coordinator. As a result of his being struck by the bullet from the hunter's rifle, the painter lost the sight in his right eye. This rendered him totally blind, causing him to lose his job. The painter subsequently asserted a negligence claim against the driver, alleging permanent loss of earning capacity in addition to other items of damage.

Which of the following is the driver's most effective argument in defense against the painter's claim for permanent loss of earning capacity?

(A) The painter was a super-sensitive plaintiff, since he was already blind in one eye.

(B) The hunter acted unreasonably by leaving a loaded rifle in the back seat of his car.

(C) The painter was outside the foreseeable zone of danger.

(D) The reasonable person would not have expected that the driver's conduct would cause any person to be rendered blind.

7. A burglar broke into the grocer's grocery store in the middle of the night. After stealing all the money that was in the cash register, she blew open the door of the safe with nitroglycerin and stole its contents as well. Then, as she was leaving, she stole a six-pack of beer. Because of poor quality control at the brewery, the beer contained a toxic ingredient. Later that night, the burglar drank the beer and was made seriously ill by the toxic ingredient that it contained. In an action by the burglar against the brewery, the court will most likely find for

(A) the burglar, because her injury was proximately caused by the negligence of the brewery.

(B) the burglar, since the brewery breached an express warranty.

(C) the brewery, since the burglar does not come into court with "clean hands."

(D) the brewery, because the burglar's theft of the beer will be regarded as unforeseeable.

8. A movie studio was filming part of a motion picture at a large residential apartment building with the permission of the building owner. To avoid interference by curious onlookers, the movie studio's security agents set up a command post in the lobby of the building. No persons were allowed to enter the building without identifying themselves and explaining their reasons for being there. A fisherman, who lived in an apartment in the building, was returning from a fishing trip late one night. Unaware of the movie studio's activities, he was stopped by the movie studio employees as he attempted to enter. Because he was not carrying identification, the fisherman was unable to establish his identity. For this reason, the employees refused to allow him to enter. After trying unsuccessfully to convince them that he lived there, the fisherman stayed with his sister, who lived a block away. The following morning, he contacted the building owner, who spoke to the movie studio officials and arranged to have them allow the fisherman to enter.

If the fisherman asserts a claim against the movie studio for false imprisonment, which of the following would be the movie studio's most effective argument in defense?

(A) The movie studio employees did not know that the fisherman was entitled to enter the building.

(B) The conduct of the movie studio employees was not unreasonable.

(C) The fisherman was not imprisoned.

(D) The fisherman sustained no damage as a result of the conduct of the movie studio employees.

9. A handyman, who owned an appliance repair shop, was at a cocktail party when he saw one of his competitors. When the handyman suggested that they work together, the competitor responded, "I wouldn't go into business with you because you're the most incompetent person I've ever known." A customer of the handyman's overheard the conversation. As a result, the following day the customer cancelled a contract that he had with the handyman.

If the handyman asserts a claim against the competitor for defamation, the handyman will be successful if .

(A) the competitor knew or should have known that the statement was defamatory when he made it.

(B) the competitor knew or should have known that the statement was false when he made it.

(C) the competitor knew or should have known that the statement would be overheard when he made it.

(D) the competitor knew or should have known that harm would result from the statement.

10. A farmer agreed to deliver all of her wheat to a bread company to be used by that company in the production of bread for sale to the general public. While harvesting the crop, she realized that a blade on her harvesting machine was broken and that fine slivers of metal were becoming mixed with the wheat. She said nothing about this when she delivered the wheat to the bread company since she knew that the bread company ordinarily cleaned its wheat before using it. The harvesting machine had been manufactured and sold by a tractor company.

The bread company used the wheat that it purchased from the farmer to manufacture a loaf of bread that it sold to a deli owner who operated a sandwich shop. The deli owner used the bread to make a sandwich. Because the bread contained slivers of the blade from the farmer's harvesting machine, a bike messenger lacerated the lining of his throat when he swallowed a bite of the sandwich.

Which of the following additional facts or inferences, if it was the only one true, would be most helpful to the farmer in defense against an action brought by the bike messenger on a theory of strict liability in tort?

(A) If the bread company acted reasonably, the slivers of metal would have been removed from the wheat before it was baked into bread.

(B) The sandwich that contained the slivers of metal had been purchased by one of the bike messenger's coworkers, who gave it to the bike messenger after changing his mind about eating it.

(C) The bread company made substantial changes to the wheat.

(D) The blade on the farmer's harvesting machine was defective when she purchased it from the tractor company.

11. The plaintiff and the defendant were drinking at the same bar when the plaintiff began insulting the defendant by calling him names that were ethnically offensive. When they started to argue with each other, the bartender asked them both to leave. The plaintiff got into his car and drove away. Angry, the defendant began chasing him in his own car. When he caught up with the plaintiff, the defendant began passing the plaintiff's car on the left. As he did so, he swerved his car toward the plaintiff's for the purpose of frightening the plaintiff. The plaintiff did not know that the car swerving toward him was the defendant's, but he became frightened that it would hit him and steered away from it, striking a fire hydrant and sustaining injury.

If the plaintiff institutes an action against the defendant, a court should hold the defendant liable for

(A) battery only.

(B) assault only.

(C) both battery and assault.

(D) neither battery nor assault.

12. The buyer was interested in purchasing the seller's house. Because the buyer knew that some of the houses in the area were infested with termites, he asked the seller whether there were any termites in his house. The seller said that there were none, believing this statement to be true. The buyer purchased the house from the seller and moved into

it. Three months later, the buyer discovered that the framework of the house had been damaged by termites, and that the termites had been damaging the framework for several years. He subsequently asserted a claim against the seller on a theory of negligent misrepresentation.

Which of the following is the seller's most effective argument in defense against the buyer's claim?

(A) The seller did not know that there were termites in the house.

(B) The seller had no duty to tell the buyer whether there were termites in the house.

(C) The seller's statement that there were no termites in the house was an expression of opinion.

(D) The seller's belief that there were no termites in the house was reasonable.

13. The plaintiff purchased a box labeled "Generic Breakfast Cereal" from a supermarket. While he was eating it, he broke a tooth on a stone that the product contained. The product sold by the supermarket and labeled "Generic Breakfast Cereal" is furnished by three different manufacturers. Each sells an approximately equal quantity to the supermarket. In addition, all package their product in identical wrappers, so that it is impossible to tell which of them furnished any given box of breakfast cereal. Although the companies compete with each other, at the supermarket's request, they worked together to design the product wrapper.

If the plaintiff is successful in an action for damages against the supermarket, it will probably be because

(A) the supermarket and manufacturers were involved in a concerted action in the manufacture and marketing of the product.

(B) the supermarket and manufacturers established standards on an industry-wide basis, which standards made identification of the product's manufacturer impossible.

(C) the negligence of any of the three manufacturers resulted in harm to the plaintiff under circumstances such that it was impossible to tell which of them caused the harm, and the supermarket is vicariously liable for that negligence.

(D) any of the three manufacturers manufactured a defective product, and the supermarket sold that product while it was in a defective condition.

14. A young girl planned to spend an entire weekend camping alone in the woods. A kidnapper, who knew about the girl's plan, phoned the girl's mother the day after the girl left home. The kidnapper said, "We have your daughter. We've already beaten her up once, just to hear her scream. Next time, we might kill her." The kidnapper instructed the girl's mother to deliver a cash ransom to a specified location within one hour. Since there was no way to locate the girl's campsite in the woods, the girl's mother could not find out whether the kidnapper was telling the truth. Horrified that her daughter might be beaten and injured or killed, she delivered the ransom as instructed. She remained in a hysterical state until the girl returned from her camping trip and the girl's mother realized that the ransom demand had been a hoax. The girl's mother, who already suffered from a heart ailment, had a heart attack the day after the girl's return.

If the girl's mother asserts a claim against the kidnapper for assault, the court should find for

(A) the girl's mother, because the kidnapper was aware that his conduct would frighten her.

(B) the girl's mother, because the court will transfer the kidnapper's intent.

(C) the kidnapper, because the girl's mother did not perceive injury being inflicted upon the girl.

(D) the kidnapper, because the girl's mother had no reason to expect to be touched by the kidnapper.

15. An actor owned a leopard, which the actor had trained and which had appeared with him in motion pictures. The leopard had always been tame and gentle, even when young. When the actor retired, the leopard was old, almost blind, somewhat slow-moving, and the size of a large dog. The actor brought the animal to live with him, keeping it in the fenced yard alongside his house. A young girl delivered newspapers to the actor. One day, she came to the actor's home to collect for the past week's deliveries. Since she knew the leopard, the girl opened the gate and called the animal so that she could pet him. The leopard bounded toward the place from which the sound had come, but because he was almost blind, he bumped into the girl. The girl fell to the ground, fracturing her ankle.

If the girl asserts a claim against the actor on a theory of strict liability, the court should find for

(A) the actor, because the injury did not result from a trait that made it dangerous to keep a leopard.

(B) the actor, because the leopard was not a wild animal.

(C) the girl, because it was unreasonable for the actor to keep the leopard in his yard.

(D) the girl, because the actor should have anticipated that a child would attempt to pet the leopard.

16. While the plaintiff was visiting her daughter, the two of them decided to go swimming at a nearby public pool. Since she had not brought a bathing suit along on her visit, the plaintiff went to a department store to purchase one. While looking at the suits on the bargain counter, she found one that had been manufactured by the defendant. The package that contained it bore a label that read, "Disposable Bathing Suit. This garment is made completely from recycled paper. Although it is strong enough to be worn several times and is even washable, it's inexpensive enough to be thrown away after one use. Buy several, and take them with you on trips to the beach." The plaintiff bought the bathing suit and wore it at the public swimming pool. After swimming for a few minutes, the wet paper bathing suit suddenly dissolved and fell from her in shreds, leaving her completely naked.

If the plaintiff asserts a claim against the defendant for damages resulting from her embarrassment, the defendant's best argument in defense is that

(A) the defendant made no representations to the plaintiff.

(B) the plaintiff sustained no physical injury or symptoms.

(C) the plaintiff purchased the suit from the department store.

(D) the defendant acted reasonably in manufacturing and labeling the bathing suit.

17. A mother needed butter for the cookies that she was baking, so she asked her seven-year-old son to go to the store. Because traffic was sometimes heavy, the boy was not usually permitted to ride his bicycle on the roadway there. The mother needed the butter right away, however, so she told him that he could ride in the roadway if he was sure to stay on the left side. A driver was driving his car when he was momentarily blinded by the sun. He did not see the boy, who was riding toward him in the roadway, and struck him, causing the boy to sustain serious injuries.

The boy subsequently asserted a claim for negligence against the driver. The driver raised a defense based on contributory negligence. In a jurisdiction that applies the all-or-nothing rule of contributory negligence, the driver's defense will succeed only if

(A) the boy acted unreasonably.

(B) the mother acted unreasonably.

(C) either the mother or the boy acted unreasonably.

(D) both the mother and the boy acted unreasonably.

18. A company manufactured a leash for training dogs. The leash had been submitted to all reasonable tests and inspections before being marketed. A professional dog trainer was working with a dog in her unfenced front yard and was using a brand new leash. The dog was of average size and strength. A walker was walking past the yard when the dog began to snarl and lunge at him. When the trainer yanked on the leash, it suddenly broke, freeing the dog. The dog sprang forward, biting the walker.

If the walker asserts a claim against the company alleging that the leash used by the trainer was defective, the court should find for

(A) the company, because the walker was not a purchaser or consumer of the product.

(B) the company, because the leash had been submitted to all reasonable tests and inspections before being marketed.

(C) the walker, because the dog was a dog of average size and strength.

(D) the walker, because it was foreseeable that the leash would eventually weaken and break when used as it was meant to be used.

19. On a boy's first birthday, his aunt bought him a rag doll as a gift. The toy was made of plush material, with buttons sewn on for eyes. While playing with the toy, the boy pulled one of the buttons off, put it in his mouth, and choked to death on it. The boy's father commenced an action against the aunt under the state's wrongful death statute.

If the father is successful in his action against the aunt, it will probably be because

(A) the aunt was negligent in giving the rag doll to the boy.

(B) the rag doll was unfit for ordinary use.

(C) the rag doll was defective when the aunt gave it to the boy.

(D) the rag doll was unreasonably dangerous when the aunt gave it to the boy.

20. Because the plaintiff had a headache, he took two headache tablets from a bottle that had been purchased by his wife at the grocery store. The tablets had been manufactured by the company, which sold them to the grocery store in sealed bottles for resale. Because of a toxic ingredient that the tablets contained, the plaintiff became ill as a result of taking them.

If the plaintiff asserts a claim based on negligence against the grocery store for his damages, the court should find for

(A) the plaintiff, because the company's negligence is imputed to the grocery store.

(B) the plaintiff, because a retailer has an absolute duty to provide safe products.

(C) the grocery store, because the bottle containing the tablets was sealed when the grocery store received it.

(D) the grocery store, because the tablets had been purchased by the plaintiff's wife.

21. A driver was looking for an address as he drove down the street and was not watching the road in front of him. As a result, he did not see the pedestrian crossing the street

in front of him and struck her with his car, knocking her down. The driver immediately got out of his car to help the pedestrian. When he saw that she was unconscious, he became afraid to move her, and he left her in the roadway while he ran to a nearby phone. While the driver was gone, a taxi driver drove down the same street. Because he was intoxicated by the drug PCP, the taxi driver did not see the pedestrian in the roadway and drove over her, fracturing her leg.

If the pedestrian brings an action against the taxi driver for damages resulting from her fractured leg, the taxi driver's liability will most probably turn on whether it was foreseeable that

(A) the driver would drive negligently and would leave the pedestrian lying in the roadway after striking her.

(B) a person struck by an automobile would be involved in a second accident within a short period of time.

(C) a person would be in the roadway.

(D) the taxi driver would drive while intoxicated by the drug PCP.

22. The power company operated a nuclear power plant on the seashore just outside the city and sold electricity generated by its operations to city residents. To cool its equipment, the power company drew water from the ocean and piped it through portions of its plant. Because this operation made the water highly radioactive, the power company stored used water in a series of large concrete holding ponds. The water stored in this fashion was subjected to a series of procedures designed to "neutralize" it by removing the radioactivity before it was returned to the ocean. Because of an earthquake, one of the concrete holding ponds cracked, permitting several million gallons of neutralized water to escape. Although the escaping water was not radioactive, it caused substantial damage to the fields of a farmer as it passed over them.

If the farmer asserts a claim against the power company for damage to his realty, the court should find for

(A) the farmer, because operating a nuclear power plant is an abnormally dangerous activity.

(B) the farmer, because water is a substance that is likely to do great harm if it should escape from captivity.

(C) the farmer, because it was unreasonable to operate a nuclear power plant in an area where an earthquake could occur.

(D) the power company, because the damage resulted from an Act of God.

23. The company was a manufacturer of explosives. Its warehouse, which contained large quantities of explosives, was located a short distance from the town. A group of political extremists were planning to set off a series of bombs in public places in the town. Several members broke into the company's warehouse for the purpose of stealing explosives to use in making bombs. Their entry set off an alarm that brought the police. Rather than surrender to the police, the terrorists committed suicide by detonating the explosives that they had stolen. The blast caused the entire warehouse to explode. A house located a half mile away was damaged by the explosion.

If the homeowner asserts a claim for damages against the company on the ground that storing explosives was an abnormally dangerous activity, which of the following would be the company's most effective argument in defense?

(A) The explosion did not result from unreasonable conduct by the company.

(B) The damage did not result from a physical invasion of the homeowner's realty by any tangible object in the control of the company.

(C) The conduct of the terrorists was an intervening cause of harm.

(D) It was not foreseeable that terrorists would deliberately detonate explosives in the warehouse.

24. The seller kept an antique hay wagon in front of her house as a yard ornament. On several occasions, she offered to sell the hay wagon to her neighbor, the buyer, for $500. Although the buyer admired it, he had always been unwilling to pay the seller's price. After reading a magazine article about the increasing popularity of farm antiques, the buyer concluded that the value of the seller's hay wagon was likely to increase, and that it would therefore be a good investment. One day he approached her, saying, "If you're still interested in selling that hay wagon, I'll pay $500." The seller was surprised that he had changed his mind, but did not ask him why because she was afraid that he would change it back again. Instead, she said, "I'll take your offer," and sold him the wagon. Two months later, an antique dealer who saw the wagon in the buyer's yard bought it from him for $2,000.

If the seller asserts a misrepresentation claim against the buyer, the court should find for

(A) the seller, because the buyer knew more about the value of antique hay wagons than the seller did.

(B) the seller, because the buyer purchased the hay wagon for the undisclosed purpose of profiting from his investment.

(C) the buyer, because he was not required to disclose his purpose in purchasing the hay wagon.

(D) the buyer, because the seller was initially satisfied with the price that the buyer paid her for the hay wagon.

25. A state statute provides that no person shall transport passengers for hire in an airplane unless that person shall be licensed as a commercial airplane pilot. A pilot owned a small private airplane but did not have a commercial pilot's license. A businessman offered the pilot $200 to fly him to a distant city in the pilot's plane. The pilot agreed, after informing the businessman that he did not have a commercial pilot's license as required by law. While they were flying over another city, the pilot realized that he had miscalculated the amount of fuel that he needed for the trip. As a result, he was forced to land at the other city's airport. After landing and while waiting to be refueled, the pilot's plane was struck by a plane that was being negligently operated by another pilot. The first pilot and the businessman were both injured in the collision. The jurisdiction applies the all-or-nothing rule of contributory negligence.

The businessman asserted a claim against the first pilot, alleging that the first pilot was negligent in miscalculating the quantity of fuel needed to make the trip. Which of the following arguments would be the first pilot's most effective argument in defense?

(A) The businessman assumed the risk, because he knew that the first pilot did not have a commercial pilot's license.

(B) The businessman was contributorily negligent in accepting a ride with the first pilot, whom he knew to be unlicensed.

(C) The first pilot's miscalculation was not a legal cause of the injury sustained by the businessman, because the first pilot's plane was safely on the ground when struck by the plane operated by the second pilot.

(D) The first pilot's miscalculation was not a factual cause of the injury sustained by the businessman, because the harm would not have occurred if the second pilot had not been negligent.

26. A manufacturer made a colorless alcohol used by physicians for cleaning the skin of patients before administering injections. Another of its products was a red liquid for cleaning glass microscope slides used in medical and research laboratories.

Because the slide cleaner contained a strong solvent that was damaging to human skin, the label normally affixed to bottles in which it was sold contained language advising users to wear rubber gloves while handling the product.

As a result of an oversight at the company's plant, skin cleaner labels were erroneously placed on several bottles of slide cleaner. One of the mislabeled bottles was delivered to a doctor's office. In giving an injection to a patient, the doctor used the slide cleaner, believing it to be the skin cleaner. As a result, the patient sustained damage to his skin.

In a negligence action by the patient against the manufacturer, if one of the following facts or inferences were true, which would provide the manufacturer with its strongest argument in defense?

(A) It was unforeseeable that a doctor with the doctor's training and experience would mistake the chemicals, since they were two different colors.

(B) If the doctor had been acting reasonably, she would have realized that the product that she was using was not the skin cleaner, since it was red instead of colorless.

(C) The doctor's failure to notice that the product that she was using was red, and therefore was not the skin cleaner, amounted to gross negligence.

(D) The doctor's conduct was an intervening cause of the patient's injury.

27. Which of the following persons is most likely to recover in an action against the manufacturer of a hypodermic needle?

(A) A doctor's child, who found the needle in the doctor's medical bag and was injured when a defect caused it to break while the child was playing with it.

(B) A doctor's patient, who was injured when a defect caused the needle to break while the doctor was injecting him with it.

(C) A dentist, who lost profits when she was unable to inject a patient with the needle because a defect caused it to break.

(D) A narcotics addict, who contracted hepatitis because the needle was infected with the microbe that caused that disease.

28. A crop duster sprayed insecticides onto growing crops from an airplane that she flew within 15 feet of the ground. In locating the fields of her customers, she used a map that the county published for that purpose and that identified every parcel of real estate in the area by a parcel number. A farmer hired the crop duster to spray his fields with insecticide. The farmer knew that his farm was identified on the county map as parcel 612, but by mistake he told the crop duster that it was parcel 621. As a result, the crop duster sprayed the farm that the county map identified as parcel 621. That farm belonged to a gardener, who had contracted to grow his crop without chemical insecticides and to sell it to an organic produce distributor. As a result of the crop duster's spraying, the gardener was unable to fulfill his contract and sustained serious economic losses.

If the gardener asserts a claim against the crop duster for damages resulting from trespass to land, the court should find for

(A) the gardener, because crop dusting is an abnormally dangerous activity.

(B) the gardener, because the crop duster intentionally flew through the airspace above his land.

(C) the crop duster, because she reasonably believed that the farm that she was spraying belonged to the farmer.

(D) the crop duster, because there was no damage to the gardener's land.

29. A state senator was chair of a committee looking into accusations of corruption in the governor's office. Because reports of committee agents were beginning to indicate that there was a sound basis for the accusations, the senator kept them locked in her office safe to prevent them from becoming public knowledge before the investigation could be completed. A reporter broke into the senator's office, picked the lock on her safe, and photographed the documents that it contained. The following day, realizing that the security of the documents had been compromised, the senator conducted a press conference in which she made their contents known. Before she had completed the conference, however, newspapers containing the reporter's story about the papers in the senator's safe were being sold.

   If the senator instituted an action against the reporter for invasion of privacy, the court should find for

   (A) the reporter, since the documents in the senator's safe were newsworthy.

   (B) the reporter, since he was protected by the First Amendment to the United States Constitution.

   (C) the reporter, since the senator made the documents a matter of public record at the press conference.

   (D) the senator, since the reporter entered her office without her permission and broke into her safe.

30. A boy, who was 11 years of age, was playing with the plaintiff, who was 10 years of age. While they were playing together, the boy offered to show the plaintiff his new air rifle. The air rifle was manufactured by a local company. The boy purchased it from the defendant with money that he earned by mowing the lawns of several of his neighbors. While demonstrating the air rifle to the plaintiff, the boy accidentally shot him with it, severely injuring the plaintiff's eye. The plaintiff subsequently asserted a negligence claim against the defendant.

   If the plaintiff is successful in his claim against the defendant, it will be because a jury finds that

   (A) any negligence by the company in the design of the air rifle should be imputed to the defendant.

   (B) the air rifle was defectively designed.

   (C) the air rifle was defectively manufactured.

   (D) it was unreasonable for the defendant to sell the air rifle to the boy.

31. A car dealer used a mechanic for all of his auto repairs. He used the mechanic because he was cheap, although the car dealer sometimes had to send cars back for repairs three or four times until the mechanic got it right. One of the car dealer's cars had a leaking carburetor, which the car dealer knew made it unsafe to drive. He had it repaired by the mechanic and then rented the car to the plaintiff. One hour later, while the plaintiff was driving the car, the carburetor began leaking again. As a result, the car exploded, injuring the plaintiff.

   If the plaintiff asserts a claim against the car dealer, the plaintiff's most effective argument in support of her claim would be that

   (A) the car dealer is vicariously liable for the negligence of his employee.

   (B) the duty to maintain a safe car was non-delegable.

   (C) the mechanic was an independent contractor.

   (D) it was unreasonable for the car dealer to hire the mechanic to repair the car.

32. Which statement most correctly completes the following sentence? A retailer owes its customers

(A)  no duty to inspect products furnished by reputable manufacturers.

(B)  a duty to inspect the packages of all products sold, but no duty to inspect the contents of those packages.

(C)  a duty to inspect only those products that are furnished by manufacturers whose products are not well known to the retailer.

(D)  a duty to make a reasonable inspection of all products that are sold by that retailer.

33.  After an employee's resignation, the employer wrote him a letter in which he said, "You were never any good as a mechanic, and in addition, you were the most dishonest employee this company ever had." These statements were false. The employee's mother, who lived with the employee and frequently opened his mail, read the letter as soon as it arrived. In an action by the employee against the employer for defamation, a court should find for

(A)  the employee, because the employer's statements were published to the employee's mother.

(B)  the employee, only if the employer had reason to know that someone other than the employee would open and read the letter.

(C)  the employer, because the statements contained in the letter were communicated only to the employee.

(D)  the employer, because of the employer's privilege.

34.  A pilot was injured when the helicopter that he was flying ran out of fuel and fell from the air. The day after the pilot purchased the helicopter, he noticed that the fuel gauge gave incorrect readings. He complained to an officer of the helicopter maker, who told him to have it fixed and to send the helicopter maker the bill. A week before the accident, the pilot hired an independent mechanic to repair the fuel

gauge. The mechanic worked on the gauge but failed to repair it properly. The day before the accident, the pilot's partner flew the helicopter, using most of the fuel in the tank. Although the pilot's partner noticed that the fuel gauge continued to indicate that the tank was full, he neither mentioned it to the pilot nor replaced the fuel in the tank. On the day of the accident, the fuel gauge indicated that the tank was full, although it was actually almost empty.

If the pilot wishes to assert a claim for damages on a theory of strict liability in tort, he is most likely to recover against

(A)  the helicopter maker only.

(B)  the helicopter maker and the pilot's partner only.

(C)  the helicopter maker and the mechanic only.

(D)  the helicopter maker, the pilot's partner, and the mechanic.

35.  A gravel pit owner was aware of the fact that neighborhood children used a steep slope on his realty for sledding during the snow season, and he feared that one of the children would be injured by sledding onto the public road adjacent to the property. Although he could have prevented this from happening by erecting a small fence at a cost of under $200, the gravel pit owner was unwilling to expend that sum. Instead, he posted a sign that read, "No Sledding, Keep Out." Three weeks later, an eight-year-old boy was sledding down the hill on the gravel pit owner's property when his sled coasted onto the adjacent public road. The boy sustained serious injuries when he was struck by a car.

If the boy asserts a negligence claim against the gravel pit owner, the court should find for

(A)  the boy, because danger invites rescue.

(B)  the boy, if the gravel pit owner's failure to erect a fence to prevent the accident was unreasonable.

(C) the gravel pit owner, because the car driver had the last clear chance to avoid injuring the boy.

(D) the gravel pit owner, if the car driver's conduct was an intervening cause of harm.

36. The seller knew that his car's engine was cracked. Because he wanted to sell the car, he filled the crack with putty and painted it so that the crack would not show. Then he brought the car to the buyer, a used car dealer, and offered to sell it for $1,000 cash. The buyer placed the car on a lift so that he could inspect it from underneath. He noticed the filled crack but thought that he would be able to resell the car in spite of it. The buyer offered $500, which the seller accepted. The next day, the buyer was showing the car to a customer when the crack caused the engine to explode, necessitating $500 in repairs and injuring the customer.

If the buyer institutes an action against the seller for misrepresentation, which of the following would be the seller's most effective argument in defense?

(A) The seller made no representation concerning the engine.

(B) The buyer did not rely on the seller's representations concerning the engine.

(C) The buyer was not justified in relying on the seller's representations concerning the engine.

(D) The buyer did not sustain damage.

37. A driver stepped on his brake pedal. Because the brakes were not working properly, he could not stop, and he continued into an intersection. A second driver saw the first driver go through the red light. Because the light was green in his favor, however, the second driver did not stop; he continued into the intersection, believing that he could avoid striking the first driver by steering around him. The two vehicles collided in the intersection. The jurisdiction has a statute that prohibits entering an intersection against a red traffic signal light and another statute that adopts the all-or-nothing rule of contributory negligence.

In an action by the second driver against the first driver, the court should find for

(A) the first driver, since the second driver had the last clear chance to avoid the accident.

(B) the first driver, because it was unreasonable for the second driver to enter the intersection when he did.

(C) the second driver, because the first driver's violation of statute was a substantial factor in producing the damage.

(D) the second driver, since the first driver's conduct was negligence per se.

38. A store owner wrote on a refrigerator "AS IS—$25." A customer bought the refrigerator. As she was loading it onto the customer's pickup truck, the store owner said, "I hope you know that this refrigerator doesn't work." The customer said that he did. When the customer got the refrigerator home, he plugged it in and received a severe electrical shock while attempting to open its door.

In an action by the customer against the store owner for damages resulting from his injury, the court will probably find for

(A) the customer, because it was unreasonable for the store owner to sell the refrigerator without warning him about the wiring defect.

(B) the customer, since the refrigerator was unfit for ordinary use.

(C) the store owner, since the customer purchased the refrigerator "AS IS."

(D) the store owner, because the customer had the "last clear chance" to avoid being injured.

39. The plaintiff was hunting on the defendant's land. The defendant told the plaintiff to leave, but the plaintiff refused to do so. The defendant then placed his hand on the plaintiff's chest and pushed him gently backward, repeating his demand that the plaintiff leave. The plaintiff shoved the defendant away from him and pointed his shotgun at the defendant. The defendant immediately drew a pistol and fired at the plaintiff, striking him in the arm and causing him to drop his shotgun.

If the plaintiff asserts a claim against the defendant for battery, the court should find for

(A) the defendant, because he fired at the plaintiff to defend his realty against a trespass.

(B) the defendant, because he fired at the plaintiff to defend himself against the plaintiff's threat with the shotgun.

(C) the plaintiff, because the defendant struck the first blow.

(D) the plaintiff, because the defendant did not use force against him until his entry onto the realty was complete.

40. A man kept a wildcat he had tamed as a pet. His neighbor was walking past the man's house when the wildcat tore through a window screen, jumped into the street, and attacked the neighbor, seriously injuring him. The neighbor subsequently asserted a claim against the man for his damages.

If the neighbor is successful in his claim against the man, it will probably be because

(A) the neighbor's damages resulted from the man's keeping a wild animal.

(B) it was foreseeable that the wildcat would do something unforeseeable.

(C) the thing speaks for itself (*res ipsa loquitur*).

(D) the man's keeping the wildcat amounted to a private nuisance.

41. A company manufactured a safety helmet in hopes of selling it to the military for general utility purposes, but it was unsuccessful in doing so. Instead, it sold the helmets to the general public. The helmets were packaged in boxes that showed pictures of three persons wearing the helmet: one riding a horse, one riding a motorcycle, and one doing construction work. A motorcyclist found a helmet that someone had discarded in its original box. He wore it the next day while riding his motorcycle and sustained a severe head injury when he fell.

The motorcyclist asserted a claim against the company for his injuries in a jurisdiction that has adopted a rule of "pure comparative negligence." At the trial, the motorcyclist proved that the helmet was not suitable for use as a motorcycle helmet, and that if it had been, he would not have sustained injury.

The court should find for

(A) the company, because the motorcyclist found the helmet.

(B) the company, if the helmets were not designed or intended for use as motorcycle helmets.

(C) the motorcyclist, unless his fall from the motorcycle resulted from his own unreasonable conduct.

(D) the motorcyclist, because the box in which the helmet was sold contained a picture of a person wearing the helmet while riding a motorcycle.

42. When the owner brought his car to the mechanic's shop for repairs, the mechanic told him that he would test-drive the car after repairing it. While the mechanic was test-driving the car, he struck a pedestrian. A statute in the jurisdiction provides that "The owner of any motor vehicle operated on the roads of this state shall be vicariously liable for the negligence of any person operating said motor vehicle with said owner's permission." The pedestrian instituted an action

against the owner and the mechanic and obtained a judgment against both of them for $10,000.

If the owner pays the judgment in full, which of the following is correct regarding the owner's rights against the mechanic?

(A) The owner may recover $10,000 from the mechanic.

(B) The owner may recover $5,000 from the mechanic.

(C) The owner may recover $7,500 from the mechanic.

(D) The owner may not recover from the mechanic.

43. A breeder of exotic birds preferred to mix feed for his birds according to his own formula instead of using commercially available mixes. For this purpose, he purchased a sealed 50-pound package of seeds from the dealer, who was in the business of selling supplies for bird and livestock breeders. The dealer had bought the sealed package from the wholesaler, a wholesaler of seed and grain. Because of negligence at the wholesaler's plant, the seeds in the package were poisonous. The breeder fed the seeds to several of his birds, which died as a result.

If the breeder brings an action in strict liability against the wholesaler for the value of the birds that died, a court is most likely to find for

(A) the breeder, because the poisonous nature of the seeds was a defect.

(B) the breeder, because it was reasonable for the dealer to resell the seeds without inspection.

(C) the wholesaler, since the wholesaler had no contractual relationship with the breeder.

(D) the wholesaler, because the breeder will be unable to recover damages from the dealer.

44. Although he had been warned that swimming within one hour after eating was likely to cause a cramp, a swimmer went swimming in the lake immediately after lunch. He had been swimming for a few minutes when he developed severe cramps. Finding himself unable to swim any further, he began calling for help. The swimmer's cries attracted the attention of a rescuer, who happened to be walking near the lake. The rescuer jumped into the water, swam to the swimmer's side, and, grabbing the swimmer by the hair, towed him to safety. In getting out of the lake, however, the rescuer cut his leg on a fragment of glass that was embedded in the lake bottom.

If the rescuer asserts an action against the swimmer for personal injuries, the court should find for

(A) the rescuer, because it was negligent for the swimmer to swim so soon after eating.

(B) the rescuer, because his injury occurred while he was attempting to rescue the swimmer.

(C) the swimmer, because danger invites rescue.

(D) the swimmer, because the glass fragment is an intervening cause of the rescuer's injury.

45. The company was a manufacturer of computer hardware. The defendant was a retailer who purchased products from the company. At an industrial convention, the defendant told the company that he heard that their mutual friend, the plaintiff, was about to go into personal bankruptcy. The company did not believe what the defendant was telling him and resolved to mention it to the plaintiff as soon as the opportunity presented itself. The following day, the plaintiff called the company to discuss computer hardware. The company told the plaintiff what the defendant had said at the party. The plaintiff laughed, assured the company that he was in excellent

financial condition, and they both laughed at the rumor.

If the plaintiff asserts a defamation claim against the defendant, which of the following would be the defendant's most effective argument in defense?

(A) The plaintiff did not experience mental suffering.

(B) The plaintiff did not sustain damage to his reputation as a result of the statement.

(C) The defendant was only repeating what he had heard.

(D) The defendant did not publish any statement about the plaintiff.

46. The plaintiff was employed as an insulation installer by various builders and general contractors for a period of 35 years. During that time, he was repeatedly exposed to an insulating material manufactured by the defendant. Last year, it was discovered for the first time that exposure to the material is a cause of cancer and that the plaintiff had contracted cancer as a result of his contact with the product.

In a jurisdiction that applies the all-or-nothing rule of contributory negligence, if the plaintiff asserts a negligence claim against the defendant for damages resulting from the plaintiff's exposure to the material, the defendant's most effective defense would be based on the argument that

(A) the plaintiff assumed the risk.

(B) the defendant did not know that contact with the material would result in cancer.

(C) the reasonable person in the defendant's situation would not have anticipated that exposure to the material would result in cancer.

(D) the plaintiff's only remedy is that created by workers' compensation statutes.

47. A gardener's flower and plant shop was located across the street from a factory, in a building that the gardener rented from a landlord. Gases from the factory caused some of the potted plants that the gardener had for sale in his shop to die. One of the gardener's employees suffered from allergies. As a result, he found the gases so irritating to his eyes that he was unable to continue working at the gardener's shop and had to quit his job. Who may successfully assert a private nuisance claim against the factory?

(A) The landlord only.

(B) The landlord and the gardener only.

(C) The gardener and the employee only.

(D) The landlord, the gardener, and the employee.

48. When the defendant entered a restaurant for lunch, she hung her coat on the coatrack. When she was leaving, she removed from the rack a coat that looked like hers, but which actually belonged to the plaintiff. At the time she took it, the defendant believed it to be her coat, but when she had driven two miles from the restaurant, she realized that it was not hers. She turned around and was driving back to the restaurant when she was involved in an automobile accident. The accident occurred because the defendant was not paying close attention to her driving. The plaintiff's coat was completely destroyed in the accident.

If the plaintiff asserts a claim against the defendant for trespass to chattel, the court should find for

(A) the plaintiff, because the coat was completely destroyed after the defendant took it.

(B) the plaintiff, because the automobile accident in which the coat was destroyed was the defendant's fault.

(C) the defendant, because she believed the coat to be her own when she took it.

(D) the defendant, because she was making a reasonable effort to return the coat when it was destroyed.

49. A trucker was eating cherry pie in a restaurant when a cherry pit contained in the pie stuck in his throat. Unable to breathe, the trucker began choking. A doctor, who was eating in the restaurant, ran to the trucker's aid and performed an operation known as an emergency tracheotomy. She did this by cutting the skin of the trucker's throat with a pocket knife and creating an opening in his windpipe through which the trucker was able to breathe. Then, at the doctor's direction, the trucker walked across the street to a hospital so that the opening that the doctor created could be cleaned and bandaged. Because hospital employees negligently failed to enter the trucker's name in the emergency room register, he sat in the emergency room for six hours without further attention. At that time, an earthquake caused a portion of the hospital's structure to fall, striking the trucker in the head and fracturing his skull. The state had a "Good Samaritan" statute. An earthquake had never occurred in the state before.

In an action by the trucker against the hospital for damages resulting from his fractured skull, the court is most likely to find for

(A) the hospital, due to the "Good Samaritan" statute.

(B) the hospital, because the doctor's conduct was unforeseeable.

(C) the hospital, because it was unforeseeable that the trucker would be injured by an earthquake if left waiting for six hours.

(D) the trucker, since a hospital owes its patients a duty to protect them against natural disasters.

50. A homeowner went to a garden supply store to purchase fertilizer for the apple trees that grew in his backyard. Since he did not know what brand was best for his purposes, he asked the store's owner to recommend a fertilizer that was especially good for apple trees. The store owner suggested a product that he said was good for all fruit trees. The homeowner purchased the product and applied it as the label directed. While doing so, he got some of the product on his hands. Because of an allergy that he had, the product irritated his skin, causing him considerable pain and disabling him for a period of time.

In an action by the homeowner against the store owner for damages resulting from breach of warranty, which of the following comments is most correct?

(A) There was no implied warranty that the product was fit for the homeowner's particular purpose because his purpose was the same as the product's ordinary use.

(B) There was no implied warranty of merchantability since the homeowner relied on the store owner's recommendation in purchasing the product.

(C) There was neither an implied warranty that the product was fit for a particular purpose nor an implied warranty of merchantability.

(D) There was an implied warranty that the product was fit for the homeowner's particular use and there was an implied warranty of merchantability.

51. The defendant is a supplier of telephone service to the city. Many of the wooden poles from which the defendant's wires are strung have been standing for more than 40 years and are in a rotted condition. A driver lost control of his automobile because he was driving while intoxicated, and he collided with one of the defendant's rotten poles. As a result of the collision, the pole fell over, striking a parked car and injuring the plaintiff, who was sitting in it. The force of the collision would have caused even a reasonably good pole to fall.

In an action by the plaintiff against the defendant, the court should find for

(A) the plaintiff, because it was unreasonable for the defendant to permit its poles to become rotten.

(B) the plaintiff, since it was foreseeable that if a pole fell, it would injure a person sitting in a parked car.

(C) the defendant, since the driver's conduct either amounted to gross negligence or was criminal.

(D) the defendant, because the force of the collision would have caused even a reasonably good pole to fall.

52. A truck and a car collided in an intersection. The drivers asserted negligence claims against each other for damage to their vehicles. In answer to specific questions posed by the court, the jury found that the accident was 60 percent the fault of the truck driver and 40 percent the fault of the car driver. In addition, the jury found that damage to the truck amounted to $1,000 and that damage to the car amounted to $10,000.

The jurisdiction had a statute that provided that "In any negligence action, a plaintiff's recovery shall not be barred by that plaintiff's fault, but the recovery of said plaintiff shall be diminished in proportion to that plaintiff's fault." Which of the following correctly states the sum to which the car driver is entitled?

(A) $6,000 ($10,000 less 40 percent).

(B) $4,000 ($10,000 less 60 percent).

(C) $10,000.

(D) 0.

53. A boy, who was 11 years old, received a sled manufactured by the sled company from his uncle as a Christmas present. Since he already had a better sled, the boy sold the sled to his neighbor, the plaintiff. The plaintiff was riding the sled down a snow-covered hill when one of the bolts that held it together broke, causing the sled to overturn and injure the plaintiff severely. The bolt broke because of a crack that existed when the sled left the sled factory but which was too minute to be discovered by reasonable inspection. If the plaintiff brings an action against the sled company, the court should find for

(A) the plaintiff, because the cracked bolt was a defect.

(B) the plaintiff, because the boy did not use the sled before selling it to the plaintiff.

(C) the sled company, since the sale by the boy was outside the regular course of business.

(D) the sled company, because the crack was too minute to be discovered upon reasonable inspection.

54. The landlord was the owner of a four-story office building. The entire second floor of the building was leased to an attorney, and the other floors were divided into offices and leased to various other tenants. The attorney was riding in the building elevator when it suddenly and without warning plunged swiftly downward, shaking the attorney up severely. The lease required the landlord to keep the elevator in good repair. Minutes later, the attorney led one of his clients to the elevator. When they were riding in the elevator to the attorney's office the elevator suddenly plunged swiftly downward, stopping short when it reached the bottom of the elevator shaft. The client was severely injured in the fall.

The client asserted a negligence claim against the attorney for damages resulting from the elevator accident. The court should find for

(A) the client, because the attorney knew or should have known that the elevator might not be working properly.

(B) the client, because the entire second floor had been leased to the attorney.

(C) the attorney, because the lease required the landlord to keep the elevator in good repair.

(D) the attorney, because he was only a tenant in the building.

55. A trucker was driving a truckload of gravel over a highway in a rural part of the state when, through no fault of her own, one of the tires on her truck blew out, causing the truck to go out of control. The truck overturned, spilling the gravel onto the land of the landowner, which was adjacent to the road. The trucker, who was unhurt, returned later with another truck and a tractor equipped with a power shovel. Using the power shovel, the trucker scooped up the spilled gravel and loaded it onto the other truck.

If the landowner asserts a claim against the trucker for trespass to land, the court should award the landowner a judgment for

(A) nominal damages only.

(B) all damages resulting from the spilling of gravel onto the landowner's land.

(C) only the damages caused by the trucker's removal of the gravel from the landowner's land.

(D) no damages.

56. A horseman owned and bred horses and was an excellent rider. He purchased a horse he had heard was wild and dangerous because he hoped that he would be able to "break" or train him. Each time the horseman attempted to approach the horse, however, it reared and kicked at him. Finally, the horseman hired a professional horse trainer to break the horse. After explaining that the horse had repeatedly attacked him, the horseman showed the trainer to the corral. While the horseman stood outside watching, the trainer entered the corral, holding out his hand and making soft murmuring noises to attract the horse's attention. When the horse saw the trainer, the horse kicked him, fracturing the trainer's leg.

If the trainer asserts a claim for damages against the horseman, the court should find for

(A) the trainer, since the horseman knew that the horse had a propensity to attack human beings.

(B) the trainer, since the horse was a wild animal.

(C) the trainer, since the horseman acted unreasonably in permitting the trainer to enter the corral under the circumstances.

(D) the horseman, since the trainer knew that the horse was dangerous when he entered the corral.

57. A man bought a used car from the car dealer. Although the car dealer assured the man that he believed the car to be in good condition, the contract of sale signed by both the man and the car dealer contained the phrase "This Vehicle Sold AS IS" in large black letters. The man was driving the car the following day when the steering jammed, causing the car to collide with a power pole. The man's wife, who was sitting beside him in the car, was injured in the crash.

If the wife asserts a claim for damages against the car dealer on the grounds that the car dealer breached the implied warranty of merchantability, the court should find for

(A) the car dealer, because the contract of sale contained the phrase, "This Vehicle Sold AS IS."

(B) the car dealer, because he did not enter into any contractual relationship with the wife.

(C) the wife, because the vehicle was unfit for ordinary use.

(D) the wife, because the car dealer said that he believed the car to be in good condition.

58. The plaintiff brought her car to the defendant, a used car dealer, asking him to sell it for her. The defendant said that he would attempt to do so on consignment, at a commission consisting

of 20 percent of the sale price. The plaintiff said that the terms were acceptable to her, but that because she had recently spent $800 for a custom two-tone, black-and-silver paint job, she wanted the car kept out of the sun. The defendant agreed, and the plaintiff left the car with him.

The defendant left the car in the sun, which caused its paint to fade. Believing that a new paint job would make the car easier to sell, the defendant had it painted red without consulting the plaintiff. Before it was repainted, the defendant drove the plaintiff's car 4,000 miles on his own personal business. After it was painted, the defendant's customers drove it an additional 1,000 miles while deciding whether to purchase it. Although the value of the plaintiff's car did not change while it was in the defendant's possession, the defendant was unable to sell the car. The plaintiff subsequently asserted a conversion claim against the defendant.

If the plaintiff is successful in her conversion action, the most she will be entitled to recover is

(A) the value that the car had at the time the plaintiff delivered it to the defendant.

(B) the cost of restoring its paint to the condition that existed at the time she delivered it to the defendant.

(C) the reasonable value of the car's use for 4,000 miles.

(D) nothing.

59. A company made a strong insecticide. The container bore a label that read: "For killing termites. Caution: This product is intended for use by professional exterminators only. Unauthorized use by any other persons may be dangerous." The shop owner placed the container on a shelf in his shop, where it was discovered by an independent contractor who the shop owner periodically hired to clean his shop. Since the cleaner thought there were termites in his house, he opened the container and poured some of it into a plastic bag that he then brought home. The next day, the

cleaner's three-year-old daughter found the plastic bag and ate some of the insecticide, becoming seriously ill as a result. A statute in the jurisdiction adopted the all-or-nothing rule of contributory negligence.

In a negligence action by the girl against the company, the company's most effective argument in defense would be that

(A) the cleaner was contributorily negligent.

(B) the shop owner's conduct was an intervening cause of harm.

(C) the cleaner's conduct was an intervening cause of harm.

(D) the company did not act unreasonably.

60. A warehouse owner was the owner of a warehouse that was usually unattended at night. As a result, burglars had broken in on several occasions and had stolen valuable merchandise from the warehouse. The warehouse owner looked into the possibility of hiring a security guard but decided that it would be too expensive. Instead, he installed an explosive device in the doorway, rigging it to explode if anyone opened the door without first inserting a key in a specially constructed slot. A burglar was attempting to break into the warehouse owner's warehouse for the purpose of stealing when the explosive device detonated while he was trying to open the door. The burglar was seriously injured in the explosion.

If the burglar is successful in an action against the warehouse owner, it will most probably be because the court finds that

(A) it was negligent for the warehouse owner to install the explosive device, since it was foreseeable that a person entering on legitimate business might be injured by it.

(B) the warehouse owner used excessive force to defend his property, since the explosive device was liable to inflict serious or deadly injury.

(C) the use of a mechanical device is not permitted in defense of property.

(D) the explosive device was just as likely to injure an innocent bystander as a thief.

61. After living together for several months, a man and his girlfriend began to argue frequently. The following Saturday, the girlfriend took all the man's possessions, including his television set, which was valued at $600, to a swap meet in hopes of selling them. At the swap meet, she put up a sign that said, "Moving. Everything Must Be Sold Today."

A neighbor was browsing at the swap meet when she saw the television set at the girlfriend's booth. She asked whether it was in good condition, and when the girlfriend said that it was, she asked the price. The girlfriend said, "$50." The neighbor immediately handed the girlfriend the cash, placed the television in her station wagon, and hurried home.

In an action by the man against the neighbor for conversion, a court should find for

(A) the man, since the neighbor desired to make the television her own, and did so.

(B) the man, since the price of $50 should have made the neighbor aware that there was something suspicious about the sale.

(C) the neighbor, since it was reasonable for her to believe that the girlfriend owned the television set and that the price was low because the girlfriend needed to sell it in a hurry.

(D) the neighbor, since the television was not in the man's possession when she acquired it.

62. The plaintiff and the defendant lived on the same street and worked in the same office, so they formed a car pool, each driving his own car on alternate days. One day while the defendant was driving, the car in front of his stopped suddenly and without warning. Since the defendant had taken his eyes off the road for a moment to look at the plaintiff, he was unable to stop in time and collided with the rear of the stopped car. The plaintiff was injured as a result of the collision.

A statute in the jurisdiction provides that "No person shall maintain an action for damages resulting from negligence in the operation or ownership of an automobile if said person was a guest in said automobile at the time said damages allegedly occurred." In an action by the plaintiff against the defendant for damages resulting from his injuries, which of the following arguments is most likely to result in a judgment for the plaintiff?

(A) The fact that most drivers have insurance makes the statute obsolete.

(B) The plaintiff was not a guest, since his driving on alternate days was consideration for the ride.

(C) The defendant's conduct was reckless and therefore constituted aggravated negligence, a lawsuit that is not prohibited by the statute.

(D) Enforcement of the statute will leave the plaintiff without a remedy.

63. The company is the manufacturer of a device that was designed for use by professional rescuers in removing accident victims who have become pinned in automobiles.

A fire department purchased the device from a firefighter supply store. Subsequently, the fire department was called to the scene of an accident in which a woman was trapped in her car. The fire chief directed a volunteer firefighter to use the device to free the woman from her car, although he knew that the volunteer firefighter had not been trained in its use and had never heard of it before.

Due to a crack caused by a manufacturing defect, the device operated improperly, injuring the volunteer firefighter. If the volunteer firefighter institutes an action against the company, the company's most effective argument in defense would be that

(A) it had acted reasonably in its marketing and sale of the device.

(B) the firefighter supply store substantially changed the device before selling it to the fire department.

(C) the volunteer firefighter assumed the risk, since he attempted to use the device without proper training.

(D) the volunteer firefighter's attempt to use the machine without training was an independent intervening cause of harm that broke the chain of proximate causation.

64. As a result of her neighbor's negligence, a baker's shoulder and eye were both injured. The baker went immediately to her eye doctor. The eye doctor treated the injury to the baker's eye but suggested that she see an orthopedist for treatment of her shoulder. The following day, the baker visited an orthopedist, who treated the baker's shoulder.

Because of negligent treatment by the eye doctor, the baker's nose became infected, and because of negligent treatment by the orthopedist, she lost the use of her elbow.

In an action by the baker against the eye doctor, a court is most likely to hold the eye doctor liable for

(A) nothing, since all the injuries were caused by the negligence of the neighbor.

(B) the injury to the baker's nose, since it is the only one of her injuries that was caused by his negligence.

(C) the injury to the baker's nose and the injury to the baker's elbow, since both were caused by his negligence.

(D) the injuries to the baker's nose, shoulder, and elbow, since all were caused by his negligence.

65. After taking and failing the state bar exam on 12 different occasions, an attorney decided to practice law without a license. Moving to a small town, he hung out a shingle that proclaimed him to be an attorney and ran advertisements in the local newspaper referring to himself as an attorney. Having seen one of the advertisements, a client retained the attorney to defend him against a charge of driving while intoxicated. The attorney attempted to negotiate a plea to a lesser charge, but because he was unable to do so, a trial was held. The attorney appeared on behalf of the client, but the client was convicted. During the course of the trial, the district attorney became suspicious of the attorney's credentials because he did not defend his client in the way a reasonable attorney would have done. Following an investigation that the district attorney instituted, the attorney was charged with violation of a state law that made it a crime to practice law without a license. He pleaded guilty and was sentenced to six months in jail.

If the client brings an action against the attorney for negligence in the way the attorney handled his defense, a court should find for

(A) the client, because the attorney failed to defend him the way a reasonable attorney would have done.

(B) the client, since it was unreasonable for the attorney to practice law without a license.

(C) the client, since the law that prohibited practicing law without a license was designed to keep unqualified persons from practicing law.

(D) the attorney, since not even a licensed attorney guarantees results.

66. The plaintiff was attending a nightclub at which a hypnotist was performing. Before the show began, a request was made for a volunteer to assist the hypnotist with his act, and the plaintiff volunteered. She was taken backstage to the hypnotist's dressing room, where she and the hypnotist had a conversation. Following their conversation, the plaintiff agreed to participate in the hypnotist's show. During the course of the performance, the hypnotist attempted to hypnotize the plaintiff on stage. He then touched her skin with an electric cattle prod (a device that produces an electric shock and is used for handling stubborn cattle), causing her great pain and discomfort.

    The plaintiff subsequently instituted an action against the hypnotist. In it, she alleged that he committed various intentional torts against her by touching her with the cattle prod. If one of the following facts were established at the trial, which one would be most helpful to the plaintiff in responding to the hypnotist's defense of consent?

    (A) During the conversation in the hypnotist's dressing room, the hypnotist stated that he was going to attempt to hypnotize the plaintiff on stage, he was usually successful in hypnotizing volunteers, and if he was successful, the cattle prod would cause her no discomfort.

    (B) During the conversation in the hypnotist's dressing room, the hypnotist promised to pay her $100 for participating in the show; he never did pay her; and, in fact, when he promised that he would pay her, he did not intend to do so.

    (C) During the conversation in the hypnotist's dressing room, the hypnotist stated that the electric cattle prod produced a mild electric shock that would cause no real discomfort, when he knew that this was not true.

    (D) When the plaintiff consented to participating in the hypnotist's act, she did not know that contact with the electric cattle prod would result in great pain and discomfort.

67. A professor publicly stated her opposition to the consumption of alcohol. As a result, she is much in demand as a lecturer on the evils of intoxication. One of her slogans is, "When you drink, make it fruit juice." The company, a producer of packaged apple juice, invited the professor to participate in a promotional apple-juice-drinking contest that it was holding. The professor, who succeeded in drinking one and one-half quarts of chilled apple juice without stopping for a breath, was declared the winner.

    The student newspaper ran a photo of the professor holding the winner's trophy over a caption that read, "Prof. drinks them all under the table, winning first prize at the company's drinking contest." A story that described the fruit-juice drinking contest in detail appeared on the same page as the photo but some distance from it. The day after the photo and story appeared, an organization that had hired the professor to lecture on the evils of alcohol canceled its contract with the professor because, after seeing the photo and caption in the newspaper, some members believed that the professor was a drinker of alcohol.

    If the professor sues the newspaper for defamation, the court should instruct the jury that the statements made by the newspaper in the photo and caption were *not* defamatory if

    (A) the reasonable person would have read the story.

    (B) the organization members who saw the photo and caption did not read the story.

    (C) a substantial group of respectable persons would have read the story.

(D) the reasonable person would not have read the story.

68. An athlete appeared in a television commercial. While films of his medal-winning performances showed in the background, the athlete ate a candy bar. He said that he had been eating candy bars for energy ever since he was a child. He ended the commercial by smiling and saying, "Who knows? Maybe candy bars gave me the power to win."

The plaintiff purchased a case of 24 candy bars after seeing the commercial several times on television. After tasting one, however, he found he did not like the flavor. If the plaintiff brings an action against the athlete for misrepresentation, which of the following arguments will be most helpful in the athlete's defense?

(A) The athlete is not in the business of selling candy bars.

(B) The script for the commercial was not written by the athlete.

(C) The plaintiff was not in privity with the athlete.

(D) The plaintiff has not sustained damage as the result of a false assertion by the athlete.

69. A demolition contractor was hired by a builder to demolish a building located a half-mile from a horse breeder's farm. The demolition contractor was using dynamite for that purpose. The breeder called the contractor and warned him that sounds from the explosions were scaring his horses. The day after the breeder called, sounds of the explosions so frightened one of the breeder's horses that the horse tried to jump over a fence, injuring herself in the process.

If the breeder institutes an action against the demolition contractor on a strict liability theory, which of the following would be the demolition contractor's most effective argument in defense?

(A) The breeder's farm was not within the foreseeable zone of danger.

(B) The possibility that noise will frighten animals is not one of the risks that makes blasting an ultra-hazardous activity.

(C) The demolition contractor used reasonable care in setting off the blast.

(D) The demolition contractor was working under contract to the builder.

70. The landlord was the owner of a small office building. Her own office was located on the ground floor of the building, the second floor was leased to a company, and the third and fourth floors were divided into smaller offices that were rented to various tenants on a month-to-month basis. Although the building was equipped with an elevator, occupants of the building frequently used a stairway over which the landlord retained control. One day, while one of the company's employees was walking down the stairs from the second floor, she cut her hand on a jagged part of the handrail that ran alongside the stairs. She commenced an action against the landlord, alleging that the handrail was jagged because of negligence by the landlord.

Which of the following is an accurate statement about the case of the injured employee vs. the landlord?

(A) The company's employee was an invitee since she was an employee of one of the landlord's tenants.

(B) The company's employee was contributorily (or comparatively) negligent if the reasonable person in her situation would have noticed the jagged condition of the handrail and would have avoided being injured by it.

(C) The company's employee was an invitee, and she was contributorily (or comparatively) negligent if the reasonable person in her situation would have noticed the jagged condition of the handrail and would have avoided being injured by it.

(D) The company's employee was neither an invitee nor was she contributorily (or comparatively) negligent.

71. A building inspector was employed by the city to conduct periodic inspections of business premises located in a territory to which she was assigned. The instruction manual that the city furnished to its inspectors contained instructions on testing draperies for fire-retardant properties. In large boldface letters, the manual stated, "NEVER EXPOSE DRAPERIES TO FLAME WHILE THEY ARE HANGING IN PLACE."

One of the businesses in the building inspector's territory was a nightclub. On one of her inspections of the nightclub, the building inspector asked the manager of the business whether the window draperies were fire-retardant as required by the city's building code. The manager responded that they were. Although the building inspector was familiar with the instructions in the manual, she was in a hurry. Taking a cigarette lighter from her pocket, she held its flame under one of the draperies where it was hanging. The drapery caught fire, which spread, completely destroying the building. A passerby was injured in the fire.

If the passerby brings an action for damages against the city on a theory of *respondeat superior,* the passerby will

(A) lose, since the building inspector was acting in violation of specific instructions from her employer.

(B) lose, since the building inspector's duties involve the exercise of unsupervised discretion.

(C) win, because the building inspector was negligent.

(D) win, whether or not the building inspector was negligent.

72. A statute provides that every motor vehicle must be equipped with an ignition lock, and that it shall be a misdemeanor for any person to park a motor vehicle without locking it and removing the ignition key. The statute was enacted after many accidents involving stolen cars. The defendant left his car parked on a public street with the ignition key in it, in violation of the statute. A small monkey that had escaped from a nearby circus got in the car, managed to turn the key, and drove the car down the street before hitting the plaintiff. If the plaintiff sues the defendant, the plaintiff will:

(A) win, because it was unreasonable for the defendant to leave his keys in the ignition.

(B) win, because the statute was designed to prevent accidents involving stolen cars.

(C) lose, because the intervention of the monkey was likely unforeseeable.

(D) lose, because the intervention of the monkey was likely foreseeable.

73. The state governor was attending a major league baseball game when a member of the home team hit a home run. The governor jumped to his feet and cheered loudly, along with the rest of the crowd. A freelance photographer took his picture while he was cheering. When the photograph was developed, the photographer had it imprinted on targets. With toy plastic darts, the photographer marketed and sold several thousand. The governor sued the photographer for invasion of privacy.

On which of the following theories is the governor most likely to be successful in his action against the photographer?

(A) Appropriation of identity.

(B) Public disclosure.

(C) Intrusion.

(D) False light.

74. A professor was disturbed by the fact that students frequently left the room during her lectures, so she instructed her teaching assistant to lock the door of her classroom 10 minutes after the class began and not to unlock it again until 10 minutes before the class was scheduled to end. On Thursday, a student attended the professor's four o'clock class. By five minutes past four, the student was sound asleep in his seat. At ten minutes past four, the teaching assistant locked the classroom door as instructed by the professor, unlocking it at ten minutes to five. When the class ended at five, the student, who had slept through the class, was awakened by a classmate and left the room. The classroom had been painted the previous day with a paint to which the student was allergic, although neither the professor, the teaching assistant, nor the student knew about it. As a result of his exposure to the paint in the room, the student developed allergic symptoms later that day that required hospitalization.

If the student institutes an action for false imprisonment against the professor, who will win?

(A) The student, because his illness resulted from the professor's intentional confinement of him.

(B) The student, since a professor owes her students a duty to refrain from exposing them to unreasonable risks of foreseeable harm.

(C) The professor, since she did not know with substantial certainty that harm would result from locking the door.

(D) The professor, since she did not confine the student against his will.

75. The Lovers of God is a small religious sect. During the 19th century, they were prosecuted for engaging in religious rituals that involved public nudity and group sex. Some non-members of the sect continue to associate it with illicit sex and continue to call its members "Makers," a term coined by 19th-century journalists who campaigned against the sect.

A minister ordained in the Church of Love, a religious organization that is not associated in any way with the Lovers, spoke at a local meeting. The following day, a local daily newspaper printed an article about the meeting. The article referred to the minister as "a minister of the Church of Love, better known as the Makers (Lovers of God)." The minister sued the newspaper, alleging that the reference to him as a minister of "the Makers (Lovers of God)" was defamatory.

In his lawsuit, the minister must prove that the newspaper

(A) knew, or that the reasonable publisher would have known, that the minister was not affiliated with the Lovers of God.

(B) entertained serious doubts about whether or not the minister was affiliated with the Lovers of God.

(C) knew that "the Makers (Lovers of God)" were associated with shame or disgrace in the minds of some readers.

(D) made the statement, but the minister is not required to prove fault since the minister is not a public person.

76. The defendant owned a small hardware store. One of the products he sold were circular saws made by a local manufacturer. The defendant sold the saws in their original boxes. One day, the defendant sold the plaintiff a saw. Two years later, the plaintiff hurt herself badly when the blade detached from the saw and cut her in the face. The blade broke free after delivery to the plaintiff and was due to poor design by the manufacturing company. There was no research available that would have indicated to the defendant that there was a risk of such injury or that the product was badly designed. The plaintiff sued the defendant for her injuries. Assuming the saw design constituted a dangerous defect, the court should find

(A) in favor of the defendant, because there was no indication the defendant behaved negligently.

(B) in favor of the defendant, because there was no way the defendant could have discovered the risk of such breakage before selling the product to the plaintiff.

(C) in favor of the plaintiff, because the defendant sold the saw.

(D) in favor of the plaintiff, because selling the defective saws was unreasonable.

77. A driver was driving her automobile in the rain on a curvy road known for numerous accidents when she rounded a bend and saw a cow standing directly in her path. She immediately jammed on her brakes and pulled the steering wheel to the right in an attempt to avoid striking the cow. As a result, she lost control of her car, which skidded off the road and into the homeowner's yard. The homeowner, who was in the process of installing an automatic watering system, had dug a trench across the yard for pipes. When the wheels of the driver's car hit the trench, the car stopped abruptly, throwing the driver forward into the windshield and causing her to be injured.

In an action by the driver against the homeowner for negligence, will a court decide that the homeowner owed the driver a duty of reasonable care?

(A) Yes, because it was foreseeable that persons driving on the road might lose control of their vehicles and skid into the homeowner's yard.

(B) Yes, because the homeowner knew that drivers used the neighboring road.

(C) No, because it was not unreasonable for the homeowner to dig a trench on his own land.

(D) No, because the driver was a trespasser.

78. A carpenter who was building a house on his own property had posted a sign that said, "No Trespassing." While he was working, he threw his hammer off the roof. The hammer hit a truck driver who was walking across the property because he mistakenly thought he was supposed to deliver a load of wood to the carpenter. Even though he saw the hammer hit, the carpenter failed to call for help. A passerby called an ambulance, and after the ambulance picked up the truck driver, the ambulance had an accident resulting in the truck driver's death.

The representative of the truck driver's estate instituted an appropriate action against the carpenter, alleging that the carpenter's failure to call for medical assistance after he saw the hammer strike the truck driver was negligence. Which of the following comments is most accurate regarding that allegation?

(A) The carpenter owed the truck driver no duty to call for help if the truck driver was a trespasser.

(B) The truck driver's estate is entitled to punitive (exemplary) damages if the carpenter was substantially certain that there was a possibility of harm resulting from his failure to act.

(C) The carpenter's failure to call for medical aid was not a factual cause of harm to the truck driver since someone did call a moment later.

(D) the truck driver was an invitee since he was a user of the public street who had entered upon adjacent private land.

79. The company had been operating a soap factory in the county for 50 years. When the factory was first opened, the nearest residential settlement was the town, six miles away. Because the factory has been in existence for 50 years, county zoning ordinances were drafted to allow its continued operation. In the past 50 years, however, the town has

expanded in size. Now the edge of town is only a quarter of a mile from the company's factory. On days when the wind is blowing from the direction of the factory, residents of the town are annoyed by the noxious odor emanating from the factory chimneys. A homeowner, who moved to the town three years ago, has asked the town attorney to seek an injunction to prohibit the company from emitting foul odors, but the town attorney has refused.

If the homeowner sues the company for damages resulting from the odors on a theory of public nuisance, which of the following will be the company's most effective argument in defense?

(A)  The company's operation preceded the growth of the town.

(B)  The homeowner came to the nuisance.

(C)  The homeowner's damages are no different from those of other residents of the town.

(D)  A lawful activity cannot constitute a public nuisance.

80.  The defendant and the plaintiff had been friends for years and worked in the same office. Ever since they were children, they had enjoyed playing practical jokes on each other. One day, planning to have some fun with the plaintiff, the defendant bought a large rubber spider from a toy store. Knowing that the plaintiff was terrified of spiders, the defendant came into work early and placed the toy spider in the top drawer of the plaintiff's desk. Later, when the plaintiff arrived at work, he opened his top drawer and saw the rubber spider. Believing it to be real and terrified that it would bite him, the plaintiff screamed in fear, fainted, and fell to the floor. As he fell, he struck his head on the corner of his desk, sustaining a serious fracture of the skull.

If the plaintiff asserts a claim for assault against the defendant for the injury that he

sustained in the fall, which of the following arguments would be most effective in the defendant's defense?

(A)  The plaintiff's fear of being bitten by a spider was not apprehension of a battery.

(B)  The reasonable person in the plaintiff's position would not have become apprehensive at the sight of a spider.

(C)  The plaintiff impliedly consented to the prank by engaging in a course of practical joking with the defendant.

(D)  The defendant was not substantially certain that the plaintiff would be injured as a result of the joke.

81.  The plaintiff commenced an action against the defendant, and proved the following:

The defendant and his friend were both slingshot enthusiasts known for the accuracy of their aim. Without consulting the other, each went independently to the woods outside of town to practice his or her skill. Since not many people frequented the area, the defendant and his friend were both somewhat casual about their targets, each shooting at anything that moved without properly checking to make sure of what they were shooting at. The plaintiff, who had gone to the woods to read in solitude, was struck by a steel ball shot from one of the slingshots. Since the defendant and his friend were using the same kind of ammunition, it is impossible to determine which of them fired the ball that struck the plaintiff, but it is certain that one of them did.

If the court finds for the defendant, it will probably be for which one of the following reasons?

(A)  The defendant did not owe the plaintiff a duty of reasonable care since not many people frequented the area.

(B)  There is no evidence that the defendant acted unreasonably.

(C) The evidence does not establish that the defendant's conduct was a factual cause of the injury.

(D) Even if the defendant's conduct was a factual cause of the injury, it is impossible to tell whether it was a legal cause of the injury.

82. Statutes in the state provide that persons under the age of 20 years are incompetent to enter into contracts, may not marry without the written consent of their parents, may not lawfully purchase alcoholic beverages, and are subject to local curfew regulations. A 19-year-old girl was fishing for pleasure from a pier in the state when she accidentally struck a fisherman in the eye with a fishhook on the end of her line. The fisherman commenced a negligence action against the girl. The trial court should find that the girl was negligent because

(A) she failed to act like a reasonable 19-year-old with her experience and intelligence.

(B) fishing is an adult activity.

(C) at 19 she is old enough to be treated as an adult by the law of torts.

(D) the risk of injury caused by her use of the fishhook outweighs the utility of fishing for pleasure.

83. A company manufactured several kinds of cooked-fruit desserts.

A man bought one of the company's desserts at a grocery store, opened the package and began eating the contents with a spoon. After consuming more than half of the product, the man noticed parts of a rat's tail mixed with the cooked fruit.

If the man asserts a claim against the company on the theory of strict liability in tort, which of the following would be the man's most effective argument?

(A) The presence of a rat's tail was a defect that made the product unreasonably dangerous.

(B) The man was in horizontal privity with the grocery store, and there is no need for vertical privity.

(C) The labeling and packaging implied a promise that the contents of the package purchased by the man were fit for human consumption.

(D) The doctrine of *res ipsa loquitur* applies, since the product was sold in a sealed package.

84. A driver swerved to avoid a car and hit a boy walking along the road. The boy's mother had told the boy that she did not want him riding his bicycle on the road because it was a heavily travelled roadway with no sidewalks. She gave him permission, however, to walk his bicycle carefully along the road shoulder.

The jurisdiction applies the all-or-nothing rule of contributory negligence.

If the boy's mother asserts a negligence claim against the driver for the medical bills that she incurred as a result of the boy's injury, which of the following may the driver assert in defense?

(A) The accident resulted from the boy's negligence.

(B) The accident resulted from the boy's mother's negligence.

(C) The accident resulted from both the boy's and his mother's negligence.

(D) The driver cannot claim that either the boy or his mother was negligent.

85. The defendant was towing a small travel-trailer with his automobile when the hitch that attached the trailer to the car broke, causing the trailer to collide with the vehicle of the plaintiff, which was parked at the

curb. A statute in the jurisdiction provides that "No person shall operate a motor vehicle or trailer on the roads of this state unless said motor vehicle or trailer is covered by a valid policy of liability insurance." The defendant was in violation of that statute in that he knew that his trailer was not covered by a valid policy of liability insurance at the time of the accident. Is his violation of statute relevant to the issue of negligence in an action brought against him by the plaintiff?

(A) Yes, because the statute was designed to protect the victims of automobile and trailer accidents.

(B) Yes, because the reasonable person does not knowingly violate a statute.

(C) No, because the law encourages the purchase of automobile insurance and therefore absolutely prohibits disclosure to the jury about whether or not a defendant was insured.

(D) No, because compliance with the statute does not prevent automobile or trailer accidents.

86. One night, police officers received a message that a burglary was in progress at a grocery store. In the ensuing attempt to make an arrest, the officers knocked over several stacks of merchandise, including cases of bottled soda-pop manufactured by the company. This caused minute cracks in all the bottles. A woman purchased one of the bottles but did not notice the minute crack in it.

That evening, the woman was placing the bottle on the dinner table when the bottle exploded. The woman was cut by flying glass.

In an action by the woman against the company, may she successfully rely on the doctrine of *res ipsa loquitur*?

(A) Yes, because it applies in exploding bottle cases.

(B) Yes, because the company was in exclusive control of the bottling process.

(C) No, because the bottles were knocked over by the officers.

(D) No, because the bottles were not in the company's possession at the time the woman's injury occurred.

87. A contractor did some renovations on a customer's apartment. In order to put in a new window, the contractor used a glue made by a local manufacturer. Due to a design defect, the glue released highly toxic fumes that floated into a neighbor's apartment and caused severe lung injuries. The neighbor can recover

(A) in strict liability against the contractor.

(B) in strict liability against the manufacturer.

(C) in strict liability against the contractor or manufacturer.

(D) in negligence only.

88. One day, while a well-known collector was visiting the dealer's art gallery, the dealer showed him a new painting that she had received that day.

"The artist didn't sign it," the dealer said. "But I'm sure it was painted by Degas. That would make it worth at least $250,000."

The collector answered, "It's by Degas, all right. It's worth every cent you're asking. But I already have several paintings by Degas in my collection, and I don't need another."

The buyer, who was browsing in the dealer's gallery, overheard the conversation between the collector and the dealer. The buyer knew very little about art. Because he knew that the collector and the dealer were art experts, he believed what he heard them saying. After the collector left the gallery, the buyer purchased the painting for $225,000. The buyer subsequently learned that it had not been painted by Degas and was worth only $600.

If the buyer asserts a tort claim for misrepresentation against the dealer, which of the following would be the dealer's most effective argument in defense?

(A) A statement of opinion cannot be construed as a misrepresentation, since there is no such thing as a false idea.

(B) The buyer did not sustain damage as a result of his reliance on a statement by the dealer.

(C) The dealer did not know that the buyer would rely on the statements that she made to the collector.

(D) The value of any work of art is a matter of opinion.

89. As a joke, the defendant knocked on the plaintiff's door wearing a police officer's uniform that he had rented from a costume shop. When the plaintiff came to the door, the defendant told her that her husband had just been killed in a highway accident, and that she would have to come with him to claim the body. The plaintiff, who recognized the defendant and knew that he was not a police officer, slammed the door in his face and told him to leave her alone. She was outraged at his attempt to play such a joke on her, but she sustained no physical or mental injury.

If the plaintiff asserts a claim against the defendant for intentional infliction of emotional distress, the court should find for

(A) the plaintiff, because the defendant's conduct exceeded all bounds normally tolerated by decent society.

(B) the plaintiff, because the defendant's conduct was calculated to cause severe mental suffering.

(C) the defendant, because his intention was merely to play a joke on the plaintiff.

(D) the defendant, because the plaintiff sustained no physical or mental injury as a result of the defendant's conduct.

90. Which of the following most correctly states the duty owed to customers by a druggist who dispenses prescription drugs?

(A) To know all the harmful side effects of the drugs being dispensed.

(B) To warn of all the harmful side effects of the drugs being dispensed.

(C) To sell only those drugs that are not defective.

(D) To make whatever inspection of the drugs is reasonable before dispensing them.

91. A plaintiff asserted a claim for damages against a man and his friend. The man and his friend had been trying to see who could hit a golf ball farthest. The plaintiff succeeded in proving that a golf ball that struck him had been driven by one of them, but he was unable to show which one. The court found that both the man and his friend had acted negligently, and that they were involved in a concert of action.

Which of the following statements is most correct about the relationship of the parties?

(A) Either the man or his friend may avoid liability by proving that his ball was not the one that struck the plaintiff.

(B) Neither the man's nor his friend's conduct was a factual cause of harm because each one's conduct was a substantial factor in producing the plaintiff's injury.

(C) The man's conduct and his friend's conduct were legal causes of harm, but neither was a factual cause of harm.

(D) The man and his friend may each be held vicariously liable for the other's conduct.

92. A cancer patient was given a drug that caused her to have an allergic reaction that blinded

her in one eye. The patient subsequently retained an attorney to commence a malpractice action against the doctor for the damages that resulted from her allergic reaction. Although the statute of limitations on such an action fixed a period of one year, more than one year passed before the attorney commenced an action against the doctor. As a result, no such action could ever be brought. The patient eventually sued the attorney, alleging that the attorney's failure to bring the action on time was negligent.

Which one of the following additional facts or inferences, if it was the only one true, would be most effective as part of the attorney's defense?

(A) The attorney had been admitted to the bar only three weeks before being retained by the patient.

(B) The attorney honestly believed that the statutory period of limitations for the commencement of medical malpractice actions was two years.

(C) After discussing the case with the doctor's attorney, the attorney came to the conclusion that the patient's case against the doctor was weak.

(D) Cancer would have led to the patient's death within a few months if left untreated, and the drug was the only drug available for its treatment.

93. The defendant was an elderly man who lived in a house with a swimming pool in the backyard. Although the defendant enjoyed swimming in the pool, his age and physical infirmity made him unable to clean or maintain the pool himself. Instead, he agreed to allow his 14-year-old neighbor, the plaintiff, to swim in the pool anytime she wanted without notifying the defendant or asking his permission, in exchange for the plaintiff's services in cleaning and maintaining the pool.

On Friday morning, the plaintiff thoroughly cleaned the defendant's pool. Later that day, the defendant drained all the water from the pool and did not refill it. Saturday morning, the plaintiff woke up early and decided to go swimming in the defendant's pool. She put on her bathing suit and went into the defendant's yard, running onto the diving board of his swimming pool and diving in without looking first. The plaintiff was severely injured when she fell to the concrete bottom of the empty swimming pool.

If the plaintiff asserts a negligence claim for her injuries against the defendant in a jurisdiction that has a pure comparative negligence statute, the court should find for

(A) the plaintiff, because the pool constituted an attractive nuisance.

(B) the defendant, because the plaintiff was a trespasser.

(C) the plaintiff, because it was unreasonable for the defendant to drain the pool without warning her.

(D) the defendant, because a reasonable person in the plaintiff's position would have known the risk of diving into an empty swimming pool.

94. A playground was directly adjacent to a company's property, separated from it by a 6-foot wire mesh fence. The company officials were aware that a large gaping hole in this fence had existed for approximately one year, and that children frequently crept through the hole to play on the company's property.

One morning, the plaintiff, a 12-year-old student, entered the company's property through the hole in the fence. The plaintiff began climbing spikes that had been driven into a pole. When she reached a wooden platform located 12 feet aboveground, she put her head through the hole in its center to see what was above it. Her head came into contact with a high-voltage wire that had been strung over the platform, causing her to sustain serious injuries.

In a negligence action by the plaintiff against the company, which one of the following additional facts or inferences, if it were the only one true, would provide the company with its most effective argument in defense?

(A) The plaintiff entered the premises without the company's permission.

(B) To the company's knowledge, no child had ever before attempted to climb the pole.

(C) The plaintiff was old enough to comprehend the dangers associated with an attempt to climb the pole.

(D) The fence that separated the company's property from the schoolyard was located completely on realty occupied by the school.

95. Several cases of explosives made by a company were shipped to a buyer in another state to be stored in a warehouse pending delivery. While the explosives were there, the warehouse facility was struck by lightning, causing the explosives to explode. The cases containing the explosives did not bear any description of their contents. If the warehouse employees knew that the cases contained explosives, they would have stored them in a way that would have prevented the explosion. A homeowner who sustained property damage as a result of the explosion has asserted a claim against the company.

Which of the following facts or inferences, if it were the only one true, would provide the company with its most effective argument in defense?

(A) The company did not do anything unreasonable or irresponsible in manufacturing, packaging, or labeling its product.

(B) When the company shipped the cases of explosives, they had been properly labeled with firmly affixed labels identifying their contents, but the labels had somehow come off in transit.

(C) The company had assigned an employee to make sure that all cases of explosives shipped by the company were properly labeled, but the employee had forgotten to inspect this shipment.

(D) The storage of explosives by the warehouse was an ultra-hazardous activity.

96. A restaurant opened on the edge of a college bar area, which abutted a residential neighborhood. The restaurant had a walk-up window where people could purchase food and drinks without going inside. The restaurant and window were open until 4 A.M. every night. College students soon started to congregate in front of the restaurant. On many nights, the students were loud, and some even engaged in the use of illegal drugs or drank alcohol underage. The plaintiff, who lived in a house next to the new restaurant, complained and told the restaurant it was bringing down his property value. He demanded that the restaurant close at 11 P.M., like many other restaurants in the area. The restaurant refused.

If the plaintiff chooses to sue, which of the following legal theories would be most likely to result in a judgment for the plaintiff?

(A) Invasion of privacy.

(B) Intentional infliction of emotional distress.

(C) Trespass to land.

(D) Private nuisance.

97. During a comedian's long career in the entertainment business, the comedian's trademark was always a cigar that he clenched between his teeth or held in his hand while delivering his jokes. As part of an interview on a television show, the interviewer asked the comedian whether he really smoked cigars. The comedian replied, "Sure. I always smoke these cigars. They're the best cigars made."

The following day, the manufacturer of the cigars placed several advertisements in newspapers. All the advertisements said, "Jimmy Stoker the Famous Comedian says our cigars are the best cigars made. He always smokes them, and you should too."

If the comedian asserts a claim against the cigar company for invasion of privacy by misappropriation of identity, the court should find for

(A) the cigar company, because the comedian had in fact made the statement that appeared in the advertisement.

(B) the cigar company, because the advertisement constituted a constitutionally protected form of commercial expression.

(C) the comedian, because when he made the statement on the television show, it was unforeseeable that the cigar company would use it in its advertising.

(D) the comedian, because the cigar company used his name to sell its product without his permission.

98. The defendant grew fruit trees on her farm outside the village. In addition, she operated a fruit store in the village. Every day during the harvest season, in a trailer that she towed with her pickup truck, she hauled fresh fruit from her orchards to her store. One day, as she was towing the trailer filled with fruit up a hill on her way to the village, the hitch that fastened the trailer to the pickup truck failed, permitting the trailer to break loose and roll down the hill, striking and damaging the home of the plaintiff. Subsequent investigation revealed that the hitch failed because one of its parts was made of defective steel.

If the plaintiff asserts a claim against the defendant for damage to his house, the court's decision is most likely to turn on whether

(A) the defendant acted reasonably.

(B) the hitch was defective in manufacture or in design.

(C) the defendant was a merchant.

(D) the plaintiff could have foreseen the damage.

99. The pilot was a helicopter pilot employed by a radio station as a traffic reporter. One day, while flying in his helicopter, he hovered over the home of a woman. Using powerful binoculars, he looked into her window to watch her while she was exercising in the nude. If the woman institutes an action against him, which of the following facts or inferences must she establish to make out a *prima facie* case of trespass to land?

(A) The altitude at which the pilot hovered over her house.

(B) Damage to her land, or to her right to enjoy it, that resulted from the pilot's conduct.

(C) That she had a reasonable expectation of privacy while exercising nude in her own home.

(D) That she was in lawful possession of the premises at the time that the pilot hovered over her house.

100. When a woman discovered that her car had been stolen, she reported the theft to the police. Then, while she was walking home from the police station, she saw her car in a homeowner's driveway, where the person who stole it had abandoned it after using it in a bank robbery. When she began walking toward the automobile, the homeowner ran out of his house shouting, "Hey, you! Where do you think you're going?" The woman explained that she was attempting to retrieve her car, but the homeowner pushed her, saying, "Get off my land." The woman, who sustained no physical or mental injury as a result of the homeowner's contact with her, got into her car and drove it away. The woman subsequently commenced a battery action against the homeowner. If, in response to the woman's claim, the homeowner asserts the privilege to defend realty, the court should find for

(A) the homeowner, because the woman was not in hot pursuit of her car when she entered the homeowner's realty.

(B) the homeowner, because the woman was not injured as a result of his contact with her.

(C) the woman, because force is never permitted in defense of realty.

(D) the woman, because she was privileged to enter and retake her automobile.

101. A husband's wife died when she jumped in front of a train owned by the railroad. Two weeks later, a railroad employee contacted the husband. The employee said that although the railroad was not legally responsible for the wife's death, the railroad was willing to pay $1,000 in full settlement of all claims arising from the wife's death. When the husband said he wanted to speak with an attorney, the employee told him that if an attorney got involved, the railroad would not pay anything because the husband "had no legal claim." The husband doubted that the employee was telling the truth, so he consulted with an attorney. The attorney didn't think the husband had a claim and declined representation. Consequently, the husband accepted the $1,000 and executed a general release. The husband then retained another attorney and instituted a wrongful death action against the railroad. The court dismissed, citing the release.

Which of the following additional facts must the husband prove to establish a cause of action for misrepresentation against the employee?

(A) If the husband's wrongful death suit was not dismissed, it would have resulted in a judgment for the husband in excess of $1,000.

(B) When the employee made the statements to the husband, the employee knew or should have known that the statements were false.

(C) The husband's wrongful death suit would have resulted in a judgment for the husband in excess of $1,000, and the employee knew or should have known the statements were false.

(D) The husband doesn't have to prove that his lawsuit would have resulted in a judgment in excess of $1,000, or that the employee knew or should have known his statements were false.

102. The company, a manufacturer of dog whistles, operated a factory for that purpose. The whistles manufactured by the company issued a sound so high-pitched that it could not be heard by human ears; only dogs could hear it. For this reason, before leaving the assembly line, each whistle was tested by a machine that blew air through it and metered the sound that it made. After the company's factory had been in operation for 15 years, a breeder moved onto the adjoining realty and began operating a kennel. Two weeks after moving onto the realty, the breeder discovered that the dogs in his kennel were being disturbed by the testing of dog whistles in the company's factory. Although he told the company about the problem, the company did not stop testing the whistles. The breeder commenced a private nuisance action against it. Which of the following would be the company's most effective argument in defense against the breeder's claim?

(A) The operation of a dog-whistle factory is a lawful business.

(B) The breeder came to the nuisance.

(C) The company did not intend to cause harm to the breeder or to the breeder's business.

(D) The breeder's damage resulted from the fact that the breeder was making an unusually sensitive use of the land.

103. The plaintiff purchased a bottle of dishwashing detergent from the defendant, a self-

service supermarket. The plaintiff selected the product from the defendant's shelves, carried it to a checkout counter, and paid the cashier. The plaintiff then placed the bottle in a bag furnished by the defendant and carried it home. The product purchased by the plaintiff was manufactured by a local company. The product had a label stating that it would not harm a user's skin. After using the product for washing dishes, the plaintiff experienced a serious rash on his hands and wrists as the result of an allergic reaction to a chemical in the product.

If the plaintiff asserts a claim against the defendant for breach of express warranty, a court should find for

(A) the plaintiff, because the label stated that the product would not harm the skin of a user.

(B) the plaintiff, because the product was unfit for ordinary use.

(C) the defendant, because the plaintiff's injury resulted from reliance on a statement that the company caused to be printed on the label of its product.

(D) the defendant, because no employee of the defendant knew what statements were contained on the company's detergent label.

104. The defendant bought a new sailboat, although he had never been on one before. Although the defendant had not received any instruction at all, and although he heard a weather report that warned of severe storms, he decided to take the boat out for a test sail by himself. A few minutes after he left the dock with his boat, the storm struck, causing high and dangerous waves. Fearful that the defendant would be killed at sea, the defendant's wife stood crying on the shore. The plaintiff, an experienced sailor who knew the defendant and the defendant's wife, heard the defendant's wife crying about her husband's predicament. Without saying anything to the defendant's wife, the plaintiff went out in his own boat to look for the defendant. The defendant returned unhurt an hour later, but the plaintiff's boat capsized in the storm, severely damaging his boat and causing the plaintiff to sustain injury.

If the plaintiff asserts a claim against the defendant for the damage that he sustained, the court should find for

(A) the plaintiff, because his damage resulted from the defendant's failure to act reasonably.

(B) the plaintiff, because a rescuer is entitled to indemnity from the person whom he or she was attempting to rescue.

(C) the defendant, because the plaintiff was an officious intermeddler.

(D) the defendant, because the defendant was unaware that the plaintiff would attempt to rescue him.

105. The defendant was driving to visit her fiancé. Before she left, her friend asked her to deliver a small package to someone. The package contained a bottle of caustic chemicals. Because she was afraid that the defendant would refuse to carry it if she knew its contents, the friend wrapped the package in brown paper and did not tell the defendant what was in it. The defendant placed the package in the glove compartment of her car and began driving. Along the way, the defendant saw the plaintiff hitchhiking by the side of the road. The defendant offered the plaintiff a ride. While the plaintiff was sitting in the front seat, the plaintiff opened the glove compartment and removed the wet package. As soon as the caustic liquid touched the plaintiff's hand, it burned his skin severely.

If the plaintiff commences a negligence action against the defendant in a jurisdiction that has no automobile guest statute and that applies the all-or-nothing rule of contributory negligence, which of the following would be the defendant's most effective argument in defense?

(A) The plaintiff was a mere licensee and was entitled only to a warning of those conditions that the defendant knew were dangerous.

(B) The defendant could not have known or anticipated that the contents of the package would cause harm to a passenger in her car.

(C) The plaintiff was contributorily negligent in touching the wet package.

(D) The plaintiff assumed the risk of injury resulting from contact with the wet package.

106. The plaintiff decided to have a rosebud tattooed on her shoulder. While the defendant was tattooing the plaintiff's shoulder, the tattoo needle broke off in the plaintiff's skin, injuring the plaintiff. If the plaintiff asserts a strict liability claim against the defendant on the ground that the tattoo needle that the defendant used was defective, the defendant's most effective argument in defense would be that

(A) the defendant did not sell the needle to the plaintiff.

(B) the defendant was not the manufacturer of the needle and therefore had no control over its quality.

(C) the plaintiff assumed the risk of injury.

(D) a tattoo needle is not an inherently dangerous product.

107. When a policeman saw a walker hurrying down the street in the early morning darkness, he pulled his car over to the curb and ordered the walker to stop and identify himself. The walker showed the policeman his license, told him that he lived only a few blocks away, and explained that he was just taking a walk. When the policeman told the walker to get into the back of the patrol car, the walker asked whether he was under arrest. The policeman replied, "No, but if you know what's good for you, you'll get into the car and shut up while I decide what to do with you." The walker got into the car and sat quietly in the backseat with the door open while the policeman called the walker's description in to police headquarters over the radio. About 15 minutes later, satisfied that the walker was not wanted for violating any law, the policeman told him that he could go. When he was leaving the car, the walker scraped his finger. If the walker asserts a claim against the policeman for false imprisonment, the court should find for

(A) the policeman, because the rear door of the policeman's patrol car remained open all the time that the walker sat in the car.

(B) the policeman, because the walker did not object to sitting in the patrol car.

(C) the walker, because the language used by the policeman induced the walker to obey the policeman's order.

(D) the walker, because he sustained damage as a result of his detention by the policeman.

108. A driver hit a pole, causing a power failure. At the time of the power failure, a patient was undergoing facial surgery in a hospital operating room. The hospital's emergency generator went on automatically, supplying enough electrical power to light the operating room dimly. The doctor who was operating on the patient was able to complete the surgery on the patient's face, but the operation left the patient with permanent and disfiguring scars. If the power had not failed, the doctor would have been able to prevent the scarring.

If the patient asserts a claim for negligence against the driver, which of the following additional facts or inferences, if it were the only one true, would provide the driver with his most effective defense?

(A) The reasonable surgeon in the doctor's position would not have proceeded with the operation while the operating room was dimly lit by the hospital's emergency generator.

(B) The reasonable person in the driver's position would not have anticipated that hitting a pole would affect any person at the hospital.

(C) The doctor was guilty of aggravated negligence in continuing to operate on the patient under the circumstances then existing.

(D) The patient's scarring was caused by the conduct of the doctor.

109. The plaintiff and the defendant were sportswriters who wrote for competing newspapers in the city. Because most of the plaintiff's articles praised his home team, and most of the defendant's articles praised his home team, a rivalry developed between the plaintiff and the defendant. One of the defendant's recent columns contained the following statement:

> [Plaintiff]'s team can't play ball, and [plaintiff] can't write his way out of a paper bag. The only thing more boring than reading [plaintiff]'s stuff is reading it while watching his team play.

If the plaintiff commences an action for defamation against the defendant, which of the following would be the defendant's most effective argument in defense?

(A) The plaintiff is a public figure.

(B) The statements made by the defendant were expressions of opinion.

(C) The defendant's occupation makes him a media defendant.

(D) The defendant's statements were privileged by the defense of competition.

110. A manufacturer built and sold a machine to a steel mill. Two years later, the steel mill sold the machine to a small computer parts startup. The manufacturer discovered that a screw in the machine would wear down and break within three years. It learned the startup had purchased the machine, and offered to repair the defective screw for $1,000, which was what it would cost the manufacturer to make the repair. The startup did not want to spend that much money to fix the machine. Six months later, the screw snapped and an employee was injured.

The employee sued the manufacturer on a theory of strict liability. During trial, the jury found the worn screw made the machine defective when it was sold to the steel mill, the machine had not been substantially changed since the first sale, and the defective screw was the proximate cause of the employee's injury. The jury should find in favor of

(A) the employee, because he was injured by the defective screw.

(B) the employee, because the manufacturer's demand for $1,000 was unreasonable.

(C) the company, because the machine was removed from the stream of commerce when the steel mill sold it.

(D) the company, because the startup's refusal to pay the cost of the repair was unreasonable.

111. At 9 A.M., a man parked his car on a road in front of the play yard of the elementary school. At the time that he parked the car, the man knew that he was violating a statute that prohibited parking within two blocks of any elementary school. At 10 A.M. on the same day, because she was driving at an unreasonably fast rate of speed, a woman lost control of her car and struck the man's parked vehicle. The impact caused a passenger in the woman's car to be thrown against the windshield, severely cutting her face and rendering her unconscious. If the man's car had not been parked where it was, the woman would have collided with a six-foot

concrete wall that surrounded the school play yard.

If the passenger asserts a negligence claim against the man, which of the following additional facts or inferences, if it was the only one true, would be most likely to lead to a judgment for the man?

(A) The statute that prohibited parking within two blocks of any elementary school was designed to protect schoolchildren.

(B) The accident would not have occurred if the woman had not been operating her vehicle in an unreasonable manner.

(C) If the woman's car had hit the concrete wall, the passenger would have sustained injuries as serious as those sustained in the collision with the man's car.

(D) The woman's unreasonable driving was an intervening cause of harm.

112. A jury found that the plaintiff was damaged to the extent of $100,000. The jury further found that the plaintiff's damage was caused 20 percent by the plaintiff's negligence, 40 percent by one defendant's negligence, and 40 percent by another defendant's negligence. The jurisdiction had a statute that read as follows:

> In a negligence action, no plaintiff shall be barred from recovery because of that plaintiff's contributory negligence, but such plaintiff's recovery shall be diminished in proportion to plaintiff's own fault.

The court held that the two defendants were jointly and severally liable for the plaintiff's damage and entered judgment for the plaintiff consistent with the jury's verdict.

The first defendant became insolvent following the entry of judgment. How much money is the plaintiff entitled to collect from the second defendant?

(A) $100,000.

(B) $80,000 ($100,000 less 20 percent).

(C) $40,000 (40 percent of $100,000).

(D) None.

113. While the plaintiff was shopping at a sporting goods store owned by the defendant, another customer assaulted the plaintiff with a baseball bat. The plaintiff sued the defendant for his damages. The could should find

(A) the defendant liable under the principle of vicarious liability.

(B) the defendant liable under the principle of general liability.

(C) the defendant liable under the principle of strict liability.

(D) the defendant not liable.

114. A magazine contained an article about the recent sale of an old house that had once been owned by a United States President. The article stated that the home had been purchased by the plaintiff for $950,000. It described the plaintiff as a bank president earning a salary of $100,000 per year and stated that she had purchased the home with part of the $1 million fortune that she inherited from her mother.

Writers of the article had obtained information about the sale from public records of the Office of the County Recorder. Information about the plaintiff's employment and salary had been obtained from public records of the state Department of Banks, and information about her inheritance from public records of the state Probate Court. All statements made in the article were accurate.

The plaintiff asserts a claim for invasion of privacy on the ground that the article publicly disclosed facts about her salary and inheritance. The court should find for

(A) the plaintiff, because most members of the general public were unfamiliar with records of the state Department of Banks and the state Probate Court.

(B) the plaintiff, because there is no right to publish information regarding the personal wealth of a person who is not a public employee.

(C) the magazine, because liability cannot be imposed for publication of the truth.

(D) the magazine, because the plaintiff's salary and inheritance were a matter of public record.

115. A landowner lived in a cabin in the area. After a nearby factory began using unbagged cement, cement dust from the factory's operation continually settled on the cabin that the landowner occupied. Although the dust did no physical harm to the cabin or to the landowner, the landowner complained to officials of the factory that the dust annoyed her. Because the factory received no other complaints from other area residents, however, it continued using unbagged cement.

If the landowner wishes to assert a tort claim against the factory on account of the cement dust that continually settles on the cabin, which of the following would be her most effective theory?

(A) Invasion of privacy.

(B) Public nuisance.

(C) Trespass to land.

(D) Strict liability for engaging in an abnormally dangerous activity.

116. An employee was driving a pickup truck owned by the company when he collided with an automobile owned and operated by a driver. A passenger in the driver's car

subsequently asserted a claim against the company, the employee, and the driver for injuries sustained in the accident. At trial, the jury fixed the amount of the passenger's damages and found that the employee was 40 percent at fault, the driver was 60 percent at fault, and the passenger was not at fault. In issuing a judgment for the passenger, the court held that the employee and the driver were jointly and severally liable for the passenger's injuries and that the company was vicariously liable for the employee's tort. The jurisdiction had statutes that adopted pure comparative negligence and recognized a right of contribution between joint tortfeasors.

In enforcing the judgment, what portion of her damages is the passenger entitled to collect from the employee?

(A) 0 percent

(B) 40 percent

(C) 50 percent

(D) 100 percent

117. In a negligence action by the plaintiff against two defendants, the court found that the plaintiff's injuries were proximately caused by the combined negligence of the two defendants and that they were jointly and severally liable to the plaintiff in the sum of $100,000. The court also found that in producing the plaintiff's injury, the first defendant was 40 percent at fault and the second defendant was 60 percent at fault. The jurisdiction has a statute recognizing the right of contribution between joint tortfeasors, and that contribution shall be based on apportionment of fault.

After the entry of judgment, the plaintiff succeeded in collecting $10,000 from the first defendant. Which of the following correctly states the amount that the plaintiff is entitled to collect from the second defendant?

(A) $50,000 (60 percent of $100,000 minus $10,000 already collected).

(B) $60,000 (60 percent of $100,000).

(C) $90,000 ($100,000 minus $10,000 already collected).

(D) $100,000.

118. A plaintiff was in an auto accident with the defendant. After a jury trial, the jury found that the plaintiff's damage was $100,000. The jury also found the accident was 25 percent the fault of the defendant, and 75 percent the fault of the plaintiff. A statute in the relevant jurisdiction imposes a system of pure comparative negligence.

Based on the jury's findings, the court should enter judgment for

(A) the defendant, because he was only 25 percent at fault.

(B) the plaintiff, in the amount of $25,000.

(C) the plaintiff, in the amount of $75,000.

(D) the plaintiff, in the amount of $100,000.

119. During the course of an argument about politics, the defendant slapped the plaintiff in the face. Angry, the plaintiff pointed an unloaded pistol at the defendant. The defendant immediately drew a knife and stabbed the plaintiff with it, injuring him severely. The plaintiff subsequently asserted a battery claim against the defendant. The only defense raised by the defendant was self-defense.

In determining the defendant's liability to the plaintiff, the most important issue that must be decided is whether

(A) the use of a knife by the defendant constituted deadly force.

(B) the defendant knew or should have known that he could safely and easily retreat without sustaining harm.

(C) the defendant was the initial aggressor.

(D) the plaintiff knew that his pistol was unloaded.

120. The defendant kept an extremely tame lion as a pet. The lion had worked in a circus for most of its life and had never attacked anyone in all the years it was performing. Now, the lion was old, practically blind, and had lost all of its teeth. Without any negligence by the defendant, the lion escaped from the defendant's backyard and walked to the plaintiff's home, which was over one mile away. Finding the front door open and smelling some steak cooking, the lion walked through the front door and into the plaintiff's kitchen. When the plaintiff saw the lion she panicked and dropped a boiling pot of grease onto her foot. She suffered severe burns as a result. The plaintiff sued the defendant for damages. The court should find

(A) the defendant not liable because the lion had never shown any propensity to harm a person.

(B) the defendant not liable because the defendant was not negligent.

(C) the defendant not liable because the injury was not the result of the lion's dangerous propensities.

(D) the defendant liable for the plaintiff's injuries.

121. The owner of a supermarket purchased an automatic door-opener from its manufacturer. The device included rubber step-plates that were to be installed on the floor on both sides of the door. When a person stepped on one of the step-plates, the machine was designed to swing the door away from him or her.

The store owner hired a contractor to install the automatic door-opener while the store was closed for the night. The contractor read the instructions furnished by the manufacturer but disregarded the warnings. When he finished installing the device, he did not test it by stepping on one of the step-plates but advised the store's night manager that the job was complete. The following morning when the store opened, a customer was injured by the door.

The customer asserted a claim for his injuries against the store owner. Which one of the following additional facts or inferences, if it was the only one true, would be most likely to result in a judgment for the customer?

(A) The customer's injury resulted from a defect in the step-plate.

(B) The contractor was not negligent in his installation of the automatic door-opener.

(C) A reasonable inspection by the store owner would have disclosed that the door opened improperly.

(D) The customer made a purchase from the store owner before being struck by the door.

122. The plaintiff, an adult, took his neighbor's seven-year-old son to see the circus. During the show, many children left their seats to watch the performance from the edge of the area on which it took place. The boy did so with the plaintiff's permission. When the circus's trained lions were performing, one of the animals got away from its enclosure and struck the boy with its paw, injuring him. Horrified, the plaintiff ran from his seat and chased the lion away from the boy. The plaintiff was not touched by the lion but became highly nervous as a result of the incident. The circus knew that the lions would often attack people. The jurisdiction applied the doctrine of transferred intent.

If the plaintiff asserts a claim for battery against the circus, the court should find for

(A) the plaintiff, because the jurisdiction applies the doctrine of transferred intent.

(B) the plaintiff, because the plaintiff experienced mental suffering as a result

of harmful contact inflicted upon the boy.

(C) the circus, because the plaintiff was not touched by the lion.

(D) the circus, because the circus knew that the lions would attack a member of the audience when the circus exhibited them.

123. One weekend, while the plaintiff's son was visiting with her ex-husband, a friend of the plaintiff's phoned her. The friend said that she heard that the ex-husband was planning to remove the boy from the state permanently.

Panicked, the plaintiff ran to the home of the ex-husband's father and pounded on the door. When the ex-husband's father came to the door, the plaintiff demanded, in a loud voice, that the ex-husband's father tell her where her ex-husband and her son were. The ex-husband's father knew that the ex-husband had taken the boy to the movies and would soon be returning. Because the plaintiff's manner frightened him, however, the ex-husband's father said that he had no idea where they were or when they were coming back and refused to talk to the plaintiff any further.

As a result, the plaintiff became highly upset. She visited her physician, who prescribed a mild tranquilizer, but she remained nervous until the ex-husband brought the boy to her home that evening.

The plaintiff asserted a claim against the ex-husband's father for false imprisonment. The court should find for

(A) the ex-husband's father, because the plaintiff sustained no physical injury as a result of the incident.

(B) the ex-husband's father, because he did not prevent the plaintiff from leaving his home.

(C) the plaintiff, because she was legally entitled to custody of the boy.

(D) the plaintiff, because the ex-husband's father prevented her from seeing or communicating with the boy.

124. The defendant's car struck and killed a boy, flinging the child and his tricycle through the air.

The plaintiff was standing in her living room when she heard the screech of the defendant's brakes. Glancing out through her window, she saw the boy's bloody body fly through the air and land on her front lawn. The plaintiff was so shocked by what she saw that she suffered a heart attack and needed to be hospitalized for several weeks.

If the plaintiff asserts a claim against the defendant for damages resulting from mental distress that she experienced because of the incident, which one of the following additional facts or inferences, if it was the only one true, would be most likely to result in a judgment for the plaintiff?

(A) The reasonable person would have expected someone to be in the plaintiff's position and to experience mental suffering as a result of the incident.

(B) The jurisdiction applies the doctrine of transferred intent.

(C) The jurisdiction applies the doctrine of transferred consequences.

(D) The reasonable person would regard the defendant's speed as outrageous.

125. A homeowner hired a painter to paint the outside of the homeowner's house. While doing so, the painter left his ladder unattended on the front lawn.

Two days later, a government employee was walking across the homeowner's lawn while delivering mail. On several occasions in the past, the homeowner had asked her to use the sidewalk and not to walk on his lawn. The homeowner saw the employee walking toward the painter's ladder on his lawn but did not warn the employee because he believed that she saw it. Although the lawn had recently been mowed and the ladder was in plain view, the employee did not see the ladder and tripped over it, injuring her knee.

The jurisdiction applies the all-or-nothing rule of contributory negligence.

If the employee asserts a negligence claim against the homeowner for damages resulting from her injury, which of the following would be the homeowner's most effective argument in defense?

(A) The homeowner did not know with certainty that the employee would be injured.

(B) The dangerous condition was created by the painter.

(C) The homeowner believed that the employee knew that the ladder was there.

(D) A landowner owes no duty to government employees entering on official business.

126. Six months after a doctor performed surgery on her, a patient was X-rayed by another doctor. The X-ray disclosed a surgical instrument inside the patient's chest. The first doctor was the only person who had ever performed surgery on the patient. The patient subsequently asserted a medical malpractice claim against the doctor, alleging that the doctor had negligently left the surgical instrument inside her while operating on her.

If an expert testifies that surgeons do not usually leave instruments inside a patient's body unless they are acting unreasonably, may the patient rely on *res ipsa loquitur* in her claim against the doctor?

(A) No, because the doctrine of *res ipsa loquitur* is not applicable to a claim for professional malpractice.

(B)  No, because a jury of laypersons is not competent to infer that a physician was negligent.

(C)  Yes, because a surgeon is under an absolute duty not to leave instruments inside a patient's body.

(D)  Yes, because the doctor was the only person who had ever performed surgery on the patient.

127.  The defendants were driving their vehicles in an unreasonable manner when they collided. The collision caused the first driver's vehicle to strike and injure a pedestrian who was crossing the street in the middle of the block. The pedestrian was hospitalized as a result of the accident, but he had hospitalization insurance that paid $10,000 toward his hospital bill.

The pedestrian subsequently asserted a claim against both defendants. At the trial, in response to the judge's instructions, the jury found that the pedestrian sustained damages of $100,000, and that the accident resulted 40 percent from the negligence of the first driver, 40 percent from the negligence of the second driver, and 20 percent from the negligence of the pedestrian. The judge ruled that the defendants were jointly and severally liable to the pedestrian and entered judgment in accordance with the jury's verdict.

Which of the following statements correctly describes the amount that the pedestrian is entitled to collect from the first driver in a jurisdiction that has a pure comparative negligence statute?

(A)  $100,000 reduced by 20 percent.

(B)  $100,000 reduced by $10,000 and further reduced by 20 percent.

(C)  40 percent of $100,000.

(D)  40 percent of the amount derived by subtracting $10,000 from $100,000.

128.  The defendant, a power company, built a large nuclear power plant. It did so with utmost care, and the plant went far beyond the safety measures required by federal guidelines. The plant sat on the edge of a small harbor that had a beach that was extremely popular for fishing. The plaintiff went to the harbor every day to fish. Because the plaintiff was also extremely proud of his dark tan, he fished with his shirt off, surrounded by mirrors he placed in the sand so the sun reached all sides of his body evenly. After three years, the plaintiff developed an extremely rare form of cancer that was linked to radiation escaping from the plant. The radiation leak was so small that it could not be detected, and in fact was only discovered because the plaintiff became sick. If the plaintiff had not fished surrounded by mirrors, it was unlikely he would have gotten sick or that the leak would have been discovered at all. The plaintiff sued the defendant for his injuries. During trial, the defendant proved that it was not negligent in any way. The jurisdiction used common law contributory negligence principles. The court should rule in favor of

(A)  the defendant, because the defendant was not negligent.

(B)  the defendant, because the plaintiff's use of the mirrors was contributory negligence.

(C)  the defendant, because the leak was impossible to discover before the plaintiff was injured.

(D)  the plaintiff.

129.  One evening in a tavern, a 17-year-old girl drank alcoholic beverages. The girl then left and went to the tavern next door, where she drank alcoholic beverages. The girl attempted to ride home on her motorcycle. Because the girl was intoxicated, she struck and injured a pedestrian. The pedestrian subsequently asserted claims against both taverns under a state law that provides as follows: "If a minor under the age of 20 years injures another while intoxicated, any

person who sold said minor the alcohol that resulted in said minor's intoxication shall be liable to the injured person."

The first tavern did not sell the girl enough alcohol to make the girl intoxicated, and the alcohol that the second tavern sold the girl would have made the girl intoxicated even if the first tavern had sold the girl no alcohol at all. In determining the pedestrian's claim against the second tavern, the court should find that

(A) the second tavern's conduct was not the cause of the girl's intoxication because the first tavern's conduct was a substantial factor in making the girl intoxicated.

(B) the second tavern is liable under the statute even if the second tavern's conduct did not cause the girl to become intoxicated.

(C) the second tavern's conduct was a cause of the pedestrian's injury because the girl would not have become intoxicated if the second tavern did not sell the girl alcoholic beverages.

(D) the second tavern's conduct was a cause of the girl's intoxication but was not a cause of the pedestrian's injury because the girl's driving superseded it.

130. A contractor told the landowner that she did not think that one pillar would provide sufficient support for the landowner's staircase. When the landowner discussed the contractor's objection with the architect, however, the architect insisted that one pillar would be sufficient. The landowner told this to the contractor and convinced the contractor to rely on the architect's plan.

The contractor completed the building as agreed and turned it over to the landowner on April 1. Two weeks later, the landowner hired a mover to move a piano onto the second floor of the house. While the mover was carrying the piano up the staircase, the staircase collapsed, causing the mover to sustain injury. If the staircase had been supported by two columns, it would not have collapsed.

If the mover asserts a negligence claim against the contractor, the court should declare that

(A) the contractor assumed the risk because she supported the stairway with only one pillar even though she was aware of the danger of doing so.

(B) the contractor is not liable because she had turned the building over to the landowner prior to the accident.

(C) the contractor is not liable because it was reasonable for her to rely on the architect's instructions in constructing the stairway.

(D) the contractor absolved herself of the risk by objecting to supporting the stairway with only one pillar.

131. A man was obviously intoxicated when he entered a bartender's tavern one night and ordered a drink of whiskey. A statute in the jurisdiction prohibits serving alcoholic liquor to any intoxicated person. The bartender knew that the man was intoxicated, but because the man was a good customer, the bartender opened a new bottle and poured him some of it. After drinking the liquor, the man left the tavern and began driving home.

Before the whiskey left the factory, an angry employee added a poison to it that could not have been discovered by reasonable inspection. While the man was driving in a reasonable manner, the poison caused him to die. As a result, the man's car struck a pedestrian, injuring her.

If the pedestrian asserts a claim against the factory, the court should find for

(A) the factory, because the employee deliberately poisoned the liquor before it left the factory.

(B) the factory, because the pedestrian did not purchase or consume the factory's product.

(C) the pedestrian, because the liquor contained poison when it left the factory.

(D) the factory, because the poison could not have been detected by reasonable inspection.

132. Pursuant to a contract with the federal government, a rocket company manufactured and launched rockets used for placing communications satellites into space. Shortly after the rocket company launched one of its rockets, the rocket exploded in the air. It then crashed into a storage building owned by a medical company that contained antibiotics with a value of $180 million, totally destroying the building and its contents. No one could determine the cause of the explosion. Although the rocket company used reasonable care in all aspects of the manufacturing and launching process, a few of the rocket company's rockets had exploded in the past shortly after launch. Each time this happened, the rocket involved was completely destroyed while in the air and caused no damage on the ground.

If the medical company asserts a claim against the rocket company for the loss of its building and contents, the court should find for

(A) the medical company, because the construction and launching of rockets is an abnormally dangerous activity.

(B) the medical company, under the doctrine of *res ipsa loquitur*.

(C) the rocket company, because the reasonable person would not expect antibiotics worth $180 million to be stored in one building.

(D) the rocket company, because none of the rocket company's rockets caused any damage on the ground in the past.

133. Due to an error at its factory, a company sold an airline a belt truck that did not have an acceleration suppressor.

Two months later, the airline went out of business and sold the belt truck to a second airline. An independent contractor hired by the second airline to maintain the second airline's equipment set the belt idle above 15. Doing so can cause the truck to lurch forward unless it is equipped with an acceleration suppressor. The company was aware that people who maintain the trucks often set the idle above 15. Subsequently, an employee of the second airline attempted to activate the belt while standing beside the belt truck. She was injured when the belt truck lurched forward and struck her.

The employee asserts a claim against the company on the ground that the absence of an acceleration suppressor made the belt truck defective. The court should find for

(A) the company, because the first airline was negligent in failing to discover that the belt truck was not equipped with an acceleration suppressor.

(B) the company, because if the contractor had acted reasonably in setting the belt idle, the employee would not have been injured.

(C) the employee, because persons who maintain belt trucks frequently set the belt idle above 15.

(D) the employee, because the negligence of the contractor is imputed to the company.

134. A company operated a manufacturing plant just outside the town, making an insecticide that was very important to the state's orange crop. Breezes frequently carried fumes from the company's plant into the town.

Although the fumes did not violate state air pollution laws, they caused many buildings in the town to need frequent repainting and led many homeowners to complain about it to the company. The company did nothing about it, however, because the cost of eliminating the fumes was extremely high.

A homeowner, who owned a house in the town in which he resided with his son, had to repaint his house several times because of the fumes.

The homeowner asserted a private nuisance claim against the company for the damage to his paint, asserting that the company was negligent in failing to eliminate the fumes. Which of the following would be the company's most effective argument in defense against the homeowner's claim?

(A) The operation of the company's plant did not result in a physical invasion of the homeowner's realty.

(B) The fumes affected others in substantially the same way as they affected the homeowner.

(C) The company officials did not know that the fumes would affect the paint of the homeowner's house.

(D) The cost of eliminating the fumes would have driven the company out of business.

135. A company was the manufacturer of a product that was sold over the counter for the treatment of dandruff and dry scalp conditions. The plaintiff purchased a bottle at a local drugstore. A statement on the label read, "This product will not harm normal scalp or hair." The plaintiff used the product as directed. Because of a scalp condition making him allergic to one of the ingredients, the product irritated his scalp, causing him much pain and discomfort.

In an action by the plaintiff against the company on the theory of strict liability in tort,

which of the following additional facts or inferences, if it was the only one true, would be most helpful to the plaintiff's case?

(A) Injuries of the kind sustained by the plaintiff do not ordinarily result from the use of a product like this one unless the manufacturer was negligent.

(B) Prior to the plaintiff's purchase of the product, an article regarding the allergy from which he suffered had appeared in a widely read journal of the hair-care industry.

(C) The ordinary consumer would not have expected the use of the product to result in an irritation of the scalp of someone with the plaintiff's allergy.

(D) At the time it manufactured the product purchased by the plaintiff, the company was aware that its ingredients could irritate the scalp of persons with allergies like the plaintiff's.

136. The city sidewalk in front of the defendant's business was often covered with leaves that made the sidewalk slippery. To try to fix matters, the defendant made a deal with the city, giving the defendant possession and control of the trees. The defendant then swept the leaves off the sidewalk every morning. One morning, the defendant failed to sweep, and the plaintiff, who was walking into the business on his way to a meeting, slipped on the leaves and fell, cracking his head open. The plaintiff was texting on his phone when he fell, but he had walked into the building every day for weeks and reasonably believed that the leaves would be swept because of the past conduct of the defendant. The plaintiff sued, and the defendant defended himself by asserting he had no duty to sweep the leaves off the sidewalk under the circumstances.

How should the court rule?

(A) In favor of the defendant, because the sidewalk was city property.

(B) In favor of the defendant, because the plaintiff was texting when he fell.

(C) In favor of the plaintiff, because the defendant had possession and control of the trees.

(D) In favor of the plaintiff, because the defendant's past conduct made the plaintiff reasonably believe the leaves would be swept

137. A farmer owned 500 acres of land on which she grew wheat. By a valid written contract, she agreed to deliver all her wheat to a company to be used by that company in the production of bread for sale to the general public. While harvesting the crop, she realized that a blade on her harvesting machine was broken and that fine slivers of metal were becoming mixed with the wheat. She said nothing about this when she delivered the wheat to the company, since she knew that the company ordinarily cleaned its wheat before using it.

The bread company used the wheat that it purchased from the farmer to manufacture a loaf of bread that it sold to a sandwich shop. The sandwich shop owner used the bread to make a sandwich. Because the bread contained slivers of the blade from the farmer's harvesting machine, the customer who bought the sandwich lacerated the lining of his throat when he tried to eat it.

In an action by the customer against the bread company, can the customer successfully rely on the doctrine of *res ipsa loquitur*?

(A) Yes, because the exercise of reasonable care in the baking process would ordinarily have eliminated all metal slivers from the wheat.

(B) Yes, because the presence of metal slivers made the bread defective.

(C) No, because the presence of the metal slivers in the wheat resulted from

the farmer's failure to use reasonable care.

(D) No, because it was unforeseeable that a broken blade on the farmer's harvesting machine would result in the presence of metal slivers in the wheat.

138. A kidnapper falsely claimed he was holding a girl hostage. In reality, the girl was on a camping trip. The girl's mother remained in a hysterical state until the girl returned from her camping trip and the girl's mother realized that it had been a hoax. The girl's mother, who already suffered from a heart ailment, had a heart attack the day after the girl's return.

If the girl's mother asserts a claim against the kidnapper for damages resulting from her heart attack on a theory of intentional infliction of emotional distress, the court should find for

(A) the kidnapper, because the heart attack occurred the day after the girl's return.

(B) the kidnapper, because the mother's preexisting condition made her especially susceptible to heart attack.

(C) the girl's mother, because the heart attack was caused by the kidnapper's outrageous conduct.

(D) the girl's mother, because the kidnapper should have foreseen that his conduct would result in harm.

139. While the plaintiff was visiting her daughter, the two of them decided to go swimming at a nearby public pool. Since she had not brought a bathing suit along on her visit, the plaintiff went to a department store to purchase one. While looking at the suits on the bargain counter, she found one made by a bathing suit company. The package that contained it bore a label that read, "Disposable Bathing Suit. This garment is made completely from recycled paper.

Although it is strong enough to be worn several times and is even washable, it's inexpensive enough to be thrown away after one use." The plaintiff bought the suit and then went to the beach. The first time she was hit by a wave, however, the suit completely disintegrated.

Which of the following additional facts or inferences, if it was the only one true, would be most helpful to the department store's defense in an action by the plaintiff against the department store?

(A) The department store had sold the bathing suit company's products for several years and had never heard of any problem like the one experienced by the plaintiff.

(B) A sign on the bargain counter where the plaintiff found the suit said, "Sale Merchandise. All sales final."

(C) The plaintiff knew that paper bathing suits like the one she had purchased sometimes dissolved when they became wet.

(D) The department store could not implead the bathing suit company into the action because the company had gone out of business.

140. A 13-year-old boy and his family lived on a farm in a very remote portion of the state. Because of the lack of automobile traffic, the boy's parents let him ride a motorcycle between the family farm and the local grocery store. There was no statute or ordinance that prohibited the boy's use of the motorcycle. One morning, there was heavy fog on the ground when the boy drove the motorcycle to the store. The speed limit was 35 miles per hour. While a reasonable adult would have known to drive under the speed limit because of the poor visibility, a reasonable 13-year-old would not normally have such knowledge. The boy drove the motorcycle at 35 miles an hour and crashed into a car when he was unable to slow down

in time. The boy did not expect a car to be on the road, because cars were so rarely around. The car owner sued the boy for negligence. The court should rule in favor of

(A) the car owner, because the boy was driving a motorcycle.

(B) the car owner, because a reasonable adult would have known to drive under the speed limit.

(C) the boy, because a reasonable 13-year-old would not normally know to drive under the speed limit.

(D) the boy, because he was driving at the speed limit.

141. The company manufactured a device for training dogs. A professional dog trainer was working with a dog in her unfenced front yard and was using the company's brand new device. A man was walking past the yard when the dog began to snarl and lunge at him. When the trainer yanked on the leather strap of the device, it suddenly broke, freeing the dog. The dog sprang forward, biting the walker.

If the walker asserts a claim against the dog trainer, the walker's most effective argument in support of his claim would be that

(A) the dog trainer is strictly liable for damage resulting from her use of a defective product.

(B) it was unreasonable for the dog trainer to work the dog in her front yard.

(C) the dog trainer's conduct was a concurring cause of harm.

(D) the dog trainer was a professional dog trainer.

142. Because the plaintiff had a headache, he took two headache tablets from a bottle that had been purchased by his wife at the grocery store. The tablets had been manufactured by the company, which sold them to the grocery store in sealed bottles for resale.

Because of a toxic ingredient that the tablets contained, the plaintiff became ill as a result of taking them.

If the plaintiff asserts a claim against the company based on a theory of strict liability in tort, the ruling should turn on the question of whether

(A) the company knew that the tablets contained a toxic ingredient.

(B) headache tablets that contain a toxic ingredient are inherently dangerous.

(C) it was reasonable for the company to market the tablets.

(D) the presence of the toxic material was a defect.

143. A driver was looking for an address as he drove down the street and was not watching the road in front of him. As a result, he did not see a pedestrian crossing the street in front of him and struck her with his car, knocking her down. The driver immediately got out of her car to help the pedestrian. When he saw that she was unconscious, he became afraid to move her and left her in the roadway while he ran to a nearby phone. While the driver was gone, a taxi drove down the same street. The taxi did not see the pedestrian in the roadway, and drove over her, fracturing her leg.

In an action by the pedestrian against the driver for damages resulting from her fractured leg, a court is most likely to find for

(A) the pedestrian, because the driver's negligence was a factual and legal cause of the pedestrian's fractured leg.

(B) the pedestrian, since the negligence of the taxi is imputed to the driver.

(C) the driver, since his conduct was a legal cause but not a factual cause of the pedestrian's fractured leg.

(D) the driver, because the pedestrian would not have been injured but for the taxi striking her.

144. An employee resigned after being told he wouldn't be compensated for extra work hours. At the same time, he told his former employer he would retain a set of tools issued to him until he received payment. The employee applied for a job with another company, and that company wrote to the former employer asking for an evaluation of the employee's honesty and ability. The former employer wrote a letter to the other company that stated, "When the employee left my company, he stole a valuable set of tools." As a result, the other company did not hire the employee. If the employee asserts a claim against his former employer for defamation, the employee should

(A) lose, because the employee did not return the tools that he took when he left the employer's employ.

(B) lose, because the employer's statement was made in response to a specific request by the employee's prospective employer.

(C) win, because the employer's statement could not have benefitted the employer's business interests.

(D) win, because the employer's statement accused the employee of stealing tools.

145. The defendant operated a train carrying high explosives used to blow tunnels through mountains. As the train was passing through a city, it hit the plaintiff, who had ducked through the lowered train-crossing bars and was trying to get across the tracks to the other side before he was blocked by the train. The plaintiff was severely injured. The plaintiff sued the defendant for his damages. During trial, the defendant proved that it was not negligent in any way. The jurisdiction followed comparative negligence principles. The court should rule in favor of

(A) the plaintiff, under the doctrine of strict liability.

(B) the defendant, because the plaintiff assumed the risk of getting hit by the train.

(C) the defendant, because it was not negligent.

(D) the defendant, because the plaintiff was contributorily negligent by trying to cross the tracks.

146. The seller knew that his car's engine was cracked. Because he wanted to sell the car, he filled the crack with putty and painted it so that the crack would not show. He then sold the car to a used car dealer. The next day, the used car dealer was showing the car to a customer when the crack caused the engine to explode, injuring the customer.

If the customer asserts a claim against the seller for injuries that he sustained when the engine exploded, which of the following would be the customer's most effective theory?

(A) Battery, because the seller knew that the engine was cracked.

(B) Intentional misrepresentation, because the seller knew that the engine was cracked.

(C) Negligent misrepresentation, because the seller had a duty to disclose that the engine was cracked.

(D) Negligence, because the seller should have anticipated that a customer of the used car dealer would be injured as a result of the cracked engine.

147. The defendant negligently burned down a restaurant when he used a highly flammable cleaner to clean the restaurant's deep fryer. The defendant was an independent contractor hired to clean the restaurant and he owned no interest in the restaurant. The plaintiff, a waiter at the restaurant, was laid off because of the fire damage and could not

get a job for six months. The plaintiff sued the defendant for his financial losses from his joblessness. The court should rule in favor of

(A) the defendant, because the plaintiff suffered only economic harm.

(B) the defendant, because he owned no interest in the restaurant.

(C) the plaintiff, because the defendant's negligence caused him to be laid off.

(D) the plaintiff, because the defendant's negligence burned down the restaurant.

148. A natural gas factory was located on the edge of the city. When the wind blew from the east, foul-smelling waste gases from the factory's chimneys were blown over the city, causing most of the residents to experience a burning of the eyes and throat. On several occasions, a city resident attempted to persuade the city attorney to seek an injunction against the factory. The city attorney refused, however, because the city council was afraid that doing so would drive the factory from the area. If the resident seeks an injunction by asserting a claim against the factory on a theory of public nuisance, which of the following would be the factory's most effective argument in defense?

(A) The city attorney's decision is binding.

(B) The resident has not sustained harm different from that of the general public.

(C) A private citizen may not seek an injunction against environmental polluters.

(D) A private citizen may not sue on a theory of public nuisance.

149. A trucker was eating cherry pie in a restaurant when a cherry pit contained in the pie stuck in his throat. Unable to breathe, the trucker began choking. A doctor who was eating in the restaurant ran to the trucker's

aid and performed an operation known as an emergency tracheotomy. Then, at the doctor's direction, the trucker walked across the street to a hospital. The hospital's emergency room had famously long waits. Because hospital employees negligently failed to enter the trucker's name in the emergency room register, he sat in the emergency room for six hours without further attention. At that time, an earthquake caused a portion of the hospital's structure to fall, striking the trucker in the head and fracturing his skull. An earthquake had never occurred in the state before.

Assume that the doctor's conduct in performing the emergency tracheotomy was unreasonable, and if the doctor had acted reasonably, the trucker would have coughed up the pit without any injury. In an action by the trucker against the doctor for damages resulting from his fractured skull, will the trucker win?

(A) Yes, since he would not have been in the hospital if the doctor had not performed the tracheotomy.

(B) Yes, because it was foreseeable that the trucker would be required to wait six hours in the hospital's emergency room.

(C) No, since he would not have been injured were it not for the cherry pit contained in the pie.

(D) No, because the earthquake was a superseding cause of the trucker's injury.

150. In answer to specific questions posed by the court, the jury found that an accident was 60 percent the fault of the plaintiff and 40 percent the fault of the defendant. In addition, the jury found that damage to plaintiff's car amounted to $1,000, and that damage to the defendant's car amounted to $10,000.

The jurisdiction had a statute that provided that "In any negligence action, a plaintiff's recovery shall not be barred by that plaintiff's fault, but the recovery of said plaintiff shall be diminished in proportion to such plaintiff's fault, unless that plaintiff's fault shall be greater than that of the defendant, and in such event the plaintiff's recovery shall be barred." Which of the following correctly states the sum to which the plaintiff is entitled?

(A) $600 ($1,000 less 40 percent).

(B) $400 ($1,000 less 60 percent).

(C) $1,000.

(D) 0.

151. The landlord was the owner of a four-story office building. An attorney in the landlord's building knew that the elevator was broken, but decided to take one of his client's up in it anyway. The landlord had promised the attorney he would fix it, but the landlord did not do so. When the attorney and the client were riding in the elevator, it suddenly dropped, injuring the client.

The client asserted a claim against the landlord for damages resulting from his injuries, alleging that the landlord was negligent in failing to fix the elevator or warn the client about it. Which of the following would be the landlord's most effective argument in defense?

(A) The landlord did not owe the client a duty to repair the elevator since the landlord's promise was not made to the client.

(B) The client was a mere licensee since his presence did not confer a benefit on the landlord.

(C) It was not foreseeable that the attorney would permit the client to use the elevator since the attorney knew it was not working properly.

(D) It was unreasonable for the attorney to permit the client to use the elevator since the attorney knew that it was not working properly.

152. A licensed exterminator bought a large container of insecticide. The label said it should only be used by professional exterminators. The exterminator placed the container on a shelf in his shop, where it was discovered by a janitor. Since the janitor thought there were termites in his house, he opened the container and poured some of the chemical pellets into a plastic bag that he then brought home. The next day, the janitor's three-year-old daughter found the plastic bag containing the pellets and ate some of them, becoming seriously ill as a result. A statute in the jurisdiction adopted the all-or-nothing rule of contributory negligence.

In an action by the daughter against the exterminator, which of the following would be the daughter's most effective argument?

(A) The exterminator should have foreseen that the insecticide would cause injury to someone in the daughter's position if left on an exposed shelf in his shop.

(B) The insecticide was defective since its label did not adequately warn of the dangers connected with its use.

(C) The insecticide is an inherently dangerous product.

(D) The janitor's theft of the pellets was a concurring cause of his daughter's harm.

153. After living together for several months, a man and his girlfriend began to argue frequently. On Monday, after an argument, the man left their apartment in anger, saying that he didn't know when he was coming back. The following Saturday, the girlfriend took all the man's possessions, including his television set, to a swap meet in hopes of selling them. At the swap meet, she sold the television to a neighbor.

If the man instituted an action against his former girlfriend for trespass to chattel, which one of the following additional facts

or inferences, if it was the only one true, would be most helpful to the girlfriend's defense?

(A) The man's leaving the apartment constituted implied consent to the girlfriend's sale of his possessions.

(B) The girlfriend's interference with the man's right to the television was serious enough to justify a forced sale.

(C) The neighbor committed a conversion by purchasing the television set at the swap meet.

(D) At the time the man's action against her was instituted, the girlfriend could not reacquire possession of the television set from the neighbor.

154. The plaintiff and the defendant lived on the same street and worked in the same office, so they formed a car pool, each driving his own car on alternate days. One day while the defendant was driving, the car in front of him stopped suddenly and without warning. Since the defendant had taken his eyes off the road for a moment to look at the plaintiff, he was unable to stop in time and collided with the rear of the stopped car. The plaintiff was injured as a result of the collision.

There was no automobile guest statute in the jurisdiction. In an action by the plaintiff against the defendant, which of the following would be the defendant's most effective argument in defense?

(A) The plaintiff assumed the risk since he knew that it was possible that the defendant's car would be involved in an accident while traveling to work.

(B) The defendant's conduct was not a cause-in-fact of harm since the accident would not have occurred if the car in front of him had not stopped suddenly.

(C) The defendant did not owe the plaintiff a duty of reasonable care since the plaintiff was a licensee.

(D)  It was not negligent for the defendant to take his eyes off the road for a moment.

155. After an accident, a woman was trapped in her car. The fire chief told a volunteer firefighter to use a new device to free her. He knew the device could be dangerous, and that the volunteer firefighter had not been trained in how to use it. The volunteer firefighter used the device improperly, injuring the woman.

If the woman instituted an action against the fire chief, the woman's best theory would be

(A)  negligence.

(B)  battery.

(C)  strict products liability.

(D)  *res ipsa loquitur.*

156. As a result of her neighbor's negligence, the plaintiff's shoulder and eye were both injured. The plaintiff went immediately to her eye doctor. The eye doctor treated the injury to the plaintiff's eye but suggested that she see an orthopedist for treatment of her shoulder. The following day, the plaintiff visited an orthopedist, who treated the plaintiff's shoulder.

Because of negligent treatment by the eye doctor, the plaintiff's nose became infected, and because of negligent treatment by the orthopedist, she lost the use of her elbow.

In an action by the plaintiff against her neighbor, which of the following parts of the plaintiff's body is a court most likely to find were injured as a proximate result of the neighbor's negligence?

(A)  Her nose.

(B)  Her elbow.

(C)  Both her nose and elbow.

(D)  Neither her nose nor her elbow.

157. A newspaper incorrectly stated that a local minister was a minister for a group that was historically perceived as a cult engaged in unlawful activities. Which of the following is a court most likely to find about the statement?

(A)  The statement is not defamatory if the group can be classified as a religion under the First Amendment to the United States Constitution.

(B)  The statement is not defamatory if members of the group do not currently engage in improper activities.

(C)  The statement is not defamatory if a substantial group of right-thinking people know that members of the group no longer engage in improper activities.

(D)  The statement is defamatory if many people continue to believe that members of the group engage in improper activities.

158. A company was in the business of developing and manufacturing machinery used in other industries.

A warehouse employee was injured when a pin in one of the company's machines wore out. The company knew that a pin failure was dangerous. The employee instituted a negligence action against the company that made the machine. The company's defense was based on the assertion that prior to the accident, the company neither knew nor reasonably could have known that the pin would wear out. If the jury believes this assertion, the employee will

(A)  win, since the company is deemed to be an expert in its field and has a duty to know all relevant facts about the product that it makes.

(B)  win, since it is foreseeable that if the pin did wear out, someone would be hurt.

(C)  win, since a manufacturer is strictly liable for defects in its product, whether
or not it could have prevented those
defects.

(D)  lose.

159.  A carpenter was working on the framework of his roof when he found that he had
brought the wrong hammer onto the roof
with him. Without looking to see if anyone
was around, he tossed the hammer to the
ground, shouting, "Heads up!"

A man who was crossing the property was
killed when the hammer hit him in the head.

The representative of the man's estate
instituted an appropriate action against the
carpenter, in a jurisdiction that applies the
all-or-nothing rule of contributory negligence, alleging that the carpenter's throwing
of the hammer without looking was negligence. If it were the only one true, which of
the following additional facts or inferences
would be most effective in the carpenter's
defense against that allegation?

(A)  It was reasonable for the carpenter to
believe that no one would be struck
by the hammer.

(B)  It is customary in the construction
industry for people working on a roof
to toss unwanted tools and objects to
the ground without looking, so long
as they shout, "Heads up!"

(C)  The man could have avoided being
struck by the hammer if he had seen it
coming.

(D)  The blow of his hammer would not
have caused a serious injury to
a normal person, but it seriously
injured the man because his head was
extraordinarily sensitive.

160.  A man bought a sealed pie from a grocery
store. The pie was made by a local manufacturer. After opening and eating half of

the pie, the man discovered that it was full
of worms. A reasonable inspection by the
grocery store would have discovered the
worms.

If the man asserts a claim for negligence
against the grocery store, the court should
find for

(A)  the man, because any negligence by the
manufacturer of a product is imputed
to a retailer selling that product.

(B)  the man, because the product was
defective when the man purchased it
from the grocery store.

(C)  the man, because the grocery store
failed to act reasonably in selling the
product to the man.

(D)  the grocery store, because a retailer
is under no duty of reasonable care
when selling products packaged in
sealed containers.

161.  A mother negligently allowed her nine-
year-old son to ride his bike on a busy road.
While doing so, the boy negligently swerved
side-to-side until he was hit by a car driven
by a driver. The driver was acting unreasonably when he struck the boy. The jurisdiction applies the all-or-nothing rule of
contributory negligence.

If the boy asserts a negligence claim against
the driver for his injuries, the court should
find for

(A)  the boy, because a nine-year-old is
presumed incapable of contributory
negligence.

(B)  the boy, under the doctrine of *res ipsa
loquitur.*

(C)  the driver, because the accident
resulted from the boy's unreasonable
conduct.

(D)  the driver, because it was unreasonable
for the boy's mother to give her son

permission to ride his bicycle along the roadway.

162. While attempting to make an arrest at a grocery store, police officers knocked over several stacks of merchandise, including cases of bottled soda-pop. This caused minute cracks in all the bottles. The following day, store employees cleaned up the mess, restacking the cases of soda-pop without checking any of the bottles for damage. A woman purchased one of the bottles but did not notice the minute crack in it.

That evening, the woman was placing the bottle on the dinner table when the bottle exploded because of the crack in it, sending fragments of glass flying in all directions. The woman was injured.

In an action by the woman against the grocery store, a court is most likely to find for

(A) the woman, because she could not have done anything to protect herself against the kind of injury that occurred.

(B) the woman, because the grocery store's conduct in restacking and selling the bottles without some sort of inspection was unreasonable under the circumstances.

(C) the grocery store, because the conduct of the police officers was a proximate cause of the injury sustained by the woman.

(D) the grocery store, because the woman and the grocery store were not in privity.

163. While standing in an art gallery, a buyer overheard a conversation between a collector and an art dealer. The dealer stated that a particular painting was worth $250,000. After the collector left the gallery, the buyer purchased the painting for $225,000 from the dealer. The buyer subsequently learned that the painting was worth only $600.

If the buyer is successful in a tort action for misrepresentation against the dealer, the court is likely to award him a judgment for

(A) $250,000 (the value that the dealer stated).

(B) $250,000 (the value that the dealer stated), on condition that the buyer return the painting to the dealer.

(C) $225,000 (the price that the buyer paid to the dealer).

(D) $224,400 (the price that the buyer paid to the dealer, less the value of the painting).

164. A man lent his friend his car. The man knew his friend had had his license revoked for reckless driving, but his friend promised he was only driving his mother to a doctor's appointment and would return the car as quickly as possible. In fact, the friend drove the car several hundred miles away to visit his girlfriend. On the way back, the friend was speeding and swerving between cars when he crashed into a woman's car. Because the man's friend had no money, the woman sued the man for negligence. May she recover?

(A) Yes, because the man loaned his friend the car.

(B) Yes, because the man owned the car.

(C) No, because the friend lied to the man about how he would use the car.

(D) No, because the woman is only suing the man because his friend has no money.

165. The plaintiff purchased a bottle of dishwashing detergent made by the defendant at a supermarket. After using the product for washing dishes, the plaintiff experienced a serious rash on his hands and wrists as the result of an allergic reaction to a chemical in the product.

If the plaintiff asserts a claim against the defendant on the ground that the product was not merchantable, which of the following additional facts or inferences, if it were the only one true, would provide the defendant with its most effective defense?

(A) The plaintiff's allergic reaction was the only such reaction that ever occurred.

(B) The supermarket purchased the product from an independent wholesaler that purchased it from the defendant.

(C) Before marketing the product, the defendant made a reasonable effort to determine whether the product would be harmful to normal skin.

(D) Prior to manufacturing and marketing the product, the defendant received approval for its sale from the federal Food and Drug Administration.

166. A statute required all high-rise construction sites to be surrounded by a temporary fence. The purpose of the statute was to protect people from being hurt by falling construction debris. A construction company failed to fence in one of its sites near an elementary school. One of the schoolchildren wandered onto the site and was poisoned when he drank water from a puddle on the site. The child's injury was severe. The child sued the construction company, and the court found the child would not have been able to get onto the site if the proper fence had been in place. It also found that a reasonable child of the child's age, intelligence, and experience would not have drunk the water from the puddle. The child's attorney then asked the judge to instruct the jury that the violation of the statute was negligence per se. Should the court do so?

(A) Yes, because the child would not have been hurt but for the violation of the statute.

(B) Yes, because the puddle was under the construction company's control.

(C) No, because the child was poisoned.

(D) No, because the child failed to adhere to the proper standard of care.

167. The plaintiff and the defendant were at an extremely loud rock concert. During an argument about gun control, the defendant called the plaintiff a "dope smoking moron" who only supported gun rights because he was a "habitual thief." The plaintiff had never done drugs or stolen from anyone. A fellow concertgoer overheard the remark and understood it, although it was so loud that the defendant had no reason to believe anyone else at the concert could hear him arguing with the plaintiff. The plaintiff sued the defendant for defamation. During trial, the court found that the defendant was not negligent in his making of the statement. The court should find the defendant

(A) liable for libel.

(B) liable for slander.

(C) liable for defamation.

(D) not liable.

168. The plaintiff was injured in a car accident and received $100,000 worth of damages. The jury further found that the plaintiff's damage was caused 20 percent by the plaintiff's negligence, 40 percent by one defendant's negligence, and 40 percent by another defendant's negligence. The jurisdiction had a statute that read as follows:

In a negligence action, no plaintiff shall be barred from recovery because of that plaintiff's contributory negligence, but such plaintiff's recovery shall be diminished in proportion to plaintiff's own fault.

The court held that the defendants were jointly and severally liable for the plaintiff's damage and entered judgment for the plaintiff consistent with the jury's verdict.

Prior to the entry of judgment, the plaintiff collected $10,000 from an insurance company under a policy in which it agreed to pay any medical bills that the plaintiff might incur as the result of an automobile accident. Which of the following correctly reflects the sum that the plaintiff is entitled to collect from the defendants?

(A) $90,000, because the plaintiff's damage of $100,000 should be diminished by the sum the plaintiff received from the insurance company.

(B) $80,000, because the plaintiff's damage of $100,000 should be diminished by a sum proportional to the plaintiff's own fault, without regard to sums that the plaintiff has received under the insurance policy.

(C) $70,000, because the plaintiff's damage of $100,000 should be diminished by a sum proportional to the plaintiff's own fault and further diminished by the sum that the plaintiff received under the insurance policy.

(D) $60,000, because the plaintiff's damage of $100,000 should be diminished by a sum proportional to the plaintiff's own fault, and the two defendants' proportional shares should each be further diminished by the sum that the plaintiff received under the insurance policy.

169. Although a man realized that his neighbor was drunk, the man asked the neighbor for a ride home. The neighbor agreed and left with the man at once. Because he was drunk, the neighbor lost control of his car.

The man asserts a negligence claim for his injuries against his neighbor in a jurisdiction that applies the all-or-nothing rule of contributory negligence. Which of the following arguments would be likely to provide the neighbor with an effective defense to that claim?

(A) The man was contributorily negligent in accepting a ride from his neighbor

when he knew his neighbor was drunk.

(B) The man assumed the risk by accepting a ride from his neighbor when he knew his neighbor was drunk.

(C) It did not matter that the man knew his neighbor was drunk.

(D) The man was contributorily negligent and assumed the risk by accepting the ride when he knew his neighbor was drunk.

170. A monthly publication of interest primarily to persons who deal in the purchase and sale of historic buildings as an investment stated that a property had been purchased by the plaintiff for $1,450,000. It described the plaintiff as a bank president earning a salary of $200,000 per year and stated that she had purchased the property with part of the $1 million fortune that she inherited from her mother.

The plaintiff asserted a claim for invasion of privacy on the ground that the publication appropriated her identity by publishing the article about her without her permission. Which of the following would be the publication's most effective argument in defense?

(A) Information about the purchaser of the property was of interest to readers of the publication.

(B) The article about the plaintiff did not enrich the publication because the plaintiff was not a celebrity.

(C) The sale of the property to the plaintiff was a matter of public record.

(D) Publication of the article was not the result of actual malice.

171. For many years, powdered cement used by a factory was delivered in 90-pound sacks. Recently, however, factory officials determined that it would be considerably less expensive to purchase unbagged cement.

A landowner lived in the area. After the factory began using unbagged cement, cement dust from the factory's operation continually settled on the cabin that the landowner occupied. Although the dust did no physical harm to the cabin or to the landowner, the landowner complained to officials of the factory that the dust annoyed her. Because the factory received no other complaints from area residents, however, it continued using unbagged cement.

The landowner asserts a negligence claim against the factory. Which of the following would be the factory's most effective argument in defense?

(A) Changing from bagged cement to unbagged cement resulted in substantial financial savings to the factory.

(B) The factory's conduct was not a factual cause of the landowner's discomfort because no other residents complained about the dust.

(C) The landowner assumed the risk by continuing to live in the area.

(D) The landowner sustained no damage as a result of the factory's conduct.

172. In a negligence action by the plaintiff, the court found that the defendants were jointly and severally liable to the plaintiff in the sum of $100,000. The court also found that in producing the plaintiff's injury, the first defendant was 40 percent at fault and the second defendant was 60 percent at fault. The jurisdiction has a statute recognizing the right of contribution between joint tortfeasors, and that contribution shall be based on apportionment of fault.

After the entry of judgment, the plaintiff succeeded in collecting $100,000 from the first defendant. In an action for contribution by the first defendant against the second defendant, which of the following correctly states the amount that he is entitled to collect from the second defendant?

(A) 0.

(B) $40,000 (40 percent of $100,000).

(C) $50,000 (50 percent of $100,000).

(D) $60,000 (60 percent of $100,000).

173. An employee was driving a pickup truck owned by the company when he collided with an automobile owned and operated by a driver. The plaintiff, a passenger in the car, sued. At trial, the jury fixed the amount of the plaintiff's damages and found that the employee was 40 percent at fault, the driver was 60 percent at fault, and the plaintiff was not at fault. It was also found that the employee was acting within the scope of his duties as an employee of the company when the accident occurred. In issuing a judgment for the passenger, the court held that the employee and the driver were jointly and severally liable for the passenger's injuries and that the company was vicariously liable for the employee's tort. The jurisdiction had statutes that adopted pure comparative negligence and recognized a right of contribution between joint tortfeasors.

In enforcing the judgment, the plaintiff succeeded in collecting $100,000 from the company. If the company asserts a claim against the employee seeking compensation for the company's payment to the plaintiff, the company is entitled to recover

(A) nothing, because the company was found to be vicariously liable for the employee's tort.

(B) $40,000 as partial indemnity.

(C) $50,000 as contribution.

(D) $100,000 as complete indemnity.

174. A biker was riding her bicycle in a reasonable manner when she was struck by a car negligently driven by a driver. As a result, the biker was thrown to the ground, breaking her left leg. A moment later, while lying in the road, the biker was struck by a car

negligently driven by a second driver, breaking the biker's right leg.

If the biker asserts a claim against the second driver, the second driver will be held liable for damages resulting from

(A) the biker's broken right leg.

(B) the biker's broken right and left legs.

(C) the biker's broken right and left legs, but only if the first driver's conduct was foreseeable.

(D) neither leg.

175. As a result of a minor earthquake, the framework of a building that the builder was erecting collapsed. When the builder began the building, he knew that the steel that he was using for that purpose was of poor quality but decided to use it anyway. If the steel had not been of poor quality, the earthquake would not have caused the building to collapse.

A driver was employed by a gas company to operate a gasoline truck. She had parked the truck in front of the builder's construction site moments before the earthquake. When the building collapsed, falling debris struck the truck, causing it to rupture and causing its cargo of gasoline to leak. A stream of gasoline that leaked from the truck flowed for three blocks until it reached another nearby street. There, unaware of the presence of gasoline, a man tossed a lit cigarette into the street. The cigarette caused the gasoline to explode, injuring a woman standing nearby.

If the woman asserts a claim against the gas company driver, alleging that it was negligent for the driver to park a gasoline truck in front of a construction site, which of the following would be the driver's most effective argument in defense against the woman's claim?

(A) The builder's use of poor-quality steel was a superseding cause of the woman's injury.

(B) The explosion would not have occurred if the man did not throw a lit cigarette into the street.

(C) The driver could not have anticipated that falling debris from the construction site would cause the truck to rupture and leak.

(D) The explosion that injured the woman was proximately caused by the earthquake.

176. The owner of a supermarket purchased an automatic door-opener from its manufacturer. The device included rubber step-plates that were to be installed on the floor on both sides of the door.

The store owner hired a contractor to install the automatic door-opener while the store was closed for the night. The contractor read the instructions furnished by the manufacturer but disregarded a warning regarding testing the step-plates. When he finished installing the device, he did not test it by stepping on one of the step-plates, but advised the store's night manager that the job was complete. The following morning, a customer was injured by the door.

The customer asserted a claim against the manufacturer on the ground that the step-plate was defective when sold by the manufacturer. Which of the following would be the manufacturer's most effective argument in defense?

(A) It was not foreseeable that a person installing the automatic door-opener would disregard the warning contained in the instructions.

(B) The manufacturer did not act unreasonably in designing or manufacturing the automatic door opener or in furnishing the instructions that came with them.

(C) The customer was not a purchaser of the automatic door-opener.

(D) The store owner was negligent in selecting the contractor to install the automatic door-opener.

177. The plaintiff owned a local coffee shop. The defendant wrote a newspaper story that the plaintiff had been accused by a customer of drugging her coffee and locking her in a dungeon in the basement. The customer really made the accusation, but the accusation was false and the customer was well-known throughout town for making false accusations against shop owners she didn't like. The plaintiff sued the defendant for defamation. At trial, it was established the plaintiff was not a public figure, and the plaintiff presented evidence that the defendant knew or should have known of the customer's habit of making false accusations. The court should rule in favor of

(A) the defendant, because the plaintiff did not establish that the defendant believed the accusations were false.

(B) the defendant, because the plaintiff did not establish that the defendant recklessly disregarded whether the accusations were true.

(C) the defendant, because the plaintiff did not establish that the defendant intended to cause harm to the plaintiff's reputation.

(D) the plaintiff.

178. A homeowner hired a painter to paint the outside of the homeowner's house.

Two days later, a government employee was walking across the homeowner's lawn while delivering mail. The homeowner saw the employee walking toward the painter's ladder on his lawn but did not warn the employee because he believed that she saw it. Although the lawn had recently been mowed and the ladder was in plain view, the employee did not see the ladder and tripped over it, injuring her knee.

The jurisdiction applies the all-or-nothing rule of contributory negligence.

If the government employee asserts a negligence claim against the painter for damages resulting from her injury, which of the following would be the painter's most effective argument in defense?

(A) The ladder was in plain view.

(B) The employee was trespassing at the time the accident occurred.

(C) The painter owed no duty to licensees of the homeowner.

(D) The homeowner was negligent in not warning the employee about the ladder.

179. The plaintiff was involved in an accident after he was hit by a drunk driver. The amount of alcohol that one defendant sold the driver would have made her intoxicated even if a second defendant sold the driver no alcohol at all, and the amount of alcohol that the second defendant sold the driver would have made the driver intoxicated even if the first defendant sold the driver no alcohol at all. Which of the following statements is most correct?

(A) The first defendant did not cause the plaintiff's injury because the second defendant subsequently sold the driver enough alcohol to make her intoxicated.

(B) The second defendant did not cause the plaintiff's injury because the first defendant had previously sold the driver enough alcohol to make her intoxicated.

(C) Neither defendant caused the injury.

(D) Both defendants caused the injury.

180. A landowner hired a professional architect to draw plans for a two-story residence to be constructed on the landowner's realty. The plans that the architect prepared called

for a staircase to be supported by a single concrete pillar. The landowner then hired a licensed building contractor to construct a house in accordance with the architect's design. Upon examining the plans, the contractor told the landowner that she did not think that one pillar would provide sufficient support for the staircase. When the landowner discussed the contractor's objection with the architect, however, the architect insisted that one pillar would be sufficient. The landowner told this to the contractor and convinced the contractor to rely on the architect's plan.

The contractor completed the building as agreed and turned it over to the landowner on April 1. Two weeks later, the landowner hired a mover to move a piano onto the second floor of the house. While the mover was carrying the piano up the staircase, the staircase collapsed, causing the mover to sustain injury. If the staircase had been supported by two columns, it would not have collapsed.

If the mover asserts a negligence claim against the architect, which of the following would be the architect's most effective argument in defense?

(A)  It was reasonable to support the staircase with only one pillar.

(B)  The architect owed the mover no duty since the architect was employed by the landowner.

(C)  The contractor had the last clear chance to avoid the accident.

(D)  The use of a single pillar to support the staircase was a matter exclusively within the architect's professional judgment as an architect.

181.  A man was obviously intoxicated when he entered a bartender's tavern one night and ordered a drink. A statute made it unlawful to serve liquor to any intoxicated person. Even so, the bartender served the man. After

drinking the liquor, the man left the tavern and began driving home.

Before the liquor left the manufacturer's factory, an angry employee added a poison to it that could not have been discovered by reasonable inspection. While the man was driving in a reasonable manner, the poison caused him to die. As a result, the man's car struck a pedestrian, injuring her.

If the pedestrian asserts a claim against the bartender based on the bartender's violation of the above statute, which of the following would be the bartender's most effective argument in defense against that claim?

(A)  The bartender did not serve the man enough liquor to make him intoxicated.

(B)  The statute was not meant to prevent people from drinking liquor that had been poisoned.

(C)  Serving the liquor to the man was not a cause of the pedestrian's injuries.

(D)  The angry employee's conduct was a superseding cause of the pedestrian's injuries.

182.  An airline went out of business and sold a belt truck to a second airline. An independent contractor hired by the second airline to maintain the second airline's equipment set the truck's belt idle above 25. Due to a mistake at the factory, the belt truck was not equipped with an acceleration suppressor. An acceleration suppressor would keep the truck from lurching no matter where the idle was set. Subsequently, an employee of the second airline attempted to activate the belt while standing beside the belt truck. Because the idle was set above 25, she was injured when the belt truck lurched forward and struck her.

The employee asserted a negligence claim against the independent contractor. Which one of the following additional facts or inferences, if it were the only one true, would be most likely to result in a judgment for the independent contractor in a jurisdiction that applies the all-or-nothing rule of contributory negligence?

(A) Belt trucks are usually equipped with acceleration suppressors.

(B) If the employee had been in the driver's seat when she started the belt truck, she would not have been injured.

(C) The omission of an acceleration suppressor was a manufacturing defect in the belt truck.

(D) The first airline failed to notify the second airline about the need for an acceleration suppressor.

183. A company operated a manufacturing plant just outside the town. Breezes frequently carried fumes from the company's plant into the town.

A homeowner's son developed a respiratory illness as the result of an unusual reaction to the fumes. The homeowner complained to the company about his son's illness. When the company responded by offering to buy the homeowner's house, the homeowner refused.

The homeowner asserted a public nuisance claim on behalf of his son in which he sought an order directing the company to eliminate the fumes. Which of the following would be the company's most effective argument in response to this claim?

(A) The claim is not for special damages.

(B) The son's illness was the result of an unusually sensitive reaction to the fumes.

(C) The homeowner assumed the risk by refusing to sell the property to the company.

(D) The fumes did not violate state pollution laws.

184. The manufacturer made a product that was sold over the counter for the treatment of dandruff and dry scalp conditions. A doctor purchased a bottle at a drugstore. A statement on the label read, "This product will not harm normal scalp or hair." The doctor used the product as directed. Because of a scalp condition making him allergic to one of the ingredients, the product irritated his scalp, causing him much pain and discomfort.

In an action by the doctor against the drugstore, which of the following would be the doctor's most effective argument?

(A) Any negligence by the manufacturer is imputed to the drugstore.

(B) The product was defective as labeled.

(C) The drugstore breached an express warranty.

(D) A drugstore is under a special duty to be aware of possible allergic reactions to products that it sells.

185. After the plaintiff sued the defendants for injuries caused in an auto accident, the jury found that the accident was 60 percent the fault of the first defendant and 40 percent the fault of the second defendant. The court ruled that the defendants were jointly and severally liable for the plaintiff's injuries, which amounted to $100,000.

The jurisdiction had a statute that provided that "In any negligence action, a plaintiff's recovery shall not be barred by that plaintiff's fault, but the recovery of said plaintiff shall be diminished in proportion to such plaintiff's fault unless that plaintiff's fault shall be greater than that of the defendant, and in such event the plaintiff's recovery shall be barred." Which of the following correctly states the sum that the plaintiff is entitled to receive from the second defendant?

(A)  $60,000 (60 percent of $100,000).

(B)  $40,000 (40 percent of $100,000).

(C)  $100,000.

(D)  0.

186.  A daily newspaper printed an article about a minister's speech. The article referred to the minister's speech as "inspiring, considering the fact the minister suffers from leprosy." After seeing the article, the minister sued the newspaper for defamation.

The newspaper moved to dismiss the minister's action on the grounds that his complaint contained no allegation of damage. Which of the following additional facts or inferences, if it were the only one true, would be most helpful to the minister in opposing the motion to dismiss?

(A)  Leprosy is a loathsome disease.

(B)  The minister was so upset upon reading the newspaper's statement about him that he became physically ill.

(C)  Editors of the newspaper disliked the minister.

(D)  The minister is neither a public official nor a public figure.

187.  A man was eating one of the company's prepackaged desserts when he found a cockroach in it.

In an action by the man against the company, which of the following additional facts or inferences, if it were the only one true, would provide the company with its most effective defense?

(A)  The company did not act unreasonably in manufacturing, packaging, or marketing the product purchased by the man.

(B)  The man sustained no injury as a result of the presence of a cockroach in the product.

(C)  The company complied with all statutory requirements for quality control in the production of the product.

(D)  The man purchased the product on the recommendation of a sales clerk at the grocery store.

188.  A pilot was flying his airplane when one of its engines stopped working. Although the pilot thought he could probably make it back to the airport, he decided it would be safer to make an emergency landing in a farmer's field. The plane ended up causing $500 worth of damage to the farmer's crops, although the pilot's actual landing of the plane was done in accordance with federal aviation rules and was not negligent. The farmer sued the pilot to recover his $500. The court should rule in favor of

(A)  the pilot, because the broken engine created a private necessity.

(B)  the pilot, because the pilot was not negligent.

(C)  the farmer, because the pilot damaged his crops.

(D)  the farmer, because the pilot probably could have made it back to the airport.

189.  Two political candidates were known for insulting and playing pranks on each other. During a nationally televised debate, the defendant lit a firecracker as a joke and tossed it onto the plaintiff's podium right as the plaintiff was making a speech regarding his toughness and bravery in foreign policy. When the firecracker went off, the plaintiff covered his head and fell onto the floor. Although the plaintiff sustained no physical injury, the audience laughed and he was embarrassed by the incident.

The plaintiff filed a claim against the defendant for intentional infliction of emotional distress. The court should rule in favor of

(A) the defendant, because the plaintiff was only embarrassed.

(B) the defendant, because he was only joking.

(C) the plaintiff, because he fell onto the floor.

(D) the plaintiff, because throwing a firecracker at someone is outrageous.

190. A store owner hired a contractor to install an automatic door-opener while the store was closed for the night. The contractor read the instructions furnished by the manufacturer but disregarded a warning related to its installation. The following morning, a customer was injured by the door when it short-circuited. In a claim by the customer against the contractor, which of the following would be the customer's most effective argument?

(A) The contractor's liability is established by *res ipsa loquitur.*

(B) It was unreasonable for the contractor to disregard the warning contained in the instructions furnished by the manufacturer.

(C) The automatic door-opener was installed in a way that made it unfit for ordinary use.

(D) The short circuit made the automatic door-opener defective.

191. A driver was driving her automobile in the rain when she rounded a bend and saw a cow standing directly in her path. She immediately jammed on her brakes and pulled the steering wheel to the right in an attempt to avoid striking the cow. As a result, she lost control of her car, which skidded off the road and into the homeowner's yard.

In an action by the homeowner against the driver for negligence, which of the following arguments would be most effective as a defense for the driver?

(A) Her conduct did not result in damage.

(B) She was not required to act reasonably because she was confronted by an emergency.

(C) She was privileged by the doctrine of necessity.

(D) It was foreseeable that users of the road would deviate onto adjacent private land in connection with their use of the road.

192. A doctor owned a large machine for putting patients to sleep during surgery. The doctor sent the machine to the manufacturer for repairs. While making the repairs, the manufacturer accidentally filled the anesthetic gas can with plain oxygen and the plain oxygen can with anesthetic. During a surgery, the doctor wanted to administer pure oxygen to the patient. However, because of the mistake in the cans, the patient got pure anesthetic instead. As a result, the patient died.

The patient's family sued the doctor for damages resulting from the death of the patient. During trial, the court found the doctor acted unreasonably in her treatment of the patient. The court should find the doctor is

(A) liable, because the doctor was unreasonable in her treatment of the patient.

(B) liable, because of *res ipsa loquitur.*

(C) not liable, because the death was caused by the manufacturer's negligence.

(D) not liable, because the negligence occurred while the machine was in the care of the manufacturer.

# ANSWERS
## TORTS

# ANSWERS TO
# TORTS QUESTIONS

1. **B**    If the risk of injury to the doctor was not foreseeable, then the manufacturer could not be said to have acted unreasonably in the face of a foreseeable risk. Since negligence is usually defined as failure to act reasonably in the face of a foreseeable risk, this would mean that the manufacturer was not negligent.

Conduct is a cause of harm if the harm would not have occurred without it. Thus, if the label contained a warning that the doctor disregarded or failed to read, his conduct could be contributory or comparative negligence that helped cause his injury. Since the label did not contain any warning, however, his injury would have occurred whether he read it or not. For this reason, his failure to read it was not causally related to the harm that he suffered and does not provide the manufacturer with a defense. If the doctor sued for breach of warranty, he might be required to show that he relied on some statement contained on the label, and his failure to read it might prevent him from establishing such reliance. Since his lawsuit is based on negligence, however, **A** is incorrect. Even if the product was manufactured by another, the manufacturer would be under a duty to use reasonable care in marketing it, so that fact alone would not protect the manufacturer against liability to the doctor. **C** is therefore incorrect. **D** is incorrect because the manufacturer's lack of awareness might have been negligent if the reasonable person in the manufacturer's shoes would have been aware.

2. **A**    Negligence is unreasonable conduct in the face of a foreseeable risk. The defendant's awareness of the high incidence of crime in the neighborhood would make the risk foreseeable and might result in a finding that it was unreasonable for her to open the door under the circumstances. While it is not certain that a court would come to this conclusion, the fact in **A** is the only one listed that would help support the plaintiff's case.

The plaintiff's knowledge would not impose any duty on the defendant, so **B** is incorrect. Although the defendant's intention to sell furniture to the plaintiff might make the plaintiff an invitee, and thereby impose upon the defendant a duty to act reasonably, the duty would not be breached unless the defendant had some reason to know that there was a danger in opening the door. **C** is therefore incorrect. **D** is incorrect because unless the defendant knew or should have known of the incident, it would have no relevance to the reasonableness of the defendant's conduct.

3. **D**    A misrepresentation is a false assertion of material fact made with the intent to induce the plaintiff's reliance. If the defendant knew that the statement was false, and if the plaintiff justifiably relied upon it, the defendant is liable for damage that results. If a party to a transaction is under a legal obligation to disclose a fact, nondisclosure may be an assertion that the fact does not exist. Thus, since the developer had an obligation to disclose that the highway was coming, her silence was an assertion that there was no highway coming. Since she knew this assertion to be false, she is liable for misrepresentation if the farmer's reliance on it was justified. Consequently, **D** is correct.

Since real estate investors are usually experts in determining the value of real estate, the fact that the farmer knew the developer to be a real estate investor might have justified his reliance on her misrepresentation. **A** is incorrect because this would be likely to result in a victory for the farmer rather than the developer. If the developer's nondisclosure was a misrepresentation, she probably repeated the misrepresentation by permitting an appraiser to determine value without disclosing the coming of the highway. **B** is therefore incorrect. A fiduciary relationship is one based on trust. Since buyer and seller are adversaries, neither is the other's fiduciary. **C** is therefore incorrect.

4.  **D**     Negligence is the failure to act reasonably in the face of a foreseeable risk. If selling a pistol for less than $50 created a foreseeable risk to the woman, it might be found that the gun maker's conduct in doing so was unreasonable and that the gun maker is liable to the woman for negligence. While it is not certain that a court would come to this conclusion, the argument in **D** is the only one listed that could possibly support the woman's claim.

Intent is an essential element of battery. In a battery case, intent means that the defendant desired (or knew with substantial certainty) that harmful or offensive contact with the plaintiff would occur. **A** is incorrect because the fact that harm is foreseeable (rather than substantially certain) is not sufficient to result in liability for battery. In every sale by a merchant, there is an implied warranty that the product sold is merchantable, or fit for ordinary use. There is no indication, however, that the pistol did not function as a pistol ordinarily functions. **B** is therefore incorrect. It is sometimes said that violation of a criminal statute establishes negligence if the statute was designed to protect a class of persons to which the plaintiff belongs against risks like the one that led to the harm. **C** is incorrect, however, because there is no indication that the gun maker violated a criminal statute.

5.  **C**     One whose conduct creates a foreseeable risk to any person owes that person a duty of reasonable care. One who helps an intoxicated person get his or her car started is creating a foreseeable risk to all who are likely to be endangered by that person's driving. If the injury to the pedestrian occurred 200 miles away from the place where the dentist assisted the man, however, it may successfully be argued that the reasonable person in the man's situation would not have anticipated harm to him because the man could be expected to sober up in the time it took to drive that distance. While it is not certain that a court would come to this conclusion, the argument in **C** is the only one listed that could possibly support the dentist's defense.

Although a statute like the one mentioned in **A** might impose liability on the bartender, it would not have the effect of relieving any other person of liability, so **A** is incorrect. **B** is incorrect because being in the road service business does not exempt any person from his or her common law duty to act reasonably in the face of a foreseeable risk. **D** would establish that the man's intoxication was a cause of the accident but would not establish that the dentist's actions were not. If anything, it would prove the cause-and-effect relationship between the dentist's conduct and the accident. **D** is therefore incorrect.

6.  **C**     Negligence liability requires a breach of the duty of reasonable care that is a proximate cause of the plaintiff's damage. To say that the plaintiff was outside the foreseeable zone

of danger is simply another way of saying that because of where the plaintiff was located, the injury to him or her was not foreseeable. This argument could help support the driver's defense in two ways. First, if harm to the painter was not foreseeable, the driver did not owe him a duty of reasonable care. This would mean that, although the driver's conduct might have been negligent as to the hunter, it could not have been negligent as to the painter. Second, unless some injury to the painter was a foreseeable result of the driver's conduct, that conduct was not a proximate cause of it. Although a court might not agree that the painter was outside the foreseeable zone of danger, the argument in **C** is the only one listed that could possibly support the driver's defense.

It is generally understood that if an injury to the plaintiff was foreseeable, all its complications are foreseeable too, no matter how improbable those complications actually were. For this reason, **A** and **D** are incorrect. Joint tortfeasors are two or more persons whose torts proximately caused the same injury. In most jurisdictions, they are jointly and severally liable for the full extent of the plaintiff's injury. The argument in **B** would establish that the hunter was negligent, but this would not provide the driver with a defense since he and the hunter might be found to be joint tortfeasors.

7. **A**      All persons are liable for the harm that proximately results from their negligence. Thus, if the burglar's injury was proximately caused by the brewery's negligence, the brewery is liable to her.

         An express warranty is an assertion of fact that becomes part of the basis of the bargain. **B** is incorrect because there is no indication that an express warranty was made. **C** is incorrect because the clean hands doctrine, which is relevant in equity proceedings, is not applicable to an action for money damages. Since it is foreseeable that the burglar could obtain the beer in some manner, the precise manner in which the burglar obtained the beer is immaterial. **D** is therefore incorrect.

8. **C**      False imprisonment occurs when the defendant intentionally confines the plaintiff. The plaintiff is confined when his or her will to leave a place with fixed boundaries is overcome in a way that would similarly overcome the will of the reasonable person in the plaintiff's situation. Since the fisherman was not prevented from leaving, he was not confined (*i.e.*, imprisoned).

         In a false imprisonment case, the term *intent* means a desire or knowledge that the defendant's act will result in a confinement of the plaintiff and does not depend on whether the defendant knew that the plaintiff's rights were being violated. Thus, if the acts of the movie studio's employees had resulted in a confinement of the fisherman, the fact that they did not know they were violating the fisherman's rights would not provide them with an effective defense. **A** is therefore incorrect. **B** is incorrect because false imprisonment is an intentional tort of which unreasonable conduct is not an essential element. **D** is incorrect because damage is not an essential element of liability for false imprisonment.

9. **C**      Although liability ordinarily results from the publication of false defamatory statements about the plaintiff, the courts have always required that publication be either intentional

or the result of negligence. The competitor's statement to the handyman was not a publication since the handyman is the plaintiff. The fact that it was overheard by the customer does not satisfy the requirement of publication unless either the competitor intended that the customer hear it or the customer heard it as a result of the competitor's unreasonable conduct in the face of the foreseeable risk that the customer would hear it. If the competitor knew that the customer would hear it, he intended the publication. If he should have known that the customer would hear it, he acted unreasonably in saying it.

When the plaintiff is not a public figure, courts do not require proof that the defendant knew the statement to be defamatory, so **A** is incorrect. The United States Supreme Court has held that in some defamation cases, the plaintiff must prove that the defendant knew or should have known that the statement was false when he made it. **B** is incorrect, however, because the requirement has not been applied to a defamation action brought by a private person against a non-media defendant. **D** is incorrect because knowledge that harm will result is not an essential element of any defamation case.

10. **C**    Strict liability is imposed on the seller of a product that is in a defective condition when sold and that reaches the consumer in a condition that is substantially unchanged. Although the farmer could still be held liable, **C** would be her most effective argument.

**A** is incorrect because intervening negligence, unless it was unforeseeable, is not sufficient to relieve the supplier of a defective product from liability. Although privity or some substitute is relevant to warranty liability, strict liability in tort may be applied to benefit any plaintiff whose contact with the product was foreseeable. **B** is therefore incorrect. Since strict liability is not based on fault, proof that the defect resulted from some circumstance beyond the defendant's control is not sufficient to free that defendant from liability. **D** is therefore incorrect.

11. **C**    Assault results when the defendant, with the intention of causing either offensive contact or apprehension of offensive contact, induces apprehension of such contact in the plaintiff. Battery results when the defendant, with the intention of causing either offensive contact or apprehension of offensive contact, causes offensive contact with the plaintiff. The defendant, intending to cause apprehension of offensive contact, induced such apprehension, making him liable for assault. With intent to induce apprehension, he also caused offensive contact, making him liable for battery. Therefore, **A**, **B**, and **D** are all incorrect.

12. **D**    A negligent misrepresentation is a false assertion of fact that is made without knowledge of its falsity but under circumstances such that a reasonable person in the defendant's situation would have had such knowledge. Thus, if the seller's belief that there were no termites in the house was reasonable, his misrepresentation was not negligent. Although there are not enough facts to determine whether a court would come to this conclusion, **D** is the only argument listed that could possibly support the seller's position.

**A** is incorrect because lack of such knowledge would be negligent if the reasonable person would have known. Whether or not the seller had a duty to disclose the presence of termites, when he discussed termites, he had a duty to do so honestly and reasonably. **B** is therefore incorrect. A statement is of opinion if it concerns a subjective matter or contains an expression of doubt. Since the seller's statement was neither, it was not of opinion. **C** is therefore correct.

13.   **D**   Strict liability is imposed on the seller of a product that is in a defective condition when sold. Thus, if the supermarket sold the product while it was defective, the supermarket would be held strictly liable no matter who manufactured it.

Parties who work together to accomplish a particular result are involved in a concert of action that may make any one of them vicariously liable for torts committed by the others. **A** is incorrect, however, because the facts indicate that the manufacturers and retailer did not work together on manufacturing or marketing the product. It has been held that where there are a small number of manufacturers in a particular industry, where all belong to an industry-wide association that establishes industry standards, where those standards result in their products' being defective, and where all members of the industry and the association are named as defendants, liability may be imposed on an industry-wide basis. **B** is incorrect, however, because there is no indication that the number of cereal manufacturers is small or that they belong to an industry-wide association that sets standards or that their standards made the product defective or that all members of the industry and their association have been named as defendants. Under the alternate liability theory, where two or more defendants commit identical acts of negligence under circumstances that make it impossible to tell which one injured the plaintiff, it will be presumed that all of them factually caused the plaintiff's injury. **C** is incorrect, however, because there is no indication that all the parties named committed identical acts of negligence or that any of them was negligent at all.

14.   **D**   Assault occurs when, with the intent to induce such apprehension, the defendant induces in the plaintiff a reasonable apprehension that a harmful or offensive contact with the plaintiff will occur. Since the girl's mother did not fear contact with herself, she was not assaulted.

**A** and **B** are incorrect because the kidnapper's conduct did not induce the girl's mother to apprehend contact with herself. If the kidnapper's conduct did give the girl's mother reason to apprehend contact with herself, it would not matter whether she had perceived contact with the girl. **C** is therefore incorrect.

15.   **A**   Strict liability is imposed on the keeper of a wild animal, but only for harm that proximately results from an aspect of the animal that made keeping it dangerous. Leopards are dangerous because they bite or attack. The risk that they may clumsily knock someone over is not one that makes them more dangerous than a dog or other domestic animal.

**B** is incorrect because an animal is "wild" if it comes from a species that cannot ordinarily be safely kept without special training or restraint. Since this is true with leopards, the leopard's tameness does not prevent it from being so classified. **C** and **D** are incorrect because strict liability does not depend on the reasonableness of a defendant's conduct.

16.   **B**   A claim for damages resulting from contact with a product manufactured or sold by the defendant may be based on several theories, including negligence, misrepresentation,

breach of warranty, and strict liability in tort. In most jurisdictions, however, mental suffering is not a recoverable item of damage in a claim based on any of these theories unless the mental suffering is the result of a physical injury or has a physical manifestation. Although a few jurisdictions permit recovery even in the absence of physical injuries, the argument in **B** is the only one listed that could possibly support the defendant's defense.

**A** is incorrect for two reasons: First, even without a representation, the defendant could be held liable on negligence, implied warranty, or strict liability theories, and second, the statement that the suit was "strong enough to be worn several times" was probably a representation. **C** is incorrect because none of the theories requires that the plaintiff be in privity with the manufacturer. Although the argument in **D** might provide an effective defense to a negligence claim, **D** is incorrect because the other theories that are available do not depend on unreasonable conduct by the defendant.

17. **A**    Under the all-or-nothing rule of contributory negligence, unreasonable conduct by the plaintiff that contributes to the happening of an accident is a complete bar to recovery by the plaintiff. Thus, if the boy's conduct was unreasonable, the driver's defense of contributory negligence will succeed.

B, C, and D are incorrect because the negligence of a parent in supervising a child is not imputed to the child. The reasonableness of the mother's conduct is therefore not in issue.

18. **C**    Strict liability is imposed on the seller of a product that is in a defective condition when sold. A product is defective if its condition would defeat the reasonable expectations of the reasonable consumer. Since the reasonable consumer probably would not expect a brand new training leash to break when used on a dog of average size and strength, one that did was probably defective.

Strict liability may be applied to benefit any person whose contact with the defective product was foreseeable, so **A** is incorrect. **B** is incorrect because strict liability does not depend on the reasonableness of the defendant's conduct. **D** is incorrect because the risk that it describes as foreseeable is not the one that led to the harm in this case since the device was brand new when it broke.

19. **A**    A person is liable for all harm that proximately results from his or her negligence. Thus, if the aunt was negligent in giving the doll to the boy, she may be held liable for the injury that resulted. It is possible that a court would come to this conclusion since it may have been foreseeable that a child of the boy's age would swallow the button and be injured. Although the result is not certain, the argument in **A** is the only one listed that could possibly result in a judgment for the father.

In every sale by a merchant, there is an implied warranty that the product sold is fit for ordinary use. If the product is unfit, breach of warranty liability is imposed without regard to fault. Similarly, if a product is defective or unreasonably dangerous, strict tort liability may be imposed on the supplier. **B**, **C**, and **D** are incorrect, however, because these theories are available only against a defendant who is a professional supplier of products, which the aunt was not.

20.　**C**　The key to this question is that the plaintiff is basing his claim on negligence, not strict products liability. Since negligence is a breach of the duty to act reasonably, the grocery store could be held liable under that theory only if it acted unreasonably. Since the tablets were delivered in a sealed bottle, and since the reasonable merchant does not ordinarily open sealed products before selling them, the grocery store probably did not breach the duty that it owed to the plaintiff. While the grocery store could be held liable if the trier of fact found that the reasonable merchant would ordinarily open sealed products before selling them, **C** is the best answer out of the choices given.

**A** is incorrect because a manufacturer's negligence is not imputed to a retailer. **B** is based on an incorrect statement of the law. A retailer's duty is *to use reasonable care*. The breach of this duty is negligence. Although a retailer may be held liable without fault under a theory of strict liability, this liability is based not on the breach of "an absolute duty," but on a policy that attempts to distribute the risks of being injured by defective products. **D** is incorrect because negligence liability depends on the foreseeability of the risk, not upon the existence of any contractual relationship.

21.　**C**　A defendant owes a plaintiff a duty of reasonable care if the defendant's conduct creates a foreseeable risk to the plaintiff. Thus, if it was foreseeable that a person would be in the roadway, the taxi driver owed that person a duty to drive as a reasonable person. Once it is established that such a duty existed, its breach by driving while intoxicated is obvious.

Since the pedestrian's presence in the roadway was part of the set stage (*i.e.*, preexisted the defendant's tortious act), it does not matter whether the circumstances that put her there were foreseeable. **A** and **B** are therefore incorrect. Although a plaintiff must establish that his or her injury was a foreseeable result of the defendant's negligent conduct, he or she is never required to establish that the defendant's negligence was foreseeable. **D** is therefore incorrect.

22.　**B**　Strict liability is often imposed on one who uses his or her land in a non-natural manner for the storage of a substance that is likely to do harm upon its escape from storage. The storage of water frequently leads to the application of this principle.

Although strict liability is imposed on one who engages in an abnormally dangerous activity, it is imposed only for damage that results from the dangerous nature of the activity. Although the operation of a nuclear power plant may be an abnormally dangerous activity, **A** is incorrect because harm in this case did not result from any of the aspects of operating a nuclear power plant that make it abnormally dangerous. If the power company knew or should have known that an earthquake might occur in the area of the nuclear power plant, it might have been unreasonable to operate it there. But absent such actual or constructive knowledge, the power company's conduct cannot be presumed to be unreasonable. **C** is therefore incorrect. The intervention of an Act of God does not free an antecedent wrongdoer from liability unless that intervention was unforeseeable. **D** is therefore incorrect.

23.  **D**    Strict liability may be imposed for damage resulting from participation in abnormally dangerous activities such as the manufacture and storage of explosives. Even under a theory of strict liability, however, a defendant is not liable for harm unless it was proximately caused by the defendant's activity. Conduct that is a factual cause of harm is a proximate cause of that harm if the harm was a foreseeable result and was not brought about by unforeseeable intervention. Thus, if the intervening conduct of the terrorists was not foreseeable, the harm sustained by the homeowner was not proximately caused by the conduct of the company. While it is not certain that a court would come to this conclusion, **D** is the only argument listed that could possibly support the company's defense.

A is incorrect because strict liability may be imposed regardless of fault and regardless of whether the defendant's conduct was reasonable. Most jurisdictions hold that there can be no liability for trespass to land unless there was a physical invasion of the plaintiff's realty. **B** is incorrect, however, because the company may be held liable on a strict liability theory, which does not require a physical invasion. Even though a defendant's conduct was a factual cause of harm, that defendant will not be held liable if there was an unforeseeable intervening cause of the harm. **C** is incorrect, however, because the intervening cause will not prevent such liability unless the intervention was unforeseeable.

24.  **C**    Nondisclosure of a fact is not an assertion (*i.e.*, representation) unless the fact is one that is essential to the transaction and the circumstances are such that the other party is reasonably entitled to expect disclosure of it. Since the buyer had no special expertise, his reason for purchasing the hay wagon was not a fact essential to the transaction, and there were no circumstances that entitled the seller to expect disclosure of his hope of making a profit.

A and B are incorrect because slight differences in knowledge concerning the subject of a particular transaction are not sufficient to impose a duty of disclosure. **D** is incorrect because the seller's initial satisfaction would not prevent her from recovering if it had been induced by a misrepresentation by the buyer.

25.  **C**    A defendant's conduct is not a proximate cause of harm if the harm was brought about by an independent intervening cause. An intervening cause is "independent" if it did not result from one of the normal risks resulting from the defendant's conduct. Since the first pilot's plane was safely on the ground at an airport when struck by the second pilot's plane, it can be argued that the collision was independent of the risks created by the first pilot's miscalculation. While it is not certain that a court would come to this conclusion, the argument in **C** is the only one listed that could possibly be effective in the first pilot's defense.

A plaintiff may be barred from recovery by assumption of the risk when the harm results from a danger of which the plaintiff was aware and which he or she voluntarily encountered. Since there is no indication that the first pilot's miscalculation resulted from his lack of a commercial pilot's license, the harm did not result from a risk of which the businessman knew. **A** is therefore incorrect. Under the all-or-nothing rule, a plaintiff's negligence may prevent recovery if it was causally related to the harm which he or she sustained. Since there is no indication that the first pilot's miscalculation resulted from his lack of a commercial pilot's license, any negligence by the businessman in accepting a ride from him was not causally related to the accident. **B** is therefore incorrect. Conduct is a factual cause of harm if the harm would not have occurred without it. The argument in **D** states that the harm would not have occurred if the second pilot had not been negligent. This is obviously true and establishes that the second pilot's negligence was a factual cause of the accident. The argument also states, however, that the first pilot's miscalculation was therefore not a factual cause of the accident. Since the accident would not have occurred if the first pilot's plane had not been on the ground, and since the first pilot's plane would not have been on the ground had the first pilot not miscalculated, the first pilot's miscalculation was also a factual cause of the accident. **D** is therefore incorrect.

26.  **A**   The patient's injury would not have occurred without the manufacturer's negligence, so the manufacturer's negligence was a cause of it. Since the patient's injury would not have occurred without the doctor's error, and since the doctor's error came between the manufacturer's conduct and the patient's injury, the doctor's error was an intervening cause of the patient's injury. If negligence that is a cause of harm is followed by an intervening cause of harm that was not foreseeable, the intervention is regarded as a superseding cause that relieves the antecedent wrongdoer of liability. Thus, if the doctor's error was unforeseeable, the manufacturer would not be liable to the patient.

If the doctor's conduct was foreseeable, it would constitute a concurring cause of harm and, as such, would not shield the antecedent wrongdoer from liability. This is true whether that intervention was reasonable or not, and whether it is classified as gross negligence or not. **B**, **C**, and **D** are therefore incorrect.

27.  **B**   Almost all theories of products liability require that the plaintiff's contact with the product be foreseeable. Since hypodermic needles are commonly used by doctors to give injections to patients, the patient's contact with the needle is foreseeable.

It is less foreseeable, if it is foreseeable at all, that a child would play with a hypodermic needle, so **A** is incorrect. **C** is incorrect because none of the products liability theories permit the recovery of losses that are unrelated to personal injury or property damage. **D** is incorrect because there is no indication that the needle was infected when sold by the manufacturer or that the infection resulted from the manufacturer's negligent conduct.

28.  **B**   Trespass to land is defined as intentional entry on the plaintiff's realty without authorization. Since realty includes the airspace immediately above the land, the crop duster entered the gardener's realty when she flew through the air 15 feet above his land. Although she believed that she had authority to do so, she did not have such authority. Her overflight was, thus, a trespass if her entry onto the realty was intentional. A defendant has the necessary intent to be liable for trespass to land if he or she desires or knows that his or her act will result in an entry onto the realty that he or she entered. This is so regardless of whether he or she knows whose realty he or she is entering, or that the entry is unauthorized. Since the crop duster did desire to fly over parcel 621, she had the necessary intent and will be liable for trespass to the land of the gardener.

Without intent, there is no trespass liability. **A** is incorrect because participation in an abnormally dangerous activity does not satisfy the requirement of intent. **C** is incorrect because intent means a desire to enter the land or airspace above it (without regard to knowledge of the plaintiff's right). **D** is incorrect because damage to the realty is not an essential element of trespass to land.

29.  **D**    The tort known as invasion of privacy can be committed in various ways. One, called "intrusion," is committed by intentionally invading the plaintiff's right to solitude in a manner that would offend the reasonable person. An invasion of the plaintiff's solitude occurs when the defendant causes a physical entry into the plaintiff's private space. Since the reporter deliberately entered the senator's private office, opened the senator's private file, and copied the senator's private documents, there is no doubt that the reporter intentionally invaded the senator's solitude. Although it can never be certain that a court or jury will decide that the reasonable person would have been offended by any particular conduct, **D** is the only answer listed that could possibly be correct.

**A** and **B** are incorrect because freedom of the press under the First Amendment does not privilege invasions of privacy for the purpose of obtaining documents, even if they are newsworthy. **C** is incorrect for two reasons: First, the documents were not made public until after the reporter invaded the senator's privacy by obtaining them, and second, the privilege to publish facts that are matters of public records does not include a privilege to invade privacy for the purpose of obtaining them.

30.  **D**    The facts specify that the plaintiff's claim is for negligence. Negligence is unreasonable conduct. It may be unreasonable to sell a device as dangerous as an air rifle to an 11-year-old because the risk that he or she will use it to shoot another child is foreseeable. In any event, **D** is the only finding listed that could result in a judgment for the plaintiff.

**A** is incorrect because negligence of a manufacturer is not imputed to a retailer. **B** and **C** are incorrect for two reasons: First, there is no indication that the air rifle was defective, and second, negligence liability requires unreasonable conduct, and there is no indication that the defendant acted unreasonably. Thus, even if the air rifle was defective, there would be no reason to impose negligence liability on the defendant.

31.  **D**    Since the car dealer knew that the mechanic's repairs were frequently not successful until the third or fourth attempt, it was probably unreasonable for the car dealer to trust him with the repair of a condition that the car dealer knew made the car unsafe to drive. While it is not certain that a court would come to this conclusion, the argument in **D** is the only one listed that could possibly result in a judgment for the plaintiff.

Under the doctrine of *respondeat superior,* an employer is vicariously liable for torts of an employee committed within the scope of employment. In determining whether one who renders services to the defendant is an employee, courts generally hold that if the employer has a right to control the details of performance, the worker is an employee, while if the employer does not have a right to control the details of performance, the worker is an independent contractor. Since the car dealer did not control the details of the mechanic's performance, the mechanic probably was not an employee. **A** is therefore incorrect. Statutory duties are sometimes held to be "non-delegable," but **B** is incorrect because no statute is given. Since employers of independent contractors are not ordinarily held vicariously liable for the torts of those contractors, **C** is incorrect.

32. **D**     Like other suppliers of products, a retailer owes its customers a duty to act reasonably. This includes a duty to make whatever inspection is reasonable. Sometimes the circumstances make it reasonable for a retailer to make no inspection at all, but in such a case, no inspection constitutes a reasonable inspection.

    **A**, **B**, and **C** are incorrect because under some circumstances the conduct specified would not be reasonable. (**Note:** Beware of statements that are overly broad or general. For example, some writers and judges have stated that "a retailer owes the customer no duty to inspect products furnished by reputable manufacturers." Do you think that this statement would be true if the retailer knew that a shipment of glassware furnished by a reputable manufacturer was dropped by the delivery company, or that many customers had found dead rats in the jars of peanut butter that were furnished by a reputable manufacturer? It is safer to recognize that a retailer, like any other supplier of products, owes customers a duty to act reasonably, and that under some circumstances, failure to inspect merchandise furnished by reputable manufacturers is reasonable, while under other circumstances, it is not.)

33. **B**     There can be no liability for defamation unless the defendant intentionally or negligently communicated the defamatory statement to a person other than the plaintiff. Communication of the accusation to the employee's mother would satisfy this requirement only if the employer knew or should have known that she would see the letter that contained them.

    **A** is therefore incorrect. **C** is incorrect because the statements actually were communicated to the employee's mother, who read the letter. Courts have sometimes held that an employer who defames a former employee in a communication with a prospective employer of that former employee is privileged if he or she believes reasonably and in good faith that his or her statements are true. This reasoning does not apply to the facts given, however, because the employer's statements were not being made to a prospective employer of the employee. **D** is therefore incorrect.

34. **A**     Strict liability is imposed on the professional seller of a product that is in defective condition when sold. Neither the pilot's partner nor the mechanic sold the helicopter, so **B**, **C**, and **D** are incorrect.

35. **B**     A trespassing child is entitled to reasonable care if it was foreseeable that a child would trespass and be injured, and if the child's age made it likely that he or she would fail to recognize the danger. Thus, although the boy was a trespasser, the fact that the gravel pit owner could foresee his presence and foresee that he would be injured by the proximity of the hill to the road imposed upon the gravel pit owner the duty to act reasonably and to keep the premises reasonably safe. If the gravel pit owner's failure to erect a fence was unreasonable, the gravel pit owner was negligent and probably is liable to the boy.

The phrase "danger invites rescue" is usually used to explain why a person who created a danger to another owed a duty of reasonable care to a rescuer who came to the aid of that other. **A** is incorrect because it has no application to these facts. "Last clear chance" is a doctrine that accomplishes only one thing: Under the proper circumstances, it negates the effect of a plaintiff's contributory negligence. Only the plaintiff raises it, and only for the purpose of negating the effect of his or her own negligence. **C** is incorrect because it would put the argument at the disposal of a defendant. An intervening cause does not free an antecedent wrongdoer from liability unless its occurrence was unforeseeable. Thus, the mere fact that the car driver's conduct was an intervening cause would not lead to a judgment for the gravel pit owner. **D** is therefore incorrect.

36.  **B**    A misrepresentation is a false assertion of material fact made for the purpose of inducing the plaintiff's reliance. If the defendant knows that the assertion is false, and damages result from the plaintiff's justified reliance on it, the defendant may be held liable. It may be argued successfully that by concealing the crack, the seller falsely asserted that it did not exist. No liability will result from that assertion, however, unless the buyer relied on it. A plaintiff relies on a misrepresentation when it is a significant factor in the plaintiff's decision. Since the buyer discovered the crack, the assertion that it did not exist could not have been a factor in his decision to buy the car. For that reason, he did not rely on it and is not entitled to recover damages.

A is incorrect because a court would probably hold that the affirmative act of concealing the crack was an assertion that it did not exist. Since the buyer did not rely on the seller's representation, it does not matter whether such reliance would have been justified. **C** is therefore incorrect. Since the facts indicate that the buyer was required to spend $500 on repairs, **D** is an inaccurate statement of fact and is therefore incorrect.

37.  **B**    Under the all-or-nothing rule of contributory negligence, a plaintiff is completely barred from recovering damages if his or her own unreasonable conduct contributed to the occurrence. Since the second driver saw the first driver in the intersection, it was probably unreasonable, and therefore contributorily negligent, for him to enter the intersection when he did.

The doctrine of last clear chance does no more than negate the effect of a plaintiff's contributory negligence. If a defendant had "the last clear chance" to avoid injuring the plaintiff, the defendant might be held liable in spite of the plaintiff's negligence. The plaintiff never loses a case, however, simply because that *plaintiff* had "the last clear chance" to avoid being injured. **A** is therefore incorrect. **C** and **D** are incorrect for two reasons: First, the presumption that results from a defendant's violation of a statute (sometimes called *negligence per se*) may ordinarily be rebutted by proof that the violation resulted from circumstances beyond the defendant's control, and second, even if the first driver could not rebut the presumption that he was negligent, the second driver's contributory negligence is still available to him as a defense.

38.  **A**    Although the phrase "AS IS" disclaims implied warranties of merchantability or fitness for a particular purpose, it does not free a seller from the duty of acting reasonably. Since

it probably was foreseeable that the purchaser of a refrigerator would plug it in even after being advised that it did not work, the store owner had a duty to take reasonable precautions against the harm that might result. If her failure to warn the customer was unreasonable, it was negligence that was a proximate cause of harm and would result in liability.

**B** is incorrect because the phrase "AS IS" is an effective disclaimer of the implied warranty of merchantability (*i.e.*, fitness for ordinary use). **C** is incorrect because the store owner is still liable under a negligence theory. **D** is based on a misinterpretation of the doctrine of last clear chance, which accomplishes nothing more than undoing the effect of a plaintiff's contributory negligence. (If a defendant had "the last clear chance" to avoid injuring the plaintiff, the defendant might be liable in spite of the plaintiff's negligence. The plaintiff never loses a case, however, simply because that plaintiff had "the last clear chance" to avoid being injured.)

39. **B**     Self-defense is a privilege to use reasonable force to defend oneself against a threatened contact. Reasonable force is that force that would appear necessary to the reasonable person. Courts generally hold that it is reasonable to use deadly force in defense against what reasonably appears to be a threat of deadly force.

**A** is incorrect because it is never reasonable to use deadly force for the sole purpose of preventing a trespass to land or chattel. **C** is incorrect because the defendant's initial use of gentle force was privileged in defense of property, making the plaintiff's response to it a threatened battery. The plaintiff's trespass did not end when he completed his entry but continued so long as he refused to leave in response to the defendant's demand. **D** is therefore incorrect.

40. **A**     One who keeps a wild animal is strictly liable for harm that proximately results from keeping it. An animal is "wild" if it comes from a species that cannot ordinarily be kept safely without special training or restraint. For this purpose, the wildcat was a wild animal even though it had been tamed.

The terms *foreseeable* and *unforeseeable* are mutually exclusive. Thus if the cat's behavior was unforeseeable, it could not have been foreseeable. **B** is incorrect for this reason, and because the foreseeability of harm is not in itself sufficient to result in liability. **C** is incorrect for several reasons: First, *res ipsa* does not apply in strict liability cases; second, there is no reason to believe that the injury would not ordinarily have occurred without negligence; and third, *res ipsa* does not apply when there is direct evidence of the defendant's conduct. **D** is incorrect because private nuisance is an interference with the plaintiff's right to use and enjoy realty, and there was no interference with the plaintiff's right to use or enjoy realty.

41. **D**     If a product fails to live up to an express assertion of fact that a supplier made about it, the supplier may be liable without regard to fault on theories of breach of express warranty and misrepresentation. For this purpose, an assertion of fact may be made by the use of models or pictures. The photo on the box probably was an express assertion that the helmet was suitable for use as a motorcycle helmet. Since it was not suitable for such use,

the company is liable for breach of express warranty and misrepresentation. In addition, strict products liability may be imposed for damage that results from a defect in a product supplied by a defendant. For this purpose, a product is defective if its condition would defeat the reasonable expectations of the reasonable consumer. Since the photo on the box showed the helmet being used as a motorcycle helmet, the reasonable person probably would have expected it to be suitable for such use. Since it was not, the company is strictly liable for damage.

**A** is incorrect because the misrepresentation and strict products liability theories discussed above do not require privity between defendant and plaintiff, and because under the express warranty theory, it has been held that the necessary privity exists between anyone who made the express assertion and anyone who relied on it. **B** is incorrect because even if the product was not intended for use as a motorcycle helmet, the photo on the box probably was an assertion that it was suitable for such use. **C** is incorrect for three reasons: First, the jurisdiction's "pure comparative negligence" system would diminish the plaintiff's recovery in proportion to his own fault, but it would not completely bar that recovery; second, since the purpose of a motorcycle helmet is to protect the user in an accident, the defendant's assertion and the reasonable person's expectation might have been that the helmet would be effective even if the accident was the wearer's own fault; and third, most jurisdictions hold that comparative negligence is not a defense to actions that are not based on fault (*i.e.*, breach of warranty, misrepresentation, or strict products liability).

42. **A**  The statute given is typical of the "owner-consent" statute that exists in a number of jurisdictions. It requires the owner to pay for the tort committed by the driver. Whenever the law imposes vicarious liability on one for damage that another has caused, the one who pays is entitled to complete indemnity from the one who should have paid.

**B** would be correct if the accident resulted from some fault by the owner in addition to that of the mechanic, but it is incorrect because there is no indication that the owner acted unreasonably. **C** is incorrect because there is no factual basis for determining that the owner is himself responsible for any portion of the loss. **D** is incorrect because of the owner's right of indemnity.

43. **A**  Commercial suppliers, such as the wholesaler, are strictly liable if they sell a defective product that injures a foreseeable plaintiff, such as a purchaser. Here, the seeds were defective since they were poisonous, and the breeder was a foreseeable plaintiff.

Since the dealer sold the seeds in the same package in which they came, the dealer's failure to inspect them was foreseeable whether or not it was reasonable. **B** is incorrect because a foreseeable intervention, even if unreasonable, does not free an antecedent wrongdoer from liability. Although liability for breach of warranty may require privity, the theories of negligence and strict liability in tort do not. **C** is therefore incorrect. **D** is incorrect because strict liability is imposed on the seller of a product that is in a defective condition when sold, without regard to the possibility that some other seller of the same product might be liable. Thus, a manufacturer and retailer of a defective product may be jointly and severally liable as joint tortfeasors.

44. **A**    Since the coming of a rescuer is generally viewed as a foreseeable result of peril, negligence that causes peril is often held to be a breach of a duty owed to a rescuer. Thus, if the swimmer's negligence caused the need for the rescuer to rescue him, it was a breach of duty owed to the rescuer.

         **B** is incorrect because if the swimmer had not acted negligently, there would be no basis for holding him liable to the rescuer. The phrase "danger invites rescue" is often used to explain why one who imperils another owes a duty of reasonable care to a rescuer attracted by that peril. If that principle had any application to these facts, it would be to establish liability, not to free the swimmer from such liability. **C** is therefore incorrect. An intervening cause does not prevent an antecedent wrongdoer from being liable unless the intervention was unforeseeable. **D** is therefore incorrect.

45. **B**    There is some question about whether it is defamatory to say that a person is impoverished or on the verge of bankruptcy. But even if the defendant's statement was defamatory, it was oral and, therefore, classified as slander. Ordinarily, there is no liability for slander unless the plaintiff establishes actual damage to his or her reputation. Since the company did not believe what the defendant told him, there was no damage to the plaintiff's reputation, and the defendant will not be held liable for saying it.

         **A** is incorrect because mental suffering is not an essential element of defamation. Since liability for defamation is imposed on the publisher of a defamatory statement, the fact that the defendant was only repeating what he heard would not in itself protect him against liability. **C** is therefore incorrect. Since publication is defined as communication to any person other than the plaintiff, **D** is incorrect.

46. **C**    Since negligence is defined as a failure to act reasonably in the face of a foreseeable risk, the defendant cannot be called negligent if the reasonable person in the defendants' situation would not have acted any differently than the defendant did.

         Assumption of the risk requires that the plaintiff have knowledge of the risk that he or she is voluntarily encountering. Since there is no indication that the plaintiff knew of the risks associated with exposure to the material, **A** is incorrect. **B** is incorrect because the defendant's lack of knowledge would not prevent liability if the reasonable person in the defendant's situation would have known. Workers' compensation may be the exclusive remedy against an injured party's employer, but since the plaintiff did not work for the defendant, **D** is incorrect.

47. **B**    A claim for private nuisance can be asserted only by a plaintiff who claims that the defendant's conduct interfered with his or her use and enjoyment of realty in which he or she has a present or future possessory interest. Since the gardener held a leasehold interest and the landlord a reversion, they can successfully assert a private nuisance claim.

         **A** is incorrect because as a tenant, the gardener had sufficient interest in the realty. **C** and **D** are incorrect because, since the employee was only an employee of the gardener, he lacked the property interest necessary to the assertion of the claim.

48.   **A**    Trespass to chattel is intentional interference with the plaintiff's chattel resulting in damage. For this purpose, intent consists of a desire or knowledge that the chattel will be involved, without regard to whether the defendant knows that the chattel is the plaintiff's or that the plaintiff's rights are being violated. Interference can consist of any act regarding the chattel that only its rightful possessor is entitled to perform. Since the defendant desired to take that particular coat, she had the necessary intent, regardless of her belief that the coat was her own. Since only the plaintiff was entitled to take the coat, the defendant interfered with it. Since the coat was destroyed while the defendant possessed it, her interference resulted in damage to the plaintiff. The defendant is therefore liable to the plaintiff for trespass to chattel.

**B** is incorrect because the tort was committed when the defendant took the coat and the tort led to the coat's destruction. In trespass to chattel, intent does not require knowledge that the chattel belongs to another, or that the defendant's act will affect the rights of another. **C** is therefore incorrect. Trespass to chattel was committed when the defendant took the coat. If she had succeeded in returning the coat, damages might have been mitigated (*i.e.*, reduced), but the tort would not have been undone. **D** is incorrect because her unsuccessful attempt to return the coat could not even mitigate damages.

49.   **C**    Liability is imposed on a defendant for damage that was proximately caused by the defendant's negligence. Since it is given that the hospital was negligent in keeping the trucker waiting six hours, it is necessary to determine whether that negligence was a proximate cause of his injury in the earthquake. Conduct is a proximate cause of harm if it was a factual and legal cause of that harm. Conduct is a factual cause of harm if the harm would not have occurred without it. Since the trucker would not have been struck by the debris that fell in the earthquake if he had not been present, the delay occasioned by the hospital's negligence was a factual cause of his injury. If conduct is a factual cause of harm, it is a legal cause if the harm was foreseeable. Thus, if it was foreseeable that the trucker would be injured by an earthquake, the hospital's negligence was a legal cause of that injury and the hospital is liable for it. Otherwise, the hospital is not liable. Here, the fact that an earthquake had never occurred before likely made the earthquake unforeseeable.

"Good Samaritan" statutes, where they exist, only protect doctors who voluntarily render emergency aid at the scenes of accidents. **A** is, therefore, incorrect. Although the liability of an antecedent wrongdoer might depend on whether subsequent intervention was foreseeable, since the doctor's conduct preceded the hospital's, the hospital's liability does not depend on whether the doctor's conduct was foreseeable. **B** is therefore incorrect. **D** is too absolute a statement to be correct. Even if a hospital owes its patients some duty with respect to natural disasters, that duty is only to act reasonably in the face of them.

50.   **D**    If the seller of a product knows the buyer's purpose in buying it, and he knows also that the buyer is relying on the seller's skill in selecting a product to suit that purpose, the sale is accompanied by an implied warranty that the product is fit for the buyer's particular purpose (UCC §2-315), even where that purpose is identical to the ordinary use of such a product. Similarly, even where the implied warranty of fitness for the buyer's particular

purpose is present, the implied warranty of merchantability accompanies every sale by a merchant (UCC §2-314) unless it is effectively disclaimed.

51.  **D**    The defendant is not liable for harm unless its conduct was a factual and legal cause of it. Its conduct was a factual cause of harm only if the harm would not have occurred without it. If the force of the collision would have caused a good pole to fall, then the fact that the pole was rotten is not a factual cause of its falling.

**A** and **B** are incorrect because they do not establish that the defendant's conduct was a factual cause of harm, and liability cannot be imposed unless it was. If the defendant's conduct was a factual cause of harm, the driver's intervention might be a superseding cause that protects the defendant from liability, but only if the intervention was unforeseeable. This does not necessarily depend on whether it was criminal or grossly negligent. **C** is therefore incorrect.

52.  **A**    The statute given is typical of the "pure comparative negligence" approach. Since the car driver's loss amounted to $10,000, and since it was 40 percent his own fault, 40 percent of $10,000 (or $4,000) must be deducted from his recovery. The balance that he is entitled to collect is $6,000. Therefore, **B**, **C**, and **D** are incorrect.

53.  **A**    Strict liability is imposed on the seller of a product that is in a defective condition when sold. Since the bolt was cracked when the sled left the sled factory, the sled company would be held liable if the crack constituted a defect.

**B** and **C** are incorrect because the use or sale by the boy would not prevent the imposition of strict liability if the sled was defective when it left the sled factory, so long as such use or sale did not substantially change its condition. **D** is incorrect because strict liability in tort does not depend on unreasonable conduct by the defendant.

54.  **A**    Negligence is the failure to act as a reasonable person would act in the face of risks that are foreseeable or known to exist. Since a reasonable person would not ordinarily subject others to unnecessary risks, it would probably have been unreasonable (*i.e.*, negligent) for the attorney to subject the client to the danger of a defective elevator if the attorney knew or should have known of the danger. Here, leading the client to the elevator minutes after it plunged downward was likely unreasonable.

However, if the attorney did not act unreasonably, he would not be negligent even though he occupied the entire second floor. Thus, **B** is incorrect. Ordinarily, obligations in a lease flow only between parties to that lease. Some jurisdictions hold that a landlord's lease obligation to keep premises in good repair may impose on the landlord a duty to invitees of tenants. **C** is incorrect, however, because the attorney continues to be liable for the proximate results of his own negligence even though the landlord might also be liable. While a tenant might not have an obligation to repair the leased premises, **D** is incorrect because the attorney might be liable for his negligence in allowing the client to use the elevator.

55.   **C**    One who enters the realty of another to retrieve a chattel that got there through no fault of his or her own has a qualified privilege to do so, but he or she must compensate the landholder for any actual damage that results.

A and **D** are therefore incorrect. Unless damage to the realty of another results from participation in an abnormally dangerous activity, liability for it is imposed only if the entry resulted from fault (*i.e.*, was intentional or negligent). Since transporting gravel is not an abnormally dangerous activity, and since the gravel was spilled without any fault on the part of the trucker, the trucker is not liable for damage resulting from spilling the gravel. **B** is therefore incorrect.

56.   **D**    One who voluntarily encounters a known risk assumes that risk and is not entitled to damages resulting from it.

**A, B**, and **C** are all incorrect since assumption of risk is available as a defense in claims based on negligence or strict liability. In addition, **B** is incorrect because horses are not regarded as wild animals, and **C** is incorrect because the fact that the trainer had been warned of the animal's propensity indicates that the horseman's conduct was reasonable.

57.   **A**    The phrase "AS IS" disclaims the implied warranty of merchantability. In addition, it may be argued that it modifies any express warranties or representations that resulted from the car dealer's assurance that he believed the car to be in good condition, and that it would have placed the reasonable consumer on notice that the car might not be in good condition. In any event, **A** contains the only combination of conclusion and reason that are reasonably related to each other.

**B** is incorrect because all jurisdictions permit an action for breach of the implied warranty of merchantability to be brought by any member of the purchaser's household. **C** and **D** are incorrect because the phrase "AS IS" disclaimed the implied warranty that the car was fit for ordinary use.

58.   **A**    In an action for conversion, the defendant is liable for the full value of the chattel at the time of conversion. Consequently, the plaintiff can recover the value of the car at the time she delivered it to the defendant. **B, C**, and **D** are therefore incorrect.

59.   **D**    Negligence is unreasonable conduct. If the company did not act unreasonably, it could not have been negligent. Although a court might not come to this conclusion, the argument in **D** is the only one listed that could possibly support the company's defense.

**A** is incorrect because contributory negligence is unreasonable conduct by a *plaintiff*. In this case, the plaintiff is the girl, not the cleaner. **B** and **C** are incorrect because an intervening cause of harm does not cut off a wrongdoer's liability unless that intervening cause was unforeseeable.

60.   **B**    A landholder is entitled to use reasonable force to prevent a trespass. Serious or deadly force is not regarded as reasonable, however, since human life is much more valuable than mere property. The use of such force is therefore a battery.

Negligence is the breach of a duty of reasonable care owed by the defendant to the plaintiff. Ordinarily, a defendant owes a plaintiff a duty of reasonable care if the defendant's conduct creates a foreseeable risk to the plaintiff. Thus, if the risk to persons entering on legitimate business was foreseeable, the warehouse owner owed a duty of reasonable care to such persons. This does not mean that he owed such a duty to everyone, however, or that he owed it to the burglar. **A** is incorrect for this reason and because of a rule applied by most jurisdictions that a landholder owes no duty of reasonable care to trespassers. **C** is incorrect because no rule of law prohibits the use of mechanical devices unless they inflict excessive force. Although courts have made statements like that in **D**, it is irrelevant here since the device did not injure an innocent bystander. **D** is therefore incorrect.

61. **A**   An intentional exercise of dominion and control over a chattel by a defendant is a conversion if the plaintiff was lawfully entitled to possession of the chattel, and if he or she was thereby damaged. In a conversion case, "intent" means a desire (or knowledge with certainty) that the defendant's act will affect the particular chattel involved. In this case, the neighbor's desire to make the television hers and to carry it off satisfies the intent requirement, even though it was reasonable for her to believe that the sale was legitimate.

   **B** and **C** are therefore incorrect. **D** is incorrect since the plaintiff need not be in possession of the chattel at the time of conversion, so long as he or she had a right to possess it.

62. **B**   A guest rides free. If something of value — like rides on alternate days — is given in return for passage, courts will conclude that the passenger was not a guest for purposes of the automobile guest statute.

   In a negligence claim, the existence of insurance coverage is not relevant in determining liability. **A** is incorrect for this reason and because the "guest" statute was originally created to protect insurance companies against collusive claims. Recklessness or aggravated negligence is usually held to be actionable in the face of a statute that prohibits actions for negligence. **C** is incorrect, however, because the facts do not indicate the conscious disregard of an obvious and serious risk that aggravated negligence requires. **D** is probably an accurate statement. It is incorrect, however, because it does not justify non-enforcement of the statute.

63. **B**   A defendant manufacturer can be relieved of strict products liability if an intermediate handler of the product substantially changes the product before sending it on through the stream of commerce.

   Strict liability may be imposed regardless of whether the defendant was negligent. Since the basis of the volunteer firefighter's action is a claim that the product was defective (*i.e.*, strict liability in tort), the fact that the company acted reasonably would not furnish it with an effective defense. **A** is therefore incorrect. A plaintiff assumes the risk when he or she knows of it and voluntarily encounters it. Since the volunteer firefighter had never heard of the device before, he could not have known of the risk or assumed it. **C** is therefore incorrect. An intervening cause of harm is one that came between the defendant's conduct and the plaintiff. It is "independent" if it is not related to the risk created by the defendant.

**D** is incorrect because a plaintiff's own conduct is not usually regarded as an intervening cause of harm.

64.　**B**　Since it is given that the injury to the baker's nose resulted from the eye doctor's negligence, the eye doctor is liable for it.

It is, of course, possible for harm to have more than one proximate cause. Thus, even if the neighbor's conduct was a proximate cause of the injury, the eye doctor's conduct may also be a cause of it, making the eye doctor liable as a joint tortfeasor. (In most jurisdictions, joint tortfeasors are jointly and severally liable.) **A** is therefore incorrect. Conduct is a factual cause of harm if the harm would not have occurred without it. Since the injuries to the baker's elbow and shoulder would have occurred even without the negligence of the eye doctor, his conduct was not a factual cause of those injuries, and the eye doctor could not be held liable for them. **C** and **D** are therefore incorrect.

65.　**A**　One who holds himself or herself out to be an attorney, even if unlicensed, is required to act like a reasonable attorney. If the attorney did not, he will be held liable for damages that proximately resulted.

Negligence does not lead to liability unless it is a cause of damage. Thus, although violation of a statute sometimes results in a presumption of negligence, it does not result in liability unless it was a cause of the plaintiff's damage. Negligence is not a cause of damage that would have occurred without it. Since licensed attorneys sometimes lose cases, it cannot be said that the attorney would not have lost the case if he had had a license. **B** and **C** are incorrect for this reason and because courts usually hold that violation of a licensing statute does not result in a presumption of negligence. **D** is incorrect because even though an attorney does not guarantee results, he or she is liable for damages that result from his or her negligence.

66.　**C**　Consent means willingness, and the affirmative defense of consent is effective because of the rule that a plaintiff who is willing for a particular thing to happen to him or her has no right to complain when it does. For this reason, a defendant does not commit a tort when he or she does something to which the plaintiff has consented. If the defendant induces his or her consent by fraud, however, the consent does not have this effect and does not privilege the defendant's conduct. A defendant induces consent by fraud when he or she knowingly misrepresents the nature of the act to which the plaintiff is consenting. Thus, if the hypnotist told the plaintiff that the cattle prod would produce no real discomfort when he knew that this was false, he fraudulently induced her consent to contact with it and was not privileged by her consent.

In **A**, the plaintiff consented to the contact even though she was aware that the hypnotist was not always successful in hypnotizing volunteers, and that if he was not successful in hypnotizing her, the cattle prod might cause discomfort. Since she knew the nature of the act to which she was consenting, her consent would furnish the hypnotist with a privilege. **A** is therefore incorrect. In **B**, although the hypnotist defrauded the plaintiff by promising money that he did not intend to pay, the fraud did not relate to the nature of the act to which she was consenting. He would, therefore, be privileged by her consent, and **B** is therefore incorrect. A mistake that induces consent does not destroy the effect of that consent unless the defendant is aware of the mistake. Since there is no indication in **D** that the hypnotist was aware of the plaintiff's mistake regarding the effect of a cattle prod, her consent privileged him, and **D** is therefore incorrect.

67.   **A**   A statement is defamatory if it is likely to cause a substantial group of respectable people to lose respect for the person about whom it is made. A statement that the professor drank a large quantity of alcohol might be defamatory because many people regard such conduct as disreputable, and because it implies that the professor's public statements were dishonest. A statement that she drank a large quantity of fruit juice clearly would not be defamatory. If an allegedly defamatory statement is ambiguous (*i.e.*, has two possible meanings), it is held to mean what the reasonable person would think it means. Thus, the statements made in the photo and caption would not have been defamatory if the reasonable person would have believed them to mean that the professor drank fruit juice. If the reasonable person would have read the story, he or she would have known that this was what the statements in the photo and caption meant.

B and C are incorrect because the standard used to determine the meaning of an ambiguous statement is objective and does not depend on what any particular group of persons thought. **D** is incorrect because if the reasonable person would not have read the story, the photo and caption might mean that the professor had drunk a large quantity of alcohol, and thus it might be a defamatory statement.

68.   **D**   Liability for misrepresentation may be imposed upon a defendant who makes an intentionally (or, in some jurisdictions, negligently) false assertion of fact upon which the plaintiff justifiably relies to his or her detriment. The athlete's only assertion of fact was that he ate candy bars for energy. There is no indication, however, that this assertion was false. The athlete made no assertion about the flavor of the candy bar, so even if the plaintiff's dislike of the flavor can be regarded as damage, it is not damage that proximately resulted from his reliance on an assertion by the athlete.

A is incorrect because misrepresentation liability can be imposed on anyone who makes a misrepresentation, and also because the facts indicate that the athlete is in the business of selling candy. If the athlete's statements were misrepresentations, the fact that he said them could result in liability even though they were written by someone else. **B** is therefore incorrect. **C** is incorrect because liability for intentional misrepresentation may be imposed to benefit anyone who was damaged by his or her justified reliance on the misrepresentation, regardless of privity.

69.   **B**   Although blasting is generally recognized to be an ultra-hazardous activity, strict liability applies only to harm that resulted from the risks that made the activity ultra-hazardous. The possibility of noise frightening animals accompanies a great many activities that are not ultra-hazardous, so it is probably not one of the risks that makes blasting ultra-hazardous.

A is incorrect because the breeder's phone call announcing that harm was occurring on his farm made it foreseeable that harm would continue to occur there if the activity was continued. **C** is incorrect because strict liability may be imposed even though the defendant acted reasonably. While the demolition contractor's relationship with the builder might impose liability on the builder as well, it would not relieve the demolition contractor from liability for his acts. **D** is therefore incorrect.

70.  **C**    An invitee is one whose presence confers an economic benefit on the landholder. That which enables a tenant to do business on the premises confers economic benefit on the landholder by making the premises attractive to the tenant. This applies to the presence of a tenant's employees, and makes them invitees of the landlord. Contributory (comparative) negligence is unreasonable conduct by the plaintiff. If the reasonable person in the employee's shoes would have seen and avoided the dangerous condition, then the employee's failure to do so was negligent.

71.  **C**    Under the doctrine of *respondeat superior,* an employer is vicariously liable for the negligence of an employee committed within the scope of employment. An employee is acting within the scope of employment if his or her conduct is intended to further the interests of his or her employer and if his or her employer has a right to control his or her conduct. Since the building inspector was attempting to find out whether the drapes were fire-retardant, which was part of what the city hired her to do, and since the city had the right to tell her how to test drapes, she was acting within the scope of her employment even if she was violating specific instructions that she received from the city.

     **A** is therefore incorrect. **B** is a fabrication with no basis in law, since even when an employee's conduct is unsupervised, *respondeat superior* may result in the imposition of vicarious liability on his or her employer. **D** is incorrect because under *respondeat superior,* an employer is vicariously liable only for that for which the employee is liable.

72.  **C**    It may have been unreasonable for the defendant to leave his keys in the ignition. If so, he was negligent. Even if his conduct was not unreasonable, his violation of the ignition key statute may result in a presumption of negligence if the statute was designed to prevent accidents involving stolen cars. Negligence does not result in liability, however, unless it is a proximate (*i.e.*, factual and legal) cause of harm. Conduct is a factual cause of harm if the harm would not have occurred without it. Since the monkey probably would not have moved the defendant's car and struck the plaintiff with it had the defendant not left his key in the ignition, the defendant's conduct was a factual cause of the plaintiff's injury. A factual cause of harm is a legal cause if the harm was foreseeable and not brought about by an unforeseeable intervening cause (*i.e.*, a superseding cause). Since the accident would not have occurred without the monkey's conduct, and since the monkey's conduct came between the defendant's conduct and the plaintiff's injury, it was an intervening cause. If it was unforeseeable, it was a superseding cause of the plaintiff's harm, and the defendant's conduct was not a proximate cause of it. Thus, the plaintiff will lose his case against the defendant unless it is found that the monkey's intervention was foreseeable. This is unlikely.

     Even if the defendant's conduct was reasonable, his violation of the statute might result in a presumption of negligence. **A** is therefore incorrect. Even if the violation of the statute does not result in a presumption of negligence, the defendant's conduct might have been unreasonable and therefore negligent. **B** is therefore incorrect. **D** is incorrect because an intervening cause of harm is not superseding unless it was unforeseeable.

73. **A**    Appropriation of identity is committed when the defendant, without the plaintiff's permission, uses the plaintiff's identity for a commercial purpose. Since the photographer sold games that were imprinted with the governor's likeness, a court could conclude that he is liable for appropriation.

Public disclosure is committed when the defendant publicly discloses a private fact about the plaintiff, the disclosure of which would offend the reasonable person in the plaintiff's position. Since a photo of the governor's face as it appeared in a public place is obviously not a private fact, **B** is incorrect. Intrusion is committed by intentionally invading the plaintiff's private space in a manner that would offend the reasonable person in the plaintiff's position. Since the photographer snapped the photo in a public place, he did not invade the governor's private space, and **C** is incorrect. False light is committed by publishing false statements about the plaintiff that, although not defamatory, are in some way embarrassing or damaging. Since the photographer did not publish any statements about the governor, **D** is incorrect.

74. **D**    False imprisonment requires intentional confinement, which is an overcoming of the plaintiff's will to leave. Since a sleeping person has no will to leave, the student was not confined by the locked door.

**A** is therefore incorrect. **B** is based on an inaccurate statement since the risk probably was not a foreseeable one, but it is incorrect in any event because false imprisonment requires intent. If the professor intentionally confined the student, she would be held liable for all the harm that foreseeably resulted. **C** is incorrect, however, because she did not confine him.

75. **A**    In a defamation action by a private person against a professional publisher (media defendant), the plaintiff must prove either actual malice or negligence. If the newspaper knew the statement to be false, it had actual malice. If the reasonable publisher would have known the statement to be false, the newspaper acted negligently.

**B** describes actual malice and is incorrect because a plaintiff who is not a public person is not required to prove actual malice. **C** is incorrect because no liability can be imposed unless the newspaper knew, or reasonably should have known, that the statement was false. **D** is incorrect since liability without fault cannot be imposed in an action for defamation against a professional (media defendant) publisher.

76. **C**    Strict liability means that the seller of a product is liable without fault for personal injuries or other physical harm caused by the product if the product is sold in a defective condition. Once a defect is found, the seller is liable even if he or she used all possible care. Importantly, strict liability applies not only to the manufacturer, but also to the retailer and any other person in the distribution chain who is in the business of selling such products.

Consequently, a retailer is strictly liable for selling the defective product even if the retailer is non-negligent and even if the retailer could not have discovered the defect. Here, since the defendant sold the defective product, he is liable even though he sold the saws without opening the boxes and could not have possibly discovered the defect before the plaintiff was injured. **A** and **B** are therefore incorrect.

There was no indication that selling saws made by the manufacturer was unreasonable. **D** is therefore incorrect.

77.  **A**   Holders of land owe a duty of reasonable care to travelers who foreseeably deviate onto the land for reasons related to their use of the adjacent public way. Here, the fact that the road was curvy and known for numerous accidents likely made the driver's accident foreseeable.

     **B** is incorrect because the mere fact that the homeowner knew drivers used the neighboring road is not enough. **C** is incorrect because although the reason given explains why the homeowner's conduct was not negligent, it fails to explain why he had no duty. Although a landholder generally owes no duty of reasonable care to a trespasser, **D** is incorrect because a strayed traveler as described above is entitled to reasonable care as an exception to the general rule.

78.  **C**   Conduct is a factual cause of harm if the harm would not have occurred without it. Since medical assistance was summoned just a moment later, and since the facts do not indicate that the truck driver was worse off for the momentary delay, the carpenter's failure to summon aid was not a cause of harm.

     Most jurisdictions agree that a landholder owes no duty of reasonable care to a trespasser. When the landholder knows of the trespasser's presence, however, and knows that the trespasser has been imperiled by some affirmative act of the landholder, the landholder does have a duty to act reasonably to protect the trespasser from that act. Since the carpenter knew that his act of throwing the hammer created the need for aid, he probably did owe the truck driver a duty to act reasonably in summoning it. **A** is therefore incorrect. Punitive damages may be available against a defendant who intended harm by his or her act. Intent requires a substantial certainty that the harm will probably occur, however. Knowledge that harm is *possible* is not intent and is not sufficient to result in liability for punitive damages. **B** is therefore incorrect. A user of the public way who enters upon private land foreseeably and in connection with his or her use of the public way is entitled to some measure of reasonable care. **D** is incorrect, however, because he or she does not thereby become an invitee, and, further, because the truck driver's entry onto the carpenter's realty was not connected with the truck driver's use of the public way.

79.  **C**   A private individual may sue for public nuisance only if his or her damages were different in kind from those sustained by the general public.

     **A** and **B** are incorrect because the fact that the defendant's conduct preexisted the plaintiff's presence is not, by itself, a defense to nuisance unless it can be shown that the plaintiff came to the nuisance specifically for the purpose of instituting litigation. **D** is an incorrect statement of the law; even a lawful activity may constitute a public nuisance if it is conducted in a way that unreasonably interferes with the rights of the public.

80. **C**   Consent—the plaintiff's willingness—is a complete defense to most intentional tort actions. Consent is implied if the reasonable person would infer from the plaintiff's conduct and the surrounding circumstances that the plaintiff is willing for the defendant's act to occur. The fact that the defendant and the plaintiff have been enjoying each other's jokes for years could result in the inference that the plaintiff was willing to have a joke played upon him. Although it is not certain that a court would come to this conclusion, the argument in **C** is the only one listed that could support the defendant's defense.

**A** is incorrect because assault requires apprehension of harmful contact but not necessarily of battery. Ordinarily, the apprehension experienced by the plaintiff must be such as a reasonable person in his or her shoes would experience. **B** is incorrect, however, because an exception to this objective standard is made when the plaintiff has a special sensitivity about which the defendant knows, and the defendant knew that the plaintiff was terrified of spiders. **D** is incorrect because assault requires an intent to cause apprehension, not necessarily an intent to cause injury.

81. **C**   Conduct is a factual cause of harm if the harm would not have occurred without the conduct. Since there is no way of knowing whether the defendant's shot struck the plaintiff, it cannot be established that the plaintiff's harm was factually caused by the defendant's conduct. (**Note:** Do not confuse these facts with the rule of *Summers v. Tice, 199 P.2d 1 (1948)* where *both* negligent persons were named as defendants.)

The defendant's duty of reasonable care might not require the same vigilance that would be required in an urban area, but **A** is incorrect because the possibility that someone would come by required some vigilance. Since it is likely that a person struck by a pellet shot from a slingshot would be seriously injured, it is probably unreasonable to shoot a slingshot without taking some precaution against hitting other persons. **B** is therefore incorrect. If the defendant's conduct was a factual cause of the harm, it was a legal cause of the harm if the harm was foreseeable. Since it is clearly foreseeable that a person struck by a slingshot pellet will sustain an injury, **D** is incorrect.

82. **C**   Although the law recognizes a special standard for judging the negligence of children, it is applied only when the youth of the defendant is likely to prevent him or her from exercising the same mature judgment as an adult. When a child is old enough to have acquired the judgment of an adult with respect to a particular activity, the child standard no longer applies. It is rare for a court to apply the child standard to persons over the age of 14 years.

**A** is therefore incorrect. An adult activity is one that is substantially more likely to be dangerous when performed by a child than by an adult, or one in which only adults traditionally engage. **B** is incorrect because fishing is neither. The balancing test that is sometimes used to determine whether conduct is negligent weighs the risks that foreseeably result from acting a certain way against the utility of acting that particular way. **D** is incorrect because it distorts that rule by weighing the risk of handling a fishhook in whatever way the girl was handling it against the utility of fishing in general.

83.  **A**      Strict liability in tort is imposed on the supplier of a product for damages that result from a defect in the product that existed at the time it left that supplier's hands and that made the product unreasonably dangerous. Since a defect is a condition that would defeat the reasonable expectations of the reasonable consumer, and since the reasonable consumer probably does not expect to find a rat's tail in food products, the presence of a rat's tail was probably a defect. Since a product is unreasonably dangerous if the benefits of its condition are outweighed by its disadvantages, and since the presence of a rat's tail has no advantage and is likely to be a source of disease and disgust in a person eating it, the presence of a rat's tail in a food product probably makes that product unreasonably dangerous.

**B** is incorrect because strict liability in tort may be imposed for the benefit of any plaintiff whose contact with the product was foreseeable, without regard to the existence of a con-tractual relationship (*i.e.*, privity). Although the sale of a product by a merchant implies a warranty that the product is merchantable (*i.e.*, fit for ordinary use), **C** is incorrect because the question stem specifies the theory of strict liability in tort, and this theory does not depend on the existence of an implied promise. The doctrine of *res ipsa loquitur* is applied to establish an inference that the defendant acted unreasonably. Since the reasonableness of the defendant's conduct is not relevant to the imposition of strict liability, **D** is incorrect.

84.  **C**      A parent's claim for medical bills incurred as a result of injuries negligently inflicted on a child is a derivative one, subject to any defenses that could have been raised in response to an action by the child. Here, the boy's negligence could be asserted by the driver in response to a claim by the boy. Additionally, since the mother is the plaintiff, her negli-gence can be asserted by the driver. Consequently, the driver can raise both the boy's and the boy's mother's negligence as a defense.

85.  **D**      Violation of a statute is relevant to the question of negligence only if the statute violated was designed to protect a class of persons to which the plaintiff belongs against risks like the one that resulted in harm to the plaintiff. Since insurance would not have prevented the trailer hitch from failing, the statute was not designed to protect against the risk that it would. Its violation is therefore not relevant.

**A** is therefore incorrect. **B** is incorrect because the violation is not relevant unless the statute was designed to protect against the risk involved. Public policy generally prohibits disclosing to a jury that a defendant was or was not insured. Such disclosure is not *abso-lutely* prohibited, however, since there are circumstances under which such disclosure could be made to a jury (*e.g.*, to establish ownership of a vehicle). **C** is thus based on an over-inclusive statement of the law and is therefore incorrect.

86.  **C**      An inference of negligence may be established under the doctrine of *res ipsa loquitur* when the accident was one that would not ordinarily have occurred without negligence,

and the circumstances eliminate the probability that the negligence was anyone's but the defendant's. Bottles don't *usually* explode unless the company that was in exclusive control of the bottling process acted negligently, so *res ipsa* frequently is applied in exploding bottle cases. But where, as here, some other event was as likely a cause of the explosion, *res ipsa* cannot be applied.

**A** and **B** are therefore incorrect. **D** is incorrect because the fact that the bottles were not in the defendant's possession when the accident occurred is not in itself sufficient to eliminate the probability that the negligence was anyone's other than the defendant's.

87. **B**   A person who sells services rather than goods does not generally fall within standard strict liability. Consequently, since the contractor was not selling the glue itself, he could not be held strictly liable for its defect. However, the neighbor could recover in strict liability against the manufacturer, because the glue was defective, was sold by the manufacturer, and proximately caused the injury to the neighbor.

**A**, **C**, and **D** are therefore incorrect.

88. **C**   An essential element of tort liability for misrepresentation is the defendant's intent to induce the plaintiff's reliance with his or her statement. If the dealer did not know that the buyer would rely on the statements that she made to the collector, she could not have intended to induce the buyer's reliance on those statements. Since there is no indication that the dealer was aware that the buyer had overheard her conversation with the collector, **C** is correct.

**A** is over-inclusive and therefore incorrect. Statements of opinion, especially when made by experts, may be regarded as assertions of fact (*i.e.*, the fact that the speaker actually held that particular opinion). Since the buyer paid $225,000 for something worth only $600 based on his belief in what he had overheard, he did sustain damage as a result of his reliance on the dealer's statement. **B** is therefore incorrect. **D** is incorrect for two reasons. First, as indicated above, an expert may incur misrepresentation liability by stating that he or she holds an opinion that he or she doesn't actually hold. Second, the dealer's statement was not only an evaluation of the painting's value, but also a statement about who had painted it.

89. **D**   Intentional infliction of emotional distress requires intentional, outrageous conduct that results in severe mental suffering. Since the plaintiff did not experience any mental injury, the defendant is not liable to her for this tort.

Conduct is "outrageous" if it exceeds all bounds normally tolerated by decent society and is calculated to cause mental suffering. Conduct is "calculated to cause mental suffering" if suffering in the mind of a reasonable person is an almost inevitable result. The defendant's conduct probably was both. **A** and **B** are incorrect, however, because the plaintiff sustained no mental injury. Outrageous conduct is "intentional" if the defendant desired or knew with substantial certainty that it would result in mental suffering in the plaintiff. **C** is incorrect because the defendant might have had such a desire or knowledge, even though his motive was only to play a joke.

90.   **D**       A seller of products owes his or her customers the duty to act reasonably. If it would be reasonable to inspect a product before selling it, then the druggist owes his customers a duty of doing so.

                  **A, B,** and **C** are over-inclusive statements. Since some of the harmful side effects or defects associated with a particular drug might be unknown even to the reasonable druggist, a druggist cannot be said to have a duty to know them all. (**Note:** A druggist who sells a defective drug may be held strictly liable for damages that result. This is because strict liability is not based on fault, however, and does not justify the conclusion set forth in **C.**)

91.   **D**       Persons engaged in a concert of action are regarded as members of a joint enterprise. As such, they are vicariously liable for torts committed by other members of the enterprise. Thus, the man and his friend may each be held liable for the other's tort.

                  To recover against either or both of them, the plaintiff need prove only that his injury was caused by the negligence of some member of the enterprise. **A** is therefore incorrect. **B** suggests that one thing cannot be a cause of harm if some other thing is. Since any effect may have more than one cause, **B** is incorrect. **C** is incorrect because nothing can be a legal cause of harm unless it is a factual cause of that harm.

92.   **D**       Negligence does not result in liability unless it was a proximate cause of damage. Although the attorney's failure to commence the patient's action against the doctor was probably negligent, no liability will result unless the attorney's negligence was a proximate cause of damage. If the patient would have lost her lawsuit against the doctor anyway, the attorney's failure to institute it did not result in damage since the patient lost nothing as a result. If the doctor's use of the drug did not result in damage to the patient, the doctor would not have been liable to her even if her conduct was negligent. If the drug saved the patient's life at the expense of her eye, it probably did not result in damage, since what the patient gained from its use exceeded what she lost. This means that the patient would have lost her lawsuit against the doctor, and that the attorney's failure to assert it did not result in damage.

                  **A** is incorrect because even an inexperienced lawyer is required to act as the reasonable attorney. The attorney's honest belief is no defense unless the reasonable attorney would have held it. **B** and **C** are therefore incorrect.

93.   **C**       Under pure comparative negligence statutes, a plaintiff's recovery in a negligence action is diminished in proportion to the plaintiff's fault, but it is not barred by the plaintiff's own negligence. Thus, the plaintiff would be entitled to recover part of any damages that she sustained as a result of the defendant's conduct if the defendant's conduct was unreasonable.

                  In most jurisdictions, a landholder owes a duty of reasonable care to an invitee but owes no duty of reasonable care to a trespasser. For this purpose, an invitee is one whose presence confers an economic benefit on the landholder, and a trespasser is one who enters without permission. Since the plaintiff's use of the defendant's pool was consideration for valuable services that she rendered, she was an invitee. Under the "attractive nuisance" doctrine, a trespassing child may be entitled to reasonable care, but it is inapplicable here because the plaintiff was an invitee rather than a trespasser. **A** and **B** are therefore incorrect. If the plaintiff's conduct was unreasonable, the amount of her damages would be diminished accordingly. The language of option **D** may suggest defenses based on comparative negligence and on assumption of the risk. If it suggests a comparative negligence defense, it is incorrect because in a pure comparative negligence system, the plaintiff's recovery is diminished in proportion to his or her own fault but is not barred completely. In most jurisdictions, assumption of the risk is a complete bar to recovery by the plaintiff. A plaintiff assumes the risk when he or she voluntarily encounters a risk of which he or she knows. The knowledge requirement is subjective, meaning that unless the plaintiff himself or herself was aware of the risk, the fact that the reasonable person would have been aware is irrelevant. **D** is also incorrect for this reason, and because the facts indicate that the plaintiff dove in without looking and was thus unaware that the pool was empty.

94. **C**    Since the plaintiff entered without the company's permission, she was a trespasser. Ordinarily, a landholder owes trespassers, even if they are children, no duty of reasonable care with respect to dangerous conditions of the premises. A trespassing child may be entitled to reasonable care, however, if it was foreseeable that children would trespass, it was foreseeable that a child who trespassed would be injured, and if the child was too young to comprehend the danger. Thus, if the plaintiff was old enough to comprehend the danger associated with an attempt to climb the pole, the company owed no duty of reasonable care to protect her against it. Although a minority of jurisdictions holds that a landholder owes a duty of reasonable care to all who enter, **C** is correct because it is the only argument listed that could provide the company with an effective defense in any jurisdiction.

**A** is incorrect because under the rule stated above, a duty of reasonable care may be owed to a trespassing child. The fact that no child had ever before attempted to climb the pole would not prevent the rule from being applied if it was foreseeable that a child would do so in the future. **B** is therefore incorrect. **D** is incorrect because even if the company could not repair the fence, there may have been other steps that the reasonable person in the company's position would have taken to prevent the danger that resulted in the plaintiff's injury.

95. **B**    The homeowner's lawsuit may be founded either on negligence or upon strict products liability. Negligence involves unreasonable conduct. If the explosives were properly labeled, the company's conduct was not unreasonable. Strict liability is imposed only if the product that caused harm left the defendant in a defective condition. A product may be defective because of the way in which it is labeled, but if the labels were properly affixed when the cases left the company's plant, the product was not defective at the time it left the company's hands.

**A** is incorrect because strict liability may be imposed even though the defendant acted reasonably. **C** is incorrect because the negligence of a company employee would be imputed to the company. Although the storage of explosives is usually regarded as an ultra-hazardous activity, resulting in the imposition of strict liability upon one storing it, **D** would not furnish the company with a defense since the imposition of liability on the warehouse would not prevent liability from being imposed on the company.

96.  **D**  A private nuisance is liability-forming conduct by the defendant that unreasonably interferes with the plaintiff's right to use and enjoy his or her property. Liability is formed if the defendant intends to invade the plaintiff's rights. After speaking with the plaintiff, the defendant now intends his invasion because he is now acting with either desire or substantial certainty that the interfering conduct will occur. Consequently, if the interference is unreasonable, the defendant is liable. This is the only theory listed that could result in a judgment for the plaintiff.

A is incorrect because the theory requires some physical intrusion into the plaintiff's presence, and there is no indication the restaurant or the college kids are doing so. **B** is incorrect because the plaintiff is not complaining of or seeking damages for severe mental suffering. **C** is incorrect because trespass requires tangible entry onto the plaintiff's land, and none has occurred.

97.  **D**  Misappropriation of identity is an invasion of privacy that consists of the unauthorized use of the plaintiff's identity for a commercial purpose. Since the cigar company used the comedian's name without his permission for the purpose of selling its product, it has committed this tort against the comedian.

Although the truth of the statement made in the advertisements might justify its publication for some purposes, its use for a commercial purpose is not privileged. **A** is therefore incorrect. Although the protection of the First Amendment to the United States Constitution has been extended to commercial expression, it has not been extended to the unauthorized use of another's identity for a commercial purpose. **B** is therefore incorrect. **C** is incorrect because liability for misappropriation of identity does not depend on the foreseeability of the defendant's conduct.

98.  **A**  Tort liability may be imposed only for harm that resulted from intent, negligence, or any activity for which strict liability may be imposed. Since there is no indication that the defendant intended the harm, and since her activity was not an abnormally dangerous one, the only theory available to the plaintiff is negligence. Negligence is a breach of the duty of reasonable care. The duty exists if the defendant's conduct creates a foreseeable risk to the plaintiff. Since the operation of a motor vehicle on a roadway creates foreseeable risks to persons owning property along the roadway, the operator of a vehicle owes a duty of reasonable care to such persons. The question of whether the defendant breached that duty depends on whether the defendant acted reasonably.

A professional seller of products (*i.e.*, a merchant) may be held liable for damage resulting from a defect in a product that he or she supplied on theories of strict liability in tort or breach of the implied warranty of merchantability. Since the defendant did not supply the trailer, however, neither of these theories can be applied to her. Thus, the questions of whether the hitch was defective or whether the defendant was a merchant are not relevant. **B** and **C** are therefore incorrect. Although negligence liability is often made to depend on whether the reasonable person in the position of the *defendant* would have foreseen the harm, **D** is incorrect because it is never necessary that the harm be foreseeable to the *plaintiff*.

99.   **A**    The old rule that "he or she who holds the land holds upward unto heaven" is no longer true. All jurisdictions agree that a flight over land is a trespass to the land only if it was below a certain altitude (although they frequently disagree about what that altitude is). Thus, unless the woman can prove the altitude at which the pilot hovered, she cannot establish a trespass.

   **B** is incorrect because damage is not an essential element of an action for trespass to land. **C** is incorrect since an action for trespass is not one for invasion of privacy, but rather for invasion of the right to exclusive possession of realty. **D** is incorrect because even one whose possession is unlawful may sue for trespass.

100.   **D**    A person entitled to possess a chattel who enters the realty of another for the purpose of recovering that chattel is privileged to make such entry, provided that he or she does so in a reasonable manner (and provided further that the chattel did not get onto the realty through any fault of his or her own). The woman's entry onto the homeowner's realty was therefore privileged. Since the woman's entry was privileged, the homeowner was not entitled to use force against her to defend his realty, and his use of such force constituted a battery.

   A privilege to use force *against the wrongful dispossessor* of a chattel exists only when that force is used in hot pursuit of the dispossessor. **A** is incorrect, however, because hot pursuit is not a prerequisite to the privilege *to enter realty* to recover a chattel. **B** is incorrect because injury is not an essential element of battery. **C** is incorrect because a possessor of realty is privileged to use reasonable force to prevent a trespass to that realty.

101.   **C**    An action for misrepresentation requires proof that the defendant made a statement that he or she knew or should have known was false, for the purpose of inducing plaintiff's reliance, and that the plaintiff was damaged by his or her justified reliance on the statement. The facts given establish that the employee made statements to the husband for the purpose of inducing him to settle his claim. The husband's independent consultation with the attorney would at least create a jury question about whether the husband was acting in reliance on the employee's statements. The fact that the wrongful death suit would have resulted in a judgment for the husband in excess of $1,000 would have to be proven to establish that the employee's statements were false and that the husband's reliance on them led to damages. The fact that the employee knew or should have known that the statements were false would have to be proven to show that the employee had the necessary fault.

102.   **D**    Private nuisance may consist of an intentional and unreasonable interference with the plaintiff's right to use and enjoy his or her realty. Interference is intentional if the

defendant is substantially certain that it will occur. Since the company continued testing dog whistles after the breeder notified it that the testing procedure was interfering with the breeder's business, the interference with the breeder's use and enjoyment of land was intentional. The interference was not unreasonable, however, unless the company's conduct would have interfered with ordinary use or enjoyment of the breeder's realty. So, if the breeder's damage resulted from an unusually sensitive use of the breeder's land, it would not be the result of an unreasonable interference. Since only dogs could hear the sound, and since most people are not in the business of keeping dogs, the argument in **D** might be successful. Of the arguments listed, it is the only one that could possibly be successful.

**A** is incorrect because even a lawful business may constitute a private nuisance if it is operated in a way that unreasonably interferes with the use and enjoyment of the plaintiff's realty. **B** is incorrect because if a defendant's activity unreasonably interferes with plaintiff's use and enjoyment of his or her realty, the fact that the defendant was engaging in it before the plaintiff arrived is not in itself sufficient to prevent that activity from being characterized as a nuisance. Since the intent requirement is satisfied by the company's knowledge that its activity was interfering with the breeder's use of his land, **C** is also incorrect.

103.   **A**      An express warranty is a representation regarding a condition of the product sold. Liability for breach of express warranty is imposed on the warrantor, regardless of fault, if the product's failure to be what it was represented to be results in damage. If the label said that the product would not harm the skin, the fact that it harmed the plaintiff's skin would be a breach of warranty.

Although liability may be imposed for the breach of an implied warranty of fitness for ordinary use (*i.e.*, merchantability), express warranty liability requires some assertion of fact about the product. **B** is therefore incorrect. Liability for breach of express warranty is imposed on whoever made the warranty that was breached. A retailer who delivers a product makes whatever warranties are printed on its label. **C** is therefore incorrect. **D** is incorrect because liability for breach of express warranty is imposed without regard to fault.

104.   **A**      As a general rule, the courts hold that the coming of a rescuer is foreseeable. This is what is meant by the well-known phrase "Danger invites rescue." For this reason, one who unreasonably creates a danger to any human being—including himself or herself—creates a risk to a potential rescuer as well and owes a potential rescuer a duty of reasonable care. Thus, if the defendant's conduct was unreasonable, it was a breach of a duty he owed the plaintiff.

**B** is based on an over-inclusive statement of law—a rescuer's right to collect from the person whom he or she rescued must be based either on the breach of duty to act reasonably or on an implied contract. An officious intermeddler is a person who acts without a legitimate reason. **C** is incorrect because a human life was at stake, giving the plaintiff a legitimate reason to act. The rule that is characterized by the phrase "Danger invites rescue" makes **D** incorrect because the rescuer's attempt to rescue the defendant is regarded as foreseeable for the reason given.

105. **B**   Negligence is a failure to act reasonably in the face of a foreseeable risk. If it was not foreseeable that the contents of the package would cause harm to a passenger in her car, the defendant's conduct with respect to the package could not have been negligent. Although it is not certain that a court would come to this conclusion, the argument in **B** is the only one listed that is supported by the facts.

    **A** is incorrect because the rule limiting the duty owed to a licensee applies only to conditions of realty occupied by a defendant. Contributory negligence is unreasonable conduct by the plaintiff that contributes to the happening of the accident. Since the plaintiff could not have known that the contents of the package were caustic, there is no reason to conclude that his conduct was unreasonable. **C** is therefore incorrect. A plaintiff is said to have assumed the risk when he or she voluntarily encounters a known risk. **D** is incorrect because the plaintiff did not know that the contents of the package were caustic, and touching it did not, therefore, constitute an encounter with a known risk.

106. **A**   Strict liability in tort may be imposed upon a professional supplier of products who places a defective product into the stream of commerce. Since a tattoo artist does not sell tattoo needles to his or her customers, he or she does not place them in the stream of commerce, and he or she cannot be held strictly liable for damage that results from his or her customer's contact with them.

    **B** is incorrect because strict liability is imposed regardless of fault and therefore may be imposed on a defendant although he or she did not exercise any control over the quality of the product. A plaintiff assumes a risk when he or she knows of it and voluntarily encounters it. Although the defendant informed the plaintiff that the process was likely to be a painful one, there is no indication that the plaintiff knew that the needle would break off in her skin. **C** is therefore incorrect. Strict liability may be imposed upon the supplier of defective products without regard to whether those products would be dangerous without the defect (*i.e.*, inherently dangerous). **D** is therefore incorrect.

107. **C**   False imprisonment consists of the intentional confinement of the plaintiff. Confinement is an overcoming of the plaintiff's will to leave in a manner that would overcome the reasonable person's will to leave. Since the reasonable person usually obeys the directions of a police officer, the police officer's words would have been sufficient to overcome the reasonable person's will to leave. For this reason, if the police officer's language overcame the walker's will to leave, it confined him.

    **A** is incorrect because if it was reasonable for the walker to believe that an attempt to leave would result in some harm to him, then he was confined even though no physical barriers prevented him from getting out of the police car. **B** is incorrect because the police officer's assertion of legal authority and threatening language would have made any protest by the walker a futile—and thus unnecessary—gesture. **D** is incorrect because damage is not an essential element of false imprisonment.

108.   **B**     A defendant owes a duty of reasonable care to a plaintiff if the defendant's conduct creates a foreseeable risk to that plaintiff. A foreseeable risk is a danger that a reasonable person would anticipate. If the driver's conduct created no foreseeable risks to persons in the hospital, the driver did not owe such persons a duty of reasonable care and could not be held liable to them for negligence.

The intervening act of a third person may be a superseding cause of harm, relieving the original wrongdoer of liability for the plaintiff's injuries. This is so, however, only if the intervention was unforeseeable. **A** is incorrect because the negligence of a surgeon is usually regarded as foreseeable. **C** is similarly incorrect because even aggravated negligence may be foreseeable. Since any result may have several causes, the fact that the scars were caused by the conduct of the doctor does not establish that they were not also caused by the negligence of the driver. **D** is therefore incorrect.

109.   **B**     There can be no liability for making defamatory statements unless those statements are false. Statements that are expressions of the writer's feelings regarding subjective matters are statements of opinion, and opinions are neither true nor false. Since the quality of the plaintiff's writing is a subjective matter, the defendant's statements are opinions. Statements of opinion can be defamatory only if the reasonable person would interpret the statements as fact. Here, the nature of the defendant's statements makes them unlikely to be interpreted as facts.

A media defendant may be held liable for defaming a public figure if the defamatory statements were made with actual malice. **A** and **C** are therefore incorrect. Although a businessperson may be privileged to compete by making unflattering reference to his or her competitor's products, **D** is incorrect because the privilege is qualified by the requirement of good faith.

110.   **A**     A professional supplier who sells a product in a defective condition is strictly liable for harm that proximately results from the defect. Here, since the jury found the machine was the proximate cause of the employee's injury, the manufacturer is strictly liable for it.

**B** is incorrect because the manufacturer's liability would not be based on whether it was reasonable in its offers to make a repair. **C** is incorrect because the machine was defective when it was placed in the stream of commerce, and nothing happened to change its condition. **D** is incorrect because the unreasonable conduct of an intervenor is not a superseding cause of harm unless it is unforeseeable. Here, an owner of the machine not wanting to pay $1,000 for a repair is likely foreseeable.

111.   **C**     A defendant is liable only for harm caused by his or her conduct. Conduct is a cause of harm only if the harm would not have occurred without that conduct. If the passenger's harm would have occurred without the man's conduct, the man's conduct could not have been a cause of the passenger's harm.

Although the violation of a statute is relevant to the issue of negligence if the statute was designed to protect persons like the plaintiff against risks like that which produced the plaintiff's harm, **A** would not be an effective defense for two reasons. First, the fact that the statute was designed to protect schoolchildren does not prove that it was not also designed to protect automobile passengers. Second, even if the statutory violation is not relevant to the issue of negligence, the passenger might succeed in establishing common law negligence (*i.e.*, that the man failed to act reasonably). An intervening cause of harm may be a superseding cause that shifts responsibility from the original wrongdoer to the intervenor, but only if the conduct of the intervenor was unforeseeable. Since the negligence of motorists is a common occurrence, the woman's negligence was probably foreseeable. **B** and **D** are therefore incorrect.

112.　**B**　Since the two defendants were found to be jointly and severally liable, the plaintiff can collect the entire amount of his judgment from either of them or from both of them in any combination. Under the pure comparative negligence statute that existed in the jurisdiction, the plaintiff's judgment should be for the amount of his damages, diminished in proportion to his own fault. Since the plaintiff's injury was found to have resulted 20 percent from the plaintiff's own negligence, his judgment should be for $100,000 less 20 percent, or $80,000.

　　　　　 **A** is incorrect because it does not diminish the plaintiff's recovery in proportion to his fault. **C** is incorrect because joint tortfeasors are jointly and severally liable. In an all-or-nothing contributory negligence jurisdiction, a plaintiff who was contributorily negligent will receive nothing, even though the defendant may have been negligent as well. Under the "pure comparative negligence" statute given, however, the plaintiff's recovery is not completely barred by his negligence. **D** is therefore incorrect.

113.　**D**　Vicarious liability only occurs when there is an employment relationship (or, occasionally, an independent contractor relationship) between the defendant and the tortfeasor. While the defendant could be liable for inadequate security or negligently allowing the tortfeasor to come onto the premises, the defendant cannot be found liable under the principle of vicarious liability for torts committed by a customer. **A** is therefore incorrect. "General liability" is not a principle for holding a party liable. **B** is therefore incorrect. Strict liability comes into play with defective products, keeping wild or other dangerous animals, or carrying out abnormally dangerous activities. Here, the question involves none of these three scenarios. **C** is therefore incorrect.

114.　**D**　Invasion of privacy by public disclosure of private facts consists of publishing offensive and previously unknown facts about the plaintiff. The United States Supreme Court has held, however, that First Amendment guarantees of free expression prohibit imposing liability for the publication of facts that are already matters of public record. The Court said that this rule applies even to facts that are not commonly known, since the press often serves as eyes and ears for a public too busy to search public records for itself.

　　　　　 **A** and **B** are incorrect for the above reason. **B** is also incorrect because a privilege to publish information about one who is involved in a matter of public interest may exist even though that person is not a public employee. **C** is incorrect because although publication of the truth cannot lead to liability for defamation, publication of private facts that are not newsworthy may result in liability when it would offend the reasonable person, even if those facts are true.

115.  **C**    Trespass to land consists of intentional unauthorized entry on realty possessed by the plaintiff. There is no requirement of damage. Since the landowner's complaint gave the factory knowledge that dust from its operation was settling on the cabin, and since the factory thereafter continued operating as it had been, the necessary intent is present (*i.e.*, the factory was substantially certain that entry would occur). Some cases have held that the settling of dust constitutes a tangible entry on affected realty; other cases have held that it does not. For this reason, it is not certain that a court would find that a trespass occurred. Of all the theories listed, however, trespass to land is the only one that might possibly result in a judgment for the landowner.

Invasion of privacy by intrusion involves an interference with the plaintiff's interest in solitude and requires some kind of prying into the plaintiff's affairs or private life. This did not occur here. Other privacy theories—appropriation, public disclosure, false light—are not even remotely applicable. **A** is therefore incorrect. Unlike trespass, which requires no damage, nuisance liability is imposed only where the plaintiff has sustained some substantial harm. An individual may assert a *public* nuisance claim only if the harm that he or she sustained differed from that sustained by the general public. **B** is incorrect for these reasons. An abnormally dangerous activity is one that necessarily involves a serious risk of harm that cannot be eliminated by acting reasonably. Since there are no facts indicating that the use of unbagged cement is such an activity, **D** is incorrect.

116.  **D**    When tortfeasors are jointly and severally liable, a plaintiff is entitled to collect all his or her damages from any one of them (*i.e.*, "severally"), or to collect his or her damages from them together (*i.e.*, "jointly") in any combination whatsoever. Since the court held the company, the employee, and the driver to be jointly and severally liable to her, the passenger is entitled to collect 100 percent of her damages from the employee if she chooses to do so.

**A, B,** and **C** are therefore incorrect. (**Note:** Comparative negligence statutes determine the effect of the plaintiff's fault. Since the jury found the plaintiff to be free of fault, the existence of a comparative negligence statute is irrelevant. Statutory and common law contribution systems give joint tortfeasors certain rights against each other, but do not affect a plaintiff's right to collect from them jointly and/or severally.)

117.  **C**    That joint tortfeasors are "jointly and severally liable" means that the plaintiff may collect all his or her damages from either of them or from both of them in any combination. Obviously, however, the fact that there are multiple tortfeasors does not entitle a plaintiff to collect his or her damages more than once. Since the defendants were jointly and severally liable to the plaintiff for $100,000, the plaintiff is entitled to collect $100,000 from either or both of them in any combination. Since the plaintiff has already received $10,000 from the first defendant, she is entitled to collect the remaining $90,000 from the second defendant.

**A** and **B** are incorrect because a statute basing contribution on apportionment of fault affects the rights that joint tortfeasors have against each other, but it does not affect their joint and several liability to the plaintiff. **D** is incorrect because the plaintiff has already received $10,000 from the first defendant, and to allow her to collect an additional $100,000 from the second defendant would result in her collecting her damages more than once.

118.　**B**　In jurisdictions that follow pure comparative negligence, the plaintiff's recovery is reduced in proportion to the plaintiff's fault. Consequently, the $100,000 in damages was 75 percent the fault of the plaintiff, so he should only recover 25 percent of the damages, or $25,000.

**A** is incorrect because in a pure comparative fault jurisdiction, the fact that the plaintiff was responsible for more of the damages does not relieve the defendant from liability. **C** is incorrect, because the plaintiff would not be entitled to damages that could be attributed to his negligence. **D** is incorrect, because the plaintiff's damages would be reduced by the amount of his negligence.

119.　**B**　Self-defense is a privilege to use reasonable force to protect oneself against a threatened tortious contact or confinement. Some jurisdictions hold that it is never reasonable to use deadly force when it is reasonably safe to retreat. But even in those jurisdictions that do not *require* retreat, the defendant's privilege is likely to turn on whether he knew or should have known that he could safely retreat. In connection with the privilege of self-defense, "reasonable force" means the force that would have appeared necessary to the reasonable person in the defendant's situation. If the defendant knew or should have known that he could safely and easily retreat without sustaining harm, the reasonable person in his situation would probably not have considered it necessary to use any force at all in self-defense. On the other hand, if the defendant could not have known that he could safely and easily retreat, the reasonable person in his situation might have considered the use of a knife necessary because of the extreme danger facing a person who has a pistol pointed at him.

Deadly force may be reasonable in self-defense if the person using it is being threatened by what reasonably appears to be deadly force. Since the plaintiff was threatening the defendant with a pistol, the use of a knife—even if it was deadly force—may have been privileged in self-defense. For this reason, **A** is incorrect. If the defendant initiated the aggression by slapping the plaintiff, then the plaintiff was privileged to use reasonable force to defend himself against the possibility of further blows by the defendant. Thus, if the force with which the plaintiff threatened the defendant was reasonable, it would have been privileged and therefore not tortious. If that was so, then the defendant would not have been privileged to use force to defend himself against it. (This reasoning accounts for the rule that an initial aggressor is not privileged to use force to defend himself or herself against a reasonable response to his or her aggression.) If, however, the plaintiff's use of a pistol was unreasonable (*i.e.*, excessive force), it was not privileged by self-defense. Then, the contact with which the plaintiff threatened the defendant would have been tortious, and the defendant would have been privileged to defend himself against it by using reasonable force. Thus, even if the defendant was the initial aggressor, he might have been privileged to use a knife to defend himself against the plaintiff's use of a gun. **C** is therefore incorrect. Since reasonable force depends on what the reasonable person in the defendant's situation would have considered necessary, the defendant's privilege depends on how *the defendant* perceived or should have perceived the threat with which he was confronted. Whether or not *the plaintiff* knew that the pistol was loaded, the defendant's use of a knife might have been reasonable if *the defendant* believed that the pistol was loaded. **D** is therefore incorrect.

120. **D** A person who keeps a wild animal is strictly liable for all damage done by that animal so long as that damage results from a dangerous propensity that is typical of the animal's species. Importantly, the fact that the average person fears a particular type of animal is part of that animal's dangerous propensities. Here, although the lion may not have harmed the plaintiff in any way, the defendant is strictly liable because humans' fear of unrestrained lions is part of what makes lions dangerous. Importantly, that fear caused the plaintiff to drop the pot of grease onto her foot. **C** is therefore incorrect. Whether an animal is known to be dangerous comes into play when determining liability for domestic animals. A lion is certainly not a domestic animal (like a cat, dog, or hamster). **A** is therefore incorrect. Because the defendant can be held strictly liable, the defendant's negligence is irrelevant. **B** is therefore incorrect.

121. **C** The law of torts knows only three possible bases of liability: intent, negligence, and strict liability. Since intent is desire or knowledge with substantial certainty that harm will occur, and since the store owner did not desire or know that any person would be struck by the door, no recovery is possible on an intent theory. Although strict liability is imposed on the sellers of defective products, strict liability is not available against the store owner because the store owner did not sell the product that injured the customer. The only remaining theory is negligence, which involves unreasonable conduct in the face of a duty of reasonable care. Since the customer entered the premises for the purpose of making a purchase, he is an invitee. The duty owed to an invitee is to keep the premises reasonably safe by making reasonable inspections and reasonable repairs. Thus, if a reasonable inspection would have disclosed the problem, then the store owner was either negligent in not inspecting or negligent in failing to discover what a reasonable inspection would have disclosed.

**A** is incorrect because only a professional seller of products like the one that caused injury can be held strictly liable for defects in that product. The liability of a defendant does not depend upon the availability of remedies against others. Thus, even if the fact that the contractor was not negligent might leave the customer without a remedy, it would not affect the liability of the store owner. **B** is therefore incorrect. A landholder owes an invitee a duty of reasonable care to keep the premises reasonably safe, while he or she owes a lesser duty to licensees and trespassers. For this reason, it might be relevant to determine whether the customer entered the store owner's premises as an invitee. An invitee is one whose presence is likely to confer an economic benefit on the landholder or one who has entered the premises in response to a public invitation. Supermarkets ordinarily invite the public (either expressly or impliedly) to enter their premises for the purpose of examining their wares. In addition, the courts usually hold that a person who is likely to buy confers an economic benefit by entering business premises, even if he or she does not actually make a purchase while there. For these two reasons, the customer was an invitee whether or not he made a purchase before leaving. **D** is therefore incorrect.

122. **C** Battery is committed by intentionally causing harmful or offensive contact with another person. Since there was no contact with the plaintiff, he could not successfully maintain a battery claim.

**A**, **B**, and **D** are incorrect for the above reason.

123. **B** False imprisonment is committed by intentionally confining another person. For this purpose, "confining" means overcoming the plaintiff's will to leave. If the ex-husband's father did not prevent the plaintiff from leaving, he did not confine her and could not be liable to her for false imprisonment.

**A** is incorrect because damage is not an essential element of false imprisonment. Although the ex-husband's father's conduct may have prevented the plaintiff from obtaining physical custody of her son, the plaintiff cannot maintain an action for false imprisonment unless she herself was confined. **C** and **D** are therefore incorrect.

124. **A** Since the facts do not indicate that the defendant intended contact with the boy or harm of any kind to the plaintiff, the only claim that could possibly succeed against him would be one founded on negligence. Negligence is a breach of the duty of reasonable care. Generally, a defendant owes a duty of reasonable care to a plaintiff only if his or her conduct created a risk to that plaintiff that was foreseeable to the reasonable person. Thus, if the reasonable person would not have expected (*i.e.*, foreseen) harm to the plaintiff, the defendant would have owed her no duty of reasonable care and could not be held liable to her for negligence. Many jurisdictions apply the "zone of danger" rule, which holds that a plaintiff may not recover for mental suffering that he or she experienced upon seeing another person sustain a physical injury unless he or she was in the same zone of physical danger as the injured person. In those jurisdictions, the plaintiff could not succeed against the defendant even if the harm to her was foreseeable. **A** is correct, however, because of all the additional facts listed, it is the only one that could possibly result in a judgment for the plaintiff.

**B** is incorrect because the doctrine of transferred intent applies only when the defendant's intent was tortious to begin with. Since the facts do not indicate that the defendant desired or knew with certainty that his car would strike the boy, he had no tortious intent. **C** is incorrect because there is no rule of tort law that transfers consequences that is known as the "doctrine of transferred consequences." Liability for intentionally inflicting emotional distress requires outrageous conduct by the defendant. This tort also requires that the defendant intend to cause mental suffering or be reckless in creating the risk of emotional distress, however. Since the defendant lacked such intent (while he was speeding, "reckless" requires the defendant to act in deliberate disregard of a high degree of probability that emotional distress will occur, and there are no facts indicating this), he could not be held liable for intentionally inflicting mental distress even if his conduct was outrageous. **D** is therefore incorrect.

125.  **C**    ⸱ Negligence is the breach of a duty of reasonable care. In some jurisdictions, the duty that a landholder owes to a plaintiff who enters the land depends on the plaintiff's status as trespasser, licensee, or invitee. In other jurisdictions, the duty does not depend on the plaintiff's status. All jurisdictions agree, however, that a defendant does not owe a plaintiff anything more than reasonable care, no matter what the plaintiff's status. Since the lawn had recently been mowed, and since the ladder was in plain view, it probably was reasonable for the homeowner to believe that the employee saw it. If so, the homeowner's failure to warn the employee about it probably was reasonable as well, and therefore probably was not negligent. While it is not certain that a court would come to this conclusion, the argument in **C** is the only one listed that could possibly support the homeowner's defense.

The fact that the homeowner did not know with certainty that the employee would be injured means that he did not intend her injury. **A** is incorrect, however, because negligence liability does not require intent or knowledge with certainty that harm will result. **B** is incorrect because a landholder's obligation to warn or protect others against dangerous conditions of his or her land may extend to conditions that he or she did not create. **D** is an incorrect statement of the law; in general, a government employee entering on official business is at least a licensee, entitled to be warned of dangerous conditions known to the landholder and hidden from the licensee's view.

126.  **D**    Under the doctrine of *res ipsa loquitur*, an inference that the defendant acted unreasonably can be drawn if the injury involved was one that does not usually occur without unreasonable conduct and the defendant was the only person whose conduct could have caused the injury (*i.e.*, the defendant had exclusive control of the circumstances). If an expert witness testifies that surgeons do not usually leave instruments inside a patient unless they are acting unreasonably, the patient can rely on the inference established by *res ipsa loquitur* if she can show that the doctor was the only person who could have left the instrument inside her. Since the doctor was the only person who had ever performed surgery on the patient, the doctor is the only person who could have left the instrument inside her.

**A** is incorrect because it is based on an inaccurate statement of law; there are many medical malpractice cases in which the plaintiff was permitted to rely on *res ipsa loquitur*. (**Note**: These frequently involve foreign objects that were left in the plaintiff's body during surgery). Ordinarily, in drawing an inference of negligence under the doctrine of *res ipsa loquitur*, a jury relies on what it knows about human experience to determine whether a particular accident is of a kind that does not usually occur without negligence. Because of its lack of specialized knowledge, a jury is not competent to decide whether the particular result of a professional's conduct is one that would not usually occur without negligence. Once a jury has heard testimony to that effect from an expert witness, however, it may base an inference of negligence on its decision about whether or not it believes that witness. This is a decision that a jury is uniquely competent to make. For this reason, **B** is incorrect. **C** is incorrect because *res ipsa loquitur* is not dependent on the existence of any "absolute duty," but rather on circumstantial evidence that justifies the inference that a particular defendant acted unreasonably.

127. **A**   In an all-or-nothing contributory negligence jurisdiction, a plaintiff whose own negligence contributed to the accident cannot recover any damages for injuries that he or she sustained. Under pure comparative negligence statutes, a plaintiff's negligence does not bar his or her recovery, but results in a reduction of damages in proportion to his or her own fault. Since the jury found the pedestrian's damage to be $100,000 and found the pedestrian to be 20 percent at fault, the pedestrian is entitled to collect $100,000 reduced by 20 percent. When two defendants are "jointly and severally" liable to the plaintiff, the plaintiff may collect the entire amount of his or her judgment from either of them (several liability), or may collect it from both of them in any combination whatsoever (joint liability). Since the court found both defendants to be jointly and severally liable to the pedestrian, the pedestrian can collect the full amount of his judgment from the first driver alone.

**B** is incorrect because of the "collateral source rule," which provides that money that a plaintiff receives from parties other than tortfeasors or their representatives is irrelevant in determining his or her damages. For this reason, the sum of $10,000 that the pedestrian received from his own hospitalization insurer plays no part in determining the amount that he can collect from the defendants. **C** is incorrect because the court found the defendants to be jointly and severally liable to the pedestrian as explained above. **D** is incorrect under the collateral source rule as explained above.

128. **D**   A person is strictly liable for any damages that occur while he or she is conducting an abnormally dangerous activity. An activity is abnormally dangerous if there is a high degree of risk of some harm to others, the harm that results is likely to be serious, the risk cannot be eliminated by the exercise of reasonable care, the activity is not common, the activity is not appropriate for the place where it is carried on, and the danger outweighs the activity's value to the community. There are some types of activities that are generally held to be abnormally dangerous, such as the use or storage of explosives, crop dusting or spraying with pesticides, and the operation of a nuclear reactor. Here, since the defendant is operating a nuclear reactor, it is strictly liable for the harm done to the plaintiff. **A** and **C** are therefore incorrect. Ordinary contributory fault will not usually bar a plaintiff from recovery under strict liability. **B** is therefore incorrect.

129. **C**   Under the "but for" rule of causation, a defendant's conduct is a cause of a plaintiff's injury if the plaintiff's injury would not have occurred without it. Since the pedestrian would not have been injured without the girl's intoxication, and since the girl would not have become intoxicated without the second tavern's conduct, the second tavern's conduct was a cause of the pedestrian's injury.

**A** is incorrect for two reasons. First, given the facts, it is uncertain whether the first tavern's conduct was a substantial factor in making the girl intoxicated. Second, even if the first tavern's conduct was a cause of the harm (*i.e.*, a substantial factor in producing it), the second tavern's conduct was also a cause of that harm. **B** is incorrect because the language of the statute (". . . any person who sold said minor the alcohol which resulted in said minor's intoxication . . .") indicates that liability depends on a causal relationship between the defendant's conduct and the minor's intoxication. Since the pedestrian's injury would not have occurred without the girl's intoxication, any cause of the girl's intoxication must also have been a cause of the pedestrian's injury. **D** is therefore incorrect.

130.   **C**   Negligence is unreasonable conduct in the face of a foreseeable risk. If the contractor acted reasonably in relying on the architect's instructions, she could not have been negligent.

A plaintiff may be prevented from recovering for damages resulting from a defendant's negligence if the plaintiff "assumed the risk" by voluntarily encountering a risk of which he or she knew. **A** is incorrect because this concept applies only to the conduct of a plaintiff. **B** is incorrect because a defendant owes a duty of reasonable care to all persons who are placed at a foreseeable risk as a result of that defendant's conduct. Since it was foreseeable that the landowner would hire a mover to bring furniture into the new house, the contractor thus owed the mover a duty to act reasonably in building the house and could be liable to the mover for breaching it. **D** is incorrect because a ritualistic protest is not sufficient to absolve a person of liability for the results of his or her conduct if that conduct is unreasonable.

131.   **C**   The manufacturer of a product is strictly liable for damage that results from a defect in the product that existed at the time the manufacturer placed that product in the stream of commerce. In this connection, a product is defective if its condition would defeat the expectations of the reasonable consumer. Since a reasonable consumer would not expect liquor to contain poison, the liquor was defective. Since that defect existed when the liquor left the factory, the factory is strictly liable for the pedestrian's injuries.

**A** is incorrect because strict liability is imposed regardless of the reason for the existence of the defect. **B** is incorrect because strict liability is applied for the benefit of any foreseeable plaintiff regardless of whether he or she was a purchaser, consumer, or bystander. **D** is incorrect because strict liability (*i.e.*, liability *without fault*) does not depend on the defendant's unreasonable conduct.

132.   **A**   Strict liability (*i.e.*, liability without fault) may be imposed on one who engages in an abnormally dangerous activity. In this connection, an activity is sufficiently dangerous to result in strict liability if it is not a common activity and necessarily involves a serious risk of harm that cannot be eliminated by reasonable care. While it is not certain that a court would come to this conclusion, **A** is the only option that could possibly be correct.

Although the doctrine of *res ipsa loquitur* may permit an inference of negligence to be drawn from circumstantial evidence, it does not impose negligence liability on a defendant who was not negligent. Since the facts indicate that the rocket company acted reasonably, negligence liability should not be imposed. **B** is therefore incorrect. Although tort liability is sometimes limited by the concept of foreseeability, the *amount* of damage need not be specifically foreseeable so long as the *type* of damage is foreseeable. **C** is therefore incorrect. **D** is incorrect because a type of harm may be foreseeable even though it never happened before (*e.g.*, it is foreseeable that a person will die even though he or she has never died before). The fact that no such damage had ever occurred in the past is therefore not sufficient to make that damage unforeseeable.

133.  **C**  A manufacturer is strictly liable for injuries that result from a defect in its product if the defect existed when the manufacturer placed the product in the stream of commerce. The company will thus be strictly liable if the absence of an acceleration suppressor was a defect. A defect is a condition that would defeat the expectations of the reasonable consumer. Unless the belt truck is equipped with an acceleration suppressor, it will lurch forward if the belt idle is adjusted improperly. The reasonable consumer probably does not expect a vehicle to lurch forward when it is being used for its intended purpose. Since persons who maintain belt trucks frequently adjust the belt idle improperly, belt trucks will frequently lurch in the absence of an acceleration suppressor. Its absence, therefore, is probably a defect.

The absence of an acceleration suppressor was a factual cause of the employee's injury because the employee would not have been injured if the truck had been equipped with one. The fact that the injury would not have occurred without the subsequent acts of others (*i.e.*, intervening causes) would not prevent the company from being liable unless those subsequent acts (*i.e.*, intervening causes) were unforeseeable (*i.e.*, superseding causes). Since humans are frequently negligent, the unreasonable conduct of the first airline and the contractor may have been foreseeable. For this reason, **A** and **B** are incorrect. **D** is incorrect because it is based on an inaccurate statement. Sometimes the relationship between two persons makes one of them responsible for conduct of the other (*i.e.*, conduct of one is imputed to the other). There is no relationship between the contractor and the company that would result in such an imputation, however.

134.  **D**  Private nuisance involves a tortious invasion of the plaintiff's right to use and enjoy realty. Although the fumes invaded the homeowner's right to use and enjoy his realty, their emission was not a nuisance unless it resulted from liability-forming (*i.e.*, tortious) conduct by the company. Since the homeowner has alleged that the company's conduct was liability-forming in that it was negligent, liability will depend on whether the company's conduct was unreasonable (*i.e.*, negligent). Ordinarily, in determining whether conduct is unreasonable, it is necessary to weigh the risks resulting from such conduct against the burdens of eliminating those risks. Additionally, courts will weigh the social value and utility of the defendant's activity against the harm done to the plaintiff. Here, the company is making an insecticide that is very important to the state's orange crop, and the plaintiff is having the paint on his home damaged. If the cost (*i.e.*, the burden) of eliminating the fumes would drive the company out of business, a court might find that the burden was so much heavier than the risk that it would eliminate that it was not unreasonable for the company to continue emitting the fumes, and that the company, therefore, was not negligent. While it is not certain that a court would come to this conclusion, **D** is the only argument listed that could possibly provide the company with an effective defense.

**A** is incorrect because nuisance requires an invasion of plaintiff's rights in realty, but it does not require a physical invasion of the realty itself. For an individual to prevail in a claim for public nuisance, he or she must show that the harm that he or she sustained was substantially different from that sustained by the general public. **B** is incorrect, however, because no such showing is required in a claim for private nuisance. If the homeowner's claim were based on intent, it would be necessary for him to show that the company knew that its activity was interfering with his right. Since his claim is based on negligence, however, it is sufficient for him to show that such interference was foreseeable. **C** is therefore incorrect.

135. **C**    Strict liability in tort is imposed, regardless of fault, on a professional supplier who sells a product while it is in a defective condition. If a product is more dangerous than would be contemplated by the ordinary consumer, the product is defectively dangerous. If the ordinary consumer would not have expected the product to irritate the scalp of a person with the plaintiff's allergy, then the product's condition would defeat the reasonable expectation of the ordinary consumer and was defective.

Under the doctrine of *res ipsa loquitur*, an inference of negligence can be drawn from the fact that a particular kind of accident does not usually occur without negligence. **A** is incorrect, however, because the plaintiff's theory is strict liability in tort, and since strict liability is imposed without regard to fault, an inference that the defendant was negligent is not relevant to it. The facts in **B** and **D** would suggest that the company knew or should have known about the plaintiff's allergy. This knowledge is not sufficient, however, to establish that the product's condition would have defeated the reasonable expectation of the ordinary consumer (*i.e.*, that the product was defective). For this reason, **B** and **D** are incorrect.

136. **D**    Negligence can be based on an unreasonable omission, so long as the potentially negligent party had a duty to act. Generally, a person has a duty to act only when his or her conduct causes a need for such action. This can happen when a person's conduct causes a plaintiff to fail to protect himself or herself against already existing risks because he or she reasonably believes that the person would protect him or her. Consequently, since the defendant's past conduct had caused the plaintiff to reasonably believe there would be no leaves on the sidewalk, the defendant could be found negligent under these circumstances. This would be so whether or not the danger was created by the defendant or located on his or her property. Therefore, **A** and **C** are incorrect. **B** is incorrect because the plaintiff's potential negligence would not necessarily insulate the defendant from liability.

137. **A**    *Res ipsa loquitur* permits an inference of unreasonable conduct to be drawn where the accident is one that would not ordinarily have occurred without negligence, and the defendant was in exclusive control of the circumstances that produced the harm. Since the bread company was in exclusive control of the baking process, *res ipsa loquitur* would apply if reasonable care in baking would ordinarily have eliminated the slivers (*i.e.*, if the accident would not ordinarily have occurred without negligence).

**B** is incorrect because liability for negligence (which is the only theory to which *res ipsa loquitur* applies) does not depend on whether a product is defective. The customer's harm was caused by the presence of the metal slivers in the bread. **C** is incorrect because even if the farmer's negligence caused the slivers to be in the wheat, the bread company may be liable for the harm if its negligence caused them to be in the bread. If reasonable care would have prevented the slivers from getting in the bread, it does not matter how they got into the wheat. Thus, even if the breaking of the farmer's blade was unforeseeable, the bread company might be liable to the customer for its negligence in failing to keep the slivers out of the bread. **D** is therefore incorrect.

138. **C**    A defendant is liable for intentional infliction of emotional distress if, with the intent to cause mental distress, he or she engages in outrageous conduct that causes severe mental distress. The defendant intends the plaintiff's mental distress if he or she desires or knows that it will result from his or her conduct. Because of the affection normally associated with the mother-daughter relationship, the kidnapper probably intended that his threats to injure or kill the girl would cause her mother to experience mental distress. If his conduct was outrageous and caused her to experience mental distress, the kidnapper is liable to her for the mental distress and any physical manifestations of it.

A is incorrect because the passage of time is not sufficient to prevent liability for an injury that was caused by the defendant's tortious conduct. If the reasonable person would not have experienced any suffering as a result of the kidnapper's conduct, then a plaintiff who did experience suffering might not be permitted to recover for it because the law does not seek to benefit a supersensitive plaintiff. If the reasonable person would have experienced some suffering, however, a plaintiff will be permitted to recover for his or her suffering even if a preexisting condition makes it unusually severe. **B** is therefore incorrect. **D** is incorrect because liability for intentional infliction of mental distress requires intent, not merely a foreseeable risk.

139. **C**    Assumption of the risk is a defense in all approaches to products liability (although some jurisdictions have merged it with the concept of comparative fault), and it occurs when the plaintiff voluntarily encounters a known risk. If the plaintiff knew that the paper suit was likely to dissolve when wet and wore it anyway, she voluntarily encountered (and therefore assumed) a known risk.

A is incorrect because the department store may be held liable without fault for selling a defective product. **B** is incorrect because a sign like the one described is not sufficient to apprise the buyer that the product is being sold without any warranty of merchantability or to prevent the reasonable consumer from expecting the bathing suit to hold together when wet. Although a product retailer who is held liable for selling a defective product has a right to be indemnified by the product's manufacturer, the right of the injured plaintiff to recover does not depend on this right of the retailer. **D** is therefore incorrect.

140. **B**    Normally, a minor child is held to the same standard of care as a reasonable child of similar "age, intelligence, and experience." However, if the child engages in an adult activity, the child is held to an adult standard of care. An adult activity is one normally undertaken only by adults and for which adult qualifications are required. Driving a motorcycle is such an activity (usually, it requires a license and has age restrictions). Consequently, the boy would be held to an adult standard of care. According to the question, a reasonable

adult would have known to slow down, so the boy is liable for not adhering to that standard.

**A** is incorrect because the boy is not automatically liable for the simple fact he is driving a motorcycle. **C** is incorrect because it states the wrong standard of care. **D** is incorrect because following the posted speed limit would not necessarily absolve him from liability.

141. **B**    Negligence is a failure to act reasonably. Thus, if it was unreasonable for the dog trainer to work the dog in her front yard, her conduct was negligent and could result in liability. While it is not certain that a court would come to this conclusion, the argument in **B** is the only one listed that could possibly support the walker's claim.

Strict liability for damage resulting from a product defect is imposed only against a professional supplier who placed the product in the stream of commerce. Since the dog trainer was a user of the device rather than a supplier of it, **A** is incorrect. Conduct that causes damage can result in tort liability only if the damage was intended, resulted from negligence, or resulted from an activity for which strict liability is imposed. Without establishing one of these bases of liability, calling the dog trainer's conduct a cause of harm would not be sufficient to result in liability. For this reason, the argument in **C** is incomplete, making **C** incorrect. Although some special standard of care might be imposed because of the dog trainer's profession, **D** is incorrect because there is no indication that the standard was breached.

142. **D**    Strict liability is imposed on the seller of a product that is in a defective condition when sold. If the presence of the toxic material was a defect, the company would be strictly liable.

**A** is incorrect because strict liability is imposed regardless of fault or knowledge by the defendant. Although the classification of a product as "inherently dangerous" was significant during a certain historical period in the development of the law of torts, this is no longer the case. **B** is therefore incorrect. **C** is incorrect because strict liability in tort does not depend on the reasonableness of the defendant's conduct.

143. **A**    A person whose conduct is negligent is liable for damage that is proximately caused by that negligence. Conduct is a proximate cause of harm if it is a factual and legal cause of that harm. Thus, because the driver's negligence was a factual and legal cause of the pedestrian's broken leg, the driver is liable for it.

**B** is incorrect because there was no relationship between the driver and the taxi that would result in such an imputation. **C** is an impossibility since nothing can be regarded as a legal cause of harm unless it was a factual cause of that harm. The reasoning of **D** establishes that the taxi's conduct was a cause of harm, but it does not establish that the other driver's conduct was not. **D** is therefore incorrect.

144. **D**    A statement is defamatory if it would tend to hold the plaintiff up to shame, disgrace, or ridicule in the minds of a substantial group of respectable people. Since most respectable

people believe that theft is disgraceful, an accusation that the plaintiff is a thief is probably defamatory.

Because the employee did not return the tools, the employer's statement is literally true. However, the literal truth of the statement would not prevent the employer from being liable since there is some dispute as to whether the employee was justified in taking the tools. **A** is therefore incorrect. A defendant may be privileged to make defamatory statements in a reasonable and good faith attempt to protect a legitimate interest. In deciding whether a former employer was acting in good faith when making a defamatory statement to a plaintiff's prospective employer, courts frequently look to whether the former employer made the statement gratuitously (making it less likely that he or she was acting in good faith) or in response to a request for information (making it more likely that he or she was acting in good faith). **B** is incorrect, however, because this fact alone is not sufficient to privilege a defendant's publication. **C** is incorrect because if the defendant was acting reasonably and in good faith, the interest that a former employer has in common with a prospective employer might be sufficiently legitimate to make the privilege apply.

145.  **C**    While a defendant can be held strictly liable for carrying on an abnormally dangerous activity such as transporting high explosives, the defendant is only strictly liable for damage that results from the kind of risk that made the activity abnormally dangerous. While transporting high explosives may be abnormally dangerous, the plaintiff's injuries did not result from the kind of risk that made this activity abnormally dangerous (namely explosions). **A** is therefore incorrect. **B** is incorrect because assumption of the risk involves situations where the plaintiff has voluntarily consented to take his or her chances that a harm will occur. This usually involves situations where the plaintiff is engaging in some type of activity, such as going to a baseball game, bungee jumping, skiing, etc. Here, the plaintiff's actions were more correctly categorized as contributory negligence. Importantly, in a jurisdiction that follows comparative negligence principles, this negligence will not completely bar the plaintiff's recovery. It will only lessen the amount recovered. **D** is therefore incorrect.

146.  **D**    Negligence is the failure to act reasonably in the face of a foreseeable risk created by the defendant's conduct. Since it probably was foreseeable that the used car dealer would show a customer the car after buying it for resale, the seller owed such customers a duty of reasonable care that probably was breached by his failure to disclose the crack. Although it is not certain that a court would come to this conclusion, **D** is the only argument listed that could possibly lead to recovery by the customer.

Battery is committed by intentionally causing a harmful or offensive contact with the plaintiff. In a battery case, intent means a desire or knowledge that there will be harmful or offensive contact with the plaintiff or that the plaintiff will become apprehensive of such contact. Although the seller knew that the engine was cracked, there is no indication that he desired or knew that the crack would result in harmful or offensive contact with any person, or that it would cause apprehension of such contact. Although these risks may have been foreseeable, battery liability cannot be imposed without intent. For this reason, **A** is incorrect. Misrepresentation liability is imposed only for the benefit of a plaintiff who justifiably relied on the defendant's false representation. Since the customer did not rely on any express or implied statement made by the seller, **B** and **C** are incorrect.

147.   **A**   When a defendant negligently causes physical injury or property damage to one party, but only pure economic loss to the plaintiff, the traditional rule is that the plaintiff may not recover anything. This is because a defendant could have open-ended liability (for example, the restaurant's suppliers could sue, other waiters, etc.). Some courts recognize case-by-case exceptions to this rule, but only in cases where the injury to the plaintiff was relatively foreseeable, relatively few plaintiffs would be permitted to sue, and the defendant's conduct was relatively blameworthy. As stated above, if plaintiffs are allowed to sue for pure economic loss in this case, there is a potentially limitless number of plaintiffs. **C** and **D** are therefore incorrect. Because the defendant would be liable in certain exceptional cases, **B** is incorrect.

148.   **B**   A private individual can successfully assert a claim for public nuisance only if the harm that he or she sustained was different from that sustained by the general public (*i.e.*, "particular" harm). Since no fact indicates this to be so of the resident, she may not assert the public nuisance claim.

       **A** is incorrect because if the resident had sustained "particular" harm, the decision of the city attorney would not prevent her from suing for damages. Although it is generally held that a private individual may not seek an injunction on a public nuisance theory, **C** is incorrect because there are other theories on which a private individual may receive an injunction against environmental polluters. **D** is incorrect because a private individual who sustains particular harm as result of a public nuisance may sue for damages.

149.   **D**   It is given that the doctor's conduct was negligent. Even if a defendant's conduct was negligent, however, the defendant is not liable for the plaintiff's injuries unless they were proximately caused by that conduct. Conduct is a proximate cause of an injury if it is a factual and legal cause of the injury. Conduct is a factual cause of injury if the injury would not have occurred without it. Since the trucker would not have been in the hospital and injured by the falling of the hospital structure except for the doctor's conduct, the doctor's conduct was a factual cause of the trucker's injury. If conduct was a factual cause of harm, it was a legal cause of that harm if the harm was foreseeable and not brought about by superseding causes. A superseding cause of harm is an intervening cause that is unforeseeable or independent of the risks created by the defendant's conduct. Thus, because the earthquake was a superseding cause of the trucker's fractured skull, it prevented the doctor's negligence from being a legal or proximate cause of the fractured skull.

       **A** establishes that the doctor's conduct was a factual cause of the fractured skull, but it is incorrect because it does not deal with the problem of legal cause. The doctor's conduct was not a legal cause of the fractured skull unless the *fractured skull* was a foreseeable result of it. The fact that the wait might have been foreseeable does not make the fractured skull foreseeable. **B** is therefore incorrect. **C** establishes that the presence of the cherry pit was a factual cause of the trucker's injury, but it does not establish that the doctor's conduct was not also a cause of it. **C** is therefore incorrect.

150.  **D**  The statute given is typical of the "modified" comparative negligence approach. A deduction is made from the plaintiff's recovery based on the percentage of fault which was the plaintiff's. But if the plaintiff's fault exceeds the defendant's, the plaintiff receives nothing. Since the jury found the plaintiff to be 60 percent at fault, he can recover nothing. **A**, **B**, and **C** are therefore incorrect.

151.  **C**  Even if a defendant's conduct is negligent, the defendant is not liable for the plaintiff's injuries unless they were proximately caused by that conduct. Conduct is a proximate cause of harm if it was a factual and legal cause of the harm. Conduct is a factual cause of harm if the harm would not have occurred without it. Since the client would not have been hurt if the landlord had fixed or warned him about the elevator, the landlord's failure to do so was a factual cause of the client's injuries. Conduct that is a factual cause of harm is a legal cause if the harm was a foreseeable result of it and not brought about by an unforeseeable intervening cause (*i.e.*, a superseding cause). Since the client would not have been hurt if the attorney had not permitted him to use the elevator, the attorney's conduct was also a cause of the client's injury. Thus, if it was not foreseeable that the attorney would permit the client to use the elevator, the attorney's conduct was a superseding cause of the client's injury. While it is not certain that a court would come to this conclusion, **C** is the only argument listed that could possibly support the landlord's defense.

Although the landlord's promise to repair the elevator might not be enforceable by the client, **A** is not an effective argument because, apart from the promise, one who holds realty owes a duty of reasonable care to invitees. An invitee is a person whose presence confers an economic benefit on the landholder. The client was the attorney's client, and the attorney would not have rented space in the building unless his clients could come to see him there. For this reason, the client's presence did confer an economic benefit on the landlord, and the client was the landlord's invitee. (**Note:** It is usually held that invitees of a tenant are also invitees of the landlord.) **B** is therefore incorrect. Although an *unforeseeable* intervening cause may be superseding (*i.e.*, prevent the antecedent wrongdoer from being liable), the fact that it was *unreasonable* is not sufficient to make it superseding. **D** is therefore incorrect.

152.  **A**  If the harm to the daughter was foreseeable, then the exterminator had a duty to act reasonably in the face of it. His failure to do so would constitute negligence, for which he may be liable to the daughter. Although a court might not come to this conclusion, the argument in **A** is the only one listed that could possibly support the daughter's claim.

Strict liability is imposed on the seller of a defective product, but since the store owner did not sell the pellets to the janitor, **B** is incorrect. Courts impose a duty to act reasonably in designing or producing a product on the manufacturers of all products. For this reason, the question of whether a product is inherently dangerous is of no importance, and **C** is incorrect. Unless the exterminator was negligent, questions of causation are irrelevant. **D** is therefore incorrect.

153. **A**    Consent (*i.e.*, willingness) is a defense to all intentional torts. While it is not likely that this inference would be drawn, it would give the girlfriend a complete privilege if it was.

**B** is incorrect because the plaintiff has a right to elect whether to sue for conversion or trespass to chattel. **C** is incorrect because the neighbor's liability would not prevent the girlfriend from being liable as well. The remedy for trespass to chattel is money damages. **D** is therefore incorrect.

154. **D**    Negligence means failing to act like the reasonable person. If the defendant can convince the trier of fact that the reasonable person occasionally takes his or her eyes off the road while driving, and that his conduct was therefore not negligent, the plaintiff's negligence action against him will fail. While a court might not come to this conclusion, **D** is the only argument listed that might be effective in the defendant's defense.

**A** is incorrect because assumption of the risk requires a voluntary encounter with a known risk. For this purpose, a risk is "known" if the plaintiff is substantially certain that harm will probably occur. Recognition of a mere possibility of harm is not sufficient. **B** is incorrect because although it establishes that the other car's sudden stop was a cause of the accident, that does not mean that the defendant's conduct was not also a cause. **C** is incorrect since the special rules about duties owed to licensees apply only to accidents that occur on a defendant's land.

155. **A**    It was probably unreasonable for the fire chief (who knew the device could be dangerous) to permit the volunteer firefighter (whom he knew to be untrained) to use it. Although a court might not find that the fire chief was negligent, **A** is the only theory listed that could result in a judgment for the woman.

Unless the fire chief had a substantial certainty that harm would result, he lacked the intent to make him liable for battery. **B** is therefore incorrect. Strict products liability is imposed only on a professional supplier of a defective product. Since the fire chief was not in the business of supplying the device, **C** is incorrect. **D** is incorrect because *res ipsa* permits an inference of negligence to be drawn from the circumstances only when there is no direct evidence of the defendant's conduct.

156. **C**    A defendant is liable for damage that was proximately caused by his or her negligence. A defendant's conduct is a proximate cause of harm if it is a factual and legal cause of that harm. Conduct is a factual cause of harm if the harm would not have occurred without it. Since the plaintiff would not have sustained any injuries at all were it not for her neighbor's negligence, her neighbor's negligence is a factual cause of all her injuries. Conduct that is a factual cause of harm is a legal cause of that harm if the harm was foreseeable and not brought about by unforeseeable or independent interventions. Courts usually hold that in treating injuries inflicted by a defendant, the malpractice of a physician is neither unforeseeable nor independent of the conduct that caused the initial injuries. For

this reason, all complications caused by the malpractice of the doctors were proximately caused by the neighbor, making the neighbor liable for them. **C** is therefore correct. (**Note**: The negligent doctors may also be held liable as joint tortfeasors.)

157. **D** A statement is defamatory if it would expose the plaintiff to hatred, contempt, disgrace, or ridicule. Here, if many people continue to believe that members of the group engage in improper activities, the statement would do so.

**A** is incorrect since a judgment for the minister will not violate either the Establishment Clause or the Free Exercise Clause. **B** is incorrect because what matters is what a substantial group of people would believe about the plaintiff as a result of the statement. The fact that a substantial group of right-thinking people would not associate the plaintiff with shame or disgrace does not prevent the statement from being defamatory if there is also a substantial group of people who would. **C** is therefore incorrect.

158. **D** Negligence is the failure to act reasonably in the face of a foreseeable risk. If the risk was not foreseeable, the company's failure to guard against it was not negligence.

**A** is incorrect since an expert is expected to know only that which the reasonable expert would know. If the risk that it will wear out was not foreseeable, knowledge that harm would occur if it did wear out does not result in a duty to protect against its wearing out. **B** is therefore incorrect. **C** is incorrect because the employee's action is based on negligence.

159. **A** Negligence is a breach of the duty of reasonable care. Most cases hold that a defendant does not owe a duty of reasonable care unless it is foreseeable (*i.e.*, the reasonable person would anticipate) that his or her act will cause harm. If it was reasonable for the carpenter to believe that his act would cause no harm, he owed no duty of reasonable care. If the carpenter owed no duty of reasonable care, the carpenter could not have been negligent.

**B** is incorrect because custom does not determine what reasonable care is. Although the man's contributory negligence might prevent him from recovering, there is no indication that the man's failure to see the hammer was negligent. **C** is therefore incorrect. **D** is incorrect because of the rule that a defendant takes the plaintiff as he or she finds him or her. (**Note**: What this means is that if an injury to the plaintiff is foreseeable, the full extent of that injury is foreseeable even though some special sensitivity of the plaintiff was a contributing factor to its extent.)

160. **C** Negligence consists of a failure to act reasonably. Since the question specifies an action for negligence, the man cannot win without establishing that the grocery store was negligent (*i.e.*, acted unreasonably).

**A** is incorrect because it is based on an inaccurate statement of law: The negligence of a manufacturer is not ordinarily imputed to a retailer selling products made by that manufacturer, although a retailer may be held strictly liable for damages resulting from a defect that existed when the product was sold by that retailer. **B** is incorrect because *negligence* liability is not imposed unless the defendant acted unreasonably. **D** is incorrect because it is based on an inaccurate statement of law; a retailer owes its customers a duty of acting reasonably, which, depending on the circumstances, may require the inspection of products packaged in sealed containers.

161.  **C**    Negligence is unreasonable conduct. Thus, if the driver was acting unreasonably, he was negligent and should be liable for the boy's injuries. Under the all-or-nothing rule of contributory negligence, however, a plaintiff is completely barred from recovery if his or her own negligence contributed to the happening of the accident. Contributory negligence is unreasonable conduct by a plaintiff. Thus, if the boy's injury resulted from his own unreasonable conduct (*i.e.*, contributory negligence), he will not recover in spite of the fact that the driver was also negligent.

A child is said to have been negligent if he failed to act like a reasonable child of the same age, experience, and intelligence. **A** is therefore incorrect. *Res ipsa loquitur* permits an inference that the defendant was negligent to be drawn from certain circumstantial evidence. Since the driver's negligence is given, *res ipsa loquitur* is inapplicable, and **B** is incorrect. Unreasonable conduct by a third person is not imputed to a plaintiff as contributory negligence, even when the third person is the minor plaintiff's parent. **D** is therefore incorrect.

162.  **B**    A defendant's conduct is a proximate cause of harm if it was a factual and legal cause of that harm. Conduct is a factual cause of harm if the harm would not have occurred without it. Since the woman would not have been injured by the bottle if the grocery store had not restacked and sold the bottles, the grocery store's conduct was a factual cause of the woman's injury. Conduct that is a factual cause of harm is a legal cause of that harm if the harm was a foreseeable result of it. Since the contents of bottles of soda-pop are under pressure, it is probably foreseeable that a crack in the bottle will result in an explosion and injury. The grocery store's conduct was thus a proximate cause of the woman's injury. A defendant is liable for the proximate results of his or her negligence. For this reason, since the grocery store's conduct was negligent, the woman is likely to win her lawsuit against it.

**A** is incorrect because the plaintiff's helplessness is not in itself a basis of the defendant's liability. **C** is incorrect because harm may have more than one proximate cause. The fact that the conduct of the officers was a proximate cause of the plaintiff's harm does not mean that the negligence of the grocery store was not. Since privity is not an essential element of a negligence action, **D** is also incorrect.

163.  **D**    Since the buyer received something for his money, the measure of his damages must consider the value that he has received. In some jurisdictions, damage for misrepresentation is measured by the difference between what the plaintiff received and what the defendant told him or her he or she would be receiving ("benefit of the bargain" theory). In this case, that would be $250,000 less $600, or $249,400. In other jurisdictions, the damage is measured by the difference between what the plaintiff paid and what he or she actually received ("out-of-pocket" theory). In this case, that would be $225,000 less $600 or $224,400. **D** is therefore correct.

**A** and **C** are incorrect because they ignore the value of what the buyer actually received. **B** is incorrect because it describes a rescission remedy, which may be available in a claim for breach of contract but is not available in this tort claim for damages.

164. **A** If the likelihood of injury is great, a defendant may be required to anticipate the negligence of others. Here, a reasonable person would not have lent the car to the friend, considering the fact he had his license revoked for reckless driving.

**B** is incorrect because the man's liability in this instance is based on his loan of the car, not his ownership of it. **C** is incorrect because the man was negligent when he lent the car to his friend, so the fact the friend lied to him about his intentions does not change the analysis. **D** is incorrect because the woman's motivation for suing the man does not affect the man's liability for negligence.

165. **A** The term *merchantable* means "fit for ordinary use." Proof that the plaintiff's allergic reaction was the only one that ever occurred indicates that it was an unusual one. If the plaintiff's allergy was unusual enough to be regarded as extraordinary, the product may have been fit for ordinary use (*i.e.*, by ordinary persons) although unfit for use by the plaintiff. While a court might not come to this conclusion, **A** is the only fact listed that could possibly support the defendant's defense.

Most jurisdictions hold all members of the chain of commercial product distribution liable for a condition of the product that breaches the implied warranty of merchantability. **B** is therefore incorrect. Although reasonable inspection may have revealed that the product was safe for persons with "normal" skin, **C** is incorrect for two reasons. First, warranty liability does not depend on unreasonable conduct by the defendant, and second, ordinary use may include use by persons with skin that is not normal. **D** is incorrect because government approval or compliance with government requirements does not prevent common law liability.

166. **C** For the violation of a statute to constitute negligence per se, the type of harm that occurred must be the type of harm the statute intended to protect against. Here, the purpose of the statute was to protect people from falling debris, not poisoning, so the construction company's violation of it would not constitute negligence per se in this instance. Therefore, **A** is incorrect.

**B** and **D** are incorrect because issues of control or the child's negligence would not change the initial negligence per se analysis.

167. **D** Defamation is a tort that protects a person's interest in their reputation. It is split into two sub-torts, libel and slander. Libel consists mainly of all written and printed matter, while slander involves oral statements. To establish a prima facie case for either libel or slander, the plaintiff must prove there was a false and defamatory statement concerning the plaintiff, a communication of that statement to some person other than the plaintiff, fault on the part of the defendant, and either special harm or other actionability. Importantly, the communication of the statement has to be either intentional or negligent. There is no strict liability. Here, since the defendant was not negligent in making the statement and did not intend for others to hear it, he is not liable for either form of defamation. **A**, **B**, and **C** are therefore incorrect.

168. **B** Under the given "pure comparative negligence" statute, the plaintiff's damage should be diminished by 20 percent, since 20 percent of his injury resulted from his own negligence.

Under the collateral source rule, applied in most jurisdictions, money that the plaintiff has received from collateral sources (*i.e.*, those other than tortfeasors) is not relevant to his or her rights against tortfeasors who caused his or her injury. The insurance money that the plaintiff received was from a collateral source and should therefore not play any role in determining the damages.

**A, C**, and **D** are therefore incorrect.

169.  **D**      Contributory negligence is unreasonable conduct by the plaintiff without which his or her injury would not have occurred. Since the man would not have been injured if he had not accepted a ride from his neighbor, and since doing so was obviously unreasonable, the man was contributorily negligent. Assumption of the risk occurs when the plaintiff voluntarily encounters a known risk. Since the man knew that his neighbor was drunk and voluntarily rode with him, the man assumed all the risks that normally accompany riding in a car driven by a person who is drunk. Both of these would be effective arguments in the neighbor's defense.

170.  **A**      Tortious appropriation of identity is committed by making commercial use of the plaintiff's name, likeness, or identity without his or her permission. It has been repeatedly held, however, that newsworthy publications about the plaintiff do not constitute commercial use and therefore cannot result in liability for this tort. It has also been held that information may be regarded as "newsworthy" for this purpose, even though the group to which it is of interest is a limited one.

Since the use of a non-celebrity's identity might be put to commercial gain (*e.g.*, the photograph of an unknown but muscular person in an advertisement for exercise equipment), it is not necessary that the plaintiff be a public figure. Many of the cases imposing liability for this tort have involved plaintiffs who were not celebrities. **B** is incorrect for this reason and because every article of interest to a publication's readers enriches the publisher by increasing the demand for its product. Although the publication of facts that are contained in public records is protected by the First Amendment, the *commercial* use of such information is not necessarily protected. For this reason, although **C** would be an effective defense against a claim of public disclosure, it is not necessarily an effective defense against a claim of appropriation. The United States Supreme Court has indicated that liability for false light privacy invasions cannot be imposed without a showing of actual malice, but no such requirement exists for the tort of appropriation. **D** is therefore incorrect.

171.  **D**      Damage is an essential element of a negligence action. There are circumstances under which a plaintiff's mental suffering, although unrelated to physical injury, may be regarded as damage. Mere annoyance, however, is probably not damage sufficient to justify recovery for negligence. While it is not certain that this argument would defeat the claim of the landowner, **D** is the only argument listed that could possibly lead to a judgment for the factory.

The reasonableness of a defendant's conduct is ordinarily determined by weighing the risks that it creates against the benefits that it confers. The argument set forth in **A** is not an effective defense, however, because it considers only the benefit resulting from the use of unbagged concrete without balancing it against the resulting risks. **A** is therefore incorrect. Conduct is a factual cause of any result that would not have occurred without it. Since the landowner would not have experienced annoyance if the factory had not used unbagged cement, the use of unbagged cement was a factual cause of the landowner's annoyance. **B** is therefore incorrect. A plaintiff assumes a risk when he or she knows of it and voluntarily encounters it. **C** is incorrect because there is no indication that the landowner's encounter with the dust was voluntary.

172.  **D**     Although the plaintiff can still collect her judgment from either of them or from both of them in any combination, as between themselves, the defendants' contributive shares will be in proportion to their fault. Thus, the plaintiff could collect $100,000 from the first defendant. After paying this sum, however, the first defendant is entitled to contribution from the second defendant in a sum proportionate to the second defendant's fault. Since the second defendant was 60 percent at fault, the first defendant is entitled to collect 60 percent of what he paid, or $60,000.

A is incorrect because the jurisdiction recognizes a right of contribution. **B** is incorrect because the court found that the second defendant was 60 percent at fault. **C** is incorrect because the given statute based contribution on apportionment of fault.

173.  **D**     The doctrine of *respondeat superior* makes an employer vicariously liable to a plaintiff for torts committed by an employee acting within the scope of employment. But the concept of indemnity may shift the burden of payment from the one who actually did pay to the one who should have paid. Therefore, an employer who has been required to pay for a tort committed by an employee is entitled to complete indemnity (*i.e.*, repayment) from the employee.

The concept of vicarious liability determines a plaintiff's rights against a tortfeasor's employer, but it does not determine the rights of that employer against its employee. **A** is therefore incorrect. When parties are found to be jointly and severally liable to a plaintiff, the plaintiff may collect all of his or her damages from any one of them or from all of them in any combination whatsoever. For this reason, one of the joint tortfeasors may be required to pay more than its fair share of the plaintiff's damages. After this happens, most jurisdictions allow the one who has paid to seek partial repayment from the others so that each ends up paying a fair share. The majority of jurisdictions apply the equal apportionment approach, determining fair shares by dividing the amount paid by the number of joint tortfeasors (treating an employee and employer who is vicariously liable for his or her tort as a single unit for this purpose). In these jurisdictions, joint tortfeasors who pay more than their fair share are said to seek "contribution." Other jurisdictions apply the apportionment of fault approach, basing the determination of fair shares on the relative fault of the joint tortfeasors. In these jurisdictions, joint tortfeasors who pay more than their fair share are said to seek "partial indemnity." **B** and **C** are both incorrect, however, because all jurisdictions recognize that a party who pays only because he or she is vicariously liable for the tort committed by another person is entitled to complete indemnity from that person.

174.  **A**     One who is negligent is liable for all harm proximately caused by that negligence. Negligence is a proximate cause of harm if that negligence was a factual cause of the

harm and if the harm was a foreseeable consequence of the negligence. Since the biker's right leg would not have been broken without the second driver's negligence, and since a broken leg is a foreseeable consequence of being run over by a car, the second driver's negligence was a proximate cause of the biker's broken right leg. However, since the biker's left leg would have been broken without the second driver's negligence, the second driver's negligence was not a factual cause of it, and the second driver cannot be held liable for it.

175.   **C**    A defendant's conduct is a proximate cause of the plaintiff's harm if it was both a factual and legal cause of that harm. Conduct is a factual cause of harm if the harm would not have occurred without it. Since the truck would not have leaked gas if it had not been parked in front of the builder's construction site where it was struck by falling debris, the driver's parking it there was a factual cause of the woman's harm. Conduct is a legal cause of harm if the harm was a foreseeable result of it and was not brought about by an unforeseeable intervention. Since the explosion would not have occurred if debris had not fallen onto the truck after the driver parked it, the falling debris was an intervening cause of the woman's harm. If that intervening cause was foreseeable, however, the driver's conduct could still be regarded as a legal cause of the explosion. On the other hand, if the intervention of the falling debris was unforeseeable, the driver's conduct would not be regarded as a legal cause of the explosion, and the driver could not be held liable for the resulting damage. Whether the driver could have anticipated that debris would fall and damage the truck cannot be determined from the facts, but **C** is the only argument listed that could possibly be effective in the driver's defense.

A superseding cause of harm is an unforeseeable intervening cause. An intervening cause is something that happened after the defendant's conduct, and without which the accident would not have occurred. Although the builder's use of poor-quality steel was a cause of the woman's injury (because the injury would not have occurred without it), it preceded the driver's conduct and thus was not an *intervening* cause. It could not, therefore, have been a superseding cause. For this reason, **A** is incorrect. The fact that the explosion would not have occurred if the man had not thrown a lit cigarette into the street proves that the man's conduct was a cause of the woman's harm. The fact that the man's act occurred after the driver's conduct makes the man's act an intervening cause. **B** is incorrect, however, because unless its occurrence was unforeseeable, the fact that there was an intervening cause is not sufficient to prevent the driver's conduct from being a proximate cause of the woman's injury. Since any result may have several proximate causes, it is never correct to conclude that one thing was not a proximate cause because another thing was. **D** is incorrect because the driver's conduct and the earthquake could both have been proximate causes of the woman's injury.

176.   **A**    Although the manufacturer of a defective product may be held liable without fault to a person injured, it is necessary for the plaintiff to show that his or her injury was proximately caused by the product's defect. If there was a superseding intervening cause of the harm, the defect was not the proximate cause. An intervening cause of harm is a superseding cause if its occurrence was unforeseeable. Thus, if it was unforeseeable that the contractor would disregard the warning, the contractor's conduct would be a

superseding cause of the customer's injury. Although cases have held that intervening negligence is foreseeable, many cases have held that when the intervention involves the disregard of a known risk, it is unforeseeable. For this reason, it is impossible to tell whether the contractor's intervening conduct would be found to be unforeseeable. Of all the arguments listed, however, **A** is the only one that could possibly be effective in the manufacturer's defense.

**B** is incorrect because strict liability may be applied to make the manufacturer of a defective product liable without regard to whether it acted reasonably. **C** is incorrect because strict products liability may be imposed to benefit any injured person whose contact with the defective product was foreseeable, without regard to the existence of a business relationship between the defendant and plaintiff. **D** is incorrect for two reasons: First, there is no fact indicating that the reasonable person in the store owner's position would not have selected the contractor to do the job, and second, intervening negligence by a third party is not a superseding cause of harm unless it was unforeseeable.

177. **D** If the plaintiff is a public figure, he or she can recover in defamation only if he or she shows that the statement was made either with knowledge that the statement was false or with reckless disregard to its truth. However, if the plaintiff is a private figure, he or she is not required to prove that the defendant knew the statement was false or recklessly disregarded its truth or falsity. However, even if the plaintiff is a private figure, he or she has to show at least negligence by the defendant regarding the truth of the statement. If the plaintiff does prove that defendant was negligent in not ascertaining that the communication was false, most states allow the plaintiff to recover if the plaintiff is not a public figure. Here, the plaintiff has shown that the defendant was at least negligent in making the statement. **A** and **B** are therefore incorrect. **C** is incorrect because a plaintiff in a defamation case does not have to prove that the defendant actually intended to cause harm to the plaintiff's reputation.

178. **A** Under the all-or-nothing rule of contributory negligence, unreasonable conduct by a plaintiff is a complete bar to recovery. Since the ladder was in plain view, it was probably unreasonable (*i.e.*, contributorily negligent) for the employee not to see it. Although it is not certain that a jury would come to this conclusion, **A** is the only argument listed that could possibly provide the painter with an effective defense.

**B** is incorrect because the special rules that limit the duty owed to trespassers protect only the landholder, and no one but he or she or a member of his or her household may successfully assert them in defense. **C** is incorrect because a defendant owes a duty of reasonable care to any person who may foreseeably be injured by his or her conduct, whether such persons are licensees of another or not. One whose negligence proximately causes an injury to another is liable for damages even though there were other causes of that injury. For this reason, **D** is incorrect.

179. **D** Under the "substantial factor" rule of causation, a defendant's conduct is a cause of a particular consequence if it was a substantial factor in bringing that consequence about. Conduct that would have produced a particular consequence all by itself was a

substantial factor in producing that consequence even if other factors happened to combine with that conduct to bring the consequence about. Since either defendant's conduct alone would have made the driver intoxicated, each was a substantial factor in making the driver intoxicated. Each was, therefore, a cause of the driver's intoxication. Under the "but for" rule of causation, a condition is a cause of harm if the harm would not have occurred without that condition. Since the plaintiff's injury would not have occurred had the driver not been intoxicated, the driver's intoxication was a cause of the plaintiff's injury. Since the conduct of both defendants were causes of the driver's intoxication, and since the driver's intoxication was a cause of the plaintiff's injury, the conduct of both drivers were causes of the plaintiff's injury.

180.   **A**   The fact that an accident occurred is not enough to prove that the architect was negligent, even if he could have avoided the accident by using two pillars. Negligence is unreasonable conduct. If the architect's conduct was reasonable, it could not have been negligent. Since the facts are not sufficient to permit a conclusion as to whether or not the architect's conduct was reasonable, it is not certain that a jury would be convinced by the architect's contention. **A** is the only argument listed, however, that could possibly provide the architect with an effective defense.

A defendant owes a duty of reasonable care to all persons who are placed at foreseeable risk as a result of that defendant's conduct. Since it was foreseeable that the landowner would hire a mover to bring furniture into the new house, the architect thus owed the mover a duty to act reasonably in designing the house and could be liable to the mover for breaching it. **B** is therefore incorrect. The doctrine of "last clear chance" has become obsolete in most jurisdictions. All it ever did (and all it does in those jurisdictions in which it survives) is excuse a *plaintiff* from the consequences of his own contributory negligence. It was never an argument that a defendant would advance because it never benefitted any party but a plaintiff. For these reasons, it is inapplicable to this problem, and **C** is incorrect. **D** is incorrect because the unreasonable exercise of professional judgment in making a decision is negligence (or malpractice) and may result in liability.

181.   **B**   Violation of a statute may establish the violator's negligence (or liability) in a particular case if the statute was designed to protect against the risk that led to the plaintiff's harm. The pedestrian was not hurt because the man was drunk but because the man had been poisoned. (Note that the facts indicate that the man was driving reasonably.) If the statute was not meant to protect against the risk of drinking poison, then its violation would not be relevant in the case of an injury that resulted from drinking poison. Since poison could as easily be drunk in non-alcoholic drinks, it is unlikely that the statute in this case was designed to protect against drinking poison.

**A** is incorrect because the language of the statute appears to prohibit the sale of alcohol to a person who is already intoxicated without regard to how he got intoxicated. **C** is based on an inaccurate statement. Conduct is a cause of harm if that harm would not have occurred without the conduct. Since the man's death and the resulting accident would not have occurred if the man had not drunk the poisoned liquor, service of the liquor was a cause of the pedestrian's injuries. **C** is therefore incorrect. If an intervening cause of harm was unforeseeable, it may be called a superseding cause and relieve a defendant of liability because his or her conduct was not a "legal" or "proximate" cause of the injury. Causes that existed or occurred prior to the defendant's conduct are not intervening causes, however, and therefore cannot be superseding causes of harm. **D** is incorrect because the employee's conduct preceded the bartender's service of liquor to the man.

182. **A**   Negligence is unreasonable conduct in the face of a foreseeable risk. Thus, unless the risk that the contractor created was foreseeable, it was not negligent for the contractor to create it. Adjusting the belt idle improperly does not cause a belt truck to lurch if it is equipped with an accelerator suppressor. Thus, if belt trucks are usually equipped with acceleration suppressors, it might not be foreseeable that adjusting the belt idle improperly would cause a belt truck to lurch. If this risk was not foreseeable, the contractor was not negligent in creating it. Although it is not certain that a jury would come to this conclusion, the additional fact listed in **A** is the only one that could possibly result in a judgment for the contractor.

Under the all-or-nothing rule, a plaintiff whose own negligence contributed to the accident is prevented from recovering. **B** is incorrect, however, because there is no fact indicating that it was negligent for the employee to attempt to activate the belt while standing on the ground. **C** and **D** are incorrect because a defendant is liable for damage that was proximately caused by his or her negligence even though there are other causes or other parties who may also be liable.

183. **A**   Public nuisance is a tortious invasion of some right of the general public. Ordinarily, a public nuisance action is brought on behalf of the general public as an entity, and it may result in a judgment for damage, an injunction, or both. An individual may bring a public nuisance action on his or her own behalf, but only by showing that the public nuisance that the defendant created caused the individual plaintiff to sustain harm so different from that of the general public that his or her damages would not be included in a judgment on behalf of the general public. Most jurisdictions hold that in such an action, the plaintiff's only remedy is a judgment for those damages. Since the son's claim is for an injunction rather than for the son's special damage, public nuisance is not an appropriate vehicle for it.

An activity that does not disturb anyone but a super-sensitive plaintiff is probably not a public nuisance since it does not interfere with a public right. If an activity does disturb the general public, however, and is therefore a public nuisance, the fact that the plaintiff's damage resulted from a special sensitivity will not prevent him or her from recovering for that damage. (**Note**: This is the essence of the famous "eggshell skull" hypothetical, in which the defendant accidentally drops an object that strikes the head of a plaintiff whose skull is as thin as an eggshell. If it was not foreseeable that dropping the object would injure the ordinary person, the defendant was not negligent in dropping it. But if it was foreseeable that dropping it would injure the ordinary person, then the defendant was negligent in dropping it and would be liable for the full extent of the plaintiff's injury even though the ordinary person in the plaintiff's shoes would not have sustained an injury as serious as that of the plaintiff.) **B** is therefore incorrect. A plaintiff "assumes the risk" when he or she voluntarily encounters a risk of which he or she has knowledge. Although assumption of the risk is a complete defense in many jurisdictions, **C** is incorrect because the claim was asserted on behalf of the son, and the homeowner could not "assume the risk" for his son. **D** is incorrect, because, although violation of a statute sometimes helps to establish tort liability, compliance with a statute does not ordinarily prevent a defendant from being liable in tort.

184.    **B**     A seller of a product that is defective at the time it was sold is held strictly liable for damages that result. Thus, if the product was defective when the drugstore sold it, the drugstore would be strictly liable to the doctor. A product is "defective as labeled" if its condition would defeat the expectations that the reasonable person would form upon reading its label. While it is not certain that a court would come to this conclusion about the product, the argument in **B** is the only one listed that could possibly support the doctor's claim.

           **A** is incorrect because the negligence of a manufacturer is not ordinarily imputed to a retailer. **C** is incorrect because any express warranty that was made referred to "normal hair or scalp" and would therefore be inapplicable to the doctor. Although a drugstore might be under the type of duty set forth in **D**, there is no indication that the drugstore failed to act reasonably in pursuit of such a duty. **D** is therefore incorrect.

185.    **C**     The statute given is typical of the "modified" comparative negligence approach. Since the plaintiff was not at fault at all, however, it has no relevance to her rights. No matter what approach a jurisdiction takes to contributory or comparative negligence, most agree that joint tortfeasors are jointly and severally liable to the injured plaintiff. In this case, the court specifically held that the defendants are jointly and severally liable. This means that the plaintiff can collect all her damage from the first defendant, or the second defendant, or the two of them in any combination.

186.    **A**     In general, the plaintiff in a defamation case must allege and prove special damages to his or her reputation that occurred because of the defendant's statements. However, if the defendant accuses the plaintiff of having a "loathsome" disease (such as leprosy, venereal diseases, or AIDS), the plaintiff is not required to show damages.

           Consequently, **B**, **C**, and **D** are incorrect.

187.    **B**     All the products liability theories require proof that the plaintiff sustained damage as a result of his or her contact with the product. If the man did not, he cannot succeed against the company on any theory.

           **A** is incorrect because some of the approaches to products liability (*i.e.*, strict liability in tort and breach of warranty) do not depend on the unreasonableness of the defendant's conduct. **C** is incorrect because compliance with a statute is not a defense to any products liability theory. A seller who recommends a particular product, knowing why the purchaser wants it and that the purchaser is relying on the seller's judgment, may be held liable for breach of warranty if the product is unfit for the buyer's particular purpose. **D**

is incorrect, however, because imposing liability on the grocery store would not prevent its being imposed on the company.

188.  **C**  Under the private necessity doctrine, a person may enter another person's property if the entry is necessary to protect someone from serious harm. This is a complete defense to a trespass claim. However, the person still has to pay for any damage caused. Here, while the pilot was protecting himself from a plane crash, he would still be liable for the damage to the crops. Therefore, **A** is incorrect.

B is incorrect because the pilot's lack of negligence in actually landing the plane would not change the analysis in regards to private necessity. **D** is incorrect because although the pilot could probably have made it back to the airport, the private necessity doctrine would not require the pilot to be 100 percent sure that he could only avoid serious harm by trespassing in the farmer's field.

189.  **A**  Intentional infliction of emotional distress requires outrageous behavior that intentionally results in severe mental suffering. Because the plaintiff was only embarrassed by the incident, the defendant's actions likely did not result in liability.

B is incorrect because even if the defendant was only joking, he may still have had the required mental state to satisfy the intent requirement if he desired or knew that mental suffering would result from his act. **C** is incorrect because although some jurisdictions require some physical manifestation of the mental suffering, the question stated the plaintiff was only embarrassed and suffered no physical injury. **D** is incorrect because, although throwing a firecracker at someone could be outrageous, the plaintiff still did not suffer the necessary harm.

190.  **B**  Negligence is a breach of the duty to act reasonably. A defendant owes such a duty to a plaintiff when the defendant's conduct creates a foreseeable risk to the plaintiff. Since the installation of an automatic door-opener creates obvious risks to future users of the device, the installer owes them a duty to install it in a reasonable manner. If the contractor failed to do so, he was negligent. Whether or not it was unreasonable to disregard the warning is probably a question of fact for the jury. The argument in **B** is the only one listed, however, that could possibly support the customer's claim.

When the defendant's conduct is unknown, the doctrine of *res ipsa loquitur* allows an inference that the defendant acted unreasonably to be established circumstantially by proof that the accident was one that would not ordinarily have occurred without negligence. It is inapplicable when the defendant's conduct was known and the question to be determined is whether that conduct was unreasonable. **A** is incorrect for this reason, and because there is no fact indicating that this kind of accident would not ordinarily occur without negligence by the installer. According to UCC §2-314, every sale by a merchant implies a warranty that the product sold is fit for its ordinary use (*i.e.*, merchantable). **C** is incorrect, however, because the contractor did not sell the automatic door-opener and therefore did not impliedly warrant its fitness. The seller of a defective product may be held strictly liable for damage resulting from the product's defect. **D** is incorrect, however, because the contractor was not the seller of the automatic door-opener.

191.  **A**    Although damage is not an essential element of an action for trespass to land, it is an essential element of a negligence action. Since there is no indication that the homeowner was damaged, **A** is correct.

          **B** is incorrect because, even in an emergency, a person is expected to act as the reasonable person would under the circumstances (although conduct that would ordinarily be regarded as unreasonable might be reasonable in an emergency). While necessity is a defense to actions for intentional tort, it is not a defense to actions founded in negligence. **C** is therefore incorrect. **D** is probably an accurate statement, but its effect is to impose a duty of reasonable care on the homeowner, not to relieve the driver of liability for negligence.

192.  **A**    The doctor can only be liable if he or she acted unreasonably in treating the patient. Here, the court found the doctor acted unreasonably, so the doctor would be liable for the patient's damages.

          If there is no evidence as to what the defendant did, the doctrine of *res ipsa loquitur* might allow an inference regarding the defendant's conduct. This doctrine applies when the accident is one that would not ordinarily occur without negligence and the defendant is in exclusive control of whatever caused the harm. Here, the defendant's conduct is known, and the defendant was not in exclusive control of the tanks when the manufacturer filled them. Therefore **B** is incorrect. **C** and **D** are incorrect, because under the circumstances, the fact the patient's death likely resulted from the manufacturer's negligence did not establish that the death did not also result from the doctor's negligence.

# QUESTIONS

## PRACTICE MBE—A.M. EXAM

# PRACTICE MBE—A.M. QUESTIONS

1. A man was looking out through the open window of his house when he saw a robber knock down an old woman and snatch her handbag. As the robber ran off with the woman's purse, the man grabbed a wooden board and jumped through his window. After chasing the robber for two blocks, the man caught up with him and struck him on the head with the wooden board. The man retrieved the purse and returned it to the woman. The robber subsequently died as the result of being struck by the man.

   If the man is prosecuted for criminal homicide, his most effective argument in defense would be that he used force that

   (A) the woman would have been privileged to use to defend herself.

   (B) the reasonable person in the man's position would have used to defend the woman.

   (C) the reasonable person in the woman's position would have used to defend her property.

   (D) the reasonable person in the man's position would have used to prevent the robber's escape from a crime.

2. At the trial of an action brought by the plaintiff against the defendant for damages resulting from breach of contract, the plaintiff's attorney called the witness as a witness on the plaintiff's direct case. After the witness was sworn, the plaintiff's attorney asked only one question: "Are you employed by the defendant in this case?" The witness answered, "Yes." The plaintiff's attorney then said, "I have no further questions."

   On cross-examination, the defendant's attorney asked the witness, "Do you have any personal knowledge of the contract that is the basis of this lawsuit?"

   If the plaintiff's attorney objects to the question, which of the following would be the most effective argument in support of that objection?

   (A) The defendant may not impeach its own witness.

   (B) The question is leading.

   (C) The question is argumentative.

   (D) The question goes beyond the scope of cross-examination.

3. After being informed that members of a college fraternity were engaged in the unlawful sale of cocaine, police officers obtained a warrant to search the fraternity house. While searching, the officers discovered the defendant, a guest of one of the fraternity's members, sitting on a bed in a room of the house. Under the bed was a locked trunk. Inside the trunk, the officers found a box of cocaine. They immediately placed the defendant under arrest for possession of cocaine and, upon searching her, found a plastic bag in her pocket containing marijuana. Subsequently charged with the unlawful possession of marijuana, the defendant moved to suppress use of the marijuana as evidence against her.

   Which of the following would be the prosecution's most effective argument in response to the defendant's motion?

   (A) Marijuana found in the defendant's possession could properly be seized as "fruit of the poisonous tree."

   (B) The defendant's proximity to the trunk gave the officers probable cause to believe that she was guilty of possessing cocaine.

   (C) The officers searching the fraternity house were entitled to frisk all persons present to protect themselves against the possibility of physical attack.

(D) A warrant authorizing the search of specified premises permits the arrest of all persons present at the time the warrant is executed.

4. Upon inheriting her aunt's ranch, the seller subdivided it into 1,000 separate numbered parcels of realty and offered them for sale. After inspecting a parcel that had no building on it, the buyer and his attorney went to see the seller in her sales office. After negotiation, the seller accepted the buyer's offer to purchase the parcel for $15,000. At the buyer's request, the attorney prepared a contract of sale, using a printed form that the attorney had brought with her. While doing so, the attorney asked the seller how to identify the parcel involved. Although its correct identification was "Parcel 241," the seller inadvertently referred to it as "Parcel 341." None of them were aware of the seller's error. As soon as the attorney finished preparing it, the seller and the buyer signed a contract that described the realty as Parcel No. 341.

Although Parcels No. 241 and No. 341 were the same size, Parcel No. 341 had a valuable building on it that made it worth $80,000. Prior to the date set for closing, the seller realized her mistake. She immediately informed the buyer of the error. If the buyer sues the seller for an order directing her to convey Parcel No. 341 to him for $15,000, which of the following would be the seller's most effective argument in defense?

(A) The buyer should have known that realty with a building on it was more valuable than realty without a building on it.

(B) The buyer selected the attorney to prepare the contract.

(C) Parcel No. 341 was substantially more valuable than Parcel No. 241.

(D) Both the seller and the buyer were mistaken about the identity of the parcel described in the contract.

5. A state law provides that no person may hold elective state office while acting as a practicing member of the clergy of any religious organization. The plaintiff, a practicing member of the clergy, asked the state commissioner of elections to enter his name as a candidate for the office of state legislator. The commissioner advised the plaintiff that under the state law described above, she could do so only if the plaintiff resigned his position.

If the plaintiff challenges the constitutionality of the state law on the ground that it violates the Free Exercise Clause of the First Amendment, which of the following arguments best supports the conclusion that the statute is unconstitutional?

(A) A state may not set qualifications for elective state office that are different from those for elective federal office.

(B) The state may not set qualifications for practicing members of the clergy of religious organizations.

(C) The statute creates political divisiveness along religious lines.

(D) The statute discriminates against persons because of their religious affiliations.

6. A girl's mother, a citizen of State A, brought suit in federal district court in State A against a saddle maker, a citizen of State B, after the girl fell during a riding lesson. The mother bought the saddle from the saddle maker online, and the saddle maker shipped it to her directly in State A. State A's long-arm statute stated that service could be made on out-of-state individuals by first-class mail, so long as the alleged injury occurred within State A. State B did not allow service by mail.

Is service proper if the girl's mother sends it to the saddle maker by first-class mail?

(A) Yes, because the federal district court sits in State A.

(B) Yes, because it is allowed under federal law.

(C) No, because it is not allowed under federal law.

(D) No, because State B does not allow it.

7. The victim, who was employed as a security guard, was required to carry a loaded pistol on the job. While traveling to and from his job, however, he kept the pistol unloaded. Driving to work one day, the victim's car was struck from behind by a car operated by the defendant. In the discussion that ensued, the defendant used language that the victim found offensive. At that point, the victim turned his back on the defendant and attempted to walk away. Angry, the defendant ran after the victim and slapped him in the face. Although the victim did not intend to shoot the defendant, he pulled his pistol from its holster and began loading it, hoping that the defendant would become frightened and leave him alone. When the defendant saw the victim loading the pistol, he thought of running away, but he was afraid that the victim would shoot him if he tried to do so. Drawing a knife from his pocket, the defendant stabbed the victim in the chest. The defendant was subsequently arrested and charged with assaulting the victim with a deadly weapon.

If the defendant asserts the privilege of self-defense, he should be found

(A) guilty, because as the initial aggressor, the defendant had no privilege to use deadly force.

(B) guilty, because the defendant could have successfully escaped in his car without being shot by the victim.

(C) not guilty, because the defendant's fear of being shot by the victim was reasonable.

(D) not guilty, because the victim should have known that by loading his pistol, he was inviting the use of deadly force by the defendant.

8. The plaintiff was a passenger on a motorcycle operated by her friend when it collided with a car operated by the defendant. As a result of the collision, the plaintiff sustained injuries that required her hospitalization. Although the plaintiff's hospital bills were high, they were paid in full by the insurance company under a policy that the plaintiff had purchased previously. In litigation by the plaintiff against the defendant for negligence, a jury found for the plaintiff in the sum of $50,000. Prior to the entry of judgment, the defendant's attorney made an appropriate motion asking the court to reduce the damage award by the amount that the plaintiff had already received from the insurance company.

The motion to reduce the plaintiff's damage award should be

(A) denied, because the insurance company was not acting for any person liable to the plaintiff for negligence.

(B) denied, because payment by the insurance company was not the result of a judicial determination.

(C) granted, because the plaintiff should not be permitted to receive a double recovery.

(D) granted, because the defendant is entitled to partial indemnity.

9. The defendant operated a computer repair business, servicing the computers of several large organizations with the assistance of her daughter. When the defendant decided to retire, she sold the entire business to her daughter. As part of the sale, she assigned to her daughter a written contract to repair and service all the plaintiff's computers for a period of three years in return for a fixed monthly payment.

The day after her assignment to her daughter, the defendant notified the plaintiff about it by telephone. Because the plaintiff knew that the daughter had worked on his computers in the past, he consented to the assignment and orally agreed to release the defendant from all further obligation or liability under their contract.

The plaintiff subsequently became dissatisfied with the daughter's service, however, and asserted a claim against the defendant for breach of contract.

If the defendant's only defense is that the plaintiff agreed to release her from all further obligation or liability under their contract, which of the following would be the plaintiff's most effective argument in response to that defense?

(A) The defendant is attempting to use parol evidence to contradict or modify the terms of an unambiguous written agreement.

(B) There was no consideration for the plaintiff's agreement to release the defendant of further obligation or liability under the contract.

(C) The agreement to release the defendant of further obligation or liability under the contract was not in writing.

(D) The defendant's delegation to her daughter and the plaintiff's agreement to release the defendant constituted an accord and satisfaction.

10. A doctor sued a truck driver in state court in State A for injuries he received in an automobile accident. Under State A law, any negligence on a plaintiff's part barred the plaintiff from recovery. The court found in favor of the doctor and awarded him $100,000 in damages. The truck driver then brought a negligence suit against the doctor in state court in State A to recover the damages done to his truck. State A law did not require any claim to be a compulsory counterclaim.

May the truck driver bring his action against the doctor?

(A) No, because the issue of the doctor's negligence was already litigated.

(B) No, because the property damage arose from the same transaction or occurrence.

(C) Yes, because State A does not require any claim to be a compulsory counterclaim.

(D) Yes, because the truck driver is bringing his action in a state court in State A.

11. Congress passes a law providing that no one who has been a member of an organization that uses unlawful means to deprive any group of persons of their rights under the United States Constitution is eligible for employment by the federal government. If the constitutionality of that law is challenged, it should be held

(A) unconstitutional, because it is an *ex post facto* law.

(B) unconstitutional, because it prohibits members of certain organizations from holding public office without regard to whether those members knew the purpose of the organizations to which they belonged.

(C) constitutional, because employment by the federal government is not a right but a privilege.

(D) constitutional, because the federal government has the right to protect itself by not employing persons who hold views inconsistent with the United States Constitution.

12. A river is located entirely within the state. Acting under authority granted by Congress, the Federal Transportation Commission awarded a contract to the company for the construction of a bridge over the river so road users could enter a neighboring state for business. The contract required that all materials used in constructing the bridge be purchased within the state.

A state statute imposes a 6 percent sales tax, to be paid by the buyer, on any purchases made within the state. Upon purchasing steel in the state for use in the construction of the bridge, the company refused to pay the sales tax. As a result, the state prosecuted the company for violating the sales tax statute.

If the company's only defense is that in fulfilling a contract with the federal government, it was immune from the state sales tax statute, the court should find the company

(A) not guilty since the bridge was to be used in interstate commerce.

(B) not guilty, because the state lacks power to tax activities of the federal government.

(C) guilty, because independent contractors working for the federal government are subject to state taxes.

(D) guilty, because the company's contract with the Federal Transportation Commission was not on a cost-plus-fixed-profit basis.

13. When the plaintiff applied for a job as a nurse at a hospital, the hospital's personnel department sent questionnaires to doctors on its staff, requesting information about the plaintiff. The defendant, a doctor on staff, knew the plaintiff from when they had both been employed at another clinic. Since the defendant had heard another doctor who was very well respected as a trainer and mentor of nurses at that clinic accuse the plaintiff of incompetence resulting in the death of a patient, the defendant disliked the plaintiff. In fact, however, the doctor who made the accusation had mistaken the plaintiff for another nurse, and the plaintiff had been cleared of blame by a clinic board of inquiry.

Hoping that the plaintiff's job application would be rejected, the defendant wrote on the questionnaire, "I once heard that the plaintiff's incompetence resulted in the death of a patient." The hospital did not hire the plaintiff.

If the plaintiff asserts a defamation claim against the defendant for the defendant's statement in the questionnaire, the court should find for

(A) The defendant, because the defendant reasonably believed that the plaintiff's

incompetence resulted in the death of a patient.

(B) The defendant, because the statement clearly indicated that the defendant had heard the accusation from another.

(C) The plaintiff, because the defendant's dislike of the plaintiff and the defendant's hope that the plaintiff's job application would be rejected amounted to actual malice.

(D) The plaintiff, because the statement resulted in the hospital not hiring the plaintiff.

14. In December 2009, the seller, a manufacturer of packaging materials, entered into a written agreement with the buyer, a wholesaler of melons. The agreement provided that the buyer would purchase from the seller all the boxes required by the buyer for packaging melons in 2012, but that in no event would the number of boxes required be less than 2,000.

After the agreement was executed, the price of melons fell from $1 per melon to $0.80 per melon. As a result, the buyer notified the seller in January 2012 that he intended to package melons in bags instead of boxes and that he would not order any boxes from the seller in 2012.

In January 2012, the seller instituted an action against the buyer for damages. If the buyer asks the court to dismiss the seller's action, should the court do so?

(A) Yes, because the buyer might still order 2,000 boxes by the end of 2012.

(B) Yes, because the provision that required the seller to furnish all the boxes required by the buyer in 2012 makes it impossible for the court to determine the seller's damages.

(C) No, because damages are presumed to result from every breach of contract.

(D) No, because the buyer has stated that he will not fulfill his obligations under the contract.

15. A riot broke out during a political rally in the town. Subsequently, a newspaper published an editorial about the rally and the ensuing disruption. The editorial stated that "Police present at the rally beat and kicked innocent bystanders and engaged in other acts of sense-less and unnecessary brutality." Following publication of the editorial, the four police officers who were present at the rally asserted a defamation claim against the newspaper.

The only argument raised by the newspaper in defense is that the statements contained in the editorial did not identify the plaintiffs. The court should find for

(A) the plaintiffs, because the number of police present at the rally was so small that readers who knew the plaintiffs would believe that the statement had been made about them.

(B) the plaintiffs, because they were engaged in their official duties as police officers.

(C) the plaintiffs, because the statement was *slander per se.*

(D) the newspaper, because the statement did not specifically name the plaintiffs.

16. A woman was called as a juror in a claim brought in federal district court. The action involved a man's claim that he was unlawfully targeted and beaten by several local police officers because of his race. During voir dire, the woman stated she would find it hard to keep an open mind because she believed that police officers and departments habitually discriminated against minorities. However, she said she had no strong feelings or prior knowl-edge about the case or the parties involved. Both the woman and the man were black, while the police officers involved were white.

Based on her statements during voir dire, would it be proper for the juror to be excused?

(A) No, because the juror cannot be excused based on her race.

(B) No, because the juror stated she had no strong feelings or prior knowledge about the case or parties.

(C) Yes, because the juror stated it would be hard to keep an open mind.

(D) Yes, because the juror had an implied bias in the man's favor.

17. The plaintiff asserted a tort claim against the defendant for battery but died of cancer before the trial. At the trial, the witness was called as a witness by the attorney for the plaintiff's estate. The witness testified that she was a police officer called to the scene of a shooting, and that when she arrived, she found the plaintiff lying on the ground in a pool of blood. The witness stated that when she asked the plaintiff to tell her what hap-pened, the plaintiff replied, "Tell my wife to meet me at the hospital and tell her that the defendant shot me."

The defendant objected. If the court finds that the plaintiff's statement to the witness was not a dying declaration, it will probably be because

(A) the plaintiff did not believe that he was dying when he made the statement.

(B) the plaintiff did not die as a result of the shooting.

(C) the witness's testimony was not being offered at the trial of a criminal prosecution.

(D) the plaintiff's statement was not made spontaneously.

18. A man was injured when a boiler in his building exploded. The man sued the owner of the building. The man hired an accident investigator who talked to one of the build-ing's maintenance workers. The maintenance worker told the investigator that the boiler exploded because the building owner failed to make necessary repairs. The man also hired an expert in boiler explosions. The expert read the investigator's report. The expert then

testified on behalf of the man, saying the boiler exploded because the building owner failed to make necessary repairs. She based her testimony in part on the maintenance worker's statement because other experts in boiler explosion analysis would do so.

Assuming the maintenance worker's statement is inadmissible hearsay, may the expert base part of her testimony on the statement?

(A) No, because the maintenance worker's statement is not substantively admissible.

(B) No, because the expert did not interview the maintenance worker herself.

(C) Yes, because the expert's use of the statement in her testimony makes the statement substantively admissible.

(D) Yes, because other experts in the field would rely on the maintenance worker's statement.

19. After serving a portion of his sentence in a state prison, the plaintiff applied for parole in accordance with state law. His application was denied following a State Parole Board hearing at which the plaintiff was not permitted to appear either in person or by counsel. The plaintiff subsequently instituted a proceeding in a state court in which he claimed that the hearing violated his right to due process under the federal and state constitutions. The state court found for the plaintiff. On appeal by the State Parole Board, the highest appellate court in the state affirmed. In its decision, the court refused to consider claims under the federal constitution but concluded that the state constitution had been violated.

On application by the State Parole Board, is judicial review by the United States Supreme Court available?

(A) No.

(B) Yes, by certiorari only.

(C) Yes, by appeal only.

(D) Yes, by either certiorari or appeal.

20. The defendant was charged with violating a state law that made it a crime to knowingly issue a worthless check. On the presentation of its direct case at trial, the prosecution offered into evidence a properly authenticated judgment showing that the defendant had been convicted of violating the same law three years earlier. The defendant's counsel objected. Which of the following statements is correct about the judgment of conviction?

(A) It is admissible as substantive evidence of *modus operandi.*

(B) It is admissible to impeach the defendant's credibility.

(C) It is admissible both as substantive evidence of *modus operandi* and to impeach the defendant's credibility.

(D) It is inadmissible.

21. A landowner conveyed a large nature area "to the county, but if the land ceases to be used as a nature park, to my friend and his heirs." What interests are created by this conveyance?

(A) The county has a fee simple absolute.

(B) The county has a fee simple subject to an executory limitation, and the friend has an executory interest.

(C) The county has a fee simple subject to a condition subsequent, and the friend has a right of entry.

(D) The county has a fee simple determinable, and the friend has a possibility of reverter.

22. A landowner decided to make a gift to his son of a parcel of land he owned. He properly prepared a deed for the transfer of the land according to state law and handed it to his son, saying "I want you to own this land." Nine months later, the landowner met

a woman and fell deeply in love with her. Soon thereafter, he had a fight with his son about the woman. He told his son to return or destroy the deed because he was "revoking his gift." The son made a photocopy of the deed and gave the deed back to the landowner. The landowner then threw the deed in a fire. Two months later, the landowner died, leaving all of his real and personal property to the woman.

Who owns the land?

(A) The woman, because the son returned the deed to the landowner.

(B) The woman, because the landowner told the son he was revoking his gift.

(C) The son, because he kept a photocopy of the deed.

(D) The son, because the landowner gave him the deed.

23. A woman purchased a food and beverage processing machine as a gift for her husband. The machine was manufactured by the company and was purchased by the woman from a store, a retailer. When the woman got home, she unpacked the machine, placed it on the kitchen counter, and plugged it into an electrical outlet. When she started the machine, however, she noticed a jarring vibration. She immediately switched the machine off and telephoned the store. After she described the vibration to a store employee, the employee said, "If the processor vibrates like that, it is defective. Don't try to use it. It's inherently dangerous."

The woman left the processing machine on the counter, still plugged in, and went out for the evening. The husband arrived home soon afterwards. With him was a neighbor. When the husband saw the processing machine on the counter, he decided to use it to mix drinks for the neighbor and himself. After placing the necessary ingredients in the machine's glass container, the husband switched it on. The machine immediately began to vibrate,

causing the glass container to shatter. The neighbor was seriously injured by flying glass.

The neighbor asserts a claim against the store for damages resulting from a defect in the processing machine. Which of the following would be the store's most effective argument in defense against that claim?

(A) The neighbor was a bystander.

(B) The woman had assumed the risk by leaving the processing machine plugged into the electrical outlet.

(C) The processing machine was defective at the time it left the company's factory.

(D) The woman's conduct in leaving the processing machine plugged into the electrical outlet was a superseding cause of harm.

24. The plaintiff challenges the constitutionality of a state law that provides that no contraceptive device that requires insertion into a cavity of the human body may be sold without a prescription. If the only argument used by the plaintiff is that the statute violates the Equal Protection Clause of the Fourteenth Amendment because only women use such devices, which of the following would be the most effective argument in opposition to the plaintiff's claim?

(A) Gender is not a suspect classification.

(B) The statute has a rational basis because devices inserted into the human body are more likely to cause harm than devices manufactured solely for external use.

(C) The right to protect citizens against their own lack of judgment is included in the state's police powers.

(D) The statute bears a substantial relationship to an important government interest because devices inserted into the human body are more likely to cause harm than devices manufactured solely for external use.

25. On January 10, the plaintiff, a builder, entered into a written contract with the defendant to construct a building on the defendant's realty. The contract required the plaintiff to build to specifications furnished by the architect and required the defendant to make periodic payments to the plaintiff during construction. A final payment of $30,000 was to be made when the building was complete. The contract provided, however, that "In no event shall said final payment be required unless the plaintiff obtains and presents to the defendant prior to July 30 a Certificate of Satisfactory Completion issued by the architect following final inspection by the architect."

On July 15, after making all periodic payments required by the contract, the defendant asked the architect to delay issuing a Certificate of Satisfactory Completion until after July 30. The architect agreed to do so. On July 20, the plaintiff notified the architect that the building was complete and requested final inspection. The architect did not inspect the building or issue a Certificate of Satisfactory Completion until August 15. On August 16, the plaintiff requested final payment from the defendant, presenting the Certificate. The defendant refused to make payment on the ground that the plaintiff did not obtain the Certificate prior to July 30, as required by the contract.

In an action by the plaintiff against the defendant for breach of contract, which of the following would be the plaintiff's most effective argument?

(A) The contract between the plaintiff and the defendant imposed upon the architect an obligation to act reasonably in issuing the Certificate of Satisfactory Completion.

(B) The plaintiff substantially performed all conditions of the contract by completing the building prior to July 30.

(C) As a result of the defendant's request that the architect delay issuing the Certificate of Satisfactory Completion, the plaintiff was not required to obtain it prior to July 30.

(D) Applying an objective standard, satisfactory completion was achieved prior to July 30.

26. At the defendant's trial on criminal charges, undisputed evidence established that the defendant and his friend had planned to take a certain fur coat from the victim's fur shop by threatening the victim with a pistol carried by the friend; that when they did so, the victim began shooting at them; and that the friend shot back with his pistol, intentionally killing the victim.

Testifying on behalf of the prosecution, the friend stated that the defendant knew that the friend's pistol would be loaded. He also stated that the victim had handed the defendant the coat; that the friend had returned his own gun to his pocket; and that he and the defendant were on their way out of the victim's shop when the victim began shooting at them.

The defendant testified that the coat in question had previously been stolen from her by the victim, and that she and the friend were trying to retrieve it.

Statutes in the jurisdiction define first degree murder as the intentional unlawful killing of a human being, and second degree murder as the unintentional killing of a human being by the defendant or an accomplice during the course of a burglary, robbery, rape, kidnapping, or arson committed by the defendant.

The defendant is charged with first degree murder on the ground that as a co-conspirator and accomplice, she is vicariously liable for the friend's shooting of the victim. If the jury does not believe the testimony of the friend or of the defendant, the defendant should be found

(A) guilty, because she and the friend planned to take the coat by threatening the victim with the friend's pistol.

(B) guilty, because she was present when the friend shot the victim.

(C) not guilty, because the victim shot first.

(D) not guilty, because she did not aid or abet the friend in shooting the victim.

27. On February 1, the landowner conveyed a parcel of realty to his friend as a gift. The landowner executed the deed in the presence of a notary public, and the notary affixed his seal as required by law. On March 1, after the landowner learned that his friend had not recorded his title, the landowner purported to convey the same parcel of realty to his neighbor for value. The neighbor was unaware that the landowner's friend held any interest in the realty. On March 15, the friend recorded the deed that he had received from the landowner in February. In June, the neighbor executed a deed conveying the realty to the notary. The notary immediately recorded the deed.

A statute in the jurisdiction provides that "No transfer of an interest in real property shall be good against a subsequent purchaser for value without notice of such transfer unless it shall have been recorded." In litigation between the friend and the notary, who should be declared owner of the realty?

(A) The friend, because the notary had notice that the realty had first been conveyed to him.

(B) The friend because the landowner conveyed the property to him first.

(C) The neighbor, because he purchased the property for value.

(D) The notary, because the neighbor purchased the realty from the landowner before the friend recorded his deed.

28. A boy and a girl were dating when they decided it was time for them to try sexual intercourse. The girl was 17 years old. A statute in the jurisdiction provided that any male who has sexual intercourse with a female whom he knows to be under the age of 18 shall be guilty of second degree rape.

If the boy is charged with second degree rape under the above statute, which of the following facts or inferences, if it was the only one true, would provide the boy with his most effective defense to that charge?

(A) The boy was 17 years of age at the time of the alleged crime.

(B) The boy did not know that the girl was below the age of 18 years when he had sexual intercourse with her.

(C) The boy was intoxicated at the time he had sexual intercourse with the girl.

(D) The girl was not intoxicated, and, in fact, consented to having sexual intercourse with the boy.

29. A man sued a moving company for $100,000 in state court in State A after the man was injured by one of the moving company's trucks. His claim was based on State A motor vehicle law. The man was a citizen of State A. The moving company was incorporated in State B and had 70 percent of its business operations in State A. However, all of the company's directors and top management worked in State C.

Because of a large amount of local bad press, the moving company had a good faith belief that any action against it in State A would be unfair. May it remove the action to federal district court?

(A) No, because the man's claim was based on State A motor vehicle law.

(B) No, because the moving company was a citizen of State A.

(C) Yes, because the moving company's directors and top management worked in State C.

(D) Yes, because the moving company had a good faith belief that any action against it in State A would be unfair.

30. The defendant was driving her truck across a bridge when the bridge collapsed, causing a car driven by the plaintiff to fall into the river. The plaintiff subsequently asserted a negligence claim against the defendant for injuries that he sustained in the fall.

A statute in the jurisdiction prohibits the operation of a vehicle weighing more than 20,000 pounds at a speed in excess of 25 miles per hour on any bridge in the state. At the trial, it was proven that the defendant's truck weighed 30,000 pounds, and that the defendant was driving it at a speed of 40 miles per hour when the bridge collapsed. It was also proven that a truck weighing 30,000 pounds would have been more likely to cause the bridge to collapse if driven across it at a speed under 25 miles per hour than at a speed over 25 miles per hour.

The court should find for

(A) the plaintiff, because the defendant's violation of the statute was negligence per se.

(B) the plaintiff, because the defendant's violation of the statute raises a presumption that the defendant's negligence was a proximate cause of the plaintiff's injuries.

(C) the defendant, because the defendant's violation of statute was not a factual cause of the plaintiff's injury.

(D) the defendant, because the defendant did not violate a statute that was designed to protect a class of persons to which the plaintiff belonged.

31. The landowner conveyed a lakefront parcel of realty to the buyer "unless the realty is used for non-residential purposes, in which case grantor or his successors may re-obtain possession." Two years later, by a properly executed document that was subsequently recorded, the buyer granted a fisherman a license to enter the realty for a period of five years to fish from the lake on which it fronted. If the landowner commences an appropriate proceeding seeking possession of the realty, the buyer's most effective argument in defense would be that

(A) the condition contained in the landowner's deed to the buyer violates the Rule Against Perpetuities.

(B) fishing is a residential use of the realty.

(C) the landowner's deed created a fee simple subject to a condition subsequent.

(D) the condition contained in the landowner's deed to the buyer is void as a restraint on alienation.

32. A sculptor and a famous architect entered into a contract to design a new studio for the sculptor. The sculptor told the architect that she was hiring her because she believed in her unique vision. The written contract also provided that "neither party shall assign or delegate this contract without the other party's written approval."

The sculptor subsequently hired a builder who began construction of the architect's design. As work progressed, the sculptor and the architect argued frequently. When the building was 85 percent complete, the architect refused to continue working for the sculptor and executed a document purporting to assign the contract to another architect. The architectural work that remained involved personal services. The sculptor immediately ordered the builder to stop construction and sued the architect for an order directing her to specifically perform her obligations under the contract.

Should the court grant the relief requested by the sculptor?

(A) Yes, because the architectural work that remained to be completed at the time of the architect's assignment involved personal services.

(B)   Yes, because the agreement between the sculptor and the architect prohibited assignment.

(C)   No, because an agreement not to assign destroys the power but not the right to make a valid assignment.

(D)   No, because the architectural work that remained to be completed at the time of the architect's assignment involved personal services.

33.   At the trial of a breach of contract action brought by the plaintiff against the defendant, the plaintiff testified in her own behalf. The plaintiff stated that a man who called her on the telephone said that he was the defendant and ordered goods from her at an agreed price. She said that when she tried to deliver the goods, the defendant refused to accept them. The plaintiff stated further that she had never spoken to the defendant before or after that telephone conversation, but that she had heard his voice in the judge's chambers immediately before the trial began and that she recognized it as the voice of the person to whom she had spoken on the telephone.

If the defendant's attorney asks the court to exclude the plaintiff's testimony regarding the identification of the voice on the telephone, the plaintiff's statement should be

(A)   admitted, because the plaintiff heard the defendant's voice in the judge's chambers before testifying.

(B)   admitted, because the person to whom the plaintiff spoke on the telephone identified himself as the defendant.

(C)   excluded, because the plaintiff had never spoken to the defendant prior to the telephone conversation.

(D)   excluded, because the plaintiff had not dialed the defendant's telephone number before speaking to him on the telephone.

34.   A chemical used in the manufacture of munitions is frequently found floating, as dust, in the air of munitions factories. Since prolonged inhalation of the chemical can cause lung disease, Congress passes an Act to limit use of the chemical. Among other things, the Act prohibits the operation of any munitions factory in which the chemical's airborne levels exceed specified standards. The Act also establishes an Agency, authorizes it to inspect munitions factories, and empowers it to issue Closure Orders, enforceable by the Department of Justice, and directing the closing of any factory operating in violation of the Act. Section 34 of the Act provides that Closure Orders do not become effective until 10 days after their approval by the National Defense Committee of the Senate.

After determining that airborne levels of the chemical exceed statutory standards in a munitions factory operated by the company, the Agency issues a Closure Order, sending copies to the United States Department of Justice and to the Senate National Defense Committee as required by the Act. The Senate National Defense Committee refuses to approve the Closure Order.

If the Department of Justice challenges the constitutionality of Section 34 of the Act in an appropriate proceeding, the court should find this section

(A)   constitutional, because circumstances known only to the Senate National Defense Committee might make the continued operation of a particular munitions factory necessary to national security.

(B)   constitutional, because after delegating its power to an administrative agency, Congress may continue to act in a supervisory capacity.

(C)   unconstitutional, because Congress may not delegate to an administrative agency the power to impose criminal or quasi-criminal sanctions.

(D) unconstitutional, because Section 34 would allow the passage of legislation by a committee of Congress.

35. The victim, who lived alone, was a collector of antiques. One day, the defendant followed the victim to work. Knowing that the victim's valuable antiques collection was stored in her home, the defendant phoned the victim at work and told her that he had placed a bomb in her home. He said that if she immediately paid him $1,000 in cash, he would give the police information necessary for them to defuse the bomb. If she did not pay him, he said would detonate the bomb, destroying her home and her collection of antiques. The victim paid the defendant as instructed. In reality, the defendant had not placed a bomb in the victim's home.

What is the most serious offense of which the defendant is likely to be convicted?

(A) Robbery.

(B) Extortion.

(C) Larceny by trick.

(D) Embezzlement.

36. A state law requires a permit for the use of certain recreational facilities in state parks and fixes the annual fee for such permits at $25 for residents and $200 for non-residents. If a non-resident of the state challenges the law as unconstitutional, the **LEAST** effective argument in support of that claim would be that the law violates

(A) the Equal Protection Clause of the Fourteenth Amendment.

(B) the Obligation of Contracts Clause of Article I.

(C) the Privileges and Immunities Clause of Article IV.

(D) the Commerce Clause of Article I.

37. The seller and the buyer entered into a valid written contract for the sale of the seller's

home to the buyer. Subsequently, the seller's neighbor, the defendant, telephoned the seller and said, "If you don't back out of your contract with the buyer, there's going to be an accident and one of your children is going to be seriously hurt. Understand?" Before the seller had a chance to answer, the defendant hung up. The seller became so frightened by the defendant's threat that he suffered an immediate heart attack.

If the seller asserts a claim against the defendant for assault, which of the following would be the defendant's **LEAST** effective argument in defense against that claim?

(A) The defendant's statement did not justify apprehension of immediate harm.

(B) The defendant told the seller that he could avoid harm by complying with a specified condition.

(C) The defendant's threat was not directed against the person of the seller.

(D) The defendant committed no physical act.

38. At his trial on a charge of arson committed in the city, the defendant testified that on the day of the fire, he was not in the city but was actually 1,000 miles away in another state. The prosecution subsequently called a witness who testified that on the day of the fire, she was in a liquor store in the city when the defendant came into the store with a gun and robbed its owner. Over timely objection by the defendant's attorney, the witness's testimony should be

(A) admitted for impeachment only.

(B) admitted as substantive evidence only.

(C) admitted for impeachment and as substantive evidence.

(D) excluded.

39. The landowner was the owner of a parcel of realty on which there were several buildings and a gold mine. The landowner lived in one

of the buildings and personally worked the gold mine, earning a comfortable living by selling the gold that he removed. The other buildings were vacant. When the landowner died, his will devised the realty "to my friend, but if my friend should die without issue from his wife, to the mailman." The land-owner's friend and his wife did not have any children.

Which of the following statements is correct about the mailman's interest in the realty?

(A) The landowner's will gave the mailman a vested remainder in the property.

(B) The landowner's will gave the mailman a contingent remainder in the property.

(C) The landowner's will gave the mailman a shifting executory interest in the realty.

(D) The mailman has no interest in the realty.

40. After she was fired from her job, a sales-woman brought an action against her former employer in federal district court in State A. The saleswoman sought $50,000 in damages. The saleswoman was a citizen of State A, while her former employer was incorporated in State B and had its primary place of business in State C. The saleswoman's action included claims for violation of federal employment laws and for breach of contract under State A law. The employer moved to dismiss the breach of contract claim.

How should the court rule?

(A) Grant the motion, because the contract claim is based on state law.

(B) Grant the motion, because the sales-woman is only claiming $50,000 in damages.

(C) Deny the motion, because the sales-woman can bring all claims she has against the company in her action.

(D) Deny the motion, because all of her claims arose from the saleswoman's loss of her job.

41. At the defendant's trial on a charge of rape, the victim testified that on March 1, the defendant forced her to have sexual inter-course with him against her will. Testifying in his own defense, the defendant admitted that he had engaged in sexual intercourse with the victim on that date, but he claimed that the victim had consented. The defendant stated further that the victim had not accused him of rape until April 3, when she discov-ered that he was married and was living with his wife.

The prosecutor subsequently offered a prop-erly authenticated public record indicating that the defendant had been convicted of state income tax fraud in another jurisdiction two years earlier. In both the jurisdiction where the defendant was convicted and the juris-diction where the defendant was being tried for rape, state income tax fraud was a felony. On objection by the defendant's attorney, the record should be

(A) admitted.

(B) admitted, because state income tax fraud is a felony in the jurisdiction where the defendant was convicted.

(C) admitted, because state income tax fraud is a felony in the jurisdiction where the defendant was being tried for rape.

(D) excluded.

42. The defendant had been convicted of fraud on three separate occasions and served three different prison sentences as a result. Soon after his most recent release, the defen-dant proclaimed himself to be a minister and began conducting prayer meetings on Sunday nights. During these meetings, the defendant stated that his vows as minister prevented him from working for money, and he asked the people present to make cash contributions to provide for his personal

needs. After collecting several hundred dollars in this fashion, the defendant was arrested and charged with fraud under a state law that prohibits any person from making statements that he or she knows to be false for the purpose of obtaining money from others.

In defense, the defendant asserted that a court could not convict him without questioning the sincerity of his religious beliefs, and that the prosecution therefore violated his First Amendment rights to freedom of religion. He asked that the court dismiss the prosecution on that ground.

Should the prosecution be dismissed?

(A) Yes.

(B) No, because a court may determine the sincerity of a person's religious beliefs without violating First Amendment rights to freedom of religion.

(C) No, because First Amendment rights to freedom of religion cannot be used to justify what would otherwise be a criminal act.

(D) No, because First Amendment rights to freedom of religion protect beliefs, but not actions.

43. In which one of the following fact situations is the defendant most likely to be properly convicted of violating a state law that prohibits depriving any person of a right conferred by the Equal Protection Clause of the Fourteenth Amendment to the United States Constitution?

(A) The defendant, the president of a university operated by a religious organization, refused to admit certain students solely because of their religion.

(B) The defendant, a federal court official, prevented certain persons from serving on federal juries solely because of their race.

(C) The defendant, the principal of a public high school, expelled certain students solely because they were pregnant.

(D) The defendant, the vice president of a bank, refused to grant loans to certain applicants solely because of their place of national origin.

44. The defendant was the manufacturer of a chemical used by photo processors. A professional photographer customarily used the chemical in his processing laboratory. On August 15, 2012, while working in his laboratory, the photographer read the label of a bottle of the chemical that he had purchased several months earlier. The label said, "Best when used prior to June 1, 2012." Although the manufacturer knew that the chemical's fumes were extremely toxic, the label contained no other statements. The photographer poured the contents of the bottle down a drain that emptied into a municipal sewer. Because the sewer was cracked, toxic fumes entered the home of the plaintiff, causing the plaintiff to become seriously ill. The plaintiff's home was located a half-mile from the photographer's laboratory.

The plaintiff subsequently asserted a claim for damages against the defendant manufacturer on the ground that the absence of a warning on the bottle made the product defective and unreasonably dangerous.

Which of the following additional facts or inferences, if it was the only one true, would provide the defendant with its most effective defense to the plaintiff's claim?

(A) The reasonable person would not have anticipated that the plaintiff would come into contact with the chemical or its fumes.

(B) The photographer acted negligently in pouring the chemical down the drain.

(C) The plaintiff's damage would not have occurred but for the crack in the municipal sewer.

(D)  The photographer had purchased the chemical from a retail store that had purchased it from a wholesaler that had purchased it from the defendant.

45.  A man was injured when he was hit by a taxi. He sued the taxi driver in federal district court in State A. Under the applicable statute of limitations, the action had to be commenced by June 16 and an action was deemed commenced when it was filed with the court. The man filed his action on June 11. On June 12, he served the complaint on the taxi driver. On June 13, he received a call from the owner of the taxi company asking whether he would be brought into the action as well. The man filed an amended complaint on June 17 that added the owner as a co-defendant. On June 22, the man served the amended complaint on both the taxi driver and the owner. The owner moved to dismiss the complaint, arguing it was barred by the statute of limitations.

How should the court rule?

(A)  Grant the motion, because the complaint was served on the owner more than 10 days after the action commenced.

(B)  Grant the motion, because the complaint was amended on June 17.

(C)  Deny the motion, because both claims related to the taxi accident.

(D)  Deny the motion, because the owner called to ask about the original complaint.

46.  A woman was the owner of a parcel of realty on which she lived with her husband. The woman was admitted to a hospital following a severe heart attack. While her husband was visiting her in the hospital, the woman said, "I know I'm dying, and I want to be sure that you have the land after I'm gone. Please have our lawyer take care of it." The following day, the husband asked the family attorney to prepare a quitclaim deed to the land for execution by the woman. The husband brought the document to the woman in the hospital, where she executed it according to the requirements of law. After signing the quitclaim deed, the woman handed the document to the husband and said, "Please put it in the safe deposit box at the bank." The husband did so, but he never recorded the quitclaim.

The woman subsequently recovered from her heart attack and was moved from the hospital to a rest home, where she resided until 30 years later, when she died from other causes. At the woman's request, the husband continued to occupy, maintain, and pay taxes on the land throughout that period of time. During the last nine years of her life in the rest home, the woman was attended by a nurse. When the woman died, her will purported to leave the land "to my faithful nurse." The husband and the nurse subsequently asserted conflicting claims to the land.

Which of the following additional facts or inferences, if it was the only one true, would be most likely to result in a judgment for the husband?

(A)  The woman intended the quitclaim deed to be a testamentary substitute.

(B)  The quitclaim deed to the husband was a gift *causa mortis.*

(C)  The safe deposit box into which the woman asked the husband to put the quitclaim deed was held jointly by the woman and the husband.

(D)  The statutory period for adverse possession is less than 30 years.

47.  Assuming that the appropriate objection is made, in which of the following fact situations is the offered evidence **LEAST** likely to be excluded under the original document rule?

(A)  In an action for breach of contract, the plaintiff offers a photocopy of the contract, asserting that the original is kept at the plaintiff's branch office, which is located in a foreign country.

(B)  In a prosecution of the defendant
     for forging a check, the prosecu-
     tion—without producing the check
     or explaining its absence—offers to
     call a witness who will testify that the
     defendant paid the witness for mer-
     chandise with a check to which the
     defendant signed the name "James
     Grant."

(C)  In a personal injury action, the defen-
     dant—without producing the X-ray
     or explaining its absence—calls a
     medical expert who testifies that based
     solely on the examination of an X-ray,
     it is her opinion that the plaintiff did
     not sustain a fracture of the skull.

(D)  In a lawsuit by the plaintiff against the
     state tax collector, the plaintiff offers
     to testify to the contents of her state
     income tax return, asserting that she
     sent the original to the state tax collec-
     tor as required by law, and that she did
     not keep a copy.

48.  A woman from the Southern District of State
     A was injured in a boating accident in the
     Eastern District of State B. The woman sued
     two other boaters involved in the accident
     in a federal action based on diversity. The
     first was a doctor from the Western District
     of State C. The second was a nurse from the
     Eastern District of State C.

     In which judicial districts would venue be
     proper for the woman's action?

     (A)  The Eastern District of State B.

     (B)  The Southern District of State A and the
          Eastern District of State B.

     (C)  The Western District of State C and the
          Eastern District of State C.

     (D)  The Eastern District of State B, the
          Western District of State C, and the
          Eastern District of State C.

49.  The defendant was employed by an attorney
     to clean his office and to sweep the parking
     lot every night. While sweeping one evening,

the defendant found the attorney's wallet
where he had dropped it in the parking lot.
The wallet contained $300. Planning to return
it to the attorney the next morning, the defendant took the wallet home for safekeeping.
That night, however, realizing that nobody
knew that she had it. the defendant decided
to keep the attorney's wallet. She went out
and spent $4 of the attorney's money on ice
cream. The following morning, the defendant felt guilty about keeping the attorney's
money. She replaced what she had spent and
returned the wallet and cash to the attorney.

If the defendant is prosecuted for crimes
resulting from the above incident, she may
properly be convicted of

(A)  larceny only.

(B)  embezzlement only.

(C)  neither larceny nor embezzlement.

(D)  larceny and embezzlement.

50.  The defendant purchased property in a popu-
     lar resort area and constructed a restaurant on
     it. The defendant's restaurant was equipped
     with a walk-up window so that people who
     chose to do so could purchase food and soft
     drinks without entering the restaurant. The
     defendant kept his restaurant and walk-up
     window open every night until 2 A.M. Soon,
     large noisy crowds of young people began
     congregating in front of the defendant's res-
     taurant, making occasional purchases at the
     walk-up window and remaining there until
     it closed. On many nights, members of the
     crowd openly smoked marijuana and used
     profane language in loud voices. The plain-
     tiff, who resided in a house next to the restau-
     rant, telephoned the defendant. The plaintiff
     complained that the value of his home was
     being diminished by the walk-up window and
     by noise from the restaurant. He asked the
     defendant to close the restaurant each night at
     11 P.M., but the defendant refused.

     If the plaintiff subsequently asserts a claim
     against the defendant for damages result-
     ing from the reduction of his home's value,

which of the following theories would be most likely to result in a judgment for the plaintiff?

(A)  Trespass to land.

(B)  Intentional infliction of emotional distress.

(C)  Private nuisance.

(D)  Invasion of privacy.

51.  Because of severe economic recession, the state has enacted a statute imposing a tax on corporations that have gross sales within the state in excess of $1 million during a calendar year. The statute applies to all such corporations, whether incorporated inside or outside the state. It establishes a sliding-scale tax schedule with a maximum tax rate of 10 percent of gross sales in excess of $1 million.

Which of the following persons or entities is most likely to have standing to challenge the constitutionality of the statute on the ground that it violates the Commerce Clause of the United States Constitution?

(A)  The governor of a neighboring state.

(B)  The stockholders of a state corporation with annual gross sales of $1.5 million in the state.

(C)  The stockholders of an out-of-state corporation with annual gross sales of $500,000 in the state.

(D)  A taxpayer in the state.

52.  When the landowner died, she left a one-half interest in a parcel of realty to her niece and the niece's husband, as joint tenants with full right of survivorship, and a one-half interest in the realty to the 13-year-old unmarried daughter of the landowner. One year later, the niece, the husband, and the daughter were killed simultaneously in an automobile accident.

Which of the following statements correctly describes ownership of the realty following their deaths?

(A)  The heirs of the daughter hold a one-half interest, the heirs of the niece hold a one-quarter interest, and the heirs of the husband hold a one-quarter interest.

(B)  The entire property is held by the heirs of the daughter.

(C)  The heirs of the daughter hold a one-third interest, the heirs of the niece hold a one-third interest, and the heirs of the husband hold a one-third interest.

(D)  The heirs of the niece hold a one-half interest and the heirs of the husband hold a one-half interest.

53.  The landowner was the owner of a large tract of realty located in a heavily forested area. In January 2012, the landowner leased the realty to a friend for a period of 20 years. In March 2012, the landowner sold the realty to an artist, executing a general warranty deed containing covenants of seisin, quiet enjoyment, the right to convey, and a covenant against encumbrances. In April 2012, the artist conveyed the realty to a baker by a deed containing covenants substantially identical to those contained in the deed that the artist had received from the landowner. In May 2012, the artist became insolvent. In June 2012, the baker attempted to move onto the realty and was prevented from doing so by the friend, who claimed a superior right.

If the baker subsequently asserts a claim for damages against the landowner, the baker's most effective theory would be that the landowner breached the warranty

(A)  of seisin.

(B)  against encumbrances.

(C)  of the right to convey.

(D)  of quiet enjoyment.

54.  The defendant was the operator of a summer camp for children. The plaintiff was a nine-year-old child staying at the camp, her

parents having paid the defendant a fee. The plaintiff was playing softball with other children on a field that the defendant set aside for this purpose. When one of the children hit the ball, it rolled into a group of bushes alongside the field. Running into the bushes after the ball, the plaintiff tripped on a tree root that was covered by a pile of leaves. The tree root would have been discovered and removed by a reasonable summer camp operator.

The plaintiff asserted a claim against the defendant, alleging that the defendant's negligence was a proximate cause of injuries that the plaintiff sustained when she tripped on the tree root. The court should find for

(A) the defendant, because the tree root was a natural condition of the land.

(B) the defendant, because the plaintiff assumed the risk by chasing the ball into the grove of bushes.

(C) the plaintiff, because the defendant owed her an absolute duty to keep the premises safe.

(D) the plaintiff, because a reasonable person in the defendant's position would have discovered and removed the tree root.

55. The seller owned a 10-acre parcel of realty. On March 6, the seller offered to sell the land to the buyer for $80,000. The buyer said that he might be interested but that he would not be in a position to make up his mind until July. The seller said that she would hold the realty for the buyer until then and signed a paper on which she wrote:

> I hereby offer to sell Blackacre to the buyer for $80,000 cash. In return for $1 that I have on this date received, I promise to hold this offer open until July 15.

On July 1, the buyer told the seller that he was ready to purchase the land, but the seller told him that she had changed her mind and

did not want to sell. The buyer asserted a claim against the seller based on her written promise to keep the offer open until July 15. At the trial, the seller proved that she never actually received $1 from the buyer in return for her promise. In deciding the buyer's claim, the court should find for

(A) the buyer, because the parol evidence rule prevents the seller from relying on oral evidence that she did not actually receive $1.

(B) the buyer, because the buyer detrimentally relied on the seller's promise to keep the offer open until July 15.

(C) the seller, because the realty is obviously worth more than $1.

(D) the seller, because nothing was bargained for or given in exchange for the seller's promise to keep the offer open until July 15.

56. A woman sued a company in federal district court in State A. She claimed that she had been injured by one of the company's products and could no longer work. The company's attorney did not believe the woman was as injured as she claimed and would like to have the woman physically examined by a doctor.

What should the company's attorney do?

(A) File notice of request to take a physical examination.

(B) Serve the woman with a notice of deposition.

(C) Obtain a court order requiring the woman to undergo an examination.

(D) Subpoena the woman to appear at a physical examination.

57. The plaintiff, who was four years of age, was the plaintiff in a battery action against the defendant, who was seven years of age. At trial, the plaintiff's attorney called the plaintiff to testify on the plaintiff's direct

case. After interviewing her, the trial judge ruled that because of the plaintiff's youth, she was unable to appreciate her duty to testify truthfully and therefore was not a competent witness. The plaintiff's attorney subsequently called a witness, the plaintiff's neighbor. The witness testified that, immediately after the incident in question, the plaintiff had come running up to her on the street, crying and with her nose bleeding. The witness testified further that at that time the plaintiff said, "The defendant pushed me and gave me a bloody nose."

If the defendant's attorney objects to the witness's statement about what the plaintiff said to her, the court should rule that evidence

(A) admissible as an excited utterance.

(B) admissible because the plaintiff's incompetence to testify made her a presently unavailable declarant.

(C) inadmissible because it is hearsay.

(D) inadmissible because the plaintiff was incompetent to testify.

58. The plaintiff asserted a claim against the defendant for injuries that the plaintiff received when she was struck by a truck owned by the defendant and driven by one of the defendant's employees. At trial, the plaintiff's attorney called a woman as a witness on the presentation of the plaintiff's direct case. In response to questions asked by the plaintiff's attorney, the witness stated that she was presently employed by the defendant and that she had been driving the defendant's truck on the day of the accident. The plaintiff's attorney then asked, "You were going faster than 35 miles per hour, weren't you?" The defendant's attorney objected to the question on the ground that it was leading.

If the objection of the defendant's attorney is overruled, it will probably be because

(A) the witness is employed by an adverse party.

(B) the witness is a hostile witness.

(C) leading questions are permitted on cross-examination.

(D) the question was not leading.

59. The defendant, the owner of a gasoline delivery service, operated a tank truck for delivering gasoline. The defendant's truck was 35 feet in length and had the words "DANGER — GASOLINE" printed on it. One day, while on the way to a gasoline delivery, the defendant stopped at a bank. Although she saw an official sign that prohibited parking in that location, the defendant parked her truck directly in front of the bank. A statute in the jurisdiction prohibited parking any vehicle longer than 30 feet on a city street. Another statute prohibited parking any vehicle directly in front of a bank. The defendant was aware of both statutes.

While the defendant was in the bank, a driver, who was driving down the street, lost control of her car and struck the defendant's truck. As a result, a large quantity of gasoline in the defendant's delivery tank exploded, injuring the driver. The plaintiff, a bank employee who was sitting at his desk inside the bank, was also injured in the explosion.

The plaintiff asserts a claim against the defendant for his injuries. If the plaintiff's claim is successful, it will most likely be because

(A) the statute that prohibited parking vehicles longer than 30 feet on a city street was a traffic safety statute.

(B) the defendant was aware that a statute prohibited parking any vehicle in front of a bank.

(C) the reasonable person would not park a vehicle in violation of an official sign that prohibits parking.

(D) transporting large quantities of gasoline is an abnormally dangerous activity.

60. A seven-year-old girl was admitted to a hospital unconscious. Doctors who examined her asked the girl's parents to consent to a blood transfusion for the girl, stating that the girl would probably die otherwise. The girl's parents refused, saying that they did not believe in blood transfusions.

A state statute provides that if a child is admitted to a hospital with a life-threatening disease or injury, and the parents of that child refuse to consent to treatment that in the opinion of hospital officials is necessary to save the child's life, the court shall designate the hospital administrator to act as the child's guardian for the purpose of consenting to such treatment. The hospital administrator immediately commenced a proceeding in a state court to have herself declared the girl's guardian under that statute. The girl's parents petitioned a federal court to enjoin the state court from granting the hospital administrator's application on the ground that the state law is unconstitutional on its face. Prior to the disposition of either proceeding, the girl died.

If the statute is found to be unconstitutional, it will most likely be because the statute

(A) violates the Equal Protection Clause of the Fourteenth Amendment.

(B) is vague.

(C) violates the Free Exercise Clause of the First Amendment.

(D) interferes with a fundamental right.

61. After a man died without a will, the state treasurer instituted a proceeding for a declaration that the man's assets should escheat to the state, on the ground that there were no living persons eligible to inherit. A woman opposed the proceeding, claiming that she was the man's niece and therefore his heir under the state law of intestate distribution. In support of her claim, the niece offered a Bible. She testified that the Bible had belonged to her deceased mother, and that her mother had made notations in it indicating that her husband, the niece's father, was the man's brother, and indicating the date of birth of her daughter, the niece. The state treasurer objected to admission of the Bible.

If the notation in the Bible is admitted into evidence, it will probably be as

(A) an ancient document.

(B) a statement of the mother's personal history or pedigree.

(C) a transaction recorded under the "dead man's statute."

(D) a record of vital statistics.

62. The defendant and his friend agreed to rob a bank and planned the robbery for several weeks. According to their plan, the defendant's car would be used as the getaway vehicle. The defendant was to drive to and from the robbery and wait in the car while his friend went into the bank to hold it up. While driving to the bank with his friend on the day the robbery was to take place, however, the defendant began to have second thoughts. After a brief conversation with his friend, the defendant stopped the car. Taking his car keys with him, he told his friend he wasn't going through with it and went into a store, where he telephoned the police and told them about the planned robbery. While the defendant was in the store, his friend left and robbed the bank himself. The information provided by the defendant's call led to the apprehension and conviction of his friend.

If the defendant is subsequently arrested and prosecuted for conspiracy to commit bank robbery, he should be found

(A) not guilty, because he removed his keys from the car when he got out to phone the police.

(B) not guilty, because he notified his friend that he had changed his mind about going through with the plan.

(C) not guilty, because the defendant's telephone call to the police led to the apprehension and conviction of his friend.

(D) guilty.

63. The defendant was the owner and operator of a hotel. Because electrical wiring in the hotel was beginning to deteriorate, the defendant hired a licensed electrician to repair it. The electrician was hired as an independent contractor. If the defendant had done any investigation regarding the electrician, he would have discovered many complaints and citations regarding poor work done by the electrician. While repairing the wiring, the electrician negligently connected the wiring in room 201 to a dangerous high-voltage supply line instead of to a safe low-voltage supply line. Reasonable inspection by the defendant would not have disclosed the error. The following day, when the plaintiff registered at the hotel, the defendant assigned him to room 201. That evening, while the plaintiff was attempting to adjust the electric heater in room 201, he received a severe electric shock as a result of the fact that the room had been connected to a high-voltage supply line.

If the plaintiff asserts a claim against the defendant for damage resulting from the electric shock, the court should find for

(A) the defendant, because the defendant hired the electrician as an independent contractor.

(B) the defendant, because reasonable inspection by the defendant would have failed to disclose the electrician's error.

(C) the plaintiff, because the defendant failed to use adequate care in hiring the electrician.

(D) the plaintiff, because the electrician's error made the wiring in room 201 ultra-hazardous.

64. When the landowner's mother died, she left him a 640-acre parcel of realty known as the Smith and Baker tract. Soon afterwards, the landowner executed a general warranty deed to his sister, conveying realty described as "the north 40 of the parcel of land known as the Smith and Baker tract." The landowner thereafter executed a quitclaim deed in favor of his wife to "all my rights, title, and interest in a parcel of realty known as the Smith and Baker tract." The Smith and Baker tract was a famous piece of land in the area, and was easily identifiable by its name. However, the jurisdiction was one in which reference to government survey markers was customarily used in describing realty in general warranty deeds. If the wife subsequently institutes a proceeding against the sister seeking to declare herself the owner of the entire Smith and Baker tract, should the court grant the relief requested by the wife?

(A) No, because one who executes a quitclaim deed does not warrant that he or she holds any interest in the property described.

(B) No, because the description in the landowner's deed to the sister was reasonably sufficient to identify the property conveyed.

(C) Yes, because the jurisdiction is one in which reference to government survey markers is customarily used in describing realty in general warranty deeds.

(D) Yes, because a deed that conveys a portion of a parcel of realty must describe the portion conveyed in terms of "metes and bounds" or other survey terminology.

65. A newspaper published an article stating that the plaintiff had once been convicted of armed robbery. In fact, the plaintiff had never been convicted of any crime. If the plaintiff asserts a defamation claim against the newspaper, which one of the following additional facts or inferences, if it was the only one true, would be most likely to result in a judgment for the newspaper?

(A) Official government records indicating that the plaintiff had never been convicted of robbery were available for public inspection.

(B) Officials of the newspaper responsible for publishing the article reasonably believed the statement to be true.

(C) The plaintiff was a public figure.

(D) The plaintiff failed to prove that damage resulted from the statement.

66. A woman was the owner of a house in which she lived with her 23-year-old son, the defendant. After receiving a tip that the defendant was involved in the unlawful sale of drugs, two police officers went to the woman's home for the purpose of questioning the defendant. When they arrived, the defendant was not in, but the woman admitted them to the house. The officers explained why they had come and asked whether they could see the defendant's room. The woman showed them to the defendant's room and permitted them to enter, saying that the defendant never locked his door. When the officers saw a footlocker in the room, they asked the woman whether they could look inside it. She told them that the defendant was the only one who had a key to the footlocker, but she said if they could find some way to open it, she had no objection to their looking inside. While the woman watched, one of the officers picked the lock and opened the footlocker. In it, they found a plastic bag containing cocaine. The officers left the plastic bag there and returned later with a search warrant that they obtained by swearing that they had seen cocaine in the defendant's footlocker. After seizing the cocaine, they arrested the defendant for unlawful possession of a dangerous drug. Prior to trial, the defendant asked the court to suppress use of the cocaine as evidence.

The defendant's motion should be

(A) denied, because the woman gave the police permission to open the footlocker.

(B) denied, because the woman had apparent authority to permit the search of the defendant's room.

(C) granted.

(D) denied, because the officers had probable cause to believe that they would find cocaine in the footlocker.

67. After negotiation, the buyer and the seller entered into a valid written contract for the sale to the buyer of the seller's realty. The contract provided for closing of title "on or before June 15" because the buyer was moving into the area on June 15 and needed to move into the realty immediately. The contract also stated that "time is of the essence." On June 12, the seller informed the buyer that she would not be able to close until June 16. On June 16, the seller tendered a conveyance. Although the seller complied with the requirements of the contract in all other respects, the buyer refused to accept the conveyance on the ground that the date for performance had passed.

If the seller asserts a claim against the buyer as a result of the buyer's refusal to accept the seller's conveyance on June 16, the court should find for

(A) the buyer, because circumstances contemplated by the parties at the time the contract was formed made it essential that the conveyance occur on or before June 15.

(B) the buyer, because the contract contained the phrase "time is of the essence."

(C) the seller, because there was no indication that a conveyance after June 15 would cause damages to the buyer.

(D) the seller, because she made a reasonable effort to comply with the terms of the contract.

68. The defendant was the manufacturer of a gas sold for commercial use. The defendant produced the gas at its factory and stored it in a large tank located behind the factory building. Although the defendant made reasonable inspections of its storage tank at reasonable intervals, a leak in the tank allowed some gas

to escape. A wind carried the escaped gas to the home of the plaintiff, located a half-mile from the defendant's factory. The plaintiff died as a result of his exposure to the gas.

In a strict liability claim against the defendant for damages resulting from the plaintiff's exposure to gas, which of the following must the plaintiff's personal representative prove to prevail?

(A) The tank in which the defendant stored the gas was defective.

(B) The gas was defectively designed.

(C) The gas was defectively manufactured.

(D) The gas is extremely deadly.

69. After a man died in a plane crash, the man's family sued the airline in federal district court. The family's attorney hired an expert in airplane accidents to create a model of the man's accident. Based on his research, the expert planned to testify that the accident was caused by pilot negligence.

The airline's attorney would like to know the details of the expert's research before trial. How may the airline's attorney do so?

(A) The airline's attorney doesn't have to do anything to learn the details of the expert's research.

(B) The airline's attorney may serve interrogatories on the expert.

(C) The airline's attorney may depose the expert.

(D) The airline's attorney may not know the details of the expert's research because it is protected work product.

70. The plaintiff asserted a negligence claim against the defendant for personal injuries sustained when the plaintiff fell down a stairway while leaving the defendant's restaurant. The defendant asserted a defense of contributory negligence. At trial, the defendant's attorney called a witness. After answering

several preliminary questions, the witness testified that she observed the plaintiff leaving the restaurant just before the accident and that the plaintiff appeared to be intoxicated. The witness said she based her opinion on the fact she heard the plaintiff slurring her words and the plaintiff appeared to almost walk into a wall. The plaintiff's attorney objected, and the judge found that the witness's opinion appeared to be rationally based on the witness's personal perceptions. The witness's statement that the plaintiff appeared to be intoxicated should be

(A) admitted.

(B) excluded, because the witness is not an expert on intoxication.

(C) admitted, but the judge should instruct the jury to disregard it unless the jury decides that the witness is an expert on intoxication.

(D) admitted, but the judge should instruct the jury to disregard it unless the jury decides that the witness's opinion is rationally based on her personal perceptions.

71. The Department of Sanitation was established for the purpose of providing free sanitation services to the people of the state. Since its inception, the Department's activities have included garbage collection and street cleaning. The plaintiff, an alien residing within the state, applied for a job as a Director of Public Policy with the Department of Sanitation. The Director had broad discretion regarding policies in the Department of Sanitation. Although he qualified in all other respects, the state Personnel Division rejected the plaintiff's application on the sole ground that he was not a United States citizen. A statute of the state provides in part that "no person shall be eligible for employment as Director of Public Policy in the Department of Sanitation who is not a citizen of the United States." The plaintiff challenged the constitutionality of that statute in an appropriate proceeding.

The statute should be found constitutional

(A) because street cleaning is a traditional government activity in the state.

(B) because there is a rational basis for restricting employment by the state to citizens of the United States.

(C) because the job the plaintiff applied for appears to involve policy-making functions and includes broad discretion in the execution of public policy.

(D) unless employment by the state is found to be a fundamental right.

72. A shoe company sued an athlete in federal district court in State A. The case was tried in front of a jury.

Which of the following statements is correct?

(A) The jury must have at least five members.

(B) The jury can have no more than nine members.

(C) A jury can hear the case if the company seeks an injunction.

(D) The jury verdict must be unanimous.

73. A woman, a citizen of State A, sued a company for violations of the federal National Labor Relations Act in federal district court in State A. The company was incorporated in State B and had most of its factories in State A (including the factory where the woman's claim arose). The company president and most of its decision-makers worked in an office in State C just across the border from State B. The woman claimed $80,000 in damages.

Does the federal district court in State A have subject matter jurisdiction over the claim?

(A) No, because most of the company's factories are in State A.

(B) No, because the woman's claim arose from a company factory in State A.

(C) Yes, because the woman is suing under the National Labor Relations Act.

(D) Yes, because the company president and most of its decision-makers work in an office in State C.

74. The defendant kept a pet cougar in a yard that was surrounded by a wire chain-link fence. The plaintiff, who lived in the vicinity, frequently walked on the public sidewalk adjacent to the defendant's yard. One day, while the plaintiff was standing on the public sidewalk looking at the cougar through the defendant's fence, the cougar sprang toward the plaintiff. Because the fence was badly deteriorated, it collapsed under the cougar's weight and fell on the plaintiff, inflicting serious injuries. The defendant knew the fence was in need of repair.

If the plaintiff asserts a negligence claim against the defendant as a result of her injuries, the court should find for

(A) the plaintiff, because the keeping of a wild animal is *prima facie* negligent.

(B) the plaintiff, because a reasonable person in the defendant's position would have repaired the fence.

(C) the plaintiff, because the defendant knew that the fence was in need of repair.

(D) the defendant, because the plaintiff assumed the risk by standing by the fence and looking at the cougar.

75. On March 1, a farmer entered into a written contract with the worker. By its terms, the worker agreed to plow the farmer's fields by April 1, using the worker's own tractor. In return, the farmer promised to pay $2,000 upon completion of the work. On March 25, while the worker was plowing the farmer's field, her tractor broke down. The worker informed the farmer that because the tractor needed extensive repairs, it would be impossible to finish the job by April 1 unless she rented another tractor. The worker said that she could rent one for $600, but she would not do so unless the farmer agreed to add the

rental charge to the worker's fee for preparing the field. The farmer agreed without complaint, afraid that the value of his crop would be reduced if the field was not plowed in time. The worker returned to work after renting a tractor for $600.

After the worker finished plowing the farmer's field, however, the farmer refused to pay her any more than $2,000.

If the worker asserts a claim against the farmer on account of the farmer's promise to pay an additional $600 for the rental of a tractor, which of the following would be the farmer's most effective argument in defense?

(A) The farmer's promise to pay for the tractor rental was not in writing.

(B) The farmer's promise to pay for the tractor rental was unsupported by consideration.

(C) The farmer's promise to pay for the tractor rental was induced by economic duress.

(D) The farmer detrimentally relied on the worker's original promise to complete plowing of the field by April 1 at a price of $2,000.

76. A landowner conveyed a parcel of land "to my son for life, remainder to my daughter." Two years later, without the landowner's permission, the son quitclaimed all of his interest in the land to his wife.

What is the state of the land's title?

(A) Life estate in daughter, remainder in fee simple to landowner.

(B) Fee simple absolute in daughter.

(C) Life estate per autre vie in wife, remainder in fee simple in daughter.

(D) Life estate in wife, remainder in fee simple in daughter.

77. A man went to a car dealer. The dealer showed him a car that he said was "brand new." The man checked the odometer, which showed it had been driven 10 miles, and checked the interior and engine, which looked new. After the man bought the car for $2,000 less than the suggested list price, he discovered the car was actually a used car that had been completely submerged in a flood. On further investigation, he learned the car dealer had rolled back the odometer back from 10,000 miles and had covered up the flood damage with paint.

What crime, if any, can the car dealer be charged with?

(A) Larceny by trick.

(B) False pretenses.

(C) Embezzlement.

(D) No crime.

78. In determining what law to apply in a case brought in federal court based on diversity, which of the following statements is incorrect?

(A) A court of appeals should defer to a district court's decision regarding unsettled state law.

(B) A district court should apply the substantive law of the state in which it sits.

(C) A district court should apply federal procedural law.

(D) A district court should apply the statute of limitations rules of the state in which it sits.

79. A police officer was walking by a home when he heard screaming. The officer ran to the front door, announced himself, and then entered the house. When he went into the kitchen, the officer saw a large amount of cocaine and a scale sitting in an open kitchen

cupboard. He placed both of the men under arrest.

At their trial for drug crimes, the men argued that the court should suppress the evidence against them because their arrests were the result of a warrantless search. What result?

(A) The evidence should be suppressed because the warrantless entry violated the men's Fourth Amendment rights.

(B) The evidence should not be suppressed because the officer could enter the premises without a warrant based on the plain view doctrine.

(C) The evidence should not be suppressed because there were exigent circumstances supporting the officer's warrantless entry.

(D) The evidence should not be suppressed because there was probable cause for the officer to enter the premises to make the arrests.

80. A lumber supplier entered into a contract with a new home builder. The contract stated that the builder would purchase all the wood required by the builder for new homes he was building in 2013, but that in no event would the amount be less than 20,000 board-feet of wood. In making the agreement, neither party contemplated a decline in new home starts. After the agreement, new home starts fell dramatically. As a result, the builder informed the supplier he would not be ordering any wood in 2013.

The supplier sued the builder for damages. At trial, the builder tried to testify that in the home-building industry it was generally understood that minimum requirements set forth in contracts for the supply of wood were of no effect when new home starts fell dramatically. The supplier objected. Should the builder's testimony be admitted?

(A) Yes, because evidence of a regularly observed business practice may be

offered to explain the terms of a written agreement.

(B) No, because the written agreement was intended by the parties to be a final expression of their agreement.

(C) No, because the parties did not contemplate a decline in new home starts.

(D) No, because the fact that the parties specified a minimum requirement of 20,000 board-feet shows that they did not intend to be bound by any preexisting industry standards.

81. A local newspaper published an editorial claiming that the majority of firefighters at the local fire department were dangerously out of shape and had recently failed their physicals. Following publication, several firefighters sued the newspaper for defamation.

All parties agree that the newspaper lacked actual malice in making the statement and that this is the only defense raised by the newspaper. Which of the following arguments would be most likely to result in a judgment for the newspaper?

(A) There is no such thing as a false idea.

(B) The plaintiffs were in a position of apparent control over public affairs.

(C) The editorial and resulting lawsuit made the public familiar with the plaintiffs.

(D) The plaintiffs were public employees.

82. The plaintiff, a manufacturer of police equipment, obtained a patent for a bulletproof vest made entirely of recycled aluminum cans. On April 1, a police department entered into a written contract with the plaintiff providing for the purchase and sale of 30 of the plaintiff's bulletproof vests per month for the next year at a specified price. For the following three months, both parties performed as required by the agreement. On July 5, soon after the third delivery, the plaintiff's only factory burned completely to the ground without any fault on the part of the plaintiff.

On July 10, officials of the police department wrote to the plaintiff, asking whether the plaintiff would continue to deliver as agreed. When the plaintiff failed to respond within a reasonable time, the police department entered into an agreement with another company for the purchase of 30 bulletproof vests per month.

After the police department contracted with another company for the purchase of bulletproof vests, the plaintiff delivered 30 bulletproof vests to the police department, but the police department refused to accept them. If the plaintiff asserts a claim against the police department for breach of contract, which of the following would be the police department's most effective argument in defense against that claim?

(A) The destruction of the plaintiff's factory reasonably appeared to frustrate the purpose of the contract between the police department and the plaintiff.

(B) The plaintiff's failure to respond to the police department's letter of July 10 resulted in a prospective inability to perform.

(C) The plaintiff's contract with the police department was divisible.

(D) The police department's contract to purchase bulletproof vests from another company was a repudiation of its contract with the plaintiff.

83. A group of teenagers hired a stretch limousine for their prom. While driving to the prom, the limousine driver saw a dog crossing the road in front of the vehicle. He swerved to avoid it and ended up crashing into a tree. Several of the teenagers were injured. A state statute required that all limousine drivers carry at least a $100,000 minimum accident liability policy. The limousine driver was uninsured. If the limousine driver is found liable for the teenagers' injuries, it will be

(A) under the doctrine of *res ipsa loquitur*, because an accident like this would not normally occur without negligence.

(B) under the doctrine of *negligence per se*, because the driver violated the state insurance statute.

(C) because his conduct in swerving to avoid the dog was unreasonable.

(D) because he owed a special duty to the teenagers in his care.

84. At the defendant's trial on criminal charges, undisputed evidence established that the defendant and his friend had planned to take a certain coat from the victim's shop by threatening the victim with a pistol carried by the friend; that when they did so, the victim began shooting at them; and that the friend shot back with his pistol, intentionally killing the victim.

Testifying on behalf of the prosecution, the friend stated that the defendant knew that the friend's pistol would be loaded. He also stated that the victim had handed the defendant the coat; that the friend had returned his own gun to his pocket; and that he and the defendant were on their way out of the victim's shop when the victim began shooting at them.

The defendant testified that the coat in question had previously been stolen from her by the victim, and that she and the friend were trying to retrieve it.

Statutes in the jurisdiction define first degree murder as the intentional unlawful killing of a human being, and second degree murder as the unintentional killing of a human being by the defendant or an accomplice during the course of a burglary, robbery, rape, kidnapping, or arson committed by the defendant.

The jury believes the testimony of the defendant but does not believe the testimony of the friend. Which of the following would be the defendant's most effective argument in defense against a charge of second degree murder?

(A) It was unforeseeable that the victim would begin shooting.

(B) The defendant did not know that the friend's pistol would be loaded.

(C) The victim's death did not occur during the course of one of the crimes specified in the applicable statute.

(D) The statute was not intended to impose criminal liability on one person for the acts of another.

85. On February 1, the landowner conveyed a parcel of realty to his cousin as a gift. The landowner executed the deed in the presence of a notary public, and the notary affixed his seal as required by law. On March 1, after the landowner learned that his cousin had not recorded his title, the landowner purported to convey the same parcel of realty to his barber for value. The barber was unaware that the landowner's cousin held any interest in the realty. On March 15, the landowner's cousin recorded the deed that he had received from the landowner in February. On March 17, the barber recorded his deed. In June, the barber executed a deed conveying the realty to the notary. The notary immediately recorded the deed.

A statute in the jurisdiction provides that "Every conveyance of real estate which shall not be recorded is void as against any subsequent purchaser of the same real estate in good faith and for a valuable consideration whose conveyance shall be first duly recorded." In litigation between the landowner's cousin and the notary, who should be declared owner of the realty?

(A) The notary, because the landowner's cousin did not purchase the realty from the landowner for value.

(B) The notary, because the barber recorded his deed prior to conveying the realty to the notary.

(C) The landowner's cousin, because the barber recorded his deed after the landowner's cousin recorded his deed.

(D) The landowner's cousin, because any recording by the barber was outside the chain of title.

86. One night, the defendant looked out his window and saw a robber taking something from his garage. The defendant went outside with a pistol and saw that the robber was already backing down the defendant's driveway in his getaway car. The defendant yelled, "Stop or I'll shoot you right through the windshield!" The robber stopped and started to get out of the car with a large axe in his hand. Before the robber could get to his feet, the defendant shot the robber in the head, killing him instantly. The defendant was charged with manslaughter. At trial, the defendant claimed he acted in self-defense. If the defendant is found guilty of manslaughter, it will because

(A) the harm being defended against was not reasonably imminent.

(B) the defendant used more force than necessary.

(C) the robber had already withdrawn.

(D) the defendant provoked the robber.

87. A man's brother went away for a week on business. The man agreed to stay in his brother's apartment to watch his dogs. While he was staying in the apartment, he smoked marijuana several times. The neighbors called the police to complain about the marijuana smell and told the police the owner was away. The police went to the apartment and knocked on the door. When the man answered the door, the police forced their way in. Once they entered the apartment, they immediately saw a large amount of marijuana on the kitchen table and arrested the man. At trial, the man argued that the search of the apartment was unlawful and the marijuana should be suppressed.

How should the court rule?

(A) The evidence should be suppressed, because the man was staying at the apartment for a week.

(B) The evidence should not be suppressed, because the police officers saw the marijuana in plain view.

(C) The evidence should not be suppressed, because the neighbors smelled the marijuana.

(D) The evidence should not be suppressed, because the man did not own the apartment.

88. The landowner was the owner of a parcel of realty on which there were several buildings and a gold mine. The landowner lived in one of the buildings and personally worked the gold mine, earning a comfortable living by selling the gold that he removed. The other buildings were vacant. When the landowner died, his will devised the realty "to my best friend, but if my best friend should die without issue from his wife, to my accountant." Soon after the landlord's death, the landowner's friend entered into a contract with a mining company. Pursuant to the contract, the company was to work the gold mine for 10 years and to pay the landowner's friend 50 percent of the gross proceeds from the sale of gold removed from the mine. In addition, the landowner's friend leased all the buildings on the realty to the company for 10 years for use by the company employees as living quarters. He never had any children with his wife.

His wife died two years later, and the accountant then demanded that the landowner's friend pay the accountant all funds that the friend would subsequently receive from the company as proceeds of the company's gold mining operation on the realty and as rent on the buildings. The accountant is entitled to receive

(A) proceeds of the gold mining operation only.

(B) rent on the buildings only.

(C) proceeds of the gold mining operation and rent on the buildings.

(D) neither the proceeds of the gold mining operation nor rent on the buildings.

89. A concert promoter sued a rock singer for breach of contract in federal district court after the rock singer failed to perform at a charity concert in State A. The federal district court ruled in favor of the rock singer, finding his signature had been forged on the contract. The concert promoter appealed, arguing the signature was really the rock singer's.

What standard of review should the appellate court use?

(A) De novo, because the validity of the signature is a question of law.

(B) Clearly erroneous, because the validity of the signature is a question of fact.

(C) Abuse of discretion, because the validity of the signature is a question of law.

(D) Abuse of discretion, because the validity of the signature is a question of fact.

90. At the defendant's trial on a charge of rape, the victim testified that on March 1, the defendant forced her to have sexual intercourse with him against her will. Testifying in his own defense, the defendant admitted that he had engaged in sexual intercourse with the victim on that date, but he claimed that the victim had consented. The defendant stated further that the victim had not accused him of rape until April 3, when she discovered that he was married and was living with his wife.

The prosecutor subsequently called the victim's neighbor to the stand. The neighbor testified that while she was conversing with the victim on March 7, the victim suddenly burst into tears and told her that she had been raped by the defendant a week before. Upon objection by the defendant's attorney, the neighbor's statement should be

(A) admitted, because the victim's statement was an excited utterance.

(B) excluded, because it is hearsay not within any exception.

(C) admitted, because it contradicts the defendant's claim that the victim did not accuse him of rape until she learned that he was married.

(D) admitted, because the victim's statement was a present sense impression.

91. A woman was the owner of a parcel of realty on which she lived with her husband. The woman was admitted to a hospital following a severe heart attack. While her husband was visiting her in the hospital, the woman said, "I know I'm dying, and I want to be sure that you have the land after I'm gone. Please have our lawyer take care of it." The following day, the husband asked the family attorney to prepare a quitclaim deed to the land for execution by the woman. The husband brought the document to the woman in the hospital, where she executed it according to the requirements of law. After signing the quitclaim deed, the woman handed the document to the husband and said, "Please put it in the safe deposit box at the bank." The husband did so but never recorded the quitclaim.

The woman subsequently recovered from her heart attack and was moved from the hospital to a rest home, where she resided until 30 years later, when she died from other causes. At the woman's request, the husband continued to occupy, maintain, and pay taxes on the land throughout that period of time. During the last nine years of her life in the rest home, the woman was attended by a nurse. When the woman died, her will purported to leave the land "to my faithful nurse." The husband and the nurse subsequently asserted conflicting claims to the land.

Which of the following arguments would be most likely to lead to a judgment for the nurse?

(A) The husband did not record the quitclaim.

(B) A quitclaim deed is relevant only in disputes between grantor and grantee.

(C) No warranties of seisin or quiet enjoyment are created by a quitclaim deed.

(D) The woman did not intend for the quitclaim to be effective until after her death.

92. A boy decided to play a prank on his babysitter. He took one of his play swords and swung it at his babysitter's head, acting like he was going to hit her (although he had no intention of doing so). The babysitter raised her arms in defense. At the same moment, the boy's little sister walked out of the bathroom, saw her brother swinging the sword, and ducked, thinking she was about to be hit by the sword. Due to a manufacturing defect in the sword, the blade flew off and struck the babysitter in the head. Which statement is most correct?

(A) The boy could not be held liable for battery of the babysitter because he did not have the necessary intent.

(B) The boy's sister could claim assault under the doctrine of transferred intent.

(C) Since the boy only intended to frighten the babysitter, he did not have the necessary intent for assault.

(D) Because the boy did not bear malice or hostility toward the babysitter, he could not be held liable for battery.

93. On March 1, the buyer, a well-known collector of antique automobiles, mailed to a newspaper an advertisement that read, in part: "I will pay $100 for information leading to purchase of an antique car." On March 2, before the advertisement appeared in the newspaper and without knowing about it, the seller phoned the buyer collect and offered to sell him an antique car. The advertisement was published on March 3.

On March 3, a man saw the advertisement and remembered meeting someone who owned an antique car. After calling a few friends, the man obtained the owner's name and address and mailed it to the buyer with a request for the $100 reward.

On March 4, the buyer looked at the seller's antique car and purchased it. Later that day, the buyer mailed to the newspaper for publication a second advertisement that in part read: "No reward for antique car. I hereby withdraw my previous request for information about an antique car." The second advertisement did not appear in the newspaper until March 6.

On March 5, the buyer received the man's letter, but discarded it because he had purchased the seller's antique car.

If the man asserts a claim against the buyer for $100, the court should find for

(A) the buyer, because he mailed the second advertisement before receiving the man's letter.

(B) the buyer, because the man's letter did not lead to the purchase of an antique car.

(C) the man, because he mailed the letter to the buyer before the buyer purchased an antique car.

(D) the man, because the buyer received the man's letter before the second advertisement was published.

94. A man who suffered from severe skin allergies purchased a topical cream online. A statute required the drug manufacturer to insert into the cream's packaging a warning of its potential adverse side effects. The manufacturer failed to insert an appropriate warning of a particular side effect, skin discoloration, into the cream's packaging. The man used the cream for several months until his skin began to turn a dark blue color. Even though the man continued to use the cream, the man

sued. At trial, the man testified that neither he nor anyone in his household ever read warnings that accompanied drugs.

How should the court rule?

(A) In favor of the manufacturer, because no one in the man's household read drug warnings.

(B) In favor of the manufacturer, because the man continued to use the cream.

(C) In favor of the man, because the manufacturer violated the statute by failing to include the warning.

(D) In favor of the man, because the type of harm caused could have been avoided by an adequate warning.

95. A seven-year-old girl was admitted to a hospital unconscious. Doctors who examined her asked the girl's parents to consent to a blood transfusion for the girl, stating that the girl would probably die otherwise. The girl's parents refused, saying that they did not believe in blood transfusions.

A state statute provides that if a child is admitted to a hospital with a life-threatening disease or injury, and the parents of that child refuse to consent to treatment that in the opinion of hospital officials is necessary to save the child's life, the court shall designate the hospital administrator to act as the child's guardian for the purpose of consenting to such treatment. The hospital administrator immediately commenced a proceeding in a state court to have herself declared the girl's guardian under that statute. The girl's parents petitioned a federal court to enjoin the state court from granting the hospital administrator's application on the ground that the state law is unconstitutional on its face. Prior to the disposition of either proceeding, the girl died.

If the proceeding instituted by the girl's parents is dismissed, it will most likely be because

(A) the girl's death has turned the controversy into a non-justiciable political question.

(B) the girl's death has made the proceeding moot.

(C) the court lacks jurisdiction under the Eleventh Amendment.

(D) the issues are not ripe since the highest state court has not yet ruled on the constitutionality of the statute.

96. Because of a deficit in the city budget, the city institutes a "pay-to-throw" system where people must buy special trash bags if they want to throw out their trash. The bags cost $2 a piece, and are burdensome on low-income families. If a person or organization with standing challenges the new system, its constitutionality will be based on

(A) whether the new system has a rational basis.

(B) whether it is necessary to serve a compelling interest of the state.

(C) whether it is found to interfere with a fundamental right.

(D) whether it is found to discriminate against a discrete class of persons.

97. A man was at the beach when he saw a small dog being washed out to sea. He jumped into the ocean and rescued the dog. As soon as the man and the dog were back on the beach, the dog's owner ran up to the man and said, "That's my prize show dog! I promise to pay you $1,000 for rescuing him!" The man accepted. In celebration, the man bought himself a new motorcycle on credit based on his expected reward money. Several months passed, and the man called the dog's owner to ask when he might be paid so he could pay off the motorcycle. The dog owner refused to pay the $1,000 he had promised, claiming it was unsupported by any consideration. Which of the following would be the man's most effective argument in support of his claim?

(A) The dog owner's promise was given in exchange for the man's rescue of his dog.

(B) The dog owner was morally obligated to compensate the man for rescuing his dog.

(C) Allowing the dog owner to avoid compensating the man for rescuing the dog would unjustly enrich the dog owner.

(D) The man detrimentally relied on the dog owner's promise by buying the motorcycle.

98. At the defendant's trial for murder, the prosecution proved that the defendant was driving while intoxicated when his car struck another car, killing all its occupants. The defendant appealed his conviction for voluntary manslaughter.

Which of the cases below is most applicable as precedent?

(A) Believing that the victim was attacking her, the defendant swung a tennis racket at the victim, hoping to frighten the victim away but not meaning to strike the victim with it. The tennis racket struck the victim in the head, causing his death. At the defendant's trial, over the defendant's objection, the judge instructed the jury to find the defendant guilty of involuntary manslaughter if the force used by the defendant was excessive. The defendant's conviction for involuntary manslaughter was affirmed.

(B) The defendant's wife was admitted to the intensive care unit of a hospital following an automobile accident. While visiting her, the defendant overheard doctors saying that there was no hope of saving the life of a certain patient who would be in intense pain and paralyzed for as long as she lived. Mistakenly believing that they were talking about his wife, the defendant subsequently smothered her to death with a pillow while she was asleep in the hospital bed. The defendant was convicted of murder after the court refused to charge the jury that if the defendant believed that his wife was hopelessly ill and in intense pain, they could find him guilty of voluntary manslaughter. The defendant's conviction for murder was reversed.

(C) While the defendant was robbing a tavern, the bartender attempted to grab the defendant's gun. During the struggle, the gun accidentally went off, seriously injuring the bartender. At the defendant's trial for attempted murder, the court instructed the jury to return a verdict of not guilty if they found that the defendant did not intend to cause the bartender's death. The defendant's acquittal was affirmed.

(D) After the defendant quarreled with her lover, she fired a gun at him while he was with his wife. The bullet missed the defendant's lover but struck and killed his wife. At the defendant's trial, it was established that she fired with the intention of frightening both her lover and his wife, but that she did not mean to strike either of them. The defendant was convicted of murder after the court refused to charge the jury on involuntary manslaughter. The conviction was affirmed.

99. After receiving a warrant, police officers went to the defendant's address to arrest him. They arrested the defendant on the street outside his residence and placed him in a police car. The officers then knocked on the front door of the house, and the defendant's girlfriend answered. She gave the officers consent to search a back bedroom she shared with the defendant "most of the time." Inside the bedroom, the officers found drugs and guns.

At trial, the defendant moved to suppress the evidence on the grounds that his girlfriend had no authority to search the bedroom. How should the court rule?

(A) Grant the motion, because the girlfriend only shared the bedroom "most of the time."

(B) Grant the motion, because by her statements it was clear she was not the owner of the property.

(C) Deny the motion, because the girlfriend had joint authority over the bedroom.

(D) Deny the motion, because the police could reasonably believe she could give consent to search the bedroom.

100. A buyer signed a sales contract to buy a new house from the seller. The contract stated that it was "subject to and conditional upon the buyer obtaining a 30-year mortgage from a bank or other lending institution in the amount of $200,000 at an interest rate of less than 2 percent." The buyer went to several banks in the area, but no bank would lend him the money at an interest rate of less than 2 percent. The seller offered to set up a private financing plan between the two parties that would bring the interest rate down to less than 2 percent for the buyer over the course of the loan. The buyer refused to close the deal. The seller argued that with the private financing in place, the net result of the loan was the same and the contract should be enforced.

What is the result of the buyer's failure to obtain an interest rate of less than 2 percent?

(A) The buyer is discharged from his duty to close the sale.

(B) Since the net result of the private financing is the same, the buyer is required to close the sale.

(C) The seller can sue the buyer for specific performance to complete the sale.

(D) The seller can sue the buyer for any damages he suffered under the contract due to the buyer's failure to obtain a loan at less than 2 percent interest.

# QUESTIONS
## PRACTICE MBE—P.M. EXAM

# PRACTICE MBE—P.M. QUESTIONS

101. The homeowner, who owned a home in a residential development, decided to have his driveway paved. He called the plaintiff, a licensed contractor who specialized in residential driveways, and asked for an estimate on the job. Although the standard market price to pave a driveway the size of the homeowner's was $2,750, the plaintiff was willing to do the job for $2,500 since business was slow. The homeowner agreed to hire him to do the job at that price and filled out and signed a detailed work order for the plaintiff's work crew. Since the homeowner was planning to go on vacation for two weeks, he and the plaintiff agreed that the job would be finished by the time the homeowner returned.

Three days later, the plaintiff's work crew went out to do the job described in the homeowner's work order. By mistake, they paved the neighbor's driveway, which was identical to the homeowner's except that it was on a different street. The neighbor was out of town at the time. The job cost the plaintiff $2,600 in labor and materials and increased the value of the neighbor's realty by $2,100. The homeowner did not communicate with the plaintiff while away on vacation. When he returned and discovered that his driveway had not yet been paved, he demanded that the plaintiff perform as agreed, but the plaintiff refused.

The plaintiff asserts a claim against the neighbor on a quasi-contract theory. If the plaintiff is successful, he is entitled to

(A) $2,100 (the increase in the value of the neighbor's realty).

(B) $2,500 (the agreed price in the contract between the plaintiff and the homeowner).

(C) $2,600 (the plaintiff's cost in paving the neighbor's driveway).

(D) $2,750 (the standard price of the paving job).

102. The plaintiff and the defendant, both residents of the state, entered into an installment contract for the sale of goods. When a dispute arose between them under the contract, the plaintiff asserted a claim for $52,000 against the defendant in a United States district court in the state. The defendant moved to dismiss the claim on jurisdictional grounds. A state statute grants concurrent state and federal jurisdiction over contract disputes, and a federal statute grants jurisdiction to hear such a claim to the United States district court.

Did the United States district court have jurisdiction to adjudicate the claim?

(A) Yes, because a statute of the state grants concurrent state and federal jurisdiction over contract disputes.

(B) Yes, because a federal statute grants jurisdiction to hear such a claim to the United States district court.

(C) No, under Article III of the United States Constitution.

(D) No, under the Eleventh Amendment to the United States Constitution.

103. The company was a major corporation with shares of stock traded on several stock exchanges. When rumors began to circulate that the company was experiencing financial difficulties, the price of the company stock fell drastically. The reporter was a journalist who wrote a financial news column for a daily newspaper.

One day, while the reporter was discussing the company rumor with her friend, the friend said, "I wouldn't be surprised if the whole thing was some kind of stunt to manipulate the price of stock." The reporter was aware that the friend knew nothing about the stock market or about the company. The following day, based solely upon what she had heard from the friend, the reporter made the following statement in her column:

> Don't be fooled by rumors that the company is in trouble. Insiders say that the whole thing is a stunt to manipulate the price of the stock. I say the company is still a good investment.

After reading the column, the plaintiff invested in the company's stock in reliance on the reporter's statement. Two days later, the company filed a petition in bankruptcy, and its stock became worthless. If the plaintiff asserts a claim against the reporter for misrepresentation, which one of the following facts or inferences, if it were the only one true, would be most likely to result in a judgment for the reporter?

(A) At the time the plaintiff purchased the company's stock, the company's financial condition was a matter of public record.

(B) The reporter's statement "I think the company is a good investment" was an expression of opinion.

(C) The plaintiff did not purchase the edition of the newspaper that contained the reporter's statement, but read it after finding it on a bus.

(D) The reporter did not know that any person would rely on her statement.

104. Upon borrowing money from her accountant, the landowner executed a note and a mortgage on her realty in favor of her accountant. The accountant immediately and properly recorded the mortgage. One month later, the landowner borrowed money from her brother, executing a note and a mortgage on the realty in her brother's favor. The landowner's brother immediately and properly recorded the mortgage. The landowner died soon afterwards, leaving a will that devised the realty to her nephew for life, remainder to her niece. Her nephew subsequently moved onto the realty. Neither the accountant nor the landowner's brother received payment as required by the notes executed by the landowner.

Without notifying or serving process on the landowner's nephew and niece, the accountant asks a court to order a foreclosure sale of the realty. The court should

(A) order the sale of a life estate only.

(B) order the sale of a remainder only.

(C) order the sale of a fee interest.

(D) deny the accountant's request.

105. The defendant and the victim, who resided in the city, purchased rifles. Because neither of them had ever fired a rifle before, they decided to take them to the municipal dump to try them out. Although both believed that the dump was outside city limits, it was actually within city limits. At the dump, the defendant shot his rifle in the victim's direction, aiming slightly to the right to miss the victim. The bullet struck a rock and ricocheted, hitting the victim in the back and causing his death.

A city ordinance provides that "Any person who shall discharge a firearm knowing that he or she is within the municipal limits shall be guilty of a misdemeanor punishable by a maximum fine of $100." Which of the following is the most serious crime of which the defendant may properly be convicted?

(A) Murder.

(B) Voluntary manslaughter.

(C) Attempted murder.

(D) Discharging a firearm within the municipal limits.

106. The plaintiff asserted a personal injury claim against the defendant for injuries that she sustained when their cars collided at an intersection. At the trial, the witness, an eye-witness to the accident, testified that when it occurred, the traffic light at the intersection was red against the plaintiff. In a prior deposition given under oath, the witness had stated that, at the time of the accident, the light was green in the plaintiff's favor.

The witness was called by the defendant and her testimony was given on direct examination by the defendant's attorney. On cross-examination, the witness authenticated the deposition described above, and the plaintiff's attorney offered it in evidence. Over the defendant's objection, the deposition should be

(A) admitted for impeachment only.

(B) admitted as substantive evidence only.

(C) admitted for impeachment and as substantive evidence.

(D) excluded.

107. A waiter worked for a catering service owned by a chef. One night while the waiter was working a dinner party in State A, he dumped hot soup on a professor. The professor was a citizen of State B and the chef was a citizen of State A. The professor sued the chef in federal district court in State A based on diversity jurisdiction. The professor claimed $100,000 in damages. The professor had the summons served on the chef personally at her kitchen in State A. The chef wanted to implead the waiter as a third-party defendant. The waiter lived in State C, 60 miles away from the district court in State A. The chef had the summons served on the waiter personally at her home. Under State A's long-arm statute, state courts did not have personal jurisdiction over defendants who could not be personally served within the state itself.

Would the federal district court in State A have personal jurisdiction over the chef's third-party claim?

(A) No, because the district court must follow the long-arm statute of State A.

(B) No, because there is no indication the waiter would be liable for at least $75,000 in damages.

(C) Yes, because the waiter lived 60 miles away.

(D) Yes, the chef is diverse from the waiter.

108. Which of the following constitutional provisions is most likely to give Congress the power to pass a law making it a federal crime for persons or corporations in the construction industry to practice racial discrimination in their hiring practices?

(A) The Due Process Clause of the Fifth Amendment.

(B) The Involuntary Servitude Clause of the Thirteenth Amendment.

(C) The Equal Protection Clause of the Fourteenth Amendment.

(D) The Previous Condition of Servitude Clause of the Fifteenth Amendment.

109. On March 1, the seller entered into a written agreement with a licensed real estate broker. By its terms, the seller agreed to pay the broker a commission equal to 6 percent of the price if, prior to April 15, the broker procured a buyer ready, willing, and able to pay $50,000 for the seller's realty. In return, the broker agreed to make reasonable efforts to sell it.

After the agreement was executed, the broker advertised the seller's property and showed it to several prospective buyers. On April 10, the buyer signed a document agreeing to purchase the seller's realty for

$50,000 but stating that her agreement was contingent upon her success in obtaining the necessary financing. The same day, the broker presented to the seller the document that the buyer had signed. The seller read it, thought for a moment, and handed it back to the broker, saying, "I won't even consider a deal built around a contingency." Although the broker protested that the agreement between him and the seller did not specify a sale without contingencies, the seller refused to discuss the matter any further.

On April 11, the broker informed the buyer of the seller's response. The buyer then obtained a cashier's check for $50,000 payable to the seller. She delivered the check to the broker, together with a signed document in which she agreed to purchase the seller's realty for that sum. On April 14, the broker presented the second document to the seller with the cashier's check. The seller said, "I've changed my mind. I'm not interested in selling."

If the broker asserts a claim against the seller for a commission, the court should find for

(A)  the seller, because he did not agree to sell the realty to the buyer.

(B)  the seller, because his rejection of the buyer's offer on April 10 terminated his agreement with the broker.

(C)  the broker, because the seller's oral rejection of the buyer's written offer of April 10 was invalid under the Statute of Frauds.

(D)  the broker, because on April 14 the buyer was ready, willing, and able to purchase the seller's realty for $50,000.

110.  The defendant was speeding in her car 15 miles per hour above the speed limit when the car's steering mechanism failed, causing her to lose control of the vehicle. The vehicle spun approximately 250 degrees

before skidding across the plaintiff's lawn and colliding with the side of the plaintiff's house, causing serious structural damage to the building.

If the plaintiff asserts a claim against the defendant for damage to his realty, the court should find for

(A)  the plaintiff, because the defendant entered his realty without his permission.

(B)  the plaintiff, because the defendant negligently operated her car by speeding.

(C)  the plaintiff, because the defendant had the last clear chance to avoid damaging his realty.

(D)  the defendant, because she was privileged by necessity to enter the plaintiff's realty.

111.  In an action by the plaintiff against the defendant, the plaintiff claimed that the defendant breached a contract to market the plaintiff's products. At trial, the plaintiff testified that she and the defendant had reached an agreement at a conference held in the office of the plaintiff's attorney on October 15. She stated that she and the defendant discussed five separate products on that occasion. On direct examination of the plaintiff, the attorney asked her to name the products that had been discussed. The plaintiff named four of them, but said she could not remember the fifth. After having them properly marked for identification, the attorney offered to show the plaintiff notes that the attorney had made during the conference, asking whether looking at them would refresh the plaintiff's recollection. The defendant's attorney objected to the plaintiff's looking at the notes. The objection should be

(A)  sustained, because the notes had not been made by the plaintiff.

(B)  sustained, because the notes were not in evidence.

(C) sustained, because the attorney's question was leading.

(D) overruled.

112. A state law empowers any municipality within the state to collect a property tax from its landowners if a plan to do so is proposed by its governing body and approved by a majority of its eligible voters. The township is a municipality governed by a Township Council. Pursuant to the above law, the Township Council proposed a property tax plan and scheduled a special election for August 15 to submit the plan for voter approval. The Township Council declared that only persons owning land within the township were eligible to vote in the special election and that eligible voters were required to register for that purpose at the Township Hall between the hours of 1 P.M. and 3 P.M. on Tuesday, July 15. The constitutionality of the special election was challenged in an appropriate proceeding by a petitioner with standing.

If the special election is found to be unconstitutional, it will probably be because

(A) the eligibility requirements violated the Fifteenth Amendment by excluding a discrete class of persons.

(B) the registration requirement had the effect of imposing a residence qualification for voter eligibility.

(C) all persons who did not own land were excluded from the voting process.

(D) conducting the special election on an at-large basis could have the effect of diluting the political power of a particular interest group.

113. The plaintiff was the manufacturer of a chair that she usually sold only to furniture dealers. When the plaintiff recently stopped making the product, she found that she had only 75 of the chairs left. As a result, the plaintiff published the following advertisement in a popular magazine:

For Sale to the Public. Chairs at $100 each (or $80 each in orders of 10 or more). Act fast. There are only 75 left. When they're gone, don't ask for any more.

On February 12, the defendant, a furniture dealer, saw the advertisement and wrote to the plaintiff, "We will purchase all 75 Chairs at the wholesale price."

On February 15, the plaintiff received the defendant's letter and wrote to the defendant, saying, "This will confirm our agreement to the sale of 75 Chairs at $80 each. Shipment to follow immediately."

On February 20, the defendant telephoned the plaintiff to say that he had changed his mind and did not want the chairs after all. Within the next two weeks, the plaintiff sold all the chairs for $80 each to individuals who purchased one chair each.

If the plaintiff asserts a claim against the defendant for damages resulting from breach of contract, the court should award the plaintiff

(A) a sum equivalent to the profit that the plaintiff would have made by selling all the chairs to the defendant.

(B) a sum equivalent to the total of the difference between $100 per chair and the price that the plaintiff actually received.

(C) a sum equivalent to the difference between the price that the defendant had agreed to pay and the actual market value of the chairs.

(D) nothing, because the plaintiff sustained no loss as a result of the defendant's failure to purchase the chairs.

114. The plaintiff brought an action against the defendant for injuries that he sustained when a gas stove that he purchased from the defendant exploded while he was attempting

to use it. At trial, the plaintiff produced a snapshot photograph that he said had been taken by him prior to the accident and which he said was an accurate representation of the stove. On behalf of the defendant, the defendant's employee testified that he had installed the stove. The employee produced a photograph from an advertising brochure and stated that it fairly and accurately represented the stove that the plaintiff had purchased from the defendant and that the employee had installed. The stove in the photograph offered by the defendant was clearly different from the stove in the photograph offered by the plaintiff.

Both photographs were offered into evidence, and each party's attorney objected to admission of the other party's photograph. In response to the objections, the court should

(A)  admit both photographs and allow the jury to decide whether either of them accurately represents the stove in question.

(B)  admit only the photograph offered by the plaintiff.

(C)  admit only the photograph offered by the defendant.

(D)  not admit either photograph.

115.  The landlord, the owner of a seven-story office building, leased the entire sixth floor to an attorney for a period of five years by a written lease that fixed the rent at $2,000 per month. There were only two offices on the sixth floor, identified as Office 6A and Office 6B. A clause in the lease provided that in the event it ever became necessary to determine how the rent payments were apportioned, it was understood that $900 of each month's rent was to be applied to Office 6A, $900 was to be applied to Office 6B, and $200 was to be applied to the hallways and other common areas. The lease prohibited assignment by the attorney without the landlord's written permission and

provided that such permission would not be unreasonably withheld.

One year after executing the lease, the attorney entered into a written agreement with a second attorney. Under its terms, the second attorney was to occupy Office 6A for the balance of the attorney's term at a monthly rental of $1,500 payable to the attorney. The second attorney was an attorney with a better reputation and a more lucrative practice than the first attorney's.

The landlord refused to consent to the attorney's arrangement with the second attorney. The landlord subsequently asserted a claim against the attorney for breaching the lease provision prohibiting assignment. Which of the following would be the attorney's most effective argument in response to that claim?

(A)  The attorney's agreement with the second attorney was not an assignment because the rent paid by the second attorney was not in the same sum as the rent paid by the first attorney.

(B)  The attorney's agreement with the second attorney was not an assignment because it only gave the second attorney the right to occupy part of the sixth floor.

(C)  The clause prohibiting assignment was an invalid restraint on alienation.

(D)  The landlord's refusal to consent was not reasonable because the second attorney's credit was as good as the first attorney's.

116.  The defendant wrote a column about life in suburbia that appeared regularly in a newspaper of general circulation. In one of his columns, the defendant mentioned his neighbor, the plaintiff, by name, and referred to him as "a silly pig." If the plaintiff asserts a defamation claim against the defendant as a result of this reference, which of the following would be the defendant's most effective argument in defense?

(A) The defendant did not have actual malice when he made the statement.

(B) Reasonable persons would not believe that the statement asserted a fact about the plaintiff.

(C) Reasonable persons would not believe the statement to be true.

(D) At the time the defendant made the statement, he was of the opinion that it was an accurate assertion of fact.

117. A brick supplier wrote to a builder, stating "We will sell you bricks at $1 per brick for as many bricks as you would like to purchase, up to 100,000 per quarter." The brick supplier signed the letter. The builder did not refrain from entering any other deals or otherwise rely on the letter, but he did write back, "I accept your offer to sell any bricks I need to me for $1. We will likely order some bricks this summer." The builder signed the letter. Six months later, the builder placed an order for 50,000 bricks at a $1 per brick. The brick supplier responded that due to transportation costs outside of its control, the price of bricks was now $1.50.

The builder sued the supplier for breach of contract. May the builder recover?

(A) Yes, because the offer was in writing and signed by the supplier.

(B) Yes, because the acceptance was in writing and signed by the builder.

(C) No, because the revocation was based on increased transportation costs.

(D) No, because the builder did not provide sufficient consideration.

118. After inheriting a large tract of land, the landowner subdivided it into 60 numbered lots pursuant to state law, filing a plat map and development scheme that indicated that all lots in the subdivision would be restricted to residential use. The landowner thereafter conveyed Lot 1 to his brother and Lot 2 to his sister by deeds containing a condition restricting the lots to residential use.

The landowner's sister announced her intention to erect a motorcycle repair shop on Lot 2, and her brother instituted a proceeding seeking to prevent his sister from doing so. Which of the following additional facts or inferences, if it was the only one true, would be most likely to result in a decision in the brother's favor?

(A) The brother's deed to Lot 1 was recorded prior to his sister's purchase of Lot 2.

(B) The brother purchased Lot 1 before his sister purchased Lot 2.

(C) The brother was aware of the landowner's development scheme when he purchased Lot 1 from the landowner.

(D) The sister was aware of the landowner's development scheme when she purchased Lot 2 from the landowner.

119. The plaintiff was hired as a probationary employee by an agency of the state pursuant to a written contract. The contract provided that at the end of one year, the parties could agree to renew the contract for an additional one-year period, but that either party could, without cause, elect not to renew.

Eleven months after hiring him, the agency informed the plaintiff in writing that his contract would not be renewed at the end of the year. The plaintiff asked the agency for a hearing on his fitness to be rehired, but his request was denied. The plaintiff subsequently instituted a proceeding to challenge the decision of the agency on the ground that its failure to hold a hearing before deciding not to rehire him violated his right to due process.

Which of the following would be the agency's most effective argument in response to the plaintiff's challenge?

(A) Due process was not required, since the decision not to rehire the plaintiff did not deprive him of life, liberty, or property.

(B) State employment is a privilege rather than a right, since no person is guaranteed employment by the state.

(C) There would be no point in holding a hearing in the plaintiff's case, since the hearing officer would be an employee of the agency and the findings would necessarily support the decision already made by the agency.

(D) The plaintiff's constitutional rights could not have been violated by the decision not to renew his contract, since the contract provided that the decision could be made without cause.

120. The plaintiff purchased realty in the county in 2000 and has lived on it since then. The realty is located approximately one mile from a private airport owned and operated by the defendant. At the time of the plaintiff's purchase, county ordinances restricted the use of the defendant's airport to aircraft of a particular type. Noise from the airport was not disturbing to the plaintiff. Recently, however, the county adopted an ordinance allowing other kinds of aircraft to use the airport. Since then, noise levels from the airport have increased, disturbing the quiet atmosphere of the plaintiff's home.

If the plaintiff desires to assert a claim against the defendant on account of noise from the airport, which of the following would be his most effective theory of recovery?

(A) Private nuisance.

(B) Prescriptive aeronautical easement.

(C) Inverse condemnation.

(D) Continuing trespass.

121. While the defendant and his wife were standing in line outside a movie theater, the defendant whispered to his wife that he had committed a series of robberies the previous week. The defendant was subsequently arrested and charged with the robberies in a jurisdiction that holds that confidential marital communications are privileged.

A prosecution witness attempted to testify that he overheard the defendant's whispered statement to his wife while standing behind them in the movie line. If the defendant objects to this testimony, his objection should be

(A) sustained, because communications made within a marriage are presumed to be confidential.

(B) sustained, because the statement is inadmissible hearsay.

(C) overruled, because the statement is admissible as an admission.

(D) overruled, because a communication concerning a crime is not subject to the marital privilege.

122. After he was fired, a man filed suit in state court in State A against a company. The man's complaint alleged a single federal discrimination claim and a number of state law claims. The company removed the case to federal district court. The man then amended his complaint to remove the discrimination claim because he believed it was untenable and moved to have the case remanded to state court.

May the federal district court remand the case to state court?

(A) No, because the case must be dismissed.

(B) No, because the state claims were in federal court based on pendent jurisdiction.

(C) Yes, because the claim was originally brought in state court.

(D) Yes, because of judicial economy.

123. The defendant was charged with assaulting the victim. At the trial, the victim testified that he accidentally bumped into the defendant while walking on a crowded street, and that the defendant responded by repeatedly hitting and punching him. As part of his defense, the defendant denied that he had ever struck any person intentionally and testified that any contact between the victim and him had been accidental.

The prosecutor subsequently called a witness. The witness testified that she and the defendant were divorced, but that she had been married to him for 10 years. She stated that during the period of their marriage, the defendant had frequently struck her with his fists in public places. The jurisdiction recognized a privilege for marital communications. If the defendant's attorney objects and asks the court to exclude the witness's testimony, the testimony should be

(A) excluded, because the jurisdiction recognizes a privilege for marital communications.

(B) excluded, because it is not relevant to a material issue.

(C) admitted, because it bears on the defendant's reputation for truth and veracity.

(D) admitted, because the defendant testified in his own defense.

124. The plaintiff showed his silver coins to the defendant and asked whether the defendant would be interested in trading them for chickens. After inspecting the coins, the defendant and the plaintiff placed them in a bag that they sealed together and left with a banker whom they both knew. Then, in a writing signed by both of them, they agreed to the trade.

Pursuant to the terms of their agreement, the defendant was to deliver 6,000 fryer chickens to the plaintiff on July 1, at which time the bag of coins would be turned over to the defendant as payment in full. In May, weather conditions were such that the price of fryer chickens increased to three times what it had been when the agreement was signed. Although it was foreseeable that the market price for fryer chickens would change dramatically, neither party knew that the marker price of fryer chickens would change,

On July 1, the defendant refused to deliver 6,000 fryer chickens to the plaintiff. If the plaintiff asserts a claim against the defendant for breach of contract, the court should find for

(A) the defendant, because neither party knew that the market price of fryer chickens would change.

(B) the defendant, because the likelihood of fluctuation in the value of money makes this contract aleatory.

(C) the plaintiff, because it was foreseeable that the market price of fryer chickens would change dramatically.

(D) the plaintiff, because the transaction was not a sale as defined by the UCC.

125. The defendant, a water supply company, owned a well adjacent to the plaintiff's land. By a conveyance that properly described the size and location of the easement, the plaintiff granted the defendant an easement across his realty "for the installation of underground pipe or pipes for the transport of water to customers of the defendant." Pursuant to the easement, the defendant subsequently installed a single underground pipe across the plaintiff's land. After the installation, the defendant regularly entered the plaintiff's land to service its underground pipe, occasionally excavating for that purpose. Twenty years after the easement had been granted, construction of a nearby housing

development caused the number of the defendant's customers to double, making it necessary for the defendant to transport more water than the single pipe could carry. The defendant notified the plaintiff that it planned to install a second underground pipe alongside the first within the area over which the defendant had an easement. The plaintiff objected and instituted an appropriate proceeding to stop the defendant from installing a second underground pipe.

Which of the following arguments would be most likely to result in a judgment for the plaintiff?

(A) Twenty years of continuous use by the defendant established the scope of the easement.

(B) The initial installation of a single pipe by the defendant established the scope of the easement.

(C) When the easement was granted, neither party could have anticipated that the number of the defendant's customers would double.

(D) The plaintiff's grant to the defendant did not specify the number of pipes that could be installed.

126. By a contract calling for the delivery of marketable title, the seller agreed to sell the buyer a parcel of realty consisting of four adjacent lots. On the date set for closing, the seller informed the buyer that one of the four lots was encumbered by a utility company easement. The seller said that it was unlikely that the utility company would ever attempt to exercise its easement and offered to either execute a general warranty deed to the entire parcel, including a covenant against encumbrances, or to convey the remaining three lots to the buyer, deducting from the purchase price the reasonable value of the encumbered lot. The buyer refused both offers.

In litigation between the seller and the buyer for breach of contract, a court should find for

(A) the seller, because a covenant against encumbrances would have given the buyer sufficient protection.

(B) the seller, because title to the remaining three lots was marketable and abatement of the purchase price would assure the buyer of receiving the value for which he had bargained.

(C) the buyer, because the seller knew of the easement at the time the contract of sale was formed.

(D) the buyer, because the seller failed to deliver marketable title.

127. At the trial of a personal injury action brought by the plaintiff against the defendant and arising out of an automobile accident, the plaintiff attempted to testify that immediately following the accident, the defendant offered to pay $500 to fix the plaintiff's car. Over objection by the defendant's attorney, the plaintiff's statement should be

(A) excluded, because to admit such evidence would violate public policy.

(B) admitted, because the court could give the defendant an opportunity to explain his offer.

(C) admitted, as a declaration against the defendant's pecuniary interest.

(D) admitted, as an implied admission of a party.

128. The defendant was out walking when she saw the plaintiff, a seven-year-old child, suddenly chase a ball into the street in the path of a car driven by a driver. Afraid that the plaintiff would be hit by the car, the defendant ran into the roadway and pushed the plaintiff out of the way. The driver's car struck the defendant. The plaintiff was not hit by the driver's car, but he hurt his knees when he fell to the ground as a result of being pushed by the defendant. The jurisdiction applies the all-or-nothing rule of contributory negligence.

If the plaintiff asserts a negligence claim against the defendant for the injuries to his knees, which one of the following additional facts or inferences, if it was the only one true, would be most likely to result in a judgment for the defendant?

(A) The plaintiff's injury was proximately caused by the negligence of the driver.

(B) If the defendant had not pushed him out of the way, the plaintiff would have been struck by the driver's car and killed.

(C) The defendant was severely injured as a result of being struck by the driver's car.

(D) The situation confronted the defendant with an emergency.

129. At a jury trial, the defendant was convicted of aggravated assault. On appeal, the defendant's conviction was reversed on the ground that, as a matter of law, the evidence against her was insufficient to establish guilt beyond a reasonable doubt. Subsequently, the prosecutor attempted to try the defendant again on the same charge. If the defendant asserts that the subsequent prosecution violates the constitutional protection against double jeopardy and moves to dismiss it, her motion should be

(A) denied, because the reversal of her conviction ended any jeopardy that attached as a result of the initial prosecution.

(B) denied, because the reversal amounted to a declaration that the trial was a nullity and that she had, therefore, never been in jeopardy as a result of the initial prosecution.

(C) denied, because the defendant waived the constitutional protection against double jeopardy by appealing her conviction.

(D) granted.

130. After he was injured during surgery, a man sued a doctor in federal district court. The doctor's lawyer hired a private investigator, who interviewed several witnesses to the surgery, including the head nurse. The investigator filmed all of the interviews with his phone and made transcripts of them. During the head nurse's interview, she stated certain facts regarding what happened during the surgery that were only known to the head nurse. Shortly after the interview, the head nurse died. Is the man entitled to a copy or transcript of the interview?

(A) Yes, because the head nurse is dead.

(B) Yes, because the investigator was the one who filmed and transcribed the interviews.

(C) No, because the interview was prepared in anticipation of litigation.

(D) No, because the interview was prepared by another on the attorney's behalf.

131. The state published an advertisement calling for bids "for a contract to be the exclusive supplier of fuel for state vehicles." The plaintiff submitted a bid and, after negotiation, entered into a written contract to supply at a specified price per gallon for a period of one year "all fuel ordered by the state." Several months after executing the contract, the plaintiff learned that the state was purchasing substantial amounts of fuel from other suppliers.

The plaintiff asserted a claim against the state for breach of contract. At the trial, state attorneys offered the written contract into evidence and pointed out that its language did not specifically state that the plaintiff was to be the exclusive supplier. When the plaintiff attempted to offer a copy of the advertisement calling for bids into evidence, state attorneys objected on the ground that the advertisement was inadmissible under the parol evidence rule. The plaintiff's most effective argument in response to the state's objections would be that the advertisement

(A)  tends to show that the written contract was ambiguous.

(B)  was in writing.

(C)  was a communication that led to a written contract.

(D)  was an invitation to negotiate.

132.  In 2008, the landowner conveyed a parcel of realty to her oldest son in fee simple absolute as a gift. At the landowner's request, the oldest son did not record the conveyance. In 2010, the landowner borrowed $10,000 from a neighbor, executing a note purporting to be secured by a mortgage on the land. The neighbor did not record the mortgage. In 2012, the landowner purported to convey the land in fee simple to her youngest son as a gift. The youngest son immediately recorded the deed. On default by the landowner, the neighbor now seeks to foreclose on the land.

A statute in the jurisdiction provides that "No transfer of an interest in real property shall be good and effectual in law or equity against creditors or subsequent purchasers for value and without notice unless it shall be recorded."

Is the neighbor entitled to foreclose on the land?

(A)  No, because his mortgage was not recorded.

(B)  No, because the youngest son recorded his deed in 2012.

(C)  Yes.

(D)  No, because the oldest son owns the land in fee simple absolute.

133.  The plaintiff bought from the defendant, a car dealer, a new car manufactured by the manufacturer. The vehicle was equipped with a seat belt warning indicator, although the law did not require such a device. The indicator was designed to cause a bright red light on the dashboard to begin glowing when the engine was started and to remain lit until the driver's seat belt was fastened. When the car was delivered to the plaintiff, an employee of the defendant explained to the plaintiff that the seat belt warning indicator was not working, but that the defendant would repair it without charge as soon as the necessary parts were received.

The following day, the plaintiff was involved in an accident while driving the new car. As a result of the impact, she was thrown from the vehicle and sustained an injury when her head struck the pavement. If she had been wearing a seat belt at the time, she would not have been injured.

The plaintiff subsequently asserted a claim against the defendant for her injuries on the ground that the failure of the seat belt warning indicator made the vehicle defective. Which of the following would be the defendant's most effective argument in response to that allegation?

(A)  When the plaintiff drove the vehicle, she was aware that the seat belt warning indicator was not working.

(B)  The law did not require the vehicle to be equipped with a seat belt warning indicator.

(C)  It is impossible to prove with certainty that the plaintiff would have worn a seat belt if the seat belt warning indicator had been working.

(D)  The failure of the seat belt warning indicator was the result of the negligence of the manufacturer.

134.  A man owned a home worth $200,000. He had three mortgages on the property. The first mortgage was for $150,000 and was owed to first bank. The second mortgage was for $30,000 and was owed to second bank. The third mortgage was for $10,000 and was owed to third bank. The first

mortgage was foreclosed, and the bid at the foreclosure sale was $200,000. The attorney's fees and foreclosure expenses were $15,000, and the accrued interest on the first mortgage was $5,000.

How will the funds from the foreclosure sale be distributed?

(A) $5,000 to the accrued interest, $15,000 to attorneys and foreclosure expenses, $150,000 to the first mortgage, $30,000 to the second mortgage, and nothing to the third mortgage.

(B) $5,000 to the accrued interest, $15,000 to attorneys and foreclosure expenses, $150,000 to the first mortgage, $20,000 to the second mortgage, and $10,000 to the third.

(C) $5,000 to the accrued interest, $15,000 to attorneys and foreclosure expenses, $140,000 to the first mortgage, $30,000 to the second mortgage, and $10,000 to the third mortgage

(D) $15,000 to attorneys and foreclosure expenses, $150,000 to first mortgage, $30,000 to second mortgage, $5,000 to third mortgage, nothing to the accrued interest.

135. After the plaintiff instituted litigation against the defendant, the defendant's attorney demanded that the plaintiff furnish the answers to a list of interrogatories as provided by the state code of civil procedure. Interrogatory #4 was "List the plaintiff's gross sales receipts for each month during the four-year period in controversy." In response to this interrogatory, the plaintiff responded, "Gross receipts for the period in question are contained in an industry publication." The court provided judicial notice that the industry publication was a reputable source that reasonably well informed people regarded as accurate.

At trial, the defendant's attorney attempted to offer into evidence those portions of the industry publication listing the plaintiff's gross receipts for the months in question. Upon objection by the plaintiff's attorney, the court should rule those portions of the industry publication

(A) inadmissible, because the contents of the industry publication have not been shown to be accurate.

(B) inadmissible as hearsay not within any exception.

(C) admissible as an admission of a party.

(D) admissible, because the industry publication was shown to be a reputable source that reasonably well informed people regard as accurate.

136. After the victim lost all his money to the defendant in a dice game, the two men began to argue. During the course of the argument, the defendant stabbed the victim in the leg with a knife. The victim staggered home and pounded on the door, begging his wife to let him in. The wife realized that the victim needed medical attention because he was bleeding badly, but she was so angry at him for gambling that she refused to open the door or call a doctor. The victim collapsed on the doorstep and died an hour later from loss of blood. The wife could have secured immediate medical attention for the victim, and if she had done so, the victim would not have died.

If the defendant is prosecuted for the murder of the victim, which of the following would be his most effective argument in defense?

(A) The defendant did not cause the victim's death because the victim would not have died if the wife had secured prompt medical attention.

(B) Leg wounds do not usually result in death.

(C) It was unforeseeable that the wife would refuse to secure medical attention for the victim when she knew that he needed it so badly.

(D)  The wife's omission to secure medical attention was a substantial factor in producing the victim's death.

137.  A state statute grants state employees an annual 5 percent salary increase. Another statute provides that upon retirement, a state employee shall receive an annual pension equivalent to 60 percent of the salary received during the year immediately prior to retirement. The state also maintains a group health insurance plan for state employees. After determining that the health insurance plan could be operated less expensively if it did not include persons over the age of 65, the state legislature passed a compulsory retirement law requiring state employees to retire at the age of 65.

The plaintiff, who was employed by the state as a station engineer, reached the age of 65 several years after the compulsory retirement law was passed. His job did not require any skills or abilities related to age. When he was informed that he was required to retire, the plaintiff challenged the constitutionality of the mandatory retirement law. In support of his challenge, the plaintiff proved that a federal law permits station engineers employed by the federal government to continue working until they are 70.

In deciding the plaintiff's claim, the court should hold that the state's mandatory retirement law is

(A)  invalid under the Supremacy Clause.

(B)  invalid, because the plaintiff's job did not require skills or abilities that were related to age.

(C)  valid, because the state could operate its employee health insurance plan on a more economically efficient basis by mandating retirement at 65.

(D)  valid, because the federal government may not impose economic burdens on the state.

138.  A banker, a citizen of State A, was injured in a car accident with a doctor, a citizen of State A, and a lawyer, a citizen of State B. The banker sued both the doctor and the lawyer in state court for $100,000. The banker then voluntarily dismissed the doctor. Twenty-five days later, the lawyer sought removal to the federal district court.

May the lawsuit be removed to federal court?

(A)  Yes, because there is now complete diversity of citizenship.

(B)  Yes, because the lawyer sought removal within 30 days of the doctor's dismissal.

(C)  No, because the lawyer did not seek removal within 14 days of the doctor's dismissal.

(D)  No, because the banker voluntarily dismissed the doctor.

139.  The Department of Highway Transportation is the agency of state government responsible for maintaining state highways. While driving on a state highway, the defendant attempted to pass the plaintiff's vehicle on the right. As she did so, one of the defendant's wheels struck a pothole, causing her car to go out of control and strike the plaintiff's car. The pothole existed because the Department of Highway Transportation was negligent in maintaining the road surface, and there were many potholes in the area. The defendant would not have lost control of her car if she had not hit the pothole while driving at an unreasonably fast rate of speed. A statute in the jurisdiction prohibits passing on the right. The jurisdiction has also abolished the concept of governmental immunity.

The plaintiff subsequently asserted a negligence claim against the defendant for injuries sustained in the accident. If the defendant's only argument in defense is that the pothole was a superseding cause of harm, the court should find for

(A) the plaintiff, because the defendant's attempt to pass the plaintiff on the right was a violation of an automobile safety statute.

(B) the plaintiff, because potholes are often found on the road surfaces where the accident occurred.

(C) the plaintiff, because the concept of governmental immunity has been abolished in the jurisdiction.

(D) the defendant, because the accident would not have happened but for the existence of the pothole.

140. The plaintiff had an exclusive five-year contract to sell products manufactured by the defendant. When the defendant canceled the contract in its third year, the plaintiff entered into a similar contract with another manufacturer. The plaintiff then asked an attorney to sue the defendant for breach of contract. Because the compensation plans in the plaintiff's contracts with the defendant and the other company were extremely complex, the attorney was unable to determine whether the defendant's breach had damaged the plaintiff. Before agreeing to represent the plaintiff, the attorney therefore arranged for the plaintiff to meet with the witness, an accountant. At the attorney's request, the witness interviewed the plaintiff, obtained certain facts from her, and made mathematical calculations that she submitted to the attorney.

The attorney subsequently commenced a lawsuit against the defendant on the plaintiff's behalf. At the trial, the defendant's attorney called the accountant as a witness and attempted to question her about her interview with the plaintiff. If the attorney objects to the examination of the witness, the most effective argument in support of her objection would be that statements made by the plaintiff to the witness are

(A) privileged as part of an attorney's work product.

(B) records kept in the course of business.

(C) inadmissible hearsay.

(D) confidential communications between client and attorney.

141. A man and a woman were residents of a local housing project in the center of the city. Because the housing project was thought of as a hotbed of crime and gang activity, the city wanted to tear down the project and relocate the project's 800 residents to several smaller apartment buildings spread out among the far suburbs. The man and the woman filed suit against the city housing authority in federal district court, claiming that the city's plan violated their federal due process rights. The man and the woman wanted to certify a class made up of the current project residents. The best law firm in the city agreed to take the case, and the man and the woman were longtime residents of the project who each owned small successful businesses. Their action sought an injunction to stop the planned demolition and relocation from going forward.

Can the action go forward as a class action?

(A) Yes, because the injunction would likely be worth more than $75,000.

(B) Yes, because the requested injunction is appropriate to the class as a whole.

(C) No, because a class action cannot be based on a request for an injunction.

(D) No, because joinder of the project residents would be more appropriate.

142. A man was negligently flying his new drone when it hit a woman walking on the sidewalk nearby. According to Federal Aviation Authority law, drones were aircraft that needed to be registered. The man's drone was not. The drone did not hit the woman very hard, but it did cause her to fall on the ground. Although an ordinary person would have suffered at most slight scrapes or bruises, the woman had a rare brain condition that made any fall extremely dangerous to her optic nerves. Because of the fall, the woman's optic nerves disconnected and she became blind. The woman sued the man for damages related to loss of her sight.

May the woman recover?

(A) Yes, because the man failed to register his drone.

(B) Yes, because the man negligently hit her with the drone.

(C) No, because the blindness was caused by the woman's rare medical condition.

(D) No, because an ordinary person would only have suffered slight scrapes or bruises.

143. At the jury trial of an action by a bank against the defendant on a promissory note, the defendant testified that the signature on the note was not his. An employee of the bank testified that she recognized the signature as the defendant's. The judge believed the signature on the promissory note was the defendant's. Accordingly, the judge decided that the evidence was sufficient to support a finding that the signature on the note was the defendant's. The jury was also given an authenticated sample of the defendant's signature so that they could decide whether the signature on the promissory note was the defendant's.

If the bank's attorney offers the promissory note into evidence, it should be

(A) admitted, because any dispute regarding the genuineness of a signature should be decided by the jury.

(B) admitted, because the judge decided that the evidence was sufficient to support a finding that the signature on the note was the defendant's.

(C) admitted, because the jury was given an authenticated sample of the defendant's signature so that they could decide whether the signature on the promissory note was the defendant's.

(D) admitted, because the judge believed that the signature on the promissory note was the defendant's.

144. A plaintiff belongs to an ethnic minority that constitutes 10 percent of the general population of the city. Approximately 10 percent of the motorists driving on a particular road are members of the plaintiff's ethnic minority. One day, while the plaintiff was driving her automobile on the road, a police officer stopped her and issued a traffic summons charging her with driving in excess of the statutory speed limit. In her defense, the plaintiff asserted that the traffic statute was unconstitutional as applied.

Which one of the following additional facts or inferences, if it were the only one true, would best support the plaintiff's assertion?

(A) In the past two years, the plaintiff has received three such summonses from the officer, but she has never received one from another officer.

(B) In the past two years, the officer has issued a total of 300 summonses for driving in excess of the statutory speed limit on the road, all of which were issued to members of the plaintiff's ethnic group.

(C) Properly compiled statistics indicate that members of the plaintiff's ethnic group do not customarily drive faster than members of any other ethnic group.

(D) At the time the officer issued the summons to the plaintiff, many people who did not belong to the plaintiff's ethnic group were driving on the road at speeds in excess of the plaintiff's speed, and the officer did not issue summonses to any of them.

145. A defendant knew that he often became intoxicated upon drinking small quantities of alcoholic beverages. He frequently visited the neighborhood tavern because he liked the atmosphere, but he usually ordered orange juice or some other non-alcoholic beverage. While at the tavern one night, the defendant drank half of a friend's glass of beer. Soon afterwards, he began shouting and throwing objects about the tavern. A chair that he hurled across the room struck the bartender, injuring her severely. As a result, the defendant was subsequently arrested and prosecuted. At the defendant's trial, the defense attorney called a psychiatrist to the witness stand to testify that the defendant suffered from a mental illness that made him extremely susceptible to the effects of alcohol. The psychiatrist offered to testify further that even a small quantity of beer was likely to make the defendant become physically violent, and that when this happened to him, he was not aware that his conduct would result in injury to others.

The defendant's prosecution was for criminal battery. If the prosecutor moves to exclude the psychiatrist's testimony, the motion should be

(A) granted, because the defendant knew that he often became intoxicated upon drinking small quantities of alcoholic beverages.

(B) granted, because the sanity of a defendant is a question of fact to be determined by a jury.

(C) denied, because a jury might find that the defendant's intoxication prevented

him from forming the intent to injure the bartender.

(D) denied, because that testimony could establish that the defendant's intoxication was involuntary.

146. The buyer and the seller signed a written document agreeing to the sale of the seller's realty to the buyer. The document adequately described the realty, required the seller to deliver marketable title by a general warranty deed, and set the date for closing. It also stated that the price would be determined by agreement of the parties prior to the date of closing. The value of real estate in the area could be objectively determined rather easily. Three weeks before the date set for closing, the buyer telephoned the seller to discuss the price of the realty. At that time, the seller told the buyer that she had changed her mind and would not sell the realty to the buyer at any price. If the buyer asserts a claim against the seller for breach of contract, the court should find for

(A) the seller, because the Statute of Frauds requires a contract for the sale of realty to be in writing and to state the price.

(B) the seller, because the parties did not agree on a method for determining the price.

(C) the buyer, because the value of real estate in the area can be objectively determined.

(D) the buyer, because where a written contract omits the price term, the price is to be a reasonable price.

147. The defendant was a college student preparing to take an important exam. Before the exam, she sneaked into the professor's office, hoping to steal a copy of the exam answer. The exam answer was locked securely in the dean's safe, however, and the defendant was therefore unable to find it. While she was looking, the professor discovered her in his office, and the defendant told him her reason for being there.

A state statute prohibits the theft of certain specifically defined "information," which specifically included "exam answers." The defendant did not believe an exam answer was "information" under the statute. If the defendant is charged with attempting to violate the statute, she should be found

(A) not guilty, because the exam answers were, in fact, securely locked in the dean's safe and the defendant could not possibly have stolen them.

(B) not guilty, because an exam answer is "information" as defined by the statute, but the defendant believed that it was not.

(C) guilty, because the theft of an exam answer by one preparing to take the exam is "inherently immoral."

(D) guilty, because an exam answer is "information" as defined by the statute, even though the defendant believed that it was not.

148. A group of friends were playing a pickup soccer game. The plaintiff was dribbling the ball down the field when the defendant kicked the ball away, tripping the plaintiff and injuring him. If the plaintiff sues the defendant for battery, the defendant's best defense is

(A) by playing in the game, the plaintiff assumed the risk of the contact.

(B) by playing in the game, the plaintiff consented to the contact.

(C) the defendant did not intend to injure the plaintiff

(D) being tripped in a soccer game is not offensive to a reasonable sense of dignity.

149. A will devised a parcel of real estate to a brother and his sister as joint tenants with full right of survivorship. The brother died after quitclaiming his interest in the realty to his wife. Subsequently, the sister died, leaving a will that purported to devise her interest in the realty to her daughter. Which of the following statements most accurately describes the rights of the wife and the daughter after the deaths of the brother and the sister?

(A) The wife is the sole owner of the realty.

(B) The daughter is the sole owner of the realty.

(C) The wife and the daughter hold the realty as joint tenants.

(D) The wife and the daughter hold the realty as tenants in common.

150. Congress authorizes a federal agency to lease federally owned land to livestock ranchers for grazing purposes at specified rental rates. The plaintiff also owns land in the area that it leases for grazing purposes. The plaintiff complains that the rates charged by the federal agency are significantly lower than those charged by the plaintiff and that this has resulted in unfair competition that will cause the plaintiff an immediate loss of revenue. In an appropriate proceeding, the plaintiff challenges the constitutionality of the federal lease.

Which of the following arguments would be most effective **IN OPPOSITION TO** the plaintiff's claim?

(A) The Property Clause of Article IV of the Constitution empowers Congress to dispose of federal land as it sees fit.

(B) The lease of federal land is valid under the Commerce Clause.

(C) The plaintiff lacks standing because the activities of the federal agency do not affect it directly.

(D) The federal government is immune from claims based on allegations of unfair competition.

151. A breeder agreed to sell a farmer a cow, which both parties believed to be barren.

The contract price was $200. Prior to delivery of the cow, the breeder realized the cow was pregnant and refused to deliver her because her value as a breeding cow was at least $1,000. May the breeder rescind the contract?

(A) Yes, because the characteristic on which the parties were mistaken was a basic assumption of the contract.

(B) Yes, because the cow is worth much more as a breeding cow.

(C) No, because the mistake merely went to the adequacy of price.

(D) No, because the farmer merely received an unexpected benefit in the deal.

152. At the trial of a robbery prosecution, a witness for the prosecution testified that the robber walked with a limp. While the witness was on the stand, the prosecutor asked the defendant to walk across the courtroom. If the defendant objects, asserting his Fifth Amendment privilege against self-incrimination, his objection should be

(A) sustained, because the defendant has not waived the privilege by testifying in his own behalf.

(B) sustained, because the jury is likely to interpret a refusal by the defendant to walk across the courtroom as evidence that he is guilty.

(C) overruled, because the Fifth Amendment privilege applies only to testimony.

(D) overruled, because the defendant has waived the privilege by personally appearing in the courtroom.

153. Following her indictment by a grand jury for bank robbery, the defendant voluntarily surrendered at police headquarters.

The officers went to lunch and returned to headquarters an hour later. Upon their return, they ordered the defendant to appear in a lineup for identification purposes in connection with the bank robbery. At first, the defendant refused. When the officer threatened to use force to compel her appearance, however, the defendant appeared without resisting. Witnesses at the lineup identified her as the bank robber.

If the defendant objects to the admission of evidence of the lineup identification, which of the following would be her most effective argument in support of her objection?

(A) The defendant was deprived of her right to have an attorney present during the lineup.

(B) The lineup deprived the defendant of the right to confront her accusers.

(C) The lineup violated her right against self-incrimination.

(D) Police officers coerced the defendant into appearing in the lineup.

154. A man was snowmobiling with his friend as a passenger. The man negligently cut across a road and an oncoming car struck the snowmobile. The friend was severely injured. The driver of the car called an ambulance, and the ambulance picked up the friend. Because of the serious nature of the friend's injuries, the ambulance drove in excess of the speed limit and crashed into a pole. The friend was killed in the crash. The friend's estate sued the man.

Assuming the estate may recover for the injuries sustained during the initial car crash, can it recover for the friend's death?

(A) No, because the ambulance broke the chain of liability.

(B) No, because the ambulance was negligent by speeding.

(C) Yes, because the ambulance's rescue attempt was foreseeable.

(D) Yes, because the death was preceded by the friend's serious injuries.

155. By a properly executed and recorded deed, the landowner conveyed a parcel of real estate with a building on it as follows:

> to the church for as long as the land is used by the church for church purposes; and when the land ceases to be so used, to the hospital for as long as the land shall be used by the hospital for hospital purposes; and when the land ceases to be so used, to my son if my son is then living.

The church moved onto the real estate, using the building as a house of worship.

If the validity of the interest held by the son is challenged on the sole ground that it violates the Rule Against Perpetuities, the interest of the son should be declared

(A) valid, because the church and the hospital are charitable institutions.

(B) valid.

(C) void, because there is no assurance that the interest of the son will vest during the period established by the Rule Against Perpetuities.

(D) void, because the interest of the hospital is void.

156. After a nuclear power plant was built in the state, the state passed the Nuclear Waste Act. The Act regulates the storage of radioactive wastes and authorizes the construction of radioactive waste storage facilities at specified locations within the state. Section 40 of the Act provides that "No radioactive waste storage facility in the state shall store or accept for storage any radioactive waste resulting from activities conducted more than five miles from said storage facility." All storage facilities within the state that are authorized by the Nuclear Waste Act are located more than five miles from the state line.

If the constitutionality of Section 40 is challenged in an appropriate proceeding, it is **LEAST** likely to be declared unconstitutional under the

(A) Privileges and Immunities Clause of Article IV.

(B) Privileges and Immunities Clause of the Fourteenth Amendment.

(C) Equal Protection Clause of the Fourteenth Amendment.

(D) Due Process Clauses of the Fifth and Fourteenth Amendments.

157. A married couple lived in State A. The wife moved to State B and filed for divorce in State B state court. The husband was visiting State B on business and to see his daughters when he was served with the divorce papers. In a special appearance, the husband moved to quash service, arguing he had insufficient contacts with State B to confer personal jurisdiction.

Does the State B court have personal jurisdiction over the husband?

(A) Yes, because the divorce action was filed in state court in State B.

(B) Yes, because the husband was personally served in State B.

(C) No, because the husband was only in State B on business and to see his daughters.

(D) No, because there is no indication the husband consented to jurisdiction.

158. The security guard of a warehouse was making his rounds after closing time one night when he found the defendant walking around inside the warehouse. When the guard asked him what he was doing there, the defendant replied that he had been driving past the warehouse when he noticed that its door was open, and that he had entered to report this to the guard. The guard called the police, and the defendant was arrested and charged with violating a statute providing that "any person entering the building

of another for the purpose of committing a crime therein is guilty of burglary."

At the defendant's trial, the prosecutor tried to prove that the defendant's van, parked outside the warehouse at the time of the defendant's arrest, had license plates on it that had been stolen from an out-of-state vehicle the day before the defendant's arrest.

Over objection by the defendant's attorney, evidence that the license plates had been stolen should be

(A) inadmissible, because the defendant was not on trial for stealing license plates.

(B) inadmissible, because the defendant was not convicted of stealing license plates.

(C) admissible, because it tends to establish that the defendant was likely to engage in criminal behavior.

(D) admissible, because it tends to establish that the defendant made special preparations for the commission of a crime.

159. The farmer was the owner of a peach orchard. On May 15, the seller contracted in writing to sell the land to the buyer for $200,000 under terms specified. The agreement called for the delivery of marketable title and set July 15 as the date for closing. The seller did not own the land on May 15 but planned to acquire title to it prior to the closing. On June 1, the buyer assigned his rights under the contract to an attorney. On June 15, the seller acquired title to the land by purchasing it from the farmer for $150,000. On July 15, the seller tendered a general warranty deed, but the buyer and the attorney both refused to go through with the transaction.

If the seller asserts a breach of contract claim for damages against the buyer, the court should find for

(A) the seller, because at the time of closing, the seller held marketable title to the realty.

(B) the seller, under the doctrine of estoppel by deed.

(C) the buyer, because at the time of contracting, the seller did not hold title to the land.

(D) the buyer, because at the time of closing, the seller's interest was outside the chain of title.

160. A businessman, a citizen of State A, sued a real estate company in federal district court in State A for breach of contract. The real estate company was incorporated in State B and was run by a group of executives based in State A. However, the majority of its apartments were located in State C. The businessman claimed that after he was injured in one of the company's luxury apartments, the company gave him a free apartment for life in exchange for his promise not to file suit. However, three years after giving him the free apartment, the company started charging him rent. The company defended its decision to start charging the businessman rent by pointing to a new law enacted by Congress that made gifts of free apartments illegal because of concerns free apartments were being used to bribe foreign businessmen and other officials. After a trial, the district court ruled in favor of the businessman. The company appealed, arguing the case should have been dismissed for lack of jurisdiction.

How should the court rule?

(A) The case should be dismissed, because the company was a citizen of State A.

(B) The case should be dismissed, because the majority of the company's apartments were in State C.

(C) The case should not be dismissed, because the company did not challenge jurisdiction in the initial trial.

(D)  The case should not be dismissed,
     because the company's defense is
     based on a law passed by Congress.

161. After police officers arrested the defen-
     dant for driving with a suspended license,
     the officers handcuffed the defendant and
     placed him in their patrol car. The police
     officers then searched the defendant's car
     and discovered cocaine in the pocket of a
     jacket on the backseat. At trial, the defen-
     dant argued that the search of his car was
     unlawful. If the court rules in the defen-
     dant's favor, it will be because

     (A)  searches conducted without prior
          approval by a judge or magistrate are
          *per se* unreasonable under the Fourth
          Amendment.

     (B)  the defendant could not have accessed
          his car to retrieve weapons or evi-
          dence at the time of the search.

     (C)  the search of the car was not the result
          of a valid inventory search.

     (D)  the interior of a car is always within
          the immediate control of an arrestee.

162. An insurance salesman sued a company in
     federal district court after he was passed
     over for a promotion. The salesman's claim
     arose under federal employment law. In the
     salesman's complaint, he gave a short state-
     ment claiming he was entitled to relief, but
     the complaint did not contain details regard-
     ing the alleged employment discrimination
     and it set out three different claims that were
     inconsistent with each other. In response,
     the company filed a motion to dismiss for
     failure to state a claim.

     How should the court rule?

     (A)  Deny the motion, because the com-
          plaint contained a short and plain
          statement of the claim.

     (B)  Deny the motion, because the com-
          plaint gave the company notice of the
          lawsuit.

     (C)  Grant the motion, because the com-
          plaint did not adequately allege a
          prima facie case.

     (D)  Grant the motion, because the com-
          plaint contained inconsistent claims.

163. A man told his friend, a druggist, that he
     was planning to kill his wife and asked the
     druggist to help him by furnishing a poi-
     son. Although the druggist did not actually
     intend to help the man kill his wife, he said
     that he would because he did not want his
     friend to be angry at him. The druggist gave
     the man a commonly used antibiotic, telling
     him that it was a deadly and undetectable
     poison. The druggist knew that the antibiotic
     was not supposed to be dispensed without a
     prescription and that about 2 percent of the
     people who received it developed an aller-
     gic reaction to it, but he did not believe that
     it would hurt the wife. That night while the
     wife was asleep, the man injected her with
     the antibiotic that the druggist had given
     him. Because she was allergic to the drug,
     the wife became seriously ill and nearly
     died.

     If the druggist is prosecuted for attempted
     murder, he should be found

     (A)  guilty, because giving the man the
          antibiotic without a prescription with
          knowledge that the man would give it
          to his wife shows a reckless disregard
          for human life.

     (B)  guilty, because he did not attempt to
          stop the man from killing his wife.

     (C)  guilty, because he furnished the drug
          knowing that the man would use it to
          attempt to kill his wife.

     (D)  not guilty, because he did not believe
          that the wife would die.

164. The defendant was arrested and charged in
     a state court with the unlawful possession
     of a dangerous drug. As his defense, the
     defendant asserted that he was an under-
     cover officer in a special division of the

state police department and that he had possessed the drug lawfully as part of an undercover assignment. During the presentation of its case, the prosecution called the witness, an official of the state police department. The witness testified that he was the custodian of a personnel file that contained the names of all undercover officers employed by the special division of the state police department and that he had studied the file before coming to court. He said that all entries in the file were made by the person who selected its personnel and issued their assignments when the special division was formed and as new personnel were added.

The prosecution then offers to have the witness testify that the file contains no mention of the defendant. The defendant's attorney objects. Which of the following additional facts and inferences, if it was the only one true, would be most likely to result in the admission of the witness's testimony?

(A) The file itself is unavailable.

(B) The person who makes the entries in the file is unavailable.

(C) The person who made the entries in the file is dead.

(D) The personnel file is available for inspection by the public.

165. The homeowner, who owned a home in a residential development, decided to have his driveway paved. He called the plaintiff, a licensed contractor who specialized in residential driveways, and asked for an estimate on the job. Although the standard market price to pave a driveway the size of the homeowner's was $2,750, the plaintiff was willing to do the job for $2,500 since business was slow. The homeowner agreed to hire him to do the job at that price and filled out and signed a detailed work order for the plaintiff's work crew. Since the homeowner was planning to go on vacation for two weeks, he and the plaintiff agreed

that the job would be finished by the time the homeowner returned.

Three days later, the plaintiff's work crew went out to do the job described in the homeowner's work order. By mistake, they paved the neighbor's driveway, which was identical to the homeowner's except that it was on a different street. The neighbor was out of town at the time. The job cost the plaintiff $2,600 in labor and materials and increased the value of the neighbor's realty by $2,100. The homeowner did not communicate with the plaintiff while away on vacation. When he returned and discovered that his driveway had not yet been paved, he demanded that the plaintiff perform as agreed, but the plaintiff refused.

After the driveway was paved, the neighbor promised to pay the plaintiff $2,000 for the job. In a jurisdiction that adopts the view of the Restatement (2d) of Contracts, if the neighbor then refused to pay and the plaintiff sued him for breaching his promise, which of the following additional facts or inferences, if it was the only one true, would be most likely to result in a judgment for the plaintiff?

(A) When the neighbor promised to pay, the neighbor knew that the plaintiff had already paved his driveway.

(B) When the neighbor promised to pay, the neighbor did not know that the plaintiff had already paved his driveway.

(C) The neighbor decided to have his driveway paved before speaking with the plaintiff.

(D) The neighbor did not decide to have his driveway paved until speaking with the plaintiff.

166. The landlord leased an apartment to a new tenant. The lease provided that the tenant could not assign or sublease without the landlord's consent. Soon thereafter, the

tenant assigned the lease to his friend. The landlord accepted the friend's first rent payment without any protest.

The landlord then realized he didn't like the idea of having the friend as a tenant, so he declared the lease terminated. May he do so?

(A) Yes, because assignments were prohibited by the lease.

(B) Yes, because the landlord protested within a reasonable time.

(C) Yes, because the landlord had a superior property interest to the tenant and the friend.

(D) No, because the landlord waived his right to terminate the lease.

167. The defendant suffered from severe anxiety. One day, he had a job interview at a new company. Because he was so nervous about the interview, he took three times the amount of anxiety pills that were prescribed for him and drank a bottle of beer. The pills and the beer made him severely intoxicated. On the way to the interview, the defendant was driving his car when a man in another car ran a red light. The resulting collision ended up killing the man. A police investigation showed the defendant was driving at the correct speed and obeyed all other traffic regulations.

The defendant was charged with involuntary manslaughter. How should the court rule on the involuntary manslaughter charge?

(A) Guilty, because the defendant was grossly negligent in taking three times the drugs prescribed for him and drinking a beer before driving.

(B) Guilty, because the defendant was negligent under the totality of the circumstances.

(C) Guilty, because driving while intoxicated is *malum in se*.

(D) Not guilty.

168. The defendant's husband owed money to the plaintiff. This was evidenced by a promissory note. When the note became due, the defendant signed the back of it and promised to pay the note if her husband did not. In return, the plaintiff promised he would not put the note in his bank for immediate collection. Instead, he agreed to "hold it until the time I want my money." The plaintiff did not collect on the note for two years. The plaintiff then sued the defendant based on her endorsement. If the court does not enforce the agreement, it will be because

(A) there was no consideration for the promise.

(B) the plaintiff did not detrimentally rely upon the promise.

(C) the defendant's husband was the primary debtor.

(D) the agreement was unconscionable.

169. On March 1, the seller entered into a written agreement with a licensed real estate broker. By its terms, the seller agreed to pay the broker a commission equal to 6 percent of the price if, prior to April 15, the broker procured a buyer ready, willing, and able to pay $50,000 for the seller's realty. In return, the broker agreed to make reasonable efforts to sell it.

After the agreement was executed, the broker advertised the seller's property and showed it to several prospective buyers. On April 10, the buyer signed a document agreeing to purchase the seller's realty for $50,000 but stating that her agreement was contingent upon her success in obtaining the necessary financing. The same day, the broker presented to the seller the document that the buyer had signed. The seller read it, thought for a moment, and handed it back to the broker, saying, "I won't even consider a deal built around a contingency." Although the broker protested that the agreement between him and the seller did not specify a sale without contingencies, the seller refused to discuss the matter any further.

On April 11, the broker informed the buyer of the seller's response. The buyer then obtained a cashier's check for $50,000 payable to the seller. She delivered the check to the broker, together with a signed document in which she agreed to purchase the seller's realty for that sum. On April 14, the broker presented the second document to the seller with the cashier's check. The seller said, "I've changed my mind. I'm not interested in selling."

If the buyer institutes a proceeding against the seller for an order directing the seller to sell her the realty for $50,000, the court should find for

(A) the seller, because he did not agree to sell the realty to the buyer.

(B) the seller, because his attempt to orally modify his written agreement with the broker was invalid.

(C) the buyer, because she can show that the realty is unique.

(D) the buyer, because her written agreement to purchase was delivered with the cashier's check prior to April 15.

170. In an action by the plaintiff against the defendant, the plaintiff claimed that the defendant breached a contract to market the plaintiff's products. At trial, the plaintiff testified that she and the defendant had reached an agreement at a conference held in the office of the plaintiff's attorney on October 15. She stated that she and the defendant discussed five separate products on that occasion. On direct examination of the plaintiff, the attorney asked her to name the products that had been discussed. The plaintiff named four of them but said she could not remember the fifth. After having them properly marked for identification, the plaintiff's attorney offered to show the plaintiff notes that the attorney had made during the conference, asking whether looking at them would refresh the plaintiff's recollection.

The defendant's attorney did not object to the plaintiff's looking at the notes, and the plaintiff stated that looking at the notes refreshed her recollection. After looking at the notes, the plaintiff named the fifth product, and the plaintiff's attorney then offered the notes in evidence. If the defendant's attorney objects to admission of the notes in evidence, the objection should be

(A) overruled, because the notes constitute a business record.

(B) overruled, because the plaintiff used the notes to refresh her recollection while testifying.

(C) sustained, because the notes are hearsay not within any exception.

(D) sustained, because the notes constitute an attorney's work product.

171. A state law empowers any municipality within the state to collect a property tax from its landowners if a plan to do so is proposed by its governing body and approved by a majority of its eligible voters. The township is a municipality governed by a Township Council. Pursuant to the above law, the Township Council proposed a property tax plan and scheduled a special election for August 15 to submit the plan for voter approval. The Township Council declared that only persons owning land within the township were eligible to vote in the special election and that eligible voters were required to register for that purpose at the Township Hall between the hours of 1 P.M. and 3 P.M. on Tuesday, July 15. The constitutionality of the special election was challenged in an appropriate proceeding by a petitioner with standing.

The petitioner argued that the registration schedule was discriminatory, proving that a substantial percentage of persons who owned land in the township were males who commuted to work in a city 45 miles away and were unable to register during the scheduled hours without missing a day's work and incurring a loss of income. In response, the Township Council argued that the registration schedule had a rational basis, proving that its timing allowed the process to be carried out with volunteer labor that would save the Township the cost of hiring special registration personnel. If these are the only arguments made, the court should declare the registration schedule invalid because

(A) it discriminates against commuters on the basis of their lifestyle.

(B) it discriminates on the basis of wealth by excluding those who cannot afford to lose a day's work.

(C) it results in benign sex discrimination.

(D) the right to vote is a fundamental right.

172. The landlord, the owner of a seven-story office building, leased the entire sixth floor to an attorney for a period of five years by a written lease that fixed the rent at $2,000 per month. There were only two offices on the sixth floor, identified as Office 6A and Office 6B. A clause in the lease provided that in the event it ever became necessary to determine how the rent payments were apportioned, it was understood that $900 of each month's rent was to be applied to Office 6A, $900 was to be applied to Office 6B, and $200 was to be applied to the hallways and other common areas. The lease prohibited assignment by the attorney without the landlord's written permission and provided that such permission would not be unreasonably withheld.

One year after executing the lease, the attorney entered into a written agreement with a second attorney. Under its terms, the second attorney was to occupy Office 6A for the balance of the attorney's term at a monthly rental of $1,500 payable to the attorney. The second attorney was an attorney with a better reputation and a more lucrative practice than the first attorney's.

The landlord consented to the arrangement between the two attorneys, but one month before the term expired, the second attorney vacated the premises and made no further payments. After the second attorney moved

out, the office that the second attorney had occupied remained vacant. For the final month of the lease term, the first attorney paid only $1,100 to the landlord, although the landlord demanded an additional $900. In an appropriate proceeding, the landlord can collect $900 from

(A) the first attorney only.

(B) the second attorney only.

(C) Either attorney.

(D) Neither attorney.

173. A woman sued a company in federal district court in State A after she was injured by one of the company's products. After trial, the jury ruled in favor of the woman and awarded her damages.

If the trial judge believed the compensatory damages awarded by the jury were inadequate because the jury was prejudiced against the woman, what should she do?

(A) Amend the judgment through additur.

(B) Offer the defendant a choice between a higher damage award or a new trial.

(C) Order a new trial.

(D) Enter judgment as a matter of law.

174. The owner of one piece of land granted an easement to his neighbor, the owner of the adjacent piece of land. The easement allowed the neighbor to use a 12-foot-wide strip of the owner's land to drive his car from his property to the public highway. The strip crossed a bridge, but the easement document was silent regarding any repairs to it. After the grant of the easement, the bridge washed out. The neighbor asked the owner who granted him the easement to repair the bridge, and he refused to do so. Does the owner who granted the easement have a duty to repair the bridge?

(A) No, because the owner of the servient estate is not required to repair or maintain the property used in the easement.

(B)  No, but he will have to reimburse his neighbor if his neighbor chooses to repair it.

(C)  Yes, because without the bridge, the neighbor has no way to get to the public highway.

(D)  Yes, because he expressly granted an easement for his neighbor to be able to reach the highway.

175.  The plaintiff was hired as a probationary employee by an agency of the state pursuant to a written contract. The contract provided that at the end of one year, the parties could agree to renew the contract for an additional one-year period, but that either party could, without cause, elect not to renew.

Eleven months after hiring him, the agency informed the plaintiff in writing that his contract would not be renewed at the end of the year. The plaintiff asked the agency for a hearing on his fitness to be rehired, but his request was denied. The plaintiff subsequently instituted a proceeding to challenge the decision of the agency on the ground that its failure to hold a hearing before deciding not to rehire him violated his right to due process.

If it was the only one true, which of the following additional facts or inferences would be most likely to lead to an order requiring the agency to hold a hearing before deciding not to rehire the plaintiff?

(A)  During the same year, the agency held hearings before deciding whether to rehire certain other probationary employees.

(B)  The decision not to rehire the plaintiff was based in part on the fact that, while employed by the agency, he had actively campaigned for a political candidate.

(C)  The decision not to rehire the plaintiff was likely to damage the plaintiff's reputation.

(D)  The job held by the plaintiff was vital to the efficient operation of the agency.

176.  While the defendant and his wife were standing in line outside a movie theater, the defendant whispered to his wife that he had committed a series of robberies the previous week. The defendant was subsequently arrested and charged with the robberies in a jurisdiction that holds that confidential marital communications are privileged.

The wife is called as a prosecution witness, and the prosecutor attempts to question her about the statement that the defendant made to her while they were waiting in the movie line. Which of the following statements is most correct?

(A)  The court should exclude this testimony if the wife is willing to testify but the defendant objects to her testimony.

(B)  The court should exclude this testimony even if the defendant and his wife make no objection to it.

(C)  The court should exclude this testimony even if the defendant and his wife make no objection to it, or if the wife is willing to testify but the defendant objects to her testimony.

(D)  The court should admit the testimony.

177.  The defendant showed his silver coins to the plaintiff and asked whether the plaintiff would be interested in trading them for chickens. After inspecting the coins, the defendant and the plaintiff placed them in a bag that they sealed together and left with a banker whom they both knew. Then, in a writing signed by both of them, they agreed to the trade.

Pursuant to the terms of their agreement, the plaintiff was to deliver 6,000 fryer chickens to the defendant on July 1, at which time the bag of coins would be turned over to the plaintiff as payment in full. In May, weather conditions were such that the price of fryer chickens increased to three times what it had been when the agreement was signed.

In May, the plaintiff notified the defendant that because of the increase in the price of chickens, the plaintiff would not be able to accept the bag of coins as payment for 6,000 fryer chickens in July. The defendant immediately sold the coins to a third person. On July 1, the plaintiff attempted to deliver 6,000 fryer chickens to the defendant, but the defendant refused to accept delivery. If the plaintiff asserts a claim against the defendant for breach of contract, the court should find for

(A) the defendant, because the plaintiff said that she would not accept the coins as payment for the chickens.

(B) the defendant, because the defendant's sale of the coins has resulted in the defendant's prospective inability to perform.

(C) the plaintiff, because the sale of the coins by the defendant has made performance by the defendant impossible.

(D) the plaintiff, because the plaintiff tendered the chickens as required by the contract.

178. While out hunting for wolves, the defendants saw a large furry animal that they believed was a wolf running through the trees. The defendants opened fire, killing the creature. When they got closer, they realized they had just shot a dog that was owned by a local farmer. The dog did in fact look exactly like a wolf. The farmer sued the defendants for damages, and the defendants countered that they shot the dog by mistake and were acting in good faith. What result?

(A) The defendants are not liable for the farmer's damages because their mistake was made in good faith.

(B) The defendants are not liable for the farmer's damages because their mistake was reasonable.

(C) The defendants are liable for the farmer's damages because it is unreasonable to mistake a dog for a wolf.

(D) The defendants are liable for the farmer's damages even though they may have been acting in good faith.

179. After many residents of the state complained of being annoyed by calls received from robocall computers, the state legislature enacted a statute that prohibited operating such a device from within the state.

The company, a manufacturing company doing business in the state, planned to use the robocall computer to market its products within the state. After passage of the law, the company attempted to hire an out-of-state company to set up a robocall computer system connected to phone lines outside the state for the purpose of making calls to telephones within the state. When the company learned that the cost of doing so would far exceed the cost of setting up such a system inside the state, the company challenged the constitutionality of the state law.

The company's only claim is that the statute violates the First Amendment protection of freedom of expression. The company's most effective argument in support of that conclusion is that the statute is

(A) overbroad because it could interfere with non-commercial communications as well as with commercial communications.

(B) content-related because it is more likely that the telephone solicitation computer would be used for commercial communications than for non-commercial communications.

(C) likely to have a chilling effect on expression because of the increased cost of using the telephone solicitation computer from locations outside the state.

(D) not justified because prohibiting use of the telephone robocall computer from locations within the states does not directly advance a substantial government interest.

180. The farmer was the owner of a small farm that had been in his family for many generations and which had become a well-known community landmark. The farmer had a son and a daughter. Because the farmer was advanced in age, he was concerned about what would happen to the property after his death. He wanted to keep it in the family for as long as possible, and he wanted the son to have the use of it throughout his lifetime.

The farmer died, leaving a will that devised the property "to my son for life, but if within 40 years my son attempts to sell or mortgage his interest, to my daughter for life." If, in an appropriate proceeding, the son challenges the validity of the restrictions on his estate, his most effective argument would be that the restrictions

(A) constitute a disabling restraint on alienation.

(B) constitute a forfeiturial restraint on alienation.

(C) constitute a promissory restraint on alienation.

(D) violate the Rule Against Perpetuities.

181. A police officer was going door-to-door in a neighborhood handing out flyers related to several recent burglaries. A homeowner invited the police officer in for some coffee. The police officer sat down in the living room while the homeowner went into the kitchen to get the coffee. While the officer was sitting there, he noticed a large gun case on the floor. The case wasn't locked, so he opened it. Inside was a fully automatic machine gun, which was unlawful in the state. The police officer arrested the homeowner. The homeowner moved to have the evidence against her suppressed.

Should the evidence be suppressed?

(A) Yes, because the homeowner was not in the room when the officer opened the case.

(B) Yes, because the homeowner did not give the officer permission to open the case.

(C) No, because the homeowner had invited the officer into her home.

(D) No, because the illegality of the evidence was readily apparent.

182. After determining that the health insurance plan could be operated less expensively if it did not include persons over the age of 65, the state legislature passed a compulsory retirement law requiring state employees to retire at the age of 65.

The plaintiff, an employee of the state, sued, claiming that she reached 65 several years after the passing of the new law.

The plaintiff's only argument was that the mandatory retirement law violated the Obligation of Contracts Clause of Article I of the United States Constitution. If it was the only one true, which of the following additional facts or inferences would best support the plaintiff's claim?

(A) The plaintiff was a state employee prior to the time the mandatory retirement law was passed.

(B) The plaintiff borrowed money for the purchase of a retirement home, planning to pay it back from his salary as a state employee.

(C) The plaintiff is as physically fit as the average person who is 60 years of age.

(D) The plaintiff's job as a state employee does not require any physical labor or strain.

183. After executing a contract with the defendant, the plaintiff advertised that he would be showing the defendant's world-famous hog at the state fair. All his advertising emphasized that the hog, the American champion, would be exhibited at the fair. On June 20, the hog contracted a highly contagious and frequently fatal disease of hogs. The defendant notified the plaintiff on June 22 that, because of the disease, he could not exhibit the hog as agreed. When the plaintiff advised the public that the hog would not be appearing, many people who had planned to purchase tickets changed their minds and did not do so. The plaintiff subsequently asserted a claim against the defendant for damages resulting from the defendant's refusal to exhibit the hog as agreed.

Which of the following additional facts, if it were the only one true, would be most likely to result in a judgment in favor of the plaintiff?

(A) On May 1, the defendant was aware that many hogs in the area had contracted the hog disease.

(B) On June 21, the state learned that the hog had contracted the hog disease and issued an order prohibiting the exhibition of the hog.

(C) On June 22, the defendant owned a hog with qualities equivalent to the other hogs.

(D) On the day of the trial, the plaintiff could prove exactly how much revenue the plaintiff lost as a result of the defendant's failure to exhibit the hog.

184. The tenant leased a parcel of real estate from the landlord for one year at a monthly rent of $2,000 with an option to buy it for a specified price at the termination of the lease. After moving onto the realty, the tenant erected a storage building on it.

The construction cost of the building was $6,000, but when it was completed, its value was $8,000. The tenant's employer subsequently transferred him to a company office located in a different state. As a result, the tenant vacated the realty four months before the expiration of the lease, advising the landlord that he would not exercise his purchase option. On the same day, the landlord conveyed the property to the buyer.

The buyer moved onto the realty on the day the tenant vacated it, and all parties agreed that therefore the tenant would have no further obligation to pay rent. If the tenant wishes to remove the storage building, but the landlord and the buyer object, which of the following statements is correct?

(A) The landlord and the buyer may prevent removal of the building by declaring it to be realty and tendering its reasonable value to the tenant.

(B) If a court prevents the tenant from removing the building, declaring it has been annexed to the realty, the tenant is entitled to receive its reasonable value from the landlord or the buyer.

(C) The landlord and the buyer may prevent the removal of the building by declaring it to be realty and tendering its reasonable value to the tenant, and if a court prevents the tenant from removing the building, declaring it has been annexed to the realty, the tenant is entitled to receive its reasonable value from the landlord or buyer.

(D) If the building has become part of the realty, the landlord and the buyer owe nothing.

185. The company is the manufacturer of an agricultural insecticide. Since the county in which the company is located is primarily devoted to farming, the company has manufactured the agricultural insecticide at its factory there for the past 50 years. Although the insecticide is an important product

commonly used by farmers for the control of an insect highly destructive to food crops, only three other companies have a similar product.

Due to the manufacture of the insecticide, fumes that issue from the company factory frequently have an unpleasant odor. These fumes cause no physical harm to persons, property, or crops, but residents of the county frequently complain about the foul smell. All the factories that manufacture a product similar to the insecticide produce the same odor.

The farmer began growing crops on a field near the company factory less than a year ago. The farmer leases the field from its owner in return for a percentage of his crop. When he telephoned the company to complain about the bad smell emanating from its factory, a company official told him that nothing could be done about it.

The farmer asserts a claim against the company based on private nuisance, seeking damages for discomfort that he experiences as a result of the bad smell produced by the company's factory. Which one of the following additional facts or inferences, if it was the only one true, would be most likely to result in a judgment for the company?

(A) There is no other factory within 1,000 miles that manufactures a product similar to the insecticide.

(B) The farmer does not own realty in or reside in the county.

(C) It is impossible to manufacture a product similar to the insecticide without producing a bad smell.

(D) The farmer's discomfort does not differ substantially from the discomfort experienced by other residents of the county.

186. At the jury trial of an action by the bank against the defendant on a promissory note, the defendant testified that the signature on

the note was not his. An employee of the bank testified that she recognized the signature as the defendant's.

The defendant's attorney asserts that the promissory note is hearsay. The bank's most effective response to that assertion would be that

(A) the promissory note is a business record.

(B) the promissory note is an original document.

(C) the promissory note is not being offered to prove that any statement that it contains is true.

(D) the defendant is in court.

187. Three men all agreed to carry loaded fully automatic machine guns for a robbery of a pharmacy. The men entered the pharmacy, and to scare everyone, one of the men fired about 30 bullets into the ceiling. The pharmacy was in an antique building with a tin ceiling. A bullet ricocheted off the metal and killed a customer. All three men were arrested and charged with murder. The jurisdiction does not apply the felony-murder rule. What is the most severe crime committed by the two men who did not shoot into the ceiling?

(A) Conspiracy.

(B) Involuntary manslaughter.

(C) Voluntary manslaughter.

(D) Depraved-indifference murder.

188. A stockbroker brought an action in federal district court in State A against a car salesman after the stockbroker was injured while taking a test drive in a new car he was thinking about buying. The stockbroker, a citizen of State A, sought $1 million in damages. The salesman was a citizen of State B. The salesman brought a counterclaim against the stockbroker for damages he claimed he received during the same accident. The salesman joined to the

counterclaim the car dealer he was working for at the time of the accident. The car dealer was a citizen of State B. The salesman claimed the car dealer and the stockbroker were both liable to him for $50,000 in damages based on the accident. The salesman also joined to the counterclaim a claim for breach of contract against the car dealer because the car dealer fired him shortly after the accident.

May the court hear the salesman's claim for breach of contract?

(A) Yes, because the claim is part of the same case or controversy.

(B) Yes, because the federal court would have supplemental jurisdiction over the related claim.

(C) No, because the counterclaim would contain additional facts from the main claim.

(D) No, because the salesman and the dealer are citizens of the same state.

189. An astronaut, who is a resident of the Western District of State A, sued an engineer, who was a resident of the Eastern District of State B, and a videogame designer, who was a resident of the Southern District of State C, in federal district court for damages related to an automobile accident. The accident occurred in the Western District of State D. The astronaut brought suit in the Western District of State A. After the defendants submitted their answers, they realized venue was improper and moved to have the case transferred to the Western District of State D. However, the district judge found that in the interest of convenience, the district court in the Western District of State A should hear the case.

Is venue proper in the Western District of State A?

(A) No, because neither the defendants nor the accident have any connection to the Western District of A.

(B) No, because neither defendant is a citizen of State A.

(C) Yes, because the defendants have already filed their answers.

(D) Yes, because venue decisions are discretionary.

190. The defendant and the victim are adults. During an argument, the defendant slammed a glass door against the victim, causing the victim to sustain serious cuts on her hand. After the victim received medical treatment for her injuries, she spoke to the defendant's mother about it. The victim told the mother that she was thinking of suing the defendant for her medical expenses, but that if the mother would agree to pay the victim $250, the victim would make no claim against the defendant for medical expenses. The mother agreed in writing that she would do so.

Two weeks later, the defendant was prosecuted criminally as a result of the injuries that he had inflicted on the victim. The victim told the defendant's mother that the prosecutor had asked the victim to testify against the defendant at the proceeding. The mother begged her not to. Finally, the victim said that if the mother gave her an additional $1,000 for her pain and suffering, she would not testify against the defendant. The defendant's mother orally agreed to do so.

The defendant's mother paid $250 to the victim, but refused to pay an additional $1,000. If the victim asserts a claim against the defendant's mother on account of the mother's failure to pay the additional $1,000, which of the following would be the mother's most effective argument in defense?

(A) The defendant's mother was not legally obligated to pay for damage done by her adult son.

(B)  The defendant's mother's promise to pay an additional $1,000 to the victim was not supported by consideration.

(C)  The defendant's mother's payment of $250 to the victim was an accord and satisfaction.

(D)  The defendant's mother's promise to pay the debt of the defendant was not in writing.

191.  Following her indictment by a grand jury for bank robbery, the defendant voluntarily surrendered at police headquarters. After booking her, police officers advised the defendant that she had a right to remain silent, that anything she said might be used against her, that she was entitled to have an attorney present during questioning, and that if she could not afford an attorney, one would be furnished without cost to her. The defendant said that she did not wish to answer any questions until her attorney arrived.

The officers went to lunch and returned to headquarters an hour later. Upon their return, they ordered the defendant to appear in a lineup for identification purposes in connection with the bank robbery. At first, the defendant refused. When the officer threatened to use force to compel her appearance, however, the defendant appeared without resisting. Witnesses at the lineup identified her as the bank robber.

Following the lineup, the officers asked the defendant whether she knew anything about a series of residential burglaries. Although they did not think that she had committed the burglaries, they thought that she might know the people who had. The defendant admitted participating in the burglaries, however. She was subsequently prosecuted for bank robbery and the burglaries.

If the defendant moves to exclude evidence that she admitted participating in the burglaries, her motion should be

(A)  denied, because the police did not suspect her of being involved in the burglaries when they asked her about them.

(B)  denied, because she received *Miranda* warnings before being questioned about the burglaries.

(C)  granted, because she stated that she did not wish to answer any questions until her attorney arrived and did not in any other manner waive her *Miranda* rights.

(D)  granted, because the police did not advise her that she was suspected of committing the burglaries before they questioned her about them.

192.  By a properly executed and recorded deed, the landowner conveyed a parcel of real estate with a building on it as follows:

> to the church for so long as the land is used by the church for church purposes; and when the land ceases to be so used, to the hospital for so long as the land shall be used by the hospital for hospital purposes; and when the land ceases to be so used, to my son if my son is then living.

The church moved onto the real estate, using the building as a house of worship.

Five years after the landowner's conveyance, the size of the congregation of the church increased, creating the need for more space. As a result, church officials sold the realty, planning to use the proceeds to buy a bigger church, and executed a deed purporting to convey the realty to a real estate development company. In subsequent litigation to determine the rights of the church, the hospital, and the company, which of the parties should be found to have a present possessory interest in the realty?

(A)  The company, because the church plans to use the proceeds of the sale to purchase realty for church use.

(B) The company, because the hospital's interest is void under the Rule Against Perpetuities.

(C) The hospital, because the conveyance to the company terminated the estate of the church.

(D) The church, because its conveyance to the company was invalid under the grant from the landowner.

193. After a nuclear power plant was built in the state, the state passed the Nuclear Waste Act. The Act regulates the storage of radioactive wastes and authorizes the construction of radioactive waste storage facilities at specified locations within the state. Section 40 of the Act provides that "No radioactive waste storage facility in the state shall store or accept for storage any radioactive waste resulting from activities conducted more than five miles from said storage facility." All storage facilities within the state that are authorized by the Nuclear Waste Act are located more than five miles from the state line.

The constitutionality of Section 40 is challenged on the sole ground that it violates the Commerce Clause. Which of the following additional facts or inferences, if it was the only one true, would be most likely to result in a conclusion that Section 40 is constitutional?

(A) Prohibiting the storage of radioactive wastes generated outside the state reduces the expense of operating nuclear power plants within the state.

(B) The transportation of radioactive wastes within the state over distances greater than five miles would pose a significant health and safety hazard to state residents.

(C) There are only a few locations within the state where radioactive wastes can be stored safely.

(D) There are many locations outside the state where radioactive wastes can be stored safely.

194. The security guard of a warehouse was making his rounds after closing time one night when he found the defendant walking around inside the warehouse. When the guard asked him what he was doing there, the defendant replied that he had been driving past the warehouse when he noticed that its door was open, and that he had entered to report this to the guard. The guard called the police, and the defendant was arrested and charged with violating a statute providing that "any person entering the building of another for the purpose of committing a crime therein is guilty of burglary."

At the defendant's trial, the prosecutor tried to prove that the defendant's van, parked outside the warehouse at the time of the defendant's arrest, had license plates on it that had been stolen from an out-of-state vehicle the day before the defendant's arrest.

The prosecutor subsequently offered evidence that the defendant had previously been convicted of a crime other than burglary. Which of the following additional facts or inferences, if it was the only one true, would be most likely to result in the exclusion of that evidence?

(A) The defendant testified in his own behalf at the burglary trial and stated that he had never been convicted of a crime.

(B) The defendant did not testify in his own behalf at the burglary trial.

(C) The defendant's prior conviction was for involuntary manslaughter.

(D) The defendant's prior conviction was rendered in the court of another state.

195. A man sued a boxer in federal district court in the Western District of State A for injuries the man sustained during a bar fight. The boxer's attorney wanted to get a copy of the police report. The police department was located in the Western District of State A, the same District in which the fight occurred.

How can the boxer's attorney get a copy of the police report?

(A) Serve a request to produce documents on the police department.

(B) Cause the court clerk to issue a subpoena duces tecum on the police department.

(C) Serve a notice of deposition on the police officer that wrote the report.

(D) Serve interrogatories on the police officer that wrote the report.

196. The plaintiff, a dentist, owned an apparatus for putting patients to sleep while she operated on their teeth. The apparatus consisted of two canisters, one filled with oxygen and the other filled with anesthetic gas. By manipulating valves attached to the canisters, the plaintiff used the apparatus to mix and administer a proper combination of gases to patients. Noticing that one of the valves was beginning to wear out, the plaintiff sent the apparatus to its manufacturer for repairs. After fixing the valve, the manufacturer negligently filled the oxygen canister with anesthetic gas and the anesthetic gas canister with oxygen.

After the manufacturer returned the apparatus to the plaintiff, she attempted to use it on a patient. While treating the patient, the plaintiff decided that it was necessary to administer pure oxygen and manipulated the valves accordingly. Because of the manufacturer's error in refilling the oxygen canister with anesthetic gas, however, the plaintiff administered pure anesthetic instead. As a result, the patient died in the plaintiff's office.

If the plaintiff asserts a claim against the manufacturer for mental suffering that she experienced as a result of the patient's death in her office, which of the following would be the plaintiff's most effective argument in support of her claim?

(A) The manufacturer's error was outrageous because it created a high probability of serious harm.

(B) It was likely that the manufacturer's error would lead the plaintiff to experience mental suffering.

(C) The plaintiff assumed all risks associated with using anesthetic gas.

(D) There was substantial certainty that the plaintiff would use the apparatus on a patient.

197. A man told his friend, a druggist, that he was planning to kill his wife and asked the druggist to help him by furnishing a poison. Although the druggist did not actually intend to help the man kill his wife, he said that he would because he did not want his friend to be angry at him. The druggist gave the man a commonly used antibiotic, telling him that it was a deadly and undetectable poison. The druggist knew that the antibiotic was not supposed to be dispensed without a prescription and that about 2 percent of the people who received it developed an allergic reaction to it, but he did not believe that it would hurt the wife. That night while the wife was asleep, the man injected her with the antibiotic that the druggist had given him. Because she was allergic to the drug, the wife became seriously ill and nearly died.

If the man is prosecuted for conspiracy to murder his wife, which of the following would be his most effective argument in defense?

(A) His wife did not die.

(B) The druggist did not believe that the wife would die.

(C) The drug that the man gave his wife was not likely to cause her death.

(D) The inchoate crime and the substantive crime merge when the defendant's overt act brings him or her substantially close to achieving his or her intended result.

198. The defendant was arrested and charged in a state court with the unlawful possession of a dangerous drug. As his defense, the defendant asserted that he was an undercover officer employed by the Special Division of the State Police Department and that he had possessed the drug lawfully as part of an undercover assignment. During the presentation of its case, the prosecution called the witness, an official of the State Police Department. The witness testified that he was the custodian of a personnel file that contained the names of all undercover officers employed by the Special Division of the State Police Department and that he had studied the file before coming to court. He said that all entries in the file were made by the person who selected its personnel and issued their assignments when the Special Division was formed and as new personnel were added.

The prosecution offers the file itself into evidence for the purpose of showing that it contains no mention whatsoever of the defendant. If the defendant's attorney objects, the personnel file should be

(A) admitted as a business record.

(B) admitted as past recollection recorded.

(C) excluded, because government documents may only be used against the government.

(D) excluded, because it calls for an inference to be drawn from negative evidence.

199. A company brought a claim for violations of federal securities laws against a bank in federal district court. The case was tried before a jury. The company's case consisted of one witness: the company president, who presented a few emails that allegedly proved the company had been harmed by insider trading committed by the bank. The bank then presented its case, which included dozens of documents and several expert witnesses regarding the financial actions taken by the bank. The experts all agreed that the bank's actions were legal. The case was then submitted to the jury. The jury found in favor of the company. The bank made a motion for judgment as a matter of law, arguing there was no way a reasonable jury could have ruled in favor of the company.

How should the court rule?

(A) Deny the motion, because the bank provided no new evidence to dispute the claim.

(B) Deny the motion, because the bank did not move for judgment as a matter of law before the case was submitted to the jury.

(C) Grant the motion, based on the insufficiency of the company's evidence.

(D) Grant the motion, because the jury's decision was clearly erroneous.

200. A pipe company filed a complaint in state court in State A for breach of contract against a builder. The company did not serve the builder then, but emailed a "courtesy copy" of the complaint to one of the builder's vice presidents. The company officially served the builder two weeks later. Twenty-nine days after service, but 44 days after receiving the email, the builder removed the case to federal district court in State A. The company moved to remand the case to state court.

How should the court rule?

(A) Deny the motion, because the builder removed the claim within 30 days after it was served.

(B) Deny the motion, because the "courtesy copy" was not sent by certified mail.

(C) Grant the motion, because the builder did not remove the claim within 30 days of receiving notice of the complaint.

(D) Grant the motion, because the builder did not challenge notice when it received the initial email.

# ANSWERS

## PRACTICE MBE—A.M. EXAM

# PRACTICE MBE—ANSWERS TO A.M. QUESTIONS

1. **D**     A private citizen or police officer is privileged to use whatever non-deadly force he or she reasonably believes is necessary to prevent the escape of a criminal from a crime. Although there is some doubt whether the force used by the man against the robber was reasonable, or indeed whether it was non-deadly, **D** is the only argument listed that could possibly result in an acquittal.

In some jurisdictions, a person defending another against a threat of immediate bodily harm is privileged to use whatever force the person being defended would have been privileged to use. In other jurisdictions, a person defending another against a threat of immediate bodily harm is privileged to use the force that reasonably appears necessary to the defendant himself or herself. Both **A** and **B** are incorrect, however, because the robber was in the process of running away at the time of the man's blow, and therefore the man was not defending the woman against a threat of bodily harm. A person who owns or is in charge of property may use reasonable force to protect it. This may privilege the use of force to stop a person who is in the process of unlawfully carrying that property off. **C** is incorrect, however, because the man was not the owner or custodian of the woman's handbag and therefore had no privilege to protect it.

2. **D**     Under FRE 611(b), as well as the common law majority rule, cross-examination is limited to matters to which the witness testified on direct examination. Because the witness did not testify about the contract, the question asked by the defendant's attorney probably exceeds the scope of cross-examination. Since the trial court is given discretion in determining how far the scope of cross-examination extends, it is not certain that the court would sustain the objection on this ground. Of all the arguments listed, however, the one set forth in **D** is the only one that could possibly be effective in support of the objection.

**A** is incorrect for two reasons: First, the witness was called by the plaintiff, and therefore she is not the defendant's witness, and second, under FRE 607, a party may impeach its own witness. A leading question is one that contains a suggestion that would cause the ordinary person to believe that the questioner desires one answer instead of another. **B** is incorrect because the question asked by the defendant's attorney contains no such suggestion and because leading questions are permitted on cross-examination. Argumentative questions are those that are used to emphasize some point to the jury rather than to elicit information. Although argumentative questions are improper, **C** is incorrect because the question asked by the defendant's attorney did not seek to emphasize any particular point to the jury.

3. **B**     For the purpose of discovering weapons or preventing the destruction of evidence, officers may make an incidental search of a person who has been lawfully arrested. Thus, if the defendant's arrest was lawful, the search of her person was lawful as an incident to that arrest. An officer may make an arrest without a warrant if there is probable cause to believe that the person arrested has committed or is in the process of committing a felony. Thus, if the defendant's proximity to the trunk gave the officers probable cause to believe that she was guilty of possessing cocaine, her arrest and incidental search were lawful.

Probable cause means a belief that the defendant is guilty, supported by facts that would lead a reasonable person to entertain such a belief. While it is not certain that the officers had probable cause to believe the defendant guilty, the argument set forth in **B** is the only one listed that might provide the prosecution with an effective argument in response to the defendant's motion.

It is sometimes said that evidence discovered by violating a defendant's rights is inadmissible because it is "fruit of the poisonous tree." **A** is incorrect because evidence so classified is excluded, not admitted. Many states hold that officers executing a warrant to search premises are entitled to frisk all persons present for weapons. The frisk, however, consists of a patting down of the outside of the clothing and does not justify reaching into pockets unless the patdown has revealed something that feels like a weapon. Since there is no indication that the bag of marijuana felt like a weapon, **C** is incorrect. **D** is incorrect because although a warrant to search premises might authorize a search of persons present, it does not justify their arrest unless there is probable cause to believe that they have committed or are committing a felony.

4.  **D**   To be enforceable, a contract requires mutuality of assent. If both parties are mistaken about a basic assumption of their agreement (*i.e.*, there is a bilateral mistake), there is no mutuality of assent and no enforceable agreement can be formed. Both the seller and the buyer believed that they were contracting for the purchase and sale of one parcel of realty, when in fact the written contract identified a different parcel of realty. Their bilateral mistake thus prevented the mutuality of assent necessary to make their "contract" enforceable.

If the mistake had been the seller's alone (*i.e.*, unilateral), it would not have prevented the formation of a contract unless the buyer knew or should have known about it. For this reason, if the buyer had known that the parcel described in the writing (#341) had a building on it, while the parcel that he had inspected (#241) did not, the seller's mistake would have prevented the formation of a contract. **A** is incorrect, however, because the buyer did not know this at the time the writing was signed. If the only mistake in the formation of a contract is made by an intermediary chosen by one of the parties, that mistake is charged to the party who selected the intermediary. (If, for example, the attorney had said, "My client wants to buy #341," and the seller and the buyer had agreed on a price for #341, then the buyer would have been obligated to buy #341 because his unilateral mistake would not have prevented the formation of a contract.) In this case, however, the error was bilateral—both the seller and the buyer believed that they were contracting for the purchase of a different parcel. For this reason, **B** is incorrect. **C** is incorrect for two reasons: First, if the seller's mistake had been unilateral, the fact that she would suffer a substantial loss as a result would not be enough to free her of obligations under the contract, and second, the bilateral mistake regarding a basic assumption of the contract prevented the formation of an enforceable contract for the sale of #341 whether it was more valuable than #241 or not.

5.  **D**   The First Amendment prohibits laws that interfere with the free exercise of religion. A law that makes a benefit available to some people but denies it to others because of their religious affiliations may violate this provision because it imposes a burden on the exercise of a religious belief. In 1978, the United States Supreme Court specifically held (*McDaniel*

*v. Paty, 435 U.S. 618 (1978)*) that a statute that prohibited members of the clergy from running for public office was invalid for this reason. Even without this decision, however, the argument set forth in **D** is the only one listed that could possibly support the plaintiff's position.

Although a state may not set qualifications for state office that violate rights protected by the United States Constitution, there is no constitutional requirement that qualifications for state office be consistent with qualifications for federal office. **A** is therefore incorrect. **B** is incorrect because the statute in question does not attempt to set qualifications for practicing members of the clergy. **C** is incorrect for two reasons: First, although the creation of political divisiveness along religious lines may make a law invalid under the Establishment Clause, this is not relevant to rights protected by the Free Exercise Clause, and second, prohibiting members of the clergy from holding public office is not likely to have that effect.

6.  **A**    If the long-arm statute of the state in which the federal district court sits permits a certain type of service against an out-of-state defendant, the federal district court will permit that type of service as well. *See Fed. R. Civ. P. 4(e)(1).*

Therefore, **B**, **C**, and **D** are incorrect.

7.  **C**    The privilege of self-defense excuses a defendant from criminal liability when he or she is using reasonable force to protect himself or herself against the commission of a crime. One is never justified in using deadly force in self-defense, however, unless he or she reasonably believes that he or she is in imminent danger of death or great bodily injury. The defendant was not justified in slapping the victim's face; however, if the victim exceeded his privilege of self-defense when he began loading his pistol in apparent retaliation, this made him the aggressor. If the defendant then had a reasonable (even though mistaken) belief that his life was in danger, he was justified in using deadly force to defend himself.

During the course of a fight, the role of aggressor may shift from one person to the other. Although a person is not privileged to defend himself or herself against a privileged (*i.e.*, reasonable) response to his or her own aggression, he or she is privileged to defend himself or herself against an unprivileged attack. Although the defendant was the initial aggressor, he may have been privileged to use force to defend himself against the victim's response to the slap if the victim's response was excessive (*i.e.*, unprivileged). **A** is therefore incorrect. What force is reasonable in self-defense depends not so much on the facts as upon the way the facts were perceived by the defendant and how they would have been perceived by the reasonable person in the defendant's position. Thus, even in jurisdictions that require a defendant to make reasonable attempts to escape before using lethal force in self-defense, the fact that the defendant could have escaped would not be relevant unless the reasonable person in his shoes would have realized that. **B** is therefore incorrect. **D** is incorrect because a determination of what force is reasonable in self-defense depends on the state of mind of the defendant, not on that of the victim.

8.  **A**    Under the collateral source rule, sums that a plaintiff receives from anyone other than a tortfeasor or a tortfeasor's representative are not relevant in determining the amount of

damages to which the plaintiff is entitled. This is because a benefit that is given to an injured person should not be used to the advantage of the person who injured him or her. Since the insurance company paid under a policy that the plaintiff had purchased, the defendant should not derive a benefit from it by the reduction of damages that he is required to pay.

If a plaintiff has received payment from a tortfeasor (*e.g.*, in settlement), the amount of such payment may be deducted from the plaintiff's damage to reduce the liability of other tortfeasors. **B** is incorrect since this is true whether or not such payment was made pursuant to a judicial determination. **C** is incorrect under the collateral source rule for the reasons stated above. Ordinarily, when one joint tortfeasor pays more than his or her fair share of a judgment, he or she is entitled to recover part of it from other joint tortfeasors. Some jurisdictions base this recovery on equal apportionment, referring to it as "contribution" between joint tortfeasors. Other jurisdictions base this recovery on the relative fault of the joint tortfeasors, referring to it as "partial indemnity." Since the insurance company was not a joint tortfeasor with the defendant, use of the term *partial indemnity* is not applicable. **D** is therefore incorrect.

9.  **B**     Ordinarily, a promise is not enforceable unless it was supported by consideration. Consideration is something of value given in exchange for the promise. Since the defendant gave nothing of value in return for the plaintiff's agreement to release her, his agreement was unsupported by consideration and is therefore unenforceable. A novation is an agreement to substitute the performance of a third party for that of a promisor coupled with the promisee's express agreement to release the original promisor from further obligation. In a novation, the third party's promise to perform for the promisee is consideration for the promisee's agreement to release the original promisor. (For example, X and Y have a contract requiring Y to perform. X, Y, and Z then agree that Z will perform instead of Y, and Y is released from further obligation. Z's promise to perform is consideration for X's agreement to release Y.) A court could find that there was no novation in this case because the daughter's promise to perform had already been made, and, therefore, it was not given in return for (*i.e.*, as consideration for) the plaintiff's agreement to release the defendant. While it is not certain that a court would come to this conclusion, the argument given in **B** is the only one listed that might be effective in response to the defendant's claim.

The parol evidence rule prohibits evidence of a *prior or contemporaneous* oral agreement to contradict or modify the terms of certain writings. Since the plaintiff's oral agreement to release the defendant was made *after* their written contract, the parol evidence rule does not apply to it. **A** is therefore incorrect. The original contract between the plaintiff and the defendant was for a three-year period (*i.e.*, could not be performed within a year). For that reason, the Statute of Frauds required it to be in writing. Since the plaintiff's agreement to release the defendant had instant effect, however, the Statute of Frauds does not apply to it. **C** is therefore incorrect. Accord occurs when contracting parties agree to substitute a new obligation for an existing one; satisfaction occurs when that new obligation is fulfilled. Since the defendant's delegation to her daughter did not create any new obligation between the plaintiff and the defendant, it was not an accord; thus, there could have been no satisfaction. **D** is therefore incorrect.

10.  **A**   **I**ssue preclusion (also known as collateral estoppel) bars a party from re-litigating issues that were actually litigated and necessary for the judgment in the first action. Here, the doctor's potential negligence was litigated in the first case and it was necessary to the decision because State A rules stated that any negligence on the doctor's part would bar him from recovery. Since the court found in favor of the doctor, it necessarily found that the doctor was not negligent in any way.

**B** is incorrect because a subsequent action may not necessarily be barred even if it arose from the same transaction or occurrence. **C** is incorrect because, although the action did not have to be brought as a compulsory counterclaim, the truck driver could still be collaterally estopped from forcing the doctor to re-litigate the negligence issue. **D** is incorrect because the fact the truck driver is bringing his action in the same state court would not allow the truck driver to re-litigate the negligence issue.

11.  **B**   Freedom of association is a corollary of the First Amendment freedoms of expression and assembly. For this reason, it has been held that neither the federal nor the state government can impose a disability on a person as a result of membership in an organization unless the organization advocates illegal conduct and the person is an active member who knows the organization's unlawful purposes and specifically intends to further them. Since the law in question would impose a disability (*i.e.*, ineligibility for federal employment) solely because of membership in an organization, without regard to knowledge of the organization's purposes or the intent to further those purposes, it is unconstitutional.

An *ex post facto* law is one that imposes a criminal penalty on the basis of something that occurred before the law was passed. Since the law in question does not impose a criminal penalty, it is not an *ex post facto* law. **A** is therefore incorrect. Whether government employment is a privilege or a right, ineligibility for it is a disability. Since the disability cannot be constitutionally imposed for mere membership in an organization, **C** is incorrect. **D** may be incorrect for several reasons, but at least because the law does not take into account the views held by the persons to which it applies.

12.  **C**   The federal government is immune from taxation by the states. It is generally understood, however, that this immunity does not shield private parties from state tax liability, even though they have a contractual relationship with the federal government. Although Congress has the power to specifically exempt a particular contractor from state sales tax liability, there is no fact here indicating that Congress exercised that power.

A state attempt to regulate interstate commerce may violate the Commerce Clause of the United States Constitution. **A** is incorrect, however, because a sales tax imposed on the purchase of materials used to build a bridge does not regulate interstate commerce, even though interstate vehicles may eventually use the bridge. While the state lacks power to tax the federal government, **B** is incorrect because so long as it does not discriminate against them, the state is free to tax persons doing business with the federal government. This has been held to be so even though the cost of such taxes may eventually be passed along to the federal government via cost-plus-fixed-profit contracts. **D** is therefore incorrect.

13. **A**     A person seeking to protect a legitimate interest is privileged to make defamatory statements that he or she reasonably believes to be true, under circumstances where the publication is reasonable in its scope. Clearly, a doctor has a legitimate interest in attempting to prevent the hiring of incompetent nurses by a hospital. Since the defendant's response to the personnel department questionnaire was likely to reach only those people who could decide whether or not to hire the plaintiff, it was probably reasonable in scope. Also, because the other doctor was a well-respected trainer and mentor of nurses, it was likely reasonable to believe his statements regarding the nurse's competence. Therefore, because the defendant reasonably believed the statement, it was privileged, and the defendant would not be liable for defamation.

The publication of a false defamatory statement—unless privileged—ordinarily results in liability, even though the publisher heard the statement from another and so indicates when making the statement. **B** is therefore incorrect. The Supreme Court of the United States has held that a plaintiff who is a public person may prevail in a defamation action only by proving that the defendant had "actual malice." **C** is incorrect, however, because the Court has stated that, in a defamation action, "actual malice" means that when publishing the statement, the defendant either knew that it was false or entertained serious doubts about its truth. **C** is also incorrect because actual malice alone is not sufficient to result in defamation liability. In some defamation actions, the plaintiff must prove that the defendant's publication resulted in actual damage to the plaintiff. Proof of damage, however, is not sufficient to result in defamation liability where other elements of the plaintiff's case have not been established or where the defendant was privileged. **D** is therefore incorrect.

14. **D**     A positive statement by the promisor to the promisee indicating that the promisor will not perform his or her contractual duty is a repudiation of the contract. Even though performance was not yet due at the time of repudiation, the non-repudiating party may usually sue on a theory of anticipatory breach as soon as the repudiation occurs. Therefore, the seller acquired an immediate right of action as soon as the buyer communicated that he would not order any boxes in 2012.

**A** is therefore incorrect. **B** is incorrect for two reasons: First, UCC §2-306 specifically recognizes the validity of "requirements" contracts and specifies the manner in which their terms should be construed, and second, damages for failing to order the specified minimum requirement could be fixed with certainty. A party who seeks damages for breach of contract is required to prove those damages; they are not presumed. **C** is incorrect for this reason, and because—strictly speaking—a repudiation is not a "breach," but an "anticipatory breach."

15. **A**     To prevail in an action for defamation, a plaintiff must prove that the defendant published a defamatory statement about the plaintiff. A defamatory statement is about the plaintiff if the reasonable person who knows the plaintiff would recognize the plaintiff from the statement. For this reason, a defamatory statement made about a group to which the plaintiff belongs identifies the plaintiff so long as the group is small enough to lead the reasonable person who knows that the plaintiff is a member of the group to believe that the statement about the group is being made about the plaintiff.

The issue here is what was said in the newspaper, not whether the police officers were engaged in their official duties or not. This makes **B** incorrect. A spoken defamation is called "slander per se" if it accuses the plaintiff of a crime of moral turpitude, of having a loathsome disease, of being an unchaste woman, or of being unfit for the plaintiff's occupation. In certain cases of slander per se, the plaintiff may be relieved of the need to prove actual damage. **C** is incorrect for two reasons: First, the statement cannot be called slander because it was in writing, and second, calling a statement slander per se does not eliminate the need to prove that the statement was made about the plaintiff. If the group of police officers present at the rally was small enough, the statement about the group identifies the plaintiffs (for reasons given above) even though it does not name them. **D** is therefore incorrect.

16. **C**      If questioning during voir dire reveals a juror is biased, the juror may be excused for cause. A juror has an actual bias if the juror indicates he or she would use predetermined beliefs or principles instead of the facts presented to determine a case. Since the woman stated she would have a hard time keeping an open mind because she believed the police habitually discriminated against minorities, she can be excused for cause.

     **A** is incorrect because the question specifically asks about her statements. There is no indication any of the attorneys want the juror dismissed based on her race. **B** is incorrect because although she said she had no strong feelings or private knowledge, she did indicate she had an actual bias regarding the issue presented by the case. **D** is incorrect because an implied bias refers to the situation where a juror states he or she is not biased, but an average person in that juror's position would likely be partial to one of the parties (for example, if one of the parties was related to the juror). Here, the woman stated an actual bias.

17. **A**      Under FRE 804(b)(2), a statement is admissible as a dying declaration if it was made about the cause and circumstances of death by a presently unavailable declarant with a sense of impending death, was based upon the declarant's personal knowledge, and is offered at the trial of a criminal homicide prosecution or of any civil action. Since the plaintiff asked the witness to tell his wife to meet him at the hospital, it is possible that a court would find that he did not believe himself to be dying. This conclusion is, of course, not certain (since he may have been telling her where to claim his body), but **A** is the only reason listed that could possibly justify finding that the plaintiff's statement was not a dying declaration.

     **B** is incorrect because while the Federal Rules of Evidence (FRE) require the declarant to be unavailable, it does not require that he have died from the incident described in his statement, or even that he is dead. Although some controversy exists at common law about whether a dying declaration is admissible in anything but a criminal homicide prosecution, the FRE specifically permit its use in a civil action. **C** is therefore incorrect. The common law provides that an excited utterance may be admissible under an exception to the hearsay rule, but only if the statement was spontaneous (*e.g.*, not in response to a question). The FRE exception for excited utterance does not specifically mention spontaneity, but some cases indicate that excited utterances should be excluded under the FRE if they were made in response to a question. **D** is incorrect, however, because neither the common law nor the FRE require that a *dying declaration* be made spontaneously.

18.  **D**      Under FRE 703, "[i]f experts in the particular field would reasonably rely on those kinds of facts or data in forming an opinion on the subject, they need not be admissible for the opinion to be admitted." Consequently, if other experts in the field would rely on the maintenance worker's statement, the expert may do so even if it is inadmissible. Therefore, **A** is incorrect.

               **B** is incorrect because the fact the expert did not interview the maintenance worker herself does not change the analysis. **C** is incorrect because the expert's use of the statement in her testimony does not change the inadmissible statement to an admissible one.

19.  **A**      Although the United States Supreme Court interprets the federal constitution, it does not have the power to interpret state constitutions. Therefore, if it reviewed the decision of the state court, it could not disturb the holding that the due process requirement of the state constitution was violated. Since that holding alone is sufficient to support the state court's finding on behalf of the plaintiff (*i.e.*, the finding is based on an adequate and independent state ground), the United States Supreme Court lacks the power to overturn the state court decision. For this reason, review by the United States Supreme Court is not available. **B**, **C**, and **D** are therefore incorrect.

20.  **D**      Under FRE 803(22), a judgment of conviction may be admissible as an exception to the hearsay rule. For any evidence to be admissible, however, it must be logically and legally relevant. Whether a past conviction for passing bad checks is *logically* related to any material issues in the defendant's prosecution is uncertain, but there is little doubt about the *legal relevancy* of such evidence. Because of its capacity for arousing prejudice, evidence bearing on a person's character is not admissible as circumstantial evidence that his or her conduct on a particular occasion was consistent with that character. Thus, the defendant's conviction for passing worthless checks is inadmissible if offered to support an inference that because he passed bad checks that time, it is likely that he did it again this time. If the crime charged had been committed in a highly distinctive way, evidence that the defendant previously used that same distinctive *modus operandus* (MO) would tend to establish that he was familiar with it. It could be admissible since its purpose would not be to circumstantially establish conduct by showing character. **A** is incorrect, however, because there is no fact indicating that the crime with which the defendant is now charged and the crime of which he was previously convicted involved the same distinctive MO. Since the fact that a person has committed a crime involving dishonesty suggests that his or her statements are not worthy of belief, evidence that a witness has been convicted of such a crime may be admissible for the purpose of impeaching that witness's credibility. Since the defendant has not testified, however, his credibility is not in question. **B** is therefore incorrect.

21.  **A**      A fee simple subject to an executory limitation allows for an estate to pass to a third person upon the happening of a stated event. The third person who may gain the estate holds an executory interest. However, the issue here is that executory interests are subject to the Rule Against Perpetuities. The Rule Against Perpetuities states "No interest is good unless it must vest, if at all, not later than 21 years after some life in being at the creation of the interest." Here, since the friend's interest might not vest until more than 21 years after

all lives in being at the time the landowner conveyed the interest, the executory interest violates the Rule Against Perpetuities and is void. Consequently, the county is simply left with a fee simple absolute. **B** is incorrect because of the executory interest's violation of the Rule Against Perpetuities. **C** is incorrect because, although a fee simple subject to a condition subsequent also takes into account the happening of a certain event, it does not automatically end when the event occurs. In addition, it is the grantor, not a third party, who has the right to take back the property. Phrases that create a fee simple subject to a condition subsequent use words such as "upon express condition that" or "provided that." **D** is incorrect because a fee simple determinable is created by using phrases such as "so long as" or "until." Importantly, the grantor is left with a possibility of reverter if the stated event occurs.

22. **D**    Title passes immediately from the grantor to the grantee once a deed is validly executed and delivered. Consequently, returning or destroying the deed has no effect on the conveyance. If the landowner wanted to get the land back, he should have required his son to execute and deliver a new deed to him. Therefore, **A** and **B** are incorrect.

C is incorrect because whether or not the son made a photocopy wouldn't change the analysis.

23. **D**    A professional seller who supplies a defective product is strictly liable for damage that proximately results from the product's defect. A defect is a proximate cause of harm if it was both a factual and a legal cause of it. A defect is a factual cause of harm if the harm would not have occurred without it. Assuming that the vibrations resulted from a defect, the defect was a factual cause of the neighbor's injury since the injury would not have occurred without it. A defect is a legal cause of harm if the harm was a foreseeable result of the defect, not the result of unforeseeable interventions (*i.e.*, superseding causes). Thus, if the intervening conduct of the woman was a superseding cause of the harm, then the product defect—although a factual cause of the injury—was not a legal cause of it. Although it might take a jury to determine whether the woman's conduct was unforeseeable (*i.e.*, a superseding cause), **D** is the only argument listed that might result in a judgment for the store.

If all other requirements are satisfied, strict liability may be imposed to benefit any plaintiff whose contact with the product was foreseeable, regardless of whether the plaintiff is classified as a bystander. **A** is therefore incorrect. A plaintiff who voluntarily encounters a known risk assumes that risk. **B** is incorrect, however, because the woman was not the plaintiff, and only a plaintiff is said to assume a risk. If the processing machine was defective when it left the company's factory, the company might be strictly liable for the neighbor's injuries that proximately resulted. **C** is incorrect, however, because if the product was defective when it left the company's factory, it must have been defective when it left the store's premises, making the store strictly liable as well.

24. **D**    A statutory system of classification that regulates social or economic interests is valid under the Equal Protection Clause if it has a rational basis. On the other hand, if it discriminates against a suspect class of persons, it is valid only if it is necessary to serve a

compelling state interest. (**Note:** To withstand a constitutional challenge based on the claim that a statute interferes with a fundamental right, the statute must be necessary to serve a compelling state interest. Since the plaintiff's challenge is not based on that claim, however, the compelling state interest standard does not apply.) Although it has been held that a statutory classification based on gender does not discriminate against a suspect class, the United States Supreme Court has developed a third, or middle, level of scrutiny (sometimes called "rational basis with a bite") for such classifications. It has been held that gender classifications are valid only if they are substantially related to an important governmental interest. Since the plaintiff's sole claim is that the statute discriminates against women, the statute would be valid if it satisfied this middle level of scrutiny. Although it is not certain that the statute would satisfy the requirements of this test, the argument set forth in **D** is the only one listed that might possibly be effective in opposition to the plaintiff's claim.

**A** is incorrect because the fact that a system of classification does or does not discriminate against a suspect class determines the standard to be applied, but it does not itself determine whether the statute is constitutional. **B** is incorrect because a rational basis is not sufficient to make constitutional a statute that discriminates on the basis of gender. **C** is incorrect because police powers, like all other powers of the state, may not be exercised in a way that is inconsistent with the United States Constitution.

25.   **C**   The terms of a contract may provide that a party's performance is not required until the happening of a specified event (*i.e.*, a condition precedent). If so, the duty to perform does not become absolute until that event has occurred (*i.e.*, the condition precedent has been satisfied). In this contract, the defendant's duty to make final payment was conditioned upon the plaintiff's obtaining a Certificate of Satisfactory Completion from the architect prior to July 30. Thus, the defendant's duty to pay would not become absolute until the plaintiff satisfied the condition precedent by obtaining the certificate by that date. It is understood, however, that a party who wrongfully interferes with the other party's fulfillment of a condition may not rely on that unfulfilled condition to avoid performing. Sometimes this conclusion is based on what is referred to as a breach of the "implied promise to cooperate." Sometimes courts simply say that wrongful interference excuses performance of the condition precedent. Either way, since the defendant's request caused the architect to delay issuing the certificate, the defendant's duty to make final payment may become absolute in spite of the plaintiff's failure to fulfill that condition of the contract.

**A** is incorrect because the architect was not a party to the contract between the defendant and the plaintiff, and that contract therefore could not have imposed duties on the architect. It is sometimes said that express conditions of a contract must be fully satisfied, but that "substantial performance" satisfies constructive conditions. Since the condition requiring the plaintiff to obtain a Certificate of Satisfactory Completion by July 30 was express, substantial performance would not have been sufficient. **B** is therefore incorrect. Sometimes in a contract calling for performance to the satisfaction of the other party, a dispute arises as to whether that satisfaction is to be subjective or based on objective standards. Usually, in the absence of a clear agreement to the contrary, the standard is understood to be an objective one. In this case, however, the express condition required not only satisfactory completion, but the obtaining of a certificate by a particular date. For this reason, the application of an objective standard would not be sufficient to defeat the defendant's claim. **D** is therefore incorrect.

26. **A** One who intentionally aids, abets, or facilitates the commission of a crime is an accomplice and not only is guilty of the crime that he or she aided, but also is vicariously liable for all its reasonably foreseeable consequences. One who agrees with another to commit a crime is guilty of conspiracy and is vicariously liable for any crimes committed by a co-conspirator in furtherance of the conspiracy. Since the jury did not believe the defendant's testimony, the friend was committing a robbery when he used a threat of force to steal the coat from the victim. Since the defendant assisted him in doing so, she was an accomplice. Since she agreed to do so, she was a co-conspirator. As an accomplice, she is probably liable vicariously for the friend's intentional killing of the victim because her knowledge that the friend would be using a gun to coerce the victim into handing over the coat probably made it foreseeable that he would shoot the victim with the gun. As a co-conspirator, she is vicariously liable for the shooting since it was clearly in furtherance of the robbery that she agreed to commit.

   **B** is incorrect because being present while a crime is committed is not sufficient to make a defendant an accomplice or a co-conspirator. Self-defense is a privilege to use reasonable force to defend oneself against the use of force. A person who is being shot at may, therefore, be privileged to defend himself or herself by shooting back. **C** is incorrect, however, because self-defense does not privilege the use of force in response to force which itself was privileged by self-defense. Since the friend was menacing the victim with a pistol, the victim was privileged to use a pistol in self-defense. Since the victim's use of force was privileged, the friend was not privileged to use any force in defense against it. **D** is incorrect because as a co-conspirator and accomplice to the crime of *robbery*, the defendant is vicariously liable for the shooting that was a foreseeable consequence and done in furtherance of the robbery.

27. **D** Since the notary received his interest from the neighbor, the validity of the notary's title depends on the validity of the neighbor's title. For this reason, if the neighbor's title is superior to the friend's, then the notary's title is superior to the friend's. The validity of the neighbor's title depends on the recording statute. The statute given is a typical "notice" statute. According to its provisions, the interest of a subsequent grantee for value and without notice is superior to that of a prior grantee unless the prior grantee's interest was recorded prior to the time the subsequent grantee received his or her interest. Since the friend's deed was not recorded prior to the landowner's conveyance to the neighbor, the neighbor's interest is superior to the friend's. Since the notary derives his interest from the neighbor's grant, the notary's interest is also superior to the friend's.

   As a result of this reasoning, it is correct to say that one who derives his or her interest from a bona fide purchaser for value (*i.e.*, BFP) is protected by a recording statute even if he or she is not a BFP himself or herself. Thus, the notary's possible knowledge would not deprive him of the protection of the recording statute, and **A** is incorrect. **B** is incorrect because it fails to take into account the effect of the recording statute. While the neighbor did purchase for value, he clearly executed a deed conveying the property to the notary. **C** is therefore incorrect.

28. **B**    Under the common law, rape consists of sexual intercourse with a female not the wife of the defendant without that female's consent. Under most statutory rape laws, a female below a given age is determined to be incapable of consent, meaning that any male who has sexual intercourse with her does so without her consent. For this reason, knowledge of the victim's age is not ordinarily an element of statutory rape. Under the statute given in this question, however, knowledge of the female's age is specifically required. For this reason, the boy could not be convicted if he did not know that the girl was under the age of 18 years.

So long as a male defendant is old enough to be convicted of a crime, he may be convicted of statutory rape even though his age is the same as or younger than that of the female victim. **A** is therefore incorrect. Intoxication is a defense to a criminal charge only if it made the defendant incapable of possessing the necessary state of mind required. **C** is incorrect because there is no indication that the boy's intoxication affected his knowledge regarding the girl's age or prevented him from knowing that he was having sexual intercourse with her. Statutory rape, of which the crime charged is a form, is based on the concept that certain persons are incapable of consenting to sexual intercourse. For this reason, the victim's consent never furnishes a defense, and **D** is incorrect.

29. **C**    If a plaintiff brings an action in state court that could have originally been brought in federal court, a defendant can have it removed to federal court. *See 28 U.S.C.§1441.* Federal courts have subject matter jurisdiction over claims where the plaintiff and defendant are citizens of different states and the amount in controversy is over $75,000. The man is claiming $100,000, so he meets the jurisdictional amount. He is also a citizen of State A. A corporation is a citizen of the state it is incorporated in and a citizen of the state where it has its principal place of business. Courts determine "principal place of business" by looking at where the corporation's top management direct the corporation's business activities. Consequently, the moving company is a citizen of State B based on incorporation, and a citizen of State C based on its principal place of business. Thus, there is diversity of citizenship between the parties, and the moving company can remove the claim to federal court because it could have originally been brought there.

**A** is incorrect because the claim can still be removed even if it is based on State A motor vehicle law. **B** is incorrect because although the moving company did 70 percent of its business in State A, it is not a citizen of State A. **D** is incorrect because the company's belief regarding fairness would not create federal subject matter jurisdiction.

30. **C**    Although a defendant's violation of a statute may help the plaintiff establish that the defendant was negligent, that negligence does not result in liability unless it was a factual and legal cause of the plaintiff's damage. Conduct is a factual cause of harm if the harm would not have occurred without it. Since obeying the speed limit was more likely to cause the collapse than exceeding it, the accident would have occurred if the statute had

been obeyed. Since the collapse would have occurred without it, the violation was not a factual cause of the collapse.

In some jurisdictions, the violation of a statute may be negligence per se; in others, it may raise a rebuttable presumption of negligence; and in others, it may merely raise an inference of negligence. **A** is incorrect, however, because negligence does not result in liability unless it was a factual cause of harm, and the defendant's violation of a statute—even if it establishes negligence—was not a cause of the plaintiff's harm. Although violation of a statute may raise a presumption of negligence, it does not result in any presumption as to causation and is usually not relevant to issues of causation. **B** is therefore incorrect. Unless the statute violated was designed to protect a class of persons that includes the plaintiff, its violation is not relevant to the question of negligence at all. **D** is incorrect, however, because it is generally understood that traffic laws are at least designed to protect other users of the roads.

31. **B**  Since the condition imposed by the landowner's deed prohibited non-residential use, the buyer's grant of a license to fish does not violate it if fishing is a residential use. Whether or not this is so is uncertain, but **B** is the only argument listed that could possibly provide the buyer with an effective defense.

Under the Rule Against Perpetuities, no interest is good if it can vest after a particular period of time. The *creation* of an interest that might vest after the period is thus void under the Rule, but the Rule has no effect on the *termination* of an existing interest. **A** is incorrect for this reason and because the Rule Against Perpetuities is not applicable to future interests of a grantor. The fee simple determinable and the fee simple subject to a condition subsequent are possessory interests that may be terminated on the happening of a specified event. The most important difference between them is that the fee simple determinable terminates automatically on the happening of that event, and the fee simple subject to a condition subsequent does not terminate without some action being taken. The language of the landowner's deed makes it difficult to determine which of those interests was conveyed to the buyer, but the difference is insignificant to the buyer since his interest is subject to termination in either event. For this reason, **C** is incorrect. A restraint on alienation is a condition that attempts to control the alienability (*i.e.*, power to convey an interest) of realty. If the condition attempts to do so *directly* (*e.g.*, the condition prohibits selling or mortgaging the realty), it may be declared void under certain circumstances. Although use restrictions are likely to affect the alienability of realty, policy does not require that they be declared void for this reason alone because their effect is *indirect*. **D** is therefore incorrect.

32. **D**  Ordinarily, specific performance is available as a remedy for breach of contract when damages would not be an adequate remedy. For several reasons, however, courts do not grant specific performance of contracts calling for personal service. These reasons include the constitutional protections against involuntary servitude and of freedom of association, as well as practical considerations that make it unwise for courts to become unduly involved in the supervision of performance. Thus, if the architectural work that remained to be completed involved personal services, specific performance would not be granted.

**A** is therefore incorrect. An agreement not to assign usually destroys the right but not the power to make an effective assignment. This means that an assignment made in the face of such an agreement is usually valid, although the assignor might be liable for damages resulting from the assignment and from his or her own failure to perform. For this reason, damages are usually the only remedy available for breach of a promise not to assign. **B** is therefore incorrect. **C** is a misstatement of the above rule. While an agreement not to assign may destroy the right to make a valid assignment (*i.e.*, one who violates it may be liable for breach of contract), it does not ordinarily destroy the power to assign (*i.e.*, an assignment made in violation of the assignor's promise may be valid). For this reason, **C** is incorrect. (**Note:** The obligation to perform personal services is not usually assignable or delegable. This rule is not relevant here, however, because the question asks not about the validity of the assignment, but about the availability of specific performance as a remedy.)

33. **A**    Under FRE 901(5) (and at common law), a voice may be identified by any person who testifies that he or she recognizes it based upon hearing the voice under circumstances connecting it with the alleged speaker. Although the plaintiff may not have known whose voice she was hearing when she had the telephone conversation, if she subsequently heard the defendant's voice and recognized it as the same voice that she heard on the telephone, she is competent to testify that it was the defendant's voice that she heard on the telephone. This is true even though her first real opportunity to connect the defendant with the voice occurred on the morning of trial.

If a person's telephone number is listed in the telephone book, there is a presumption that one who properly dialed that number reached the premises of the person listed. Under FRE 901(6), this presumption combined with other circumstances, including self-identification of the speaker as the person listed, may justify the admission of voice-identification testimony by a witness who dialed the number. Since the plaintiff did not look up the defendant's number in the telephone book or dial it, the defendant's self-identification is insufficient to make the plaintiff's testimony admissible. **B** is therefore incorrect. **C** is incorrect because the plaintiff's subsequent hearing of the defendant's voice is sufficient to make her voice-identification testimony admissible. The fact that the plaintiff had not dialed the defendant's number before speaking to him would prevent her voice-identification testimony from being admissible under the special FRE provision discussed above regarding telephone identifications. **D** is incorrect, however, because the fact that she recognized the telephone voice as the defendant's after hearing the defendant's voice in the judge's chambers is sufficient to make her testimony admissible without that special provision.

34. **D**    Since the Act prohibits the operation of munitions factories in which airborne levels of the chemical exceed statutory standards, it would take a new law to permit the company's factory to operate in violation of those standards. In effect, by giving the Senate National Defense Committee the power to permit such operation, Section 34 purports to give it the power to make a law. Article I of the United States Constitution provides that federal legislation must be passed by both houses of Congress and then presented to the President for approval. An attempt to legislate without fulfilling these requirements violates the Constitution.

The committee system in Congress exists, in part, because it enables certain questions to be considered by bodies that have had an opportunity to develop expertise in certain areas. The principle of bicameralism established by Article I prevents those committees from legislating, however. For this reason, **A** is incorrect. Although Congress may supervise the activities of administrative agencies that it has created, the scope of such supervision is, of course, limited by the provisions of the Constitution. As indicated above, the system of supervision created by Section 34 exceeds constitutional limitations because it purports to give a Senate committee the power to legislate. **B** is therefore incorrect. **C** is incorrect for two reasons: First, Congress *may* authorize an administrative body to impose quasi-criminal sanctions (although not to create them), and second, Section 34 does not give an administrative agency the power to impose sanctions but purports to limit that power.

35.  **B**    Extortion consists of obtaining property from another by threatening future harm to persons, property, or economic interests. Since the defendant obtained money from the victim by threatening to blow up her real and personal property, he can be convicted of extortion.

Robbery consists of obtaining property from another by using or threatening force against a person. Since the defendant made no threat of harm to a person, **A** is incorrect. Larceny by trick is a larceny committed by making a misrepresentation that induces the victim to part with temporary possession of personal property. Since the victim did not expect her cash to be returned, she was not parting with temporary possession of it, and **C** is incorrect. Embezzlement is a criminal conversion of personal property by one in lawful custody of it. Since the defendant was not in lawful custody of the victim's money, **D** is incorrect.

36.  **B**    Article I, Section 10, provides in part that no state shall pass any law impairing the obligation of contracts. This prevents states from repudiating their own contractual obligations or interfering with private contractual obligations except by regulations that are reasonable and appropriate to a significant state purpose. Since the statute in question does not result in a repudiation of the state's contractual obligations or interfere with private contractual obligations, it does not violate the Obligation of Contracts Clause.

The Equal Protection Clause prohibits states from invidiously discriminating. Since the statute requires higher fees from non-residents, it discriminates against them. Although some such discrimination has been held to be valid, it is possible that this statute is not. **A** therefore could be an effective argument in support of the constitutional challenge, making **A** incorrect. The Privileges and Immunities Clause of Article IV of the United States Constitution provides that "The citizens of each state shall be entitled to all privileges and immunities of the citizens in the several states." Since this has been held to prohibit certain discrimination against out-of-staters, **C** also could be an effective argument in support of the constitutional challenge and is therefore incorrect. The Commerce Clause prohibits the states from discriminating against or imposing undue burdens on interstate commerce. Violations have been found on both grounds in laws that denied to out-of-staters advantages that were available to state residents. For this reason, **D** also could be an effective argument and is therefore incorrect.

37. **B**    An assault is committed by intentionally inducing the plaintiff's reasonable apprehension of immediate harmful or offensive contact. It has been held that a threatening act is not an assault if accompanied by words that make clear that the threat will not be carried out, since any apprehension experienced by the plaintiff would not be reasonable. It is understood, however, that a defendant is not free to avoid assault liability by demanding compliance with a condition that he or she has no legal right to impose. Since the defendant had no legal right to require the seller to back out of his contract with the buyer, the fact that he told the seller that he could avoid the threatened harm by doing so would not prevent the defendant from being liable for assault. **B** is therefore not an effective argument in the defendant's defense and is therefore correct.

Since it was obvious from the defendant's statement that the threatened harm would not occur until sometime in the future, **A** would be an effective defense and is therefore incorrect. Since the threat was of harm to the seller's children and not to the seller, **C** would be an effective defense and is therefore incorrect. Courts have generally argued (although this argument is not always credible) that apprehension induced by the defendant's mere use of words is not reasonable. This has led to a rule that there can be no assault liability unless the defendant has performed some physical act. **D** is therefore an effective defense and is therefore incorrect.

38. **C**    Although extrinsic evidence of unconvicted bad acts is not usually admissible for the purpose of proving that a person has a bad character or was inclined to commit other bad acts, such evidence may be admissible for other purposes. Proof that a fact is not as stated by the defendant may be admissible for the purpose of impeachment (*i.e.*, to show that his or her testimony is not to be believed). If such proof is extrinsic (*i.e.*, not from the defendant's own mouth) it may be used to impeach, but only if it relates to a material issue in the controversy. Since the defendant claimed to be 1,000 miles away from where the crime of arson was committed, his whereabouts on the day of the crime are of consequence (*i.e.*, material) in the arson prosecution. The witness's testimony is therefore admissible to impeach the defendant. In general, evidence is admissible as substantive proof if it is relevant to some fact of consequence in the controversy. Since the defendant's whereabouts on the day of the crime are material to the arson prosecution, the witness's testimony — which tends to establish that the defendant was in the city on the day of the fire — is admissible as substantive evidence.

39. **C**    Since a will speaks upon the death of the testator, the mailman's interest was created upon the death of the landowner. An executory interest is a future interest in a grantee that will become possessory only upon the termination of a prior estate, the termination of which is not inevitable. Since, according to the devise, the friend's interest was to terminate only if he died without issue from his wife, and since it was not inevitable that this would happen, it was executory. Since the mailman's interest was to replace that of the friend, it was a shifting interest.

Consequently, **A**, **B**, and **D** are incorrect.

40. **D**    If a claim is brought in federal court based on a question of federal law, the federal court will also have jurisdiction over any state law claims arising from the same case or

controversy. *See Hurn v. Oursler, 289 U.S. 238 (1933)*. Because both the federal law claim and the breach of contract claim arise from the woman's loss of her job, the federal court would have jurisdiction over the breach of contract claim even if it is based on state law. Therefore, **A** is incorrect.

**B** is incorrect because there is no amount in the controversy requirement for federal question jurisdiction. **C** is incorrect because the saleswoman would not be able to bring a claim against the company if it did not arise from the same case or controversy.

41. **A**    Under FRE 609, evidence that a witness has been convicted of a crime is admissible for the purpose of attacking his or her credibility under two distinct sets of circumstances. Such evidence is admissible if the crime was a felony *and* the court determines that the probative value outweighs the prejudicial effect to the defendant. Such evidence is also admissible, however, if the crime is one that involved dishonesty. Since tax fraud is a crime involving dishonesty, the evidence is admissible whether or not the crime was a felony, and without an affirmative finding that its probative value outweighs its prejudicial effect.

**B**, **C**, and **D** are therefore incorrect.

42. **B**    In *Wisconsin v. Yoder, 406 U.S. 205 (1972),* the United States Supreme Court specifically held that in determining whether a defendant's conduct is privileged by First Amendment rights to freedom of religion, it was proper to consider whether the defendant's religious beliefs were sincere.

**A** is therefore incorrect. Ordinarily, a state may prohibit specified activities whenever such prohibition serves a rational basis. Under the Free Exercise Clause of the First Amendment, however, a state may not interfere with acts performed in the exercise of religious beliefs unless the interference bears a rational relationship to a compelling state interest. This means that there are some acts that the state may validly declare to be criminal and prohibit because the prohibition has a rational basis, but which may still be performed by persons who are doing so in the exercise of their religious beliefs if the prohibition does not bear a rational relationship to a compelling state interest. Thus, First Amendment rights to freedom of religion might justify acts that would otherwise be criminal. For this reason, **C** and **D** are both incorrect.

43. **C**    The Equal Protection Clause provides that no state shall deny to any person within its jurisdiction the equal protection of the law. This means that any state agency that employs a system of classification granting rights or privileges to some persons while denying them to others may be violating rights conferred by the Equal Protection Clause. Some systems of classification are valid if they have a rational basis; other systems are valid only if they are necessary to serve a compelling state interest. It is uncertain whether the exclusion of pregnant students from a public high school system is valid. Of the fact situations given, however, **C** is the only one that could possibly involve a violation of rights granted by the Equal Protection Clause. This is because the Equal Protection Clause regulates only state action, and **C** is the only fact situation involving state action.

The defendant in **A** is employed by a religious organization. The defendant in **B** is a federal official. The defendant in **D** works in private enterprise. Since none of them is an agency of the state, **A**, **B**, and **D** are incorrect.

44. **A** Strict liability is imposed on the professional supplier of a product that is defective and unreasonably dangerous, if that defect proximately causes harm to a plaintiff whose contact with the product was foreseeable. If the reasonable person could not have anticipated the plaintiff's contact with the chemical (*i.e.*, the plaintiff's contact with it was unforeseeable), strict liability cannot be imposed to benefit the plaintiff.

If the plaintiff's harm was produced by an unforeseeable intervening event, the product defect was not a proximate cause of it. **B** is incorrect, however, because intervening negligence may be (and usually is) regarded as foreseeable. If the plaintiff's injury would not have occurred but for the crack in the sewer, the crack was also a cause of harm. The existence of an additional cause of harm is not sufficient to relieve any defendant of liability, however, unless that additional cause was unforeseeable. Since there is no indication that the crack in the sewer was unforeseeable, **C** is incorrect. **D** is incorrect because strict products liability does not depend on the existence of a commercial relationship (*i.e.*, privity) between the defendant and any other person.

45. **D** Under Fed. R. Civ. P. 15(c), if a party wants to amend a pleading to change the party against whom a claim is asserted, the amendment will relate back to the date of the original pleading if the claim arises out of the same occurrence as the original pleading, so long as the new party is served within 90 days after the complaint is filed (Fed. R. Civ. P. 4(m)) and "(i) received such notice of the action that it will not be prejudiced in defending on the merits; and (ii) knew or should have known that the action would have been brought against it, but for a mistake concerning the proper party's identity." The owner was served on June 22, so it was within 90 days. Additionally, the man's amended complaint arose from the same accident and the owner knew that an action would be brought against him (based on his phone call to the man). Therefore, **B** is incorrect.

**A** is incorrect because it states the wrong deadline for service. **C** is incorrect because it is not enough that the claim arose from the same occurrence. Importantly, the new party must have had some notice or knew of the likelihood of being sued.

46. **C** An *inter vivos* conveyance of realty is not effective without delivery. Delivery occurs when the grantor, by some words or act, manifests an intent that the deed have a present operative effect. While the woman indicated that she wanted to be sure that the husband had the property after her death, she may have intended the quitclaim deed to transfer an interest immediately. If, instead of handing the document to the husband, she had locked it in a safe deposit box to which only she had access, it would be clear that she did not intend an immediate transfer. On the other hand, if she simply handed it to the husband, it would be clear that she did intend an immediate transfer. Here, because she was unable to leave the hospital, she could not personally place it in a safe deposit box. When she handed it to the husband with the request that he put it in the box, she may have intended to "deliver" it to him, or, without intending any present effect, she may have been asking him to lock it away for her since she was physically unable to do so herself. From the facts given, it is impossible to determine

with certainty what her intention was. If the safe deposit box was held jointly by the woman and the husband, however, it is likely that she intended an immediate transfer, since putting the quitclaim deed in the box would place it in the husband's immediate possession. **C** is correct since it is the only fact listed that could possibly result in a judgment for the husband.

Since the formal requirements for wills are usually more demanding than those for deeds, a deed that is intended to take effect only on the death of a grantor (*i.e.*, a testamentary substitute) is invalid. **A** is therefore incorrect. **B** is incorrect because a gift *causa mortis* is revoked by operation of law if the donor recovers from the illness that threatened his or her life at the time the gift was made. **D** is incorrect because adverse possession requires possession inconsistent with the rights of the owner, and the husband's possession of the land was at the woman's request.

47. **A**    Under the best evidence rule (aka the original document rule), secondary evidence of a writing is not admissible to prove the contents of the writing unless the original or a qualified duplicate is shown to be unavailable. If the writing involved is in the hands of a person located outside the jurisdiction of the court, it may be regarded as unavailable. This is not so, however, if the person who has it is the party offering secondary evidence. Since the original contract is in the hands of the plaintiff, it therefore cannot be regarded as unavailable. Nevertheless, the copy that the plaintiff offers in **A** will not be excluded under the best evidence rule, since the FRE treat all photocopies as originals.

In **B**, the defendant is charged with forging a check. This obviously places the contents of the check in issue. Since the check has not been shown to be unavailable, the best evidence rule will exclude oral testimony as to its contents. Ordinarily, an expert witness may base his or her opinion on things that are not in evidence. In **C**, however, the expert has based her opinion solely on her examination of the X-ray. In effect, this means that all she is really doing is telling the court what the X-ray says. By doing so, she placed the contents of the X-ray in issue. Under the best evidence rule, her testimony is thus inadmissible unless the X-ray is produced or its absence explained. If the writing in question is in the control of an adverse party who has failed to produce the original after receiving notice to do so, the document may be regarded as unavailable. In **D**, however, there is no indication that the state tax collector was asked to produce the plaintiff's original tax return or refused to do so. Until the plaintiff establishes this, or otherwise establishes that the tax return is unavailable, the best evidence rule will prevent the admission of secondary evidence of its contents.

48. **D**    Under 28 U.S.C. §1391, venue is proper in "(1) a judicial district in which any defendant resides, if all defendants are residents of the State in which the district is located; (2) a judicial district in which a substantial part of the events or omissions giving rise to the claim occurred, or a substantial part of property that is the subject of the action is situated; or (3) if there is no district in which an action may be otherwise brought as provided in this section, any judicial district in which any defendant is subject to the court's personal jurisdiction with respect to such action." Because both the doctor and the nurse are citizens of State C, either of the districts in State C are proper. Additionally, since the accident occurred in the Eastern District of State B, that is also a proper venue.

Therefore, **A**, **B**, and **C** are incorrect.

49.   **B**   Embezzlement is criminal conversion of personal property known to be another's with intent to defraud, committed by one in lawful possession of that property. (**Note:** Some jurisdictions require that there be a fiduciary relationship between victim and defendant. Since the defendant's possession of the wallet resulted from her employment relationship with the attorney, she may be found to have possessed it as his fiduciary.) When the defendant spent some of the attorney's money on ice cream, she converted it. Since she planned to keep the money (*i.e.*, use it as her own) she had the intent to defraud. At the time, she was in lawful possession of the wallet. Her use of the attorney's money for the purchase of ice cream was, therefore, an embezzlement. Once a crime has been committed, it cannot be uncommitted. Thus, her returning the money to the attorney would not prevent her from being convicted.

C is therefore incorrect. Larceny is a trespassory taking and carrying off of personal property known to be another's with the intent to permanently deprive. A taking is trespassory if it violates the rights of the owner. When the defendant found the attorney's wallet in the parking lot and carried it off, she did not commit a trespassory taking since her purpose prevented the taking from violating the rights of the attorney. For this reason, and because she then lacked the intent to permanently deprive the attorney, she did not commit larceny by taking the wallet home. When she formed the intent to permanently deprive the attorney, and when she acted on that intent by spending some of the money, the wallet was already in her possession, so she did not "take" or carry it off. For this reason, she did not commit larceny. **A** and **D** are therefore incorrect.

50.   **C**   Private nuisance involves liability-forming conduct by the defendant that unreasonably interferes with the plaintiff's right to use and enjoy his or her realty. A defendant's conduct may be liability-forming if it involves an intentional invasion of the plaintiff's rights. A defendant "intends" a particular result if he or she acts with the desire or substantial certainty that it will occur. Here, as a result of his conversation with the plaintiff, the defendant knew with substantial certainty that his conduct was interfering with the plaintiff's use and enjoyment of his realty — and, therefore, by definition he intended the interference. Thus, if the interference was an unreasonable one, the defendant is liable for nuisance. Although the (un)reasonableness of the invasion depends on many factors not given, private nuisance is the only theory listed that could possibly result in a judgment for the plaintiff.

Trespass to land requires an intentional unauthorized entry onto the plaintiff's realty by something tangible. Since there was no tangible entry onto the plaintiff's land, **A** is incorrect. Intentional infliction of emotional distress requires outrageous conduct by which the defendant intentionally inflicts severe mental suffering upon the plaintiff. **B** is incorrect because the plaintiff does not seek damages for mental suffering but for reduction in the value of his realty. Although an invasion of privacy may be committed by intentionally and offensively interfering with the plaintiff's solitude, **D** is incorrect because this theory requires some physical intrusion into the plaintiff's presence.

51.   **B**   The requirement of standing exists to assure that a person making a constitutional challenge will have incentive to fully and vigorously litigate the issues. For this reason, standing requires that a person challenging the constitutionality of a statute show some actual or immediately threatened concrete personal injury that will be avoided if the court grants

the relief requested. Since the tax will reduce their profits, the stockholders of a corporation with sales in the state in excess of $1 million will suffer an actual injury under the statute. Since a finding that it violates the Commerce Clause would result in a declaration that the statute is invalid and will therefore prevent the tax from being collected, the injury will be avoided if the court grants the relief requested. These stockholders therefore have standing to challenge the statute.

**A** is incorrect because there is no fact indicating that the people of the neighboring state face any injury under the statute, and additionally because a state government does not have standing as a representative of its residents. Since the corporation in **C** does not have annual gross sales in excess of $1 million within the state, the statute imposes no tax on it. Thus, the corporation's stockholders lack standing because they face no actual or immediately threatened injury under the statute. **C** is therefore incorrect. Some cases have held that state taxpayers have standing to challenge certain expenditures of state funds. **D** is incorrect, however, because this statute provides for acquisition rather than expenditure of state funds.

52.  **A**    A transfer of realty to co-owners is presumed to convey equal interests unless its language specifies otherwise. Since the landowner's will made the niece and the husband joint tenants with full right of survivorship as to a one-half interest, each is presumed to have received an equal interest in the one-half interest, or a one-quarter interest in the whole. Joint tenancy is a form of co-ownership best known for the right of survivorship. This means that upon the death of a joint tenant, his or her interest passes to the surviving joint tenant. Since a one-half interest was held by the niece and the husband as joint tenants with full right of survivorship, the death of either spouse would cause his or her one-quarter interest in the realty to pass to the surviving spouse. Since neither spouse survived the other, however, the interest of each passes to his or her heirs. A conveyance to co-owners that does not specify the form of co-ownership is presumed to create a tenancy in common. Since the landowner's will did not specify the form of the daughter's co-ownership, it made her a tenant in common with the niece and the husband. Co-owners do not have a right to survive to the interest of a tenant in common. For this reason, the daughter's one-half interest passes to her heirs.

**B** is incorrect because the daughter's tenancy in common with the niece and the husband gave her no right to their interest. **C** is incorrect because the landowner's will did not make the shares of the co-owners equal but specified that the daughter held a one-half interest, and that the other one-half interest was held by the niece and the husband. **D** is incorrect because the landowner's will gave the daughter a one-half interest.

53.  **D**    The covenant of quiet enjoyment is a promise that the grantee shall peaceably and quietly enjoy possession without interference by the grantor or anyone with a lawful claim. This covenant is breached only when an actual eviction or other interference with possession occurs. For this reason, it flows from the covenantor to the grantee *and his or her successors*. Since the friend interfered with the baker's possession under a lawful claim of right, the warranty was breached. Since it flowed from the landowner to successors of the artist, the landowner may be liable to the baker for damages resulting from the breach.

The covenant of seisin is a promise that the grantor has title to and possession of the realty. The covenant against encumbrances is a promise that no other person has encumbrances or liens against the realty. If the realty is not as covenanted, these covenants are breached the moment a deed containing them is delivered to a grantee. Since the covenants are breached upon delivery of the deed, however, they do not flow to successors of the covenantor's grantee. Since the landowner did not have a right to possession (*i.e.*, he had leased the realty to a friend), and since the friend held a lien on the realty (resulting from the lease), these covenants were breached by the landowner when he conveyed the realty to the artist in March. Since they do not flow to the artist's successors, however, the baker could not succeed against the landowner on these theories. **A** and **B** are therefore incorrect. **C** is incorrect because a covenant of the right to convey does not include a promise that the grantor is entitled to possession, and this covenant was not breached by the landowner at any time.

54.  **D**    Negligence is the breach of a duty of reasonable care owed to the plaintiff by the defendant. Ordinarily, a defendant owes a plaintiff a duty of reasonable care if the defendant's conduct creates a foreseeable risk to the plaintiff. Most jurisdictions limit this duty if the plaintiff is a trespasser on the defendant's land. Since the plaintiff's parents had paid a fee for her to stay at the defendant's camp, however, she was an invitee to whom a duty of reasonable care was owed. Since the defendant set aside a particular area for use by children as a playing field, she owed the children who used it (*i.e.*, her invitees) the duty of making reasonable inspections and taking reasonable steps to protect the children against dangerous conditions. Thus, because the reasonable person would have discovered and removed the tree root, the defendant's failure to do so was negligent (*i.e.*, unreasonable).

Many jurisdictions have held that a landholder is not obligated to protect even invitees against dangers that result *solely* from natural conditions of the land. Since the way softball is played and the nature of children make it foreseeable that children using the field would run into the bushes, however, the defendant's designation of the field as a playing field for children resulted in a risk greater than that created by nature (*i.e.*, the tree root's existence). Her creation of this risk imposed upon her a duty to act reasonably to protect the children against it. **A** is therefore incorrect. A plaintiff assumes the risk when he or she voluntarily encounters a danger of which he or she actually (*i.e.*, subjectively) knows. Since the pile of leaves covering the tree root prevented the plaintiff from knowing about it, she did not assume the risk by encountering it. **B** is therefore incorrect. Some writers have said that an invitee is owed "the highest duty of care." This is a much-misunderstood statement, however. All it really means is that the duty owed to invitees is generally higher than that owed to trespassers or licensees. Basically, it is a duty of reasonable care, not an absolute duty to keep invitees safe. It simply makes landholders liable if they fail to act reasonably. **C** is therefore incorrect.

55.  **D**    Ordinarily, a promise is not enforceable unless it is supported by consideration. Consideration is a bargained-for exchange of something of value for the promise. Because parties should be free to strike whatever bargains appeal to them, courts do not usually inquire into the relative values of the promise and the thing given in return for it. For this reason, the payment of $1 could be consideration for a promise to hold open an offer to

sell realty for $80,000. This is true, however, only if the payment of $1 was bargained-for and given *in exchange* for that promise. Since the seller did not ask for or receive anything in exchange for her promise, it was unsupported by consideration and therefore unenforceable. In a few jurisdictions, a recital like the seller's might be held to create a promise to pay $1, and that promise might be held to be consideration for the seller's agreement to keep the offer open. **D** is correct, however, because it contains the only reason listed that could possibly support the conclusion that accompanies it.

The parol evidence rule prevents the use of extrinsic evidence of prior negotiations or agreements to modify the terms of an unambiguous written contract that the parties intended as a complete record of their agreement. Since the written statement that she had received $1 was not a term of agreement but merely a recital of fact, the parol evidence rule does not prevent the use of extrinsic evidence to contradict it. **A** is therefore incorrect. When a promisee justifiably relies to his or her detriment on a promise, his or her detrimental reliance may make the promise enforceable without consideration. **B** is incorrect, however, because there are no facts indicating that the buyer changed his position as a result of the seller's promise (*i.e.*, relied on the promise), the reasonable person would have relied on it (*i.e.*, that reliance was justified), or the buyer was damaged (*i.e.*, suffered detriment) as a result of such reliance. **C** is incorrect for two reasons: First, courts do not ordinarily consider whether consideration was equal in value to a promise that it purports to support, and second, the dollar was not consideration for the realty itself, but for an option to buy it.

56.  **C**   A party can only require another party to undergo a physical or mental examination by obtaining a court order. *See Fed. R. Civ. P. 35(a)*. An order to submit to a physical or mental examination may only be made if the other party's physical condition is "in controversy" and there is a showing of "good cause."

Therefore, **A**, **B**, and **D** are incorrect.

57.  **A**   Under FRE 803(2), a statement is admissible as an excited utterance if it was made about a startling event while the declarant was under the stress of excitement caused by that event. Since being pushed down and injured is a startling event, and since the plaintiff's bleeding and crying indicate that she was under the stress of excitement that it produced, her statement qualifies as an excited utterance.

The fact that a declarant is presently unavailable is never in itself sufficient to permit the admission of his or her out-of-court statements. **B** is incorrect for this reason, and because the excited utterance exception does not require that the declarant be unavailable. **C** is incorrect, because although the plaintiff's statement is hearsay, it is admissible under the excited utterance exception to the hearsay rule. The court found that the plaintiff was incompetent to testify because she could not appreciate her duty to testify truthfully. The reason that hearsay is customarily excluded is the fact that the hearsay declarant was under no duty to speak truthfully when making the out-of-court statement. The excited utterance exception to the hearsay rule, however, is based on the inherent trustworthiness of certain statements made even while the declarant was under no legal duty to tell the truth. For this reason, the plaintiff's inability to appreciate her *duty* to tell the truth does not prevent her excited utterance from being inherently trustworthy. **D** is therefore incorrect.

58.  **A**  Leading questions are those that would give the ordinary person the impression that the questioner desires one answer rather than another and are ordinarily improper if asked on direct examination. FRE 611 recognizes an exception to this rule, permitting leading questions to be asked in direct examination of a witness associated with an adverse party. Since the witness is employed by the plaintiff's adversary, the defendant, the objection should be overruled.

Leading questions may also be asked of hostile witnesses. **B** is incorrect, however, because a hostile witness is one who has manifested hostility or prejudice under examination, and there is no indication that the witness did so. While leading questions are permitted on cross-examination, **C** is incorrect because the question was asked on direct examination. (**Note:** The facts indicate that the witness was called by the plaintiff's attorney to testify on the presentation of the plaintiff's direct case.) Since the question made it clear that the examiner wanted an affirmative answer, it was a leading question. Thus, **D** is incorrect.

59.  **D**  One who engages in an abnormally dangerous activity is strictly liable for harm that proximately results from the dangerous nature of that activity. Most jurisdictions hold that transporting large quantities of any explosive substance is such an activity.

If a statute is designed to protect a class of persons to which the plaintiff belongs against risks like the one that resulted in harm, its violation may raise an inference or a presumption of negligence and may even be termed negligence per se. Since the statute prohibited parking without regard to a vehicle's contents, it was obviously not designed to protect against risks resulting from the explosion of a large quantity of gasoline. **A** and **B** are therefore incorrect. Since the "No Parking" sign was also not designed to protect against this risk, its violation is not relevant to determining whether the defendant was negligent. For this reason, **C** is also incorrect.

60.  **B**  The state statute could result in depriving the girl's parents of the liberty to decide what treatment their daughter should receive. The Due Process Clauses of the Fifth and Fourteenth Amendments require that a law that regulates a liberty interest must be clear enough to be understandable by the person of ordinary intelligence. Otherwise, the law may be void for vagueness. The statutory use of the phrase "life-threatening" could violate this requirement, since the meaning of that phrase may depend on the opinion of the person using it. The statutory reference to "hospital officials" may also be vague since it is impossible to tell which officials the statute designates. Although the court might find that the statute is not vague, the argument set forth in **B** is the only one listed that could possibly result in the conclusion that it is unconstitutional.

The Equal Protection Clause prohibits invidious discrimination by the states. **A** is incorrect because there is no indication that the statute discriminates against any particular group. The Free Exercise Clause prohibits the government from interfering with the exercise of religious beliefs. **C** is incorrect because the girl's parents have not claimed that their refusal to consent to the blood transfusion was related to any religious belief that they held. (**Note:** Beware of reading into a question facts that the examiners did not write into it.) Determining whether a statute does or does not interfere with a fundamental right is relevant in selecting the standard that it must meet to be valid. **D** is incorrect, however, because the fact that a statute interferes with a fundamental right is never in itself sufficient to justify the conclusion that it is unconstitutional.

61. **B**   Statements by a now-unavailable declarant concerning—among other things—the declarant's marriage, or relationship by blood or marriage, are admissible under the FRE hearsay exception for statements of personal history, and under the common law exception for statements of pedigree. Since the mother was deceased at the time of trial, she was unavailable. Since the notations contained in the Bible were statements by the mother about her marriage to the man's brother, about her relationship by marriage to the man, and about her relationship by blood to the niece, it qualifies for admission under both FRE 803(13) and the common law.

The FRE permit the admission, as an "ancient document," of a properly authenticated writing that is at least 20 years old. Common law usually requires 30 years. **A** is incorrect under both systems, however, because there is no fact indicating the age of the mother's notation in the Bible. In some jurisdictions, a law known as the "dead man's statute" prevents the admission of certain evidence regarding certain transactions with a person who is now deceased. Although the dead man's statute may *prevent* the admission of evidence, it never *justifies* the admission of evidence. **C** is therefore incorrect. Under FRE 803(9), "records of vital statistics," including birth, death, and marriage, may be admissible if such records were kept by a public office pursuant to the requirements of law. **D** is incorrect because the notation that the niece offered into evidence was not reported to or kept by a public office pursuant to the requirements of law.

62. **D**   Criminal conspiracy consists of an agreement between two or more persons to commit a crime. When the defendant and the friend agreed to rob a bank, the crime of conspiracy was complete—whether or not they ever actually went through with the plan.

In most jurisdictions, once a defendant has become guilty of a conspiracy (by agreeing to commit a crime), he or she cannot avoid criminal responsibility for the crime of conspiracy by withdrawing from or renouncing their plan. **A**, **B**, and **C** are therefore incorrect.

63. **C**   A defendant is liable for harm that proximately results from his or her breach of a duty of reasonable care. Since a hotel keeper obviously owes a duty of reasonable care to hotel guests, the defendant's failure to use adequate care in hiring the electrician would be a breach of that duty, making the defendant liable for injuries resulting from the electrician's error.

Although one who employs an independent contractor is not vicariously liable for torts committed by the contractor, the employer may be liable for his or her own negligence in failing to use adequate care in selecting the contractor. **A** is therefore incorrect. If reasonable inspection by the defendant would have failed to disclose the electrician's error, then the defendant's failure to discover the electrician's error would not be negligence. This alone would not be enough to result in a judgment for the defendant, however, because the defendant may have committed some other act of negligence (*e.g.*, failing to use adequate care in selecting the electrician) for which liability can be imposed. **B** is therefore incorrect. Strict liability may be imposed upon one who engages in (or employs another to engage in) an ultra-hazardous activity. Strict liability does not apply, however, to an ordinary activity that has become ultra-hazardous because of a negligent error made by the person engaging in it. **D** is therefore incorrect.

64.  **B**      A quitclaim deed conveys the interest held by the grantor at the time of its execution. The wife could not own the entire Smith and Baker tract if the landowner had already conveyed part of it to the sister. Although certain methods of describing realty are popular or traditional, any description is adequate if it identifies the land conveyed with reasonable clarity. Thus, if the description contained in the landowner's deed to the sister was reasonably sufficient to identify the property conveyed, it effectively conveyed that property.

A conveyance by deed usually implies a warranty of title which, if breached, may give the grantee a right of action against the grantor. A quitclaim deed does not. But although one who receives a quitclaim deed has no right of action for breach of warranty against the grantor, the quitclaim deed may effectively convey whatever interest the grantor did possess. Thus, if the landowner's deed to the sister did not effectively convey part of the Smith and Baker tract, his conveyance to his wife by quitclaim could have been sufficient to make her the owner of the entire Smith and Baker tract. **A** is therefore incorrect. **C** and **D** are incorrect because a description is sufficient if it identifies the realty conveyed with reasonable clarity.

65.  **B**      The United States Supreme Court has held that a public person suing for defamation must prove "actual malice," and that a private person suing a media defendant for defamation must prove either "actual malice" or negligence. A defendant had "actual malice" if, at the time he or she made a defamatory statement, he or she knew the statement to be false or entertained serious doubts about its truth. A defendant was negligent if at the time he or she made a defamatory statement, he or she did not know that the statement was false, but would have known had he or she been acting reasonably. If officials of the newspaper believed the statement was true, they lacked "actual malice." If their belief was reasonable, they were not acting negligently. Thus, if they had a reasonable belief in the truth of the statement, the newspaper would not be liable for defamation.

Although some states recognize a privilege to publish false statements that are contained in public records, there is no privilege to misstate the contents of a public record. **A** is therefore incorrect. A defendant who defamed a public figure may be liable if he or she had "actual malice" as defined above. Thus, the fact that the plaintiff was a public figure would not be sufficient in itself to protect the newspaper against liability for defaming him. **C** is therefore incorrect. A plaintiff asserting a claim for written defamation (*i.e.*, libel) is not required to prove damage to make out a case if the written statement was defamatory on its face. Thus, the plaintiff's failure to prove damage is not sufficient to prevent recovery. For this reason, **D** is incorrect.

66.  **C**    The Fourth Amendment guarantee against unreasonable search and seizure is ordinarily violated when a search is conducted without a warrant. To enforce this guarantee, the United States Supreme Court has ruled that the fruits of an unlawful search should be excluded from evidence. A search occurs when there has been an invasion of an area as to which a defendant had a reasonable expectation of privacy. Since the defendant was the only person who had a key to the footlocker, it was reasonable for him to expect that its contents would remain private. For this reason, the officers' first look into the footlocker was a search. Since the warrant was issued because of what the officers found, its issuance was one of the fruits of that first unlawful search. For this reason, the defendant's motion to suppress the cocaine must be granted. (**Note:** There are some special exceptions to the rule that a warrantless search is unlawful. The facts in this case do not satisfy the requirements of *any* of these exceptions, but the nature of the question only makes it necessary to eliminate those listed in the options.)

Consent by a third party to search the property of a defendant makes a warrantless search lawful, but only if the person who consented had rights in the property that were equal to those of the defendant. Since the defendant was the only person who had a key to the footlocker, the woman did not have rights to its contents that were equal to the defendant's. Thus, her consent did not eliminate the need for a warrant to search it. **A** is therefore incorrect. Even the consent of a person who does not have an equal right to the premises might justify a warrantless search if the police officers reasonably believed that he or she had such a right (*i.e.*, the person who consented had the "apparent authority" to do so). **B** is incorrect, however, because even if the woman had apparent authority to consent to a search of the *room*, the fact that the defendant had the only key to the footlocker should have made it obvious to the officers that the woman's authority did not extend to its contents. Probable cause justifies an arrest without a warrant but does not justify a search without a warrant. Thus, probable cause could not justify the first search. Although a search warrant may be issued upon a showing of probable cause, it is invalid if that probable cause was itself the fruit of an unlawful search. Thus, probable cause does not justify the issuance of the warrant or the second search that was conducted pursuant to it. **D** is therefore incorrect.

67.  **A**    Although a breach of contract may entitle the wronged party to suspend his or her own performance, it does not always give him or her the right to terminate the contract entirely. Fairness and the courts ordinarily require that the breaching party be allowed a reasonable period of time in which to cure the breach. If it is cured within that period, the breaching party may enforce the contract against the non-breaching party, although he or she may be liable for damages resulting from his or her breach. In determining whether the breach was cured in a reasonable time, the courts consider the nature of the contract itself and the circumstances surrounding its formation. Because the circumstances contemplated by the parties made it essential that the conveyance occur on or before June 15, the court is likely to determine that a conveyance on June 16 did not cure the breach.

Sometimes the phrase "time is of the essence" is inserted in a contract to make it clear that the circumstances contemplated by the parties did make it essential that performance occur by a certain date. Since those circumstances may be found to exist even without the insertion of specific language, however, its insertion is not the only thing that would result in a judgment for the buyer. **B** is therefore incorrect. Even if the seller's breach resulted in damage to the buyer, a court could find that the breach was cured within a reasonable time, and that therefore the buyer's only remedy is damages. **C** is therefore incorrect. **D** is incorrect because contract liability does not depend on fault and may be imposed in spite of reasonable efforts to comply with the contract.

68. **D**     One who engages in an ultra-hazardous or abnormally dangerous activity is strictly liable for damage that proximately results therefrom. Since most jurisdictions agree that storing poisonous gases is an ultra-hazardous or abnormally dangerous activity, proof that the gas is extremely deadly would be sufficient to result in the imposition of strict liability on the defendant.

One who places a defective product — whether defective in design or in manufacture — in the stream of commerce may be held strictly liable for damage resulting from the product defect. **A** is incorrect, however, because the defendant did not place the tank in the stream of commerce. **B** and **C** are incorrect because the defendant did not place the gas that injured the plaintiff in the stream of commerce.

69. **A**     Under Fed. R. Civ. P. 26(a)(2)(b), the party using an expert witness must automatically supply a written report containing "(i) a complete statement of all opinions the witness will express and the basis and reasons for them; (ii) the facts or data considered by the witness in forming them; [and] (iii) any exhibits that will be used to summarize or support them." Consequently, the airline's attorney does not need to do anything to know the details of the expert's research before trial.

Therefore, **B**, **C**, and **D** are incorrect.

70. **A**     Lay witnesses are generally permitted to testify only to facts. When it would be helpful to a clear understanding of the witness's testimony, however, the opinion of a lay witness may be admissible if it is rationally based on the perceptions of the witness. The decision as to whether this is so and as to whether the lay opinion is admissible is made in the court's discretion. Therefore, if the judge decides that the witness's opinion is rationally based on her perceptions, it is admissible. Conversely, unless the judge so decides, the witness's opinion should be excluded.

So long as they do not go beyond matters in common knowledge, lay opinions about the physical and mental condition of another are usually admissible. For this reason, an opinion that another person was intoxicated is admissible (so long as it is rationally based on the witness's perceptions) even if the witness is not an expert on intoxication. **B** and **C** are therefore incorrect. The admissibility of opinion evidence is a question of law for the judge. This means that the judge cannot admit the witness's opinion testimony unless he or she finds it to be rationally based on the witness's perceptions, and he or she cannot delegate that responsibility to the jury. **D** is therefore incorrect.

71. **C**     The Fourteenth Amendment to the United States Constitution prohibits a state from denying persons within its jurisdiction the equal protection of the law. A system of classification

contained in social or economic legislation is usually presumed to comply with this requirement so long as it has some rational basis. When the classification is a "suspect" one, the presumption of constitutionality is inverted, and the statute is unconstitutional unless it is necessary to serve a compelling state interest. Since alienage is a "suspect classification," a statute that discriminates against aliens is ordinarily required to meet the compelling state interest test. Under the "political function" exception, however, a statute that prevents aliens from holding a particular state job may be constitutionally valid if the job is one that should be performed only by people familiar with and sympathetic to American traditions. The Supreme Court has held that the only jobs falling into this category are those that invest the public employee with the power to make policy or with broad discretion in executing public policy.

**A** is incorrect because not all "traditional" government activities fall into this category. Since alienage is a suspect classification, **B** is incorrect because a rational basis is not sufficient to justify a classification based on alienage. Statutes that interfere with fundamental interests—like those based on "suspect classifications"—are also subject to the compelling state interest standard. **D** is incorrect, however, because a classification based on alienage is "suspect," making the compelling state interest standard applicable even if the right with which the statute interferes is not a fundamental one.

72. **D**    Unless the parties stipulate otherwise, a jury verdict must be unanimous. *See Fed. R. Civ. P. 48(b).*

A and **B** are incorrect because the jury must have between 6 and 12 members. **C** is incorrect because the Seventh Amendment generally does not give a right to a jury trial for parties seeking an equitable claim such as an injunction.

73. **C**    Federal courts have subject matter jurisdiction over claims that arise under federal law. *See 28 U.S.C. §1331.* Since the woman is making a claim based on the federal National Labor Relations Act, the federal district court in State A has jurisdiction over the matter.

Because the woman is bringing a federal claim, any issues regarding the citizenship of the parties are irrelevant. Therefore, **A**, **B**, and **D** are incorrect.

74. **B**    Negligence is a breach of the duty of reasonable care. This duty is breached by a defendant's failure to act like the reasonable person. Thus, unless the reasonable person would have repaired the fence, the defendant's failure to do so was not negligent.

In most jurisdictions, a person who keeps a wild animal is strictly liable for damage that it causes. The jurisdictions that do not apply this rule generally hold that keeping a wild animal is *prima facie* negligent. Neither rule is applied, however, unless the injury sustained by the plaintiff resulted from the wild and dangerous nature of the animal involved. Since even a domestic animal might knock over a fence that has become badly deteriorated, the plaintiff's injury did not result from the wild and dangerous nature of the defendant's cougar. For this reason, **A** is incorrect. In deciding whether a defendant's conduct was negligent, it is compared to that of the reasonable person. What matters is not what the defendant actually knew about the risks, but what the reasonable person in the defendant's position would have known about those risks. **C** is incorrect because the issue was whether a reasonable person would repair the fence. A plaintiff assumes a risk when, knowing that it exists, he or she voluntarily encounters it. **D** is incorrect because there is no fact indicating that the plaintiff knew that the fence was deteriorated enough to create a risk that the cougar would injure her.

75.  **B**    Ordinarily, a promise is unenforceable unless it is supported by consideration. Consideration is a bargained-for exchange of something of value given in return for and to induce a promise. It usually consists of some benefit conferred upon the promisor or of some detriment incurred by the promisee. Consistent with this definition is the rule that a promisee's undertaking to do something that he or she is already legally obligated to do (*i.e.*, performance of a preexisting duty) is not consideration for a new promise by the promisor because it does not confer on the promisor any benefit that he or she was not already entitled to receive and does not impose on the promisee any detriment that he or she had not already incurred. Since all that the worker gave the farmer in return for his promise to pay for the tractor rental was her promise that she would finish plowing by April 1, and since she was already legally obligated to do so, the farmer may successfully argue that his promise was unsupported by consideration. [**Note:** Although UCC §2-209(1) permits the modification of a sales contract between merchants to be enforced without consideration, it is inapplicable here because this was not a contract for sale.]

Although the Statute of Frauds makes an oral contract for the purchase of goods with a price of $500 or more unenforceable over objection, **A** is incorrect because the agreement between the farmer and the worker was not for the sale of goods. Duress is some compulsion or restraint that deprives a contracting party of the ability to exercise free will and usually involves some physical force or threat. A few cases have recognized the possibility of economic duress, but this defense is rarely applied, and when it is, it involves much more desperate economic threats than any indicated by the facts in this case. **C** is incorrect for this reason and because a party to a contract is expected to show reasonable firmness in asserting his or her contract rights. Since the farmer failed to object to the additional charge, it is unlikely that a court would conclude that he did so under duress. When a promise would ordinarily be unenforceable because it is unsupported by consideration or because it fails to satisfy the Statute of Frauds, justified detrimental reliance by the promisee may result in enforcement on a theory of promissory estoppel. **D** is incorrect, however, because the farmer's reliance on the worker's promise is not relevant to the worker's attempt to enforce the farmer's promise.

76.  **C**    The landowner's conveyance made his son a life tenant. A life tenant may convey that interest. When the son quitclaimed his interest in the land, the wife gained a life estate per autre vie, or a life estate measured by the life of another. Here, the wife would get what the son had, specifically a life estate measured by the son's life. The daughter continued to hold a remainder in fee simple, since the conveyance gave "the remainder to my daughter" without any limitation. Ultimately, the daughter would get the land from the wife when the son died. The fact that the landowner did not give the son permission to quitclaim his interest does not change the analysis.

Therefore, **A**, **B**, and **D** are incorrect.

77.  **B**     False pretenses consists of obtaining title to another's property by a knowing false statement of present or past fact with the intent to defraud. Here, the dealer obtained title to the man's money by knowingly lying about the fact the car was not a new car. Consequently, he could be charged with this crime, and **D** is incorrect.

**A** is incorrect because larceny by trick happens when a victim merely transfers custody of his or her property, not title. **C** is incorrect because embezzlement requires the person to convert property he or she is already in lawful possession of. Here, the dealer was clearly not already in lawful possession of the man's money before the man gave it to him based on his belief he was buying a new car.

78.  **A**     Federal courts of appeal review a district court's determination regarding unsettled state law *de novo*. Consequently, a court of appeals should not defer to a district court's decision.

**B** is incorrect because a federal court sitting in diversity must apply the substantive law of the state in which it is sitting. *See Erie Railroad v. Tompkins, 304 U.S. 64 (1938).* **C** is incorrect because federal courts follow federal procedural law. **D** is incorrect because statutes of limitations are substantive law when determining whether to apply federal or state law. *See Guaranty Trust Co. v. York, 326 U.S. 99 (1945).* Consequently, a federal court should follow the statute of limitations rules of the state in which it is sitting.

79.  **C**     Exigent circumstances justify a warrantless entry into a home if police officers are assisting an injured occupant or preventing imminent injury. Exigent circumstances also include preventing the imminent destruction of evidence and searching in "hot pursuit" for a suspect. Here, the officer heard the men fighting, and entered the home to prevent imminent injury. He then discovered the drug evidence in plain view. **A** is incorrect because exigent circumstances were present. **B** is incorrect because the plain view doctrine applies to situations where police see evidence of a crime from a location where they have a right to be. Here, the plain view doctrine does not address the officer's initial entry into the house. **D** is incorrect because the issue here is exigent circumstances, not probable cause. Additionally, the validity of a search does not depend on whether there was probable cause for the suspect's ultimate arrest.

80.  **A**     UCC §1-205 defines usage of trade as a practice or method of dealing that is regularly observed in a particular industry. UCC §2-202 permits evidence of usage of trade to explain the terms of a written contract, even when the contract was intended to be a final expression of the agreement of the parties.

**B** is therefore incorrect. Ordinarily, parties to a contract are understood to accept the economic risks resulting from subsequent events that were within their contemplation at the time the contract was formed. This means that if the parties *did* contemplate a decline in new home starts, a strong argument could be made that the builder should be bound by the 20,000-board-feet minimum set forth in the contract. The fact that they did *not* contemplate such a decline in new homes, if relevant at all, is thus more likely to support the builder's position than it is to support the supplier's. In any event, although the contemplation of the parties might help determine the meaning of the terms that they used, it is not the only factor to be considered. In fact, the UCC specifically permits evidence of trade usage to be considered as well. **C** is therefore incorrect. Ordinarily, in construing contracts, courts consider the manifest intentions of the parties and do so by examining the language of the written agreement between them. A problem may arise, however, since the words used may have meant different things to the different parties. Since trade usage may indicate the meaning that certain terms generally have for people in the industry involved, the UCC provision regarding trade usage is designed to help determine what the parties meant by the terms they used. If, for example, it was generally understood in the trade that minimum requirements were inapplicable in times of falling prices, the parties might have specified a minimum number, meaning it to be applicable only if prices did not fall, even though this intention would not be apparent to persons not in the trade. The argument set forth in **D**, however, is based on what the language means to people who are unaware of its special trade usage. For this reason, **D** is incorrect.

81.  **B**     The United States Supreme Court has held that the First Amendment of the United States Constitution requires a public official or public figure suing for defamation to prove that the defendant had actual malice in making the defamatory statement. The Court defined a public official as a public employee who has or reasonably appears to have substantial control over the conduct of public affairs. The plaintiffs are clearly public employees. Whether they reasonably appear to have substantial control over the conduct of public affairs may be a question of fact, but **B** is the only argument listed that could possibly result in a judgment for the newspaper.

The United States Supreme Court has said that there is no such thing as a false idea. Since defamation liability cannot be imposed for publication of the truth, this statement by the Supreme Court prevents defamation liability from being imposed for the publication of an opinion. **A** is incorrect, however, because—even though it was contained in an editorial—the statement that the majority of firefighters were dangerously out of shape and had recently failed their physicals is obviously an assertion of fact. The Supreme Court has defined a public figure as either one who has achieved such "pervasive fame and notoriety" that he or she is known to the great mass of humanity, or one who has voluntarily "mounted the rostrum" in an attempt to influence public opinion on a matter of public controversy. **C** is incorrect because there is no fact indicating that either definition applies to the plaintiffs. In addition, **C** is incorrect because the Supreme Court has held that a defendant may not successfully argue that the plaintiff has become a public figure as a result of the defamatory statements that the defendant published about the plaintiff. **D** is incorrect since the Supreme Court's definition of "public official" makes it clear that not all public employees fit into this category.

82.  **B**     Under UCC §2-609, whenever it reasonably appears that a party to a sales contract will be unable to perform as required, the other party may demand an adequate assurance of performance. If the party on whom such demand is made fails to respond within a reasonable period of time, the party making that demand may treat the other party's prospective inability to perform as a repudiation. Since the destruction of the plaintiff's only factory raised reasonable questions about whether the plaintiff would be able to perform as required, the police department was entitled to demand assurances as it did in its letter of

July 10. When the plaintiff failed to respond within a reasonable time, the police department was relieved of any further obligation to perform.

When unforeseen circumstances eliminate the underlying reasons for contracting, the doctrine of frustration of purpose may excuse performance by the parties. (If, for example, all the criminals in the city stopped using guns so that there was no longer any reason for the police department to need bulletproof vests, the doctrine of frustration of purpose might relieve it of its obligation to continue purchasing vests from the plaintiff.) **A** is incorrect because the underlying reasons for the agreement between the police department and the plaintiff (*i.e.*, the police department's need for bulletproof vests) continued to exist even though the plaintiff's factory was destroyed. An agreement calling for a series of performances by the parties may be regarded as a single contract or as a series of separate ones. Calling it "divisible" simply means that the court will treat it as a series of separate contracts. It is difficult to tell from the facts whether the contract between the defendant and the police department is or is not "divisible." In either event, however, whether it is a breach of a single agreement calling for a series of performances, or of one of the separate agreements that result from calling the contract divisible, the defendant's failure to deliver bulletproof vests might be a breach. Therefore, determining that the contract was divisible is not relevant in determining whether failure to perform constitutes a breach, so **C** is incorrect. Even before the time of performance, a party may treat the other party's repudiation as a breach. Thus, a repudiation by the police department might provide the plaintiff with an argument in support of its position, but it would not provide the police department with support for its position. **D** is therefore incorrect.

83. **C**    Negligence is unreasonable conduct when one has a duty to act reasonably. Importantly, a person cannot be negligent if he or she acted reasonably. Consequently, only unreasonable conduct on the limousine driver's part can result in a judgment against him. Here, if a court finds it was unreasonable for the driver to swerve to avoid the dog, he would be liable for negligence. **A** is incorrect because the doctrine of *res ipsa loquitur* is used in cases where the defendant's conduct is unknown. In that case, it allows a plaintiff to create an inference that the defendant acted unreasonably by relying on circumstantial evidence. In that case, the evidence has to show that the accident was one that would not normally have occurred without negligence, under circumstances that eliminated all probabilities other than the negligence of the defendant. Here, such circumstantial evidence is unnecessary because the limousine driver's conduct in swerving to avoid the dog was known. Under *negligence per se*, the defendant is negligent if, without excuse, he or she violates a statute that is designed to protect against the type of accident that the defendant's conduct causes, and the accident victim is within the class of persons the statute is designed to protect. The important point is that the violation must cause the accident. Since the accident would have happened even if the limousine driver had insurance, there is no causal link between the violation and the statute. Thus, **B** is incorrect. **D** is incorrect because even if the limousine driver owed some special duty to the teenagers, he still would have had to act unreasonably before he could be found liable.

84. **C**    Under the statute, the defendant can be guilty of second degree murder only if the victim dies during the course of the commission of one of the enumerated felonies. Nothing in the facts suggests that the defendant or the friend was committing a rape, kidnapping,

burglary, or arson. Robbery is a larceny that is committed by force or a threat of force against a human being. Larceny is a trespassory taking and carrying off of personal property known to be another's with the intent to permanently deprive the other of it. Since the jury believed the defendant's testimony, the coat that she was attempting to obtain from the victim was her own. Her taking it could not, therefore, constitute a larceny, and her use of force to take it was not a robbery.

**A** and **B** are incorrect because if a death occurs during the course of one of the felonies specified, the felony murder rule is frequently applied even though the death was unforeseeable. Since the statute provides that an unintentional killing is second degree murder if perpetrated by the defendant *or an accomplice* during the course of a listed crime, **D** is obviously incorrect.

85. **C**    Since the notary received his interest from the barber, the validity of the notary's title depends on the validity of the barber's title. For this reason, if the barber's title is superior to that of the landowner's cousin, then so is the notary's. The validity of the barber's title (and therefore of the notary's) depends on the recording statute. The statute given is a typical "race-notice" statute. According to its provisions, the interest of a subsequent grantee for value and without notice is superior to that of a prior grantee unless the prior grantee's interest is recorded before the subsequent grantee's interest is *recorded*. Thus, since the landowner's cousin's interest was recorded before the barber's, it was superior to the barber's (and therefore to the notary's).

**A** is incorrect because although the statute makes the payment of value a condition for the superiority of a *subsequent* grantee's interest, it does not impose such a requirement on the prior grantee. Since the "race" aspect of the statute makes priority depend on who *recorded* first, the fact that the barber recorded before selling to the notary would not defeat the landowner's cousin's interest since the barber recorded after the cousin did. **B** is therefore incorrect. Recording is "outside the chain of title" if it could not have been discovered by a reasonable title search. (For example, since the cousin recorded before the barber, a reasonable title search might not have disclosed a record of the deed from the landowner to the barber. This is because after finding a record of the landowner's grant to the cousin, the searcher would have expected that the next grant of an interest in the property was by the cousin and would have no reason to search for a subsequent grant by the landlord.) Most jurisdictions hold that a recording outside the chain of title is no recording at all since it does not give the reasonable searcher notice of the transaction. **D** is incorrect, however, because if the barber recorded prior to the cousin, the recording of the landowner's grant to the barber would have been within the chain of title.

86. **D**    If the defendant is the initial aggressor, he or she may not claim self-defense. Importantly, the defendant can be an aggressor, and lose the right of self-defense, even if the defendant did not actually strike the first blow. If a defendant does an unlawful act that intentionally provokes the physical conflict, the defendant becomes the aggressor. Here, the defendant provoked the robber by telling the robber that the defendant would shoot him through the windshield if the robber tried to leave. Consequently, the defendant became the aggressor and lost his claim of self-defense.

For a self-defense claim, the harm being defended against must be reasonably imminent. While the danger that someone will be attacked tomorrow is likely insufficient to support a claim of self-defense, courts will not make the defendant wait until the absolute last second before he or she can defend himself or herself. Here, even though the robber was still getting out of his car, a court would likely find the danger was reasonably imminent. Thus, **A** is incorrect. In a self-defense claim, the defendant may not use more force than seems reasonably necessary in the circumstances. Here, a large axe is likely a use of deadly force. Consequently, the defendant's use of the pistol was not more force than was necessary and **B** is incorrect. While the robber had already attempted to withdraw, the real issue is the defendant's provocation, so **C** is incorrect.

87. **A**    In *Minnesota v. Olson, 495 U.S. 91 (1990)*, the United States Supreme Court held that an overnight guest has a legitimate interest in privacy in the residence where he or she is staying. Consequently, the police had to obtain a search warrant before they could lawfully enter the apartment because the man was staying there for a week and was thus an overnight guest. Therefore, **D** is incorrect.

**B** is incorrect because the plain view exception only applies when the police see evidence from a place they are lawfully able to be. Here, the police only saw the marijuana once they unlawfully entered the apartment. **C** is incorrect because even if the neighbors smelled the marijuana, this was not an exigent circumstance or other exception that would relieve the police from having to obtain a search warrant.

88. **D**    One who holds a present possessory interest in real estate is entitled to make all normal uses of the land and to keep the profits from those uses so long as he or she does not unreasonably decrease its value to the holders of future interests. This means, among other things, that the holder of a present possessory interest in realty is permitted to rent the realty and to keep the rent. For this reason, the accountant has no right to the rents. On the other hand, since the permanent removal of minerals from the land will inevitably reduce the value of the realty, limitations on the removal of minerals are imposed on holders of certain present possessory interests. If, however, the grantor had been actively removing minerals from the realty, it is presumed that in granting a present possessory interest, the grantor intended to grant the right to continue removing minerals as well. Since the landowner had been mining the gold on the land, it is presumed that he intended to grant the friend the right to continue doing so, even though the friend's interest in the realty was less than a fee. Thus, the accountant is not entitled to proceeds from the mining operation, either.

For the combination of reasons given above, **A**, **B**, and **C** are incorrect.

89. **B.**    A question of fact is an issue in the case that is decided by looking at the facts in evidence. The validity of the rock singer's signature would be a question of fact. A trial court's findings regarding a question of fact will not be disturbed unless they are "clearly erroneous." *See Fed. R. Civ. P. 52(a)(6).*

**A** is incorrect because a question of law is an issue that must be decided by applying legal principles (for example, whether a police officer had probable cause to arrest a suspect). **C**

and **D** are incorrect because abuse of discretion is the standard applied to the discretionary decisions of a trial court, such as leaves to amend.

90.  **C**    FRE 801(d)(1)(B) specifies that a prior consistent statement of a declarant is not hearsay if the declarant has testified and is available for cross-examination, and if the statement is offered to rebut a claim of recent fabrication. Since the victim testified that the defendant raped her, and since the defendant claimed that the victim's complaint was fabricated on April 3, evidence that the victim made that same complaint to the neighbor on March 7 tends to rebut the defendant's claim. The neighbor's testimony is therefore admissible.

Under FRE 803(2), a statement is admissible as an excited utterance if it was made about a startling event while the declarant was under the stress of excitement caused by that event. Ordinarily, this requires the statement to have been made either during the event or immediately thereafter. Since a week passed between the alleged rape and the victim's statement to the neighbor, it probably does not qualify as an excited utterance. **A** is therefore incorrect. Hearsay is defined as an out-of-court statement offered for the purpose of proving the truth of the matter asserted in that statement. If the victim's out-of-court statement to the neighbor is not offered to prove the truth of what she asserted (*i.e.*, that the defendant raped her) but is offered to prove that she did not fabricate her complaint after learning that the defendant was married, it is not hearsay. FRE 801(d)(1)(B) specifically provides that such a statement "is not hearsay." This means that in addition to being admissible for the purpose of rebutting the defendant's claim of recent fabrication, the victim's statement may be admissible as substantive evidence as well. **B** is therefore incorrect. FRE 803(1) recognizes a hearsay exception for a statement of the declarant's sense impressions. This exception applies, however, only when the declarant's statement describing an event is made during or immediately after the event. Since the victim's statement to the neighbor was made a week after the incident that it purported to describe, **D** is incorrect.

91.  **D**    Since the formal requirements for wills are more demanding than those for deeds, a deed that is intended to take effect only on the death of the grantor (*i.e.*, a testamentary substitute) is invalid. Thus, if the woman intended for the quitclaim deed to have no effect until after her death, it is invalid. Although the facts make it impossible to determine with certainty what the woman's intention was, **D** is the only argument listed that could possibly result in a judgment for the nurse.

**A** is incorrect because recording statutes protect only those who purchase for value. Since the nurse received by will and without consideration, the husband's failure to record would not give the nurse a priority. Although a quitclaim deed does not imply any warranties or covenants, it does serve to transfer whatever interest the grantor held at the time of its execution. **B** and **C** are therefore incorrect.

92.  **B**    Assault is the intentional causing of an apprehension of harmful or offensive contact. Importantly, the doctrine of transferred intent applies to assault. Under this doctrine, if the defendant had the necessary intent with respect to one person, he or she will be held to have committed an intentional tort against any other person who happens to be injured. Here, the boy clearly intended to frighten the babysitter. Thus, even though the boy intended

to scare his babysitter, the fact that his sister was nearby and was put in apprehension of harmful or offensive contact (*i.e.*, she ducked) was enough for liability. **A** is incorrect because the boy could also have been held liable for battery since he did in fact hit the babysitter. Importantly, a defendant has the necessary intent for battery if he intended to cause an imminent apprehension on the plaintiff's part of a harmful or offensive contact. Basically, the intent to commit an assault is sufficient for battery. **C** is incorrect because if the defendant intends to frighten the plaintiff, he has the necessary intent for assault. **D** is incorrect because in the case of battery or assault, it is not necessary that the defendant bear malice or hostility toward the plaintiff.

93. **B**   It has been said that the offeror is monarch of the offer. This means, of course, that the person who institutes the contractual process by making an offer is in complete control of that offer's terms and, upon acceptance, is not bound to any terms other than those. Since the buyer's offer was to pay $100 for information "leading to purchase of an antique car," he is not required to pay unless the information furnished actually leads to the purchase of an antique car. Since the man's letter did not, it does not qualify the man to receive the reward.

   **A** is incorrect because an offer to the general public that is made by advertisement ordinarily is not revoked until a withdrawal is given approximately equal publicity. **C** and **D** are incorrect because the buyer only offered to pay for information leading to purchase, and the man's did not.

94  **A**   When a safety statute is violated, courts will find an unexcused violation of that statute *negligence per se*. There are three main requirements for application of *negligence per se*: 1) the defendant violated a statute, 2) the statute was designed to protect against the same type of accident that occurred, and 3) the accident victim is a member of the class of persons the statute was designed to protect. Here, all three elements were satisfied because the manufacturer failed to provide a warning, the warning would have protected against the man's skin discoloration, and the man was a member of the class (a user of the cream) that the statute was designed to protect. However, even when *negligence per se* applies, the plaintiff must still show a causal link between the violation and the injury. Here, since the man admitted that no one in his household read the warnings, there was no causal link, since the harm would have occurred even if the warning was inside the packaging. **B** is incorrect because the main issue here is the lack of the warning in the package, not the man's continued use of the cream. **C** is incorrect, because there was no causal link between the harm and the failure to provide the warning. **D** is incorrect because it fails to take into account whether the man would have read or even followed the warning.

95. **B**   A proceeding is moot when there are no contested material issues for the court to decide. Since the girl has died, the state court can no longer appoint the hospital administrator her guardian. Since the purpose of the federal proceeding was to stop the state proceeding, and since the state proceeding must terminate in any event, there is no longer any contested issue before the federal court. The issues have thus become moot. An exception to the mootness rule exists when a controversy is capable of repetition and evading judicial review. Under this exception, the federal court might decide to hear the case even though

the girl's death has made it moot. Mootness, however, is the only argument listed that could possibly result in dismissal of the proceeding brought by the girl's parents.

A non-justiciable political controversy is a case in which a federal court is asked to interfere with the operation of a co-equal branch of the federal government. **A** is incorrect because the challenge raised by the girl's parents is to a state law, not to an action of the federal government. The Eleventh Amendment prohibits federal courts from hearing certain claims against state governments. **C** is incorrect, however, because the Eleventh Amendment does not prevent the federal courts from hearing claims that state action violates the United States Constitution. Where a pending state court proceeding might result in an interpretation of or a conclusion about a state statute that would resolve a federal challenge to it, federal courts are usually unwilling to enjoin enforcement of that statute. The reason given is sometimes said to be "equitable restraint." It is not related, however, to the question of ripeness. So long as there is someone who can actually benefit from a resolution of the issues, and so long as the issues are fully developed and clearly defined, those issues are ripe. Thus, although the issues in this case may no longer be "ripe," this is not because the highest state court has not decided, but because there is no longer any person who will actually benefit from a resolution of the issues. **D** is therefore incorrect.

96.  **A**    Economic regulation by the state is constitutionally valid if it has a rational basis. The "pay-to-throw" program is an economic regulation and therefore is subject to the rational basis standard. Obviously, any legal requirement of payment may have the effect of discriminating in favor of the wealthy against the poor. However, the United States Supreme Court has rejected arguments that classifications based on wealth are "suspect." Consequently, **B** is incorrect. **C** is incorrect because even interference with a fundamental right may be constitutional if it is necessary to serve a compelling state interest. All laws discriminate against somebody (*e.g.,* penal codes discriminate against criminals). Thus, unless a law has no rational basis (in the case of certain kinds of regulation) or is not necessary to serve a compelling interest of the state (as in other kinds of regulation), the fact that it discriminates against a discrete class of persons is not enough to make it unconstitutional. Thus, **D** is incorrect.

97.  **B**    Ordinarily, a promise is not enforceable unless there was consideration for it (*i.e.,* something given in exchange for and to induce the promise). Since the man had already rescued the dog without expectation of payment, the rescue was not given in exchange for or to induce the dog owner's promise and is therefore not consideration for it. Some cases have held, however, that a promise to do that which the promisor is morally obligated to do should be enforceable even without consideration. Although this is an infrequently applied exception to the requirement of consideration, the argument set forth in **B** is the only one listed that could possibly provide the man with effective support for his claim.

Since the man had already rescued the dog without expecting compensation, the rescue was not given in exchange for or to induce the dog owner's promise. **A** is therefore incorrect. In determining whether to rescind a contract because of mutual mistake, fraud, duress, or undue influence, the court may attempt to decide whether its failure to rescind would unjustly enrich one of the parties. Ordinarily, however, the fact that a party will be unjustly enriched by something is not in itself sufficient to result in the imposition of contractual duty on the party. **C** is incorrect for this reason and because the fact that the man rescued the dog without expectation of payment probably prevents the dog owner's enrichment from being unjust. Sometimes a promise that is unsupported by consideration will be enforced under the doctrine of promissory estoppel if the promisee justifiably relied upon it to his or her detriment. **D** is incorrect, however, because while the man did rely on the promise to his detriment, there is no indication the dog owner should have foreseen such reliance.

98. **D** Since there is no evidence that the defendant in the question scenario intended to cause death or great bodily harm, the issue in the defendant's case is whether a person who lacks such intent can be convicted of voluntary manslaughter. Although voluntary manslaughter requires such intent, murder does not. In **D**, the defendant was convicted of murder after bringing about the death of another person without the intent to kill or inflict injury. The affirmance of her murder conviction established that the trial court was correct in refusing to charge on voluntary manslaughter where the defendant lacked the intent to kill. Since this has a direct bearing on whether the defendant (who also lacked the intent to kill) can be convicted of voluntary manslaughter, **D** is applicable to the defendant's case.

The effect of **A** is to hold that one who acts unreasonably may be guilty of *involuntary* manslaughter. Since it does not say anything about what it would take to justify a conviction for *voluntary* manslaughter, it is inapplicable to the defendant's case, and **A** is therefore incorrect. Since the defendant in **B** had the intent to kill and the defendant in the question scenario did not, the decision in **B** that the court should have charged on voluntary manslaughter is inapplicable to the defendant's case. **B** is therefore incorrect. Like voluntary manslaughter, attempted murder requires the specific intent to cause death or great bodily harm. For this reason, **C** appears at first glance to raise an issue similar to that raised in the defendant's case. Since the crimes charged in the two cases were different, however, **C** is not really applicable as a precedent in the defendant's case. (That is, a holding that the defendant cannot be guilty of *attempted murder* without specific intent does not logically relate to the question of whether a defendant can be guilty of *voluntary manslaughter* without specific intent.) **C** is therefore incorrect.

99. **C** People have joint authority over a place when there is mutual use of the property by persons generally having joint access or control for most purposes. Here, the girlfriend stated that she shared the bedroom with the defendant "most of the time." Consequently, she had joint authority over the bedroom and could give valid consent to search it. **A** is incorrect because "most of the time" does not lessen the fact that she appears to have joint access or control for most purposes. In fact, "most of the time" could mean 99.9 percent of the time because the girlfriend did not limit her statement in any way. **B** is incorrect because she does not need to be the owner of the property to give valid consent, as long as she actually has or is reasonably believed by the police to have joint authority over the premises. **D** is incorrect because the girlfriend's statement made it clear she had joint authority over the premises. There is no indication in the question that the police made any kind of mistake regarding her ability to consent to a search, so the police would not have to argue that they were reasonable in their belief regarding the girlfriend's ability to consent.

100.  **A**      Contracts are sometimes subject to a condition precedent. A condition precedent is any event, other than a lapse of time, that must occur before performance under the contract is due. Importantly, strict compliance with an express condition is ordinarily necessary. Here, since the buyer could not find adequate financing, he is discharged from any of his obligations under the sales contract. **B** is incorrect because even if the seller helped subsidize the interest payments, the express condition precedent still failed to occur. **C** is incorrect because the failure of the express condition precedent meant no contract was formed. Finally, **D** is incorrect because there was no contract until the condition was fulfilled, so the seller could not suffer any damages under it.

# ANSWERS
## PRACTICE MBE — P.M. EXAM

101. **A**   A person who renders a measurable benefit to another, with the reasonable expectation of payment and not as an officious intermeddler, may be entitled to recovery on a theory of quasi-contract (*i.e.*, restitution for unjust enrichment). (**Note:** Since the neighbor did not request the plaintiff's performance, and since the neighbor did not become aware of it until after it had occurred, it is not at all certain that a court would find in favor of the plaintiff on this theory. But since the question calls for the assumption that the plaintiff would be successful in his claim, it is necessary to consider the relief to which he would be entitled if successful.) Ordinarily, recovery on this theory is based on the benefit received by the person from whom payment is sought. This benefit may be measured in terms of net enrichment or cost avoided. If these amounts are unequal, the court will usually award the lower of the two. In this case, the neighbor's net enrichment is the increase in his realty's value — $2,100. The cost avoided is what he would have had to pay another for the job (*i.e.*, the standard market price) — $2,750. Since the net enrichment is the lesser of these two figures, the plaintiff would be entitled to receive $2,100.

    **B** and **C** are incorrect because the benefit received by the neighbor is unrelated to the plaintiff's agreement with the homeowner or to the plaintiff's cost. **D** is incorrect because it exceeds the net enrichment that the neighbor received.

102. **C**   Article III of the United States Constitution vests federal judicial power in the United States Supreme Court and in such inferior federal courts as Congress shall establish. In addition, by specifying what cases they may hear, Article III establishes limits on the jurisdiction that may be exercised by the federal courts. Although it gives federal courts the power (*i.e.*, jurisdiction) to hear controversies between citizens of *different* states, or between citizens of the same stat*e claiming lands under grants of different states*, it does not give the federal courts any power to hear contract disputes between residents of the same state. Since the United States Constitution is the supreme law of the land, neither Congress nor a state legislature can confer this power on the United States district courts.

    **A** and **B** are therefore incorrect. The Eleventh Amendment only prohibits the federal courts from hearing certain claims against a state and is inapplicable because the plaintiff's claim is not against the state. **D** is therefore incorrect.

103. **D**   A misrepresentation is a false assertion of material fact intended to induce the plaintiff's reliance. A defendant intends to induce the plaintiff's reliance if he or she knows with substantial certainty that a class of persons to which the plaintiff belongs will rely on his or her statement. If the reporter did not know that any person would rely on her statement, she could not have intended to induce any person's reliance. Her statement would therefore not be a misrepresentation.

    In addition, misrepresentation liability cannot be imposed unless the plaintiff was justified in relying (*i.e.*, the reasonable person in the plaintiff's situation would have relied) on the defendant's false statement. Since the reasonable person might believe a newspaper account instead of personally checking public records, however, **A** is incorrect. **B** is incorrect for two reasons: First, an expert's statement of opinion may be a misrepresentation because it asserts as a fact that the expert actually holds that opinion, and second, the reporter's statement that "Insiders say . . . (etc.)" is an assertion of fact on which misrepresentation liability could be based. In actions for negligent misrepresentation, it is frequently held that, without privity, the defendant owes the plaintiff no duty of reasonable care. In this case, however, since the reporter knew that there was no basis for her statement, her misrepresentation was intentional. **C** is incorrect because privity is not a prerequisite to liability for intentional misrepresentation.

104.  **D**   One who inherits an interest in realty takes it subject to any existing prior interests. Since the landowner's accountant and brother received interests prior to the death of the landowner, and since both of those interests were immediately recorded, the landowner's nephew and niece took their interests in the realty subject to those of the accountant and the brother. Thus, the accountant is entitled to succeed in a foreclosure proceeding. Because of the constitutional requirement of due process, however, persons who may be deprived of property as the result of a judicial proceeding must be given notice of an opportunity to be heard in that proceeding. For this reason, all persons with existing present or future interests in the realty are necessary parties who must be served with process in a foreclosure proceeding. Deciding who must be served thus requires nothing more than determining who holds a property interest — present or future — in the realty. Since the landowner's nephew is the holder of a life estate (*i.e.*, has a present interest), and the landowner's niece is the holder of a remainder (*i.e.*, has a future interest), both are necessary parties. Since neither has been served or brought into the proceeding, the accountant's request for a foreclosure sale must be denied.

      **A**, **B**, and **C** are therefore incorrect.

105.  **A**   Murder is the unlawful killing of a human being with malice aforethought. Malice aforethought consists of a wanton disregard for human life, or of the intent to kill, inflict great bodily harm, resist a lawful arrest, escape from custody, or commit a dangerous felony. Because it was very likely to lead to death or serious injury, the defendant's firing slightly to the right of the victim probably showed a wanton disregard for human life. This is particularly so in view of the fact that the defendant had never fired a rifle before, and therefore he could not have been sure that he would miss the victim. Thus, since the defendant caused the unjustified killing of the victim with malice aforethought, he could properly be convicted of murder. While it is not certain that he would be convicted, murder is the only crime listed of which he could possibly be properly convicted.

      Voluntary manslaughter is the intentional killing of a human being under mitigating circumstances. Since the defendant did not intend to hit the victim with the bullet, he cannot be guilty of voluntary manslaughter. Thus, **B** is incorrect. A person is guilty of a criminal attempt when, with the intent of bringing about a criminally prohibited result, he comes largely close to achieving that result. Thus, while murder does not require the intent to kill or inflict great bodily harm, attempted murder does. The defendant did not intend to inflict harm upon the victim, so he cannot be guilty of attempted murder. Thus, **C** is incorrect. **D** is incorrect because knowledge that the location is within the municipal limits is an essential element of guilt, and the defendant did not know the dump was within these limits.

106. **C**    The fact that a witness has made prior statements that are inconsistent with her testimony suggests that her testimony is not worthy of belief. For this reason, such statements are admissible for purposes of impeachment. In general, substantive evidence is admissible if it tends to establish a fact in issue. Since the color of the traffic light is material to the determination of the plaintiff's rights against the defendant (*i.e.*, is a fact in issue), the deposition in which the witness said that the light was green for the plaintiff is relevant evidence. Hearsay is ordinarily defined as an out-of-court statement offered to prove the truth of the matter that it asserts. FRE 801(d)(1)(A) specifically provides, however, that a deposition given under oath is not hearsay so long as the person who gave it is available for cross-examination. Thus, the witness's deposition is not hearsay although it was made out of court and is offered to prove the truth of a matter asserted in it. For this reason, it is admissible as substantive evidence. **A**, **B**, and **D** are therefore incorrect.

107. **C**    Under Fed. R. Civ. P. 4(k)(1)(B), "serving a summons or filing a waiver of service establishes personal jurisdiction over a defendant . . . who is a party joined under Rule 14 or 19 and is served within a judicial district of the United States and not more than 100 miles from where the summons was issued." Here, the chef is impleading the waiter under Fed. R. Civ. P. 14(a)(1), since the waiter may be liable to the chef for all or part of the professor's claim. Consequently, since the waiter lives within 100 miles of the court where the summons was issued, the federal district court in State A has personal jurisdiction over her.

   **A** is incorrect because of the 100-mile rule stated above. **B** and **D** are incorrect because the amount in controversy and the citizenship of the parties is irrelevant to the question of whether the federal district court in State A would have personal jurisdiction over the parties.

108. **B**    The Thirteenth Amendment provides that, except as a punishment for crime, "Neither slavery nor involuntary servitude . . . shall exist within the United States," and grants Congress the power to enforce that provision. The United States Supreme Court has held that the prohibition against slavery was directed at individuals as well as at government action. This, the Court stated, gives Congress the power to define badges of servitude and to eliminate them by enacting legislation regulating private conduct. The Court further ruled that racial discrimination could constitute a badge of slavery.

   The Due Process Clause of the Fifth Amendment has been held to protect certain substantive individual rights. Since the Fifth Amendment protects only against action by the federal government, however, it could not justify the regulation of private conduct. Thus, **A** is incorrect. Since the Equal Protection Clause prohibits only invidious discrimination by states, **C** is incorrect for the same reason. The Fifteenth Amendment provides that the right to vote shall not be denied on account of race or previous condition of servitude. Since the legislation in question does not protect the right to vote, it cannot be justified by the Fifteenth Amendment. **D** is therefore incorrect.

109. **D**    A contract may make the happening of a particular event a condition precedent to the performance of a contractual duty. If so, one party's strict compliance with the condition makes the other party's conditional duty absolute. The terms of the commission

agreement made the broker's delivery prior to April 15 of a buyer ready, willing, and able to pay $50,000 for the realty a condition precedent to the seller's duty to pay a commission. Since the broker complied with that condition by presenting the buyer's offer on April 14, the seller's duty to pay has become absolute.

**A** is incorrect because the commission agreement did not make completion of the sale a condition precedent to the seller's obligation to pay a commission. If an agreement specifies its own duration, then the obligations that it creates are understood to exist for the period specified. The commission agreement required the broker to make reasonable efforts to sell the realty until April 15 and required the seller to pay a commission if the broker procured a buyer prior to that date. Those obligations, therefore, continued to exist until April 15. The seller's rejection of the buyer's offer of April 10 terminated the buyer's offer but did not affect the obligations created by the seller's contract with the broker. **B** is therefore incorrect. The Statute of Frauds simply provides that certain agreements are unenforceable over objection unless they are in writing and signed by the party to be charged. The Statute of Frauds would thus prevent the enforcement of any contract that is claimed to have been formed as a result of the buyer's April 10 offer. **C** is incorrect for this reason and because while the Statute of Frauds may prevent an alleged oral contract from being enforced, it does not have any effect on the validity of the rejection of an offer.

110.  **B**    There are only three potential bases of liability in a tort action—intent, negligence, and liability without fault (*i.e.*, strict liability). It is clear from the facts that the defendant's entry onto the plaintiff's realty was not intentional. Operating an automobile is not one of the activities for which strict liability is imposed. The only possible basis of liability is therefore negligence. Thus, the defendant can be liable only if she was negligent. Here, she was negligent because she was driving 15 miles per hour above the speed limit.

**A** is incorrect because an unauthorized entry onto realty is not a trespass unless it is intentional. The doctrine of "last clear chance" is practically obsolete, but where it is applicable, its only effect is to relieve a plaintiff of the consequences of his or her own contributory negligence. Since the defendant is not the plaintiff, whether or not she had the "last clear chance" to avoid an accident is irrelevant. **C** is therefore incorrect. The privilege of necessity permits the reasonable violation of property rights in the face of an emergency. **D** is incorrect, however, for two reasons: First, necessity is available only as a defense to intentional tort, and second—even under the privilege of necessity—one who invades the property rights of another to protect his or her own interests must pay for any actual damage that results from that invasion.

111.  **D**    It is generally understood that even while testifying, a witness may look at any document (in fact, at anything at all) that serves to refresh his or her recollection about the matters to which he or she is testifying. Although there are dangers connected with this rule, it is thought that these can be averted by investing the judge with discretion to determine, while listening to the testimony, whether the witness's recollection has really been refreshed by consulting such a document, or whether the witness has no real present recollection but is simply reading from the document. Since the plaintiff had not yet looked

at the notes or stated that looking at them would refresh her recollection, the judge is not yet in a position to exercise this discretion and must overrule the objection.

**A** is incorrect because any material may be used to refresh the recollection of a witness, without regard to the origin of that material. **B** is incorrect because even material that has not been admitted or is not capable of being admitted may be used to refresh a witness's recollection. A leading question is one that suggests a particular answer. **C** is incorrect for two reasons: First, there are occasions when a direct examiner is permitted to stimulate a witness's memory through the use of leading questions, and second, since the attorney's question did not suggest a particular answer, it was not leading.

112.   **C**   The United States Supreme Court has held that constitutional requirements of equality in the electoral process prohibit the use of property ownership as a qualification for voter eligibility in general elections. An exception to this rule has been recognized for special-purpose elections on matters that relate only to the interests of landowners. The election in question does not fit this exception, however, since municipal revenues and their source are of interest to all residents of the municipality. For this reason, the land ownership requirement probably makes the special election invalid.

The Fifteenth Amendment only prohibits exclusion of persons from the electoral process on the basis of race, color, or previous condition of servitude. **A** is incorrect because there is no indication that any persons will be excluded from voting in the special election on this basis. **B** is incorrect because the United States Supreme Court has held that states can constitutionally limit the vote to residents and has specifically upheld residence requirements of up to 50 days, and because persons owning land within the township are not necessarily residents of the township. **D** is incorrect for two reasons: First, unlike the election of representatives, which may be conducted by district, this is an election that could not be conducted in any other way but at-large, and second, in the absence of a specific intent to dilute the power of a particular interest group, at-large elections are valid even if they have that effect.

113.   **D**   Upon breach by a buyer, UCC §2-706 provides that the seller may resell the goods in a commercially reasonable manner and recover damages equivalent to the difference between the contract price and the price that the seller actually received upon the resale. Here, since the plaintiff resold the chairs at the same price that she had agreed to accept from the defendant, she has sustained no damage at all. (**Note:** If the plaintiff incurred extra expense in making 75 individual sales of one chair each, rather than a single sale of 75 chairs as agreed by the defendant, recovery for the extra expense might be available as incidental damages. **D** is correct, however, because the facts do not indicate that any extra expense was actually incurred, and because no other answer listed correctly describes damages that might be available.)

Where the goods that a breaching buyer contracted to buy are in unlimited supply, the seller may be entitled to recover the profit that the seller would have realized if not for the breach. Since there were a limited number of chairs, however, and since the plaintiff succeeded in selling them all, she is not entitled to this remedy. **A** is therefore incorrect.

**B** is incorrect because the defendant did not agree to pay $100 per chair, and **C** is incorrect because when the seller resells under UCC §2-706, the damages are measured by the difference between the contract price and the price that she actually received.

114.　**A**　　Generally it is the judge's function to decide whether offered evidence may be considered by the jury (*i.e.*, is admissible), and the jury's function to decide what weight to give evidence that the judge decides they may consider. To find them admissible, a judge must determine whether photographs offered into evidence have been properly authenticated. A party seeking to authenticate a photograph must establish that the photograph is an accurate representation of what it purports to picture. The plaintiff has authenticated his photo by testifying that he took it of the stove in question and that it accurately represents the stove. The employee has authenticated his photo by testifying that it accurately represents the stove in question. Both photos have thus been sufficiently authenticated to be admitted into evidence. It will then be the jury's job to decide which witness it believes — if any — and which photo it therefore believes to be an accurate representation of the stove in question.

　　　　　　　　**B** is incorrect because the employee's testimony that his photo fairly and accurately represents the stove sufficiently authenticates it even though he was not the photographer. **C** is incorrect because the plaintiff's testimony that he took the snapshot and that it accurately represents the stove sufficiently authenticates it. **D** is incorrect for a combination of the reasons that make **B** and **C** incorrect.

115.　**B**　　Restraints on the alienation of leasehold interests are generally regarded as valid but are strictly construed. For this reason, a restraint against assignment is held not to prohibit sublease. Assignment of a lease takes place when a lessee transfers to another his or her entire remaining interest in the premises. If any interest less than this is transferred, the transfer is a sublease rather than an assignment. Since the attorney retained a right to one of the offices, his transfer to the second attorney was not an assignment and did not breach the lease provision prohibiting assignments.

　　　　　　　　**A** is incorrect because if a transfer of the lessee's entire remaining interest occurs, the transfer is an assignment even though the terms in the agreement between assignor and assignee are not identical to the terms in the agreement between the landlord and assignor. Although courts generally disfavor restraints on the alienation of fee interests in realty, **C** is incorrect because clauses prohibiting the assignment of leasehold interests are generally regarded as valid. The financial status of a prospective tenant is only one of the factors which a landlord considers in deciding whether to rent to him or her. (For example, a landlord might be unwilling to rent to a person with a good credit rating if that person has a history of damaging leased premises or engages in an occupation inconsistent with other uses of the premises.) **D** is therefore incorrect.

116.　**B**　　The United States Supreme Court has held that because defamation liability can be imposed only for a false statement, and because there is no such thing as a false opinion, defamation liability cannot be imposed for an assertion of opinion. The Supreme Court also ruled that a statement is an assertion of opinion if reasonable readers would recognize that it was an expression of the writer's feelings and would not believe that it was intended to assert a fact. Thus, if reasonable readers would not believe that the statement asserted a fact, it was an expression of opinion and therefore not subject to defamation liability.

Although the Supreme Court has held that a public person suing for defamation must prove actual malice (*i.e.*, knowledge of falsity or reckless disregard for truth), this requirement has not been imposed on private persons. For this reason, the defendant could be liable for publishing a defamatory statement about the plaintiff that he negligently believed to be true, even if he did not have actual malice when he made it. **A** is therefore incorrect. A statement, even if it is defamatory, will not subject its publisher to defamation liability unless it is false. But a defamatory statement is said to be false if it is not substantially true, without regard to whether or not the reasonable person would believe it. If damage results from the publication of a statement found to be defamatory (which *does* depend on what the reasonable person would think it means) and false (which does *not* depend at all on what the reasonable person would think), defamation liability is imposed. Although the amount of damage will probably be related to the number of people who believed the defamatory statement and held it against the plaintiff, it does not depend on whether or not those who did so were reasonable people. The argument in **C** would not therefore be an effective defense for the defendant. Although (for reasons stated above) defamation liability is not imposed for stating an opinion, it may be imposed for a false assertion of fact even though the maker of that statement believed it to be true. Thus, if the defendant's statement was defamatory, and if it was a false assertion of fact, the defendant could not escape liability by proving that he believed it (*i.e.*, in his opinion it was accurate) unless his belief was reasonable. **D** is therefore incorrect.

117. **D**  An illusory promise is a statement that appears to make a promise but does not commit the promisor to do anything. Illusory promises are insufficient consideration to support a contract. Here, the builder has not bound himself to do anything since he's only agreed to buy bricks for $1 if he decides to buy bricks. Because the builder's promise did not actually bind him in any way, it did not provide consideration for the brick supplier's promise. Consequently, the brick supplier could not be bound to its promise.

**A** is incorrect because it appears to be referencing the rules for a firm offer under UCC § 2-205. Under that section, a promise to keep an offer open is enforceable without consideration if the promisor is a merchant, offering to buy or sell goods in a signed writing, and the writing gives assurances that it will be held open. In that case, the offer is not revocable for lack of consideration during the time stated, or if no time is stated, for a reasonable time (in no event exceeding three months). Here, it doesn't seem that the supplier is giving any assurances regarding holding the offer open, the supplier's letter includes no promised time, and the builder made his order six months later, so the rules regarding a firm offer could not apply. Importantly, this is not the situation of a requirements contract, as the builder made no promise to buy his required brick from the brick supplier. **B** is incorrect because the letter sent by the builder was not an acceptance. As stated above, it was an illusory promise. **C** is incorrect because the reason for the price increase is irrelevant to the analysis.

118.   **C**   Since the restriction to residential use was contained in the deed by which the sister received her interest in Lot 2, there is no question about whether the restriction is enforceable *against* her. But since her brother was not a party to the transaction in which the restriction on his sister's use was created (*i.e.*, the conveyance of Lot 2), a question exists about whether that restriction is enforceable *by the brother*. The facts are unclear about who purchased first. (If the sister purchased before her brother, the question would be an easier one. Then, the benefit that the landowner received from the restriction in his sister's deed probably ran with the landowner's land and probably passed to the brother with the conveyance of Lot 1. Unfortunately, this is not one of the options.) Even if the brother purchased first, he may be able to enforce the restriction in his sister's deed if, at the time of his purchase, he relied on a representation by the landowner that Lot 2 would be similarly restricted. In that event, the brother might succeed on two theories: first, that he was an intended creditor beneficiary of his sister's covenant, and second, that there were implied reciprocal servitudes. One way of establishing reliance on such a representation would be to show that at the time of his purchase, the brother was aware that the restriction was part of the landowner's development scheme. The additional fact in **C** might thus result in a decision for the brother.

If the brother purchased before his sister, the benefit that the landowner received from the restriction in his brother's deed probably passed to his sister with Lot 2 because that benefit ran with the land. For this reason, the facts in **A** and **B** might be relevant if the sister was trying to enforce the restriction contained in her brother's deed. They are irrelevant to the brother's attempt to enforce the restriction contained in his sister's deed, however. For this reason, **A** and **B** are incorrect. If the sister purchased before her brother, she might be able to enforce the restriction in her brother's deed by showing that she was aware of the landowner's development scheme when he purchased. But since the question involves the brother's attempt to enforce the restriction in his sister's deed, **D** is incorrect.

119.   **A**   The Fifth and Fourteenth Amendments of the United States Constitution provide in part that no person shall be deprived of life, liberty, or property without due process of law. Since the plaintiff's claim is that the agency's decision violated his right to due process, his claim must fail unless the decision deprived him of life, liberty, or property. If it did not, he was not entitled to due process in the decision-making process. Cases have held that if a state employee's contract provides that the state may decide not to rehire him or her without cause, the employee's expectation of being rehired is not a sufficient property interest to require due process. Thus, the argument in **A** would probably be successful. Even without these cases, however, **A** would be the only argument listed that could possibly be an effective response to the plaintiff's challenge.

Although no person has a right to state employment (*i.e.*, no person is guaranteed employment by the state), the distinction between right and privilege is unimportant where the interest involved is an ''entitlement'' that is seen to be a property interest. **B** is therefore incorrect. **C** is incorrect because the hearing officer would presumably act properly in considering whatever evidence the plaintiff might submit and therefore might not come to the same conclusion as the agency. **D** is incorrect because it is based on an over-inclusive statement; even though the contract provided that the decision not to renew could be made without cause, it could still have been made for a reason (*e.g.*, based on race) or in a manner inconsistent with the requirements of the Constitution, thus violating the plaintiff's constitutional rights.

120.   **A**   Private nuisance is a tortious interference with the plaintiff's right to use and enjoy realty, and it may be committed without any physical intrusion onto the realty. Although the county ordinance permitted use of the airport by certain aircraft, the defendant could still be liable for private nuisance if he was operating the airport in a manner other than that contemplated by the ordinance. While it is not certain that the plaintiff would recover on this theory, private nuisance is the only theory listed that could possibly result in a judgment in his favor.

It is sometimes held that repeated overflights for a given period of time result in a prescriptive aeronautical easement. **B** is incorrect, however, because this conclusion would privilege the continuing overflights, thus providing the defendant with a defense to an action brought by the plaintiff. The Fifth Amendment to the United States Constitution prohibits the taking by government of private property for public use without just compensation. If the county ordinance resulted in a reduction in the value of the plaintiff's realty, the Fifth Amendment might require that the county pay just compensation to the plaintiff. Although this right would be enforceable in an inverse condemnation proceeding, **C** is incorrect because this theory is available only against an agency of the government. Trespass to land and the variant known as continuing trespass require a physical or tangible entry onto the realty. **D** is incorrect because noise is not tangible.

121.   **C**   An "admission" is a statement by a party offered against that party. Under the common law, it is admissible as an exception to the hearsay rule; under FRE 801(d)(2), it is not hearsay. Since the defendant's statement to his wife is offered against the defendant, it is an admission and therefore admissible.

The marital privilege is designed to protect the confidentiality of the marital relationship. For this reason, it prevents either spouse from testifying over objection by the other to a confidential communication made during the marriage. For the same reason, however, it does not prevent a stranger to the marriage from testifying to a communication that he or she overheard between the spouses. Thus, although communications made within the marriage are presumed to be confidential, **A** is incorrect because the witness did not receive the communication within the marriage (*i.e.*, as a marriage partner). **B** is incorrect because an admission is not hearsay under FRE 801(d)(2) and it is admissible as an exception to the hearsay rule under common law. Communications that advance a crime are not protected by privilege. The defendant's statement did not advance a crime, however, because it was about a crime that had already been committed. The fact that it concerned a crime is not enough to take it out of the protection of the marital privilege, making **D** incorrect.

122.   **D**   If an action is in federal court based on federal question jurisdiction, a federal court has discretion to remand the case to state court once all the federal questions have been

resolved based on principles of fairness and judicial economy. *See Carnegie-Mellon University v. Cohill, 484 U.S. 343 (1988).* Here, considering the action was originally brought in state court and only state claims remain, it would be more practical and fair to remand the case to the state court. Therefore, **A** and **B** are incorrect.

**C** is incorrect because the district court's discretion to remand the case to state court is not based on the simple fact the case was originally brought in state court.

123. **B**     A basic principle of the law of evidence is that only evidence that is relevant to a material issue may be received in evidence. Evidence is logically relevant to a material issue if it has any tendency to prove or disprove a fact of consequence. Since the defendant is charged with assaulting the victim, not the witness, his beating of the witness could not tend to prove or disprove a fact of consequence in the prosecution. (It might *seem* logical to argue that the witness's testimony tends to establish that the defendant is the kind of person who is likely to have committed the crime with which he is charged. All jurisdictions agree, however, that evidence of a defendant's character is not admissible to create the inference that he or she engaged in particular conduct on a particular occasion.)

In some jurisdictions, confidential marital communications are privileged and cannot be revealed — even after the marriage has terminated — over the objection of the spouse against whom they are offered. There is some disagreement about whether this privilege applies to acts as well as communications. It is generally agreed, however, that communications or acts are privileged only if they were intended to be confidential. The fact that the acts to which the witness testified occurred in public places indicates that they were not intended to be confidential, and the privilege therefore does not apply. **A** is incorrect for this reason and because, as explained above, the testimony may be excluded even if the jurisdiction did not recognize the marital privilege. The credibility of a witness may be impeached by evidence relating to his or her reputation for truth and veracity. **C** is incorrect, however, for two reasons: First, the witness's testimony does not logically relate to the defendant's *reputation* at all, and second, FRE 608(b) specifically provides that extrinsic evidence (except for convictions) of specific conduct may not be used to impeach the credibility of a witness. Although a defendant who testifies in his or her own behalf may be impeached by cross-examination (*i.e.*, intrinsically) regarding past conduct, FRE 608(b) prevents the use of extrinsic evidence of specific acts of unconvicted bad conduct. **D** is therefore incorrect.

124. **C**     Under the doctrine of impossibility of performance, a party may be excused from obligations under a contract if an unforeseeable change in circumstances has made performance vitally different than that which was contemplated by the parties at the time the contract was formed. On the other hand, if the change that occurred was foreseeable, the fact that it increases a party's burden of performance is not in itself sufficient to excuse that performance. Because contracts must remain stable even when the market does not, it is generally understood that, for this purpose, fluctuations in market price are foreseeable. In any event, *if* dramatic fluctuation in the price of chickens *was* foreseeable, then the increase in market price would not excuse the defendant's performance.

A is incorrect because if the change was foreseeable, it does not matter whether the parties actually knew that it would occur. In an "aleatory" contract, one party agrees to confer a benefit on the other upon the happening of a fortuitous event over which neither party has control (*e.g.*, X agrees to pay Y if Y's roll of the dice comes up 7). Since the agreement between the plaintiff and the defendant was not conditioned upon the happening of any event over which neither had control, it was not aleatory. **B** is therefore incorrect. (**Note:** Under the reasoning of option **B**, all contracts for the future payment of money would be aleatory and invalid.) **D** is incorrect for two reasons: First, the rights of the parties would be the same under common law as under the UCC, and second, the transaction is deemed a sale by the language of the UCC, which defines a sale as a passing of title from the seller to the buyer for a price.

125.  **C**    When an easement is created by grant, the language of the grant determines the scope of the easement. When that language is unclear, the courts most often determine the scope of the easement on the basis of what could reasonably have been anticipated at the time the easement was created. Although there are insufficient facts to determine whether the argument in **C** would result in a judgment for the plaintiff, it is the only argument listed that could possibly support his position.

If an easement is created by adverse use over a specified period of time (*i.e.*, by prescription), the use over that period determines the scope of the easement. If the easement is created by grant, however, its scope is determined by the language of the grant, construed in the light of what the parties contemplated at the time of its creation. **A** is therefore incorrect. The initial installment of a single pipe by the defendant might be evidence of what the parties contemplated at the time the easement was created. It is not conclusive, however, because the scope of an easement is usually understood to include those changes in the activities of the dominant estate that could reasonably have been foreseen. Thus, although the defendant installed only one pipe, it may be found that the parties anticipated that the installation of a second pipe might one day be necessary. If so, that anticipation would be relevant in determining the scope of the easement granted by the language given. **B** is therefore incorrect. **D** is incorrect because where the granting language is not sufficiently specific, the scope of the easement is determined as explained above.

126.  **D**    Since the sales contract called for delivery of marketable title to a parcel consisting of four lots, the buyer could not be required to accept anything less. Outstanding encumbrances—including easements—make a title unmarketable. Since one of the four lots was encumbered by an easement, the seller was unable to deliver marketable title and was, therefore, in breach of contract.

A covenant against encumbrances is breached if an encumbrance exists at the time of conveyance, and it gives rise to an action against the covenantor for any damage resulting from the existence of such an encumbrance. **A** is incorrect, however, because marketable title means a title that can be enjoyed without the likelihood of litigation, and title to encumbered realty is likely to lead to litigation. Since there may be reasons why the buyer would want to purchase a parcel consisting of four lots but not a parcel consisting of three lots, he cannot be required to accept less than what he bargained for. Having bargained for a parcel consisting of four lots, he cannot therefore be compelled to accept a deed to only three of them. **B** is therefore incorrect. In a *tort* action for intentional misrepresentation, it would be necessary for the buyer to show that the seller knew that the easement existed when he promised to deliver marketable title. *Breach of contract* liability is not based on fault, however, and may be imposed simply because the promisor has failed to keep a promise that he or she made. Since the seller promised to deliver marketable title (*i.e.*, title free of encumbrances), he may be liable for breaching that contract without regard to whether he knew that it would be breached when he made it. For this reason, **C** is incorrect.

127.   **A**    For various reasons, the law recognizes a policy to encourage settlements. Since a party might refrain from making a settlement offer if he or she believed that his or her offer could be used as circumstantial evidence of his or her liability, this policy prohibits the admission as evidence of the offerer's liability of an offer to settle or compromise a claim.

Since the offerer's explanation for his or her offer would not always prevent the offerer from convincing a jury of his or her liability, policy would prevent the admission of evidence of the offer even if the offerer was given an opportunity to explain it. **B** is therefore incorrect. Although a declaration against pecuniary interest may be an exception to the hearsay rule, and although the admission of a party is an exception to the hearsay rule under common law, and not hearsay at all under FRE 801(d)(2), **C** and **D** are incorrect since the settlement offer is being excluded, not because it is hearsay, but because of the policy to encourage settlements.

128.   **B**    The plaintiff in a negligence action must establish that the defendant breached a duty of reasonable care and that the breach was a proximate cause of damage. In concept, a plaintiff has sustained *damage* as a result of a defendant's act if the plaintiff would have been better off without that act. If the plaintiff otherwise would have died, then the defendant's act saved the plaintiff's life at the expense of his injured knees. Since the plaintiff's life was more important (*i.e.*, valuable) than his knees, he would not have been better off without the defendant's act and therefore sustained no damage.

Since a result might have several proximate causes, any damage that the plaintiff did sustain could have been proximately caused by the negligence of the defendant *and* by the negligence of the driver. This would make the defendant and the driver joint tortfeasors — in most jurisdictions, jointly and severally liable for the plaintiff's damage. For this reason, the fact that the driver's negligence was a proximate cause of the plaintiff's injury is not likely to result in a judgment for the defendant. **A** is therefore incorrect. If the plaintiff was damaged as a proximate result of the negligence of the defendant, the defendant would be liable for the plaintiff's damage. This is true regardless of any injuries that the defendant might have sustained. **C** is therefore incorrect. Ordinarily, a person who acts is required to act as the reasonable person would in the same circumstances. Since emergencies call for quick response without time for cool reflection, a person confronted with an emergency is not required to act as he or she would if not confronted by an emergency. He or she is, however, required to act like the reasonable person would if confronted with the same emergency. Thus, the fact that an emergency existed does not excuse a defendant from the obligation of acting reasonably. **D** is therefore incorrect.

129. **D**    The Fifth Amendment to the United States Constitution provides that no person shall for the same offense be placed twice in jeopardy of life or limb. In general, this prevents a person from being tried twice for the same crime. Since the defendant has already been tried, the subsequent prosecution violates this constitutional protection. **D** is correct for this reason, and because none of the reasons listed in the other options is sufficient to result in a denial of her motion.

For the protection against double jeopardy to be violated by prosecution for a crime, it must be found that the defendant has already been in danger (*i.e.*, jeopardy) of losing his or her liberty as a result of a prosecution for the same crime and that the danger has ended. If the danger to the defendant that was created by the first prosecution has ended, subsequent prosecution would place her in danger again, thus violating the Double Jeopardy Clause. **A** is therefore incorrect. It is sometimes argued that a reversal based on a legal flaw in the trial results in the conclusion that the trial was a nullity and that jeopardy therefore never attached in the first place. If this were so, subsequent prosecution would not violate the Double Jeopardy Clause because the defendant was never in danger as a result of the previous prosecution. **B** is incorrect, however, because the reversal by the appellate court was not based on a legal flaw but on insufficiency of the evidence that is equivalent to an acquittal after trial. Usually a convicted defendant who appeals his or her conviction thereby waives the constitutional protection against double jeopardy. A reversal based on insufficiency of the evidence, however, indicates that the initial trial should have resulted in an acquittal, which would have barred re-prosecution, and so in such a case, the defendant does not waive his or her rights under the Double Jeopardy Clause. **C** is therefore incorrect.

130. **A**    Under Fed. R. Civ. P. 26(b)(3), a statement prepared by a party "in anticipation of litigation" is protected by work-product immunity. However, since the statement is simply the statement of the head nurse and does not appear to contain any mental conclusions or impressions by the investigator, it is probably only protected by qualified immunity. In that case, the man can get the statement if he shows he has "substantial need for the materials . . . and [he] cannot, without undue hardship, obtain their substantial equivalent by other means." Since the head nurse related information that was known only to her regarding what happened during the surgery, the fact she has died means the man is likely entitled to the information. Therefore, **C** is incorrect.

**B** is incorrect because work-product immunity applies both to work prepared by the lawyer and work prepared by the party's "representative (including the other party's attorney, consultant, surety, indemnitor, insurer, or agent)." Consequently, the fact it was the investigator who did the interview and not the lawyer is irrelevant. **D** is incorrect because the issue doesn't revolve around the question of whether the information was obtained by another working on the attorney's behalf.

131.   **A**      Under the parol evidence rule, extrinsic evidence of prior agreements or negotiations is not admissible to contradict or modify an unambiguous written contract that the parties intended as a complete expression of their agreement. The rule does not prevent the use of extrinsic evidence for other purposes, however. Virtually all jurisdictions permit its use to show that the written contract is ambiguous and to clear up the ambiguity. Since the phrase "all fuel ordered by the state" might mean all the fuel that the state chooses to order from the plaintiff, or all the fuel that the state orders at all during that period, the contract is probably ambiguous on its face. If it is not ambiguous on its face, the fact that the advertisement calling for bids indicated that the contract would be exclusive tends to show an ambiguity since it might mean that the parties intended the plaintiff to be the exclusive supplier even though the written contract does not specifically say so. The advertisement is probably admissible for this reason. Although it is not certain that a court would come to this conclusion, the argument set forth in **A** is the only one listed that might provide the plaintiff with an effective response to the state's objection.

**B** is incorrect because the parol evidence rule may prevent the admission of extrinsic evidence, whether it is oral or written. **C** and **D** are incorrect because the parol evidence rule excludes extrinsic evidence of statements made prior to and during negotiations if offered to modify the terms of an unambiguous written contract.

132.   **C**      At common law, priorities were determined by the dates of the transactions involved. The person who received his or her interest first had priority over all others. In all jurisdictions in the United States, recording statutes have modified the common law rule. Under the statute given (typical of the "notice" variety) an unrecorded interest does not defeat the rights of a subsequent taker for value and without notice. Since the youngest son received the property as a gift (*i.e.*, did not give value), however, he is not protected by the statute. For this reason, the interest of the neighbor, since it was created before that of the youngest son, has priority over it. Since the neighbor did give value for his interest, and since the facts do not indicate that he was aware of the oldest son's interest, the neighbor is protected by the recording statute. Under the statute, the oldest son's interest is not good against the neighbor, since the oldest son's deed was not recorded. Thus, the interest of the neighbor has priority, and the neighbor is entitled to foreclose.

Although the neighbor did not record his mortgage, it has priority over the youngest son's interest because the youngest son—not having given value—is not protected by the recording statute. Under the statute, the interest of the neighbor—which is protected by the recording statute—has priority over the previously created interest of the oldest son because the oldest son's interest was unrecorded when the neighbor received the mortgage. **A** is therefore incorrect. **B** is incorrect because the youngest son is not protected by the recording statute for the reasons given above. Since the neighbor's interest is superior to the oldest son's under the recording statute, the oldest son's interest is subject to the mortgage held by the neighbor. **D** is therefore incorrect.

133.   **A**      The plaintiff's allegation that the vehicle was defective means that her claim is based on the theory of strict liability in tort. Assumption of the risk may be raised as an effective defense to such a claim. Since a plaintiff assumes the risk when he or she voluntarily

encounters a danger of which he or she knows, the plaintiff may have assumed the risk by driving with the knowledge that the seat belt warning indicator light was not working.

**B** is incorrect because a product might be defective even though it does not violate a safety statute. If the plaintiff would have ignored the seat belt warning indicator light, its failure to operate was not a factual cause of her harm, and the defendant could not be liable for her injury. Factual cause is a question of fact for the jury, however, and a plaintiff needs to prove it only by a fair preponderance of the evidence. Thus, even if the plaintiff cannot prove *with certainty* that she would have worn the seat belt had the indicator been working, she may still win her case if the jury finds it more likely than not that she would have. **C** is therefore incorrect. A professional seller who supplies a defective product is strictly liable for resulting harm whether or not the defect resulted from that seller's fault. **D** is therefore incorrect.

134. **A**    In a foreclosure sale, the proceeds are first used to pay the attorney's fees and other expenses of the sale, the principal and interest on the foreclosed loan, and then any junior mortgages in the order of their priority. If there is anything left over, it goes to the mortgagor. On the other hand, if the proceeds are insufficient to pay the mortgage debt, the mortgagee can bring a personal action against the mortgagor unless such an action is prohibited by state law. Here, **A** correctly states these rules. If it is not prohibited by state law, the third bank may sue for a personal judgment against the man to recover the $10,000 it is owed under the third mortgage.

**B** is incorrect because junior mortgage holders do not split the remaining proceeds. **C** is incorrect because the junior mortgage holders do not have priority over the foreclosed mortgage. **D** is incorrect because the principal and interest on the first mortgage must be paid before any proceeds can go to other mortgagees.

135. **C**    An admission is a declaration by a party offered against that party. Under the common law, admissions are admissible as exceptions to the hearsay rule; under FRE 801(d)(2), admissions are not hearsay. Matters to which a party has stipulated on the record are known as "judicial admissions" and are conclusive in the proceeding in which they were made. Since the plaintiff specified that the information contained in the industry publication was to be used as its response to the defendant's interrogatories, the appropriate portions of the industry publication may be regarded as a judicial admission.

**A** is therefore incorrect. **B** is incorrect because an admission is either admissible hearsay (under common law) or not hearsay at all (under the FRE). A court may take judicial notice of facts contained in a reference work that is shown to be a reputable source beyond reasonable dispute. Since the portions of the industry publication are admissible as admissions, however, judicial notice is not the *only* way that they would be admissible. **D** is therefore incorrect.

136. **C**    Murder is the unlawful killing of a human being with malice aforethought. Among other things, malice aforethought may consist of the intent to cause serious bodily harm or of a reckless disregard for human life. Stabbing with a knife is evidence of both these states

of mind. Therefore, if the defendant's stabbing of the victim proximately caused the victim's death, it was probably murder. An act is a proximate cause of death if it was a factual and legal cause of the death. The defendant's act was a factual cause of the victim's death because the victim's death would not have occurred without it. Conduct is a legal cause of death if the death was a foreseeable result of it, and if there were no superseding intervening causes. The wife's conduct was also a cause of the victim's death, since the victim's death would not have occurred if the wife had secured medical attention. Further, her failure to do so was an intervening cause of the victim's death because it came after the defendant's act and before the victim's death. If the wife's conduct was unforeseeable, it can be called a superseding intervening cause of death. Under the definition given above, this would prevent the defendant's conduct from being a legal (or proximate) cause.

As indicated above, the defendant's conduct was a factual cause of the victim's death, since the death would not have occurred if the defendant had not stabbed the victim. The wife's failure to secure prompt medical attention was also a factual cause of the victim's death, since it would not have occurred if she had secured prompt medical attention. Any result may have several causes; the fact that the wife's conduct was a cause does not establish that the defendant's was not. **A** is therefore incorrect. If the victim's death was an unforeseeable result of the defendant's act, the defendant's act was not a proximate cause of it. The term *foreseeable,* however, means "that which the reasonable person would anticipate." Thus, even an unusual result may be foreseeable. For this reason, the fact that leg wounds do not usually cause death does not necessarily justify the conclusion that the victim's death was an unforeseeable result of the defendant's act. **B** is therefore incorrect. If the wife's conduct was a substantial factor in producing the victim's death, it was a factual cause of that death. Any result may have several proximate causes, however. **D** is incorrect because the defendant's act was also a cause of the victim's death.

137.   **C**   Unless it involves a fundamental right (*i.e.,* voting, or marriage and procreation) or discriminates on the basis of a suspect classification, state regulation of social or economic interests is valid if it has a rational basis. Since the United States Supreme Court has held that age is not a suspect classification, the state mandatory retirement law is valid if it has a rational basis. Under this test, if any state of facts can be imagined that would make the legislative choice a reasonable way to achieve a legitimate legislative purpose, the law will be upheld. Since providing state employees with the best insurance protection at the lowest cost is a legitimate legislative purpose, the mandatory retirement law probably has a rational basis that makes it valid. (**Note:** Although it is possible to conclude that the law does not have a rational basis because mandatory retirement is not a reasonable means of achieving this objective, **C** is the only answer that could possibly be correct.)

Under the Supremacy Clause, a state law is invalid if it conflicts with a valid federal law covering the same subject matter. Since the federal law fixes the retirement age for federal employees, and the state law fixes the retirement age for state employees, the two laws do not cover the same subject matter and are therefore not inconsistent with each other. **A** is thus incorrect. A law may have a rational basis even though its application to one particular person does not advance its objective. Thus, if many other state jobs require skills or abilities that are related to age, the fact that the plaintiff's does not will not be sufficient to invalidate the law. **B** is therefore incorrect. **D** is too general a statement to be correct; the federal government may impose some economic burdens on the states (*e.g.*, may tax certain state activities).

138.  **B**   If a case is initially not removable to federal court, a defendant has 30 days to file a notice of removal after the case becomes removable. *See 28 U.S.C. §1446(b)(3)*. Here, the case became removable to federal court once the doctor was dismissed because there is now complete diversity between the plaintiff and defendant and the amount in controversy is over $75,000. Because the lawyer sought removal within 30 days, the case can be removed.

   **A** is incorrect because although there is now complete diversity of citizenship, the lawyer would still need to seek removal within 30 days of the doctor's dismissal. Consequently, **B** is a better answer. **C** is incorrect because the lawyer has 30 days to seek removal. **D** is incorrect because the fact the banker voluntarily dismissed the doctor does not change the analysis.

139.  **B**   An intervening cause is an event without which the accident would not have occurred and which took place after the defendant's negligence. The defendant's encounter with the pothole was, thus, an intervening cause of the collision. A superseding cause is an unforeseeable intervening cause. In this context, the word *unforeseeable* may be used to mean either something that the reasonable person would not have anticipated, or something which, in retrospect, appears to have been extraordinary. If potholes are frequently found on road surfaces in the area, the presence of the pothole was foreseeable (in either sense of the word), and could not have been a superseding cause of harm.

   **A** is incorrect because although violation of a statute may establish that the defendant was negligent, it does not establish that the defendant's conduct was causally related to the plaintiff's injury. A superseding cause may relieve a defendant of liability by justifying the conclusion that his or her conduct was not a legal cause of harm, whether or not the person responsible for the superseding cause can be required to compensate the plaintiff. Thus, the plaintiff's liability does not depend on whether the Department of Highway Transportation is liable for its negligence or on whether governmental immunity has been abolished. **C** is therefore incorrect. The fact that the accident would not have occurred without the pothole proves that the pothole was one of its factual causes. Unless the presence of the pothole was an unforeseeable intervening cause, however, it was not a superseding cause of the plaintiff's harm and would not relieve the plaintiff of liability.

140.  **D**   The majority of jurisdictions recognize a client's privilege to prevent disclosure of a confidential communication that he or she made to his or her attorney while seeking legal advice even before retaining him or her. In addition, the privilege applies to confidences that the client communicates to an agent of the attorney in connection with the subject of the attorney-client relationship. Since the plaintiff's communication with the witness

was at the attorney's request to enable the attorney to make decisions relative to her representation of the plaintiff, it is protected by the attorney-client privilege.

A document prepared by or for an attorney that contains the attorney's mental impressions may be privileged as an attorney's work product. **A** is incorrect, however, because the conversation between the plaintiff and the witness was not a document and did not contain the attorney's mental impressions. **B** is incorrect because there is no rule of privilege that protects records kept in the course of business simply because of that fact. (**Note:** Records kept in the course of business are sometimes *admissible* under an exception to the hearsay rule.) An admission is a declaration by a party that is offered against that party. Under common law, admissions are admissible hearsay; under FRE 801(d)(2), admissions are not hearsay at all. Since the defendant seeks to offer the plaintiff's statements against the plaintiff, they cannot be classified as inadmissible hearsay. **C** is therefore incorrect.

141.  **B**      Under Fed. R. Civ. P. 23(a), the requirements for a class action are numerosity, common questions of law or fact, typicality of claim or defenses, and adequate representation. Here, there are 800 residents who are all being forcibly removed from their homes by the city, which is apparently doing so in an effort to combat crime. The best law firm in the city has taken the case, and the two named members are longtime residents and business owners. Consequently, it seems as if the four requirements are met. Importantly, an injunction can be the basis of a class action under Fed. R. Civ. P. 23(b)(2) so long as "the party opposing the class has acted or refused to act on grounds that apply generally to the class, so that final injunctive relief or corresponding declaratory relief is appropriate respecting the class as a whole." Here, an injunction to stop the city's plans would be appropriate respecting the class as a whole. Therefore, **C** is incorrect.

A is incorrect because the action would be heard in federal court based the alleged violation of federal law, not based on diversity of the parties. **D** is incorrect because 800 residents are likely too large a group of people to make joinder feasible.

142.  **B**      Generally, if a tortfeasor negligently causes an injury, the tortfeasor is liable for the full consequences of the injury even though a unique or rare medical condition causes the injury to be much worse than it would have been for an ordinary person. Since the man's negligent flying of the drone knocked over the woman, the fact her medical condition caused blindness when the injury would not have done so in an ordinary person does not relieve the man from liability. Therefore, **C** and **D** are incorrect.

A is incorrect because the man's failure to register the drone had no relation to his negligently hitting the woman with it. Negligence per se only applies when a violation of a law leads to the plaintiff being injured (*i.e.*, speed limits).

143.  **B**      Ordinarily, a relevant object is admissible into evidence if a witness testifies that he or she recognizes it. Because writings are particularly subject to fraud, however, special rules have developed regarding their admission. Where the legal significance of a writing depends upon its authorship, the writing cannot be admitted unless the court (*i.e.*, judge) finds that there is sufficient evidence to warrant a finding regarding its authorship.

Unless the court determines that there has been sufficient authentication, the jury should not be given an opportunity to see the document. **A** is therefore incorrect. FRE 901(b)(3) and the common law permit the jury to consider an authenticated exemplar of a party's signature in determining whether a document in question was signed by the party. **C** is incorrect, however, because this is not the *only* way of getting the promissory note before the jury. **D** is incorrect because once the court determines that there is sufficient evidence to justify a finding by the jury regarding the genuineness of a signature, the question of whether it actually is genuine is one of fact for the jury.

144. **B**   A statute that establishes a system of classification that discriminates against members of a particular ethnic group may violate the Equal Protection Clause of the Fourteenth Amendment to the United States Constitution. Even if a statute does not establish such a system of classification, however, it may be enforced in a way that makes it unconstitutional *as applied*. In determining whether the *application* of a statute violates the Equal Protection Clause, the United States Supreme Court has examined statistical evidence that the statute is being enforced in a discriminatory manner. Since the fact that 100 percent of the officer's speeding tickets were issued to members of an ethnic minority constituting only 10 percent of the population suggests a discriminatory application of the speed limit statute, that fact furnishes effective support for the plaintiff's assertion.

On the other hand, the fact that the plaintiff has received such summonses only from the officer does not indicate a discriminatory application of the statute by the officer unless it is coupled with information about other summonses issued by the officer. **A** is incorrect for this reason and because three incidents are probably not enough to justify any generalization. Coupled with the facts in option **B**, the facts in option **C** might support the conclusion that discrimination was behind the apparent inequity in the officer's issuing of speeding tickets. Standing alone, however, the fact that members of the plaintiff's minority do not drive any differently from members of other groups does nothing to show that the summons was issued to the plaintiff on a discriminatory basis. **C** is therefore incorrect. It is, of course, physically impossible for a police officer to apprehend all violators of a particular statute. This means that some will be apprehended, while others will not. For this reason, the fact that one member of a particular ethnic group was apprehended while some persons who did not belong to that ethnic group were not apprehended is not in itself sufficient to indicate that the apprehension of the plaintiff was the result of discrimination. **D** is therefore incorrect.

145. **A**   Criminal battery consists of the intentional, reckless, or criminally negligent application of force to the body of another person. One who knows that he or she often becomes intoxicated upon drinking small quantities of alcoholic beverages may be guilty of recklessness or criminal negligence by drinking half a glass of beer in the company of other people. Since this is all the *mens rea* required for a battery conviction, the fact that it was the alcohol that made the defendant become violent would not be relevant to any material issue in the case. For this reason, the psychiatrist's testimony should be excluded.

The psychiatrist's testimony had no bearing on the defendant's sanity under any definition of that term currently applied in the United States, but it might be admissible for some other reason. **B** is therefore incorrect. **C** is incorrect because criminal battery may be committed recklessly or criminally negligently without the intent to injure (*i.e.*, criminal battery is a general-intent crime). A defendant's intoxication is involuntary if the intoxicant was taken against his or her will or without knowledge of its intoxicating properties. Since the defendant was aware that even a small quantity of alcohol could intoxicate him, he cannot be said to have become intoxicated involuntarily. The psychiatrist's testimony would simply confirm what the defendant already knew about himself when he drank the beer, and therefore it could not establish that the intoxication was involuntary. **D** is therefore incorrect.

146.  **B**      To be enforceable, a contract must be definite and certain in all its basic terms. One way of determining whether a purported agreement is sufficiently definite and certain is to ask whether its terms make it possible for a court to fashion a remedy for its breach. Most of the time, this requires that the agreement identify the parties and show that they have agreed to the subject matter, the time for performance, and the price. The writing between the buyer and the seller leaves the price to be determined by a later agreement. But if the parties have not agreed as to how that subsequently-to-be-agreed-on price shall be determined, there is no way that a court could fashion a remedy for its breach. The writing would thus fail because it is not sufficiently definite and certain.

The Statute of Frauds requires that an agreement to transfer an interest in real estate be in writing. A writing might satisfy its requirements even though it does not specify a price, so long as it indicates the method that the parties have agreed to use in setting the price. For example, if the parties have agreed to set "a reasonable price" in the future, the writing might satisfy the Statute of Frauds even though it does not specify what the price will be. **A** is therefore incorrect. **C** is incorrect because the parties did not agree to be bound by the objective value of the property, even if it could be determined. **D** is incorrect for two reasons: First, the UCC provision that deems an omitted price term to call for a reasonable price applies only to transactions in goods, and second, this contract did not omit the price term but provided that it would be set by mutual agreement in the future.

147.  **D**      A person is guilty of an attempt when, with the intent to bring about a result that is criminally prohibited, he or she commits some act that brings him or her substantially close to accomplishing that result. If the result that the defendant intended is criminally prohibited, and if the defendant came substantially close to accomplishing it, she is guilty of attempting it. If an exam answer is "information" as defined by the statute, its theft would be a crime whether the defendant knew it or not. Similarly, if she intended to steal it and came substantially close to doing so, she is guilty of an attempt to violate the statute even though she did not know that what she was attempting to do was a crime.

A person may be guilty of attempting to commit a crime even though facts unknown to him or her would have made successful completion of the crime impossible. **A** is therefore incorrect. As a matter of policy, all persons are irrebuttably presumed to know the law. Thus, a defense cannot be based on the defendant's ignorance of the statute that prohibits his or her conduct (*i.e.*, ignorance of the law is no excuse). **B** is therefore incorrect. Since criminal attempt requires the intent to bring about a result that is criminally prohibited, a person cannot be guilty simply because the result that he or she intended to achieve was immoral. **C** is therefore incorrect.

148.  **B**     Battery is the intentional infliction of a harmful or offensive bodily contact. However, consent is a complete defense to battery, and a plaintiff's consent can be implied by the plaintiff's actions. Here, by taking part in the soccer game, the plaintiff impliedly consented to having the ball kicked away from him (a common occurrence in the game). While the defense of consent can be lost if the defendant goes beyond the consented-to level of contact, the defendant's actions here do not seem to rise to that level (*e.g.*, if he had punched the plaintiff or intentionally kicked him directly in the leg). **A** is incorrect because assumption of the risk is a defense in negligence actions that generally applies in clearly dangerous situations where the plaintiff voluntarily takes his or her chances that a particular harm will occur (*e.g.*, sky diving). **C** is incorrect, because a defendant does not need to intend to injure the plaintiff, so long as he or she intends to cause a harmful or offensive contact. **D** is incorrect because the contact here was truly "harmful" in that it injured the plaintiff. "Offensive to a reasonable sense of dignity" involves situations where the plaintiff is not actually harmed by the contact.

149.  **D**     The right of survivorship is the best known characteristic of a joint tenancy. It means that if one of the joint tenants dies, the survivor becomes the owner of the deceased tenant's share. Thus, if the brother died while he and his sister were joint tenants, the sister would have become the sole owner of the realty. When a joint tenant conveys his or her interest, however, the joint tenancy is severed, and his or her grantee becomes a tenant in common with the remaining co-owner. Tenants in common do not have a right of survivorship. Since a quitclaim deed conveys the grantor's interest, the brother's quitclaim to his wife severed his joint tenancy with his sister and made his wife and his sister tenants in common. When the sister died, her daughter inherited the sister's interest, thus becoming a tenant in common with the wife.

**A** and **B** are incorrect for the reasons given above. **C** is incorrect because the brother's quitclaim deed to his wife severed the joint tenancy.

150.  **A**     Article IV, Section 2, paragraph 2 of the United States Constitution contains what is known as the Property Clause: "Congress shall have power to dispose of and make all needful rules and regulations respecting . . . property belonging to the United States." The United States Supreme Court has held that the Property Clause leaves the lease or other disposition of federal property within the discretion of Congress.

Although the Commerce Clause gives Congress the power to regulate interstate commerce, **B** is incorrect because there is no fact indicating that the lease of grazing land was for that purpose or would have that effect. A person has standing to assert a constitutional challenge if he or she is faced with some actual or immediately threatened concrete harm that the court could avoid by granting the relief requested. If the low rate will cause the plaintiff to lose revenue, the plaintiff faces an immediately threatened concrete harm. If the court declares the federal lease unconstitutional, the problems created by competition with the federal government will be solved, and the harm will be averted.

**C** is therefore incorrect. This proceeding challenges the constitutionality of the action of Congress and the agency to which it delegated power. The authority of Congress and the federal government is limited by the Constitution. If the federal government were immune from such a challenge, constitutional limitations on its exercise of power would be meaningless. Whether the federal government is immune from tort claims based on allegations of unfair competition is irrelevant. **D** is therefore incorrect.

151.   **A**   Under the Restatement approach, whether the breeder could rescind the contract would depend on whether the characteristic on which the parties were mistaken was a "basic assumption." Here, the belief of the parties that the cow was barren, and the huge price difference between a barren and breeding cow, shows that the characteristic was a basic assumption of the contract. **B** is incorrect because that answer choice only mentions the price difference, and does not take into account whether it was a basic assumption of the contract. **C** is incorrect because the mistake concerned a basic assumption of the contract, not merely the price. **D** is incorrect for the same reason.

152.   **C**   The Fifth Amendment to the United States Constitution provides in part that "No person . . . shall be compelled in any criminal case to be a witness against himself." The privilege only prohibits the government from requiring a testimonial communication, however. It does not protect a person against being required to participate in identification procedures that might lead to his or her conviction. For this reason, the Fifth Amendment privilege does not protect the defendant against being required to walk across the courtroom.

A defendant who testifies in his or her own behalf thereby waives the privilege and may even be required to utter testimonial communications that might tend to incriminate him or her. Since the Fifth Amendment privilege does not include non-testimonial communications, however, the question of waiver is irrelevant. **A** is therefore incorrect. A prosecutor may not comment on a defendant's assertion of the Fifth Amendment privilege; the jury may not draw inferences from it. **B** is incorrect, however, because the Fifth Amendment does not privilege the defendant to refuse to walk across the courtroom. Since no penalty can be imposed for the assertion of a constitutional right, and since a criminal defendant has a constitutional right to be present at his or her own trial, the defendant's presence in the courtroom cannot be a waiver of any other right. **D** is therefore incorrect.

153.   **A**   The United States Supreme Court has held that because manipulation of circumstances surrounding a lineup could create considerable likelihood of inaccuracy, and because it would be difficult at trial to fully develop evidence regarding such manipulation, the Sixth Amendment requires the presence of counsel at a post-indictment lineup. For this reason, the defendant's objection would probably be sustained for the reason given in **A.**

The constitutional right to confront witnesses requires that a defendant be given an opportunity to cross-examine such witnesses at a trial. It does not require, however, that the defendant be given an opportunity to question those witnesses at any other stage of the proceeding (*i.e.*, at a lineup). **B** is therefore incorrect. The Fifth Amendment protection against self-incrimination applies only to testimonial communication. For this reason, it does not prohibit compelling a defendant to show himself or herself to witnesses for identification purposes. **C** is therefore incorrect. Since a defendant has no constitutional right to refuse to appear in a lineup, police may compel or coerce him or her to do so by the use or threat of reasonable force. **D** is therefore incorrect.

154. **C**    A negligent defendant is liable for additional damage caused by foreseeable rescue efforts. This is true even if these rescue efforts are negligent in themselves. When faced with a severally injured person, it is foreseeable that an ambulance driver would drive faster than the speed limit and negligently crash into a pole. Consequently, the man is also liable for his friend's death in the ambulance accident.

A is incorrect because a foreseeable rescue does not break the chain of liability. **B** is incorrect because it was foreseeable that the ambulance might drive negligently and crash into a pole. **D** is incorrect because the simple fact the death happened after the friend's injuries would not make the man liable for the friend's death. Importantly, there is no connection between the accident injuries and the actual death.

155. **B**    Under the Rule Against Perpetuities, no interest is good unless it must vest *if at all* within a period measured by a life or lives in being plus 21 years. Thus, a future interest that might never vest at all is valid under the Rule so long as the language that created it will prevent it from vesting after the prescribed period (*i.e.*, *if* it vests, it will do so during the prescribed period). Since the church might never cease using the land for church purposes, and since, even if it did, the hospital might never cease using the land for hospital purposes, it is possible that the son's interest as created by the landowner's deed will never vest at all. The language of the landowner's deed provides, however, that in no event is the interest of the son to vest unless the son is alive when the conditions precedent are satisfied. Thus, since the interest of the son must vest if at all during a period measured by a life in being (*i.e.*, the son's life), it does not violate the Rule Against Perpetuities.

Many jurisdictions recognize an exception to the Rule Against Perpetuities for the interest of a charitable organization that follows the interest of another charitable organization. The son is not a charitable organization, however, so this exception would not prevent the Rule Against Perpetuities from applying to the son's interest. **A** is therefore incorrect. **C** is incorrect because the Rule Against Perpetuities does not require that the interest in question will vest during the prescribed period, but that if it vests at all, it will be during that period. In a jurisdiction that does not recognize an exception for the interest of a charity that follows the interest of another charity, the hospital's interest would be void under the Rule Against Perpetuities. This is because the condition that would make its interest vest (*i.e.*, cessation of use for church purposes) might occur after the period established by the rule. Since the landowner's deed provides that the interest of the son cannot vest unless it does so during the life of the son, however, the interest of the son would not violate the Rule even if the interest of the hospital did. **D** is therefore incorrect.

156. **D**    Although the Due Process Clause of the Fifth Amendment (applied to state action by the Fourteenth Amendment) prohibits the arbitrary regulation of economic interests, it

is almost never used to justify the conclusion that an economic regulation is unconstitutional. In general, so long as such a regulation employs a means reasonably related to accomplishing a purpose within the scope of a state's general police power and does not amount to a "taking," it will be regarded as valid under the Due Process Clause. Since regulating the storage of radioactive wastes is reasonably related to the legitimate police power objective of protecting the public good, and since there is no indication that Section 40 drastically interferes with the operation of out-of-state power plants, the Section does not violate the Due Process Clauses. Although it is not certain that Section 40 would be declared unconstitutional, due process is the only argument listed that could not possibly result in such a declaration.

The Privileges and Immunities Clause of Article IV prohibits a state from arbitrarily discriminating against out-of-staters. Since Section 40 effectively denies the use of state storage facilities to out-of-staters, it might violate this clause. **A** is therefore incorrect. The Privileges and Immunities Clause of the Fourteenth Amendment prohibits a state from interfering with any of the rights that go with United States citizenship. One of these is the right to travel freely from state to state. Since the Section effectively prevents the importation of radioactive wastes from outside the state, it may be unconstitutional because it interferes with this freedom. For this reason, **B** is incorrect. The Equal Protection Clause prohibits invidious discrimination by a state. Since Section 40 effectively disqualifies out-of-state producers of radioactive waste from using facilities available to in-state producers, it discriminates against them. If that discrimination is invidious, the section is unconstitutional. **C** is therefore incorrect.

157.  **B**    The United States Supreme Court has upheld a state court's personal jurisdiction over a defendant when the defendant is personally served with process while he or she is within the state's borders. *See Burnham v. Superior Court, 495 U.S. 604 (1990).* This is true even if the defendant is only in the state for a short time. Therefore, **C** and **D** are incorrect.

A is incorrect because the fact the action was filed in state court in State B would not automatically confer personal jurisdiction over a defendant.

158.  **D**    In general, all evidence is admissible if it is relevant to a fact of consequence in the litigation. The fact that there were stolen license plates on the defendant's van tends to establish that he was attempting to avoid recognition, and therefore that he was planning to commit some crime. Since the burglary statute requires an intent to commit a crime inside the entered premises, the defendant's plan is relevant to a fact of consequence. For this reason, evidence of the stolen license plates may be admissible in the burglary prosecution.

A is therefore incorrect. It is generally understood that evidence of unconvicted bad acts by a defendant is inadmissible for the purpose of establishing that he or she had a criminal disposition. Where such evidence is offered not merely to prove that defendant had a criminal disposition, however, but to establish an inference that he or she committed the act charged, it may be admissible. Here, evidence that the defendant made special preparations for a crime justifies the inference that he entered the warehouse to commit a crime therein. **B** is therefore incorrect. **C** is incorrect because evidence of unconvicted acts is inadmissible for the purpose of establishing a criminal disposition.

159. **A**    Generally, in the absence of an agreement by the promisee to release the promisor from his or her obligations under a contract, the promisor continues to be bound by his or her promise even after assigning his or her rights. Thus, any rights that the seller had against the buyer under the contract of sale survived the assignment by the buyer to the attorney. Even in the absence of a specific provision requiring it, a contract for the sale of real property is understood to impose upon the seller an obligation to deliver marketable title. But the seller satisfies this obligation if his or her title is marketable at the time set for performance (*i.e.*, the closing). Since the seller acquired title to the land prior to the closing, he is entitled to enforce the contract of sale against the buyer.

The doctrine of estoppel by deed provides that when a seller acquires title to realty that he or she has already purported to grant to another person, he or she acquires it on behalf of that grantee and is estopped from denying the validity of his or her previous conveyance. It is inapplicable to this case because the seller obtained title to the land before attempting to convey it to the buyer. **B** is therefore incorrect. **C** is incorrect because the contract did not require the seller to deliver marketable title until July 15, and on that date he did hold marketable title. An interest is said to be outside the chain of title if it could not have been discovered by a reasonable title searcher. Sometimes this occurs when a person claims to have received an interest from a grantor after a transfer of that same interest by the same grantor had previously been recorded. (For example, O transfers to A. O then transfers to B. B records before A. A's interest may be outside the chain of title, because a reasonable title searcher finding O's transfer to B in the record would not look for any subsequent transfers of the same interest by O.) **D** is incorrect, however, for two reasons: First, this argument is normally relevant only in determining the priority of two different interests, and second, there is no indication that the farmer had previously conveyed the land to another person or that such a conveyance had been recorded before the farmer's conveyance to the seller.

160. **A**    An action must be dismissed if the federal court does not have subject matter jurisdiction over the action. For a federal court to have subject matter jurisdiction over an action, the plaintiff and defendant must be citizens of different states or the action must arise under federal law. Here, the businessman is a citizen of State A. A corporation is a citizen of where it is incorporated and where its principal place of business is located. A corporation's principal place of business is where the corporation's high-level officers control the business. Consequently, the company is a citizen of State B, where it is incorporated, and State A, where its executives are based. Because both the businessman and the company are citizens of State A, the action should be dismissed.

**B** is incorrect because the issue presented here is not one regarding personal jurisdiction, and the location of the majority of the company's apartments does not affect its citizenship in regards to determining subject matter jurisdiction. **C** is incorrect because the appeals court would be required to dismiss the action for lack of subject matter jurisdiction even if the company did not challenge jurisdiction. **D** is incorrect because federal question jurisdiction cannot be based on a defendant's defense.

161. **B**    Police may search a vehicle incident to a recent occupant's arrest only if the arrestee is within reaching distance of the passenger compartment at the time of the search or it is reasonable to believe the vehicle contains evidence of the offense of arrest. When these justifications are absent, a search of an arrestee's vehicle will be unreasonable unless police obtain a warrant or show that another exception to the warrant requirement applies. Here, the defendant was secured in the police car at the time of the search, and there is unlikely to be any evidence relating to his offense. While searches conducted without prior approval are unlawful, this statement is too broad because it fails to note the exceptions to this rule. **A** is therefore incorrect. **C** is incorrect because an inventory search is not the only way a police officer can lawfully discover evidence contained in a car. **D** is incorrect because there is no rule stating that the interior of a car is always within the immediate control of an arrestee.

162. **A**    Generally, the federal rules only require that a complaint contain "a short and plain statement of the claim showing that the pleader is entitled to relief." *See Fed. R. Civ. P. 8(a)(2).* Under Fed. R. Civ. P. 9, certain other matters, such as fraud, mistake, and special damages require a party to give more detail. Here, since the man is simply making a claim under federal employment law, he does not need to do more than make a short and plain statement of the claim.

              **B** is incorrect because the relevant analysis requires more than mere notice. For example, a plaintiff could not simply file a complaint that stated "I'm suing defendant!" In that case, while the defendant would certainly have notice, the defendant would know nothing about the claim. **C** is incorrect because the salesman does not need to set out a prima facie case. **D** is incorrect because "a party may state as many separate claims or defenses as it has, regardless of consistency." *See Fed. R. Civ. P. 8(d)(3).*

163. **D**    A person is guilty of a criminal attempt when, with the specific intent to bring about a criminally prohibited result, he or she does some significant act that brings him or her substantially close to accomplishing that result. Thus, although a person may be guilty of murder without actually intending to bring about a death, he or she cannot be guilty of attempted murder without the intent to bring about a death. Since the druggist did not really believe that the wife would die, he could not have intended to bring about her death and cannot be guilty of attempting to murder her.

              Murder is the unlawful killing of a human being with malice aforethought. Malice aforethought includes a reckless disregard for human life. If the druggist's conduct showed a reckless disregard for human life, and if it resulted in the death of the wife, then the druggist would be guilty of murder. **A** is incorrect, however, because no person can be guilty of attempted murder without the specific intent to bring about a death or to cause great bodily harm. **B** is incorrect for the same reason, and because ordinarily a person is under no duty to stop another from committing a crime. Since the druggist did not believe the drug that he furnished would harm the wife, he lacked the specific intent necessary to make him guilty of attempting to kill her. **C** is therefore incorrect.

164. **A**   Under FRE 803(8), the file itself may be admissible as an official written statement since it was made at or near the time of the matter recorded by a public official regarding matters in the declarant's personal knowledge in the course of the declarant's duties. (**Note:** The file may also be admissible as a business record.) Even if the personnel file's contents are admissible, however, the witness's testimony about its contents might not be. Under the common law and FRE 1002, the best evidence rule prohibits secondary evidence to prove the terms of a writing unless the writing itself is shown to be unavailable. Since the purpose of the witness's testimony is to prove the contents of the file, he will not be permitted to do so unless the file is shown to be unavailable.

If the requirements of the best evidence rule are satisfied, the witness's testimony would be as admissible as the file itself. Since the FRE make business records and official written statements admissible without regard to the availability of the person who made entries in them, **B** and **C** are incorrect. **D** is incorrect because the official written statement exception, although it is sometimes called the "public document" exception, does not require that the record be one that is available for public inspection.

165. **A**   Ordinarily, a promise is not enforceable unless something of value (*i.e.*, consideration) was given in return for it. Since the plaintiff paved the driveway before the neighbor promised to pay, he could not have done so in return for the promise. The paving job, therefore, could not have been consideration for the neighbor's promise. Under the view of the Restatement (2d) of Contracts, however, a promise made in recognition of a benefit previously received by the promisor from the promisee is binding to the extent necessary to prevent injustice. Thus, if the neighbor knew that the plaintiff had paved his driveway and made the promise to pay in recognition of this benefit, the promise would be enforceable.

**B** is incorrect because the neighbor's promise could not have been given in recognition of the paving job if the neighbor did not know about it at the time he made the promise. Since the paving job done by the plaintiff was not given in return for the neighbor's promise, it would not be consideration for that promise no matter when the neighbor decided to have the job done. **C** and **D** are therefore incorrect.

166. **D**   A landlord's failure to take prompt action when he or she learns of an attempted assignment or sublease constitutes a waiver of the right to block it. Here, the landlord will probably not be permitted to terminate the lease since he likely waived his right to do so by accepting rent and failing to take prompt action when he discovered the assignment. Consequently, **A** is incorrect. **B** is incorrect because, by accepting rent and waiting to protest, the landlord did not appear to be protesting within a reasonable time. **C** is incorrect because the issue involves the landlord's actions, not the nature of the property interests.

167. **D**   If a person's behavior is grossly negligent, he or she may be liable for involuntary manslaughter if his or her conduct results in the death of another person. Nearly all states hold that the defendant's negligence must be something more than ordinary negligence. "Gross negligence" usually means the defendant disregarded a substantial danger of serious bodily harm or death. However, there must be a causal link between the gross

negligence and the death. Consequently, if the death would have occurred even without the defendant's gross negligence, involuntary manslaughter wouldn't apply. Here, the facts state that the defendant drove the correct speed and obeyed all traffic regulations. Consequently, his gross negligence, specifically his intoxication, was not the cause in fact or proximate cause of the man's death. Thus, **A** is incorrect. **B** is incorrect because, even though courts look at the totality of the circumstances in determining gross negligence, the important point is that the defendant's gross negligence was not the cause of the accident. **C** is incorrect because, even if a violation is *malum in se* (dangerous in itself), there still needs to be a causal relation between the negligence and the death.

168.  **A**    An illusory promise is a statement which appears to promise something, but in fact does not commit the promisor to anything. Importantly, such a promise will not give sufficient consideration to support a contract. Here, there was no consideration for the endorsement because the plaintiff could have sued immediately if he decided he wanted his money. Thus, he really didn't promise to do anything at all. The fact that the plaintiff in fact did not collect on the note for two years is irrelevant. Under promissory estoppel, a promise is binding if ". . . (c) the promisor should reasonably expect the promise to induce action or forbearance of a substantial character on the part of a promisee or a third person, and the promise does induce such action or forbearance." Here, a court might find that the defendant's guarantee should reasonably have been expected to induce the plaintiff to refrain from suing, that it did have this effect, and that this was of a substantial character. In such an event, the defendant would have been bound. Based on the facts here, a court could find that the plaintiff did in fact rely to his detriment on the promise. Thus, **B** is incorrect, and **A** is a stronger answer. **C** is incorrect because the fact that the husband is the primary debtor does not change the analysis. Unconscionability arises in situations where an agreement is grossly unfair. Here, there is no indication of any unfairness in the agreement, so **D** is incorrect.

169.  **A**    Specific performance is a remedy available for breach of a contract for the sale of something unique. Since each parcel of realty is regarded as unique, specific performance is usually available as a buyer's remedy for a seller's breach of a contract for the sale of realty. Unless such a contract has been formed and breached, however, no remedy is available at all. A contract is formed by the acceptance of an offer. An offer is an expression of an unequivocal willingness to enter into a contract with another on specified terms. Since the seller never indicated a willingness to enter into a contract with the buyer on any particular terms, he never made an offer to the buyer. The buyer twice made offers to the seller, but the seller did not accept either of them. Thus, no contract was ever formed between the seller and the buyer or breached by the seller. The buyer is therefore without any remedy.

Whether the seller's statement to the broker on April 10 was an attempt to modify an existing agreement is not at all certain under the facts regarding that agreement. **B** is incorrect in any event because the agreement between the seller and the broker did not require the seller to accept an offer procured by the broker, and it is not relevant to the buyer's rights against the seller. Specific performance is not usually available as a remedy for the breach of a contract for sale unless the subject of the contract is unique or damages would be an inadequate remedy. **C** is incorrect, however, because—for the reasons given above—there has been no breach, and the buyer therefore has no remedy at all. Since the seller made no offer to the buyer, the document that was presented to the seller on April 14 was nothing more than an offer. Since the seller did not accept it, no contract between him and the buyer was formed. **D** is therefore incorrect.

170. **C**    Hearsay is defined as an out-of-court statement offered for the purpose of proving the truth of the matter asserted in that statement. Since the plaintiff's attorney's notes were made out of court, and since the only apparent reason to offer them is to establish the truth of their contents, they are hearsay.

FRE 803(6) recognizes a hearsay exception for properly authenticated business records recorded as part of the regular course of business, while the transaction recorded was fresh in the entrant's mind, regarding facts within the entrant's personal knowledge or from an inherently reliable source. Since the facts do not indicate what information was contained in the attorney's notes, there is no way to determine whether all the information actually contained in them was within the attorney's personal knowledge or from an inherently reliable source. An additional question exists as to whether an attorney's notes regarding a negotiation between a client and another party are kept in the regular course of business. No matter how these questions are resolved, however, the attorney's notes cannot be admitted as a business record unless they are authenticated by a person who testifies to the record's identity and its mode of preparation. Since no one has testified as such, **A** is incorrect. Documents that have been used to refresh a witness's recollection while testifying may be consulted by an adverse party in cross-examining that witness. In addition, an *adverse* party may introduce into evidence those portions of the document that are relevant to the witness's testimony. **B** is incorrect, however, because the fact that a party used a document to refresh his or her recollection is not sufficient to justify its introduction by the party that used it. Under certain circumstances, an attorney may resist discovery of his or her own work product and prevent it from being received in evidence. This privilege belongs to the attorney (and his or her client), however, not to his or her adversary. For this reason, the defendant's attorney could not successfully object on the ground that the document was the plaintiff's attorney's work product. **D** is therefore incorrect.

171. **D**    The Equal Protection Clause prohibits invidious discrimination by the state, but not all discrimination is invidious. Ordinarily, statutory systems of classification (*i.e.*, discrimination) are valid so long as they have a rational basis. If the discrimination is based on a suspect classification or interferes with a fundamental right, however, it is presumed invalid unless it is proven to be necessary to achieve a compelling state interest. The Supreme Court has held that the right to vote is a fundamental right. For this reason, the Township Council's assertion that the registration schedule had a rational basis would not be sufficient to prevent it from being declared unconstitutional.

Discrimination on the basis of lifestyle or wealth has been held not to involve a suspect classification. **A** and **B** are therefore incorrect. Some forms of sex discrimination, referred to as "benign" because they are aimed at compensating for the demonstrated economic disadvantages of women, have been found constitutional. Some forms of sex discrimination, called "benign" because they are based on old thought patterns about sex roles and the dependency of women, have been found unconstitutional. Thus, the term "benign sex discrimination" is not relevant in determining whether a statute is constitutional, and **C** is incorrect.

172.   **C**   Unless a landlord specifically agrees to release a tenant from further obligations under a lease, assignment or sublease does not relieve the original tenant from those obligations. For this reason, the landlord can collect unpaid rent from the first attorney. Since the landlord was an intended third-party creditor beneficiary of the agreement between the attorneys, the landlord can also collect from the second attorney. **A**, **B**, and **D** are therefore incorrect.

173.   **C**   Under Fed. R. Civ. P. 59(d), a district court can order a new trial on its own for any reason that would justify granting one on a party's motion. Because inadequate damages could be the basis for a new trial, the trial judge can order a new trial.

A and **B** are incorrect because additur, or offering a defendant a choice between a higher damage award or a new trial, had been found to be a violation of the Seventh Amendment (although this does not apply to state courts). **D** is incorrect because a motion for judgment as a matter of law must be made by a party before the case is submitted to a jury.

174.   **A**   Unless the parties expressly agree otherwise, the owner of the servient estate is not required to repair or maintain the property used in the easement. Here, there was no express agreement regarding repair between the parties, so the owner who granted the easement has no duty to repair the bridge. **B** is incorrect, because, although the holder of the easement has an implied right to maintain the property used in the easement, if the servient estate holder does not enjoy any of the benefits of the easement, he is under no obligation to reimburse for repairs. Here, there is no indication that the owner who granted the easement uses the easement. **C** is incorrect because the owner of the servient estate has no obligation of repair, even if the lack of maintenance means that the easement holder cannot use the easement as the parties intended. **D** is incorrect because the fact that this was an express easement does not change the analysis.

175.   **B**   State action that imposes a penalty for the exercise of a constitutional right is a deprivation of liberty. If the decision not to renew the plaintiff's contract was based on his speech (an exercise of First Amendment rights), it interfered with a liberty interest. Since the Fifth and Fourteenth Amendments protect against deprivation of liberty without due process, the additional fact set forth in **B** could result in a finding that a hearing (*i.e.*, due process) was required.

A is incorrect because there is no indication that the contracts of the probationary employees who received hearings permitted non-renewal without cause, as did the plaintiff's. **C** is incorrect because the United States Supreme Court has specifically held that state action does not require a prior hearing merely because it interferes with reputation, particularly since a tort action for defamation is available to prevent abuse. Sometimes urgency plays a role in the court's decision about whether a prior hearing is required for a particular action. For example, it has been held that because the denial of welfare benefits could leave a person in a desperate financial situation, a prior hearing is required. Similarly, if delaying governing action until after a hearing is held is likely to result in serious harm to the government, it might be appropriate to act without holding a prior hearing. The fact set forth in **D** might justify the conclusion that keeping the plaintiff on the job until a hearing is held would result in serious harm to the state. In that case, it would hurt rather than help the plaintiff's cause.

176. **A** In jurisdictions that recognize the spousal privilege, a spouse is not permitted to testify to a confidential communication received during marriage if the spouse who made the communication objects to the testimony. For this reason, the court should exclude his wife's testimony if the defendant objects to it.

In general, all evidence that tends to establish a material fact is relevant and should be admitted unless excluded by some rule of law. Since the defendant's statement that he committed the crimes he is charged with tends to establish that he did so, it is relevant. Hearsay is an out-of-court statement offered to prove the truth of the matter asserted in that statement and is inadmissible unless it falls within an exception to the hearsay rule. A statement by a party offered against that party is an admission, however. An admission is admissible under common law as an exception to the hearsay rule and is not hearsay under FRE 801(d)(2). Thus, the defendant's statement should be admitted unless excluded by the spousal privilege. A privilege may only be asserted by one who holds it. In some jurisdictions (and the FRE follow local state law as to privileges), the spousal privilege can be asserted only by the spouse who made the confidential communication. In other jurisdictions, the privilege may also be asserted by the spouse who received the communication. But all jurisdictions agree that the communication may be excluded only if a person holding it objects. Therefore, if *neither* spouse asserts the privilege, it cannot be used to exclude the wife's testimony. **B**, **C**, and **D** are therefore incorrect.

177. **A** A party's unequivocal statement that he or she will not perform is an anticipatory repudiation and entitles the other party to all rights resulting from a breach. The plaintiff's statement that she would not accept the coins in payment for the chickens was such a statement. Its result was to free the defendant from any further obligation under the contract and to give the defendant a right to an immediate action against the plaintiff for breach of contract.

A prospective inability to perform occurs when a party engages in some conduct that divests that party of the ability to perform. All jurisdictions agree that one party's prospective inability to perform excuses the other party's performance, and some jurisdictions hold that it gives him or her an immediate right to sue. **B** is incorrect, however, because *the defendant's* prospective inability to perform would not in any jurisdiction give *the defendant* a right of action. For the reason stated above, the defendant's refusal to accept delivery of the chickens was excused by the plaintiff's anticipatory repudiation and was therefore not a breach. **C** is therefore incorrect. (**Note:** **C** may be confusing because of its use of the word *impossible*. If an unforeseeable change in circumstances makes it impossible for a party to perform his or her obligation under a contract, his or her failure to perform might be excused under the doctrine of impossibility of performance. Since the defendant's refusal to accept delivery did not result from an unforeseen change in circumstances but rather from his decision to treat the plaintiff's repudiation as an immediate breach, the doctrine of impossibility of performance is not relevant to this case. If it were relevant, it would tend to defeat the plaintiff's claim, not support it.) Since the defendant chose to treat the plaintiff's anticipatory repudiation as an immediate breach, the plaintiff cannot subsequently undo the breach by offering to perform. **D** is therefore incorrect.

178.  **D**    A defendant's conduct is not privileged solely by virtue of the fact that he or she made a mistake. Consequently, while the defendants may have made a good faith mistake in mistaking the farmer's dog for a wolf, they will still be liable for the farmer's damages.

       **A**, **B**, and **C** are therefore incorrect.

179.  **D**    Expression with a primarily commercial purpose may be regulated so long as the regulation directly advances a substantial government interest by the least burdensome means necessary. Whether protecting the public against annoyance by computerized telephone calls is a substantial government interest and whether the prohibition against the use of the robocall computer within the state directly advances that interest are two questions open to debate. If the answer to either question is "no," then the statute violates the First Amendment. It is far from certain that a court would come to this conclusion, but the argument set forth in **D** is the only one listed that could possibly support the company's position.

       Because of the importance of free expression, the rules of standing are ordinarily relaxed for First Amendment challenges based on a claim of overbreadth. Thus, a person whose speech can be constitutionally punished may challenge the constitutionality of a statute that punishes it on the ground that the statute is "overbroad" in that it also punishes speech that cannot be constitutionally punished. The purpose of this rule is to prevent the "chilling" of First Amendment rights by state regulations. Since it is believed that advertisers are unlikely to be chilled by such regulations, however, this rule does not apply in commercial speech cases. **A** is therefore incorrect. The selection of a standard to be applied in deciding the constitutional validity of a law regulating expression may depend on whether the regulation is content-related. This fact alone, however, is never sufficient to justify the conclusion that the regulation is invalid. **B** is therefore incorrect. A statute is said to have a "chilling" effect on freedom of expression if its terms are so unclear that the reasonable person could not tell what forms of expression are prohibited and might therefore be afraid to engage in unprohibited forms of expression. Although the high cost of using telephone solicitation computers outside the state to call numbers inside the state might discourage people from doing so, this will not be because they are uncertain about what expression the law forbids. Thus, the law cannot be said to have a chilling effect for this reason, making **C** incorrect.

180.  **A**    A direct restraint on alienation is a covenant or condition that attempts to control the alienability of the estate granted. A disabling restraint purports to withhold the grantee's power to alienate. A promissory restraint consists of a covenant not to alienate. It does

not withhold the covenantor's power to alienate but subjects the covenantor to liability for damages for breaching the covenant by alienating. A forfeitural restraint terminates the estate upon an attempt to alienate it, causing the property to vest in someone else. Direct restraints on the alienation of *fee simple estates* are generally void and unenforceable, whether they are disabling, promissory, or forfeiturial. While disabling restraints on the alienation of life estates are similarly void, promissory or forfeiturial restraints on the alienation of *life estates* may be valid if reasonable. From the language of the farmer's will, it is difficult to determine whether the restraint that it creates is disabling or forfeiturial. The argument presented in **A** is the only one listed, however, that might possibly support the son's claim.

**B** and **C** are incorrect because promissory and forfeiturial restraints on the alienation of life estates may be enforceable. **D** is incorrect in spite of the 40-year period that it specifies, because the son could not possibly alienate his interest except during his own lifetime. Thus, the vesting of the daughter's interest could not possibly occur beyond a period measured by a life in being (the son's) plus 21 years, making the Rule Against Perpetuities inapplicable to it.

181. **B** The "plain view" doctrine allows a police officer to seize evidence falling into the officer's "plain view" when that officer sees the evidence from a place where it is lawful for the officer to be. Here, by consenting to have the officer in her home, the police officer was lawfully in the living room. However, the question in such circumstances is what the homeowner would have reasonably believed her consent amounted to. Importantly, if one consents to have another person in his or her home, that does not mean there is consent for the person to open things he or she finds in the home. People do not expect casual guests to open boxes, dig through closets, etc. Therefore, the plain view doctrine would not apply because the homeowner did not give her consent to open the gun case. Therefore, **C** is incorrect.

**A** is incorrect because the homeowner leaving the room did not change the analysis. **D** is incorrect because the police officer simply saw a gun case. In many instances, guns and gun cases are perfectly lawful. Here, the police officer did not know about the illegality until the case was opened.

182. **A** Article I, Section 10 of the United States Constitution prohibits the states from passing laws impairing the obligation of contracts. This prevents a state from unjustifiably repudiating its own contractual obligations or interfering with the contract rights of individuals. If the plaintiff was a state employee prior to the time the mandatory retirement law was passed, the state owed him certain obligations under the employment contract. Under the laws that then existed, these included the obligations to grant an annual salary increase and to pay a retirement pension based on the salary he earned the year immediately prior to this retirement. Accompanying all contract obligations is the implied warranty that the promisor will not willfully prevent the promisee from enjoying the benefits thereunder. By mandating retirement at 65, the state has prevented the plaintiff from further increasing his annual salary and thus increasing the amount of his retirement pension. Since he had this right under the employment contract that existed prior

to passage of the mandatory retirement law, the law may be held to impair an obligation of contracts.

On the other hand, unless the plaintiff was a state employee prior to the passage of the mandatory retirement law, he has no contractual expectation of continued employment after 65. This is true even though he undertook financial obligations in contemplation of continued employment, because although he might have detrimentally relied on that expectation, such reliance was not justified. **B** is therefore incorrect. The fact that the plaintiff was fit for continued employment after the age of 65 would not result in a finding that the mandatory retirement law impairs the obligation of contracts because his fitness did not create a contractual expectation unless he was employed prior to passage of the law. **C** and **D** are therefore incorrect.

183.   **A**     There are various theories that might exclude performance because of a change in circumstances, but all require that the change in circumstances be unforeseeable at the time the contract was formed. If the defendant knew on May 1 that many hogs in the area had contracted the disease, it was probably foreseeable to him that the hog would contract it also. If the hog's disease was foreseeable to the defendant, it would not excuse his performance under any theory.

There are various theories that might exclude performance because of a change in circumstances, but all require that the change in circumstances be unforeseeable at the time the contract was formed. If the defendant knew on May 1 that many hogs in the area had contracted the disease, it was probably foreseeable to him that the hog would contract it also. If the hog's disease was foreseeable to the defendant, it would not excuse his performance under any theory.

If performance required by a contract becomes illegal after the contract is formed, both parties are excused from further performance. Thus, if the state issued an order prohibiting the exhibition of the hog, the defendant would be excused from exhibiting him, and the court would find *against* the plaintiff. **B** is therefore incorrect. **C** is incorrect because the contract called for the exhibition of the hog, and not merely for the exhibition of a hog with the other hog's qualities, so the fact that the defendant had a hog like him is irrelevant. **D** is incorrect because if the change of circumstances that resulted in the plaintiff's loss was unforeseeable, the plaintiff cannot collect for that loss even if it can be established with particularity.

184.   **D**     Under the doctrine of accession, the owner of realty becomes the owner of anything that becomes part of it as well. Thus, if the storage building has become part of the realty, the tenant may not remove it. Unless the parties agree, however, the decision as to whether the building has become part of (*i.e.*, annexed to) the realty can be made only by a court. **A** is incorrect because the landlord does not have the power to decide it unilaterally. **B** is incorrect because if the building has become part of (*i.e.*, annexed to) the realty, the landlord is already its owner by accession, and cannot be required to pay for it. For the above reasons, **C** is also incorrect.

185.   **C**     Private nuisance is a tortious interference with the plaintiff's right to use and enjoy real property in which he or she has a present or future possessory interest. In effect, a plaintiff suing a defendant for private nuisance is claiming that the defendant's use of its realty unreasonably violates the plaintiff's right to use his or her realty. For this reason, in deciding a claim for private nuisance, the courts must balance the rights of the plaintiff and defendant in an attempt to determine which right is more worthy of protection. In doing so, courts consider many factors, including the relative importance of the

plaintiff's and the defendant's activities, the appropriateness of each to the location, and the ability of each to avoid the harm complained of. Because the insecticide is an important agricultural product, the fact that it cannot be manufactured without producing bad smells could lead a court to conclude that the production of bad smells is not a nuisance. It is by no means certain that a court would come to this conclusion, but of all the additional facts listed, **C** is the only one that might result in a judgment for the company.

There was a time when a 1,000-mile distance might have made it impossible for farmers to obtain the insecticide from other manufacturers. Then, in balancing the rights of the company against those of the farmer, a court might have concluded that the importance of the company's activity outweighed the importance of the farmer's, and that the manufacture of the insecticide was therefore not a nuisance. Modern transportation makes that argument unpersuasive, however. **A** is therefore incorrect. **B** is incorrect because a tenant (*i.e.*, the holder of a leasehold interest) has sufficient possessory interest in realty to maintain an action for private nuisance against one who interferes with his or her right to use or enjoy it. A private individual may not maintain an action for public nuisance unless his or her harm is substantially different from that sustained by the general public. No such requirement is imposed on the plaintiff in a private nuisance action, however. He or she must show only that the defendant tortiously interfered with his or her right to use and enjoy his or her realty. **D** is therefore incorrect.

186. **C**     Hearsay is defined as an out-of-court statement offered for the purpose of proving the truth of the matter asserted in that statement. The language of a promissory note creates an indebtedness. It is offered into evidence for the purpose of establishing that indebtedness (*i.e.*, for its independent legal significance), not for the purpose of establishing the truth of any facts that it incidentally communicates. For this reason, it is not hearsay.

A is incorrect because there is no indication that the note was prepared in the regular course of business, which is one of the requirements of a business record. Under the best evidence rule, secondary evidence to prove the terms of a writing is not admissible unless the writing itself is shown to be unavailable. This rule is thus a rule of exclusion. Although it may prevent the admission of a document that is not an original, it does not keep an original document from being hearsay or permit the admission of an original document that is inadmissible for other reasons. **B** is therefore incorrect. If an out-of-court statement is offered to prove the truth of a matter that it asserts, it is hearsay. The fact that the declarant (*i.e.,* the person who made the statement) is in court does not prevent it from being hearsay or permit its admission. **D** is therefore incorrect.

187. **D**     Most courts impose accomplice liability on a defendant when one person commits a killing with reckless indifference to human life, and the defendant, acting with the same reckless indifference, encourages the person in the conduct leading to the death. A scenario that is likely to involve accomplice liability for depraved-indifference murder is when multiple defendants all carry very dangerous weapons into a crime scene. Even in jurisdictions not applying the felony-murder rule, these defendants may have accomplice liability imposed upon them. Here, all three men carried extremely dangerous weapons into the pharmacy, and all three aided and abetted each other in the crime. The one robber

then acted with depraved indifference by shooting 30 bullets into the metal ceiling, where there was a large risk of the sort of ricochet that caused the death. Consequently, the two men who did not fire their weapons are accomplices to the killing, making them guilty of depraved-indifference murder. Thus, **A**, **B**, and **C** are incorrect.

188. **D**      Under Fed. R. Civ. P. 18(a), joinder of the additional contract claim against the dealer would be proper. However, a claim joined under Fed. R. Civ. P. 18(a) cannot be brought into federal court based on supplemental jurisdiction unless the claims are part of the same case or controversy. Because the contract claim involves a different "common nucleus of operative fact" than the accident, it must independently meet the requirements for federal subject matter jurisdiction. Here, since the salesman and the dealer are citizens of the same state, the claim would fail to do so.

      **A** is incorrect because although the accident and the firing are tangentially related, they are not part of the same case or controversy. One claim involves the facts and evidence related to the car accident, while the other involves facts and evidence related to the salesman's contract. **B** is incorrect because the accident and the firing are not part of the same case or controversy, as stated above. **C** is incorrect because all counterclaims would necessarily contain additional facts from the main claim.

189. **C**      The defense of improper venue is waived if it is not made either as a pre-answer motion under Fed. R. Civ. P. 12 or as part of the defendant's answer. When the defendants' submitted their answers without the defense, they waived it. Once that happened, "nothing . . . shall impair the jurisdiction of a district court of any matter involving a party who does not interpose timely and sufficient objection to the venue." *See 28 U.S.C. §1406(b).* Consequently, the court in the Western District of State A will get to hear the case even though venue is technically improper.

      Therefore, **A**, **B**, and **D** are incorrect.

190. **B**      The defendant's mother's promise to pay $1,000 is enforceable only if it is supported by consideration. Consideration is something of value—either benefit to the promisor or detriment to the promisee—given in exchange for the promise. A promise to do something that the promisor has no legal right to do cannot be regarded as consideration because it has no value. Unless a privilege exists, no person has the right to refuse to testify in a criminal prosecution. Certainly, no person may do so in return for payment. Thus, the victim's promise not to testify was a promise to do something that she had no right to do. For this reason, it would not have been consideration for the mother's promise to pay $1,000.

      **A** is incorrect because although the defendant's mother was not legally obligated to pay for damage caused by her adult son, she may have made an enforceable promise to do so. An accord is an agreement to substitute a new obligation for one that already existed. Satisfaction occurs when the accord is completely performed. Since the defendant may have had a duty to pay all the victim's medical expenses resulting from his act, and since the victim agreed to accept $250 instead, there may have been an accord that was satisfied when the defendant's mother paid as promised. But this accord existed only with respect to the obligation to pay medical expenses. Since the obligation to pay for pain and suffering is a separate obligation, it is not extinguished by satisfaction of the accord regarding medical expenses. **C** is therefore incorrect. A promise to pay the debt of another is unenforceable unless it is written. But a promise to pay in return for the promisee's forbearance to sue (even a third person) is not a promise to pay the debt of another but rather a personal obligation of the promisor. As such, it need not be in writing. **D** is therefore incorrect.

191. **C**    The Fifth Amendment right against self-incrimination protects a defendant against being coerced into answering questions asked by the police. Because police interrogation of a person in custody is inherently coercive, a person in custody is entitled to *Miranda* warnings like those given the defendant when she was first taken into custody. If, after receiving such warnings, the person in custody asserts his or her right to have an attorney present during questioning, all interrogation must stop and may not be continued without the presence of an attorney or a subsequent valid waiver. Because any further interrogation is regarded as coercive, a confession obtained in its course is not admissible in evidence. Although these rights were once held to apply only to a person who was a suspect, it is now clear that they apply to any person in custody.

**A** is therefore incorrect. **B** is incorrect because upon receiving the warnings, the defendant asserted her right to have an attorney present during questioning. Although the police are required to advise a defendant of his or her rights when he or she is in custody, they are not required to advise him or her of their suspicions or of their reasons for asking a particular question. **D** is therefore incorrect.

192. **C**    The grant of an interest in realty "for so long as" a certain condition continues to exist or "until" a certain condition shall exist is traditionally held to create a fee simple determinable. One of the characteristics of this particular interest is that it terminates automatically upon the happening of the specified event or condition. Since the conveyance to the church was "for so long as" the land is used for church purposes, it was a fee simple determinable, and it was terminated automatically when the church conveyed the land. According to the language of the deed, the interest of the hospital was to become possessory at that time. Although this might not have occurred within the period prescribed by the Rule Against Perpetuities, the hospital's interest is valid because in most jurisdictions, the rule does not apply to the future interest of a charity that follows the interest of another charity. **C** is correct for this reason and because it is the only option that could possibly be correct in any jurisdiction.

The estate system, and in particular the law of future interests, was developed so that a grantor could exercise some control over the subsequent use of the land conveyed. For that reason, restrictive language such as that contained in the landowner's deed is understood to relate to the way the conveyed land itself is used. Although the sale by the church might serve to enable the church to continue operation elsewhere, it violates the special limitation contained in the landowner's deed since it results in a cessation of the use of the land itself for the purpose stated in that limitation. For this reason, **A** is incorrect. **B** is incorrect for two reasons. First, as explained above, an exception prevents the interest of the hospital from being void under the Rule Against Perpetuities. Second, the Rule Against Perpetuities prevents the vesting of certain interests but does not prevent the divesting of any interest. Thus, even if the interest of the hospital was void under the Rule, the violation of the special limitation contained in the landowner's grant would terminate the interest of the church no matter when it occurred. The language of the landowner's grant limited the use for which the realty conveyed could be put. Restrictions of this kind are enforceable, even though they *indirectly* restrain alienation. The effect of the language used by the landowner is to divest the church of its interest when the church ceases to use the land for church purposes. Since the sale would have that effect, the church is divested of its interest, and **D** is incorrect. (**Note:** Sometimes the language of a conveyance attempts to *directly* restrain subsequent alienation of the interest conveyed by prohibiting such alienation. Most of the time, courts hold that direct restraints on alienation are invalid. If a restraint on alienation is held to be valid, it might make the person who violated it liable for damages, but it does not void the alienation. Thus, even if the conveyance created a direct restraint on alienation, it would not make the subsequent conveyance by the church invalid.)

193.  **B**  Although the Commerce Clause gives Congress the power to regulate interstate commerce, some regulation by the states is permitted so long as the effect is not to discriminate against or impose an undue burden on interstate commerce. Even state regulations that do discriminate against interstate commerce or impose a burden on it may be constitutional if they are aimed at a legitimate health or safety objective that cannot be achieved by less drastic means. It is possible that the additional fact set forth in **B** would result in a finding that Section 40 is valid because it protects the health and safety of the people of the state in the least drastic way possible. It is far from certain that a court would come to this conclusion, but **B** is the only one of all the additional facts listed that could possibly result in a finding of constitutionality.

One of the purposes of the Commerce Clause is to ban artificial barriers to interstate competition. Since the fact in **A** would make creation of a business advantage for in-state nuclear power plants a purpose of the Section, it would show that the statute is designed to create exactly the kind of artificial barrier that the Commerce Clause was designed to prevent. **A** is therefore incorrect. The shortage of storage facilities within the state underscores the competition for the use of such facilities. Thus, **C** would not justify finding Section 40 to be constitutional since its terms effectively eliminate out-of-staters from that competition. Even if there are many safe storage locations outside the state, there may be sound business reasons why out-of-staters prefer to use state locations. The discrimination resulting from the provisions of Section 40 would thus not be justified by the existence of out-of-state locations. **D** is therefore incorrect.

194.  **B**  It is generally understood that evidence of a person's bad character is inadmissible for the purpose of proving that he or she acted in a particular way on a particular occasion. Since evidence of a criminal conviction is evidence of character, it is usually excluded by this rule. Under FRE 609, a judgment of conviction may be admitted for the purpose

of impeaching the credibility of a witness, however, because it tends to establish that the person convicted is untrustworthy. If the defendant did not testify, there is no reason to impeach his credibility, and evidence of his prior conviction would be inadmissible.

On the other hand, if he did testify, evidence of his conviction would be admissible under the FRE. **A** is therefore incorrect. Under FRE 609, evidence of a conviction for a felony in any state or nation is admissible to impeach a witness without regard to the nature of the felony. Since involuntary manslaughter is a felony, **C** is incorrect. Since the FRE make a conviction from any state or nation admissible, **D** is incorrect.

195. **B**    To get a copy of the police report, the boxer's attorney must cause the clerk of the court to issue a subpoena duces tecum (an order requiring the recipient to appear before the court and produce documents) on the police department under Fed. R. Civ. P. 45.

A is incorrect because a request to produce documents may only be served on a party to the suit. *See Fed. R. Civ. P. 34.* **C** is incorrect because it is unnecessary to take the deposition of the police officer in order to get the police report. **D** is incorrect because only parties to an action are required to respond to interrogatories. *See Fed. R. Civ. P. 33(a).*

196. **B**    A plaintiff who experiences mental suffering as a result of witnessing the infliction of a physical injury on another may recover from a person who negligently inflicted that physical injury. Although the majority of jurisdictions permit such recovery only when the plaintiff is in the same zone of physical danger as the person who sustained physical injury, an important minority permit the plaintiff to recover if his or her mental suffering was a foreseeable result of the physical injury that he or she witnessed. In this minority of jurisdictions, the plaintiff might recover from the manufacturer for her mental suffering at witnessing the patient's death if it was likely (*i.e.*, foreseeable) that the manufacturer's negligence in causing the patient's death would lead to the plaintiff's mental suffering. Because this is a minority rule, there is no guarantee that it would lead to a judgment for the plaintiff. Of those listed, however, **B** is the only argument that could possibly be effective in support of the plaintiff's claim.

A defendant who engages in outrageous conduct with the intent to cause the plaintiff to experience mental suffering may be liable for mental suffering that the plaintiff experiences as a result. **A** is incorrect, however, for two reasons: First, outrageous conduct is conduct that exceeds bounds normally tolerated by decent society, not conduct that creates a high probability of harm, and second, there is no fact indicating that the manufacturer intended to cause the plaintiff to experience mental suffering. When a plaintiff voluntarily encounters a risk of which he or she knows, he or she assumes that risk. Since the plaintiff did not know that the oxygen tank contained anesthetic gas, she could not have assumed the risk resulting from that fact. **C** is incorrect for this reason and because assumption of the risk would prevent the plaintiff from recovering. A defendant who intends mental suffering to result from its outrageous conduct may be liable for the intentional infliction of mental harm. In this regard, a substantial certainty that the suffering will occur is equivalent to an intent to bring it about. **D** is incorrect, however, because even if the manufacturer was certain that the apparatus would be used on a patient, it did not intend the plaintiff's suffering unless it was certain that the patient would die and that the plaintiff would suffer as a result.

197.   **B**      A conspiracy occurs when two or more persons with the specific intent to commit a crime agree to commit it. Since the druggist did not believe that the wife would be hurt by the drug that he furnished, he did not have the requisite specific intent and did not really agree to commit murder. For this reason, there was never an actual agreement between him and the man, and therefore no conspiracy.

Conspiracy, if it exists, is separate from the substantive crime and is complete when the unlawful agreement is made. For this reason, a defendant may be guilty of conspiring to commit a particular crime even though he or she never succeeded and was not likely to succeed in committing it. **A** and **C** are therefore incorrect. **D** is incorrect because it is an inaccurate statement of law: The inchoate crime of conspiracy never merges with the substantive crime; a defendant can be convicted of both.

198.   **A**      Under FRE 803(6), a properly authenticated writing may be admitted under the business record exception to the hearsay rule if it was made in the regular course of business while fresh in the declarant's mind about facts that the declarant knew or learned from an inherently reliable source. Since the witness's testimony satisfied all these requirements, the personnel file should be admitted as a business record. (**Note:** Do not be confused about a controversy that exists over whether police records *describing an accident* are kept in the "regular course of business." Police department personnel records clearly are.)

**B** is incorrect because to be admissible as "past recollection recorded," a writing must have been made by the witness himself or herself, and because under FRE 803(5) and the common law, the writing may be read aloud but not physically admitted into evidence. **C** is incorrect because business records and official written statements may be used by any party. Although negative evidence presents some special problems, FRE 803(7) specifically permits the absence of a business record to be admissible as evidence that an unrecorded transaction did not occur.

199.   **B**      A motion for judgment as a matter of law is made before the case is submitted to a jury and asks the court for judgment in the moving party's favor based on the argument that no reasonable person could come to a different conclusion. A renewed motion for judgment as a matter of law comes after entry of judgment and can only be made if the moving party made a motion for judgment as a matter of law during the trial. Because the bank did not make a motion for judgment as a matter of law during trial, it cannot now try to make one after the entry of judgment.

**A** is incorrect because a motion for judgment as a matter of law does not need to be supported by new evidence. **C** and **D** are incorrect because the bank had to have made a motion for judgment as a matter of law before the jury verdict to have the court grant the bank's attempt at a renewed motion for judgment as a matter of law after the verdict.

200. **A**     Under 28 U.S.C. §1446(b), a defendant must file notice of removal within 30 days after formal service of the complaint. Since the builder removed 29 days after formal service, the builder's removal was timely. *See Murphy Brothers v. Michetti Pipe Stringing, Inc., 526 U.S. 344 (1999).*

**B** is incorrect because there is no special rule regarding notice by certified mail. **C** is incorrect because the 30-day period begins when the defendant receives official service. **D** is incorrect because there is no rule regarding challenging notice received by email.